Lennox and Addington Room 644

Mohamed

: Less managing. More teaching. Greater learning.

INSTRUCTORS...

Would you like your **students** to show up for class **more prepared**?
(Let's face it, class is much more fun if everyone is engaged and prepared...)

Want an **easy way to assign** homework online and track student **progress**?
(Less time grading means more time teaching...)

Want an **instant view** of student or class performance?
(No more wondering if students understand...)

Need to **collect data and generate reports** required for administration or accreditation?
(Say goodbye to manually tracking student learning outcomes...)

Want to **record and post your lectures** for students to view online?
(The more students can see, hear, and experience class resources, the better they learn...)

With McGraw-Hill's *Connect*,™

INSTRUCTORS GET:

- Simple **assignment management**, allowing you to spend more time teaching.
- **Auto-graded** assignments, quizzes, and tests.
- **Detailed Visual Reporting** where student and section results can be viewed and analyzed.
- Sophisticated **online testing** capability.
- A **filtering and reporting** function that allows you to easily assign and report on materials that are correlated to learning objectives and Bloom's taxonomy.
- An easy-to-use **lecture capture** tool.
- The option to **upload course documents** for student access.

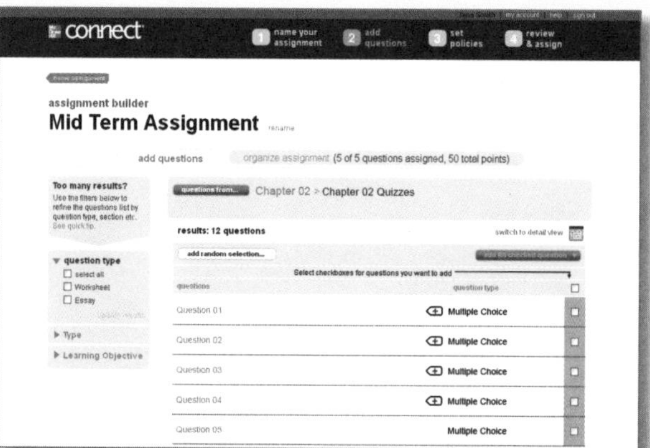

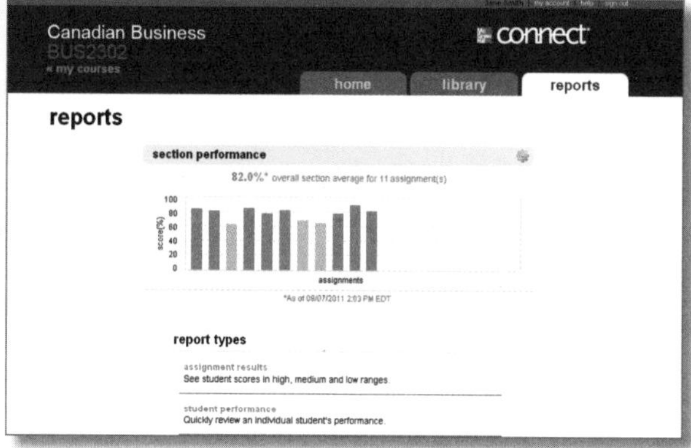

UNDERSTANDING CANADIAN BUSINESS

8 edition

William G. Nickels
University of Maryland

James M. McHugh
St. Louis Community College at Forest Park

Susan M. McHugh
Applied Learning Systems

Rita Cossa
McMaster University

Bob Sproule
University of Waterloo

The McGraw-Hill Companies

Understanding Canadian Business
Eighth Edition

ISBN-13: 978-0-07-105161-3
ISBN-10: 0-07-105161-9

1 2 3 4 5 6 7 8 9 10 TCP 1 9 8 7 6 5 4 3 2

Printed and bound in Canada.

Editorial Director: *Rhondda McNabb*
Publisher: *Kim Brewster*
Marketing Manager: *Cathie Lefebvre*
Developmental Editors: *Tracey Haggert, Becky Ranger, and Lori McLellan*
Senior Editorial Associate: *Christine Lomas*
Supervising Editor: *Graeme Powell*
Copy Editor: *Cat Haggert*
Permissions Editor: *Allison McDonald, McDonald Editorial Services*
Production Coordinator: *Sheryl MacAdam*
Cover and Interior Design: *Kyle Gell*
Page Layout: *Laserwords Private Limited*
Printer: *Transcontinental Printing Group*

Library and Archives Canada Cataloguing in Publication

Understanding Canadian Business / William G. Nickels ... [et al.]. — 8th ed.
Includes bibliographical references and indexes.
ISBN 978-0-07-105161-3
1. Industrial management—Textbooks. 2. Business—Textbooks. 3. Industrial management—Canada—Textbooks. 4. Business—Canada—Textbooks. I. Nickels, William G
HD31.U5135 2013 650 C2012-904950-6

DEDICATION

With gratitude to my husband, Stephen, and our children, Mattia and Leila, for their love and support. A special thank you to my students for sharing their questions and enthusiasm as they gained an appreciation and understanding of Canadian business.

Rita Cossa

To my wife for her ongoing support and encouragement of me as a teacher. To my children for keeping me connected to today's students. To my students, who provide me with the opportunity to support their learning.

Bob Sproule

To Marsha, Joel, Casey, Dan, Molly, Michael, and Colin—you have been our strength in the past, our joy in the present, and our hope for the future.

Bill Nickels, Jim McHugh, Susan McHugh

ABOUT THE AUTHORS

Bill Nickels is professor emeritus of business at the University of Maryland, College Park. He has over 35 years' experience teaching graduate and undergraduate business courses, including introductory courses in business, marketing, and promotion. He has won the Outstanding Teacher on Campus Award four times and was nominated for the award many other times. He received his MBA degree from Western Reserve University and his PhD from The Ohio State University. He has written a marketing communications text and two marketing principles texts in addition to many articles in business publications. He has taught many seminars to business people on subjects such as power communications, marketing, non-business marketing, and stress and life management.

Jim McHugh holds an MBA degree from Lindenwood University and has had broad experience in education, business, and government. As chairman of the Business and Economics Department of St. Louis Community College/Forest Park, Jim coordinated and directed the development of the business curriculum. In addition to teaching several sections of Introduction to Business each semester for nearly 30 years, Jim taught in the marketing and management areas at both the undergraduate and graduate levels. Jim enjoys conducting business seminars and consulting with small and large businesses. He is actively involved in the public service sector and served as chief of staff to the St. Louis County Executive.

Susan McHugh is a learning specialist with extensive training and experience in adult learning and curriculum development. She holds an MEd degree from the University of Missouri and completed her coursework for a PhD in education administration with a specialty in adult learning theory. As a professional curriculum developer, she has directed numerous curriculum projects and educator training programs. She has worked in the public and private sectors as a consultant in training and employee development.

Rita Cossa is an Assistant Professor at the DeGroote School of Business, McMaster University. This textbook marks her fifth edition as an author for *Understanding Canadian Business*. For over ten years she has enjoyed teaching Business Environment & Organization to undergraduate students. Rita has also taught Business Policy & Strategic Management and Introduction to Marketing courses at both the undergraduate and master's levels, as well as Marketing in the Non-Profit Sector. Highlights include a nomination to *TVOntario's Best Lecturer Competition*, multiple nominations for a McMaster Student Union Teaching Award, and notations in the *Maclean's Guide to Canadian Universities* as a Popular Prof for Marketing. Prior to her teaching career, Rita held several management-level positions in the financial services industry.

Bob Sproule is a faculty member in the School of Accounting and Finance at the University of Waterloo. Teaching in some capacity for over 30 years, Bob has been challenged by and enjoyed being part of the learning journey of thousands of students. Most recently he received two international teaching awards recognizing his innovation in teaching, one from the Society for Teaching and Learning in Higher Education and the other from Desire to Learn. He has been the Associate Director of Teaching and Learning and a member of the Teaching Excellence Council at the University of Waterloo. He is a trained facilitator for the Instructional Skills Workshop and has leadership roles both nationally and internationally in a number of organizations supporting teaching and learning.

BRIEF CONTENTS

CONTENTS

PREFACE

As authors, it is thrilling to see the results of the work we love embraced by colleagues in colleges and universities throughout Canada and around the world. We firmly believe that no course is more important than the Introduction to Business course. That's why we enjoy teaching it so much and why we are willing to spend so much time helping others make this the best course on campus. We thank all the dedicated instructors who have supported us through the years and welcome new instructors to the *Understanding Canadian Business* team. We look forward to a continuing relationship with all of you and to sharing what we consider the most exciting classroom experience possible: teaching students to understand business.

Bill Nickels **Jim McHugh** **Susan McHugh** **Rita Cossa** **Bob Sproule**

KEEPING UP WITH WHAT'S NEW

Users of *Understanding Canadian Business* have always appreciated the currency of the material and the large number of examples from companies of *all* sizes and industries (e.g., service, manufacturing, profit, and non-profit) in Canada and around the world. Accordingly, this edition features the latest business practices and other developments affecting business, including:

- Green marketing
- Social networking media
- Cloud computing
- International financial reporting standards
- Significant revisions in the coverage of finance based on the many changes in the industry
- Expanded coverage of leadership based on its ongoing importance in all aspects of business

TO OUR FELLOW INTRODUCTION TO BUSINESS INSTRUCTORS

How quickly things are changing! The ways instructors teach, the ways students learn, and the ways information is delivered are all changing rapidly. This evolution is affecting courses across the country. As authors, we must consider all of these changes, both in the types of resources we offer and in the way we provide them to you.

We Have 3 Goals In This Edition

- To sustain the celebrated quality of the text and its supporting resources.
- To address the changing course environment and methods for information delivery.
- To help you build your course by providing what YOU need most.

We remain dedicated to listening vigilantly to what you tell us you need in this course. We have made changes and enhancements in this revision that are all based on what we heard from you. As you look through the next few pages, you'll find what you need to navigate your way most effectively through this book and its supplements.

INTEGRATION OF IMPORTANT CONCEPTS THROUGHOUT THE TEXT

Understanding Canadian Business, Eighth Edition, is revised, updated, and filled with new examples of business in Canada and around the world. Each chapter begins with a focus on a business professional. Take some time to consider their career choices and how they spend their time applying the business principles that are introduced in the subsequent pages.

The following key topics are incorporated as themes throughout the text:

- Constant and dynamic change
- Small business and entrepreneurship
- Ethics and social responsibility
- "Green" business
- Global business
- Technology and change
- Pleasing customers
- Teams
- Quality
- Cultural diversity

These themes reflect a strong consensus among instructors of introductory business courses that certain topics deserve and need special emphasis. Among these, instructors encouraged us to add particular focus in the areas of small business/entrepreneurship, ethics, global business, environmental issues, and dealing with change. In response, this edition incorporates many examples throughout including chapter feature boxes titled "Spotlight on Small Business," "Making Ethical Decisions," and "Green Box." In addition, we have included the following two boxes—"Reaching Beyond Our Borders" and "Dealing with Change"—at the end of each text Part.

Learning Objectives ▸

Tied directly to the summaries at the end of the chapter and to the Test Bank questions, the Learning Objectives help students preview what they should know after reading the chapter, and then test that knowledge by answering the questions in the summary. These Learning Objectives are also incorporated in the margins throughout the chapter, at the start of the discussion that pertains to the Learning Objective so students can quickly see where the content aligns with each objective.

LEARNING OBJECTIVES

After you have read and studied this chapter, you should be able to:

LO 1 Describe basic economics.

LO 2 Explain what capitalism is and how free markets work.

LO 3 Define socialism and its benefits and negative consequences.

LO 4 Evaluate communism and the challenges of such a system.

LO 5 Describe the mixed economy of Canada.

LO 6 Illustrate the significance of key economic indicators and the business cycle.

PROFILE

GETTING TO KNOW: HERNANDO SOTO: ECONOMIST FOR THE PO

A crowd of anxious fans pushes to get a g of a celebrity visiting a poor community i Who is this person who has the town so e A rock singer, a famous athlete, a movie sta Would you believe he's an economist? Her de Soto, a noted economist, wrote one of bestselling books and the crowds were to hear his ideas about improving the co economy—and thus their own lives.

Hernando de Soto was born in Peru. He went on in Canada, the United States, and Switzerland. E

Getting to Know Business Professionals ▾

Each chapter begins with a profile of a business person whose career relates closely to the material covered in that chapter. Not all of the personalities are famous, since some of them work in small businesses and non-profit organizations. Getting to know these business professionals provides the perfect transition to the text material.

PART 1

CHAPTER 1

TAKING RISKS AND MAKING PROFITS WITHIN THE DYNAMIC BUSINESS ENVIRONMENT

LEARNING OBJECTIVES

PROFILE

GETTING TO KNOW RON FOXCROFT OF FOX 40 INTERNATIONAL INC.

URLs Within the Chapter Content ▸

At the first mention of a relevant company we have included the company's URL for your reference—these will be hotlinked in your eBook so you can quickly jump to the company's web site for additional information.

Companies also continuously review their global operations to ensure that they are operating at a profit. One Canadian industry that has been particularly hard hit as a result of global trends is the auto industry. Factors such as the increasing price of gas and weakening demand for trucks and sport utility vehicles (SUVs) have forced companies to consider restructuring plans. As a result, thousands of Canadian jobs have been eliminated. Layoffs have occurred at General Motors Canada <*www.gm.ca*>, Chrysler Canada <*www.chryslercanada.ca*>, Ford Motor Company of Canada <*www.ford.ca*>, and many parts suppliers.[8] The global market is truly dynamic, and progressive companies continuously scan the business environment to ensure that they take advantage of the opportunities and minimize the impact of threats.

Because the global market is so large, it is important to understand the language of international trade. Canada is a large exporting nation. **Exporting** is selling products (i.e., goods and services) to another country. **Importing** is buying products from

Photo and Illustration Essays ▸

More and more students have expressed that they are visually oriented learners; therefore, increased emphasis on the pedagogical value of illustrations is essential. Some photos and illustrations in the text are accompanied by a short essay that highlights the relevance of the visuals to the material in the text.

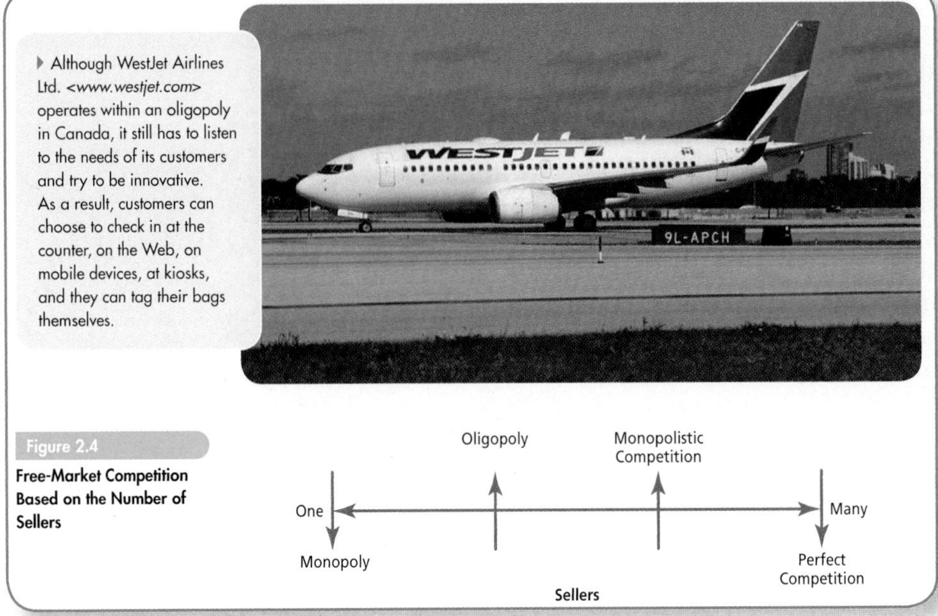

▸ Although WestJet Airlines Ltd. <*www.westjet.com*> operates within an oligopoly in Canada, it still has to listen to the needs of its customers and try to be innovative. As a result, customers can choose to check in at the counter, on the Web, on mobile devices, at kiosks, and they can tag their bags themselves.

Figure 2.4
Free-Market Competition Based on the Number of Sellers

Progress Assessments ▾

To ensure that students understand and retain the material, Progress Assessments stop them and show them what they need to review before proceeding. The Progress Assessment is a proven learning tool that helps students comprehend and retain material.

PROGRESS ASSESSMENT

- How do business people know what to produce and in what quantity?
- How are prices determined?
- Describe the four degrees of competition.
- What are some of the limitations of free markets?

Interactive Summaries ▸

The end-of-chapter summaries are directly tied to the Learning Objectives and are written in a question-and-answer format—great for chapter review and studying.

SUMMARY

Describe basic economics.

Economics is the study of how society chooses to employ resources to produce goods and services and distribute them for consumption among various competing groups and individuals.

What are the two branches of economics?

There are two major branches of economics: macroeconomics studies the operation of a nation's economy as a whole, and microeconomics studies the behaviour of people and organizations in particular markets (e.g., why people buy smaller cars when gas prices go up).

Explain what capitalism is and how free markets work.

Capitalism is an economic system in which all or most of the means of production and distribution (e.g., land, factories, railroads, and stores) are privately owned and operated for profit.

Who decides what to produce under capitalism?

In capitalist countries, business people decide what to produce; how much to pay workers; how much to charge for goods and services; whether to produce certain goods in their own countries, import those goods, or have them made in other countries; and so on.

Key Terms

Important terms, highlighted in blue type throughout the text with an accompanying definition in the margin, are listed in alphabetical order at the end of the chapter and in the glossary with page numbers for ease of reference.

KEY TERMS

brain drain
business cycles (economic cycles)
capitalism
command economy
communism
consumer price index (CPI)
deflation
demand
depression
disinflation
economics
free-market economy
gross domestic product (GDP)
inflation
invisible hand
macroeconomics
market price
microeconomics
mixed economies
monopolistic competition
monopoly
oligopoly
perfect competition
recession
resource development
socialism
stagflation
supply
unemployment rate

Critical Thinking Questions

Found in each chapter, Critical Thinking questions ask students to pause and think about how the material they are reading applies to their own lives.

CRITICAL THINKING

Many say that business people do not do enough for society. Some students choose to work for non-profit organizations instead of for-profit organizations because they want to help others. However, business people say that they do more to help others than non-profit groups because they provide jobs for people rather than giving them charity, which often precludes them from searching for work. Furthermore, they believe that businesses create all the wealth that non-profit groups distribute. Can you find some middle ground in this debate that would show that both business people and those who work for non-profit organizations contribute to society and need to work together more closely to help people? Could you use the concepts of Adam Smith to help illustrate your position?

Developing Workplace Skills

The Developing Workplace Skills section has activities designed to increase student involvement in the learning process. Some of these mini-projects require library or Internet searches, while others can be used as team activities either in or out of the classroom.

DEVELOPING WORKPLACE SKILLS

1. Show your understanding of the principles of supply and demand by looking at the oil market today. Why does the price of gas fluctuate so greatly? What will happen as more and more people in China and India decide to buy automobiles? What would happen if more Canadian consumers decided to drive electric cars?
2. This exercise will help you understand socialism from different perspectives. Form three groups. Each group should adopt a different role in a socialist economy: one group will be the business owners, another group will be workers, and the third will be government leaders. Within your group, discuss and list the advantages and disadvantages to you of lowering taxes on businesses. Then have each group choose a representative to debate the tax issue with the representatives from the other groups.
3. Draw a line and mark one end "capitalism" and the other end "socialism." Mark where Canada is now on that line. Explain why you marked the spot you did. Students from other countries may want to do this exercise for their own countries and explain the differences to the class.
4. Break into small groups. In your group, discuss how the following have affected people's purchasing behaviour and attitudes toward Canada and its economy: development of the Alberta oil sands; the Atlantic seal hunt; mad cow disease; and the growth of the Internet. Have a group member prepare a short summary for the class.

Analyzing Management Decisions ▸

Each chapter concludes with a case that allows students to analyze management decision making. These cases are intentionally brief and are meant to initiate discussion rather than take up the entire class period.

ANALYZING MANAGEMENT DECISIONS

The Rule of 72

No formula is more useful for understanding inflation than the rule of 72. Basically, the rule allows you to quickly compute how long it takes the cost of goods and services to double at various compounded rates of growth. For example, if houses were increasing in cost at 9 percent a year, how long would it take for the price of a home to double? The answer is easy to calculate. Simply divide 72 by the annual increase (9 percent) and you get the approximate number of years it takes to double the price (eight years). Of course, the same calculation can be used to predict how high food prices or auto prices will be 10 years from now.

Here's an example of how you can use the rule of 72. If the cost of going to college goes up by 6 percent a year, how much might you have to pay to send your child to college in 24 years (this assumes you will have a child six years from now) if college costs are now $10,000 a year? To find the answer, you divide 72 by 6, which shows that the cost of an education would double in 12 years. It would double twice in 24 years. Your son or daughter can expect to pay $40,000 per year to attend college.

Discussion Questions

1. If the cost of a university education is about $20,000 per year now, what will it cost your children per year if costs go up 9 percent a year and your children go to university 16 years from now?
2. If the value of a home doubles in 12 years, what is the annual rate of return? (Hint: Use the rule of 72 in reverse.)
3. If you put $1,000 into a savings account and earned 6 percent per year, how much money would you have in the account after 48 years?

Video Cases ▸

Video cases from CBC programs and custom segments from the McGraw-Hill Management Library filmed specifically for the Nickels text are provided for each chapter. They feature companies, processes, practices, and managers that highlight and bring to life the key concepts, and especially the themes, of the eighth edition. These videos are available through Connect or on DVD for in-class viewing.

CHAPTER 2 The Bank of Canada: Count on Us

The Bank of Canada contributes to the well-being of the Canadian economy through the implementation of monetary policy, its role in the Canadian financial system, and its management of Canada's bank notes. Located in Ottawa, Ontario, the Bank of Canada is our country's central bank. It is not a commercial bank and it does not offer banking services to the public. Its principal role, as defined in the Bank of Canada Act, is "to promote the economic and financial welfare of Canada." The Bank was founded in 1934 as a privately owned corporation. In 1938, it became a Crown corporation belonging to the federal government. (Crown corporations will be discussed in Chapter 4.)

Take a second and think of your bank balance. What makes that money valuable? According to the Bank of Canada Governor, Mark Carney, you don't have to worry about your money or the financial system in Canada due to the work of the Bank of Canada.

The Bank of Canada's main job is to direct monetary policy, which involves setting the interest rates that people and businesses pay when they borrow money. The Bank's objective is to influence interest rates so that the economy can remain healthy and create jobs. A healthy and stable economy helps families and businesses adapt to the changing conditions in the world economy.

As long as inflation is low, stable, and predictable we can remain confident in the future value of our money. The Bank of Canada and the Government of Canada aim for an annual inflation rate of 2 percent. This is known as the inflation target. The Bank of Canada sets the policy interest rate, which influences commercial interest rates. For consumers, low interest rates mean that it costs less to borrow money. For businesses, low-cost loans help them buy new equipment and expand their operations. All of this economic activity helps to push rates up. On the reverse, when everyone spends less due to higher interest rates, inflation tends to come down.

From buyers to sellers, from sellers to banks, and from banks back to businesses and consumers, it is easy to take all of these millions of transfers for granted. Money moves through a financial system. The Bank of Canada oversees these large complex systems that are used for making these daily financial transfers.

Since Canada is an open economy (i.e., we depend more on international trade and capital flows than many other countries), it is important to understand the global economic environment as well. To this end, the Bank of Canada works to ensure that the financial system stays strong and secure by working with the G20 (the 20 largest countries in the world), the IMF (International Monetary Fund), and the BIS (Bank of International Systems) to raise the standard of regulation and also ensure that other countries are applying these regulations and supervision through their banks, insurance companies, and financial systems so that Canada is not impacted by shocks from abroad.

When the Bank of Canada was established, it was given the sole authority to issue bank notes in Canada and to preserve the value of money. Bank notes are designed to be attractive, easy to use, durable, and difficult to counterfeit. If it was hard to tell a real Canadian bank note from a fake, confidence in our currency would disappear. All of our bank notes have security features that are easy to check.

Discussion Questions

1. The Bank of Canada has the mandate to contribute and enhance the well-being of Canadians. What three areas are targeted by the Bank of Canada as a way to do this?
2. How does the Bank of Canada try to keep the inflation in check?
3. What is the impact of high interest rates for consumers and businesses? How about low interest rates?

NEW End-of-Part Running Case ▸

This new six-part running case, found at the end of each text Part, provides realistic business scenarios based on Fox 40 International Inc. The discussion questions at the end of the case encourage students to consider how this company has applied some of the concepts that were introduced in the text Part.

RUNNING CASE

Ron Foxcroft: The Dream for a Pealess Whistle

For successful Canadian entrepreneur and inventor Ron Foxcroft, it all started in 1982 when he purchased Fluke Transport, a Southern Ontario trucking business. The company slogan—If It's On Time . . . It's A "FLUKE"—was soon recognized throughout North America. Over the years, Ron diversified into new ventures and the Foxcroft Group of Companies now includes Fluke Transportation Group, Fluke Warehousing Inc., Foxcroft Capital Group, and Fox 40 International Inc.

The formation of Fox 40 International Inc. (Fox 40) is the result of a dream for a pealess whistle. When developing his first whistle, Ron was motivated by his knowledge and experience as an international

Discussion Questions

1. In addition to employees and customers, what other stakeholders does the company consider as part of its business activities?
2. What is the primary reason why the company is unlikely to consider other global market-entry strategies (e.g., licensing)?
3. Visit the company's Web site at www.fox40world.com. What are some of its newest green initiatives? Can you recommend any new ones? (Hint: Review the Green Initiatives under the About Us tab.)
4. Do you have a dream for a product that has not yet been produced? If yes, how do you plan to develop this idea and turn it into reality?

STUDENT RESOURCES

Connect

McGraw-Hill Connect™ is a web-based assignment and assessment platform that gives students the means to better connect with their coursework, with their instructors, and with the important concepts that they will need to know for success now and in the future.

With Connect, instructors can deliver assignments, quizzes and tests online. Nearly all the questions from the text are presented in an auto-gradeable format and tied to the text's learning objectives. Instructors can edit existing questions and author entirely new problems. They can track individual student performance—by question, assignment or in relation to the class overall—with detailed grade reports. Integrate grade reports easily with Learning Management Systems (LMS) such as WebCT and Blackboard. And much more.

By choosing Connect, instructors are providing their students with a powerful tool for improving academic performance and truly mastering course material. Connect allows students to practice important skills at their own pace and on their own schedule. Importantly, students' assessment results and instructors' feedback are all saved online—so students can continually review their progress and plot their course to success.

Connect also provides 24/7 online access to an eBook—an online edition of the text—to aid them in successfully completing their work, wherever and whenever they choose.

Mc Graw Hill connect™

LearnSmart

No two students are alike. McGraw-Hill LearnSmart™ is an intelligent learning system that uses a series of adaptive questions to pinpoint each student's knowledge gaps. LearnSmart then provides an optimal learning path for each student, so that they spend less time in areas they already know and more time in areas they don't. The result is LearnSmart's adaptive learning path helps students retain more knowledge, learn faster, and study more efficiently.

Mc Graw Hill LearnSmart™

INSTRUCTORS' RESOURCES

Understanding Canadian Business, Eighth Edition, offers a complete, integrated supplements package for instructors to address all your needs.

Instructor's Manual: The instructor's manual, prepared by Kashif Memon, University of Waterloo, accurately represents the text's content and supports instructors' needs. Each chapter includes the learning objectives, glossary of key terms, a chapter synopsis, complete lecture outline, and solutions to the end-of-chapter discussion questions.

Computerized Test Bank: This flexible and easy-to-use electronic testing program allows instructors to create tests from book-specific items. Created by Thomas McKaig, University of Guelph and University of Guelph-Humber, the test bank has undergone a rigorous auditing and revision process for the eighth edition. It contains a broad selection of multiple choice, true/false, and essay questions. Instructors may add their own questions as well. Each question identifies the relevant page reference and difficulty level. Multiple versions of the test can be created and printed.

PowerPoint Presentations: These robust presentations offer high-quality visuals from the text and highlight key concepts from each chapter to bring key business concepts to life. Two different presentations offer instructors choice on how they like to present the material to their classes. The basic set was authored by Valerie Miceli, Seneca College, and the advanced set was authored by Tim Richardson, Seneca College and the University of Toronto.

Videos for All Chapters: Complementary videos from CBC programs and customized business segments from the McGraw-Hill Management Library filmed specifically for the Nickels text are available on DVD and also can be accessed on the password-protected area of Connect. Detailed teaching notes written by the text authors are available in the instructor's manual and on the instructor area of Connect.

Management Asset Gallery—for Instructors and Students

The Management Asset Gallery is a one-stop shop for a wealth of McGraw-Hill management assets, making it easier for instructors to locate specific materials to enhance their courses, and for students to supplement their knowledge (via the Student Asset Gallery). The Instructor Asset Gallery includes non–text-specific management resources (Self-Assessments, Test Your Knowledge exercises, videos*, Manager's HotSeat, and additional group and individual exercises), along with supporting PowerPoint and instructor's manual materials.

The **Manager's HotSeat** is a resource within the Asset Gallery that allows students to watch over 14 real managers apply their years of experience to confront daily issues such as ethics, diversity, teamwork, and the virtual workplace. Students are prompted for their feedback throughout each scenario and can then submit a report critiquing the manager's choices, while defending their own. The Manager's HotSeat is ideal for group or classroom discussions.

Business Plan Pro

Business Plan Pro is available as a bundled option that includes more than 250 sample business plans and 400 case studies to give you a wide variety of examples as you create your own business plan. It helps you set up your business by answering questions that help the software customize your plan. Then you enter your financial data to generate financial worksheets and statements.

Superior Learning Solutions and Support

The McGraw-Hill Ryerson team is ready to help you assess and integrate any of our products, technology, and services into your course for optimal teaching and learning performance. Whether it's helping your students improve their grades or putting your entire course online, the McGraw-Hill Ryerson team is here to help you do it. Contact your iLearning Sales Specialist today to learn how to maximize all of McGraw-Hill Ryerson's resources!

For more information on the latest technology and Learning Solutions offered by McGraw-Hill Ryerson and its partners, please visit us online: **www.mcgrawhill.ca/he/solutions**.

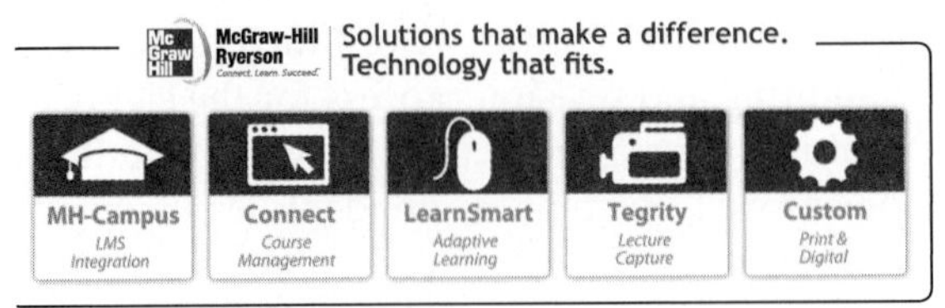

*The "Management in the Movies" videos are not licensed for distribution outside of the United States; however, adopting instructors are able to access the instructor notes.

ACKNOWLEDGEMENTS

Development of the Text and Supporting Resources

To ensure continuous improvement of our product, we have used an extensive review and development process for each of our editions. Building on that history, the development process for this eighth edition included evaluation by a broad panel of instructors where new ideas were exchanged. Thank you to all of our reviewers and participants—your suggestions to improve the quality, coverage, and the supplements package were invaluable. We extend our deepest thanks for your time and involvement.

Reviewers who were vital in helping us develop this edition include:

Dave Barrett, *Conestoga College*
Edith Callaghan, *Acadia University*
Brahm Canzer, *John Abbott College*
Kerry Couet, *Concordia University*
Ken Desroches, *University of Prince Edward Island*
Linda Donville, *Centennial College of Applied Arts and Technology*
David Fleming, *George Brown College*
Mark Fuller, *St. Francis Xavier University*
Tom Gallagher, *Mount Royal University*
Don Hill, *Langara College*
Stephen Hunt, *Canadore College*
Lorne Jeal, *Medicine Hat College*
Michael Khan, *University of Toronto*
Amy Macarthur, *Crandall University*
Pelham Matthews, *Algoma University*
Bill McConkey, *University of Toronto*
Valerie Miceli, *Seneca College*
Paul Myers, *St. Clair College*
Ardith Plant, *University of Winnipeg*
Gordon Preston, *King's University College*
Jeff Ryan, *Grant MacEwan University*
Susanne Thiessen, *Camosun College*
Carl Weston, *Mohawk College*

The eighth edition continues to be the market's gold standard due to involvement of these committed instructors. We thank them all for their help, support, and friendship.

Many thanks are also due to the following people who worked hard to make this book a reality: Kim Brewster, Publisher; Tracey Haggert, Lori McLellan, and Becky Ranger, Developmental Editors; Kara Stahl and Graeme Powell, Supervising Editors; Margaret Henderson, Manager, Editorial and Design Services; Sheryl MacAdam, Production Coordinator; Cat Haggert, Copy Editor; Allison McDonald, Permissions and Photo Researcher; and Kyle Gell, Designer.

The authors would also like to extend their appreciation to Ron Foxcroft and his son, Dave Foxcroft, for allowing them to highlight Fox40® International Inc. (Fox 40), a proudly Canadian company, in this edition's new running case. Ron, a Canadian entrepreneur and inventor, started Fox 40 twenty-five years ago as the result of his dream for a pealess whistle. Today, this privately held, family-run organization continues to dominate the global whistle industry. Read the case at the end of each part to learn how Ron, Dave, and their management team apply the business principles that are discussed throughout this textbook.

UNDERSTANDING CANADIAN BUSINESS

8 edition

PART 1

CHAPTER

1

TAKING RISKS AND MAKING PROFITS WITHIN THE DYNAMIC BUSINESS ENVIRONMENT

LEARNING OBJECTIVES

After you have read and studied this chapter, you should be able to:

LO 1 Describe the relationship of businesses' profit-to-risk assumption.

LO 2 Illustrate the importance of stakeholders and non-profit organizations to business activities.

LO 3 Explain how entrepreneurship is critical to the wealth of an economy, and list the five factors of production that contribute to wealth.

LO 4 State the six elements that make up the business environment and explain why the business environment is important to organizations.

LO 5 Give examples of how the service sector has replaced manufacturing as the principal provider of jobs, but why manufacturing remains vital for Canada.

PROFILE

GETTING TO KNOW RON FOXCROFT OF FOX 40 INTERNATIONAL INC.

For successful Canadian entrepreneur and inventor Ron Foxcroft, it all started in 1982 when he purchased Fluke Transport, a Southern Ontario trucking business. The company slogan—If It's On Time . . . It's A "FLUKE"—was soon recognized throughout North America. Over the years, Foxcroft diversified into new ventures and the Foxcroft Group of Companies now includes Fluke Transportation Group <*www.fluke.ca*>, Hamilton Terminals Inc., Foxcroft Capital Corp., and Fox 40 International Inc. <*www.fox40world.com*>.

The formation of Fox 40 International Inc. is the result of a dream for a pealess whistle. When Foxcroft began developing the whistle, he was motivated by his knowledge and experience as an international basketball referee. Frustrated with faulty pea whistles, he spent three years of development with design consultant Chuck Shepherd, resulting in the creation of the Fox 40 Classic Whistle. (The whistle was named for Foxcroft and that he was 40 when his invention was being developed). Introduced in 1987, this finely tuned precision instrument doesn't use a pea to generate sound. In fact, there are no moving parts whatsoever. There is nothing to obstruct sound, nothing to stick, freeze, or fail. The patented design moves the air blast through three tuned chambers. Fox 40 whistles are entirely constructed of high-impact ABS plastic so they are impervious to moisture. A quick rinse in disinfectant eliminates bacteria. Every time, they deliver on faultless performance (e.g., loudness), and they never fail.

In 1987, Shepherd said to Foxcroft, "Ron, we have just developed the 'best whistle in the world.' You must pledge to me that you will dedicate your life to making the Fox 40 whistle better." To this day, Foxcroft and the company employees continue to honour this pledge. Fox 40 International Inc., a proudly Canadian company, dominates the global whistle industry. Tens of thousands of Fox 40 whistles are produced monthly for shipment to 140 countries. These whistles can be heard in arenas, stadiums, and gymnasiums and it is estimated that 98 percent of all referees around the world use a Fox 40 whistle. It is the sanctioned whistle for referees and officials in several professional and amateur sports leagues including the NBA, NFL, NHL, FIFA, and the NCAA. Fox 40 whistles are also used by fire and rescue professionals around the world, lifeguards, school crossing guards, boaters, and for individual safety use.

Ron Foxcroft's philosophy of "be the best at what you do" has contributed to his success both on and off the basketball courts. He has been named one of the 52 most influential persons in North American Officiating of all time. *PROFIT* magazine voted him to be one of the top ten Canadian businessmen in the 1990s. In 2010, the National Association of Sports Officials named him—the only Canadian—to a group of 30 who have made a difference in the world of sports officials. In 2011, he was honoured as Entrepreneur of the Year by the Burlington Economic Development Corporation. Foxcroft continues his active role as Founder and Chief Executive Officer (CEO) of Fox 40 International Inc. and Chairman and CEO of Fluke Transportation. On the courts, he is in his eighth season as an Observer Evaluator of the Officials for the NBA.

Foxcroft credits his customers and employees for the improvements to the original whistle. In his words, "When you are the best, you need to be better." This all starts with watching people to understand their needs. It involves developing products and services that customers might want. Making decisions along the way is challenging, but if you are successful, you can make a lot of customers very happy. Throughout this process, you need to have a vision, be focused, adapt to change, and never give up. His advice for future entrepreneurs, in the words of Walt Disney, is to "Get a good idea and stay with it. Dog it, and work it until it's done and done right."

The purpose of this text is to introduce you to the exciting and challenging world of business. Each chapter will begin with a story similar to this one. You will meet more successful entrepreneurs who have started a business. You will also learn about people who work for companies and have succeeded far beyond their original expectations. You will learn about all aspects of business: management, human resource management, marketing, accounting, finance, and more. You will also learn about businesses of all sizes. We begin by looking at some key terms and exploring the rapidly changing business environment so that you can prepare to meet tomorrow's challenges today.

Sources: Ron Foxcroft, Founder and CEO, Fox 40 International Inc., in-person interview, 19 December 2011; "Who We Are: The Fox 40 Story," Fox 40 International Inc., 18 December 2011, www.fox40world.com/index.cfm?pagepath=ABOUT_US/Who_We_Are__The_Fox_40_Story&id=4099; "BEDC Inducts Mr. Ron Foxcroft into the Entrepreneur Hall of Fame," Burlington Economic Development Corporation, 10 June 2011, www.bedc.ca/sites/default/files/PDF/businessnews/MediaRelease—BEDCInductsMr.RonFoxcroftintotheEntrepreneurHallofFame.pdf; John Kernaghan, "Fox 40 founder Foxcroft feted," *The Hamilton Spectator,* 18 October 2010, www.thespec.com/sports/local/article/268488—fox-40-founder-foxcroft-feted; REFEREE Staff, "Not An Inadvertent Whistle," *REFEREE Magazine,* July 2007, 45–47; and Global TV, "Ron Foxcroft," Summit of Life, Summer 2005.

ENTREPRENEURSHIP AND WEALTH BUILDING

One thing that you can learn from the chapter-opening Profile is that success in business if often based on the strategy of finding a need and filling it. Ron Foxcroft saw the need for a pealess whistle and he filled it. This strategy lets you help the community in several ways. You provide needed goods, jobs, and services to people in the area. **Goods** are tangible products such as computers, food, clothing, cars, and appliances. **Services** are intangible products (i.e., items that cannot be held in your hand) such as education, health care, insurance, recreation, and travel and tourism.

goods
Tangible products such as computers, food, clothing, cars, and appliances.

services
Intangible products (i.e., products that can't be held in your hand) such as education, health care, insurance, recreation, and travel and tourism.

Although you don't need to have wealth as a primary goal, one result of successfully filling a market need is that you can make money for yourself, sometimes a great deal, by giving customers what they want. Thousands of people have learned that one of the best ways to become a success in Canada, or almost anywhere else in the world, is to have a career in business. A **business** is any activity that seeks to provide goods and services to others while operating at a profit. An **entrepreneur** is a person who risks time and money to start and manage a business. You will read more about successful entrepreneurs throughout this text.

business
Any activity that seeks to provide goods and services to others while operating at a profit.

entrepreneur
A person who risks time and money to start and manage a business.

An entrepreneur learns early that there is a need for a reliable accountant, a good lawyer, and strong managers. Entrepreneurs may have to go to financial institutions (e.g., banks) or to venture capital firms to borrow more money. In today's economy, borrowing from a financial institution is harder than usual.[1] Therefore, later on in the text, we will talk about ways to get closer to financial institutions so that they will be more inclined to give you a loan. Entrepreneurs will also need to learn more about business, including how to deal with unions, what kind of insurance to buy, and how to find the right people to hire. Usually that means studying business at a community college or university.[2] That is much easier today now that so many courses are available online.[3] Taking this course and reading this text are good ways to start building a foundation for understanding business. In this chapter, we'll give you an overview to help you organize what you'll be learning.

Revenues, Profits, and Losses

Describe the relationship of businesses' profit-to-risk assumption.

Revenue is the total amount of money that is received during a given period for goods sold, services rendered, and other financial sources. **Profit** is the amount of money a business earns above and beyond what it spends for salaries and other expenses. Since not all businesses make a profit, starting a business can be risky. A **loss** occurs when a business's expenses are more than its revenues. If a business loses money over time, it will likely have to close, putting its employees out of work. It should be no surprise, therefore, that thousands of businesses enter and exit the marketplace throughout the year.[4] Some owners close down one business to start another one or to retire. Even though such closings are not failures, they are reported as exits by Industry Canada. Only a small proportion of firms that exit the marketplace end up filing for *bankruptcy,* which refers to the liquidation of the business debtor's assets and the end of the commercial entity's operations.[5]As discussed later in this textbook, most business failures are due to poor management or problems associated with cash flow.

revenue
The total amount of money that is received during a given period for goods sold, services rendered, and other financial sources.

profit
The amount a business earns above and beyond what it spends for salaries and other expenses.

loss
When a business's expenses are more than its revenues.

The business environment is constantly changing. What seem like a great opportunity one day—for example, online grocery shopping—may become a failure when the economy changes. Starting a business may come with huge risks. But huge risks can result in huge profits. We'll explore that concept next.

Matching Risk with Profit

Starting a business involves risk. Generally speaking, **risk** refers to the chance of loss, the degree of probability of loss, and the amount of possible loss. Risk is the chance an entrepreneur takes of losing time and money on a business that may not prove profitable. Profit, remember, is the amount of money a business earns *above and beyond* what it pays

risk
Refers to the chance of loss, the degree of probability of loss, and the amount of possible loss (i.e., time and money).

▸ How well do you know yourself? Are you more excited at the prospect of starting your own small business or would you prefer to work for a large- or medium-sized business? The answer to this question may start with understanding your personal risk tolerance.

out for salaries and other expenses. For example, if you were to start a business selling hot dogs in the summer, you would have to pay for the cart rental, for the hot dogs and other materials, and for someone to run the cart while you were away. After you paid your employee and yourself, paid for the food and materials you used, paid the rent on the cart, and paid your taxes, any money left over would be profit.

Keep in mind that profit is over and above the money you pay yourself in salary. You could use any profit you make to rent or buy a second cart and hire other employees. After a few summers, you might have a dozen carts employing dozens of workers.

Even among companies that do make a profit, not all make the same amount. Those companies that take the most risk may make the most profit. There is high risk, for example, in making a new kind of automobile.[6] With a small loan from his parents and a contract with General Motors, Mike Lazaridis founded Research In Motion Ltd. <*www.rim.com*> in 1984 and built it into a world leader in the mobile telecommunications market.[7] Big risks, big profits.

As a potential business owner, you need to do research (e.g., talk to other business people and read business publications) to find the right balance between risk and profit for you. Different people have different tolerances for risk. To decide which is the best choice for you, you have to calculate the risks and the potential rewards of each decision. The more risks you take, the higher the rewards may be. In Chapter 7, you will learn more about the risks and rewards that come with starting a business.

Standard of Living and Quality of Life

Entrepreneurs such as Mike Lazaridis not only became wealthy themselves, they also provide employment for many other people. Businesses and their employees pay taxes to the different levels of government (federal, provincial, and municipal). This money is used to build hospitals, schools, libraries, playgrounds, roads, and other public facilities. Taxes also help to keep the environment clean, support people in need, and provide police and fire protection. Thus, the wealth businesses generate and the taxes they pay help everyone in their communities. A country's businesses are part of an economic system that contributes to the standard of living and quality of life for everyone in the country (and, potentially, the world). How has the most recent economic slowdown affected the standard of living and quality of life in Canada?

Having a high quality of life means having the freedom, safety, health, and leisure to enjoy the satisfaction that goods and services can provide. How does a country's standard of living contribute to its citizens' quality of life?

The term **standard of living** refers to the amount of goods and services people can buy with the money they have. For example, Canada has one of the highest standards of living in the world, even though workers in some other countries may on average make more money per hour. How can that be? Prices for goods and services might be higher than in Canada, so a person in that country can buy less than what a person in Canada can buy with the same amount of money. For example, a bottle of domestic beer may cost $5.79 in Japan and $4.98 in Canada.[8]

Often, goods cost more in one country than another because of higher taxes and stricter government regulations. Finding the right level of taxes and regulation is important in making a country or city prosperous. We'll explore that issue more deeply in Chapter 2. At this point, it is enough to understand that Canada enjoys a high standard of living partly because of the wealth created by its businesses.

standard of living
The amount of goods and services people can buy with the money they have.

The term **quality of life** refers to the general well-being of a society in terms of its political freedom, natural environment, education, health care, safety, amount of leisure, and rewards that add to the satisfaction and joy that other goods and services provide. Maintaining a high quality of life requires the combined efforts of businesses, non-profit organizations (to be discussed soon), and government agencies. The more money businesses create, the more is potentially available to improve the quality of life for everyone. It's important to be careful, however. Working to build a higher standard of living may lower the quality of life if it means less time with family or more stress.[9]

Illustrate the importance of stakeholders and non-profit organizations to business activities.

Responding to the Various Business Stakeholders

Stakeholders are all of the people who stand to gain or lose by the policies and activities of a business and whose concerns the business needs to address. As noted in Figure 1.1, stakeholders include many different groups such as customers, employees, financial institutions (e.g., banks and credit unions), investors (e.g., shareholders), environmentalists, and government. Don't forget that businesses can also influence government policies through the activities and efforts of their associations, lobbyists, and trade unions.

The challenge of the twenty-first century will be for organizations to balance, as much as possible, the needs of all stakeholders. For example, the need for the business to make profits must be balanced against the needs of employees for sufficient income. The need to stay competitive may call for offshoring jobs to other countries, recognizing that this sound business strategy might do harm to the community because jobs would be lost.[10] **Offshoring** entails sourcing part of the purchased inputs outside of the country.[11] **Outsourcing** means contracting with other companies to do some or all of the functions of a firm, such as production or accounting.[12]

quality of life
The general well-being of a society in terms of its political freedom, natural environment, education, health care, safety, amount of leisure, and rewards that add to the satisfaction and joy that other goods and services provide.

stakeholders
All the people who stand to gain or lose by the policies and activities of a business.

offshoring
Sourcing part of the purchased inputs outside of the country.

You may be wondering, how are the terms outsourcing and offshoring that different? A Statistics Canada <*www.statcan.gc.ca*> report highlights the distinction. As stated, "Outsourcing decisions affect the boundaries of the firm—what production takes place within the firm and what is purchased from outside the firm. Changes in offshoring may be, but are not necessarily, related to changes in outsourcing. They involve decisions both to purchase outside of the firm and to do so from abroad. Considerations to do the latter are at the heart of the study of international trade. Interest in outsourcing arises because it may foretell changes in industrial structure. Interest in offshoring arises because it may signify changes in international trading patterns."[13]

Companies have gone from outsourcing production jobs to offshoring research and development and design functions. Such decisions may prove disastrous to these firms

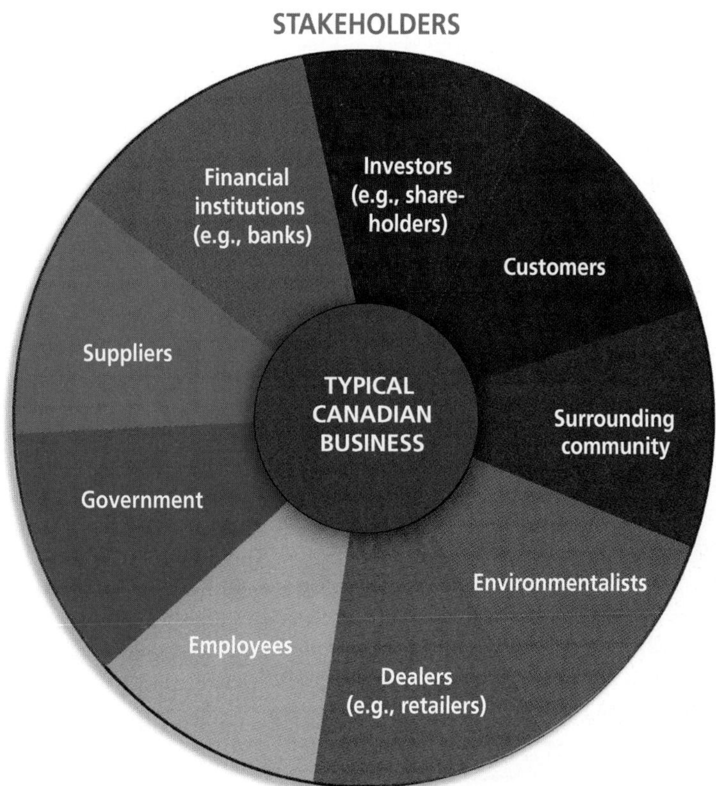

Figure 1.1

A Business and Its Stakeholders

Often the needs of a firm's various stakeholders will conflict. For example, paying employees more may cut into shareholders' profits. Balancing such demands is a major role of business managers.

doing the offshoring if the overseas companies use the information to produce their own competitive products.[14] In Canada, most of the offshoring that occurs is with the United States, though there has been some increase over the last decade with developing countries.[15]

outsourcing
Assigning various functions, such as accounting, production, security, maintenance, and legal work to outside organizations.

It is legal to outsource and offshore, but is that best for all stakeholders, including workers? Business leaders must make decisions based on all factors, including the need to make a profit. As you can see, pleasing all stakeholders is not easy and it calls for trade-offs that are not always pleasing to one or another stakeholder. Keep in mind that regardless of temptations, company officials do have a responsibility to their stakeholders.

Such trade-offs are also apparent in the political arena. As will be discussed in Chapter 4, governments make policies that affect many stakeholders. However, budget limitations force governments to make difficult choices, and these decisions are often not popular. Consequently, after years of insufficient funding, any changes in the areas of the environment, health care, and education generate a lot of attention. As you will learn, balancing the demands of stakeholders is not limited to for-profit businesses.

Using Business Principles in Non-Profit Organizations

Despite their efforts to satisfy all of their stakeholders, businesses cannot do everything that is needed to make a community all it can be. Non-profit organizations—such as schools, hospitals, and charities—also make a major contribution to the welfare of society. A **non-profit organization** is an organization whose goals do not include making a personal profit for its owners or organizers. Non-profit organizations often do strive for financial gains, but such gains are used to meet their social or educational goals rather than for personal profit.

non-profit organization
An organization whose goals do not include making a personal profit for its owners or organizers.

Non-profit organizations also include the different levels of government in our country. They are increasingly involved in business decisions and operations even though the primary purpose is not to generate a profit. We will consider the role of government in business in Chapter 4.

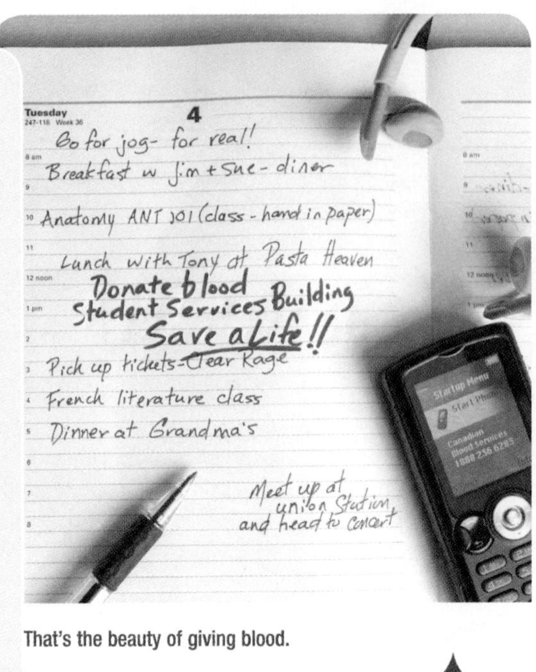

▸ Non-profit organizations use for-profit business principles to achieve results. Canadian Blood Services <*www.blood.ca*> is a national not-for-profit charitable organization whose mission is to manage the blood and blood products supply for Canadians. Did you know that approximately every minute of every day, someone in Canada needs blood? The good news is that one blood donation—in just one hour—can save up to three lives. This is a poster that has been used in schools across Canada with the purpose of encouraging people to donate blood.

Social entrepreneurs are people who use business principles to start and manage non-profit organizations and help address social issues. Muhammad Yunus won the Nobel Prize for starting the Grameen Bank <*www.grameen.com*>, a microlending organization that provides small loans to entrepreneurs too poor to qualify for traditional loans. Yunus has started 30 of what he calls social businesses that do not have profit as their goal. One, for example, provides cataract operations for a fraction of the usual cost.[16] The Spotlight on Small Business box features the Canadian Social Entrepreneurship Foundation. Would you consider becoming a social entrepreneur?

Your interests may lead you to work for a non-profit organization. Millions of professionals, staffers, volunteers, and donors work for Canada's approximately 200,000 charities and non-profit organizations.[17] This doesn't mean, however, that you shouldn't study business. If you want to start or work in a non-profit organization, you'll need to learn business skills such as information management, leadership, marketing, and financial management. Therefore, the knowledge and skills you acquire in this and other business courses will be useful for careers in any organization, including non-profits. We shall explore entrepreneurship right after the Progress Assessment.

SPOTLIGHT ON SMALL BUSINESS

Social Entrepreneurship

The Canadian Social Entrepreneurship Foundation (CSEF) site <*www.csef.ca*> was created by Jason Carvalho to spur innovation and "bridge the gap" that was developing between the non-profit, business, and government sectors. The motto of the CSEF is taken from a famous line which is as follows: "Some men and women see things as they are and say, 'Why?' I dream things that never were and say, 'Why not?'"

To begin to bridge this gap, CSEF looks for social entrepreneurs who are under the age of 40 and who want to develop and take a new service or product to market. Although social entrepreneurs share some characteristics and techniques with traditional business entrepreneurs—for example, an emphasis on innovation and the utilization of time-tested business theories and practices—their work and impact span the sectors noted earlier.

CSEF, which is sixty percent a virtual organization, provides access to funding, media resources, mentorship and support, and an online community. It invests in Canadian social enterprises that produce revenue and focus on specific areas such as (social) inventors, children and youth (e.g., employing at-risk youth), the environment (e.g., clean technologies and energy efficiency), and civic engagement.

Can you see yourself as a social entrepreneur? You could become a small-business owner in Canada, but you could also use the business skills you learn in this course to be a social entrepreneur in Canada and other countries. Think of the possibilities.

Source: The Canadian Social Entrepreneurship Foundation. Copyright 2010, www.csef.ca. Used with permission.

PROGRESS ASSESSMENT

- What is the difference between revenue and profit?
- What is risk, and how is it related to profit?
- What is the difference between standard of living and quality of life?
- What do the terms stakeholders, offshoring, and outsourcing mean?

ENTREPRENEURSHIP VERSUS WORKING FOR OTHERS

Explain how entrepreneurship is critical to the wealth of an economy, and list the five factors of production that contribute to wealth.

There are two ways to succeed in business. One is to rise up through the ranks of large companies such as Royal Bank of Canada <*www.rbcroyalbank.com*> or Manulife Financial <*www.manulife.ca*>. The advantage of working for others is that somebody else assumes the entrepreneurial risk and provides you with benefits such as paid vacation time and health insurance. It's a good option and many people choose it.

The other, riskier path, is to start your own business and become an entrepreneur. While you may hear about success stories, keep in mind that many small businesses fail each year; thus, it takes a brave person to start a small business or to turn a business around. Furthermore, as an entrepreneur you don't receive any benefits such as paid vacation time and health insurance. You have to provide them for yourself!

Before you take on the challenge of entrepreneurship it makes sense to study the experiences of those who have succeeded to learn the process. Consider the example of Ron Joyce, who in 1963 purchased a Dairy Queen outlet <*www.dairyqueen.com/ca*> Two years later, he invested $10,000 to become a franchisee in the first Tim Hortons <*www.timhortons.com*> (we will discuss franchising in Chapter 6). By 1967, he became a full partner in the company with Tim Horton. In the early years, both partners worked on expanding the business. When Horton died in 1974, Joyce became the sole owner of the chain. In the following years, he continued to develop the business, spending hundreds of hours piloting his plane in search of new franchise opportunities and doing everything from training new store owners to baking donuts. When Joyce sold the chain to Wendy's for US$450 million in 1995, there were more than 1,000 Tim Hortons restaurants. Today, Tim Hortons is Canada's largest publicly-traded quick service restaurant chain, with 3,871 systemwide restaurants, including 3,225 in Canada and 645 in the United States.[18] What you can learn from successful entrepreneurs like Ron Joyce is that you need to find something that you love to do. Before he became an entrepreneur, Joyce was a police officer. He started to get experience in business with his Dairy Queen outlet, and from there went on to great success with his Tim Hortons restaurants. While there were many challenges along the way, he was willing to put in the long hours needed to be successful. In addition to the original coffee and donut offerings, he continuously added new products to the restaurants to meet his customers' needs.

This is also the case for Ron Foxcroft, the focus of the chapter-opening Profile. Twenty-five years after introducing the Fox 40 Classic Whistle, Fox 40 International Inc. sells an expanded whistle product line, pro coaching boards, mouthguards, and Fox 40 marine products (e.g., first aid and safety kits).

Small businesses and entrepreneurs contribute enormously to the Canadian economy. While these terms have been briefly mentioned in this chapter, be aware that more time will be spent discussing their significance in Chapters 6 and 7. After all, without the initial ideas and risks taken by entrepreneurs, we would not have successful businesses today.

The Importance of Entrepreneurs to the Creation of Wealth

Have you ever wondered why some countries are relatively wealthy and others are poor? Economists have been studying the issue of wealth creation for many years. They began the process by studying potential sources of wealth to determine which are the most important. Over time, they came up with five factors that seemed to contribute to wealth, which they called **factors of production**. Figure 1.2 describes those five factors, which are:

factors of production
The resources used to create wealth: land, labour, capital goods, entrepreneurship, and knowledge.

1. Land (or natural resources)
2. Labour (workers)
3. Capital Goods (This includes machines, tools, buildings, or whatever else is used in the production of goods. It does not include money. Money is used to buy factors of production but is not always considered to be a factor by itself.)
4. Entrepreneurship
5. Knowledge

Traditionally, business and economics textbooks have emphasized only four factors of production: land, labour, capital, and entrepreneurship. But management expert and business consultant Peter Drucker said that the most important factor of production in our economy is and always will be *knowledge.*

What do we find when we compare the factors of production in rich and poor countries? Some poor countries often have plenty of land and natural resources. Russia, for example, has vast areas of land with many resources such as timber and oil, but it is not considered a rich country (yet). In contrast, Japan is a relatively rich country but is poor in land and other natural resources. Therefore, land isn't the critical element for wealth creation.

Most poor countries such as Mexico have many labourers, so labour is not the primary source of wealth today. Labourers need to find work to make a contribution; that is, they need entrepreneurs to provide jobs for them. Furthermore, capital—machinery and tools—is now easy for firms to find in world markets, so capital isn't the missing ingredient. Capital is not productive without entrepreneurs to put it to use.

What makes countries rich today is a combination of *entrepreneurship* and the effective use of *knowledge.* Entrepreneurs use what they've learned (knowledge) to grow their businesses and increase wealth. Economic and political freedom also matter.

Figure 1.2

The Five Factors of Production

Land	Land and other natural resources are used to make homes, cars, and other products.
Labour	People have always been an important resource in producing goods and services, but many people are now being replaced by technology.
Capital Goods	Capital includes machines, tools, buildings, and other means of manufacturing.
Entrepreneurship	All the resources in the world have little value unless entrepreneurs are willing to take the risk of starting businesses to use those resources.
Knowledge	Information technology has revolutionized business, making it possible to quickly determine wants and needs and to respond with desired goods and services.

The business environment either encourages or discourages entrepreneurship. That helps explain why some provinces and cities in Canada grow rich while others remain relatively poor. In the following section, we'll explore what makes up the business environment and how to build an environment that encourages growth and job creation.

PROGRESS ASSESSMENT

- What are some of the advantages of working for others?
- What benefits do you lose by being an entrepreneur, and what do you gain?
- What are the five factors of production? Which ones seem to be the most important for creating wealth?

To create wealth for its citizens, a country requires more than natural resources like timber. No matter how vast its forests or other inputs like labour, fuel, and waterways, a country needs the efforts of entrepreneurs and the skill and knowledge to produce goods and services. How can the government support entrepreneurship and the spread of knowledge?

THE BUSINESS ENVIRONMENT

The **business environment** consists of the surrounding factors that either help or hinder the development of businesses. Figure 1.3, which summarizes some of the points discussed in this chapter, shows the six elements in the business environment:

1. The legal environment
2. The economic environment
3. The technological environment
4. The competitive environment
5. The social environment
6. The global environment

Businesses that create wealth and jobs grow and prosper in a healthy environment. Thus, creating the right business environment is the foundation for social benefits of all kinds, including good schools, clear air and water, good health care, and low rates of crime. Businesses normally cannot control their environment, but they need to monitor it carefully and do what they can to adapt as it changes.

business environment
The surrounding factors that either help or hinder the development of businesses.

The Legal Environment

State the six elements that make up the business environment and explain why the business environment is important to organizations.

People are willing to start new businesses if they believe that the risk of losing their money isn't too great. Part of that decision is affected by how governments work with businesses. Governments can do a lot to lessen the risk of starting and running a business through the laws (also known as Acts) that are passed by its elected officials. The Constitution Act defines the powers that can be exercised by the different levels of government. In Chapter 4, we will review some of the responsibilities of these different levels.

Each legislation authorizes an agency (such as Industry Canada) to write regulations that interpret the law in more detail and indicate how it will be implemented and enforced. Consequently, **regulations** consist of restrictions that provincial and federal laws place on businesses with respect to the conduct of their activities.[19] Regulations exist to protect consumers as well as businesses.[20] In Chapter 4, you will be introduced to some government departments that deal with businesses.

regulations
Restrictions that provincial and federal laws place on businesses with respect to the conduct of their activities.

Figure 1.3

Today's Dynamic Business Environment

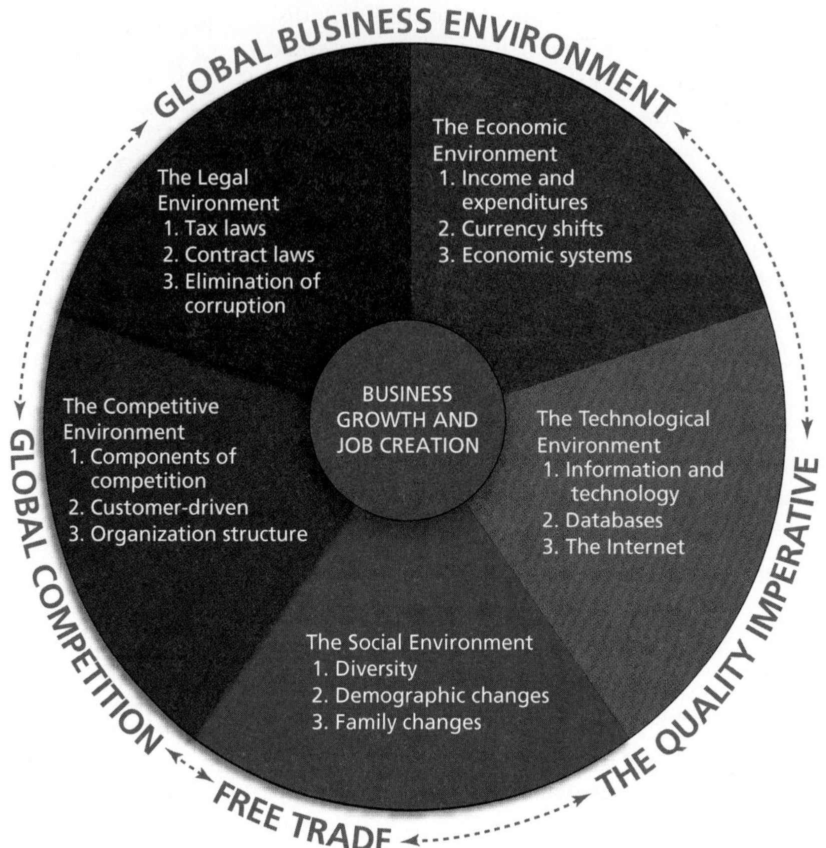

Laws Affect Business

Businesses need to be aware of the laws that are in place (or may be passed) that will affect their operations. For example, government can keep taxes and regulations to a minimum, thereby encouraging entrepreneurship and increasing wealth. Entrepreneurs are looking for a high return on investment (ROI), including the investment of their time. If the government takes away much of what the business earns through high taxes, ROI may no longer be worth the risk. Provinces and territories that have high taxes and restrictive regulations tend to drive entrepreneurs out, while areas with low taxes and less restrictive regulations can attract entrepreneurs.

The government can also lessen the risks of entrepreneurship by passing laws that enable business people to write contracts that are enforceable in court. You can read more about the importance of business law in Canada in the appendix at the end of Chapter 4.

There are many laws in Canada that are intended to minimize corruption, and businesses can flourish when these laws are followed. Nonetheless, corrupt and illegal activities at some companies do negatively affect the business community and the economy as a whole. The news media widely reports these scandals.[21] Ethics is so important to the success of businesses and the economy as a whole that we feature ethics boxes in each chapter and devote Chapter 5 to the subject.

The capitalist system relies heavily on honesty, integrity, and high ethical standards. Failure of those fundamentals can weaken the whole system as was the case with the subprime mortgage scandal in the United States.[22] The faltering economy of 2008–2009 was due in large part to such failure. Some mortgage lenders, for instance, failed to do the research necessary to ensure their borrowers' creditworthiness. Many subprime borrowers forfeited their loans. The ripple effects of these unpaid debts not only cost many people their homes but also reduced the value of housing across the country and made it difficult even for business borrowers to get new loans. Part of the blame for this economic disaster can be placed on the borrowers who didn't tell the truth about their income or who otherwise deceived the lenders. This subprime mortgage crisis will be discussed in Chapter 4.

It is easy to see the damage caused by the poor moral and ethical behaviour of some business people. What is not so obvious is the damage caused by the moral and ethical lapses of the everyday consumer—that is, you and me. The Making Ethical Decisions box discusses that issue in more depth.

Starting a business in some countries is much harder than in others. In India, for example, a person has to go through an extraordinary and time-consuming bureaucratic process to get permission to start a business—and with no certainty of success. Nonetheless, those businesses that do get started can become a major source of wealth and employment. This jewellery business is one example. Can you imagine the opportunities and wealth that might be created with just a little more freedom in this country of over one billion people?

The Economic Environment

The economic environment affects both businesses and consumers. For our discussion, the focus will be on businesses. The economic environment looks at income, expenditures, and resources that affect the cost of running a business. Businesses review the results of major economic indicators such as consumer spending, employment levels, and productivity. This analysis will give them a sense of what is happening in the marketplace and what actions they may need to take. Since Chapter 2 is dedicated to how economic issues affect businesses, the discussion here will be very brief.

The movement of a country's currency relative to other currencies also pertains to this environment. Currency movements are especially critical for countries, such as Canada, that generate a great deal of business activity from exports. For instance, a lower Canadian dollar value relative to the U.S. dollar makes our exports cheaper and more attractive to the U.S. market, as consumers can buy more products with their higher-valued currency. The opposite is also true. For example, in the late 2000s the Ontario economy was negatively impacted as a result of the strong Canadian dollar, which surpassed parity with the U.S. dollar in the fall of 2007. The province lost tens of thousands of manufacturing jobs in just a few years as manufacturers shifted operations overseas. Some of the province's flagship employers, like General Motors, closed factories and trimmed production at others.[23]

MAKING ETHICAL DECISIONS

How Ethical Are You?

It is easy to criticize the ethics of people whose names appear in the headlines. It is more difficult to see the moral and ethical misbehaviour of your own social group. Do you find some of the behaviours of your friends morally or ethically questionable?

A survey found that the number of employees calling in sick had reached a five-year high, and three-fifths were not sick at all. Other employees have been caught conducting personal business at work, such as paying their bills or going on Facebook. And others play video games on their work computers. We're sure you can add many more examples.

Many companies today are creating ethics codes to guide their employees' behaviour. We believe the trend toward improving ethical behaviour is so important that we've made it a major theme of this book. Throughout the text you'll see boxes like this one, called Making Ethical Decisions, that pose ethical dilemmas and ask what you would do to resolve them. The idea is for you to think about the moral and ethical dimensions of every decision you make.

Here is your ethical dilemma. You are doing a home project that requires paper, pens, and other materials available at work. You have noticed other employees taking home such materials, and are thinking about doing the same. What is the problem in this situation? What are your alternatives? What are the consequences of each alternative? Which alternative will you choose? Is your choice ethical?

One way for governments to actively promote entrepreneurship is to allow private ownership of businesses. In some countries, the government owns most businesses; thus, there's little incentive for people to work hard or create a profit. Around the world today, however, some governments are selling those businesses to private individuals to create more wealth. In Chapter 2, we will discuss the different economic systems around the world.

You should soon realize, as we continue with our brief introduction to the other business environments, that the activities occurring in one environment have an impact on the others. In short, all of the environments are linked. For example, if a new government regulation decreases business taxes, then the impact will be seen in the economic environment when one considers expenditures. Therefore, as a business person you need to scan all of the environments to make good business decisions.

The Technological Environment

Since prehistoric times, humans have felt the need to create tools that make work easier. Few technological changes have had a more comprehensive and lasting impact on businesses, however, than the emergence of information technology (IT): computers, networks, cellphones, and especially the Internet. The iPod, the iPhone, the BlackBerry and other personal digital assistants, and even social networks like MySpace and Facebook have completely changed the way people communicate with one another. Advertisers and other business people have created ways of using these tools to reach their suppliers and customers.[24]

IT is such a major force in business today that we discuss its impact on businesses throughout the entire text and in more detail in Appendix A. New technologies are dramatically changing business practices and the way businesses and customers buy and sell.[25]

Rogers Wireless, a division of Rogers Communications Inc. *<www.rogers.com>*, provides wireless voice and data services to approximately nine million customers. Are you a customer of a telecommunications firm?

How Technology Benefits Workers and You

One of the advantages of working for others is that the company often provides the tools and technology to make your job more productive. **Technology** refers to inventions or innovations from applied science or engineering research.[25] Technology can include (but is not limited to) everything from phones and copiers to computers, medical imaging devices, personal digital assistants, and the various software programs that make business processes more effective, efficient, and productive. *Effectiveness* means producing the desired result. *Efficiency* means producing goods and services using the least amount of resources. Effectiveness is usually more important than efficiency.

technology
Inventions or innovations from applied science or engineering research.

Productivity is the amount of output you generate given the amount of input (e.g., hours worked). The more you can produce in any given period of time, the more money you are worth to companies. Technology affects people in all industries. For example, Don Glenn, a farmer, uses his personal computer to compare data from the previous year's harvest with infrared satellite photos of his farm that show which crops are flourishing. He has a desktop terminal called a DTN that allows him to check the latest grain prices, and he uses AgTalk, a Web-based bulletin board, to converse with other farmers from all over the world. He also bids for bulk fertilizer on <*XSAg.com*>, an online agricultural exchange. High-tech equipment tells Glenn how and where to spread fertilizer and seed, tracks yields yard by yard, and allows him to maintain high profit margins. Companies look to technology to allow them to be more efficient, effective, and productive.

productivity
The amount of output that is generated given the amount of input.

The Growth of Electronic Commerce (E-commerce)

E-commerce is the buying and selling of goods and services over the Internet. There are two major types of e-commerce transactions: business-to-consumer (B2C) and business-to-business (B2B). According to Statistics Canada, in 2010 Canadians used the Internet to place orders for goods and services valued at $15.3 billion, up from $12.8 billion in 2007. The increase resulted from more online shoppers and a higher volume of orders.[26]

e-commerce
The buying and selling of goods and services over the Internet.

As important as the Internet has been in the consumer market, it has become even more important in the B2B market, which consists of selling goods and services from one business to another. Considered one of Canada's fastest-growing companies, such is the case for Richmond, British Columbia's Talent Technology Corporation <*www.talenttech.com*>; it's largest clients, such as Oracle and SAP, pay up to $50,000 a year for its hosted recruitment software.[27]

Traditional businesses have been learning how to deal with the competition from B2B and B2C firms, and vice versa. Some new parents would just as soon buy used items posted on Craigslist <*www.craigslist.org*> than shop in a baby-goods store.[28] Starting a business on eBay has never been easier.[29] Just consider one country: over 215 million Chinese citizens are using the Internet.[30] And what did people do before they could Google? E-commerce has become so important that we will discuss it throughout the text.

Do not confuse e-commerce with electronic business (e-business). Mostly done with Web technologies, the term **e-business** refers to any information system or application (e.g., business software) that empowers business processes.[31] While e-commerce is frequently mixed up with the term e-business, e-commerce only covers one aspect of e-business (i.e., the use of an electronic support for the commercial relationship between a company and individuals).[32]

e-business
Any information system or application that empowers business processes.

Using Technology to Be Responsive to Customers

A major theme of this text is that those businesses most responsive to customer wants and needs will succeed.[33] That realization points to one way in which even traditional retailers can use Internet technology. For example, businesses use bar codes to identify products you buy and their size, quantity, and colour. The scanner at the checkout counter can read that information and put it into a **database**, an electronic storage file in which information is kept.

database
An electronic storage file for information.

Alvin Amparo displays a selection of some of the paper shredders available at a Toronto office supply store. Whenever a TV show airs anything on identity theft, a flood of shoppers comes in to buy paper shredders, one of the best ways to guard against the crime. Once an identity thief has obtained your social insurance number, credit card number, address, and other such information, he or she can charge goods and services to your account. Do you know the limit you are liable for?

Databases enable stores to carry only the merchandise their local population wants. But because companies routinely trade database information, many retailers know what you buy and from whom you buy it. Thus they can send you catalogues and other direct mail advertising offering the kind of products you might want, as indicated by your past purchases. We discuss other ways businesses use technology to be responsive to consumers throughout the text and in more detail in Appendix A.

Unfortunately, the legitimate collection of personal customer information also opens the door to identity theft. **Identity theft** is the act of obtaining personal information about a person, such as social insurance number and/or credit card number, and using that information for illegal purposes, such as buying things with them. In response to consumer complaints, federal privacy laws have been created. The Personal Information Protection and Electronic Documents Act (PIPEDA) sets out ground rules for how private sector organizations may collect, use, or disclose personal information in the course of commercial activities.[34] If you think an organization covered by the Act is not living up to its responsibilities under the law, you have the right to lodge an official complaint.

What you should learn from these examples is to limit those to whom you give personal information. You also need antivirus software on your computer as well as a firewall and anti-spyware software. You may also want to monitor your credit report. Appendix A discusses identity theft, security, privacy, stability and other important IT issues.

Social Media Marketing[35]

In Chapter 14, you will read how some Canadian companies are in the midst of the emergence of the social media marketing era. The most common tools or platforms used by both consumers and organizations are social networking sites (e.g., Twitter and Facebook), blogs, wikis, podcasts, and other shared media sites (e.g., YouTube). To survive in this new social media world, organizations must understand, navigate, and adapt to this new landscape. Some organizations are heeding this advice. A recent study showed that twenty-five percent of businesses, in particular, small businesses and entrepreneurs, are leveraging social media as a way to connect and communicate with current and potential customers.

identity theft
Obtaining personal information about a person and using that information for illegal purposes.

PROGRESS ASSESSMENT

- List the six elements of the business environment.
- What are four ways in which the government can foster entrepreneurship?
- How does technology benefit workers and customers?

The Competitive Environment

Competition among businesses has never been greater than it is today. Some companies have found a competitive edge by focusing on quality. The goal for many companies is zero defects—no mistakes in making the product. However, simply

Figure 1.4

How Competition Has Changed Business

Traditional Businesses	Modern Businesses
Customer satisfaction	Delighting the customer[1]
Customer orientation	Customer and stakeholder orientation[2]
Profit orientation	Profit and social orientation[3]
Reactive ethics	Proactive ethics[4]
Product orientation	Quality and service orientation
Managerial focus	Customer focus

[1]*Delight* is a term from total quality management. *Bewitch* and *fascinate* are alternative terms.
[2]Stakeholders include customers, employees, investors, suppliers, dealers (e.g., retailers), and the community; the goal is to please *all* stakeholders.
[3]A social orientation goes beyond profit to do what is right and good for others.
[4]*Proactive* means doing the right thing before anyone tells you to do it. *Reactive* means responding to criticism after it happens.

making a high-quality product isn't enough to allow a company to stay competitive in world markets. Companies now have to offer both high-quality products and good value—that is, outstanding services and products at competitive prices. Figure 1.4 shows how competition has evolved to a new, world-class model.

Components of Competition[36]

When developing their strategies, companies must consider the factors that drive competition: entry, bargaining power of buyers and suppliers, existing rivalries, and substitution possibilities. Scanning the competitive environment requires a look at all of these factors.

Entry In considering the competition, a firm must assess the likelihood of new entrants. Additional producers increase industry capacity and tend to lower prices. *Barriers to entry* are business practices or conditions that make it difficult for new firms to enter the market. Barriers to entry can be in the form of capital requirements, product identity, distribution access, or switching costs. The higher the expense of the barrier, the more likely it will deter new entrants, and vice versa (e.g., barriers to exit).

Power of Buyers and Suppliers Powerful buyers exist when they are few in number, there are low switching costs, or the product represents a significant share of the buyer's total costs. This last factor leads the buyer to exert significant pressure for price competition. A supplier gains power when the product is critical to the buyer and when it has built up switching costs.

Existing Competitors and Substitutes Competitive pressure among existing firms depends on the rate of industry growth. In slow-growth settings, competition is more heated for any possible gains in market share. High fixed costs also create competitive pressures for firms to fill production capacity. (We will discuss production in Chapter 10.) For example, airlines offer discounts for making early reservations and charge penalties for changes or cancellations in an effort to fill seats, which represent a high fixed cost.

Competing by Exceeding Customer Expectations

Manufacturers and service organizations throughout the world have learned that today's customers are very demanding. Companies have to offer both high-quality products and outstanding service at competitive prices (value). Business is becoming customer-driven, not management-driven as in the past. This means that customers' wants and needs must come first.

Customer-driven organizations include Disney amusement parks <*http://disney.go.com*>, where the parks are kept clean and appeal to all ages, and Moto Photo

<*www.motophoto.com*>, which it does its best to please customers with fast, friendly service. Such companies can successfully compete against Internet firms if they continue to offer better and friendlier service. Successful organizations must now listen more closely to customers to determine their wants and needs, then adjust the firm's products, policies, and practices to meet those demands. We will explore these concepts in more depth in Chapter 14.

Competing by Restructuring and Empowerment

To meet the needs of customers, firms must give their front-line workers (e.g., office clerks, front-desk people at hotels, and salespeople) the responsibility, authority, freedom, training, and equipment they need to respond quickly to customer requests. They must allow workers to make other decisions essential to producing high-quality goods and services. The process is called **empowerment**, and we'll be talking about it throughout this book. To implement a policy of empowerment, managers must train front-line people to make decisions within certain limits, without the need to consult managers.

empowerment
Giving front-line workers the responsibility, authority, and freedom to respond quickly to customer requests.

As many companies have discovered, it sometimes takes years to restructure an organization so that managers are willing to give up some of their authority and employees are willing to assume more responsibility. We'll discuss such organizational changes and models in Chapter 9.

The Social Environment

Demography is the statistical study of the human population with regard to its size, density, and other characteristics such as age, race, gender, and income. In this book, we're particularly interested in the demographic trends that most affect businesses and career choices. The Canadian population is going through major changes that are dramatically affecting how people live, where they live, what they buy, and how they spend their time. Furthermore, tremendous population shifts are leading to new opportunities for some firms and to declining opportunities for others.

demography
The statistical study of the human population with regard to its size, density, and other characteristics such as age, race, gender, and income.

The Aging Population

The Canadian population has been aging for several decades. More people are living longer due to better medical knowledge and technology and better health habits, more exercise, and a reduction in the number of people who smoke. The portion of the population that is very young continues to decrease because of birth rates that have declined since the mid-1960s. The **baby-boom echo** (those born in the period from 1980 to 1995) represents the children of the large number of **baby boomers** (those born in the period from 1947 to 1966).[37] Some students are part of this echo generation.

baby-boom echo
A demographic group of Canadians that were born in the period from 1980 to 1995; the children of the baby boomers.

baby boomers
A demographic group of Canadians that were born in the period from 1947 to 1966.

Figure 1.5 shows the population projections for Canada. You will notice that the 5 to 19 age group is declining, while the 65 years and over age group is increasing steadily. Based on these projections, it is expected that seniors will become more numerous than children sometime around 2015. The median age of Canada's population will continue to rise as a direct result of the pronounced baby boom.

Figure 1.5
Population Distribution by Age Group

Year	0–4	5–19	20–34	35–64	65 and Above
2011	5%	17%	21%	43%	14%
2016	5%	16%	20%	42%	16%
2021	5%	16%	19%	41%	19%
2026	5%	15%	18%	40%	21%
2031	5%	15%	17%	39%	23%

Source: Adapted from "Population Projections for Canada, Provinces and Territories 2005–2031," Cat. No. 91-520-XIE, December 2005.

What do such demographics mean for you and for businesses in the future? In his book *Boom Bust & Echo: Profiting from the Demographic Shift in the 21st Century,* economist and demographer David Foot writes that demographics play a pivotal role in the economic and social life of our country. According to Foot, demographics explain about two-thirds of everything—including which products will be in demand in five years.[38]

Think of the goods and services that the middle-aged and elderly will need—anything from travel and recreation to medicine, assisted-living facilities, and smaller apartments. Don't forget the impact of aging baby boomers; more grandparents with more money in their pockets will be buying more gifts for their grandchildren. We will discuss some of the human resource management issues related to an aging population in Chapter 12.

Managing Diversity[39]

Canada has a strong multicultural population. In the last ten years, it has welcomed close to 2.7 million permanent residents. Between 2005 and 2010 alone, over 1.5 million newcomers—or an annual average of 255,123 individuals—were admitted as permanent residents. Looking at Canada's overall population, 19.8 percent of the entire population (6,186,950) is made up of people who were born outside of Canada. The high level of annual admission of immigrants and the relatively slow rate of natural growth of the population explain why the proportion of the foreign-born in the Canadian population has been increasing since the 1990s.

Companies have responded to this diverse customer base by hiring a more diversified workforce to serve them. For example, one of NAV CANADA's goals <*www.navcanada.ca*> as an employer is to recruit and retain people who have not only talent and skill but a range of backgrounds and perspectives. Company officials believe that diversity in the workplace makes everyone a higher performer and it makes the company stronger by promoting new ideas and new ways of thinking. This generates creativity and adaptability, which are basic elements in at least two areas critical to NAV CANADA's future as a global leader: problem solving and innovation.[40]

The Family Portrait (2011 Census)[41]

Every five years, Statistics Canada conducts a national census. The census provides demographic and statistical data that is used by businesses and government. For example, information that refers to living arrangements is valuable to federal, provincial, and municipal governments as it shows which parts of Canada have rising seniors populations and which parts have more young families. The data can be used to guide decisions on public services (i.e., where to build new schools and parks), immigration, health care, and labour mobility.

Canadian families are smaller, increasingly urban, and made up of an ever-broadening mix of relationships. The 2011 Census confirms what Canadians see in their day-to-day lives: married couples are still the predominant family structure (accounting for two-thirds of all families), but it is a category that continues a decades-long decline. In contrast, the proportion of common-law couples and lone parent families both increased. For the first time, common-law couples (16.7 percent) outnumbered lone-parent families (16.3 percent). Companies have implemented a host of programs in response to such trends. For example, employee plans may include parental leave, flexible work schedules, and referral services for child care or elder care.

There are now more one-person households (27.6 percent) than couple households with children (26.5 percent). About 4 in 10 young adults aged 20 to 29 live with their parents. On the topic of children, 44.5 percent of couples are without children compared to 39.2 percent with children. The numbers indicate a widening gap in a growing trend that first appeared in the 2006 Census. (The statistics are partly explained by the nature of the couples being counted. Baby boomers with children who no longer live at home are being counted in the "without children" category.) In Canada, one in five women will not have a child in their lifetime, which is a continuation of something that has been going on since the 1970s. Monica Zeniuk, who

▸ Kids & Company Ltd. *<www.kidsandcompany.ca>* is in the business of providing backup and full-time child care to employees of dozens of corporate clients such as AGF, BP, and CIBC. The services are promoted as an employee benefit and an employee-retention tool.

belongs to Babes without Babes, an Edmonton social club for child-free women, says, "The benefits of not having children are in the driveway, in our closet, and stamped in our passports...Kids are expensive. And the marriage mortality rate is huge, without the added pressure of financing a child through its life."

While this information is not exhaustive, it should give you an idea of some of the demographic trends that business people track as they develop their products and services. Can you think of some opportunities that are not currently being met as a result of some of these trends?

PROGRESS ASSESSMENT

- Describe the components of competition.
- What is empowerment?
- What social trends are evident in Canada?

The Global Environment

The global environment of business is so important that we show it as surrounding all other environmental influences in Figure 1.3. Two important environmental changes in recent years have been the growth of global competition and the increase of free trade among nations.

World trade, or *globalization,* has grown thanks to the development of efficient distribution systems (we'll talk about these later in the text) and communication advances such as the Internet. Globalization has greatly improved living standards around the world. China and India have become major competitors. For example, Lenovo <*www.lenovo.com*>, a Chinese firm, bought IBM's PC unit <*www.ibm.com*>. Shop at Walmart <*www.walmart.ca*> and most other retail stores, and you can't help but notice the number of "Made in China" stickers you see. Call for

GREENBOX

Getting Involved Personally

There are an increasing number of terms that recognize today's preoccupation with how individual and business actions impact us nationally and internationally. Some examples include *carbon footprint* (defined as the impact of human activity measured in terms of the amount of carbon dioxide it causes to be emitted into the atmosphere), *food miles* (the distance travelled from the place where food is produced to the place where it is eaten, considered in terms of the environmental damage that transporting it entails), *green tax* (a tax imposed with the intention of discouraging activities that may damage the environment), and *eco-village* (a small-scale, environmentally friendly settlement designed for sustainable living). There is little doubt humans can take action to protect the environment. What can we do now to start?

It's not necessary to change your lifestyle radically to make a difference. Simply heating or cooling your apartment or house more efficiently is a good start. Why not buy a reusable grocery bag? It is also a good idea to change your light bulbs. A 25-watt compact fluorescent bulb produces about as much light as a 100-watt conventional bulb but uses one-quarter of the energy. You can recycle paper and containers. You can walk or ride a bike instead of driving. You can reduce your use of electrical equipment and of water (pumping water takes a lot of electricity). Buy produce that is grown locally to save the energy used in shipping food from faraway places. If you're in the market for a car, you could "go green" by buying a hybrid or a small, fuel-efficient car.

The idea is to become more ecologically aware and join others throughout the world in using less energy and emitting less carbon into the atmosphere. Everyone benefits when the air is cleaner. That's part of what the green movement is all about.

Sources: Mya Frazier, "Who's in Charge of Green?" *Advertising Age*, 9 June 2008; Anne Underwood, "10 Fixes for the Planet," *Newsweek*, 14 April 2008; Rebecca Smith, "A Little Knowledge . . . ," *The Wall Street Journal*, 30 June 2008; Arden Dale, "Green Products Gain from New Price Equation," *The Wall Street Journal*, 24 June 2008; and Associated Press, "Wardrobe Malfunction Joins the Credit Crunch," *Toronto Star*, 16 August 2008, www.thestar.com/article/478662.

computer help, and you are as likely to be talking with someone in India as someone in Canada.

World trade has its benefits and costs. You'll read much more about its importance in Chapter 3 and in the Reaching Beyond Our Borders boxes in each text part.

How Global Changes Affect You

As businesses expand to serve global markets, new jobs will be created in both manufacturing and service industries. Global trade also means global competition. The students who will prosper will be those prepared for the markets of tomorrow. Rapid changes create a need for continuous learning, so be prepared to continue your education throughout your career. You'll have every reason to be optimistic about job opportunities in the future if you prepare yourself well.

Climate Change

Few issues have captured the attention of the international business community more than climate change.[42] **climate change** is the movement of the temperature of the planet up or down over time. The issue now is global warming, but the issue may become global cooling if the sun starts giving off less heat. Some of the world's largest firms—including General Electric <*www.ge.com/ca*>, Coca-Cola <*www.cocacola.ca*>, Shell <*www.shell.ca*>, Nestlé <*www.nestle.ca*>, DuPont <*http://www2.dupont.com/inclusive-innovations/en-us/gss/sustainability.html*>, Johnson & Johnson <*www.jnjcanada.com*>, British Airways <*www.britishairways.com*>, and Shanghai Electric <*www.shanghai-electric.com/en*>—say the evidence for climate change is overwhelming. Saving energy and producing products that cause less harm to the environment is a trend called **greening**. Greening has become such a pervasive issue that we devote boxes to that subject throughout the text. See the Green Box for things you can do to contribute to the cause.

climate change
The movement of the temperature of the planet up or down over time.

greening
The trend toward saving energy and producing products that cause less harm to the environment.

Give examples of how the service sector has replaced manufacturing as the principal provider of jobs, but why manufacturing remains vital for Canada.

THE EVOLUTION OF CANADIAN BUSINESS

Many managers and workers are losing their jobs in major manufacturing firms. Businesses in Canada have become so productive that, compared to the past, fewer workers are needed in industries that produce goods. If global competition and improved technology are putting skilled people out of work, should we be concerned about the prospect of high unemployment rates and low incomes? Where will the jobs be when you graduate? These important questions prompt us to look briefly at the manufacturing and service sectors.

Progress in the Agricultural and Manufacturing Industries

Canada has seen strong economic development since the nineteenth century. The agricultural industry led the way, providing food for Canadians and people in other parts of the world. Inventions such as the harvester and cotton gin did much to make farming successful, as did ongoing improvements to such equipment. The modern farming industry has become so efficient through the use of technology that the number of farms has dropped. Due to increased competition, many of the farms that existed even 50 years ago have been replaced by some huge farms, some merely large farms, and some small but highly specialized farms. The loss of farm workers over the past century is not a negative sign. It is instead an indication that Canadian agricultural workers are more productive.

Most farmers who lost their jobs went to work in factories. The manufacturing industry, much like agriculture, used technology to become more productive. The consequence, as in farming, was the elimination of many jobs. Again, the loss to society is minimal if the wealth created by increased productivity and efficiency creates new jobs elsewhere. This is exactly what has happened over the past 50 years. Many workers in the industrial sector found jobs in the service sector. Most of those who can't find work today are people who need retraining and education to become qualified for jobs that now exist.

Canada's Manufacturing Industry

The goods-producing sector includes the manufacturing, construction, utilities, agriculture, forestry, fishing, mining, quarrying, and the oil and gas industries. Of this sector, manufacturing employs a little over ten percent of Canada's working population, as noted in Figure 1.6. Manufacturing is diverse in Canada and it includes food, beverage, clothing, chemical, machinery, wood, and petroleum and coal products manufacturing.[43]

Tens of thousands of Canadian jobs were lost in the late 2000s. The rising Canadian dollar and increasing global competition were two of the reasons for these

Figure 1.6

The Importance of the Services-Producing and Goods-Producing Sectors in Canada

Canada is a service economy, where the majority of jobs are generated in the services-producing sector. This table highlights the importance of each sector, as well as the two largest-employer industries in each.

	Number of Employed (thousands)	Total Workforce (percent)
Total Employed in Canada	**17,306.2**	**100.0**
Services-Producing Sector	**13,501.3**	**77.7**
Trade	2,669.9	15.4
Health Care and Social Assistance	2,091.5	12.1
Goods-Producing Sector	**3,804.9**	**22.3**
Manufacturing	1,760.2	10.2
Construction	1,262.2	7.3

Source: Statistics Canada, "Employment by Industry," CANSIM Table 282-0008, http://www40.statcan.gc.ca/l01/cst01/labor10a-eng.htm, 6 January 2012. Reproduced and distributed on an "as is" basis with the permission of Statistics Canada.

▶ The entire process of growing food and getting it to our tables is so smooth that it's easy to take the agriculture industry for granted. But behind those well-stocked supermarkets is an army of farmers and distributors who supply our needs. Use of technology has led to increased productivity and made farmers more efficient, resulting in larger farms. This trend has meant less expensive food for us, but a continual reduction in the number of small, family-run farms. Is it still possible for small farms to be successful, and if so, how?

losses. Despite such losses, manufacturing still remains an important contributor to the Canadian economy. The Canadian Manufacturers & Exporters association highlights some of the reasons why this sector is important to Canada:

- Manufacturing sales topped $540 billion in 2010;
- Every $1 of manufacturing in Canada generates $3.05 in total economic activity; and
- Manufacturing accounts for two-thirds of all business investment in research and development in Canada.[44]

While the manufacturing sector is much smaller today than it was 25 years ago, it is still clearly an integral part of our business economy. We will discuss the manufacturing sector and production in more detail in Chapter 10.

Progress in Service Industries

In the past, the dominant industries in Canada produced goods such as steel, railroads, and machine tools. The shift in Canada's employment makeup began slowly early in the twentieth century, and has accelerated rapidly since the 1950s. Today, the leading firms are in services (such as legal, health, telecommunications, entertainment, financial services, etc.). As noted in Figure 1.6, the services-producing sector employs almost 78 percent of the working population.

There are several reasons why there has been growth in this sector. First, technological improvements have enabled businesses to reduce their payrolls while increasing their output. Since staffing has been downsized by many companies, business has become more complex and specialized companies have relied more heavily on outside services firms. Secondly, as large manufacturing companies seek to become more efficient, they contract out an increasing number of services, creating more opportunities for business people. Other service firms have risen or expanded rapidly to provide traditional services that used to be performed by women at home. Since many women have entered the workforce, there is increased demand for food preparation, child care, and household maintenance, to name just a few services.

Chances are very high that you'll work in a service job at some point in your career. Another bit of good news is that there are *more* high-paying jobs in the services-producing sector than in the goods-producing sector. High-paying service-sector jobs abound in health care, accounting, finance, entertainment, telecommunications, architecture, law, software engineering, and more. Projections are that some areas of the service sector will grow rapidly, while others may have much slower growth. The strategy for graduates is to remain flexible, find out where jobs are being created, and move when appropriate. Such was the case for Toronto-based Mood Media Corporation <*www.moodmedia.com*>, which was singled out by PROFIT 200 as Canada's Fastest-Growing Company:

> The company provides in-store media. What, you may ask, is in-store media? It's the background music, video, signage and even customized scents intended to make customers stay longer and open their wallets wider. "When you walk into a store, the music you're listening to is likely from us," says Lorne Abony, Chief Executive Office. The same may be true for the promos and music you hear while on hold with your bank, or the advertising displays at a Burger King. "We help our customers sell more," says Abony. "By making the store sound good, look good, and in some cases smell good, consumers feel better and stick around." [45]

Your Future in Business

Despite the growth in the service sector, the service era now seems to be coming to a close as a new era is beginning. We're now in the midst of an information-based global revolution that will alter all sectors of the economy. It's exciting to think about the role you'll play in that revolution. You may be a leader; that is, you may be one of the people who will implement the changes and accept the challenges of world competition based on world quality standards. This book will introduce you to some of the concepts that will make such leadership possible, not just in business but also in government agencies and non-profit organizations. Business cannot prosper in the future without the co-operation of government and social leaders throughout the world.

PROGRESS ASSESSMENT

- What changes have affected the global environment?
- Give examples of how the service sector has replaced manufacturing as the principal provider of jobs, but why manufacturing remains vital for Canada.
- Why is the services-producing sector important to the economy?

SUMMARY

Describe the relationship of businesses' profit-to-risk assumption.

A business is any activity that seeks to provide goods and services to others while operating at a profit.

What are the relationships between risk, profit, and loss?

Profit is money a business earns above and beyond the money it spends for salaries and other expenses. Business people make profits by taking risks. Risk is the chance an entrepreneur takes of losing time and money on a business that may not prove profitable. A loss occurs when a business's costs and expenses are more than its revenues.

Illustrate the importance of stakeholders and non-profit organizations to business activities.

Stakeholders include customers, employees, investors (e.g., shareholders), suppliers, dealers, people in the local community, environmentalists, and government.

How do non-profit organizations differ from profit-seeking organizations?
A non-profit organization is an organization whose goals do not include making a personal profit for its owners or organizers.

Which stakeholders are most important to a business?
The goal of business leaders is to try to balance the needs of all stakeholders and still make a profit. Some businesses put the needs of shareholders above the other interests, but most businesses today seek a balance among the needs of the various stakeholders.

Explain how entrepreneurship is critical to the wealth of an economy, and list the five factors of production that contribute to wealth.

Entrepreneurs are people who risk time and money to start and manage a business.

What importance does entrepreneurship hold in the list of the five factors of production?
Businesses use five factors of production: land (natural resources), labour (workers), capital goods (buildings and machinery), entrepreneurship, and knowledge. Of these, the most important are entrepreneurship and knowledge, because without them land, labour, and capital are not of much use.

State the six elements that make up the business environment and explain why the business environment is important to organizations.

The business environment consists of the surrounding factors that either help or hinder the development of businesses. The six elements are the legal environment, the economic environment, the technological environment, the competitive environment, the social environment, and the global environment.

Explain why the business environment is important to organizations.
Scanning the business environment on a continual basis is important to organizations so that they can take advantage of trends. These trends could affect the organization's ability to achieve its objectives, steer clear of threats, or take advantage of new opportunities.

Give examples of how the service sector has replaced manufacturing as the principal provider of jobs, but why manufacturing remains vital for Canada.

Canada has evolved from an economy based on manufacturing to one based on services.

Why is manufacturing still a vital industry for Canada?
While the services-producing sector employs almost 78 percent of the working population, the manufacturing industry employs approximately 10 percent of workers. Every $1 of manufacturing in Canada generates $3.05 in total economic activity. Manufacturing accounts for two-thirds of all business investment in research and development in Canada.

KEY TERMS

baby-boom echo
baby boomers
business
business environment
climate change
database
demography
e-business
e-commerce
empowerment
entrepreneur
factors of production
goods
greening
identity theft

loss
non-profit organization
offshoring
outsourcing
productivity
profit
quality of life
regulations
revenue
risk
services
stakeholders
standard of living
technology

CRITICAL THINKING

Imagine that you are thinking of starting a restaurant in your community. Answer the following questions.

1. You need to consider whether you will purchase locally-grown produce versus foreign-grown produce. What are the advantages and disadvantages of using either, especially if the foreign-grown produce is cheaper or of better quality?
2. What are some of the things you could do to benefit your community other than provide jobs and generate tax revenue?
3. You are considering paying your employees the minimum wage. Do you think that you would attract better employees if your wages were higher?
4. How might you be affected by the six environmental factors outlined in this chapter? Which factor(s) might have the biggest impact on your business?

DEVELOPING WORKPLACE SKILLS

1. Make a list of non-profit organizations in your community that might offer you a chance to learn some of the skills you'll need in the job you hope to have when you graduate. How could you make time in your schedule to volunteer or work at one or more of those organizations? Write a letter to a non-profit organization to inquire about such opportunities. Hint: You can identify organizations and events in your city by going to 411 Local Search <*www.411.ca*> and inputting "non profit organizations and events *your city name*" in the cell under Business, near the top. A less targeted source is the Charity Village Web site <*www.charityvillage.com*>. Charity Village supports Canada's charities and non-profit organizations as well as the stakeholders who support them.
2. Form into teams of four or five and discuss creating an entirely new product or service. What value does this new product or service create? Who are the stakeholders for this new product or service? Could an entrepreneur readily produce it or would its chance of success be higher if it was produced by a large company? Explain.
3. Imagine that you are a local business person who has to deal with the various issues involved with outsourcing. You want to begin with the facts. How many jobs have been lost to outsourcing in your area, if any? Are there any foreign firms in your area that are creating jobs (insourcing)? You may want to use the Internet to find the data you need.
4. Form into teams of four or five and discuss the technological and e-commerce revolutions. How many students now shop for goods and services online? What have been their experiences? What other technological aids (e.g., cellphones and personal digital assistants) do they use? What products do they plan on buying in the next year?

ANALYZING MANAGEMENT DECISIONS

Canada's Fastest-Growing Companies

Every year, *PROFIT* magazine publishes a list of Canada's fastest-growing companies. The importance of many of the points we discussed in this chapter is evident in a recent issue, especially when one considers the breakdown among the types of companies. Services providers dominate the marketplace, which reinforces that Canada is a service economy. Here is a breakdown of the Top 100:

Focus	Number of Firms
Business services	42
Manufacturing	19
Software development	12
Consumer services	7
Construction	6
Natural resource production and services	6
Wholesale/distribution	5
Retail	3

While the companies were located across Canada, Ontario continued to support the largest share of these companies:

Ontario	42
Alberta	23
British Columbia	19
Quebec	12
Manitoba	2
Atlantic Canada	2

Clearly, great teams start with great people. Interesting statistics about the Top 100 company leaders include:

1. The age ranges from 27 to 67, with an average age of 43 years.
2. A substantial share (28 percent) are foreign-born.
3. An overwhelming 94 percent are male.
4. The average yearly compensation was $398,000.

What makes these companies leaders is that they grew rapidly, with a minimum explosive growth of 627 percent over the past five years. It does not matter whether they are high-tech or old-economy companies, manufacturing or service companies, they all are exceptional. A remarkable assortment of products and services are offered by these companies. Examples include child-care centres, IT staffing services, smoothies, air purifiers, custom clothing, and organic cranberries and blueberries. Seventy-five of the companies are exporters with 69 percent of sales ($7.9 billion) being thus generated. The top export markets are the United States, the United Kingdom, other Western European countries, Eastern Europe (excluding Russia), Australia, the Pacific Rim (excluding China and Japan), Africa, and the Middle East.

Source: Jim McElgunn, "Sights for Sore Eyes," PROFIT, June 2008, 38–58.

Discussion Questions

1. Which of these data support the information discussed in the chapter? Explain your answer.
2. Why do certain provinces or regions have so many (e.g., Ontario) or few (e.g., Atlantic Canada) companies?
3. Review the most recent edition of PROFIT 200 for information on the companies that have made the list. Are there any surprises? How much has changed since these results were posted?

Practise and learn online with Connect.

APPENDIX

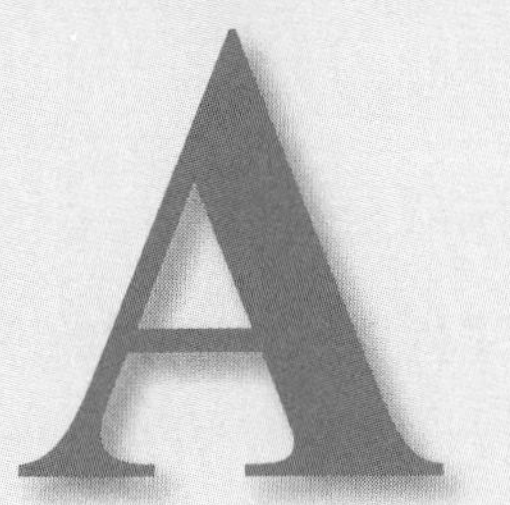

USING TECHNOLOGY TO MANAGE INFORMATION

THE ROLE OF INFORMATION TECHNOLOGY

The importance of business knowledge is nothing new—what is new is the recognition of the need to manage it like any other asset. To manage knowledge, a company needs to learn how to share information throughout the organization and to implement systems for creating new knowledge. This need is leading to new technologies that support the exchange of information among staff, suppliers, and customers. Who wins and who loses will be decided by who harnesses the technology that provides the pipeline of interaction and information flows between individuals and organizations.

In the 1970s, business technology was known as data processing. (Although many people use the words *data* and *information* interchangeably, they are different. Data are raw, unanalyzed, and unorganized facts and figures. Information is the processed and organized data that can be used for managerial decision making.) The primary purpose of data processing was to improve the flow of financial information. Data processing employees were support staff who rarely came in contact with customers.

In the 1980s, business technology became known as information systems when it moved out of the back room and into the centre of the business. Its role changed from supporting the business to doing business. Customers began to interact with a wide array of technological tools, from automated teller machines (ATMs) to voice mail. As business increased its use of information systems, it became more dependent on them.

Until the late 1980s, business technology was just an addition to the existing way of doing business. Keeping up-to-date was a matter of using new technology on old methods. But things started to change when businesses applied new technology to new methods. Business technology then became known as **information technology (IT)**, and its role became to change business.

information technology (IT)
Technology that helps companies change business by allowing them to use new methods.

Obviously, the role of the IT staff has changed as the technology itself has evolved. The chief information officer (CIO) has moved out of the back room and into the boardroom and now spends less time worrying about keeping the systems running and more time finding ways to use technology to boost business by applying technology to purchasing decisions, operational strategy, and marketing and sales. Today the role of the CIO is to help the business use technology to communicate better with others while offering better service and lower costs.[1]

How Information Technology Changes Business

Time and place have always been at the centre of business. Customers had to go to the business during certain hours to satisfy their needs. We went to the store to buy clothes. We went to the bank to arrange for a loan. Organizations decided when and where we did business with them. Today, IT allows businesses to deliver goods and services whenever and wherever it is convenient for the customer. You can order books and clothes, arrange a home mortgage loan, and buy music or a car online anytime you choose.

Consider how IT has changed the entertainment industry. If you wanted to see a movie forty years ago, you had to go to a movie theatre. Thirty-five years ago, you could wait for it to be on television. Twenty-five years ago, you could wait for it to be on cable television. Twenty years ago, you could go to a video store and rent it. Now you can order video on demand by satellite or cable, or download it to watch on your TV, computer, cell phone, iPod, or other device whenever and wherever you wish.[2]

As IT broke time and location barriers, it created new organizations and services that were independent of location. That independence brought work to people instead of people to work. Smart phones, laptop computers, netbooks, and personal digital assistants allow employees to have access to people and information as if they were in the office.[3] For example, the TSX Venture Exchange is an electronic stock exchange where buyers and sellers make trades electronically.

The way people do business drastically changes when companies increase their technological capabilities. Electronic communications can provide substantial time savings. E-mail has put an end to tedious games of telephone tag and is far faster than paper-based correspondence. Instant messaging (IM) and texting, best known as the preferred ways for millions of teenagers to communicate, is now a favourite business real-time communication tool. Internet and intranet communications using shared documents and other methods allow contributors to work on a common document without time-consuming meetings. See Figure A.1 for other examples of how information technology changes business.

The Move Toward Business Intelligence

Knowledge is information charged with enough intelligence to make it relevant and useful. Knowledge technology adds a layer of intelligence to filter appropriate information and deliver it when it is needed. In the early 2000s, as this technology became more sophisticated, it became better known as **business intelligence (BI)**. BI refers to a variety of software applications that analyze an organization's raw data and take useful insights from it. BI activities include data mining (which we will discuss later in this appendix), online analytical process, querying, and reporting.[4]

business intelligence (BI)
BI refers to a variety of software applications that analyze an organization's raw data and take useful insights from it.

Business people that use BI can focus on what's important: deciding how to react to problems and opportunities. For example, imagine you are a sales rep who

Figure A.1

How Information Technology Is Changing Business

This table shows a few ways that information technology is changing businesses, their employees, suppliers, and customers.

Organization	Technology is breaking down corporate barriers, allowing functional departments or product groups (even factory workers) to share critical information instantly.
Operations	Technology shrinks cycle times, reduces defects, and cuts waste. Service companies use technology to streamline ordering and communication with suppliers and customers.
Staffing	Technology eliminates layers of management and cuts the number of employees. Companies use computers and telecommunication equipment to create "virtual offices" with employees in various locations.
New products	Information technology cuts development cycles by feeding customer and marketing comments to product development teams quickly so that they can revive products and target specific customers.
Customer relations	Customer service representatives can solve customers' problems instantly by using companywide databases to complete tasks from changing addresses to adjusting bills. Information gathered from customer service interactions can further strengthen customer relationships.
New markets	Since it is no longer necessary for customers to walk down the street to get to stores, online businesses can attract customers to whom they wouldn't otherwise have access.

just closed a big deal. While you celebrate your success, someone in the finance department is upset because your customer never pays on time, which costs the company a lot of money. By using BI that provides the right information to the right person at the right time, you could have negotiated different payment terms with the customer, thus connecting the sales activity to the financial requirements in a seamless process.[5]

Technology changes react with one another to create more change. Maintaining the flexibility to successfully integrate these changes is crucial to business survival. Packard Bell <*www.packardbell.co.uk*> and RCA <*www.rca.com*> once dominated their industries but failed to compete effectively and lost market share. They had size and money, but not flexibility. Knowledge sharing is at the heart of keeping pace with change.

TYPES OF INFORMATION

Today, information flows into and through an organization from many different directions. The types of information that are available to businesses today include the following:[6]

- *Business Process Information.* This includes all transaction data gathered at the point of sale as well as information gained through operations like enterprise resource planning, supply chain management (these will be discussed in Chapter 10), and customer relationship management systems.
- *Physical-World Observations.* These result from the use of radio frequency identification (RFID) devices, miniature cameras, wireless access, global positioning systems (GPSs), and sensor technology—all of which have to do with where people or items are located and what they are doing. Computer chips cost pennies apiece and can be found in a wide range of products including credit cards, printer ink cartridges, baseballs, tire valves, running shoes, and vacuum

cleaners. For example, the Montreal Transit Corporation <*www.stm.info/English/a-somm.htm*> has installed RFID readers in several terminal entrances and exits.[7] As soon as a bus enters the terminal, a large electronic display board is updated so that waiting passengers know their bus is about to pull up; if a bus doesn't pass the entrance on time, the board indicates that it is delayed.[8]

- *Biological Data.* Forms of identification include improved fingerprinting technology and biometric devices that scan retinas, recognize faces and voices, and analyze DNA data. Although such information usually serves security purposes, it may customize products and services in the future.
- *Public Data.* Free and accessible, public data includes electronic traces that people leave when posting to the Internet, sending e-mail, and using IM. More and more, public data are being stored, shared, or sold.
- *Data that Indicate Personal Preferences or Intentions.* Internet shoppers leave a trail of information that can reveal personal likes and dislikes.

Managing Information

Even before the use of computers, managers had to sift through mountains of information to find what they needed to help them make decisions. Today, business people are deluged with so much data that this information overload is referred to as *infoglut,* an overabundance of data. Too much information can confuse issues rather than clarify them.

How can managers keep from getting buried in the infoglut? Stepping back to gain perspective is the key. Identify the four or five key goals you wish to reach, and eliminate information not related to them. That can cut the information flow by half. As we were gathering information to include in this appendix, we collected several hundred journal articles. Feeling the pressure of information overload, we identified the goals we wanted the appendix to accomplish and eliminated all of the articles that didn't address those goals. As we further refined our goals, the huge stack of paper gradually dropped to a manageable size.

Obviously, not all of the information that ends up on your desk will be useful. The usefulness of management information depends on four characteristics:

1. *Quality.* Quality means that the information is accurate and reliable. When the clerk at a fast-food restaurant enters your order into the cash register, it may be automatically fed to a computer, and the day's sales and profits can be calculated as soon as the store closes. The sales and expense data must be accurate, or the rest of the calculations will be wrong. Quality can be a real problem when a large number of calculations are based on questionable sales forecasts rather than actual sales.
2. *Completeness.* There must be enough information to allow you to make a decision but not so much as to confuse the issue. Today, as we have noted, the problem is often too much information rather than too little.
3. *Timeliness.* Information must reach managers quickly. E-mail and IM can let marketing, engineering, and production know about a problem with a product the same day the salesperson hears about it, so customer complaints can be handled instantly if possible, or certainly within a day. Product changes can be made on the spot using computer-integrated manufacturing, as discussed in Chapter 10.
4. *Relevance.* Different managers have different information needs. Since information systems often provide too much data, managers must learn which questions to ask to get the answers they seek.

Remember, though, that you can never read everything available. Set goals for yourself, and do the best you can.

Organizing E-mail and Electronic Files

Today's information management tools make it easier than ever for individuals and small businesses to organize information. Here are some tips for sorting e-mail and electronic files so that you can find what you need easily and quickly:[9]

1. *Use your e-mail program's organizing tools.* Most e-mail programs allow you to create folders for specific topics, projects, or clients. As you work through your inbox, move the messages you want to keep to the appropriate folders. Archive your old e-mail monthly.
2. *Use consistent file names.* Save related materials across multiple software programs under the same name, and file them together. Perhaps you've been assigned to work with a team of other students to create a sample business plan for this course. You could save all files (whether e-mail, spreadsheets, or Word documents) with a file name that begins "Business Plan Project" and store them in one folder in "My Documents."
3. *Use online backup services.* Backup, backup, backup—we've all heard how important it is to back up our files, but we often forget to follow through. Don't risk an avoidable loss. Some online services like Mozy < *www.mozy.com*> will do the job for you for only a few dollars a month. Small and midsized companies that need more storage space can use vendors such as E-Vault <*www.symantec.com/enterprise-vault*> and Iron Mountain <*www.ironmountain.ca*>.
4. *Use desktop search software.* Finding files can be easier with a desktop search software program like Google Desktop or Windows Live Search. Google Desktop has an enterprise version for midsize companies. Larger companies also have access to Google but may need to pay for additional tech support.

Storing and Mining Data

It doesn't matter how interesting your information is if people can't find it or aren't paying attention to it. How do businesses organize a data glut into useful information? The answer for many companies is a data warehouse. A *data warehouse* stores data on a single subject over a specific period of time.

The whole purpose of a data warehouse is to get data out. *Data mining* is looking for hidden patterns in a data warehouse. Data mining software discovers previously unknown relationships among the data. For example, Walmart has massive data warehouses that track sales on a minute-by-minute basis and can reveal regional and local sales trends. Using this information, Walmart customizes each store's offerings on the basis of local demand, keeping it and its suppliers informed about how each of the 70,000 products in the stores is selling and what it anticipates will sell next.

The success of data mining depends on a number of factors, but perhaps the most important is having data to mine in the first place. If organizations have a multitude of data storage systems that run on incompatible platforms, they must integrate these in some way. That's possible, but getting departments and divisions to hand over the keys to their data can be difficult.[10] The following is one such example:

> Canada Post transformed its systems to become more competitive. This did not happen overnight as it took six years and $442 million to accomplish this task. According to Aaron Nichols, general manager of Canada Post Corp.'s internal IT department, ". . . those custom-built systems were so unwieldy that every time we wanted to raise the price of stamps, it took a year to make the changes to all the systems." Surprisingly, the greatest resistance to Canada Post's transformation was from middle management: hoarding knowledge was previously a source of power for this group, and they were unused to providing all levels of staff with access to operating information.[11]

THE ROAD TO KNOWLEDGE: THE INTERNET

You already know that the Internet is a network of computers that evolved from a one-to-one communications tool to a one-to-many broadcast communications tool. Today it is the heart of *knowledge management.* Internet users can point and click their way from site to site with complete freedom. But what if you don't want just anybody to have access to your Web site? You might create an intranet.

An **intranet** is a companywide network, closed to public access, that uses Internet-type technology. To prevent unauthorized outsiders (particularly the competition) from accessing their sites, companies can construct a firewall between themselves and the outside world to protect corporate information from unauthorized users. A firewall can consist of hardware, software, or both. Firewalls allow only authorized users to access the intranet. Some companies use intranets only to publish information for employees, such as phone lists and employee policy manuals, while others create interactive applications that fully exploit the technology's possibilities. They allow employees to update their addresses or submit company forms such as supply requisitions, time sheets, or payroll forms online, eliminating paper handling and speeding decision making.

intranet
A companywide network, closed to public access, that uses Internet-type technology.

Many businesses choose to open their intranets to other, selected companies through the use of extranets. An **extranet** is a semi-private network that uses Internet technology and allows more than one company to access the same information or allows people on different servers to collaborate. One of the most common uses of extranets is to extend an intranet to outside customers. Extranets change the way we do business. No longer are the advantages of electronic data interchange (EDI) available only to the large companies that can afford such a system. Now almost all companies can use extranets to share data and process orders, specifications, invoices, and payments.

extranet
A semi-private network that uses Internet technology and allows more than one company to access the same information or allows people on different servers to collaborate.

Notice that we described an extranet as a semi-private network. This means that outsiders cannot access the network easily, but since an extranet does use public lines, knowledgeable *hackers* (people who break into computer systems for illegal purposes such as transferring funds from someone's bank account to their own without authorization) can gain unauthorized access. Most companies want a network that is as private and secure as possible, so they use *dedicated lines* (lines reserved solely for the network). There are two problems with this method: it's expensive and it limits use to computers directly linked to those lines. What if your company needs to link securely with another firm or individual for just a short time? Installing dedicated lines between companies in this case would be too expensive and time-consuming. Virtual private networks are a solution.

A **virtual private network (VPN)** is a private data network that creates secure connections, or "tunnels," over regular Internet lines.[12] It gives users the same capabilities as an extranet at a much lower cost by using shared public resources rather than private ones. Just as phone companies provide secure shared resources for voice messages, VPNs provide the same secure sharing of public resources for data. This allows for on-demand networking; an authorized user can join the network for any desired function at any time, for any length of time, while keeping the corporate network secure.

virtual private network (VPN)
A private data network that creates secure connections, or "tunnels," over regular Internet lines.

The Front Door: Enterprise Portals

How do users log on to an organization's network? Frequently, through an enterprise portal that centralizes information and transactions. Portals serve as entry points to a variety of resources, such as e-mail, financial records, schedules, and employment and benefits files. They can even include streaming video of the company's day care centre. Portals are more than simply Web pages with links. They identify users and allow them access to areas of the intranet according to their roles: customers, suppliers, employees, and so on. They make information available in one place so that users don't have to deal with a dozen different Web interfaces.

The challenge to the CIO is to integrate resources, information, reports, and so on—all of which may be in a variety of places—so that they appear seamless to the user and save money for the firm.

Broadband Technology

broadband technology
Technology that offers users a continuous connection to the Internet and allows users to send and receive mammoth files that include voice, video, and data much faster than ever before.

Internet2
The new Internet system that links government supercomputer centres and a select group of universities; it runs more than 22,000 times faster than today's public infrastructure and supports heavy-duty applications.

The more traffic on the Internet, the slower connections become. In 2010, eight out of ten Canadian households had access to the Internet, and over one-half of connected households used more than one type of device to go online (e.g., a computer and handheld device).[13] Tools to unlock these traffic jams include **broadband technology**, a continuous connection to the Internet that allows users to send and receive mammoth files that include voice, video, and data much faster than ever before. Broadband is dramatically faster than dial-up connections. It should be no surprise then to learn that about 96 percent of Canadian households with home Internet access reported a high-speed connection.[14]

Even with broadband technology, scientists and other scholars who access, transmit, and manipulate complex mathematical models, data sets, and other digital elements need a faster solution. Their answer? Create a private Internet, reserved for research purposes only. **Internet2** runs more than 22,000 times faster than today's public infrastructure and supports heavy-duty applications such as videoconferencing, collaborative research, distance education, digital libraries, and full-body simulations known as tele-immersion. A key element of Internet2 is a network called very-high-speed backbone network service (vBNS), which was set up in 1995 as a way to link government supercomputer centres and a select group of universities. The power of Internet2 makes it possible for a remote medical specialist to assist in a medical operation over the Internet without having the connection deteriorate as, say, home users check sports scores.[15]

Although Internet2 initially became available to only a few select organizations, there are now more than 325 member universities.[16] Whereas the public Internet divides bandwidth equally among users (if there are 100 users, they each get to use 1 percent of the available bandwidth), Internet2 is more capitalistic. Users who are willing to pay more can use more bandwidth.

Some fear that Internet2 may soon be overrun by undergrads engaged in music swapping and other resource-hogging pursuits. But, the designers of Internet2 are thinking ahead. Not only do they expect Internet history to repeat itself, they are counting on it. They are planning to filter the Internet2 technology out to the wider Internet community in such a way that there is plenty of room on the road for all of us—at a price, of course.

Social Networking and Web 2.0

Every day millions of people worldwide develop their own online identities on social networking sites like Facebook <*www.facebook.com*> and MySpace <*www.myspace.com*> by sharing pictures and videos or just sending a quick hello to an old friend. While sites focused on general socializing remain the most popular, there are hundreds of other social networking sites for nearly any purpose. LinkedIn <*www.linkedin.com*> encourages professionals to post résumés and develop business relationships, while Patients Like Me <*www.patientslikeme.com*> lets members share experiences of their illnesses and network with people affected by the same ailments. Ning <*http://ca.ning.com*> even allows users to create their own social networking site on whatever subject they choose.

For businesses, social networking provides an array of opportunities and challenges. It's an inexpensive way to gain exposure. Most important, it gives businesses tools to collaborate with consumers on product development, service enhancement, and promotion.

In a recent survey, 93 percent of social media users felt companies should have a social media presence.[17] However, while increasing numbers of companies are trying to woo customers, their employees' productivity may go down as they succumb to social media's many time-wasting aspects. Some companies ban employees from using social networking sites at work. Another challenge is that a single disparaging remark on a social networking forum can have devastating effects on the company's reputation.[18]

For all its strengths and weaknesses, social networking is the best example of what tech publisher Tim O'Reilly in 2004 dubbed "Web 2.0." **Web 2.0** is the set of tools that allow people to build social and business connections, share information, and collaborate on projects online with user-generated sites like blogs, wikis, social networking sites and other online communities, and virtual worlds.[19] (In this context, *Web 1.0* refers to corporate-generated sites like Google <*www.google.ca*> and Amazon <*www.amazon.ca*>.) YouTube <*www.youtube.com*> and the microblogging site Twitter <*twitter.com*> are among the largest Web 2.0 businesses, where ordinary people create all the content. But despite their enormous popularity, Web 2.0 companies have made little or no profit; almost all rely on advertising to generate revenue.[20]

Web 2.0
The set of tools that allow people to build social and business connections, share information, and collaborate on projects online (including blogs, wikis, social networking sites and other online communities, and virtual worlds).

Today's Web 2.0 companies may be transformed by yet another generation of Web innovators that expand the utility of the Web, create location-based services, and tie financial payment systems to existing sites. Translation: they make money. Location-based services are tied to devices that can track a user's whereabouts and suggest places, like restaurants or shops, in the area. If you happen to have a GPS device in your car, this location-based technology is not new to you, but now that same location-tracking power can be put in a portable device like your cell phone. Someday, you could get a message from Starbucks offering you a discount on a latte as you walk by its door. Experts predict that portable location-based services will become a $13 billion industry by 2013.[21] It looks like the start of Web 3.0.

THE ENABLING TECHNOLOGY: HARDWARE

We hesitate to discuss the advances that have been made in computer hardware because what is powerful as we write this may be obsolete by the time you read it. Rather than add potentially outdated facts to your information overload, we offer you a simple overview of the current computer technology. Hardware includes computers, mobile phones, printers, scanners, fax machines, and personal digital assistants (PDAs).

Cutting the Cord: Wireless Information Appliances

Some experts think we are moving away from a PC-dominant environment toward an array of post-PC appliances designed to connect us to the Internet and to e-mail. They include PDAs (e.g., smart phones/mobile phones such as BlackBerry and iPhone), netbooks, and in-dash computers for cars.[22] "We are entering a golden age of mobility," says Bob Iannucci, chief technology office for Nokia Corp. "Web 1.0 made lots of information available to a lot of people. Web 2.0 democratized information. Web 3.0 is about all that, anywhere, where mobility and connectivity converge in our lifestyle."[23]

The standardization of wireless networking has set the common PC free as well. Laptop users have the mobility and flexibility to work anywhere they can tap into a wireless network, using technology call wi-fi, from *wireless fidelity*.

Computer Networks

In older systems, mainframe computers performed all tasks and sent the results to a "dumb" terminal that could not perform those tasks itself. In a **network computing system** (also called **client/server computing**), personal computers (clients) can obtain

network computing system (client/server computing)
Computer systems that allow personal computers (clients) to obtain needed information from huge databases in a central computer (the server).

needed information from huge databases in a central computer or server. Networks connect people to people and people to data. They allow companies to save time and money, provide easy links across functional boundaries, and allow employees to see complete information.

Networks have drawbacks as well. Maintaining a fleet of PCs can be expensive. The cost of the computer itself is just the down payment. Computing costs and productivity losses go up as you upgrade and troubleshoot equipment and train employees to use it. By the time you've recouped your costs, it's time for another upgrade. Some companies that tried networking PCs are now looking at other options.

One option is a hybrid of mainframe and network computing. In this model, applications and data reside on a server, which handles all of the processing needs for all of the client machines on the networks. The client machines look like the PCs that most people use, but they lack the processing power to handle applications on their own. Called *thin-client networks,* these networks may resemble the ill-tempered dumb terminals of the 1980s, but the execution is much better. Users can still use the Windows applications they had been using. In a thin-client network, software changes and upgrades need to be made only on the server, so the cost of ownership can be reduced by 20 percent.

Another option is to rent software and hardware access by way of the Internet as needed instead of trying to maintain your own network. Back in the Web boom, companies called application service providers (ASPs) ran software at data centres and rented access to these functions to customers who didn't want to buy expensive servers and software. Most ASPs went out of business because CIOs were slow to hand over their critical data to companies with no track record or little experience in their specific industries. However, the fall of little ASPs didn't stop the flow of outsourcing IT functions to big service providers such as IBM. In fact, the trend today is toward two types of outsourced networking that look like highly developed descendants of earlier forms of networking and ASPs: virtualization and cloud computing. We'll discuss those next.

Virtualization and Cloud Computing

For every computer a company has in its network, an array of potential problems lurks in the shadows, from time-wasting crashes to crippling viruses. To remedy this, some companies have begun to adopt **virtualization**, a process that allows networked computers to run multiple operating systems and programs through one central computer at the same time.[24]

virtualization
A process that allows networked computers to run multiple operating systems and programs through one central computer at the same time.

Virtualization's centralized storage system gives companies ready access to update system software and fix problems, a practice as cost-effective as it is convenient. That is, the cost to operate a virtual desktop at a typical company is less than the cost of operating a PC.[25] Virtual desktops are also safer from thieves or hackers since the hub can cut off access to the computer if it becomes compromised.

Companies that want to virtualize but not to store all that data in their own offices need only look to the sky for a solution called **cloud computing**. This technology stores a company's data and applications at offsite data centres, accessed over the Internet (the cloud). The data aren't necessarily stored in a single data centre; portions could be in a series of centres anywhere in the world. The data are easily accessible from any computer with an Internet connection.[26] Vendors like Amazon, Google, and IBM offer cloud computing to businesses for a monthly pay-as-you-go fee. While cloud computing's universal accessibility and hassle-free data management may seem preferable to in-house virtualization, the monthly payment system may commit businesses to an escalating payment system just to access their own data.

cloud computing
A form of virtualization in which a company's data and applications are stored at offsite data centres that are accessed over the Internet (the cloud).

Green IT

Keeping your technology "green" is often as simple as turning it off. Leaving your computer on after work hours needlessly wastes energy, so simply hit the off button before you leave. Or purchase software like Surveyor <*www.verdiem.com*> to power down all the computers in the office with one click. But prepare your overhead for a major dent. Surveyor costs $25 per computer with a minimum license of 5,000 machines.[27] On second thought, turning off your computer at the end of the day isn't so hard, is it?

SOFTWARE

Computer software provides the instructions that tell your computer what to do. The type of software you want dictates the kind of equipment you need.

Although most software is distributed commercially through suppliers such as retail stores or electronic retailers, some software, called **shareware**, is copyrighted but distributed free of charge. Users are asked to send a specified fee to the developer if the program meets their needs and they decide to use it. **Public domain software** (or **freeware**) is software that is free for the taking.

shareware
Software that is copyrighted but distributed to potential customers free of charge.

public domain software (freeware)
Software that is free for the taking.

The quality of shareware and freeware varies greatly. To learn more, find a Web site that rates such programs. For example, Shareware Junkies <*www.sharewarejunkies.com*> lists the programs downloaded most often, editors' picks, and links to downloadable programs.

Business people most frequently use software for writing (word processors), manipulating numbers (spreadsheets), filing and retrieving data (databases), presenting information visually (graphics), communicating (e-mail and IM), and accounting. Integrated software or a software suite can perform many functions. Another class of software program, called *groupware,* is used on networks.

EFFECTS OF INFORMATION TECHNOLOGY ON MANAGEMENT

The increase of information technology has affected management greatly and will continue to do so. Four major issues arising out of the growing reliance on information technology are in the areas of human resources changes, security, privacy, and stability.

Human Resources Issues

We will talk in Chapter 9 about tall versus flat organization structures. Computers often eliminate middle-management functions and thus flatten organization structures.

Human resources managers need to recruit employees who know how to use the new technology or train those who already work in the company.[28] Companies often hire consultants instead of internal staff to address these concerns. Outsourcing technical training allows them to concentrate on their core businesses.

Perhaps the most revolutionary effect of computers and the Internet is **telecommuting**, also known as **telework**. Using computers linked to the company's network, mobile employees can transmit their work to the office from anywhere as easily as they can walk to the boss's office. Naturally, that decreases travel time and overall costs and often increases productivity. Having fewer employees in the office also means that a company can get by with smaller, and therefore less expensive, office space than before.

telecommuting (telework)
Using computers linked to the company's network, mobile employees can transmit their work to the office from anywhere.

Telecommuting enables men and women to work while staying home with small children or elders. It has also been a tremendous boon for workers with disabilities. Employees who can work after hours on their home computers rather than staying late at the office report lowered stress and improved morale. Telecommuting is most successful among people who are self-starters, who don't have home distractions, and whose work doesn't require face-to-face interaction with co-workers.

Electronic communication can never replace face-to-face communication for creating enthusiasm and team spirit, however. Even as telecommuting has grown in popularity, some telecommuters report that a consistent diet of long-distance work leaves them feeling dislocated or left out of the loop. Some miss the energy of social interaction or dislike the intrusion of work into what is normally a personal setting. Often people working from home don't know when to turn the work off. Some companies are therefore using telecommuting only as a part-time alternative. For additional information about telecommuting and home-based workers, review Chapters 7 and 12.

Security Issues

"Secure" information may be at risk from hackers who break into companies' networks, from employees who steal it, or from companies' own incompetence, poor gatekeeping, or sloppy procedures.[29] Computer security is more complicated than ever as hackers target Web-enabled smart phones and the 3G networks they run on, social networks and online games, and USB storage devices (flash drives and memory cards).[30] When information was processed on mainframes, the single data centre was easier to control because there was limited access to it. Today, however, computers are accessible not only in all areas within the company but also in all areas of other companies with which the firm does business.

Some of the most common security breaches involve viruses and phishing. A **virus** is a piece of programming code inserted into other programming to cause some unexpected and, for the victim, usually undesirable event. Users pick up viruses by unknowingly downloading infected programming over the Internet or by sharing an infected USB storage device. Often the source of the infected file is unaware of the virus.[31] The virus lies dormant until circumstances cause its code to be executed by the computer. Some viruses are playful ("Kilroy was here!"), but some can be quite harmful, erasing data or causing your hard drive to crash. Programs such as Norton Antivirus inoculate your computer so it doesn't catch a known virus. But because new viruses are being developed constantly, antivirus programs may have only limited success. Keep your antivirus protection up-to-date and, more important, practise safe computing by not downloading files from unknown sources.

virus
A piece of programming code inserted into other programming to cause some unexpected and, for the victim, usually undesirable event.

Phishing involves e-mails embellished with a stolen logo for a well-known enterprise (often from financial institutions) that make the messages look authentic. The messages often state something like "Dear Customer" (rather than your name), "Account activation required" or "Your account will be cancelled if you do not verify." When the victims click the link contained in the message, they are sent to phony Web sites that take personal data and use it to commit fraud. The best way to avoid this scam is to never access a Web site through a link in an e-mail message. Instead, open a new window and go to the Web site directly.[32] Canadian banks are working together through the Canadian Bankers Association <*www.cba.ca*> to share information to fight back against threats to online commerce. Phishing is on top of the group's list because attackers have targeted bank customers directly. "We're able to shut these things down within one to three hours by working closely with the RCMP," says Mark Saunders, then senior vice-president of enterprise infrastructure at the Bank of Montreal. "But these threats come in every hour and they're not selective, so they'll go after all the financial institutions, which is likely why we've been seeing a lot of phishing over the last year or two."[33]

phishing
E-mails embellished with a stolen logo for a well-known enterprise (often from financial institutions) that make the messages look authentic, but which are used to collect personal data and use it to commit fraud.

Cybercrimes cost companies billions of dollars a year. Companies that insure businesses against security breaches are demanding that strong measures be put in place, and it's also becoming the law.[34] Privacy regulations such as Sarbanes-Oxley in the United States and the European Data Protection Act stipulate that organizations doing business in their jurisdiction have systems in place to protect and preserve data from misuse, alteration, or destruction.[35]

Existing laws do not address all of the problems with today's direct, real-time communication. As more and more people log on to the Internet, the number of legal issues likely will increase. Today, copyright and pornography laws are crashing into the virtual world. Other legal questions—such as those involving intellectual property and contract disputes, online sexual and racial harassment, and the use of electronic communication to promote crooked sales schemes—are being raised as millions of people go online.

Privacy Issues

The increasing use of technology creates major concerns about privacy. For example, e-mail is no more private than a postcard. You don't need to be the target of a criminal investigation to have your e-mail snooped. Companies today scan employees' e-mails regularly and legally. Just as employers can log and listen to employees' telephone conversations, they can track e-mail in a search for trade secrets, non-work-related traffic, harassing messages, and conflicts of interest. Also, most e-mail travels over the Internet in unencrypted plain text. Any hacker with a desire to read your thoughts can trap and read your messages. Some e-mail systems, such as Lotus Notes, can encrypt messages so that you can keep corporate messages private. If you use browser-based e-mail, you can obtain a certificate that has an encryption key from a company such as VeriSign <*www.verisign.com/ca/*>. Legitimate users who want to decrypt your mail need to get an unlocking key.

The Internet presents increasing threats to your privacy, as more and more personal information is stored in computers and people are able to access that data, legally or illegally. Some Web sites allow people to search for vehicle ownership from a licence number or to find individuals' real estate property records. One key question in the debate over protecting our privacy is: Isn't this personal information already public anyway? Civil libertarians have long fought to keep certain kinds of information available to the public. If access to such data is restricted on the Internet, wouldn't we have to re-evaluate our policies on public records entirely? The privacy advocates don't think so. After all, the difference is that the Net makes obtaining personal information too easy. Would your neighbours or friends even consider going to the appropriate local agency and sorting through public documents for hours to find your driving records or to see your divorce settlement? Probably not. But they might dig into your background if all it takes is a few clicks of a button.

Many Web servers track the online movements of users willing to swap personal details for free access to online information. Site owners can send **cookies** to your computer that stay on your hard drive. These are pieces of information—such as registration data (name and password) or user preferences—that the browser sends back to the server whenever you return to that Web site. Other cookies track your movements around the Web and then blend that information with a database so that a company can tailor the ads you receive. Some software, known as *spyware,* can be installed on your computer without your knowledge. The spyware can then infect your system with viruses and track your online behaviour.

cookies
Pieces of information, such as registration data or user preferences, sent by a Web site over the Internet to a Web browser that the browser software is expected to save and send back to the server whenever the user returns to that Web site.

Do you mind someone watching over your shoulder while you're on the Web? Tim Berners-Lee, the researcher who invented the World Wide Web, led the development of a way to prevent you from receiving cookies without your permission.

His Platform for Privacy Preferences, or P3, allows a Web site to automatically send information on its privacy policies. With P3 you can set up your Web browser to communicate only with those Web sites that meet certain criteria. You need to decide how much information about yourself you are willing to give away. Remember, we are living in an information economy, and information is a commodity—that is, an economic good with a measurable value.

Stability Issues

Although technology can provide significant increases in productivity and efficiency, instability has a significant impact on business. Candy maker Hershey <*www.hersheycanada.com*> discovered that the Halloween trick was on it one year when the company couldn't get its treats to the stores on time. Failure of its new $115-million computer system disrupted shipments, and retailers were forced to order Halloween treats from other companies. Consequently, Hershey suffered a 12 percent decrease in sales that quarter.

What's to blame for instability? Experts say it is a combination of computer error, human error, malfunctioning software, and an overly complex marriage of software, hardware, and networking equipment. Some systems are launched too quickly to be bug-proof, and some executives don't have the technical knowledge to challenge computer specialists. As critical as technology is to business, some of it is not built for rigorous engineering, and some people aren't properly trained to use it. As things become more complex, we will probably be prone to more errors.

TECHNOLOGY AND YOU

If you are beginning to think that being computer illiterate may negatively affect your career, you are getting the point. As information technology eliminates old jobs while creating new ones, it is up to you to learn and maintain the skills you need to be certain you aren't left behind.

KEY TERMS

broadband technology
cloud computing
cookies
extranet
information technology (IT)
Internet2
intranet
network computing system (client/server computing)
phishing
public domain software (freeware)
shareware
telecommuting (telework)
virtual private network (VPN)
virtualization
virus
Web 2.0

Practise and learn online with Connect.

CHAPTER

2

HOW ECONOMIC ISSUES AFFECT BUSINESS

LEARNING OBJECTIVES

After you have read and studied this chapter, you should be able to:

Describe basic economics.

Explain what capitalism is and how free markets work.

Define socialism and its benefits and negative consequences.

Evaluate communism and the challenges of such a system.

Describe the mixed economy of Canada.

Illustrate the significance of key economic indicators and the business cycle.

PROFILE

GETTING TO KNOW: HERNANDO DE SOTO: ECONOMIST FOR THE POOR

A crowd of anxious fans pushes to get a glimpse of a celebrity visiting a poor community in Peru. Who is this person who has the town so excited? A rock singer, a famous athlete, a movie star? No. Would you believe he's an economist? Hernando de Soto, a noted economist, wrote one of Peru's bestselling books and the crowds were eager to hear his ideas about improving the country's economy—and thus their own lives.

Hernando de Soto was born in Peru. He went on to study in Canada, the United States, and Switzerland. Eventually he earned a graduate degree in international economics and law at the University of Geneva. He was successful enough to become managing director of Universal Engineering Corporation, a Swiss consulting firm. He made enough money to retire, but instead decided to devote his time to studying what makes some countries rich and others poor. He returned to Peru and studied the entrepreneurs there to see what held them back. What he learned was that the business owners were locked out of the formal, legal economy because there were no laws that provided property titles. That is, people could have houses, but no titles to them; farms, but no deeds to them; and businesses, but no statutes of incorporation. The lack of formal titling prevented owners from using their property as collateral, and thus prevented the capital embedded in these assets to be used for other purposes. This meant that entrepreneurs could not sell their property and use the money to invest. They also could not borrow money from banks to expand or improve their businesses. De Soto's book, *The Other Path,* outlined his findings.

De Soto found that another barrier to wealth in Peru and other less developed countries is government bureaucracy. It took de Soto and others 6.5 years and 207 administrative steps in 52 government offices to obtain legal authorization to build a house on state-owned land. It took 289 six-hour days and $1,231 (about 31 times the monthly minimum wage) in fees to legally open a garment workshop. In short, it is often very difficult and very expensive to become an entrepreneur in less developed countries.

De Soto estimates that the value of real estate held, but not owned, by the poor in less developed countries is at least $9.3 trillion. That's a lot of money that could be used to start or expand businesses, hire more people, and create wealth. De Soto's second book, *The Mystery of Capital,* goes into more detail about how property ownership leads to the creation of wealth.

De Soto is now the president of the Institute for Liberty and Democracy <*www.ild.org.pe*>, a Lima, Peru–based think tank. He says that two-thirds of humanity is not in a position to participate in a modern market economy, and that is his biggest challenge. De Soto finds this to be true around the world and in countries such as Peru, Egypt, Russia, and the Philippines. He found, for example, that it takes 25 years of red tape to gain through legal means the kind of home in Manila that people now obtain through squatting. Roughly half of the world's people live in makeshift homes in squatter settlements and work in shadow economies. In many countries, more than 80 percent of all homes and businesses are unregistered. In the Philippines, the figure is 65 percent and in Tanzania, 90 percent. More than one-third of the developing world's gross domestic product is generated in the underground economy, a figure that has increased steadily over the past decade. He cites Switzerland and Japan as two countries that went from relative poverty to wealth by modifying their property laws.

As you can imagine, de Soto has his share of detractors. Articles have been written challenging his thinking, and his life has been threatened. But such challenges only help him bring the issue of poverty to the forefront and urge countries to change their laws to make prosperity a reality.

Many people don't realize the importance of the economic environment to the success of business. That is what this chapter is all about. You will learn to compare different economic systems to see the benefits and drawbacks of each. You will learn that the mixed economy is the system in Canada. By the end of the chapter, you should understand the direct effect that economic systems have on the wealth and happiness of communities throughout the world.

Sources: "Hernando de Soto's Biography," The Cato Institute, [2012?], http://www.cato.org/special/friedman/desoto/; Madeleine Albright, "Giving The Poor Their Rights," *Time,* 5 July 2007, www.ild.org.pe/en/hernando-de-soto/blog/time/jul07; Hernando de Soto, *The Mystery of Capital: Why Capitalism Triumphs in the West and Fails Everywhere Else* (New York: Basic Books, 2003); Hernando de Soto, *The Other Path: The Invisible Revolution in the Third World* (New York: Harper and Row, 1989); Jeremy Main, "How to Make Poor Countries Rich," *Fortune,* 16 January 1989; N. Stephan Kinsella (ed.), book review, *Journal of Libertarian Studies,* Winter 2002; and www.nytimes.com/books/00/12/24/reviews/00124.24skidelt.html.

HOW ECONOMIC CONDITIONS AFFECT BUSINESS

If you want to understand the underlying situation and conditions in which Canadian businesses operate, it is essential that you (1) have some grasp of economics, (2) be aware of the impact of the global environment, and (3) understand the role of the federal and provincial governments in Canada.

The Canadian economy is an integral part of the world economy. Business firms use labour from other countries, export to and import from other countries, buy land in other countries for their facilities, and receive money from foreign investors. To understand events in the Canadian economy, therefore, one has to understand the world economy.

Why is South Korea comparatively wealthy and North Korea suffering economically, with many of its people starving? Why is China's income per person lower than Taiwan's? Such questions are part of the subject of economics. In this chapter, we explore the various economic systems of the world and how they either promote or hinder business growth, the creation of wealth, and a higher quality of life for all.[1]

A major part of business success is due to an economic and social climate that allows businesses to operate freely. Foreign investors like Canada because we have a stable economic and political environment. Investing is risky enough without having to worry about unpredictable governments, massive corruption, and weak laws. Therefore, any change in our economic or political system can have a major influence on businesses.

Describe basic economics.

What Is Economics?

economics
The study of how society chooses to employ resources to produce goods and services and distribute them for consumption among various competing groups and individuals.

Economics is the study of how society chooses to employ resources to produce goods and services and distribute them for consumption among various competing groups and individuals. Remember from Chapter 1 that these resources (land, labour, capital goods, entrepreneurship, and knowledge) are called *factors of production.*

Businesses may contribute to an economic system by inventing products that greatly increase available resources. For example, businesses may discover new energy sources, new ways of growing food, and new ways of creating needed goods and services.[2] Ballard Power Systems <*www.ballad.com*>, a global leader in the design, development, and manufacture of hydrogen fuel cells, is doing just this. Among other initiatives, Ballard is working with auto manufacturers to develop the next generation of efficient and clean engines for buses, automobiles, and trucks.[3]

Your buying behaviour falls under the study of microeconomics. How does understanding spending patterns benefit a country's economy?

This is a close-up of a salmon farm in British Columbia. Environmental groups are concerned that some current mariculture practices create negative environmental impacts such as water pollution (e.g., due to chemicals used to control diseases), transfer of disease from caged species to wild populations, and the death of sea birds, turtles, and marine mammals that get tangled in nets.

There are two major branches of economics: **macroeconomics** looks at the operation of a nation's economy as a whole, and **microeconomics** looks at the behaviour of people and organizations in particular markets. For example, while macroeconomics looks at how many jobs exist in the whole economy, microeconomics examines how many people will be hired in a particular industry or a particular region of the country. Topics discussed in this chapter that are part of macroeconomics include gross domestic product, unemployment rate, and price indexes. Chapter topics that deal with microeconomic issues include pricing and supply and demand.

macroeconomics
The part of economic study that looks at the operation of a nation's economy as a whole.

microeconomics
The part of economic study that looks at the behaviour of people and organizations in particular markets.

Some economists define economics as the allocation of "scarce" resources. They believe that resources are scarce and that they need to be carefully divided among people, usually by the government. There's no way to maintain peace and prosperity in the world by merely dividing the resources we have today among the existing nations. There aren't enough known resources available to do that. **Resource development** is the study of how to increase resources (say by getting oil from shale and oil sands) and to create the conditions that will make better use of them (like recycling and oil conservation).[4]

resource development
The study of how to increase resources and the creation of the conditions that will make better use of those resources (e.g., recycling).

Businesses can contribute to an economic system by inventing products that greatly increase available resources such as discovering new energy sources (e.g., hydrogen fuel for cars), new ways of growing food (e.g., hydroponics), and new ways of creating needed goods and services (e.g., nanotechnology).[5] For example, people are starting to raise more fish in pens out in the ocean.[6] Such *mariculture* (the farming of aquatic plants and animals in land-based tanks and ponds or in sea cages) could lead to more food for everyone and more employment. The Green Box recognizes one company for its eco-winery philosophy.

The Secret to Creating a Wealthy Economy

Imagine the world when kings and other rich landowners had most of the wealth, and the majority of the people were peasants. The peasants had many children, and it may have seemed a natural conclusion that if things went on as usual there would soon be too many people and not enough food and other resources. Economist Thomas Malthus made this argument in the late 1700s and early 1800s, leading the writer Thomas Carlyle to call economics "the dismal science."

GREENBOX

Stratus Winery Is LEEDing the Way

There are close to 500 wineries in Canada that provide jobs, preserve valuable agricultural land, and create tourist destinations. The sale of just one litre of Canadian wine provides over $4 in economic value to the Canadian economy. Wine sales in Canada are approaching $5 billion annually, and 40 percent of this total comes from Canadian brands. Canada's wine industry is characterized by new investments in world-class wineries, aggressive new plantings of vinifera varietals, diversified wine offerings, new technology, expanding exports, and greater recognition of the industry's ability to produce fine wines at competitive prices.

Stratus Vineyards <*www.stratuswines.com*>, established in 2000, is one company that is achieving success with its eco-winery philosophy. Committed to responsible stewardship of the land, environmental sustainability is a core value of every decision involved in the design and operation of Stratus. Stratus is a sustainable, innovative winery located in Niagara-on-the-Lake. Its goal is to make limited quantities of premium wine with as minimal a carbon footprint as possible. The winery is the first building in Canada to achieve LEED® (Leadership in Energy and Environmental Design) certification from the Canada Green Building Council <*www.cagbc.org*> and it is the only winery in the world to achieve this designation fully.

To qualify for LEED certification, the winery had to meet numerous criteria that reduced negative impacts on the environment, both during construction and on a permanent, operational basis. Primary features include geothermal technology to heat and cool the building, the use of recycled materials in the construction and design, resource and energy-efficient electrical and plumbing systems, a toxin-free waste management program, herbicide-free vineyards, and a landscape plan that is organic and based on indigenous grasses and plants. For example, it is estimated that 80 percent of the energy that is used is free. The company also uses a hybrid, gas-electric vehicle for winery deliveries.

Stratus is a strong example of the sustainable "triple bottom-line": people, planet, and profit. Its wines are critically acclaimed and have become benchmarks of quality within the Canadian wine industry.

Sources: Frederick G. Crane et al., *Marketing*, 8th Canadian ed. (Toronto: McGraw-Hill Ryerson Ltd., 2011), 22–24; Terri Meyer, "Case Studies in Canadian Sustainable Design: Stratus Winery," University of Waterloo, 27 June 2006, www.architecture.uwaterloo.ca/faculty_projects/terri/sustain_casestudies/stratus_gallery.html; and "Stratus Vineyards Becomes First Winery Worldwide to Achieve LEED Certification," CSRwire, 15 May 2005, www.csrwire.com/News/3943.html.

Followers of Malthus today (who are called neo-Malthusians) still believe there are too many people in the world and that the solution to poverty is radical birth control, including forced abortions and sterilization.[7] The latest world statistics, however, show population growing more slowly than expected. In some industrial countries—like Japan, Germany, Italy, and Russia—population growth may be so slow that eventually there will be too many old people and too few young people to care for them. In the developing world, on the other hand, population will climb relatively quickly and may lead to greater poverty and more unrest. Studies about the effects of population growth on the economy are part of macroeconomics.

Some macroeconomists believe that a large population, especially an educated one, can be a valuable resource. You've probably heard the saying "Give a man a fish and you feed him for a day, but teach a man to fish and you feed him for a lifetime." You can add to that: "Teach a person to start a fish farm, and he or she will be able to feed a village for a lifetime." *The secret to economic development is contained in this last statement.* Business owners provide jobs and economic growth for their employees and communities as well as for themselves.

The challenge for macroeconomists is to determine what makes some countries relatively wealthy and other countries relatively poor, and then to implement policies and programs that lead to increased prosperity for everyone in all countries.[8] One way to begin understanding this challenge is to consider the theories of Adam Smith.

Growth Economics and Adam Smith

Rather than believing that fixed resources had to be divided among competing groups and individuals, Scottish economist Adam Smith envisioned creating more resources so that everyone could become wealthier. The year was 1776. Adam Smith's book, *An Inquiry into the Nations and Causes of the Wealth of Nations* (simply called *The Wealth of Nations*), was later considered the foundation of the study and understanding of the newly developing capitalist industrial society.

Smith believed that *freedom* was vital to the survival of any economy, especially the freedom to own land or property and the freedom to keep profits from working the land or owning a business. He believed that people will work hard if they have incentives for doing so—that is, if they know that they will be rewarded. According to Smith, as long as farmers, labourers, and business people (entrepreneurs) could see economic rewards for their efforts (i.e., receive enough money in the form of profits to support their families), they would work long hours and work hard. As a result of these efforts, the economy would prosper—with plenty of food and all kinds of products available to everyone. Smith's ideas were later challenged by Malthus and others who believed economic conditions would only get worse, but Smith, not Malthus, is considered the *father of modern economics.*

How Businesses Benefit the Community

In Adam Smith's view, business people don't necessarily deliberately set out to help others. They work primarily for their own prosperity and growth. Yet as people try to improve their own situation in life, Smith said, their efforts serve as an "invisible hand" that helps the economy grow and prosper through the production of needed goods, services, and ideas. Thus, the **invisible hand** turns self-directed gain into social and economic benefits for all.

invisible hand
A phrase coined by Adam Smith to describe the process that turns self-directed gain into social and economic benefits for all.

How is it that people working in their own self-interest produce goods, services, and wealth for others? The only way farmers in a given area can become wealthy is to sell some of their crops to others. To become even wealthier, farmers would have to hire workers to produce more food. As a consequence, people in that area would have plenty of food available and some would have jobs on the farms. So the farmers' self-centred efforts to become wealthy lead to jobs for some and food for almost all. Stop and think about that process for a minute because it is critical to your understanding of economic growth in Canada and other countries in the world. The same principle applies to other products as well—everything from clothing to iPhones.

Smith assumed that as people became wealthier, they would naturally reach out to help the less fortunate in the community.[9] This has not always happened. Today, however, more business people are becoming concerned about social issues and their obligation to return to society some of what they've earned. As we mentioned in Chapter 1, it is important for businesses to be ethical as well as generous.[10] Unethical practices undermine the whole economic system. The Making Ethical Decisions box explores an ethical question.

MAKING ETHICAL DECISIONS

Corruption Destroys Economies

Numerous forces can hinder economic growth and development. One of those forces is corruption. In many countries, a business person must bribe government officials to get permission to own land, build on it, and conduct normal business operations.

Imagine you need a permit to add liquor to your restaurant menu to increase your profit. You have tried for years to get one, with no results. You have a friend in the government who offers to help you if you make a large contribution to his re-election campaign. Would you be tempted to make a campaign contribution? What are your alternatives? What are the consequences of each?

PROGRESS ASSESSMENT

- What is the difference between macroeconomics and microeconomics?
- What does Adam Smith's term *invisible hand* mean? How does the invisible hand create wealth for a country?

Explain what capitalism is and how free markets work.

UNDERSTANDING FREE-MARKET CAPITALISM

Basing their ideas on free-market principles, such as those of Adam Smith, business people began to create more wealth than had ever been created before. They hired others to work on their farms and in their factories and nations began to prosper as a result. Business people soon became the wealthiest people in society. While there were great disparities between the wealthy and the poor, there was always the promise of opportunities to become wealthy.

The economic system that has led to wealth creation in much of the world is known as capitalism. Under **capitalism**, all or most of the factors of production and distribution—such as land, factories, railroads, and stores—are owned by individuals (i.e., not owned by the government). They are operated for profit, and business people, not government officials, decide what to produce and how much, what to charge, and how much to pay workers. They also decide whether to produce goods in their own countries or have them made in other countries. Capitalism is the popular term used to describe free-market economies.

A free-market system is evident at a farmer's market. As a buyer, what can you do to ensure that you pay the best price for produce?

No country is purely capitalist, however. Often the government gets involved in issues such as determining minimum wages and subsidizing certain sectors, as the federal government does in Canada for the agriculture sector. Today, capitalism is the foundation for the economies of Canada, England, Australia, the United States, and most other developed nations. We will discuss Canada's mixed economy in some detail later in this book.

The root word of *capitalism* is "capital." The Spotlight on Small Business box shows how a little capital can help small businesses grow in the poorest countries of the world.

capitalism
An economic system in which all or most of the factors of production and distribution are privately owned and operated for profit.

How Free Markets Work

The free market is one in which decisions about what to produce and in what quantities are made by the market—that is, by buyers and sellers negotiating prices for goods and services. Consumers (such as you and me) send signals to tell producers what to make, how many, in what colours, and so on. We do that by choosing to buy (or not to buy) certain goods and services. Note that just as no country is purely capitalist, no market is truly free. "Free" markets work not just from the interaction of buyers and sellers, but also from government signals (e.g., laws and regulations, taxes, warnings, advice, etc.).

How Prices Are Determined

In a free market, prices are not determined by sellers; they are determined by buyers and sellers negotiating in the marketplace. A seller may want to receive $50 for a

SPOTLIGHT ON SMALL BUSINESS

The Key to Capitalism is Capital

The Foundation for International Community Assistance (FINCA) <*www.finca.org*> is a non-profit organization. FINCA provides financial services to the world's lowest-income entrepreneurs so they can create jobs, build assets, and improve their standard of living. Small loans and other products are offered to those turned down by traditional banks. With these loans, families can invest in, and build, their own small businesses and their income-earning capacity. FINCA has loaned more than $447 million to over 600,000 small-scale entrepreneurs in some of the world's poorest countries. Worldwide, clients (borrowers) have repayment rates of over 97 percent.

The story of one small entrepreneur will help you understand the process. Pros Magaga lives in Kampala, Uganda. She had a tiny shop in town, but it carried very little inventory. She did not make enough to send her four children to school or to feed them more than once a day. FINCA lent her $50; she used it to buy a refrigerator, which allowed her to carry fresh foods and cold snacks. Later she added a freezer. Now her children are all in school, and the family enjoys two meals a day. Magaga has built a small home with two rooms and plans to add another room soon. She can borrow more money from FINCA because she has already paid back her $50 loan.

Sources: "About FINCA, "The Foundation for International Community Assistance," [2012?], www.finca.org/site/c.6flGIXMFJnJ0H/b.6088399/k.75E7/ABOUT_FINCA.htm; David Armstrong, "Is Bigger Better?" *Forbes*, 2 June 2008; Constance Loizos, "Muhammad Yunus," *Portfolio*, May 2008; Opportunity International's quarterly newsletter, Summer 2008; and Sheridan Prasso, "Saving the World One Cup of Yogurt at a Time," *Fortune*, 19 February 2007.

With 75,000 hotel rooms and an estimated 300,000 visitors, some Vancouverites rented out their homes during the 2010 Vancouver Olympics. Would you have paid $36,000 for a two-bedroom condo for one month?

T-shirt, but the quantity demanded at that price may be quite low. If the seller lowers the price, the quantity demanded is likely to increase. How is a price that is acceptable to both buyers and sellers determined? The answer is found in the microeconomic concepts of supply and demand.

The Economic Concept of Supply

Supply refers to the quantity of products that manufacturers or owners are willing to sell at different prices at a specific time. Generally speaking, the amount supplied will increase as the price increases because sellers can make more money with a higher price.

supply
The quantity of products that manufacturers or owners are willing to sell at different prices at a specific time.

Economists show this relationship between quantity supplied and price on a graph. Figure 2.1 shows a simple supply curve for T-shirts. The price of the T-shirts in dollars

Figure 2.1

The Supply Curve at Various Prices

The supply curve rises from left to right. Think it through. The higher the price of T-shirts goes (the left margin), the more sellers will be willing to supply.

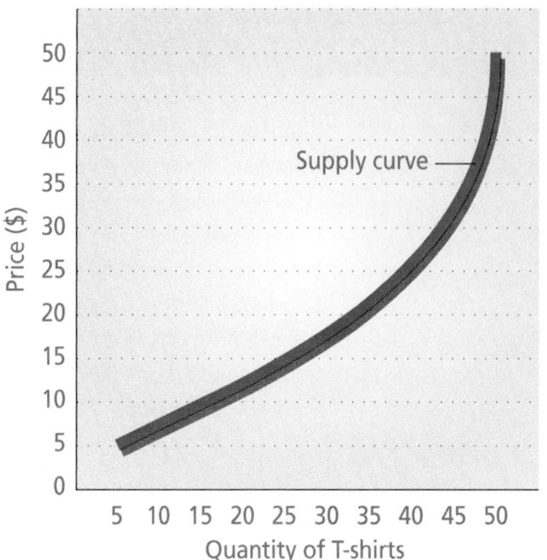

is shown vertically on the left of the graph. The quantity of T-shirts that sellers are willing to supply is shown horizontally at the bottom of the graph. The various points on the curve indicate how many T-shirts sellers would provide at different prices. For example, at a price of $5 a T-shirt, a vendor would provide only five T-shirts, but at $50 a T-shirt the vendor would supply 50 shirts. The supply curve indicates the relationship between the price and the quantity supplied. All things being equal, the higher the price, the more the vendor will be willing to supply.

The Economic Concept of Demand

demand
The quantity of products that people are willing to buy at different prices at a specific time.

Demand refers to the quantity of products that people are willing to buy at different prices at a specific time. Generally speaking, the quantity demanded will increase as the price decreases. Again, the relationship between price and quantity demanded can be shown in a graph. Figure 2.2 shows a simple demand curve for T-shirts. The various points on the graph indicate the quantity demanded at various prices. For example, at a price of $45, the quantity demanded is just five T-shirts, but if the price were $5, the quantity demanded would increase to 35 T-shirts. The line connecting the dots is called a demand curve. It shows the relationship between quantity demanded and price. The Dealing with Change box (placed at the end of this text part, which is Chapter 5) highlights how demand can impact supply.

The Equilibrium Point and the Market Price

market price
The price determined by supply and demand.

It should be clear to you after reviewing Figures 2.1 and 2.2 that the key factor in determining the quantity supplied and the quantity demanded is *price*. Sellers prefer a high price, and buyers prefer a low price. If you were to lay one of the two graphs on top of the other, the supply curve and the demand curve would cross. At that crossing point, the quantity demanded and the quantity supplied are equal. Figure 2.3 illustrates that point. At a price of $15, the quantity of T-shirts demanded and the quantity supplied are equal (25 shirts). That crossing point is known as the *equilibrium point* or the *equilibrium price*. In the long run, that price would become the market price. Market price, then, is determined by supply and demand.

Figure 2.2

The Demand Curve at Various Prices

This is a simple demand curve showing the quantity of T-shirts demanded at different prices. The demand curve falls from left to right. It is easy to understand why. The lower the price of T-shirts, the higher the quantity demanded.

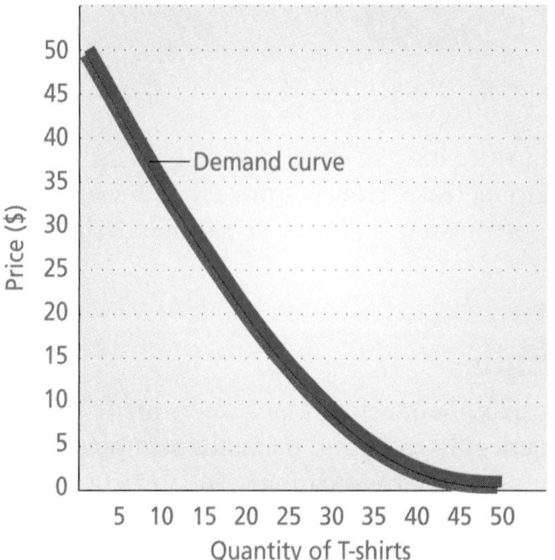

Supporters of a free market would argue that because supply and demand interactions determine prices, there is no need for government involvement or government planning. If surpluses develop (i.e., if quantity supplied exceeds quantity demanded), a signal is sent to sellers to lower the price. If shortages develop (i.e., if quantity supplied is less than quantity demanded), a signal is sent to sellers to increase the price. Eventually, supply will again equal demand if nothing interferes with market forces.

Such price swings were evident when the oil supply was cut because of Hurricane Katrina. When supplies were low because of the hurricane, the price of gasoline went up (dramatically). When supplies were again plentiful, the price of gas fell a little. Then it rose again as demand increased globally, especially in China and India. Food prices went up when more corn was being used for ethanol fuel and less for food.[11]

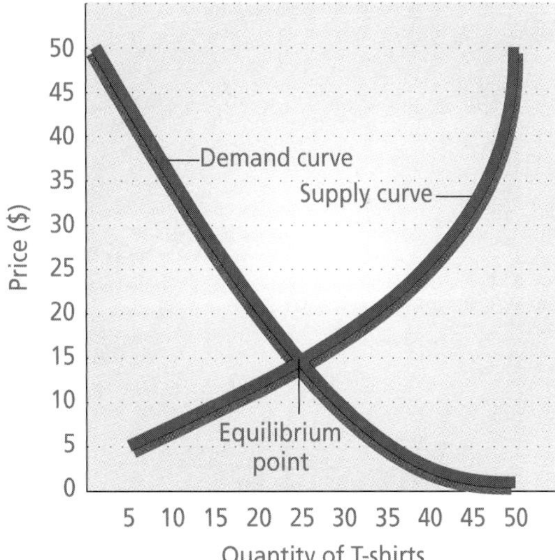

Figure 2.3

The Equilibrium Point

The place where quantity demanded and supplied meet is called the equilibrium point. When we put both the supply and demand curves on the same graph, we find that they intersect at a price where the quantity supplied and the quantity demanded are equal. In the long run, the market price will trend toward the equilibrium point.

In countries without a free market, there is no such mechanism to reveal to businesses (via price) what to produce and in what amounts, so there are often shortages (not enough products) or surpluses (too many products). In such countries, the government decides what to produce and in what quantity, but the government has no way of knowing what the proper quantities are. Furthermore, when the government interferes in otherwise free markets, such as when it subsidizes farm goods, surpluses and shortages may also develop.

Competition Within Free Markets

Economists generally agree that four different degrees of competition exist: (1) perfect competition, (2) monopolistic competition, (3) oligopoly, and (4) monopoly.

Perfect competition exists when there are many sellers in a market and no seller is large enough to dictate the price of a product. Under perfect competition, sellers produce products that appear to be identical. Agricultural products (e.g., apples, corn, potatoes) are often considered to be the closest examples of such products. You should know, however, that there are no true examples of perfect competition. Today, government price supports and drastic reductions in the number of farms make it hard to argue that even farming is an example of perfect competition.

perfect competition
The market situation in which there are many sellers in a market and no seller is large enough to dictate the price of a product.

Monopolistic competition exists when a large number of sellers produce products that are very similar but are perceived by buyers as different (e.g., hot dogs, candy, and T-shirts). Under monopolistic competition, *product differentiation* (the creation of real or perceived product differences) is a key to success. The fast-food industry, in which there are often promotional battles between hamburger restaurants, offers a good example of monopolistic competition.

monopolistic competition
The market situation in which a large number of sellers produce products that are very similar but that are perceived by buyers as different.

An **oligopoly** occurs when a few sellers dominate a market. Oligopolies exist in industries that produce products in the areas of oil and gas, tobacco, automobiles, aluminum, and aircraft. One reason some industries remain in the hands of a few sellers is that the initial investment required to enter the business is tremendous. In an oligopoly, prices for products from different companies tend to be close to the same. The reason for this is simple. Intense price competition would lower profits for all competitors, since a price cut on the part of one producer would most likely be matched by the others. As in monopolistic competition, product differentiation, rather than price, is usually the major factor in market success.

oligopoly
A form of competition in which just a few sellers dominate the market.

A **monopoly** occurs when there is only one seller for a good or service, and that one seller controls the total supply of a product and the price. Traditionally, monopolies

monopoly
A market in which there is only one seller for a product or service.

Although WestJet Airlines Ltd. <*www.westjet.com*> operates within an oligopoly in Canada, it still has to listen to the needs of its customers and try to be innovative. As a result, customers can choose to check in at the counter, on the Web, on mobile devices, at kiosks, and they can tag their bags themselves.

Figure 2.4

Free-Market Competition Based on the Number of Sellers

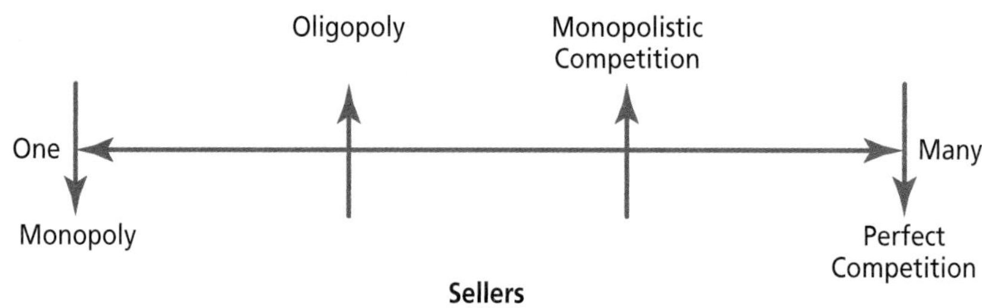

were common in areas such as water, electricity, and telephone services that were considered essential to a community.[12] Legislation has ended the monopoly status of utilities in some areas, letting consumers choose among providers. The intention of such deregulation is to increase competition among utility companies and, ultimately, lower prices for consumers. Figure 2.4 highlights where these forms of free-market competition fall when one considers the number of sellers (i.e., competitors) in the marketplace.

Benefits and Limitations of Free Markets

One benefit of the free market is that it allows open competition among companies. Businesses must provide customers with quality products at fair prices with good service. If they don't, they lose customers to businesses that do. Do government services have the same incentives?

The free market—with its competition and incentives—was a major factor in creating the wealth that industrialized countries now enjoy. Some people even talk of the free market as an economic miracle. Free-market capitalism, more than any other economic system, provides opportunities for poor people to work their way out of poverty. Capitalism also encourages businesses to be more efficient so they can successfully compete on price and quality.

Yet even as free-market capitalism has brought prosperity, it has brought inequality as well. Business owners and managers make more money and have more wealth than workers. There is much poverty, unemployment, and homelessness. People who are old, disabled, or sick may not be able to support themselves.

Smith assumed that as people became wealthier, they would naturally reach out and help the less fortunate in the community. As was discussed earlier, while this has not always happened, business people are becoming more concerned about social issues and their obligation to return to society some of what they've earned.

For example, Warren Buffet, Chairman and Chief Executive Officer of Berkshire Hathaway <*berkshirehathaway.com*> and ranked as one of the world's wealthiest people, has pledged to give away most of his money to the Bill and Melinda Gates Foundation.[13] In another example, every year an amount equivalent to 1 percent of Cirque du Soleil's earnings is dedicated to various social and cultural programs managed by Cirque <*www.cirquedusoleil.com*>, as well as to the ONE DROP Foundation.[14]

One of the dangers of free markets is that some people let greed dictate how they act. Criminal charges brought against some big businesses in banking, oil, accounting, telecommunications, insurance, and pharmaceuticals indicate the scope of the potential problem. Some business people have deceived the public about their products; others have deceived shareholders about the value of their stock, all in order to increase executives' personal assets.[15] Clearly, some government rules and regulations are necessary to make sure that all of a business's stakeholders are protected and that people who are unable to work get the basic care they need. To overcome the limitations of capitalism, some countries have adopted an economic system called socialism. It, too, has its good and bad points. We explore the advantages and disadvantages of socialism after the Progress Assessment questions.

PROGRESS ASSESSMENT

- How do business people know what to produce and in what quantity?
- How are prices determined?
- Describe the four degrees of competition.
- What are some of the limitations of free markets?

UNDERSTANDING SOCIALISM

Define socialism and its benefits and negative consequences.

Socialism is an economic system based on the premise that some, if not most, basic businesses—such as steel mills, coal mines, and utilities—should be owned by the government so that profits can be evenly distributed among the people. Entrepreneurs often own and run the smaller businesses, and individuals are often taxed relatively steeply to pay for social programs.

socialism
An economic system based on the premise that some, if not most, basic businesses should be owned by the government so that profits can be evenly distributed among the people.

Socialists acknowledge the major benefit of capitalism—wealth creation—but believe that wealth should be more evenly distributed than occurs in free-market capitalism. They believe that the government should be the agency that carries out the distribution and be much more involved in protecting the environment and providing for the poor.[16]

The Benefits of Socialism

The major benefit of socialism is supposed to be social equality. Ideally, it comes about because the government takes income from wealthier people, in the form of taxes, and redistributes it to poorer people through various government programs. Free education, free health care, and free child care are some of the benefits socialist governments, using the money from taxes, may provide to their people. Workers in socialist countries usually get longer vacations, worker fewer hours per week, and have more employee benefits (e.g., generous sick leave) than those in countries where free-market capitalism prevails.

The Negative Consequences of Socialism

Socialism may create more equality than capitalism, but it takes away some of business people's incentives to work hard, as their profits will be heavily taxed. For example, tax rates in some nations once reached 85 percent.

▸ Socialism has been much more successful in some countries than in others. This shows Denmark's modern and clean transportation system. In France, on the other hand, street riots erupted when young people protested legislation that would have allowed businesses to fire younger workers. The legislation was withdrawn. What other factors might lead to slower growth in socialist countries?

Today, doctors, lawyers, business owners, and others who earn a lot of money pay very high tax rates. As a consequence, some of them leave socialist countries for capitalistic countries with lower taxes, such as the United States. This loss of these educated people to other countries is called a **brain drain**.

Imagine an experiment in socialism in your own class. Imagine that after the first exam, those with grades of 90 and above have to give some of their points to those who make 70 and below so that everyone ends up with grades in the 80s. Would those who got 90s study as hard for the second exam? What about those who got 70s? Can you see why workers may not work as hard or as well if they all get the same benefits regardless of how hard they work?

Socialism also results in fewer inventions and less innovation because those who come up with new ideas usually don't receive as much reward as they would in a capitalist system. Generally speaking, over the past decade or so, most socialist countries have simply not kept up with more capitalist countries in new inventions, job creation, or wealth creation.[17]

Communism may be considered a more intensive version of socialism. We shall explore that system next.

UNDERSTANDING COMMUNISM

Evaluate communism and the challenges of such a system.

Communism is an economic and political system in which the state (the government) makes almost all economic decisions and owns almost all of the major factors of production. Communism affects personal choices more than socialism does. For example, some communist countries have not allowed their citizens to practise certain religions, change jobs, or move to the town of their choice.

One problem with communism is that the government has no way of knowing what to produce because prices don't reflect supply and demand as they do in free markets. As a result, shortages of many items may develop, including shortages of food and basic clothing. Another problem with communism is that it doesn't inspire business people to work hard, because the government takes most of their earnings. Therefore, although communists once held power in many nations around the world, communism is slowly disappearing as an economic form.

Most communist countries today are suffering severe economic depression. In North Korea, many people are starving. In Cuba, people suffer from a lack of goods and services readily available in most other countries, and some fear the government. Even so, there seems to be a movement toward communist principles in Venezuela, following the Cuban model.[18]

While some parts of the former Soviet Union remain under communist ideals, Russia itself now has a flat tax of 13 percent. Even this low tax rate increased the government's tax revenues by nearly 30 percent, because more people were willing to pay. The trend toward free markets is growing in Vietnam and parts of China as well.

brain drain
The loss of educated people to other countries.

communism
An economic and political system in which the state (the government) makes all economic decisions and owns almost all of the major factors of production.

The regions of China that are most free have prospered rapidly, while the rest of the country has grown relatively slowly. Remnants of China's communist system, such as political and religious oppression, still exist, however.

THE TREND TOWARD MIXED ECONOMIES

The nations of the world have largely been divided between those that followed the concepts of capitalism and those that adopted the concepts of communism or socialism. Thus, to sum up the preceding discussion, the two major economic systems vying for dominance in the world today can be defined as follows:

1. A **free-market economy** exists when the market largely determines what goods and services are produced, who gets them, and how the economy grows. *Capitalism* is the popular term used to describe this economic system.
2. A **command economy** exists when the government largely decides what goods and services are produced, who gets them, and how the economy will grow. *Socialism* and *communism* are the popular terms used to describe variations of this economic system.

free-market economy
An economy in which the market largely determines what goods and services are produced, who gets them, and how the economy grows.

command economy
An economy in which the government largely decides what goods and services are produced, who gets them, and how the economy will grow.

Experience has shown that neither of these systems has resulted in optimum economic conditions. Free-market mechanisms haven't been responsive enough to the needs of the poor, the old, or the disabled. Some people also believe that businesses in free-market economies have not done enough to protect the environment. Over time, voters in free-market countries, such as Canada, have therefore elected officials who have adopted social and environmental programs such as medicare, unemployment compensation, and various clean air and water acts.

Socialism and communism, for their part, haven't always created enough jobs or wealth to keep economies growing fast enough. As a consequence, communist governments are disappearing and socialist governments have been cutting back on social programs and lowering taxes for businesses and workers. The idea is to generate more business growth and thus generate more revenue.[19]

The trend, then, has been for so-called socialist countries to move toward more capitalism. We say "so-called" because no country in the world is purely capitalist or purely socialist. All countries have some mix of the two systems. Thus, the long-term global trend is toward a blend of capitalism and socialism. This trend likely will increase with the opening of global markets as a result of the Internet.[20] The net effect of capitalist systems moving toward socialism and socialist systems moving toward capitalism is the emergence throughout the world of mixed economies.

Mixed economies exist where some allocation of resources is made by the market and some is made by the government. Most countries don't have a name for such a system. If the dominant way of allocating resources is by free-market mechanisms, then the leaders of such countries still call their system capitalism. If the dominant way of allocating resources is by the government, then the leaders call their system socialism. Figure 2.5 compares the various economic systems.

mixed economies
Economic systems in which some allocation of resources is made by the market and some by the government.

PROGRESS ASSESSMENT

- What led to the emergence of socialism?
- What are the benefits and drawbacks of socialism?
- What are the characteristics of a mixed economy?

	Capitalism (United States)	Socialism (Sweden)	Communism (North Korea)	Mixed Economy (Canada)
Social and economic goals	Private ownership of land and business. Freedom and the pursuit of happiness. Free trade. Emphasis on freedom and the profit motive for economic growth.	Public ownership of major businesses. Some private ownership of smaller businesses and shops. Government control of education, health care, utilities, mining, transportation, and media. Very high taxation. Emphasis on equality.	Public ownership of all businesses. Government-run education and health care. Emphasis on equality. Many limitations on freedom, including freedom to own businesses, change jobs, buy and sell homes, and assemble to protest government actions.	Private ownership of land and business with government regulation. Government control of some institutions (e.g., mail). High taxation for the common welfare. Emphasis on a balance between freedom and equality.
Motivation of workers	Much incentive to work efficiently and hard, because profits are retained by owners. Workers are rewarded for high productivity.	Capitalist incentives exist in private businesses. Government control of wages in public institutions limits incentives.	Very little incentive to work hard or to produce quality products.	Incentives are similar to capitalism except in government-owned enterprises, which have few incentives.
Control over markets	Complete freedom of trade within and among nations. No government control of markets.	Some markets are controlled by the government and some are free. Trade restrictions among nations vary and include some free trade agreements.	Total government control over markets except for illegal transactions.	Some government control of trade within and among nations (trade protectionism).
Choices in the market	A wide variety of products is available. Almost no scarcity or oversupply exists for long because supply and demand control the market.	Variety in the marketplace varies considerably from country to country. Choice is directly related to government involvement in markets.	Very little choice among competing products.	Similar to capitalism, but scarcity and oversupply may be caused by government involvement in the market (e.g., subsidies for farms).

Figure 2.5

Comparisons of Key Economic Systems

Describe the mixed economy of Canada.

CANADA'S MIXED ECONOMY

Like most other nations of the world, Canada has a mixed economy. The degree of government involvement in the economy today—in areas such as health care, education, and business regulation, just to name a few—is a matter of some debate. (In Chapter 4, we will discuss the role of government in more detail.) The government's perceived goal is to grow the economy while maintaining some measure of social equality. The goal is very hard to attain. Nonetheless, the basic principles of freedom and opportunity should lead to economic growth that is sustainable.

Several features have played a major role in Canada becoming an independent economic entity with high government involvement in the economy. First, we are one of the largest countries in the world geographically, but we have a small population (over 34.8 million).[21] We have one of the lowest population densities in the world.

Most important, our neighbour to the south has ten times the population and an economy even greater than that proportion, speaks our language, is very aggressive economically, and is the most powerful country in the world. The United States

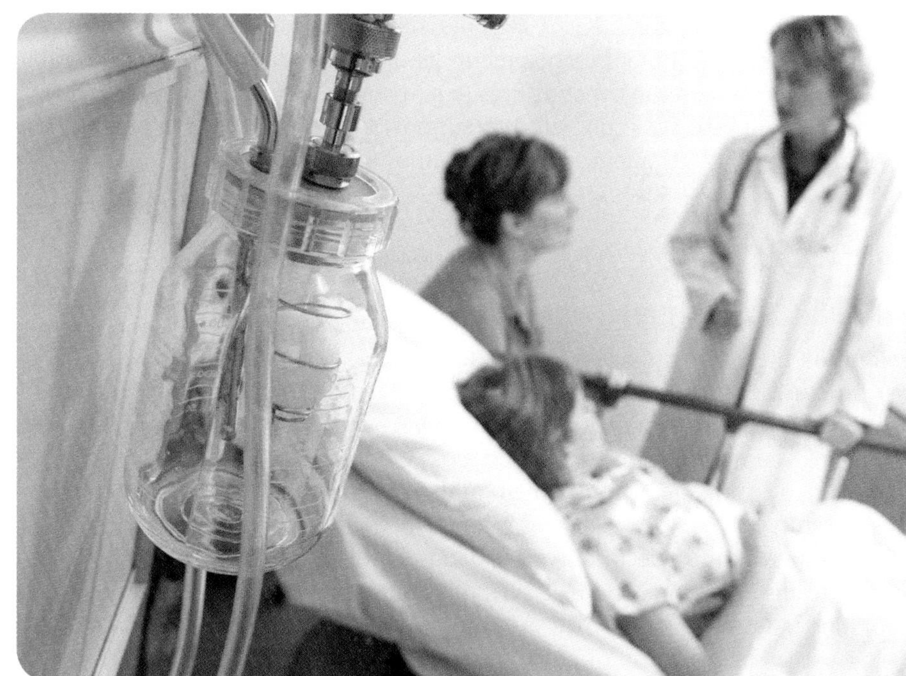

Governed by the Canada Health Act, public care is designed to make sure that all eligible people in the country have reasonable access to insured health services on a prepaid basis, without direct charges at the point of service. Private care covers anything beyond what the public system will pay for. Who would benefit from private health coverage? What happens if someone is not eligible for private coverage?

exerts a very powerful influence on Canada as our largest trading partner. (We will discuss details in Chapter 3.) To control our destiny, Canadian governments have passed many laws and regulations to ensure that significant economic and cultural institutions, such as banks, insurance companies, and radio and TV stations, remain under Canadian control. (Even powerful countries like the United States and Japan have similar regulations.)

All of these factors led to the Canadian capitalist system taking on many characteristics of a mixed economy. Massive government support was necessary to build our first national rail line, the CPR, in the 1880s. When air transport was beginning in the 1930s no company wanted to risk investing heavily in such a large country with only 10 million people spread thinly across the land. So the government set up Air Canada (then called Trans Canada Airlines) to transport mail, people, and freight. There are many such examples of government action to protect the national interest.

In the 1980s, many countries, including Canada, began to reduce government involvement in, and regulation of, the economy. This trend toward deregulation was widespread. In Canada, airlines, banks, and the trucking industry have all seen a marked reduction in regulatory control.

This trend continues today as groups lobby the government to relax regulations to allow them to be more competitive. For example, to encourage competitiveness, the Competition Policy Review Panel <*www.competitionreview.ca*> recommends lowering barriers to foreign investment in a number of industries, including telecommunications and air transportation.[22] The Conference Board of Canada <*www.conferenceboard.ca*> has released a report that warns that Canadian industries need to do a better job competing for global investment dollars, attracting foreign investors, and establishing new investments overseas.[23]

There are also many new players entering the Canadian marketplace that are competing with publicly funded (i.e., government-funded) institutions. One such industry is health care, where private health care supporters continue to lobby for a greater presence in Canada.

In the years to come, we can expect to see more examples of our mixed economy moving toward a more capitalist system, as the private sector will play a greater role in delivering some goods and services (e.g., health care) that have historically been managed by public institutions. Keep in mind that during tough economic times, voters demand more government involvement. Thus, it is a traditional and desirable role of government to increase expenditures (e.g., provide financial aid to industries, increase spending on infrastructure, etc.) to support and stabilize the economy. The question is how much involvement, debt, etc. is appropriate.

UNDERSTANDING CANADA'S ECONOMIC SYSTEM

The strength of the economy has a tremendous effect on business. When the economy is strong and growing, most businesses prosper and almost everyone benefits through plentiful jobs, reasonably good wages, and sufficient revenues for the government to provide needed goods and services. When the economy is weak, however, businesses are weakened, employment and wages fall, and government revenues decline as a result.

Because business and the economy are so closely linked, business literature is full of economic terms and concepts. It is virtually impossible to read business reports with much understanding unless you are familiar with the economic concepts and terms being used. One purpose of this chapter is to help you learn additional economic concepts, terms, and issues—the kinds that you will be seeing daily if you read the business press, as we encourage you to do.

Illustrate the significance of key economic indicators and the business cycle.

Key Economic Indicators

Three major indicators of economic conditions are (1) the gross domestic product (GDP), (2) the unemployment rate, and (3) the price indexes. Another important statistic is the increase or decrease in productivity. When you read business literature, you'll see these terms used again and again. It will greatly increase your understanding if you learn the terms now.

Gross Domestic Product

gross domestic product (GDP)
The total value of goods and services produced in a country in a given year.

Gross domestic product (GDP) is the total value of final goods and services produced in a country in a given year. Either a domestic company or a foreign-owned company may produce the goods and services included in the GDP as long as the companies are located within the country's boundaries. For example, production values from Japanese automaker Toyota's factory <*www.toyota.ca*> in Cambridge, Ontario, would be included in the Canadian GDP. Likewise, revenue generated by Magna International's manufacturing and assembly plants in Brazil would be included in Brazil's GDP, even though Magna <*www.magna.com*> is a Canadian company.

If GDP growth slows or declines, there are often many negative effects on business. What can account for increases in GDP? A major influence on the growth of GDP is how productive the workforce is—that is, how much output workers create with a given amount of input. This is linked to the combination of creating jobs, working longer hours, or working smarter. Working smarter means being more productive through the use of better technology and processes and employing a more educated and efficient workforce. In the past, GDP growth has been affected by rising employment (to be discussed soon), low inflation, and low interest rates.[24]

The more you produce, the higher the GDP and vice versa. The economy benefits from a strong GDP. Money that is earned from producing goods and services goes to the employees that produce them in the form of wages. People who own the business generate a return on their investment, and government benefits from tax collection.

A strong economy usually leads to a high standard of living for Canadians. In your opinion, have too many people in Canada sacrificed their quality of life to have a higher standard of living by working more? Since productivity is central to a country's GDP, we will look at this next.

Productivity in Canada

An increase in productivity means a worker can produce more goods and services than before in the same time period, usually thanks to machinery or other equipment. Productivity in Canada has risen because computers and other technology have made production faster and easier. Improved productivity can decrease production costs which can then result in lower prices. Therefore, business people are eager to increase productivity.

The Canadian economy is a service economy. Productivity is an issue because service firms are very labour-intensive. Spurred by foreign competition, productivity in the goods-producing sector is rising rapidly. In the service sector, however, productivity is growing more slowly because service workers—like teachers, clerks, lawyers, and barbers—have fewer new technologies available than there are for factory workers.

Productivity in the Services-Producing Sector

One problem with the services-producing sector is that an influx of machinery may add to the *quality* of the service provided but not to the *output per worker.* For example, you've probably noticed how many computers there are on campus. They add to the quality of education but they don't necessarily boost professors' productivity. The same is true of some equipment in hospitals, such as CAT scanners, PET scanners (more modern versions of the X-ray machine), and MRI scanners. They improve patient care but they don't necessarily increase the number of patients doctors can see. In other words, today's productivity measures in the services-producing sector fail to capture the improvement in quality caused by new technology.

Clearly Canada and other countries need to develop new measures of productivity for the service economy, measures that include quality as well as quantity of output. Productivity is extremely important to a country, as it is a measure of its economic prosperity. Canadian businesses are criticized for not spending enough on research and development, relative to other advanced countries. By not doing so, these businesses will fall behind in the fierce global competitive battle. We will discuss the importance of research and development in Chapter 10.

Of course, technological advances usually lead to people being replaced by machines, often contributing to unemployment. We will now examine this important issue.

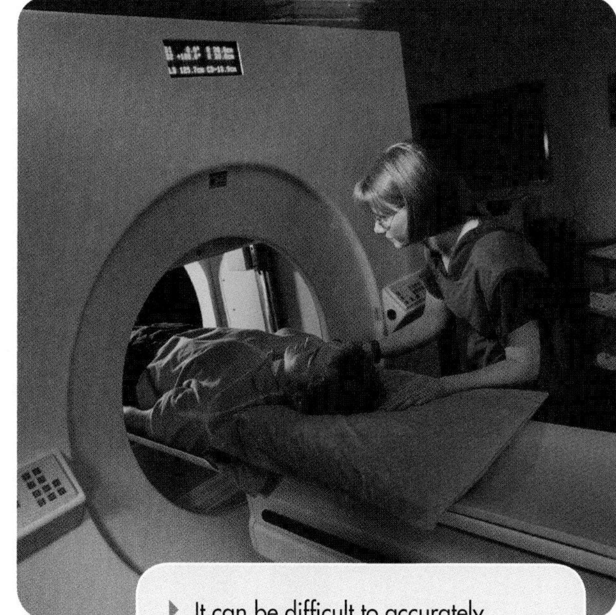

▸ It can be difficult to accurately measure productivity in service industries because new technologies, like high-tech medical scanning, can greatly improve the quality of services provided without necessarily increasing the number of people served. A doctor can make much more accurate diagnoses with better scans, for instance, but can still see only so many patients in a day. How can productivity measures try to capture improvements in service quality?

The Unemployment Rate

unemployment rate
The percentage of the labour force that actively seeks work but is unable to find work at a given time.

The **unemployment rate** refers to the percentage of the labour force (15 years and over) that actively seeks work but is unable to find work at a given time.[24] Figure 2.6 describes different types of unemployment and highlights Canada's unemployment rate over five years. The real rate is higher because Statistics Canada does not include people who have given up looking for jobs, those who were unable

▸ According to the Conference Board of Canada, businesses need to work smarter to improve productivity. This includes producing higher-value-added products and services that are worth more in the marketplace. This report card summarizes country ratings in a variety of areas.

REPORT CARD

	Economy	Innovation	Environment	Education and Skills	Health	Society
Australia	B	D	D	B	B	C
Austria	C	D	C	C	B	B
Belgium	B	C	C	B	n.a.	B
Canada	B	D	C	B	B	B
Denmark	B	C	C	C	D	A
Finland	B	C	A	A	B	B
France	D	C	B	C	B	B
Germany	D	B	C	B	B	B
Ireland	A	A	C	C	C	C
Italy	D	D	B	D	B	C
Japan	C	B	C	B	A	D
Netherlands	A	B	C	B	C	A
Norway	A	D	A	C	B	A
Sweden	A	B	A	B	B	A
Switzerland	A	A	A	B	A	B
U.K.	B	B	B	C	D	C
U.S.	B	A	D	C	D	D

Note: Data for the most recent year available used.
Source: Used with permission of the Conference Board of Canada, 2009.

to work, those who stay in or return to school because they cannot find full-time work, and various other categories of people. The unemployment rate is a key indicator of the health of the economy and of society more generally. That is, when economic growth is strong, the unemployment rate tends to be low and a person who wants a job is likely to experience little trouble finding one. On the other hand, when the economy is stagnating or in recession (to be discussed soon), unemployment tends to be higher.[25]

Figure 2.6

Canadian Unemployment Rate, 2007–2011

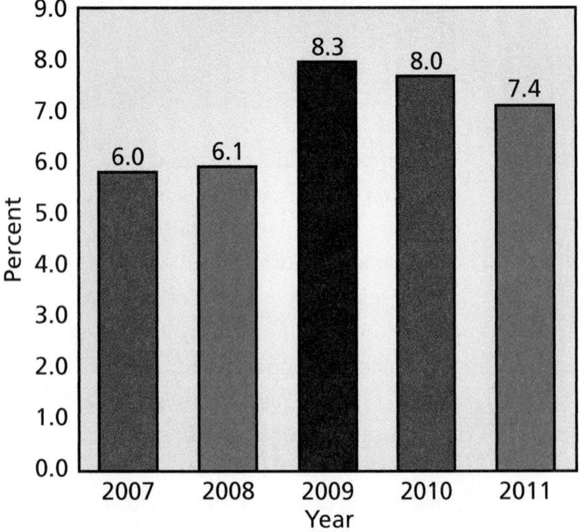

Statistics Canada, "Labour force characteristics," Statistics Canada, 6 January 2012, http://www.statcan.gc.ca/tables-tableaux/sum-som/l01/cst01/econ10-eng.htm. Reproduced and distributed on an "as is" basis with the permission of Statistics Canada.

The types of unemployment are:

- *Frictional unemployment* refers to those people who have quit work because they didn't like the job, the boss, or the working conditions and who haven't yet found a new job. It also refers to those people who are entering the labour force for the first time (e.g., new graduates) or are returning to the labour force after significant time away (e.g., parents who raised children). There will always be some frictional unemployment because it takes some time to find a first job or a new job.
- *Structural unemployment* refers to unemployment caused by the restructuring of firms or by a mismatch between the skills (or location) of job seekers and the requirements (or location) of available jobs (e.g., coal miners in an area where mines have been closed).
- *Cyclical unemployment* occurs because of a recession or a similar downturn in the business cycle (the ups and downs of business growth and decline over time). This type of unemployment is the most serious.
- *Seasonal unemployment* occurs where demand for labour varies over the year, as with the harvesting of crops.

People are unemployed in Canada for various reasons. Perhaps their employer goes out of business or their company cuts staff. Young persons enter the job market looking for their first job and other employees quit their jobs but have trouble finding new ones. Companies merge and jobs are consolidated or trimmed. Companies transfer their operations to another country, or a branch of a foreign company is closed down. When a job is lost, not only is it a loss to society and the economy, but the loss of income can also create hardship for individuals and families.

According to Statistics Canada, the unemployed include persons who (during the reference period) were as follows: (1) without work but had looked for work in the past four weeks ending with the reference period and were available for work; (2) were on temporary layoff due to business conditions and were available for work; or (3) were without work, had a job to start within four weeks from the reference period and were available for work.[26] Unemployment insurance only goes so far to relieve such unemployment.

The Price Indexes

The price indexes help measure the health of the economy by measuring the levels of inflation, disinflation, deflation, and stagflation. **Inflation** refers to a general rise in the prices of goods and services over time. Rapid inflation is scary. If the cost of goods and services goes up by just 7 percent a year, everything will double in cost in just ten years or so. Inflation increases the cost of doing business. When a company borrows money, interest costs are higher, employees demand increases to keep up with the rise in the cost of living, suppliers raise their prices, and as a result the company is forced to raise its prices. If other countries succeed in keeping their inflation rates down, then Canadian companies will become less competitive in the world market.

Disinflation describes a condition where price increases are slowing (the inflation rate is declining). **Deflation** means that prices are actually declining.[27] It occurs when countries produce so many goods that people cannot afford to buy them all. That is, too few dollars are chasing too many goods. **Stagflation** occurs when the economy is slowing but prices are going up regardless.[28]

The **consumer price index (CPI)** is a monthly statistic that measures the pace of inflation or deflation. To calculate the consumer price index, costs of a "basket" of goods and services for an average family—including food, shelter, transportation, and clothing and footwear—are calculated to see if they are going up or down. For example, Canadian consumers paid, on average, 2.5 percent more for such a basket in January, 2012, than twelve months earlier; this was led by increases in energy prices (6.5 percent) and food prices (4.2 percent).[29] The CPI is an important figure because it affects nearly all Canadians, either directly or indirectly. For example, government benefits (such as Old Age Security and Canada Pension Plan), rental agreements, some labour contracts, and interest rates are based on it.

Other indicators of the economy's condition include housing starts, retail sales, motor vehicle sales, consumer confidence, and changes in personal income. You can learn more about such indicators by reading business periodicals, contacting government agencies, listening to business broadcasts, and exploring the Internet.

inflation
A general rise in the prices of goods and services over time.

disinflation
A situation in which price increases are slowing (the inflation rate is declining).

deflation
A situation in which prices are declining.

stagflation
A situation in which the economy is slowing but prices are going up regardless.

consumer price index (CPI)
A monthly statistic that measures the pace of inflation or deflation.

The Business Cycle

Business cycles (also known as **economic cycles**) are the periodic rises and falls that occur in economies over time.[30] These fluctuations are often measured using the real gross domestic product.[31] Economists look at a number of types of cycles, from seasonal cycles that occur within a year to cycles that occur every 48 to 60 years. Economist Joseph Schumpeter identified the four phases of long-term business cycles as boom, recession, depression, recovery:

1. An economic boom is just what it sounds like—business is booming. Periods of economic boom bring jobs, growth, and economic prosperity.

business cycles (economic cycles)
The periodic rises and falls that occur in economies over time.

recession
Two or more consecutive quarters of decline in the GDP.

depression
A severe recession.

2. Two or more consecutive quarters of decline in the GDP result in a **recession**. In a recession, prices fall, people purchase fewer products, and businesses fail. A recession has many negative consequences for an economy: high unemployment, increased business failures, and an overall drop in living standards. The 2009 recession is an example.
3. A **depression** is a severe recession usually accompanied by deflation. Business cycles rarely go through a depression phase. In fact, while there were many business cycles during the twentieth century, there was only one severe depression (in the 1930s).
4. A recovery occurs when the economy stabilizes and starts to grow. This eventually leads to an economic boom, starting the cycle all over again.

One goal of some economists is to predict such ups and downs. That is very difficult to do. Business cycles are identified according to facts, but we can explain those facts only by using theories. Therefore, one cannot predict with certainty. But one thing is certain: over time, the economy will rise and fall as it has done in recent years.

Since dramatic swings up and down in the economy cause all kinds of disruptions to businesses, the government tries to minimize such changes. The government uses fiscal policy and monetary policy to try to keep the economy from slowing too much or growing too rapidly. We will discuss both of these policies in Chapter 4.

PROGRESS ASSESSMENT

- What factors have contributed to the decision to have a mixed economy in Canada?
- Name three economic indicators and describe how well Canada is doing using each one.
- What's the difference between a recession and a depression?

SUMMARY

Describe basic economics.

Economics is the study of how society chooses to employ resources to produce goods and services and distribute them for consumption among various competing groups and individuals.

What are the two branches of economics?
There are two major branches of economics: macroeconomics studies the operation of a nation's economy as a whole, and microeconomics studies the behaviour of people and organizations in particular markets (e.g., why people buy smaller cars when gas prices go up).

Explain what capitalism is and how free markets work.

Capitalism is an economic system in which all or most of the means of production and distribution (e.g., land, factories, railroads, and stores) are privately owned and operated for profit.

Who decides what to produce under capitalism?
In capitalist countries, business people decide what to produce; how much to pay workers; how much to charge for goods and services; whether to produce certain goods in their own countries, import those goods, or have them made in other countries; and so on.

How does the free market work?

The free market is one in which decisions about what to produce and in what quantities are made by the market—that is, by buyers and sellers negotiating prices for goods and services. Buyers' decisions in the marketplace tell sellers what to produce and in what quantity. When buyers demand more goods, the price goes up, signalling suppliers to produce more. The higher the price, the more goods and services suppliers are willing to produce. Price, then, is the mechanism that allows free markets to work.

What is supply and demand?

Supply refers to the quantity of products that manufacturers or owners are willing to sell at different prices at a specific time. Demand refers to the quantity of products that people are willing to buy at different prices at a specific time. The key factor in determining the quantity supplied and the quantity demanded is price.

What is the relevance of the equilibrium point?

The equilibrium point, also referred to as the equilibrium price, is the point where the quantity demanded is the same as the quantity supplied. In the long run, that price becomes the market price.

Define socialism and its benefits and negative consequences.

Socialism is an economic system based on the premise that some businesses should be owned by the government.

What are the advantages and disadvantages of socialism?

Socialism creates more social equality. Compared to workers in capitalist countries, workers in socialist countries not only receive more education and health care benefits but also work fewer hours, have longer vacations, and receive more benefits in general, such as child care. The major disadvantage of socialism is that it lowers the profits of owners, thus cutting the incentive to start a business or to work hard. Socialist economies tend to have a higher unemployment rate and a slower growth rate than capitalist economies.

Evaluate communism and the challenges of such a system.

Under communism, the government owns almost all major production facilities and dictates what gets produced and by whom.

How else does communism differ from socialism?

Communism is more restrictive when it comes to personal freedoms, such as religious freedom. With communism, one can see shortages in items such as food and clothing, and business people may not work as hard as the government takes most of their earnings. While many countries practise socialism, only a few (e.g., North Korea) still practise communism.

Describe the mixed economy of Canada.

A mixed economy is one that is part capitalist and part socialist. That is, some businesses are privately owned, but taxes tend to be high to distribute income more evenly among the population.

What countries have mixed economies?

Canada has a mixed economy, as do most other countries of the world.

What does it mean to have a mixed economy?

A mixed economy has most of the benefits of wealth creation that free markets bring plus the benefits of greater social equality and concern for the environment that socialism offers.

Illustrate the significance of key economic indicators and the business cycle.

Three major indicators of economic conditions are (1) the gross domestic product (GDP), (2) the unemployment rate, and (3) the price indexes.

What are the key terms used to describe the Canadian economic system?

Gross domestic product (GDP) is the total value of goods and services produced in a country in a given year. The unemployment rate represents the number of unemployed persons expressed as a percentage of the labour force. The consumer price index (CPI) measures changes in the prices of a basket of goods and services that consumers buy. It is a monthly statistic that measures the pace of inflation (consumer prices going up) or deflation (consumer prices going down). Productivity is the total volume of goods and services one worker can produce in a given period. Productivity in Canada has increased over the years due to the use of computers and other technologies.

What are the four phases of business cycles?

In an economic boom, businesses do well. A recession occurs when two or more quarters show declines in the GDP, prices fall, people purchase fewer products, and businesses fail. A depression is a severe recession. Finally, recovery is when the economy stabilizes and starts to grow.

KEY TERMS

brain drain
business cycles (economic cycles)
capitalism
command economy
communism
consumer price index (CPI)
deflation
demand
depression
disinflation
economics
free-market economy
gross domestic product (GDP)
inflation
invisible hand
macroeconomics
market price
microeconomics
mixed economies
monopolistic competition
monopoly
oligopoly
perfect competition
recession
resource development
socialism
stagflation
supply
unemployment rate

CRITICAL THINKING

Many say that business people do not do enough for society. Some students choose to work for non-profit organizations instead of for-profit organizations because they want to help others. However, business people say that they do more to help others than non-profit groups because they provide jobs for people rather than giving them charity, which often precludes them from searching for work. Furthermore, they believe that businesses create all the wealth that non-profit groups distribute. Can you find some middle ground in this debate that would show that both business people and those who work for non-profit organizations contribute to society and need to work together more closely to help people? Could you use the concepts of Adam Smith to help illustrate your position?

DEVELOPING WORKPLACE SKILLS

1. Show your understanding of the principles of supply and demand by looking at the oil market today. Why does the price of gas fluctuate so greatly? What will happen as more and more people in China and India decide to buy automobiles? What would happen if more Canadian consumers decided to drive electric cars?
2. This exercise will help you understand socialism from different perspectives. Form three groups. Each group should adopt a different role in a socialist economy: one group will be the business owners, another group will be the workers, and the third will be government leaders. Within your group, discuss and list the advantages and disadvantages to you of lowering taxes on businesses. Then have each group choose a representative to debate the tax issue with the representatives from the other groups.
3. Draw a line and mark one end "capitalism" and the other end "socialism." Mark where Canada is now on that line. Explain why you marked the spot you did. Students from other countries may want to do this exercise for their own countries and explain the differences to the class.
4. Break into small groups. In your group, discuss how the following have affected people's purchasing behaviours and attitudes toward Canada and its economy: development of the Alberta oil sands; the Atlantic seal hunt; mad cow disease; and the growth of the Internet. Have a group member prepare a short summary for the class.

ANALYZING MANAGEMENT DECISIONS

The Rule of 72

No formula is more useful for understanding inflation than the rule of 72. Basically, the rule allows you to quickly compute how long it takes the cost of goods and services to double at various compounded rates of growth. For example, if houses were increasing in cost at 9 percent a year, how long would it take for the price of a home to double? The answer is easy to calculate. Simply divide 72 by the annual increase (9 percent) and you get the approximate number of years it takes to double the price (eight years). Of course, the same calculation can be used to predict how high food prices or auto prices will be 10 years from now.

Here's an example of how you can use the rule of 72. If the cost of going to college goes up by 6 percent a year, how much might you have to pay to send your child to college in 24 years (this assumes you will have a child six years from now) if college costs are now $10,000 a year? To find the answer, you divide 72 by 6, which shows that the cost of an education would double in 12 years. It would double twice in 24 years. Your son or daughter can expect to pay $40,000 per year to attend college.

Discussion Questions

1. If the cost of a university education is about $20,000 per year now, what will it cost your children per year if costs go up 9 percent a year and your children go to university 16 years from now?
2. If the value of a home doubles in 12 years, what is the annual rate of return? (Hint: Use the rule of 72 in reverse.)
3. If you put $1,000 into a savings account and earned 6 percent per year, how much money would you have in the account after 48 years?

Practise and learn online with Connect.

CHAPTER 3

COMPETING IN GLOBAL MARKETS

LEARNING OBJECTIVES

After you have read and studied this chapter, you should be able to:

LO 1 Describe the importance of the global market and the roles of comparative advantage and absolute advantage in global trade.

LO 2 Explain the importance of importing and exporting and define key terms used in global business.

LO 3 Illustrate the strategies used in reaching global markets and explain the role of multinational corporations in global markets.

LO 4 Evaluate the forces that affect trading in global markets.

LO 5 Debate the advantages and disadvantages of trade protectionism, define tariff and non-tariff barriers, and give examples of common markets.

LO 6 Discuss the changing landscape of the global market.

PROFILE

GETTING TO KNOW GUY LALIBERTÉ OF CIRQUE DU SOLEIL

From a group of 20 street performers at its beginnings in 1984, Cirque du Soleil, a Quebec-based organization, now generates annual sales in excess of US$700 million. The company's performances have brought wonder and delight to more than 100 million spectators in more than 300 cities in over 40 countries on six continents. In 2012, Cirque du Soleil is expecting close to 15 million spectators in its 22 different shows around the world.

Guy Laliberté, an accordionist, stilt-walker, and fire-breather, founded Quebec's first internationally renowned circus with the support of a small group of accomplices. The company was formed on a dream to create a Quebec circus and take it around the world. Each show is a theatrical blend of circus arts and street performance, with spectacular costumes and fairyland sets. Creativity is the cornerstone of the organization's identity. Every concept and scenic element is created at the Studio, a training facility in Montreal. There, close to 2,000 employees work together to create new shows and costumes.

Laliberté juggles the demands of creative and financial types and walks a tightrope among the 5,000 employees from close to 50 different countries. With such diversity, you can see why the company's great strength is its ability to develop material that resonates with audiences worldwide.

Since the very beginnings of Cirque du Soleil, Laliberté has insisted on having a social approach as part of the development of the company. He has dedicated 1 percent of all revenues generated by Cirque du Soleil to social and cultural programs worldwide. Another initiative, ONE DROP Foundation <*www.onedrop.org*>, was created to fight poverty around the world by providing sustainable access to safe water. In 2009, he became the first Canadian private explorer when he boarded the Soyuz TMA-16 spacecraft with Expedition 21 from the Russian Federal Space Agency. His journey was the first social/artistic mission in space with the objective of raising awareness of water issues facing the world.

Due to open markets and global trade, there are many opportunities for Canadian companies beyond our borders. This chapter will introduce some of the topics that explain the opportunities that exist in global markets and the challenges that business people such as Guy Laliberté face as they continue to look globally for growth and success.

Sources: "Press Room," Cirque du Soleil, 22 February 2012, www.cirquedusoleil.com/en/press/default.aspx; "First poetic social mission in space: Guy Laliberté, founder of Cirque du Soleil and the ONE DROP Foundation, begins training for travel on board SOYUZ TMA-16 to ISS," Cirque du Soleil, 4 June 2009, www.cirquedusoleil.com/en/press/news/2009/news127.aspx; Lori McLeod and Gordon Pitts, "From Quebec's Streets to Dubai," *The Globe and Mail*, 7 August 2008, B4; "Cirque du Soleil At a Glance," Cirque du Soleil, 26 July 2008, www.cirquedusoleil.com/cirquedusoleil/pdf/pressroom/en/cds_en_bref_en.pdf; Telios Demos, "Cirque du Balancing Act," *Fortune*, 12 June 2006, http://money.cnn.com/magazines/fortune/fortune_archive/2006/06/12/8379232/index.htm; and Shirley Won, "Cirque Faces New Balancing Act," *The Globe and Mail*, 7 April 2006, B3.

Describe the importance of the global market and the roles of comparative advantage and absolute advantage in global trade.

THE DYNAMIC GLOBAL MARKET

Have you ever dreamed of travelling to exotic cities such as Paris, Tokyo, Rio de Janeiro, or Cairo? Today, over 90 percent of the companies doing business globally believe it's important for their employees to have experience working in other countries.[1] The reason is not surprising. Although Canada is a market of more than 34.8 million people, there are over 7 billion potential customers in the 195 independent countries that make up the global market.[2] (See Figure 3.1 for a map of the world and important statistics about the world's population.[3])That's too many people to ignore.

Canadian companies, both large and small, continuously look for opportunities to grow their businesses. For example, Bombardier Inc. <*www.bombardier.com*> is a world-leading manufacturer of innovative transportation solutions in the areas of aerospace and rail transportation.[4] Headquartered in Montreal, the company has 69 production and engineering sites in 23 countries, and a worldwide network of service centres.[5] Small-business Lija Style Inc. <*www.lijastyle.com*> was started in 1997 by Linda Hipp after she became frustrated with the unflattering golfwear available for women.[6] Today, the company's products are serviced by four Canadian, sixteen U.S., and four international representative forces/agencies in the European Union, South Africa, Dubai, and Australia.[7]

Companies also continuously review their global operations to ensure that they are operating at a profit. One Canadian industry that has been particularly hard hit as a result of global trends is the auto industry. Factors such as the increasing price of gas and weakening demand for trucks and sport utility vehicles (SUVs) have forced companies to consider restructuring plans. As a result, thousands of Canadian jobs have been eliminated. Layoffs have occurred at General Motors Canada <*www.gm.ca*>, Chrysler Canada <*www.chryslercanada.ca*>, Ford Motor Company of Canada <*www.ford.ca*>, and many parts suppliers.[8] The global market is truly dynamic, and progressive companies continuously scan the business environment to ensure that they take advantage of the opportunities and minimize the impact of threats.

exporting
Selling products to another country.

importing
Buying products from another country.

Because the global market is so large, it is important to understand the language of international trade. Canada is a large exporting nation. **Exporting** is selling products (i.e., goods and services) to another country. **Importing** is buying products from

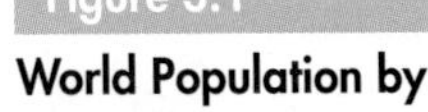

Figure 3.1

World Population by Continent

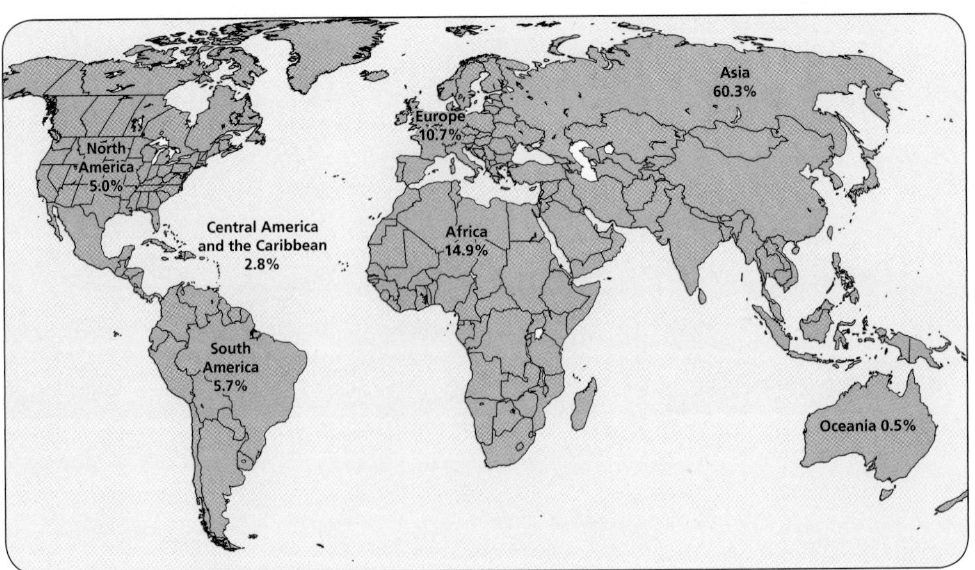

Source: "World Population by Estimates," Nations Online, 24 September 2011, www.nationsonline.org/oneworld/.

another country. Competition in exporting is very intense and Canadian companies face aggressive competition from exporters around the world who also have the same objectives of growing their businesses.

This chapter will familiarize you with global business and its many challenges. As competition in global markets increases, the demand for students with training in global business is almost certain to grow. If you choose such a career, prepare yourself to work hard and always be ready for new challenges.

Why Trade with Other Nations?

No country, not even a technologically advanced one, can produce all of the products that its people want and need. Even if a country did become self-sufficient, other nations would seek to trade with that country to meet the needs of their own people. Some nations, like Venezuela and Russia, have an abundance of natural resources but have limited technological know-how. Other countries, such as Japan and Switzerland, have sophisticated technology but few natural resources. Global trade enables a nation to produce what it is most capable of producing and to buy what it needs from others in a mutually beneficial exchange relationship. This happens through the process of free trade.

free trade
The movement of goods and services among nations without political or economic barriers.

Free trade is the movement of goods and services among nations without political or economic barriers. It is often a hotly debated concept. Figure 3.2 offers some of the pros and cons of free trade.

comparative advantage theory
A theory that states that a country should sell to other countries those products that it produces most effectively and efficiently, and buy from other countries those products that it cannot produce as effectively or efficiently.

The Theories of Comparative and Absolute Advantage

Global trade is the exchange of goods and services across national borders. Exchanges between and among countries involve more than goods and services, however. Countries also exchange art, sports, cultural events, medical advances, space exploration, and labour. Comparative advantage theory, suggested in the early nineteenth century by English economist David Ricardo, was the guiding principle that supported this idea of free economic exchange.[9]

Comparative advantage theory states that a country should sell to other countries those products that it produces most effectively and efficiently, and buy from

Figure 3.2

The Pros and Cons of Free Trade

Pros	Cons
The global market contains more than 7 billion potential customers for goods and services.	Domestic workers (particularly in manufacturing-based jobs) can lose their jobs due to increased imports or production shifts to low-wage global markets.
Productivity improves when countries produce goods and services in which they have a comparative advantage.	Workers may be forced to accept pay cuts from employers who can threaten to move their jobs to lower-cost global markets.
Global competition and less-costly imports keep prices down, so inflation does not curtail economic growth.	Moving operations overseas because of intense competitive pressure often means the loss of service jobs and white-collar jobs.
Free trade inspires innovation for new products and keeps firms competitively challenged.	Domestic companies can lose their comparative advantage when competitors build advanced production operations in low-wage countries.
Uninterrupted flow of capital gives countries access to foreign investments, which helps keep interest rates low.	

Canada became a diamond producer in 1998 when the Ekati diamond mine opened about 300 kilometres northeast of Yellowknife. Here you see the Diavik Diamond Mine, located on a 20-square-kilometre island in the same area. Today Canada is the world's third-largest diamond producer on a value basis, after Botswana and Russia.[10]

other countries those products it cannot produce as effectively or efficiently. (Recall that these two terms were introduced in Chapter 1.) Japan has shown this ability with cars and electronic items. Canada has such an advantage with certain forestry and agricultural products, and various minerals. In contrast, Canada lacks a comparative advantage in growing coffee; thus, we import most of the coffee we consumer. By specializing and trading, Canada and its trading partners can realize mutually beneficial exchanges.[11]

In practice, this theory application does not work so neatly. For various reasons, many countries decide to produce certain agricultural, industrial, or consumer products despite a lack of comparative advantage. To facilitate this plan, they restrict imports of competing products from countries that can produce them at lower costs. The net result is that the free movement of goods and services is restricted. We will return to the topic of trade protectionism later in the chapter.

absolute advantage
The advantage that exists when a country has a monopoly on producing a specific product or is able to produce it more efficiently than all other countries.

A country has an **absolute advantage** if it has a monopoly on producing a specific product or is able to produce it more efficiently than all other countries. However, an absolute advantage in natural resources does not last forever. For instance, South Africa once had an absolute advantage in diamond production but this is no longer the case. Global competition also causes other absolute advantages to fade. Today there are very few instances of absolute advantage in global markets.

Explain the importance of importing and exporting and define key terms used in global business.

GETTING INVOLVED IN GLOBAL TRADE

People interested in finding a job in global business often think of firms like Bombardier, Magna International, and Sony <*www.sony.ca*>, which have large multinational accounts. The real job potential, however, may be with small businesses. Small businesses contribute slightly more than 30 percent to Canada's gross domestic product and employ approximately five million individuals (or 48 percent of the total labour force in the private sector). As well, about 86 percent of Canadian exporters were small businesses.[12] With the help of government agencies, such as Foreign Affairs and International Trade Canada <*www.international.gc.ca*/> and Export

China produces and exports 80 percent of the toys manufactured in the world. What products do you use that are imported from China?

Development Canada <*www.edc.ca*>, many small businesses are becoming more involved in global markets.

Getting started globally is often a matter of observation, determination, and risk. What does that mean? First, it is important to observe and study global markets. Your library, the Internet, and your fellow classmates are good starting points for doing your research. Second, if you have the opportunity, travelling to different countries is a great way to observe foreign cultures and lifestyles and see if doing business globally appeals to you.

Importing Goods and Services[13]

The Canada Border Services Agency <*www.cbsa-asfc.gc.ca*> deals with importers across the whole range of goods and services that enter our country. These products (also referred to as items) are subject to compliance with certain conditions imposed by the federal and, sometimes, provincial government(s). Some of the conditions may include the following:

- Is the article prohibited entry into Canada (e.g., hate literature)?
- Is the article allowed in only under the authority of an import permit? Examples include textiles and clothing, steel, wheat, barley and their products, certain farm products (e.g., dairy, chicken, eggs, and turkey), and firearms.
- Is the article subject to some other federally-imposed condition? For example, goods for retail sale have to comply with labelling laws; motor vehicles have to meet emission control standards; and food and agricultural products have to pass the necessary health and sanitary checks.
- Is the article subject to some privately-certified standard? For example, all electrical appliances and equipment must be certified by a recognized certification body before they can be sold in Canada.
- Is there a provincial rule to comply with? For example, imports of liquor, wine, and beer require prior authorization from the appropriate liquor commission.

Review Figure 3.3 for categories and examples of goods and services that are imported, as well as exported.

Figure 3.3

Categories and Examples of Canada's Merchandise and Service Trade

Categories	Examples
Merchandise Trade	
Industrial Goods and Materials	Metals and metal ores, chemicals and plastics, and other industrial goods and materials
Machinery and Equipment	Industrial and agricultural machinery, aircraft and other transportation equipment, and other machinery and equipment
Energy Products	Crude petroleum and other energy products such as natural gas, petroleum, and coal products
Automotive Products	Passenger autos and chassis, trucks and other motor vehicles, and motor vehicle parts
Agricultural and Fishing Products	Wheat, fruits and vegetables, and other agricultural and fishing products such as live animals, feed, beverages, and tobacco
Forestry Products	Lumber and sawmill products, wood pulp and other wood products, and newsprint and other paper products
Other Consumer Goods	Apparel and footwear, and miscellaneous consumer goods such as watches, sporting goods and toys, and television and radio sets
Service Trade Categories	
Travel Services	Business travel and personal travel
Transportation Services	Air transport, water transport, land, and other transport
Commercial Services	Communication, construction, insurance, computer and information, architectural, engineering, research and development, and other financial services
Government Services	Military activities and business support

Sources: "Exports of goods on a balance-of-payments basis, by product," Statistics Canada, 13 August 2008, http://www40.statcan.ca/l01/cst01/gblec04.htm; "Imports of goods on a balance-of-payments basis, by product," Statistics Canada, 13 August 2008, http://www40.statcan.ca/l01/cst01/gblec05.htm; and "Canada's Balance of International Payments," Statistics Canada, 29 May 2008, http://www40.statcan.ca.libaccess.lib.mcmaster.ca/l01/cst01/econ01a.htm?sdi=services. Reproduced and distributed on an "as is" basis with the permission of Statistics Canada.

▸ Nickelback began as a cover band in Hanna, Alberta, and to date has sold millions of records worldwide. Other Canadian-born entertainers that have global appeal include Justin Bieber, Celine Dion, Drake, and Nelly Furtado. Do you prefer to support Canadian talent?

Exporting Goods and Services[14]

You may be surprised at what you can sell in other countries. The fact is, you can sell just about any good or service that is used in Canada to other countries—and often the competition is not nearly as intense for producers in global markets as it is at home. You can, for example, sell snowplows to Saudi Arabians who use them to clear sand off their driveways. (Review the Spotlight on Small Business box for a unique exporting business.) Don't forget that services can be exported as well.

While Canada has a small population, it produces vast quantities of products. Based on the most recent data, Canadian exports represented 2.5 percent (US$452 billion) of world merchandise trade and 1.8 percent (US$74 billion) of world services trade. Why is trade so important? Trade with other countries enhances the quality of life for Canadians and contributes to our country's economic well-being. Exports alone account for one in three Canadian jobs.

Canadian goods and services can be sold abroad directly as an export from a Canadian company or they can be sold indirectly via a foreign-located subsidiary of a Canadian company. Sales by majority-owned foreign affiliates of Canadian businesses are an important means by which Canadian companies engage in international commerce, and they are equivalent to slightly over 90 percent of the value of goods and services exports.

Spend some time reviewing Figure 3.3. By understanding this information, you will realize why you hear so much about these categories in the news. After all, such activities are vital to our economy. It is also important for businesses to be aware of these great opportunities. But don't be misled. Selling in global markets is not by any means easy. Adapting goods and services to specific global markets is potentially profitable but can be very difficult. We shall discuss a number of forces that affect global trading later in this chapter.

balance of trade
A nation's ratio of exports to imports.

trade surplus
A favourable balance of trade; occurs when the value of a country's exports exceeds that of its imports.

Measuring Global Trade

In measuring the effectiveness of global trade, nations carefully follow two key indicators: balance of trade and balance of payments. The **balance of trade** is a nation's ratio of exports to imports. A *favourable* balance of trade, or **trade surplus**, occurs when the value of the country's exports exceeds that of its imports. An unfavourable balance of

SPOTLIGHT ON SMALL BUSINESS

Ice Means Business

In 1996, Julian Bayley and his wife Ann turned an ice-carving hobby and sales of ice-punch bowls for local weddings into a successful business. Iceculture Inc. *<http://iceculture.com>*, located in Hensall, Ontario, is the ultimate Canadian cliché. Using water from Hensall's town well, the water is transformed into icy wonders that are carved by computer-guided lathes. Freezer containers ship these items to the far corners of the world. Hot spots include South Africa, Australia, and Dubai, and cold corners include Iceland and Norway.

This multi-million-dollar family business (daughter Heidi is the President) exports massive blocks of crystal-clear carving ice, ice sculptures, ice lounges (rooms where the walls and all the furniture and décor are made out of ice), carving equipment and much more. Its first export order was for raw ice blocks to the United Kingdom. Other examples include Dubai's first ice restaurant, the building of some 20 permanent ice lounges from Australia to South Africa, and sculptures that have been supplied to some of the biggest events in the world, like the Super Bowl. Today, some 80 percent of the company's production is exported.

Sources: Ian Harvey, "8 wacky Canadian entrepreneurs," MSN Money, 24 May 2012, http://money.ca.msn.com/small-business/gallery/8-wacky-canadian-entrepreneurs#image52; "Who We Are," Ice Culture Inc., [2012?], http://iceculture.com/about-us; "Iceculture carves out exports in five continents," Export Development Canada, [2012], www.edc.ca/EN/Knowledge-Centre/Success-Stories/Pages/export-success-story-ice-culture.aspx; and "Sharing the Iceculture Lounge Experience," Ice Culture Inc., 7 September 2011, http://iceculture.com/press-releases.

trade deficit
An unfavourable balance of trade; occurs when the value of a country's imports exceeds that of its exports.

balance of payments
The difference between money coming into a country (from exports) and money leaving the country (for imports) plus money flows from other factors such as tourism, foreign aid, military expenditures, and foreign investment.

trade, or **trade deficit**, occurs when the value of the country's imports exceeds that of its exports. In 2009, Canada registered its first trade deficit in 15 years and this continued to be the case for 2010 and 2011.[15] It is easy to understand why countries prefer to export more than they import. If I sell you $200 worth of goods and buy only $100 worth, I have an extra $100 available to buy other things. However, I'm in an unfavourable position if I buy $200 worth of goods from you and sell you only $100.

The **balance of payments** is the difference between money coming into a country (from exports) and money leaving the country (for imports) plus money flows coming into or leaving a country from other factors such as tourism, foreign aid, military expenditures, and foreign investment. The goal is always to have more money flowing into the country than flowing out of the country; in other words, a *favourable* balance of payments. Conversely, an *unfavourable* balance of payments is when more money is flowing out of a country than coming in.

Trading in Global Markets: The Canadian Experience

At first glance, Canada's foreign trade statistics are impressive. As a country, we rank thirteenth in the world as leading exporter and eleventh in the world as leading importer in world merchandise trade.[16] While our abundant natural resources are a major area for exports, developing countries continue to give Canada stiff competition in these areas. When we look carefully at the numbers in Figure 3.4, we see that we are dependent on one country, the United States. Over the long-term, Derek Burleton, TD deputy chief economist, expects that Canada's economic prosperity will be increasingly driven by trade with economies other than the United States'. He predicts that by 2020, the United States will account for only two-thirds of Canada's exports, down from a peak of 85 percent in 2002.[17] Read the next section to learn about these priority markets.

Canada's Priority Markets[18]

Technological advances in most fields, primarily in the area of transmission and storage of information, have shattered the archaic notions of how things ought to function, from production and trade to war and politics. The new ways of communicating, organizing, and working are inviting the most remote corners of the world to be actors on the global economic stage. These *emerging economies* are enjoying high growth rates, rapid increases in their living standards, and a rising global prominence. Tapping into these markets is crucial. For example, in thirty years a gain of just 0.1 percent in the Canadian share of the import markets of Brazil, Russia, India, and China (BRIC countries) would mean an export gain of $29 billion.

Based on extensive consultation with government, academic, and Canadian business and industry representatives, the federal government identified 13 priority markets around the world where Canadian opportunities and interests have the

Figure 3.4
Canada's Goods and Services Trade by Region, 2011

	Exports %	Imports %
United States	69.5	60.8
European Union	10.4	11.0
Japan	2.4	1.9
Rest of World	17.7	26.3

Source: Canada's State of Trade: Trade and Investment Update 2012 - Table 4-1 Canada's Good and Services Trade by Region, 2011 ($ millions and annual % change)," Foreign Affairs and International Trade Canada, 2012, http://www.international.gc.ca/economist-economiste/assets/pdfs/performance/SoT_2012/SoT_2012_Eng.pdf, 42. Affairs and International Trade. Reproduced with the permission of the Minister of Public Works and Government Services Canada, 2012.

One objective of the federal government's Science and Technology program is to identify and incorporate world-leading research into the development of innovative processes, goods, and services in Canada. What are some other benefits of such collaboration?

greatest potential for growth. The priority markets are as follows: the Association of South East Asian Nations (Brunei Darussalam, Burma, Cambodia, Indonesia, Laos, Malaysia, Philippines, Singapore, Thailand, and Vietnam), Australia and New Zealand, Brazil, China, Europe, Gulf Cooperation Council (Saudi Arabia, United Arab Emirates, Kuwait, Qatar, Bahrain, and Oman), India, Japan, Korea, Latin America and the Caribbean, Mexico, Russia, and the United States.

China and India are of particular interest as they are growing and emerging markets due to their size and economic transformation. A Conference Board of Canada report notes that by 2050, India will be the world's third-largest economy, with a GDP approaching US$30 trillion, behind only the United States and China, which will top the list. Steps already taken to encourage a stronger Canadian presence in the global marketplace include tax cuts, increased support for research and development, and critical investments in infrastructure at Canada–U.S. border crossings and Canada's Asia-Pacific Gateway.

PROGRESS ASSESSMENT

- How do world population and market statistics support the expansion of Canadian businesses into global markets?
- What is comparative advantage? How does this differ from absolute advantage?
- How are a country's balance of trade and balance of payments determined?

STRATEGIES FOR REACHING GLOBAL MARKETS

Illustrate the strategies used in reaching global markets and explain the role of multinational corporations in global markets.

Businesses use many different strategies to compete in global markets. The key strategies include licensing, exporting, franchising, contract manufacturing, creating international joint ventures and strategic alliances, and engaging in foreign direct investment. Each of these strategies provides opportunities for becoming involved in global markets, along with specific commitments and risks. Figure 3.5 places the

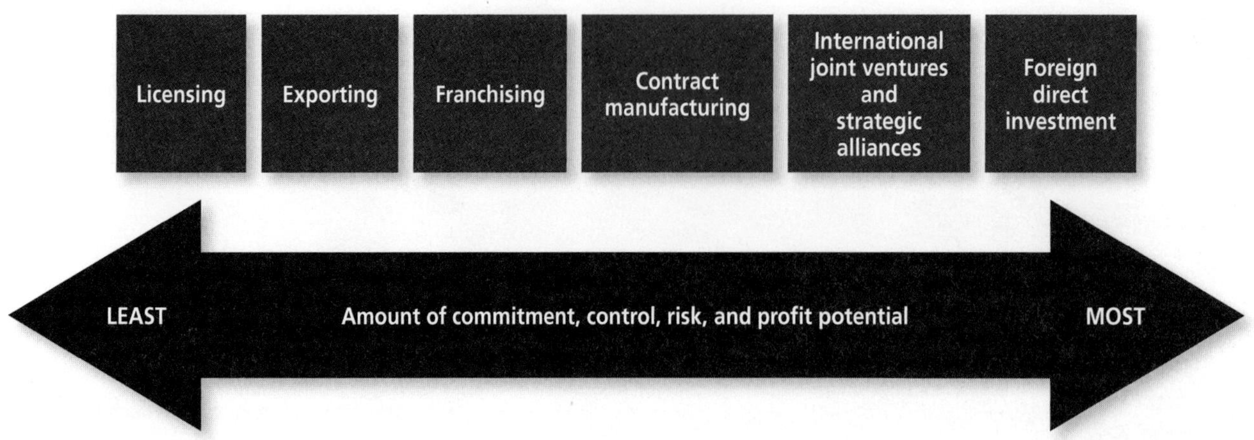

FIGURE 3.5

Strategies for Reaching Global Markets

strategies discussed on a continuum showing the amount of commitment, control, risk, and profit potential associated with each one. Take a few minutes to look it over before you continue.

Licensing

licensing
A global strategy in which a firm (the licensor) allows a foreign company (the licensee) to produce its product in exchange for a fee (a royalty).

A firm (the licensor) may decide to compete in a global market by **licensing** the right to manufacture its product or use its trademark to a foreign company (the licensee) for a fee (a royalty). A company with an interest in licensing generally needs to send company representatives to the foreign producer to help set up the production process. The licensor may also assist or work with a licensee in such areas as distribution, promotion, and consulting.

A licensing agreement can benefit a firm in several ways. First, the firm can gain revenues it would not otherwise have generated in its home market. Also, foreign licensees must often purchase start-up supplies, component materials, and consulting services from the licensing firm. Disney and Coca-Cola entered global licensing agreements that have extended into long-term service contracts. For example, Oriental Land Company <*www.olc.co.jp/en*> owns and operates Tokyo Disneyland and Tokyo Disney Sea Park under a licensing agreement that pays Disney management and consulting fees.[19] Disney and competitors like Universal Studios <*www.universalstudios.com*> and Marvel Entertainment <*www.marvel.com*> are seeking to sign licensing agreements for theme parks in the oil-rich Middle East.[20]

A final advantage of licensing is that licensors spend little or no money to produce and market their products. These costs come from the licensee's pocket. Therefore, licensees generally work hard to succeed. However, licensors may also experience some problems. Often, a firm must grant licensing rights to its product for an extended period, 20 years or longer. If a product experiences remarkable growth in the foreign market, the bulk of the revenues earned belong to the licensee. Perhaps even more threatening is that a licensing firm is actually selling its expertise. If a foreign licensee learns the company's technology or product secrets, it may break the agreement and begin to produce a similar product on its own. If legal remedies are not available, the licensing firm may lose its trade secrets, not to mention promised royalties.

Exporting

Canadian companies export goods and services (e.g., call centres, IT consultants, and cultural and performing artists). As you will see in the chapters on marketing, many decisions have to be made when a company markets a new product or goes into

▸ Warner Bros. <*www.warnerbros.com*> has licensed with hundreds of companies to make products related to its series of hit films based on the best-selling Harry Potter books, which have been translated into dozens of languages. Do you think Potter-licensed products will maintain their global popularity with new generations of young readers and viewers?

new markets with existing products. Often the first export sales occur as a result of unsolicited orders received. Regardless of how a company starts exporting, it must develop some goals and some strategies for achieving those goals.

Canadian firms that are still hesitant can engage in indirect exporting through specialists called export-trading companies (or export-management companies) that assist in negotiating and establishing trading relationships. An export-trading company not only matches buyers and sellers from different countries but also deals with foreign customs offices, documentation, and even weights and measures conversions to ease the process of entering global markets. It also helps exporters get paid. If you are considering a career in global business, export-trading companies often provide internships or part-time opportunities for students.

Franchising

Franchising is a contractual agreement whereby someone with a good idea for a business sells the rights to use the business name and sell a product or service in a given territory in a specified manner. Franchising is popular domestically and internationally. (We will discuss it in depth in Chapter 6.) Canadian franchisors such as Molly Maid <*www.mollymaid.ca*> and Tim Hortons have global units operated by foreign franchisees.

In 1986, brothers Michael and Aaron Serruya, then aged 19 and 20, wanted to buy a franchise, but no one would take a chance on them. So, they started their own frozen yogurt shop, Yogen Früz <*www.yogenfruz.com*>. Today, Yogen Früz has grown to be a world leader in the frozen yogurt category, with over 1,200 locations operating in 25 countries around the world.[21] Another Canadian business, BeaverTails Pastry <*www.beavertailsinc.com*>, was started in 1978. The company produces whole-wheat pastries that are stretched by hand to resemble the tail of a beaver, one of Canada's best-known national symbols. The pastries are then float cooked on high quality canola oil and served piping hot, topped with butter and a choice of delectable flavours. The company operates over 80 franchised and licensed outlets across Canada, together with two locations in Saudi Arabia and two stores in Colorado's ski country.[22]

▸ Tired of studying and want a quick snack? How about a piping hot Domino's pizza with squid and sweet mayonnaise to satisfy your craving? Domino's serves pizzas around the globe that appeal to different tastes. Franchises like Domino's and McDonald's <*www.mcdonalds.ca*> know the world is a big place with wide differences in food preferences. How can franchises ensure their products are appropriate for global markets?

Franchisors have to be careful to adapt their good or service in the countries they serve. For example, KFC's <*www.kfc.ca*> first eleven Hong Kong outlets failed within two years. Apparently the chicken was too greasy, and eating with fingers was too messy for the fastidious people of Hong Kong. Pizza Hut <*www.pizzahut.ca*> and Domino's Pizza <*www.dominos.ca*> learned that preferences in pizza toppings differ globally. Japanese customers enjoy squid and sweet mayonnaise pizza.

Contract Manufacturing

contract manufacturing
A foreign country's production of private-label goods to which a domestic company then attaches its brand name or trademark; also called outsourcing.

Contract manufacturing involves a foreign company's production of private-label goods to which a domestic company then attaches its own brand name or trademark. (This practice falls under the broad category of *outsourcing,* which we introduced in Chapter 1 and will discuss in more depth later in this chapter.) For example, Dell Computer <*www.dell.com*> contracts with Quanta Computer of Taiwan <*www.quantatw.com*> to make notebook PCs, on which it then puts the Dell brand name, while Nike <*www.nike.com*> has almost 700 contract factories around the world that manufacture its footwear and apparel.[23]

Contract manufacturing enables a company to experiment in a new market without incurring heavy start-up costs such as building a manufacturing plant. If the brand name becomes a success, the company has penetrated a new market with relatively low risk. A firm can also use contract manufacturing temporarily to meet an unexpected increase in orders and, of course, labour costs are often very low.

One company, featured in *PROFIT* magazine's ranking of Canada's emerging growth companies, has used contract manufacturing successfully. FouFou Dog <*www.foufoudog.com*> is a dog apparel company whose collection includes canine track suits, hoodies, jewelled collars and leashes, as well as chew toys. At the age of 24, Cheryl Ng, owner of a Maltese dog named Ernie, started the company because she liked how Paris Hilton dressed her dog. Today, the company exports 95 percent of its products. According to Ng, "All our stuff is made in Argentina. In China, quality control can be hit-and-miss or downright sloppy—you could have a disaster on your hands—but it's been consistently good from my suppliers." And she has other reasons for heading south instead of east: "My suppliers will make me a small quantity if I want to try something out. You can't get that from China anymore, and I don't want to be stuck with a colour or style nobody wants; besides, they let me check out the textiles before I buy and they always have good stuff." She also likes the shorter flights and the fact that she only has to cross two time zones.[24]

▸ The Bank of Nova Scotia <*www.scotiabank.com*> formed a joint venture with the Bank of Beijing <*www.bankofbeijing.com.cn/en2011/index.html*>. The Bank of Beijing Scotiabank Asset Management Co. Ltd. markets mutual funds to retail and institutional customers through the Chinese bank's national branch network.

International Joint Ventures and Strategic Alliances

A **joint venture** is a partnership in which two or more companies (often from different countries) join to undertake a major project. Joint ventures are often mandated by governments as a condition of doing business in their country, as often occurs in China. For example, Colgate-Palmolive <*www.colgate.com*> entered a joint venture with one of China's largest toothpaste producers. Since then it has doubled its oral hygiene revenues in China and now exports its Chinese products to 70 countries.[25]

Joint ventures are developed for many different reasons. Campbell Soup Company's <*www.campbellsoup.ca*> joint venture with Japan's Nakano Vinegar Company <*http://mizkan.com*>, called Campbell Nakano Inc., was designed to expand Campbell's rather low share of the soup market in Japan. Elite Foods is a joint venture between PepsiCo <*www.pepsico.ca*> and Elite Industries <*www.strauss-group.com*> to market Frito-Lay snacks in Israel.

The benefits of international joint ventures are clear:

1. Shared technology and risk.
2. Shared marketing and management expertise.
3. Entry into markets where foreign companies are often not allowed unless goods are produced locally.

joint venture
A partnership in which two or more companies (often from different countries) join to undertake a major project.

The drawbacks are not so obvious but are important. One partner can learn the other's technology and practices, and then use what it learned to its own advantage. Also, a shared technology may become obsolete or the joint venture may become too large to be as flexible as needed.

The global market is also fuelling the growth of strategic alliances. A **strategic alliance** is a long-term partnership between two or more companies established to help each company build competitive market advantages. Unlike joint ventures, strategic alliances don't share costs, risks, management, or even profits. Thanks to their flexibility, strategic alliances can effectively link firms from different countries and firms of vastly different sizes. Hewlett-Packard <*www.hp.com*> has strategic alliances with Hitachi <*www.hitachi.ca*> and Samsung <*www.samsung.com*>, and Chevron <*www.chevron.com*> has alliances with the Western Australian Energy Research Alliance <*www.waera.com.au*>.

strategic alliance
A long-term partnership between two or more companies established to help each company build competitive market advantages.

Foreign Direct Investment

Foreign direct investment (FDI) is buying permanent property and businesses in foreign nations. As the size of a foreign market expands, many firms increase FDI and establish a foreign subsidiary. A **foreign subsidiary** is a company owned in a foreign country by another company (called the *parent company*). The subsidiary operates like a domestic firm, with production, distribution, promotion, pricing, and other business functions under the control of the subsidiary's management. The subsidiary must observe the

foreign direct investment (FDI)
The buying of permanent property and businesses in foreign nations.

foreign subsidiary
A company owned in a foreign country by the parent company.

legal requirements of both the country where the parent firm is located (called the *home country*) and the foreign country where the subsidiary is located (called the *host country*).

The primary advantage of a subsidiary is that the company maintains complete control over any technology or expertise it may possess. The major shortcoming is the need to commit funds and technology within foreign boundaries. Should relationships with a host country falter, the firm's assets could be *expropriated* (taken over by the foreign government). Swiss-based Nestlé has many foreign subsidiaries. The consumer-products giant spent billions of dollars acquiring foreign companies such as Ralston Purina <*www.purina.com*>, Chef America (maker of Hot Pockets), and Dreyer's Ice Cream <*www.dreyers.com*>, as well as Perrier <*www.perrier.com*> in France. It employs around 280,000 people in factories and operations in almost every country in the world.[26]

multinational corporation An organization that manufactures and markets products in many different countries and has multinational stock ownership and multinational management.

Nestlé is a **multinational corporation**, one that manufactures and markets products in many different countries and has multinational stock ownership and management. Multinational corporations are typically extremely large corporations like Nestlé, but not all large global businesses are multinationals.[27] A business could export everything it produces, deriving 100 percent of its sales and profits globally, and still not be a multinational corporation. Only firms that have *manufacturing capacity* or some other physical presence in different nations, such as Magna International, can truly be called multinational.[28]

Canadian subsidiaries of foreign-based companies have played a major role in developing the Canadian economy. There are, however, several disadvantages to foreign investment. One is that Canada has been criticized for having a "branch plant economy." This occurs when many subsidiaries are owned by foreign companies and profits are returned to the home country rather than reinvested in Canada. There are concerns that decisions made by the parent company are not primarily based on the needs of Canadians. For example, if a U.S. company decides to reduce its workforce or close a plant, it may more readily do that to a Canadian subsidiary rather than in its home country.

In the early 1990s, Michael Porter, the competition guru from Harvard University Business School, released a report titled *The Competitive Advantage of Nations* that was commissioned by the Canadian government. While this report is now more than 20 years old, some of his points still ring true today:

> One of Canada's competitive problems is the high concentration of foreign-owned firms that perform little sophisticated production or R&D. It matters a lot where a multinational calls home, because a company's home base is where the best jobs exist, where core R&D is undertaken, and where strategic control rests . . . Home bases are important to an economy because they support high productivity and productivity growth.

Regardless of these concerns, more countries are welcoming subsidiaries as a way to develop their economies.

Getting involved in global business requires selecting an entry strategy that best fits your business goals. The different strategies discussed reflect different levels of ownership, financial commitment, and risk. However, this is just the beginning. You should also be aware of market forces that affect a business's ability to trade in global markets. After the Progress Assessment, we will discuss them.

PROGRESS ASSESSMENT

- What are the advantages to a firm of using licensing as a method of entry in global markets? What are the disadvantages?
- What is the key difference between a joint venture and a strategic alliance?
- What makes a company a multinational corporation?

▸ Bombardier Transportation won a contract to supply Bombardier Flexity Swift high-floor light rail vehicles to the Bursa Metropolitan Municipality, Turkey. The vehicles will be built at Bombardier's manufacturing facility in Bautzen, Germany. Bodies will come from the Siegen site, while the electrical equipment will be supplied by the Mannheim plant.

FORCES AFFECTING TRADING IN GLOBAL MARKETS

LO 4 Evaluate the forces that affect trading in global markets.

The hurdles to success are higher and more complex in global markets than in domestic markets. Such hurdles include dealing with differences in sociocultural forces, economic and financial forces, legal forces, and physical and environmental forces. Let's take a look at each of these global market forces to see how they challenge even the most established and experienced global businesses.

Sociocultural Forces

The word **culture** refers to the set of values, beliefs, rules, and institutions held by a specific group of people.[29] Culture can also include social structures, religion, manners and customs, values and attitudes, language, and personal communication. An attitude that one's own culture is superior to all others is known as **ethnocentricity**. If you hope to get involved in global trade, it's critical to be aware of the cultural differences among nations.

culture The set of values, beliefs, rules, and institutions held by a specific group of people.

ethnocentricity An attitude that one's own culture is superior to all others.

Different nations have very different ways of conducting business. Canadian businesses that wish to compete globally must adapt to those ways. In North America, we like to do things quickly. We tend to call each other by our first names and try to get friendly even on the first encounter. In Japan, China, and other countries these actions would be considered surprising and even rude. Canadian negotiators will say no if they mean no, but Japanese negotiators usually say maybe when they mean no.

Religion is an important part of any society's culture and can have a significant impact on business operations. Consider the violent clashes between religious communities in India, Pakistan, Northern Ireland, and the Middle East—clashes that have wounded these areas' economies. Companies sometimes ignore religious implications in business decisions. Both McDonalds and Coca-Cola offended Muslims in Saudi Arabia by putting the Saudi Arabian flag on their packaging. The flag's design contains a passage from the Quran (Islam's sacred scripture), and Muslims feel that their holy writ should never be wadded up and thrown away.

Successful companies are those that can understand these differences and develop goods and services accordingly. The focus may be on a large global market or a smaller yet profitable global market. Understanding sociocultural differences can also be important when managing employees. In Latin American countries, workers believe that managers are placed in positions of authority to make decisions and be responsible for the well-being of their workers. Consider what happened to one North American manager in Peru who was unaware of this characteristic and believed that workers should participate in managerial functions. This manager was convinced that he could motivate his workers to higher levels of productivity by instituting a more democratic decision-making style than the one already in place. Soon workers began quitting their jobs in droves. When asked why, the workers said the new manager did not know his job and was asking the workers what to do. All stated that they wanted to find new jobs, since obviously this company was doomed due to incompetent managers.

Many companies still fail to think globally. A sound philosophy is: *Never assume that what works in one country will work in another.* Companies such as Roots *<canada.roots.com>*, Nike, and Toyota have developed brand names with widespread global appeal and recognition. However, even these successful global marketers often face difficulties. To get an idea of the problems companies have faced with advertising translations, take a look at Figure 3.6.

Economic and Financial Forces

Economic differences can also make entering global markets more challenging. It's hard for us to imagine buying chewing gum by the stick instead of by the package. Yet this buying behaviour is commonplace in economically depressed nations like Haiti, where customers can afford only small quantities. You might suspect that with more than 1 billion people, India would be a dream market for companies like PepsiCo and Hershey's. However, Indians consume an average of only three soft drinks per person a year, and most cannot afford chocolate due to India's low per-capita income.

Global financial markets unfortunately do not have a worldwide currency. Mexicans shop with pesos, South Koreans with won, Japanese with yen, and Canadians with dollars. Globally, the U.S. dollar is considered a dominant and stable currency. However, it doesn't always retain the same market value.[30] In an international transaction today, one dollar may be exchanged for eight pesos; tomorrow, you may only get seven. The **exchange rate** is the value of one nation's currency relative to the currencies of other countries.

exchange rate
The value of one nation's currency relative to the currencies of other countries.

Changes in a nation's exchange rates can have important implications in global markets. A *high value of the dollar* means that a dollar would be traded for more foreign currency than normal. The products of foreign producers would be cheaper

Figure 3.6

Oops, Did We Say That?

A global marketing strategy can be very difficult to implement. Look at the problems these well-known companies encountered in global markets.

PepsiCo attempted a Chinese translation of "Come Alive, You're in the Pepsi Generation" that read to Chinese customers as "Pepsi Brings Your Ancestors Back from the Dead."

Coor's Brewing Company put its slogan "Turn It Loose" into Spanish and found it translated as "Suffer from Diarrhea."

KFC's patented slogan "finger-lickin' good" was understood in Japanese as "Bite Your Fingers Off."

On the other side of the translation glitch, Electrolux, a Scandinavian vacuum manufacturer, tried to sell its products in the North American market with the slogan "Nothing Sucks Like an Electrolux."

because it takes fewer dollars to buy them, but the cost of Canadian-produced goods would become more expensive to foreign purchasers because of the dollar's high value. Conversely, a *low value of the dollar* means that a dollar is traded for less foreign currency than normal. Therefore, foreign goods become more expensive because it takes more dollars to buy them, but Canadian goods become cheaper to foreign buyers because it takes less foreign currency to buy Canadian goods.[31]

Global financial markets operate under a system called *floating exchange rates,* in which currencies "float" according to the supply and demand for them in the global market for the currency. This supply and demand is created by global currency traders, who develop a market for a nation's currency based on the perceived trade and investment potential of the country.

Changes in currency values cause many problems globally. For instance, labour costs for multinational corporations like Bombardier, Nestlé, General Electric, and Sony can vary considerably as currency values shift, causing them to juggle production from one country to another.[32]

Currency valuation problems can be especially harsh on developing economies. At certain times a nation's government will intervene and adjust the value of its currency, often to increase the export potential of its products. **Devaluation** is lowering the value of a nation's currency relative to other currencies. Sometimes, due to a nation's weak currency, the only way to trade is *bartering,* which is the exchange of merchandise for other merchandise, or service for other service, with no money involved.[33]

devaluation
Lowering the value of a nation's currency relative to other currencies.

Countertrading is a complex form of bartering in which several countries may be involved, each trading goods for goods or services for services. It has been estimated that countertrading accounts for over 20 percent of all global exchanges. Let's say that a developing country such as Jamaica wants to buy vehicles from Ford Motor Company in exchange for bauxite, a mineral compound that is a source of aluminum ore. Ford does not need Jamaican bauxite, but does need compressors. In a countertrade agreement, Ford may trade vehicles to Jamaica, which then trades bauxite to another country—say, India—which then exchanges compressors with Ford. All three parties benefit in the process, and avoid some of the financial problems and currency constraints in global markets.

countertrading
A complex form of bartering in which several countries may be involved, each trading goods for goods or services for services.

When the dollar is "up," foreign goods and travel are a bargain for Canadian consumers. When the dollar trades for less foreign currency, however, foreign tourists (like these viewing Niagara Falls) often flock to Canadian cities to enjoy relatively cheaper vacations and shopping trips. Do Canadian exporters profit more when the dollar is up or when it is down?

Legal Forces

In any economy, the conduct and the direction of business are firmly tied to the legal environment. In Canada, federal and provincial laws heavily affect business practices. In global markets, no central system of law exists, so different systems of laws may apply. This makes conducting global business difficult as business people navigate a sea of laws that are often inconsistent. Antitrust rules, labour relations, patents, copyrights, trade practices, taxes, child labour, product liability, and other issues are governed differently country by country.[34]

Canadian businesses must follow Canadian laws in conducting business globally. For example, bribery is not considered legal in Canada. The problem is that this runs contrary to beliefs and practices in many countries where corporate or government bribery not only is acceptable, but also may be the only way to secure a lucrative contract.[35] The Organization for Economic Cooperation and Development (OECD) <*www.oecd.org*> and Transparency International <*www.transparency.org*> have led a global effort to fight corruption and bribery in foreign markets, with limited success. Figure 3.7 shows a partial list of countries where bribery or other unethical business practices are most common.

The co-operation and sponsorship of local business people can help a company penetrate the market and deal with laws and bureaucratic barriers in their country.

Physical and Environmental Forces

Certain technological forces can also have an important impact on a company's ability to conduct business in global markets. In fact, technological constraints may make it difficult given the nature of exportable products. For example, houses in most developing countries do not have electrical systems that match those of Canadian homes, in kind or in capacity. How would the differences in electricity available (110 versus 220 volts) affect a Canadian appliance manufacturer wishing to export?

Also, computer and Internet usage in many developing countries is rare or nonexistent. You can see how this would make for a tough business environment in general and would make e-commerce difficult, especially as this is becoming a critical element of business. After the Progress Assessment, we will explore how trade protectionism affects global business.

Figure 3.7

The Corruption Perceptions Index

The corruption perceptions index ranks countries and territories according to their perceived level of public sector (government) corruption. This list starts with the most corrupt countries.

1. Somalia and North Korea (tie)
2. Myanmar and Afghanistan (tie)
3. Uzbekistan, Turkmenistan, and Sudan (tie)
4. Iraq and Haiti (tie)
5. Venezuela, Equatorial Guinea, and Burundi (tie)

. . .

173. Canada (10th least corrupt country in the world)

. . .

182. New Zealand (least corrupt country in the world)

Sources: Suzane Muhereza, "The 2011 Corruption Perceptions Index: Demanding better government," One, 5 December 2011, www.one.org/blog/2011/12/05/the-2011-corruption-perceptions-index-demanding-better-government/; Simon Rogers and Claire Provost, "Corruption index 2011 from Transparency International: find out how countries compare," *Guardian News*, 1 December 2011, www.guardian.co.uk/news/datablog/2011/dec/01/corruption-index-2011-transparency-international#data; and "Corruption Perceptions Index 2011," Transparency International, 2011, http://cpi.transparency.org/cpi2011/results/.

PROGRESS ASSESSMENT

- What are the major hurdles to successful global trade?
- What does ethnocentricity mean, and how can it affect global success?
- How would the low value of the dollar affect Canadian exports?

trade protectionism
The use of government regulations to limit the import of goods and services.

TRADE PROTECTIONISM

Debate the advantages and disadvantages of trade protectionism, define tariff and non-tariff barriers, and give examples of common markets.

As we discussed in the previous section, sociocultural, economic and financial, legal, and physical and environmental forces are all challenges to global trade. What is often a much greater barrier to global trade, however, is trade protectionism. **Trade protectionism** is the use of government regulations to limit the import of goods and services. Supporters of trade protectionism believe that it allows domestic producers to survive and grow, producing more jobs. Those against trade protectionism argue that it not only impedes global trade, but that it also adds millions of dollars to the price of products, costing consumers billions of dollars.

Countries often use protectionist measures to guard against practices such as dumping. **Dumping** is selling products in a foreign country at lower prices than those charged in the producing country. This tactic is sometimes used to reduce surplus products in foreign markets or to gain a foothold in a new market. Some governments may offer financial incentives to certain industries to sell goods in global markets for less than they sell them at home. China, Brazil, and Russia, for example, have been penalized for dumping steel in North America.[36] To understand how trade protectionism affects global business, let's briefly review a bit of global economic history.

Business, economics, and politics have always been closely linked. What we now call economics was once referred to as the *political* economy, indicating the close ties between politics (government) and economics. In the seventeenth and eighteenth centuries, business people and governments advocated an economic policy called *mercantilism*. The overriding idea of mercantilism was for a nation to sell more goods to other nations than it bought from them; that is, to have a favourable balance of trade. According to the mercantilists, this resulted in a flow of money to the country that sold the most globally. This philosophy led governments to implement **tariffs**, which are taxes on imports, thus making imported goods more expensive to buy.

There are two kinds of tariffs: protective and revenue. *Protective tariffs* (import taxes) are designed to raise the retail price of imported products so that domestic products will be more competitively priced. These tariffs are meant to save jobs for domestic workers and to keep industries—especially infant industries that have companies in the early stages of growth—from closing down entirely because of foreign competition. Such tariffs are usually met with resistance. After the Canada Border Services Agency ruled that grain was being subsidized in

Believing that the annual seal hunt off the East Coast is inhumane, the European Union has imposed an import ban (or trade embargo) on all products from Canada's seal hunt. The Canadian government believes that it is a trade law violation and has appealed this decision to the World Trade Organization. Which perspective do you support?

dumping
Selling products in a foreign country at lower prices than those charged in the producing country.

tariff
A tax imposed on imports.

import quota
A limit on the number of products in certain categories that a nation can import.

embargo
A complete ban on the import or export of a certain product or the stopping of all trade with a particular country.

General Agreement on Tariffs and Trade (GATT)
A 1948 agreement that established an international forum for negotiating mutual reductions in trade restrictions.

World Trade Organization (WTO)
The international organization that replaced the General Agreement on Tariffs and Trade, and was assigned the duty to mediate trade disputes among nations.

the United States and then sold in Canada below its true cost, the federal government imposed a duty of US$1.65 a bushel on U.S. corn imports.[37] *Revenue tariffs* are designed to raise money for the government.

An **import quota** limits the number of products in certain categories that a nation can import. Canada has import quotas on a number of products including textiles and clothing, agricultural products, steel, and softwood lumber.[38] The goal is to protect Canadian companies and to preserve jobs. Products subject to export controls include softwood lumber, firearms, sugar and sugar-containing products, peanut butter, and B.C. logs.[39]

An **embargo** is a complete ban on the import or export of a certain product or the stopping of all trade with a particular country. Political disagreements have caused many countries to establish embargoes, such as Canada's embargo against Burma, reflecting its condemnation of the Burmese regime's complete disregard for human rights and ongoing repression of the democratic movement.[40]

Non-tariff barriers are not as specific or formal as tariffs, import quotas, and embargoes but can be as detrimental to free trade.[41] One example is restrictive standards that detail exactly how a product must be sold in a country. For example, Denmark requires companies to sell butter in cubes, not tubs. Other non-tariff barriers include safety, health, and labelling standards. The United States has stopped some Canadian goods from entering because it said that the information on the labels was too small. The discovery of mad cow disease resulted in a temporary import ban of Canadian beef by the United States, Japan, South Korea, Australia, and other countries.[42]

Would-be exporters might view trade barriers as good reasons to avoid global trade, but overcoming trade constraints creates business opportunities. Next, we'll look at organizations and agreements that attempt to eliminate barriers.

The GATT and the WTO

In 1948, government leaders from 23 nations formed the **General Agreement on Tariffs and Trade (GATT)**, a global forum for reducing trade restrictions on goods, services, ideas, and cultural programs. In 1986, the Uruguay Round of the GATT convened to renegotiate trade agreements. After eight years of meetings, 124 nations voted to lower tariffs an average of 38 percent worldwide, and expand new trade rules to areas such as agriculture, services, and the protection of patents.

The Uruguay Round also established the **World Trade Organization (WTO)** <*www.wto.org*> to mediate trade disputes among nations. The WTO, headquartered in Geneva, Switzerland, is an independent entity of 153 member nations, and its purpose

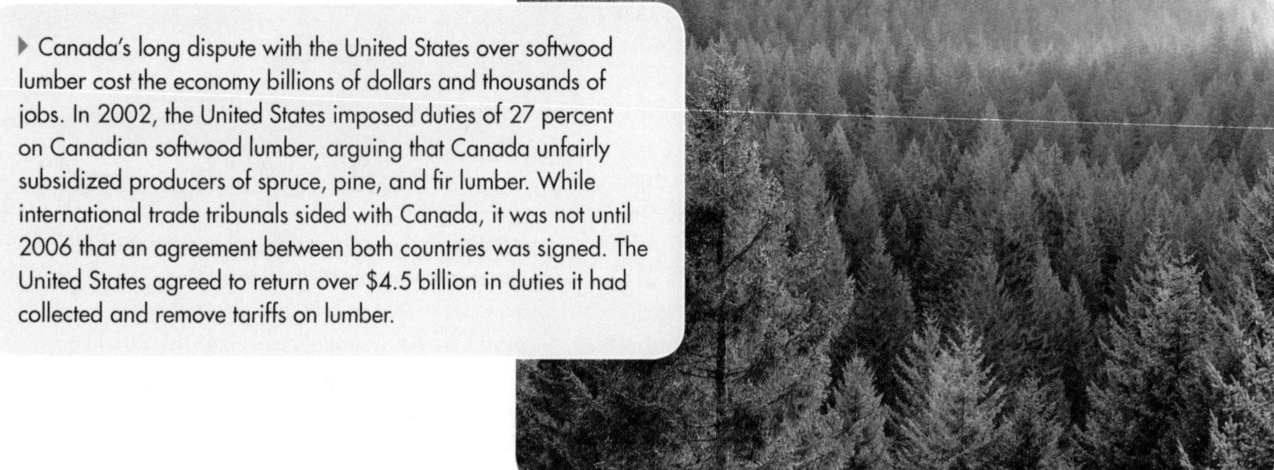

▸ Canada's long dispute with the United States over softwood lumber cost the economy billions of dollars and thousands of jobs. In 2002, the United States imposed duties of 27 percent on Canadian softwood lumber, arguing that Canada unfairly subsidized producers of spruce, pine, and fir lumber. While international trade tribunals sided with Canada, it was not until 2006 that an agreement between both countries was signed. The United States agreed to return over $4.5 billion in duties it had collected and remove tariffs on lumber.

is to oversee cross-border trade issues and global business practices among those nations.[43] Trade disputes are presented by member nations with decisions made within a year, rather than languishing for years, as in the past.

The WTO has not solved all global trade problems. Legal differences (discussed earlier) often impede trade expansion. And a wide gap separates developing nations (80 percent of the WTO membership) and industrialized nations like Canada.[44] The WTO meetings in Doha, Qatar, began in 2001 to address dismantling protection of manufactured goods, eliminating subsidies on agricultural products, and overturning temporary protectionist measures. Unfortunately, the Doha Round ended in 2008 with no significant agreements.[45]

▸ Failure to reach agreement on whether to allow tariff protection for farmers in developing nations marked the end of the recent Doha Round of trade talks among WTO members. Some disappointed observers feared the failure could also endanger global agreements on other issues like global warming. Do you agree? Why or why not?

The IMF and the World Bank

The **International Monetary Fund (IMF)** <*www.imf.org*> was created in 1944. The IMF is an international bank supported by its members that usually makes short-term loans to countries experiencing problems with their balance of trade. The IMF's basic objectives are to promote exchange stability, maintain orderly exchange arrangements, avoid competitive currency depreciation, establish a multilateral system of payments, eliminate exchange restrictions, and create standby reserves. The IMF makes long-term loans at low interest rates to the world's most destitute nations to help them strengthen their economies. The function of the IMF is very similar to that of the World Bank.

The **World Bank** <*www.worldbank.org*>, an autonomous United Nations agency, is concerned with developing infrastructure (e.g., roads, schools, hospitals, power plants, etc.) in less-developed countries. The World Bank borrows from more prosperous countries and lends at favourable rates to less-developed countries. (In recent years, the IMF and the World Bank have forgiven some loans to highly indebted countries, such as Mozambique.) To qualify for the program, numerous macroeconomic policies (such as inflation and poverty reduction) have to be implemented. These new requirements allow the lending organizations to continue to fulfill their objectives.

Some countries believe that their economies will be strengthened if they establish formal trade agreements with other countries. Some of these agreements, involving forming producers' cartels and common markets, are discussed next.

International Monetary Fund (IMF)
An international bank that makes short-term loans to countries experiencing problems with their balance of trade.

World Bank
An autonomous United Nations agency that borrows money from the more prosperous countries and lendvs it to less-developed countries to develop their infrastructure.

Producers' Cartels

Producers' cartels are organizations of commodity-producing countries. They are formed to stabilize or increase prices, optimizing overall profits in the long run. The most obvious example today is the Organization of the Petroleum Exporting Countries (OPEC). Similar attempts have been made to manage prices for copper, iron ore, bauxite, bananas, tungsten, rubber, and other important commodities. These cartels are all contradictions to unrestricted free trade and letting the market set prices.

producers' cartels
Organizations of commodity-producing countries that are formed to stabilize or increase prices to optimize overall profits in the long run.

Common Markets

An issue not resolved by the GATT or the WTO is whether common markets create regional alliances at the expense of global expansion. A **common market** (also called a **trading bloc**) is a regional group of countries that have a common external tariff, no

common market (trading bloc)
A regional group of countries that have a common external tariff, no internal tariffs, and a coordination of laws to facilitate exchange; also called a trading bloc.

internal tariffs, and the coordination of laws to facilitate exchange among member countries. Two examples are the North American Free Trade Agreement and the European Union. Let's look briefly at both.

▸ Officially, almost all trade in the NAFTA region now flows tariff-free. But several major areas of dispute have yet to be resolved including trucking, immigration, the environment, and agricultural tariffs.

The North American Free Trade Agreement (NAFTA)

A widely debated issue of the early 1990s was the ratification of the **North American Free Trade Agreement (NAFTA)**, which created a free-trade area among Canada, the United States, and Mexico. In January, 1993, NAFTA came into effect, replacing the previous Free Trade Agreement between Canada and the United States. The objectives of NAFTA were to (1) eliminate trade barriers and facilitate cross-border movement of goods and services among the three countries; (2) promote conditions of fair competition in this free-trade area; (3) increase investment opportunities in the territories of the three nations; (4) provide effective protection and enforcement of intellectual property rights (e.g., patents, copyrights, etc.) in each nation's territory; (5) establish a framework for further regional trade co-operation; and (6) improve working conditions in North America.

North American Free Trade Agreement (NAFTA) Agreement that created a free-trade area among Canada, the United States, and Mexico.

NAFTA was driven by the desire of Mexico to have greater access to the U.S. market. Improved access would spur growth, provide more employment for Mexicans, and raise the low standard of living in Mexico. The U.S. government was hoping to create jobs in Mexico and stop the flow of illegal immigrants that were crossing its border. Canada was really a minor player in this deal; the Canadian government was concerned that it would be left out or penalized indirectly unless it joined the bloc. Canadians do have something to gain by having freer access to the growing Mexican market, but the country is still a minor customer for Canada.

Today, the three NAFTA countries have a combined population of over 457 million and a gross domestic product of more than $17.6 trillion.[46] The agreement permits all three countries to reduce trade barriers with one another while maintaining independent trade agreements with other countries.

There is continuing concern by some groups (e.g., unions) in Canada and the United States that NAFTA has contributed to employment losses and that economic benefits were not realized. Some Canadian business people remain opposed because they did not like many of the details in NAFTA. In addition, Mexico has a poor policy on environmental problems, bad working conditions, and a poor record on human rights and political freedom. The country has repeatedly been condemned by many organizations in North America and abroad for serious flaws on all these counts. Others believe that NAFTA will force Mexico to gradually improve these conditions. This has been happening, but at a very slow pace.

The European Union

The European Union (EU) began in the late 1950s as an alliance of six trading partners (then known as the Common Market and later the European Economic Community). Today the EU is a group of 27 member nations, located primarily in Europe, with a population of over 502 million citizens and a GDP of almost $18.0 trillion.[47] The EU sees continued economic integration as the major way to compete for global

GREENBOX

The Politics of Oil

Canada has the second-largest oil sands reserve on the planet, estimated at 170 billion barrels. The oil sands are the largest proven reserve of oil outside of Saudi Arabia, and the world's largest reserve of "unconventional" oil, which requires much more energy and water to extract and process than conventional oil.

The tar-like bitumen has to be melted out of the ground and processed in a highly energy-intensive way before it can be refined like regular oil. The U.S. Environmental Protection Agency says that "GHG emissions from the Canadian oil sands crude would be approximately 82 percent greater than the average crude refined in the U.S. on a well-to-tank basis." And in confidential briefing notes, the Canadian government has acknowledged that the emissions-per-barrel will likely increase as the industry is forced to pursue harder-to-access reserves deeper underground. Further expansion of the oil sands—which are the fastest growing source of greenhouse gas emissions in Canada, and the biggest energy project in the world—would lock Canada into a high-carbon economy for decades to come.

The EU has adopted a "Fuel Quality Directive" aimed at making those who sell and supply fuel reduce the carbon footprint of their products by 6 percent over the next decade. The EU is ranking fuels to help sellers and buyers identify those fuels with the largest carbon footprint. In line with that, some members of the EU are pushing to rate oil sands fuel as more environmentally damaging than fuel from conventional crude oil.

The federal government and the government of Alberta have lobbied the EU to prevent that from happening. A "dirty oil" classification would amount to a European ban on oil sands crude. It would impose financial disincentives to discourage refiners and marketers from using fuel derived from oil sands bitumen in favour of lower-carbon sources of fuel.

A EU vote delayed a decision on whether to declare oil sands output more harmful to the environment than conventional crude. The vote was a setback in Europe and North America for supporters of low-carbon fuel regulations that are aimed at reducing greenhouse gas emissions in the transportation sector.

However, both sides declared victory after the vote was delayed. Canada's Finance Minister was encouraged that some of the EU countries "are taking another look at this potential kind of discriminatory action toward the oil sands and toward Canada. There's no question this resource is going to be used in the world over the course of the next many years." The environmentalist group Greenpeace called the delay welcome given "fierce" lobbying by Ottawa, Alberta, and multinational energy companies with investments in oil sands projects. The fight moves to the EU political arena after the vote by a technical committee in Brussels, with European environment ministers expected to rule on the matter. "If they want to stand up and say they sided with Shell and BP instead of the climate, then that's going to be a pretty uncomfortable position to take in Europe," said Keith Stewart, Climate and Energy Campaigner with Greenpeace Canada.

What decision did the EU ultimately make? How did both parties—the Canadian government and environmentalists—react? What is the status of this issue today?

Sources: Lorne Gunter, "A European reprieve for Canada's oil sands," *The Globe and Mail*, 24 February 2012, A14; "EU delays decision on whether oil sands crude more harmful to environment," *The Toronto Star*, 23 February 2012, www.thestar.com/business/article/1135590–eu-committee-undecided-on-labeling-oil-sands-as-worse-for-environment-than-other-crude; Shawn McCarthy, "France, Netherlands key to EU oil sands decision," *The Globe and Mail*, 23 February 2012, www.theglobeandmail.com/report-on-business/industry-news/energy-and-resources/france-netherlands-key-to-eu-oil-sands-decision/article2347236/; Satu Hassi, "European Union & Oil Sands," CBC Radio-Canada, 7 April 2011, www.cbc.ca/thecurrent/episode/2011/04/07/euoil-sands/; and Brian Blomme, "Canada's tar sands and climate change," Greenpeace Canada, 2010, www.greenpeace.org/canada/Global/canada/report/2010/11/Tar%20Sands%20and%20Climate%20Change.pdf.

business. Canada is in the midst of negotiating 14 international free trade agreements, including a major one with the EU that is expected to be completed in 2012.[48] A study estimated that Europe would gain $18.5 billion a year and Canada about $13 billion by cutting restrictions on services trade, removing tariffs, and reducing non-tariff barriers.[49] While both parties—Canada and the EU—see the benefits of more open trade, perspectives do vary on certain issues. The Green Box highlights one such example.

The path to European unification was not easy, but a significant step was taken in 1999 by adopting the euro as a common currency. Seventeen out of the 27 members have adopted this currency.[50] Businesses in these seventeen countries have saved billions by eliminating currency conversions. The euro has proven a worthy challenger to the U.S. dollar's dominance in global markets due to its economic strength.

The EU Debt Crisis[51]

Being part of an integrated global economy means that financial issues in other countries could affect the Canadian economy. Such was the case in the early years of this decade when there was speculation that the global financial conditions stemming from the debt crisis in Europe could create problems for Canada's economy.

What triggered this crisis? A handful of smaller European countries in the EU—such as Greece, Ireland, and Portugal—overspent and over-borrowed. Several countries had already received bailout funds from the IMF and other bodies, but larger economies were moving to the centre of the crisis, increasing the impact on the global economy. These countries were grappling with a sovereign debt crisis that threatened the euro and the EU itself.

Without a full restructuring of this debt by the solvent EU members, these smaller economies faced default because they could no longer service their debt as interest rates increased. Default would threaten the euro (i.e., they would leave the euro and return to their own currencies) and the European Union itself. One downside of a euro collapse would be that countries would become more protectionist. Protectionism would have a major effect on a country like Canada that relies on exports. The debt crisis became the currency crisis, which became an EU political crisis when not all of the economies could agree on how to solve this problem.

The Bank of Canada's semi-annual financial stability review stated that Canadians needed to start worrying about the worsening debt mess in Europe. "Should the crisis deepen and spread further to the larger European economies, transmission to Canada could become more severe . . . An adverse outcome for Europe would also raise the risk of a significant impairment of funding conditions for Canadian institutions." The spillover effects on the global economy would touch almost every aspect of Canada's economic and financial system, from trade, to the financial system, to consumer and business confidence.

What is the update to this debt crisis? Has it been resolved? Have new policies been put in place to prohibit a crisis from happening again? Did any members leave the EU as a result of this crisis? How, if at all, was Canada impacted in the years following this crisis?

Other Trade Agreements: UNASUR and ASEAN[52]

Modelled after the EU, twelve nations belong to the Union of South American Nations (UNASUR). UNASUR is an intergovernmental union integrating two existing common markets—Mercosur (which united Argentina, Brazil, Paraguay, Uruguay, and Venezuela) and the Andean Community of Nations (Bolivia, Colombia, Ecuador, and Peru)—into an economic free-trade zone spanning South America. Other members include Chile, Guyana, and Suriname. UNASUR has a population of over 396 million citizens and a GDP of over $7.9 trillion

The Association of Southeast Asian Nations (ASEAN) was established in 1967. It currently includes ten member countries: Brunei, Cambodia, Indonesia, the Lao People's Democratic Republic, Malaysia, Myanmar, the Philippines, Singapore, Thailand, and Vietnam. This trade association has a population of 601 million citizens and a GDP of over $3.1 trillion.

Common markets and free-trade areas will be debated far into the twenty-first century. Some economists resoundingly praise such unions, while others express concern that the world is dividing into major trading blocs (e.g., NAFTA, EU, etc.) that will exclude poor and developing nations. After the Progress Assessment, we'll look at the future of global trade.

PROGRESS ASSESSMENT

- What are the advantages and disadvantages of trade protectionism?
- What is the difference between protective tariffs and revenue tariffs?
- What is the primary purpose of the WTO?
- State four objectives of NAFTA.
- What is the primary objective of a common market like the EU?

GLOBALIZATION AND YOUR FUTURE

Discuss the changing landscape of the global market.

Global trade opportunities grow more interesting, yet challenging, each day. New and expanding markets present great potential for trade and development. Changes in technology, especially through the Internet, have transformed the landscape of business. Internet usage and advances in e-commerce enable companies worldwide to bypass historical distribution channels to reach a large market that is only a mouse click away. Take for example, small company Build-A-Bear Workshops <*www.buildabear.ca*>. Using the Internet, the company was able to find new customers online and enjoy an expanded global presence.

The lure of more than 7 billion customers is hard to pass up, especially since the Internet makes the global market instantly accessible. However, nowhere on this planet is the lure to global markets keener than in the world's most populous country, China. With more than 1.3 billion people and incredible exporting and importing prowess, China has transformed the world economic map. China is the world's largest exporter (10.4 percent of world merchandise trade, which is ahead of the U.S. and Germany) and the world's second-largest importer (9.5 percent of world merchandise trade).[53] The world's largest importer is the United States at 12.3 percent of world merchandise trade.[54] China is the largest global consumer of steel, copper, coal, and cement, and is second only to the United States in the consumption of oil. Manufacturers now use the term *China price* to mean the lowest price possible.

Many view China as the fulfillment of a free trader's dream, where global investment and entrepreneurship are leading the nation to wealth and economic

China's economy is booming, and a highly educated middle class with money to spend is emerging, especially in the cities. Many observers believe China will continue its rapid growth and play a major role in the global economy. Are Canadian firms prepared to compete?

interdependence with the rest of the world. However, concerns remain about China's one-party political system, human rights abuses, and increasing urban population growth.[55] One significant problem is China's underground economy, which generates significant product piracy and counterfeiting. Counterfeit Rolex watches, Calloway golf clubs, and Louis Vuitton bags are readily available.[56] Although China has been more responsive to these latter problems since its 2001 admission to the WTO, few expect the pirating problems to disappear anytime soon. In a relatively short period of time, China has become an economic phenomenon. With its openness to trade and investment, educated workforce, and stable infrastructure, China is expected to be a key driver of the world economy.

While China clearly attracts most of the attention in Asia, it's important not to forget the rest of the continent. For example, India's 1.1 billion population (600 million of whom are under 25 years of age) and Russia's 150 million potential customers represent opportunities too good to pass up. Both nations are emerging markets that present business opportunities. India has seen huge growth in information technology, pharmaceuticals, and biotechnology.[57] Still, it remains a nation with difficult trade laws. For example, foreign retailers like Walmart cannot sell directly to consumers. They can, however, direct wholesale operations and give support to Indian retailers.[58]

Russia is an industrialized nation with large reserves of oil, gas, and gold.[59] Unfortunately, political, currency, and social problems still persist in Russia. The developing nations of Asia, including Indonesia, Thailand, Singapore, the Philippines, Korea, Malaysia, and Vietnam also offer great potential for businesses—and possibly for you.

As you learned in Chapter 1, outsourcing means contracting with other companies to do some or all of the functions of a firm, rather than providing them within the company. In Canada, companies have outsourced payroll functions, accounting, and some manufacturing operations for many years. However, the shift in outsourcing manufacturing and services from domestic businesses to primarily low-wage markets outside of Canada is getting more attention. This shift is referred to as offshoring. The Making Ethical Decisions box offers an example of this practice.

To remain competitive, Canada must stay aware of the global challenges and focus on innovation and entrepreneurship. It's increasingly important for Canadian workers to get the proper education and training needed to stay ahead in the future.[60] The Reaching Beyond Our Borders box that follows Chapter 5 highlights how Canada shapes up as a global competitor.

Whether you aspire to be an entrepreneur, a manager, or some other type of business leader, it's becoming increasingly important to think globally in planning your

MAKING ETHICAL DECISIONS

How Much Information Is Necessary?

Imagine that you're having a problem with your computer. Not able to fix the problem yourself, you take out the operator's manual and dial customer service. Your call is answered by a service technician who identifies himself as Jeff. You explain to Jeff the problem you are having and wait for his reply. Unfortunately, Jeff cannot solve your problem and transfers your call to his colleague Jennifer. Jennifer analyzes the situation and promptly provides a suggestion that fixes your computer. Impressed, you ask Jennifer for her direct line so you can call her if you have additional questions. She says she is unable to give you her direct number, according to company policy. Upset, you call customer relations and inquire why a service technician cannot give her direct number to a customer. The company representative says, "Because the service centre is overseas. You were talking to people trained to identify themselves as Jeff and Jennifer." Should a company let customers know if its service facilities are being outsourced or as in this case, offshored? Should service people be required to give their real names when dealing with customers? What are the consequences of each alternative?

career. By studying foreign languages, learning about foreign cultures, and taking business courses (including a global business course), you can develop a global perspective on your future.[61] As you progress through this textbook, keep two things in mind: globalization is real, and economic competition promises to intensify.

Also keep in mind that global market potential does not belong only to large, multinational corporations. Small and medium-sized businesses have a world of opportunity in front of them. In fact, these firms are often better prepared to leap into global markets and react quickly to opportunities than are large firms. Finally, don't forget the potential of franchising, which we will examine in more detail in Chapter 6.

PROGRESS ASSESSMENT

- How has the Internet affected doing business in global markets?
- What are the economic risks of doing business in countries like China?
- What might be some important factors that will have an impact on global trading?
- What can you do in the next few years to ready yourself for a career in global business?

SUMMARY

Describe the importance of the global market and the roles of comparative advantage and absolute advantage in global trade.

Canada has a population of more than 34 million people. The world market for trade is huge. Over 99 percent of the people in the world live outside Canada. Major Canadian companies routinely cite expansion to global markets as a route to future growth.

Why should nations trade with other nations?

Nations should trade globally as (1) no country is self-sufficient, (2) other countries need products that prosperous countries produce, and (3) natural resources and technological skills are not distributed evenly around the world.

What is the theory of comparative advantage?

The theory of comparative advantage contends that a country should make and then sell those products it produces most efficiently but buy those it cannot produce as efficiently.

What is absolute advantage?

Absolute advantage means that a country has a monopoly on a certain product or can produce the product more efficiently than any other country. There are few examples of absolute advantage.

Explain the importance of importing and exporting and define key terms used in global business.

Anyone can get involved in world trade through importing and exporting. Business people do not have to work for big multinational corporations.

What kinds of products can be imported and exported?

Just about any kind of product can be imported and exported. Companies can sometimes find surprising ways to succeed in either activity. Selling in global markets is not necessarily easy, though.

What terms are important in understanding world trade?

Exporting is selling goods and services to other countries. Importing is buying goods and services from other countries. The balance of trade is the relationship of exports to imports. The balance of payments is the balance of trade plus other money flows such as tourism and foreign aid. Dumping is selling products for less in a foreign country than in your own country.

Illustrate the strategies used in reaching global markets and explain the role of multinational corporations in global markets.

A company can participate in world trade in a number of ways.

What are some ways in which a company can get involved in global business?

Ways of entering world trade include licensing, exporting, franchising, contract manufacturing, joint ventures and strategic alliances, and foreign direct investment.

How do multinational corporations differ from other companies that participate in global business?

Unlike other companies that are involved in exporting or importing, multinational corporations also have manufacturing facilities or some other type of physical presence in different nations.

Evaluate the forces that affect trading in global markets.

Many forces affect foreign trade.

What are some of the forces that can discourage participation in global business?

Potential stumbling blocks to global trade include sociocultural forces (e.g., religion), economic and financial forces (e.g., disposable income), legal forces (e.g., laws on bribery), and physical and environmental forces (e.g., Internet usage).

Debate the advantages and disadvantages of trade protectionism, define tariff and non-tariff barriers, and give examples of common markets.

Political differences are often the most difficult hurdles to international trade.

What is trade protectionism?

Trade protectionism is the use of government regulations to limit the import of goods and services. Supporters believe that it allows domestic producers to survive and grow, producing more jobs. The key tools of protectionism are tariffs, import quotas, and embargoes.

What are tariff and non-tariff barriers?

Tariffs are taxes on foreign products. There are two kinds of tariffs: (1) protective tariffs, which are used to raise the price of foreign products, and (2) revenue tariffs, which are used to raise money for the government. Non-tariff barriers include safety, health, and labelling standards.

What are some examples of trade organizations that try to eliminate trade barriers and facilitate trade among nations?

The World Trade Organization (WTO) replaced the General Agreement on Tariffs and Trade (GATT). The purpose of the WTO is to mediate trade disputes among nations. The International Monetary Fund (IMF) is an international bank that makes short-term loans to countries experiencing problems with their balance of trade. The World Bank is a United Nations agency that borrows money from the more prosperous countries and lends it to less-developed countries to develop their infrastructures.

What is a common market? State some examples.

A common market is a regional group of countries that have a common external tariff, no internal tariff, and a coordination of laws to facilitate exchange. The idea behind a common market is the elimination of trade barriers that existed prior to the creation of this bloc. Examples include NAFTA, the EU, UNASUR, and ASEAN.

Discuss the changing landscape of the global market.

The landscape of global business is changing.

How is business changing?

New and expanding markets present great potential for trade and development. For example, changes in technology, especially through the Internet, allow access to global customers.

What countries offer opportunities for Canadian businesses?

Expanding markets such as China, India, and Russia present great potential for trade and development.

KEY TERMS

absolute advantage
balance of payments
balance of trade
common market (trading bloc)
comparative advantage theory
contract manufacturing
countertrading
culture
devaluation
dumping
embargo
ethnocentricity
exchange rate
exporting
foreign direct investment (FDI)
foreign subsidiary
free trade
General Agreement on Tariffs and Trade (GATT)
import quota
importing
International Monetary Fund (IMF)
joint venture
licensing
multinational corporation
North American Free Trade Agreement (NAFTA)
producers' cartels
strategic alliance
tariff
trade deficit
trade protectionism
trade surplus
World Bank
World Trade Organization (WTO)

CRITICAL THINKING

1. What can businesses do to prevent unexpected problems in dealing with sociocultural, economic and financial, legal, and physical and environmental forces in global markets?
2. Countries like Canada that have a high standard of living are referred to as industrialized nations. Countries with a low standard of living and quality of life are called developing countries. (Terms formerly used were *underdeveloped* or *less-developed countries*.) What factors prevent developing nations from becoming industrialized nations?
3. How would you justify the use of revenue or protective tariffs in today's global market?

DEVELOPING WORKPLACE SKILLS

1. Find out firsthand the impact of global trade on your life. How many different countries' names appear on the labels in your clothes? How many languages do your classmates speak? List the ethnic restaurants in your community. Are they family-owned or corporate chains?

2. Prepare a short list of the advantages and disadvantages of trade protectionism. Share your ideas with others in the class and debate the following statement: Canada should increase trade protectionism to save Canadian jobs and companies.

3. The economies of Ontario and British Columbia depend heavily on exports. Ontario relies primarily on trade to the United States and Europe, while British Columbia relies heavily on trade with Asia. In a group of four, research these statements. Use Excel to develop two graphs that break down the exporting countries that trade with each of these provinces. Present your findings to the class.

4. In a group of four, list the top five Canadian-based multinationals. When researching, create a table that will include the following pieces of information: the company names, the year each was created, the number of global employees, the industry or industries in which they operate, annual revenues, and number of countries in which they have offices. Present your findings to the class.

ANALYZING MANAGEMENT DECISIONS

The Challenge of Offshoring

Outsourcing, as noted in Chapter 1, is the process of assigning various functions, such as accounting, production, security, maintenance, and legal work to outside organizations. In Canada, companies have outsourced payroll functions, accounting, and some manufacturing operations for many years. However, the shift to primarily low-wage global markets, called offshoring (or offshore outsourcing), has become a major issue. Export Development Canada believes that there are about 4,000 Canadian companies with some sort of overseas presence, an increase from ten years ago.

Canadian companies such as Bombardier Inc. (manufactures state-of-the-art planes and trains) and Gildan Activewear Inc. <*gildan.com*> (one of the world's largest T-shirt makers) have outsourced manufacturing offshore for years. Fundamentally, as lower-level manufacturing became more simplified, Canadian companies shifted focus from assembling products to design and architecture. Today, economists agree that we are moving into the "second wave" of offshoring that involves sizable numbers of skilled, well-educated middle-income workers in service-sector jobs such as accounting, law, financial and risk management, health care, and information technology that were thought to be safe from foreign market competition. This shift is potentially more disruptive to the Canadian job market than was the first, which primarily involved manufacturing jobs. To take a look at the pros and cons of offshoring, review the following table.

Pros	Cons
Less strategic tasks can be outsourced globally so companies can focus on where they can excel and grow.	Jobs are lost permanently and wages fall due to low-cost competition offshore.
Outsource work allows companies to create efficiencies that in fact let them hire more workers.	Offshoring may reduce product quality, which can cause permanent damage to a company's reputation.
Consumers benefit from lower prices generated by effective use of global resources and developing nations grow, thus fuelling global economic growth.	Communication within the company, with its suppliers, and with its customers becomes much more difficult.

China and India are oftentimes named as country providers of offshoring. Currently, China is primarily involved with manufacturing at the low end of the technology scale, and India focuses on call centres, telemarketing, data entry, billing, and low-end software development. However, China is intent on developing advanced manufacturing technology and India has a deep pool of scientists, software engineers, chemists, accountants, lawyers, and physicians. The technology talent in these nations also keeps growing: China graduates 250,000 engineers each year and India about 150,000.

When you consider the impact of offshoring on Canada, research supports that more than two-thirds of imported services are from the United States, not China and India. A Statistics Canada paper finds that services offshoring doesn't seem to affect productivity or employment. It does seem to reduce wages in the services-producing sector, though not in the goods-producing sector. Finally, on an industry-by-industry basis, rising offshoring of services seems to be associated with rising value-added activities. In the financial sector, for instance, low value-added activities such as general accounting are outsourced while high value-added activities such as strategizing are kept in-house and in-country.

Sources: Christine Dobby, "Offshore opportunities 'too good to pass up'," *The Financial* Post, 22 November 2011, FP16; William Watson, "Myth-Busting Offshoring," *National Post*, 30 May 2008, http://network.nationalpost.com/np/blogs/fpcomment/archive/2008/5/30/myth-busting-offshoring.aspx; Pete Engardio, "The Future of Outsourcing," *BusinessWeek*, 30 January 2006, 50–58; and Richard Ernsberger, "The Big Squeeze: A 'Second Wave' of Offshoring Could Threaten Middle-Income, White-Collar and Skilled Blue-Collar Jobs," *Newsweek International*, 30 May 2005.

Discussion Questions

1. Why are more Canadian companies investigating offshoring as a possible business strategy?
2. Do you think that offshoring is detrimental to the Canadian economy? Explain.
3. In your opinion, what are some business activities that should not be offshored? Explain.

Practise and learn online with Connect.

CHAPTER 4

THE ROLE OF GOVERNMENT IN BUSINESS

LEARNING OBJECTIVES

After you have read and studied this chapter, you should be able to:

LO 1 List the six categories of government activities that can affect business.

LO 2 Trace the historical role of government in the Canadian economy and explain why Crown corporations were created.

LO 3 Demonstrate why understanding laws and regulations at all levels of government is critical to business success.

LO 4 Explain how taxation and financial policies affect the Canadian economy.

LO 5 Describe how government expenditures benefit consumers and businesses alike.

LO 6 Illustrate how purchasing policies and services assist Canadian businesses.

PROFILE

GETTING TO KNOW RITA CHENG OF SUPERIOR TOFU

In this chapter, you will learn how government activities can assist businesses of all sizes. To this end, there are many government agencies mandated to provide support for entrepreneurs. One example is the Business Development Bank of Canada (BDC) <*www.bdc.ca*>. BDC is a financial institution that is owned by the Government of Canada. This Crown corporation plays a leadership role in delivering financial, investment, and consulting services to Canadian entrepreneurs, with a focus on small and medium-sized enterprises (SMEs). As an example, let us consider how it has supported Superior Tofu Ltd. <*http://superiortofu.com*>.

Rita Cheng started Superior Tofu Ltd. with her parents. Cheng had grown up with stories of her grandparents' tofu store, which they started in Vancouver in the 1940s. Her grandfather made tofu by hand and sold it in buckets that he delivered using a little red wagon through the streets of Vancouver's Chinatown.

Superior Tofu's first location was a small 1,200 sq. ft. store. Cheng and her parents would make tofu at the rear end of the store and sell their products at the front. They worked tirelessly crafting perfect blocks of tofu to sell in the neighbourhood. On their first day of business, they made $2.00 in sales! Fortunately, word got around the neighbourhood about the quality of the tofu, and Superior Tofu soon became a thriving business. Cheng recognized that to be successful, the company would need to be in continuous development mode. For Superior Tofu, this meant blending traditional recipes with new and inventive production methods. To achieve success, the decision was made to purchase a building that would allow for improved operations. To this end, the company received financing from BDC for production equipment. BDC Consulting has also helped the company increase efficiency and productivity. This support has allowed Superior Tofu to achieve Kosher status and become export-ready by obtaining the GMP/HACCP food safety certification. Today, the company is an established Vancouver-based manufacturer of premium and organic tofu, soymilk, and desserts with annual sales in the millions.

With BDC's help, Superior Tofu has expanded to four locations, leading the industry with the highest standards of tofu manufacturing and serving an ever-increasing base of satisfied customers. With ongoing innovation in its palette of products, Superior Tofu has expanded its domestic distribution outside the Lower Mainland market and also exports its products to Asia.

Sources: "Company History," Superior Tofu Ltd., 2012, http://superiortofu.com/about/company-history; "Superior Tofu Ltd.," Export Development Canada, 2012, http://www.bdc.ca/EN/about/testimonials/Pages/superiortofultd.aspx; and "To Bean or Not to Bean," Vancouver Foundation Presents, 2008, www.vancouverfoundationstories.ca/videoStory.php?recordID=155.

List the six categories of government activities that can affect business.

GOVERNMENT AFFECTS BUSINESS

Government activities that affect business may be divided into six categories: Crown corporations, laws and regulations, taxation and financial policies, government expenditures, purchasing policies, and services. Because all of these activities are scattered among different levels of government and many departments, agencies, and corporations, it is not possible to present this information in such neatly divided categories. However, as you make your way through the rest of the chapter you will be able to see elements of these different aspects of government actions affecting business.

Since the focus of this chapter is on the role of government in business, there will be limited discussion on how business affects government. It should become obvious as you read that governments are trying to respond to businesses's needs. This can be anything from creating laws that create a level playing field to providing services that support business initiatives. Reviewing Figure 4.1 will give you a sense of the scope of this relationship.

Trace the historical role of government in the Canadian economy and explain why Crown corporations were created.

Government Involvement in the Economy

As noted in Chapter 2, the Canadian economic system is described as a mixed economy—that is, an economic system in which some allocation of resources is made by the market and some is made by the government. If you look at the Government of Canada section (and equivalent provincial government sections) in a city telephone directory, you will get some idea of the degree of government involvement in our economy today. Every country's government is involved in its economy, but the specific ways in which the governments participate vary a great deal. There are particular historical reasons why Canada developed into a nation in which governments play very important roles.

When Canada was formed as a country in 1867, the federal government was given the power to "regulate trade and commerce." When the western provinces later joined this Confederation, it became clear that it would take special efforts to build a unified Canada. The very small population was scattered across a huge country, and there was no railway to connect it. Trading patterns were in a north

Figure 4.1

Government Involvement with Business

Government activities that affect business can be divided into six categories.

1. **Crown Corporations.** There are hundreds of such companies, and they play an important role in the economy. Crown corporations sometimes compete with for-profit businesses.
2. **Laws and Regulations.** These cover a wide range, from taxation and consumer protection to environmental controls, working conditions, and labour–management relations. Review Appendix B for some examples.
3. **Taxation and Financial Policies.** All levels of government collect taxes—income taxes, the GST or HST, provincial sales taxes, and property taxes. Taxation is also fine-tuned by government to achieve certain goals or to give effect to certain policies. This is called fiscal policy.
4. **Government Expenditures.** Governments pay out billions of dollars to Canadians. When these recipients spend this money, businesses benefit. All levels of government provide a host of direct and indirect aid packages as incentives to achieve certain goals. These packages consist of tax reductions, grants, loans, and loan guarantees.
5. **Purchasing Policies.** Governments are very large purchasers of ordinary supplies, services, and materials to operate the country. Because the federal government is the single largest purchaser in Canada, its policies regarding where to purchase have a major effect on particular businesses and the economy.
6. **Services.** These include a vast array of direct and indirect activities, among them helping companies go international, bringing companies to Canada, and training and retraining the workforce.

to south configuration because, like today, most people lived near the U.S. border.

The United States developed much faster and with a much larger population and a bigger economy—which provided products not available in the provinces, either because they were not made in Canada or because there was no transportation to distribute them.

This led the Canadian governments, starting with our first prime minister, Sir John A. Macdonald, to develop what was called a National Policy. The Policy placed high tariffs on imports from the United States to protect Canadian manufacturing, which had higher costs. In addition, the federal government began to grapple with the difficult question of building a costly rail line to the west coast.

These two issues set the tone for the continuing and substantial involvement of Canadian governments in developing and maintaining the Canadian economy. As you make your way through this chapter and learn about these complex activities, you should not be surprised to learn that the different levels of government are large employers in the country. The federal government and the provinces with the largest populations and levels of economic activity—namely, Ontario, Quebec, British Columbia, and Alberta—in particular have been excellent sources of employment for graduates in the past.

I WANT TO GAIN EXPERIENCE

FEDERAL STUDENT WORK EXPERIENCE PROGRAM

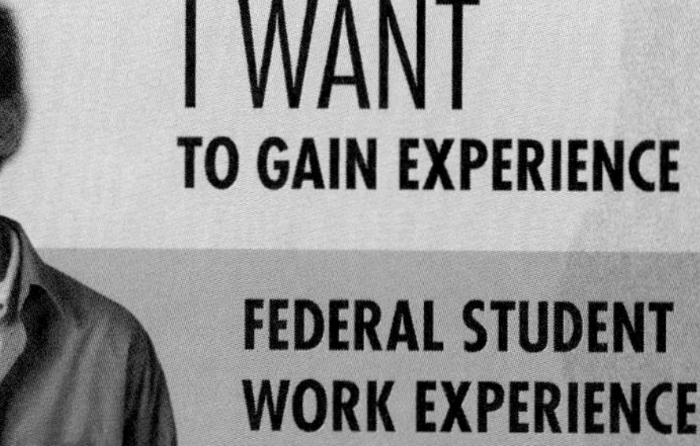

▶ The Federal Student Work Experience Program provides thousands of full-time students with work experience. With only one application, you can be considered for temporary jobs in various federal organizations across the country.

National Policy
Government directive that placed high tariffs on imports from the United States to protect Canadian manufacturing, which had higher costs.

As you will see in this chapter, we also have an interventionist government that through its activities (e.g., regulatory and fiscal policy) tries to create a stable economy for businesses. In Chapter 3, you learned that trade agreements, such as the North American Free Trade Agreement (NAFTA) and the European Union (EU) have focused on eliminating tariffs between countries. But the work has not stopped, and the federal government is in the midst of negotiating 14 international free trade agreements.[1]

Before we go into more detail, let us briefly review how government affects business. You never know, one day you may have a job in one of these areas.

CROWN CORPORATIONS

In Canada, an important aspect of the role of government is expressed through Crown corporations, which are companies that are owned by the federal or provincial governments. Review Figure 4.2 for a brief list of the top Crown corporations in

Crown corporations
Companies that are owned by the federal or provincial government.

Rank	Company	2010 Revenue ($ Billions)
1	Caisse de Dépôt et Placement du Québec	18.0
2	Hydro-Québec	12.3
3	Canada Mortgage and Housing Corp.	10.6
4	Canada Post Corp.	7.3
5	Ontario Lottery and Gaming Corp.	6.3

Source: Material reprinted with the express permission of the *National Post*, a division of Postmedia Network Inc.

Figure 4.2
Canada's Largest Crown Corporations by Revenue

▶ Set up in 1978, VIA Rail Canada <www.viarail.ca> serves some 450 Canadian communities throughout the country. Have you ever taken advantage of the student savings offered by VIA Rail?

Canada. Crown corporations were set up for several reasons. They provided services that were not being provided by businesses, which is how Air Canada <*www.aircanada.com*> came into being in the 1930s. Crown corporations were created to bail out a major industry in trouble, which is how the Canadian National Railway (CNR) <*www.cn.ca*> was put together in 1919. Lastly, they provided some special services that could not otherwise be made available, as in the case of the Bank of Canada.

Each province also owns a variety of Crown corporations. Typically, a Crown corporation owns the province's electric power company. Some examples are NB Power <*www.nbpower.com*> in New Brunswick and Hydro-Québec <*www.hydroquebec.com*> in Quebec. Alberta owns a bank called ATB Financial <*www.atb.com*>. It was originally set up to help farmers in bad times. The province of Saskatchewan owns all the liquor stores, the power company that supplies the entire province, the provincial telecom, all auto and home insurance, as well as a TV station and all sorts of corporations that assist farmers.[2] Two other examples are discussed next.

The Financial Role of Two Special Provincial Crown Corporations

The Alberta Heritage Savings Trust Fund <*www.finance.alberta.ca/business/ahstf*> was established in the 1970s, when the Alberta economy was prospering as a result of the oil boom. The government set aside a part of its oil royalty revenue to start the fund. In 2011 the Fund's assets were valued at $15.4 billion.[3] It must operate on a sound financial basis, but, as much as possible, it makes investment decisions that will benefit Alberta.

Quebec has the Caisse de dépôt et placement du Québec <*www.lacaisse.com*> (which means Quebec Deposit and Investment Fund), a giant fund that was established to handle the funds collected by the Quebec Pension Plan. With $159.0 billion in total net assets under management, it is one of the largest pools of funds in North America.[4] This plan was set up parallel to the Canada Pension Plan in 1966. The fund also handles other Quebec government funds, and it is a very powerful investment vehicle that is used to guide economic development in Quebec. Although it, too, must operate on a sound financial basis, it has a lot of scope to make decisions that will benefit the Quebec economy.

The Role for Government

privatization
The process of governments selling Crown corporations.

deregulation
Government withdrawal of certain laws and regulations that seem to hinder competition

Since the 1990s, federal and provincial governments have embarked upon a series of measures designed to reduce the role of government in the economy. Over the years, former large corporations like Teleglobe Canada, Air Canada, and CNR were sold. The national system of air traffic control, the management of airports, hundreds of ports and ferries, and other Maritime installations were also sold.

This disposal of government assets and companies signalled a minor revolution in Canadian history. The whole process of selling publicly-owned corporations is called **privatization**. As well, during this time, industries that had been regulated, such as airlines, oil and gas, and trucking, were partially or completely deregulated. **Deregulation**

▶ The federal government sold its remaining stake in Petro-Canada <*www.petro-canada.ca*>, an oil and gas company, in 2005. Here you see the Hanlan Robb gas plant near Edson, Alberta.

means that the government withdraws certain laws and regulations that seem to hinder competition. Review Appendix B for a discussion on deregulation.

Similar activities were undertaken by provincial governments. Alberta privatized its liquor board. Saskatchewan reduced its interest in giant uranium producer Cameco Corporation <*www.cameco.com*> and the British Columbia provincial government sold the British Columbia Railway Co. <*www.bcrco.com*>. The Ontario provincial government has considered selling Crown corporations such as Hydro One Inc. <*www.hydroone.com*>, the Ontario Lottery and Gaming Corp. <*www.olg.ca*>, and the Liquor Control Board of Ontario <*www.lcbo.com*> to decrease the province's deficit.[5] Deficits will be discussed later in this chapter.

Municipal governments are also looking to privatize services such as water systems, garbage collection, and cleaning. Everywhere you look, government agencies, like for-profit organizations, are looking at ways to lower costs and improve efficiencies.

It may seem odd that this introduction on the role of government includes a discussion on how the different levels of government are selling some of their Crown corporations and getting out of these services. What is important to note is that Crown corporations exist and that they provide important services to both businesses and consumers.

PROGRESS ASSESSMENT

- What are the six categories of government involvement with business?
- What are Crown corporations? Why were they created?
- What does privatization refer to? Can you cite any examples?

LAWS AND REGULATIONS

Demonstrate why understanding laws and regulations at all levels of government is critical to business success.

In Chapter 1 you were introduced to the importance of the legal environment. These laws (and resulting regulations) are created by elected politicians. Consequently, the political parties in power can greatly affect the business environment. This is why it is important to be aware of the beliefs of the different parties. Some think the

The Supreme Court of Canada has the final decision on constitutional questions and on important cases of civil and criminal law. It deals also with appeals from decisions of the provincial courts of appeal.

government should have more say in business, while others think that less government intervention is best. Regardless of the political party, public perception and changing opinion can affect government policy making. This is why all stakeholders should be considered when laws and regulations are created, modified, approved, and implemented.

How Canadians Govern Themselves is a publication that describes Canada's Constitution, the judicial system, and government powers. It is an excellent resource tools if you wish to learn more about Canada's system of government.

The power to make laws is based on the British North America Act, 1867 (BNA Act). The BNA Act was passed by the British Parliament in 1867. It is the law that created the Canadian Confederation and it sets the legal ground rules for Canada. In 1982, the BNA Act became part of the new Constitution and was renamed the Constitution Act, 1867.

Laws are derived from four sources: the Constitution, precedents established by judges, provincial and federal statutes, and federal and provincial administrative agencies.[6] As a business person, you will be affected by current (and potential) laws and regulations. Appendix B, following this chapter, considers the importance of working within the legal environment of business.

Canada has a legislature in each province and territory to deal with local matters. The Parliament in Ottawa makes laws for all Canadians. The Constitution defines the powers that can be exercised by the federal and provincial governments. In the event of a conflict, federal powers prevail.

Federal Government Responsibilities[7]

The federal government is responsible for issues that affect citizens across Canada. Its primary responsibility is to ensure and support the country's economic performance. This includes overseeing such industries as aeronautics, shipping, railways, telecommunications, and atomic energy. Some other responsibilities that have an impact on business operations are listed below:

- trade regulations (interprovincial and international)
- incorporation of federal companies
- taxation (both direct and indirect)
- the banking and monetary system
- hospital insurance and medicare
- the public debt and property
- national defence
- unemployment
- immigration
- criminal law
- fisheries

Let us consider hospital insurance and medicare, as here we see some overlap with federal, provincial, and territorial government responsibilities. The national Parliament, in effect, established nationwide systems of hospital insurance and medical care by making grants to the provinces and territories on condition that their plans reach certain standards of service. This has been largely successful, despite some differences in modes of financing and program coverage.

The Canada Health Transfer (CHT) is the largest major transfer to provinces and territories. It provides long-term predictable funding for health care, and supports the principles of the federally regulated Canada Health Act, which are universality, comprehensiveness, portability, accessibility, and public administration. The CHT cash transfer will reach $29 billion in 2012–13 and is expected to reach at least $38 billion in 2018–19. In summary, while the federal government is responsible for health care, it is still up to the provinces and territories to implement these policies, and their co-operation is critical for success.

Industry Canada is the federal agency that administers a variety of laws affecting businesses and consumers. One of the most relevant pieces of legislation is the Competition Act, which aims to ensure that mergers of large corporations will not restrict competition and that fair competition exists among businesses. (Some of the major consumer protection laws are shown in Figure 4.3.) The Act covers many laws, including discriminatory pricing, price fixing, misleading advertising, and the refusal to deal with certain companies.

Consider the clothes you wear. They are required to have a label showing the country of origin, size, type of fabric, and washing instructions. When you buy 25 litres of gasoline, you can feel confident that you have received a true measure because of the sticker on the equipment showing when it was last inspected. There are laws that give consumers the right to cancel contracts or return goods within a certain period of time. It is not possible to go through a day and not find an instance where laws have helped you in some way.

Figure 4.3

Some Major Federal Consumer Protection Laws

These laws all provide consumers with information and protection in various ways. There are also provincial consumer protection laws.

Canadian Agricultural Products Standards Act covers a wide range of farm products such as meat, poultry, eggs, maple syrup, honey, and dairy products.
Consumer Packaging and Labelling Act applies to all products not specifically included in other Acts.
Food and Drugs Act covers a whole range of regulations pertaining to quality, testing approval, packaging, and labelling.
Hazardous Products Act covers all hazardous products.
Textile Labelling Act includes apparel sizing and many other special areas.
Weights and Measures Act applies to all equipment that measures quantities such as scales, gas pumps, and so forth.

▸ Gasoline prices can vary from place to place because of a number of factors that may affect prices in local markets. These factors include the following: differences in local supply and demand conditions, including the number, size, and type of competitors in each market; differences in taxes; differences in marketing, distribution, and transportation costs; and/or the presence of one or more aggressive price competitors in a local market.[10] Has the price of gas ever deterred you from buying a car?

As noted in Chapter 1, competition has never been greater than it is today, both internationally and domestically. For example, despite trade agreements, new government policies (e.g., the "Buy American" provisions which encouraged priority for contracts with U.S. firms) can create barriers to trade.[8] The federal government lobbies other country governments to decrease such trade barriers in an attempt to create business opportunities for Canadian firms. This flip side to this is that these countries may request the same of Canada.

The Competition Bureau: Gas Price Fixing Example[9]

The Competition Bureau, as an independent law enforcement agency, ensures that Canadian businesses and consumers prosper in a competitive and innovative marketplace. Under the Competition Act, it is a criminal offence when two or more competitors or potential competitors conspire, agree, or arrange to fix prices, allocate customers or markets, or restrict output of a product.

Price-fixing conspiracies are difficult to detect and prove. High or identical prices are not in and of themselves evidence of criminal activity. There must be evidence that competitors have made an illegal agreement to set those prices. When there are substantiated allegations of wrongdoing in the marketplace, the Competition Bureau will investigate.

The Competition Bureau has charged Suncor Energy Products Inc. (Suncor) <*www.suncor.com*> with fixing the price of retail gasoline over seven months in Belleville, Ontario. The Ontario Superior Court sentenced Suncor to pay a fine of $500,000. "We are committed to pursuing those who engage in anti-competitive behaviour that harms Canadian businesses and consumers," said Melanie Aitken, Commissioner of Competition. "Illegal agreements between competitors to fix prices deny consumers the benefits of competitive prices and choice." Earlier in the year, Pioneer Energy LP <*www.pioneer.ca*>, Canadian Tire Corporation <*www.canadiantire.ca*>, and Mr. Gas <*www.mrgasltd.ca*> pleaded guilty to fixing the price of retail gasoline over the same period of time in Kingston and Brockville, Ontario, and were fined a total of $2 million.

Similar cases, some involving managers and owners, have occurred across Quebec as well. Since 2008, charges were laid against 38 individuals and 14 companies in stations throughout Quebec, including Victoriaville, Thetford Mines, Magog, and Sherbrooke. Of those, 27 individuals and 14 companies pleaded guilty, resulting in fines of over $3 million. Six of those individuals have been sentenced to imprisonment with a total time of 54 months.

marketing boards Organizations that control the supply or pricing of certain agricultural products in Canada.

Marketing Boards

In Canada, we have a special system of **marketing boards** that control the supply or pricing of certain agricultural products. Consequently, they often control trade. This supply management is designed to give some stability to an important area of the economy that is normally very volatile. Farmers are subject to conditions that are rather unique and that have a great effect on their business and on our food supply. Weather and disease are major factors in the operation of farms and are beyond the control of the individual farmer. So are unstable prices and changes in supply resulting from uncoordinated decision making by millions of farmers around the world, or the exercise of market power by concentrated business organizations.

In the past farmers have experienced periods of severe drought, flooding, severe cold, and diseases that affected crops, livestock, and poultry. The situation regarding international markets and supply has a serious impact on Canada's grain farmers, since Canada exports much more wheat than it consumes domestically. This market fluctuates greatly depending on the supply in other major grain-exporting countries such as the United States, Argentina, and Australia. The market also depends on demand from major importers such as China and Russia, whose abilities to meet their own requirements are subject to wide variation. Often the Canadian government (like other governments) grants substantial loans with favourable conditions to enable these countries to pay for their imports of our wheat and other agricultural products.

Because we export billions of dollars of agricultural products annually, the ability to hold our own in international markets has a major impact on the state of the Canadian economy. When farmers are flourishing, they buy new equipment and consumer goods and their communities feel the effects of ample cash flow. So does the transportation industry. Conversely, when farmers are suffering, all of these sectors hurt as well.

To smooth out the effects of these unusual conditions on this sector of our economy, and to ensure a steady supply of food to consumers at reasonable prices, some government agencies were set up to control dairy products and poultry. The Canadian Dairy Commission <*www.cdc-ccl.gc.ca*> controls the output and pricing of milk and other dairy products. The Egg Farmers of Canada <*www.eggs.ca*>, Chicken Farmers of Canada <*chicken.ca*>, the Turkey Farmers of Canada <*www.turkeyfarmersofcanada.ca*> and the Canadian Hatching Egg Producers <*www.chep-poic.ca*> consist of representatives from the provinces that produce these items. These organizations control the amount of production for all of the products under their supervision by allocating quotas to each province that produces them. Provincial agencies administer these quotas and set prices for their province. Each agency controls products that are sold only in its province.

The Canadian system of marketing boards has been under attack by various organizations because it does not permit normal competitive conditions to operate in this field. This, they argue, distorts the whole industry and raises prices for Canadian consumers. Defenders of the system argue that other countries have different systems that have the same effect as our marketing boards but are just less visible. The EU spends billions of dollars on subsidies for their farmers. The United States, which often complains about other countries' unreasonable trade barriers, has its own restrictions, such as on sugar imports.

In Chapter 3, we referred to the World Trade Organization, whose main purpose is to reduce barriers to trade among countries. If the organization is successful, we may see a very different picture emerging worldwide over the next decade: limited protection for domestic markets, reduced tariffs and other restrictions, and the market having a much greater impact on prices and production. The effect on Canadian farmers and on the agricultural industry in general would be enormous, as everyone would be trying to cope with the necessary adjustments to such new conditions.

The Canadian Wheat Board[11] There is a perception that Canadian farmers are more subsidized than farmers in other countries. According to information gathered by the Organisation for Economic Co-operation and Development (OECD), Canadian farmers received 17 percent of their income from subsidies. American wheat

▶ A group of former Canadian Wheat Board directors were appealing the law to end the monopoly. Why where they against this change? Were they successful?

producers received 49 percent of their income from subsidies, while EU wheat farmers received 43 percent of their income from subsidies.

The Canadian Wheat Board <*www.cwb.ca*>, a farmer-controlled organization that marketed wheat and barley grown by western Canadian producers, was one of the world's largest grain-trading companies. In 2012, a law was implemented to stop the Canadian Wheat Board's monopoly over the sale of all wheat and barley grown in Western Canada. The federal government will keep backing the Wheat Board financially for five years but farmers are free to sell their grain to the Wheat Board or to private companies.

Provincial Government Responsibilities[12]

Each province has its own government, while the territories are still governed federally. Issues that affect provincial residents but do not necessarily affect all Canadians are governed at the provincial level. Provincial government responsibilities include the following areas:

- regulation of provincial trade and commerce
- natural resources within their boundaries
- incorporation of provincial companies
- direct taxation for provincial purposes
- licensing for revenue purposes
- the administration of justice
- health and social services
- municipal affairs
- property law
- labour law
- education

The retention of a high degree of provincial autonomy in the provision of elementary and secondary school education and the accommodation of religious and linguistic preferences has resulted in a variation in school systems. Both government levels also fund programs for post-secondary education.

One trend that we are seeing today is the merging of public and private philosophies in public-private partnerships (P3s or PPPs). P3s represent a method of privatizing public services or public infrastructure. In a Nanos Research Poll, 70 percent of Canadians were open to the private sector delivering services in partnership with the government in areas such as roads, hospitals, schools, public transit systems, and safe water systems. Let us consider health-care facilities (e.g., hospitals). In a typical P3 deal, the government allows for-profit private corporations to finance, design, build, and operate health facilities. The government commits to lease the facility and use certain services for a period of as much as 30 years or more. Some provinces enter into P3 arrangements to build needed hospitals, promising that the P3s will save money and be more efficient. P3 opponents say that some P3s cost more to build and operate, take private profits from the public health budget, hide their costs, and erode the quality of services. With more than 50 P3 hospitals in operation or development, governments, health-care leaders, and communities are clearly P3 supporters.

Free Trade Between Provinces[13]

While interprovincial trade is a $300-billion industry in Canada, many Canadian companies and individuals face obstacles when trying to do business outside of their home province or territory. Some trade barriers exist because governments created

The federal government works with participating provinces and territories to implement the Canada Student Grants Program and the Canada Student Loans Program. Quebec, the Northwest Territories, and Nunavut offer their own student financial aid programs and do not participate in the Canada Student Loans Program.

them to protect their economies from outside competition. Governments also put policies in place to protect the environment, establish workforce standards, or achieve other regulatory purposes. Estimates on the costs of these interprovincial barriers in Canada are $14 billion per year. Interprovincial trade barriers are damaging to the economy and to Canadians' standards of living. While it is clear why they were created (i.e., to protect provincial jobs), these protectionist barriers discourage competition, distort market forces, and reduce efficiency.

The Agreement on Internal Trade (AIT) is an intergovernmental trade agreement signed by Canadian First Ministers. Its purpose is to reduce and eliminate barriers to the free movement of persons, goods, services, and investment within Canada. The objective is to reduce extra costs to Canadian businesses by making internal trade more efficient, increasing market access for Canadian companies, and facilitating work mobility for tradespeople and professionals. For example, the Certified General Accountants of New Brunswick <*www.gga-nb.org*> successfully appealed to the Internal Trade Secretariat to have the government of Quebec stop restricting access to those that were recognized as qualified to practice accounting in that province.

AIT amendments have removed barriers that have made it difficult, and sometimes impossible, for workers from one province or territory to work in another. While it is not expected that such amendments will address all barriers, it is a step in the right direction. Amendments to the AIT will lead to full labour mobility for workers and professionals, except where protection of public health or safety justifies barriers. (They will also provide for an effective dispute resolution mechanism, including monetary penalties for ignoring a trade panel ruling.) For example, British Columbia may benefit from the removal of such barriers, since a shortage of 350,000 workers is forecast between now and 2015. It is estimated that Alberta will create 400,000 jobs over the next decade and labour mobility is seen as key to filling these jobs.

Municipal Government Responsibilities[14]

Municipal governments—cities, towns, villages, counties, districts, and metropolitan regions—are set up by the provincial legislatures. Their authority is defined by the specific province in which they operate. There are roughly 4,000 municipal governments in Canada that provide a variety of services. Municipalities provide services such as water supply, sewage and garbage disposal, roads, sidewalks, street lighting, building codes, parks, playgrounds, libraries, and so forth. Schools are generally looked after by school boards or commissions elected under provincial education acts.

Municipalities also play a role in consumer protection. For example, they have regulations and laws regarding any establishment that serves food. Inspectors regularly examine the premises of all restaurants for cleanliness. Local newspapers often publish lists of restaurants fined for failing to maintain required standards. There are similar laws (called zoning laws) about noise, odours, signs, and other activities that may affect a neighbourhood. Certain zones are restricted to residences, and others permit only certain quiet businesses to operate.

Zoning requirements also limit the height of buildings and define how far they must be set back from the road. Most Canadian cities require that all high-rise buildings have a certain ratio of garage space so that cars have off-street parking spots. Parking problems in residential areas due to overflow of vehicles from adjacent businesses have led to parking being limited to residential permit holders on certain streets, so that stores and other places of business must offer commercial parking lots for their customers. And, of course, there are speed limits set by municipal or provincial authorities.

All businesses usually must obtain a municipal licence to operate so the appropriate department can track them to ensure they are following regulations. Many municipalities also have a business tax and a charge for water consumption.

In summary, each level of government has its own roles and responsibilities. Sometimes there is overlap and in other instances there is downloading of responsibilities. Such is the case with some municipal services. An understanding of these responsibilities will contribute to a better understanding of who is responsible for developing, implementing, and overseeing policies that are important to business.

Explain how taxation and financial policies affect the Canadian economy.

TAXATION AND FINANCIAL POLICIES

Mention the word taxes and most people frown. That's because taxes affect almost every individual and business in the country. Taxes are how all levels of government redistribute wealth. The revenue that is collected allows governments to discharge their legal obligations. This revenue is used to pay for public services (e.g., fire, police, and libraries), pay down debt, and fund government operations and programs. Taxes have also been used as a method of encouraging or discouraging taxpayers. For example, if the government wishes to reduce the use of certain classes of products (e.g., cigarettes and alcohol), it passes what is referred to as a *sin tax*. It is hoped that the additional cost of the product from increased taxes discourages additional consumption.

In other situations the government may encourage business to hire new employees or to purchase new equipment by offering a tax credit. A tax credit is an amount that can be deducted from a tax bill. For example, when Research In Motion (RIM) opened a technical support operations centre in Halifax, the Nova Scotia government offered RIM $19 million in subsidies (some consider this a tax credit), including $14 million in payroll rebates and $5 million for training and recruitment.[15]

Taxes are levied from a variety of sources. Income (personal and business), sales, and property are the major bases of tax revenue. The federal government receives its largest share of taxes from personal income. "Taxes from all levels of government make up the single largest expenditure facing Canadian families," says Charles Lammam, the Fraser Institute's Associate Director of Tax and Budget Policy Research.[16] In a recent study (some results from the report are summarized in Figure 4.4), the total

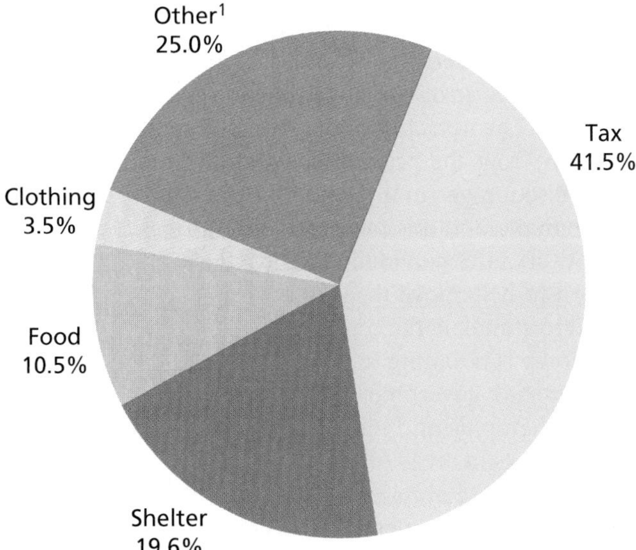

Figure 4.4

The Average Canadian Family's Total Expenditures as a Percentage of Cash Income, 2011

[1]Other expenditures include household operations (e.g., communications, child care expenses, and pet expenses), transportation, health care, recreation, education,tobacco products and alcoholic beverages, among other expenses.

Source: Used with the permission of The Fraser Institute, www.fraserinstitute.org.

tax bill of the typical Canadian family was calculated by adding up the various taxes that a family pays to federal, provincial, and local governments. This includes income taxes, sales taxes, Employment Insurance and Canadian Pension Plan contributions, and "hidden" taxes such as import duties, excise taxes on tobacco and alcohol, amusement taxes, and gas taxes.[17] Lammam hopes the study will promote a debate among Canadians about how much they pay in taxes and what they get in return. He said the public should be demanding that the government find ways to deliver public programs more efficiently.

Queen's University Faculty of Law Professor Kathleen Lahey believes that the report is limited and that it looks at only one component of the tax system. Public outcry at personal income tax rates (as a possible outcome of this report's perspective) could make it easier for the government to cut these rates. However, the result would shift more of the tax burden to taxes such as sales taxes, employment insurance premiums, and Canada Pension Plan (CPP) contributions. Those forms of taxation weigh most heavily on low-income families, couples and individuals, disabled people, and those with unequal access to well-paying jobs, such as women and aboriginal and immigrant workers, says Lahey. She believes that the report ignores the impact that corporate tax cuts had on tax revenue. For example, in the past six years corporate tax cuts have taken $41.3 billion out federal revenues and $23.3 billion in personal income tax cuts have largely benefited those with the highest incomes.[18]

Can you see how it is important to consider all aspects when information is released? Start by asking yourself some questions. What is the purpose of this information? From what perspective is this report written? What is the call to action? As you can read from the above, there are always different perspectives that should be explored before making business decisions that will impact many stakeholders.

PROGRESS ASSESSMENT

- What are four responsibilities of the federal government?
- What are responsibilities of the provincial governments?
- Why are there interprovincial trade barriers?
- What are responsibilities of the municipal governments?

Stabilizing the Economy Through Fiscal Policy

fiscal policy The federal government's effort to keep the economy stable by increasing or decreasing taxes or government spending.

Fiscal policy refers to the federal government's effort to keep the economy stable by increasing or decreasing taxes or government spending. The first half of fiscal policy involves taxation. Theoretically, high tax rates tend to slow the economy because they draw money away from the private sector and are remitted to the government. High tax rates may discourage small business ownership because they decrease the profits businesses can make, and this can make the effort less rewarding. It follows then that, theoretically, low tax rates would tend to give the economy a boost.[19] The government can use taxation to help move the economy in a desired direction. For example, taxes may be lowered to stimulate the economy when it is weak. Similarly, taxes may be raised when the economy is booming to cool it off and slow down inflation.

Federal and provincial governments constantly use the lever of fiscal policy to stimulate specific geographic and industrial areas. They offer special tax credits to companies that open plants in areas of chronically high unemployment, such as Cape Breton or Newfoundland and Labrador. All companies that invest in specific activities considered desirable by the government (such as the technology sector) may be eligible to receive a tax credit that reduces the income tax they have to pay. Unfortunately, some of these programs have been scaled back or eliminated due to budget constraints.

The second half of fiscal policy involves government spending. The government spends money in many areas, including social programs, highways, the environment, and so on. If the government spends over and above the amount it gathers in taxes for a specific period of time (namely, a fiscal year), then it has a **deficit**.

deficit Occurs when a government spends over and above the amount it gathers in taxes for a specific period of time (namely, a fiscal year).

One way to lessen annual deficits is to cut government spending. This is difficult to do. Every year, there is demand by the provinces and territories for increased transfer payments (to be discussed soon), the need for funds due to unexpected situations (such as the massive flooding in New Brunswick in 2012), more pressure from international bodies to increase peacekeeping support, and so on. Some people believe that spending by the government helps the economy grow. Others believe that the money the government spends comes out of the pockets of consumers and business people—especially when taxes have been increased—and that this slows growth. What do you think? Let us look at government actions that have been taken over the past decade.

The National Debt (Federal Debt)

For many years, the Canadian government spent more than it received in revenues, and it had to borrow heavily. However, it did not reduce spending when times were good to pay back these loans. The **national debt** (also known as the **federal debt**) is the accumulation of government surpluses and deficits over time. At the time this chapter was updated, this debt was over $583 billion. According to the Canadian Taxpayers Federation, the federal government is adding $58 million a day to our national debt and by 2015–16, the debt is expected to reach $614 billion.[20]

national debt (federal debt) The accumulation of government surpluses and deficits over time.

Increased government borrowing and spending stimulates an economy. Such was the case when the federal government tried to stimulate the economy in 2009 through initiatives such as increased spending (e.g., infrastructure) and decreased taxes. This was in response to some economic challenges during that time: a falling world GDP, a continuing U.S. recession, and a drop in commodities prices.[21] (You can see how an understanding of economics and global business is critical when reviewing the federal budget.) The changes to spending and taxes contributed to the first deficit in over ten years.

Cuts in spending have the opposite effect as they slow down the economy. Such decisions impact many stakeholders. The Making Ethical Decisions box highlights how cuts in government spending can negatively impact individuals.

Why is it important to control the debt? Financial security is critical to a country's investment in its people and businesses. A lower debt means that less money will need to go toward paying down the national debt and any outstanding interest. Reducing

MAKING ETHICAL DECISIONS

Tackling the Deficit

In the late 1990s the federal government was under strong pressure from the business community to reduce or wipe out the annual deficit in the annual budget. Business was convinced that these constant deficits and the resulting accumulated debt were dragging the Canadian economy down and making Canada uncompetitive with other major countries. As a result, the federal government drastically cut its expenditures.

There were significant reductions in funding to the provinces for health care, post-secondary education, and other important activities. Combined with other budget-cutting measures (e.g., lower and fewer payments to the unemployed and laying off employees), the result was an increase in poverty levels, especially among children and women.

These facts lead to some ethical questions. How could such severe budget cuts have been avoided? Does the business community bear some responsibility for the increase in poverty in Canada? In other words, was it ethical for businesses to allow our national debt to grow so large and not challenge the government's annual deficits much earlier? What do you think?

government spending on interest charges will allow the government to spend more money on social programs or to lower taxes. Lower taxes will stimulate the economy, as companies will have higher net profits and individuals will have more disposable income.

With a lower debt, Canada could also be considered a more attractive country to invest in—a healthy and educated workforce is able to work and buy products. In addition, employers like well-funded social programs as there is less risk that they will be asked to increase employee benefits. A lower debt load also means that in times of economic slowdown or when unexpected events occur (such as SARS) the government may have funds available to alleviate the ensuing pressures. Of course, if the debt is high, there is less money that can be dedicated to social programs and initiatives to assist businesses in becoming more competitive.

Reductions in the national debt have been the result of surpluses—a **surplus** is an excess of revenues over expenditures. As the debt comes down the annual interest costs are also reduced. This reduction in the national debt translates into a savings of billions of dollars each year on debt interest payments.

surplus
An excess of revenues over expenditures.

The Federal Budget

On an annual basis (around spring time), the federal finance minister releases a blueprint for how the government wants to set the country's annual economic agenda. This document, called the **federal budget**, is a comprehensive report that reveals government financial policies and priorities for the coming year. This political document shows how much revenue the government expects to collect, any changes in income and other taxes, and whether a deficit or a surplus is expected. The federal budget answers questions that affect businesses and Canadians, such as: How much money will go to pay down the debt? How much money will go to social programs such as health care? Will there be more money for research and development? Will taxes go up or down?

federal budget
A comprehensive report that reveals government financial policies for the coming year.

The budget is reviewed carefully by businesses, consumers, and other countries because the information it contains affects all of these stakeholders. It reflects revenues (from taxation) and expenditures (e.g., Canada Pension Plan payments) for the past year. In addition, the government will communicate program changes for the future, as well as forecasted growth projections. From this document, stakeholders can get an idea of what issues are important to the government. For example, in the 2012 federal budget, Finance Minister Jim Flaherty expected that the government would be in a surplus position by 2015. The fiscal plan called for a savings of $5.2 billion per year, with a total reduction of 19,200 public-sector jobs.[22]

Provincial governments also release their own budgets. A province's financial stability affects political decisions and, ultimately, the business environment within the province's boundaries.

▸ In 2012, more than 300,000 Quebec students joined the province-wide general strike opposing a proposed tuition increase of $1,625 over five years. If approved, the result would nearly double tuition fees to $3,800 per year, still resulting in one of the lowest rates in the country.[23] Would you participate in a general strike if such an increase was proposed in your province? How might tuition increases impact a province's budget?

Using Monetary Policy to Keep the Economy Growing

Have you ever wondered who lends the federal government money when it spends more than it collects in taxes? One source is the Bank of Canada <*www.bankofcanada.ca*>, a Crown corporation. Its role is to "promote the economic and financial well-being of Canada." The day-to-day administration of monetary policy is the responsibility of the Bank of Canada, in co-operation and in consultation with the federal finance minister.

monetary policy
The management of the money supply and interest rates.

Monetary policy is the management of the money supply and interest rates. It is controlled by the Bank of Canada. When the economy is booming, the Bank of Canada tends to raise interest rates in an attempt to control inflation. This makes money more expensive to borrow. Businesses thus borrow less, and the economy

▸ The Bank of Canada is Canada's central bank. It is not a commercial bank and it does not offer banking services to the public. Rather, it has the responsibilities for Canada's monetary policy, bank notes, financial system, funds management, and retail debt.

slows as business people spend less money on everything, including labour and machinery. The opposite is true when the Bank of Canada lowers interest rates. When this happens, businesses tend to borrow more, and the economy improves. Raising and lowering interest rates should therefore help control the business cycles.

The Bank of Canada also controls the money supply. A simple explanation of how this works is that the more money the Bank of Canada makes available to business people and others, the faster the economy grows. To slow the economy, the Bank of Canada lowers the money supply. (If you are eager to learn more about the money supply, you can turn to Chapter 18 now.) One example of the Canadian government stepping in to stimulate the economy is its reaction to the U.S. subprime mortgage crisis that impacted the global economy. Read about this in the next section.

In summary, the government makes two major efforts to control the economy: fiscal policy (taxes and spending) and monetary policy (control over interest rates and the money supply). The economic goal is to keep the economy growing so that more people can climb up the economic ladder and enjoy a satisfying quality of life.[24]

The Subprime Mortgage Crisis[25]

Subprime mortgages are loans targeted at people who do not qualify for regular mortgages because their credit records are not good enough or because they do not have a credit history. Some mortgages are interest-only loans that are lower in cost because no principal is paid down. Initially, these loans come with very low rates (thus, subprime).

In the situation that developed in the United States, people holding subprime mortgages found that at the end of the term (e.g., two years), interest rates were much higher and they couldn't afford to make their payments. As housing prices started to fall, they often found that they could no longer afford to sell the homes either. The fallout was decreasing home sales and prices, and rising foreclosures. The resulting crisis contributed to approval of a US$700 billion bank bailout by the U.S. Congress in October 2008 to stabilize the financial sector and reinforce hundreds of financial institutions. Additional bailout funds were approved the following year. Bank bailouts soon followed in England, Germany, France, Italy, and Spain.

While Canadian financial institutions did not face the high default rates experienced in the United States, they were having trouble borrowing money because banks and other lenders in other countries were more cautious. This credit squeeze sent stock markets (to be discussed in Chapter 17) crashing and there were worries of a global meltdown. In response to these conditions, the federal government announced in October 2008 that it would take over $25 billion worth of bank-held mortgages to ease the growing liquidity problems faced by the country's financial institutions. This would provide more money to financial institutions. To further stimulate the economy and encourage banks to continue lending money, the Bank of Canada continued to lower its lending rate.

The government did not agree with critics who characterized this action as a bailout of an industry that generated record profits. "This is not a bailout; this is a market transaction that will cost the government nothing," said Prime Minister Harper. "We are not going in and buying bad assets. What we're doing is simply exchanging assets that we already hold the insurance on and the reason we're doing this is to get out in front. The issue here is not protecting the banks." He believed that the problem Canada's financial institutions faced was not solvency but the availability of credit. This action was expected to make loans and mortgages more available and more affordable for ordinary Canadians and businesses. One month later, another $50 billion allocation was announced.

Fast forward to 2012. A report from the Canadian Centre for Policy Alternatives (CCPA) <*www.policyalternatives.ca*> claimed that Canadians were never told the true cost of a $114-billion "secret bailout" for the country's biggest banks during the financial

▸ This Occupy Vancouver sign communicates a demonstrator's perspective. Do you agree or disagree with each of these statements? A common slogan of the Occupy Movement is "We are the 99." Do you know what this means?

crisis. Study author and CCPA economist David MacDonald wrote "During the worst of the crisis—2008 to 2010—the official line was that Canada's banks did not require the extraordinary bailout measures that were being offered in other countries, particularly in the U.S. . . . At its peak in March 2009, support for Canadian banks reached $114 billion." Finance Minster Jim Flaherty's spokesperson, Chisholm Pothier, said MacDonald got it wrong and that "There was no 'secret bailout.'" All of the loans provided by the government as part of its relief program for Canadian lenders have been paid back in full, said Pothier.

To some extent, the report and the rebuttal to it are a matter of how the facts are interpreted. Where MacDonald says "bailout," a finance ministry official says "liquidity support." Do you agree that this was not a bailout? What would have been the implications for business people and consumers if money had not been made available by financial institutions?

This is an ideal time to pause and to recognize the need and importance for regulatory oversight. The lesson of the subprime mortgage crisis is that not all regulation is bad. That is, the right regulation is in fact necessary to create an environment that encourages entrepreneurship. This being said, the government is expected to be transparent in its actions.

The Occupy Movement is an international protest movement against economic and social inequality. It was created partially in response to the late-2000s financial crisis and the subprime mortgage crisis. One prime concern is the claim that large corporations and the global financial system control the world in a way that disproportionately benefits a minority, undermines democracy, and is unstable. Occupy Wall Street was initiated by Adbusters <*www.adbusters.org*>, a Canadian activist group. From there, demonstrations spread to over 900 cities around the world.

PROGRESS ASSESSMENT

- How does the government manage the economy using fiscal policy?
- What is Canada's national debt? What actions can the government take to decrease it?
- Explain the purpose of the federal budget.
- What does the term monetary policy mean? What organization is responsible for Canada's monetary policy?

Describe how government expenditures benefit consumers and businesses alike.

GOVERNMENT EXPENDITURES

Governments in Canada help disburse tens of billions of dollars annually in old-age pensions, allowances to low-income families or individuals, employment insurance, welfare, workers' compensation, and various other payments to individuals. These transfers give Canadians more purchasing power and, therefore, the creation of a more viable market for businesses.

As people spend their money, large numbers of Canadian companies and their employees benefit as a result of this purchasing power. Increasing or lowering the rates or eligibility for these payments results in further fine-tuning of the economy. Again, government cutbacks have resulted in the reduction of such payments in recent years.

Governments also spend huge sums of money on education, health, roads, ports, waterways, airports, and various other services required by businesses and individuals. They also provide aid through direct and indirect government programs designed to help businesses. The Canadian Subsidy Directory lists more than 3,000 sources of financing and government programs for anyone searching for Canadian grants, loans, and government programs.[26] Governments also intervene on an ad hoc (special or unplanned) basis in important cases. Aid to Saskatchewan and Alberta farmers and Newfoundland and B.C. fishers when their industries faced severe hardships are examples.

Financial Aid

All levels of government offer a variety of direct assistance programs to businesses, including grants, loans, loan guarantees, consulting advice, information, and other aids that are designed to achieve certain purposes. For example, the Newfoundland government created a program worth up to $18 million to help crab workers affected by the late start to the fishery; the program focused on employment projects to help the approximately 8,500 workers.[27]

Some government aid is designed to help industries or companies that are deemed to be very important—at the cutting edge of technology, providing highly skilled jobs, and oriented toward exports. Bombardier Inc., which makes the Learjet, plans to use $315 million in aid from the United Kingdom, $350 million from Canada, and further help from Quebec authorities to create a new commercial jet to compete with the smaller offerings of Boeing <*www.boeing.com*> and Airbus <*www.airbus.com*>. The company said that plants in Belfast (Northern Ireland), Saint-Laurent and Mirabel (Quebec), and Kansas City (Missouri) will be involved in designing and constructing the new aircraft.[28]

Major companies often hint or announce outright that they are planning to close a plant that they claim is not efficient enough to be competitive. They often suggest that they will consolidate operations with other plants in Canada or the United States. These announcements naturally result in a flurry of efforts by all affected parties to prevent the closure. Unions, municipalities, and provincial and federal

Ford Motor Company invested $1 billion to redevelop its Oakville, Ontario, plant as a state-of-the-art flexible manufacturing system. Project Centennial also received $200 million from the Ontario provincial government and from the Government of Canada. The Government of Canada's $100 million contribution is part of a larger commitment to the automotive industry that was supported with the creation of a $1 billion, five-year incentive fund for other automakers and manufacturers. What are the benefits of such government support?

governments all work to save the jobs and economies of the area. Such examples are evident in a variety of businesses, including auto plants, pulp and paper mills, food-processing plants, oil refineries, shipbuilding yards, meat-packing plants, and steel mills.

While in many cases the closures could not have been prevented, some have been saved by such concerted action. For example, in 2009 GM Canada received an auto bailout of $10.8 billion ($7.1 billion from the federal government and $3.5 billion from Ontario provincial government). What Canada gets is five GM plants in Ontario remaining open, while GM is shutting down many plants in the United States, and a guarantee that at least 16 percent of its North America assembly will be done in this country, including a new hybrid, as well as a promise of $2.2 billion in new investments over the next seven years. All of this effort was to save fewer than 5,000 jobs in the assembly plants. This works out to an investment of $1.4 million to save each job. However, in addition to saving these auto assembly jobs, auto parts suppliers can also continue to remain in Canada.[29]

Some of these rescue efforts end in costly failures. For example, in 2004 the PEI government bought Polar Foods, as its bankruptcy put at risk tens of millions of dollars in government investments and brought into question where Island lobsters would be sold.[30] It was estimated that the government lost close to $27 million when it later sold the company. To assist the approximately 800 unemployed fish plant workers, the government set aside close to $1 million in an aid package. Was it worthwhile to spend such sums to provide hundreds of jobs in chronically depressed areas? Was it the best way to help the unemployed in areas of high unemployment? How do you decide what businesses or industries to help and which ones to ignore? These questions are constantly being asked in Canada.

Equalization Program[31]

Canada is a very large country with uneven resources, climate, and geography, which has led to uneven economic development. **Transfer payments** are direct payments from governments to other governments or to individuals. Federal transfer payments to individuals include elderly benefits and employment insurance. Such payments provide social security and income support.

transfer payments
Direct payments from governments to other governments or to individuals.

Equalization is the federal government's transfer program for reducing fiscal disparities among provinces. These payments enable less prosperous provincial governments to provide their residents with public services that are roughly comparable to those in other provinces, at roughly comparable levels of taxation. While provinces are free to spend the funds on public services according to their own priorities, these payments are intended to fund medicare, post-secondary education, and smaller programs.

equalization
A federal government program for reducing fiscal disparities among provinces.

The 2012 budget allocated a total of $15.4 billion in equalization payments to six provinces in 2012–13 (Manitoba, Ontario, Quebec, New Brunswick, Nova Scotia, and Prince Edward Island). Did you notice that this program does not include the territories? The Territorial Formula Financing program provides territorial governments with funding to support public services, in recognition of the higher cost of living in the north.

PROGRESS ASSESSMENT

- Explain how governments in Canada spend tax dollars to help Canadians.
- Give two examples of how government has provided financial aid to businesses.
- Who benefits from equalization transfer payments?

PURCHASING POLICIES

Illustrate how purchasing policies and services assist Canadian businesses.

Most governments are very large purchasers and consumers of goods and services; indeed, in Canada they are the largest buyers. The federal and provincial governments use this enormous purchasing power to favour Canadian companies. The provinces favour those companies within their boundaries and have even set up trade barriers between provinces (as discussed earlier). When advanced technology items—civilian or military—must be obtained from foreign companies, our governments usually insist that a certain minimum portion be manufactured in Canada. This enables Canadian companies to acquire advanced technology know-how and to provide employment.

Contracts are often awarded to help Canadian businesses even if they are sometimes more expensive than bids by non-Canadian companies. This is particularly true in the military acquisitions programs. Whatever can be produced or serviced in Canada—ships, electronics, trucks, artillery, ammunition—is acquired from Canadian companies. (See the Spotlight on Small Business box for an example of a company that benefits from a government contract). These federal and provincial policies are being modified as a result of the general movement to freer trade due to NAFTA.

Be aware that government procurement has some challenges. It is a demanding bidding process that is strictly regulated. In some provinces, government organizations may also include government boards, councils, committees, commissions and publicly funded academic, health and social service organizations.[32] It can be demanding to fully understand government procurement and to properly target potential niches. In large cities alone—such as Montreal, Toronto and Vancouver—there are several hundred public organizations that function differently for their procurement. If a firm is interested in conducting business in the Canadian public sector, MERX Canadian Public Tenders service <*www.merx.com*> is an easy, fast, and efficient prospecting tool. New opportunities are listed daily for access to billions of dollars in Canadian public-sector business opportunities. They range from the private sector to all levels of government, and include the MASH (Municipal, Academic, School Boards and Hospitals) sector from across Canada.[33]

SPOTLIGHT ON SMALL BUSINESS

Ink Isle

Located in Charlottetown, Prince Edward Island, Ink Isle <*http://inkisleonline.ca*> is the only business of its kind in the province that remanufactures inkjet cartridges and resells other generic inkjet and toner cartridges. This is an environmentally-friendly alternative to throwing out unused inkjet and toner cartridges.

A proud Mi'kmaq member of the Abegweit First Nation, entrepreneur Jacob Jadis discovered his business idea during several exciting travel opportunities for Aboriginal youth across Canada, Australia, and the United States. During these trips he noticed several seemingly successful ink refilling kiosks, located mostly in malls. This was a type of business that had not yet reached PEI, and with further research it became evident that he could create a better business by remanufacturing, instead of just refilling, ink cartridges. Jadis spent a year on business-planning activities, including researching the industry, writing a business plan, seeking start-up funding, receiving specialized training in Colorado, searching for a storefront location, and finally purchasing the equipment and products he needed to start Ink Isle. Not only is he fulfilling one of his lifetime goals of being an entrepreneur, but he also enjoys having his future in his own hands.

Since he started his business in 2005, Jadis has been receiving orders for toners from a large federal government agency on the Island. As you can infer, the different levels of government not only provide funding for small businesses, but they are also a good source of potential revenue generation. Jadis has also been recognized as the 2007 Prince Edward Island Best Business Award Winner, Winner of the 2006 Aboriginal Entrepreneur of the Year Award for Prince Edward Island, and second place for Atlantic Canada Youth Aboriginal Entrepreneur of the Year.

Source: © Thomas I. White.

SERVICES

The federal government has departments that provide services to businesses and consumers. We will look at two of these important departments: Industry Canada and Foreign Affairs and International Trade Canada. There are corresponding departments in many of the provinces, especially the four largest and most developed ones (British Columbia, Alberta, Ontario, and Quebec).

Industry Canada

For many years, the federal government has implemented a variety of programs to help small businesses get started. These programs are part of a larger one, called Canada Business Network, that involves setting up Canada Business service centres in every province and territory. These centres are operated jointly with provincial governments and certain local organizations. Industry Canada publishes brochures, booklets, and guides informing business people of the help available and how and where to get it. Industry Canada also participates in the production of publications to promote Canadian businesses internationally.

Other programs are designed to encourage businesses to establish themselves or expand in economically depressed areas of the country. These are populated regions that are industrially underdeveloped, have high unemployment, and have lower standards of living. The programs include help for the tourism industry and for Aboriginal residents of remote areas who want to establish businesses.

National Research Council

The National Research Council (NRC) is a federal agency that began in 1916. It reports to Parliament through Industry Canada. The NRC plays a significant role in research that helps Canadian industry remain competitive and innovative. Its vision is to be the most effective research and development organization in the world, stimulating sustainable domestic prosperity.[34]

This organization of over 3,500 researchers, technologists, and support staff represents Canada's principal science and technology agency. NRC also benefits from the efforts of guest workers drawn from Canadian and foreign universities, companies, and public- and private-sector organizations. Located in every province, areas of research and industry support include aerospace, biotechnology, engineering and construction, fundamental sciences, information and communications technologies, and manufacturing.

▸ NRC researchers are using thermographic cameras to design tools for physicians to rapidly identify tissue damage. Thermographic video cameras record infrared radiation, or heat, rather than visible light. This heat-imaging camera is thus able to identify differences in blood flow. Warmer areas have greater blood flow, and areas of tissue damage will register abnormally low levels of flow and thus heat. Here, a healthy subject's nose has less blood flow and is cooler (bluer) than her cheeks and the sides of her neck, which are warmer (redder).

Foreign Affairs and International Trade Canada

Because exports are particularly important to Canada's economic well-being, the government has a very large and elaborate system to assist companies in their exporting and foreign-investment activities. The federal government and most provincial and all large municipal governments have various ministries, departments, and agencies that provide a variety of such services. These include information, marketing, financial aid, insurance and guarantees, publications, and contracts. All major trading countries provide similar support to their exporters.

Government Source	Mission	Web Site
Business Development Bank of Canada (BDC)	BDC provides small and medium-sized businesses with flexible financing, affordable consulting services, and venture capital. BDC has a particular focus on the emerging and exporting sectors of the economy.	www.bdc.ca
Canada Business Network	Canada Business is a government information service for businesses and start-up entrepreneurs in Canada. It serves as a single point of access for federal and provincial/territorial government services, programs, and regulatory requirements for business.	www.canadabusiness.ca
Export Development Canada (EDC)	EDC provides Canadian exporters with financing, insurance, and bonding services as well as foreign market expertise.	www.edc.ca
Industry Canada	The Department's mission is to foster a growing, competitive, knowledge-based Canadian economy. Program areas include developing industry and technology capability, fostering scientific research, and promoting investment and trade.	www.ic.gc.ca
National Research Council (NRC)	NRC helps turn ideas and knowledge into new processes and products. Businesses work with partners from industry, government, and universities.	www.nrc-cnrc.gc.ca

Figure 4.5

Some Government Resources Available to Assist Canadian Businesses

See Figure 4.5 for a list of government sources that are available to assist Canadian businesses. Most of them also provide some support for those that wish to succeed in global markets. We have discussed some of these organizations already in this textbook.

PROGRESS ASSESSMENT

- Why do federal and provincial governments tend to favour Canadian companies when contracts are approved?
- How does the NRC contribute to technology advancement in Canada?
- List some organizations that aim to help exporters.

ROLE OF THE CANADIAN GOVERNMENT—SOME FINAL THOUGHTS

What should be clear is that government always has a critical role to play. This is especially the case during economic downturns or if the Canadian economy is being impacted by foreign events such as the financial crisis that started in the late 2000s.

Some people believe that the best way to protect the Canadian economy is for the federal government to reverse its current direction of privatization. Instead of withdrawing from active direction and participation in the economy, it should develop a long-term industrial policy of leadership and an active role in shaping the future of the economy. An **industrial policy** is a comprehensive, coordinated government plan to guide and revitalize the economy. An industrial policy requires close consultation with business and labour to develop a comprehensive program for long-term sustainable industrial development.

industrial policy
A comprehensive, coordinated government plan to guide and revitalize the economy.

Others are opposed in principle to such government involvement. As mentioned earlier in this chapter, the 1980s witnessed the start of a movement toward deregulation, privatization, and less government involvement within Canada and other countries. Some believe that these were the right steps for the government to take, and that it should continue with these activities. Interestingly enough, when events such as mad cow disease or a recession appear, some groups that normally lobby for less

GREENBOX

The Environment and the Economy

Governments have many policy options available to reduce greenhouse gas emissions. Some are more politically acceptable and easier to implement than others, and not all approaches are likely to be equally effective. Experience in addressing other environmental issues has shown that using a mix of policy measures is more likely to succeed and to spread the responsibility around fairly. It has been a challenge for governments in Canada to come up with effective policy options to address climate change, partly because all three levels of government (federal, provincial, and municipal) have a stake in this issue as well as responsibilities and opportunities. Not all policy options are suitable for all levels of government, so co-operation and collaboration is important to make sure that effective measures are put in place without overlap and duplication.

The National Round Table on the Environment and the Economy has recommended that Canada immediately put in place a hard cap regime on emissions by 2015, with auctioning of carbon permits to businesses by 2020. To do otherwise would face dire environmental and economic consequences. Round table chairman Bob Page says the United States is moving quickly on capping emissions and will penalize Canadian exports if Canada does not follow suit. "It is the most serious protectionist challenge we've had to face. Now we're going to see in place of the softwood lumber issue, we're going to see the issue that cuts right across manufacturing in Ontario and Quebec, and natural resource products like the oil sands in Alberta and Saskatchewan . . . those products will be subject to a carbon intensity surcharge at the American border unless Canada meets new American standards." Alberta won't like it, but will likely agree, since the oil sands producers are likely concerned about being shut out of the United States and possibly world markets, said Page, a professor of sustainable development at the University of Calgary.

The report says it is imperative that Canada move from the patchwork approach adopted by different provinces and for Ottawa to have a unified policy with identical standards across jurisdictions and industries. And it says it is critical that Canadian policy be compatible with that of its largest trading partners, particularly the United States. The cap-and-trade system is designed to put a price on pollution, but instead of taxing energy use by individuals directly, the cost is borne first by large emitters, who are expected to pass it on to consumers. Emissions permits can be traded on an open market between firms that need extra quota and those who have quota to sell.

While this system will involve a major transformation on the cost, the usage, and even the nature of energy in Canada, it is expected that the Canadian economy will continue to grow through the transformation period and that new industries will be created.

Sources: "Control Greenhouse Emissions or Face Trade Sanctions, Panel Tells Governments," The Canadian Press, 16 April 2009, www.cbc.ca/news/story/2009/04/16/tech-090416-cap-and-trade-greenhouse-gas.html; and "Government Policy Options," The Pembina Foundation, 2009, www.greenlearning.ca/climate/policy/canadian-policy-directions/2.

government involvement in their industries suddenly believe that government should step in and provide financial assistance. While this is contrary to free-market principles, troubled times are usually followed by calls for more government involvement.

The Constitution Act outlines the powers of all levels of government. Each level of government is focused on creating a competitive environment for businesses of all sizes. As we move forward, the federal government will continue to focus on international trade initiatives to provide opportunities for Canadian businesses. This chapter has highlighted some of the resources that are available to businesses to assist them in their operations.

It is natural for disputes to arise as industries and countries attempt to act in their best interests. These disputes arise even between established trading partners such as Canada and the United States, as evidenced by the long-running lumber dispute. However, in most instances, trade agreements create opportunities. Did you know, for example, that 95 percent of Canada–U.S. trade due to NAFTA is problem-free?[35] While disputes will not be resolved overnight, they are being addressed in a global arena, and this is at least a step in the right direction. Since Canada is a large exporter of goods and services, it must also be aware how its policies on the environment may impact future trade. Read the Green Box for more information.

SUMMARY

List the six categories of government activities that can affect business.

There are six categories of government involvement in Canada.

What are the government activities that affect business?
The six categories of government activities are Crown corporations, laws and regulations, taxation and financial policies, government expenditures, purchasing policies, and services. See Figure 4.1 for a brief description of each activity.

What is the relationship between Canada's economic system and government involvement?
As noted in Chapter 2, Canada has a mixed economy, which is an economic system in which some allocation of resources is made by the market and some by the government. As a result of the Constitution Act, the different levels of government have responsibilities and jurisdiction over certain matters of the economy and population.

Trace the historical role of government in the Canadian economy and explain why Crown corporations were created.

The Canadian government played a key role from the beginning of the country in 1867 in protecting young manufacturing industries and getting the railroad built to the west coast, helping to bind the country together.

Why did the government have to do what it did?
It had the legal power and responsibility to do so as a result of the Constitution Act. The United States threatened to overwhelm our industries, which were not strong enough by themselves to resist or to build the railway.

Why were Crown corporations necessary?
Companies were not willing or able to assume certain responsibilities or fill some needs in the marketplace. CNR, Air Canada, and Hydro-Québec are some important examples. (CNR and Air Canada are no longer Crown corporations.)

What is the recent trend with Crown corporations?
In recent years, we have seen an increasing trend where governments (both federal and provincial) have been selling Crown corporations. This is called privatization. Some examples include the sale of remaining Petro-Canada shares and the sale of BC Rail Ltd.

Demonstrate why understanding laws and regulations at all levels of government is critical to business success.

Businesses need to understand the laws and regulations that affect them. The Constitution Act defines the powers that can be exercised by the federal government and provincial governments. In the event of a conflict, federal powers prevail.

What are some federal government responsibilities?
The federal government's responsibilities include trade regulations, the incorporation of federal companies, national defence, immigration, and the fisheries.

What are some provincial government responsibilities?
Among other areas, provincial governments oversee natural resources within their boundaries, the administration of justice, municipal affairs, and education.

What are some municipal government responsibilities?

Municipal governments—cities, towns, villages, counties, districts, metropolitan regions—are set up by the provincial legislatures. Municipalities provide services such as water supply, sewage and garbage disposal, roads, sidewalks, street lighting, building codes, parks, playgrounds, libraries, and so forth. They play a role in consumer protection (e.g., inspectors examine restaurants) and the establishment of zoning requirements.

Explain how taxation and financial policies affect the Canadian economy.

Each level of government collects taxes from companies. These taxes allow governments to discharge their legal obligations and to fund social programs.

What is fiscal policy?

Fiscal policy refers to the federal government's effort to keep the economy stable by increasing or decreasing taxes or government spending.

What is the national debt?

The national debt, also known as the federal debt, is the accumulation of past government surpluses and deficits.

How is monetary policy different from fiscal policy?

Controlled by the Bank of Canada, monetary policy is the management of the money supply and interest rates. When the economy is booming, the Bank of Canada tends to raise interest rates in an attempt to control inflation. Since money is more expensive to borrow, businesses borrow less, and the economy slows as business people spend less money on everything.

Describe how government expenditures benefit consumers and businesses alike.

Government expenditures benefit consumers and businesses alike.

How do governments assist consumers with their tax dollars?

Governments disburse tens of millions of dollars annually in social program spending (e.g., old-age pensions, employment insurance, allowances to low-income families, etc.). These transfers give consumers more purchasing power.

How do businesses benefit from government expenditures?

All levels of government provide direct and indirect aid packages as incentives to achieve certain goals. These packages can consist of tax reductions, tariffs and quotas on imports, grants, loans, and loan guarantees.

Illustrate how purchasing policies and services assist Canadian businesses

Purchasing policies and services assist Canadian businesses.

Why is preferential treatment given to Canadian companies when they bid for a government contract?

Contracts are often awarded to help Canadian businesses. This way, companies are employing Canadians and contributing to a strong economy.

What are two government departments that are particularly focused on assisting Canadian businesses?

Industry Canada and the Department of Foreign Affairs and International Trade Canada assist businesses domestically and internationally.

KEY TERMS

Crown corporation
deficit
deregulation
equalization
federal budget
fiscal policy
industrial policy
marketing boards
monetary policy
national debt (federal debt)
National Policy
privatization
surplus
transfer payments

CRITICAL THINKING

1. The issue of how much government should be involved in the economy has been the subject of much debate in Canada. In the United States, ideology has played a major role in influencing Americans to believe that, in principle, government should "butt out." This thinking ignores the significant role that the U.S. government has played and continues to play in the country's economy. (In comparison, the governments in France and Sweden are more socialistic in nature.) In Canada, we are less negative and perhaps more pragmatic: If it works, let's do it. But where do we go from here? Do we need less or more government involvement? Is it a question of the quality of that involvement? Could it be smarter rather than just less? How can the cost of government involvement decrease?
2. What are the implications of a majority federal government to the Canadian political scene? How does this differ from a minority government? (A minority government exists when no one party has a majority of seats in a legislative assembly. To pass legislation and other measures, that government would need the support of at least some members of other parties in the assembly.[36]) Explain.
3. If you represented the federal government, how would you respond to industries that have been seeking government action (e.g., bailout money or changes to policies) but to no avail? (For example, take the position of the Canadian forestry industry, which in six years lost about 130,000 jobs.[37]) Keep in mind that other industries (e.g., auto) have received such support (i.e., bailout money).

DEVELOPING WORKPLACE SKILLS

1. Scan your local newspapers, the *Globe and Mail,* the *National Post,* or a Canadian magazine such as *Canadian Business* for references to government programs that help Canadian businesses or have assisted a specific company. Bring these articles to class and discuss.
2. Many foreign governments have developed strong marketing campaigns to attract Canadian businesses. They also offer many incentives, including financial ones, to lure businesses to move there. Should anything be done about this? Many provincial and municipal governments have similar programs to attract foreign companies to their jurisdictions. Check out your provincial and municipal governments' Web sites for examples. Bring your information to class to discuss this kind of government expenditure.
3. In a group of four, choose an industry (e.g., telecommunications, auto, health care, etc.). Find out if there have been any recent changes in federal and/or provincial legislation that will impact businesses. For example, has the Canadian Radio-television and Telecommunications Commission (CRTC) <*www.crtc.gc.ca*> deregulated the industry? What are advantages and disadvantages of these changes? Have any of the provinces moved closer to a two-tier heath care system? Present your findings in a report or to the class.
4. Although unemployment remains high, especially among young people, business people complain that they cannot find trained employees to fill existing vacancies. Job candidates lack math and science backgrounds and their written English-language skills are weak. (In Quebec, there are similar complaints, but the language problems are with French.) Further, too many candidates are high-school dropouts. What can be done about this serious problem? Should business or government be working harder on it? What exactly should they be doing? Discuss this in a group of three.

ANALYZING MANAGEMENT DECISIONS

Gambling: A Cash Cow for Provincial Governments

Starting slowly in Quebec in the late 1960s, but catching on quickly across the country, lotteries, casinos, bingo, video-lottery terminals (VLTs), and other forms of gambling had become, by the end of the twentieth century, a major source of revenue for many provincial governments.

You can get some idea of how large the gambling business has become by looking at the revenues and profits for the Ontario and Quebec governments for their respective 2011 year ends. The Ontario Lottery and Gaming Corporation generated \$3.7 billion in economic activity. Total revenue at Loto-Québec <*lotoquebec.com*> was also approximately \$3.7 billion. Over the years, both organizations have generated billions of dollars for their respective governments. Both operations also allot millions of dollars to help gamblers whose obsession with gambling has proven destructive to themselves or their families.

Sources: "Towards a New Balance 2011 Annual Report," Loto-Québec, 2011, http://lotoquebec.com/corporatif/nav/en/about-loto-quebec/annual-report; and "OLG Gives Back," Ontario Lottery and Gaming Corporation, 2012, www.olg.ca/about/economic_benefits/index.jsp.

Discussion Questions

1. Some people and organizations argue that governments should not be in the gambling business, that encouraging gambling is a bad idea. Others argue that private enterprise should run that kind of business, and argue further that companies would generate more profit (leading to more tax revenues for governments). Governments reply that they want to prevent organized crime from controlling gambling, so they must own and run such operations. What do you think? Is it okay for governments to be in the gambling business?
2. Governments seem to believe that gambling is a great way to raise money because Canadians don't seem to mind creating revenue by having some fun and a chance at big winnings, instead of just paying higher taxes. Besides, they argue, nobody is forced to gamble, so it's a kind of voluntary tax. How do you feel about that? Do you buy that argument? Explain.
3. Some churches and other institutions concerned with personal and family welfare point to the rising number of family and personal breakdowns caused by people becoming gambling addicts. Also, easy access to VLTs is very bad for young persons. Do you agree with either of these concerns? Why? What can be done to improve the situation?
4. Suppose that you agree with those who are totally opposed to governments encouraging gambling. Wouldn't taxes have to be raised to replace these revenues? Would you mind paying more taxes? Do you think your parents or family members would mind? Do you have any other suggestions?

Practise and learn online with Connect.

APPENDIX B

WORKING WITHIN THE LEGAL ENVIRONMENT OF BUSINESS*

THE NEED FOR LAWS

Imagine a society without laws. Just think, no speed limits to control how fast we drive, no age restrictions on the consumption of alcoholic beverages, no limitations on who can practise medicine—a society in which people are free to do whatever they choose, with no interference. Obviously, the more we consider this possibility, the more unrealistic we realize it is. Laws are an essential part of a civilized nation. Over time, though, the direction and scope of the body of laws must change to reflect changes in the needs of society.

In the Canadian system of government, which uses the English model, there are three branches of government. Each has a distinct role in the legal system, though sometimes the lines get blurred. The primary function of the legislative branch, composed of the Parliament of Canada and the legislatures of the provinces, is to make the laws. Municipal councils also make laws, but their legislative power is limited to the scope delegated to them by their provincial legislature. The executive branch (e.g., government departments, administrative boards, and police departments) administers the laws, putting them into practice. The judicial branch (i.e., the courts) applies the law and interprets it when there is a dispute.

The Canadian court system has both federal and provincial courts, with jurisdiction that parallels the constitutional division of power between the central and provincial governments. The

*Written by Ray Klapstein, Dalhousie University

courts hear cases involving both criminal and civil law. Criminal law defines crimes, establishes punishments, and regulates the investigation and prosecution of people accused of committing crimes. Civil law involves legal proceedings that do not involve criminal acts; it includes laws regulating marriage, payment for personal injury, and so on. There are also appeal courts that hear appeals of decisions made at the initial trial, brought by the losing party in the case. Appeal courts can review and overturn decisions made by the trial court. The highest level appeal court for all matters is the Supreme Court of Canada.

criminal law
Defines crimes, establishes punishments, and regulates the investigation and prosecution of people accused of committing crimes.

civil law
Legal proceedings that do not involve criminal acts.

The law also governs the activities and operations of business in general. In fact, business people often complain that the government is stepping in more and more to govern the behaviour of business. We have laws and regulations regarding sexual harassment on the job, hiring and firing practices, leave for family emergencies, environmental protection, safety, and more. As you may suspect, business people prefer to set their own standards of behaviour. However, the business community has not been perceived as implementing acceptable practices quickly enough. To hasten the process, governments have expanded their control and enforcement procedures. In this appendix we will look at some of the laws and regulations now in place and how they affect business.

Business law refers to rules, statutes, codes, and regulations that are established to provide a legal framework within which business must be conducted and that are enforceable by court action. A business person should be familiar with laws regarding product liability, sales, contracts, fair competition, consumer protection, taxes, and bankruptcy. Let's start at the beginning and discuss the foundations of the law. It's hard to understand the law unless you know what the law is.

business law
Rules, statutes, codes, and regulations that are established to provide a legal framework within which business must be conducted and that are enforceable by court action.

STATUTORY AND COMMON LAW

There are two major kinds of law: statutory law and common law. Both are important for business people.

Statutory law includes the laws that are made by the Parliament of Canada and the provincial legislatures, international treaties, and regulations and bylaws—in short, written law established by or through the legislative branch of government. You can read the statutes that make up this body of law, but they are often written in language whose meaning must be determined in court. That's one reason why there are so many lawyers in Canada! Common law is the body of law that comes from decisions handed down by judges. Common law is often referred to as unwritten law because it does not appear in any legislative enactment, treaty, or other such document. Under common law principles, what judges have decided in previous cases is very important to today's cases. Such decisions are called precedents, and they guide judges in the handling of new cases. Common law evolves through decisions made in trial courts, appellate courts, and special courts. Lower courts (trial courts) must abide by the precedents set by higher courts (appeal courts) such as the Supreme Court of Canada. In law classes, therefore, students study case after case to learn about common law as well as statutory law.

statutory law
Federal and provincial legislative enactments, treaties of the federal government, and bylaws and ordinances—in short, written law.

common law
The body of law that comes from decisions handed down by judges; also referred to as unwritten law.

precedent
Decisions judges have made in earlier cases that guide the handling of new cases.

The Canadian legal system is complicated by the fact that federal law and provincial (including municipal) law in nine provinces operate under the English common law system, while provincial law in the Province of Quebec operates under the French civil law system. The difference lies more in principle than in practice: the common law system recognizes that courts actually make law through their decisions, while the civil law system restricts courts to interpreting the law that is provided by legislation that takes the form of the provincial civil code.

Laws Made Under Delegated Authority: Administrative Agencies

administrative agencies
Federal or provincial institutions and other government organizations created by Parliament or provincial legislatures with delegated power to pass rules and regulations within their mandated area of authority.

Different organizations within the government issue many rules, regulations, and orders. **Administrative agencies** are federal or provincial institutions and other government organizations created by Parliament or provincial legislatures with delegated power to pass rules and regulations within their mandated area of authority. Legislative bodies can both create administrative agencies and dissolve them. Some administrative agencies hold quasi-legislative, quasi-executive, and quasi-judicial powers. This means that an agency is allowed to pass rules and regulations within its area of authority, conduct investigations in cases of suspected rule violations, and hold hearings to determine whether the rules and regulations have been violated.

Administrative agencies actually issue more rulings affecting business and settle more disputes than courts do. There are administrative agencies at the federal, provincial, and local levels of government. For example, these include:

1. *At the federal level:* The Canadian Radio-television and Telecommunications Commission (CRTC) regulates the use of the airwaves, the Office of the Superintendent of Financial Institutions (OSFI) <*www.osfi-bsif.gc.ca*> regulates the operation of banks and other financial institutions, and the Commissioner of Competition is responsible for investigating complaints that the Competition Act has been violated.
2. *At the provincial level:* Public utility commissions and boards regulate prices for services such as electricity, licensing boards set the qualifications required for practising trades and professions (e.g., the practice of medicine or law), and labour relations boards oversee the certification of unions and relations between employers and unionized employees.
3. *At the local level:* Zoning boards and planning commissions control land use and development, and there are school boards and police commissions.

TORT LAW

tort
A wrongful act that causes injury to another person's body, property, or reputation.

The tort system is an example of common law at work. A **tort** is a wrongful act that causes injury to another person's body, property, or reputation. This area of law comes within provincial jurisdiction, so legislation dealing with the topic comes from the provincial legislatures.

negligence
In tort law, behaviour that does not meet the standard of care required and causes unintentional harm or injury.

Criminal law focuses its attention on punishing and rehabilitating wrongdoers. Tort law, though, focuses on the compensation of victims. There are two kinds of torts. An intentional tort is a wilful act that results in injury. On the other hand, the unintentional tort of **negligence** provides compensation when the wrongdoer should have acted more carefully even though the harm or injury was unintentional. Decisions involving negligence can often lead to huge judgments against businesses. In a highly publicized U.S. case, McDonald's lost a lawsuit to a person severely burned by its hot coffee. The jury felt the company failed to provide an adequate warning on the cup, and awarded a very large amount as compensation. Product liability is another example of tort law that's often very controversial. This is especially true regarding torts related to business actions. Let's look briefly at this issue.

Product Liability

product liability
Part of tort law that holds businesses liable for harm that results from the production, design, sale, or use of products they market.

Few issues in business law raise as much debate as product liability. Critics believe that product liability laws have gone too far and deter product development. Others feel that these laws should be expanded to include products such as software and fast food. **Product liability**, covered under tort law, holds businesses liable for harm that results from the production, design, sale, or use of products they market. At one time, the legal standard for measuring product liability was whether a producer knowingly placed a hazardous product on the market. Today, many provinces have extended product liability to the level of **strict product liability**. Legally, this means without regard to fault. Thus, a company could be held liable for damages caused by placing a defective product on the market even if the company did not know of the defect at the time of sale. In such cases, the company is required to compensate the injured party financially.

strict product liability
Legal responsibility for harm or injury caused by a product regardless of fault.

The rule of strict liability has caused serious problems for businesses. For example, companies that produced lead-based paint in the past could be subject to expensive legal liabilities even though lead paint has not been sold for many years. The manufacturers of chemicals and drugs are also often susceptible to lawsuits under strict product liability. A producer may place a drug or chemical on the market that everyone agrees is safe. Years later, a side effect or other health problem could emerge. Under the doctrine of strict liability, the manufacturer could still be held liable. Businesses and insurance companies have called for legal relief from huge losses awarded in strict product liability suits. They have lobbied to set limits on the amounts of damages for which they are liable should their products harm consumers.

Intellectual Property: Patents, Copyrights, and Trademarks

Many people, perhaps including you, have invented products that may have commercial value. The question that obviously surfaces is what to do next. One step may be to apply for a patent. A **patent** gives inventors exclusive rights to their inventions for 20 years from the date they file their patent application. The Canadian Intellectual Property Office receives the application and grants the patent. In addition to filing forms, the inventor must ensure that the product is truly unique. Most inventors rely on lawyers who specialize in the field to manage the filing process.

patent
A form of intellectual property that gives inventors exclusive rights to their inventions for 20 years.

Patent owners have the right to sell or license the use of a patent to others. Foreign companies are also eligible to file for Canadian patents. Recent changes in the Patent Act and an international patent co-operation treaty permit any inventor who applies within 12 months of filing in his or her own country to obtain a uniform filing date in all participating countries.

The penalties for violating a patent can be very severe, but the defence of patent rights is solely the job of the patent holder. In a rather famous U.S. case (where the law regarding patents is much the same as in Canada), the camera and film company Polaroid <*www.polaroid.com*> was able to force Kodak <*www.kodak.ca*> to recall all of its instant cameras because Polaroid had several patents that Kodak violated. Kodak lost millions of dollars, and Polaroid maintained market leadership in instant cameras for many years. The possible remedies for patent infringement include compensation in the form of money damages, injunctions prohibiting further infringements, and an accounting for all profits gained from the infringement.

Just as a patent protects an inventor's right to a product or process, a **copyright** protects a creator's rights to materials such as books, articles, photos, paintings, and cartoons. Copyright is protected by the Copyright Act, a federal statute. The protection of a copyright extends for the life of the original author plus 50 years after his or her death. Registration of the copyright is not required, but provides the benefit of public notice of its existence and provides proof of the copyright holder's ownership of the work.

copyright
A form of intellectual property that protects a creator's rights to materials such as books, articles, photos, and cartoons.

A **trademark** is a brand that has been given legal protection for both the brand name and the pictorial design. Trademarks generally belong to the owner forever, as long as they are properly registered and renewed every 15 years. Some well-known trademarks include the Pillsbury <*www.pillsbury.com*> Doughboy, the Disney Company's Mickey Mouse, the Nike swoosh, and the golden arches of McDonald's. Like

trademark
A brand that has been given exclusive legal protection for both the brand name and the pictorial design.

a patent, a trademark is protected from infringement. Companies fight hard to protect trademarks, especially in global markets where pirating can be extensive. Like patents, there are specific requirements imposed by the Trademarks Act, the most difficult one being that the trademark must be "distinctive."

industrial design
A form of intellectual property that protects the owner's exclusive right to use the visible features of a finished product that identify it.

The fourth type of intellectual property protected by federal legislation in Canada is an **industrial design**. Industrial designs differ from things that can be copyrighted by the fact that they are produced by an industrial process. For example, fine china dinnerware would be a product that would fall into this category. As with the other types of intellectual property, the design of the subject matter must be original.

THE SALE OF GOODS

Each of Canada's provinces has a statute called the Sale of Goods Act. With limited exceptions (i.e., contracts where the price is below the minimum set by the individual province's Act), this Act applies to all contracts for the sale of goods. A sale contract is different from others in that there must be a transfer of ownership of goods in return for money consideration. Except in Ontario and British Columbia, a contract for the sale of goods must be written. There are exceptions, though, where part of the goods has actually been received by the buyer, there has been partial payment of the price, or an "earnest" has been given to demonstrate sincerity. The Sale of Goods Act establishes the rules and requirements associated with the deal, establishing the respective rights and obligations of the parties of the contract.

Warranties

express warranties
Specific representations by the seller that buyers rely on regarding the goods they purchase.

implied warranties
Guarantees legally imposed on the seller.

A warranty guarantees that the product sold will be acceptable for the purpose for which the buyer intends to use it. There are two types of warranties. **Express warranties** are specific representations by the seller that buyers rely on regarding the goods they purchase. The warranty you receive in the box with a clock or toaster is an express warranty. **Implied warranties** are legally imposed on the seller. It is implied, for example, that the product will conform to the customary standards of the trade or industry in which it competes. For example, it's expected that a toaster will toast your bread to your desired degree (light, medium, dark) or that food bought for consumption off an establishment's premises is fit to eat.

Warranties offered by sellers can be either full or limited. A *full warranty* requires a seller to replace or repair a product at no charge if the product is defective, whereas a *limited warranty* typically limits the defects or mechanical problems that are covered. Many of the rights of buyers, including the acceptance and rejection of goods, are spelled out in the Sale of Goods Act, so both buyers and sellers should be familiar with its provisions.

NEGOTIABLE INSTRUMENTS

negotiable instruments
Forms of commercial paper (such as cheques) that are transferable among businesses and individuals and represent a promise to pay a specified amount.

Negotiable instruments are forms of commercial paper, and come in three types: promissory notes, cheques, and bills of exchange. A *promissory note* is a written contract with a promise to pay a sum of money in the future. A *cheque* is an instruction to a bank to make a payment. A *bill* (or *draft*) is an order to make a payment. All three types are regulated by the federal Bills of Exchange Act. All three types are transferable among businesses and individuals and represent a promise to pay a specified amount. They must be (1) written and signed by the maker or drawer, (2) payable on demand or at a certain time, (3) payable to the bearer (the person holding the instrument) or to a specific order, and (4) contain an unconditional promise to pay a specified amount of money. Negotiable instruments are transferred (negotiated for payment) when the payee signs the back. The payee's signature is referred to as an endorsement.

CONTRACT LAW

If I offer to sell you my bike for $35 and later change my mind, can you force me to sell the bike, saying we had a contract? If I lose $120 to you in a poker game, can you sue in court to get your money? If I agree to sing at your wedding for free and back out at the last minute, can you claim that I violated a contract? These are the kinds of questions that contract law answers.

A **contract** is a legally enforceable agreement between two or more parties. **Contract law** specifies what constitutes a legally enforceable agreement. Basically, a contract is legally binding if the following conditions are met:

contract
A legally enforceable agreement between two or more parties.

contract law
Set of laws that specify what constitutes a legally enforceable agreement.

1. *An offer is made.* An offer to do something or sell something can be oral or written. If I agree to sell you my bike for $35, I have made an offer. That offer is not legally binding, however, until other conditions are met.
2. *There is a voluntary acceptance of the offer.* Both parties to a contract must voluntarily agree on the terms. If I used duress in getting you to agree to buy my bike, the contract would not create enforceable rights and obligations. Duress occurs if there is coercion through force or threat of force. You couldn't use duress to get me to sell my bike, either. Even if we both agree, though, the contract is still not legally binding without the next four conditions.
3. *Both parties give consideration.* **Consideration** means something of value, and there must be a flow of consideration in both directions. If I agree to sell you my bike for $35, the bike and the $35 are consideration, and we have a legally binding contract. If I agree to sing at your wedding and you do not agree to give me anything in return (consideration), we have no contract.
4. *Both parties are competent.* A person under the influence of alcohol or drugs, or a person of unsound mind (e.g., one who has been legally declared incompetent), cannot be held to a contract. In many cases, a minor may not be held to a contract either. For example, if a 15-year-old agrees to pay $10,000 for a car, the seller will not be able to enforce the contract due to the buyer's lack of competence.
5. *The contract must be legal.* A contract to do something illegal cannot be enforced. For example, a contract for the sale of illegal drugs or stolen merchandise would not be enforceable, since both types of sales are violations of criminal law.
6. *The contract is in proper form.* Provincial legislation in each province requires that an agreement for the sale of goods for more than a fixed amount (e.g., $200) must be in writing. Contracts that cannot be fulfilled within one year and contracts regarding real property (land and everything attached to it) must be in writing as well.

consideration
Something of value; consideration is one of the requirements of a legal contract.

Breach of Contract

Breach of contract occurs when one party fails to follow the terms of a contract. Both parties may voluntarily agree to end a contract. While in force, however, if one person violates the contract, the following remedies may be available.

breach of contract
When one party fails to follow the terms of a contract.

1. *Specific performance.* The person who violated the contract may be required to live up to the agreement if money damages would not be adequate. For example, if I legally offered to sell you a rare painting, I may be required to actually sell you that painting.

damages
The monetary settlement awarded to a person who is injured by a breach of contract.

2. *Payment of damages.* The term **damages** refers to the monetary settlement awarded by the court to a person who is injured by a breach of contract. If I fail to live up to a contract, you can sue me for damages, usually the amount you would lose from my non-performance. If we had a legally binding contract for me to sing at your wedding, for example, and I failed to come, you could sue me for the cost of hiring a new singer of the same quality and reputation.
3. *Discharge of obligation.* If I fail to live up to my end of a contract, you could agree to drop the matter. Generally you would not have to live up to your end of the agreement either.

Lawyers would not be paid so handsomely if the law were always as simple as implied in these rules of contracts. In fact, it is always best to have a contract in writing even if not required under law. The offer and consideration in a contract should be clearly specified, and the contract should be signed and dated. A contract does not have to be complicated as long as it has these elements: it is in writing, mutual consideration is specified, and there is a clear offer and agreement to accept it.

LAWS TO PROMOTE FAIR AND COMPETITIVE PRACTICES

One objective of legislators is to pass laws that the courts will enforce to ensure a competitive atmosphere among businesses and to promote fair business practices. In Canada, the Competition Bureau and other government agencies serve as watchdogs to ensure that competition among sellers flows freely and that new competitors have open access to the market. The scope of the governments' approach on this is broad and extensive.

There was a time when big businesses were able to drive smaller competitors out of business with little resistance; however, governments have responded to these troubling situations and continue to establish new rules to govern how businesses must deal with the new challenges facing them today.

The changing nature of business from manufacturing to knowledge technology has called for new levels of regulation on the part of both federal and provincial agencies. For example, Microsoft's <*www.microsoft.com*> competitive practices have been the focus of intense investigation in countries around the globe. One of the major accusations against the computer software firm has been that it has hindered competition by refusing to sell the Windows operating system to computer manufacturers unless they agree to sell Windows-based computers exclusively. This requirement has forced computer manufacturers to make a difficult choice: buy only Windows or don't buy Windows at all! Given that many consumers wanted Windows, the computer companies had little choice but to agree.

LAWS TO PROTECT CONSUMERS

consumerism
A social movement that seeks to increase and strengthen the rights and powers of buyers in relation to sellers.

Consumerism is a social movement that seeks to increase and strengthen the rights and powers of buyers in relation to sellers. Although consumerism is not a new movement, it has taken on new vigour and direction in the early twenty-first century because of the corporate scandals and greed involving companies such as Enron and WorldCom. Consumers have been particularly critical of government for its lack of oversight and action in the securities markets.

The protection of consumers has only recently come into vogue as a suitable topic for legislation. In earlier times, legislators deemed it appropriate to leave this to the common law, supplemented by the provisions of the Sale of Goods Act. The modern phenomenon of concentration of economic power in large manufacturing and distributing companies and in financial institutions has dramatically eroded the relative bargaining power of the consumer. The technical sophistication of modern products makes it impossible for consumers to detect product defects in advance. Price, quality, and safety have become matters that are often not negotiable: the consumer's choice is to accept or not accept the product, as is. Because of the inequality of bargaining power held by consumers in comparison to large retailers, manufacturers, and financial institutions, legislators have deemed it appropriate to intervene, readjusting the balance by protecting the consumer. The topics that have received the most attention are product performance and business practices.

Product Performance

The Parliament of Canada has enacted several major statutes dealing with consumer safety and product performance. The Consumer Packaging and Labelling Act establishes requirements for disclosing ingredients and quantities, and includes provision for some standardization of package sizes. The Textile Labelling Act requires disclosure of the fabrics and fibres in wearing apparel, together with recommended cleaning procedures. The Weights and Measures Act establishes a uniform system for weighing and measuring goods sold to consumers. The Food and Drugs Act provides for inspection and regulation of food and drugs, requires purity and sanitary storage, and restricts the distribution of potentially harmful substances. The Hazardous Products Act establishes a list of dangerous products that it is illegal to manufacture, and regulations governing the manufacture, packaging, and distribution of other products that can be harmful. The Motor Vehicle Safety Act and the Aeronautics Act establish national standards, specifying safety features that must be provided in motor vehicles and aircraft.

This federal legislation is supplemented by provincial legislation in all provinces. Some provinces have been much more active in this regard than others. In most, this legislation appears in a provincial Consumer Protection Act, but provisions designed to protect consumers appear in other Acts as well.

Business Practices

With respect to door-to-door sales, most provinces have legislation permitting the consumer to rescind a purchase contract within a specified "cooling off" period. All provinces also have registration and licensing requirements for door-to-door sellers and collection agencies, designed to prevent the use of harassment and pressure. Most also provide that a consumer who receives unsolicited goods through the mail is not liable to pay for them, or even to return them. Most provinces have also established statutory warranties with regard to contracts for the purchase and sale of consumer durables, voiding attempts to negate the warranties implied by the Sale of Goods Act.

Misleading Advertising

One of the major topics addressed by the Competition Act, mentioned earlier in this appendix, is misleading advertising. False or misleading representations about the characteristics of a product are prohibited. These include statements, warranties, and guarantees about the performance, efficacy, or length of life of a product that are not based upon adequate or proper testing, and by placing the onus on anyone making such representations to prove that they are based on testing. Misleading representations about the "ordinary" price of a product are also prohibited, as is the advertising of products for sale at a "bargain" price when the advertiser does not have reasonable quantities available for sale.

Most provinces supplement the federal legislation in this area, in much the same way as they do with regard to product performance requirements. The Ontario Business Practices Act, for example, prohibits false representations about product performance.

DOING BUSINESS AS A CORPORATION

A company or corporation is a legal entity, separate from its owners (who are called shareholders or stockholders), in the eyes of the law. The shareholders elect a small group of individuals (called directors) who are given ultimate decision-making authority for the corporation. In turn, the directors appoint the officers (e.g., president), who are placed in charge of the day-to-day management of the corporation. Shareholders do not participate in the normal management processes of the corporation.

The rules for how a corporation is governed and the nature of its rights and obligations are established by statute law (e.g., The Canada Business Corporations Act) and by the principles of common law and equity. The directors and officers of a corporation have obligations to the shareholders, but also have responsibilities to non-shareholder groups, including employees, creditors, customers, and the public at large. Issues in the area of corporate governance have gained much attention in recent years. Notable cases—such as those involving Nortel, Livent, Enron, and WorldCom—have demonstrated clearly the need for corporate officers and directors to act with utmost good faith in discharging their obligations.

BANKRUPTCY AND INSOLVENCY

bankruptcy
The legal process by which a person, business, or government entity unable to meet financial obligations is relieved of those obligations by a court that divides debtor assets among creditors, allowing creditors to get at least part of their money and freeing the debtor to begin anew.

The **bankruptcy** process recognizes that a debtor can reach a point where he or she will never be able to meet all obligations to creditors. The process is designed to minimize the negative impact of this situation for both debtor and creditor. The Bankruptcy and Insolvency Act, a federal statute, establishes a uniform national system for dealing with the problem. It is designed to achieve a reasonable and fair distribution of the debtor's assets among creditors, and to release the honest debtor in this position from ongoing obligations that cannot possibly be met, allowing him or her to resume productive business activity without them.

The provinces continue to have jurisdiction over an individual's financial affairs until he or she becomes insolvent or bankrupt. Once a person becomes bankrupt, the central government has jurisdiction to enact laws governing the rights and obligations of bankrupts and their creditors.

voluntary bankruptcy
Legal procedures initiated by a debtor.

involuntary bankruptcy
Bankruptcy procedures filed by a debtor's creditors.

Bankruptcy can be either voluntary or involuntary. In **voluntary bankruptcy** cases the debtor applies for bankruptcy, whereas in **involuntary bankruptcy** cases the creditors start legal procedures against the debtor. Most bankruptcies today are voluntary because creditors often want to wait in hopes that they will be paid all of the money due them rather than settle for only part of it.

The Bankruptcy and Insolvency Act establishes the scheme of distribution to be followed by the trustee in settling the claims of a bankrupt person's creditors. There are three basic categories of creditors for these purposes.

The highest priority is given to *secured creditors,* who have a direct claim against a specified asset of the debtor. When a debtor goes through bankruptcy proceedings, secured creditors are entitled to the entire proceeds realized on the sale of the asset in which they hold security, up to the secured amount owed to them by the debtor.

The second class of creditors is *preferred creditors,* and they have priority over general or unsecured creditors. This category includes trustees and lawyers involved in the process, unpaid employees of the bankrupt individual, and unpaid taxes.

The third group is the *unsecured creditors,* who do not have a direct claim against any asset and are not given preferred treatment by the Act. Unsecured claims include amounts owed to secured or preferred creditors that are in excess of the amount secured or preferred. All unsecured claims are treated equally by the Act, with each entitled to receive the same amount per dollar owed from the trustee in settlement of the amount claimed.

The bankrupt's contractual obligations to his or her creditors are discharged once he or she has complied fully with the terms of the arrangement that has been made by the trustee and accepted by the court. Payment of the established proportion of unsecured obligations, rather than payment in full, is sufficient to discharge all obligations. However, the discharge of a bankrupt is not automatic; it is a matter within the court's discretion. Whether a discharge is granted depends on matters like whether the person is a first-time bankrupt. Also, a discharge doesn't cover absolutely all obligations. Some obligations continue anyway. These include fines, child support payments, and amounts gained through fraud.

The Companies' Creditors Arrangement Act

The Companies' Creditors Arrangement Act (CCAA) is a federal statute that provides a second option in the commercial context for insolvent debtors to avoid bankruptcy proceedings. It makes provision for the restructuring of business debt when a company is unable to meet its financial obligations. The CCAA enables a company to submit a proposal to its creditors for an arrangement without bankruptcy proceedings. It permits a company to remain in business even though insolvent, and protects it from proceedings by creditors who might wish to force it into bankruptcy. The benefit to creditors is orderly conduct of the debtor's affairs, by maintaining the status quo while the debtor attempts to gain its creditors' approval of the plan and, if the plan is approved, payment by its terms. The attempts to financially restructure Air Canada and Stelco (now U.S. Steel Canada <*www.ussteelcanada.com*>) in the early years of this decade have been made under the CCAA.

The CCAA and the Bankruptcy and Insolvency Act work in concert with each other. The Bankruptcy and Insolvency Act expressly provides that it does not affect the operation of the CCAA, and allows the court to order continuation of a proposal made under the Bankruptcy and Insolvency Act under the CCAA.

DEREGULATION

Canada now has laws and regulations covering almost every aspect of business. In recent years, public concern that there are too many laws and regulations, and that these laws and regulations cost the public too much money, has developed. Thus began the movement toward deregulation. As you may recall from Chapter 4, deregulation means that the government withdraws certain laws and regulations that seem to hinder competition. Perhaps the most publicized examples of deregulation were those in the airline and telecommunications industries. Government used to severely restrict airlines with regard to where they could land and fly. When such restrictions were lifted, the airlines began competing for different routes and charging lower prices. This has provided a clear benefit to consumers, but puts tremendous pressure on the airlines to be competitive. Airlines such as WestJet have taken advantage of the opportunities, while Air Canada has had difficulty adapting. Similar deregulation in telecommunications has given consumers a flood of options in the telephone service market.

It seems that some regulation of business is necessary to ensure fair and honest dealings with the public. Still, businesses have adapted to the laws and regulations, and have done much toward producing safer, more effective products. However, corporate scandals since the turn of the century have soured what appeared to be better dialogue and co-operation between business and government. Many in government and society called for even more government regulation and control of business operations to protect investors and workers. With global competition increasing and small and medium-sized businesses striving to capture selected markets, business and government need to continue to work together to create a competitive environment that is fair and open. If businesses do not want additional regulation, they must accept their responsibilities to all their stakeholders.

KEY TERMS

administrative agencies
bankruptcy
breach of contract
business law
civil law
common law
consideration
consumerism
contract
contract law
copyright
criminal law
damages
express warranties
implied warranties
industrial design
involuntary bankruptcy
negligence
negotiable instruments
patent
precedent
product liability
statutory law
strict product liability
tort
trademark
voluntary bankruptcy

CHAPTER

5

ETHICS AND SOCIAL RESPONSIBILITY

LEARNING OBJECTIVES

After you have read and studied this chapter, you should be able to:

LO 1 Explain why obeying the law is only the first step in behaving ethically.

LO 2 Ask the three questions to answer when faced with a potentially unethical action.

LO 3 Describe management's role in setting ethical standards.

LO 4 Distinguish between compliance-based and integrity-based ethics codes, and list the six steps that can be considered when setting up a corporate ethics code.

LO 5 Define corporate social responsibility and compare corporations' responsibilities to various stakeholders.

LO 6 Discuss the importance of ethical behaviour and social responsibility in global markets.

PROFILE

GETTING TO KNOW STEVE ELLS OF CHIPOTLE MEXICAN GRILL

In the mind of burrito baron Steve Ells, founder and CEO of Chipotle Mexican Grill, Inc. <*www.chipotle.com*>, a fast-food restaurant shouldn't have to sacrifice quality or ethical responsibility to be inexpensive and, well, *fast*. Customers agree as they line up for the company's gourmet burritos, made with fresh ingredients right before their eyes. Chipotle (pronounced chi-POAT-lay) only serves a few things: burritos, burrito bowls (a burrito without the tortilla), tacos, and salads. But because customers can choose from four different meats, two types of beans, and a variety of extras such as salsas, guacamole, cheese and lettuce, there's enough variety to extend the menu to provide countless choices. Dedication to quality has made Chipotle a hit, with annual revenues over $2.2 billion.

But it's not just big burritos or towering sales that make Chipotle an exceptional restaurant chain. In 2000, Ells visited one of his meat suppliers and could not believe the horrible conditions of the supplier's factory farm. As a result of this eye-opening visit, Ells launched Chipotle's "Food With Integrity" campaign, with "a philosophy that we can always do better in terms of the food we buy," said Ells.

"If people know that the food is based on abusing animals, how satisfying can that dining experience be?" said Ells. Since

2010, all of Chipotle's pork comes from family farms with open pastures, bedded pens, and vegetarian meals for the pigs, with no antibiotics or growth hormones. Although there are not yet enough producers of naturally raised chicken and beef to supply all of Chipotle's meat, the supply is growing. The company's ultimate goal is to serve naturally raised chicken and beef in 100 percent of its restaurants. This support of family farms has made Chipotle the leading restaurant buyer of humanely raised meats.

Thanks to its high-quality food and humane treatment of animals, diners are going hog wild for Chipotle. The average annual revenue for a Chipotle restaurant that has been open more than a year is $1.7 million. There are 1,262 restaurants in the United States, Canada, and the United Kingdom, with expectations to open 155 to 165 new restaurants in 2012.

The company's environmentally friendly attitude has even rubbed off on fast-food giants Wendy's and Burger King, which have begun to incorporate humanely raised pork in their food. But despite such strides, Ells's mission to serve "Food With Integrity" is far from complete.

"Have we achieved our mission? No. Will we ever accomplish it? Never, because 'Food With Integrity' is a constant process of searching and improving. But the changes will be noticeable, positive, and significant," said Ells.

Though they may not receive as much press as their corrupt colleagues, ethical entrepreneurs are the backbone of the business world. In this chapter, we explore the responsibility of businesses to their stakeholders, which include customers, investors, employees, and society. We look at the responsibilities of individuals as well. After all, responsible business behaviour depends on responsible behaviour of each individual in the business.

Sources: "Chipotle Story," Chipotle Mexican Grill, Inc., 6 May 2012, www.chipotle.com/en-US/chipotle_story/chipotle_story.aspx; "Chipotle Mexican Grill, Inc. Announces First Quarter 2012 Results," Chipotle Mexican Grill, Inc., 31 March 2012, http://ir.chipotle.com/phoenix.zhtml?c=194775&p=irol-newsArticle&ID=1685193&highlight=; "2011 Annual Report and Proxy," Chipotle Mexican Grill, Inc., 2012?, http://ir.chipotle.com/phoenix.zhtml?c=194775&p=irol-reportsAnnual; "Chipotle Commits to Serving More Than 50 Million Pounds of Naturally Raised Meat in 2008," Business Wire, 7 January 2008; Adrianne Cohen, "Ode to a Burrito," *Fast Company,* April 2008; and Anna Kuchment, "A Chain That Pigs Would Die For," *Newsweek,* 12 May 2008.

Explain why obeying the law is only the first step in behaving ethically.

ETHICS IS MORE THAN LEGALITY

It is not uncommon to hear of instances where business people are involved in unethical behaviour. Some examples of Canadian companies that have been caught in such scandals include Livent, CIBC World Markets <*www.cibcwm.com*>, Nortel, and WestJet. After two years of denying accusations, WestJet Airlines Ltd. admitted to spying on Air Canada. In a news release, WestJet apologized for accessing a confidential Air Canada Web site designated for reservations: "This practice was undertaken with the knowledge and direction of the highest management levels of WestJet and was not halted until discovered by Air Canada. This conduct was both unethical and unacceptable and WestJet accepts full responsibility for such misconduct."[1] As part of the settlement, WestJet paid Air Canada's investigation and litigation costs of \$5.5 million and it made a \$10 million donation in the name of both airlines to children's charities across Canada.[2] The Canadian business environment has also been impacted by notable scandals in other countries such as Enron, Arthur Andersen, Tyco, and Parmalat <*www.parmalat.com*>, just to name a few.

It is not just for-profit business people that are accused of unethical behaviour. Government employees have also been implicated. For example, Elections Canada launched an investigation after the 2011 federal election. Voters in 200 ridings complained that they had received phone calls on behalf of Elections Canada directing them to the wrong polling stations.[3] A pattern of phone calls was reported in which voters identified as not supporting the Conservatives were targeted with robocalls or live calls directing them to the wrong polling stations.[4] At the time this chapter was being written, this was still under investigation. What was the conclusion of the investigation? Were charges laid? Review Figure 5.1 for a brief summary of some of the most-publicized scandals in recent years.

▸ The federal government was criticized in the Auditor General's Report for the way it implemented a historic land claims deal it struck with the Inuit in the western Arctic in 1984. While Ottawa paid the money it promised, it has ignored some of its other responsibilities, including preservation of native identity, improving the economic status of the Inuvialuit, and protecting the environment.

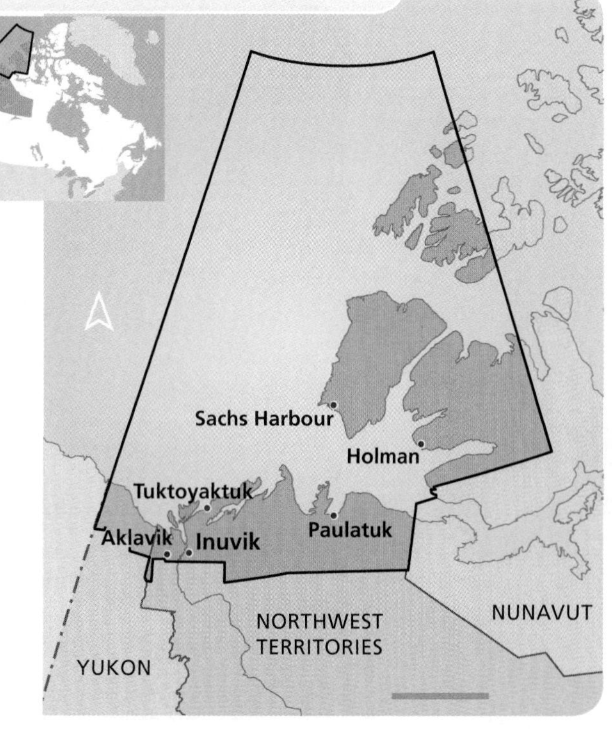

Given the ethical lapses that are so prevalent today, what can be done to restore trust in the free-market system and leaders in general? First, those who have broken the law need to be punished accordingly. New laws making accounting records more transparent (easy to read and understand) and more laws making business people and others more accountable may help. But laws do not make people honest, reliable, or truthful. If they did, crime would disappear.

One danger in writing new laws to correct behaviour is that people may begin to think that any behaviour that is within the law is also acceptable. The measure of behaviour, then, becomes: "Is it legal?" A society gets in trouble when people consider only what is illegal and not also what is unethical. Ethics and legality are two very different things. Although following the law is an important first step, ethical behaviour requires more than that. Ethics reflects people's proper relations with one another: How should people treat others? What responsibility should they feel for others? Legality is narrower. It refers to laws we have written to protect ourselves from fraud, theft, and violence. Many immoral and unethical acts fall well within our laws.[5]

Figure 5.1

Brief Summary of Some Corporate Scandals[6]

Lottery Corporations: Ontario Ombudsman Andre Marin's Report blasted the Ontario Lottery and Gaming Corporation for not cracking down on retailers who collected tens of millions of dollars in jackpots between 1999 and 2006, some of them fraudulently. As a result, police began probing allegations of fraudulent lottery prize claims by retailers. The Atlantic Lottery Corporation announced it was turning over its files to police over similar concerns of retailers stealing winning tickets from customers. The British Columbia government announced an audit of the province's lottery system following a negative report by its Ombudsman that found it was open to fraud.

Research In Motion (RIM) Stock Option Scandal: An Ontario court approved a settlement between the company and the Ironworkers of Ontario Pension Fund over allegations RIM had backdated stock options to company executives. Under terms of the settlement, RIM's co-founders Jim Balsillie and Mike Lazaridis agreed to pay $2.5 million each (in addition to the $5 million the executives had each agreed to repay earlier). The company has also ceased giving stock options to directors, added more independent directors to the board, and tightened up its executive compensation practices.

Federal Government Sponsorship Scandal: The Auditor General's 2004 Report found that $100 million was paid to a variety of communications agencies in the form of fees and commissions, and said that the program was basically designed to generate commissions for these companies rather than to produce any benefit for Canadians. Implicated in this scandal were high-level officials. Charles Guité, a former senior bureaucrat, was sentenced to 42 months in prison for defrauding the federal government. Other scandal participants who received prison sentences include Jean Brault (30 months) and Paul Coffin (18 months). Gilles-André Gosselin was charged in 2008 with nineteen criminal charges, including fraud.

Hollinger International Inc.: Conrad Black, who once headed the Hollinger International Inc. media empire, was convicted of obstruction of justice in 2007. In addition to three other former Hollinger executives, he was also found guilty of fraud for funnelling US$6.1 million from the media company. Black was sentenced to 6½ years in federal prison and ordered to pay a six-figure fine plus restitution of $6.1 million. Three former Hollinger executives also received sentences: Jack Boultbee (27 months), Peter Atkinson (24 months), and Mark Kipnis (placed on probation with six months of house arrest). David Radler, one-time CEO of Hollinger International, plead guilty to mail fraud. He received a 29-month sentence and agreed to pay a US$250,000 fine.

Ethical Standards Are Fundamental

We define **ethics** as the standards of moral behaviour; that is, behaviour that is accepted by society as right versus wrong. Many people today have few moral absolutes. Many decide situationally whether it's okay to steal, lie, or drink and drive. They seem to think that what is right is whatever works best for the individual, and that each person has to work out for himself or herself the difference between right and wrong. That is the kind of thinking that has led to the recent scandals in government and business. This is not the way it always was. However, in the past decade there has been a rising tide of criticism in Canada (and other countries) of various business practices that many Canadians consider unacceptable.

ethics
Standards of moral behaviour; that is, behaviour that is accepted by society as right versus wrong.

In a country like Canada, with so many diverse cultures, you might think it would be impossible to identify common standards of ethical behaviour. However, among sources from many different times and places—such as the Bible, Aristotle's *Ethics,* William Shakespeare's *King Lear,* the Quran, and the *Analects* of Confucius—you will find the following basic moral values: integrity, respect for human life, self-control, honesty, courage, and self-sacrifice are right; cheating, cowardice, and cruelty are wrong. Furthermore, all of the world's major religions support a version of the Golden Rule: Do unto others as you would have them do unto you.[7]

Ethics Begins with Each of Us

Ask the three questions to answer when faced with a potentially unethical action.

It is easy to criticize business and political leaders for their moral and ethical shortcomings, but we must be careful in our criticism to note that ethics begins with each of us. Ethical behaviour should be exhibited in our daily lives, not just in a business environment.

Plagiarizing material from the Internet, including cutting and pasting information from Web sites without giving credit, is the most common form of cheating in schools today. To fight this problem, many instructors now use services like Turnitin, which scans students' papers against more than 9 billion online sources to provide evidence of copying in seconds.[8] Have you seen students cheat on assignments or exams? How did this make you feel? Students use many reasons to rationalize such behaviour, such as "Everyone else is doing it" or "I ran out of time to prepare, but I will do all my own work next time." What do you think of these reasons?

In a study, most teens said they were prepared to make ethical decisions in the workforce, but an alarming 38 percent felt that lying, cheating, plagiarizing, or behaving violently is sometimes necessary.[9] Two recent studies found a strong relationship between academic dishonesty among undergraduates and dishonesty at work.[10] In response, many schools are establishing heavier consequences for cheating and requiring students to perform a certain number of hours of community service to graduate. Do you think such policies make a difference in student behaviour?

It is always healthy when discussing moral and ethical issues to remember that ethical behaviour begins with you and me. We cannot expect society to become more moral and ethical unless we as individuals commit to being moral and ethical ourselves.

The Making Ethical Decisions boxes throughout the text—like the accompanying one on video piracy —remind you to keep ethics in mind whenever you are making a business decision. The choices are not always easy. Sometimes the obvious solution from an ethical point of view has drawbacks from a personal or professional point of view. For example, imagine that your supervisor at work has asked you to do something you feel is unethical. You have just taken out a mortgage on a new house to make room for your first baby, due in two months. Not carrying out your supervisor's request may get you fired. What would you do? Sometimes there is no easy alternative in such *ethical dilemmas* because you must choose between equally unsatisfactory alternatives.

▸ Downloading from the Internet is the most common form of cheating today. Have you ever been tempted to take credit for someone else's work?

It can be difficult to balance between ethics and other goals such as pleasing stakeholders or advancing in your career. It is helpful to ask yourself the following questions when facing an ethical dilemma:[11]

1. *Is it legal?* Am I violating any law or company policy? Whether you are thinking about having a drink and then driving home, gathering marketing intelligence, designing a product, hiring or firing employees, getting rid of industrial waste, or using a questionable nickname for an employee, think about the legal implications of what you do. This is the most basic question in business ethics, but it is only the first.
2. *Is it balanced?* Am I acting fairly? Would I want to be treated this way? Will I win everything at the expense of another? Win–lose situations often become lose–lose situations and generate retaliation from the loser. Not every situation can

MAKING ETHICAL DECISIONS

To Tube or Not to Tube?

Whether you want to watch a dog playing a piano, a flashy new music video, or just a slideshow of a family vacation, you can find it on YouTube. Every minute of every day, people all across the globe upload 60 hours of video onto the Google-owned site. A lot of the content is user-generated, meaning amateurs produce it and can instantly place it online for the whole world to see. But some users upload clips from Hollywood movies or network television shows without the permission of the copyright-holding companies.

Viacom <*www.viacom.com*>—a media corporation that owns TV stations like CBS <*www.cbs.com*>, Comedy Central <*www.comedycentral.com*>, and MTV <*www.mtv.com*>, as well as the film production company Paramount <*www.paramount.com*>—does not take video sharing lightly. In 2007, when Viacom noticed that entire episodes of popular shows like *South Park* and *The Daily Show* appeared on YouTube, it filed a $1 billion lawsuit for copyright infringement. Viacom argued that featuring its content on YouTube violates the Digital Millennium Copyright Act, which requires that Web sites remove copyrighted material uploaded without the owner's permission. Viacom claims it identified 150,000 unauthorized clips viewed a total of 1.5 billion times, supporting its argument that the exposure robbed it of valuable revenue it would have received from television advertisers. Viacom holds YouTube, rather than the individuals who uploaded the video clips, responsible for carrying the illegal content.

YouTube says it diligently tries to delete any videos that generate complaints from copyright owners, but with millions of different users of the site, it is impossible to catch everything. To discourage people from posting copyrighted material, YouTube not only removes the offending videos but also bans any user who uploads copyrighted content without permission. It also provides companies with software to easily identify copyrighted material so it can be reported and removed.

YouTube worries that Viacom's suit will prevent people from uploading user-generated content, which has revolutionized worldwide communication and given anyone with a camera and a computer the chance to become a star. In their defensive statement YouTube's lawyers said, "Viacom's complaint threatens the way hundreds of millions of people legitimately exchange information, news, entertainment, and political and artistic expression."

What do you think? Who should be held accountable for copyright violations—the people who upload the material or the Web sites that carry it? If Web sites are not held legally responsible, do they still have an ethical responsibility to find and remove such material? What should they do?

Five years later, the lawsuit was still active. A U.S. appeals court revived Viacom's lawsuit (and that of various other media companies) over the use of copyrighted videos on YouTube's service without permission. The appeals court reversed a June 2010 lower court ruling that was in favour of YouTube. What is the update on this lawsuit? Has it been settled?

Sources: "Statistics," YouTube, 6 May 2012, www.youtube.com/t/press_statistics; Jonathan Stempel and Yinka Adegoke, "Viacom wins reversal in landmark YouTube case," Reuters, 5 April 2012, www.reuters.com/article/2012/04/05/net-us-google-viacom-idUSBRE8340RY20120405; Stephen Foley, "Defender of the Net, or an Infringement Factory?" *The Independent*, 1 June 2008; and Larry Neumesiter, "YouTube Suit Called Threat to Online Communication," Associated Press, 27 May 2008.

be completely balanced, but the health of our relationships requires us to avoid major imbalances over time. An ethical business person has a win–win attitude and tries to make decisions that benefit all.

3. *How will it make me feel about myself?* Would I feel proud if my family learned of my decision? My friends? Could I discuss the proposed situation or action with my supervisor? The company's clients? Will I have to hide my actions? Has someone warned me not to disclose them? What if my decisions were announced on the evening news? Am I feeling unusually nervous? Decisions that go against our sense of right and wrong make us feel bad—they corrode our self-esteem. That is why an ethical business person does what is proper as well as what is profitable.

Individuals and companies that develop a strong ethics code and use the three ethics-check questions presented above have a better chance than most of behaving ethically. If you would like to know which style of recognizing and resolving ethical dilemmas you favour, fill out the ethical orientation questionnaire in Figure 5.2.

Please answer the following questions.

1. Which is worse?
   A. Hurting someone's feelings by telling the truth.
   B. Telling a lie and protecting someone's feelings.
2. Which is the worse mistake?
   A. To make exceptions too freely.
   B. To apply rules too rigidly.
3. Which is it worse to be?
   A. Unmerciful.
   B. Unfair.
4. Which is worse?
   A. Stealing something valuable from someone for no good reason.
   B. Breaking a promise to a friend for no good reason.
5. Which is it better to be?
   A. Just and fair.
   B. Sympathetic and feeling.
6. Which is worse?
   A. Not helping someone in trouble.
   B. Being unfair to someone by playing favourites.
7. In making a decision you rely more on
   A. hard facts.
   B. personal feelings and intuition.
8. Your boss orders you to do something that will hurt someone. If you carry out the order, have you actually done anything wrong?
   A. Yes.
   B. No.
9. Which is more important in determining whether an action is right or wrong?
   A. Whether anyone actually gets hurt.
   B. Whether a rule, law, commandment, or moral principle is broken.

To score: The answers fall in one of two categories, J or C. Count your number of J and C answers using this key:
1. A = C, B = J; 2. A = J, B = C; 3. A = C, B = J; 4. A = J, B = C; 5. A = J, B = C; 6. A = C, B = J; 7. A = J, B = C; 8. A = C, B = J; 9. A = C, B = J

What your score means: The higher your J score, the more you rely on an ethic of justice. The higher your C score, the more you prefer an ethic of care. Neither style is better than the other, but they are different. Because they appear so different they may seem opposed to one another, but they are actually complementary. In fact, your score probably shows you rely on each style to a greater or lesser degree. (Few people end up with a score of 9 to 0.) The more you can appreciate both approaches, the better you will be able to resolve ethical dilemmas and to understand and communicate with people who prefer the other style.

An ethic of justice is based on principles such as justice, fairness, equality, or authority. People who prefer this style see ethical dilemmas as conflicts of rights that can be solved by the impartial application of some general principle. The advantage of this approach is that it looks at a problem logically and impartially. People with this style try to be objective and fair, hoping to make a decision according to some standard that is higher than any specific individual's interests. The disadvantage of this approach is that people who rely on it might lose sight of the immediate interests of particular individuals. They may unintentionally ride roughshod over the people around them in favour of some abstract ideal or policy.

An ethic of care is based on a sense of responsibility to reduce actual harm or suffering. People who prefer this style see moral dilemmas as conflicts of duties or responsibilities. They believe that solutions must be tailored to the special details of individual circumstances. They tend to feel constrained by policies that are supposed to be enforced without exception. The advantage of this approach is that it is responsive to immediate suffering and harm. The disadvantage is that, when carried to an extreme, this style can produce decisions that seem not simply subjective, but arbitrary.

To learn more about an ethic of justice, consult the writings of Lawrence Kohlberg. To learn more about an ethic of care, consult the research of Carol Gilligan.

Source: © Thomas I. White.

Figure 5.2

Ethical Orientation Questionnaire

PROGRESS ASSESSMENT

- What is ethics?
- How does ethics differ from legality?
- When faced with ethical dilemmas, what questions can you ask yourself that might help you make ethical decisions?

MANAGING BUSINESSES ETHICALLY AND RESPONSIBLY

Describe management's role in setting ethical standards.

Ethics is caught more than it is taught. That is, people learn their standards and values from observing what others do, not from hearing what they say. This is as true in business as it is at home. Organizational ethics begins at the top, and the leadership and example of strong managers can help instill corporate values in employees. The majority of CEOs surveyed recently attributed unethical employee conduct to the failure of the organization's leadership in establishing ethical standards and culture.[12]

Trust and co-operation between workers and managers must be based on fairness, honesty, openness, and moral integrity. The same applies to relationships among businesses and among nations. A business should be managed ethically for many reasons: to maintain a good reputation; to keep existing customers and attract ones; to avoid lawsuits; to reduce employee turnover; to avoid government intervention in the form of new laws and regulations controlling business activities; to please customers, employees, and society; and simply to do the right thing.[13]

Some managers think that ethics is a personal matter—either individuals have ethical principles or they don't. These managers feel that they are not responsible for an individual's misdeeds and that ethics has nothing to do with management. But a growing number of people think that ethics has everything to do with management. Individuals do not usually act alone; they need the implied, if not direct, co-operation of others to behave unethically in a corporation.

For example, there have been reports of cell phone service sales representatives who actually lie to get customers to extend their contracts—or even extend their contracts without the customers' knowledge. Some phone reps intentionally hang up on callers to prevent them from cancelling their contracts. Why do these sales reps sometimes resort to overly aggressive tactics? Because poorly designed incentive programs reward them for meeting certain goals, sometimes doubling or tripling their salaries with incentives. Do their managers say directly, "Deceive the customers"? No, but the message is clear. Overly ambitious goals and incentives can create an environment in which unethical actions like this can occur.[14]

Distinguish between compliance-based and integrity-based ethics codes, and list the six steps that can be considered when setting up a corporate ethics code.

Setting Corporate Ethical Standards

More and more companies have adopted written codes of conduct. Figure 5.3 offers Johnson & Johnson Inc.'s as a sample. Although ethics codes vary greatly, they can be

Written in 1943 by long-time Chairman General Robert Wood Johnson, the Johnson & Johnson Credo serves as a conscious plan that represents and encourages a unique set of values. Our Credo sums up the responsibilities we have to the four important groups we serve:

- Our customers—We have a responsibility to provide high-quality products they can trust, offered at a fair price.
- Our employees—We have a responsibility to treat them with respect and dignity, pay them fairly, and help them develop and thrive personally and professionally.
- Our communities—We have a responsibility to be good corporate citizens, support good works, encourage better health and protect the environment.
- Our stockholders—We have a responsibility to provide a fair return on their investment.

The deliberate ordering of these groups—customers first, stockholders last—proclaims a bold business philosophy: If we meet our first three responsibilities, the fourth will take care of itself . . . To ensure our adherence to Credo values, we periodically ask every employee to evaluate the company's performance in living up to them. We believe that by monitoring our actions against the ethical framework of our Credo, we will best ensure that we make responsible decisions as a company.

Figure 5.3

Overview of Johnson & Johnson Inc.'s Code of Ethics

Johnson & Johnson calls this code of ethics its Credo.

Figure 5.4

Strategies for Ethics Management

Both codes have a concern for the law and use penalties as enforcement. Integrity-based ethics codes move beyond legal compliance to create a "do-it-right" climate that emphasizes core values such as honesty, fair play, good service to customers, a commitment to diversity, and involvement in the community. These values are ethically desirable, but not necessarily legally mandatory.

Features of Compliance-Based Ethics Codes		Features of Integrity-Based Ethics Codes	
Ideal	Conform to outside standards (laws and regulations)	Ideal	Conform to outside standards (laws and regulations) and chosen internal standards
Objective	Avoid criminal misconduct	Objective	Enable responsible employee conduct
Leaders	Lawyers	Leaders	Managers with aid of lawyers and others
Methods	Education, reduced employee discretion, controls, and penalties	Methods	Education, leadership, accountability, decision processes, controls, and penalties

compliance-based ethics codes
Ethical standards that emphasize preventing unlawful behaviour by increasing control and by penalizing wrongdoers.

integrity-based ethics codes
Ethical standards that define the organization's guiding values, create an environment that supports ethically sound behaviour, and stress a shared accountability among employees.

whistleblowers
People who report illegal or unethical behaviour.

classified into two categories: compliance-based and integrity-based. **Compliance-based ethics codes** emphasize preventing unlawful behaviour by increasing control and by penalizing wrongdoers. Whereas compliance-based ethics codes are based on avoiding legal punishment, **integrity-based ethics codes** define the organization's guiding values, create an environment that supports ethically sound behaviour, and stress shared accountability among employees. See Figure 5.4 for a comparison of compliance-based and integrity-based ethics codes.

The following six-step process can help improve business ethics:[15]

1. Top management must adopt and unconditionally support an explicit corporate code of conduct.
2. Employees must understand that expectations for ethical behaviour begin at the top and that senior management expects all employees to act accordingly.
3. Managers and others must be trained to consider the ethical implications of all business decisions.
4. An ethics office must be set up. Phone lines to the office should be established so that employees who don't necessarily want to be seen with an ethics officer can inquire about ethical matters anonymously. **Whistleblowers** (people who report illegal or unethical behaviour) must feel protected from retaliation as oftentimes this exposure can lead to great career and personal cost.
5. Outsiders such as suppliers, subcontractors, distributors, and customers must be told about the ethics program. Pressure to put aside ethical considerations often comes from the outside, and it helps employees to resist such pressure when everyone knows what the ethical standards are.
6. The ethics code must be enforced. It is important to back any ethics program with timely action if any rules are broken. This is the best way to communicate to all employees that the code is serious.

This last step is perhaps the most critical. No matter how well intended a company's ethics code is, it is worthless if it is not enforced. Engineering and construction firm, SNC-Lavalin <*www.snclavalin.com*>, was in the news after the results of an internal investigation showed that a series of unauthorized payments—to the tune of $56 million—were made in connection to business in Libya.[16] The company CEO, Pierre Duhaime, resigned under the weight of the allegations; Duhaime had not been charged with any crime, but the company said his signing off on payments to undisclosed agents was a breach of the company's code of ethics.[17] In contrast,

Johnson & Johnson's response to a cyanide poisoning crisis in the 1980s shows that enforcing ethics codes can enhance the bottom line. Although not legally required to do so, the company recalled its Tylenol products and won great praise and a reputation of corporate integrity.[18]

An important factor in the success of enforcing an ethics code is selecting an ethics officer. The most effective ethics officers set a positive tone, communicate effectively, and relate well to employees at every level. They are equally comfortable as counsellors and investigators, and can be trusted to maintain confidentiality, conduct objective investigations, and ensure fairness. They can demonstrate to stakeholders that ethics are important in everything the company does.

As more organizations are recognizing the importance of this role, associations are also providing support for those in these roles. One such example is the Ethics Practitioners' Association of Canada (EPAC) <*www.epac-apec.ca*>. EPAC's mission is "to enable individuals to work successfully in the field of ethics in organizations by enhancing the quality and availability of ethics advice and services across Canada." This organization supports ethics officers, consultants, educators, students, and others who are interested in the field of ethics as applied to organizations of all kinds.

The Sarbanes-Oxley Act of 2002 (SOX)[19]

The major corporate and accounting scandals in the United Sates in the early 2000s (e.g., Enron, Tyco, Adelphia, and WorldCom) gave rise to the implementation of U.S. federal legislation known as the Sarbanes-Oxley Act (SOX). The legislation established stronger standards to prevent misconduct and improve corporate governance practices. SOX applies to all publicly traded companies whose shares are listed on the stock exchanges under the jurisdiction of the U.S. Securities and Exchange Commission. The goal of SOX is to ensure the accuracy and reliability of published financial information. Requirements deal with the proper administration routines, procedures, and control activities.

SOX also protects whistleblowers from any company retaliation as it requires that all public corporations provide a system that allows employees to submit concerns regarding accounting and auditing issues both confidentially and anonymously. The purpose is to motivate employees to report any wrongdoing. For example, the legislation provides for reinstatement and back pay to people who were punished by their employers for passing information about frauds to authorities.

In response to SOX, Canada also implemented similar corporate governance legislation.

Whistleblower Legislation in Canada[20]

One might suggest that for the six steps mentioned earlier to work, there must first be protection in place for whistleblowers. Otherwise, how effective can such a process be? Unfortunately, there is no legislation in place that protects all workers—public sector and private sector—across the country. Regarding public-sector workers, the federal government and some provinces have variations of whistleblower legislation that set up a third-party independent officer, such as the federal integrity commissioner or Saskatchewan's public interest disclosure commissioner, to whom employees can raise concerns. Let us consider one piece of legislation.

The Federal Accountability Act (FAA) applies to approximately 400,000 government employees. It lists a wide range of measures to help make the Canadian federal government more accountable and to increase transparency and oversight in government operations. Among other objectives, it is promoted as protecting federal government employees who come forward, so they need not fear reprisal. This includes direct employee access to the Commissioner to report wrongdoing in the workplace. The Commissioner has the authority to deal with reprisal complaints,

▶ Ornge, Ontario's air ambulance service, is under police investigation for financial irregularities. Ontario's Health Ministry and the province's financial investigations team were warned of serious problems three years earlier by an Ornge accountant.

conduct investigations, and attempt to conciliate a settlement between the parties. Democracy Watch <*www.dwatch.ca*>, a citizen group advocating democratic reform, government accountability, and corporate responsibility, believes that much more needs to be done to protect whistleblowers. Among some of its criticisms, it maintains that the "FAA established a system that does not provide promised adequate funding for whistleblowers' legal services, and that it requires the whistleblower to prove retaliation has occurred (instead of requiring the government to prove it has not punished the whistleblower)."

While Canadians who work for corporations listed on a U.S. stock exchange may have some protection under the U.S. Sarbanes-Oxley legislation, there is no provision to protect private-sector whistleblowers. In a KPMG survey on private corporations' policies on whistleblowers, almost two-thirds of respondents to the business ethics survey stated that they have a written policy requiring employees to report fraud or misconduct in the workplace. However, only 40 percent of respondents reported having formal systems designed to protect whistleblowers from retaliation. One-fifth of respondents lacked any type of protection system. Yet, whistleblowers add value to corporations. A PricewaterhouseCoopers study showed that whistleblowers uncovered far more fraud than internal audit and all other management control systems combined. The study, which polled 5,400 senior executives from 40 countries, found that 43 percent of corporate frauds had been initially detected by employee tip-offs.

Petro-Canada is a company that has an internal whistleblower policy. An anonymous 1-800 line is in place. A third-party service provider responds and reports all calls to the appropriate members of Petro-Canada's executive or audit committee, depending on the nature of the call. Employees are informed that they will not be discriminated against for stepping forward.

PROGRESS ASSESSMENT

- How are compliance-based ethics codes different from integrity-based ethics codes?
- What are the six steps to follow in establishing an effective ethics program in a business?
- What laws are in place to protect whistleblowers?

Define corporate social responsibility and compare corporations' responsibilities to various stakeholders.

corporate social responsibility (CSR)
A business's concern for the welfare of society.

CORPORATE SOCIAL RESPONSIBILITY

Just as you and I need to be good citizens, contributing what we can to society, corporations need to be good citizens as well. **Corporate social responsibility (CSR)** is the concern businesses have for the welfare of society, not just for their owners. CSR goes well beyond merely being ethical. It is based on a commitment to integrity, fairness, and respect.[21]

There is discussion in this chapter about ethics and CSR. It is important to note that both of these are often judgement calls, depending on which side of the issue you are on. To clarify, one person's unethical behaviour can be considered another person's sound business decision. Also, do not underestimate the impact of cultural values. Differences from country to country also contribute to varying perspectives on the same issue. This can result in decision making that is not in line with one's personal values but is congruent with what is considered ethical in a country.

You may be surprised to know that not everyone thinks that CSR is a good thing. Some critics of CSR believe that a manager's sole role is to compete and win in the marketplace. Economist Milton Friedman made a classic statement when he said that the only social responsibility of business is to make money for shareholders. He thought that doing anything else was moving dangerously toward socialism.[22] Other CSR critics believe that managers who pursue CSR are doing so with other people's money—money they invested to make more money, not to improve society. In this view, spending money on CSR activities is stealing from investors.[23]

▸ Tim Horton Children's Foundation is a private organization that is supported by Tim Hortons. Every year, thousands of children from economically challenged homes participate in camps that are run by the Foundation.

CSR defenders, in contrast, believe that businesses owe their existence to the societies they serve and cannot succeed in societies that fail. Firms have access to society's labour pool and its natural resources, in which every member of society has a stake. Even Adam Smith, the father of capitalism, believed that the self-interested pursuit of profit was wrong and that benevolence was the highest virtue. CSR defenders acknowledge that businesses have deep obligations to investors, and that businesses should not attempt government-type social responsibility projects. However, they also argue that CSR makes more money for investors in the long run. Studies show that companies with good ethical reputations attract and retain better employees, draw more customers, and enjoy greater employee loyalty.[24]

The social performance of a company has several dimensions:

- **Corporate philanthropy** includes charitable donations to non-profit groups of all kinds. Some make long-term commitments to one cause such as the Canadian Tire Foundation for Families. Since 2005, the Foundation has given over 417,000 financially disadvantaged children the chance to participate in organized recreational programs.[25]
- **Corporate social initiatives** include enhanced forms of corporate philanthropy that are more directly related to the company's competencies. For example, as part of the 2004 Asian tsunami disaster relief, UPS <*www.ups.com*> and FedEx <*www.fedex.com*> shipped emergency relief supplies for free from all over the world, Johnson & Johnson sent medical supplies, and other pharmaceutical companies sent antibiotics, nutritional supplements, and baby formula.[26]
- **Corporate responsibility** includes everything from hiring minority workers to making safe products, minimizing pollution, using energy wisely, and providing a safe work environment—that is, everything that has to do with acting responsibly within.
- **Corporate policy** refers to the position a firm takes on social and political issues. For example, Patagonia's <*www.patagonia.com*> corporate policy includes this statement: "A love of wild and beautiful places demands participation in the fight to save them, and to help reverse the steep decline in the overall environmental health of our planet. We donate our time, services and at least 1% of our sales to hundreds of grassroots environmental groups all over the world who work to help reverse the tide." [27]

corporate philanthropy
Dimension of social responsibility that includes charitable donations.

corporate social initiatives
Dimension of social responsibility that includes enhanced forms of corporate philanthropy that are more directly related to the company's competencies.

corporate responsibility
Dimension of social responsibility that includes everything from hiring minority workers to making safe products.

corporate policy
Dimension of social responsibility that refers to the position a firm takes on social and political issues.

So much news coverage has been devoted to the problems caused by corporations that people tend to develop a negative view of the impact that companies have on society. But businesses make positive contributions too. Few people know, for example, that a Xerox <*www.xerox.com*> program called Social Service Leave allows employees to take a leave of absence for up to a year to work for a non-profit organization while earning their full Xerox salary and benefits, including job security.[28] In fact, many companies allow employees to give part-time help to social agencies of all kinds.

Two-thirds of the MBA students surveyed by a group called Students for Responsible Business said they would take a reduced salary to work for a socially responsible company.[29] But when the same students were asked to define *socially responsible,* things got complicated. It appears that even those who want to be socially responsible cannot agree on what it is.

Concepts of Social Corporate Responsibility

What should be the guiding philosophy for business in the twenty-first century? For most of the twentieth century, there was uncertainty regarding the position top managers should take, and this question is still being debated today. How a company answers this question depends on its fundamental belief of how stakeholders should be treated and its responsibility to society. There are two different views of corporate responsibility to stakeholders:

1. *The Strategic Approach.* The strategic approach requires that management's primary orientation be toward the economic interests of shareholders. The rationale is this: as owners, shareholders have the right to expect management to work in their best interests; that is, to optimize profits. Furthermore, Adam Smith's notion of the invisible hand suggests that the maximum social gain is realized when managers attend only to their shareholders' interests.

   Friedman and others argue that since (in their view) only people can have social responsibilities, corporations are only responsible to their shareholders and not to society as a whole. Although they accept that corporations should obey the laws of the countries within which they work, they assert that corporations have no other obligation to society.[30] Often, the interests of other stakeholders are considered only when they would adversely affect profits, if ignored.
2. *The Pluralist Approach.* This approach recognizes the special responsibility of management to optimize profits, but not at the expense of employees, suppliers, and members of the community. This approach recognizes the moral responsibilities of management that apply to all human beings. Managers don't have moral immunity when making managerial decisions. This view says that corporations can maintain their economic viability only when they fulfill their moral responsibilities to society as a whole. When shareholders' interests compete with those of the community, as they often do, managers must decide, using ethical and moral principles.

▸ Imperial Tobacco Canada <www.imperialtobaccocanada.com> promotes itself as a socially responsible company. Among other programs, it supports Operation I.D., a youth smoking prevention program. Overall, what view of corporate responsibility do you believe this company supports?

The guiding philosophy for the twenty-first century will be some version of the pluralist approach. Managerial decision making will not be easy, and new ethical guidelines may have to be drawn. But the process toward such guidelines has been started, and a new era of more responsible and responsive management is under way.

The time when ethics matters the most is when the company is tested. That is, when it is in a crisis. This is when a company can prove that it is staying true to its values and ethics, based on its reaction to the crisis. Moving forward in this chapter, you will be introduced to two examples (highlighted in photos with some details in the captions) of companies that were faced with a crisis. Some would argue that one handled the situation much better than the other. Do some research to discover which was which.

Perhaps it would be easier to understand social responsibility if we looked at the concept through the eyes of the stakeholders to whom businesses are responsible: customers, investors, employees, society in general, and the environment.

In 2008, twenty people died after eating listeria-tainted Maple Leaf meat. The company was credited with quickly issuing a massive recall and developed new standards of food safety. "This is a terrible tragedy," publicly stated CEO Michael McCain. "To those people who have become ill, and to the families who have lost loved ones, I want to express my deepest and most sincere sympathies. Words cannot begin to express our sadness for your pain."[31]

Responsibility to Customers

Consumers have four basic rights: (1) the right to safety, (2) the right to be informed, (3) the right to choose, and (4) the right to be heard. These rights will be achieved only if business and consumers recognize them and take action in the marketplace.

A recurring theme of this book is the importance of pleasing customers by offering them real value. We recognize that this responsibility is not as easy to meet as it seems. One sure way of failing to please customers is to be less than honest with them. The payoff for socially conscious behaviour, however, can be new customers who admire the company's social efforts—a powerful competitive edge. Consumer behaviour studies show that, all else being equal, a socially conscious company is likely to be viewed more favourably than others.

It's not enough for companies to brag about their social responsibility efforts; they must live up to the expectations they raise or face the consequences. When herbal tea maker Celestial Seasonings <*www.celestialseasonings.com*> ignored its advertised image of environmental stewardship by poisoning prairie dogs on its property, it incurred customers' wrath.[32] Customers prefer to do business with companies they trust and, even more important, don't want to do business with those they don't trust. Companies earn customers' trust by demonstrating credibility over time; they can lose it at any point.

Maple Leaf Foods takes its responsibility to customers seriously. In 2009, the company announced a voluntary recall of more than 1,000 cases of wieners that were distributed without abiding by the company's new food-safety guidelines. Said McCain, "Notwithstanding the exceptionally low risk this represents, Maple Leaf is committed to maintaining the most stringent standards and we intend to live by those standards so consumers can have absolute confidence in the integrity of our products."[33]

Responsibility to Investors[34]

Some people believe that before you can do good, you must do well (i.e., make a lot of money); others believe that by doing good, you can also do well. What we do know is that ethical behaviour is good for shareholder wealth. It does not subtract from the bottom line, but rather adds to it. On the other hand, unethical behaviour does cause financial damage. Those cheated by financial wrongdoing are the shareholders themselves. Unethical behaviour may seem to work for the short term, but it guarantees eventual failure. For example, in the early 2000s, accounting irregularities reported at Nortel Networks Corp., once the most-traded stock in Canada, damaged investor trust and subsequently the company's share value. Years later, the company was still being scrutinized amid rumours of bankruptcy when its share price was under $1. In 2009, the company declared bankruptcy.

Unfortunately, we continue to read of individual business people who abuse the trust that individual investors have placed in them. Some high-profile examples in recent years include financiers Earl Jones and Bernard Madoff. Jones plead guilty to defrauding 158 clients of $50 million in a Ponzi scheme that he operated for more than two decades. He was sentenced to 11 years in prison. Madoff is serving a 150-year sentence after admitting he squandered tens of billions of dollars in investors' money. Madoff's crimes left many investors impoverished and some charities decimated.

Many investors believe that it makes financial as well as moral sense to invest in companies that plan ahead to create a better environment. By choosing to put their money into companies whose goods and services benefit the community and the environment, investors can improve their own financial health while improving society's health.

Insider Trading[35]

insider trading An unethical activity in which insiders use private company information to further their own fortunes or those of their family and friends.

A few investors, known as inside traders, have chosen unethical means to improve their own financial health. **Insider trading** uses private company information to further insiders' own fortunes, or those of their family and friends. For example, Andrew Rankin, a former executive with RBC Dominion Securities <*www.rbcds.com*>, was charged by the Ontario Securities Commission (OSC) <*www.osc.gov.on.ca*> with ten counts of tipping his friend, Daniel Duic. Investigators found that Rankin had alerted Duic to upcoming mergers and acquisitions before they were publicly known. The OSC alleges that, based on this information, Duic bought and sold investments in ten companies and saw his investment increase following the release of the merger and acquisition news. Duic agreed to pay just over $3 million in the form of a penalty, taxes, and lawyer's fees and to testify against Rankin. Under the Ontario Securities Act, Rankin was sentenced to six months in jail for Canada's first conviction for illegal stock tipping.

Responsibility to Employees

It's been said that the best social program in the world is a job. Businesses have a responsibility to create jobs if they want to grow. Once they have done so, they must see to it that hard work and talent are fairly rewarded. Employees need realistic hope of a better future, which comes only through a chance for upward mobility. Studies have shown that what most influences a company's effectiveness and financial performance is human resource management.[36] We'll discuss human resource management in Chapter 12.

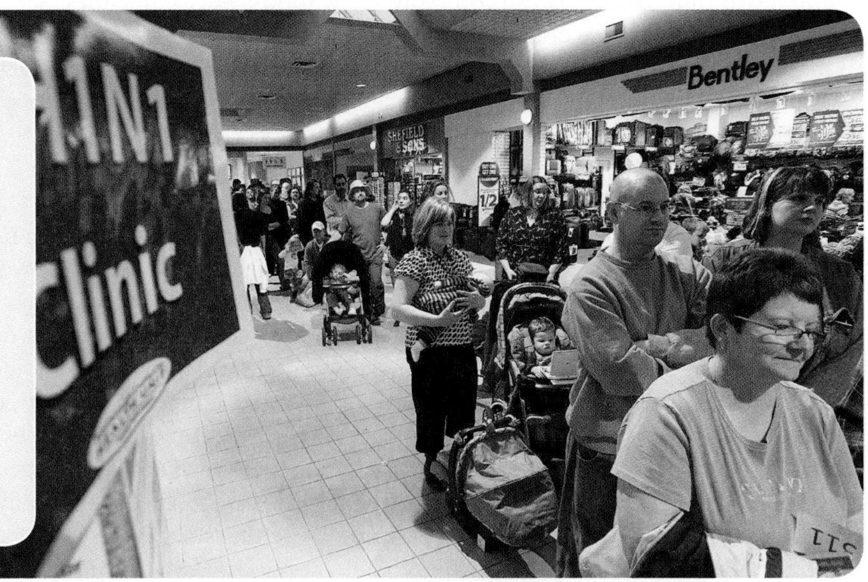

▶ High-risk groups lined up for hours at public clinics when the H1N1 vaccine was released in October 2009, while many non-high-risk Canadians (e.g., some professional athletes and private-clinic members) received the vaccine courtesy of their employers. For weeks following the initial rollout, thousands of those on the priority list did not receive the vaccine due to the shortage. Were the actions of these employers ethical?

If a company treats employees with respect, they usually will respect the company as well. That respect can make a huge difference in a company's bottom line. In their book *Contented Cows Give Better Milk,* Bill Catlette and Richard Hadden compared "contented cow" companies with "common cow" companies. The companies with the contented employees outgrew their counterparts by four to one for more than ten years. The "contented cow" companies out-earned the "common cow" companies by nearly $40 billion and generated 800,000 more jobs. The authors attribute this difference in performance to the commitment and caring that the companies demonstrate for their employees.[37]

When employees feel they have been treated unfairly, they often strike back. Getting even is one of the most powerful incentives for good people to do bad things. Not many disgruntled workers are desperate enough to resort to violence in the workplace, but a great number do relieve their frustrations in more subtle ways, such as blaming mistakes on others, not accepting responsibility for decision making, manipulating budgets and expenses, making commitments they intend to ignore, hoarding resources, doing the minimum needed to get by, making results look better than they are, or even stealing. The loss of employee commitment, confidence, and trust in the company and its management can be very costly indeed. Employee larceny costs Canadian businesses billions of dollars every year. According to the Association of Certified Fraud Examiners, fraud and theft cost employers an average of $9 a day per employee, with the average organization losing about five percent of its total annual revenue to thieves.[38] On average, most victimized firms lose around $159,000, up more than one-third since 2002.[39] Canadian retailers alone are relieved of approximately $8 million of merchandise every day, with employees out-stealing the shoplifters.[40] You will read more about issues that affect employee–management relations in Chapter 13.

Responsibility to Society

One of business's responsibilities to society is to create new wealth, which is disbursed to employees, suppliers, shareholders, and other stakeholders. But if businesses don't create wealth, who will? Non-profit organizations play an important role in distributing the funds they receive from donors, governments, and even their own investments in billions of shares in publicly-held companies. As those stock prices increase, more funds are available to benefit society. However, for stock prices to increase, the publicly-held company must be successful. For companies to prosper, they need to provide customers with safe products. Businesses today, more than ever before, need to develop long-term profitable relationships with their customers. There is no question that repeat business is based on buying safe and value-laden goods and services, at reasonable prices.

Businesses are also partially responsible for promoting social justice. Many companies believe that business has a role in building a community that goes well beyond giving back. To them, charity is not enough. Their social contributions include cleaning up the environment, building community toilets, providing computer lessons, caring for the elderly, and supporting children from low-income families.

As concern about global warming increased, the green movement emerged in nearly every aspect of daily life. What makes a product "green"? Some believe that a product's carbon footprint (the amount of carbon released during

From left to right, Chiefs Na'Moks of the Wet'suwet'en Nation, Martin Louie of Nadleh Whut'en, and Jackie Thomas of the Saik'az Nation attend Enbridge Inc.'s <www.enbridge.com> annual meeting where they voiced their opposition to the proposed $5.5 billion Enbridge Northern Gateway pipeline. The pipeline would transport crude oil from Alberta to the B.C. coastline for transport to Asian markets (e.g., China) and to the U.S. west coast. There is concern that the pipeline could damage natural resources as the pipeline would cross lands belonging to dozens of First Nations groups, as well as three fault lines.[43] Was the pipeline approved?

production, distribution, consumption, and disposal) defines how green it is. Many variables contribute to a product's carbon footprint. The carbon footprint of a package of, say, frozen corn includes not only the carbon released by the fertilizer to grow the corn but also the carbon in the fertilizer itself, the gas used to run the farm equipment and transport the corn to market, the electricity to make the plastic packages and power the freezers, and so on.

No specific guidelines define the carbon footprints of products, businesses, or individuals or outline how to communicate them to consumers. PepsiCo presents carbon information with a label on bags of cheese-and-onion potato chips, for example, that says "75 grams of CO_2."[41] Simple enough, but what does it mean? (We don't know either.)

The focus of this book is on business; however, one should not forget that government decisions also affect business and society. The Walkerton, Ontario, *E. coli* tragedy that killed seven people and made half of the town's 5,000 residents ill from contaminated water is one such example. After hearing testimony from more than 100 witnesses over nine months, Justice O'Connor concluded that the catastrophe could have been prevented if brothers Stan and Frank Koebel, who ran Walkerton's water system, had properly chlorinated the water and if the Ontario government had heeded warnings that cuts to the provincial environment ministry were resulting in ineffective testing.[42] Clearly, the Koebel brothers were responsible for their individual decisions.

Responsibility to the Environment[44]

Businesses are often criticized for their role in destroying the environment. Such was the case when images of the slow death of 500 ducks on a toxic oil sands tailings pond in northern Alberta flashed around the world. This led to federal and provincial charges against Syncrude Canada Ltd. <*www.syncrude.ca*>, which was charged under the Alberta Environmental Enhancement and Protection Act and the federal Migratory Birds Convention Act. While Syncrude attempted to rescue some of the ducks that landed in the tailings pond, only a handful were taken out of the water for cleaning and none survived. The Analyzing Management Decisions case near the end of this chapter discusses the implications of an oil spill in Alberta.

We are seeing more efforts being made to reverse years of neglect to the environment. For example, the Sydney Tar Ponds in Nova Scotia are North America's largest hazardous waste site. More than 80 years of discharges from the steel-producing coke ovens near the harbour filled Muggah Creek with contaminated sediments. By 1983, Environment Canada had pinpointed the coke ovens as the major source of pollution in the Sydney area. Fishing was banned and the Sydney lobster fishery was closed. Statistics show that the area has significantly higher levels of cancers and other debilitating diseases than anywhere else in Canada. Two decades later, there have been several attempts and more than $100 million spent to clean up this toxic site. In May 2004, the governments of Canada and Nova Scotia committed $400 million to the cleanup. It is expected that this cleanup will take ten years.

Some governments are taking more responsibility for improving the environment, as highlighted

▸ BP Oil <*www.bp.com*> will pay $7.8 billion to settle with thousands of individuals and businesses affected by the 2010 Gulf of Mexico spill. Considered to be the world's biggest accidental oil leak, the explosion killed eleven oil rig workers and unleashed an estimated 4.9 million barrels of oil before the damaged well was capped three months later. There has also been extensive damage to marine and wildlife habitat. Pollution fines under the U.S. Clean Water Act are expected to also be in the billions.

GREENBOX

To Carbon Tax or Not?

The carbon tax, sometimes called a green tax, can refer to any number of measures designed to increase the cost of burning fossil fuels like oil, gas, and coal. In basic terms, it is a tax on greenhouse gas emissions levied with the aim of reducing pollution to combat climate change. Those emissions spewing from exhaust pipes or industrial smokestacks are made up primarily of carbon dioxide, which is produced when fossil fuels containing carbon—such as coal, natural gas, or diesel—are burned. "It's a really important tool for fighting climate change," says Clare Demerse, a senior policy analyst with the Pembina Institute <*www.pembina.org*>. "It's a way to make sure pollution carries a cost."

A carbon tax would provide an incentive to stop the social harm and move to more positive alternatives. The idea is both to change behaviour (e.g., turn people and businesses away from "bad" fossil fuels and toward "good" clean alternatives) and to set aside a fund to help smooth the transition to a cleaner economy.

A carbon tax can be (1) an across-the-board levy on all fuels based on CO_2 (carbon dioxide) emissions, (2) applied to just the businesses that produce carbon emissions, leaving it up to them whether or not to pass costs along to consumers, or (3) directly levied on consumers. Another alternative is a "revenue-neutral carbon tax" in which any levies extracted from a particular sector (e.g., transportation) would be given back in some other form of subsidy or tax break, that would reward more fuel-efficient behaviour. The most common form of this has been the fairly modest tax breaks on small and hybrid cars.

The tax is described in terms of a dollar value per tonne of gas produced. This can then be translated into a cost on the fuel that emits the greenhouse gases (e.g., 10 cents a litre on gasoline). The Pembina Institute and the David Suzuki Foundation <*www.davidsuzuki.org*> say that Canada needs a carbon tax of $30 per tonne immediately, at least $50 per tonne by 2015 and $75 per tonne by 2020 for the country to do its part in cutting greenhouse gas pollution.

Opposition to carbon taxes includes suggestions that they are merely a cash grab to bolster government revenue and will just push jobs and business to cheaper jurisdictions. In Alberta, for example, where oil and gas production is such a strong segment of the economy, there is little support for any kind of across-the-board carbon tax. Depending on how the tax is introduced, and whether it is accompanied by tax cuts, financial assistance for people with lower incomes, or other incentives to encourage consumers to make choices that reduce pollution, its costs may not be distributed evenly in the economy.

Quebec was the first province to introduce a carbon tax in 2007. The levy was just under one cent for a litre of gas, with funds collected being directed to pay for energy-saving initiatives such as improvements to public transit. British Columbia followed in 2008, taxing carbon-based fuels such as gasoline, diesel, natural gas, and home heating fuel, at a rate of $10 per tonne of greenhouse gases generated. The carbon tax will reach $30 per tonne in 2012. This works out to 7.24 cents per litre. The provincial government said that all carbon tax revenue—about $1.8 billion over three years—will be returned to British Columbians through reductions in income and business taxes. To soften the impact of the carbon tax, the government gave a $100 climate action dividend to each British Columbian.

Compare these taxes to those imposed in Finland, where drivers pay a carbon surtax of about 8 cents per litre. In Sweden, people pay almost 40 cents extra per litre in carbon taxes at the pumps. What do you think? Could governments, businesses, and consumers be doing more? Do you agree or disagree with a green tax?

Sources: "Just What Is a Carbon Tax?" CBC News, 29 September 2008, www.cbc.ca/news/canadavotes/story/2008/09/19/f-carbontaxprimer.html; "Carbon Taxes: Cash Grab or Climate Saviour?" CBC News, 19 June, 2008, www.cbc.ca/canada/story/2008/06/18/f-carbon-tax.html; and "B.C. Carbon Tax Kicks in on Canada Day," CBC News, 1 July 2008, www.cbc.ca/canada/british-columbia/story/2008/06/30/bc-carbon-tax-effective.html.

in the Green Box. Businesses are also taking more responsibility for helping to make their own environment a better place. Environmental efforts may increase the company's costs, but they also may allow the company to charge higher prices, to increase market share, or both. For example, Ciba Specialty Chemicals (now a part of BASF <*www.basf.com*>), a Swiss textile-dye manufacturer, developed dyes that require less salt than traditional dyes. Since used dye solutions must be treated before they are released into rivers or streams, having less salt means lower water-treatment costs.

Patents protect Ciba's low-salt dyes, so the company can charge more for its dyes than other companies can charge for theirs. Ciba's experience illustrates that, just as a new machine enhances labour productivity, lowering environmental costs can add value to a business.

Environmental quality is a public good; that is, everyone gets to enjoy it regardless of who pays for it. The challenge for companies is to find the right public good that will appeal to their target markets. Many corporations are publishing reports that document their net social contribution. To do that, a company must measure its positive social contributions and subtract its negative social impacts. We will discuss that process next.

Social Auditing

It is nice to talk about having organizations become more socially responsible. It is also encouraging to see some efforts made toward creating safer products, cleaning up the environment, designing more honest advertising, and treating women and minorities fairly. But is there any way to measure whether organizations are making social responsibility an integral part of top management's decision making? The answer is yes, and the term that represents that measurement is *social auditing.*

social audit
A systematic evaluation of an organization's progress toward implementing programs that are socially responsible and responsive.

A **social audit** is a systematic evaluation of an organization's progress toward implementing programs that are socially responsible and responsive. One of the major problems of conducting a social audit is establishing procedures for measuring a firm's activities and its effects on society. What should be measured? Many social audits consider such things as workplace issues, the environment, product safety, community relations, and respecting the rights of local people.[45] See Figure 5.5 for an outline of business activities that could be considered socially responsible.

triple-bottom line (TBL, 3BL, or People, Planet, Profit)
A framework for measuring and reporting corporate performance against economic, social, and environmental parameters.

A commitment to corporate social responsibility implies a commitment to some form of **triple-bottom line ("TBL," "3BL," or "People, Planet, Profit")** reporting.[46] TBL is used as a framework for measuring and reporting corporate performance against economic, social, and environmental parameters.[47] Corporations that use TBL focus on the economic value they add, but also on the environmental and social value they add and destroy.[48]

There is some question as to whether positive actions should be added (e.g., charitable donations and pollution control efforts) and negative effects subtracted (e.g., layoffs and overall pollution levels) to get a net social contribution. Or should only positive actions be recorded? In general, social responsibility is becoming one of the aspects of corporate success that business evaluates, measures, and develops.

Figure 5.5

Socially Responsible Business Activities

Community-related activities such as participating in local fundraising campaigns, donating employee time to various non-profit organizations and participating in urban planning and development
Employee-related activities such as establishing equal opportunity programs, offering flextime and other benefits, promoting job enrichment, ensuring job safety, and conducting employee development programs; you will learn more about such programs in Chapter 12
Political activities (such as taking a position on nuclear safety, gun control, pollution control, consumer protection, and other social issues) and working more closely with local, provincial, and federal government officials
Support for higher education, the arts, and other non-profit social agencies
Consumer activities such as ensuring product safety, creating truthful advertising, handling complaints promptly, setting fair prices, and conducting extensive consumer education programs

In addition to the social audits conducted by the companies themselves, there are four types of groups that serve as watchdogs regarding how well companies enforce their ethical and social responsibility policies:

1. *Socially conscious investors* insist that a company extend its own high standards to all its suppliers. Social responsibility investing (SRI) is on the rise. Be aware that SRI is highly subjective. Different people have different values, so what is ethically appropriate for one may not be the case for another.
2. *Environmentalists* apply pressure by publicly identifying companies that do not abide by the environmentalists' standards.
3. *Union officials* hunt down violations and force companies to comply to avoid negative publicity.
4. *Customers* take their business elsewhere if a company demonstrates unethical or socially irresponsible practices.

What these groups look for constantly changes as the world view changes. One important thing to remember is that it is not enough for a company to be right when it comes to ethics and social responsibility. It also has to *convince* its customers and society that it's right.

Sustainable Development[49]

Sustainable development means implementing a process that integrates environmental, economic, and social considerations into decision making. This reinforces the World Commission on Environment and Development's conclusion that development should be sustainable for the benefit of current and future generations. Such a focus has created opportunities for new ventures such as Revive Enterprise <*www.reviveenterprise.co.uk*>. Corporations that wish to eliminate no-longer-needed facility assets (e.g., chairs, desks, etc.) can deal with Revive, which provides a cost-effective alternative to having these items removed. These items are then redistributed to needy non-profit organizations, schools, and health clinics that then receive critically needed equipment and supplies, and planet Earth is given relief from the pressures of expanding population and waste.

sustainable development Implementing a process that integrates environmental, economic, and social considerations into decision making.

In another example, Canada's two largest grocery chains, Loblaw Companies Limited <*www.loblaws.ca*> and Sobeys <*www.sobeys.com*>, have eliminated free plastic bags at their checkout counters. The plastic bags will be available only on request, and will cost five cents each. "It represents the next natural step forward as we continue to acknowledge and respond to Canadians' desire to support environmental initiatives," Loblaw executive chairman Galen Weston Jr. said. Most of the proceeds from the sale of Loblaw's bags will be used to cover the cost of its plastic

Ethical Funds <*www.ethicalfunds.com*> believes that the best possible returns can be achieved by investing in companies that combine strong financial performance with positive social, environmental, and governance performance. The company does not invest in corporations that derive a significant portion of their income from military weapons, tobacco, or nuclear power. Would you invest in companies on the basis of their environmental, social, and governance performance?

SPOTLIGHT ON SMALL BUSINESS

An Eco-Friendly Solution for Dog Owners

Every year, up to a trillion plastic bags are deposited into landfills, where it is estimated that they can take up to 1,000 years to breakdown, with millions still ending up in our waterways, trees, and oceans. Over 100,000 sea turtles and other marine animals die every year because they mistake plastic bags for food. Many municipalities have taken action by banning plastic bags, forcing consumers to switch to reusable cloth bags. This has left dog owners with the challenge of cleaning up after their dogs without the use of these convenient bags.

A business idea was born when grocery stores started charging for plastic bags. In 2010, co-owner Abby Gnanendran started Montreal-based Earth Rated PoopBags <*earthrated.com*>, which sells biodegradable PoopBags for dogs. Two years later, these bags are carried in 900 pet stores across North America and parts of Europe.

The company was created to help care for the environment while at the same time taking care of a dog's poop, both at an economical price. (For example, the suggested retail price for an eight-roll box containing 120 biodegradable bags is $5.99, which translates into pennies a poop.) Unscented compostable bags are made from 100 percent corn-based renewable resources, and they degrade in as little as 40 days. There are also scented biodegradable bags (with or without handles) that are completely broken apart into carbon dioxide and water in as little as 24 months. Both types of bags—compostable and biodegradable bags—meet the eco-certification standard.

Sources: "Our Products," Earth Rated PoopBags, 9 May 2012, http://earthrated.com/our-products/; "About the Bags," Earth Rated PoopBags, 9 May 2012, http://earthrated.com/about-the-bags/; and Denise Deveau, "Cleaning up in pet stores," *Financial Post,* 2 April 2012, FP1, 5.

bag reduction program. As well, "we'll take some of the money and invest it in lower food prices . . . [and] in our sustainability projects and a couple of environmental charities," said Weston.

Other companies have also implemented similar actions. The Liquor Control Board of Ontario (LCBO) has ended its use of plastic shopping bags, offering shoppers paper bags instead. Furniture retailer IKEA Canada <*www.ikea.com/ca*> charges five cents for plastic bags, donating proceeds to Tree Canada to help plant trees throughout the country. Would you shop more at a retailer that supports such initiatives?

With the elimination of plastic bags, Earth Rated PoopBags, the focus of this chapter's Spotlight on Small Business, saw an opportunity. Review the box to learn how a messy business can also be sustainable.

PROGRESS ASSESSMENT

- What is corporate social responsibility, and how does it relate to a business's major stakeholders?
- How does the strategic approach differ from the pluralist approach?
- What is a social audit, and what kinds of activities does it monitor?
- Which company—Maple Leaf Foods or BP Oil—best demonstrated socially responsible behaviour?

LO 6 Discuss the importance of ethical behaviour and social responsibility in global markets.

INTERNATIONAL ETHICS AND SOCIAL RESPONSIBILITY

Ethical problems and issues of social responsibility are not unique to Canada. Top business and government leaders in Japan were caught in a major "influence-peddling" (read bribery) scheme in Japan. Similar charges have been brought against top officials in South Korea, the People's Republic of China, Italy, Brazil, Pakistan, and Zaire.

What is new about the moral and ethical standards by which government leaders are being judged? They are much stricter than in previous years.

Government leaders are not the only ones being held to higher standards. Many businesses are demanding socially responsible behaviour from their international suppliers by ensuring that suppliers do not violate domestic human rights and environmental standards. For example, Sears <*www.sears.ca*> will not import products made by Chinese prison labour. Clothing manufacturer Phillips–Van Heusen <*www.pvh.com*> said it would cancel orders from suppliers that violate its ethical, environmental, and human rights code. McDonald's denied rumours that one of its suppliers grazed cattle on cleared rain forest land, but wrote a ban on the practice anyway.

▸ Fair-trade products can include coffee, tea, cocoa, clothing, flowers, and crafts. Do you ever look for the FAIRTRADE Mark to confirm if you are buying a fair-trade product?

Fair trade is a growing social movement dedicated to making sure that producers in developing countries are paid a fair price for the goods we consume (rather than exploiting desperately poor people), resulting in more money in their pockets.[50] Put another way, it is a strategy for poverty alleviation and sustainable development with the purpose of creating opportunities for producers who have been disadvantaged or marginalized by the traditional economic model.[51] Fairtrade Canada <*fairtrade.ca*> is responsible for certifying that Canadian products bearing the FAIRTRADE Mark meet international Fairtrade standards. If the product bears the FAIRTRADE Mark on the package, then it means that it has conformed to Fairtrade standards and it has contributed to the development of disadvantaged producers and workers.[52]

In contrast to companies that demand that their suppliers demonstrate socially responsible behaviour are those that have been criticized for exploiting workers in less-developed countries. Nike, the world's largest athletic shoe company, has been accused by human rights and labour groups of treating its workers poorly while lavishing millions of dollars on star athletes to endorse its products. Nike is working to improve its reputation, in part by joining forces with Patagonia, Gap <*www.gapinc.com*>, and five other companies and six leading anti-sweatshop groups to create a single set of labour standards with a common factory-inspection system. The goal of the Joint Initiative on Corporate Accountability & Workers' Rights is to replace the current multitude of approaches with something that is easier and cheaper to use, in the hope that more companies will adopt the standards as well.[53]

The fairness of requiring international suppliers to adhere to domestic ethical standards is not as clear-cut as you might think. For example, what could be considered a gift in one culture is considered a bribe in another. Is it always ethical for companies to demand compliance with the standards of their own countries? What about countries in which child labour is an accepted part of the society and families depend on the children's salaries for survival? What about foreign companies doing business in Canada? Should these companies have to comply with Canadian ethical standards? What about multinational corporations? Since they span different societies, do they have to conform to all of the societies' standards? None of these questions are easy to answer, but they give you some idea of the complexity of social responsibility issues in international markets.

▸ Ethical responsibility does not stop at North American borders. Many colleges and universities have adopted standards that prohibit their schools' names or logos from being displayed on apparel made in foreign sweatshops. Sweatshops are factories with very low pay and poor health and safety standards. Would you be willing to buy products from a manufacturer that produces its goods in substandard facilities in foreign nations?

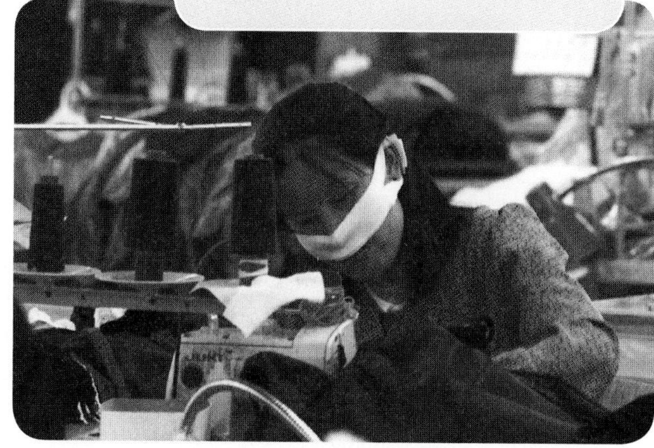

SUMMARY

Explain why obeying the law is only the first step in behaving ethically.

Ethics goes beyond obeying laws. It also involves abiding by the moral standards accepted by society.

How is legality different from ethics?

Ethics reflects people's proper relation with one another. Legality is more limiting; it refers only to laws written to protect people from fraud, theft, and violence.

What influences our ethical decision making?

Ethical behaviour begins with you and me. We are influenced by our society and what it considers to be ethical, the behaviour of others (both socially and in a work setting), and by our own personal values and beliefs.

Ask the three questions to answer when faced with a potentially unethical action.

It can be difficult to maintain a balance between ethics and other goals such as pleasing stakeholders or advancing your career.

How can we tell if our business decisions are ethical?

We can put our business decisions through an ethics check by asking three questions: (1) Is it legal? (2) Is it balanced? and (3) How will it make me feel? Companies (and individuals) that develop strong ethics codes and use these three questions have a better chance than most of behaving ethically.

Describe management's role in setting ethical standards.

Some managers think that ethics is an individual issue that has nothing to do with management, while others believe that ethics has everything to do with management.

What is management's role in setting ethical standards?

Managers often set formal ethical standards, but more important are the messages they send through their actions. Management's tolerance or intolerance of ethical misconduct influences employees more than written ethics codes do.

Distinguish between compliance-based and integrity-based ethics codes, and list the six steps that can be considered when setting up a corporate ethics code.

Business ethics can be improved if companies follow a six-step process.

What is the difference between compliance-based and integrity-based ethics codes?

Whereas compliance-based ethics codes are concerned with avoiding legal punishment, integrity-based ethics codes define the organization's guiding values, create an environment that supports ethically sound behaviour, and stress a shared accountability among employees.

What are the six steps that can improve business ethics?

The six steps are as follows: (1) top management must adopt and support an explicit corporate code of conduct; (2) employees must understand that expectations for ethical behaviour begin at the top and that senior management expects all employees to act accordingly; (3) managers and others must be trained to consider the ethical implications of all business decisions;

(4) an ethics office must be set up, and phone lines to the office should be established; (5) outsiders such as suppliers, subcontractors, distributors, and customers must be told about the ethics program; and (6) the ethics code must be enforced.

Which step is the most critical in this six-step process?
The last step is most critical because a company's ethics policy must be enforced to be taken seriously.

Define corporate social responsibility and compare corporations' responsibilities to various stakeholders.

Corporate social responsibility goes beyond merely being ethical.

Define corporate social responsibility.
Corporate social responsibility is the concern businesses have toward stakeholders.

How do businesses demonstrate corporate responsibility toward stakeholders?
Business is responsible to five types of stakeholders: (1) it must *satisfy customers* with goods and services of real value; (2) it must make money for its *investors;* (3) it must create jobs for *employees,* maintain job security, and see that hard work and talent are fairly rewarded; (4) it must create new wealth for *society* and promote social justice, and (5) it must contribute to making its *environment* a better place.

How are a company's social responsibility efforts measured?
A corporate social audit measures an organization's progress toward social responsibility. Some people believe the audit should add together the organization's positive actions and then subtract the negative effects to get a net social benefit.

Discuss the importance of ethical behaviour and social responsibility in global markets.

Social responsibility issues are complex in global markets.

How can companies influence ethical behaviour and social responsibility in global markets?
Many businesses are demanding socially responsible behaviour from their international suppliers by making sure their suppliers do not violate human rights and environmental standards. Companies like Sears and Phillips–Van Heusen will not import products from companies that do not meet their ethical and social responsibility standards.

KEY TERMS

compliance-based ethics codes
corporate philanthropy
corporate policy
corporate responsibility
corporate social initiatives
corporate social responsibility (CSR)
ethics
insider trading
integrity-based ethics codes
social audit
sustainable development
triple-bottom line (TBL, 3BL, or People, Planet, Profit)
whistleblowers

CRITICAL THINKING

1. Think of a situation in which you have been involved that tested your ethical behaviour. For example, perhaps your best friend forgot about a term paper due the next day and asked you if he could copy and hand in a paper you wrote for another instructor last semester. What are your alternatives, and what are the consequences of each one? Would it have been easier to resolve the dilemma if you had asked yourself the three questions in the ethics check? Try answering them now and see if you would have made a different choice.
2. In Chapter 4 we discussed how the granting of subprime mortgages contributed to a crisis in the financial markets. Was it ethical for firms to provide mortgages to individuals that were unlikely to be able to afford them? How about for investors?
3. Companies appear to act with corporate responsibility but the underlying motive seems to be to increase profits. Does this motive undermine the value of corporate responsibility or is it only the actions that are important? That is, do you think less of a company if you know it is being responsible only to increase its profits?
4. What do you think of the phrase, "It's not personal, it's just business?" Do you agree or disagree with this statement if it were to be used to justify a business decision? Explain.

DEVELOPING WORKPLACE SKILLS

1. Newspapers and magazines are full of stories about individuals and businesses that are not socially responsible. What about those individuals and organizations that do take social responsibility seriously? We don't normally read or hear about them. Do a little investigative reporting of your own. Identify a public interest group in your community and identify its officers, objectives, amount of financial support, and size and characteristics of membership. List some examples of its recent actions and/or accomplishments. Consider environmental groups, animal protection groups, political action committees, and so on. (If you don't know where to start, call your local Chamber of Commerce, the Better Business Bureau, or local government agencies for help). Try using one of the Internet search engines to help you find more information.
2. You are the manager of a coffee house called the Morning Cup. One of your best employees wants to be promoted to a managerial position; however, the owner is grooming his son for the promotion your employee seeks. The owner's act of nepotism may hurt a valuable employee's chances for advancement, but complaining may hurt your own chances for promotion. What do you do?
3. You are a salesperson at a clothing store. You walk into the storage room to start ticketing some clothes that came in that morning and see a co-worker quickly take some pants from a box and put them into her knapsack. Your colleague does not see you enter the room. What do you do? Do you leave and say nothing to your employer? Do you say something to your colleague? Is your responsibility to your organization, your colleague, or both? What might be the implications of your decision?
4. Contact a local corporation and ask for a copy of its written ethics code. Would you classify its code as compliance-based or integrity-based? Explain.

ANALYZING MANAGEMENT DECISIONS

CNR Charged with Spill

Canadian National Railway (CNR) was charged by Alberta Environment <*environment.alberta.ca*> with failing to take all reasonable measures to remedy and confine the spill from a train derailment into a northern Alberta lake in August 2005. In the incident, 43 cars derailed next to Wabamun Lake, west of Edmonton, spilling almost 800,000 litres of heavy fuel and a potentially cancer-causing wood preservative. The environmental offence is punishable by a maximum fine of $500,000.

Alberta Environment spokeswoman Kim Hunt said the charges were laid by Alberta Justice after a review.

"It's the law in Alberta that the polluter pays," Hunt told the Canadian Press. After the spill, Alberta Environment issued an Environmental Protection Order to CNR. The company was ordered to clean up the spill, begin long-term environmental planning and monitoring of the area, and keep the public informed on its progress. Residents of Wabamun were told in June 2006 that they could use the lake again for swimming and boating, but not for washing dishes, cleaning vegetables, or bathing. At that time, CNR said in a statement that it was committed to the monitoring and testing of the lake, and announced that the cleanup was expected to be completed by the end of the month.

The spill initially left a slick on the surface of the lake and coated migrating waterfowl. While most of the oil has been removed, residents claim that balls of tar still occasionally wash up onshore. Wabamun Lake residents' committee chairman Doug Goss said that while CNR has already spent $75 million removing the mess, he hopes in future that the provincial government will clean up spills immediately and send the bill to the company responsible.

CNR offered nearly $7.5 million on a sliding scale to the area's 1,600 residents. The payments, which ranged from $1,500 to $27,000 for those closest to the spill, were in recognition of loss of property use as a result of the derailment. The Paul First Nation, whose reserve is on the western shore of the lake, also filed a multi-million-dollar lawsuit against CNR, Ottawa, and the province, alleging that the spill destroyed its traditional way of life. In September 2008, CNR reached a $10 million settlement with the band. "This money will play a major part in implementing the band's business development plan, which we are confident will result in a much stronger economic situation for our people," said Chief Daniel Paul. Earlier in 2008, three charges were laid by Environment Canada and Fisheries and Oceans Canada <*www.dfo-mpo.gc.ca*> against CNR: one for allegedly depositing a substance harmful to migratory birds into a lake and the other two for alleged disruption of a fish habitat.

Sources: "Canadian National Railway to Pay $10M to Alta. Band in Derailment Along Lake," CANOE Inc., 12 September 2008, http://cnews.canoe.ca/CNEWS/Politics/2008/09/12/6751421-cp.html; "Oil Spill Nets CN Rail Three Charges from Feds," *Canadian Geographic,* 18 March 2008, www.canadiangeographic.ca/cea/archives/news_item.asp?articleid=493; Gordon Kent and Kelly Cryderman, "Wabamun Residents Unhappy with CN Charge," CanWest News Service, 6 June 2006, www.canada.com/topics/news/national/story.html?id=14a77881-cc1b-4ec0-90a7-fd86af5a9c7c&k=58041; and "CN Rail Charged in Oil Spill at Alta. Lake," The Canadian Press, 6 June 2006, http://sympaticomsn.ctv.ca/servlet/ArticleNews/story/CTVNews/20060605/cn_wabamun_060506.

Discussion Questions

1. What stakeholders were impacted by this incident?
2. Conduct some research into this story. As a result of this derailment, what changes were implemented by CNR and Environment Alberta?
3. Do you feel that the costs associated with this incident are excessive? Explain.

PART 1 ENDS WITH:

DEALING WITH CHANGE

Adapting to Swings in Demand

Imagine that your local professional hockey or baseball team has not been winning many games in the last few years. We're sure that many of you can identify with that. Ticket prices are set and the season begins. Because of a few new people on the team, the team begins winning game after game and the demand for tickets goes up. The owners cannot raise the prices without creating great tumult among the fans, so the price remains stable. But an informal market (among fans) grows for tickets, often on the Internet. Prices for these tickets usually go up because interested purchasers may be willing to pay more than the ticket's face value. Revenue also goes up for the owners because they sell a lot more hot dogs and beverages.

But what happens if the team starts losing again? Demand for tickets falls. The owners begin losing money at the concession stand. What can the owners do to adjust? You can see how adapting to changes in demand are often difficult to do.

The same is true with auto sales. When gas prices go up dramatically, as they did in 2008, auto dealers find themselves with many large SUVs and light trucks in their inventories. This created opportunities as sales of subcompacts, compacts, and small sport utility vehicles jumped dramatically when consumers shifted sharply to more fuel-efficient models because of the gas-price shock. For example, General Motors of Canada Ltd. reported that sales of the small Pontiac Wave and the Chevrolet Aveo models rose 19 percent and almost 23 percent respectively. Toyota Canada Inc. noted sales of its hybrid Prius rose 137 percent.

What other examples could you cite that show the lag between changes in supply and/or demand and the reaction by business people?

By scanning the business environment, proactive businesses adapt to changes in the marketplace when developing their products. With gas prices increasing in 2012, one might expect to see a decrease in demand for larger vehicles. The reverse is true. Rising gas prices are contributing to what could be the biggest annual sales increase in almost three decades. Part of the growth is coming from buyers trading in older vehicles for more fuel-efficient cars and trucks, said Reid Bigland, president of Chrysler Canada Inc. and head of U.S. sales for Chrysler. Rather than downsizing, people are "trading in SUVs for more fuel-efficient SUVs, pickup trucks for more fuel-efficient pickup trucks, because on average if you look at today's vehicle versus five years ago they are all up 20 to 30 percent in fuel economy, regardless of make," he said. "People are still demanding more fuel efficiency in their vehicles without sacrificing space and functionality."

Not everyone wants a truck. "With gas prices hitting record highs last month, we saw an increasing number of Canadian consumers choosing cars," said Dianne Craig, president and CEO, Ford of Canada. However, its fuel-efficient vehicles did well, with car sales increasing 5.1 percent year over year, offset by a nine percent decline in truck sales. "Ford has invested heavily in fuel-efficient gas engines, hybrids, plug-in hybrids, and electric vehicle technology—we like to call this the power of choice."

Sources: Sunny Freeman, "Chrysler reclaims top sales spot in April; Ford, Toyota sales fall from year-ago," Canadian Press, 1 May 2012, www.canadianbusiness.com/article/82266-chrysler-reclaims-top-sales-spot-in-april-ford-toyota-sales-fall-from-year-ago; Greg Keenan, "Gas price rise fuels strong car sales," *The Globe and Mail*, 5 April 2012, www.theglobeandmail.com/globe-investor/gas-price-rise-fuels-strong-car-sales/article2383384/; Tony Van Alphen, "Canadian Auto Sales Back in Gear," *The Toronto Star*, 2 August 2008, www.thestar.com/article/471543; and Victoria Murphy, "Seattle's Best Kept Secret," *Forbes*, 25 April 2005, 86–88.

REACHING BEYOND OUR BORDERS

How Does Canada Shape Up as an International Competitor?

How does Canada rank when compared to other industrialized countries? Canadian businesses have been criticized for not being more productive as productivity contributes to competitiveness. However, productivity is just one important component. Assessing international competitiveness is complex and open to varying opinions.

There are several indexes that attempt to measure competitiveness, and different criteria and weightings are used by the agencies that produce them. You will notice the importance of economic conditions and the role of government when evaluating a country's attractiveness. Let us consider two popular rankings.

The prestigious World Economic Forum (WEF) <*www.weforum.org*> produces the annual Global Competitiveness Report. The Growth Competitiveness Index is based on estimates of each country's ability to grow over the next five to ten years. Thus, economic conditions and institutions (e.g., government and financial markets) are reviewed. It was assessed that improving the sophistication and innovative potential of the private sector with greater R&D spending and producing goods and services higher on the value chain would enhance Canada's competitiveness and productive potential going into the future.

The International Institute for Management Development (IMD) produces the World Competitiveness Yearbook, which ranks the ability of a nation to provide an environment that sustains the competitiveness of enterprises. The ranking considers four criteria: economic performance, government efficiency, business efficiency, and infrastructure. In the past it has been assessed that while Canada ranks well on government policies conducive to competitiveness, Canada would rank higher if it had a more enterprising business community.

There is no single authority on ranking a country's competitiveness. These two examples highlight how different criteria are considered by different organizations. What should be of interest is that the criteria incorporate some of the concepts that are discussed in this textbook (e.g., economic performance).

Year	WEF's Growth Competitiveness Index	IMD's Overall Country Ranking
2012	14	6
2011	12	7
2010	10	7
2009	10	8
2008	13	8
2007	12	10
2006	14	5
2005	15	3

As a business student, be assured that the concepts that you are learning are in fact incorporated in business decision making.

The business environment is clearly influenced by factors such as economic performance and government policies. Canada's ranking is influenced not only by what happens domestically, but also by what happens internationally. Our fall in the rankings is influenced by our strengths and weaknesses (as assessed by these organizations) as measured against the strengths and weaknesses of other countries. As other countries improve their competitiveness, this will contribute to Canada's fall in the rankings if we do not improve accordingly.

Sources: "Table 3: The Global Competitiveness Index 2012–2013 rankings and 2011–2012 comparisons," World Economic Forum, 31 August 2012, http://www3.weforum.org/docs/CSI/2012-13/GCR_Rankings_2012-13.pdf; "IMD announces its 2012 World Competitiveness Rankings," IMD International, 31 May 2012, http://www.imd.org/news/IMD-announces-its-2012-World-Competitiveness-Rankings.cfm; "The World Competitiveness Scoreboard 2011," IMD International, 17 May 2011, www.imd.ch/research/publications/wcy/upload/scoreboard.pdf; "The Global Competitiveness Report 2011–2012," World Economic Forum, 7 September 2011, http://www3.weforum.org/en/initiatives/gcp/Global%20Competitiveness%20Report/index.htm; and "David Crane, "Innovation: Management Gap Means Canada Is Falling Behind," *The Montreal Gazette*, 22 May 2008, B5.

RUNNING CASE

Ron Foxcroft: The Dream for a Pealess Whistle

For successful Canadian entrepreneur and inventor Ron Foxcroft, it all started in 1982 when he purchased Fluke Transport, a Southern Ontario trucking business. The company slogan—If It's On Time . . . It's A "FLUKE"—was soon recognized throughout North America. Over the years, Ron diversified into new ventures and the Foxcroft Group of Companies now includes Fluke Transportation Group, Fluke Warehousing Inc., Foxcroft Capital Group, and Fox 40 International Inc.

The formation of Fox 40 International Inc. (Fox 40) is the result of a dream for a pealess whistle. When developing his first whistle, Ron was motivated by his knowledge and experience as an international basketball referee. Frustrated with faulty pea whistles, he spent three years of development with design consultant Chuck Shepherd, resulting in the creation of the Fox 40® Classic Whistle. (The whistle was named for Ron and that he was 40 when he applied for the patent.)

Introduced in 1987, this finely tuned precision instrument does not use a pea to generate sound. In fact, there are no moving parts. The patented design moves the air blast through three tuned chambers. This whistle, and all the subsequent whistles that have been introduced, is 100 percent constructed of high-impact ABS plastic so it is impervious to moisture. Wet or dry, Fox 40 Pealess Whistles cannot be overblown and never fail—the harder you blow, the louder the sound! They can be heard for miles and work in all conditions. They are faultless, reliable, and trusted.

Fox 40, a proudly Canadian company, dominates the global whistle industry. Tens of thousands of Fox 40 Whistles are produced monthly for shipment to 140 countries. A mould may be made offshore due to the cost savings (at least $100,000); however, Fox 40 owns all of its moulds. Approximately 90 percent of the company's products are made in Canada with select components coming from overseas markets. Final assembly occurs in Canada. While the first product was the Fox 40® Classic Whistle, the company's product lines now include (more) whistles, pro coaching boards, mouthguards, and a marine line. All of these products come with a lifetime guarantee.

When you consider the global business environment, the biggest threat is counterfeiters. There are at least five attempts per year to counterfeit the company's products. In response, Fox 40 aggressively polices its patents and trademarks. This includes monitoring offshore Web sites and catalogue publications for the misuse of Fox 40 intellectual property (IP). It is the company's responsibility to police and look for infringements to protect its IP and distributors worldwide. In addition, when a new product is introduced, an improvement to the new product is already in the vault, ready to be introduced at the first sign of counterfeiters.

Direct exporting is the strategy used to reach global markets. Rather than hiring someone to represent Fox 40 in a foreign country, Fox 40 employees attend global trade shows that service their targeted countries. At these trade shows, they look for three distributors that will deal directly with Fox 40. Orders are then directly exported to these distributors.

Even though offshoring would result in lower overall costs, the company insists on controlling the quality of its products by manufacturing them domestically. International customers especially value Fox 40's "Made in Canada" products as they connote quality. This is reinforced in international business trade shows where Fox 40 employees are often asked to confirm that their products continue to be made in Canada. At the recent ISPO MUNICH trade show, Ron observed that attendance seemed poorer than in the past in the Sourcing section. (ISPO MUNICH is an international leading sports business trade show. Every year, over 2,000 international exhibitors present their latest products to more than 80,000 visitors from over 100 countries. Exhibitors are categorized by segment: Outdoor, Ski, Action, Sportstyle, Performance Sports, and Sourcing.) This part of the trade show included association members from offshore countries such as China, Taiwan, and India. Ron believes that the lower turnout for some of the offshore exhibitors was in recognition of buyers' concerns with the decreasing quality of offshore-produced products. As a result, buyers are increasingly seeking high-standard, quality-made products from manufacturers such as Fox 40.

There has been some discussion in this textbook about the role of government in business. Ron's perspective is as follows: "Government has been a big help to me in business. I simply take what they do and do the exact opposite. They take 12 months to do what I do in 12 minutes. I have learned to have courage, 59-minute stand-up meetings, eliminate large committees, long-winded rhetoric, and keep my company lean and customer focused. If governments practiced this, they could be efficient too. However, most politicians are focused on re-election and not customer (citizen) service. Therefore, rather than make correct decisions they make popular decisions. Finally, too many rules in government inhibit innovation."

The company's GREEN PLAN highlights some of the areas where Fox 40 has taken steps to do its part to help to protect the environment. Examples include the following: reusing shipping containers whenever possible; the elimination of all clamshell packaging; bagging whistles and mouthguards in #4 biodegradable packaging; reducing the overall whistle package size by 20 percent to lessen the impact on the environment; and reducing the size of shipping boxes due to package dimension changes, resulting in less boxboard consumed and improved shipping methods. Sustainable packaging solutions include blister packaging made from recycled water and pop bottles, and using print material that contains recyclable and/or recycled post-consumer water material. Savings over nine months from the use of emission-free electricity in print production includes 93 trees preserved for the future, 128,746 litres of wastewater flow saved, and 15,289 kilograms of air emissions not generated.

Fox 40 is a strong community-conscious company and as a result invests heavily in corporate responsibility initiatives. Over the years, it has helped well over

100 organizations that include non-profits, charities, foundations (e.g., the Foxcroft Family Youth Foundation, which supports disadvantaged youth), hospitals, and educational institutions. Ron also believes that we should support the military and veterans. In recognition of Fox 40's contributions, Ron will be appointed as the 2012 Honorary Colonel in The Argyll and Sutherland Highlanders of Canada Reserve Troop.

While Ron has chaired several local high-profile capital campaigns—which include Hillfield Strathallan College, St. Joseph's Hospital, and McMaster University Athletics Capital Campaign—most of the company's contributions are anonymous. These anonymous contributions have often been directed to areas that have been deemed to have the greatest need. The Foxcrofts recognize that there are over 60,000 charities and non-profits in Ontario. By anonymously supporting some of those in need, they do not upset the many worthy ones that are left out.

Ron credits his customers and employees for the improvements to the original whistle. In his words, "When you are the best, you need to be better." This all starts with watching people to understand their needs. It involves developing products and services that customers might want. Making decisions along the way is challenging, but if you are successful, you can make a lot of customers very happy. Throughout this process, you need to have a vision, be focused, adapt to change, and never give up. His advice for future entrepreneurs, in the words of Walt Disney, are to, "Get a good idea and stay with it. Dog it, and work it until it's done and done right."

Sources: Ron Foxcroft, Founder and CEO, and Dave Foxcroft, President and COO, Fox 40 International Inc., in-person interviews, 25 June 2012, Hamilton, 905-561-4040; "Fox 40 Green Initiatives," Fox 40 International Inc., 1 June 2012, www.fox40world.com/index.cfm?pagepath=ABOUT_US/Green_Initiatives&id=4240; Roy Green, "Roy Green: A Terrifying Moment Leads to a Canadian Global Success," *The Canadian Business Journal*, 12 May 2012, www.cbj.ca/features/may_12_features/roy_green_a_terrifying_moment_leads_to_a_canadian_global_success.html; "Visitors," Messe München International, 2012, www.ispo.com/munich/en/All-Sports/Visitors; "Who We Are: The Fox 40 Story," Fox 40 International Inc., 18 December 2011, www.fox40world.com/index.cfm?pagepath=ABOUT_US/Who_We_Are_The_Fox_40_Story&id=4099; "BEDC Inducts Mr. Ron Foxcroft into the Entrepreneur Hall of Fame," Burlington Economic Development Corporation, 10 June 2011, www.bedc.ca/sites/default/files/PDF/businessnews/MediaRelease-BEDCInductsMr.RonFoxcroftintotheEntrepreneurHallofFame.pdf; John Kernaghan, "Fox 40 founder Foxcroft feted," *The Hamilton Spectator*, 18 October 2010, www.thespec.com/sports/local/article/268488-fox-40-founder-foxcroft-feted; REFEREE Staff, "Not An Inadvertent Whistle," *REFEREE Magazine*, July 2007, 45–47; and "Ron Foxcroft, Summit of Life," Global TV, Summer 2005.

Discussion Questions

1. In addition to employees and customers, what other stakeholders does the company consider as part of its business activities?
2. What is the primary reason why the company is unlikely to consider other global market-entry strategies (e.g., licensing)?
3. Visit the company's Web site at www.fox40world.com. What are some of its newest green initiatives? Can you recommend any new ones? (Hint: Review the Green Initiatives under the About Us tab.)
4. Do you have a dream for a product that has not yet been produced? If yes, how do you plan to develop this idea and turn it into reality?

PART 2

CHAPTER 6

FORMS OF BUSINESS OWNERSHIP

LEARNING OBJECTIVES

After you have read and studied this chapter, you should be able to:

LO 1 List the advantages and disadvantages of sole proprietorships.

LO 2 Describe the advantages and disadvantages of partnerships. Include the differences between general and limited partners.

LO 3 Discuss the advantages and disadvantages of corporations.

LO 4 Define and give examples of three types of corporate mergers, and explain the role of leveraged buyouts and taking a firm private.

LO 5 Outline the advantages and disadvantages of franchises, and discuss the challenges of global franchising.

LO 6 Describe the role of co-operatives in Canada.

PROFILE

GETTING TO KNOW BRIAN SCUDAMORE, FOUNDER OF 1-800-GOT-JUNK?

In 1989, 18-year-old college student Brian Scudamore could not find a summer job, so he decided to start his own business in Vancouver, British Columbia. Inspired by a junk-hauling truck he saw at a McDonald's, Scudamore bought a used truck for $700 and began a junk removal company called the Rubbish Boys (he chose the plural name even though he was the owner and sole employee). His slogan was "We'll Stash Your Trash in a Flash!" Over the following summers Scudamore's business grew, and in 1998 he changed the name to 1-800-GOT-JUNK? <*www.1800gotjunk.com*> and expanded his business through franchising.

With uniformed employees and clean, shiny trucks proudly advertising the company's name and telephone number, Scudamore set his company apart from other independent junk haulers, creating an unlikely brand out of hauling people's trash or, as Scudamore sees it, treasure. Most trash removal services require you to drag your junk down to the curb, but 1-800-GOT-JUNK? doesn't. Leave your stuff in the garage, basement, attic, or wherever, and the crew will come in and pick it up from there. They will even sort your trash into three categories: recycling, donating, and dumping, so you can rest assured that your reusable castoffs will not end up in a landfill unnecessarily.

While many companies expand their businesses by transforming into corporations and selling shares on the open market, 1-800-GOT-JUNK? expanded solely through franchising. That is, entrepreneurs opening licensed franchises in their own towns. By franchising his business and not depending on outside investors, Scudamore has been able to retain 100 percent control of the company. At the time that this profile was written, the company had 200 franchises across North America and Australia, and annual revenues were over $100 million.

Scudamore has received wide recognition in the media and business community. 1-800-GOT-JUNK? has celebrated appearances on *Undercover Boss Canada, The Dr. Oz Show, Dr. Phil,* CNN, ABC *Nightline,* the *Today Show, The Hour with George Stroumboulopoulos,* and *The View.* 1-800-GOT-JUNK? is currently the starring junk removal attraction on the hit A&E reality show, *Hoarders.* He has been inducted into the Young Presidents' Organization and served as a board member for the Young Entrepreneurs' Organization. In 2007, Scudamore was named the International Franchise Association's Entrepreneur of the Year. Other accolades include *Fortune* Small Business' Best Bosses Award, the *Globe & Mail*'s Top 40 under 40, and a three-time winner of a prestigious "Best Company To Work For" award.

Scudamore continues to look to the future. Impressed by entrepreneur Jim Bodden's concept of getting any job done in one day, the two launched 1-888-WOW-1DAY Painting *<wow1daypainters.com>*. The new company leverages several of the strengths of 1-800-GOT-JUNK?, such as a strong brand name, call centre capabilities, established training, and a franchising system to launch franchises across North America. Scudamore expects 1-800-GOT-JUNK? to double its revenues to $200 million by 2016, and sees even more potential in the new painting business. When asked what the biggest challenge facing his business was, Scudamore responded that it was, "Keeping the right people, keeping them motivated and great. As clichéd as it sounds, having the right people is all a business really is."

Just like Scudamore, all business owners must decide for themselves which form of business is best for them. Whether you dream of starting a business for yourself, going into business with a partner, forming a corporation, or someday being a leading franchisor, it is important to know that each form of ownership has its advantages and disadvantages. You will learn about them all in this chapter.

Sources: "Brian Scudamore, Founder and CEO," 1-800 GOT JUNK?, 12 May 2012, www.1800gotjunk.com/us_en/about/brian_scudamore.aspx; Jeff Beer, "Q&A: Brian Scudamore founder/CEO, 1-800-Got-Junk," *Canadian Business,* 7 May 2012, www.canadianbusiness.com/article/81127–q-a-brian-scudamore-founder-ceo-1-800-got-junk; Eric Stites, "Franchise Relations: Different Ideas, Great Solutions," *Franchising World,* 1 May 2008; and "Junk Removal Founder Awarded Entrepreneur of the Year by International Franchise Association," PR Newswire, 11 February 2008.

STARTING A SMALL BUSINESS

Like Brian Scudamore, thousands of people start new businesses in Canada every year. Chances are, you have thought of owning your own business or know someone who has. How you set up your business can make a tremendous difference in your long-term success. You can form a business in one of several ways. The three major forms of business ownership are (1) sole proprietorships, (2) partnerships, and (3) corporations. Each has advantages and disadvantages that we will discuss.

▸ Friends Michelle Strum and David Eisnor lived for many months in hostels around the world. Their business, Halifax Backpackers Hostel *<www.halifaxbackpackers.com>*, provides budget accommodations for travellers visiting Halifax.

It can be easy to get started in your own business. You can begin a word-processing service out of your home, open a car repair centre, start a restaurant, develop a Web site, or go about meeting other wants and needs in your community. A business owned, and usually managed, by one person is called a **sole proprietorship**. This is the most common form of business ownership.

Many people do not have the money, time, or desire to run a business on their own. When two or more parties legally agree to become co-owners of a business, the organization is called a **partnership**.

Sole proprietorships and partnerships are relatively easy to form, but there are advantages to creating a business that is separate and distinct from the owners. A legal entity with authority to act and have liability separate from its owners is called a **corporation**.

sole proprietorship
A business that is owned, and usually managed, by one person.

partnership
A legal form of business with two or more parties.

corporation
A legal entity with authority to act and have liability separate from its owners.

liability
For a business, it includes the responsibility to pay all normal debts and to pay because of a court order or law, for performance under a contract, or payment of damages to a person or property in an accident.

As you will learn in this chapter, each form of business ownership has advantages and disadvantages. It is important to understand these advantages and disadvantages before attempting to start a business. Keep in mind that just because a business starts in one form of ownership, it does not have to stay in that form. Many companies start out in one form, then add (or drop) a partner or two, and eventually may become corporations or franchisors.[1] The advantages and disadvantages that are highlighted in this chapter may give you an idea of why there may be a change in ownership form as the business grows.

Another topic that must be considered before proceeding is *liability*. **Liability** is often just another word for debt, but it also has a wider and important meaning, as you will see in the following pages. Liability for a business includes the responsibility to pay all normal debts and to pay:

1. Because of a court order
2. Because of a law
3. For performance under a contract (recall this from Appendix B)
4. For damages to a person or property

Let's begin our discussion by looking at the most basic form of ownership—the sole proprietorship.

List the advantages and disadvantages of sole proprietorships.

SOLE PROPRIETORSHIPS

Advantages of Sole Proprietorships

Sole proprietorships are the easiest kind of businesses for you to explore in your quest for an interesting career. Every town has sole proprietors you can visit. Talk with some of these business people about the joys and frustrations of being on their own. Most will mention the benefits of being their own boss and setting their own hours. Other advantages they mention may include the following:

1. *Ease of starting and ending the business.* All you have to do to start a sole proprietorship is to buy or lease the needed equipment (e.g., a saw, a word processor, a tractor, a lawn mower, etc.) and put up some announcements saying you are in business. It is just as easy to get out of business; you simply stop. There is no one to consult or to disagree with about such decisions. You may have to get a permit or licence from the local government, but often that is no problem.
2. *Being your own boss.* Working for others simply does not have the same excitement as working for yourself. At least, that is the way sole proprietors feel. You can start things quickly and you have the responsibility for all of the key aspects of realizing your vision. You may make mistakes, but they are your mistakes—and so are the many small victories each day.
3. *Pride of ownership.* People who own and manage their own businesses are rightfully proud of their work. They deserve all the credit for taking the risks and providing needed products.
4. *Retention of company profit.* Other than the joy of being your own boss, there is nothing like the pleasure of knowing that you can earn as much as possible and not have to share that money with anyone else (except the government, in taxes).
5. *No special taxes.* All profits of a sole proprietorship are taxed as the personal income of the owner, and the owner pays the normal personal income tax rate on that money. Another tax advantage for sole proprietors is that they can claim any business losses against other earned income. These losses would decrease the personal taxes they would need to pay. Understanding tax planning is an important factor in choosing the appropriate form of business organization and often requires the advice of professional accountants. Accounting will be discussed in Chapter 16.
6. *Less regulation.* While proprietorships are regulated by the provincial/territorial governments, and the proprietorship may have to be registered, overall they are less regulated than corporations.[2] As well, the administration of a proprietorship is less costly than that of a corporation.

Tammy Beese started *What's Up Yukon*, a free weekly magazine that features 100 percent local content. Printed on newsprint, the magazine covers Yukon news about arts and culture, sports and recreation, and "all things fun and entertainment."

Disadvantages of Sole Proprietorships

Not everyone is equipped to own and manage a business. Often it is difficult to save enough money to start a business and keep it going. The costs of inventory, supplies, insurance, advertising, rent, computers, utilities, and so on may be too much to cover alone. Other disadvantages of owning your own business include:

1. *Unlimited liability—the risk of personal losses.* When you work for others, it is their problem if the business is not profitable. When you own your own business, you and the business are considered one. You have **unlimited liability**; that

unlimited liability The responsibility of business owners for all of the debts of the business.

▸ Being the sole proprietor of a company, like a dog-walking service, means making a major time commitment to run the business, including constantly seeking out new customers and looking for reliable employees when the time comes to grow. If you were a sole proprietor, how would you need to prepare at the office if you wanted to take a week's vacation?

is, any debts or damages incurred by the business are your debts and you must pay them, even if it means selling your home, your car, or whatever else you own. This is a serious risk, and one that requires not only thought but also discussion with a lawyer, an insurance agent, an accountant, and others.

2. *Limited financial resources.* Funds available to the business are limited to the funds that the one (sole) owner can gather. Since there are serious limits to how much money one person can raise, partnerships and corporations have a greater probability of obtaining the needed financial backing to start a business and keep it going.
3. *Management difficulties.* All businesses need management; that is, someone must keep inventory records, accounting records, tax records, and so forth. Many people who are skilled at selling things or providing a service are often not so skilled at keeping records. Sole proprietors often find it difficult to attract good, qualified employees to help run the business because they cannot compete with the salary and benefits offered by larger companies.
4. *Overwhelming time commitment.* Though sole proprietors may say they set their own hours, it is hard to own a business, manage it, train people, and have time for anything else in life. This is true of any business, but a sole proprietor has no one with whom to share the burden. The owner often must spend long hours working. The owner of a store, for example, may put in 12 hours a day, at least six days a week—almost twice the hours worked by a non-supervisory employee in a large company. Imagine how this time commitment affects the sole proprietor's family life. Tim DeMello, founder of the successful company Wall Street Games Inc., echoes countless other sole proprietors when he says, "It's not a job, it's not a career, it's a way of life."
5. *Few fringe benefits.* If you are your own boss, you lose the fringe benefits that often come from working for others. You have no paid health insurance, no paid disability insurance, no sick leave, and no vacation pay.
6. *Limited growth.* Expansion is often slow since a sole proprietorship relies on its owner for most of its creativity, business know-how, and funding.
7. *Limited lifespan.* If the sole proprietor dies, the business no longer exists, unless it is sold or taken over by the sole proprietor's heirs. While the net business assets pass to the heirs, valuable leases and contracts may not.[3]
8. *Possibly pay higher taxes.* If the business is profitable, it may be paying higher taxes than if it was incorporated as a Canadian Controlled Private Corporation (CCPC).[4] (We will discuss private corporations shortly.) That is, tax rates are more advantageous if the business is incorporated. We will expand on this point later on in the chapter under the corporations discussion.

Talk with a few local sole proprietors about the problems they have faced in being on their own. They are likely to have many interesting stories to tell about problems in getting loans from a financial institution, problems with theft, problems simply keeping up with the business, and so on. These problems are also reasons why many sole proprietors choose to find partners to share the load.

PROGRESS ASSESSMENT

- What are the three forms of business ownership?
- Most people who start businesses in Canada are sole proprietors. What are the advantages and disadvantages of sole proprietorships?
- Why would unlimited liability be considered a major drawback of sole proprietorships?

PARTNERSHIPS

Describe the advantages and disadvantages of partnerships. Include the differences between general and limited partners.

A partnership is a legal form of business with two or more parties. The business can be a partnership of individuals, corporations, trusts, other partnerships, or a combination of these.[6] Two types of partnerships are general partnerships and limited partnerships. A **general partnership** is a partnership in which all owners share in operating the business and in assuming liability for the business's debts. A **limited partnership** is a partnership with one or more general partners and one or more limited partners.

A **general partner** is an owner (partner) who has unlimited liability and is active in managing the firm. Every partnership must have at least one general partner. A **limited partner** is an owner who invests money in the business but does not have any management responsibility or liability for losses beyond the investment. **Limited liability** means that limited partners are not responsible for the debts of the business beyond the amount of their investment—their liability is limited to the amount they put into the company; therefore, their personal assets are not at risk.

Another type of partnership was created to limit the disadvantage of unlimited liability. A **limited liability partnership (LLP)** limits partners' risk of losing their personal assets to the outcomes of only their own acts and omissions and those of people under their supervision. If you are a limited partner in an LLP, you can operate without fear that one of your partners might commit an act of malpractice resulting in a judgment that takes away your house, car, retirement plans, etc. as would be the case in a general partnership. LLPs are permitted for lawyers and accountants throughout Canada (except for Nunavut, the Yukon Territory, and Prince Edward Island). In British Columbia, LLPs are also permitted for other professionals as well as businesses.[7]

general partnership
A partnership in which all owners share in operating the business and in assuming liability for the business's debts.

limited partnership
A partnership with one or more general partners and one or more limited partners.

general partner
An owner (partner) who has unlimited liability and is active in managing the firm.

limited partner
An owner who invests money in the business but does not have any management responsibility or liability for losses beyond the investment.

limited liability
The responsibility of a business's owners for losses only up to the amount they invest; limited partners and shareholders have limited liability.

limited liability partnership (LLP)
A partnership that limits partners' risk of losing their personal assets to only their own acts and omissions and to the acts and omissions of people under their supervision.

Advantages of Partnerships

Often, it is much easier to own and manage a business with one or more partners. Your partner may be skilled at inventory control and accounting, while you do the selling or servicing. A partner can also provide additional money, support, and expertise as well as cover for you when you are sick or on vacation. Partnerships usually have the following advantages:

1. *More financial resources.* When two or more people pool their money and credit, it is easier to pay the rent, utilities, and other bills incurred by a business. A limited partnership is specially designed to help raise capital (money). As mentioned earlier, a limited partner invests money in the business but cannot legally have any management responsibility and has limited liability.
2. *Shared management and pooled/complementary skills and knowledge.* It is simply much easier to manage the day-to-day activities of a business with carefully chosen partners. Partners give each other free time from the business and provide different skills and perspectives. Some people find that the best partner is a spouse. That is why you see so many husband-and-wife teams managing restaurants, service shops, and other businesses.

▶ Husband-and-wife teams can make highly successful business partnerships. A case in point: art director and marketer Caterina Fake and her husband, Web designer Stewart Butterfield, founded the free photo-sharing Web site Flickr <www.flickr.com> and sold it to Yahoo a year later for $30 million. What are some of the advantages and disadvantages of being married to your business partner?

3. *Longer survival.* One study that examined 2,000 businesses started since 1960 reported that partnerships were four times as likely to succeed as sole proprietorships. Being watched by a partner can help a business person become more disciplined.
4. *Shared risk.* A partnership shares the risk among the owners. This includes financial risk in starting the business and ongoing risks as the business grows. Read the Spotlight on Small Business for how taking on a partner has allowed Inder Bedi to grow his business.
5. *No special taxes.* As with sole proprietorships, all profits of partnerships are taxed as the personal income of the owners, and the owners pay the normal income tax on that money. Similarly, any business losses can be used to decrease earned income from other sources.
6. *Less regulation.* Like a sole proprietorship, a partnership is less regulated than a corporation.

Disadvantages of Partnerships

Any time two people must agree, conflict and tension are possible. Partnerships have caused splits between relatives, friends, and spouses. Let's explore the disadvantages of partnerships next.

SPOTLIGHT ON SMALL BUSINESS

Bags That Travel

It started with a challenge to forgo animal products for thirty days. Today, matt & nat's line of vegan bags (e.g., totes, clutches, laptop carriers, and briefcases) for men and women is known to an ever-growing number of consumers in boutiques across Canada, the United States, the United Kingdom, and Japan. Celebrity followers include Brad Pitt, Eva Mendes, and Natalie Portman.

Inder Bedi started matt & nat <*mattandnat.com*> in 1995, fresh out of university. "I dreamed of something that no one else in the market was doing: a lifestyle brand that embraces a philosophy of positivity and is environmentally conscious," he says. "Being a vegetarian, I wanted the line to be cruelty-free, using no animal products. But beyond that, I wanted the product to reflect a philosophy, which is why there is a positivity message stamped on all bags, something that has universal appeal."

When he began, Bedi lived with family until he saved enough money to fund the business start-up, while learning everything he could about design and the trade. "In the first years of the company, the line was produced locally in Montreal," says Bedi. "I got to the point where I wanted to bring the business to the next level. I brought in a business partner and we took production to Asia. This allowed us to make the line more affordable, while maintaining our designer appeal. Due to the attention we give to design and details, we have managed to maintain the perception of a high-end line while taking it to mass market."

Matt & nat has successfully distinguished itself in the crowded fashion accessories industry with three key factors: fashion-forward designs, a philosophy, and reasonable pricing. The company targets boutique businesses and has, over time, defined a recognizable matt & nat style that appeals to a wide range of people. "We keep our designs as practical as possible without compromising style. Our strategy is to carefully select who we sell to and be the most affordable line in high-end stores," says Bedi.

Matt & nat has garnered attention in the fashion media for its distinctive message tags and eco-conscious offerings. "We have specifically chosen not to advertise through traditional ways," adds Bedi. "We want the brand and the product to speak for themselves."

Sources: "About Us," matt & nat, 14 May 2012, www.mattandnat.com/info/about/; and "Inder Bedi Wins BDC's Young Entrepreneur Award for Québec," Business Development Bank of Canada, 16 October 2007, www.bdc.ca/en/about/mediaroom/news_releases/2007/2007101603.htm.

1. *Unlimited liability.* Each *general* partner is liable for the debts of the firm, no matter who was responsible for causing those debts. You are liable for your partners' mistakes as well as your own. Like sole proprietors, general partners can lose their homes, cars, and everything else they own if the business loses a lawsuit or goes bankrupt.
2. *Division of profits.* Sharing risk means sharing profits, and that can cause conflicts. There is no set system for dividing profits in a partnership, and they are not always divided evenly. For example, if one partner puts in more money and the other puts in more hours, each may feel justified in asking for a bigger share of the profits.
3. *Disagreements among partners.* Disagreements over money are just one example of potential conflict in a partnership. Who has final authority over employees? Who works what hours? What if one partner wants to buy expensive equipment for the firm and the other partner disagrees? All terms of the partnership should be spelled out in writing to protect all parties and to minimize misunderstandings.[8]
4. *Difficulty of termination.* Once you have committed yourself to a partnership, it is not easy to get out of it. Sure, you can just quit. However, questions about who gets what and what happens next are often very difficult to resolve when the partnership ends. Surprisingly, law firms often have faulty **partnership agreements** (legal documents that specify the rights and responsibilities of each partner) and find that breaking up is hard to do. How do you get rid of a partner you do not like? It is best to decide such questions up front in the partnership agreement. In the absence of an agreement, or if certain provisions are not addressed in the agreement, provincial or territorial laws will determine some or all of the terms of the partnership.[9] Figure 6.1 gives you some ideas about what should be included in a partnership agreement.
5. *Possibly pay higher taxes.* Similar to a sole proprietorship, if the partnership is very profitable, it may be paying higher taxes than if it was incorporated as a CCPC.[10]

partnership agreement
Legal document that specifies the rights and responsibilities of each partner

The best way to learn about the advantages and disadvantages of partnerships is to interview several people who have experience with such agreements. They will give you insights and hints on how to avoid problems. The Making Ethical Decisions box leaves you with a dilemma to consider when it comes to making decisions in a partnership.

One fear of owning your own business or having a partner is the fear of losing everything you own if the business loses a lot of money or someone sues the business. Many business people try to avoid this and the other disadvantages of sole proprietorships and partnerships by forming corporations. We discuss this basic form of business ownership in the next section.

MAKING ETHICAL DECISIONS

Outsourcing or Outsmarting?

Imagine that you and your partner own a construction company. You receive a bid from a subcontractor that you know is 20 percent too low. Such a loss to the subcontractor could put him out of business. Accepting the bid will certainly improve your chances of winning the contract for a big shopping centre project. Your partner wants to take the bid and let the subcontractor suffer the consequences of his bad estimate. What do you think you should do? What will be the consequences of your decision?

Figure 6.1

Partnership Agreement Provisions

It's not hard to form a partnership, but it's wise for each prospective partner to get the counsel of a lawyer experienced with such agreements. Lawyers' services are usually expensive, so would-be partners should read all about partnerships and reach some basic agreements before calling a lawyer.

For your protection, be sure to put your partnership agreement in writing. The following provisions are usually included in a partnership agreement:

1. The name of the business. All provinces require the firm's name to be registered with the province if the firm's name is different from the name of any of the partners.
2. The names and addresses of all partners.
3. The purpose and nature of the business, the location of the principal office(s), and any other locations where business will be conducted.
4. The date the partnership will start and how long it will last. Will it exist for a specific length of time, or will it stop when one of the partners dies or when the partners agree to discontinue?
5. The contributions made by each partner. Will some partners contribute money, while others provide real estate, personal property, expertise, or labour? When are the contributions due?
6. The management responsibilities. Will all partners have equal voices in management, or will there be senior and junior partners?
7. The duties of each partner.
8. The salaries and drawing accounts of each partner.
9. Provision for sharing of profits or losses.
10. Provision for accounting procedures. Who'll keep the accounts? What bookkeeping and accounting methods will be used? Where will the books be kept?
11. The requirements for taking in new partners.
12. Any special restrictions, rights, or duties of any partner.
13. Provision for a retiring partner.
14. Provision for the purchase of a deceased or retiring partner's share of the business.
15. Provision for how grievances will be handled.
16. Provision for how to dissolve the partnership and distribute the assets to the partners.

PROGRESS ASSESSMENT

- What is the difference between a limited partner and a general partner?
- What are some of the advantages and disadvantages of partnerships?
- State four provisions usually included in a partnership agreement.

Discuss the advantages and disadvantages of corporations.

CORPORATIONS

Although the word corporation makes people think of big businesses such as the Bank of Montreal <*www.bmo.com*> or Irving Oil <*www.irvingoil.com*>, it is not necessary to be big to incorporate (start a corporation). Obviously, many corporations are big. However, incorporating may be beneficial for small businesses also.

A corporation is a federally or provincially chartered legal entity with authority to act and have liability separate from its owners. The corporation's owners (called shareholders/stockholders, as they hold shares/stock of ownership in the company) are not liable for the debts or any other problems of the corporation beyond the money they invest. Corporate shareholders do not have to worry about losing their houses, cars, and other personal property if the business cannot pay its bills—a very significant benefit. A corporation not only limits the liability of owners, but it also enables many people to share in the ownership (and profits) of a business without working there or having other commitments to it. We will discuss the rights of shareholders in Chapter 17.

public corporation
Corporation that has the right to issue shares to the public, so its shares may be listed on a stock exchange.

In Canada, corporations are divided into two classes: public and private. A **public corporation** has the right to issue stock (ownership in the company through shares) to the public, which means its shares may be listed on a stock exchange. This offers the possibility of raising large amounts of capital, regardless of the size of the company. That is, public corporations can be small and large companies.

A **private corporation** is not allowed to issue stock to the public, so its shares are not listed on a stock exchange, and it is limited to 50 or fewer shareholders. This greatly reduces the costs of incorporating. Many small corporations are in the private category. This is the vehicle employed by individuals or partners who do not anticipate the need for substantial financing but want to take advantage of limited liability. Private corporations can be very large. Examples include Sun Life Assurance Company of Canada <*www.sunlife.ca*>, Katz Group <*www.katzgroup.ca*>, and Honda Canada <*www.honda.ca*>.

▸ Chapman's Ice Cream <*www.chapmans.ca*> is a private corporation. Started in 1973 by Penny and David Chapman, it is Canada's largest independent ice cream manufacturer. Did you know that vanilla is the world's most popular ice cream flavour?

There are several advantages that Canadian-owned private corporations have over public corporations, especially from a taxation perspective. For example, a Canadian controlled private corporation pays a lower rate of federal tax (small-business rate) on the first $500,000 of active business income than would be paid by an unincorporated business, due to the small-business deduction. For private corporations claiming the small-business deduction, the net tax rate is 11 percent, while the net tax rate for other types of corporations is 15 percent.[11]

Another important advantage for the owner of a private corporation is that he or she can issue stock to a child, or a spouse, making them co-owners of the company. This procedure is not available to a sole proprietor. It is a simple and useful way of recognizing the contribution of these or other family members, or employees, to the company. This procedure may also be a good way for the owner to prepare for retirement by gradually transferring ownership and responsibility to those who will be inheriting the business.

private corporation
Corporation that is not allowed to issue stock to the public, so its shares are not listed on stock exchanges; it is limited to 50 or fewer shareholders.

Keep in mind that with any kind of succession planning in private corporations, conflict may arise. In the mid-1990s, brothers Wallace and Harrison McCain of McCain Foods <*www.mccain.com*> were bitterly divided over who should be picked to lead the company when they were gone. Wallace wanted his son Michael to take over, while Harrison preferred outside management. The fight ultimately wound up in a New Brunswick court, which sided with Harrison. Ousted from the company, Wallace ended up in Toronto, where he took over Maple Leaf Foods with sons Michael and Scott.[12] The Dealing with Change box at the end of this textbook part (Chapter 7) discusses some of the challenges associated with family businesses.

There is a formal procedure for forming a corporation that involves applying to the appropriate federal or provincial agency. It is always recommended that company owners seek the services of a competent lawyer and accountant prior to proceeding with any incorporation. The procedure for large or public corporations is much more complex and expensive and definitely requires hiring a legal firm. These costs can easily run into the thousands of dollars. Figure 6.2 describes various types of corporations.

Advantages of Corporations

Most people are not willing to risk everything to go into business. Yet for businesses to grow, prosper, and create economic opportunity, many people need to invest money in them. One way to solve this problem is to create an artificial being, an entity that exists only in the eyes of the law—a corporation. This entity is a technique for involving people in business without risking their other personal assets.

Figure 6.2

Some Corporation Categories

When you read about corporations you may find some confusing terms. Here are a few of the more widely used terms.

A *Crown corporation* is one that only the provincial or federal government can set up. (More details can be found in Chapter 4.)
A *domestic corporation* conducts business in its home country (e.g., Canada only).
A *multinational corporation* is a firm that operates in several countries.
A *non-profit* (or *not-for-profit*) *corporation* is one that does not seek personal profit for its owners.
A *non-resident corporation* conducts business in Canada but has its head office outside of Canada (e.g., foreign airlines).
A *private corporation* is one whose stock is held by a few people and is not available to the general public.
A *professional corporation* is a private corporation whose owners provide professional services (e.g., accountants and architects).
A *public corporation* sells stock to the general public.

A corporation has a separate legal identity from the owners—the shareholders—of the company and files its own tax returns. Let's explore some of the advantages of corporations:

1. *Limited liability.* A major advantage of corporations is the limited liability of owners. Remember, limited liability means that the owners of a business are responsible for losses only up to the amount they invest. Many corporations in Canada have the letters *Ltd.* after their name, which speaks to this limited liability. Others end their names with *Inc.* or *Corp.* to indicate their status.

   Be aware that you should not incorporate if it is your intention to use this ownership form as a way to avoid your debts. As a sole proprietorship or partnership, the debts the business incurs remain personal liabilities even after they are taken over by a corporation. Legally, it is the status existing at the time the debts were incurred that governs, not what happens subsequently.

2. *Ability to raise more money for investment.* To raise money, a corporation can sell ownership (stock) to anyone who is interested. This means that thousands of people can own part of major companies such as Rogers Communications Inc. <*www.rogers.com*>, TD Bank Group <*www.td.com*>, Manulife Financial Corp., EnCana Corp. <*www.encana.com*>, Canadian National Railway Co., Loblaw Companies Ltd., and smaller companies as well. If a company sold 1 million shares for $50 each, it would have $50 million available to build plants, buy materials, hire people, manufacture products, and so on. Such a large amount of money would be difficult to raise any other way.

   Corporations can also borrow money. They borrow from individual investors by issuing bonds, which are promises to repay the loan in the future with interest. Firms can also obtain loans from financial institutions, since lenders find it easier to place a value on the company when they can review how the shares are trading. Many small or individually owned corporations that do not trade actively may not have such opportunities, however. You can read about how corporations raise funds through the sale of stock and bonds in Chapter 17.

3. *Size.* That one word summarizes many of the advantages of some corporations. Because they can raise large amounts of money to work with, big corporations can build modern factories or software development facilities with the latest equipment. They can hire experts or specialists in all areas of operation.

▶ Companies can change their corporation status over time. For example, the TDL Group (owner of the Tim Hortons chain) was a private corporation. It merged with Wendy's International, Inc. in 1995. In 2006, Wendy's <www.aboutwendys.com> sold 17 percent of the TDL Group to raise approximately $783 million.[13] This money was used to repay debt owed by Wendy's. That same year, Tim Hortons was fully spun off as a separate company and today you can buy shares in Tim Hortons as it continues to be publicly traded.[14]

Figure 6.3

Canada's Largest Publicly Traded Corporations

Rank	Company	Profits ($ Billions)	Industry
1	Toronto-Dominion Bank	$5.8	Banks
2	Bank of Nova Scotia	$5.2	Banks
3	Royal Bank of Canada	$4.8	Banks
4	Barrick Gold	$4.4	Precious Metals
5	Suncor Energy	$4.3	Integrated Oils

Source: "Ranking Canada's Top 1000 Public Companies by Profit," *The Globe and Mail Report on Business Magazine*, 29 June 2012, www.theglobeandmail.com/report-on-business/rob-magazine/top-1000/2012-rankings-of-canadas-top-1000-public-companies-by-profit/article4371923/.

They can buy other corporations in different fields to diversify their business risks. (What this means is that a corporation can be involved in many businesses at once so that if one is not doing well, the negative impact on the total corporation is lessened.) In short, a large corporation with numerous resources can take advantage of opportunities anywhere in the world. Figure 6.3 lists some of Canada's largest publicly traded corporations.

When one considers size, different criteria can be used. This can include the number of employees, revenues, assets, and profits. Note that corporations do not have to be large to enjoy the benefits of incorporation. Professionals (such as physicians and lawyers) can incorporate. Individuals and partnerships can also incorporate.

4. *Perpetual life.* Because corporations are separate from those who own them, the death of one or more owners does not terminate the corporation.
5. *Ease of ownership change.* It is easy to change the owners of a corporation. All that is necessary is to sell the stock to someone else.
6. *Ease of attracting talented employees.* Corporations can attract skilled employees by offering benefits such as a pension plan, dental plan, and stock options (the right to purchase shares of the corporation for a fixed price). To be competitive, sole proprietorships and partnerships may offer money or other benefits to compete with such plans. Benefits will be discussed in Chapter 12.
7. *Separation of ownership from management.* Corporations are able to raise money from many different owners/shareholders without getting them involved in management. The corporate hierarchy in Figure 6.4 shows how the owners/shareholders elect a board of directors, who hire the officers of the corporation and oversee major policy issues. The owners/shareholders thus have some say in who runs the corporation but have no control over the daily operations (e.g., setting the price for a new product).

Disadvantages of Corporations

There are so many sole proprietorships and partnerships in Canada that clearly there must be some disadvantages to incorporation. Otherwise, more people would incorporate their businesses. The following are a few of the disadvantages:

1. *Initial cost.* Incorporation may cost thousands of dollars and involve the services of lawyers and accountants.
2. *Extensive paperwork.* The paperwork filed to start a corporation is just the beginning. A sole proprietor or a partnership may keep rather broad accounting records; a corporation, in contrast, must keep detailed financial records, the minutes of meetings, and more.
3. *Double taxation.* Corporate income is taxed twice. First the corporation pays tax on income before it can distribute any, as *dividends,* to shareholders. Then the

Figure 6.4

How Owners Affect Management

Owners have an influence on how business is managed by electing a board of directors. The board hires the top officers (and fires them if necessary). It also sets the pay for those officers. The officers then select other managers and employees with the help of the human resource department.

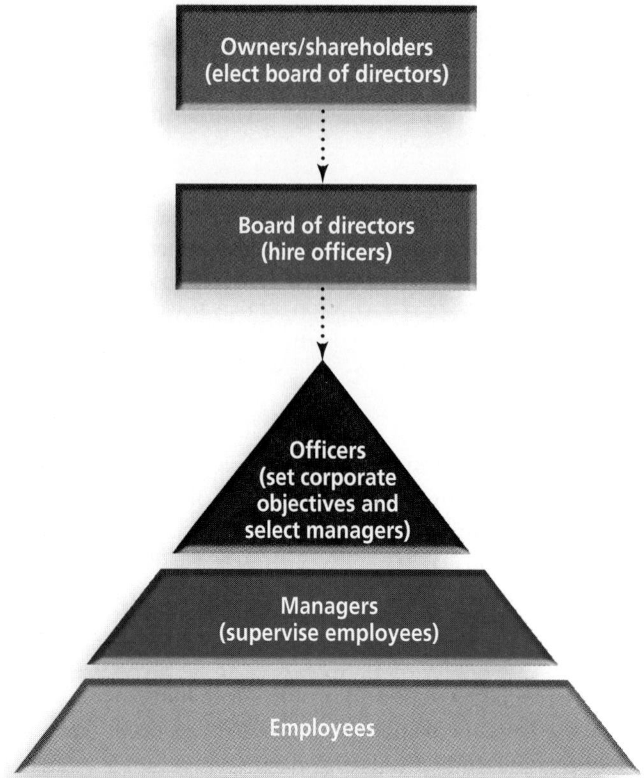

shareholders pay tax on the dividends they receive from the corporation. While this is *double* taxation, it is not *excessive* taxation, as the tax system is designed to provide some offsetting credits such as the dividend tax credit for investors.

4. *Two tax returns.* An individual who incorporates must file both a corporate tax return and an individual tax return. Depending on the size of the corporation, a corporate return can be quite complex and require the assistance of an accountant (e.g., a chartered accountant).
5. *Size.* Size may be one advantage of corporations, but it can be a disadvantage as well. Large corporations sometimes become too inflexible and too tied down in red tape to respond quickly to market changes, and their profitability can suffer.
6. *Difficulty of termination.* Once a corporation has started, it is relatively difficult to end. Legal procedures are costly and more complex than for unincorporated companies.
7. *Possible conflict with shareholders and board of directors.* Some conflict may brew if the shareholders elect a board of directors who disagree with management. Since the board of directors chooses the company's officers, entrepreneurs could find themselves forced out of the very company they founded. This happened to Tom Freston, one of the founders of MTV, and Steve Jobs, a founder of Apple Inc. (formerly Apple Computer, Inc.) <*www.apple.com*>. (Jobs later returned to the company.)

Many people are discouraged by the costs, paperwork, and special taxes that corporations must pay. However, many other business people believe that the advantages of incorporation outweigh the challenges. Figure 6.5 compares the three main types of organizations.

corporate governance
The process and policies that determine how an organization interacts with its stakeholders, both internal and external.

Corporate Governance

Corporate governance refers to the process and policies that determine how an organization interacts with its stakeholders—both internal and external. Rules outline how

		PARTNERSHIPS		CORPORATION	
	Sole Proprietorship	**General Partnership**	**Limited* Partnership**	**Public Corporation**	**Private Corporation**
Documents Needed to Start Business	None, may need permit or licence	Partnership agreement (oral or written)	Written agreement; must file certificate of limited partnership	Articles of incorporation, bylaws	Articles of incorporation, bylaws; must meet criteria
Ease of Termination	Easy to terminate: just pay debts and quit	May be hard to terminate, depending on the partnership agreement	Same as general partnership	Hard and expensive to terminate	Not difficult; pay off debts, sell off assets, withdraw cash, and pay taxes
Length of Life	Terminates on the death of owner, sale, or retirement	Terminates on the death or withdrawal of partner	Same as general partnership	Perpetual life	Perpetual life
Transfer of Ownership	Business can be sold to qualified buyer	Must have agreement of other partner(s)	Same as general partnership	Easy to change owners; just sell stock	Easy—just sell stock†
Financial Resources	Limited to owner's capital and loans	Limited to partners' capital and loans	Same as general partnership	More money to start and operate: sell stock and bonds; loans	Owners' capital and loans; no public stock issue allowed
Risk of Losses	Unlimited liability	Unlimited liability	Limited liability	Limited liability	Limited liability
Taxes	Taxed as personal income	Taxed as personal income	Same as general partnership	Corporate, double taxation	Same as public corporation
Management Responsibilities	Owner manages all areas of the business	Partners share management	Cannot participate in management	Separate management from ownership	Owners usually manage all areas
Employee Benefits	Usually fewer benefits and lower wages	Often fewer benefits and lower wages; promising employee could become a partner	Same as general partnership	Usually better benefits and wages, advancement opportunities	Same as public corporation

* There must be at least one general partner who manages the partnership and has unlimited liability.
† Unless the agreement specifies otherwise.

Figure 6.5

Comparison of Forms of Business Ownership

the organization is to be managed by the board of directors and the officers. Corporate governance is necessary because of the evolution of public ownership. In public corporations, unlike sole proprietorships and partnerships, there is a separation between ownership and management.[15] As a result, the board of directors was created.

The board assumes many of the same responsibilities that would typically rest with the sole proprietors, partners, or owners of a private corporation. Board members are often chosen based on their business experience and level of expertise. Those who serve on boards (both for-profit and non-profit) may be held personally liable for the misconduct of the organization. Having directors insurance is one way to try to limit this risk. Risk will be discussed in more detail in Appendix D.

As a result of corporate scandals, board members are under increasing scrutiny to ensure that they are effectively fulfilling their roles and responsibilities to their stakeholders. Professional development programs for board and committee members have been created to address this need. Two examples are the Directors College <*thedirectorscollege.com*> and the Institute of Corporate Directors <*www.idc.ca*>.

In the past, many boards were made up of officers of the company. It was not uncommon to have the chief executive officer hold the chairman of the board position. In the wake of corporate scandals, companies and their boards of directors are now reviewing this practice. Is the board independent from officers? Does the company have a statement of corporate governance practices? To truly represent the shareholders, are directors elected every year? These are just some of the questions that are being addressed by boards across Canada.

Business Regulations

Companies that wish to operate in Canada must follow federal and provincial business laws and regulations. Among other things, this applies to registration and to reporting and information.

Registration

Governments need to know what businesses are in operation to ensure that a wide range of laws and regulations are being followed. Guaranteeing that the names of businesses are not duplicated is important to avoid confusion. Additionally, governments have to be sure that taxes are being paid. To ensure these and other goals, every company must register its business. This is a simple, routine, and inexpensive procedure.

Companies wanting to incorporate must fill out articles of incorporation and file these with the appropriate provincial/territorial or federal authority. **Articles of incorporation** are a legal authorization from the federal or provincial/territorial government for a company to use the corporate format. The main advantage of being a federally incorporated company is that incorporation gives the company name added protection and guarantees its usage across Canada. Depending on the type of business you are considering, you may be required to incorporate federally.

articles of incorporation A legal authorization from the federal or provincial/territorial government for a company to use the corporate format.

Reporting and Information

Businesses receive many documents from governments during the course of a year. Some are just information about changes in employment insurance, the Canada or Quebec Pension Plan, or tax legislation as it affects them or their employees. Then there are various forms that all companies must complete so that governments can compile statistical reports that businesses, individuals, research organizations, and governments need to operate effectively. Statistics Canada maintains vast databases and creates useful reports from this information.

All public corporations must file annual reports containing basic data about themselves. An annual report should include the name of the officers, how many shares have been issued, and the head office location. Of course, every corporation must also file an annual tax return containing financial statements and pay the necessary taxes during the year.

PROGRESS ASSESSMENT

- What are the major advantages and disadvantages of incorporating a business?
- What is the role of owners (shareholders) in the corporate hierarchy?
- If you buy stock in a corporation and someone is injured by one of the corporation's products, can you be sued? Why or why not?

CORPORATE EXPANSION: MERGERS AND ACQUISITIONS

Define and give examples of three types of corporate mergers, and explain the role of leveraged buyouts and taking a firm private.

The last few decades saw considerable corporate expansion. It was not uncommon to read of a new merger or acquisition on a regular basis. It seemed as though each deal was intended to top the one before it. Most of the new deals involved companies trying to expand within their own fields to save costs, enter new markets, position for international competition, or adapt to changing technologies or regulations. These proved to be unattainable goals for many of the merged giants in the late 1990s, for example, as two-thirds of mergers failed to meet their goals.[16]

What's the difference between mergers and acquisitions? A **merger** is the result of two firms forming one company. It is similar to a marriage joining two individuals as one family. An **acquisition** is one company's purchase of the property and obligations of another company. It is more like buying a house than entering a marriage.

merger The result of two firms forming one company.

acquisition One company's purchase of the property and obligations of another company.

There are three major types of corporate mergers: vertical, horizontal, and conglomerate. A **vertical merger** is the joining of two firms involved in different stages of related businesses. A merger between a soft drink company and an artificial sweetener maker would ensure the merged firm a constant supply of an ingredient (i.e., sweetener) needed by the soft drink manufacturer. It could also help ensure quality control of the soft drink company's products.

vertical merger The joining of two companies involved in different stages of related businesses.

A **horizontal merger** joins two firms in the same industry and allows them to diversify or expand their products. A soft drink company and a mineral water company that merge can now supply a variety of drinking products.

horizontal merger The joining of two firms in the same industry.

A **conglomerate merger** unites firms in completely unrelated industries to diversify business operations and investments. A soft drink company and a snack food company would form a conglomerate merger. Figure 6.6 visually illustrates the three types of mergers.

conglomerate merger The joining of firms in completely unrelated industries.

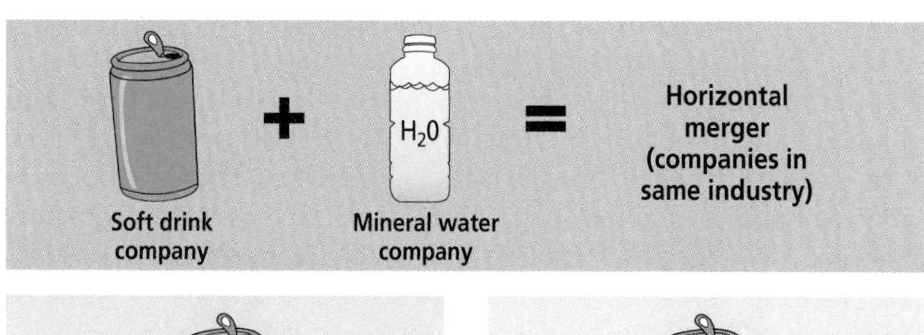

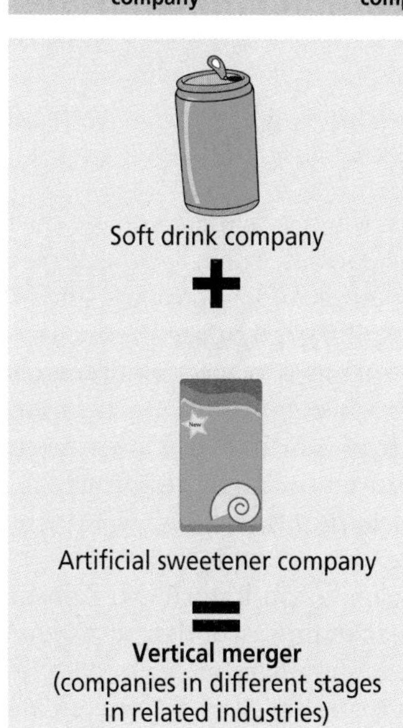

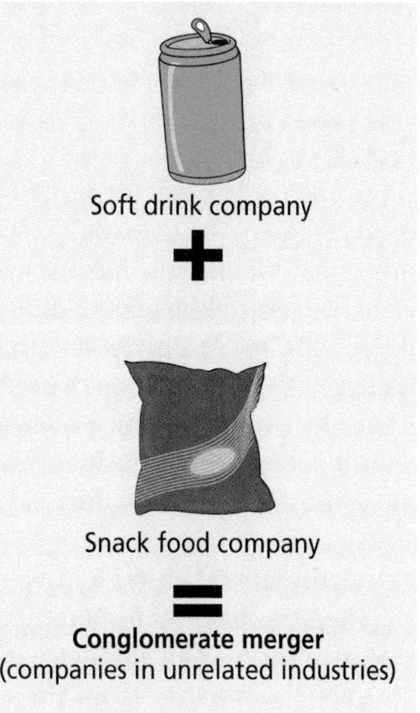

Figure 6.6

Types of Mergers

▸ Mars <www.mars.com>, the maker of M&M's, acquired the Wm. Wrigley Jr. Company. Both have long histories as family-owned businesses. Mars's president said, "The strong cultural heritage of two legendary American companies with a shared commitment to innovation, quality, and best-in-class global brands provides a great basis for this combination." What other factors might make an acquisition like this a successful one?

There are many benefits to a merger. One of them is that a merger may allow regional players to work together and compete more effectively. This was the case with the merger of salted snack food companies Old Dutch Foods Ltd. and Humpty Dumpty Snack Foods Inc. The combined entity will have $300 million in annual sales and about 25 percent of the Canadian market, says Steve Aanenson, president, CEO, and co-owner of Old Dutch Foods Inc. <*www.olddutchfoods.com*>.[17] It is estimated that the market leader, Frito-Lay <*www.fritolay.com*> (a division of PepsiCo), has more than 60 percent of the Canadian market. The merged company will also have more clout when negotiating with national retailers and undertaking marketing and promotional activities, an important consideration given ongoing consolidation in the food retail and consumer products industries.[18]

Rather than merge or sell to another company, some corporations decide to maintain control, or in some cases regain control, of a firm internally. By *taking a firm private,* management or a group of shareholders obtain all of the firm's shares for themselves by buying them back from the other shareholders. Such was the case when the former owners of Cara Operations Limited <*www.cara.com*>, the largest operator of full-service restaurants in Canada, decided to take the firm private. Cara's businesses include Swiss Chalet Rotisserie & Grill, Harvey's, Kelsey's, Montana's, Milestones Grill & Bar, and Coza! Tuscan Grill.[19]

leveraged buyout (LBO)
An attempt by employees, management, or a group of investors to purchase an organization primarily through borrowing.

franchise agreement
An arrangement whereby someone with a good idea for a business sells the rights to use the business name and sell its goods and services in a given territory.

Suppose employees believe they may lose their jobs and want to prevent that, or managers believe they could improve corporate performance if they owned the company. Does either group have an opportunity to take ownership of the company? Yes—they might attempt a leveraged buyout. A **leveraged buyout (LBO)** is an attempt by employees, management, or a group of investors to buy out the shareholders in a company, primarily by borrowing the necessary funds. The employees, managers, or investors now become the owners of the firm. LBOs have ranged in size from millions to billions of dollars and have involved everything from small family businesses to giant corporations such as Toys "R" Us <*www.toysrus.com*> and the former RJR Nabisco.[20]

Outline the advantages and disadvantages of franchises, and discuss the challenges of global franchising.

FRANCHISING

In addition to the three basic forms of business ownership, there are two special variations: franchises and co-operatives. Let's look at franchises first. A **franchise agreement** is an arrangement whereby someone with a good idea for a business (the **franchisor**) sells the rights to use the business name and to sell a good or service (the **franchise**) to others (the **franchisee**) in a given territory. As you might suspect, both franchisors and franchisees have a stake in the success of the franchise.

franchisor
A company that develops a product concept and sells others the rights to make and sell the products.

franchise
The right to use a specific business's name and sell its goods or services in a given territory.

Some people, uncomfortable with the idea of starting their own business from scratch, would rather join a business with a proven track record through a franchise agreement. A franchise can be formed as a sole proprietorship, a partnership, or a corporation.

Some students mistakenly identify franchising as an industry. It is not a specific industry. Rather, franchising is a method of distributing a good or service, or both, to achieve a maximum market impact with a minimum investment. It is not a separate form of business ownership from those already discussed in Figure 6.5 and it does not replace a form of business. How the franchisee sets up the franchise business (i.e., sole proprietorship, partnership, or corporation) and operates it, however, is dependent on the advantages and disadvantages of each form of business ownership.

Often, what looks like a chain of stores—Canadian Tire, Quiznos Sub <*www.quiznos.com*>, and Buck or Two <*www.buckortwo.com*>—is usually a franchise operation with each unit owned by a different person or company. Sometimes one person or group may own and operate more than one franchise unit. Regardless of the form of business ownership (e.g., sole proprietorship), all units are part of a franchise operation. In the following pages you will see the advantages and disadvantages of this type of business operation, and you will learn what to consider before buying a franchise unit.

SupperWorks
Taking the work out of supper
A fresh concept with all the ingredients for success!
In our kitchen, customers move through several food stations, complete with raw, prepped ingredients and recipes. In less than two hours they'll assemble twelve freezable dinners, while enjoying a social and relaxed environment. Recipes are designed to provide nutritious, delicious meals.
All for about $4 a serving!

▸ SupperWorks <*www.supperworks.com*> is a meal preparation business that has been helping families and students save time while providing nutritious, cost-effective meals. Would you consider using this company's services?

According to the Canadian Franchise Association, there are over 78,000 franchise units across Canada and they employ more than one million people. Franchised businesses account for 40 percent of all retail sales and they have been reported to account for one out of every five consumer dollars spent in Canada on goods and services.[21] You may be familiar with food franchises (e.g., Booster Juice <*www.boosterjuice.com*> and Edo Japan <*www.edojapan.com*>) and non-food franchises (e.g., Oxford Learning <*www.oxfordlearning.com*> and Home Hardware <*www.homehardware.ca*>). Have you ever considered owning one of these? The Green Box discusses a sports franchise.

franchisee
A person who buys a franchise.

GREENBOX

Root, Root, Root for the Green Team

Many people think the only thing you can buy at a franchise is fast food. Franchising, however, goes beyond a local Boston Pizza <*www.bostonpizza.com*> or Molly Maid. Any business that can be exactly replicated can be a franchise. Hotels, schools, even professional sports teams are part of the franchise system. For example, Washington, D.C., got its Major League Baseball franchise, the Nationals, when investors lured the Montreal Expos franchise to Washington.

One of the major inducements for the Expos' move was the promise of a new stadium. The D.C. city council went further and insisted that the structure be the first sports stadium to earn a Leadership in Energy and Environmental Design (LEED) rating from the U.S. Green Building Council. The $611 million stadium opened to a national TV audience and the president of the United States in 2008.

As the Nationals took the field on opening day, fans may not have noticed that 95 percent of the stadium's steel was recycled or that its low-flow toilets would save millions of gallons of water each season. They also may not have known that the wastewater system screens out organic debris such as peanut shells and hot-dog bits, or that the park's recycling centre is large enough to handle glass, metal, and plastic recyclables amassed during a three-game homestand. After all, the fans came to see baseball.

But lots of other folks, like other major league franchises, were taking notice and making their own efforts to improve the environment. The San Francisco Giants, Colorado Rockies, and Cleveland Indians have all installed solar panels in their ballparks. The Seattle Mariners started a composting project at their park. The New York Mets and Minnesota Twins have promised LEED certification at their new parks as well. Play ball! But play green!

Sources: Matthew Phillips, "Not Just Greener Grass," *Newsweek*, 14 April 2008, 66–67; and Jeff Chu, "Take Me Out to the Ballpark," *Fast Company*, April 2008, 72–73.

Advantages of Franchises

Franchising has penetrated every aspect of Canadian and global business life by offering goods and services that are reliable, convenient, and competitively priced. The worldwide growth of franchising could not have been accomplished by accident. Franchising clearly has some advantages:

1. *Management and marketing assistance.* Compared with someone who starts a business from scratch, a franchisee usually has a much greater chance of succeeding because he or she has an established product to sell, help choosing a location, and assistance in all phases of promotion and operation. It is like having your own store but with full-time consultants when you need them. Franchisors usually provide intensive management training, since they want the franchisees to succeed. For example, franchisor Boston Pizza International offers its franchisees eight weeks of training and support in its corporate training centre, one week of business management sessions, and ongoing training as needed.[22]

   Some franchisors help their franchisees with local marketing efforts rather than having franchisees depend solely on national advertising. Franchisees also have a network of fellow franchisees facing similar problems who can share their experiences. For example, The UPS Store <*www.theupsstore.com*> provides its franchisees with a software program that helps them build customer databases along with quick and personal one-on-one phone support and e-mail support. [23]
2. *Personal ownership.* A franchise operation is still your business, and you enjoy many of the incentives and profit of any sole proprietor. You are still your own boss, although you must follow more rules, regulations, and procedures than you would with your own privately owned store.
3. *Nationally recognized name.* It is one thing to open a gift shop or ice cream store. It is quite another to open a new Hallmark store <*www.hallmark.com*> or a Baskin-Robbins <*www.baskinrobbins.com*>. With an established franchise, you get instant recognition and support from a product group with established customers around the world.
4. *Financial advice and assistance.* Two major problems for small-business owners are arranging financing and learning to keep good records. Franchisees get valuable assistance and periodic advice from people with expertise in these areas. In fact, some franchisors will even provide financing to potential franchisees they believe will be valuable partners of the franchise system.
5. *Lower failure rate.* Historically, the failure rate for franchises has been lower than that of other business ventures. However, franchising has grown so rapidly that many weak franchises have entered the field, so you need to be careful and invest wisely.[24]

Disadvantages of Franchises

There are, however, some potential pitfalls to franchising. Disadvantages of franchises include the following:

1. *Large start-up costs.* Most franchises will demand a fee for the rights to the franchise. Fees for franchises can vary considerably. Start-up costs for a Kumon Math and Reading Centre <*www.kumon.ca*> include $1,000 for the franchise fee and a minimum investment ranging from $10,000 to $20,000.[25] But if you want to own a Keg Steakhouse and Bar <*www.kegsteakhouse.com*>, you will need more money. The franchise fee is $50,000 and capital requirements range from $2.0 to $3.25 million.[26]
2. *Shared profit.* The franchisor often demands either a large share of the profits in addition to the start-up fees or a percentage commission based on sales, not profit.

This share is called a *royalty*. For example, if a franchisor demands a 10-percent royalty on a franchise's sales, 10 cents of every dollar collected at the franchise (before taxes and other expenses) must be paid to the franchisor.

3. *Management regulation.* Management "assistance" has a way of becoming managerial orders, directives, and limitations. Franchisees feeling burdened by the company's rules and regulations may lose the spirit and incentive of being their own boss with their own business. Often franchisees will band together to resolve their grievances with franchisors rather than each fighting their battles alone. Tim Hortons franchise owners mounted a $2-billion lawsuit where they accused the franchisor of (1) gouging them under the company's new way of making doughnuts and (2) requiring them to sell new lunch menu items at break-even prices or sometimes at a loss.[27] The judge rejected the lawsuit saying the franchisor was well within its rights to implement new procedures and technologies to its business model.[28]
4. *Coattail effects.* What happens to your franchise if fellow franchisees fail? Quite possibly the actions of other franchisees have an impact on your future growth and profitability. Due to this *coattail* effect, you could be forced out of business even if your particular franchise has been profitable.

   Franchisees must also look out for competition from fellow franchisees. For example, TCBY franchisees' love for frozen yogurt melted as the market became flooded with new TCBY <*www.tcby.com*> *stores*. McDonald's franchisees complain that due to the company's relentless growth, some new stores have taken away business from existing locations, squeezing franchisees' profits per outlet.
5. *Restrictions on selling.* Unlike owners of private businesses, who can sell their companies to whomever they choose on their own terms, many franchisees face restrictions in the reselling of their franchises. To control quality, franchisors often insist on approving the new owner, who must meet their standards.
6. *Fraudulent franchisors.* Contrary to common belief, most franchisors are not large systems like McDonald's or Subway <*www.subway.com*>. Most franchisors are honest, but there has been an increase in complaints about franchisors that deliver little or nothing of what they promised.[29] Before you buy a franchise, make certain you check out the facts fully.[30]

▸ Canadian Tire is Canada's most-shopped retailer. To own a franchise, candidates must be willing to make a personal and financial investment. A minimum of $125,000 of accessible capital is needed and up to 25 percent of the value of the store's inventory and assets. In addition, successful dealer candidates will be charged a Dealer Training and Development Fee of $100,000 upon receiving their first store. This non-refundable fixed fee can be financed.[31]

E-Commerce in Franchising

Many brick-and-mortar franchisees are expanding their businesses online. Franchisees that started with a limited territory are now branching out globally. Many franchisors prohibit franchisee-sponsored Web sites because conflicts can erupt if the franchisor then creates its own Web site. Sometimes franchisors send "reverse royalties" to outlet owners who feel that their sales were hurt by the franchisor's Internet sales, but that does not always bring about peace. Before buying a franchise, you would be wise to read the small print regarding online sales.

PropertyGuys.com <*propertyguys.com*> is an example of a franchise that uses e-commerce as an important component of the service it offers. Formed in 1998 in Moncton, New Brunswick, PropertyGuys.com has built on the "For Sale by

▶ Holiday Inn's InterContinential Amstel hotel in Amsterdam has been celebrated as the Netherlands' most beautiful and luxurious hotel. Holiday Inn franchises try to complement the environment of the area they serve. This hotel is on the crossroads of Amsterdam's financial and exclusive shopping districts. What do you think would have been the reaction if Holiday Inn <*www.holidayinn.com*> built the typical American-style hotel in this area?

Owner (FSBO)" Internet concept. The service is a no-commission, low-cost alternative to pricey real estate commissions. PropertyGuys.com has been used to list homes, land, apartments, commercial buildings, and cottages. According to company literature, what differentiates this company from other FSBO sites is its personal touch. Company representatives will set up clients, install signage, take photos, and make themselves available during the process. Furthermore, the company does not rely solely on the Internet to display properties. Packages include a combination of print advertising, direct mail, electronic mail, seller's documentation, a "For Sale" sign, a Web site listing, and a phone answering service.

Franchising in International Markets[32]

In 1986, brothers Michael and Aaron Serruya, then aged 19 and 20, wanted to buy a franchise, but no one would take a chance on them. So, they started their own frozen yogurt shop, Yogen Früz. Today, Yogen Früz has grown to be a world leader in the frozen yogurt category, with over 1,300 locations operating in 35 countries around the world.

What makes franchising successful in international markets is what makes it successful domestically: convenience and a predictable level of service. Because of proximity and language, the United States is by far the most popular target for Canadian-based franchises. For example, Taco Del Mar <*www.tacodelmar.com*>, a Seattle-based quick-service restaurant chain specializing in Baja style "mondo burritos and rippin' tacos," has inked a deal with B.C.-based TDM Federal Holdings, Inc. to develop restaurants across Canada. The deal could produce 600 Taco Del Mar franchises in Canada by 2014.

Describe the role of co-operatives in Canada.

CO-OPERATIVES[33]

Some people dislike the notion of having owners, managers, workers, and buyers as separate individuals with separate goals. They envision a world where people co-operate with one another more fully and share the wealth more evenly. These people have formed a different type of organization that reflects their social orientation. This is called a co-operative, or co-op. A **co-operative** is an organization owned by members and customers who pay an annual membership fee and share in any profits (if it is a profit-making organization).

co-operative
An organization that is owned by members and customers, who pay an annual membership fee and share in any profits.

In their one-hundred year history in Canada, co-operatives represent a large and diverse heritage of Canadians working together to build better communities based upon co-operative principles. These principles differ from other businesses principles in several ways:

- *A different purpose.* The primary purpose of co-operatives is to meet the common needs of their members. Most investor-owned businesses have a primary purpose to maximize profit for their shareholders. Figure 6.7 summarizes some of the philosophical and community benefits of co-operatives.
- *A different control structure.* Co-operatives use the one-member/one-vote system, not the one-vote-per-share system used by most businesses. This helps the co-operative serve the common need rather than the individual need.

Figure 6.7

Benefits of Co-operatives

Philosophical Benefits	Community Benefits
Greater community autonomy	Fair market prices
Product and service development by the people for the people	Strong customer/client loyalty
Opportunities to strengthen community bonds by helping one another	Greater employment opportunities
You can define your own needs instead of letting a conglomerate do it for you	Better access to quality products and services
Modest savings for all instead of the excessive accumulation of profits by a few	Economic and social growth in the community

Source: "The Co-Operative Advantage," CoopZone Developers' Network Co-operative, accessed 15 May 2012, http://coopzone.coop/en/coop_advantage.

- *A different allocation of profit.* Co-operatives share profits among their member-owners on the basis of how much they use the co-operative, not on how many shares they hold. Profits tend to be invested in improving services for the members.

Because co-ops distribute their profits to members as a reduction in members' costs, these profits are not subject to income tax. From time to time, various business organizations assert that many co-ops are now more like large businesses and should be taxed. So far, this viewpoint does not appear to have extensive support.

Collectively, there are over 9,000 co-operatives, which provide products and services to over 18 million Canadians. Co-operatives directly employ over 155,000 people, of which over 88,000 are in non-financial co-operatives and over 32,000 are employed in the agricultural sector. Figure 6.8 illustrates the main activities of the non-financial co-operatives. Financial co-operatives (which include caisses populaires, credit unions, insurance co-operatives, and mutual companies) offer financial, loan or investment services, and insurance services to their members.

As you can see from Figure 6.8, co-operatives can be found in many sectors of the economy. The co-operative model has a long history and a proven track record in social

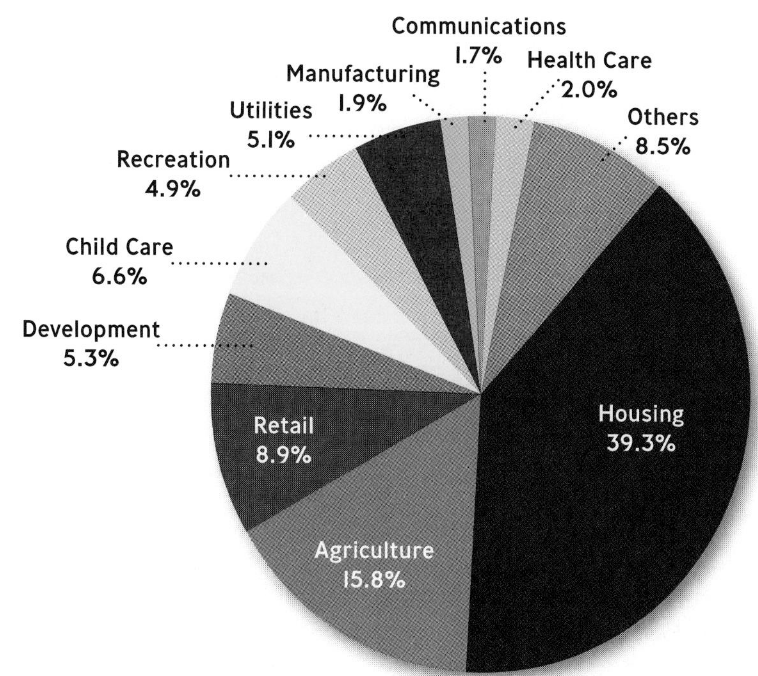

Figure 6.8

Distribution of the Non-financial Co-operatives by Sector of Activity

Source: Used with permission of the Rural and Co-operatives Secretariat.

Mountain Equipment Co-op <www.mec.ca> is Canada's largest retailer co-operative. With your $5 lifetime membership, you become part owner, and you have a voice in the governance of the company. Have you shopped at an MEC store?

and economic development, having served thousands of groups in both urban and rural areas. They are especially important to many rural and remote communities. In some communities, co-operatives are the only providers of retail and financial services, health and home care services, communications and utility services, tourism facilities, and other basic amenities.

Co-operatives also have demonstrated a higher survival rate than other forms of enterprise. A study published by the Quebec Ministry of Industry and Commerce shows that the long-term survival rate of co-operative enterprises is almost twice that of investor-owned companies. At least seven co-ops are listed in Canada's top 500 companies and several financial co-operatives have been rated the best places to work in Canada.

WHICH FORM OF OWNERSHIP IS BEST FOR YOU?

As you can see, you may participate in the business world in a variety of ways. You can start your own sole proprietorship, partnership, and/or corporation. You can purchase a franchise and structure your business as a sole proprietorship, partnership, or corporation. Co-operatives are corporations that usually have a different motivation than traditional for-profit businesses. There are advantages and disadvantages to each. However, there are risks no matter which form you choose. Before you decide which form is best for you, you need to evaluate all of the alternatives carefully.

PROGRESS ASSESSMENT

- What are some of the factors to consider before buying a franchise?
- What opportunities are available for starting a global franchise?
- What is a co-operative?

SUMMARY

List the advantages and disadvantages of sole proprietorships.

The major forms of business ownership are sole proprietorships, partnerships, and corporations.

What are the advantages and disadvantages of sole proprietorships?

The advantages of sole proprietorships include ease of starting and ending the business, being your own boss, pride of ownership, retention of profits, no special taxes, and less regulation than for corporations. The disadvantages include unlimited liability, limited financial resources, difficulty in management, overwhelming time commitment, few fringe benefits, limited growth, limited lifespan, and the possibility of paying higher taxes depending on the level of income.

Describe the advantages and disadvantages of partnerships. Include the differences between general and limited partners.

The three key elements of a general partnership are common ownership, shared profits and losses, and the right to participate in managing the operations of the business.

What are the advantages and disadvantages of partnerships?

The advantages include more financial resources, shared management and pooled knowledge, longer survival than sole proprietorships, and less regulation than corporations. The disadvantages include unlimited liability, division of profits, possible disagreements among partners, difficulty of termination, and the possibility of paying higher taxes depending on the level of income.

What are the main differences between general and limited partners?

General partners are owners (partners) who have unlimited liability and are active in managing the company. Limited partners are owners (partners) who have limited liability and are not active in the company.

Discuss the advantages and disadvantages of corporations.

A corporation is a legal entity with authority to act and have liability separate from its owners.

What are the advantages and disadvantages of corporations?

The advantages include more money for investment, limited liability, size, perpetual life, ease of ownership change, ease of drawing talented employees, and separation of ownership from management. The disadvantages include initial costs, paperwork, size, difficulty of termination, double taxation, and possible conflict with a board of directors.

What are some categories of corporations?

Corporation categories include the following: Crown, domestic, multinational, non-profit, non-resident, professional, private, and public. The figure in this chapter introduces each category.

Define and give examples of three types of corporate mergers, and explain the role of leveraged buyouts and taking a firm private.

Mergers allow companies within their own fields to save costs, enter new markets, position for international competition, or adapt to changing technologies or regulations.

What is a merger?

A merger is the result of two firms forming one company. The three major types of mergers are vertical mergers, horizontal mergers, and conglomerate mergers. A vertical merger is the joining of two companies involved in different stages of related businesses. A horizontal merger is the joining of two firms in the same industry. A conglomerate merger is the joining of firms in completely unrelated industries.

What are leveraged buyouts, and what does it mean to take a company private?
Leveraged buyouts are attempts by managers and employees to borrow money and purchase the company. Individuals who, together or alone, buy all of the stock for themselves are said to take the company private.

LO 5 Outline the advantages and disadvantages of franchises, and discuss the challenges of global franchising.

A person can participate in entrepreneurship by buying the rights to market a new product innovation in his or her area.

What are the benefits and drawbacks of being a franchisee?
The benefits include a nationally recognized name and reputation, a proven management system, promotional assistance, and pride of ownership. Drawbacks include high franchise fees, managerial regulation, shared profits, and transfer of adverse effects if other franchisees fail.

What is the major challenge to global franchises?
It may be difficult to transfer an idea or product that worked well in Canada to another culture. It is essential to adapt to the region.

LO 6 Describe the role of co-operatives in Canada.

Co-operatives have a different purpose, control structure, and allocation of profit than traditional for-profit businesses.

What is the role of a co-operative?
Co-operatives are organizations owned by members/customers. Some people form co-operatives to give members more economic power than they would have as individuals. Small businesses often form co-operatives to give them more purchasing, marketing, or product development strength.

What types of co-operatives are found in the economy?
Figure 6.8 shows the main activities of the non-financial co-operatives. Financial co-operatives (which include caisses populaires, credit unions, insurance co-operatives, and mutual companies) offer financial, loan, or investment services, and insurance services to their members.

KEY TERMS

acquisition
articles of incorporation
conglomerate merger
co-operative
corporate governance
corporation
franchise
franchise agreement
franchisee
franchisor
general partner
general partnership
horizontal merger
leveraged buyout (LBO)
liability
limited liability
limited liability partnership (LLP)
limited partner
limited partnership
merger
partnership
partnership agreement
private corporation
public corporation
sole proprietorship
unlimited liability
vertical merger

CRITICAL THINKING

1. Have you ever dreamed of opening your own business? If so, what kind of business? Could you start such a business in your own home? How much would it cost to start? Could you begin the business part-time while you attend school? What satisfaction and profit could you get from owning your own business? What could you lose? (Be aware that you must be careful not to use a name for your business that has already been used or registered by someone else. You may face some local restrictions and license requirements if you operate from your residence such as having a certain number of parking spaces, a limit on the size and type of vehicle and signage, noise bylaws, etc.)

2. Is it fair to say that franchisees have the true entrepreneurial spirit? Could you see yourself as a franchisee or franchisor? Which one? Do you have an idea that you think could eventually grow into a franchise? Explain.

DEVELOPING WORKPLACE SKILLS

1. Research businesses in your area and identify two companies that use the following forms of ownership: sole proprietorship, partnership, and corporation. Arrange interviews with managers from each form of ownership and get their impressions about their businesses. (If you are able to work with a team of fellow students, divide the interviews among team members.) Some questions that you might ask include: How much did it cost to start this business? How many hours do you work? What are some drawbacks that you have encountered with the way your business is set up (i.e., business form), if any? What are the specific benefits of this business form? Share the results with your class.

2. Have you thought about starting your own business? What opportunities seem attractive? Think of a friend or friends whom you might want as a partner or partners in the business. List all of the financial resources and personal skills you will need to launch the business. Then make separate lists of the personal skills and the financial resources that you and your friend(s) might bring to your new venture. How much capital and what personal skills do you need but lack? Develop an action plan to obtain them.

3. Let's assume you want to open one of the following new businesses. What form of business ownership would you choose for each business? Why?
   a. Wedding planning service
   b. Software development firm
   c. Computer hardware manufacturing company
   d. Dog grooming service

4. Find out how much it costs to incorporate a company in your province or territory. Then compare it to the cost of a federal incorporation. Is there a significant difference? Why might you choose not to incorporate federally?

ANALYZING MANAGEMENT DECISIONS

Going Public

George Zegoyan and Amir Gupta face a difficult decision. Their private auto parts manufacturing company has been a great success—too quickly. They cannot keep up with the demand for their product. They must expand their facilities, but have not had time to accumulate sufficient working capital, nor do they want to acquire long-term debt to finance the expansion. Discussions with their accountants, lawyers, and stockbrokers have confronted them with the necessity of going public to raise the required capital.

Zegoyan and Gupta are concerned about maintaining control if they become a public company. They are also worried about loss of privacy because of the required reporting to various regulatory bodies and to their shareholders. Naturally, they are also pleased that the process will enable them to sell some of their shareholdings to the public and realize a fair profit from their past and expected future successes. They will be able to sell 40 percent of the shares for $500,000, which is ten times their total investment in the company. It will also allow them to raise substantial new capital to meet the needs of their current expansion program.

The proposed new structure will allow them to retain 60 percent of the outstanding voting shares, so they will keep control of the company. Nevertheless, they are somewhat uneasy about taking this step, because it will change the nature of the company and the informal method of operating they are used to. They are concerned about having "partners" in their operations and profits. They are wondering whether they should remain as they are and try to grow more slowly, even if it means giving up profitable orders.

Discussion Questions

1. Do they have any other options besides going public? Is the franchise route a viable option? Explain?
2. Do you think they should try to limit their growth to a manageable size to avoid going public, even if it means forgoing profits now? Why?
3. Would you advise them to sell their business now if they can get a good price and then start a new operation? Explain.

CHAPTER

7

ENTREPRENEURSHIP AND STARTING A SMALL BUSINESS

LEARNING OBJECTIVES

After you have read and studied this chapter, you should be able to:

LO 1 Explain why people are willing to become entrepreneurs, and describe the attributes of successful entrepreneurs.

LO 2 Discuss the importance of small business to the Canadian economy.

LO 3 Summarize the major causes of small-business failure.

LO 4 List ways to learn how small businesses operate.

LO 5 Analyze what it takes to start and run a small business.

LO 6 Outline the advantages and disadvantages that small businesses have in entering global markets.

PROFILE

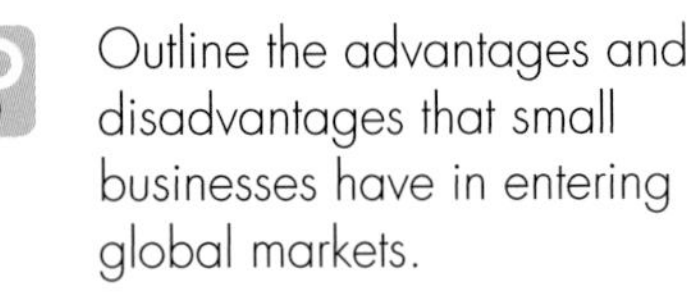

GETTING TO KNOW MARLENE ROSS OF MARLENE ROSS DESIGN

Marlene Ross has changed the face of hockey around the world. Through her company, Marlene Ross Design <*www.marlenerossdesign.com*>, she has designed and painted original pieces of "Mask Art" for Martin Brodeur, Roberto Luongo, J.S. Giguere, Marc-Andre Fleury, Grant Fuhr, and Ron Hextall, just to name a few. For over twenty years, she has been the premier artist for goalies in the NHL (National Hockey League), international and Olympic competitions, the NCAA (National Collegiate Athletic Association) and CIS (Canadian Interuniversity Sport) Leagues, major motion pictures, and for amateurs in minor hockey around the world.

Ross did not have much to do with hockey when she was growing up in Merrickville, southwest of Ottawa. The self-taught painter began her career as a cartoonist and serious portrait artist. She soon developed a reputation for being able to paint on any medium. When she was 19, a goalie playing in an adult recreational league offered her $225 to paint his mask to look like the face of Batman's nemesis, the Joker. At a hockey tournament, the mask caught the eye of everyone who saw it—including Gerry Wright, of the Chicago hockey company Itech, which makes goalie helmets. For a while, Ross painted masks for Itech, and she was offered a contract. But she wanted to remain independent, so she turned the offer down. It proved to be the right decision. Ross owns the rights to all of her designs and collects royalties from Pinnacle hockey trading cards, McDonald's restaurants, EA sports video games, and Corinthian mini masks.

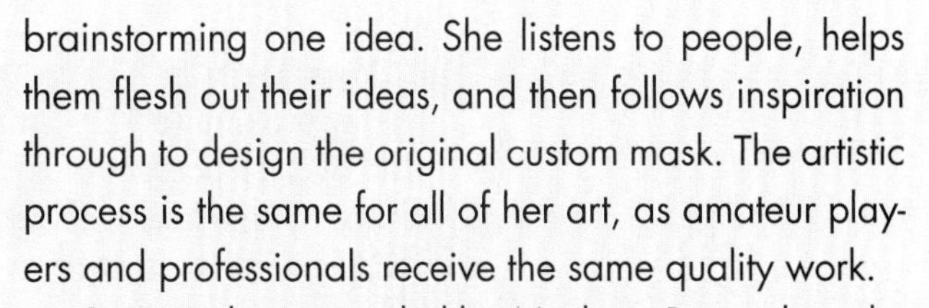

There is an eight-week wait to have a mask custom painted, each of which takes about 25 to 30 hours to paint. Each goalie is provided with detailed preliminary drawings with custom design for approval. Ross might spend anywhere from 20 to 80 hours brainstorming one idea. She listens to people, helps them flesh out their ideas, and then follows inspiration through to design the original custom mask. The artistic process is the same for all of her art, as amateur players and professionals receive the same quality work.

Stories about people like Marlene Ross who take the challenge of starting their own business are commonplace in this age of the entrepreneur. As you read about more examples in this book, maybe you will become inspired to become an entrepreneur yourself!

Sources: "Behind the Mask," Marlene Ross Design, 2008, www.marlenerossdesign.com/aboutus.html; and Jody Kingsbury, "The Woman Behind the Mask," Capital Arts Online, 1 February 2006, www.carleton.ca/sjc/capitalarts/2006/s10.shtml.

THE AGE OF THE ENTREPRENEUR[1]

The approximately 2.7 million people in Canada who are self-employed represent a little over 15 percent of all employed workers in the Canadian economy. Increasingly, young people are considering starting a small business when they graduate. Others, like Marlene Ross, start even earlier. Most young people know that it is unlikely they will get a job in a large corporation and stay 30 years. For those who want more control over their destiny, working in or starting a small business makes sense.

entrepreneurship Accepting the challenge of starting and running a business.

Schools are responding to this trend by offering more courses on the subject of entrepreneurship. **Entrepreneurship** is accepting the challenge of starting and running a business. The word entrepreneur originates from the French word, *entreprendre,* which means "to undertake." In a business context, it means to start a business. You can imagine how the concept of entrepreneurship has a wide variety of meanings. On the one extreme, an entrepreneur is a person of very high aptitude who pioneers change, possessing characteristics found in only a very small fraction of the population. On the other extreme, anyone who wants to work for himself or herself is considered an entrepreneur. It is for this reason that we discuss both topics entrepreneurship and small business in this chapter.

While many people use the terms entrepreneurship and small business interchangeably, there are significant differences. Entrepreneurial ventures differ from small businesses in the following four ways:[2]

1. *Amount of Wealth Creation.* Rather than simply generating an income stream that replaces traditional employment, a successful entrepreneurial venture creates substantial wealth, typically in excess of several million dollars of profit.
2. *Speed of Wealth Creation.* While a successful small business can generate several million dollars of profit over a lifetime, entrepreneurial wealth creation often is rapid. For example, this may occur within five years.
3. *Risk.* The risk of an entrepreneurial venture must be high. Otherwise, with the incentive of sure profits, many people would pursue the idea of entrepreneurship, making business ventures impossibly competitive.
4. *Innovation.* Entrepreneurship often involves substantial innovation beyond what a small business might exhibit. This innovation gives the venture the competitive advantage that results in wealth creation. Innovation may be in new products, new production methods, new markets, and new forms of organizations.

From this list, you can quickly gather that entrepreneurship is not always small and small business is not always entrepreneurial.

While most businesses start small, it is the intent to stay small that separates them from entrepreneurship. Explore this chapter and think about the possibilities. That is, the possibility of entrepreneurship and the possibility of starting a small business in your future. Or, the possibility of working for an entrepreneur or an agency that supports entrepreneurship.

Well-Known Canadian Entrepreneurs[3]

Entrepreneurs have played a major role in developing the Canadian economy. Consider just a few of the many entrepreneurs who have created companies that are now household names in Canada:

- Jim Pattison acquired a Pontiac Buick dealership in Vancouver in 1961 and started Jim Pattison Lease. In 1965, he was awarded a license to operate Vancouver AM radio station, CJOR. In subsequent years he continued acquisitions across the country until today the Jim Pattison Group <*www.jimpattison.com*> is the third largest private company in Canada. Headquartered in Vancouver,

British Columbia, it is comprised of over 465 locations worldwide focusing on the automotive, media, packaging, food sales and distribution, magazine distribution, entertainment, and export and financial industries.

- In 1922, two brothers, John W. and Alfred J. Billes, with a combined savings of $1,800, bought Hamilton Tire and Garage Ltd. Today, more than 80 percent of Canadians shop at Canadian Tire stores every year. Canadian Tire Corporation, Limited, is one of Canada's most-shopped general retailers and the country's largest sporting goods retailer, with more than 1,700 retail and gasoline outlets from coast-to-coast. Core businesses include PartSource, Canadian Tire Petroleum, Mark's, Canadian Tire Financial Services, and FGL Sports Ltd. (the largest national sporting goods retailer in Canada).
- Ablan Leon began his career selling clothing from a suitcase door-to-door. When he had enough money, he bought a small building in Welland, Ontario, and in 1909 the A. Leon Company was established. When he died in 1942, operation of the family business became the responsibility of his children. Today, Leon's Furniture Limited <*www.leons.ca*> is one of Canada's largest retailers, selling a wide range of merchandise including furniture, major appliances, and home electronics.
- In 1969, Jean Coutu (founder of The Jean Coutu Group <*www.jeancoutu.com*>) and his associate at the time, Louis Michaud, opened a discount pharmacy in Montreal. They offered a large array of products, high-quality professional services, and longer store-opening hours. By 1973, there were five branches of the "Jean Coutu Discount Pharmacies" and a franchise system was established. Today, The Jean Coutu Group is a leading pharmacy franchisor in Canada with 399 stores in Quebec, Ontario, and New Brunswick. The Jean Coutu Group owns Pro Doc Ltd., a manufacturer of generic drugs. It also holds a significant interest in Rite Aid Corporation, an American national drugstore chain with more than 4,700 drugstores.
- In 1907, J. W. Sobey started a meat delivery business in Stellarton, Nova Scotia. With a horse-drawn meat cart, he purchased and collected livestock from local farmers for resale. The first modern Sobeys supermarket opened in 1947. Today, Sobeys Inc. is one of Canada's two national retail grocery and food distributors. Sobeys owns or franchises more than 1,300 corporate and franchised stores in all ten provinces under retail banners that include Sobeys, IGA, Foodland, FreshCo, Price Chopper, and Thrifty Foods. The company also operates Lawtons Drug stores in Atlantic Canada.
- Kenneth Colin Irving opened Bouctouche, New Brunswick's first garage and service station in 1924. That same year, he opened a Ford dealership in Saint John and established Irving Oil <*www.irvingoil.com*>. He was 25 years old. Today, Irving Oil operates Canada's largest refinery, eight distribution terminals, a fleet of delivery trucks, and over 800 retail locations serving its wholesale, commercial and retail customers. It sells a range of finished energy products including gasoline, diesel, home heating fuel, jet fuel, and complementary products.
- Inspired by their passion for Ontario's Algonquin Park and everything it represented to them, Michael Budman and Don Green created Roots in 1973. Their goal was to translate their affinity for the Canadian wilderness and sports into

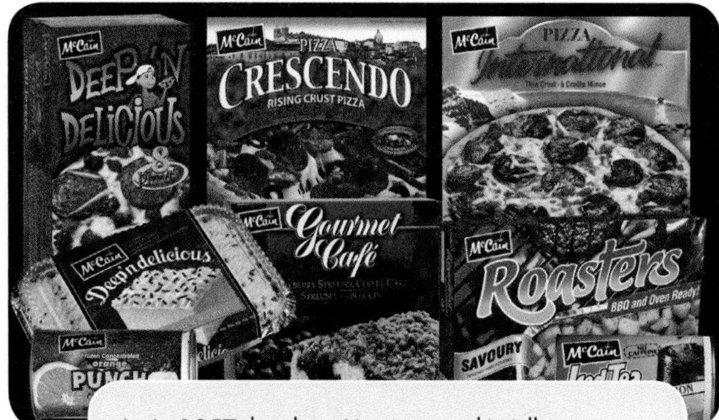

In 1957, brothers Harrison and Wallace McCain began producing frozen french fries in Florenceville, New Brunswick. Today, privately-owned McCain Foods Limited is the world's largest manufacturer of frozen potato specialties. The company's products, which include green vegetables, desserts, pizzas, juices and beverages, oven meals, entrees, and appetizers, are sold in more than 160 countries.

a distinctive line of genuine leather products and authentic athletic wear while promoting a healthy, active lifestyle and respect for the environment. The privately held company has more than 120 retail stores in Canada and the United States, and more than 40 stores in Asia. Products include leather goods, active athletic wear, yoga wear, accessories, and home furnishings.

These stories have much in common. One or a couple of entrepreneurs had a good idea, borrowed some money from friends and family, and started a business. That business now employs thousands of people and helps the country prosper.

Explain why people are willing to become entrepreneurs, and describe the attributes of successful entrepreneurs.

WHY PEOPLE TAKE THE ENTREPRENEURIAL CHALLENGE

Taking the challenge of starting a business can be scary and thrilling at the same time. One entrepreneur described it as almost like bungee jumping. You might be scared, but if you watch six other people do it and they survive, you are then able to do it yourself. There are many triggers to why people become entrepreneurial and some reasons may include the decision to leave corporate life (by choice or after downsizing), a sudden inheritance that allows them to try something different, a change in health that forces a career path adjustment, a change in family responsibility that sparks a search to increase income, or even disliking a supervisor so much that being self-employed is an attractive option. Other reasons why people are willing to take the challenge of starting a business are described in more detail below:

- *New Idea, Process, or Product.* Some entrepreneurs are driven by a firm belief, perhaps even an obsession, that they can produce a better product, or a current product at a lower cost, than anybody else. Perhaps they have gotten hold of a new widget or have conceived of an improvement that they are convinced has a large potential market. That is how Travel CUTS (Canadian Universities Travel Service) <*www.travelcuts.com*> started. In 1969, Canadian students established a national travel bureau to provide travel opportunities for students.[4] The Spotlight on Small Business highlights another business that was started by a student while he was still in school.
- *Independence.* Many entrepreneurs simply do not enjoy working for someone else. They like doing things their own way without someone standing over them. This type of person gets a great deal of satisfaction out of what he or she achieves. Melissa Harvey, whose company Will n' Roses LLC <*www.willnroses.com*> produces all-natural nut and whole-grain Kizo bars, says one of the best things about being an entrepreneur is the freedom to pursue your passion: "It's about independence. You can take something that motivates you, that inspires you and act on it without roadblocks."[5] Some corporate managers get tired of big-business life and quit their jobs to start their own small businesses. They bring with them their managerial expertise and their enthusiasm.

Company's Coming <www.companyscoming.com>, Canada's most popular name in cookbooks, began in the home of Jean Paré in Vermilion, Alberta. Since 1981, Paré has sold more than 30 million cookbooks. Even though she retired in 2011, Company's Coming is still a family business. Grant Lovig, Jean's son and co-founder of Company's Coming, remains the president.[6] Do you know of any other successful family businesses?

SPOTLIGHT ON SMALL BUSINESS

MyVoice Is My Business

Alexander Levy never planned to start a business. But while working as a student researcher at the University of Toronto, he developed a prototype mobile application. The application allows people with communication disorders—such as those caused by stroke, autism, and ALS—to make themselves understood audibly at a tiny fraction of the cost of existing hardware systems.

As Levy demonstrated the technology to clinicians and families, he found that an overwhelming percentage of them wanted to pay to use it. So, the 24- year-old launched MyVoice Inc. <*myvoiceaac.com*> in 2011 to distribute the app of the same name. More than 9,000 people in 30 countries have downloaded a free version of MyVoice, and many are converting to paid monthly subscriptions that include powerful customization tools. "Our products materially improve the lives of thousands of people with disabilities," says Levy, who now has 10 employees.

For developing a life-changing innovation, creating jobs, and building a company with the potential for explosive growth, Levy was chosen as the FuEL Entrepreneur of the Year. This award celebrates Canada's Future Entrepreneurial Leaders (FuEL). "The winners of the FuEL Awards are eager young Canadians, brimming with innovative ideas and a passion for creating a better future," says Ian Portsmouth, Editor-in-Chief of *PROFIT,* which produces the awards in co-operation with Impact Entrepreneurship Group. "They are role models for Canada's youth, and the cornerstone of the country's economic prospects."

Source: Used with permission of Rogers Publishing Limited.

- *Challenge.* Closely related to the previous factors are the excitement and the challenge of doing something new or difficult. Many people thrive on overcoming challenges. These people welcome the opportunity to run their own business.
- *Family Pattern.* Some people grow up in an atmosphere in which family members have started their own businesses, perhaps going back several generations. The talk at the dinner table is often about business matters. This background may predispose young men or women to think along the same lines. Sometimes there is a family business, and the next generation grows up expecting to take its place there in due course.
- *Profit.* It is natural for people to benefit monetarily from their ideas and dedication and to be rewarded for the money they risk and their hard work when they run a business. Yet long after a business has produced substantial profits and amassed personal fortunes for its owners, many continue to enjoy the challenge of overcoming the endless problems that every business faces and the satisfaction of continued success.
- *Immigrants.* Some immigrants who come to Canada lack education. This, combined with no Canadian job experience and weak language skills, makes it difficult for them to find employment. However, they often have the drive and desire to succeed, and if they can obtain the capital, they can start their own business. We see this in the many immigrants who run convenience stores (called dépanneurs in Quebec) as well as other types of businesses, such as importing and manufacturing. Other immigrants arrive with capital, skills, and strong entrepreneurial backgrounds. British Columbia in general has been a major beneficiary of such immigrants from Hong Kong.

What Does It Take to Be an Entrepreneur?

Would you succeed as an entrepreneur? You can learn about the managerial and leadership skills needed to run a firm. However, you may not have the personality to assume the risks, take the initiative, create the vision, and rally others to follow your lead. Those traits are harder to learn or acquire. As you review the following important entrepreneurial attributes, you may ask yourself if you have them:[7]

- *Self-directed.* You should be self-disciplined and thoroughly comfortable being your own boss. You alone will be responsible for your success or failure.
- *Self-nurturing.* You must believe in your idea even when no one else does, and be able to replenish your own enthusiasm. The best lesson Rebecca MacDonald, co-founder of Just Energy Group Inc. <*www.justenergy.com*> (formerly Just Energy Income Fund), ever learned is "to believe in yourself, because business throws you curveballs on a minute-to-minute basis. If you start second-guessing yourself, your confidence can be shaken very quickly, and lack of confidence is going to create lack of performance."
- *Action-Oriented.* Great business ideas are not enough. The most important thing is a burning desire to realize, actualize, and build your dream into reality.
- *Highly Energetic.* It is your own business and you must be emotionally, mentally, and physically able to work long and hard. For example, when starting Extreme Pita <*www.extremepita.com*>, brothers Mark and Alex Rechichi were so consumed with work that they often slept on cots in the shop's backroom after their evening shift. That way, the entrepreneurs could get a few hours of sleep before starting all over again the next morning.
- *Tolerant of Uncertainty.* Successful entrepreneurs take only calculated risks (if they can help it). Still, they must be able to take *some* risks. Remember, entrepreneurship is not for the squeamish or those bent on security. You can't be afraid to fail. The late football coach Vince Lombardi summarized the entrepreneurial philosophy when he said, "We didn't lose any games this season, we just ran out of time twice." New entrepreneurs must be prepared to run out of time a few times before they succeed.
- *Able to Learn Quickly.* Making errors is inevitable. Only those who do nothing make no mistakes. What is important is what you learn from them. Good entrepreneurs are quick to learn such lessons. They adapt and change direction as required instead of letting pride stand in the way of admitting a mistake.

While courage is not considered a skill, it is nevertheless an important element of an entrepreneur. Courage is required to challenge the status quo, to see an opportunity, and then most importantly, to try to do something about it. Entrepreneurs are doers. They do not just think and talk about an idea, they act on it! Also be aware that even if you possess many (or even all) of these attributes, there is no guarantee that you will be successful with every endeavour.

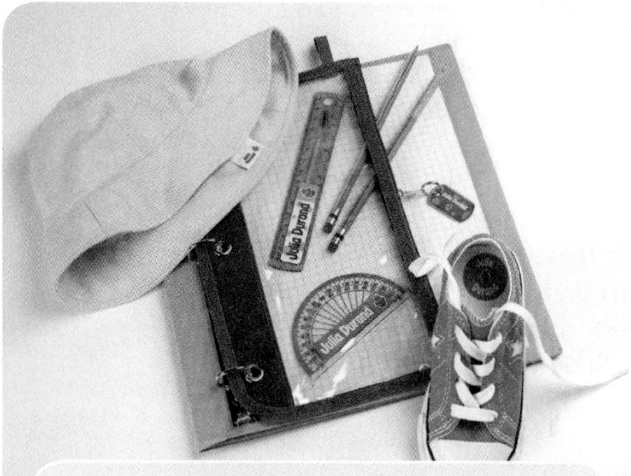

▶ Four moms started Mabel's Labels <*www.mabelslabels.com*> when they got tired of their children losing their belongings or getting them mixed up with those of their friends. Today's labels go on everything from clothing to containers, for children and adults alike. Would you put a label on your items?

Turning Your Passions and Problems into Opportunities

While many entrepreneurs' business ideas are inspired by their passions (see the Green Box for an example), many see business opportunities in their problems. For example, Anita Roddick started The Body Shop <*www.thebodyshop.com*>, which recycles its bottles and jars, because she hated paying for expensive packaging when she bought makeup.[8]

Most entrepreneurs do not get ideas for products and services from some flash of inspiration. The source of innovation is more like a *flashlight.* Imagine a search party walking in the dark, shining lights, looking around, asking questions, and looking some more. "That's how most creativity happens," says business author Dale Dauten. "Calling around, asking questions, saying 'What if?' till you get blisters on your tongue."

GREENBOX

Socially Responsible Entrepreneurship

Until recently, environmentalism and business did not mix; at least that is what Gary Hirshberg thought. After college, the anti-business Hirshberg went to work at a small ecological research centre, only to have an epiphany at an exposition funded by Kraft Foods. The expo championed the use of fossil fuels, chemicals, and everything else Hirshberg hated about big-business food production. But he realized that more people had attended the exposition in one day than had ever been to his ecological institute, so he went by the old saying "If you can't beat them, join them."

Two years later, Hirshberg started Stonyfield Farm with one question in mind: "Is it possible to run a commercial enterprise that does not hurt the planet—and still be highly profitable?" The answer is yes. By entirely offsetting all its carbon dioxide emissions, installing the largest solar photovoltaic array in New Hampshire, and generating all yogurt waste into biogas, Stonyfield runs a 100 percent organic operation. Its manufacturing process is not only environmentally sound but also profitable. Stonyfield's green attitude saves the company millions of dollars a year, and after just 15 years in business, Hirshberg surpassed his old nemesis Kraft Foods in yogurt sales. Stonyfield Farm is now a $400 million company and is the world's leading organic yogurt brand.

Stonyfield Farm was launched in Canada in 2006. Stonyfield yogurt is produced in Canada and made entirely of organic milk which comes from Canadian dairy farms. Its organic ingredient purchases keep farm acres free of chemical pesticides that can contaminate soil, rivers, and drinking water. The Canadian division contributes 10 percent of its profits from sales of Stonyfield organic yogurt to its Profit for the Planet Fund to support initiatives that will have a positive and meaningful effect on the environment.

Sources: "The Simple Way Stonyfield Farm Cut $18 Million In Expenses," *Business Insider*, 23 February 2012, http://ca.finance.yahoo.com/news/simple-way-stonyfield-farm-cut-185500825.html; "Stonyfield encourages Canadians to become greener with its Profit for the Planet Community Challenge," CNW Group, 27 January 2011, http://smr.newswire.ca/en/stonyfield/stonyfield-profit-for-the-planet-community-challenge; Gary Hirshberg, "Seven Cows and a Dream," *Newsweek*, 25 February 2008, E6; and Kris Berggren, "Compassionate Capitalists: Young Social Entrepreneurs Merge Values and Business Savvy to Change the World," *National Catholic Reporter*, 30 May 2008.

To look at problems and/or passions and see opportunities in them, ask yourself these questions: What do I want, but can never find? What product or service would improve my life? What really irritates me and what product or service would help?

Keep in mind, however, that not all ideas are opportunities. If your idea does not meet anyone else's needs, the business will not succeed. You may have a business idea that is a good opportunity if:[9]

- It fills customers' needs;
- You have the skills and resources to start a business;
- You can sell the product or service at a price customers are willing and able to pay—and still make a profit;
- You can get your product or service to customers before your window of opportunity closes (before competitors with similar solutions beat you to the marketplace); and
- You can keep the business going.

If you think you may have the entrepreneurial spirit in your blood, complete the Entrepreneurial Readiness Questionnaire that appears in the appendix at the end of this chapter.

Female Entrepreneurs[10]

A major phenomenon since the late 1970s is the large number of women who have gone into business for themselves. Throughout this book, you will see examples of such enterprises. Statistics Canada's *Labour Force Survey* reports that there were 50,000 self-employed women in Canada in 2011, accounting for about one-third of all self-employed persons. Between 2001 and 2011, the number of self-employed

▸ Christine Magee started Sleep Country Canada <www.sleepcountry.ca> with partners Steve Gunn and Gord Lownds based on their dream to give customers what they want. Today, the company is Canada's largest mattress retailer.

women grew by 23 percent, compared with 14 percent growth in male self-employment. Accommodation and food services industries have the highest share of businesses that are majority-owned by females (25 percent), whereas small businesses in agriculture and primary industries have the lowest level (9 percent).

Studies have shown a variety of reasons for the significant emergence of female entrepreneurs:

- *Financial Need.* The previous decade saw the average real incomes of Canadian employees drop and unemployment fluctuate. This has encouraged many women to start a business.
- *Lack of Promotion Opportunities.* Most positions in higher management are still dominated by men. Although the situation is improving, the pace is extremely slow. Many women who are frustrated by this pace take the entrepreneurial route.
- *Women Returning to the Workforce.* Many women who return to the job market after raising a family find that their skills are outdated. They also encounter subtle age discrimination. These factors encourage many to try self-employment.
- *Family and Personal Responsibility.* The rate of divorced women and single mothers in recent years has created a situation in which many women find themselves with children and little or no financial support. Some even refuse such support to be more independent. Affordable technology has made it possible for women to start home-based businesses.
- *Public Awareness of Women in Business.* As more publicity highlights the fact that growing numbers of women have started their own ventures, the idea catches on and gives others the confidence to try. Often two or more women will team up to form a partnership.
- *Part-Time Occupations.* Often women with some particular talent—for example, publicity, writing, designing, making clothes, cooking, organizing, or human relations—are encouraged to develop their hobby or skills on a part-time basis to see how far they can go with it. This focus has resulted in many notable success stories.
- *Higher Rate of Success for Women.* Female entrepreneurs seem to have a better success rate than men. Various factors may account for this. Women feel less pressured than men to achieve quick results. They are a little more cautious, so they make fewer mistakes. They also accept advice more readily than men, who may have a macho image of having to know it all. It will be interesting to follow this process to see if women continue to start ventures at the same rate and maintain their remarkable track record.

There are many resources available to help female entrepreneurs network and get general support. Some examples include the Canadian Women's Business Network (<*www.cdnbizwomen.com*>), Women's Enterprise Centre (<*www.wec.ca*>), and the Canadian Association of Women Executives & Entrepreneurs (<*www.cawee.net*>). Financial institutions also offer small-business products and services aimed at women, which often can be accessed on their Web sites. One example is found on the Royal Bank Web site <*www.rbcroyalbank.com/sme/women*>. In the meantime, if you wish to learn about some of Canada's top female entrepreneurs, review the annual *PROFIT/Chatelaine* W100 rankings (<*www.profitguide.com/microsite/profitw100/2011*>).

Entrepreneurial Teams

An **entrepreneurial team** is a group of experienced people from different areas of business who join together to form a managerial team with the skills needed to develop, make, and market a new product. A team may be better than an individual entrepreneur because team members can combine creative skills with production and marketing skills right from the start. Having a team also can ensure more co-operation and coordination among functions.

entrepreneurial team
A group of experienced people from different areas of business who join together to form a managerial team with the skills needed to develop, make, and market a new product.

While Steve Jobs was the charismatic folk hero and visionary of Apple Inc., it was Steve Wozniack who invented the first personal computer model and Mike Markkula who offered the business expertise and access to venture capital.[11] The key to Apple's early success was that the company was built around this "smart team" of entrepreneurs. The team wanted to combine the discipline of a big company with an environment where people could feel they were participating in a successful venture. The trio of entrepreneurs recruited seasoned managers with similar desires. All of the managers worked as a team. Everyone worked together to conceive, develop, and market products.[12]

PROGRESS ASSESSMENT

- What are key differences between entrepreneurial ventures and small businesses?
- Why are people willing to become entrepreneurs?
- What are the advantages of entrepreneurial teams?

Micropreneurs and Home-Based Businesses

Not every person who starts a business wants to grow into a mammoth corporation. Some are interested in maintaining a balanced lifestyle while doing the kind of work they want to do. The smallest of small businesses are called **micro-enterprises**, most often defined as having fewer than five employees.[13] While other entrepreneurs are committed to the quest for growth, **micropreneurs** (owners of micro-enterprises) know they can be happy even if their companies never appear on a list of top-ranked businesses.

micro-enterprises
A small business defined as having fewer than five employees.

micropreneurs
Small-business owners with fewer than five employees who are willing to accept the risk of starting and managing the type of business that remains small, lets them do the kind of work they want to do, and offers them a balanced lifestyle.

Many micropreneurs are owners of home-based businesses. According to Industry Canada, approximately 55 percent of all employer businesses (615,599 in number) were micro-enterprises, with almost 78 percent of these businesses operating in the service-producing sector.[14] Micropreneurs include writers, consultants, video producers, architects, and bookkeepers.

Many home-based businesses are owned by people who are trying to combine career and family.[15] Do not misunderstand and picture home-based workers as female child-care providers; men also run home-based businesses. In addition to helping business owners balance work and family, other reasons for the growth of home-based businesses include the following:[16]

- *Computer Technology*. Computer technology has levelled the competitive playing field, allowing home-based businesses to look and act as big as their corporate competitors. Broadband Internet connections, personal digital assistants (PDAs) such as the BlackBerry and the iPhone, and other technologies are so affordable that setting up a business takes a much smaller initial investment than it once did
- *Corporate Downsizing*. Downsizing has made workers aware that there is no such thing as job security, leading some to venture out on their own. Meanwhile, the work of the downsized employees still needs to be done and corporations are

outsourcing much of the work to smaller companies; that is, they are contracting with small companies to temporarily fill their needs.
- *Change in Social Attitudes.* Whereas home-based entrepreneurs used to be asked when they were going to get a "real" job, they are now likely to be asked instead for "how-to-do-it" advice.

Working at home has its challenges, of course. In setting up a home-based business, you could expect the following major challenges:[18]

- *Getting New Customers.* Getting the word out can be difficult because you do not have signs or a storefront, especially if the business does not have a Web presence.
- *Managing Time.* Of course, you save time by not commuting, but it takes self-discipline to use that time wisely.
- *Keeping Work and Family Tasks Separate.* Often it is difficult to separate work and family tasks. It is great to be able to throw a load of laundry in the washer in the middle of the workday if you need to, but you have to keep such distractions to a minimum. It is also difficult to leave your work at the office if the office is your home. Again, it takes self-discipline to keep work from trickling out of the home office and into the family room.
- *Abiding by City Ordinances.* Government ordinances restrict the types of businesses that are allowed in certain parts of the community and how much traffic a home-based business can attract to the neighbourhood.
- *Managing Risk.* Home-based entrepreneurs should review their homeowner's insurance policy since not all policies cover business-related claims. Some even void the coverage if there is a business in the home.

Home-based entrepreneurs should focus on finding opportunity instead of accepting security, getting results instead of following routines, earning a profit instead of earning a paycheque, trying new ideas instead of avoiding mistakes, and creating a long-term vision instead of seeking a short-term payoff. Figure 7.1 lists ten ideas for potentially successful home-based businesses. You can find a wealth of online information about starting a home-based business at <*http://sbinfocanada.about.com*> and <*www.entrepreneur.com*>.

▸ Chef Michael Smith, one of Canada's best-known chef, is host of several cooking shows on Food Network Canada and in 40 other countries. He is an award-winning cookbook author, newspaper columnist, restaurant chef, and home cook who works from his home.[17] His series, *Chef At Home,* features some of his home cooking.

Web-Based Businesses

The Internet has sprouted a world of small Web-based businesses that sell everything from staplers to refrigerator magnets to wedding dresses. These small businesses compete with other small businesses as well as large Web-based and bricks-and-mortar businesses. Take a moment and ponder the opportunities that have been created by eBay <*www.ebay.ca*> alone for entrepreneurs. This has been such a powerful channel for part-time and full-time entrepreneurs that a book has been developed, titled *eBay for Dummies,* to teach people how to successfully use this Web site to buy and sell products and services.

There are some somereal e-commerce challenges in Canada. "Despite Canada's reputation as one of the world's most wired and digitally social people, Canadians only spent $18 billion online in 2010, or 3.4 percent of total retail sales, according to Boston Consulting Group.

Many businesses can be started at home. Listed below are ten businesses that have low start-up costs, do not require an abundance of administrative tasks, and are in relatively high demand.

1. Cleaning service
2. Gift-basket business
3. Web merchant
4. Mailing list service
5. Microfarming (small plots of land for such high-value crops as mushrooms, edible flowers, or sprouts)
6. Tutoring
7. Résumé service
8. Web design
9. Medical claims assistance
10. Personal coaching

Look for a business that meets these important criteria: (1) the job is something you truly enjoy doing; (2) you know enough to do the job well or you are willing to spend time learning it while you have another job; and (3) you can identify a market for your product or service.

Figure 7.1

Potential Home-Based Businesses

This is well behind other developed countries such as the United States at 5 percent and the United Kingdom at 13.5 percent. When you consider these sales, four in ten dollars that are spent online go abroad and not into the Canadian economy. While online spending is expected to nearly double by 2015, Canada is expected to fall even farther behind: "Canada has been a little sleepy as far as getting online" to shop, said Jeffrey Grau, an analyst with U.S. market research firm eMarketer".[19]

Shop.ca <*www.shop.ca*> was started in 2012 to address some of these issues. Imagine millions of products from the greatest brands, all in one place. Take thousands of stores, twenty-six categories (e.g., health and beauty, clothing, electronic goods, and pet supplies), and free shipping on orders over $40. The company promises convenience, no more duty, customs, or return hassles, and free returns.[20] Have you heard of this site? If yes, has the company delivered on its promises?

Web-based businesses have to offer more than the same merchandise customers can buy at stores—they must offer unique products or services. For example, Marc Resnik started his Web-based distribution company after waking up one morning laughing about his business idea. Now ThrowThings.com <*throwthings.com*> makes money for him. Although the company's offerings seem like a random collection of unrelated items, everything it sells can be thrown. You can buy promotional products in the "Throw Your Name Around!" section, ventriloquist dummies in the "Throw Your Voice!" section, and sporting equipment in the "Things to Throw!" section. About two-thirds of the company's revenue comes from the promotional products section, which allows customers to add a logo to thousands of products. Why is Resnik's business so successful? As one frequent customer said, it's because of Resnik's exceptional service and quick turnaround time.[21]

One of the easiest ways to start a Web-based business is through affiliate marketing. **Affiliate marketing** is an Internet-based marketing strategy in which a business rewards individuals or other businesses (affiliates) for each visitor or customer the affiliate sends to its Web site. For example, imagine you discovered a backpack online made of an extremely lightweight, amazingly strong fabric that holds everything you need for the day, is easy to carry, and looks great. You want to tell all your friends about it, so you register as an affiliate on the seller's Web site and download to your MySpace page a *widget,* a tiny application that links your page to the seller's site. Whenever anyone clicks on the widget (an image of the product) and buys a backpack, the seller pays you a commission.

affiliate marketing
An Internet-based marketing strategy in which a business rewards individuals or other businesses (affiliates) for each visitor or customer the affiliate sends to its Web site.

A Web-based business is not always a fast road to success. It can sometimes be a shortcut to failure. Hundreds of high-flying dot-coms crashed after promising to revolutionize the way we shop. That is the bad news. The good news is that you can learn from someone else's failure and spare yourself some pain.

Entrepreneurship Within Firms

intrapreneurs
Creative people who work as entrepreneurs within corporations.

Entrepreneurship in a large organization is often reflected in the efforts and achievements of intrapreneurs. **Intrapreneurs** are creative people who work as entrepreneurs within corporations. The idea is to use a company's existing resources—human, financial, and physical—to launch new products and generate new profits.[22]

At 3M <*www.3m.com*>, which produces a wide array of products from adhesives like Scotch tape to non-woven materials for industrial use, managers are expected to devote 15 percent of their time to thinking up new products or services.[23] You know those brightly coloured Post-it Notes that people use to write messages on just about everything? That product was developed by Art Fry, a 3M employee. He needed to mark the pages of a hymnal in a way that would not damage or fall out of the book. He came up with the idea of the self-stick, repositionable paper. The 3M labs soon produced a sample, but distributors thought the product wasn't important and market surveys were inconclusive. Nonetheless, 3M kept sending samples to secretaries of top executives. Eventually, after launching a major sales and marketing program, the orders began pouring in, and Post-it Notes became a big winner. The company continues to update the product; making the notes from recycled paper is just one of many innovations. Post-it Notes have gone international as well—the notepads sent to Japan are long and narrow to accommodate vertical writing. Now you can even use Post-it Notes electronically—the software program Post-it Software Notes allows you to type messages onto brightly coloured notes and store them on memo boards, embed them in documents, or send them through e-mail.

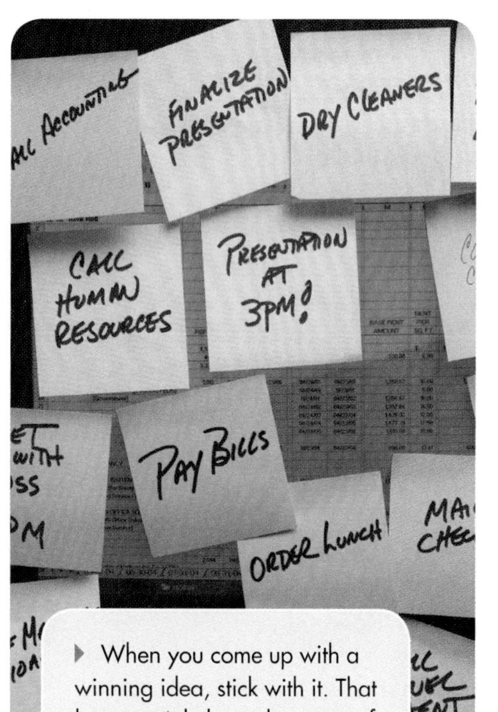

▶ When you come up with a winning idea, stick with it. That has certainly been the motto of the 3M company, the maker of Post-it Notes. 3M encourages intrapreneurship among its employees by requiring them to devote at least 15 percent of their time to thinking about new products. How has this commitment to innovation paid off for the company and its employees?

ENCOURAGING ENTREPRENEURSHIP: WHAT GOVERNMENT CAN DO[24]

The different levels of government provide many services to help entrepreneurs and small businesses to succeed. Canada Business Network <*www.canadabusiness.ca*> is a federal government information service for entrepreneurs that serves as a single point of access for federal and provincial/territorial government services, programs, and regulatory requirements for business. Canada Business's mandate is to serve as the primary source of up-to-date and accurate business-related information and to provide referrals on government programs, services, and regulations—without charge—in all regions of Canada. The mission of Canada Business is to improve the start-up, survival, and growth rates of small and medium-sized enterprises. This includes assisting with sound business planning, market research, and the use of strategic business information.

Industry Canada's SME Research and Statistics site <*www.ic.gc.ca/eic/site/061.nsf/eng/Home*> is designed to encourage small-business researchers and policy analysts across Canada to share information. It includes an extensive database of research literature on small business and entrepreneurship, recent reports on small-business financing, small-business statistics, and lists of researchers and policy development offices across Canada. The *Small Business Quarterly* (*SBQ*) provides a quick and easy-to-read snapshot of the recent performance of Canada's small-business sector. (For additional government sources, review the Services section in Chapter 4.)

Entrepreneurs and new start-ups can also find assistance from incubators. Incubators were first developed to be centres that offered new businesses low-cost offices with basic business services such as accounting, legal advice, and secretarial help. Since then, the "networked" incubator has emerged with the creation of innovation centres. The networked incubator goes beyond the simple provision of office space and provides entrepreneurs and new companies with access to more services. According to the Canadian Association of Business Incubation <*www.cabi.ca*>, **incubators** today provide hands-on management assistance, education, information, technical and vital business support services, networking resources, financial advice, as well as advice on where to go to seek financial assistance. In fact, the average survival rate of companies in Canada that go through business incubation has been shown to be higher than 80 percent after five years.

▶ Incubators offer new businesses low-cost offices with basic business services such as accounting, legal advice, and secretarial help. Do you have an incubator in your area?

The goal of an incubator is not only to ensure that the small business survives the start-up period, but also to produce confident, successful graduates who will run a productive business in the future. One example of an incubator that has received worldwide recognition is CQIB, the Quebec Biotechnology Innovation Centre <*www.cqib.org*> in Laval. It provides start-ups in life science and health technology with lab space, scientific equipment, and mentoring services.

According to the National Incubation Association, there are over 1,400 business incubators in North America (including 120 in Canada) and about 7,000 worldwide. The government can also have a significant effect on entrepreneurship by offering investment tax credits that give tax breaks to businesses that make the kind of investments that create jobs. For example, the Biotechnology Innovation Centre is a tenant in Laval's Biotech City. The Biotech City is supported by the Canadian and Quebec governments in addition to the City of Laval. These government bodies encourage research and development by granting corporations and individuals tax incentives that foster scientific and technological development. One incentive includes a 30 percent refundable tax credit on capital or rental costs for eligible equipment (up to three years).

While the government provides a great deal of assistance, it is still primarily up to the entrepreneur to make a success of the new business.

▶ The National Research Council (NRC) <*www.nrc-cnrc.gc.ca*> supports Industrial Partnership Facilities (IPFs). Similar to incubators, each IPF has a focus on a different technology sector, depending on the specialization of its host institute. IPFs offer start-ups access to specialized laboratory space and equipment, regular interaction with researchers, and the opportunity to benefit from a range of NRC technology-transfer initiatives. The NRC Plant Biotechnology Institute in Saskatoon (viewed here) strengthens the region's agricultural biotechnology cluster.

incubators
Centres that provide hands-on management assistance, education, information, technical and vital business support services, networking resources, financial advice, as well as advice on where to go to seek financial assistance.

PROGRESS ASSESSMENT

- How do micropreneurs differ from other entrepreneurs?
- What are some of the opportunities and risks of Web-based businesses?
- List some services for entrepreneurs provided by the federal government.

Discuss the importance of small business to the Canadian economy.

GETTING STARTED IN SMALL BUSINESS

Let's suppose you have a great idea for a new business, you have the attributes of an entrepreneur, and you are ready to take the leap into business for yourself. How do you start a business? How much paperwork is involved? That is what the rest of this chapter is about. We will explore small businesses, their role in the economy, and small-business management.

It may be easier to identify with a small neighbourhood business than with a giant global firm, yet the principles of management are similar. The management of charities, government agencies, churches, schools, and unions is much the same as the management of small and large businesses. So, as you learn about small-business management, you will make a giant step toward understanding management in general. All organizations demand capital, good ideas, planning, information management, budgets (and financial management in general), accounting, marketing, good employee relations, and good overall managerial know-how. We shall explore these areas as they relate to small businesses and then, later in the book, apply the concepts to large firms, even to global organizations.

business establishment Must meet at least one of the following minimum criteria: it must have at least one paid employee, it must have annual sales revenue of $30,000, or it must be incorporated and have filed a federal corporate income tax return at least once in the previous three years.

employer business Meets one of the business establishment criteria and usually maintains a payroll of at least one person, possibly the owner.

small business A business that is independently owned and operated, is not dominant in its field, and meets certain standards of size in terms of employees or annual revenues.

SMEs (small and medium-sized enterprises) Refers to all businesses with fewer than 500 employees.

Small Versus Big Business[25]

The Business Registrar of Statistics Canada maintains a count of business establishments. A **business establishment** must meet at least one of the following minimum criteria: it must have at least one paid employee, it must have annual sales revenue of $30,000, or it must be incorporated and have filed a federal corporate income tax return at least once in the previous three years. While there are a over 2.4 million business establishments in Canada, a little over 1.1 million of them are employer businesses. An **employer business** meets one of the business establishment criteria and usually maintains a payroll of at least one person, possibly the owner. The rest are classified as "indeterminate." Figure 7.2 breaks down the number of businesses by sector and number of employees.

It would be helpful to define what is meant by the term *small business*. Giant companies like TELUS Corporation or Magna International may look at most companies as small. A **small business** is often defined as a business that is independently owned and operated, is not dominant in its field, and meets certain standards of size in terms of employees or annual revenues.

Many institutions define small business according to their own needs. Generally speaking, a business with fewer than 50 employees is considered a small business. Medium-sized businesses have 50 to 499 employees, while large businesses employ more than 500 people. **SMEs (small and medium-sized enterprises)** refer to all businesses with fewer than 500 employees. In Figure 7.2, of the approximately 1.1 million employer businesses in Canada, 0.2 percent have more than 500 employees. Businesses employing fewer than 50 employees account for the vast majority (95.5 percent) of all employer businesses.

As you can see, small business is really a big part of the Canadian economy. How big a part? We'll explore that question next.

Importance of Small Businesses[26]

The small-business sector is a dynamic part of the Canadian economy. Nearly all small businesses are Canadian-owned and managed. This is in contrast to large businesses, of which many are foreign-owned and managed. Small business thus plays a major role in helping to maintain the Canadian identity and Canadian economic independence.

	Percentage of Employer Businesses	NO. OF BUSINESS LOCATIONS		
		Total	Goods-Producing Sector	Service-Producing Sector
Indeterminate1		**1,283,017**	**306,783**	**976,234**
Employer Businesses		**1,122,306**	**239,057**	**883,249**
Small businesses (1–49 employees)	95.5	1,071,978	227,589	844,389
Medium-sized businesses (50–499 employees)	4.3	47,800	11,019	36,781
Large businesses (500 + employees)	0.2	2,528	449	2,079
Total		**2,405,323**	**545,840**	**1,859,483**

Note 1: The "indeterminate" category consists of incorporated or unincorporated businesses that do not have a Canada Revenue Agency payroll deductions account. The workforce of such businesses may consist of contract workers, family members, and/or owners.

Source: Statistics Canada, "Number of Business Locations by Sector and Firm Size (Number of Employees), December 2011." Adapted from Statistics Canada, special tabulation, unpublished data, (Business Register Database), December 2011. Reproduced on an "as-is" basis with the permission of Statistics Canada.

Figure 7.2

Number of Business Locations by Sector and Firm Size (Number of Employees), December 2011

Almost 96 percent of Canadian companies are considered small businesses.

Small businesses also continue to be feeders for future large businesses. As they prosper and develop new goods and services, they are often bought out by large companies, which in turn become more competitive. Alternatively, after small businesses establish a good track record, some of them convert from private to public companies, enabling them to obtain significant financing and become larger companies.

Here are some quick facts about small businesses (in this case, defined by Industry Canada as firms that have fewer than 100 employees):

- 98 percent of businesses in Canada have fewer than 100 employees;
- Between 2002 and 2008, about 100,000 new small businesses, on average, were created in Canada each year;
- Small businesses employ approximately 5 million individuals in Canada, or 48 percent of the total private labour force;
- Small businesses contribute slightly more than 30 percent to Canada's gross domestic product; and
- About 86 percent of Canadian exporters were small businesses.

Since most of Canada's jobs are in small businesses, there is a very good chance that you will either work in a small business some day or start one. In addition to providing employment opportunities, small firms believe they offer other advantages over larger companies—more personal customer service and the ability to respond quickly to opportunities.

Bigger is not always better. Picture a hole in the ground. If you fill it with big boulders, there are many empty spaces between them. However, if you fill it with sand, there is no space between the grains. That is how it is in business. Big businesses do not serve all the needs of the market. There is plenty of room for small companies to make a profit filling those niches.

Wide Diversification

Another significant aspect of small business is the wide diversification of its activities. If you look, you will find small businesses in many sectors:

1. *Service Businesses.* You are already familiar with the services provided by car mechanics, dry cleaners, travel agencies, lawn care firms, salons, and other services that cater to you and your family. In your career search, be sure to explore opportunities provided by hotels and motels, health clubs, amusement parks, income tax preparation organizations, employment agencies, accounting firms, rental firms of all kinds, management consulting, repair services (e.g., computers), insurance agencies, real estate firms, stockbrokers, and so on. A growth area is in computer consulting and the knowledge-based industries.
2. *Retail Businesses.* You only have to go to a major shopping mall to see the possibilities in retailing. There are stores selling shoes, clothes, hats, skis, housewares, sporting goods, ice cream, groceries, and more. Much more. Watch the trends and you will see ideas such as fancy popcorn stores and cafés with Internet access areas.
3. *Construction Firms.* Drive through any big city and you will see huge cranes towering over major construction sites. Would you enjoy supervising such work? Visit some areas where construction firms are building bridges, roads, homes, schools, buildings, and dams. There is a feeling of power and creativity in such work that excites many observers. How about you? Talk to some of the workers and supervisors and learn about the risks and rewards of small construction firms.
4. *Wholesalers.* Have you ever visited a wholesale food warehouse, jewellery centre, or similar wholesale firm? If not, you are missing an important link in the small-business chain, one with much potential. Wholesale representatives often make more money, have more free time, travel more, and enjoy their work more than similar people in retailing. Wholesaling will be discussed in Chapter 15.
5. *Manufacturing.* Of course, manufacturing is still an attractive career for tomorrow's graduates. Surveys show that manufacturers make the most money among small-business owners. There are careers for designers, machinists, mechanics, engineers, supervisors, safety inspectors, and a host of other occupations. Visit some small manufacturers in your area and inquire about such jobs to get some experience before starting your own manufacturing business. Today's high-tech world opens up many opportunities, if you are interested.

There are also small farmers who enjoy the rural life and the pace of farming. Small farms have been in great trouble for the last few years, but some that specialize in exotic or organic crops do quite well. Similarly, many small mining operations attract college and university students who have a sense of adventure. People who are not sure what career they would like to follow have a busy time ahead. They should research service firms, construction firms, farms, mines, retailers, wholesalers, and all other kinds of small and large businesses to learn about the diversity and excitement available in Canadian business.

Summarize the major causes of small-business failure.

Small-Business Success and Failure

You cannot be naive about business practices, or you will go broke. There is some debate about how many new small businesses fail each year. There are many false signals about entries and exits. When small-business owners go out of business to start new and different businesses, they may be included in the "failure" category when obviously this is not the case. Similarly, when a business changes its form of ownership from partnership to corporation, it may be counted as a failure. Retirements of sole owners may also be in this category.

Thousands of businesses enter and exit the marketplace throughout the year. According to Industry Canada, survival rates for business with fewer than 250 employees

Figure 7.3

Causes of Small-Business Failure

Plunging in without first testing the waters on a small scale.	Buying too much on credit.
Underpricing or overpricing goods or services.	Extending credit too freely.
Underestimating how much time it will take to build a market.	Expanding credit too rapidly.
Starting with too little capital.	Failing to keep complete, accurate records, so that the owners drift into trouble without realizing it.
Starting with too much capital and being careless in its use.	Carrying habits of personal extravagance into the business.
Going into business with little or no experience and without first learning something about the industry or market.	Not understanding business cycles.
Borrowing money without planning just how and when to pay it back.	Forgetting about taxes, insurance, and other costs of doing business.
Attempting to do too much business with too little capital.	Mistaking the freedom of being in business for oneself for the liberty to work or not, according to whim.
Not allowing for setbacks and unexpected expenses.	

decline over time. About 85 percent of businesses that enter the marketplace survive for one full year, 70 percent survive for two years, and 51 percent survive for five years.[27] Figure 7.3 lists reasons for small-business failure. Managerial incompetence and inadequate financial planning are two of the biggest reasons for these failures.

Choosing the right type of business is critical. Many of the businesses with the lowest failure rates require advanced training to start—veterinary services, dental practices, medical practices, and so on. While training and degrees may buy security, they do not tend to produce much growth—one dentist can fill only so many cavities. If you want to be both independent and rich, you need to go after growth. Often high-growth businesses, such as technology firms, are not easy to start and are even more difficult to keep going.[28]

The easiest businesses to start have the least growth and the greatest failure rate (like restaurants). The easiest to keep alive are difficult to get started (like manufacturing). And the ones that can make you rich are the ones that are both hard to start and hard to keep going (like automobile assembly). See Figure 7.4 to get an idea of the business situations that are most likely to lead to success.

Figure 7.4

Small-Business Success Factors

The customer requires a lot of personal attention, as in a beauty parlour.	A large business sells a franchise operation to local buyers. (Don't forget franchising as an excellent way to enter the world of small business.)
The product is not easily made by mass-production techniques (e.g., custom-tailored clothes or custom auto-body work).	The owner pays attention to new competitors.
Sales are not large enough to appeal to a large firm (e.g., a novelty shop).	The business is in a growth industry (e.g., computer services or Web design).

When you decide to start your own business, think carefully. You are unlikely to find everything you want—easy entry, security, and reward—in one business. Choose those characteristics that matter most to you; accept the absence of the others; plan, plan, plan; and then go for it!

LEARNING ABOUT SMALL-BUSINESS OPERATIONS

LO 4

List ways to learn how small businesses operate.

Hundreds of would-be entrepreneurs of all ages have asked the same question: How can I learn to run my own business? Many of these people had no idea what kind of business they wanted to start; they simply wanted to be in business for themselves. There are several ways to get into your first business venture. We will introduce them to you in the next few pages. They are:

1. Learn from others.
2. Get some experience.
3. Buy an existing business.
4. Buy a franchise.
5. Inherit / take over a family business.

Here are some hints for learning about small business.

Learn from Others

Investigate your local area schools for classes on the subject. There are entrepreneurship programs in post-secondary schools throughout Canada. One of the best things about such courses is that they bring together entrepreneurs from diverse backgrounds. (Many entrepreneurs have started businesses as students—see the Analyzing Management Decisions case near the end of the chapter for an example.) An excellent way to learn how to run a small business is to talk to others who have already done it. They will tell you that location is critical. They will caution you not to be undercapitalized; that is, to start with enough money. They will warn you about the problems of finding and retaining good workers. And, most of all, they will tell you to keep good records and hire a good accountant and lawyer before you start. Free advice like this is invaluable.

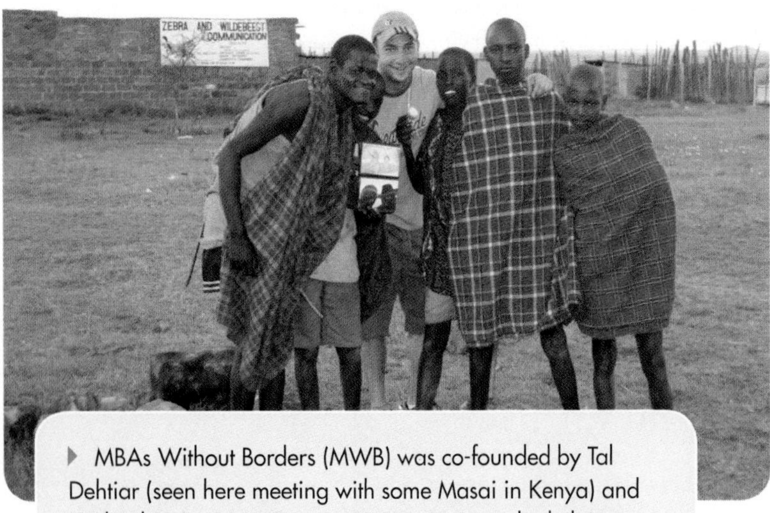

MBAs Without Borders (MWB) was co-founded by Tal Dehtiar (seen here meeting with some Masai in Kenya) and Michael Brown. MWB gave MBAs experience by helping to promote enterprise in developing nations. According to Dehtiar, "The classroom and office are great environments for education, but MWB forces MBAs to not only think outside of the box, but out of this world." CDC Development Solutions <*www.cdcdevelopmentsolutions.org*> acquired MWB with a focus on developing small and medium-sized businesses, communities, and local institutions in emerging markets.

Get Some Experience

There is no better way to learn small-business management than by becoming an apprentice or working for a successful entrepreneur. Many small-business owners got the idea for their businesses from their prior jobs. An industry standard is to have three years' experience in a comparable business.

Many new entrepreneurs come from corporate management. They are tired of the big-business life or are being laid off because of corporate downsizing. Such managers bring

MAKING ETHICAL DECISIONS

Sabotaging Your Employer

Suppose you have worked for two years in a company and you see signs that the business is beginning to falter. You and a co-worker have ideas about how to make a company similar to your boss's succeed. Rather than share your ideas with your boss, you and your friend are considering quitting your jobs and starting your own company together. Should you approach other co-workers about working for your new venture? Will you try to lure your boss's customers to your own business? What are your alternatives? What are the consequences of each alternative? What is the most ethical choice?

their managerial expertise and enthusiasm with them. Such was the case with Tom Heintzman and Greg Kiessling, co-founders of Bullfrog Power <*www.bullfrogpower.com*>. Prior to starting the company, Heintzman had experience in the private and non-governmental organizations sectors as a consultant and as the director of corporate development for ZENON Environmental. (ZENON has since been acquired by GE Water & Process Technologies.) Kiessling had 18 years of private-sector experience leading high-growth, entrepreneurial organizations.[29]

By running a small business part-time during your off hours or on weekends, you can experience the rewards of working for yourself while still enjoying a regular paycheque at another job. This is what John Stanton, founder of the Running Room <*www.runningroom.com*>, did when he first started his company. He kept his full-time job as a vice-president in the grocery sector and he opened the Running Room in a house in Edmonton. At first, he only sold cotton T-shirts and running shoes. Four years later, he was confident that the company had growth potential. He quit his job and concentrated on building the Running Room chain. Today, there are more than 111 locations across Canada and the United States.[30]

Learning a business while working for someone else may also save you money because you are less likely to make "rookie mistakes" when you start your own business. The Making Ethical Decisions box presents ethical questions about using the knowledge you have gained as an employee to start your own business.

Buy an Existing Business

Small-business management takes time, dedication, and determination. Owners work long hours and rarely take vacations. After many years, they may feel stuck in their business. They may think they cannot get out because they have too much time and effort invested. Consequently, there are some small-business owners out there eager to get away, at least for a long vacation.

This is where you come in. Find a successful business person who owns a small business. Tell him or her that you are eager to learn the business and would like to serve an apprenticeship—that is, a training period. State that at the end of the training period (one year or so), you would like to help the owner or manager by becoming assistant manager. As assistant manager, you would free the owner to take off weekends and holidays, and to take a long vacation—a good deal for him or her. For another year or so, work very hard to learn all about the business—suppliers, inventory, bookkeeping, customers, promotion, and so on. At the end of two years, make the owner this offer: the owner can retire or work only part-time and you will take over the business. You can establish a profit-sharing plan for yourself plus a salary. Be generous with yourself; you will earn it if you manage the business. You can even ask for 40 percent or more of the profits.

The owner benefits by keeping ownership in the business and making 60 percent of what he or she earned before—without having to work. You benefit by making 40 percent of the profits of a successful firm. This is an excellent deal for an owner about to retire—he or she is able to keep the firm and a healthy profit flow. It is also a clever and successful way to share in the profits of a successful small business without any personal investment of money. If you think that this is not realistic, be aware that nearly half of Canada's small-business owners plan to retire before 2020.[31]

If profit-sharing does not appeal to the owner, you may want to buy the business outright. How do you determine a fair price for a business? Value is based on (1) what the business owns, (2) what it earns, and (3) what makes it unique. Naturally, your accountant will need to help you determine the business's value.

If your efforts to take over the business through either profit-sharing or buying fail, you can quit and start your own business fully trained.

Buy a Franchise

In Chapter 6, you were introduced to franchising. Many business people first get into business via franchising. Recall that franchising is a method of distributing a good or service, or both, to achieve a maximum market impact with a minimum investment. From your investment perspective, you are not creating a product or service from scratch. Rather, you are benefiting from the experience of the franchisor. Franchising is a way that you can start a business venture, especially if you are more comfortable doing so with an established product and process.

When deciding which method is best for you in terms of getting into your first business venture, be sure to weigh the advantages and disadvantages of each option before proceeding. One example of a successful franchise business is Molly Maid International Inc., a leader in the cleaning industry. The Reaching Beyond Our Borders, located at the end of this part, introduces you to this company.

Inherit / Take Over a Family Business[32]

It is not uncommon for the dream of one to evolve into a family business. Some examples highlighted in this textbook include Company's Coming and Irving Oil. Husband and wife teams (such as Timothy Snelgrove and Teresa Snelgrove, founders of Timothy's World Coffee <*www.timothys.com*>, and David and Penny Chapman, founders of Chapman's Ice Cream) are also quite common when you review the Canadian landscape of family businesses.

▸ The late Israel Asper founded CanWest Global Communications Corp. in 1974. A major media company based in Winnipeg, it held radio, television, broadcasting, and publishing assets in several countries, but primarily in Canada. Do you know of any other family businesses that have not survived the transition to the next generation?

There are a number of factors that make family businesses unique. One is ownership. Public companies are typically owned by a large number of shareholders whose primary interest in ownership is generating the best return on investment. However, family businesses are often owned by a much smaller group whose ownership often has elements of personal identity, family legacy, and community responsibility entwined with its economic interests. This "emotional ownership" often results in family businesses having a longer-term view. Another factor that tends to separate successful family firms from their public counterparts is the concept of stewardship. Many family businesses have a clear understanding that the business is something to be preserved and grown for future generations. As Bill Ford, the chairman of Ford Motor Company once said, "I'm working for my children and grandchildren and feel I'm working for our employees' children and grandchildren as well."

As with any form of business, there are some challenges associated with a family business. Only one-third of family-owned businesses survive the transition to the second generation. And of these businesses, again only one-third will survive to the third generation, meaning that the chances your grandchildren will take over your business are about 1 in 10. For example, Israel (Izzy) Asper, founder of CanWest Global Communications Corp., once dreamed of creating a worldwide media empire. When he died in 2003, his son, Leonard, was left in charge as CanWest's CEO. Leonard stepped down as CEO in 2010 when the company was restructured due to bankruptcy.

There are two common reasons why a family does not retain its business. The first reason is straightforward—there is no qualified successor. The second major reason for unsuccessful business transitions is more unfortunate. In many cases, businesses fail or are sold off due to a lack of planning. The Dealing with Change box at the end of this chapter part discusses management problems as another factor. Regardless of such challenges, inheriting or taking over a family business is another way that one can learn about small business.

PROGRESS ASSESSMENT

- Why are small businesses important to Canada?
- What are causes of small-business failure?
- How can one get into a business venture?

MANAGING A SMALL BUSINESS

Analyze what it takes to start and run a small business.

One of the major causes of small-business failure is poor management.[33] Keep in mind, though, that the term *poor management* covers a number of faults. It could mean poor planning, poor record keeping, poor inventory control, poor promotion, or poor employee relations. Most likely it would include poor capitalization.[34] To help you succeed as a business owner, in the following sections we explore the five functions of business in a small-business setting, which are as follows:

1. Planning your business
2. Financing your business
3. Knowing your customers (marketing)
4. Managing your employees (human resource development)
5. Keeping records (accounting)

Although all of the functions are important in both the start-up and management phases of the business, the first two functions—planning and financing—are the primary concerns when you start your business. The remaining functions are the heart of the actual operations once the business is started.

Planning

Many people eager to start a small business come up with an idea and begin discussing the idea with professors, friends, and other business people. At this stage, the entrepreneur needs a business plan. A **business plan** is a detailed written statement that describes the nature of the business, the target market, the advantages the business will have in relation to competition, and the resources and qualifications of the owner(s). A business plan forces potential owners of small businesses to be quite specific about the goods or services they intend to offer. They must analyze the competition, calculate how much money they need to start, and cover other details of operation. A business plan is also mandatory for talking with bankers or other

business plan
A detailed written statement that describes the nature of the business, the target market, the advantages the business will have in relation to competition, and the resources and qualifications of the owner(s).

investors. Put another way, a business plan is a tool that is used to transition the entrepreneur from having an idea to actually developing a strategic and operational framework for the business.

If you are looking for bank financing, here are some tips. First, pick a bank that serves businesses the size of yours, have a good accountant prepare a complete set of financial statements and a personal balance sheet, and make an appointment before going to the bank. Second, go to the bank with an accountant and all of the necessary financial information and demonstrate to the banker that you are a person of good character (i.e., civic minded and respected in business and community circles). Finally, ask for all the money you need, be specific, and be prepared to personally guarantee the loan.

Writing a Business Plan

A good business plan takes a long time to write, but you have got only minutes, in the Executive Summary, to convince readers (e.g., prospective lenders and investors) not to throw it away. While there is no such thing as a perfect business plan, prospective entrepreneurs do think out the smallest details. According to Jerrold Carrington of Inroads Capital Partners, the summary has to catch the reader's interest. Bankers receive business plans every day. "You better grab me up front," says Carrington. Figure 7.5 gives you an outline of a comprehensive business plan.

Getting the completed business plan into the right hands is almost as important as getting the right information into the plan. Finding funding requires research. Next, we discuss sources of money available to new business ventures. All require a comprehensive business plan. The time and effort you invest before starting a business will pay off many times over. The big payoff is survival.

Financing Your Business

When *starting* a business, an entrepreneur can consider different types of financing, as listed in Figure 7.6. Personal savings (73 percent) and commercial or personal loans from financial institutions (51 percent) represent the most frequently used sources. When *maintaining* a business (i.e., financing current activities), the types of financial instruments vary. They include commercial or personal loans from financial institutions (64 percent), retained earnings (57 percent), personal savings (54 percent), and leasing (22 percent).[35] Retained earnings will be discussed in Chapter 17.

venture capitalists (VCs)
Individuals or companies that invest in new businesses in exchange for partial ownership of those businesses.

Investors known as **venture capitalists (VCs)** may finance your project—for a price. Venture capitalists may ask for a hefty stake (as much as 60 percent) in your company in exchange for the cash to start your business. If the VC demands too large a stake, you could lose control of the business. This may have been the case with Chris & Larry's Clodhoppers. Chris Emery and Larry Finnson started Krave's in 1996. Their Clodhopper treats are bite-sized pieces of graham wafer and chocolate candy. By the mid-2000s, they had accepted venture capital financing and management advice when their sales kept growing but they were still broke. In October 2005, Finnson stepped down as president and he and Emery turned the running of the company over to a management company so they could focus on marketing. Five months later, the assets of the company were sold to Brookside Foods. Harold Heide, vice-president of investments at ENSIS Growth Fund, which owned about 45 percent of Krave's, said the deal made sense: "The time had simply come in ENSIS's investing cycle to sell its position in Krave's."[36]

angel investors
Private individuals who invest their own money in potentially hot new companies before they go public.

An alternate source of funds, if you cannot get venture capital, is to consider finding an angel investor. **Angel investors** are private individuals who invest their own money in potentially hot new companies before they go public.[37] Angel investors usually target their support to pre-start-up and early-stage companies with high-growth prospects.[38]

If your proposed venture does require millions of dollars to start, experts recommend that you talk with at least five investment firms and their clients to find the right VCs.

Figure 7.5

Sample Outline of a Business Plan

LENGTH OF A COMPREHENSIVE BUSINESS PLAN

A good business plan is between 25 and 50 pages long and takes at least six months to write.

Cover Letter

Only one thing is certain when you go hunting for money to start a business: You will not be the only hunter out there. You need to make potential funders want to read your business plan instead of the hundreds of others on their desks. Your cover letter should summarize the most attractive points of your project in as few words as possible. Be sure to address the letter to the potential investor by name. "To Whom It May Concern" or "Dear Sir" is not the best way to win an investor's support.

Section 1—Executive Summary

Begin with a two-page or three-page management summary of the proposed venture. Include a short description of the business, and discuss major goals and objectives.

Section 2—Company Background

Describe company operations to date (if any), potential legal considerations, and areas of risk and opportunity. Summarize the firm's financial condition, and include past and current balance sheets, income and cash-flow statements, and other relevant financial records. (You will learn about these financial statements in Chapter 16.) It is also wise to include a description of insurance coverage. Investors want to be assured that death or other mishaps do not pose major threats to the company.

Section 3—Management Team

Include an organization chart, job descriptions of listed positions, and detailed resumés of the current and proposed executives. A mediocre idea with a proven management team is funded more often than a great idea with an inexperienced team. Managers should have expertise in all disciplines necessary to start and run a business. If not, mention outside consultants who will serve in these roles and describe their qualifications.

Section 4—Financial Plan

Provide five-year projections for income, expenses, and funding sources. Do not assume the business will grow in a straight line. Adjust your planning to allow for funding at various stages of the company's growth. Explain the rationale and assumptions used to determine the estimates. Assumptions should be reasonable and based on industry/historical trends. Make sure all totals add up and are consistent throughout the plan. If necessary, hire a professional accountant or financial analyst to prepare these statements.

Stay clear of excessively ambitious sales projections; rather, offer best-case, expected, and worst-case scenarios. These not only reveal how sensitive the bottom line is to sales fluctuations but also serve as good management guides.

Section 5—Capital Required

Indicate the amount of capital needed to commence or continue operations, and describe how these funds are to be used. Make sure the totals are the same as the ones on the cash-flow statement. This area will receive a great deal of review from potential investors, so it must be clear and concise.

Section 6—Marketing Plan

Do not underestimate the competition. Review industry size, trends, and the target market segment. Discuss strengths and weaknesses of the good or service. The most important things investors want to know are what makes the product more desirable than what is already available and whether the product can be patented. Compare pricing to the competition's. Forecast sales in dollars and units. Outline sales, advertising, promotion, and public relations programs. Make sure the costs agree with those projected in the financial statements.

Section 7—Location Analysis

In retailing and certain other industries, the location of the business is one of the most important factors. Provide a comprehensive demographic analysis of consumers in the area of the proposed business as well as a traffic-pattern analysis and vehicular and pedestrian counts.

Section 8—Manufacturing Plan

Describe minimum plant size, machinery required, production capacity, inventory and inventory-control methods, quality control, plant personnel requirements, and so on. Estimates of product costs should be based on primary research.

Section 9—Appendix

Include all marketing research on the good or service (off-the-shelf reports, article reprints, etc.) and other information about the product concept or market size. Provide a bibliography of all the reference materials you consulted. This section should demonstrate that the proposed company will not be entering a declining industry or market segment.

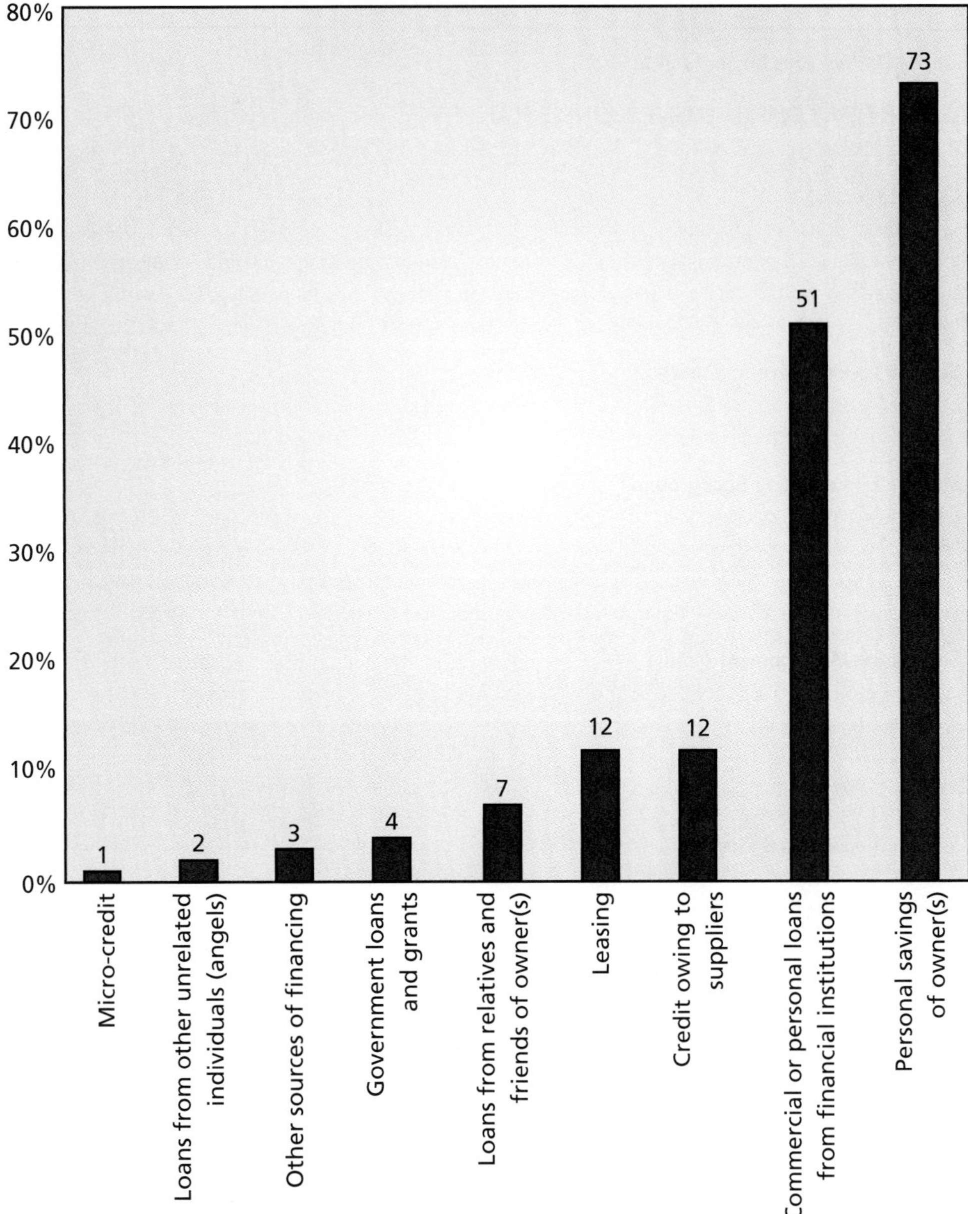

Figure 7.6

Types of Financial Instruments Used by All Start-Up SMEs (2007)

SMEs can use multiple sources of funds when they start up their businesses. Since they often lack both a credit history and the collateral needed to secure a loan, it is not surprising that personal savings constitute the largest source (73 percent).

Source: "Key Small Business Financing Statistics," Government of Canada, December 2009, 19–20, www.sme-fdi.gc.ca/eic/site/sme_fdi-prf_pme.nsf/vwapj/KSBFS-PSFPE_Dec2009_eng.pdf/$FILE/KSBFS-PSFPE_Dec2009_eng.pdf. This was the most recent data available when this chapter was written.

Online Financing Sources

There are many information sources for financing. Examples of government grants and programs include the Scientific Research and Experimental Development program and the National Research Council's Industrial Research Assistance Program.

From the comfort of your desk, you can visit government sites such as the Business Development Bank of Canada or Industry Canada's Financing site <*www.ic.gc.ca/eic/site/ic1.nsf/eng/h_00073.html*>. The Industry Canada site provides information aimed at helping small and medium-sized businesses, companies, and entrepreneurs in Canada find financing from public- and private-sector sources. You can discover funding programs for your small business through the Centre for Small Business Financing's Grant Finder program <*www.grants-loans.org/smallbusiness-funding.php*>. Another site for federal, provincial, municipal, and private funding is Fundica

<*www.fundica.com*>. Information on finances can also be found at <*www.profitguide.com/finances*>. While this list is not exhaustive, it serves to highlight that there are many sources. These are just the beginning.

Obtaining money from banks, VCs, and government sources can be a challenge for most small businesses. (You will learn more about financing in Chapter 17.) Those who do survive the planning and financing of their new ventures are eager to get their businesses up and running. Your success in running a business depends on many factors. Three important factors for success are knowing your customers, managing your employees, and keeping efficient records. These topics will be discussed next.

Dragons' Den is a CBC production where aspiring entrepreneurs pitch their business concepts and products to a panel of Canadian business moguls. If you can convince them to lend you money, they will expect ownership in the business in exchange.

Knowing Your Customers

One of the most important elements of small-business success is knowing the market. In business, a **market** consists of people with unsatisfied wants and needs who have both the resources and the willingness to buy. For example, we can confidently state that many of our students have the willingness to own a brand new car. However, few of them have the resources necessary to satisfy this want. Would they be considered a good market for a luxury car dealer to pursue?

Once you have identified your market and its needs, you must set out to fill those needs. The way to meet your customers' needs is to offer top quality at a fair price with great service. Remember, it is not enough to get customers—you have to keep them. Everything must be geared to bring the customers the satisfaction they deserve. Gérard Vroomen and Phil White founded Cervélo Cycles Inc. <*www.cervelo.com*> when they were engineering students and wished to market the new time-trial bikes they were developing. Today, the company produces road and triathlon racing bikes, and Cervélo is internationally recognized as one of the most innovative bike manufacturers. According to Vroomen, "Our basic philosophy is that we start by having very strong products. It's much easier to market a good product than a bad one."[39]

One of the greatest advantages that small businesses have over larger ones is the ability to know their customers better and to adapt quickly to their ever-changing needs. You will gain more insights about marketing in Chapters 14 and 15. Now let's consider the importance of effectively managing the employees who help you serve your market.

Here you see Cervélo Cycles founders and co-owners Phile White (left) and Gérard Vroomen (right). Cervélo Cycles is the only bike manufacturer with its own pro cycling team at the highest level. Did you know that in 2008, the Tour de France was won aboard a Cervélo bike?

Managing Your Employees

As a business grows, it becomes impossible for an entrepreneur to oversee every detail, even if he or she is working 60 hours per week. This means that hiring, training, and motivating employees is critical.

It is not easy to find good, qualified help when you offer less money, fewer benefits (if any), and less room for advancement than larger firms do. That is one reason why employee relations is such an important part of small-business management. Employees of small companies are often more satisfied with their jobs than are their counterparts in big business. Why? Quite often they find their jobs more challenging, their ideas more accepted, and their bosses more respectful.

Often entrepreneurs reluctantly face the reality that to keep growing, they must delegate authority to others. Nagging questions such as "Who should be delegated authority?" and "How much control should they have?" create perplexing problems.

This can be a particularly touchy issue in small businesses with long-term employees, and in family businesses. As you might expect, entrepreneurs who have built their companies from scratch often feel compelled to promote employees who have been with them from the start—even when those employees are not qualified to serve as managers. Common sense probably tells you this could be detrimental to the business.

The same can be true of family-run businesses that are expanding. Attitudes such as "You can't fire family" or "You must promote certain workers because they're family" can hinder growth. Entrepreneurs can best serve themselves and the business if they gradually recruit and groom employees for management positions. By doing this, entrepreneurs can enhance trust and the support of the manager among other employees and themselves.

When Heida Thurlow of Chantal Cookware <*www.chantal.com*> suffered an extended illness, she let her employees handle the work she once had insisted on doing herself. The experience transformed her company from an entrepreneurial one into a managerial one. She says, "Over the long run that makes us stronger than we were." You will learn more about managing employees in Chapters 11 to 13.

Keeping Records

Small-business owners often say that the most important assistance they received in starting and managing the business involved accounting. A business person who sets up an effective accounting system early will save much grief later. Computers simplify record keeping and enable a small-business owner to follow the progress of the business (sales, expenses, profits) on a daily basis. An inexpensive computer system can also help owners with other record-keeping chores, such as inventory control, customer records, and payroll.

Many business failures are caused by poor accounting practices that lead to costly mistakes. A good accountant can help you decide whether to buy or lease equipment and whether to own or rent the building. Help may also be provided for tax planning, financial forecasting, choosing sources of financing, and writing requests for funds.

Other small-business owners may tell you where to find an accountant experienced in small business. It pays to shop around for advice. You will learn more about accounting in Chapter 16.

Looking for Help

Small-business owners have learned, sometimes the hard way, that they need outside consulting advice early in the process. This is especially true of legal, tax, and accounting advice but may also be true of marketing, finance, and other areas. Most small and medium-sized firms cannot afford to hire such experts as employees, so they must turn to outside assistance. As a start, ask friends, other entrepreneurs, or family to recommend someone.

A necessary and invaluable aide is a competent, experienced lawyer who knows and understands small businesses. Lawyers can help with a variety of matters, including leases, contracts, and protection against liabilities. They do not have to be expensive. In fact, several prepaid legal plans offer services such as drafting legal documents for a low annual rate.

Make your marketing decisions long before a product is produced or a store is opened. An inexpensive marketing research study may help you determine where to locate, whom to select as your target market, and what would be an effective strategy for reaching those people. Thus, a marketing consultant with small-business experience can be of great help to you, especially one who has had experience with the Internet and social media.[40]

Given the marketing power of the Internet, your business will benefit from a presence on the Internet, even if you do not sell products or services directly from the Web. This applies to both small and large companies. For example, Holt Renfrew <*www.holtrenfrew.com*> and Shoppers Drug Mart only offer e-flyers and directions to their nearest stores online.[41]

Two other invaluable experts are a commercial account officer and an insurance agent. The commercial account officer can help you design an acceptable business plan and give you valuable financial advice as well as lend you money when you need it. An insurance agent will explain the risks associated with a small business and how to cover them most efficiently with insurance and other means like safety devices and sprinkler systems.

Often, local schools have business professors who will advise small-business owners for a small fee or for free. Some universities have clubs or programs that provide consulting services by master of business administration (MBA) candidates for a nominal fee. Does your school provide such services?

It also is wise to seek the counsel of other small-business owners. Other sources of counsel include local chambers of commerce, the Better Business Bureau, national and local trade associations (such as the Canadian Federation of Independent Business <*www.cfib-fcei.ca*>), the business reference section of your library, and small-business–related sites on the Internet. Some have been noted in this chapter.

GOING INTERNATIONAL: SMALL-BUSINESS PROSPECTS

Outline the advantages and disadvantages that small businesses have in entering global markets.

As we noted in Chapter 3, the world market is a much larger, much more lucrative market for small businesses than Canada alone. In spite of that potential, most small businesses still do not think internationally, and only a small percentage of small businesses export.

Technological advances have helped increase small-business exporting; PayPal <*www.paypal.com*> makes it possible for small businesses to get paid automatically when they conduct global business online. The Internet also helps small businesses find customers without the expense of international travel. As people acquire more wealth, they often demand specialized products that are not mass-produced and are willing to pay more for niche goods that small businesses offer.

Why are some companies missing the boat to the huge global markets? Primarily because the voyage involves a few major hurdles: (1) financing is often difficult to find, (2) many would-be exporters do not know how to get started, (3) potential global business people do not understand the cultural differences of prospective markets, and (4) the bureaucratic paperwork can threaten to bury a small business.

Besides the fact that most of the world's market lies outside of Canada, there are other good reasons for going international. For instance, exporting products

▸ Jennifer Ger and Suzie Chemel met while studying for their business degrees. They set out to build their company, Foxy Originals <www.*foxyoriginals.com*>, with a vision: high-style fashion jewellery accessible to young women. Upon graduation, they focused full-time on their business. Their products are found in hundreds of stores across North America and they are quickly expanding beyond. What are some challenges they might have encountered in global markets?

can absorb excess inventory, soften downturns in the domestic market, and extend product lives. It can also spice up dull routines.

Small businesses have several advantages over large businesses in international trade, which include the following:

- Overseas buyers enjoy dealing with individuals rather than with large corporate bureaucracies;
- Small companies usually can begin shipping much faster;
- Small companies can support a wide variety of suppliers; and
- Small companies can give customers more personal service and more undivided attention, because each overseas account is a major source of business to them.

The growth potential of small businesses overseas is phenomenal. This is why there are many organizations that offer assistance. Some of these have been cited in this chapter as well as in Chapter 4. Web-based business applications are helping small businesses cross boundaries like never before and, in some instances, levelling some of the advantages that large businesses traditionally have had.

PROGRESS ASSESSMENT

- What are the five functions of business in a small-business setting?
- There are nine sections in the business plan outline in this chapter. Can you describe at least four of those sections now?
- What are some of the advantages that small businesses have over large businesses in selling in global markets?

SUMMARY

Explain why people are willing to become entrepreneurs, and describe the attributes of successful entrepreneurs.

There are many reasons why people are willing to take the risks of entrepreneurship.

What are a few of the reasons people start their own businesses?

Reasons include profit, independence, opportunity, and challenge.

What are the attributes of successful entrepreneurs?

Successful entrepreneurs are self-directed, determined, action-oriented, highly energetic, tolerant of uncertainty, and able to learn quickly.

Discuss the importance of small business to the Canadian economy.

Businesses employing fewer than 50 employees account for almost 96 percent of all employer businesses.

What does the "small" in small business mean?

A small business is often defined as a business that is independently owned and operated, is not dominant in its field, and meets certain standards of size in terms of employees or annual revenues. Many institutions define small business according to their own needs.

Why are small businesses important to the Canadian economy?

Small business that have fewer than 100 employees contribute slightly more than 30 percent to Canada's gross domestic product. Perhaps more important to tomorrow's graduates, small businesses employ a large portion of the total private labour force.

Summarize the major causes of small-business failure.

Thousands of businesses enter and exit the marketplace throughout the year.

How many small businesses fail each year?

According to Industry Canada, survival rates for business with fewer than 250 employees decline over time. About 85 percent of businesses that enter the marketplace survive for one full year, 70 percent survive for two years, and 51 percent survive for five years.

Why do so many small businesses fail?

Many small businesses fail because of managerial incompetence and inadequate financial planning. See Figure 7.3 for a list of causes of small-business failure. Some of these causes include attempting to do too much business with too little capital, underestimating how much time it will take to build a market, and not allowing for setbacks and unexpected expenses.

What factors increase the chances for success?

Figure 7.4 outlines some situations for small-business success. This includes whether the product is not easily made by mass-production techniques, whether sales are not large enough to appeal to a large firm, and whether the owner pays attention to new competitors.

List ways to learn how small businesses operate.

Most people have no idea how to go about starting a small business.

What hints would you give someone who wants to learn about starting a small business?

An entrepreneur can improve the odds by learning from others. First, take courses and talk with some small-business owners. Second, get some experience working for others. Finally, study the latest in small-business management techniques, including the use of computers for things such as payroll, inventory control, and mailing lists.

Analyze what it takes to start and run a small business.

Writing a business plan is the first step in organizing a business.

What goes into a business plan?

See Figure 7.5 to see what goes into a business plan. A business plan includes a section on company background, the financial plan, and the location analysis.

What sources of funds should someone wanting to start a new business consider investigating?

A new entrepreneur has several sources of capital: personal savings, relatives, banks, finance companies, venture capital organizations, government agencies, angel investors, and more.

What are some of the special problems that small-business owners have in dealing with employees?
Small-business owners often have difficulty finding competent employees. Grooming employees for management responsibilities can be challenging.

Where can potential entrepreneurs find help in starting their businesses?
Help can be found from many sources: accountants, lawyers, marketing researchers, loan officers, insurance agents, the Business Development Bank of Canada, and your instructors.

What online sources are available to assist entrepreneurs?
Entrepreneurs can start by visiting government sources, such as the Industry Canada Web site. Financial services providers also have sites dedicated to small businesses.

Outline the advantages and disadvantages that small businesses have in entering global markets.

The future growth of some small businesses is in foreign markets.

What are some advantages small businesses have over large businesses in global markets?
Foreign buyers enjoy dealing with individuals rather than large corporations because (1) small companies can support a wide variety of suppliers and can ship products more quickly, and (2) small companies give more personal service.

Why don't more small businesses start trading internationally?
There are several reasons: (1) financing is often difficult to find, (2) many people do not know how to get started, (3) many do not understand the cultural differences in foreign markets, and (4) the bureaucratic red tape is often overwhelming.

KEY TERMS

affiliate marketing
angel investors
business establishment
business plan
employer business
entrepreneurial team
entrepreneurship
incubators
intrapreneurs
market
micro-enterprise
micropreneurs
small and medium-sized enterprises (SMEs)
small business
venture capitalists (VCs)

CRITICAL THINKING

1. There was mention in the chapter that small businesses continue to be feeders for future large businesses. As they prosper and develop new goods and services, they are often bought out by large companies. Is this good or bad? Should we do anything about it? If so, what?
2. Are there any similarities between the characteristics demanded of an entrepreneur and those of a professional athlete? Would an athlete be a good prospect for entrepreneurship? Why or why not? Could teamwork be important in an entrepreneurial effort?
3. Imagine yourself starting a small business. What kind of business would it be? How much competition is there? What could you do to make your business more attractive than those of competitors? Would you be willing to work 60 to 70 hours a week?

DEVELOPING WORKPLACE SKILLS

1. Find issues of *Canadian Business, Canadian Business Franchise,* and *PROFIT* magazines in the library, your local bookstore, or on the Internet. Read about the entrepreneurs who are heading today's dynamic new businesses. Write a profile about one entrepreneur.
2. Select a small business that looks attractive as a career possibility for you. Talk to at least one person who manages such a business. Ask how he or she started the business. Ask about financing, personnel challenges (e.g., hiring, firing, training, and scheduling), accounting problems, and other managerial matters. Prepare a summary of your findings, including whether the manager found the job to be rewarding, interesting, and challenging—and why.
3. Contact a government agency such as Export Development Canada or Business Development Bank of Canada. Write a brief summary of the services that they provide for small businesses. (Hint: Each organization has a Web site: <*www.edc.ca*> and <*www.bdc.ca*>.)
4. Contact a local bank and make an appointment to speak with a commercial accounts officer. Ask this person what a small business owner should consider if she or he is looking for financing. (This may include a discussion on the requirements of a business plan and what that bank wishes to see in this document.) Review other sources of financing that might be available to an entrepreneur. Find out what resources this bank has available to assist small-business owners. Bring this information to class and share it with your peers.
5. There has been some discussion in this chapter about entrepreneurship and traits of entrepreneurs. In a group, highlight the differences between a business person and an entrepreneur.

ANALYZING MANAGEMENT DECISIONS

Starting a Small Business While in School

Brett Sheffield, full-time student at the University of Manitoba and owner of Sheffield Farms and Stay Fit Health Club, was named the 2012 Student Entrepreneur National Champion by the national charitable organization, Advancing Canadian Entrepreneurship (ACE). Sheffield was triumphant after provincial, regional, and national rounds of competition because of his extraordinary achievements operating one flourishing business and launching a second while attending school full-time.

Sheffield Farms is a grain farm located in rural Manitoba that was founded in 2008, and Stay Fit Health Club is a 24-hour fitness centre in its first year of operation. "Sheffield's determination and proven business achievements, such as expanding his farm from 160 to 1,700 acres and pioneering a second business while maintaining his honour roll status at school, are ideal qualities of a Student Entrepreneur champion," said Amy Harder, President, ACE. "ACE is confident that Brett will make Canada proud at the Global Student Entrepreneur Awards in New York City."

Sheffield competed at the national level against five other regional finalists, to a panel of 50 industry leaders and CEOs. In addition to the national title, he received a $10,000 cash prize. "Competitions like the ACE National Exposition allow students from all corners of Canada to showcase our entrepreneurial talent," said Sheffield. "I'm honoured at being named the Student Entrepreneur National Champion and I look forward to continuing to take my business to new heights."

Sources: Sean Stanleigh, "Manitoba student wins national competition," *The Globe and Mail,* 10 May 2012, www.theglobeandmail.com/report-on-business/small-business/sb-tools/small-business-briefing/manitoba-student-wins-national-competition/article2428615/#in; "University of Manitoba Student Wins 2012 Student Entrepreneur National Champion Title," Advancing Canadian Entrepreneurship Inc., 9 May 2012, www.acecanada.ca/news/newsItem.cfm?cms_news_id=591; and Martin Cash, "U of M student farmer aces biz award," *Winnipeg Free Press,* 1 May 2012, www.winnipegfreepress.com/business/u-of-m-student-farmer-aces-biz-award-149618705.html.

Discussion Questions

1. What are the advantages and potential problems of starting a business while in school?
2. What kinds of entrepreneurs are operating around your school? Talk to them and learn from their experiences.
3. What opportunities exist for satisfying student needs at your school? Pick one idea, write a business plan, and discuss it in class (unless it is so good you do not want to share it; in that case, good luck).
4. Search and find what other Canadian competitions exist for student entrepreneurs Would you enter any of them?

PART 2 ENDS WITH:

DEALING WITH CHANGE

Some Unique Challenges of Family Businesses

According to business-heir-turned-author Thomas William Deans, the biggest problem facing family business today is not the business, it is the family. He blames the parents, not the kids in his book, *Every Family's Business*. Mom and Dad's errors include not talking business at the dinner table, not including adult children in the decision-making process, just assuming that their kids want the business, and worst of all, "gifting" the business to their kids, where they do not appreciate it.

Management problems in a family-owned business are somewhat different from similar problems in non-family businesses. When close relatives work together, emotions often interfere with business decisions. When you put up your own money and operate your own business, you prize your independence. "It's my business," you tell yourself. However, "It's our business" in a family company.

Conflicts sometimes abound because relatives look upon the business from different viewpoints. Those relatives who are silent partners, shareholders, and directors may only see dollar signs when judging capital expenditures, growth, and other major matters. Relatives who are engaged in daily operations judge major matters from the viewpoint of the production, sales, and personnel necessary to make the company successful. Obviously, these two viewpoints may conflict in some instances. This natural conflict can be aggravated by family members who have no talent for money or business.

While the majority of family business owners would like to see their businesses transferred to the next generation, it is estimated that only one-third of family-owned businesses survive the transition to the second generation. And of these businesses, again only one-third will survive to the third generation, meaning that the chances your grandchildren will take over your business are about 1 in 10. With 90 percent of businesses being family businesses, and half of all business owners planning to retire over the next decade, Canada's economic health clearly hinges on creating more successful successions.

One factor that might contribute to a successful transfer is governance. The key to effective governance for a family business is recognizing when the family business is moving from one stage to another, such as from the controlling owner (i.e., the original entrepreneur) to a sibling partnership where siblings have an ownership interest and/or some family shareholders are not working in the business. By designing revisions to the governance structure that will meet the needs of the owners for the next stage, expectations and responsibilities are likely to be clearer, contributing to a more successful business venture.

Sources: "Succession Planning for Family Business," BDO Canada LLP, [2012?], www.bdo.ca/library/publications/familybusiness/succession/planning1.cfm; "Governance for the Family Business," KPMG in Canada, 2008, www.kpmg.ca/en/services/enterprise/issuesGrowthGovernance.html; "The Parent Trap," *PROFIT*, October 2008, 13; Grant Walsh, "Family Business Succession," KPMG Enterprise™, 2008, www.kpmg.ca/en/services/enterprise/documents/3468_Succession.pdf; and "Problems in Managing a Family-Owned Business," *Canada Business*, 5 October 2005, www.canadabusiness.ca/servlet/Content Server?cid=1081945276597&pagename=CBSC_FE%2Fdisplay&lang=en&c=GuideFactSheet.

REACHING BEYOND OUR BORDERS

Canadian Franchisor Cleans Up

Molly Maid International Inc. (MOLLY MAID) set out to provide domestic cleaning services in Mississauga, Ontario, in 1979. The company is built on the fact that families are now busier than ever and need time-saving, convenient services to help manage their responsibilities at home. Since that time, MOLLY MAID has performed more than 6 million home cleanings across Canada and more than 12 million around the world. This year alone, the company is expecting to perform 2 million home cleanings.

MOLLY MAID's success should not be surprising when you scan the business environment. Much of the company's growth results from the increased participation of women in the workforce. While the majority of women between the ages of 18 and 65 now hold jobs outside the home, most are still responsible for the majority of the housework. Statistics reveal that working mothers spend as much as five hours each day on household chores—in addition to the almost eight hours spent working for employers.

Independent market research shows that MOLLY MAID is the most recognized brand in the cleaning industry. Eight of ten Canadians are familiar with the MOLLY MAID name and four of ten Canadians mention it first when asked to name a cleaning service. Today, MOLLY MAID is the largest Canadian-based cleaning company in the world with over 500 franchises and global sales in excess of $200 million. It has a presence on three continents and can be found in Canada, the United States, the United Kingdom, Portugal, and Japan.

Franchise owners have received numerous industry awards. For example, *Success* magazine ranked MOLLY MAID first in residential cleaning and fourth in the franchising industry overall in its annual Franchise Gold 200. *Income Opportunities* magazine ranked MOLLY MAID first in residential cleaning and second in the franchising industry overall. *Entrepreneur* magazine has ranked MOLLY MAID in the top 100 of its Franchise 500 for over six years.

Sources: "History," Molly Maid International Inc., 2012 and 2008, www.mollymaid.ca/news/index.php; "The Real Dirt on Canadians and Their Homes," Canada NewsWire, 19 March 2007, http://proquest.umi.com; "Molly Maid Still Cleaning Up in Canada After 25 years," *Canadian Business Franchise*, March/April 2004, 80–81; and "Pioneer in Home Cleaning Business Continues to Meet the Needs of the Modern Family," Canada NewsWire, 13 April 2004, http://proquest.umi.com.

RUNNING CASE

Fox 40 International Inc.: A Family Business

For successful Canadian entrepreneur and inventor Ron Foxcroft, it all started in 1982 when he purchased Fluke Transport, a Southern Ontario trucking business. The company slogan—If It's On Time . . . It's A "FLUKE"—was soon recognized throughout North America. Over the years, Ron diversified into new ventures and the Foxcroft Group of Companies now includes Fluke Transportation Group, Fluke Warehousing Inc., Foxcroft Capital Group, and Fox 40 International Inc. (Fox 40).

All of these companies are private corporations. Although the word corporation makes people think of big businesses, it is not necessary to be big to incorporate. As introduced in this textbook, one of the biggest advantages of incorporation is limited liability. Owners of private corporations can also make decisions more quickly than is typically the case for large, public corporations.

The formation of Fox 40 is the result of a dream for a pealess whistle. When developing his first whistle, Ron was motivated by his knowledge and experience as an international basketball referee. "I always had a problem with whistles," he explains. "They have a cork pea in them and when you blow a pea-whistle really hard, nothing comes out. When they're frozen or wet or get some dirt inside, they lose their efficiency." As a result, Ron, like many other referees, sometimes found himself unable to stop play even though he saw a clear violation take place. In a fast-moving game like basketball, a whistle that fails does not get a second chance to sound. In a really big game, even when the whistle did work, the play occasionally was not stopped because the whistle's sound was drowned out by the noise of the roaring crowds. Frustrated with faulty pea whistles, he spent three years of development with design consultant Chuck Shepherd, resulting in the creation of the Fox 40® Classic Whistle.

Although Ron was convinced a better whistle would sweep the basketball market, he was unable to obtain bank financing for the venture. Very few thought that a pealess whistle would turn out and some believed that it would only be used by a few hundred referee friends. Despite the critics, Ron managed to put together $150,000 from his own private funds and in 1987 he created Fox 40. Ron risked everything as he pursued this dream: his family's financial future (only his wife, Marie, knew how much he was risking), Fluke Transport's reputation, and Fluke Transport's money. While Ron had complete confidence in manufacturing a pealess whistle that would work, he did not know that it would be the commercial success that it is today. Twenty-five years later, Fox 40 remains a proudly Canadian company. It dominates the global whistle industry whereby tens of thousands of Fox 40® Whistles are produced monthly for shipment to 140 countries.

What about succession planning? Today, Ron plays an active role as Founder and Chief Executive Officer (CEO) of Fox 40, and Chairman and CEO of Fluke Transportation Group. While he has passed the day-to-day running of Fox 40 to his son, Dave, Ron continues to focus on the company's strategic direction. This includes listening to customers and employees (Ron insists that the best ideas still come from them), and concentrating on increasing brand recognition for the Fox 40® brand. While it is up to Ron and Dave to approve a new idea, it is up to Dave and his team to implement it. "Once you have decided on a course of action," says Ron, "failure is not an option."

Dave has listened to whistles all of his life, in addition to the people who use them. As Fox 40's President and Chief Operating Officer, he is responsible for managing Fox 40's global sales, marketing, and operations. This includes overseeing the development of the company's diverse, innovative product base and strategic acquisitions with the company's highly capable team. Outside of the company, he is involved in industry events (e.g., as a delegate for the World Federation of Sporting Goods), he actively supports several charitable associations that support youth, and he works as a professional referee in the Canadian Football League (CFL Referee #30).

To achieve sales and profit growth targets of 10 to 15 percent per year, efforts focus on the development of Fox 40 products. As a take on the "Build a better mousetrap" catchphrase, Dave believes, "You have to build it and then the world will beat a path to your door . . . but you need to still sell it, work it, and be innovative."

While Ron recognizes that very few "seconds in command" (i.e., presidents) are happy, he is quick to point out that these are the individuals that run the show. "Dave is the ideas guy," Ron emphasizes. Examples include new product introductions (e.g., the marine line, the Heat Alert Mouthguard, and the CAUL Fingergrip whistle), and social media initiatives such as Facebook contests. Dave remains modest. "My job is to keep him [Ron] as the face of the company and it will always be the case . . . Maybe it is the referee training. The good one [referee] is never seen."

Ron was motivated to become an entrepreneur for reasons that include, "My fear of working for a dumb boss and fear of being hungry." What is it like for the next generation to work in the family business? "Working for your dad is just like refereeing," says Dave. "The first game you work, they expect you to be perfect. Every game after, they expect you to improve . . . just like working for your dad."

It is evident that there is mutual respect between the Foxcrofts. When asked how they are able to successfully work together, Ron had some answers. "Don't hold grudges," he said. "We do not discuss work outside of the office. When you walk out of the building, it is over until the next morning . . . It cannot be all-consuming in your private life."

Both Ron and Dave are often approached by individuals that seek investment in their ideas or that wish to discuss their ideas. The advice that they routinely give these individuals is: "Don't give away ownership of your business or your product!" Ron adds, "We are not a distributor. We are a manufacturer distributor and we own everything we sell."

Source: Used with permission. Ron Foxcroft, Founder and CEO, Fox 40 International Inc.

Discussion Questions

1. What are some advantages of Canadian-owned private corporations over public corporations?
2. What are reasons why people are willing to take the challenge of starting a business?
3. "Immediate family members are given an opportunity to work for the company for a living," says Dave Foxcroft. What are some possible challenges in working with family members? How can these challenges be managed?

APPENDIX C

ENTREPRENEUR READINESS QUESTIONNAIRE

Not everyone is cut out to be an entrepreneur. The fact is, though, that all kinds of people with all kinds of personalities have succeeded in starting small and large businesses. There are certain traits, however, that seem to separate those who will be successful as entrepreneurs from those who may not be. The following questionnaire will help you determine in which category you fit. Take a couple of minutes to answer the questions and then score yourself at the end. A low score does not mean you will not succeed as an entrepreneur. It does indicate, however, that you might be happier working for someone else.

Each of the following items describes something that you may or may not feel represents your personality or other characteristics about you. Read each item and then circle the response (1, 2, 3, 4, or 5) that most nearly reflects the extent to which you agree or disagree that the item seems to fit you. Then return to this scoring key.

Scoring:

Give yourself one point for each 1 or 2 response you circled for questions
1, 2, 6, 8, 10, 11, 16, 17, 21, 22, 23.

Give yourself one point for each 4 or 5 response you circled for questions
3, 4, 5, 7, 9, 12, 13, 14, 15, 18, 19, 20, 24, 25.

Add your points. Find where your score falls within the following ranges to read how you rate.

21–25 Your entrepreneurial potential looks great if you have a suitable opportunity to use it. What are you waiting for?

16–20 This is close to the high entrepreneurial range. You could be quite successful if your other talents and resources are right.

11–15 Your score is in the transitional range. With some serious work you can probably develop the outlook you need for running your own business.

6–10 Things look pretty doubtful for you as an entrepreneur. It would take considerable rearranging of your life philosophy and behaviour to make it.

0–5 Let's face it. Entrepreneurship isn't really for you. Still, learning what it's all about won't hurt anything.

Looking at my overall philosophy of life and typical behaviour, I would say that . . .	RESPONSE				
	Agree Completely (1)	Mostly Agree (2)	Partially Agree (3)	Mostly Disagree (4)	Disagree Completely (5)
1. I am generally optimistic.	1	2	3	4	5
2. I enjoy competing and doing things better than someone else.	1	2	3	4	5
3. When solving a problem, I try to arrive at the best solution first without worrying about other possibilities.	1	2	3	4	5
4. I enjoy associating with co-workers after working hours.	1	2	3	4	5
5. If betting on a horse race I would prefer to take a chance on a high-payoff "long shot."	1	2	3	4	5
6. I like setting my own goals and working hard to achieve them.	1	2	3	4	5
7. I am generally casual and easy-going with others.	1	2	3	4	5
8. I like to know what is going on and take action to find out.	1	2	3	4	5
9. I work best when someone else is guiding me along the way.	1	2	3	4	5
10. When I am right I can convince others.	1	2	3	4	5
11. I find that other people frequently waste my valuable time.	1	2	3	4	5
12. I enjoy watching football, baseball, and similar sports events.	1	2	3	4	5
13. I tend to communicate about myself very openly with other people.	1	2	3	4	5
14. I don't mind following orders from superiors who have legitimate authority.	1	2	3	4	5
15. I enjoy planning things more than actually carrying out the plans.	1	2	3	4	5
16. I don't think it's much fun to bet on a "sure thing."	1	2	3	4	5
17. If faced with failure, I would shift quickly to something else rather than sticking to my guns.	1	2	3	4	5
18. Part of being successful in business is reserving adequate time for family.	1	2	3	4	5
19. Once I have earned something, I feel that keeping it secure is important.	1	2	3	4	5
20. Making a lot of money is largely a matter of getting the right breaks.	1	2	3	4	5
21. Problem solving is usually more effective when a number of alternatives are considered.	1	2	3	4	5
22. I enjoy impressing others with the things I can do.	1	2	3	4	5
23. I enjoy playing games like tennis and handball with someone who is slightly better than I am.	1	2	3	4	5
24. Sometimes moral ethics must be bent a little in business dealings.	1	2	3	4	5
25. I think that good friends would make the best subordinates in an organization.	1	2	3	4	5

Source: Kenneth R. Van Voorhis, *Entrepreneurship and Small Business Management* (New York: Allyn & Bacon, 1980).

PART 3

CHAPTER

MANAGEMENT AND LEADERSHIP

LEARNING OBJECTIVES

After you have read and studied this chapter, you should be able to:

LO 1 Describe the changes occurring today in the management function.

LO 2 Describe the four functions of management.

LO 3 Relate the planning process and decision making to the accomplishment of company goals.

LO 4 Describe the organizing function of management.

LO 5 Explain the differences between leaders and managers, and describe the various leadership styles.

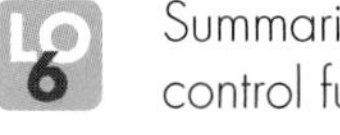

LO 6 Summarize the five steps of the control function of management.

PROFILE

GETTING TO KNOW JOHN BAKER, FOUNDER, PRESIDENT & CEO, DESIRE2LEARN

Desire2Learn (D2L, <*www.desire2learn.com*>) is a Canadian-based leader in providing innovative learning solutions. Founded in 1999, the company is focused on making knowledge more accessible, building learning environments that spark engagement, and is transforming the way the world learns. With over 8 million users of the company's technology, Desire2Learn has over 650 clients in dozens of countries around the world. Desire2Learn employs over 460 employees, with a rapidly growing global workforce and continued plans for expansion. The company has been recognized for four consecutive years as one of Canada's fastest growing technology companies as part of the Deloitte Technology Fast 50; is one of the 50 Best Small & Medium Employers in Canada for the last two years; and has received numerous global awards and recognition for ongoing contributions to learning.

The company was founded by John Baker, then a 22-year-old University of Waterloo Systems Design Engineering student. As a "problem finder," John used a third-year design workshop project to help identify his passion. He says, "I realized that helping to improve society was something I was passionate about. So I started looking around for problems where I could have an impact.

That course taught me about problem finding, not just problem solving, and that sparked something in me." From this project's success, John started working with faculty to create online content and assessments that led to his vision, starting a company focused on "building a whole learning experience that could break down barriers to high-quality education."

In his relatively short career, John has already been recognized with the Young Entrepreneur of the Year Award from the Greater Kitchener-Waterloo Chamber of Commerce, the KPMG Excellence in Technology Award, the *Waterloo Region Record* 40 Under 40, and the University of Waterloo Young Alumni Achievement Medal in 2010.

One of the four components of leadership as discussed in this chapter is planning, including creating a vision. John firmly believes that to improve the quality of society, including its productivity, everyone needs to have access to the highest quality educational experience, which is why Desire2Learn is committed to transforming teaching and learning and shaping a better future for education. He believes that learning occurs as a journey for each individual (a desire to learn) through personalizing the education experience. Innovation, collaboration, passion, and perseverance are all integral components of John's vision.

John's values as reflected in Desire2Learn's employees include: integrity, openness, hard work, dedication, and creativity. He demonstrated creativity recently through the provision of a week's free time for all research and development staff to put their current workload aside and, instead, use of all of their time to further develop any idea they had. Through Desire2Learn, John is committed to collaborating with clients to improve human potential globally by providing the most innovative technology for teaching and learning to make education accessible to all.

Source: www.communitech.ca/d2ls-john-baker-desire-to-make-a-difference; "TEDxUW—John Baker—Why We Need to Unleash the Next Generation Revolution", www.youtube.com/watch?v=dDbhwea5Kx4; and Christine Bezruki, "What are You Up to Lately", *University of Waterloo Magazine,* Spring 2012; and www.desire2learn.com

Describe the changes occurring today in the management function.

MANAGERS' ROLES ARE EVOLVING

resources
A general term that incorporates human resources, natural resources, and financial resources.

Managers must practise the art of getting things done through organizational resources. **Resources** is a general term that incorporates human resources (e.g., employees), natural resources (e.g., raw materials), and financial resources (e.g., money). Resources include the factors of production, which were introduced in Chapter 1. Every business has scarce resources, and management is about deciding how to effectively use these scarce resources. Managers also work in learning organizations. Knowledge acquisition and innovation are required to survive in the rapidly changing environment. For these reasons you will be introduced to the study of management and how the different functional areas of business (operations, human resources, and marketing are the first three covered in this book) must work together.

At one time, managers were called bosses, and their job consisted of telling people what to do and watching over them to be sure they did it. They were typically more proficient and knew more than the employees they supervised. Bosses tended to reprimand those who did not do things correctly, and generally were impersonal. Many managers still behave that way. Perhaps you have witnessed such behaviour.

Today, management is becoming more progressive. In general, management is studied as a discipline in addition to being learned on the job. Managers are educated to guide, train, support, motivate, and coach employees rather than tell them what to do.[1] When coaching, managers are trying to get the best out of their employees. Management is an assignment; coaching is a choice.[2]

Managers of high-tech firms realize that workers often know much more about technology than they do. Thus, most modern managers emphasize teamwork and co-operation rather than discipline and giving orders.[3] Managers in some high-tech firms and in progressive firms of all kinds tend to be friendly and generally treat employees as partners rather than unruly workers.

In the past, an employee would expect to work for the same company for many years, maybe even a lifetime. Similarly, companies would proudly acknowledge employees who achieved milestones in terms of duration of employment. Today, many companies do not hesitate to lay off employees, and employees do not hesitate to leave if their needs are not being met. Today's top leaders of Fortune 100 companies are younger, and more of them are female. They tend to move from one company to another as their careers unfold.[4] Traditional long-term contracts between management and employees—and the accompanying trust—are often no longer there. This increases the difficulty of the management task because managers must earn the trust of their employees, which includes rewarding them and finding other ways to encourage them to stay in the firm. This environment is subject to an added layer of complexity due to demographics. With so many baby boomers reaching retirement age, how will their wisdom be captured and who will fill their jobs?

▸ Many managers today are working in teams, and this means working *with* employees rather than simply directing them. These teams are likely to be ethnically diverse and include people of varied ages and backgrounds. Since managers will function primarily as trainers, coaches, and motivators of teams, it is expected that members of the team will do year-end evaluations of the manager and vice versa (see the discussion in Chapter 12 on Human Resource Management). How do you think most managers will react to having lower-level employees evaluate *their* effectiveness?

Future changes in the work environment will mean that work will increasingly be completed by teams, and change will come more quickly. Transparency in how managers do their job (in terms of corporate governance, found in Chapter 6) and how they address corporate social responsibility (discussed in Chapter 5) will become increasingly important.

What this means for you and other graduates of tomorrow is that successful management will demand a new kind of person: a skilled communicator and team player as well as a planner, coordinator, organizer, and supervisor. These trends will be addressed in the next few chapters to help prepare you for your future career in management.

FUNCTIONS OF MANAGEMENT

LO 2

Describe the four functions of management.

Well-known management consultant Peter Drucker says that managers give direction to their organizations, provide leadership, and decide how to use organizational resources to accomplish goals.[5] Such descriptions give you some idea of what managers do. In addition to those tasks, managers today must deal with conflict resolution, create trust in an atmosphere where trust has been badly shaken, and help create balance between work lives and family lives.[6] Managers look at the big picture, and their decisions make a major difference in organizations.[7] The following definition of management provides the outline of this chapter: **Management** is the process used to accomplish organizational goals through planning, organizing, leading, and controlling people and other organizational resources. (Figure 8.1 provides a comprehensive listing of all the critical tasks in this process.)

management
The process used to accomplish organizational goals through planning, organizing, leading, and controlling people and other organizational resources.

planning
A management function that includes anticipating trends and determining the best strategies and tactics to achieve organizational goals and objectives.

organizing
A management function that includes designing the structure of the organization and creating conditions and systems in which everyone and everything work together to achieve the organization's goals and objectives.

Planning includes anticipating trends and determining the best strategies and tactics to achieve organizational goals and objectives, for example, pleasing customers.[8] The trend today is to have *planning teams* to help monitor the environment, find business opportunities, and watch for challenges. Planning is a key management function because the other management functions depend heavily on having a good plan. Most often this plan is reflected in a set of budgets, which will be talked about more in Chapter 17.

Organizing includes designing the structure of the organization and creating conditions and systems in which everyone and everything work together to achieve the organization's goals and objectives.[9] Many of today's organizations are being designed around the customer. The idea is to design the firm so that everyone is working to please the customer at a profit. Thus, organizations must remain flexible and adaptable because customer needs change, and organizations must either change

Planning
- Setting organizational goals.
- Developing strategies to reach those goals.
- Determining resources needed.
- Setting precise standards.

Organizing
- Allocating resources, assigning tasks, and establishing procedures for accomplishing goals.
- Preparing a structure (organization chart) showing lines of authority and responsibility.
- Recruiting, selecting, training, and developing employees.
- Placing employees where they will be most effective.

Leading
- Guiding and motivating employees to work effectively to accomplish organizational goals and objectives.
- Giving assignments.
- Explaining routines.
- Clarifying policies.
- Providing feedback on performance.

Controlling
- Measuring results against corporate objectives.
- Monitoring performance relative to standards.
- Rewarding outstanding performance.
- Taking corrective action when necessary.

Figure 8.1

What Managers Do

Some modern managers perform all of these tasks with the full co-operation and participation of workers. Empowering employees means allowing them to participate more fully in decision making.

Many of today's workers are called *knowledge workers* because their tools and materials are knowledge. They have the education and skills to compete with companies anywhere in the world. Knowledge is what makes today's workers competitive. Much of that learning comes from community colleges, universities, and online learning centres of all kinds. What skills will make you more competitive in tomorrow's job market?

along with them or risk losing their business. General Motors posted their highest profit ever in 2011, two years after emerging from bankruptcy protection, in part through listening to their customers who were looking for more fuel efficient cars.[10]

Leading means creating a vision for the organization and communicating, guiding, training, coaching, and motivating others to work effectively to achieve the organization's goals and objectives. Researchers have spent a considerable amount of time studying motivation, given the direct relationship between motivation and output. This subject is explored further in Chapter 11. The trend is to empower employees, giving them as much freedom as possible to become self-directed and self-motivated. Empowerment will be further discussed in Chapter 12, Human Resource Management. This function was once known as *directing;* that is, telling employees exactly what to do. In many smaller firms, that is still the role of managers. In most large modern firms, however, managers no longer tell people exactly what to do because knowledge workers and others often know how to do their jobs better than the manager. Nonetheless, leadership is necessary to keep employees focused on the right tasks at the right time along with training, coaching, motivating, and the other leadership tasks.[11]

Controlling involves establishing clear standards to determine whether an organization is progressing toward its goals and objectives, reporting the results achieved, rewarding people for doing a good job, and taking corrective action if work is not proceeding according to plan. Basically, it means measuring whether what actually occurs meets the organization's goals.

The four functions—planning, organizing, leading, and controlling—are the heart of management, so let's explore them in more detail. The process begins with planning; we'll look at that right after the Progress Assessment.

leading
Creating a vision for the organization and guiding, training, coaching, and motivating others to work effectively to achieve the organization's goals and objectives.

controlling
A management function that involves establishing clear standards to determine whether or not an organization is progressing toward its goals and objectives, rewarding people for doing a good job, and taking corrective action if they are not.

PROGRESS ASSESSMENT

- What is the definition of management used in this chapter?
- What are the four functions of management?

PLANNING: CREATING A VISION BASED ON VALUES

Relate the planning process and decision making to the accomplishment of company goals.

Planning, the first managerial function, involves setting the organizational vision, values, goals, and objectives. Executives rate planning as the most valuable tool of their workbench. Part of the planning process involves the creation of a vision for the organization. A **vision** is more than a goal; it is an encompassing explanation of why the organization exists and where it is trying to head. A vision gives the organization a sense of purpose. **Values** are a set of fundamental beliefs that guide a business in the decisions they make. Values guide strategic planning through to day-to-day decisions by being mindful of how all stakeholders will be treated. Vision informs values, and together they unite workers in a common purpose. Managing an organization without first establishing a vision can be counterproductive. It is like motivating everyone in a rowboat to get really excited about going somewhere, but not telling them exactly where. As a result, the boat will just keep changing directions rather than speeding toward an agreed-upon goal. Without a set of values, an organization has no basis for determining how their employees should interact with stakeholders. As a result, sustainable long-term relationships will be difficult.

vision An encompassing explanation of why the organization exists and where it is trying to head.

values A set of fundamental beliefs that guide a business in the decisions they make.

Desire2Learn's vision is to provide innovative learning solutions to organizations around the world. Their values include lifelong learning for their customers through creative solutions, collaboration, enthusiasm, and commitment to make a difference.

A **mission statement** is an outline of the organization's fundamental purposes.[12] Mission statements are usually developed by top management, with some input from employees, depending on the size of the company. A meaningful mission statement should address:

mission statement An outline of the fundamental purposes of an organization.

- the organization's self-concept;
- company philosophy and goals;
- long-term survival;
- customer needs;
- social responsibility; and
- the nature of the company's product or service.

Figure 8.2 contains the mission statements for a number of well-known businesses. How well do their mission statements address all of the issues listed above?

The mission statement becomes the foundation for setting specific goals and selecting and motivating employees. **Goals** are the broad, long-term accomplishments an organization wishes to attain. Goals need to be mutually agreed on by workers and management. Thus, goal setting is often a team process.

goals The broad, long-term accomplishments an organization wishes to attain.

Objectives are specific, short-term statements detailing how to achieve the organization's goals. One of your goals for reading this chapter, for example, may be to learn basic concepts of management. An objective you could use to achieve this goal is to answer the chapter's Progress Assessment questions correctly. Objectives must be measurable. For example, you can measure your progress in answering questions by determining what percentage you answer correctly over time.

objectives Specific, measurable, short-term statements detailing how to achieve the organization's goals.

Planning is a continuous process. It is unlikely that a plan that worked yesterday would be successful in today's market. Most planning follows a pattern. The procedure you would follow in planning your life and career is basically the same as that used by businesses for their plans. Planning answers two fundamental questions for businesses: What is the gap between where an organization is now and where it wants to be? and then, How can we get there from here?

1. What is the situation now? What trends are being observed in the business environment? What opportunities exist for meeting customers' needs? What products

Figure 8.2

Sample Company Mission Statements

"Facebook's mission is to give people the power to share and make the world more open and connected."

"Apple is committed to bringing the best personal computing experience to students, educators, creative professionals, and consumers around the world through its innovative hardware, software, and Internet offerings."

"Offering a wide range of well-designed, functional home furnishing products at prices so low that as many people as possible will be able to afford them." (IKEA's)

Source: http://retailindustry.about.com/od/retailbestpractices/ig/Company-Mission-Statements/.

SWOT analysis
A planning tool used to analyze an organization's strengths, weaknesses, opportunities, and threats.

and customers are most profitable or will be most profitable? Why do people buy (or not buy) our products? Who are our major competitors? What threats are there to our business? These questions frame the **SWOT analysis**. This is an analysis of an organization's **S**trengths, **W**eaknesses, **O**pportunities, and **T**hreats—how can strengths be used and capitalized on, how can weaknesses be improved, how can opportunities be exploited, and how can threats be mitigated. Soliciting input from all key stakeholders, a company begins such a process with a general review of the business situation. Then it identifies its internal strengths and weaknesses, relative to its competitors. These strengths and weaknesses are for the most part within the control of the organization. They include elements that are referred to as PRIMO-F: people, resources, innovation and ideas, marketing, operations, and finance. Next, a business environment analysis (you were introduced to some elements, such as the legal environment, in Chapter 1) is conducted. Opportunities and threats in the marketplace are identified—and, while they cannot always be controlled or anticipated, they most definitely affect the organization. Opportunities and threats include concepts referred to as PESTLE: political, economic, social, technological, legal, and environmental. Figure 8.3 lists some of the potential issues companies consider when conducting a SWOT analysis: Where do we want to go? How much growth do we want? What is our profit goal? What are our social objectives? What are our personal development objectives? A SWOT analysis is framed by the vision and when completed may result in the vision being revisited. All of the data that is gathered is then organized to reflect where a company is today and where a company would like to be. Differences between the two represent gaps. These gaps should

Figure 8.3

SWOT Analysis

This figure identifies potential strengths, weaknesses, opportunities, and threats that organizations may discover in a SWOT analysis.

Potential Internal Strengths
- an acknowledged market leader
- core competencies in key areas
- proven and respected management team
- well-conceived functional area strategies
- cost advantages
- better advertising campaigns

Potential Internal Weaknesses
- no clear strategic direction
- weak market image
- subpar profitability
- obsolete facilities
- lack of managerial depth and talent
- too narrow a product line

Potential External Opportunities
- falling trade barriers in attractive foreign markets
- new government policies (e.g., incentives for R&D, lower taxes, industry deregulation)
- increases in market demand (due to changing buyer needs and tastes, growing incomes)
- ability to transfer skills/technology to new products
- complacency among rival firms

Potential External Threats
- recession and changing (negative) economic conditions
- introduction of substitute products (by competitors)
- costly regulatory requirements
- entry of low-cost foreign competitors
- changing buyer needs and tastes

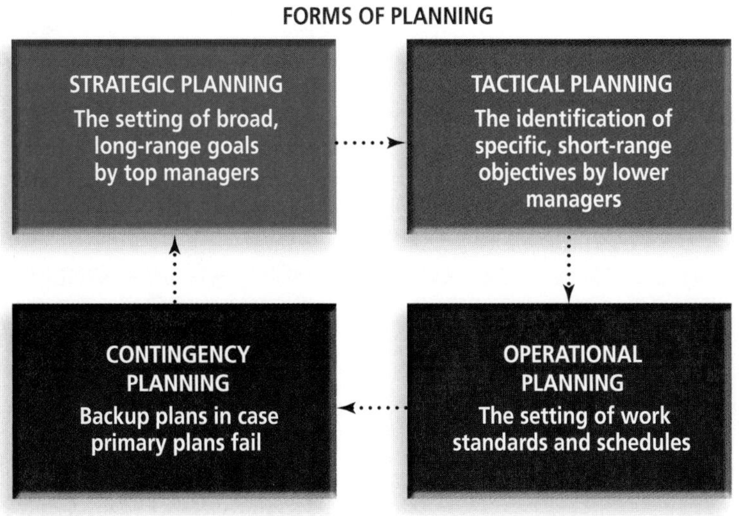

FORMS OF PLANNING

Figure 8.4

Planning Functions
Very few firms bother to make contingency plans. If something changes the market, such companies may be slow to respond. Most organization do strategic, tactical, and operational planning.

then be addressed in the planning described next. The Dealing With Change box at the end of Part 3 discusses what Change Management is all about.

2. How can we get there from here? This is the most important part of planning. It takes four forms: strategic, tactical, operational, and contingency planning. See Figure 8.4 for a visual of this. Notice the continuous connection between the four forms. Not only does this illustrate the relationship between them, but also that planning is a continuous process, which each of the forms being informed by another of the forms.

Strategic planning outlines how the company will meet its objectives and goals. It provides the foundation for the policies, procedures, and strategies for obtaining and using resources to achieve those goals. In this definition, policies are broad guides to action, and strategies determine the best way to use resources. At the strategic planning stage, the company decides which customers to serve, what goods or services to sell, and the geographic areas in which the firm will compete.[13]

strategic planning
The process of determining the major goals of the organization and the policies and strategies for obtaining and using resources to achieve those goals.

In today's rapidly changing environment, strategic planning is becoming more difficult because changes are occurring so fast that plans—even those set for just months into the future—may soon be obsolete.[14] Therefore, some companies are making shorter-term plans that allow for quick responses to customer needs and requests.[15] The goal is to be flexible and responsive to the market.

Tactical planning is the process of developing detailed, short-term statements about what is to be done, who is to do it, and how it is to be done. Tactical planning is normally the responsibility of managers or teams of managers at *lower* levels of the organization, whereas strategic planning is the responsibility of the *top* managers of the firm (e.g., the president and vice-presidents of the organization). Tactical planning, for example, involves setting annual budgets and deciding on other details and activities necessary to meet the strategic objectives. If the strategic plan of a truck manufacturer, for example, is to sell more trucks in northern Canada, the tactical plan might be to fund more research of northern truck drivers' wants and needs, and to plan advertising to reach those customers.

tactical planning
The process of developing detailed, short-term statements about what is to be done, who is to do it, and how it is to be done.

Operational planning is the process of setting work standards and schedules necessary to implement the company's tactical objectives. Operational planning focuses on the specific responsibilities of supervisors, department managers, and individual employees. Operational plans can include operational budgets. You will read about budgets in more detail in Chapter 17. The operational plan is the department manager's

operational planning
The process of setting work standards and schedules necessary to implement the company's tactical objectives.

SPOTLIGHT ON SMALL BUSINESS

I'd Rather Be Blue

Some of the best-managed organizations can be found in the most unusual situations. Consider, for example, three entrepreneurs whose product involved shaving their heads, slathering themselves with blue paint, and drumming on homemade instruments such as PVC pipe. Enter the Blue Man Group <*www.blueman.com*>. Today the original Blue Men—Matt Goldman, Phil Stanton, and Chris Wink—manage an organization of over 500 employees, 70 of whom appear nightly as Blue Men in 12 cities around the world. Their Megastar World Tour included a number of shows in central Canada featuring their unique music, comedy, and multimedia theatrics.

Like the founders of any other company, the Blue Man Group creators knew they had to tinker with their product if they wanted to expand and be successful. Planning and organization were critical. The partners locked themselves away for several days to write a detailed 132-page Blue Man operating manual. Writing the manual made the partners realize the vast market potential for their concept, but it also taught them the importance of managing the product's growth and everyday operations. They decided that company decisions would not be made on a majority vote but rather by consensus among the three of them. That policy continues today.

Sources: Liz Welch, "How We Did It: The Blue Man Group," *Inc.*, August 2008; and Blue Man Group, www.blueman.com, accessed 29 January 2009.

tool for daily and weekly operations. An operational plan could also include, say, the specific dates for certain truck parts to be completed and the quality specifications those parts must meet. You will read about operations management in more detail in Chapter 10.

contingency planning
The process of preparing alternative courses of action that may be used if the primary plans do not achieve the organization's objectives.

Contingency planning is the process of preparing alternative courses of action that may be used if the primary plans do not achieve the organization's objectives. The economic and competitive environments change so rapidly that it is wise to have alternative plans of action ready in anticipation of such changes. For example, if an organization does not meet its sales goals by a certain date, the contingency plan may call for more advertising or a cut in prices at that time. In the fall of 2011 Research in Motion was dealing with a significant shortfall of their expected sales in the computer tablet market. Their PlayBook had a very tough time competing with Apple's iPad along with a number of other entrants into this market. Starting in September of 2011 they dropped the price of this device by around 50 percent.[16] They extended the price reduction in January of 2012, based on improving sales from their earlier price reduction. With iPad sales representing over 90 percent of the market, many competitors dropped their price to below the cost of production.[17]

Some companies see opportunities where others see threats. Morneau Shepell Inc. <*www.morneaushepell.com*> provides global benefits consulting, administration systems, and outsourcing services. Morneau Shepell believes that most companies view contingency planning solely as a tool to prevent operational shutdowns. A company should be able to mitigate the potential damage and financial loss resulting from an unforeseen emergency or catastrophe, but it encourages companies to re-evaluate their thinking regarding contingency planning and the importance of anticipating health care–related emergencies (HREs). For example, while there has been widespread media attention given to events such as the SARS epidemic, other diseases such as pneumonia and influenza (also known as the flu) lead to more deaths annually in Canada. The benefits of developing an HRE contingency plan are numerous, for both newsworthy and more typical events. The main goals of such initiatives are ensuring business continuity, reducing risk to employees and their dependants, and maintaining productivity, as well as minimizing the possibility of litigation.[18]

crisis planning
Involves reacting to sudden changes in the environment.

Crisis planning is a part of contingency planning. **Crisis planning** involves reacting to sudden changes in the environment. At the 16th World Conference on Disaster

Management, Peter Power, a veteran of the anti-terrorism branch of the London Metropolitan Police, stated that "nowhere near enough" Canadian companies are ready to deal with the fallout from an environmental, accidental, technological, or terrorist-driven catastrophe.[19] Crisis planning can be especially challenging to medium-sized and smaller companies due to fewer resources, said Carolee Birchall, vice-president and senior risk officer of technology and solutions at BMO Bank of Montreal.[20] In short, crisis planning is a critical component of contingency planning that requires understanding and acceptance throughout the whole organization, regardless of its size. You will read more about risk management in Appendix D.

Planning is a key management function because the other management functions depend on having good plans. Starting with a directional plan based on broad business objectives and performance targets over three to five years, companies can then focus their efforts through strategic planning. The idea is to stay flexible, listen to customers, and seize opportunities when they come, whether or not those opportunities were expected.[21] The opportunities, however, must fit into the company's overall goals and objectives or the company could lose its focus. Clearly, then, much of management and planning involves decision making.

Before we consider decision making, let us summarize some of the points in this chapter. A vision ("WHERE we are going . . ."), in combination with values (HOW we will treat our stakeholders . . .), and the mission statement ("Our purpose IS . . ."), provides direction for the company. A company's objectives (WHAT we want to accomplish) are linked to its strategy (HOW we will accomplish the objectives). So, there is a progression from vision and values, to mission, to objectives, and to strategy. Once the strategy has been established, plans must be developed and implemented to ensure that objectives are met. There is never a strategy without there first being an objective. A SWOT analysis alone is almost useless unless you match it to the company's strategy and plan.

Clearly, then, much of management and planning requires decision making. The Spotlight on Small Business box on the previous page illustrates how one unique small business handles planning and decision making.

DECISION MAKING: FINDING THE BEST ALTERNATIVE

All management functions involve some kind of decision making. **Decision making** is choosing among two or more alternatives. It sounds easier here than it is in practice. In fact, decision making is the heart of all management functions. The *rational decision-making model* is a series of steps that managers often follow to make logical, intelligent, and well-founded decisions.[22] These steps can be thought of as the seven Ds of decision making:

decision making
Choosing among two or more alternatives.

1. Define the situation.
2. Describe and collect needed information.
3. Develop alternatives.
4. Develop agreement among those involved.
5. Decide which alternative is best.
6. Do what is indicated (begin implementation).
7. Determine whether the decision was a good one and follow up.

Managers do not always go through this seven-step process. Sometimes decisions have to be made on the spot—with little information available. Managers must make good decisions in all such circumstances.

problem solving
The process of solving the everyday problems that occur. Problem solving is less formal than decision making and usually calls for quicker action.

brainstorming
Coming up with as many solutions to a problem as possible in a short period of time with no censoring of ideas.

PMI
Listing all the pluses for a solution in one column, all the minuses in another, and the interesting in a third column.

Problem solving is the process of solving the everyday problems that occur. It is less formal than the decision-making process and usually calls for quicker action. Problem-solving teams are made up of two or more workers who are given an assignment to solve a specific problem (e.g., Why are customers not using our service policies?). Problem-solving techniques that companies use include **brainstorming** (i.e., coming up with as many solutions as possible in a short period of time with no censoring of ideas) and **PMI** (i.e., listing all the **P**luses for a solution in one column, all the **M**inuses in another, and the **I**nteresting in a third column). PMI is an tool developed by Edward de Bono as part of his work on lateral and creative thinking strategies. You can practise using the PMI system on almost all of your decisions. For example, should you stay home and study tonight? You would list all benefits of your choice (Pluses) in one column: better grades, improved self-esteem, more responsible, and so forth. In the other column, you would put the negatives (Minuses): boredom, less fun, etc. In the third column write down the outcomes of taking the action, which often helps to clarify your decision. We hope that the pluses outweigh the minuses most of the time, and that you study often, but sometimes it is best to go out and have fun. In that case, the Interesting would be that having fun would not hurt your grades or job prospects.

PROGRESS ASSESSMENT

- What's the difference between goals and objectives?
- What does a company analyze when it does a SWOT analysis?
- What's the difference between strategic, tactical, and operational planning?
- What are the seven Ds in decision making?

Describe the organizing function of management.

ORGANIZING: CREATING A UNIFIED SYSTEM

After managers have planned a course of action, they must organize the firm to accomplish their goals. Operationally, organizing means allocating resources (such as funds for various departments), assigning tasks, and establishing procedures for accomplishing the organizational objectives. When organizing, a manager develops a structure or framework that relates all workers, tasks, and resources to each other. That framework is called the organization structure. In Chapter 9, we will look at examples of several organizational structures and will review some of the challenges in developing an organization structure.

organization chart
A visual device that shows relationships among people and divides the organization's work; it shows who is accountable for the completion of specific work and who reports to whom.

Most organizations draw a chart showing these relationships. This tool is called an organization chart. An **organization chart** is a visual device that shows relationships among people and divides the organization's work; it shows who is accountable for the completion of specific work and who reports to whom. Figure 8.5 shows a simple one. Each rectangle indicates a position (and usually who holds this position) within the organization. The chart plots who reports to whom (as indicated by the lines) and who is responsible for each task. For example, in Figure 8.5, Manager B is the accounting and finance manager, and this middle manager reports directly to the president. Reporting directly to the accounting and finance manager are two first-line supervisors; two employees report directly to each of these first-line supervisors. The corporate hierarchy illustrated on the organization chart includes top, middle, and first-line managers. The problems involved in developing an organization structure will be discussed later in the text. For now, it is important to know that the corporate hierarchy usually includes three levels of management (see Figure 8.6).

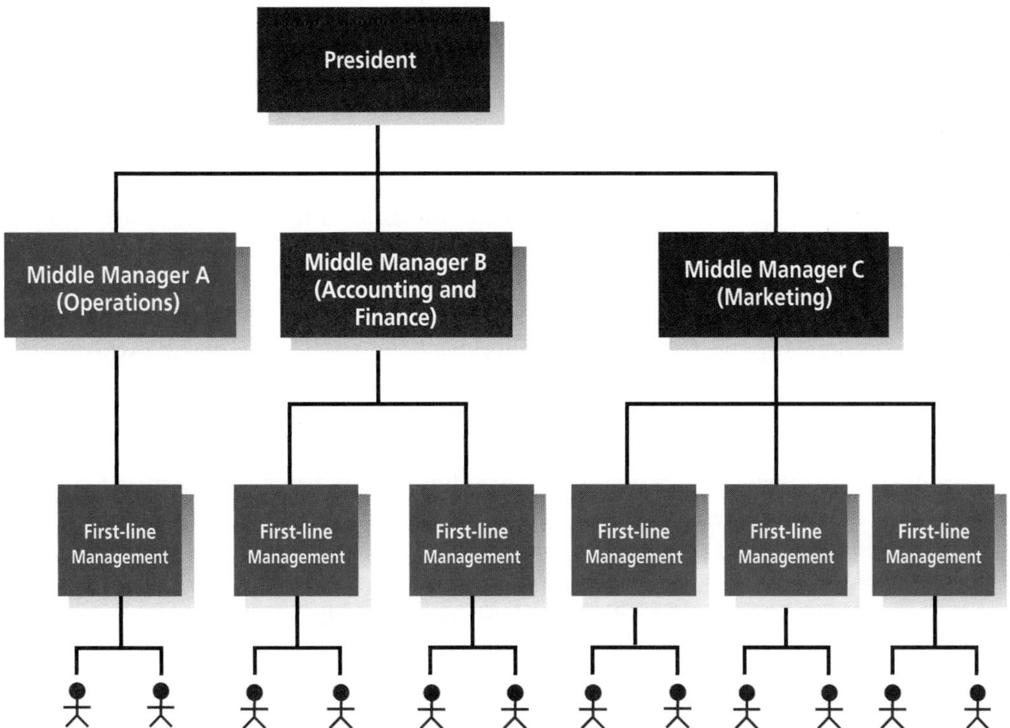

Figure 8.5

Typical Organization Chart This is a snapshot of a rather standard chart with managers for major functions and supervisors reporting to the managers In this example, each supervisor manages two employees.

top management Highest level of management, consisting of the president and other key company executives, who develop strategic plans.

Top management (the highest level of management) consists of the president and other key company executives who develop strategic plans. Terms you are likely to see often are chief executive officer (CEO), chief operating officer (COO), chief financial officer (CFO), and chief information officer (CIO), or in some companies, chief knowledge officer (CKO). The CEO is often the president of the firm and is responsible for all top-level decisions in the firm. CEOs are responsible for introducing change into an organization. The COO is responsible for putting those changes into effect. His or her tasks include structuring work, controlling operations, and rewarding people to ensure that everyone strives to carry out the leader's vision. The CFO is responsible for obtaining funds, planning budgets, collecting funds, and so on. The

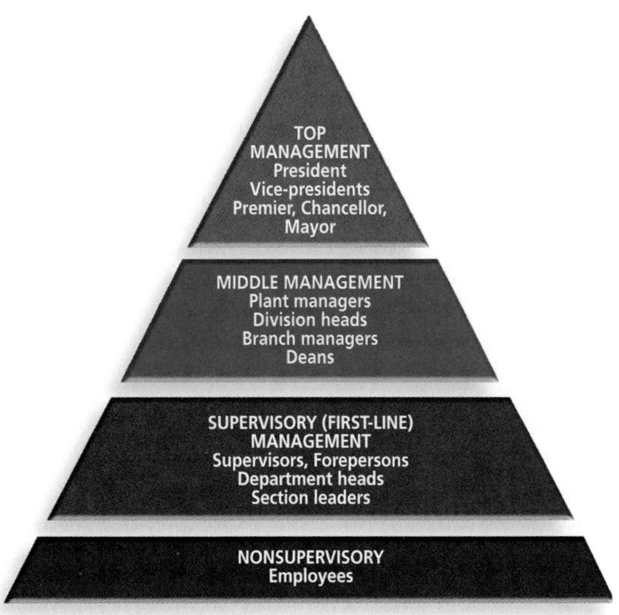

Figure 8.6

Levels of Management This figure shows the three levels of management. In many firms, there are several levels of middle management. Many firms have eliminated middle-level managers because fewer are needed to oversee self-managed teams of employees.

CIO or CKO is responsible for getting the right information to other managers so they can make correct decisions. Many companies are simplifying their executive committee by combining some of the positions, like COO and CFO, which they believe provides better focus.[23]

Loblaws has been making significant changes in their operations over the past few years. Faced with the growing presence of Walmart and general merchandising distribution problems, which resulted in significant losses for a few years, they are looking to Galen Weston Jr. to implement a series of strategic initiatives to restore their former glory. They are refocusing on their strong brands, including President's Choice, re-pricing some staple products to provide best-value-for-money, and improving efficiencies in their supply chain. While profits slowly improve they are still involved in a major overhaul of their infrastructure.[24]

middle management
The level of management that includes general managers, division managers, and branch and plant managers, who are responsible for tactical planning and controlling.

supervisory management
Managers who are directly responsible for supervising workers and evaluating their daily performance.

Middle management includes general managers, division managers, and branch and plant managers (in your school, deans and department/area heads) who are responsible for tactical planning and controlling. Many firms have eliminated some middle managers through downsizing, and have given the remaining managers more employees to supervise.

Supervisory management includes those who are directly responsible for supervising workers and evaluating their daily performance; they are often known as first-line managers (or supervisors) because they are the first level above workers.[25]

Tasks and Skills at Different Levels of Management

Few people are trained to be good managers. Usually a person learns how to be a skilled accountant or sales representative or production-line worker, and then—because of his or her technical skills—is selected to be a manager. Once someone becomes a manager they spend more of their time in supporting those people they supervise, showing them how to do things, helping them, supervising them, and generally being very active in the operating task. Robert Katz developed a model to explain the types of skills necessary to be a good manager, and the mix of these skills through the various management levels.

The further up the managerial ladder a person moves, the less important his or her original job skills become. At the top of the ladder, the need is for people who are visionaries, planners, organizers, coordinators, communicators, morale builders, and motivators.[26] Figure 8.7 shows that a manager must have three categories of skills:

technical skills
Skills that involve the ability to perform tasks in a specific discipline or department.

human relations skills
Skills that involve communication and motivation; they enable managers to work through and with people.

conceptual skills
Skills that involve the ability to picture the organization as a whole and the relationships among its various parts.

1. **Technical skills** involve the ability to perform tasks in a specific discipline (such as selling a product or developing software) or department (such as marketing or information systems).
2. **Human relations skills** involve communication and motivation; they enable managers to work through and with people. Such skills also include those associated with leadership, coaching, morale building, delegating, training and development, and help and supportiveness.
3. **Conceptual skills** involve the ability to picture the organization as a whole and the relationships among its various parts. Conceptual skills are needed in planning, organizing, controlling, systems development, problem analysis, decision making, coordinating, and delegating.

While it is not specifically stated, you can see how time-management skills are a necessary component of each one of these categories of skills. Good managers must be able to effectively handle the daily points of contact that require their attention. This includes a lot of phone calls, interruptions, meetings, and numerous e-mails.

Looking at Figure 8.7, you will notice that first-line managers need to be skilled in all three areas. However, most of their time is spent on technical and human relations tasks (assisting operating personnel, giving directions, etc.). First-line managers

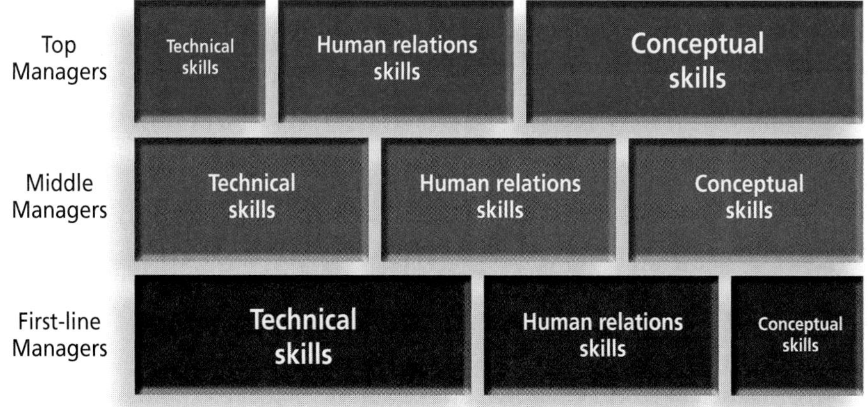

Figure 8.7

Skills Needed at Various Levels of Management

All managers need human relations skills. At the top, managers need strong conceptual skills and rely less on technical skills. First-line managers need strong technical skills and rely less on conceptual skills. Middle managers need to have a balance between technical and conceptual skills.

spend little time on conceptual tasks. Top managers, in contrast, need to use few technical skills. Instead, almost all of their time is devoted to human relations and conceptual tasks. A person who is competent at a low level of management may not be competent at higher levels, and vice versa. The skills needed are different at each level of management.

The Stakeholder-Oriented Organization

A dominating question of the past 20 years or so has been how to best organize a firm to respond to the needs of its stakeholders. Remember, stakeholders include customers, employees, suppliers, dealers, environmental groups, and the surrounding communities. The consensus seems to be that smaller organizations are more responsive than larger organizations. Therefore, many large firms are being restructured into smaller, more customer-focused units.

The point is that companies are no longer organizing to make it easy for managers to have control. Instead, they are organizing so that customers have the greatest influence. The change to a customer orientation is being aided by technology. For example, establishing a dialogue with customers on the Internet enables some firms to work closely with customers and respond quickly to their wants and needs, as in the case of WestJet Airlines, which allows customers the option to book flights via the Web. This not only generated cost savings for the company (a cost of $2 for online booking compared with as much as $20 when a travel agent booked the flight), but benefited the customers, who could collect Air Miles and get a small discount off any round-trip fare.[27]

There's no way an organization can provide high-quality goods and services to customers unless suppliers provide world-class parts and materials with which to work. Thus, managers have to establish close relationships with suppliers, including close Internet ties.[28] To make the entire system work, similar relationships have to be established with those organizations that sell directly to consumers—namely retailers.

In the past, the goal of the organization function in the firm was to clearly specify who does what within the firm. Today, the organizational task is much more complex because firms are forming partnerships, joint ventures, and other arrangements that make it necessary to organize the whole system; that is, several firms working together,

▸ Carproof <*www.carproof.com*> is a Canadian vehicle history reporting service providing detailed real-time data on used vehicles. In 2011 it was recognized as one of Canada's 50 Best Managed Companies. Dealers, auction houses, lenders, insurance companies, law enforcement agencies, and consumers all rely on data supplied by this company. Carproof and the other winners were recognized for their efforts in building a value proposition for their customers. Would you consider researching other companies that have been recognized with this award when looking for a job?

often across national boundaries.[29] One organization working alone is often not as effective as many organizations working together. Creating a unified system out of multiple organizations will be one of the greatest management challenges of the twenty-first century. This discussion will be revisited in Chapter 10, when we look at operations management.

Explain the differences between leaders and managers, and describe the various leadership styles.

LEADING: PROVIDING CONTINUOUS VISION AND VALUES

In business literature there's a trend toward separating the notion of management from that of leadership. One person might be a good manager but not a good leader. Another might be a good leader without being a good manager. One difference between managers and leaders is that managers strive to produce order and stability, whereas leaders embrace and manage change. Leadership is creating a vision for others to follow, establishing corporate values and ethics, and transforming the way the organization does business to improve its effectiveness and efficiency. Good leaders motivate workers and create the environment for workers to motivate themselves.[30] *Management is the carrying out of the leadership's vision.*

Leaders must therefore:

- *Communicate a vision and rally others around that vision.* The leader should be openly sensitive to the concerns of followers, give them responsibility, and win their trust. A successful leader must influence the actions of others.
- *Establish corporate values.* These values (as discussed earlier in this chapter) include a concern for employees, for customers, for the environment, and for the quality of the company's products. When companies set their business goals, they are defining the values of the company as well.
- *Promote corporate ethics.* Ethics include an unfailing demand for honesty and an insistence that everyone in the company is treated fairly (see the Making Ethical Decisions box). That is why we stress ethical decision making throughout this text. Many business people have made the news by giving away huge amounts to charity, thus setting a model of social concern for their employees and others.
- *Embrace transformational change.* A leader's most important job may be to transform the way the company does business so that it is more effective (does things better) and efficient (uses fewer resources to accomplish the same objectives) The Green Box illustrates how management can provide leadership in the area of sustainability.
- *Stress accountability and responsibility.* One thing we have learned from the recession of 2008–09 is that leaders need to be held accountable and need to feel responsible for their actions. A key word that has emerged from the crisis is transparency. **Transparency** is the presentation of a company's facts

transparency
The presentation of a company's facts and figures in a way that is clear, accessible, and apparent to all stakeholders.

MAKING ETHICAL DECISIONS

To Share or Not to Share

First-line managers assist in the decisions made by their department heads. The department heads retain full responsibility for the decisions—if a plan succeeds, it is their success; if a plan fails, it is their failure. Now picture this: As a first-line manager, you have new information that your department head has not seen yet. The findings in this report indicate that your manager's recent plans are sure to fail. If the plans do fail, the manager will probably be demoted and you're the most likely candidate to fill the vacancy. Will you give your department head the report? What will the consequences be of your decision?

GREENBOX

Leadership in Sustainability

Sustainability was introduced and defined in Chapter 5. Sustainability has now become a leadership issue for business. Companies are moving from an outside-in perspective (when they addressed this issue based on government mandates) to just the normal way of doing business. This is due, in part, to customers now making buying decisions based on the sustainable practices of their suppliers, and companies realizing that through sustainable practices they can also reduce their costs.

Leadership is shown by making sustainability part and parcel of how a business operates. Leadership opportunities can be found from how a business sources their inputs, to how they produce the goods or services they sell, to how they distribute and service their products. Furthermore standards are emerging that measure sustainability, including measures of energy efficiency, carbon emissions, water usage, and labour practices.

As businesses have become more mature in their view of sustainability they have moved from initially wanting to protect their value through compliance with regulations to increasing value though embedding real, measurable, ongoing commitments to sustainability that they believe will differentiate them in the market.

How could management apply each of its functions in terms of sustainability?

Source: PwC, www.pwc.com/ca/en/sustainability/publications.jhtml; Sustainability Advantage, www.sustainabilityadvantage.com/; and Simply Sustain, www.simplysustain.com/a/Sustainability/Ourviews/tabid/57/Default.aspx.

and figures in a way that is clear, accessible, and apparent to all stakeholders. Governments are trying to make companies (and themselves) more transparent so that everyone is more aware of what is happening to the economy and to specific businesses and government agencies.

All organizations need leaders, and all employees can help lead. You do not have to be a manager to perform a leadership function. That is, any employee can motivate others to work well, add to a company's ethical environment, and report ethical lapses when they occur.

Over the past ten years, there has been an increasing trend in compensation packages that involve share ownership for top executives. These packages have been justified as necessary to attract and keep good leaders, but some critics argue that they actually inhibit leadership. McGill University's Henry Mintzberg has been vocal on his disagreement with the increasing CEO compensation packages. In his view, many CEOs focus solely on the short-term increase in the share value of the company and their bonuses. "Find me a chief executive who refuses those bonuses, who takes the long-term view and says his team will share the spoils of their mandate in 10 years time, and I'll show you a leader," he said.[32] Do you agree that top executives should receive such lucrative packages in today's environment?

▸ Canada still trails the United States and the rest of the world in developing female leaders. Over 80 percent of organizations don't have a clear strategy for developing female leaders and yet studies have shown that having more senior-level women improves company's profits.[31] What should be included in leadership development programs for women?

Leadership Styles

Nothing has challenged researchers in the area of management more than the search for the "best" leadership traits, behaviours, or styles. Thousands of studies have tried to identify characteristics that make leaders different from other people. Intuitively, you would conclude about the same thing they did; leadership styles are hard to pin down. Some leaders are well groomed and tactful, while others are unkempt and abrasive—yet the latter may be just as effective as the former.

Just as no one set of traits describes a leader, no one style of leadership works best in all situations. Even so, we can look at a few of the most commonly recognized leadership styles (see Figure 8.8) and see how they may be effective:

autocratic leadership
Leadership style that involves making managerial decisions without consulting others.

1. **Autocratic leadership** involves making managerial decisions without consulting others. Such a style is effective in emergencies and when absolute "followership" is needed—for example, when fighting fires. Autocratic leadership is also effective sometimes with new, relatively unskilled workers who need clear direction and guidance. Can you think a situation where this leadership style makes sense?

participative (democratic) leadership
Leadership style that consists of managers and employees working together to make decisions.

2. **Participative (democratic) leadership** consists of managers and employees working together to make decisions. Research has found that employee participation in decisions may not always increase effectiveness, but it usually increases job satisfaction. Many progressive organizations are highly successful at using a democratic style of leadership that values traits such as flexibility, good listening skills, and empathy.

free-rein (laissez-faire) leadership
Leadership style that involves managers setting objectives and employees being relatively free to do whatever it takes to accomplish those objectives.

3. **Free-rein (laissez-faire) leadership** involves managers setting objectives and employees being relatively free to do whatever it takes to accomplish those objectives. Free-rein leadership is often the most successful leadership style in organizations in which managers supervise doctors, engineers, or other professionals. The traits needed by managers in such organizations include warmth, friendliness, and understanding. More and more firms are adopting this style of leadership with at least some of their employees.

Individual leaders rarely fit neatly into just one of these categories. Researchers illustrate leadership as a continuum with varying amounts of employee participation, ranging from purely boss-centred leadership to subordinate-centred leadership.

Other research has identified two other styles that can be included in this discussion. **Transformational leadership** occurs when visionary leaders can influence others to follow them in working to achieve a desired outcome or goal. This leadership style works best in situations where dramatic organizational change is required. Can you think of leaders who have been transformational for their organization?

Transactional leadership is associated with employees who are motivated by a system of reward. Here the leader is given power to assign tasks and their successful completion leads to rewards and reinforcement. The difference between this style and the autocratic style is that with the former the source of motivation is a reward, while with the latter it is punishment.

Figure 8.8

Various Leadership Styles

Source: Reprinted by permission of the *Harvard Business Review*. An exhibit from "How to Choose a Leadership Pattern" by Robert Tannenbaum and Warren Schmidt (May/June 1973). Copyright © 1973 by the President and Fellows of Harvard College, all rights reserved.

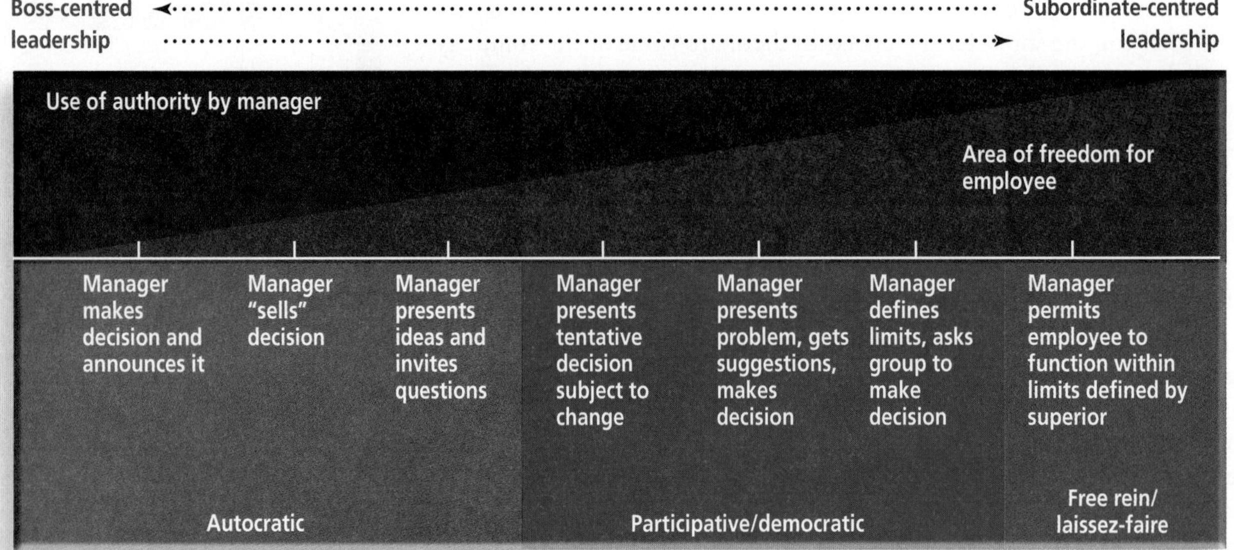

Which leadership style is best? Research tells us that successful leadership depends largely on what the goals and values of the firm are, who is being led, and in what situations. It also supports the notion that any leadership style, ranging from autocratic to free-rein, may be successful depending on the people and the situation. In fact, a manager may use a variety of leadership styles, depending on a given situation. A manager may be autocratic but friendly with a new trainee, democratic with an experienced employee who has many good ideas that can only be fostered by a flexible manager who is a good listener, and free-rein with a trusted, long-term supervisor who probably knows more about operations than the manager does.

There's no such thing as a leadership style that always works best. A truly successful leader has the ability to use the leadership style most appropriate to the situation and the employees involved.

transformational leadership
Leadership style that occurs when leaders can influence others to follow them in working to achieve a desired outcome or goal.

transactional leadership
Leadership style where the leader is given the power to assign tasks and their successful completion leads to rewards and reinforcement.

Managing Knowledge

"Knowledge is power." Empowering employees means giving them knowledge—that is, getting them the information they need to do the best job they can. Finding the right information, keeping the information in a readily accessible place, and making the information known to everyone in the firm together constitutes **knowledge management**.[33] For example, Canadian Tire was the first major Canadian retailer to use an Internet-based eLearning program. eLearning is an online training and education program that delivers product knowledge and skills training on everything from plumbing to paint mixing. The program is credited with improved customer and employee satisfaction levels. According to Janice Wismer, former vice-president of human resources, "People say the lessons have increased their confidence, that they're happier working here because the company is committing to their growth and development."[34] This is good news for store sales.

knowledge management
Finding the right information, keeping the information in a readily accessible place, and making the information known to everyone in the firm.

The first step to developing a knowledge management system is determining what knowledge is most important. Do you want to know more about your customers? Do you want to know more about competitors? What kind of information would make the company more effective or more efficient or more responsive to the marketplace? Once you have decided what you need to know, you set out to find answers to those questions.

Knowledge management tries to keep people from reinventing the wheel—that is, duplicating the work of gathering information—every time a decision needs to be made. A company really progresses when each person in the firm asks continually, "What do I still not know?" and "Whom should I be asking?" It is as important to know what is not working as what is working. Employees and managers now have e-mail, text messaging, and other means of keeping in touch with each other, with customers, and with other stakeholders. The key to success is learning how to process that information effectively and turn it into knowledge that everyone can use to improve processes and procedures. That is one way to enable workers to be more effective. (Recall that there is a brief discussion in Appendix A on information technology and knowledge management.)

PROGRESS ASSESSMENT

- What are some characteristics of leadership today that make leaders different from traditional managers?
- Explain the differences between autocratic and democratic leadership styles.
- What is the first step in developing a knowledge management system?

LO 6

Summarize the five steps of the control function of management.

CONTROLLING: MAKING SURE IT WORKS

The control function involves measuring performance relative to the planned objectives and standards, rewarding people for work well done, and then taking corrective action when necessary. Thus, the control process (see Figure 8.9) is the heart of the management system because it provides the feedback that enables managers and workers to adjust to any deviations from plans and to changes in the environment that have affected performance. Controlling consists of five steps:

1. Establishing clear performance standards. This ties the planning function to the control function. Without clear standards, control is impossible.
2. Monitoring and recording actual performance (results).
3. Comparing results against plans and standards.
4. Communicating results and deviations to the employees involved.
5. Taking corrective action when needed and providing positive feedback for work well done.

This control process is ongoing throughout the year. Continuous monitoring ensures that if corrective action is required, there is enough time to implement changes. When corrective action is necessary, the decision-making process is a useful tool to apply (recall the seven Ds of decision making). Simply, managers are encouraged to review the situation and, based on collected information, develop alternatives with their staff and implement the best alternative. Or, in some circumstances, if significant changes have occurred, management can implement a contingency plan (as discussed earlier in the chapter). The focus is to meet the standards that were initially established during the planning stage or the standards that have since been modified. This process is also ongoing. It may take several attempts before standards are successfully met.

The control system's weakest link tends to be the setting of standards. To measure results against standards, the standards must be specific, attainable, and measurable. Vague goals and standards such as "better quality," "more efficiency," and "improved performance" are not sufficient because they do not describe what you are trying to achieve. For example, let's say you are a runner and you want to improve your distance. When you started your improvement plan last year, you ran 2 kilometres a day. Now you run 2.1 kilometres a day. Did you meet your goal? You did increase your distance, but certainly not by very much. A more appropriate goal statement would be: To increase running distance from 2 kilometres a day to 4 kilometres a day by

Figure 8.9

The Control Process

The whole control process is based on clear standards. Without such standards, the other steps are difficult, if not impossible. With clear standards, performance measurement is relatively easy and the proper action can be taken.

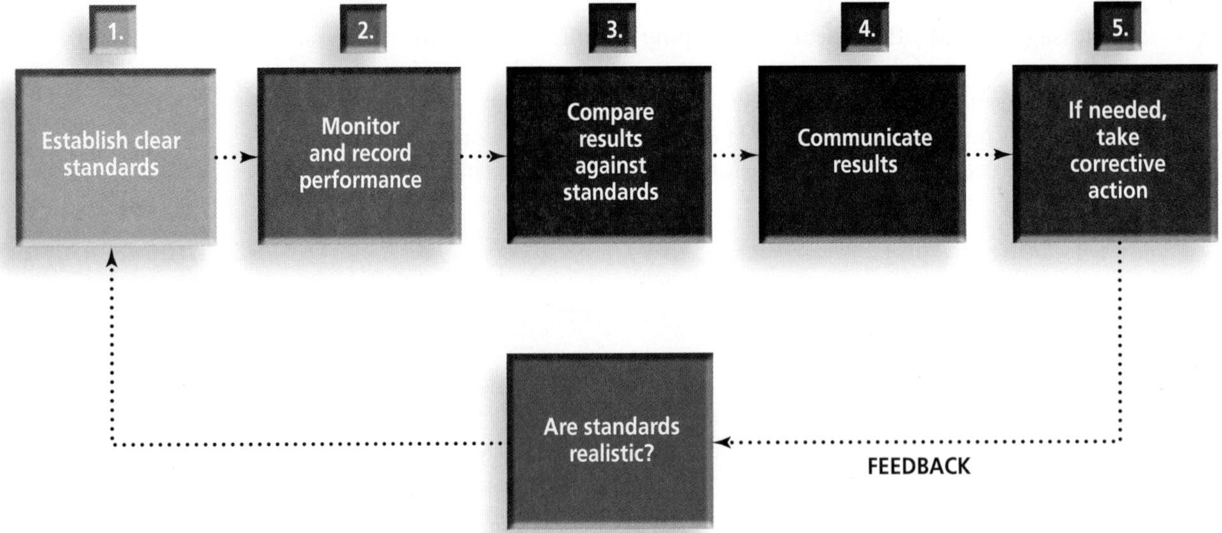

January 1. It is important to establish a time period for when specific goals are to be met. Here are examples of goals and standards that meet these criteria:

- Cut the number of finished-product rejects from 10 per 1,000 to 5 per 1,000 by March 31.
- Increase the number of times managers praise employees from 3 per week to 12 per week by the end of the quarter.
- Increase sales of product X from $10,000 per month to $12,000 per month by July 31.

One way to make control systems work is to establish clear procedures for monitoring performance. Accounting and finance are often the foundation for control systems because they provide the numbers management needs to evaluate progress. We shall explore both accounting and finance in detail later in the text.

A Key Criterion for Measurement: Customer Satisfaction

Traditional measures of success are usually financial: that is, they define success in terms of profits or return on investment. Certainly these measures are still important, but they are not the whole purpose of a firm. Other purposes may include pleasing customers, stakeholders, and customers (including both external and internal customers). One goal today is to go beyond simply satisfying customers to "delighting" them with unexpectedly good products. **External customers** include dealers, who buy products to sell to others, and ultimate customers (also known as end users) such as you and me, who buy products for their own personal use. **Internal customers** are individuals and units within the firm that receive services from other individuals or units. For example, the field salespeople are the internal customers of the marketing research people who prepare research reports for them.

Let's pause now, review, and do some exercises. Management is doing, not just reading.

external customers
Dealers, who buy products to sell to others, and ultimate customers (or end users), who buy products for their own personal use.

internal customers
Individuals and units within the firm that receive services from other individuals or units.

PROGRESS ASSESSMENT

- What are the five steps in the control process?
- What's the difference between internal and external customers?

SUMMARY

Describe the changes occurring today in the management function.

Many managers are changing their approach to corporate management.

What reasons can you give to account for these changes in management?

Business people are being challenged to be more ethical and to make their accounting practices more visible to investors and the general public. Change is now happening faster than ever, and global competition is just a click away. Managing change is an important element of success, particularly in light of today's emphasis on speed in the global marketplace. National borders mean much less now than ever before, and co-operation and integration among companies have greatly increased. Within companies, knowledge workers are demanding managerial styles that allow for freedom, and the workforce is becoming increasingly diverse, educated, and self-directed.

How are managers' roles changing?

Managers are being educated to guide, train, support, and teach employees rather than tell them what to do.

Describe the four functions of management.

Managers perform a variety of functions.

What are the four primary functions of management?

The four primary functions are (1) planning, (2) organizing, (3) leading, and (4) controlling.

Describe each of the four functions.

Planning includes anticipating trends and determining the best strategies and tactics to achieve organizational goals and objectives. Organizing includes designing the structure of the organization and creating conditions and systems in which everyone and everything works together to achieve the organization's goals and objectives. Leading involves creating a vision for the organization and guiding, training, coaching, and motivating others to work effectively to achieve the organization's goals and objectives. Controlling involves establishing clear standards to determine whether an organization is progressing toward its goals and objectives, rewarding people for doing a good job, and taking corrective action if they are not.

Relate the planning process and decision making to the accomplishment of company goals.

The planning function involves the process of setting objectives to meet the organizational goals. Goals are broad, long-term achievements that organizations aim to accomplish.

What are the four types of planning, and how are they related to the organization's goals and objectives?

Strategic planning is broad, long-range planning that outlines the goals of the organization. Tactical planning is specific, short-term planning that lists organizational objectives. Operational planning is part of tactical planning and involves setting specific timetables and standards. Contingency planning involves developing an alternative set of plans in case the first set does not work out.

What are the steps involved in decision making?

Decision making is choosing among two or more alternatives and it is the heart of all management functions. The seven Ds of decision making are (1) define the situation, (2) describe and collect needed information, (3) develop alternatives, (4) develop agreement among those involved, (5) decide which alternative is best, (6) do what is indicated (begin implementation), and (7) determine whether the decision was a good one and follow up.

Describe the organizing function of management.

Organizing means allocating resources (such as funds for various departments), assigning tasks, and establishing procedures for accomplishing the organizational objectives.

What are the three levels of management in the corporate hierarchy?
The three levels of management are (1) top management (highest level consisting of the president and other key company executives who develop strategic plans); (2) middle management (general managers, division managers, and plant managers who are responsible for tactical planning and controlling); and (3) supervisory management (first-line managers/supervisors who evaluate workers' daily performance).

What skills do managers need?
Managers must have three categories of skills: (1) technical skills (ability to perform specific tasks such as selling products or developing software), (2) human relations skills (ability to communicate and motivate), and (3) conceptual skills (ability to see organizations as a whole and how all the parts fit together). Managers at different levels need different skills.

Explain the differences between leaders and managers, and describe the various leadership styles.

Executives today must be more than just managers; they must be leaders as well.

What's the difference between a manager and a leader?
A manager plans, organizes, and controls functions within an organization. A leader has vision and inspires others to grasp that vision, establishes corporate values, emphasizes corporate ethics, and does not fear change.

Which leadership style is most effective?
Figure 8.8 shows a continuum of leadership styles ranging from boss-centred to subordinate-centred leadership. The most effective leadership style depends on the people being led and the situation.

Summarize the five steps of the control function of management.

The control function of management involves measuring employee performance against objectives and standards, rewarding people for a job well done, and taking corrective action if necessary.

What are the five steps of the control function?
Controlling incorporates (1) setting clear standards, (2) monitoring and recording performance, (3) comparing performance with plans and standards, (4) communicating results and deviations to employees, and (5) providing positive feedback for a job well done and taking corrective action if necessary.

What qualities must standards possess to be used to measure performance results?
Standards must be specific, attainable, and measurable.

KEY TERMS

autocratic leadership
brainstorming
conceptual skills
contingency planning
controlling
crisis planning
decision making
external customers
free-rein (laissez-faire) leadership
goals
human relations skills
internal customers
knowledge management
leading
management
middle management
mission statement
objectives

operational planning
organization chart
organizing
participative (democratic) leadership
planning
PMI
problem solving
resources
strategic planning
supervisory management
SWOT analysis
tactical planning
technical skills
top management
transactional leadership
transformational leadership
transparency
values
vision

CRITICAL THINKING

Many students say they would like to be a manager someday. Here are some questions to get you started thinking like a manager.

1. Would you like to work for a large firm or a small business? Private or public? In an office or out in the field? Give your reasons for each answer.
2. What type of leader would you be? What type of a leader would you most enjoy working with?
3. Do you see any problems with a participative (democratic) leadership style? Can you see a manager getting frustrated when he or she cannot control others?
4. What could be a motivator for each of the five leadership styles?

DEVELOPING WORKPLACE SKILLS

1. Allocate some time to do some career planning by doing a SWOT analysis of your present situation. What does the marketplace for your chosen career(s) look like today? What skills do you have that will make you a winner in that type of career? What weaknesses might you target to improve? What are the threats to that career choice? What are the opportunities? Prepare a two-minute presentation for the class.
2. Bring several decks of cards to class and have the class break up into teams of four or so members. Each team should then elect a leader. Each leader should be assigned a leadership style: autocratic, participative, or free-rein. Have each team try to build a house with a given design. The team that complete the task the most quickly wins. Each team member should then report his or her experience under that style of leadership.
3. Review Figure 8.8 and discuss managers you have known, worked for, or read about who have practised each style. Students from other countries may have interesting experiences to add. Which management style did you like best? Why? Which were most effective? Why?
4. Because of the illegal and unethical behaviour of a few managers, managers in general are under suspicion for being greedy and dishonest. Discuss the fairness of such charges, given the thousands of honest and ethical managers, and what could be done to improve their opinion of managers among the students in your class.

ANALYZING MANAGEMENT DECISIONS

Leading in a Leaderless Company

In an issue of *Business Week* devoted to the future of business, writer John Byrne speculated about the future of leadership. He said that the twenty-first century would be unfriendly to leaders who try to run their companies by sheer force of will, and that success would come instead to companies that are "leaderless"—or companies whose leadership is so widely shared that they resemble ant colonies or beehives. In a world that is becoming more dependent on brainpower, having teams at the top will make more sense than having a single top manager. The Internet enables companies to act more like beehives because information can be shared horizontally rather than sent up to the top manager's office and then back down again. Decisions can be made instantly by the best people equipped to make them. One of the best examples of this is Wikipedia <*www.wikipedia.org*>.

In the past, uniform thinking from the top could cripple an organization. Today, however, team leadership is ideally suited for the new reality of fast-changing markets. Urgent projects often require the coordinated contribution of many talented people working together. Such thinking does not happen at the top of the organization; it takes place down among the workers.

In the future, therefore, managers are more likely to be chosen for their team experience and their ability to delegate rather than make all key decisions themselves. Companies in the future, it is said, will be led by people who understand that in business, as in nature, no one person can be really in control.

Sources: John A. Byrne, "The Global Corporation Becomes a Leaderless Corporation," *Business Week*, 30 August 1999, 88–90; and Etienne C. Wenger and William M. Synder, "Communities of Practice: The Organizational Frontier," *Harvard Business Review*, January–February 2000, 139–145.

Discussion Questions

1. What would you look for on a resumé that would indicate that a candidate for work was a self-motivated team player? Are you that type? How do you know?
2. Given your experience with managers in the past, what problems do you see some managers having with letting employees decide for themselves the best way to do things and giving them the power to obtain needed equipment?
3. What would happen if all businesses in your area had their employees mix with customers to hear their comments and complaints? Would that be a good or bad thing? Why?
4. What are the various ways you can think of for companies to pay bonuses to team members? One way is to divide the money equally. What are other ways? Which would you prefer as a team member?

Practise and learn online with Connect.

CHAPTER 9

ADAPTING ORGANIZATIONS TO TODAY'S MARKETS

LEARNING OBJECTIVES

After you have read and studied this chapter, you should be able to:

LO 1 Outline the basic principles of organization management.

LO 2 Compare the organizational theories of Henri Fayol and Max Weber.

LO 3 Evaluate the choices managers make in structuring organizations.

LO 4 Contrast the various organizational models.

LO 5 Identify the benefits of inter-firm co-operation and coordination.

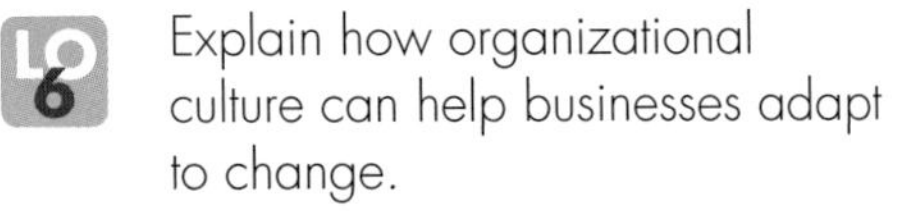

LO 6 Explain how organizational culture can help businesses adapt to change.

PROFILE

GETTING TO KNOW GALEN WESTON JR. OF LOBLAW COMPANIES LTD.

The goal of this chapter is to introduce you to the terms and concepts involved in organizing companies (and reorganizing them as well). Few challenges in business are greater than moving a large, well-established company from a management-oriented style of the past to a focus on meeting customer expectations in terms of high quality and reasonable costs. This situation is further complicated by a globally competitive market. In this case, two major international competitors are entering and attempting to take away as much business as possible from a well-established Canadian company. When the competitors are Walmart and Target you know we are talking about what has happened to the Loblaw Companies.

Back in 2006 Loblaws was facing something new. They were in the midst of dismal financial performance. They had lost their cachet or appeal as a product innovator and smart merchandiser in an industry with very tight margins that leave little room for error. They decided change was in order, starting at the top of the organization. A new management team was put in place, headed by the son of current president, W. Galen Weston. The "new kid on the block" was a Harvard-educated 34-year-old, Galen Weston Jr.

Utilizing a model of centralized authority Galen Weston Jr. lead the new team in making a number of strategic decisions, including moving into the higher-margin clothing business, introducing the Joe Fresh fashionable and affordable clothing line. They also committed to a massive, disruptive overhaul of their supply chain to better position themselves to compete against the above-mentioned global powerhouses (this initiative took fully five years to implement).

As they moved forward with these significant changes the economy entered a recession that started in 2008 and still lingered four years later. Through all of this turmoil Galen Weston Jr. has kept the company profitable. The companies have introduced a number of environmentally and socially responsible initiatives including charging for plastic grocery bags, selling re-useable cloth grocery bags, and being the first grocery chain to have unsold produce converted into energy. These are further examples of the type of initiatives that today's consumers are expecting. For these initiatives, Galen was recognized as North Toronto's Person of the Year in 2011.

By making use of the change-oriented culture and the strengths of both the formal and informal organization, the Loblaw Companies were identified as one of Canada's top 100 employers in 2010 and they were a regional winner of Canada's 10 Most Admired Corporate Cultures in the same year.

These are quite a string of accomplishments by a relatively young business person operating in a highly competitive market. And while the publicity-shy Galen is "leading the charge" he has also taken on the public image as the "pitch man," following in the steps of Dave Nichols, who was instrumental in the hugely successful launch of the President's Choice line back in the 1980s.

Sources: www.thecanadianencyclopedia.com/articles/macleans/galen-weston-jr-takes-over-at-loblaws; www.postcity.com/North-Toronto-Post/December-2009/North-Toronto-039s-person-of-the-year; and "Loblaws Companies 2010 Annual Report," www.loblaw.ca/English/investor-Centre/financial-reporting/annual-reports/default.aspx.

Outline the basic principles of organization management.

ORGANIZATION FROM THE BOTTOM UP

The principles of management are much the same, no matter the size of the business. Management, as you learned in Chapter 8, begins with planning. Let's say, for example, that you and two of your friends plan to start a lawn-mowing business. One of the first steps is to organize your business. Organizing, or structuring, begins with determining what work needs to be done (mowing, edging, trimming, etc.) and then dividing up tasks among the three of you; this is called a *division of labour.* One of you, for example, might have a special talent for trimming bushes, while another is better at mowing. The success of a firm often depends on management's ability to identify each worker's strengths and assign the right tasks to the right person. Often a job can be done quickly and well when each person specializes. Dividing tasks into smaller jobs is called job specialization. For example, you might divide the mowing task into mowing, trimming, and raking.

If your business is successful, you will probably hire more workers to help. You might then organize them into teams or departments to do the various tasks. One team, for example, might mow the lawn while another team uses blowers to clean up the leaves and cut grass. If you are really successful over time, you might hire an accountant to keep records for you, various people to do your marketing (e.g., advertising), and repair people to keep the equipment in good shape.

You can see how your business might evolve into a company with several departments: operations (mowing the lawns and everything related to that), marketing, accounting, and repair. The process of setting up individual departments to do specialized tasks is called *departmentalization.* Finally, you would need to assign authority and responsibility to people so that you could control the whole process. If something went wrong in the accounting department, for example, you would know who was responsible.

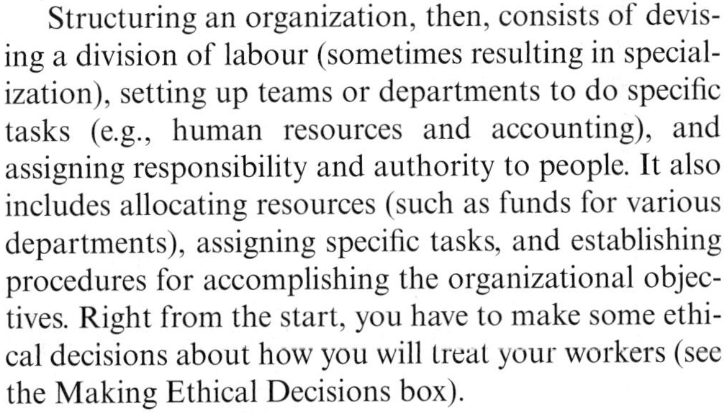

Structuring an organization, then, consists of devising a division of labour (sometimes resulting in specialization), setting up teams or departments to do specific tasks (e.g., human resources and accounting), and assigning responsibility and authority to people. It also includes allocating resources (such as funds for various departments), assigning specific tasks, and establishing procedures for accomplishing the organizational objectives. Right from the start, you have to make some ethical decisions about how you will treat your workers (see the Making Ethical Decisions box).

▶ The principles of organization apply to businesses of all sizes. Structuring the business, making an appropriate division of labour using job specialization and departmentalization, establishing procedures, and assigning authority are tasks found in most firms. How do these principles operate at your current or most recent job?

Finally, as you learned in Chapter 8, you may develop an organization chart that shows relationships among people: it shows who is accountable for the completion of specific work and who reports to whom. Finally, you have to monitor the environment to see what competitors are doing and what customers are demanding. Then, you must adjust to the new realities. For example, a major lawn care company may begin promoting its services in your area. You might have to make some organizational changes to offer even better service at competitive prices. What would be the first thing you would do if you began to lose business to competitors?

Compare the organizational theories of Henri Fayol and Max Weber.

The Changing Organization

Never before in the history of business has so much change been introduced so quickly—sometimes too quickly.[1] As you learned in earlier chapters, much of that change is due to the dynamic business environment, including more global

MAKING ETHICAL DECISIONS

Safety and Environmental Concerns Versus Profit

Imagine that you have begun a successful lawn-mowing service in your neighbourhood. To get some input on what is needed, you observe other lawn-mowing services in the area. Several seem to hire untrained workers, many of them from other countries. The companies pay the workers minimum wage or slightly more. Most often provide no safety equipment. Workers do not have ear protection against the loud mowers and blowers. Most do not wear goggles when operating the shredder. Very few workers wear masks when spraying potentially harmful fertilizers.

You are aware that there are many hazards connected with yard work. You also know that safety gear can be expensive and that workers often prefer to work without such protection. You are interested in making as much money as possible, but you also are somewhat concerned about the safety and welfare of your workers. Furthermore, you are aware of the noise pollution caused by blowers and other equipment and would like to keep noise levels down, but quiet equipment is expensive.

The corporate culture you create as you begin your service will last for a long time. If you emphasize safety and environmental concern from the start, your workers will adopt your values. On the other hand, you can see the potential for making faster profits by ignoring as many safety rules as you can and by paying little attention to the environment. What are the consequences of each choice? Which will you choose?

competition, a stagnating economy, faster technological change, and pressure to preserve the natural environment.[2] Another way to describe this situation is in the context of mechanistic versus organic organizations. The former structure works best when the environment is stable. Effectiveness and efficiency result with stable tasks and no need to make quick decisions. The latter structure makes sense when the environment is changing quickly. Decisions can be made as information is distributed quickly throughout an organization in reaction to the above noted changes (this is another way to look at a learning organization as described at the beginning of Chapter 8). Equally important to many businesses is the change in customer expectations. Customers today expect high-quality products and fast, friendly service—at a reasonable cost.[3]

Managing change, then, has become a critical managerial function. That sometimes includes changing the whole organizational structure. Many organizations in the past were designed more to facilitate management than to please the customer. Managers were typically the only members of an organization who had some level of training, and possessed most of the knowledge needed to run the business. Companies designed many rules and regulations to give managers control over employees. As you will learn later, that is called *bureaucracy.* Where did bureaucracy come from? What are the alternatives? To understand where we are, it helps to know where we have been.

The Development of Organizational Design

Until the twentieth century, most businesses were rather small, the processes for producing goods were relatively simple, and organizing workers was fairly easy. Organizing workers is still not too hard in most small firms, such as a lawn-mowing service or a small shop that produces custom-made boats. Not until the 1900s and the introduction of *mass production* (efficiently producing large quantities of goods) did business production processes and organization become complex. Usually, the bigger the plant, the more efficient production became.

Business growth led to what was called **economies of scale**. This term refers to the fact that companies can reduce their production costs if they can purchase raw materials in bulk. The average cost of goods decreases as production levels rise. The cost of

economies of scale
The situation in which companies can reduce their production costs if they can purchase raw materials in bulk and develop specialized labour; resulting in the average cost of goods going down as production levels increase.

building a car, for example, declined sharply when automobile companies adopted mass production and GM and Ford built huge factories. Over time, such innovations became less meaningful as other companies copied their processes. You may have noticed the benefits of mass production in housing and computers.

During the era of mass production, organization theorists emerged. In France, Henri Fayol published his book *Administration industrielle et générale* in 1919. It was popularized in North America in 1949 under the title *General and Industrial Management.*

Fayol's Principles of Organization

Fayol introduced such principles as the following:

- *Unity of command.* Each worker is to report to one, and only one, boss. The benefits of this principle are obvious. What happens if two different bosses give you two different assignments? Which one should you follow? To prevent such confusion, each person should report to one manager. (later we'll discuss an organizational plan that seems to violate this principle.)
- *Hierarchy of authority.* All workers should know to whom they should report. Managers should have the right to give orders and expect others to follow. (In Chapter 12 we will talk about a change to this concept, called empowerment.)
- *Division of labour.* Functions are to be divided into areas of specialization such as production, marketing, and finance. This principle, as you will read later, is now being questioned or modified.
- *Subordination of individual interests to the general interest.* Workers are to think of themselves as a coordinated team. The goals of the team are more important than the goals of individual workers. Have you heard this concept applied to hockey and football teams?
- *Authority.* Managers have the right to give orders and the power to enforce obedience. Authority and responsibility are related: whenever authority is exercised, responsibility arises. This principle is also being modified as managers are beginning to empower employees.
- *Degree of centralization.* The amount of decision-making power vested in top management should vary by circumstances. In a small organization, it is possible to centralize all decision-making power in the top manager. In a larger organization, however, some decision-making power, for both major and minor issues, should be delegated to lower-level managers and employees.
- *Clear communication channels.* All workers should be able to reach others in the firm quickly and easily.
- *Order.* Materials and people should be placed and maintained in the proper location.
- *Equity.* A manager should treat employees and peers with respect and justice.
- *Esprit de corps.* A spirit of pride and loyalty should be created among people in the firm.

▸ Henri Fayol introduced several management principles still followed today, including the idea that each worker should report to only one manager and that manager, in turn, should have the right to give orders for others to follow and the power to enforce them. Which of Fayol's principles have you observed?

These principles became synonymous with the concept of management. Organizations were designed so that no person had more than one boss, lines of authority were clear, and everyone knew to whom they were to report. Naturally, these principles tended to be written down as rules, policies, and regulations as organizations grew larger. That process of rule making often led to rather rigid organizations that did not always respond quickly to consumer requests. So, where did the idea of bureaucracy come from? We talk about that next.

Max Weber and Organizational Theory

Sociologist Max Weber (pronounced "Vay-ber") was writing about organization theory in Germany around the same time Fayol was writing his books in France. Weber's book *The Theory of Social and Economic Organizations,* like Fayol's, also appeared in North America in the late 1940s. He promoted the pyramid-shaped organization structure that became so popular in large firms. Weber put great trust in managers and felt that the firm would do well if employees simply *did what they were told.* The less decision making employees had to do, the better. Clearly, this is a reasonable way to operate if you are dealing with relatively uneducated and untrained workers. *Where are you likely to find such workers today?* Often, such workers were the only ones available at the time Weber was writing; most employees did not have the kind of educational background and technical skills that today's workers generally have.

Weber's principles of organization were similar to Fayol's. In addition, Weber emphasized:

- Job descriptions;
- Written rules, decision guidelines, and detailed records;
- Consistent procedures, regulations, and policies; and
- Staffing and promotion based on qualifications.

Weber believed that large organizations demanded clearly established rules and guidelines that were to be followed precisely. In other words, he was in favour of *bureaucracy.* Although his principles made a great deal of sense at the time, the practice of establishing rules and procedures was so rigid in some companies that it became counterproductive. However, some organizations today still thrive on Weber's theories. United Parcel Service (UPS), for example, still has written rules and decision guidelines that enable the firm to deliver packages quickly because employees do not have to pause to make decisions—procedures are clearly spelled out for them.

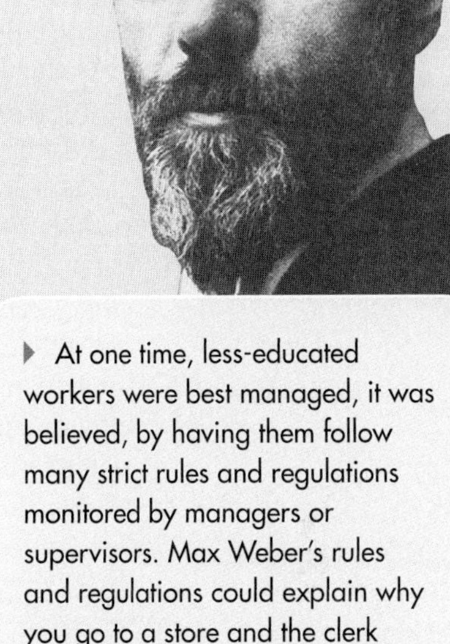

▸ At one time, less-educated workers were best managed, it was believed, by having them follow many strict rules and regulations monitored by managers or supervisors. Max Weber's rules and regulations could explain why you go to a store and the clerk says, "I'm sorry I can't do that, it's against company policy." What industries or businesses today would benefit from using such controls?

Other organizations are not as effective because they do not allow employees to respond quickly to new challenges. That is clearly the case with disaster relief in many areas, as was the case when Hurricane Katrina hit New Orleans. Later, we shall explore what can be done to make organizations more responsive. First, let's look again at some basic terms and concepts.

Turning Principles into Organizational Design

Following the concepts of theorists like Fayol and Weber, managers in the latter part of the 1900s began designing organizations so that managers could *control* workers. Many organizations are still organized that way, with everything set up in a hierarchy. A **hierarchy** is a system in which one person is at the top of the organization and there is a ranked or sequential ordering from the top down of managers and others who are responsible to that person. Since one person cannot keep track of thousands of workers, the top manager needs many lower-level managers to help. The **chain of command** is the line of authority that moves from the top of the hierarchy to the lowest level.

hierarchy
A system in which one person is at the top of the organization and there is a ranked or sequential ordering from the top down of managers who are responsible to that person.

chain of command
The line of authority that moves from the top of a hierarchy to the lowest level.

Some organizations have a dozen or more layers of management between the chief executive officer (CEO) and the lowest-level employees. If employees want to introduce work changes, they ask a supervisor (the first level of management), who asks his or her manager, who asks a manager at the next level up, and so on. It can take weeks or months for a decision to be made and passed from manager to manager until it reaches employees.

bureaucracy
An organization with many layers of managers who set rules and regulations and oversee all decisions.

Max Weber used the word *bureaucrat* to describe a middle manager whose function was to implement top management's orders. Thus, **bureaucracy** came to be the term used for an organization with many layers of managers.

When employees in a bureaucracy of any size have to ask managers for permission to make a change, the process may take so long that customers become annoyed. Has this happened to you in a department store or some other organization? Since many customers want efficient service—and they want it *now*—slow service is simply not acceptable in many of today's competitive firms.

Some companies are reorganizing to let employees make decisions on their own to please the customer no matter what. As you will see in Chapter 12, giving employees such authority and responsibility to make decisions and please customers is called *empowerment.* Remember that empowerment works only when employees are given the proper training and resources to respond.

It is important to note that well-run bureaucratic organizations can be extremely effective in certain contexts—when there is little innovation in the marketplace, consistency in demand, low-skilled workers, and a lot of time to weigh the consequences of decisions.

PROGRESS ASSESSMENT

- What do the terms division of labour and specialization mean?
- What are the principles of management outlined by Fayol?
- What did Weber add to Fayol's principles?

Evaluate the choices managers make in structuring organizations.

DECISIONS TO MAKE IN STRUCTURING ORGANIZATIONS

Henry Mintzberg, an expert on management and business, supports the current view that there is no single structure that will lead to success for all organizations. "Structure should reflect the organization's situation—for example, its age, size, type of production system, and the extent to which its environment is complex and dynamic. Small businesses with up to five employees do not need to spend time on how to structure themselves. However, the effectiveness of larger organizations or those experiencing significant change is impacted by structure. As well, a firm's design decisions (such as span of control, centralization versus decentralization, and matrix structures) need to be chosen so they can work within the chosen structure and design."[4] These design decisions will be discussed in this chapter. Mintzberg has also written a book on MBA programs entitled *Managers Not MBAs,*[5] which is a hard look at the soft practice of managing and management development.

When designing responsive organizations, firms have to make decisions about several organizational issues: (1) centralization versus decentralization, (2) span of control, (3) tall versus flat organization structures, and (4) departmentalization. The process they use is called change management. This strategic approach starts by preparing for the change, then managing the change, and concludes with re-enforcing the change. Given the risk involved with this type of change, this formal process increases the likelihood of success.

Choosing Centralization Versus Decentralization of Authority

Centralized authority occurs when decision-making authority is maintained at the top level of management at the company's headquarters. Imagine for a minute that you are a top manager for a retail company such as Roots. Your temptation may be to preserve control over all of your stores to maintain a uniform image and merchandise. You have noticed that such control works well nationally for McDonald's; why not for Roots?

centralized authority
An organization structure in which decision-making authority is maintained at the top level of management at the company's headquarters.

When a company needs radical changes, centralized decision making is often necessary, at least for a while. Such was the case of the North American based automakers starting in 2008. Ford, GM, and Chrysler's existence was questioned in the wake of rising gasoline prices and the credit crisis. Senior management made many decisions that eventually resulted in all three dramatically improving their financial results.

Decentralized authority occurs when decision-making authority is delegated to lower-level managers and employees who are more familiar with local conditions than headquarters' management could be

decentralized authority
An organization structure in which decision-making authority is delegated to lower-level managers more familiar with local conditions than headquarters management could be.

Roots customers in Kelowna, for example, are likely to demand clothing styles different from those demanded in Charlottetown or Lethbridge. It makes sense, therefore, to give store managers in various cities the authority to buy, price, and promote merchandise appropriate for each area. Such delegation of authority is an example of decentralized management. Magna International has a decentralized operating structure. Magna's manufacturing divisions operate as independent profit centres aligned by geographic region in each of the company's product areas. This decentralized structure prevents bureaucracy and makes Magna more responsive to customer needs and changes within the global automotive industry as well as within specific regions.[6] Figure 9.1 lists some advantages and disadvantages of centralized versus decentralized authority.

Choosing the Appropriate Span of Control

Span of control refers to the optimum number of subordinates a manager supervises or should supervise. There are many factors to consider when determining span of control. At lower levels, where work is standardized, it is possible to implement a wide span of control (15 to 40 workers). For example, one supervisor can be responsible

span of control
The optimum number of subordinates a manager supervises or should supervise.

Figure 9.1

Advantages and Disadvantages of Centralized Versus Decentralized Management

Advantage	Disadvantage
Centralized • Greater top-management control • More efficiency • Simpler distribution system • Consistent brand/corporate image	• Less responsiveness to customers • Less empowerment • Interorganizational conflict • Lower morale away from headquarters
Decentralized • Better adaptation to customer wants • More empowerment of workers • Faster decision making • Higher morale	• Less efficiency • Complex distribution system • Less top-management control • Diverse corporate image

for 20 or more workers who are assembling computers or cleaning up movie theatres. However, the number gradually narrows at higher levels of the organization because work is less standardized and there's more need for face-to-face communication. Variables in span of control include the following:

- *Capabilities of the manager.* The more experienced and capable a manager is, the broader the span of control can be. (A large number of workers can report to that manager.)
- *Capabilities of the subordinates.* The more the subordinates need supervision, the narrower the span of control should be. Employee turnover at fast-food restaurants, for example, is often so high that managers must constantly be training new people and thus need a narrow span of control.
- *Geographical closeness.* The more concentrated the work area is, the broader the span of control can be.
- *Functional similarity.* The more similar the functions are, the broader the span of control can be.
- *Need for coordination.* The greater the need for coordination, the narrower the span of control might be.
- *Planning demands.* The more involved the plan, the narrower the span of control might be.
- *Functional complexity.* The more complex the functions are, the narrower the span of control might be.

Other factors to consider include the professionalism of superiors and subordinates and the number of new problems that occur in a day.

The trend today is to expand the span of control as organizations adopt empowerment, reduce the number of middle managers, and hire more educated and talented lower-level employees. Information technology makes it possible for managers to handle more information, so the span can be broader still. More companies could expand the span of control if they trained their employees better and were willing to trust them more. Figure 9.2 lists some advantages and disadvantages of a narrow versus a wide span of control.

Choosing Between Tall and Flat Organization Structures

tall organization structure An organization structure in which the pyramidal organization chart would be quite tall because of the various levels of management.

In the early twentieth century, organizations grew bigger and bigger, adding layer after layer of management to create **tall organization structures**. Some organizations had as many as 14 levels, and the span of control was small (few people reported to each manager).

Imagine how a message might be distorted as it moved up through managers, management assistants, secretaries, assistant secretaries, supervisors, trainers, and so on.

Figure 9.2

Advantages and Disadvantages of a Narrow Versus a Wide Span of Control

Advantage	Disadvantage
Narrow • More control by top management • More chances for advancement • Greater specialization • Closer supervision	• Less empowerment • Higher costs • Slower decision making • Less responsiveness to customers
Wide • Reduced costs • More responsiveness to customers • Faster decision making • More empowerment	• Fewer chances for advancement • Overworked managers • Loss of control • Less specific management expertise

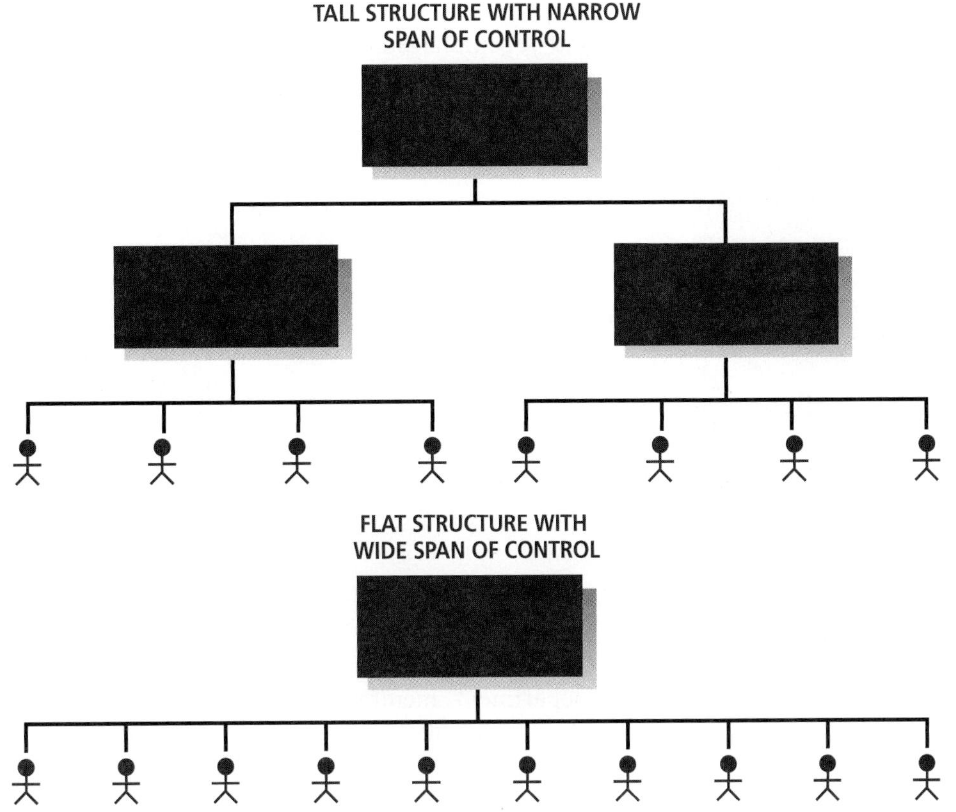

Figure 9.3

Narrow Versus Wide Span of Control

This figure describes two ways to structure an organization with the same number of employees. The tall structure with a narrow span of control has two managers who supervise four employees each. Changing to a flat surface with a wide span of control, the company could eliminate two managers and perhaps replace them with one or two employees, but the top manager would have to supervise ten people instead of two.

The cost of all of these managers and support people was quite high, the paperwork they generated was enormous, and the inefficiencies in communication and decision making often became intolerable.

More recently, organizations have adopted **flat organization structures** with fewer layers of management (see Figure 9.3) and a broad span of control (many people reporting to each manager). Flat structures can respond readily to customer demands because lower-level employees have authority and responsibility for making decisions, and managers can be spared certain day-to-day tasks. Chrysler has eliminated 6,000 white-collar jobs for just that reason.[7]

flat organization structure
An organization structure that has few layers of management and a broad span of control.

Large organizations use flat structures to try to match the friendliness of small firms, whose workers know customers by name. The flatter organizations became, the broader the span of control, which means some management positions have been eliminated.

Weighing the Advantages and Disadvantages of Departmentalization

Departmentalization divides an organization into separate units. The traditional way to departmentalize organizations is by *function,* such as design, production, marketing, and accounting. Departmentalization groups workers according to their skills, expertise, or resource use so that they can specialize and work together more effectively. It may also save costs and improve efficiency. Other advantages include the following:

departmentalization
Dividing an organization into separate units.

1. Employees can develop skills in depth and can progress within a department as they master those skills.
2. The company can achieve economies of scale by centralizing all the resource needs and locating various experts in that area.

▶ Loblaw Companies Limited, Canada's largest food distributor, operates a number of supermarket chains across Canada including Atlantic Cash & Carry, Dominion, Fortinos, Loblaws, Provigo, and Real Canadian Superstore. They have operated since the 1960s and have developed many excellent brands, including the President's Choice line of products. Since 2006 they have gone through a series of senior management shake-ups as they respond to growing competition from major U.S. merchandisers. Consolidating their distribution centres resulted in serious problems with their supply chain, costing them millions of dollars. They continued to work on this issue over the next five years. Whether this move to a more "responsive organization structure" will foster effective competition with the foreign retail Goliaths is yet to be seen.

3. Employees can coordinate work within the function, and top management can easily direct and control various departments' activities.

Disadvantages of departmentalization by function include the following:

1. Departments may not communicate well. For example, production may be so isolated from marketing that it does not get feedback from customers.
2. Employees may identify with their department's goals rather than the organization's. The purchasing department may find a good value somewhere and buy a huge volume of goods. That makes purchasing look good, but the high cost of storing the goods hurts the overall profitability.
3. The company's response to external changes may be slow.
4. People may not be trained to fulfill multiple managerial responsibilities; rather, they tend to become narrow specialists.
5. Department members may engage in groupthink (they think alike) and may need input from outside to become more creative.

Looking at Alternative Ways to Departmentalize

Functional separation is not always the most responsive form of organization. So what are the alternatives? Figure 9.4 shows five ways a firm can departmentalize. One way is by product. A book publisher might have a trade book department (for books sold to the general public), a textbook department, and a technical book department, each with separate development and marketing processes. Such product-focused departmentalization usually results in good customer relations.

Some organizations departmentalize by customer group. A pharmaceutical company might have one department for the consumer market, another that calls on hospitals (the institutional market), and another that targets doctors. You can see how the customer groups might benefit from having specialists satisfying their needs.

Some firms group their units by geographic location because customers vary so greatly by region. Japan, Europe, and Korea may involve separate departments with obvious benefits.

The decision about how to departmentalize depends greatly on the nature of the product and the customers. A few firms find that it is most efficient to separate activities by *process.* For example, a firm that makes leather coats may have one department cut the leather, another dye it, and a third sew the coat together. Such specialization enables employees to do a better job because they can focus on learning a few critical skills.

Some firms use a combination of departmentalization techniques; they would be called *hybrid forms.* For example, a company could departmentalize by function, by geography, and by customer groups.

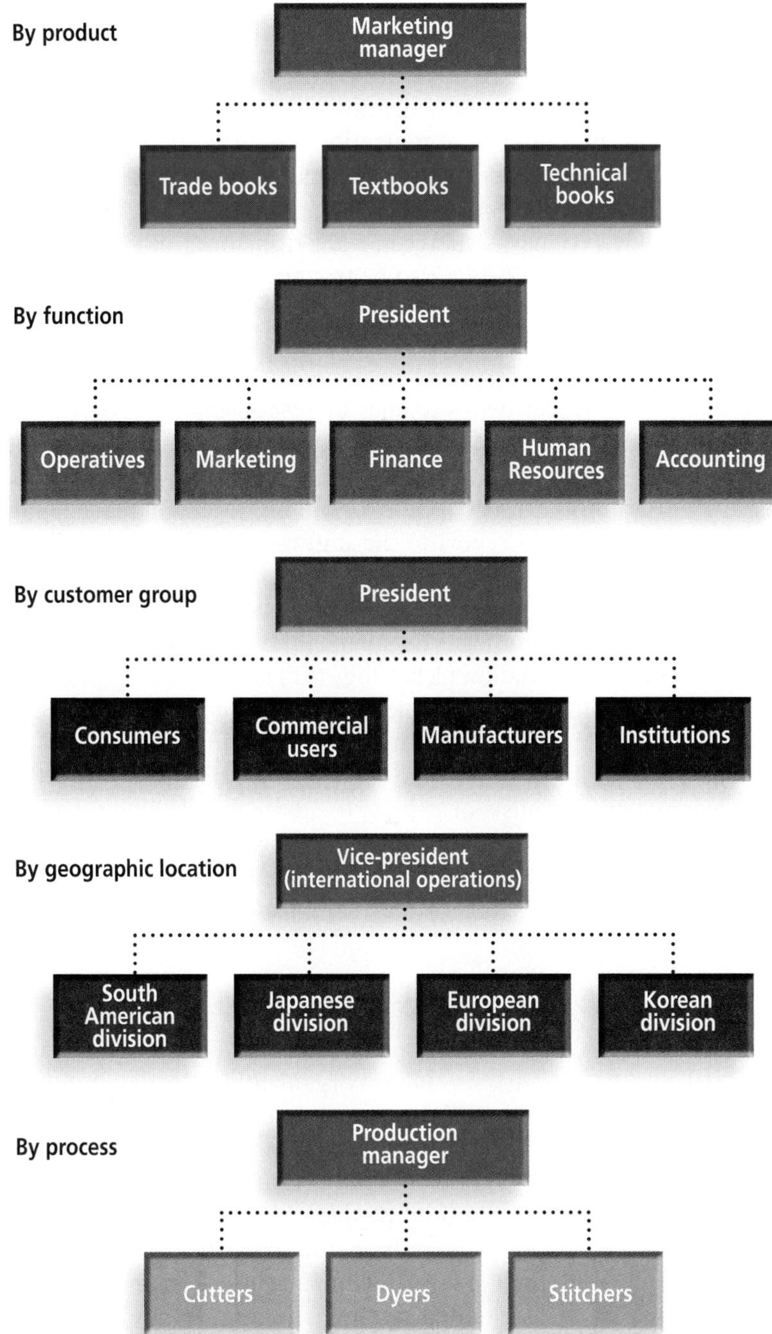

Figure 9.4

Ways to Departmentalize

A computer company may want to departmentalize by geographic location, a manufacturer by function, a pharmaceutical company by customer group, a leather manufacturer by process, and a publisher by product. In each case the structure must fit the firm's goals.

PROGRESS ASSESSMENT

- What is bureaucracy? What challenges do bureaucratic organizations face in a time of rapid change?
- Why are organizations becoming flatter?
- What are some reasons for having a narrow span of control in an organization?
- What are the advantages and disadvantages of departmentalization?
- What are the various ways a firm can departmentalize?

LO 4

Contrast the various organizational models.

ORGANIZATION MODELS

Now that we have explored the basic issues of organizational design, let's look in depth at four ways to structure an organization: (1) line organizations, (2) line-and-staff organizations, (3) matrix-style organizations, and (4) self-managed teams. You will see that some of these models violate traditional management principles. The business community is in a period of transition, with some traditional organizational models giving way to new structures. Such transitions can be not only unsettling to employees and managers but also be fraught with problems and errors.

line organization
An organization that has direct two-way lines of responsibility, authority, and communication running from the top to the bottom of the organization, with all people reporting to only one supervisor.

line personnel
Employees who are part of the chain of command that is responsible for achieving organizational goals.

staff personnel
Employees who advise and assist line personnel in meeting their goals.

Line Organizations

A **line organization** has direct two-way lines of responsibility, authority, and communication running from the top to the bottom of the organization, with everyone reporting to only one supervisor. The military and many small businesses are organized in this way. For example, Mario's Pizza Parlour has a general manager and a shift manager. All general employees report to the shift manager, and he or she reports to the general manager or owner.

A line organization does not have any specialists who provide managerial support. For example, there would be no legal department, accounting department, human resource department, or information technology (IT) department. Line organizations follow all of Fayol's traditional management rules. Line managers can issue orders, enforce discipline, and adjust the organization as conditions change.

In large businesses, a line organization may have the disadvantages of being too inflexible, of having few specialists or experts to advise people along the line, and of having lengthy lines of communication. Thus they may be unable to handle complex decisions relating to thousands of products and tonnes of paperwork. Such organizations usually turn to a line-and-staff form of organization.

DAVE CARPENTER
"SEND THIS BACK TO THE LEGAL DEPARTMENT. I THINK THEY COULD MAKE IT MUCH MORE COMPLICATED THAN THIS..."

▶ Members of a legal department are considered staff personnel in a line-and-staff organization. Staff personnel serve in an advisory role and can work with colleagues and departments at every level in the firm's hierarchy. What are some of the advantages of this type of organization model?

Line-and-Staff Organizations

To minimize the disadvantages of simple line organizations, many organizations today have both line and staff personnel. A couple of definitions will help. **Line personnel** are responsible for directly achieving organizational goals and include production workers, distribution people, and marketing personnel. **Staff personnel** advise and assist line personnel in meeting their goals and include those in marketing research, legal advising, information technology, and human resource management. See Figure 9.5 for a diagram of a line-and-staff organization. One important difference between line and staff personnel is authority. Line personnel have formal authority to make policy decisions. Staff personnel have the authority to advise the line personnel and influence those decisions, but they cannot make policy changes themselves. The line manager may choose to seek or to ignore the advice of staff personnel.

Many organizations have benefitted from the expert staff advice on safety, legal issues, quality control, database management, motivation, and investing. Staff positions strengthen the line positions and are like having well-paid consultants on the organization's payroll.

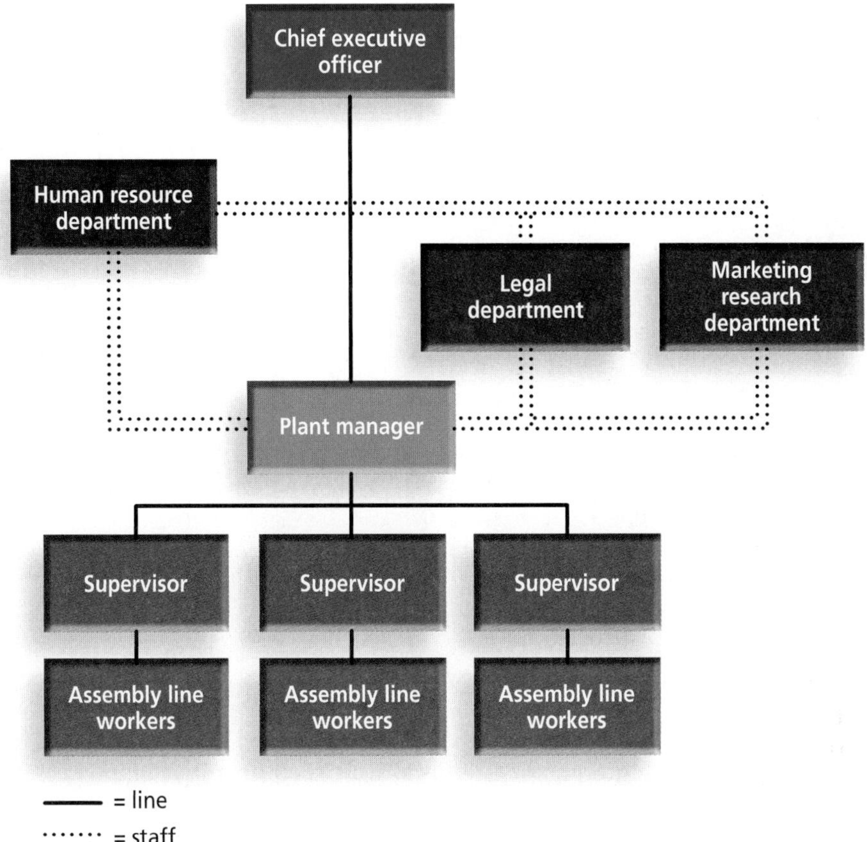

Figure 9.5

A Sample Line-and-Staff Organization

Matrix-Style Organizations

Both line and line-and-staff organization structures suffer from inflexibility. Both allow for established lines of authority and communication, and work well in organizations with stable environments and slow product development (such as firms selling household appliances). In such firms, clear lines of authority and relatively fixed organization structures are assets that ensure efficient operations.

Today's economy, however, is dominated by high-growth industries like telecommunications, nanotechnology, robotics, and biotechnology, where competition is stiff and the life cycle of new ideas is short. Emphasis is on product development, creativity, special projects, rapid communication, and interdepartmental teamwork.[8] From those changes grew the popularity of the **matrix organization**, in which specialists from different parts of the organization work temporarily on specific projects but still remain part of a line-and-staff structure (see Figure 9.6.). In other words, a project manager can borrow people from different departments to help design and market new product ideas.

matrix organization
An organization in which specialists from different parts of the organization are brought together to work on specific projects but still remain part of a line-and-staff structure.

The matrix structure was developed in the aerospace industry and is now familiar in banking, management consulting firms, accounting firms, ad agencies, and school systems. Among its advantages:

- It gives managers flexibility in assigning people to projects.
- It encourages inter-organizational co-operation and teamwork.
- It can produce creative solutions to product development problems.
- It makes efficient use of organizational resources.

As for disadvantages,

- It is costly and complex.
- It can confuse employees about where their loyalty belongs—with the project manager or their functional unit.

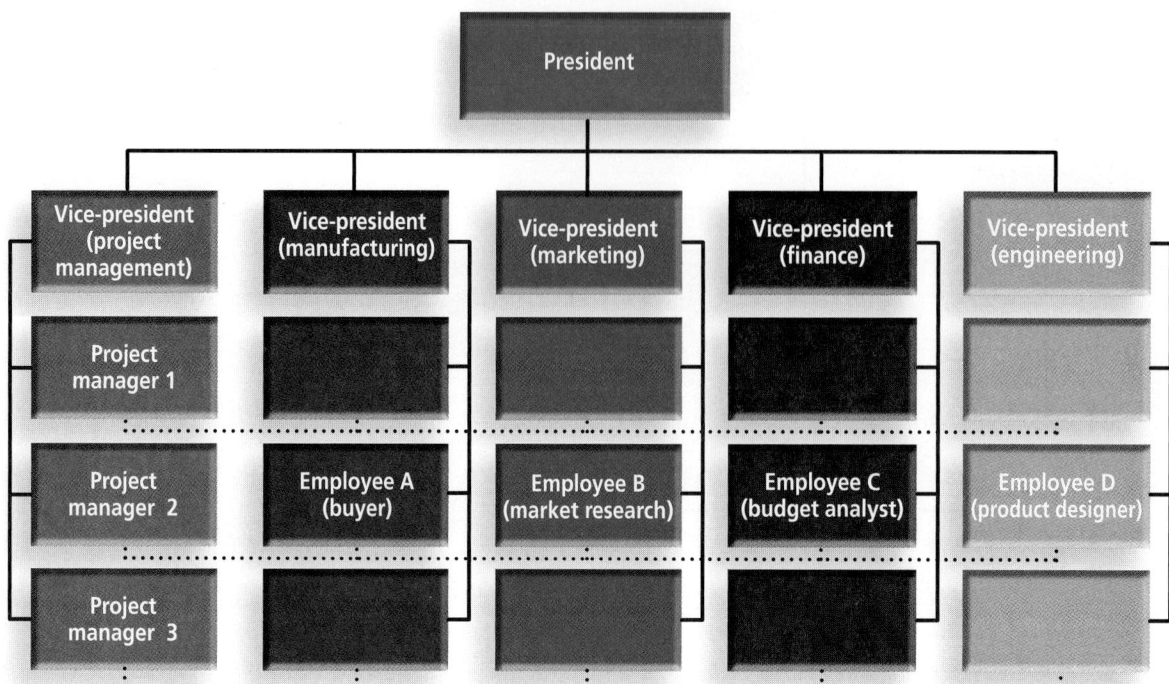

Figure 9.6

A Matrix Organization

In a matrix organization, project managers are in charge of teams made up of members of several departments. In this case, Project manager 2 supervises employees A, B, C, and D. These employees are accountable not only to Project manager 2 but also to the head of their individual departments. For example, Employee B, a market researcher, reports to Project manager 2 and to the Vice-president of marketing.

- It requires good interpersonal skills as well as co-operative employees and managers to avoid communication problems.
- It may be only a temporary solution to a long-term problem.

If you are thinking that matrix organizations violate some traditional managerial principles, you are right. Normally a person cannot work effectively for two bosses. Who has the real authority? Which directive has first priority?

In reality, however, the system functions more effectively than you might imagine. To develop a new product, a project manager may be given temporary authority to "borrow" line personnel from production, marketing, and other line functions. The employees work together to complete the project and then return to their regular positions. Thus, no one really reports to more than one manager at a time.

A potential problem with matrix management, however, is that the project teams are not permanent. They form to solve a problem or develop a new product, and then they break up. There is little chance for cross-functional learning because teams work together for such little time.

Self-Managed Teams

One solution to the disadvantage of the temporary nature of matrix teams is to establish *long-lived teams* and to empower them to work closely with suppliers, customers, and others to quickly and efficiently bring out new, high-quality products while giving great service.[9]

self-managed teams
Groups of employees from different departments who work together on a long-term basis.

Self-managed teams are groups of employees from different departments who work together on a long-term basis (as opposed to the temporary teams established in matrix-style organizations).[10] Usually the teams are empowered to make decisions without management approval.[11] The barriers among design, engineering, marketing, distribution, and other functions fall when interdepartmental teams are created. One Smooth Stone <*www.onesmoothstone.com*> (a company featured in the Video Case) is a corporate events company. They put together large, one-time functions for corporate clients. They have a team of highly skilled and trained staff that go from the planning and execution of one corporate function to another. Sometimes

	Advantage	Disadvantage
Line	• Clearly defined responsibility and authority • Easy to understand • One supervisor for each person	• Too inflexible • Few specialists to advise • Long lines of communication • Unable to handle complex questions quickly
Line and Staff	• Expert advice from staff to line personnel • Establishes lines of authority • Encourages co-operation and better communication at all levels	• Potential overstaffing • Potential overanalyzing • Lines of communication can get blurred • Staff frustrations because of lack of authority
Matrix	• Flexible • Encourages co-operation among departments • Can produce creative solutions to problems • Allows organization to take on new projects without adding to the organizational structure • Provides for more efficient use of organizational resources	• Costly and complex • Can confuse employees • Requires good interpersonal skills and co-operative managers and employees • Difficult to evaluate employees and to set up reward systems
Self-Managed Teams	• Greatly increases interdepartmental coordination and co-operation • Quicker response to customers and market conditions • Increased employee motivation and morale	• Some confusion over responsibility and authority • Perceived loss of control by management • Difficult to evaluate employees and to set up reward systems • Requires self-motivated and highly trained workers

Figure 9.7

Types of Organizations

Each form of organization has its advantages and disadvantages.

the self-managed teams are inter-firm. Toyota, for example, works closely with teams at other firms to produce its cars.

Figure 9.7 lists the advantages and disadvantages of these four types of organizations.

Going Beyond Organizational Boundaries

Self-managed teams work best when the voice of the customer is brought in, especially in product development tasks.[12] Suppliers and distributors should be on the team as well. A self-managed team that includes customers, suppliers, and distributors goes beyond organizational boundaries. When suppliers and distributors are in other countries, self-managed teams may share market information across national boundaries. Government coordinators may assist such projects, letting cross-functional teams break the barriers between government and business. Self-managed teams are only one way in which businesses can interact with other companies. In the next section we look at other ways that organizations manage their various interactions.

PROGRESS ASSESSMENT

- What is the difference between line and staff personnel?
- What management principle does a matrix-style organization challenge?
- What may hinder the development of self-managed teams?

networking between firms
Using communications technology and other means to link organizations and allow them to work together on common objectives.

MANAGING INTERACTIONS AMONG FIRMS

Identify the benefits of inter-firm co-operation and coordination.

Whether it involves customers, suppliers, distributors, or the government, **networking between firms** is using communications technology and other means to link organizations and allow them to work together on common objectives.[13] Let's explore this concept further.

GREENBOX

Ethical Consumerism

Like many companies, Loblaws is working closely with their suppliers to uphold right values in areas from labour conditions to animal welfare. They document their annual strategies and achievements in their Corporate Social Responsibility Report. Highlights from their 2011 report include the following:

- They reported on their growing sourcing of responsibly sourced farm salmon.
- They continue to transition to 100 percent cage-free eggs under their President's Choice label
- They have achieved 100 percent Global Food Safety Initiative certification with suppliers who provide Loblaws-branded products.

To ensure these achievements occur, Loblaws now requires all existing and new suppliers to be subject to, at a minimum, an annual Corporate Social Responsibility Audit. Loblaws insists that they have the right to engage qualified auditors to review all the processes and records of their suppliers. These auditors then report to Loblaws on the results of their investigation. This transparency on the part of Loblaw's suppliers is repeated in many industries so that retailers can demonstrate their social responsibility to consumers.

Source: Loblaws "2011 Corporate Social Responsibility Report", www.loblaw-reports.ca/responsibility/2011/index.php#.

real time
The present moment or the actual time in which something takes place; data sent over the Internet to various organizational partners as they are developed or collected are said to be available in real time.

Transparency and Virtual Organizations

Networked organizations are so closely linked by the Internet that each can find out what the others are doing in real time. **Real time** simply means the present moment or the actual time in which something takes place. The Internet has allowed companies to send real-time data to organizational partners as they are developed or collected. The result is transparency. Transparency occurs when a company is so open to other companies working with it that the once-solid barriers between them become see-through and electronic information is shared as if the companies were one. With this integration, two companies can work as closely as two departments once did in traditional firms. As part of the movement to increased corporate social responsibility, as discussed in Chapter 5, many businesses want to ensure that their suppliers are meeting certain standards. The Green Box describes the approach taken by Loblaws.

Can you see the implications for organizational design? Most organizations are no longer self-sufficient or self-contained. Rather, they are part of a vast network of global businesses that work closely together. An organization chart showing what people do within any one organization is simply not complete, because the organization is part of a much larger system of firms. A modern chart would show people in different organizations and indicate how they are networked. This is a relatively new concept, however, so few such charts are yet available.

virtual corporation
A temporary networked organization made up of replaceable firms that join and leave as needed.

Networked organization structures tend to be flexible. A company may work with a design expert from a different company in Italy for a year and then not need that person anymore. It may hire an expert from a company in another country for another project. Such a temporary network, made of replaceable firms that join and leave as needed, is called a **virtual corporation** (see Figure 9.8). Hosting the 2010 Winter Olympics is a dramatic example of a situation requiring a temporary networked organization. This is quite different from a traditional organization structure; in fact, traditional managers have trouble adapting to the speed of change and the impermanence of relationships when networking. We discuss adaptation to change below; first, though, we describe how organizations are using benchmarking and outsourcing to manage their interactions with other firms.

▶ The Vancouver Organizing Committee (VANOC) was responsible for the planning, organizing, financing, and staging of the 2010 Olympic and Paralympic Winter Games. With an operating budget of $1.6 billion and a capital budget of $580 million, VANOC employed and utilized 25,000 volunteers.

Benchmarking and Core Competencies

Organizations historically have tried to do all functions themselves. Each had its own department for accounting, finance, marketing, production, and so on. As we have noted, today's organizations look to other organizations to help in areas where they do not generate world-class quality.

Benchmarking compares an organization's practices, processes, and products against the world's best.[14] As one example, K2 Skis <*ktskis.com*> is a company that makes skis, snowboards, in-line skates, and related products. It studied the compact-disc industry and learned to use ultraviolet inks to print graphics on skis. It went to the aerospace industry to get piezoelectric technology to reduce vibration in its snowboards (the aerospace industry uses the technology for wings on planes). It learned from the cable television industry how to braid layers of fibre-glass and carbon, and adapted that knowledge to make skis. As another example, Suncor, one of Canada's

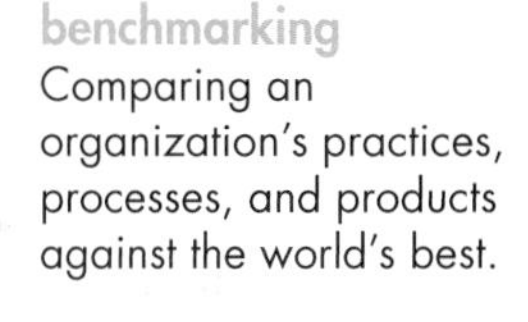

benchmarking
Comparing an organization's practices, processes, and products against the world's best.

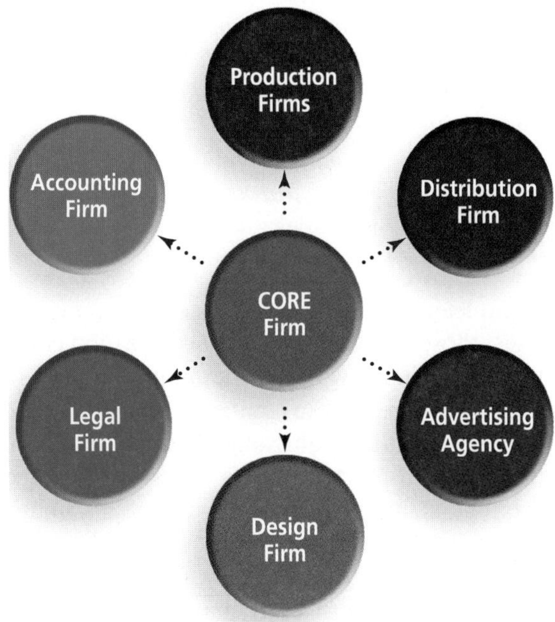

Figure 9.8

A Virtual Corporation
A virtual corporation has no permanent ties to the firms that do its production, distribution, legal, and other work. Such firms are very flexible and can adapt to changes in the market quickly.

largest emitters of greenhouse gases, continually benchmarks "best-of-class" companies in terms of sustainability reporting.[15] By doing so, they are able to evaluate their performance in reducing their carbon footprint.

Benchmarking also has a more directly competitive purpose. In retailing, Target <*www.target.ca*> may compare itself to Walmart to see what, if anything, Walmart does better. Target will then try to improve its practices or processes to become even better than Walmart. Sam Walton used to do competitive benchmarking regularly. He would visit the stores of competitors and see what, if anything, the competitor was doing better. When he found something better—say, a pricing program—he would come back to Walmart and make the appropriate changes.

Benchmarking has become a significant activity in Canada. Governments and large and small companies are all involved in procedures to discover and apply the best practices available. Industry Canada and Statistics Canada have accumulated extensive statistics on the use of benchmarking in a variety of industries. Some examples are breweries, flour mixing and cereal production, electronic computing, paperboard manufacturing, musical instruments, and the recording industry. For more information, including a link to a benchmarking tool, go to <*www.canadabusiness.ca/eng/blog/entry/3518*>.

If an organization cannot do as well as the best in, say, shipping, it will try to outsource the function to an organization like UPS or FedEx that specializes in shipping. Outsourcing, remember, means assigning one or more functions, such as accounting, production security, maintenance, and legal work, to outside organizations. Even small firms are getting involved in outsourcing.[16] We have already discussed some problems associated with outsourcing, especially when companies outsource to other countries. Jobs are lost in Canada and this has a negative impact on our economy. Some functions, such as information management and marketing, may be too important to assign to outside firms. In that case, the organization should benchmark the best firms and restructure its departments to try to be equally good.

An article titled "Offshore Outsourcing Seen Reshaping the Tech Sector" highlights this growing trend. The article states the following points:

> *Increasing global competition to decrease prices has led technology players to find low-cost partners or contract out work, according to Ramalinga Raju, chairman of Satyam Computer Services Ltd, a tech provider based in India. "Competition is something you cannot wish away. More often than not, offshore delivery has meant an offset in costs." Potential savings are dramatic. In Canada, the average computer programmer with two to three years experience earns between $33,000 and $65,000 annually. In comparison, programmers in India earn between $8,000 and $13,000 annually. Canadian partners include document management software maker Hummingbird Ltd. of Toronto and business intelligence software provider Cognos Inc. of Ottawa.*
>
> *In addition to lower costs, outsourcing frees up financial resources for better use, reports ATI Technologies Inc. of Markham, Ontario. All of the company's graphics chips are made for it by low-cost manufacturers in Taiwan, allowing the company to invest more heavily in research and development.*[17]

core competencies
Those functions that an organization can do as well as or better than any other organization in the world.

When a firm has completed its outsourcing process, the remaining functions are the firm's **core competencies**, those functions that the organization can do as well as or better than any other organization in the world. For example, Nike is great at designing and marketing athletic shoes. Those are its core competencies. It outsources the manufacturing of those shoes, however, to other companies that can make shoes better and less expensively than Nike itself can. Similarly, Dell is best at marketing computers and outsources most other functions, including manufacturing and distribution, to others. Celestica <*www.celestica.com*> has also outsourced most of their manufacturing functions.

After you have structured an organization, you must keep monitoring the environment (including customers) to learn what changes are needed. Dell, for example, recently reversed its practice of outsourcing customer support and now offers a premium service that allows Canadian customers to reach tech support in North America. The following section discusses organizational change in more detail.

ADAPTING TO CHANGE

Once you have structured an organization, you must be prepared to adapt that structure to changes in the market. That is not always easy to do. Over time an organization can get stuck in its ways. Employees have a tendency to say, "That's the way we've always done things. If it isn't broken, don't fix it." Managers also get complacent. They may say that they have 20 years' experience when the truth is that they have had one year's experience 20 times. Do you think that slow adaptation to change was a factor in the decline of the manufacturing sector in Canada?

Introducing change is one of the hardest challenges facing any manager. Nonetheless, change is what is happening at General Motors, Ford, and other companies eager to become more competitive.[18] If you have old facilities that are no longer efficient, you have to get rid of them. That is exactly what GM and other companies are doing. In fact, they have asked the government to lend them billions of dollars to help.[19]

The Internet has created whole new opportunities, not only to sell to customers directly but also to ask them questions and provide them with any information they want.[20] To win market share, companies must coordinate the efforts of their traditional departments and their Internet staff to create friendly, easy-to-mange interactions. Young people today are called digital natives because they grew up with the technology. To reach them, companies are retraining older employees to be more tech-savvy.[21] That means becoming familiar with YouTube, Facebook, wikis, Skype, Twitter, RSS, and more.[22]

Target is a highly centralized organization. Nonetheless, the company reacts effectively to changes in consumer preferences throughout the country, in part by keeping in touch with an enormous web of people of all ages, interests and nationalities—its "creative cabinet"—via the Internet. The members of the "cabinet," who never meet, so they cannot influence each other, evaluate various new initiative and recommend new programs to help Target figure out what belongs on store shelves.

restructuring
Redesigning an organization so that it can more effectively and efficiently serve its customers.

Restructuring for Empowerment

To empower employees firms must reorganize dramatically to make front-line workers their most important people. **Restructuring** is redesigning an organization so it can more effectively and efficiently serve its customers.[23] Until recently, department-store

Figure 9.9

Comparison of a Traditional Organization Structure and an Inverted Organization Structure

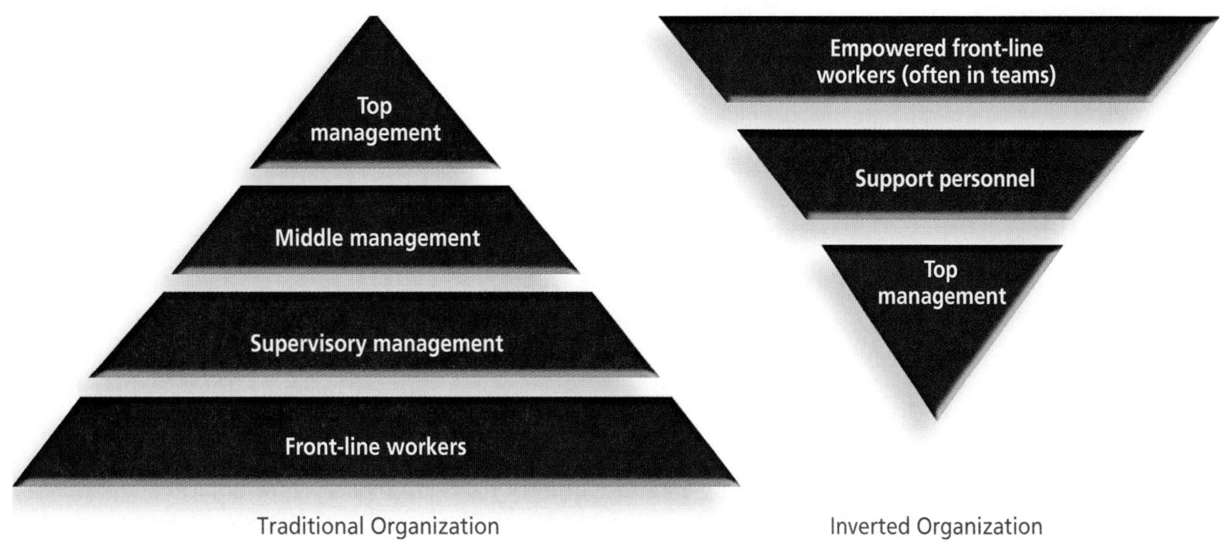

clerks, bank tellers, and front-desk staff in hotels were not considered key employees. Instead, managers were considered more important, and they were responsible for directing the work of the front-line people. The organization chart in a typical firm looked much like the pyramid in Figure 9.9.

inverted organization
An organization that has contact people at the top and the chief executive officer at the bottom of the organization chart.

A few service-oriented organizations have turned the traditional organization structure upside down. An **inverted organization** has contact people (like nurses) at the top and the chief executive officer at the bottom. Management layers are few, and the manager's job is to *assist* and *support* front-line people, not boss them around. Figure 9.9 illustrates the difference between an inverted and a traditional organizational structure.

A good example of an inverted organization is NovaCare *<www.novacare.com>*, a provider of rehabilitation care.[24] At its top are some 5,000 physical, occupational, and speech therapists. The rest of the organization is structured to serve those therapists. Managers consider the therapists to be their bosses, and the manager's job is to support the therapists by arranging contacts with nursing homes, handling accounting and credit activities, and providing training.

Companies based on this organization structure support front-line personnel with internal and external databases, advanced communication systems, and professional assistance. Naturally, this means that front-line people have to be better educated, better trained, and better paid than in the past. It takes a lot of trust for top managers to implement such a system—but when they do, the payoff in customer satisfaction and in profits is often well worth the effort.

In the past, managers controlled information—and that gave them power. In more progressive organizations, everyone shares information, often through an elaborate database system and *among* firms as well *within* them. No matter what organizational model you choose or how much you empower your employees, the secret to successful organization change is to focus on customers and give them what they want.[25]

Focusing on the Customer

No matter what organizational model you choose or how much you empower your employees, the secret to successful organization change is to focus on customers and give them what they want. That is what Ford implemented in 2006. Former CEO Bill Ford introduced a new program called "The Way Forward." "True customer focus means that our business decisions originate from our knowledge of what the customer wants," Ford said. He confessed that product plans in the past were "defined by our capacity" and vehicles were designed to use plant capacity "sometimes at the expense of creativity."[26]

One thing Ford and other auto manufacturers have learned is that customers today want more fuel-efficient (usually smaller) cars or hybrids.[27] GM, Ford, and Chrysler have lost billions of dollars over the last few years selling their gas-guzzling trucks and SUVs. Sometimes it is hard for such large companies to adapt to market changes, such as higher gas prices, but eventually they *do* change, or they go out of business. When faced with the significant economic impact of these businesses closing down, governments made the decision to invest billions of dollars based on the belief these businesses could make changes necessary to support their long-term survival.

The Restructuring Process

It is not easy to move from an organization dominated by managers to one that relies heavily on self-managed teams. How you restructure an organization depends on the status of the present system. If the system already has a customer focus, but is not working well, a total quality management approach may work.

total quality management (TQM)
Striving for maximum customer satisfaction by ensuring quality from all departments.

Total quality management (TQM) is the practice of striving for maximum customer satisfaction by ensuring quality from all departments. TQM calls for *continual improvement of present processes.* Processes are sets of activities strung together for a reason, such as the process for handling a customer's order. The process may consist of receiving the order in the mail, opening it, sending it to someone to fill, putting the order into a package, and sending it out. In Chapter 10 we will review the importance of quality control in operations management.

Continuous improvement (CI) means constantly improving the way the organization does things so that customer needs can be satisfied. Many of the companies spotlighted in this book practice it. The key focus elements for continuous improvement at Celestica are customer satisfaction, defect prevention and elimination, and process management and control. They were recognized for their focus on continuous improvement when they won the Manufacturer of the Year Award in 2011.[28]

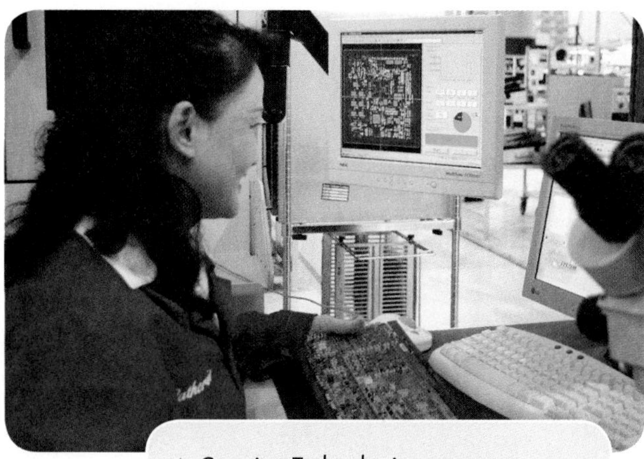

▶ Creation Technologies <www.creationtech.com> is a Canadian-based, world-class electronic manufacturing services provider to original equipment manufacturers. They build premier customer relationships, in part, through continuous improvement. All of their divisions have received ISO 9001 certification, as well as medical certification under ISO13485.

It is possible, in an organization with few layers of management and a customer focus, that new computer software and employee training could lead to a team-oriented approach with few problems. In bureaucratic organizations with many layers of management, however, TQM is not useful. Continual improvement does not work when the whole process is being done incorrectly. When an organization needs dramatic changes, only re-engineering will do.

Re-engineering is the fundamental rethinking and radical redesign of organizational processes to achieve dramatic improvements in critical measures of performance. Note the words *radical redesign* and *dramatic improvements.* At IBM's credit organization, for example, the procedure for handling a customer's request for credit once went through a five-step process that took an average of six days. By completely re-engineering the customer-request process, IBM cut its credit request processing time from six days to four hours! In re-engineering, narrow, task-oriented jobs become multidimensional. Employees who once did as they were told now make decisions on their own. Functional departments lose their reason for being. Managers stop acting like supervisors and instead behave like coaches. Workers focus more on the customers' needs and less on their bosses' needs. Attitudes and values change in response to new incentives. Practically every aspect of the organization is transformed, often beyond recognition.

Can you see how re-engineering is often necessary to change a firm from a managerial orientation to one based on self-managed teams? Re-engineering may also be necessary to adapt an organization to fit into a virtual network. Remember, re-engineering involves radical redesign and dramatic improvements. Not all organizations need such dramatic change. In fact, because of the complexity of the process, many re-engineering efforts fail. In firms where re-engineering is not feasible, restructuring may do. As discussed earlier in this chapter, restructuring involves making relatively minor changes to an organization in response to a changing environment. For example, many firms have added an Internet marketing component to the marketing department. That is a restructuring move, but it is not drastic enough to be called re-engineering.

continuous improvement (CI)
Constantly improving the way the organization does things so that customer needs can be better satisfied.

re-engineering
The fundamental rethinking and radical redesign of organizational processes to achieve dramatic improvements in critical measures of performance.

organizational (or corporate) culture
Widely shared values within an organization that provide coherence and co-operation to achieve common goals.

Creating a Change-Oriented Organizational Culture

Explain how organizational culture can help businesses adapt to change.

Any organizational change is bound to cause some stress and resistance among members. Firms adapt best when their culture is change-oriented. **Organizational (or corporate) culture** is the widely shared values within an organization that foster unity and co-operation to achieve common goals. Usually the culture of an organization is reflected in its stories, traditions, and myths.

Each McDonald's restaurant has the same feel, look, and atmosphere; in short, each has a similar organizational culture. It is obvious from visiting almost any McDonald's that the culture emphasizes quality, service, cleanliness, and value.

▸ Empowering employees who deal directly with customers to solve problems without needing a manager's approval makes a higher level of customer service possible and helps employees grow as well. What kind of guest issues do you think a front-line hotel employee should be allowed to solve on his or her own?

An organizational culture can also be negative. Have you ever been in an organization where you feel that no one cares about service or quality? The clerks may seem uniformly glum, indifferent, and testy. The mood pervades the atmosphere and patrons become unhappy or upset. It may be hard to believe that an organization, especially a profit-making one, can be run so badly and still survive. Clearly then, when you search for a job, study the organizational culture to see whether you will thrive in it.

Mintzberg notes that culture affects the way in which employees are chosen, developed, nurtured, interrelated, and rewarded. The kinds of people attracted to an organization and the way they can most effectively deal with problems and each other are largely a function of the culture a place builds and the practices and systems that support it.[29]

Some of the best organizations have cultures that emphasize service to others, especially customers.[30] The atmosphere reflects friendly, caring people who enjoy working together to provide a good product at a reasonable price. Companies that have such a culture have less need for close supervision of employees. That usually means fewer policy manuals, organization charts, and formal rules, procedures, and controls. The key to a productive culture is mutual trust. You get such trust by giving it. The very best companies stress high moral and ethical values such as honesty, reliability, fairness, environmental protection, and social involvement. One such example is TD Bank Group. They have been recognized for multiple years as one of the best workplaces in Canada. The Careers section of their home page provides numerous employee video testimonials on the culture that contributes to this success.[31] The Spotlight on Small Business box mentions organizations whose job it is to rank the best workplaces and then looks at how one small organization successfully implemented a team-oriented culture.

Thus far, we have been talking as if organizational matters were mostly controllable by management. The fact is that the formal organization structure is just one element of the total organizational system. In the creation of organizational culture, the informal organization is of equal or even greater importance. Let's explore this notion next.

SPOTLIGHT ON SMALL BUSINESS

Getting the Word Out

"A great place to work is one in which you trust the people you work for, have pride in what you do, and enjoy the people you work with"—Robert Levering, Co-founder, Great Place to Work. What Great Place to Work <*www.greatplacetowork.ca*> and Canada's Top 100 do is compile feedback from millions and millions of employees to identify those businesses where these condition exist. Following is an example of one company and what their employees have to say.

Environics Communication Inc. <*environicspr.com*> has been recognized on numerous occasions as one of the best workplaces in Canada. You may have seen their name, as they offer marketing communications and public-relations services for businesses. They build credibility by instilling with each employee the over-arching goal of doing the right thing. They support a work/life balance culture among their employees and pay for staff holidays in the 5th and 8th year of employment. They share success in part through a profit sharing plan. You can find out more about their culture through accessing their home page and clicking on Working at Environics and viewing the video.

Source: www.greatplacetowork.ca.; www.canadastop100.com; www.environicspr.com

The Informal Organization

All organizations have two organizational systems. The **formal organization** details lines of responsibility, authority, and position. It is the structure shown on organization charts. The other is the **informal organization**, the system that develops spontaneously as employees meet and form cliques, relationships, and lines of authority outside the formal organization. It is the human side of the organization that does not show on any organization chart.

formal organization
The structure that details lines of responsibility, authority, and position; that is, the structure shown on organization charts.

informal organization
The system of relationships and lines of authority that develops spontaneously as employees meet and form power centres; that is, the human side of the organization that does not appear on any organization chart.

No organization can operate effectively without both types of organization. The formal system is often too slow and bureaucratic to let the organization adapt quickly although it does provide helpful guides and lines of authority for routine situations.

The informal organization is often too unstructured and emotional to allow careful, reasoned decision making on critical matters. It is extremely effective, however, in generating creative solutions to short-term problems and creating camaraderie and teamwork among employees.

In any organization, it is wise to learn quickly who is important in the informal organization. Following formal rules and procedures can take days. Who in the organization knows how to obtain supplies immediately without the normal procedures? Which administrative assistants should you see if you want your work given first priority? Answers to these questions help people work effectively in many organizations.

The informal organization's nerve centre is the *grapevine,* the system through which unofficial information flows between and among managers and employees. Key people in the grapevine usually have considerable influence.

In the old "us-versus-them" system of organizations, where managers and employees were often at odds, the informal system hindered effective management. In more open organizations, managers and employees work together to set objectives and design procedures. The informal organization is an invaluable managerial asset that can promote harmony among workers and establish the corporate culture.

As effective as the informal organization may be in creating group co-operation, it can still be equally powerful in resisting management directives. Employees may form unions, go on strike together, and generally disrupt operations.[32] Learning to create the right corporate culture and to work within the informal organization is a key to managerial success.

PROGRESS ASSESSMENT

- What is an inverted organization?
- Why do organizations outsource functions?
- What is organizational culture?

SUMMARY

Outline the basic principles of organization management.

The basic principles of organization are much the same regardless of the size of the business.

What is happening today to Canadian businesses?
They are adjusting to changing markets. That is a normal function in a capitalist economy. There will be big winners, like Google and Facebook, and big losers as well. The key to success is remaining flexible and adapting to the changing times.

What are the principles of organization management?
Structuring an organization means devising a division of labour (sometimes resulting in specialization), setting up teams or departments, and assigning responsibility and authority. It includes allocating resources (such as funds), assigning specific tasks, and establishing procedures for accomplishing the organizational objectives. Managers also have to make ethical decisions about how to treat workers.

Compare the organizational theories of Henri Fayol and Max Weber.

Until the twentieth century, most businesses were rather small, the processes of producing goods were rather simple, and organizing workers was fairly easy. Not until the 1900s and the introduction of mass production did businesses become complex. During this era, business theorists emerged.

What were Fayol's basic principles?
Fayol introduced principles such as unity of command, hierarchy of authority, division of labour, subordination of individual interests to the general interest, authority, clear communication channels, order, and equity.

What principles did Weber add?
Weber added principles of bureaucracy such as job descriptions, written rules and decision guidelines, consistent procedures, and staffing and promotions based on qualifications.

Evaluate the choices managers make in structuring organizations.

Issues involved in structuring and restructuring organizations include (1) centralization versus decentralization, (2) span of control, (3) tall versus flat organization structures, and (4) departmentalization.

What are the latest trends in structuring?
Departments are often replaced or supplemented by matrix organizations and self-managed teams that decentralize authority. The span of control becomes larger as employees become self-directed. Another trend is to eliminate managers and flatten organizations.

Contrast the various organizational models.

Organizational design is the coordinating of workers so that they can best accomplish the firm's goals. New forms of organization are emerging that enable firms to be more responsive to customers.

What are the two major organizational models?
Two traditional forms of organization are (1) line organizations and (2) line-and-staff organizations. A line organization has clearly defined responsibility and authority, is easy to understand, and provides each worker with only one supervisor. The expert advice of staff assistants in a line-and-staff organization helps in areas such as safety, quality control, computer technology, human resource management, and investing.

What are the key alternative forms to the major organizational models?
Matrix organizations assign people to projects temporarily and encourage inter-organizational co-operation and teamwork. Self-managed teams have all the benefits of the matrix style and are long term.

Identify the benefits of inter-firm co-operation and coordination.

Networking is using communications technology and other means to link organizations and allow them to work together on common objectives.

What are the major concepts involved in inter-firm communications?
Communications technology allows firms to work together on common objectives. A virtual corporation is a networked organization of replaceable firms that join and leave as needed. Benchmarking tells firms how their performance measures up to that of their competitors in specific functions. The company may then outsource to companies that perform its weaker functions more effectively and efficiently. The functions that are left are the firm's core competencies.

What is an inverted organization?
An inverted organization places employees at the top of the hierarchy; managers are at the bottom to train and assist employees.

Explain how organizational culture can help businesses adapt to change.

Organizational culture may be defined as widely shared values that foster unity and co-operation to achieve common goals.

What is the difference between the formal and informal organization of a firm?
The formal organization details lines of responsibility, authority, and position. It is the structure shown on organization charts. The informal organization is the system that develops spontaneously as employees meet and form cliques, relationships, and lines of authority outside the formal organization. It is the human side of the organization. The informal organization is an invaluable managerial asset that often promotes harmony among workers and establishes the corporate culture. As effective as the informal organization may be in creating group co-operation, it can still be equally powerful in resisting management directives.

KEY TERMS

benchmarking
bureaucracy
centralized authority
chain of command
continuous improvement (CI)
core competencies
decentralized authority
departmentalization
economies of scale
economies of scope
flat organization structure
formal organization
hierarchy
informal organization
inverted organization
line organization
line personnel
matrix organization
networking between firms
organizational (or corporate) culture
real time
re-engineering
restructuring
self-managed teams
span of control
staff personnel
tall organization structure
total quality management(TQM)
virtual corporation

CRITICAL THINKING

1. You are thinking about setting up your own company this summer to help pay for your education and apply some of the concepts you are learning in this course. With the aging population you believe there is a need for a general home maintenance business. Define the structure and explain the rationale of your business. Include the following points.
   a. Will the decision making be centralized versus decentralized?
   b. What span of control would you have for your work teams and how tall or flat would you want your company to be?
   c. On what basis would you departmentalize your company?
2. Businesses are now trying to redesign their structures to deal with shorter product life cycles and increasing competition, which requires rapid communication and teamwork. Some businesses turn to a matrix organization. The goal, remember, is to better serve customers and to win their loyalty.
   a. How would you manage lines of authority?
   b. What tools could you use within the business to share information including knowledge gained?

DEVELOPING WORKPLACE SKILLS

1. There is no better way to understand the effects of having many layers of management on communication accuracy than to play the game of Message Relay. Choose seven or more members of the class and have them leave the classroom. Then choose one person to read the following paragraph and another student to listen. Call in one of the students from outside and have the "listener" tell him or her the information contained in the paragraph. Then bring in another student and have the new listener repeat the information to him or her. Continue the process with all those who left the room. Do not allow anyone in the class to offer corrections as each listener becomes the storyteller in turn. In this way, all students can hear how the facts become distorted over time. The distortions and mistakes are often quite humorous, but they are not so funny in organizations such as Ford, which once had 22 layers of management.

   Here is the paragraph:

   Dealers in the Maritimes have received more than 130 complaints about steering on the new Commander and Roadhandler models of our minivans. Apparently, the front suspension system is weak and the ball joints are wearing too fast. This causes slippage in the linkage and results in oversteering. Mr. Berenstein has been notified, but so far only 213 of 4,300 dealers have received repair kits.
2. Describe some informal groups within an organization with which you are familiar (at school, at work, etc.). What have you noticed about how those groups help or hinder progress in the organization?
3. Imagine that you are working for Kitchen Magic, an appliance manufacturer that produces, among other things, dishwashers for the home. Imagine further that a competitor introduces a new dishwasher that uses sound waves to clean dishes. The result is a dishwasher that cleans even the worst burnt-on food and sterilizes the dishes and silverware as well. You need to develop a similar offering fast, or your company will lose the market. Write an e-mail to management outlining the problem and explaining your rationale for recommending the use of a self-managed team to respond quickly and what type of skills you need.
4. Divide the class into teams of five. You are a producer of athletic shoes. Identify all of main functional areas of your business. Looking at your list, identify which ones you view as your core competencies, and explain why. For those that are not part of your competencies, how would you go about outsourcing them?

ANALYZING MANAGEMENT DECISIONS

IBM Is Both an Outsourcer and a Major Outsource for Others

Few companies are better known for their manufacturing expertise than IBM. Nonetheless, even IBM has to adapt to today's dynamic marketplace. In the area of personal computers, for example, IBM was unable to match the prices or speed of delivery of mail-order firms such as Dell Computer. Dell built machines after receiving orders for them and then rushed the computers to customers. IBM, in contrast, made machines ahead of time and hoped that the orders would match its inventory.

To compete against firms like Dell, IBM had to custom-make computers for its business customers, but IBM was not particularly suited to do such work. To address this issue IBM entered into a relationship with Lenovo whereby Lenovo became the manufacturer of IBM personal computers and over time replaced IBM in the personal computer market.

IBM's long-range strategy was to move away from hardware toward software development. It acquired PricewaterhouseCoopers to put more emphasis on services rather than hardware. Today IBM dominates the information technology industry. They offer outsourcing for information technology infrastructure, application development, and information technology support services. They spend over $6 billion annually on research and development and hold the most patents of any U.S. technology company.

While growing this side of their business they have outsourced a number of jobs to India in sales, semiconductor, and finance groups, resulting in the layoff of 4600 U.S. based employees in these positions in 2009.

Sources: Michael Useem and Joseph Harder, "Leading Laterally in Company Outsourcing," *Sloan Management Review*, Winter 2000, 25–36; Alison Overholt, "In the Hot Seat," *Fast Company*, January 2003, 46; "IBM Outsourcing Thousands of Jobs to India," www.peacerebelgirl.wordpress.com/2009/03/26/ibm-outsourcing-thousands-of-jobs-to-india/, March 26, 2009; and "IBM Outsourcing with Big Blue," www.itouotsourcinghq.com/it-outsourcing-to-ibm, April 12, 2011.

Discussion Questions

1. What does it say about today's competitive environment when leading companies such as IBM give up competing in an area of their business that they dominated for many years and expand significantly into a related area of business they have only been involved in for a relatively short period of time?
2. What effects will outsourcing have on trade relationships among countries?
3. If more Canadian companies unite their technologies, what will that do to competitors in other countries? Should foreign companies do more uniting with Canadian companies themselves? What about Canadian companies uniting with foreign companies?
4. How much influence will the Internet have on world trade and outsourcing among countries? What does the Internet provide that was not available before?

Practise and learn online with Connect.

CHAPTER 10

PRODUCING WORLD-CLASS GOODS AND SERVICES

LEARNING OBJECTIVES

After you have read and studied this chapter, you should be able to:

LO 1 Describe the current state of Canadian manufacturing and how companies are becoming more competitive.

LO 2 Describe the evolution from production to operations management.

LO 3 Describe operations management planning issues including facility location, facility layout, materials requirement planning, purchasing, just-in-time inventory control, quality control, and supply chain management.

LO 4 Identify various production processes and describe techniques to improve productivity including flexible manufacturing, lean manufacturing, mass customization, and computer-aided design manufacturing.

LO 5 Explain the use of PERT and Gantt charts to control manufacturing processes.

PROFILE

GETTING TO KNOW PIERRE BEAUDOIN OF BOMBARDIER INC.

After many ups and downs over the past few years due to the global economic turmoil, Bombardier has recently experienced strong financial results and solidified their ranking as the world's No. 1 passenger train maker and No. 3 civil aircraft manufacturer. The company designs and manufactures a portfolio of rail vehicles and aviation products. They have operations in 25 countries and close to 70,000 employees.

If you know anything about Bombardier, the one person who's name would come up is Laurent Beaudoin. He was the President and CEO for 35 years, the son-in-law of its founder, Joseph-Armand Bombardier. Laurent oversaw the development of this goliath—by Canadian standards—manufacturing company. So, who is Pierre Beaudoin, the 49-year-old who studied business administration and industrial relations at McGill and became President and CEO in June of 2008? Back in 1985, while Pierre was working for a sporting goods company, his father, Laurent, asked him to help develop the Sea-Doo. Pierre started as test driver for the first few prototypes of the Sea-Doo, and for the next 16 years he worked in various capacities for Bombardier Recreational Products. In 2001, he was appointed President of Bombardier Aerospace, and then in 2004 he was appointed Executive Vice President of Bombardier Inc.

In his short tenure as President of the parent company, Pierre has had to lead the company through both some very bad and good times. The collapse of the global economy in the second half of 2008 and into 2009 lead to a significant slowdown. However, Bombardier remained profitable in this difficult time and also committed to invest for the long term in research and development programs (see their ranking in Figure 10.2) such as the CSeries commercial aircraft, the Learjet 85 business jet, and the very high speed train, to prepare for the next economic cycle. The CSeries, which can seat between 110 to 149 passengers, is expected to start selling in 2013 and orders are in place in 2012 for 300 of these planes. With the introduction of this new aircraft the company will need sound supply chain management, a subject discussed in this chapter.

Pierre has supported a Code of Ethics and Business Conduct that addresses employee ethical conduct and business practices and relationships with external stakeholders. He has publicly supported the development of sustainable transportation systems including more fuel-efficient aircraft that are on target for a 20 percent reduction of carbon dioxide emissions, and rail products to increase energy efficiency by up to 50 percent.

Bombardier was an official supporter of the Vancouver 2010 Olympic and Paralympic Games, with total donations of $10 million, and the company is involved with other social responsibility projects in nine countries outside of Canada. Pierre is a twenty-first-century leader of a truly world-class, Canadian-based manufacturer.

Sources: "Bombardier in Ontario," www.bombardier.com/files/en/supporting_docs/BI-Bombardier.Ontario.pdf; Joe Castaldo, "Laurent Beaudoin Interview, Déjà vu," *Canadian Business Magazine,* 7 August 2008; "Bombardier Signs Airline for Five Q400 NextGen Airliners," *Market Wire,* 3 August 2009; "Bombardier Signs 225 Million USD Contracts to Supply, Operate and Maintain an Automated People Mover System in Phoenix, USA," CCNMatthews, 14 July 2009; and www.bombardier.com.

Describe the current state of Canadian manufacturing and how companies are becoming more competitive.

CANADA TODAY

Canada is a large industrial country with many major industries. We are one of the largest producers of forest products in the world, with plants in nearly all provinces turning out a vast array of wood, furniture, and paper products. There are giant aluminum mills in Quebec and British Columbia, automotive-related manufacturing plants in Ontario and Quebec, and aircraft plants in Ontario, Quebec, and Manitoba. Oil, natural gas, and coal are produced in Alberta, Saskatchewan, Newfoundland and Labrador, Nova Scotia, and British Columbia, and are processed there or in other provinces; a vast array of metals and minerals come from all parts of Canada. These are only some of the thousands of components, products, and natural resources produced or processed in Canada. Given that most of our industry is focused on natural resources we can experience significant growth in times when world economies are growing, offset by an equally large retraction when world economies are stagnant or in recession. Such has been the case over the past 7 to 10 years. What happens in the United States, along with the developing third world economies including China and India, has a dramatic impact on Canada, as was discussed in Chapter 3.

Canada is facing some serious challenges to its ability to remain a modern, competitive industrial country. Today's business climate is characterized by constant and restless change and dislocation, as ever-newer technologies and increasing global competition force companies to respond quickly to these challenges. Many factors account for our difficulties in the world's competitive race. Among them are inadequate improvement in productivity and unrelenting competition from the United States, Japan, Germany, and more recently from India, China, and other Southeast Asian countries; inadequate education and retraining programs for our workforce; our "branch plant economy," whereby many subsidiaries are owned by foreign parent companies and profits are mostly returned to these foreign-based companies rather then invested in Canada; and not enough money spent on research and development. Where Canada used to be able to rely on a lower-valued Canadian dollar compared to the U.S. dollar to sustain our exports, an exchange rate closer to parity has taken away this advantage. Figure 10.1 lists eight points that could improve Canada's competitiveness.

Despite these challenges, Canada still ranks fairly well in world competitiveness, as discussed in Reaching Beyond Our Borders in Chapter 5. However, one cannot expect this to continue, as other countries are becoming stronger and more competitive. In response, the federal government's innovation strategy will, among other areas, focus on research and development as a way to improve our competitiveness. Let us look at research and development next.

Figure 10.1

Making Canada More Competitive

The Canadian Manufacturers & Exporters published a report identifying eight points that would make our country more competitive.

1. Lower taxes for those businesses that invest in new products and technologies and the skills of their employees.
2. Extend the Accelerated Capital Cost Allowance program for those companies that invest in manufacturing and processing machinery and equipment.
3. Encourage innovation and the commercialization of new products and technologies.
4. Help businesses develop and take advantage of international opportunities.
5. Enhance the competitiveness of North America's integrated supply chains.
6. Improve the quality and availability of skilled workers.
7. Strengthen Canada's energy and logistics infrastructure.
8. Improve regulatory efficiency.

Source: Courtesy Canadian Manufacturers & Exporters, "An 8-point plan for a more competitive Canada by 2.5 million voters in the manufacturing and exporting sectors," www.cme-mec.ca/english/publications/cme-publications-reprots.html.

Research and Development

According to the *Canadian Oxford Dictionary,* **research and development (R&D)** is defined as work directed toward the innovation, introduction, and improvement of products and processes. When evaluating why some companies are more competitive than others, the terms *technology* and *innovation* often come up. What do these terms mean?

research and development (R&D)
Work directed toward the innovation, introduction, and improvement of products and processes.

The Centre for Canadian Studies at Mount Allison University, in co-operation with the Canadian Heritage Canadian Studies Programme, produces the *About Canada* series. Innovation in Canada is the focus of one of these documents.

> *Technology is know-how, knowing how to make and use the tools for the job. It's the combination of technology with markets that creates innovation and gives a competitive edge. An innovation is a new product or process that can be purchased. Put another way, an idea may lead to an invention, but it cannot be called an innovation until it is commercialized. When technological know-how is developed, sold, distributed, and used, then it becomes an innovation.*[1]

In the Survey of Innovation conducted by Statistics Canada, respondents indicated that the three most important objectives of innovation are to improve product quality, to increase production capacity, and to extend product range. Since that time, the Science, Innovation, and Electronic Information Division (SIEID) of Statistics Canada has piloted more surveys that focus on the importance of innovation. SIEID believes that innovation and the adoption and dissemination of innovative technologies and processes are vital to economic growth and development. It continues to elaborate by stating that, through innovation, new products are introduced in the market, new production processes are developed and introduced, and organizational changes are made. Through the adoption of newer, more advanced technologies and practices, industries can increase their production capabilities, improve their productivity, and expand their lines of new goods and services.[2]

Private industry, Canadian universities, hospitals, and government laboratories were expected to expend $29.9 billion on R&D in 2011.[3] The federal government alone—considered the principal source of R&D funds in Canada—spent an estimated $11.3 billion in 2011–12 on science and technology.[4] Figure 10.2 outlines Canada's top ten corporate R&D spenders. Corporate spending on R&D continued to decline in 2010.[5] This negative trend has been in place for five years, while revenues for the same companies have increased. Two companies are largely responsible for this decline, Nortel Networks Corporation (which is no longer in business) and TELUS Corporation <*www.telus.com*>. Offsetting the steep declines for these two companies is the significant increase in R&D by Research In Motion.

Based on its research, what does RE$EARCH Infosource Inc. <*www.researchinfosource.com*> forecast? First, the financial crisis in 2008–09 is a logical reason for a decline in this spending. However, given the drop in manufacturing and the increase in the service industry it will be difficult to reverse the trend. Where manufacturing would typically need to invest in research and development and has been supported by government, this environment does not exist in the service sector.

CANADA'S EVOLVING MANUFACTURING AND SERVICES BASE

Over the previous two decades, foreign manufacturers captured huge chunks of the North American market for basic products such as steel, cement, machinery, and farm equipment using the latest in production techniques. That competition forced

Rank			R&D Expenditures			Revenue	Research Intensity	
2010	2009	Company	FY2010 $000	FY2009 $000	% Change 2009–10	FY2010 $000	R&D as % of Revenue	Industry
1	1	Research In Motion Limited	$1,391,395	$1,202,848	26.3	$20,502,219	6.8	Comm/telecom equipment
2	3	BCE	$821,000	$806,000	1.9	$18,069,000	4.5	Telecommunications services
3	5	IBM Canada Ltd.	$551,100	$556,500	−1.0	nd	2.6	Software and computer services
4	8	Atomic Energy of Canada Limited	$476,400	$393,051	21.2	$460,935	103.4	Engineering Services
5	6	Magna International Inc.	$463,455	$553,870	−16.3	24,142,916	1.9	Automotive
6	7	Pratt & Whitney Canada Corp.	$395,000	$398,000	−0.8	$2,912,000	13.6	Aerospace
7	10	Ericsson Canada Inc.	$353,000	$197,000	79.2	$1,004,000	35.2	Comm/telecom equipment
8		AMD Canada	$241,694	$252,612	−4.3	nd		Electronic systems & parts
9	9	Alcatel-Lucent	$233,000	$224,000	4.0	nd		Comm/telecom equipment
10	14	Bombardier Inc.	$198,771	$161,022	23.4	$18,241,589	1.1	Aerospace

NOTES: nd = Not disclosed
Source: RE$EARCH Infosource Inc., Canada's Top 100 Corporate R&D Spenders 2011, www.researchinfosource.com/media/2011Top100List.pdf.

Figure 10.2

Canada's Top Corporate R&D Spenders 2010

companies to greatly alter their production techniques and managerial styles. Many firms are now as good as or better than competitors anywhere in the world. What have Canadian manufacturers done to regain a competitive edge? They have emphasized the following:

- Focusing on customers;
- Maintaining close relationships with suppliers and other companies to satisfy customer needs;
- Practising continuous improvement;
- Focusing on quality;
- Saving on costs through site selection;
- Relying on the Internet to unite companies; and
- Adopting production techniques such as enterprise resource planning, computer-integrated manufacturing, flexible manufacturing, and lean manufacturing.

As you may recall from Figure 1.6 in Chapter 1, the manufacturing and service sectors employs over 87 percent of Canada's working population. R&D spending by businesses is also critical to our economy, as they make-up 52 percent of total R&D expenditures.[6] This sector is highly innovative and technology-driven.

They continue to invest in facilities increasing their agility, expanding mass customization capabilities, and facilitating new product introductions.[7]

As we progress through this chapter, you will see that operations management has become a challenging and vital element of Canadian business. The growth of Canada's manufacturing base will likely remain a major business issue in the near future. There will be debates about the merits of moving production facilities to foreign countries. Serious questions will be raised about replacing workers with robots and other machinery. Major political decisions will be made regarding protection of Canadian manufacturers through quotas and other restrictions on free trade. Concerns about the impact of manufacturing on our environment will result in the development of new technologies as discussed in the Green Box. Regardless of how these issues are decided, however, there will be many opportunities along the way.

The service sector will also continue to get attention as it continues to become a larger part of the overall economy. Service productivity is a real issue, as is the blending of service and manufacturing through the Internet. Since many of tomorrow's graduates will likely find jobs in the service sector, it is important to understand the latest operations management concepts for this sector.

Each year companies discover new ways of automating that eliminate the need for human labour. This photo shows an automated apparatus known as a Flipper. It can pour a dozen pancakes and flip them when needed on one griddle while, at the same time, flipping burgers on another grill. Are any restaurants in your area already using equipment like this?

PROGRESS ASSESSMENT

- What are some challenges that Canada is facing in its ability to remain a competitive country?
- How is innovation related to research and development?

production
The creation of finished goods and services using the factors of production: land, labour, capital, entrepreneurship, and knowledge.

FROM PRODUCTION TO OPERATIONS MANAGEMENT

Describe the evolution from production to operations management.

Production is the creation of goods and services using the factors of production: land, labour, capital, entrepreneurship, and knowledge. Production has historically meant manufacturing and the term **production management** has described the management activities that helped firms create goods. But the nature of business has changed significantly in the last 20 years or so as the service sector, including Internet services, has grown dramatically. As discussed in Chapter 1, Canada is a service economy—that is, one dominated by the service sector. This can be a benefit to future graduates because many of the top-paying jobs are in legal services, medical services, entertainment, broadcasting, and business services such as accounting, finance, and management consulting.

production management
The term used to describe all of the activities that managers do to help their firms create goods.

Operations management is a specialized area in management that converts or transforms resources (including human resources) into goods and services. It includes inventory management, quality control, production scheduling, follow-up services, and more. In an automobile plant, operations management transforms raw materials, human resources, parts, supplies, paints, tools, and other resources into automobiles. It does this through the processes of fabrication and assembly.

operations management
A specialized area in management that converts or transforms resources (including human resources) into goods and services.

GREENBOX

Carbon Capture and Storage

One of Canada's primary resources is its fossil fuels. Abundant supplies of oil, natural gas, and coal make this country one of the world's most attractive energy centres for continuing investment and development. However, with this economic opportunity comes a challenge, to mitigate greenhouse gas (GHG) emissions and their impact on climate change. More and more evidence is being gathered by the scientific community that global emissions growth could bring rapid climate change. The challenge is to reduce GHG emissions while continuing economic progress.

Carbon dioxide capture and storage (CCS) is one way to address the carbon challenge. With CCS, carbon dioxide emissions from large industrial facilities are separated from the plant's process or exhaust system, compressed, and injected deep underground.

CCS can be built as an add-on to existing fossil energy infrastructure or incorporated into new and future facilities. The main components of this operation are: capture, transportation, and storage. Once the carbon dioxide is captured at a plant, it needs to be transported to a location with the appropriate geological formation. These stable sedimentary rock formations, that formerly securely held vast oil and gas reserves, can now be used to hold carbon dioxide, which will be injected into these formations.

Both the federal and a number of provincial governments are financially supporting the development of CCS and bringing forward legislation to reduce GHG emissions.

Carbon dioxide is also being used for enhanced oil recovery by companies including Encana. Since 2000, Encana has been injecting existing oil reserves with carbon dioxide to extract more resource. Do you have any concerns about this type of business on our environment?

Source: The Canadian CO_2 Capture and Storage Technology Network, Natural Resources Canada, www.CO2network.gc.ca; and Racel Pulfer, "Burying King Coal," *Canadian Business*, 28 April 2008, 21–22.

In a college or university, operations management takes inputs—such as information, professors, supplies, buildings, offices, and computer systems—and creates services that transform students into educated people. It does this through a process called education.

Some organizations—such as factories, farms, and mines—produce mostly goods. Others—such as hospitals, schools, and government agencies—produce mostly services. Still others produce a combination of goods and services. For example, an automobile manufacturer not only makes cars but also provides services such as repairs, financing, and insurance. And at Future Shop customers buy electronic and household goods such as TVs, computers, fridges, and stoves and can also buy extended warranties on all of these products.

Manufacturers Turn to a Customer Orientation and Services for Profit

Many manufacturers have spent an enormous amount of money on productivity and quality initiatives. Companies that have prospered and grown—General Electric and Dell, to name just a couple—have taken a similar road to success. They have expanded operations management out of the factory and moved it closer to the customer, providing services such as custom manufacturing, fast delivery, credit, installation, and repair.[8]

Another example of the growing importance of services is in the area of corporate computing. The average company spends only one-fifth of its annual personal computer budget on purchasing hardware. The rest (80 percent) goes to technical support, administration, and other maintenance activities. Because of this, IBM has shifted from its dependence on selling computer hardware to becoming a major supplier of computer services, software, and technology components.[9] Its purchase of

As this chapter's profile mentions, Bombardier is a Canadian-based, world-class manufacturing organization, which also earns substantial revenue from their service businesses. Bombardier Aerospace is involved in fractional ownership, aircraft charter and management, aircraft maintenance, and pilot training.

PricewaterhouseCoopers' tech consulting affiliate was intended to increase its presence in the service sector. General Electric is doing the same; it generates more than \$5 billion a year in worldwide revenues from Internet transactions.[10]

Companies such as Celestica and Ford have outsourced much of their production processes and are focusing more on building customer relationships and brand images.[11] As you can see, operations management has become much more focused on services, because by redirecting corporate thinking towards satisfying customer needs better than the competition, they retain their customers.

OPERATIONS MANAGEMENT IN THE SERVICE SECTOR

Operations management in the service industry is all about creating a good experience for those who use the service. For example, in a Four Seasons <*www.fourseasons.com*> hotel, operations management includes restaurants that offer the finest in service, elevators that run smoothly, and a front desk that processes people quickly. It may include placing fresh-cut flowers in the lobbies and dishes of fruit in every room. More important, it may mean spending thousands of dollars to provide training in quality management for every new employee.

Hotel customers today want in-room Internet access and a help centre with toll-free telephone service. Executives travelling on business may need video equipment and a host of computer hardware and other aids. Foreign visitors would like multilingual customer-support services. Hotel shops need to carry more than souvenirs, newspapers, and some drugstore and food items to serve today's high-tech travellers. The shops may also carry laptop computer supplies, electrical adapters, and the like. Operations management is responsible for locating and providing such amenities to make customers happy. In short, delighting customers by anticipating their needs has become the quality standard for luxury hotels, as it has for most other service businesses. But knowing customer needs and satisfying them are two different things. That is why operations management is so important: it is the implementation phase of management.

▸ Information Mapping Canada <www.infomap.ca> helps leading organizations focus on improving performance through better written communication. Clients including Xerox Canada have increased productivity through better management of customer complaints. What types of measures could you implement to track how good a job was being done in managing customer complaints?

Measuring Quality in the Service Sector

There's strong evidence that productivity in the service sector is rising, but productivity measures do not capture improvements in quality. In an example from health care, positron emission tomography (PET) scans are much better than X-rays, but the quality difference is not reported in productivity figures. The traditional way to measure productivity involves tracking inputs (worker hours) compared to outputs (dollars). Notice that there is no measure for quality improvement. When new information systems are developed to measure the quality improvement of goods and services—including the speed of their delivery and customer satisfaction—productivity in the service sector will go up dramatically.

Using computers is one way in which the service sector is improving productivity, but not the only one. Think about labour-intensive businesses such as hospitals and fast-food restaurants, where automation plays a big role in controlling costs and improving service. Today, at Burger King, for example, customers fill their own drink cups from pop machines, which allows workers to concentrate on preparing the food. And because the people working at the drive-up window now wear headsets instead of using stationary mikes, they are no longer glued to one spot and can do four or five tasks while taking an order.

Most of us have been exposed to similar productivity gains in banking. For example, people in most cities no longer have to wait in long lines for tellers to help them deposit and withdraw money. Instead, they use automated teller machines (ATMs), which usually involve little or no waiting and are available 24 hours a day.

Another service that was once very slow was grocery store checkout. The system of marking goods with universal product codes (UPC) enables computerized checkout and allows cashiers to be much more productive than before. Now, many stores have set up automated systems that enable customers to go through the checkout process on their own. Some grocery chains, such as Longo's <*www.longos.com*>, are implementing Internet services that allow customers to place orders online and receive home delivery. The potential for productivity gains in this area are enormous.

In short, operations management has led to tremendous productivity increases in the service sector but still has a long way to go. Also, service workers are losing jobs to machines just as manufacturing workers did. The secret to obtaining and holding a good job is to acquire appropriate education and training. Such education and training must go on for a lifetime to keep up with the rapid changes that are happening in all areas of business. That message cannot be repeated too frequently.

PROGRESS ASSESSMENT

- Explain the difference between production management and operations management.
- What is the biggest issue with productivity in the service sector?

OPERATIONS MANAGEMENT PLANNING

Describe operations management planning issues including facility location, facility layout, materials requirement planning, purchasing, just-in-time inventory control, quality control, and supply chain management.

Operations management planning helps solve many of the problems in the service and manufacturing sectors. These include facility location, facility layout, and quality control. The resources used may be different, but the management issues are similar.

Facility Location

Facility location is the process of selecting a geographic location for a company's operations. In keeping with the need to focus on customers, one strategy is to find a site that makes it easy for consumers to use the company's services and to communicate about their needs. For example, Hewlett-Packard (Canada) Company opened a new computer manufacturing facility in Toronto in a bid to speed new machines to Canadian business customers as fast as archrival Dell. In doing so, HP became the only major computer vendor active in Canada to actually assemble machines here.[12] Flower shops and banks are putting facilities in supermarkets so that their products are more accessible than they are in freestanding facilities. You can find a Second Cup <*www.secondcup.com*> inside some Home Depot <*www.homedepot.ca*> stores and there are Tim Hortons outlets in some gas stations. Customers can buy gas and their meals, all in one location.

facility location
The process of selecting a geographic location for a company's operations.

The ultimate in convenience is never having to leave home to get services. That is why there is so much interest in Internet banking, Internet shopping, online education, and other services. For brick-and-mortar businesses to beat such competition, they have to choose good locations and offer outstanding service. Study the location of service-sector businesses—such as hotels, banks, athletic clubs, and supermarkets—and you will see that the most successful ones are conveniently located.

Facility Location for Manufacturers

A major issue of the recent past has been the shift of manufacturing organizations from one city or province to another in Canada, or to other foreign sites. In 2005, Gildan Activewear, a Canadian company and one of the world's largest manufacturers of T-shirts, closed two plants in Canada, transferring production to North Carolina.[13] Such shifts sometimes result in pockets of unemployment in some geographic areas and lead to tremendous economic growth in others that benefit from these shifts. The Making Ethical Decisions box considers some of the issues surrounding such moves.

Why would companies spend millions of dollars to move their facilities from one location to another? In making these decisions they consider labour costs; availability of resources, including labour; access to transportation that can reduce time-to-market; proximity to suppliers; proximity to customers; crime rates; quality of life for employees; cost of living; and the need to train or retrain the local workforce.

Even though labour is becoming a smaller percentage of total cost in highly automated industries, availability of low-cost labour or the right kind of skilled labour remains a key reason many producers move their plant to Malaysia, China, India, Mexico, and other countries. Some of these firms have been charged with providing substandard working conditions and/or

▸ Facility location is a major decision for manufacturing and other companies that must take into account the availability of qualified workers; access to suppliers, customers, transportation, and local regulation including zoning and taxes. How has the growth of Internet commerce affected company location decisions?

MAKING ETHICAL DECISIONS

Financial Support or Not?

In early 2009, both General Motors and Chrysler approached the federal and Ontario governments as well as their unions, looking for financial support and major concessions. Both companies indicated that without this support, they would be forced to close their Canadian operations. They claimed they were unable to compete with the lower wage costs of non-North American owned facilities. Closure of their operations would result in tens of thousands of job losses between their plants and their suppliers' operations. They sought billions of dollars from the governments to cover losses and update their production facilities while labour leaders had to agree to re-negotiate labour contracts, significantly reducing labour costs. Do you think the governments and unions should have agreed to the demands of General Motors and Chrysler? What could have been the consequences if they did not? What would you have chosen to do?

exploiting children in the countries where they have set up factories. Others, such as Grupo M <*www.grupom.com.do*>, a textile products and services company in the Dominican Republic, are being used as role models for global manufacturing. Grupo M provides its employees with higher pay relative to local businesses, transportation to and from work, daycare centres, discounted food, and health clinics. Its operations are so efficient that it can compete in world markets and provide world-class services to its employees.

Inexpensive resources are another major reason for moving production facilities. Companies usually need water, electricity, wood, coal, and other basic resources. By moving to areas where natural resources are inexpensive and plentiful, firms can significantly lower not only the cost of buying such resources but also the cost of shipping finished products. Often the most important resource is people, so companies tend to cluster where smart and talented people are. Witness the Ottawa area, also known as Silicon Valley North.

Time-to-market is another decision-making factor. As manufacturers attempt to compete globally, they need sites that allow products to move quickly, so that they can be delivered to customers fast.[14] Access to highways, rail lines, waterways, and airports is thus critical. Information technology (IT) is also important to quicken response time, so many firms are seeking countries with the most advanced information systems.

Another way to work closely with suppliers to satisfy your customers' needs is to locate your production facilities near supplier facilities. That cuts the cost of distribution and makes communication easier.[15]

Many businesses are building factories in foreign countries to get closer to their international customers. That is a major reason why the U.S. automaker General Motors builds cars in Oshawa, Ontario, and Japanese automaker Toyota builds cars in Cambridge, Ontario. Japanese-based automaker Honda opened an engine factory plant in Alliston, Ontario, in 2008, close to its two assembly plants. Honda Canada president Hiroshi Kobayashi told a news conference that this site selection "supports Honda's global strategic manufacturing focus of bringing manufacturing and sales operations to the local market."[16] When firms select foreign sites, they consider whether they are near airports, waterways, and highways so that raw materials and finished goods can be moved quickly and easily.

Businesses also study the quality of life for workers and managers. Are there good schools nearby? Is the weather nice? Is the crime rate low? Does the local community welcome new businesses? Do the chief executive and other key managers want to live there? Sometimes a region with a high quality of life is also an expensive one, which complicates the decision. In short, facility location has become a critical issue in operations management.

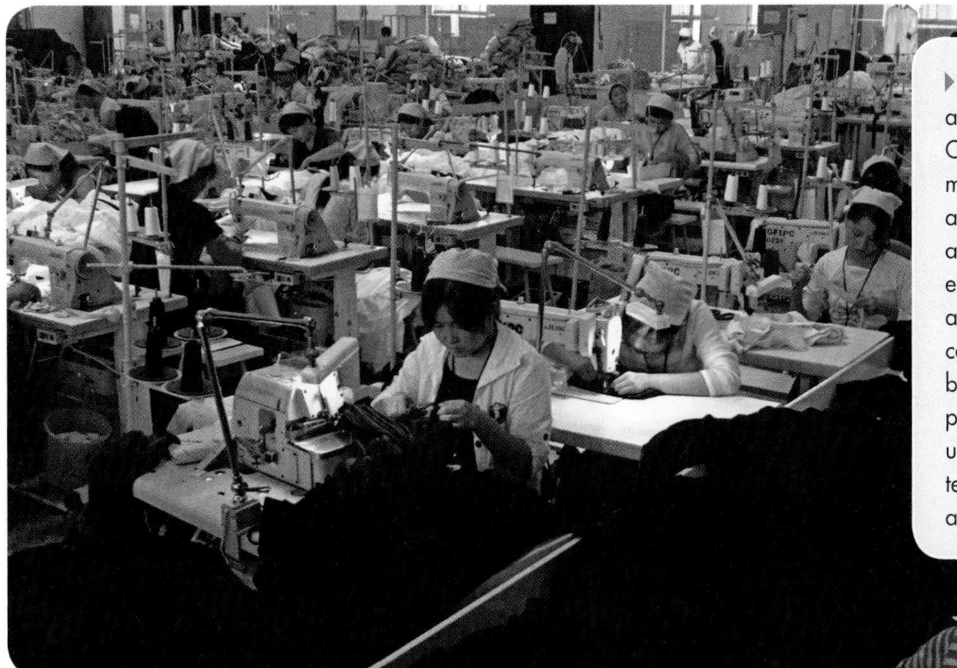

▶ With average labour costs about one-fortieth of those in Canada, China is now a leading manufacturer of not only textiles and consumer products, but also increasingly sophisticated electronic equipment, software, and other technologies. It is competing increasingly on the basis of high-end value-added products, as well as costs, using some of the world's best technologies and drawing from a pool of highly skilled talent.

Outsourcing

The previous chapter noted that many companies now try to divide their production between core competencies, work they do best in-house, and outsourcing, letting outside companies service them by doing what they are experts at. The result sought is the best-quality products at the lowest possible costs.

Outsourcing goods and services has become a hot practice in North America. Software development, call-centre jobs, and back-office jobs have been moving to developing countries for some time. The range of jobs now shifting to these countries includes accounting, financial analysis, medicine, architecture, aircraft maintenance, law, film production, and banking activities.[17] Based on a survey of its over 100,000 members, the International Association of Outsourcing Professionals has found that the percentage of companies planning on expanding their future outsourcing programs has grown from 36 percent to 56 percent from January 2009 to January 2010.[18] In the manufacturing sector, employment continues to drop lower and lower through outsourcing, in part driven by a higher Canadian dollar.

Another industry where significant outsourcing happens is software R&D. For Canadian companies needing software, hourly rates outside of Canada are much lower. Keep in mind that while outsourcing may look good on paper financially, if a company does not do its homework, outsourcing can become a problem due to language and cultural differences, differences in expectations, etc. A Canadian organization, the Centre for Outsourcing Research and Education (CORE) <*www.core-outsourcing.org*>, has been formed to provide organizations with the knowledge and skills to manage outsourcing activities.[19] More than just a cost-saving tool, outsourcing is being used as a strategic tool for focusing scarce human capital on core business activities.

One outsourcing model that is working involves the software company Macadamian Technologies Inc. <*www.macadamian.com*>. Using software engineers in eastern Europe and India, Macadamian uses a distributed model with completely transparent communication. Using wikis, every small iteration on a project is reviewed by the rest of the team members, who then post comments. A project manager gets the final say. Everyone shares their work resulting in clients getting more flexibility and quicker turnaround.

Keep in mind that Canadian companies are also benefitting from other countries' outsourcing. For example, Procter & Gamble's bar soap for North America is now

▸ The Canadian Auto Workers (CAW) <www.caw.ca> has an Auto Parts Workers United campaign. Many jobs have been lost in this sector due to imports and the global financial crisis. Should workers in this sector see cuts in their wages and pensions?

manufactured by Newmarket-based Trillium Health Care Products. This contract makes Trillium—already the leader in making private-label soap for retailers—the second- or third-largest bar soap maker on the continent.[20] Canada is one of the top IT outsourcing destinations in the world, especially for the United States. Reasons noted for why U.S. companies will outsource to Canada include: availability of highly skilled IT professionals, stable workforce without high attrition rates, similar culture and language, familiarity with American business processes, same time zones allowing for real time communication, and an excellent communication system between the two countries.[21]

There can be instances, however, when jobs do not need to be lost to foreign locations. When the Bank of Montreal (BMO) outsourced its human resource processing services to California-based Exult Inc., it negotiated an unusual condition: take our business, take our people. As part of this $75-million-a-year contract for the next ten years, more than 100 former BMO employees now work for Exult in the same office tower. Exult sees this as an excellent opportunity to expand its business in Canada, and these new employees have a mandate to bring in more Canadian clients.[22] Unfortunately, examples such as this are not the norm.

Canada's Auto Industry[23] The auto industry is critical to Canada's manufacturing economy. According to the Canadian Vehicle Manufacturers' Association, the auto sector is Canada's biggest contributor to manufacturing gross domestic product (GDP) and its largest manufacturing employer, employing one out of every seven Canadians. The industry supports jobs across Canada in 13 assembly plants, more than 540 parts manufacturers, 3,900 dealerships, and many other related industries.

It is no wonder that this industry is Canada's largest, both domestically and in exports (recall the value of these exports from Chapter 3). As well, it should be of no surprise that this industry has also faced increased competition from international players. In recent years, faced with relatively high labour and pension costs, plants have closed, eliminating thousands of jobs. Other than Toyota in Cambridge and Woodstock, and Honda in Alliston (all these locations are in Ontario), plant expansion projects have gone south of the border.

To potential investors, Canada offers cost advantages due to our public medicare program and, until a few years ago, a low currency. However, southern U.S. states such as Alabama, Georgia, and Mississippi are luring billions of dollars' worth of auto industry assembly plants with more attractive incentives, including land and training. These incentives are also starting to be offered to parts makers. To respond to the decreasing trend in new auto investments, a joint industry–government council was established. A major goal of the Canadian Automotive Partnership Council (CAPC) is to improve the future of the assembly industry. The Council has acknowledged tax cuts and provincial government support for investment in environmental research as important to the survival of this industry in Canada. Time will tell if such initiatives will improve the industry's health.

Taking Operations Management to the Internet

Many rapidly growing companies do very little production themselves. Instead, they outsource engineering, design, manufacturing, and other tasks to other companies that specialize in those functions. They create new relationships with suppliers over the Internet, making operations management an *inter-firm* process in which companies work closely together to design, produce, and ship products to customers.

Many manufacturing companies are developing Internet-focused strategies that will enable them and others to compete more effectively in the future.[24] These changes are having a dramatic effect on operations managers as they adjust from a one-firm system to an *inter-firm* environment and from a relatively stable environment to one that is constantly changing and evolving. This linking of firms is called *supply chain management*. We will briefly introduce you to this concept later in the chapter.

Facility Location in the Future

Information technology (IT), that is, computers, modems, e-mail, voice mail, text messaging, and teleconferencing, is giving firms and employees increased flexibility to choose locations while staying in the competitive mainstream. As we noted in Appendix A, telecommuting, working from home via computer and modem, is a major trend in business.[25] Companies that no longer need to locate near sources of labour will be able to move to areas where land is less expensive and the quality of life may be nicer. Furthermore, more salespeople are keeping in touch with the company and its customers through teleconferencing, using computers to talk with and show images to others.[26]

One big incentive to locate or relocate in a particular city or province is the tax situation and degree of government support. Those with lower taxes, such as Alberta, may be more attractive to companies. Some provinces and local governments have higher taxes than others, yet many engage in fierce competition by offering companies tax reductions and other support, such as zoning changes and financial aid, so they will locate there. See the Reaching Beyond Our Borders box at the end of this part to explore how one company has handled the complex role of handling production facilities all over the world.

Facility Layout

Facility layout is the physical arrangement of resources, including people, to most efficiently produce goods and provide services to customers. Facility layout depends greatly on the processes that are to be performed. For services, the layout is usually

facility layout
The physical arrangement of resources (including people) in the production process.

▸ At Cisco Systems, work spaces in some offices are fluid and unassigned, so employees with laptops and mobile phones can choose where to sit when they arrive each day. What do you think are some of the advantages of such non-traditional facility layouts? Are there any disadvantages?

designed to help the consumer find and buy things, including on the Internet. Some stores have added kiosks that enable customers to search for goods online and place orders or make returns and credit payments in the store. In short, the facilities and Internet capabilities of service organizations are becoming more customer-oriented.

Some service-oriented organizations, such as hospitals, use layouts that improve the efficiency, just as manufacturers do. For manufacturing plants, facilities layout has become critical because the possible cost savings are enormous.

Many companies are moving from an *assembly-line layout,* in which workers do only a few tasks at a time, to a *modular layout,* in which *teams* of workers combine to produce more complex units of the final product.[27] There may have been a dozen or more workstations on an assembly line to complete an automobile engine in the past, but all of that work may be done in one module today.

When working on a major project, such as a bridge or airplane, companies use a *fixed-position layout* that allows workers to congregate around the product to be completed.

A *process layout* is one in which similar equipment and functions are grouped together. The order in which the product visits a function depends on the design of the item. This allows for flexibility. The Igus <*www.igus.com*> manufacturing plant in Cologne, Germany, can shrink or expand in a flash. Its flexible design keeps it competitive in a fast-changing market. Because the layout of the plant changes so often, some employees use scooters to more efficiently provide needed skills, supplies, and services to multiple workstations. A fast-changing plant needs a fast-moving employee base to achieve maximum productivity. Figure 10.3 illustrates typical layout designs.

Figure 10.3

Typical Layout Designs

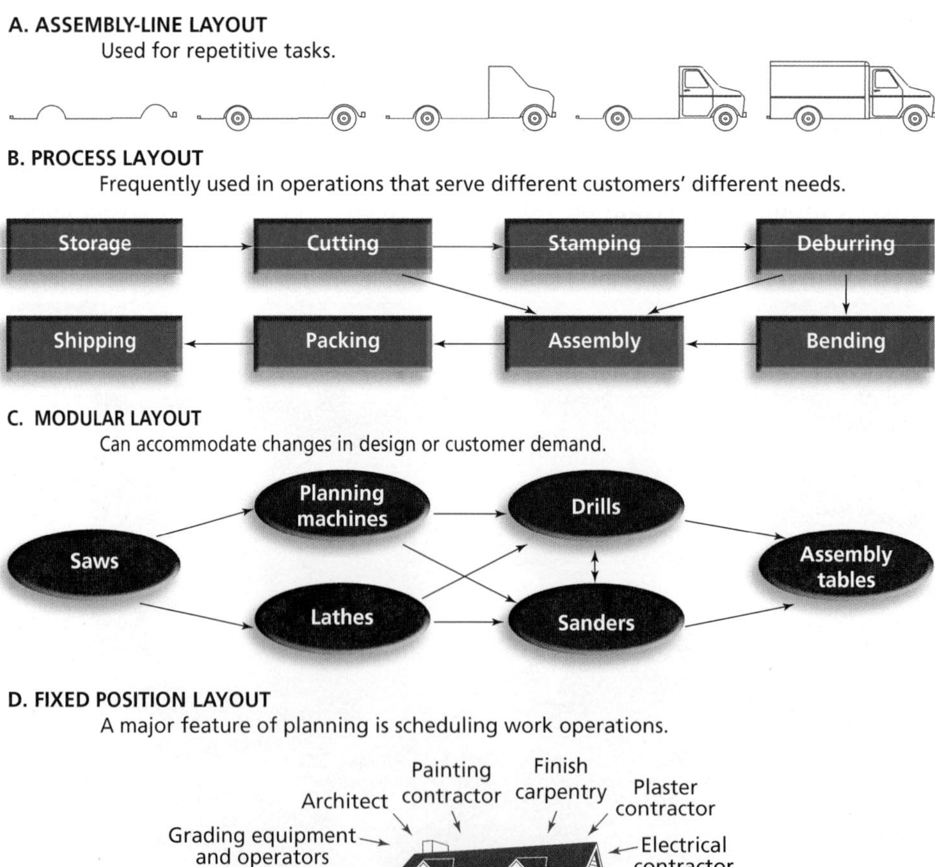

Statistical quality control (SQC) is the process that some managers use to continually monitor all phases of the production process and assure quality is being built into the product from the beginning. Statistical process control (SPC) is the process of testing statistical samples of product components at each stage of production and plotting the test results on a graph. Managers can thus see and correct any deviation from quality standards. Making sure products meet standards all along the production process reduces the need for a quality control inspection at the end because mistakes are caught much earlier in the process. SQC and SPC thus save companies much time and money. Some companies use a quality control approach called the Deming cycle (after the late W. Edwards Deming, the father of the movement toward quality).[28] Its steps are: Plan, Do, Check, Act (PDCA). Again, the idea is to find potential errors *before* they happen. Deming's approach, including implementing standards, was used for many years before the International Organization for Standardization (ISO), which we will talk about shortly, came into being.

statistical quality control (SQC)
The process that some managers use to continually monitor all phases of the production process to ensure that quality is being built into the product from the beginning.

statistical process control (SPC)
The process of taking statistical samples of product components at each stage of the production process and plotting those results on a graph. Any variances from quality standards are recognized and can be corrected if beyond the set standards.

Materials Requirement Planning (MRP)

Materials requirement planning (MRP) is a computer-based operations management system that uses sales forecasts to ensure that needed parts and materials are available at the right time and place. In a diner, for example, we could feed the sales forecast into the computer, which would specify how many eggs and how much coffee to order and then print out the proper scheduling and routing sequence. The same can be done with the seats and other parts of an automobile. In the next section, you will read how just-in-time inventory control has a similar objective.

materials requirement planning (MRP)
A computer-based production management system that uses sales forecasts to make sure that needed parts and materials are available at the right time and place.

Enterprise resource planning (ERP), a newer version of MRP, combines the computerized functions of all the divisions and subsidiaries of the firm—such as finance, human resources, and order fulfillment—into a single integrated software program that uses a single database (see Figure 10.4). The result is shorter time between orders and payment, less staff to do ordering and order processing, reduced inventories, and better customer service. For example, the customer can place an order, either through a customer service representative or online, and immediately see when the order will be filled and how much it will cost. The representative can instantly see the customer's credit rating and order history, the company's inventory, and the shipping schedule. Everyone else in the company can see the new order as well; thus when one department finishes its portion, the order is automatically routed via the ERP system to the next department. The customer can see exactly where the order is at any point by logging into the system.

enterprise resource planning (ERP)
A computer application that enables multiple firms to manage all of their operations (finance, requirements planning, human resources, and order fulfillment) on the basis of a single, integrated set of corporate data.

By entering customer and sales information in an ERP system, a manufacturer can generate the next period's demand forecast, which in turn generates orders for raw materials, production scheduling, and financial projections.

ERP software enables the firm to monitor quality and customer satisfaction as it is happening. ERP systems are going global now that the Internet is powerful enough to handle the data flows. At the plant level, dynamic performance monitoring enables plant operators to monitor the use of power, chemicals, and other resources and to make needed adjustments. In short, flows to, through, and from plants have become automated.

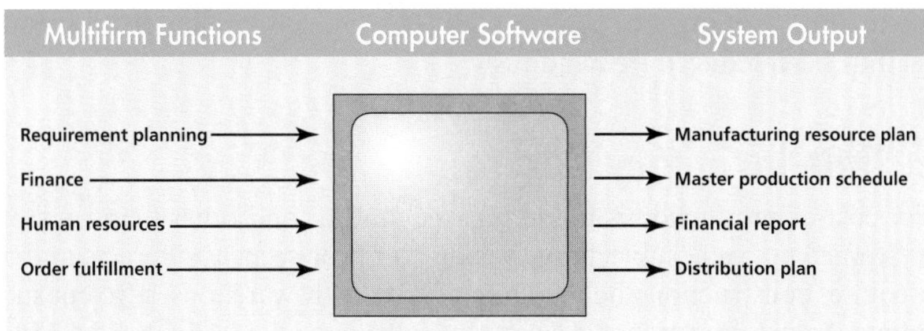

Figure 10.4
Enterprise Resource Planning

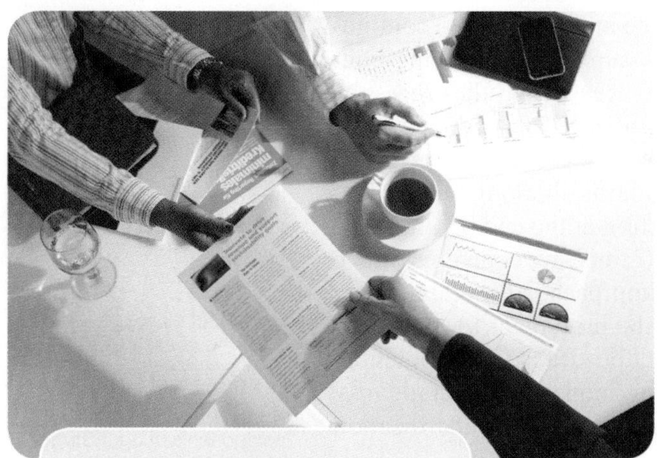

▶ SAS <*www.sas.com*> is the leading provider for business analytics that help users maximize the value of their ERP systems. SAS Business Analytics helps organizations make decisions faster with more accuracy and confidence.

Some firms are providing a service called sequential delivery. These firms are suppliers that provide components in an order sequenced to their customers' production process. For example, Ford's seat supplier loads seats onto a truck such that, when off-loaded, the seats are in perfect sequence for the type of vehicle coming down the assembly line.

While ERP can be an effective tool, it also can have its problems. The Royal Canadian Mint <*www.mint.ca*> was having difficulties extracting and manipulating data. Departments were operated independently, and because it took so long to produce reports for analysis, employees did not trust the reliability of the information once it was in their hands. "Anyone who has used an ERP system knows that reporting can be problematic," says Azfar Ali Khan, director of operations and systems at the Mint's sales and marketing departments. "They're wonderful transactional engines, but getting the richness of the data in front of the people in a context they can understand is particularly challenging."[29]

Information technology (IT) has had a major influence on the entire production process, from purchasing to final delivery. Many IT advances have been add-ons to ERP. To solve its difficulties, the Mint turned to Cognos <*www.cognos.com*> for its enterprise solution. Cognos's Analytic Applications solution made it possible for users to access data right to the day, as well as to create new reporting opportunities. The Mint's self-service, web-enabled, enterprise-wide solution has allowed it to act quickly and thereby improve customer service. According to Ali Khan, "Buying a prepackaged solution and customizing it to our own unique business requirements has saved us a lot of time and a lot of money."[30]

Purchasing

purchasing
The functional area in a firm that searches for quality material resources, finds the best suppliers, and negotiates the best price for goods and services.

Purchasing is the function that searches for high-quality material resources, finds the best suppliers, and negotiates the best price for quality goods and services. In the past, manufacturers dealt with many suppliers so that if one could not deliver, the firm could get materials from someone else. Today, however, manufacturers rely more heavily on just one or two suppliers, because the relationship between suppliers and manufacturers is much closer than before.[31] Producers share so much information that they do not want too many suppliers knowing their business. The Hudson's Bay Company <*www.hbc.com*> shifted to single merchandise buyers for a growing number of departments at its Bay, Zellers, and Home Outfitters chains. This move was designed to help improve product selection and save money through less duplication and larger purchase orders.[32]

The Internet has transformed the purchasing function. A business looking for supplies can contact an Internet-based purchasing service and find the best items at the best price. Similarly, a company wishing to sell supplies can use the Internet to find all companies looking for such supplies. The time and dollar cost of purchasing items has thus been reduced tremendously.

Just-in-Time Inventory Control

just-in-time (JIT) inventory control
A production process in which a minimum of inventory is kept on the premises and parts, supplies, and other needs are delivered just in time to go on the assembly line.

One major cost of production is holding parts, motors, and other items in storage for later use. Storage not only subjects such items to obsolescence, pilferage, and damage, but also requires construction and maintenance of costly warehouses. To cut such costs, many companies have implemented a concept called **just-in-time (JIT) inventory control**.

JIT systems keep a minimum of inventory on the premises and delivers parts, supplies, and other needs just in time to go on the assembly line. To work effectively, however, the process requires an accurate production schedule (using ERP) and excellent coordination with carefully selected suppliers, who are usually connected electronically so they know what is needed and when. Sometimes the supplier builds new facilities close to the main producer to minimize distribution time. JIT runs into problems when suppliers are farther away. Weather may delay shipments, for example.

With more than $1.9 billion in goods and more than 300,000 people moving across the Canada–U.S. border each day, the efficient flow of products and people is vital to Canada's economy.[33] Any delays require that companies adjust their JIT schedules. Today, the longer delays at borders due to increased traffic and security measures have forced companies to do just that. Other limitations are that JIT works best with standard products, demand needs to be high and stable to justify the cost and savings, and suppliers need to be extremely reliable.

JIT systems ensure that the right materials are at the right place at the right time at the cheapest cost to meet both customer and production needs. That is a key step in modern production innovation.

▸ Huge warehouses such as the one depicted in the photo would become a thing of the past if all companies implemented just-in-time (JIT) inventory control. What are the advantages and disadvantages of having large amounts of inventory available?

Quality Control

Maintaining **quality** means consistently producing what the customer wants while reducing errors before and after delivery to the customer. In the past, firms often conducted quality control at the end of the production line. Products were completed *and then tested* for quality. This resulted in several problems:

1. The need to inspect work required extra people and resources.
2. If an error was found, someone had to correct the mistake or scrap the product. This, of course, was costly.
3. If the customer found the mistake, he or she might be dissatisfied and might even buy from another firm thereafter.

Such problems led to the realization that quality is not an outcome; it is a never-ending process of continually improving what a company produces. Quality control should thus be part of the operations management planning process rather than simply an end-of-the-line inspection.

Companies have turned to the use of modern quality control standards, such as Six Sigma. **Six Sigma quality**, which sets a benchmark of just 3.4 defects per million opportunities, detects potential problems to prevent their occurrence. That is important to a company that makes 4 million transactions a day, like some banks. The Spotlight on Small Business box explores how small businesses can apply Six Sigma to their operations.

Businesses are getting serious about providing top customer service, and many are already doing it. Service organizations find it difficult to provide outstanding service every time because the process is so labour intensive. Physical goods (e.g., a gold ring) can be designed and manufactured to near perfection. However, it is hard to reach such perfection when designing and providing a service experience such as a dance on a cruise ship or a cab drive through Vancouver.

▸ What happens when you combine the zeal of technical innovators with the Six Sigma discipline of a large company like General Electric? You get a medical breakthrough. Janet Burki and her 280-person operations team developed the world's fastest CT scanner. It works ten times faster than other systems and produces clear 3-D images of the beating heart. Can you see how efforts to build in quality lead to better (and faster) products?

SPOTLIGHT ON SMALL BUSINESS

Meeting the Six Sigma Standard

Six Sigma is a quality measure that allows only 3.4 defects per million opportunities. Here is how Six Sigma works: If you can make it to the level of one sigma, two out of three products will meet specifications. If you can reach the two sigma level, then more than 95 percent of products will qualify. But when you meet six-sigma quality, as we have said, you have only 3.4 defects in a million opportunities (which means that 99.99966 percent of your products will qualify), a quality standard that approaches perfection. Service organizations are also adopting Six Sigma standards through the elimination of any activity involved with the service they provide that does not add value to the customer.

It is one thing for Motorola <*www.motorola.com*> (often cited as the driving force behind the development of this standard) or General Electric (GE) to reach for such standards given their vast resources, but what about a small company like Dolan Industries? Dolan is a 41-person manufacturer of fasteners. It spent a few years trying to meet ISO 9000 standards, which are comparable to Six Sigma. Dolan had to do that because its customers were demanding that level of quality.

Small companies can successfully implement Six Sigma if the owner is committed, the company has a routine core of work that can benefit, and the company's culture is open to change. Any change that is part of a Six Sigma project should not be so significant that any problem would have a major impact on customer relations. As a rule of thumb a small business can begin deploying Six Sigma when one employee can devote one day per week to this work, which represents 0.5 to 1 percent of employee hours (i.e., a minimum of 20 employees is required, which results in combined work hours of 800—based on 8 hour days). They should invest in software and books on the subject, access outside expertise, and pursue each project aggressively—completing most projects in four to six weeks.

Sources: Thomas Pyzdek, "A Roadmap for Deploying Six Sigma in Small Businesses," 26 February 2010, www.isixsigma.com/implementation/basics/roadmap-dploying-six-sigma-small-businesses.

quality Consistently producing what the customer wants while reducing errors before and after delivery to the customer.

Six Sigma quality A quality measure that allows only 3.4 defects per million events.

Quality Award: The Canada Awards for Excellence[34]

Excellence Canada <*www.nqi.com*> is the leading authority in Canada on workplace excellence based on quality systems and healthy workplace criteria. The Canada Awards for Excellence (CAE) are presented annually to private, public, and not-for-profit organizations that have displayed outstanding performance in the areas of quality and healthy workplace. The award has honoured hundreds of Canadian organizations, including Bombardier Inc., Canada Post <*www.canadapost.ca*>, Delta Hotels <*www.deltahotels.com*>, and Glen Park Public School. Recent recipients include Baxter Corporation <*www.baxter.ca*>, Bridgestone Canada <*www.bridgestonetire.ca*>,

▸ Excellence Canada (formally the National Quality Institute) is an independent, not-for-profit organization founded by Industry Canada. They help companies understand and apply a focus on excellence through the adoption of the Canadian Framework for Business Excellence. This approach will help companies reduce rework, waste, and costs while improving productivity and competitiveness. Do you see how this framework incorporates principles discussed in this textbook?

Hill & Knowlton Strategies <*www.hkstrategies.ca*>, and the Children's Aid Society of Peel <*www.peelcas.org*>. Other CAE awards include Healthy Workplace, Customer Service, and Health Care. For more information, visit *www.nqi.ca*.

ISO 9000 and ISO 14000 Standards

The International Organization for Standardization (ISO) is a worldwide federation of national standards bodies from more than 140 countries that set the global measures for the quality of individual products. ISO is a non-governmental organization established in 1947 to promote the development of world standards to facilitate the international exchange of goods and services. (ISO is not an acronym. It comes from the Greek word *isos,* meaning oneness.) **ISO 9000** is the common name given to quality management and assurance standards. Some of the latest standards include ISO 9004:2008.

ISO 9000
The common name given to quality management and assurance standards.

The standards require that a company must determine what customer needs are, including regulatory and legal requirements, and make communication arrangements to handle issues such as complaints.[35] Other standards involve process control, product testing, storage, and delivery. Improving quality is an investment that can pay off in better customer relations and higher sales.[36]

It is important to know that ISO did not start as a quality certification, the way many people think. In the beginning, it simply meant that your process was under control. In short, it looked to see that companies were consistently producing the same products each time. There is a difference between consistency (flawed products every time) and quality (products free from defects). Today, ISO has developed over 17,000 international standards and 1,100 new standards are published every year.[37]

What makes ISO 9000 so important is that the European Union (EU) demands that companies that want to do business with the EU be certified by ISO standards. Some major Canadian companies are also demanding that suppliers meet these standards. Several accreditation agencies in Europe and in North America will certify that a company meets the standards for all phases of its operations, from product development through production and testing to installation. SNC-Lavalin Group Inc., one of the leading groups of engineering and construction companies in the world, has met such standards. It provides engineering, procurement, construction, project management, and project financing services to a variety of industry sectors in more than 120 countries. The Quality Policy at SNC-Lavalin is to "achieve client satisfaction through the careful management of our work processes, with due attention to value creation through scope, schedule, cost control, and with emphasis on safety and the environment." To best serve its various stakeholders, the company has implemented Client Satisfaction and Continual Improvement Programs in every division, business unit, geographic office, and subsidiary. These programs are based on the applicable requirements of ISO 9001 International Standard for Quality Management Systems.[38]

ISO 14000 is a collection of the best practices for managing an organization's impact on the environment. As an environmental management system, it does not prescribe a performance level. Requirements for certification include having an environmental policy, having specific improvement targets, conducting audits of environmental programs, and maintaining top management review of the processes.

ISO 14000
A collection of the best practices for managing an organization's impact on the environment.

Certification in both ISO 9000 and ISO 14000 would show that a firm has a world-class management system in both quality and environmental standards. In the past, firms assigned employees separately to meet each set of standards. Today, ISO 9000 and ISO 14000 standards have been blended so that an organization can work on both at once. ISO is now working on ISO 26000 standards, which are designed to give guidance on social responsibility.[39]

Supply Chain Management

logistics
Those activities that focus on getting the right amount of the right products or services to the right place at the right time at the lowest possible cost.

supply chain
The sequence of firms that perform activities required to create and deliver a good or service to consumers or industrial users.

supply chain management
The integration and organization of information and logistics activities across firms in a supply chain for the purpose of creating and delivering goods and services that provide value to customers.

Before we discuss this next topic, it is important to introduce some terms. **Logistics** involves those activities that focus on getting the right amount of the right products or services to the right place at the right time at the lowest possible cost. A **supply chain** is a sequence of firms that perform activities required to create and deliver a good or service to consumers or industrial users. Some companies have been successful in attracting more customers due to their supply chain management efficiencies. **Supply chain management** is the integration and organization of information and logistics activities *across* firms in a supply chain for the purpose of creating and delivering goods and services that provide value to customers.

Facilities included in supply chain management include factories, processing centres, warehouses, distribution centres, and retail outlets (Figure 10.5). Functions and activities include forecasting, purchasing, inventory management, information management, quality assurance, scheduling, production, delivery, and customer service. Today, the major factors contributing to the importance of supply chain management include the need for improvement to remain competitive, the increase in outsourcing, shorter product life cycles and increased customization, increase in globalization, the growth of technology and e-commerce, the increase in complexity through JIT inventory, and the need for better management of inventories. When implementing supply chain management, firms are trying to improve quality, reduce costs, increase flexibility and speed, and improve customer service while reducing the number of suppliers used. Two examples follow:

- Canadian National Railway (CNR) purchased supply chain management planning software from i2 Technologies <*www.jda.com*> to manage its intermodal business. CNR has 10,000 freight cars and 7,000 containers that it owns, along with equipment belonging to shippers and other railways. While implementing this software is still a work in progress, CNR expects to increase the level of speed and reliability of hauling containers and truck trailers from ports and major cities across North America.[40]
- Only Canada's Armed Forces surpasses the Cirque du Soleil in terms of the level of supply chain and logistics planning required to deploy large amounts of equipment, supplies, and people all over the world. According to Guy Migneron, director of international headquarters operations for Cirque du Soleil, "We use computers for a lot of what we do." The planning and logistics work for each performance begins 12 to 18 months before the first act enters the tent.[41]

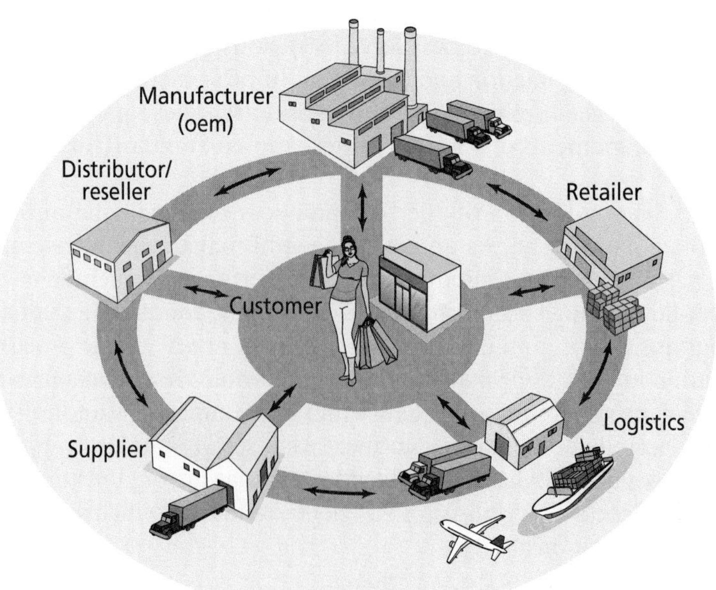

Figure 10.5

Supply Chain Management
This is an image of supply chain management showing the interrelationships between all of the types of firms involved in the provision of a good or a service to a customer.

PROGRESS ASSESSMENT

- Can you name and define three functions that are common to operations management in both the service and the manufacturing sectors?
- What are the major criteria for facility location?
- What is the difference between materials resource planning (MRP) and enterprise resource planning (ERP)?
- What is just-in-time inventory control?
- What is involved in implementing each of the following: Six Sigma, SQC, SPC, ISO 9000, and ISO 14000?

PRODUCTION PROCESSES

Identify various production processes and describe techniques to improve productivity including flexible manufacturing, lean manufacturing, mass customization, and computer-aided design and manufacturing

Common sense and some experience have already taught you much of what you need to know about production processes. You know what it takes to write a term paper or prepare a dinner. You need money to buy the materials, you need a place to work, and you need to be organized to get the task done. The same is true of the production process in industry. It uses basic inputs to produce outputs (see Figure 10.6). Production adds value, or utility, to materials or processes.

Form utility is the value producers add to materials in the creation of finished goods and services, such as the transformation of silicon into computer chips or putting services together to create a vacation package. Form utility can exist at the retail level as well. For example, a butcher can produce a specific cut of beef from a whole cow or a baker can make a specific type of cake out of basic ingredients.

form utility
The value added by the creation of finished goods and services.

To be competitive, manufacturers must keep the costs of inputs down. That is, the costs of workers, machinery, and so on must be kept as low as possible. Similarly, the amount of output must be relatively high. The question today is: How does a producer keep costs low and still increase output? This question will dominate thinking in the manufacturing and service sectors for years to come. In the next few sections, we explore production processes and the latest technology being used to cut costs.

Manufacturers use several different processes to produce goods. Andrew S. Grove, chairman of computer chip manufacturer Intel, uses a great analogy to explain production:

> *Imagine that you're a chef . . . and that your task is to serve a breakfast consisting of a three-minute soft-boiled egg, buttered toast, and coffee. Your job is to prepare and deliver the three items simultaneously, each of them fresh and hot.*

Grove says this task encompasses the three basic requirements of production: (1) to build and deliver products in response to the demands of the customer at a

Figure 10.6

The Production Process

The production process consists of taking the factors of production (land, etc.) and using those inputs to produce goods, services, and ideas. Planning, routing, scheduling, and the other activities are the means to accomplish the objective—output.

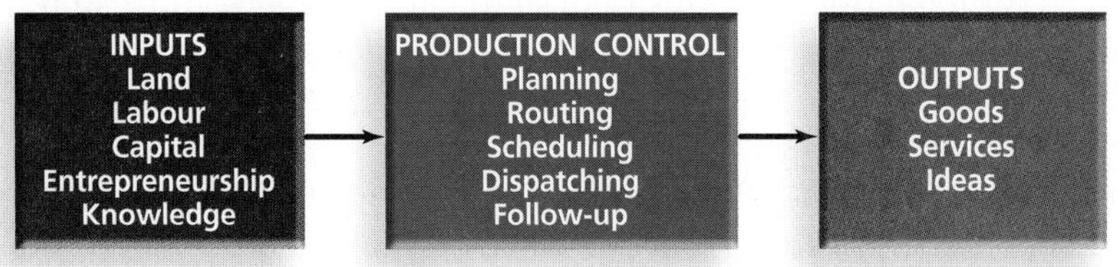

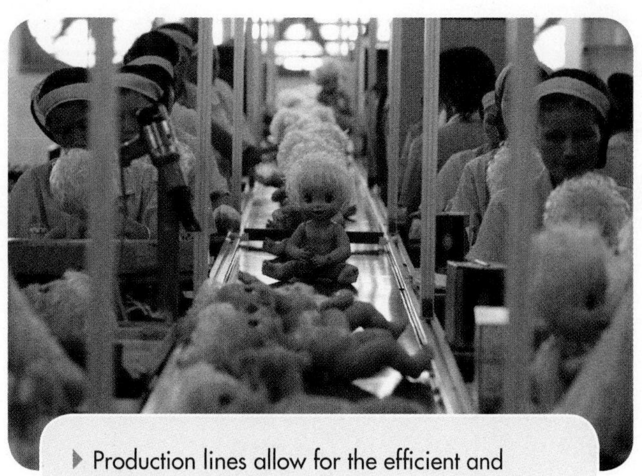

Production lines allow for the efficient and speedy production of goods that are consistent in size, weight, colour, and other measures of quality. How many products can you think of that are likely made on a production line?

scheduled delivery time, (2) to provide an acceptable quality level, and (3) to provide everything at the lowest possible cost.

Let's use the breakfast example to understand process and assembly. **Process manufacturing** physically or chemically changes materials. For example, boiling physically changes the egg. (Similarly, process manufacturing turns sand into glass or computer chips.) The **assembly process** puts together components (eggs, toast, and coffee) to make a product (breakfast). Cars are made through an assembly process that puts together the frame, engine, and other parts.

Production processes are either continuous or intermittent. A **continuous process** is one in which long production runs (lots of eggs) turn out finished goods over time. As the chef, you could have a conveyor belt that lowers eggs into boiling water for three minutes and then lifts them out. A three-minute egg would be available whenever you want. A chemical plant, for example, is run on a continuous process.

process manufacturing
That part of the production process that physically or chemically changes materials.

assembly process
That part of the production process that puts together components.

continuous process
A production process in which long production runs turn out finished goods over time.

intermittent process
A production process in which the production run is short and the machines are changed frequently to make different products.

It usually makes more sense when responding to specific customer orders to use an **intermittent process**. Here the production run is short (one or two eggs) and the producer adjusts machines frequently to make different products (like the oven in a bakery or the toaster in the diner). Manufacturers of custom-designed furniture would use an intermittent process.

An example of a product that uses both long and short production runs is Kodiak boots, which for the first time in nine years are being produced in Canada: "At the end of the day, we're going to service customers a lot better through this core Canadian production," says Kevin Huckle, president of Kodiak Group Holdings Inc., which plans to do a third of its production in Canada. Domestic production offers quick, efficient service for Canadian retailers, who may require only small numbers of boots, but need them in a hurry. With Asian production, he has to contract for long production runs—more than 1,200 pairs—and has to carry a lot of inventory. With domestic manufacturing, the plant keeps enough materials around for relatively short runs. Because of automation and location, it can turn around Canadian production orders in 21 days, compared with 90 days for orders in Asia.[42]

Today, many new manufacturers use intermittent processes. Computers, robots, and flexible manufacturing processes allow firms to turn out custom-made goods as fast as mass-produced goods were produced.[43] We'll discuss how they do that in more detail in the next few sections as we explore advanced production techniques and technology.

IMPROVING PRODUCTION TECHNIQUES AND CUTTING COSTS

The ultimate goal of operations management is to provide high-quality goods and services instantaneously in response to customer demand. As we stress throughout this book, traditional organizations were simply not designed to be so responsive to the customer. Rather, they were designed to make goods efficiently (inexpensively). The idea behind mass production was to make a large number of a limited variety of products at very low cost.

Over the years, low cost often came at the expense of quality and flexibility. Furthermore, suppliers did not always deliver when they said they would, so manufacturers had to carry large inventories of raw materials and components to keep producing. Such inefficiencies made companies vulnerable to foreign competitors that were using more advanced production techniques.

As a result of global competition, companies have had to make a wide variety of high-quality, custom-designed products at very low cost. Clearly, something had to change on the production floor to make that possible. Several major developments have made companies more competitive: (1) flexible manufacturing, (2) lean manufacturing, (3) mass customization, and (4) computer-aided design and manufacturing.

Flexible Manufacturing

Flexible manufacturing means designing machines to do multiple tasks so that they can produce a variety of products. Flexible manufacturing (also known as flex) not only leads to improved productivity, but it may also result in cost savings. Frank Gourneau, plant manager at Ford Motor Company of Canada Ltd., calls the $1-billion Oakville complex "a game changer" and a "jewel" with all the latest advances in auto technology. The first phase of the plant started production in 2006. According to Gourneau, "Undergoing major model changes in traditional plants means weeks of downtime and millions spent on new tooling and equipment. Once a flexible body shop is installed, downtime is reduced dramatically and the equipment changes consist mainly of reprogramming robots. The point is to be able to cease assembly of one model on a Friday and start a new one on a Monday, instead of six, eight or 10 weeks later."[44] Gourneau estimates productivity will improve at least 20 percent in the new plant and the company expects to achieve $2 billion in production cost savings alone during the next decade.[45]

flexible manufacturing
Designing machines to do multiple tasks so that they can produce a variety of products.

Allen-Bradley, part of Rockwell Automation, uses flexible manufacturing to build motor starters. Orders come in daily, and within 24 hours the company's 26 machines and robots manufacture, test, and package the starters—which are untouched by human hands. Allen-Bradley's machines are so flexible that managers can include a special order, even a single item, in the assembly without slowing down the process. Did you notice that these products were made without any labour? One way to compete with cheap labour is to have as few workers as possible.

Lean Manufacturing

Lean manufacturing is the production of goods using less of everything compared to mass production: less human effort, less manufacturing space, less investment in tools, and less engineering time to develop a new product. A company becomes lean by continuously increasing its capacity to produce high-quality goods while decreasing its need for resources.[46] Here are some characteristics of lean companies:[47]

lean manufacturing
The production of goods using less of everything compared to mass production.

- They take half the human effort.[48]
- They have half the defects in the finished product or service.
- They require one-third the engineering effort.
- They use half the floor space for the same output.
- They carry 90 percent less inventory.

Technological improvements are largely responsible for the increase in productivity and efficiency of Canadian plants. That technology made labour more productive and made it possible to pay higher rates. On the other hand, employees can get frustrated by innovations (e.g., they must learn new processes), and companies must constantly train and retrain employees to stay competitive.[49] The need for more productivity and efficiency has never been greater. The solution to the economic crisis depends on such innovations. One step in the process is to make products more individualistic. The next section discusses how that happens.

Mass Customization

mass customization Tailoring products to meet the needs of individual customers.

computer-aided design (CAD) The use of computers in the design of products.

computer-aided manufacturing (CAM) The use of computers in the manufacturing of products.

To *customize* means to make a unique good or provide a specific service to an individual. Although it once may have seemed impossible, **mass customization**, which means tailoring products to meet the needs of a large number of individual customers, is now practised widely. The National Bicycle Industrial Company in Japan made 18 bicycle models in more than 2 million combinations, each designed to fit the needs of a specific customer. The customer chose the model, size, colour, and design. The retailer took various measurements from the buyer and faxed the data to the factory, where robots handled the bulk of the assembly. Thus, flexible manufacturing (discussed earlier) is one of the factors that makes mass customization possible.

More and more manufacturers are learning to customize their products. For example, Indochino <*www.indochino.com*> was recently voted the most popular custom online clothing store. Consumers can order custom-made suits, shirts, blazers, and coats, along with pants and have them delivered within three weeks.[50] You can even buy custom-made M&Ms.[51]

Mass customization can be used in the service sector as well. Health clubs offer unique fitness programs for individuals, travel agencies provide vacation packages that vary according to individual choices, and some schools allow students to design their own majors. Actually, it is much easier to custom-design service programs than it is to custom-make goods, because there is no fixed tangible good that has to be adapted. Each customer can specify what he or she wants, within the limits of the service organization—limits that seem to be ever widening.

▸ 3-D tools allow designers to create cloth prototypes without a pattern's traditional stages (seaming, trying on, alternations, etc.). What advantages might this technology offer to smaller manufacturing companies?

Computer-Aided Design and Manufacturing

The one development that has changed production techniques more than any other has been the integration of computers into the design and manufacturing of products. The first thing computers did was help in the design of products, in a process called **computer-aided design (CAD)**. Today CAD systems allow designers to work in three dimensions.

The next step was to bring computers directly in the production process with **computer-aided manufacturing (CAM)**. CAD/CAM, the use of both computer-aided design and computer-aided manufacturing made it possible to custom-design products to meet the needs of small markets with very little increase in cost. A manufacturer programs the computer to make a simple design change, and that change is directly incorporated into production. In the clothing industry, a computer program establishes a pattern and cuts the cloth automatically, even adjusting to a specific person's dimensions to create custom-cut clothing at little additional cost. In food service, CAM supports on-site, small-scale, semi-automated, sensor-controlled baking in fresh-baked cookie shops to make consistent quality easy to achieve.

CAD has doubled productivity in many firms. But in the past CAD machines could not talk to CAM machines directly. Today, however, software programs unite CAD with CAM: the result is **computer-integrated manufacturing (CIM)**. The software is expensive, but it cuts as much as 80 percent of the time needed to program machines to make parts. The printing company JohnsByrne uses CIM in its Niles, Illinois, plant and has noticed a decreased cost in overhead, reduced outlay of resources, and fewer errors. You can consult the *International Journal of Computer-Integrated Manufacturing* for other examples.

computer-integrated manufacturing (CIM) The uniting of computer-aided design with computer-aided manufacturing.

program evaluation and review technique (PERT) A method for analyzing the tasks involved in completing a given project, estimating the time needed to complete each task, and identifying the minimum time needed to complete the total project.

PROGRESS ASSESSMENT

- What are three basic requirements of production?
- Define and differentiate the following: process manufacturing, assembly process, continuous process, and intermittent process.
- How does flexible manufacturing differ from lean manufacturing?
- What are CAD, CAM, and CIM?

CONTROL PROCEDURES: PERT AND GANTT CHARTS

Explain the use of PERT and Gantt charts to control manufacturing processes.

Operations managers must ensure products are manufactured and delivered on time, on budget, and to specifications. How can managers be sure all will go smoothly and be completed by the required time? One popular technique for monitoring the progress of production was developed in the 1950s for constructing nuclear submarines: the **program evaluation and review technique (PERT)**. PERT users analyze the tasks to complete a given project, estimate the time needed to complete each, and compute the minimum time needed to complete the whole project.

The steps used in PERT are (1) analyzing and sequencing tasks that need to be done, (2) estimating the time needed to complete each task, (3) drawing a PERT network illustrating the information from steps 1 and 2, and (4) identifying the critical path. The **critical path** is the sequence of tasks that takes the longest time to complete. We use the word *critical* because a delay anywhere along this path will cause the project or production run to be late.

Figure 10.7 illustrates a PERT chart for producing a music video. The squares indicate completed tasks, and the arrows indicate the time needed to complete the next task. The path from one completed task to another illustrates the relationships among tasks; the arrow from "set designed" to "set materials purchased" indicates we

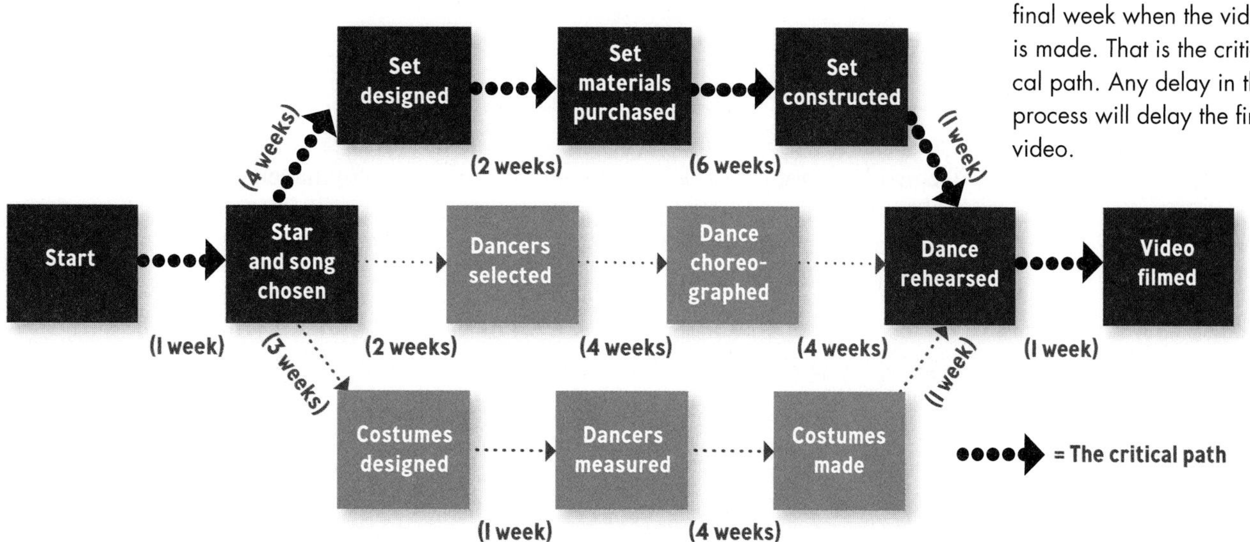

Figure 10.7

PERT Chart for a Music Video

The minimum amount of time it will take to produce this video is 15 weeks. To get that number, you add the week it takes to pick a star and a song to the four weeks to design a set, the two weeks to purchase set materials, the six weeks to construct the set, the week before rehearsals, and the final week when the video is made. That is the critical path. Any delay in that process will delay the final video.

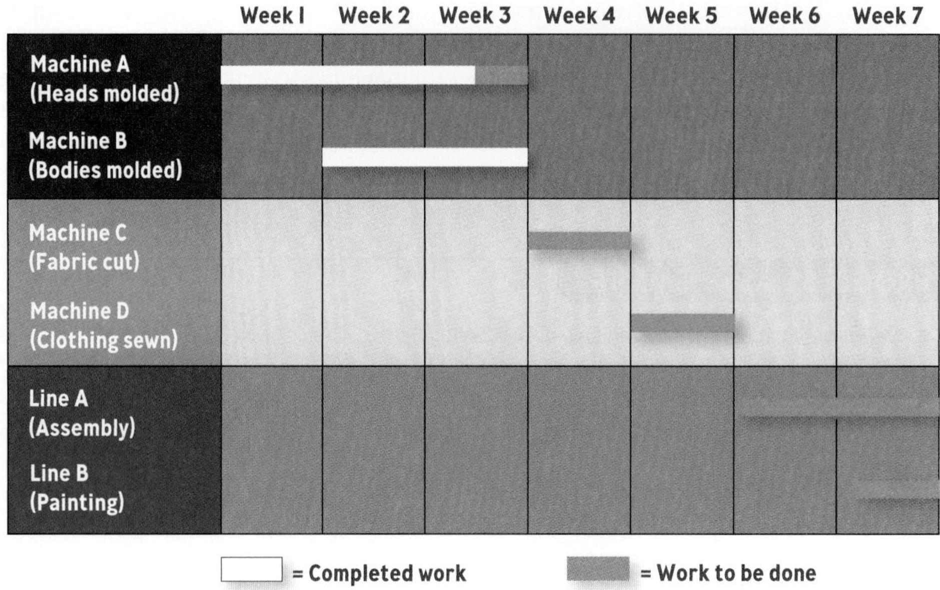

Figure 10.8

Gantt Chart for a Doll Manufacturer

A Gantt chart enables a production manager to see at a glance when projects are scheduled to be completed and what the status is now. For example, the dolls' heads and bodies should be completed before the clothing is sewn, but they could be a little late as long as everything is ready for assembly in week 6. This chart shows that at the end of week 3, the dolls' bodies are ready, but the heads are about half a week behind.

critical path
In a PERT network, the sequence of tasks that takes the longest time to complete.

Gantt chart
Bar graph showing production managers what projects are being worked on and what stage they are in at any given time.

must design the set before we can purchase the materials. The critical path, indicated by the bold black arrows, shows producing the set takes more time than auditioning dancers, choreographing dances, or designing and making costumes. The project manager now knows it is critical that set construction remain on schedule if the project is to be completed on time, but short delays in dance and costume preparation are unlikely to delay it.

A PERT network can be made up of thousands of events over many months. Today, this complex procedure is done by computer. Another, more basic strategy manufacturers use for measuring production progress is a Gantt chart. A **Gantt chart** (named for its developer, Henry L. Gantt) is a bar graph, now also prepared by computer, that clearly shows what projects are being worked on and how much has been completed at any given time. Figure 10.8, a Gantt chart for a doll manufacturer, shows that the dolls' heads and bodies should be completed before the clothing is sewn. It also shows that at the end of week 3, the dolls' bodies are ready, but the heads are about half a week behind. Using a Gantt-like computer program, a manager can trace the production process minute by minute to determine which tasks are on time and which are behind, so that adjustments can be made to allow the company to stay on schedule.

PREPARING FOR THE FUTURE

Canada is a major industrial country, but competition is growing stronger each year. Tremendous opportunities for careers in operations management as both manufacturing and service companies fight to stay competitive. Students who can see future trends and have the skills to own or work in tomorrow's highly automated factories and modern service facilities will benefit.

PROGRESS ASSESSMENT

- Draw a PERT chart for making a breakfast of three-minute eggs, buttered toast, and coffee. Define the critical path.
- How could you use a Gantt chart to keep track of production?

SUMMARY

Describe the current state of Canadian manufacturing and how companies are becoming more competitive.

Canada's industrial profile results in significant swings in activity and a number of challenges are faced in an increasingly competitive global environment.

Where is most of Canada's industry focused?
Most of our industry is focused on natural resources, which results in significant growth when world economies are growing, offset by significant retraction when the world economies are stagnant.

What have Canadian manufacturers done to achieve increased output?
Canadian manufacturers have increased output by emphasizing close relationships with suppliers and other companies to satisfy customer needs; continuous improvement; quality; site selection; and production techniques such as enterprise resource planning, computer-integrated manufacturing, flexible manufacturing, and lean manufacturing.

Describe the evolution from production to operations management.

Operations management is a specialized area in management that converts or transforms resources (including human resources) into goods and services.

What kinds of firms use operations managers?
Firms in both the manufacturing and the service sectors use operations managers.

Why is productivity so hard to measure?
The traditional way to measure productivity involves tracking inputs (worker hours) compared to outputs (dollars). Quality improvements are not weighed. New information systems must be developed to measure the quality of goods and services, the speed of their delivery, and customer satisfaction.

Describe operations management planning issues including facility location, facility layout, materials requirement planning, purchasing, just-in-time inventory control, quality control, and supply chain management.

Issues involved in both the manufacturing and the service sectors include facility location, facility layout, materials requirement planning, purchasing, just-in-time inventory control, quality control, and supply chain management.

What is facility location and how does it differ from facility layout?
Facility location is the process of selecting a geographic location for a company's operations. Facility layout is the physical arrangement of resources (including people) to produce goods and services effectively and efficiently.

Why is facility location so important, and what criteria are used to evaluate different sites?
The very survival of manufacturing depends on its ability to remain competitive, and that means either making inputs less costly (reducing costs of labour and land) or increasing outputs from present inputs (increasing productivity). Labour costs and land costs are two major criteria for selecting the right sites. Other criteria include whether (1) resources are plentiful and inexpensive, (2) skilled workers are available or are trainable, (3) taxes are low and the local government offers support, (4) energy and water are available,

(5) transportation costs are low, and (6) the quality of life and quality of education are high.

What relationship does enterprise resource planning (ERP) have with the production process?

ERP is a computer application that enables multiple firms to manage all of their operations (finance, requirements planning, human resources, and order fulfillment) on the basis of a single, integrated set of corporate data. The result is shorter time between orders and payment, fewer staff to do ordering and order processing, reduced inventories, and better customer service for all firms involved. It is an advanced form of materials requirement planning.

What is just-in-time (JIT) inventory control?

JIT involves having suppliers deliver parts and materials just in time to go on the assembly line so they do not have to be stored in warehouses.

What are the latest quality control concepts?

Six Sigma quality (just 3.4 defects per million products) detects potential problems before they occur. Statistical quality control (SQC) is the process that some managers use to continually monitor all processes in production to ensure that quality is being built into the product from the beginning. Statistical process control (SPC) is the process of taking statistical samples of product components at each stage of the production process and plotting those results on a graph. Any variances from quality standards are recognized and can be corrected.

What quality standards do firms use in Canada?

International standards that Canadian firms strive to meet include ISO 9004:2000 (ISO 9000) and ISO 14000. The first is a European standard for quality and the second is a collection of the best practices for managing an organization's impact on the environment.

Identify various production processes and describe techniques to improve productivity including flexible manufacturing, lean manufacturing, mass customization, and computer-aided design manufacturing.

There are several different processes that manufacturers use to produce goods along with varying techniques to improve productivity.

What is process manufacturing, and how does it differ from assembly processes?

Process manufacturing physically or chemically changes materials. Assembly processes put together components.

Are there other production processes?

Production processes are either continuous or intermittent. A continuous process is one in which long production runs turn out finished goods over time. An intermittent process is an operation where the production run is short and the machines are changed frequently to produce different products.

What is flexible manufacturing?

Flexible manufacturing involves designing machines to produce a variety of products.

What is lean manufacturing?

Lean manufacturing is the production of goods using less of everything compared to mass production: less human effort, less manufacturing space, less investment in tools, and less engineering time to develop a new product.

What is mass customization?

Mass customization means making custom-designed goods and services for a large number of individual customers. Flexible manufacturing makes mass customization possible. Given the exact needs of a customer, flexible machines can produce a customized good as fast as mass-produced goods were once made.

How do CAD/CAM systems work?

Design changes made in computer-aided design (CAD) are instantly incorporated into the computer-aided manufacturing (CAM) process. The linking of the two systems—CAD and CAM—is called computer-integrated manufacturing (CIM).

Explain the use of PERT and Gantt charts to control manufacturing processes

Operations managers must ensure their products or services are provided on time and on budget.

Is there any relationship between a PERT chart and a Gantt chart?

Figure 10.7 shows a PERT chart. Figure 10.8 shows a Gantt chart. Whereas PERT is a tool used for planning, a Gantt chart is a tool used to measure progress.

KEY TERMS

- assembly process
- computer-aided design (CAD)
- computer-aided manufacturing (CAM)
- computer-integrated manufacturing (CIM)
- continuous process
- critical path
- enterprise resource planning (ERP)
- facility layout
- facility location
- flexible manufacturing
- form utility
- Gantt chart
- intermittent process
- ISO 9000
- ISO 14000
- just-in-time (JIT) inventory control
- lean manufacturing
- logistics
- mass customization
- materials requirement planning (MRP)
- operations management
- process manufacturing
- production
- production management
- program evaluation review technique
- purchasing
- quality
- research and development (R&D)
- Six Sigma quality
- statistical process control (SPC)
- statistical quality control (SQC)
- supply chain
- supply chain management

CRITICAL THINKING

1. Workers on the manufacturing floor are being replaced by robots and other machines. On the one hand, that is one way in which companies compete with cheap labour from other countries. On the other hand, automation eliminates many jobs. Are you concerned that automation may increase unemployment or under-employment in Canada and around the world? Why or why not?
2. Computer-integrated manufacturing (CIM) has revolutionized the production process. What will such changes mean for the clothing industry, the

shoe industry, and other fashion related industries? What will they mean for other consumer and industrial goods industries? How will you benefit as a consumer?

3. One way to create new jobs in Canada is to have more innovation from new graduates of engineering and the sciences. How can Canada motivate more students to study in those areas?

DEVELOPING WORKPLACE SKILLS

1. Choosing the right location for a manufacturing plant or a service organization is often critical to its success. Form small groups and have each group member pick one manufacturing plant or one service organization in town and list at least three reasons why its location helps or hinders its success. If its location is not ideal, where would be a better one?
2. In teams of four or five, discuss the need for better operations management in the airline industry. Have the team develop a report listing (1) problems team members have encountered in travelling by air, and (2) suggestions for improving operations so such problems will not occur in the future.
3. Discuss some of the advantages and disadvantages of producing goods overseas using inexpensive labour. Summarize the moral and ethical issues of this practice.
4. Think of any retail outlet (e.g., bookstore or food outlet) or service centre (e.g., library, copy centre) at your school and redesign the layout (make a pencil sketch) to more effectively serve customers and allow employees to be more effective and efficient.
5. In teams of four or five, have each team build a PERT chart for a business of their choosing. First have each team identify all the tasks involved in producing the good or providing the service and then organize them into a chart. Have them identify the critical path and identify the minimum amount of time it will take to produce the good or provide the service to customers.

ANALYZING MANAGEMENT DECISIONS

Why Big Companies Fail to Innovate

Matthew Kiernan, based in Unionville, Ontario, is a management consultant whose views command attention. He has a PhD degree in strategic management from the University of London and was a senior partner with an international consulting firm, KPMG <*www.kpmg.com*>. Subsequently, he founded his own firm, Innovest Group International, with staff operating out of Geneva, London, and Toronto. He was also a director of the Business Council for Sustainable Development based in Geneva.

His book *Get Innovative or Get Dead* took aim at big corporations for their poor record on innovation. Any five-year-old could tell you that companies must innovate to survive, he said, so what's the problem? According to Kiernan, it is one thing to understand something in your head but quite another thing to really feel it in your gut. This is further complicated by the difficulty of getting a big company to shift gears, to turn its culture around so that innovation becomes the norm rather than the special effort. Look back at the discussion on innovation at the beginning of the chapter to re-visit its importance in our increasingly competitive world.

Kiernan called for a company to develop a style and atmosphere that favours individual risk-taking, the intrapreneurial approach discussed in Chapter 7. That means that if a team tries something that does not work, you do not shoot it down. Encouraging innovation, which inevitably involves taking risks with the unknown, means accepting the fact that it may take two or three attempts before something useful is developed. Recently, Matthew has applied this principle to sustainable development, including the topic of carbon finance.

The 3M company is often used as a great example of a company that encourages creativity. Its policy dictates that 30 percent of annual sales come from products less than four years old. However, 3M was not always that progressive. When the now legendary Post-it Notes were first developed by an employee, he had a hard time getting the company to see the potential in his idea. This ultimately triggered a major change in the company's policy. Kiernan pointed out that most companies give lip service to the necessity of innovation but do not act in a credible way as far as their employees are concerned. If you mean business, you must take that "bright guy out of the basement, [the one] everybody knows is a genius, but whose last two enterprise efforts came to grief, and visibly promote him."

Discussion Questions

1. Why do large companies find it difficult to innovate? Is it because they are big or because they are afraid of the unknown?
2. Do smaller companies do better at innovation? Is that because most of them are private companies and not accountable to outside stakeholders?
3. Do some research on 3M and find out how this large company encourages innovation and what it means to them.

PART 3 ENDS WITH...

DEALING WITH CHANGE

Change Management in Practice

To move a company from where it is now to where it would like to be, as discussed in Chapter 8 with respect to planning, is very much what change management is all about. One of its many definitions is found in Wikipedia, which alludes to a structured approach to shift or transition. The subject of change management was first identified in the late 1980s based on the spotty success businesses were having with successful changes. Organizational change management starts with the identification of the gaps as described earlier and then adds the capability to change. Effective change management is about employee alignment of expectations surrounding the change; broad based communication about the reasons for change, the expected benefits, and the details of the change; a proactive approach to countering resistance to change; and a set of metrics to evaluate the results of the change.

We can look at a number of business examples that demonstrate the success or lack of success with the change management process. When looking at Apple versus Microsoft over the past five years or so, we can easily identify the success that Apple has experienced versus the stagnation of Microsoft. A suggested reason for Microsoft's results is the internal struggles associated with resistance to change. In the case of Coca-Cola some of their problems in terms of change management (that has resulted in a halving of their share value over the past few years) are attributable to the product itself. Soft drinks are full of sugar and that reality is a major roadblock due to the growing awareness that those products do not contribute to a healthy lifestyle.

In Canada, Shoppers Drug Mart is an example of a company that has managed change very well. Facing growing competition from Walmart, Target, and national grocers who have added in-store pharmacies, as well as reforms in generic drugs that have significantly reduced their margins, Shoppers Drug Mart has continued to increase their profitability. Through adding front-of-the-store convenience items along with general merchandise they continue to see improvements in their sales and profits. WestJet Airlines is adding a new regional airline to provide competition to Air Canada in what they believe is an underserviced market. At the time of the writing of this edition of the textbook, WestJet is hopeful that the business model they have been so successful with in larger Canadian markets can be transferred to smaller domestic markets.

Sources: Why Apple Beats Microsoft at Change Management, www.forbes.com/2010/09/08/apple-microsoft-innovation-change-leadership-managing-human-capital-10-govindarajan.html; Change and Pressures to Innovate—The Coco Cola Case, http://changemanagement.phoenix-blogs.com/change-and-pressures-to-innovate-the-coca-cola-case/, April 3, 2010; Shoppers Boosts Dividend, Gives Rosy Outlook for 2012 Despite Drug Reforms, www.canadianbusiness.com/article/70238—shoppers-boosts-dividend-gives-rosy-outlook-for-2012-despite-drug-reforms; and Westjet Raises Dividend and Adds New Regional Airline to Take Flight in 2013, www.canadianbusiness.com/article/69966—westjet-raises-dividend-and-adds-new-regional-airline-to-take-flight-in-2013

REACHING BEYOND OUR BORDERS

Lockheed Martin Does It Again

Lockheed Martin once again is making the construction of the 5th generation F-35, multi-role combat jet airplane a global endeavour. Nine countries, 1300 suppliers and almost every state in the United States are involved in the production of this aircraft. Over 20,000 components of this aircraft are being built globally for shipment to a final assembly site in Texas.

The assembly-line layout in this mile-long site uses a production strategy based on flow-to-takt manufacturing implementation—an application of lean manufacturing. Flow-to-takt is the movement of component assemblies, like wings and forward fuselages, from one build station to the next at a rate equal to the delivery rate. This production rhythm increases efficiencies, lowers costs, and reduces span times while synchronizing the delivery of parts, timing of tasks, and positioning of personnel to achieve standard work in each line position. Lockheed Martin has early on in the building of this jet dropped the production costs by 42 percent and the delivery time has been reduced by half. After production a sophisticated supply chain network related to after-sale support and ongoing maintenance will involve companies in every country where this jet is being deployed. Canada too, is expected to be the home of their own fleet of this aircraft as a result of a decision made in 2011 to replace their aging fleet of combat aircraft.

Source: "Building the F-35," https://f35.com/building-the-F-35/.

RUNNING CASE

Leadership, Benchmarking, and Operations Management Planning at Fox 40 International Inc.

Leadership at Fox 40 is very much a reflection of the vision of the company's founder and CEO Ron Foxcroft, along with Dave Foxcroft, President and COO. Over the past 25 years of growth Ron and Dave have increasingly realized that success is very much related to both customers and employees. The importance of satisfying customer needs is central to all they do. As Ron states, "no one (i.e., any employee) needs permission to satisfy a customer." Every employee will do whatever it takes. One of the company's values is to respond to any customer question in 12 seconds, either with an answer or a commitment to, "I don't know but will find out." This vision is also reflected in a firm belief that any employee should be prepared to do any job, except take out the garbage; that is Ron's job.

They also know their vision can only be continually and consistently fulfilled if it is embodied by every employee. So, when hiring staff, Fox 40 knows the importance of hiring the right kind of people; honesty and integrity being key and a very much a reflection of how Ron and Dave behave. Starting in entry level positions, each employee's strengths and weaknesses are assessed through the assignment of tasks with specific time lines. Performance is monitored not only by management, but by peers. Strengths are channelled to customer satisfaction issues. Weaknesses are discussed and plans for improvement are identified. Senior management are directly accessible to any customer and to any employee. Ron and Dave embody the importance of front-line interaction, Ron is the first person to work every day and both of them come and leave through the front doors, passing through the main areas of the company's facility to their offices.

Fox 40 embodies benchmarking, comparing themselves to the very best. Much of their research and development is focused on "robbing and duplicating" what very successful companies have done. They have looked to companies that started with a single, simple, product and then have expanded through the addition of complementary products. Gillette <*www.gillette.com*>, started with a shaving blade, added shaving cream, and then deodorant. Wrigley's <*www.wrigley.com*> started with gum. They also focus on brand recognition and so they look to market leaders in this area, including Coke. When making decisions on potentially entering a market new to them, they are guided by a belief that no market is worth considering unless they believe they can become the number one company, in terms of sales, in the new market. They expect to be able to sell to all customers in any market they enter.

When planning on facility location, their key factors are once more impacted by their customers and employees. With sales in 140 countries they know the overriding perception of their customers of the importance of "Made in Canada." So, that is an overarching criterion. The large number of global customers supports a focus on logistics. Transportation infrastructure, including highways, shipping, airlines and close proximity to the border, are also important. The majority of their employees work in distribution and rely on public transportation to get to work. This is an equally important criterion. For their large customer base in the United States, they have chosen to do customs clearing, so they have a distribution centre in that country, located in Niagara Falls, New York, which is very close to their facilities in Hamilton, Ontario.

The importance of employee input also plays out in terms of layout decisions; they have recently moved to a new location. Their entire location is very clean and has "hospital operating room" white walls: Dave is a strong proponent of "employees act their environment."

Sources: Ron Foxcroft, Founder and CEO, Dave Foxcroft, President and COO, in-person interview, May 22, 2012

Discussion Questions

1. The leadership of Ron and Dave Foxcroft has been influenced by Donald Cooper, former founder and president of Cooper Sporting Goods. Research Donald Cooper's leadership ideas including his concept of "front-line interaction."
2. Access the company online sites for Fox40, Gillette, and Wrigley. Compare the product offerings of all three companies and comment on how Fox40 has benchmarked themselves to the other two companies.
3. Fox40 has just relocated their business to 340 Grays Road, Hamilton, Ontario. Referring to the above discussion, identify the specifics that supported a move to this location.

PART 4

CHAPTER 11

MOTIVATING EMPLOYEES

LEARNING OBJECTIVES

After you have read and studied this chapter, you should be able to:

LO 1 Relate the significance of Taylor's scientific management and the Hawthorne studies to management.

LO 2 Identify the levels of Maslow's hierarchy of needs, and relate their importance to employee motivation.

LO 3 Distinguish between the motivators and hygiene factors identified by Herzberg.

LO 4 Explain how job enrichment affects employee motivation and performance.

LO 5 Differentiate between McGregor's Theory X and Theory Y.

LO 6 Describe the key principles of goal setting, expectancy, reinforcement, and equity theories.

LO 7 Show how managers put motivation theories into action through open communication and job recognition strategies.

LO 8 Show how managers personalize motivation strategies to appeal to employees around the globe and across generations.

PROFILE

GETTING TO KNOW LISA LISSON OF FEDEX EXPRESS CANADA

Lisa Lisson, President of FedEx Express Canada (FedEx), leads a growing business of domestic and international express delivery services. The company employs more than 5,000 people across 60 locations coast-to-coast.

Lisson joined the company as a junior marketing specialist in 1992. She quickly progressed and in 2003 was appointed Vice-President of Sales, Marketing, and Corporate Communications. In 2006 Lisson gained responsibility for improving the FedEx customer experience in Canada. She was appointed to her current role in October 2010 and is the first Canadian to hold the post.

Under her leadership, FedEx has implemented critical improvements to the operation of the sales team, resulting in significant revenue growth for the company. She also drove the introduction of *fedex.ca*, shipping and tracking software, and led initiatives to increase brand awareness and market share for FedEx.

Lisson also launched a full range of new domestic and international products reinforced with award-winning advertising and new methods for measuring customer satisfaction. In the annual internal opinion survey, Lisson's own employees have ranked her above the country average in each year that she has been a manager. She is also a four-time recipient of the "Five Star Award," the highest performance accolade at FedEx.

As a single mother with a high stress job, she believes in maintaining a healthy work-life balance. FedEx is consistently listed as one of the top 50 best Canadian employers and Lisson knows that to be number one, the FedEx work environment needs to be strong. She believes that when employees are engaged, committed, and motivated by their leaders and work culture, they are driven to contribute to the company's well-being.

In an *Undercover Boss Canada* episode, Lisson went undercover to ensure employees had the tools they needed to succeed—and that FedEx not only delivered to its customers, but also to its valuable employees. Lisson disguised herself as new employee Suzanne, a mother of two re-entering the workforce. The employees she met were all real people, survivors who had come through very difficult life challenges and chosen to move forward with remarkable optimism and hope. And they did so in a corporate culture that supported them—by creating a "second family" for them. It was a powerful lesson for Lisson: if you hire the right people, train them well, engender a strong sense of belonging, listen to their ideas and expect high standards, you will achieve business success.

Says Lisson, "Going undercover was a life-changing experience for me on so many levels but, more importantly, it reinforced my strong belief in the importance of being a leader who knows the front line. Unless you walk in someone else's shoes and experience what they do, you never actually know. I encourage every FedEx manager—in fact, any manager of any company—to get out on the front line and burn the shoe leather. Go and spend a day doing what your employees do and experience what they experience day in and day out. And do it often. I always say that it's my front-line teams who create my "to-do" list.

Thousands of books and articles have been written about how to motivate a workforce. Not surprisingly, there are many conflicting points of view. Peter Drucker, considered by many to be the "father of management," believed that many workers are knowledge workers. Therefore, to motivate them, employees need autonomy and continual innovation and learning, which should be built into the job. Clearly, employees feel this under the leadership of Lisa Lisson.

In this chapter, you will be introduced to some motivation theories. These theories should be evaluated when one considers how best to motivate employees. Motivated workers are critical as they contribute to the success of an organization. As you read through this chapter, consider situations in which you have been involved. Did you witness some of the theories being applied? Looking back, could some of these situations have been handled differently to better motivate the audience?

Sources: Lisa Lisson, "Uncovering the Heart of FedEx," FedEX Express Canada, 21 May 2012, http://blog.fedex.designcdt.com/blog/uncovering-heart-fedex?page=2; Heather Connelly, "Undercover Analysis: Episode 10; FedEx CEO Lisa Lisson," *Financial Post*, 6 April 2012, http://business.financialpost.com/2012/04/06/undercover-analysis-episode-10-fedex-ceo-lisa-lisson/; "Lisa Lisson," FedEX Express Canada, 2012, http://about.van.fedex.com/executive_bios/lisa_lisson; and "FedEX," Undercover Boss Canada, 2012, www.wnetwork.com/Shows/Undercover-Boss-Canada.aspx.

THE VALUE OF MOTIVATION

"If work is such fun, how come the rich don't do it?" quipped comedian Groucho Marx. Well, the rich do work—Bill Gates did not make his billions playing computer games. And workers can have fun—if managers make the effort to motivate them. **Motivation** is a person's internal drive to act.[1] One of the most challenging skills of a manager is the ability to induce motivation in employees so that they will be committed and productive employees.[2] It is hard to overstate the importance of workers' job satisfaction. Happy workers lead to happy customers, and happy customers lead to successful businesses.[3]

motivation
A person's internal drive to act.

On the opposite side, unhappy workers are likely to leave the company and when this happens, the company usually loses out. The cost associated with losing an employee fluctuates wildly, depending on who you ask: some say it is as low as 25 percent of the departing person's salary while others peg it as high as 200 percent.[4] As the following will illustrate, turnover costs include many variables.

Direct costs include the time and cost to hire the replacement (e.g., process the paperwork, interview candidates, and pay moving expenses) and costs related to onboarding (e.g., orientation, training, and learning new material and equipment). The indirect costs are harder to quantify, but they can be substantial as these include loss of productivity. This can be of the outgoing employee, but also on the part of the team or departmental level, on the part of the colleagues who have to fill in once the employee has departed, and on the part of the new hire while he or she gets up to speed. Besides productivity, "some organizations will think about what they've invested in the person in terms of training, knowledge, and skills development that the person is now going to walk out the door with," said David Sissons, Toronto-based vice-president of HR consulting firm Hay Group <*www.haygroup.com*>. "That's a more difficult item to quantify because where do you begin—the last year, the last two years, or the last five years?"[5]

intrinsic reward
The good feeling you have when you have done a job well.

extrinsic reward
Something given to you by someone else as recognition for good work; extrinsic rewards include pay increases, praise, and promotions.

The "soft" costs are even greater: loss of intellectual capital, decreased morale, increased employee stress, and a negative reputation. Motivating the right people to join the organization and stay with it is a key function of managers. Top performing managers are usually surrounded by top-performing employees. Although the desire to perform well ultimately comes from within, good managers stimulate people and bring out their natural drive to do a good job. People are willing to work, and work hard, if they feel that their work makes a difference and is appreciated.

People are motivated by a variety of things, such as recognition, accomplishment, and status.[6] An **intrinsic reward** is the personal satisfaction you feel when you perform well and achieve goals. The belief that your work makes a significant contribution to the organization or society is a form of intrinsic reward. An **extrinsic reward** is something given to you by someone else as recognition for good work. Pay increases, praise, and promotions are examples of extrinsic rewards. Although ultimately motivation—the drive to satisfy a need—comes from within an individual, there are ways to stimulate people that bring out their natural drive to do a good job.

As an example, Canadian Tire Financial Services Ltd. designates "Customers for Life" awards to employees that have gone above and beyond the

▸ Intrinsic (inner) rewards include the personal satisfaction you feel for a job well done. People who respond to such inner promptings often enjoy their work and share their enthusiasm with others. Are you more strongly motivated by your own desire to do well, or by extrinsic (external) rewards like pay and recognition?

requirements of their jobs. The award is a way to recognize and reward employees (through a presentation, plaque, and day off) who have demonstrated superior customer service. Candidates are nominated based on outstanding conduct witnessed by fellow employees or customer feedback. The award criteria include direct customer contact, positive customer perception of the experience, and providing an experience that both meets World Class Customer Service Standards and upholds the company's values and mission statement.

This chapter will help you understand the concepts, theories, and practices of motivation. We begin with a look at some traditional theories of motivation. Why should you bother to know about these theories? Because sometimes "new" approaches are not really new; variations of them have been tried in the past. Knowing what has gone before will help you see what has worked and what has not. We discuss the Hawthorne studies because they created a new interest in worker satisfaction and motivation. Then we'll look at some assumptions about employees that come from the traditional theorists. You will see the names of these theorists over and over in business literature and future courses: Taylor, Mayo, Maslow, Herzberg, and McGregor. Finally, we'll introduce modern motivation theories and show you how managers apply them.

FREDERICK TAYLOR: THE FATHER OF SCIENTIFIC MANAGEMENT

Relate the significance of Taylor's scientific management and the Hawthorne studies to management.

Several books in the nineteenth century presented management principles, but not until the early twentieth century did there appear any significant works with lasting implications. One of the most well known, *The Principles of Scientific Management,* was written by American efficiency engineer Frederick Taylor and published in 1911. This book earned Taylor the title "father of scientific management." Taylor's goal was to increase worker productivity to benefit both the firm and the worker. The way to improve productivity, Taylor thought, was to scientifically study the most efficient ways to do things, determine the one "best way" to perform each task (all the way down to how long a step to take, how often to break, how much water to drink, etc.), and then teach people those methods.[7] This became known as **scientific management**.

scientific management
Studying workers to find the most efficient ways of doing things and then teaching people those techniques.

Three elements were basic to Taylor's approach: time, methods, and rules of work. His most important tools were observation and the stopwatch. Taylor's thinking is behind today's measures of how many burgers McDonald's expects its flippers to flip and how many callers the phone companies expect operators to assist.

A classic Taylor story involves his study of men shovelling rice coal and iron ore with the same type of shovel. Taylor felt that different materials called for different shovels. He proceeded to test a number of different shovel lengths and capacities with seasoned shovellers and, with stopwatch in hand, measured output over time in what were called time-motion studies. **Time-motion studies** were studies of the tasks performed to complete a job and the time needed to do each task. Sure enough, an average person could shovel more (in fact, from 25 to 35 tons more per day) using the most efficient motions and the proper shovel. This finding led to time-motion studies of virtually every factory job. As the most efficient ways of doing things were determined, efficiency became the standard for setting goals.[8]

time-motion studies
Studies, begun by Frederick Taylor, of which tasks must be performed to complete a job and the time needed to do each task.

Taylor's scientific management became the dominant strategy for improving productivity in the early 1900s. Hundreds of time-motion specialists developed standards in plants throughout the country. One follower of Taylor was Henry L. Gantt, who developed charts by which managers plotted the work of employees a day in advance down to the smallest detail. Engineers Frank and Lillian Gilbreth used Taylor's ideas in a three-year study of bricklaying. They developed the **principle of motion economy**,

principle of motion economy
Theory developed by Frank and Lillian Gilbreth that every job can be broken down into a series of elementary motions.

which showed that every job could be broken down into a series of elementary motions. They then analyzed each motion to make it more efficient.

Some critics of Taylor's approach compared people largely to machines that needed to be properly programmed.[9] There was little concern for the psychological or human aspects of work. While Taylor did not use this comparison, he had very precise ideas about how to introduce his system: "It is only through enforced standardization of methods, enforced adoption of the best implements and working conditions, and enforced co-operation that this faster work can be assured. And the duty of enforcing the adoption of standards and enforcing this co-operation rests with management alone."[10] A crusader for better working conditions and pay for the working class, Taylor believed that the resulting improved productivity should then benefit both the workers and the company.

Some of Taylor's ideas are still being implemented. Some companies still place more emphasis on conformity to work rules than on creativity, flexibility, and responsiveness.[11] For example, UPS tells drivers how fast to walk (three feet per second), how many packages to pick up and deliver per day (average of 400), and how to hold their keys (teeth up, third finger). Drivers wear ring scanners, which are electronic devices on their index fingers that are wired to a small computer on their wrists. The devices shoot a pattern of photons at a bar code on a package to let a customer check the Internet and know exactly where a package is at any given moment.

The benefits of relying on workers to come up with solutions to productivity problems have long been recognized, as we shall discover next.

ELTON MAYO AND THE HAWTHORNE STUDIES

One of the studies that grew out of Frederick Taylor's research was conducted at the Western Electric Company's Hawthorne plant in Cicero, Illinois. The study began in 1927 and ended six years later. Let's see why it was one of the major studies in management literature.

Elton Mayo and his colleagues from Harvard University came to the Hawthorne plant to test the degree of lighting associated with optimum productivity. In this respect, theirs was a traditional scientific management study; the idea was to keep records of the workers' productivity under different levels of illumination. However, the initial experiments revealed what seemed to be a problem: the productivity of the experimental group compared to that of other workers doing the same job went up regardless of whether the lighting was bright or dim. This was true even when the lighting was reduced to about the level of moonlight. These results confused and frustrated the researchers, who had expected productivity to fall as the lighting was dimmed.

A second series of experiments was conducted. In these, a separate test room was set up where temperature, humidity, and other environmental factors could be manipulated. In the series of 13 experimental periods, productivity went up each time; in fact, it increased by 50 percent overall. When the experimenters repeated the original condition (expecting productivity to fall to original levels), productivity increased yet again. The experiments were considered a

▶ Elton Mayo and his research team forever changed managers' fixed assumptions about what motivates employees. Mayo and his team gave birth to the concept of human-based motivation after conducting studies at the Western Electric Hawthorne plant (pictured here). Before the studies at Hawthorne, workers were often taught to behave like human robots.

total failure at this point. No matter what the experimenters did, productivity went up. What was causing the increase?

Mayo believed that some human or psychological factor was involved. He and his colleagues then interviewed the workers, asking them about their feelings and attitudes toward the experiment. The researchers' findings began a profound change in management thinking that has had repercussions up to the present. Here is what they concluded:

- The workers in the test room thought of themselves as a social group. The atmosphere was informal, they could talk freely, and they interacted regularly with their supervisors and the experimenters. They felt special and worked hard to stay in the group. This motivated them.
- The workers were involved in the planning of the experiments. For example, they rejected one kind of pay schedule and recommended another, which was adopted. They believed that their ideas were respected and they felt engaged in managerial decision making. This, too, motivated them.
- No matter the physical conditions, the workers enjoyed the atmosphere of their special room and the additional pay for being more productive. Job satisfaction increased dramatically.

Researchers now use the term **Hawthorne effect** to refer to the tendency for people to behave differently when they know they are being studied.[12] The Hawthorne study's results encouraged researchers to study human motivation and the managerial styles that lead to greater productivity. Research emphasis shifted from Taylor's scientific management toward Mayo's new human-based management.

Hawthorne effect
The tendency for people to behave differently when they know they are being studied.

Mayo's findings led to completely new assumptions about employees. One was that pay is not the only motivator. In fact, money was found to be a relatively ineffective motivator. New assumptions led to many theories about the human side of motivation. One of the best-known motivation theorists was Abraham Maslow, whose work we discuss next.

MOTIVATION AND MASLOW'S HIERARCHY OF NEEDS

Identify the levels of Maslow's hierarchy of needs, and relate their importance to employee motivation.

Psychologist Abraham Maslow believed that to understand motivation at work, one must understand human motivation in general. It seemed to him that motivation arises from need. That is, people are motivated to satisfy unmet needs; needs that have been satisfied no longer provide motivation. He thought that needs could be placed on a hierarchy of importance.

Figure 11.1 shows **Maslow's hierarchy of needs**, whose levels are as follows:

Maslow's hierarchy of needs
Theory of motivation that places different types of human needs in order of importance, from basic physiological needs to safety, social, and esteem needs to self-actualization needs.

- *Physiological Needs.* Basic survival needs, such as the need for food, water, and shelter.
- *Safety Needs.* The need to feel secure at work and at home.
- *Social Needs.* The need to feel loved, accepted, and part of the group.
- *Esteem Needs.* The need for recognition and acknowledgement from others, as well as self-respect and a sense of status or importance.
- *Self-Actualization Needs.* The need to develop to one's fullest potential.

When one need is satisfied, another higher-level need emerges and motivates the person to do something to satisfy it. The satisfied need is no longer a motivator. For example, if you just ate a full-course dinner, hunger would not (at least for several hours) be a motivator, and your attention may turn to your surroundings (safety needs) or family (social needs). Of course, lower-level needs (e.g., thirst) may emerge at any time they are not met and take your attention away from higher-level needs such as the need for recognition or status.

Figure 11.1

Maslow's Hierarchy of Needs

Maslow's hierarchy of needs is based on the idea that motivation comes from need. If a need is met, it is no longer a motivator, so a higher-level need becomes the motivator. Higher-level needs demand the support of lower-level needs. This chart shows the various levels of need.

Most of the world's workers struggle all day simply to meet the basic physiological and safety needs. In developed countries, such needs no longer dominate, and workers seek to satisfy growth needs (i.e., social, esteem, and self-actualization).

Applying Maslow's Theory

To compete successfully, firms must create a work environment that includes goals such as social contribution, honesty, reliability, service, quality, dependability, and unity—for all levels of employees. Chip Conley of Joie de Vivre <*www.jdvhotels.com*>, a chain of 17 boutique hotels, thinks about higher-level needs such as meaning (self-actualization) for all employees, including lower-level workers. Half his employees are housekeepers who clean toilets all day. How does he help them feel they are doing meaningful work? One technique is what he calls the George Bailey exercise, based on the main character in the movie *It's a Wonderful Life.* Conley asks small groups of housekeepers what would happen if they were not there every day. Trash would pile up, bathrooms would be full of wet towels, and let's not even think about the toilets. Then he asks them to come up with some other name for housekeeping. They offer suggestions like "serenity keepers," "clutter busters," or "the peace-of-mind police." In the end, these employees have a sense of how the customer's experience would not be the same without them. This gives meaning to their work that helps satisfy higher-level needs.[13]

PROGRESS ASSESSMENT

- What are the similarities and differences between Taylor's time-motion studies and Mayo's Hawthorne studies?
- How did Mayo's findings influence scientific management?
- Can you draw a diagram of Maslow's hierarchy of needs? Label and describe each level.

Distinguish between the motivators and hygiene factors identified by Herzberg.

HERZBERG'S MOTIVATING FACTORS

Another direction in managerial theory is to explore what managers can do with the job itself to motivate employees. (This is a modern-day look at Taylor's research.) In other words, some theorists ask: of all the factors controllable by managers, which are most effective in generating an enthusiastic work effort?

The most discussed study in this area was conducted in the mid-1960s by psychologist Frederick Herzberg. He asked workers to rank various job-related factors in order of importance relative to motivation. The question was: What creates enthusiasm for workers and makes them work to full potential? The results showed that the most important motivating factors were the following:

1. Sense of achievement
2. Earned recognition
3. Interest in the work itself
4. Opportunity for growth
5. Opportunity for advancement
6. Importance of responsibility
7. Peer and group relationships
8. Pay
9. Supervisor's fairness
10. Company policies and rules
11. Status
12. Job security
13. Supervisor's friendliness
14. Working conditions

▸ Herzberg believed that motivational factors such as recognition increase worker performance. How do you think Herzberg's motivational factors encourage workers to a higher level of performance on the job?

Factors receiving the most votes all clustered around job content. Workers like to feel that they contribute to the company (sense of achievement was number one). They want to earn recognition (number two) and feel that their jobs are important (number six). They want responsibility (which is why learning is so important) and to earn recognition for that responsibility by having a chance for growth and advancement. Of course, workers also want the job to be interesting. Do you feel the same way about your work?

motivators
In Herzberg's theory of motivating factors, job factors that cause employees to be productive and that give them satisfaction.

Workers did not consider factors related to job environment to be motivators. It was interesting to find that one of those factors was pay. Workers felt that the *absence* of good pay, job security, and friendly supervisors could cause dissatisfaction, but their presence did not motivate employees to work harder; it just provided satisfaction and contentment. Would you work harder if you were paid more?

hygiene (maintenance) factors
In Herzberg's theory of motivating factors, job factors that can cause dissatisfaction if missing but that do not necessarily motivate employees if increased.

Herzberg concluded that certain factors, which he called **motivators**, made employees productive and gave them satisfaction. These factors, as you have seen, mostly related to job content. Herzberg called other elements of the job **hygiene factors** (or **maintenance factors**). These related to the job environment and could cause dissatisfaction if missing but would not necessarily motivate employees if improved. See Figure 11.2 for a list of both motivators and hygiene factors.

Motivators	Hygiene (Maintenance) Factors
(These factors can be used to motivate workers.)	(These factors can cause dissatisfaction, but changing them will have little motivational effect.)
Work itself	Company policy and administration
Achievement	Supervision
Recognition	Working conditions
Responsibility	Interpersonal relations (co-workers)
Growth and advancement	Salary, status, and job security

Figure 11.2

Herzberg's Motivators and Hygiene Factors

There's some controversy over Herzberg's results. For example, sales managers often use money as a motivator. Recent studies have shown that money can be a motivator if used as part of a recognition program.

Herzberg's motivating factors led to the following conclusion—the best way to motivate employees is to make their jobs interesting, help them achieve their objectives, and recognize their achievement through advancement and added responsibility. A review of Figure 11.3 shows the similarity between Maslow's hierarchy of needs and Herzberg's theory.

Figure 11.3

Comparison of Maslow's Hierarchy of Needs and Herzberg's Theory of Motivators and Hygiene (Maintenance) Factors

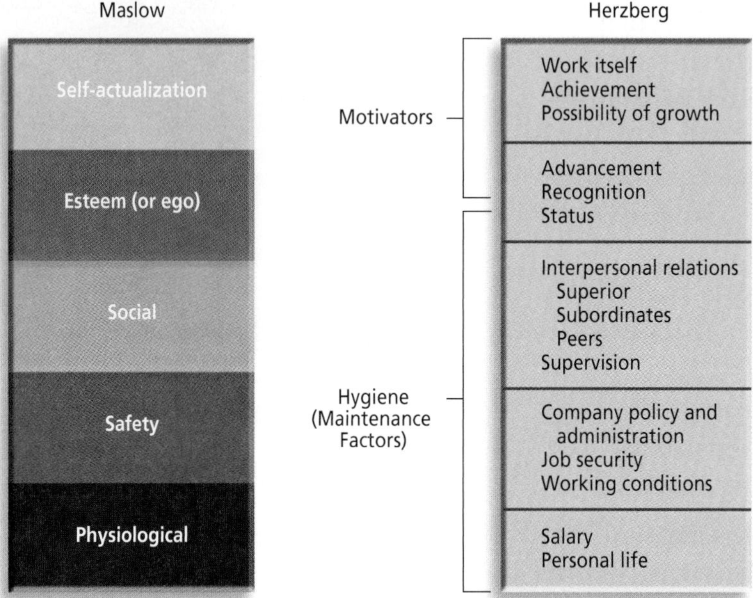

Applying Herzberg's Theories

Improved working conditions (such as better wages or increased security) are taken for granted after workers get used to them. This is what Herzberg meant by hygiene (maintenance) factors: their absence causes dissatisfaction, but their presence (maintenance) does not motivate. The best motivator for some employees is a simple and sincere "Thanks, I really appreciate what you're doing."

Mediacorp Canada Inc. <*mediacorp.ca*> annually publishes a list of Canada's Top 100 Employers. Companies are ranked based on eight key criteria: community involvement; work atmosphere and social culture; vacation and time off; performance management; health, financial, and family benefits; training and skills development; employee communications; and physical workspace.[14] The following example illustrates why Canadian Pacific Railway Ltd. <*www.cpr.ca*> has been cited on this list for its workforce planning and community involvement. Every year the company sends out its Spirit Train to support local food banks as it rattles through the communities where it operates. The company is also highly involved with the United Way and encourages its employees to take part in various initiatives throughout the year. The unique geographic spread of the company—from Vancouver to Montreal—means employees can literally work in communities across Canada. The company offers tuition subsidies of up to $10,000, a flexible health benefits program including retirees, a diverse range of working environments and roles within the firm, and its very own training facility for conductors and engineers. Mobility is what the company is all about. "You can start with this company in human resources and end up in operations, finance, public affairs—a career within a career within this railway," says Patti Clarkson, an employment advisor at the company.[15]

The Green Box highlights Vancity <*www.vancity.com*>, an organization that has also been recognized as one of Canada's Top 100 Employers. Here you will learn about some of the company's climate change initiatives.

GREENBOX

Vancity's Climate Change Solutions

Vancouver City Savings Credit Union (Vancity) is Canada's largest community credit union with $16.1 billion in assets, 479,500 members, and 59 branches throughout Greater Vancouver, the Fraser Valley, Victoria, and Squamish. Vancity also owns Citizens Bank of Canada, which serves members across the country by telephone, ATM, and the Internet.

Vancity's triple bottom line business model is driven not only by its commitment to financial success, but to environmental and social sustainability as well. The company is BC Hydro PowerSmart-certified for its energy-efficiency leadership as it is committed to supporting ways to find positive solutions to climate change. There are many individual and easy, everyday changes that can be made to reduce the impact on the environment including recycling, using less energy, and alternative forms of daily transportation. To be part of the climate change solution, here are some initiatives that are supported at Vancity:

- *Financing Member Action.* Providing financial support for the energy and environment sector is about investing in green buildings, clean technology and renewable energy, businesses that are producing green products and services, or that are actively improving their environmental performance. Activities include the purchase of hybrid and natural gas vehicles, energy-efficient home renovations, and financing green energy alternatives such as the Furry Creek small-scale hydro project.
- *Funding Community Action.* Vancity funds organizations that are involved in sustainable transportation, greening businesses, sustainable urban farming, and green energy. One example is its three-year commitment to reduce vehicle trips to the University of British Columbia and Simon Fraser University by sponsoring the student U-Pass program for transit access on buses, SkyTrain, and SeaBus.
- *Encouraging Sustainable Transportation.* Employee incentive programs offer priority parking for carpoolers and reduced-rate transit passes. Branches are located close to public transit and have bike racks. Its head office has a secure bike room, lockers, and shower facilities.
- *Leading the Way in Energy Management.* Vancity has been carbon neutral since 2008. The goal is to measure and reduce its greenhouse gas emissions, then offset emissions through the purchase of carbon offsets from emission-reducing activities that others have undertaken. As a result of energy-efficiency projects, Vancity has both saved money and avoided greenhouse gas emissions. For example, since 1992, accumulated electrical cost savings have been over $3.6 million. Accumulated emissions avoidance between 1992 and 2011 has been 3,924 tonnes.

Branches recycle approximately 64 percent of their waste; the head office recycles 79 percent of its waste. Waste audits are performed every two years and head office data is tracked annually. Would you like to work for an organization that is so committed to climate change?

Sources: "Organizations in B.C. receive funding for green building initiatives that reduce environmental impact," Vancouver City Savings Credit Union, 22 May 2012, https://www.vancity.com/AboutUs/OurNews/MediaReleases/May22/; and "Climate Change Solutions," Vancouver City Savings Credit Union, 2012, https://www.vancity.com/AboutUs/OurValues/CorporateSocialResponsibility/ClimateChangeSolutions/.

Alberta-Pacific Forest Industries Inc. (Al-Pac) <www.alpac.ca> is North America's largest single-line kraft pulp mill that produces bleached hardwood and softwood pulp. Here you see the pulp finishing area, which is the final stop for all pulp before it is transported to customers. Reasons why this company has been chosen as one of Canada's Top 100 Employers include company-wide profit sharing, comprehensive and competitive benefits, industry leading training, workplace flexibility, and subsidized community volunteering. Al-Pac also provides team members with a four-day workweek, driving range, 16-hectare trout pond, fitness centre, and walking trails.[16]

Many surveys conducted to test Herzberg's theories have supported his finding that the number-one motivator is not money but a sense of achievement and recognition for a job well done.[17] If you are skeptical about this, think about the limitations of money as a motivating force. Most organizations review an employee's performance only once a year and allocate raises at that time. To inspire and motivate employees to perform at their highest level of capability, managers must recognize their achievements and progress more than once a year.

"Employees are most productive when they feel their contributions are valued and their feedback is welcomed by management," said Max Messmer, chairman of Accountemps <*www.accountemps.ca*> and author of *Motivating Employees for Dummies*. "The reverse is also true—an unsupportive atmosphere can lead to reduced performance levels and higher turnover for businesses."[18] According to an Accountemps report, 48 percent of executives cited that better communication was the best remedy for low employee spirits, with other results such as recognition programs (19 percent), monetary awards for exceptional performance (13 percent), team-building events or meetings (5 percent), and additional days off (3 percent) lagging much farther behind. When asked what factors play a role in affecting employee morale negatively, the top reason was a lack of open, honest communication (33 percent). Other reasons included failure to recognize employee achievements (19 percent), micromanaging employees (17 percent), excessive workloads for extensive periods (16 percent), and fear of job loss (14 percent).[19]

Look back at Herzberg's list of motivating factors and identify the ones that tend to motivate you. Rank them in order of importance to you. Keep these factors in mind as you consider jobs and careers. What motivators do these job opportunities offer you? Are they the ones you consider important? Evaluating your job offers in terms of what is really important to you will help you make a wise career choice.

Explain how job enrichment affects employee motivation and performance.

job enrichment
A motivational strategy that emphasizes motivating the worker through the job itself.

JOB ENRICHMENT

Both Maslow's and Herzberg's theories have been extended by job enrichment theory. **Job enrichment** is a motivational strategy that emphasizes motivating the worker through the job itself. Work is assigned to individuals so that they have the opportunity to complete an identifiable task from beginning to end. They are held responsible for successful completion of the task. The motivational effect of job enrichment can come from the opportunities for personal achievement, challenge, and recognition.

J. Richard Hackman and Greg R. Oldham proposed the Job Characteristics Model, which is widely used as a framework to study how particular job characteristics influence work outcomes (i.e., job satisfaction, absenteeism, work motivation, etc.).[20] The five characteristics of work that are important in affecting individual motivation and performance are as follows:

1. *Skill Variety*. The extent to which a job demands different skills.
2. *Task Identity*. The degree to which the job requires doing a task with a visible outcome from beginning to end.
3. *Task Significance*. The degree to which the job has a substantial impact on the lives or work of others in the company.
4. *Autonomy*. The degree of freedom, independence, and discretion in scheduling work and determining procedures.
5. *Feedback*. The amount of direct and clear information that is received about job performance.

Variety, identity, and significance contribute to the meaningfulness of the job. Autonomy gives people a feeling of responsibility, and feedback contributes to a feeling of achievement and recognition.

Job enrichment is based on Herzberg's higher motivators such as responsibility, achievement, and recognition. It stands in contrast to *job simplification,* which produces task efficiency by breaking down a job into simple steps and assigning people to each of those steps.

Another type of job enrichment used for motivation is **job enlargement**, which extends the work cycle by adding related tasks to the job description.[21] An example might be to involve the workers in cleaning and maintaining their own plant, as well as obtaining their own materials from a central store, thereby doing tasks that were once done by service departments.[22] **Job rotation** also makes work more interesting and motivating by moving employees from one job to another. One problem with job rotation, of course, is having to train employees to do several different operations. However, the resulting increase in employee motivation and the value of having flexible, cross-trained employees offsets the additional costs.[23]

One of the hallmarks of job enrichment is the worker's ability to perform a complete task from beginning to end. Why do you think this might be more motivating than simply adding a few parts to an assembly on a production line?

MCGREGOR'S THEORY X AND THEORY Y

LO 5 Differentiate between McGregor's Theory X and Theory Y.

The way managers go about motivating people at work depends greatly on their attitudes toward workers. Management theorist Douglas McGregor observed that managers' attitudes generally fall into one of two entirely different sets of managerial assumptions, which he called Theory X and Theory Y. His research found that the assumptions of the manager provided a self-fulfilling prophecy about the behaviour of those he or she managed.

job enlargement
A job enrichment strategy that extends the work cycle by adding related tasks to the job description.

job rotation
A job enrichment strategy that involves moving employees from one job to another.

Theory X

The assumptions of Theory X management are as follows:

- The average person dislikes work and will avoid it if possible.
- Because of this dislike, workers must be forced, controlled, directed, or threatened with punishment to make them put forth the effort to achieve the organization's goals.
- The average worker prefers to be directed, wishes to avoid responsibility, has relatively little ambition, and wants security.
- Primary motivators are fear and money.

The natural consequence of such attitudes, beliefs, and assumptions is a manager who is very busy and who watches people closely, telling them what to do and how to do it. Motivation is more likely to take the form of punishment for bad work rather than reward for good work. Theory X managers give workers little responsibility, authority, or flexibility. Taylor and other theorists who preceded him would have agreed with Theory X. Time-motion studies calculated the one best way to perform a task and the optimal time to devote to it. Research assumed workers needed to be trained and carefully watched to see that they conformed to the standards that had been established as being the most efficient and effective.

▸ Theory X managers come in all sizes and shapes. Such managers may have an in-your-face style. Would you prefer to work for a Theory X or a Theory Y manager?

Many managers and entrepreneurs still suspect that employees cannot be fully trusted and need to be closely supervised. No doubt you have seen such managers in action. How did this make you feel? Were these managers' assumptions accurate regarding the workers' attitudes?

Theory Y

Theory Y makes entirely different assumptions about people. They are as follows:

- Most people like work; it is as natural as play or rest.
- Most people naturally work toward goals to which they are committed.
- The depth of a person's commitment to goals depends on the perceived rewards for achieving them.
- Under certain conditions, most people not only accept but also seek responsibility.
- People are capable of using a relatively high degree of imagination, creativity, and cleverness to solve problems.
- People are motivated by a variety of rewards. Each worker is stimulated by a reward unique to that worker (e.g., time off, money, recognition, etc.).

Rather than authority, direction, and close supervision, Theory Y managers emphasize a relaxed managerial atmosphere in which workers are free to set objectives, be creative, be flexible, and go beyond the goals set by management. (Figure 11.4 compares both Theories X and Y.) A key technique in meeting these objectives is empowerment, which includes giving employees the ability to make decisions and the tools to implement the decisions they make. For empowerment to be a real motivator, management should follow these three steps:

1. Find out what people think the problems in the organization are.
2. Let them design the solutions.
3. Get out of the way and let them put those solutions into action.

Often employees complain that although they are asked to become involved in company decision making, their managers fail to actually empower them to make decisions. Have you ever worked in such an atmosphere? How did that make you feel?

Figure 11.4

A Comparison of Theories X and Y

Theory X	Theory Y
1. Employees dislike work and will try to avoid it.	1. Employees view work as a natural part of life.
2. Employees prefer to be controlled and directed.	2. Employees prefer limited control and direction.
3. Employees seek security, not responsibility.	3. Employees will seek responsibility under proper work conditions.
4. Employees must be intimidated by managers to perform.	4. Employees perform better in work environments that are non-intimidating.
5. Employees are motivated by financial rewards.	5. Employees are motivated by many different needs.

The trend in many businesses is toward Theory Y management. One reason for this trend is that many service industries are finding Theory Y helpful in dealing with on-the-spot problems. Dan Kaplan of the Hertz Corporation <*www.hertz.ca*> would attest to this. He empowers his employees in the field to think and work as entrepreneurs. Leona Ackerly of Mini Maid <*minimaid.com*>, agrees: "If our employees look at our managers as partners, a real team effort is built."

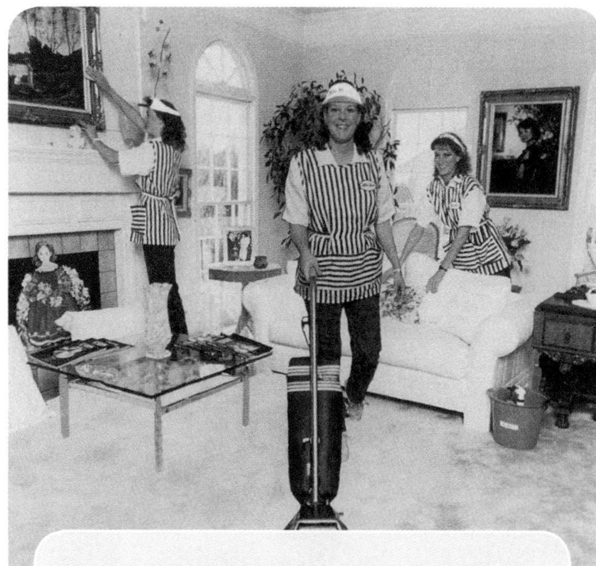

▸ At Mini Maid, the emphasis is on teamwork and employee empowerment to deal with on-the-job problems that arise. The company values the principles of Theory Y management where employees are looked on as partners. What businesses do you feel can most appropriately use the principles of Theory Y management?

PROGRESS ASSESSMENT

- Explain the difference between Herzberg's motivators and hygiene factors.
- Relate job enrichment to Herzberg's motivating factors.
- Briefly describe the managerial attitudes behind Theories X and Y.

GOAL-SETTING THEORY AND MANAGEMENT BY OBJECTIVES

Describe the key principles of goal setting, expectancy, reinforcement, and equity theories.

Goal-setting theory says setting ambitious but attainable goals can motivate workers and improve performance if the goals are accepted, accompanied by feedback, and if conditions in the organization pave the way for achievement. All organization members should have some basic agreement about both overall goals and specific objectives for each department and individual. Thus there should be a system to engage everyone in the organization in goal setting and implementation.

Notice that goal setting potentially improves employee performance in two ways: (1) by stretching the intensity and persistence of effort, and (2) by giving employees clearer role perceptions so that their efforts are channelled toward behaviours that will improve work performance.[24] At Montreal-based Messaging Architects <*www.messagingarchitects.com*>, CEO Pierre Chamberland agrees that employees need to be involved in setting company goals. "It's total disclosure, and it works to build a culture of ownership within the organization," says Chamberland. With a clearer understanding of how business works, employees can participate, whether it is asking questions or setting targets. "They are more motivated to achieve targets because they set their own," says Chamberland.[25]

goal-setting theory
The idea that setting ambitious but attainable goals can motivate workers and improve performance if the goals are accepted, accompanied by feedback, and facilitated by organizational conditions.

Management expert Peter Drucker developed such a system in the 1960s. "Managers cannot motivate people; they can only thwart people's motivation because people motivate themselves," he said. Managers, he believed, can only create the proper environment for the seed to grow. Called **management by objectives (MBO)**, Drucker's system of goal setting and implementation involves a cycle of discussion, review, and evaluation of objectives among top- and middle-level managers, supervisors, and employees. It calls on managers to formulate goals in co-operation with everyone in the organization, to commit employees to those goals, and then to monitor results and reward accomplishments.[26]

management by objectives (MBO)
A system of goal setting and implementation that involves a cycle of discussion, review, and evaluation of objectives among top- and middle-level managers, supervisors, and employees.

MBO is most effective in relatively stable situations when managers can make long-range goals and implement them with few changes. Managers must also understand the difference between helping and coaching subordinates. *Helping* means working with the subordinate and doing part of the work, if necessary. *Coaching* means acting

▶ Performance feedback is crucial for the motivation of employees. The feedback session is also ideal for setting goals.

as a resource—teaching, guiding, and recommending—but not participating actively or doing the task. The central idea of MBO is that employees need to motivate themselves.

Employee input and expectations are important.[27] Problems can arise when management uses MBO as a strategy for forcing managers and workers to commit to goals that are not really agreed on together but are instead set by top management.

Victor Vroom identified the importance of employee expectations and developed a process called expectancy theory. Let's examine this concept next.

MEETING EMPLOYEE EXPECTATIONS: EXPECTANCY THEORY

According to Victor Vroom's **expectancy theory**, employee expectations can affect an individual's motivation. That is, the amount of effort employees exert on a specific task depends on their expectations of the outcome.[28] Vroom contends that employees ask three questions before committing maximum effort to a task: (1) Can I accomplish the task? (2) If I do accomplish it, what is my reward? (3) Is the reward worth the effort? (See Figure 11.5 for a summary of this process.)

Recall from the start of the chapter when it was stated that motivation comes from within when you consider this next example. Think of the effort you might exert in your class under the following conditions. Your instructor says that to earn an A in the course you must achieve an average of 90 percent on coursework plus jump two metres high. Would you exert maximum effort toward earning an A if you knew you could not possibly jump two metres high? Or what if your instructor said that any student can earn an A in the course but you know that this instructor has not awarded an A in 10 years of teaching? If the reward of an A seems unattainable, would you exert significant effort in the course? Better yet, let's say that you read in the newspaper that businesses actually prefer hiring C-minus students to hiring A-plus students. Does the reward of an A seem worth it? Now think of the same types of situations that may occur on the job.

expectancy theory
Victor Vroom's theory that the amount of effort employees exert on a specific task depends on their expectations of the outcome.

Expectancy theory does note that expectation varies from individual to individual. Employees therefore establish their own views in terms of task difficulty and the value of the reward.[29] Researchers David Nadler and Edward Lawler modified Vroom's theory and suggested that managers follow five steps to improve employee performance:[30]

1. Determine what rewards employees value.
2. Determine each employee's desired performance standard.
3. Ensure that performance standards are attainable.
4. Guarantee rewards tied to performance.
5. Be certain that employees consider the rewards adequate.

Now that we have covered several theories, you may have realized that they try to explain all behaviour, by all people, all of the time. But this is impossible given the complexity of human behaviour. The value of being briefly introduced to different theories (you will discuss these theories in more detail in an Organizational Behaviour

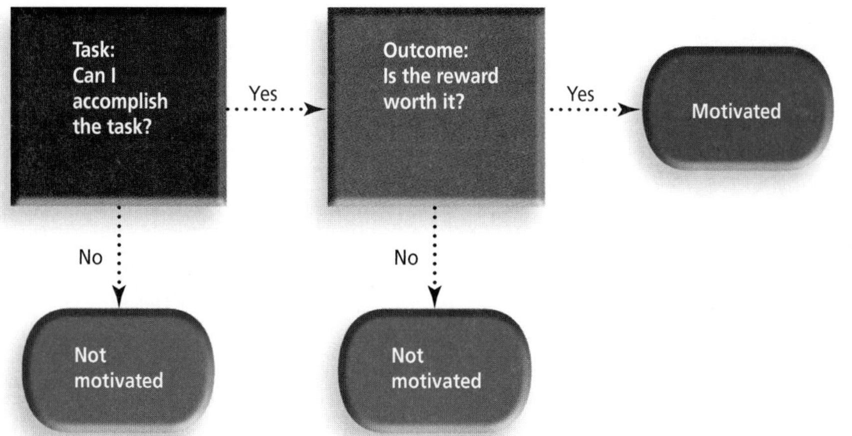

Figure 11.5

Expectancy Theory
The amount of effort employees exert on a task depends on their expectations of the outcome.

course) is that each theory offers some piece of the puzzle. No theory is complete, as people are very complex and our attempts to theorize about behaviour will never be complete. Successful leaders are sensitive to the differences between their employees and what motivates them. A starting point is understanding these theories.

REINFORCING EMPLOYEE PERFORMANCE: REINFORCEMENT THEORY

reinforcement theory
Theory that positive and negative reinforcers motivate a person to behave in certain ways.

Reinforcement theory is based on the idea that positive and negative reinforcers motivate a person to behave in certain ways. In other words, motivation is the result of the carrot-and-stick approach (reward and punishment). B. F. Skinner asserted that positive reinforcement is more effective at changing and establishing behaviour than punishment and that the main thing people learn from being punished is how to avoid punishment.[31] Put another way, individuals act to receive rewards and avoid punishment. Positive reinforcements are rewards such as praise, recognition, or a pay raise. Negative reinforcement includes reprimands, reduced pay, and layoff or firing. A manager might also try to stop undesirable behaviour by not responding to it. This is called *extinction,* because the hope is that the unwanted behaviour will eventually become extinct. Figure 11.6 illustrates how a manager can use reinforcement theory to motivate workers.

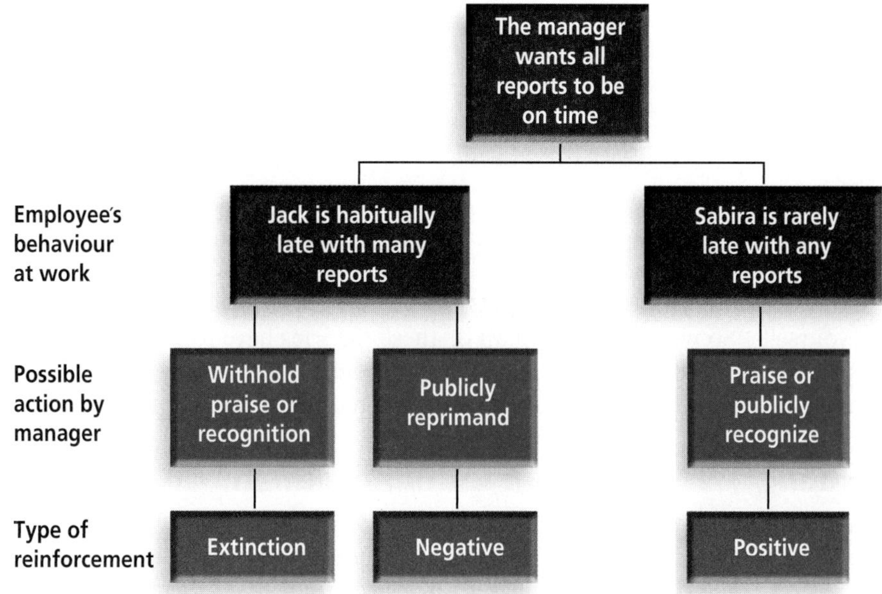

Figure 11.6

Reinforcement Theory
A manager can use both positive and negative reinforcement to motivate employee behaviour.

▸ If you attend class regularly but do not do well on your first midterm exam, how do you react? Do you stop going to class regularly as you do not think that it is worthwhile? Or, do you go and speak with your instructor to find out how to improve for the next exam?

TREATING EMPLOYEES FAIRLY: EQUITY THEORY

Equity theory deals with the questions "If I do a good job, will it be worth it?" and "What's fair?" It has to do with perceptions of fairness and how those perceptions affect employees' willingness to perform. The basic principle is that employees try to maintain equity between inputs and outputs compared to others in similar positions. Equity comparisons are made from the information that is available through personal relationships, professional organizations, and so on.[32]

When workers do perceive inequity, they will try to re-establish equitable exchanges in a number of ways. For example, suppose that you compare the grade you earned on a term paper with your classmates' grades. If you think you received a lower grade compared to the students who put out the same effort as you, you will probably react in one of two ways: (1) by reducing your effort on future class projects, or (2) by rationalizing. The latter may include saying, "Grades are overvalued anyway!" If you think that your paper received a higher grade than comparable papers, you will probably (1) increase your effort to justify the higher reward in the future, or (2) rationalize by saying, "I'm worth it!" In the workplace, inequity may lead to lower productivity, reduced quality, increased absenteeism, and voluntary resignation.

equity theory
The idea that employees try to maintain equity between inputs and outputs compared to others in similar positions.

Remember that equity judgments are based on perceptions and are therefore subject to error. When workers overestimate their own contributions—as happens often—they are going to feel that any rewards given out for performance are inequitable. Sometimes organizations try to deal with this by keeping employee salaries secret, but secrecy may make things worse; employees are likely to overestimate the salaries of others in addition to overestimating their own contribution.[33] In general, the best remedy is clear and frequent communication. Managers must communicate as clearly as possible both the results they expect and the outcomes that will occur when those results are achieved or when they are not.

PROGRESS ASSESSMENT

- Explain goal-setting theory.
- Evaluate expectancy theory. Can you think of situations in which expectancy theory could apply to your efforts or lack of effort?
- Explain the principles of equity theory.

Show how managers put motivation theories into action through open communication and job recognition strategies.

PUTTING THEORY INTO ACTION

Now that you know what a few theorists have to say about motivation, you might be asking yourself "So what?" What do all of these theories have to do with what really goes on in the workplace today? This is a fair question. Let's look at how companies put the theories into action through open communication and job recognition.

Motivating Through Open Communication

Companies with highly motivated workforces usually have several things in common. Among the most important factors are open communication systems and self-managed teams.[34] Open communication helps both managers and team members understand the objectives and work together to achieve them. Communication must flow freely throughout the organization when teams are empowered to make decisions—they cannot make these decisions in a vacuum. It is crucial for people to be able to access the knowledge they need when they need it.

Having teams creates an environment in which learning can happen, because most learning happens at the peer level—peers who have an interest in helping each other along. Empowerment works when people volunteer to share their knowledge with their colleagues. For example, when Flora Zhou, a business development manager at AES Corporation <*www.aes.com*>, was putting together a bid to the Vietnam government, she sent a detailed e-mail about what she was planning to bid and why to about 300 people within the company. She asked for and received a lot of advice and comments. Most people thought her proposal was fine, but Sarah Slusser, a group manager in Central America, sent Zhou a three-page response that contained a wealth of information about a similar situation she had encountered with a plant in the Yucatan. Slusser told Zhou what technology issues she needed to pay attention to. A few days later, Zhou made the bid. It was the lowest bid by two-tenths of a percent. Did Slusser tell Zhou the exact dollar to bid? No, but she and many others, including plant leaders and board members, gave her the best information and judgments they had to help her make her decision. They shared everything they knew with her.

Teamwork does not happen by itself. The entire organization must be structured to make it easy for managers and employees to talk to one another. Procedures for encouraging open communication include the following:[35]

- *Create an organizational culture that rewards listening.* Top managers must create places to talk, and they must show employees that talking with superiors counts—by providing feedback, adopting employee suggestions, and rewarding upward communication—even if the discussion is negative. Employees must feel free to say anything they deem appropriate. This is evident at Vancouver-based Great Little Box Company Ltd. (GLBC) <*www.greatlittlebox.com*>, a leading manufacturer of custom and stock corrugated boxes and point-of-purchase displays. To keep employees up-to-date, GLBC hosts monthly meetings (with catered lunches) that include frank discussions about all financial matters relating to the business. Uniquely, the private company opens its books for all employees every month and splits 15 percent of its profits, distributed equally every month. Employees can also provide direct feedback through a traditional suggestion box.[36]
- *Train supervisors and managers to listen.* Most people receive no training in how to listen, either in school or anywhere else, so organizations must do such training themselves or hire someone to do it.
- *Use effective questioning techniques.* We get information through questioning. Different kinds of questions yield different kinds of information. Closed questions that generate yes/no answers do not encourage the longer, more thoughtful responses that open questions do. Appropriate personal questions can create a sense of camaraderie between employee and manager.[37]
- *Remove barriers to open communication.* Having separate offices, parking areas, bathrooms, and dining rooms for managers and workers only sets up barriers in an organization. Other barriers are different dress codes and different ways of addressing one another (e.g., calling workers by their first names and managers by their last). Removing such barriers may require imagination and willingness on the part of managers to give up their special privileges.
- *Avoid vague and ambiguous communication.* Passive voice appears weak and tentative. Statements such as "Mistakes were made" leave you wondering who made the mistakes. Hedging is another way managers send garbled messages. Terms like *possibly* and *perhaps* sound wishy-washy to employees who need more definitive direction.[38]

- *Make it easy to communicate.* Encouraging organization members to eat together at large lunch tables, allowing employees to gather in conference rooms, having organizational picnics and athletic teams, and so on can help workers at all levels mix with one another.
- *Ask employees what is important to them.* Managers should not wait until the exit interview to ask an employee, "What can I do to keep you?" At that point it is too late. Instead they should have frequent *stay interviews* to find out what matters to employees and what they can do to keep them on the job.[39]

The Spotlight on Small Business box offers advice on using open communication strategies in small businesses.

Applying Open Communication in Self-Managed Teams

At Ford Motor Company, a group known as Team Mustang set the guidelines for how production teams should be formed. Given the challenge to create a car that would make people dust off their old "Mustang Sally" records and dance into

In the car business nothing works like the "wow" factor. At Ford, the 400-member Team Mustang group was empowered to create the "wow" response for the company's sleek Mustang convertible. The work team, suppliers, company managers, and even customers worked together to make the Mustang a winner in the very competitive automobile market.

SPOTLIGHT ON SMALL BUSINESS

Big Motivators for Small Businesses

Often small businesses cannot offer their employees the financial incentives larger businesses can. So how can they motivate their workers to perform their best?

Many strive to create an upbeat, relaxed company culture to encourage employees to bond with one another. For example, at Blurb <*www.blurb.com*>, a specialty publishing company, at the end of every Friday the conference room is transformed into a concert venue as employees play the video game, Rock Band. Top management provides refreshments along with the game, allowing the staff to relax and let the stress of the workweek pass into memory. Sprout Marketing <*sproutmarketing.com*>, a small marketing firm, uses a similarly laid-back strategy with weekly company trips to the movie theatre where tickets and popcorn are on the company.

But employee motivation is not just about morale-boosting leisure activities like video games and movie nights. Besides providing social interaction, management needs to communicate clearly with the staff to give purpose and direction. At the small consulting firm Sonoma Partners <*www.sonomapartners.com*>, veteran employees mentor new hires to acquaint them with the work environment and show them how to excel. Not only does this method help new employees bond with their colleagues, but it also sets them on the path to becoming productive workers.

Small businesses have a greater opportunity to motivate with open communication and broad responsibility. Individual workers can have more say in the company and not feel like just another drone in the great corporate beehive. As long as management encourages innovation from employees—and throws an occasional video game party—small businesses should have no trouble motivating their employees.

Sources: Eileen Gunn, "That's the Spirit! How to Energize Your Team—And Why It Matters," *BusinessWeek SmallBiz*, August/September 2008; and John R. Ingrisano, "Motivation: More Than Money," *Corporate Report Wisconsin*, 1 February 2008.

MAKING ETHICAL DECISIONS

Motivating Temporary Employees

Say that you work as a manager for Highbrow's, a rather prestigious department store. Each year, to handle the large number of holiday shoppers, you must hire temporary employees. Because of store policy and budget constraints, all temporaries must be discharged on January 10. As you interview prospective employees, however, you give the impression that the store will hire at least two new full-time retail salespeople for the coming year. You hope that this will serve to motivate the temporary workers and even foster some competition among them. You also instruct your permanent salespeople to reinforce the falsehood that good work during the holiday season is the path to full-time employment. Is this an ethical way to try to motivate your employees? What are the dangers of using a tactic such as this?

showrooms, the 400-member team was also given the freedom to make decisions without waiting for approval from headquarters. Everyone worked under one roof in an old warehouse where drafting experts sat next to accountants, and engineers next to stylists. Budgetary walls between departments were knocked down too as department managers were persuaded to surrender some control over their subordinates on the team.

When the resulting Mustang convertible displayed shaking problems, engineers were so motivated to finish on time and under budget that they worked late into the night, sleeping on the floor when necessary. Senior Ford executives were tempted to intervene, but they stuck with their promise not to meddle. Working with suppliers, the team solved the shaking problem and still came in under budget and a couple of months early. The new car was a hit with drivers, and sales soared.[40]

To implement such teams, managers at most companies must reinvent work. This means respecting workers, providing interesting work, developing workers' skills, allowing autonomy, decentralizing authority, and rewarding good work. In the process of reinventing work, it is essential that managers behave ethically toward all employees. The Making Ethical Decisions box illustrates a problem managers may face when filling temporary positions.

Recognizing a Job Well Done

Letting people know you appreciate their work is usually more powerful than giving a raise or bonus alone. When asked in a survey their reason for changing jobs, only 42 percent of the participants listed increased compensation and benefits, while 83 percent said they left for increased responsibilities and/or a more senior role.[41] Clearly, providing advancement opportunites is important in retaining valuable employees.

Promotions are not the only way to celebrate a job well done. Recognition can be as simple as noticing positive actions out loud, making employees feel their efforts are worthwhile and valued enough to be noticed.[42] For example: "Sarina, you didn't say much in the meeting today. Your ideas are usually so valuable; I missed hearing them." This comment lets Sarina know her ideas are appreciated, and she will be more apt to participate fully in the next meeting.

Here are just a few examples of ways managers have raised employee spirits without raising paycheques:[43]

- Kinko's <*www.fedexoffice.ca*> sent high-achieving employees to Disneyland *and* put the company's top executives in those employees' places while they were gone.
- Accounting firm KPMG gave employees a sundae surprise of gourmet ice cream and toppings.

Travelocity's Gnomie Award, based on the company's mascot, the travelling gnome, is given to employees nominated by their peers for outstanding performance. Winners receive a $750 travel voucher, a paid day off, recognition at the company's quarterly meeting, and a golden gnome. What part do you think these awards play in motivating the winners to continue their outstanding performance?

- Give More Media <*www.givemoremedia.com*> offers perks like Netflix and XM Satellite Radio memberships. It also encourages participation in its Smile and Give program, which gives employees three paid days off to work for a non-profit organization of their choice.
- Hewlett-Packard (HP) bestows its Golden Banana Award for a job well done. The award started when an engineer burst into his manager's office saying he had found the solution to a long-standing problem. In his haste to find something to give the employee to show his appreciation, the manager grabbed a banana from his lunch and said, "Well done! Congratulations!" The Golden Banana is now one of the most prestigious honours given to an inventive HP employee.

Giving valued employees prime parking spots, more vacation days, or more flexible schedules may help them feel their work is appreciated, but sometimes nothing inspires workers like the prospect of a payout down the road. Companies that offer a small equity stake or stock options often have a good chance of developing loyal employees.[44]

The same things do not motivate all employees. Next we'll explore how employees from different cultures and generations are motivated in different ways.

Show how managers personalize motivation strategies to appeal to employees around the globe and across generations.

PERSONALIZING MOTIVATION

Managers cannot use one motivational formula for all employees. They have to get to know each worker personally and tailor the motivational effort to the individual. This is further complicated by the increase in global business and the fact that managers now work with employees from a variety of cultural backgrounds. Cultural differences also exist between generational cohorts raised in the same country. Let's look at how managers personalize their strategies to appeal to employees around the globe and across generations.

Motivating Employees Around the Globe

Different cultures experience motivational approaches differently; therefore, managers study and understand these cultural factors in designing a reward system. In a *high-context culture,* workers build personal relationships and develop group trust before focusing on tasks. In a *low-context culture,* workers often view relationship building as a waste of time that diverts attention from the task. Koreans, Thais, and Saudis tend to be high-context workers who often view their North American colleagues as insincere due to their need for data and quick decision making.

Dow Chemical <*www.dow.com*> solved a cross-cultural problem with a recognition program for its 45,000 employees in over 50 countries who use a wide variety of languages and currencies. Globoforce Ltd. <*www.globoforce.com*> created a Web-based program for Dow called *Recognition@Dow* that automatically adjusts for differences created by cultural preferences, tax laws, and even local standards of living. Thus a Canadian employee might receive a gift certificate for Canadian Tire, whereas a Chinese employee receives one for online retailer *Dangdang.com*. The system even allows employees to nominate colleagues for recognition using an "award wizard" to help determine the appropriate award.[45]

Understanding motivation in global organizations and building effective global teams is still a new task for most companies. Developing group leaders who are culturally astute, flexible, and able to deal with ambiguity is a challenge businesses face in the twenty-first century.

Motivating Employees Across Generations

In your general readings you may encounter different definitions for generational cohorts. For example, Canadian demographer David Foot has studied the importance of demographic groups on business. He has categorized groups as follows:[46]

- Baby boomers (those born between 1947 and 1966)
- Generation X, a subgroup of baby boomers (those born between 1961 and 1966)
- The baby bust (those born between 1967 and 1979)
- The baby-boom echo (those born between 1980 and 1995)
- The millennium busters (those born between 1996 and 2010).

U.S. demographers often define generations as follows: baby boomers (those born between 1946 and 1964), Generation X (those born between 1965 and 1980), and Generation Y members, also known as Millennials or echo boomers (those born between 1980 and 2000). For this discussion, we will use these terms interchangeably.

Members in each generation are linked through shared life experiences in their formative years—usually the first ten years of life. The beliefs that you accept as a child affect how you view risk and challenge, authority, technology, relationships, and economics. When you are in a management position, they can affect even whom you hire, fire, or promote.

Some generalities apply to these different groups. Boomers were raised in families that experienced unprecedented economic prosperity, secure jobs, and optimism about the future. On the other hand, baby busters were raised in dual-career families with parents who focused on work. As children, they attended day care or became latchkey kids. Their parents' layoffs added to their insecurity about a lifelong job. Millennials were raised by indulgent parents, and most do not remember a time without cell phones, computers, and electronic entertainment.[47]

How do generational differences among these groups affect motivation in the workplace? Boomer managers need to be flexible with their Gen X and Millennial employees, or they will lose them. Gen X employees need to use their enthusiasm for change and streamlining to their advantage. Although many are unwilling to pay the same price for success their parents and grandparents did, their concern about undue stress and long hours does not mean they lack ambition. They want economic security as much as older workers, but they have a different approach to achieving it. Rather than focusing on job security, Gen Xers tend to focus on career security instead and are willing to change jobs to find it.

Many Gen Xers are now managers themselves, responsible for motivating other employees. What kind of managers are they? In general, they are well equipped to motivate people. They usually understand that there is more to life than work, and they think a big part of motivating is letting people know you recognize that fact. Gen X managers tend to focus more on results than on hours in the workplace. They tend to be flexible and good at collaboration and consensus building. They often think in broader terms than their predecessors because the media has exposed them to problems around the world. They also have a big impact on their team members. They are more likely to give them the goals and outlines of the project and leave them alone to do their work.[48]

▶ There's no magic formula to successfully motivating every worker. Each generation of employees has different attitudes about what is important to them in seeking a balance between a successful career and happy private life. What expectations do you have of your potential supervisor and company?

Perhaps the best asset of Gen X managers is their ability to give employees feedback, especially positive feedback. One reason might be that they expect more of it themselves. One new employee was frustrated because he had not received feedback from his boss since he was hired—two weeks earlier. In short, managers need to realize that young workers demand performance reviews and other forms of feedback more than the traditional one or two times a year.

In every generational shift, the older generation tends to say the same thing about the new: "They break the rules." The generation that lived through the Great Depression and World War II said it of the baby boomers. Boomers look at Gen Xers and say, "Why are they breaking the rules?" And now Gen Xers are looking at Millennials and saying, "What's wrong with these kids?"

As a group, Millennials tend to share a number of characteristics: they are impatient, skeptical, blunt and expressive, image-driven, and inexperienced. Like any other generation, they can transform their characteristics into unique skills. For example, Millennials tend to be adaptable, tech-savvy, able to grasp new concepts, practiced at multitasking, efficient, and tolerant. Perhaps the most surprising attribute they share is a sense of commitment.[49]

Millennials are not rushing to find lifetime careers after graduation. They are "job surfing" and are not opposed to living with their parents while they test out jobs.[50] A recent study found Millennials place a higher value on work-life balance, expect their employers to adapt to them (not the other way around), and are more likely to rank fun and stimulation in their top five ideal-job requirements.[51] What do you think are the most effective strategies managers can use to motivate Millennial workers?

One thing in business is likely to remain constant, though. Motivation will come from the job itself rather than from external punishments or rewards. Managers will need to give workers what they require to do a good job: the right tools, the right information, and the right amount of co-operation.

Motivation does not have to be difficult. It begins with acknowledging a job well done. You can simply tell those who do such a job that you appreciate them—especially if you make this statement in front of others. After all, as we said earlier in this chapter, the best motivator is frequently a sincere "Thanks, I really appreciate what you're doing."

PROGRESS ASSESSMENT

- What are several steps firms can take to increase internal communications and thus motivation?
- What problems may emerge when trying to implement participative management?
- Why is it important to adjust motivational styles to individual employees? Are there any general principles of motivation that today's managers should follow?

SUMMARY

Relate the significance of Taylor's scientific management and the Hawthorne studies to management.

Human efficiency engineer Frederick Taylor was one of the first people to study management. He did time-motion studies to learn the most efficient way of doing a job and then trained workers in those procedures.

What led to management theories that stress human factors of motivation?
The greatest impact on motivation theory was generated by the Hawthorne studies in the late 1920s and early 1930s. In these studies, Elton Mayo found that human factors such as feelings of involvement and participation led to greater productivity gains than did physical changes in the workplace.

Identify the levels of Maslow's hierarchy of needs, and relate their importance to employee motivation.

Abraham Maslow studied basic human motivation and found that motivation was based on needs. He said that a person with an unfilled need would be motivated to satisfy it and that a satisfied need no longer served as motivation.

What were the various levels of need identified by Maslow?
Starting at the bottom of Maslow's hierarchy of needs and going to the top, the levels of need are physiological, safety, social, esteem, and self-actualization.

Can managers use Maslow's theory?
Yes, they can recognize what unmet needs a person has and design work so that it satisfies those needs.

Distinguish between the motivators and hygiene factors identified by Herzberg.

Frederick Herzberg found that some factors are motivators and others are hygiene (or maintenance) factors. Hygiene factors cause job dissatisfaction if missing, but are not motivators if present.

What factors are examples of motivators?
The work itself, achievement, recognition, responsibility, growth, and advancement are motivators.

What are hygiene (maintenance) factors?
Factors that do not motivate but must be present for employee satisfaction, such as company policies, supervision, working conditions, interpersonal relations, and salary are examples of hygiene factors.

Explain how job enrichment affects employee motivation and performance.

Job enrichment describes efforts to make jobs more interesting.

What characteristics of work affect motivation and performance?
The job characteristics that influence motivation are skill variety, task identity, task significance, autonomy, and feedback.

Name two forms of job enrichment that increase motivation.
Job enrichment strategies include job enlargement and job rotation.

Differentiate between McGregor's Theory X and Theory Y.

Douglas McGregor held that managers will have one of two opposing attitudes toward employees. They are called Theory X and Theory Y.

What is Theory X?

Theory X assumes that the average person dislikes work and will avoid it if possible. Therefore, people must be forced, controlled, and threatened with punishment to accomplish organizational goals.

What is Theory Y?

Theory Y assumes that people like working and will accept responsibility for achieving goals if rewarded for doing so.

Describe the key principles of goal setting, expectancy, reinforcement, and equity theories.

Goal-setting theory is based on the notion that setting ambitious but attainable goals will lead to high levels of motivation and performance if the goals are accepted, accompanied by feedback, and facilitated by organizational conditions.

What is management by objectives (MBO)?

MBO is a system of goal setting and implementation that involves a cycle of discussion, review, and evaluation by objectives among top and middle-level managers, supervisors, and employees.

What are the key elements involved in expectancy theory?

Expectancy theory centres on three questions employees often ask about performance on the job: (1) Can I accomplish the task? (2) If I do accomplish it, what is my reward? and (3) Is the reward worth the effort?

What are the variables in reinforcement theory?

Positive reinforcers are rewards such as praise, recognition, or pay raises that a worker might strive to receive by performing well. Negative reinforcers are punishments such as reprimands, pay cuts, or firing that a worker might be expected to try to avoid.

According to equity theory, employees try to maintain equity between inputs and outputs compared to other employees in similar positions. What happens when employees perceive that their rewards are not equitable?

If employees perceive that they are underrewarded, they will either reduce their effort or rationalize that it is not important. If they perceive that they are overrewarded, they will either increase their effort to justify the higher reward in the future or rationalize by saying, "I'm worth it!" Inequity leads to lower productivity, reduced quality, increased absenteeism, and voluntary resignation.

Show how managers put motivation theories into action through open communication and job recognition strategies.

Companies with highly motivated workforces often have open communication systems and self-managed teams.

How does open communication improve employee motivation?

Open communication helps both managers and team members understand the objectives and work together to achieve them.

How can managers encourage open communication?

Top managers can create an organizational culture that rewards listening, train supervisors and managers to listen, use effective questioning techniques, remove barriers to open communication, avoid vague and ambiguous communication, and actively make it easier for all to communicate.

Show how managers personalize motivation strategies to appeal to employees around the globe and across generations.

Managers cannot use one motivational formula for all employees.

What is the difference between high-context and low-context cultures?

In high-context cultures people build personal relationships and develop group trust before focusing on tasks. In low-context cultures, people often view relationship building as a waste of time that diverts attention from the task.

How are Generation X managers likely to be different from their baby boomer predecessors?

Baby boomers tend to be willing to work long hours to build their careers and often expect their subordinates to do likewise. Gen Xers may strive for a more balanced lifestyle and are likely to focus on results rather than on how many hours their teams work. Gen Xers tend to be better than previous generations at working in teams and providing frequent feedback. They are not bound by traditions that may constrain those who have been with an organization for a long time and are willing to try new approaches to solving problems.

What are some common characteristics of Millennials?

Millennials tend to be adaptable, tech-savvy, able to grasp new concepts, practiced at multitasking, efficient, and tolerant. They often place a higher value on work-life balance, expect their employers to adapt to them, and are more likely to rank fun and stimulation in their top five ideal-job requirements.

KEY TERMS

equity theory
expectancy theory
extrinsic reward
goal-setting theory
Hawthorne effect
hygiene (maintenance) factors
intrinsic reward
job enlargement
job enrichment
job rotation
management by objectives (MBO)
Maslow's hierarchy of needs
motivation
motivators
principle of motion economy
reinforcement theory
scientific management
time-motion studies

CRITICAL THINKING

1. The textbook introduced you to the theory of scientific management. What do you think are problems that would arise as a result of breaking jobs into a series of discrete steps and treating people as cogs in a wheel? How can you motivate employees if this is how they are managed?
2. Look over Maslow's hierarchy of needs and try to determine where you are right now on the hierarchy. What needs of yours are not being met? How could a company go about meeting those needs and thus motivate you to work better and harder?

DEVELOPING WORKPLACE SKILLS

1. Talk with several of your friends about the subject of motivation. What motivates them to work hard or not work hard on projects in teams? How important is self-motivation to them?
2. Speak to a manager in the workplace. Find out what this manager does to motivate his or her direct reports.
3. Think of all of the groups with which you have been associated over the years—sports groups, friendship groups, and so on—and try to recall how the leaders of those groups motivated the group to action. What motivational tools were used, and to what effect?
4. Herzberg concluded that pay was not a motivator. If you were paid to get better grades, would you be motivated to study harder? In your employment experiences, have you ever worked harder to obtain a raise or as a result of receiving a large raise? Do you agree with Herzberg?

ANALYZING MANAGEMENT DECISIONS

Motivation Tips for Tough Times

With company cutbacks, layoffs, and economic uncertainty weighing heavily on everybody, it is no wonder some employees are dragging their feet into work. But according to Steven Stein, Toronto-based psychologist and entrepreneur, there are ways to lift and maintain motivation, even in tough times. In *Make Your Workplace Great: The 7 Keys to an Emotionally Intelligent Organization,* he offers these valuable tips for motivating employees.

- *What motivates your workers.* You may be surprised to discover how small changes, such as those in job design or reporting systems, can motivate certain people. It might not take much, but the only way to discover what your employees want, and how they react to change, is to ask them.
- *Offer ongoing feedback.* No time is better than now to open up lines of communication with your employees, if you have not already. Whether you offer feedback formally or informally, it is important to let your staff know how they are doing, where they are performing well, and where there is room for improvement regularly.
- *Emphasize personal accountability.* Self-management can be highly motivating, and if you are short-staffed, it can make a lot of sense, too. Most people will work much harder for their own sense of accomplishment than they will because they were told to do something.
- *Involve everyone in decision making.* By involving workers in certain company decisions, especially those that involve them directly, you are much more likely to get support for your initiatives. And you may even get some creative input along the way: your front-line staff might have knowledge about the impact of certain decisions that you may not be aware of.
- *Be flexible.* Time is an important commodity for people today, especially if they are taking on more work than usual. By giving your employees the opportunity to juggle their time around critical personal or family events and responsibilities, you will increase their motivation.
- *Celebrate employee and company success.* It is important to stop and recognize successes, whether individual, team, or organizational. Let everybody see that hard work is recognized and worth carrying out.

Source: "Great Ideas: Motivation Tips for Tough Times," *PROFIT,* 4 June 2009, www.canadianbusiness.com/entrepreneur/human_resources/article.jsp?content=20090603_115416_7820.

Discussion Questions

1. What other suggestions might you add to this list?
2. If you are employed now (or have been in the past), how has your supervisor motivated you? If you have never been employed before, how can a supervisor motivate you?
3. Apply each one of these tips to group work. How might you implement these suggestions so that group members, including yourself, are motivated to do well in the assigned work?

Practise and learn online with Connect.

CHAPTER

12

HUMAN RESOURCE MANAGEMENT: FINDING AND KEEPING THE BEST EMPLOYEES

LEARNING OBJECTIVES

After you have read and studied this chapter, you should be able to:

LO 1 Explain the importance of human resource management as a strategic contributor to organizational success, and summarize the five steps in human resource planning.

LO 2 Describe methods that companies use to recruit new employees, and explain some of the issues that make recruitment challenging.

LO 3 Outline the five steps in selecting employees, and illustrate the use of various types of employee training and development methods.

LO 4 Trace the six steps in appraising employee performance, and summarize the objectives of employee compensation programs.

LO 5 Describe the ways in which employees can move through a company: promotion, reassignment, termination, and retirement.

LO 6 Illustrate the effects of legislation on human resource management.

PROFILE

GETTING TO KNOW SALLY MAINQUIST, PRESIDENT AND CHIEF EXECUTIVE OFFICER OF CERTES FINANCIAL PROS

In today's business world the prospect of lifetime employment at a single company is becoming increasingly unlikely. Thanks to a sluggish economy and never-ending technological innovation, workers no longer have much of a chance to stay in one place until their retirement. As staff sizes rise and fall with the global marketplace, many companies say they require a flexible workforce of people who can come and go as they are needed. Workers in turn demand flexible schedules to help balance work and life, with non-traditional work arrangements such as part-time and temporary jobs.

That's where Sally Mainquist, president and CEO of Certes Financial Pros <*www.certespros.com*>, comes in. Her company finds senior-level financial professionals to fit flexible work environments on a project, interim, and permanent basis. Certes's 200-plus full- and part-time workers are free to shape their schedules to fit their lifestyles, allowing them to go on vacation, attend a child's sporting event, or even take the entire summer off unimpeded. In fact, Certes employees can take up to six months off and still retain benefits.

"Certes strives to implement programs and practices that create a flexible and supportive workplace, one that allows our employees to express their true needs while providing the highest level of service to our clients," Mainquist said. Besides providing an impressive array of benefits and above-average wages, Certes makes five vacation homes available to workers free of charge. Generous benefits are not typical of temporary agencies, but they have helped Mainquist attract a loyal workforce. The average tenure of a Certes employee is four years, which is exceptional in the usually turnover-heavy temporary employment industry.

Besides outstanding perks, Certes workers acquire an unusually broad range of work experience. Today's business environment demands that workers have a diverse set of skills instead of focusing on just one. Contingent workers view their temporary positions as opportunities to build their skills and gain necessary experience. Many employers in turn view temporary agencies as excellent training grounds and say hiring people for temporary work is an efficient way to test-drive employees before committing to hire them full-time. Many contingent workers find the flexibility liberating. It gives them more time with their families, along with opportunities to build new skills or switch careers.

In this chapter, you will learn how successful businesses like Certes recruit, manage, and make the most of their employees.

Sources: "Company Profile," Certes Financial Pros, 2012, www.certespros.com/news/press_kit.cfm; Elizabeth Millard, "Benefits Buffet," *Minnesota Business,* July 2008; Dr. John Sullivan, "A Flexible Force," *Workforce Management,* 14 July 2008; and Kathryn Tyler, "Treat Contingent Workers with Care," *HRMagazine,* 1 March 2008.

Explain the importance of human resource management as a strategic contributor to organizational success, and summarize the five steps in human resource planning.

human resource management (HRM)
The process of determining human resource needs and then recruiting, selecting, developing, motivating, evaluating, compensating, and scheduling employees to achieve organizational goals.

WORKING WITH PEOPLE IS JUST THE BEGINNING

Students have been known to say they want to go into human resource management because they want to "work with people." It is true that human resource managers work with people, but they are also deeply involved in planning, record keeping, and other administrative duties. To begin a career in human resource management, you need to develop a better reason than "I want to work with people." This chapter will discuss what else human resource management is all about.

Human resource management (HRM) is the process of determining human resource needs and then recruiting, selecting, developing, motivating, evaluating, compensating, and scheduling employees to achieve organizational goals. Figure 12.1 illustrates the activities associated with HRM. Janice Wismer, President and owner of Radical Simplicity Inc. (and formerly the Chief Human Resources Officer for McCain Foods Limited), believes that human resource (HR) professionals can do a lot to develop people to fulfill roles that contribute to organizational success and individual happiness. According to Wismer, "The ripple effect on our society from the way we lead and govern organizations is remarkable. In the HR profession we are not only of service to an organization, but we are also of service to the very society of which we are all a part. I can't think of a profession where we can make more of a difference. Healthy organizations are like oxygen to a vibrant community and family unit—there is an inextricable link between what happens in organizations and the prosperity of a country."[1]

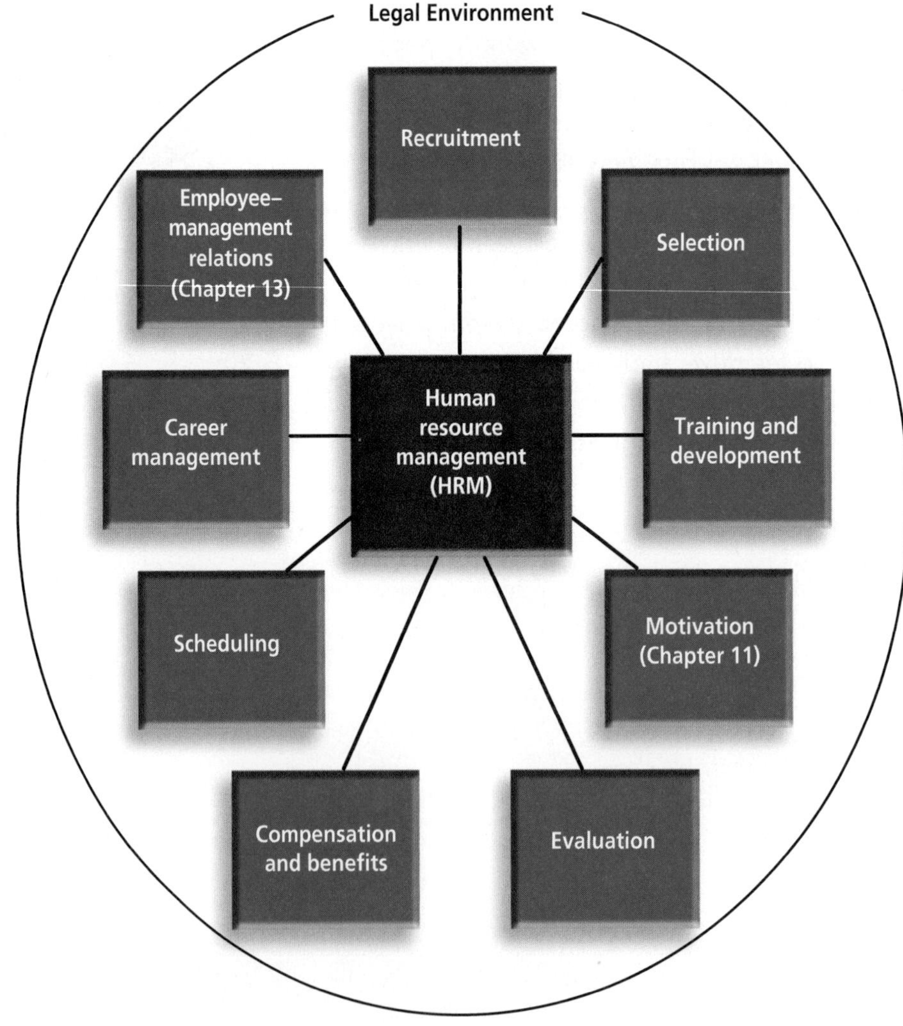

Figure 12.1

Human Resource Management
As this figure shows, human resource management is more than hiring and firing personnel. All activities are designed to achieve organizational goals within the laws that affect human resource management. (Note that human resource management includes motivation, as discussed in Chapter 11, and employee–management relations, which will be discussed in Chapter 13.)

For many years, HRM was called "personnel" and involved clerical functions such as screening applications, keeping records, processing the payroll, and finding new employees when necessary. The roles and responsibilities of HRM have evolved primarily because of two key factors: (1) organizations' recognition of employees as their ultimate resource and (2) changes in the law that rewrote many traditional practices. We will explore the first key factor next and end the chapter considering how laws affect human resource management.

Developing the Ultimate Resource

One reason why human resource management is receiving increased attention is the major shift from traditional manufacturing industries to service and high-tech manufacturing industries that require highly technical job skills. This shift means that many workers must be retrained for new, more challenging jobs.

Some people have called employees the "ultimate resource," and when you think about it, nothing could be truer. People develop the ideas that eventually become the products that satisfy consumers' wants and needs. Take away their creative minds and large leading firms such as Cirque du Soleil and Apple would be nothing. This would also be the case if you are a small business or an emerging growth company such as Mississauga-based Contingent Workforce Solutions Inc. <*www.cwsolutions.ca*> (which provides software and consulting services to help clients manage temporary and contract employees) and Montreal-based Lumenpulse Lighting Inc. <*www.lumenpulse.com*> (which sells LED lighting fixtures and controls).[2] What is the key ingredient to launching a winning start-up? According to *PROFIT* magazine's PROFIT HOT 50, "the answer is talent, talent, and more talent. When asked to score their most important success factors on a scale of one to ten, HOT 50 CEOs rated hiring good staff at 9.3 and retaining them at 9.4. These youthful firms have found smart ways to entice A-players to join their fledgling ranks: the vast majority provide bonuses, employee training, and profit-sharing plans."[3]

In the past, human resources were plentiful, so there was little need to nurture and develop them. If you needed qualified people, you simply hired them. If they did not work out, you fired them and found others. Most firms assigned the job of recruiting, selecting, training, evaluating, compensating, motivating, and, yes, firing people to the functional departments that employed them, such as accounting, manufacturing, and marketing. Today, the job of human resource management has taken on an increased role in the firm since qualified employees are scarcer, which makes recruiting and retaining people more important and more difficult.[4]

In a survey conducted by DBM <*www.dbm.com*>, an HR consulting firm, Canadian human resource professionals expect that by 2013 at least 50 percent of their HR departments' roles will be involve providing strategic input and less time and energy will be spent on HR administration.[5] According to David Weiss, a partner with international consulting firm GSW Consultants, HR should streamline its core responsibilities and align its efforts with the company's vision and customer needs. This alignment will allow HR to take advantage of unique qualifications that will enable it to provide strategic value to the company and the company's customers.[6]

In the future, human resource management may become the firm's most critical function, responsible for dealing with all aspects of a business's most critical resource—people.[7] In fact, the human resource function has become so important that it is no longer the responsibility of just one department; it is a responsibility of all managers. What are some human resource challenges all managers face? We'll outline a few next.

Human Resource Challenges[8]

Many of the changes that have had the most dramatic impact on business are the changes in the labour force. The ability to compete in global markets depends on new ideas, new products and services, and new levels of productivity. In other words, on

▸ Firms face a shortage of workers skilled in areas like computers, biotechnology, robotics, the sciences, green technology, and the development of clean energy sources like these solar panels. What other job markets do you think will grow as companies focus more on environmentally friendly policies? Which ones appeal to you?

▸ The Canadian Charter of Rights and Freedoms allows and encourages Canadians to maintain their mother tongue, traditions, and culture. However, some workers still experience harassment. What can an employer do to create a respectful environment?

people with good ideas. These are some of the challenges and opportunities in human resources:

- A third of Canada's workforce will retire over the next five years, leaving businesses scrambling to fill vacant jobs, including in skilled trades.
- An increasing number of skilled and unskilled workers from declining industries, such as steel and automobiles, who are unemployed or underemployed and need retraining. *Underemployed workers* are those who have more skills or knowledge than their current jobs require.
- A growing percentage of new workers who are undereducated and unprepared for jobs in the contemporary business environment.
- An increasing number of both single-parent and two-income families, resulting in a demand for job sharing, parental leave, and special career advancement programs for women.
- A shift in employee attitudes toward work. Leisure time has become a much higher priority, as have flextime and a shorter workweek.
- A declining economy that is taking a toll on employee morale as well as increasing the demand for temporary and part-time workers.
- A challenge from overseas labour pools whose members work for lower wages and are subject to fewer laws and regulations than Canadian workers. This results in jobs being outsourced overseas.
- An increased demand for benefits tailored to the individual, yet still cost-effective to the company. See the Green Box to learn how some companies are addressing wellness issues at work.
- A growing concern over health care, elder care, child care, and opportunities for people with disabilities.
- A decreased sense of employee loyalty, which raises employee turnover and the cost of replacing lost workers.

In a study titled *Creating People Advantage: How to Address HR Challenges Worldwide Through 2015,* more than 4,700 executives worldwide were surveyed on seventeen topics in HRM. The survey found that managing talent was the number one human resource challenge and there were predictions that it would remain at or near the top of executive agendas for the foreseeable future. In Canada, executives also identified other critical challenges: managing demographics, improving leadership development, managing work-life balance, and transforming HR into a strategic partner. To create people advantage and overcome some of the human resource challenges identified, the report suggested five major steps be taken by companies: (1) understand the external environment, (2) understand the internal environment, (3) select the most critical human resource topics and set priorities, (4) initiate projects with dedicated teams, and (5) secure support from top management. Review the Dealing with Change box at the end of this textbook part for more on the implications of an aging workforce.

GREENBOX

Green Eggs and Green Ham

In many company cafeterias, jelly doughnuts and sugary sodas are becoming distant memories. Big businesses like Google, Microsoft, and Dow Chemical have begun to supply their company eateries with healthy alternatives like dried fruit, salads, and vegan dishes, while cutting back on fatty burgers and desserts. By helping keep employees healthy, companies will not only have a fitter workforce but also save money on insurance premiums, and may even see an increase in productivity. Dow Chemical aims to reduce health risks to its 43,000 employees by 10 percent by 2014.

Besides conveying health and monetary benefits, eating right in the workplace also helps the environment. Along with eliminating trans fats from cafeteria food, San Diego State University turns 50 tons of leftovers a year into compost for the campus landscape. In a separate example, Cox Enterprises <*www.coxenterprises.com*> makes all the packaging for its health-oriented food service from sustainable sources. Plates are made of sugar cane and cups from corn; both disintegrate in 60 days. While other organizations may not be as creative, their growing use of organic and renewable sources for food are not only good for the body but also much better for the earth than chemicals and preservatives.

Sources: Stephanie Armour, "Corporate Cafeterias Go the Green, Healthy Route," *USA Today,* 8 February 2008; and Michelle Conlin, "Hide the Doritos! Here Comes HR!" *BusinessWeek,* 17 April 2008.

Given the issues mentioned, and others that are sure to develop, you can see why HRM has taken a more central position in management thinking than ever before. While the HR challenges are greater than ever before, so too are the opportunities for companies to excel through their HR strategies.

DETERMINING YOUR HUMAN RESOURCE NEEDS

All management, including human resource management, begins with planning. Five steps are involved in the human resource planning process:

1. *Preparing a human resource inventory of the organization's employees.* This inventory should include ages, names, education, capabilities, training, specialized skills, and other relevant information (e.g., languages spoken). Such information reveals whether the labour force is technically up to date and thoroughly trained.
2. *Preparing a job analysis.* A **job analysis** is a study of what is done by employees who hold various job titles. It is necessary to recruit and train employees with the necessary skills to do the job. The results of job analysis are two written statements: job descriptions and job specifications. A **job description** specifies the objectives of the job, the type of work to be done, the responsibilities and duties, the working conditions, and the relationship of the job to other functions. **Job specifications** are a written summary of the minimum qualifications (e.g., education and skills) required of workers to do a particular job. In short, job descriptions are statements about the job, whereas job specifications are statements about the person who does the job. See Figure 12.2 for hypothetical examples of a job description and job specifications.
3. *Assessing future human resource demand.* Because technology changes rapidly, effective human resource managers are proactive; that is, they forecast the organization's requirements and train people ahead of time or ensure trained people are available when needed.[9]
4. *Assessing future human resource supply.* The labour force is constantly shifting: getting older, becoming more technically oriented, and attracting more women.

job analysis
A study of what is done by employees who hold various job titles.

job description
A summary of the objectives of a job, the type of work to be done, the responsibilities and duties, the working conditions, and the relationship of the job to other functions.

job specifications
A written summary of the minimum qualifications required of workers to do a particular job.

Figure 12.2

Job Analysis

A job analysis yields two important statements: job descriptions and job specifications. Here you have a job description and job specifications for a sales representative.

Job Analysis	
Observe current sales representatives doing the job. Discuss job with sales managers. Have current sales reps keep a diary of their activities.	
Job Description	**Job Specifications**
Primary objective is to sell the company's products to stores in Territory Z. Duties include servicing accounts and maintaining positive relationships with clients. Responsibilities include: • introducing the new products to store managers in the area • helping the store managers estimate the volume to order • negotiating prime shelf space • explaining sales promotion activities to store managers • stocking and maintaining shelves in stores that wish such service	Characteristics of the ideal person qualifying for this job include: • bilingual • self-motivated • positive attitude • strong written and communication skills • have a valid Driver's Licence • two years sales experience • a diploma or degree in Business

Some workers will be scarcer in the future, like computer and robotic repair workers, and others will be oversupplied, like assembly-line workers.

5. *Establishing a strategic plan.* The plan must address recruiting, selecting, training, developing, appraising, compensating, and scheduling the labour force. For this plan to have impact, the HR department must have upper management support for its acceptance and implementation. Because the first four steps lead up to this one, we'll focus on them in the rest of the chapter.

Some companies use advanced technology to perform the human resource planning process more efficiently. For example, IBM manages its global workforce of about 100,000 employees and 100,000 subcontractors with a database that matches employee skills, experiences, schedules, and references with jobs available. If a client in Nova Scotia has a month-long project requiring a consultant who can speak English and French, has an advanced degree in engineering, and has experience with Linux programming, IBM's database can find the best-suited consultant available and put him or her in touch with the client.[10]

LO 2

Describe methods that companies use to recruit new employees, and explain some of the issues that make recruitment challenging.

RECRUITING EMPLOYEES FROM A DIVERSE POPULATION

Recruitment is the set of activities used to obtain a sufficient number of the right people at the right time. The end result is to have a pool of qualified applicants. One would think that with a continuous flow of new people into the workforce recruiting would be easy. On the contrary, recruiting has become very difficult, for several reasons:

recruitment
The set of activities used to obtain a sufficient number of the right people at the right time.

- Some organizations have policies that demand promotions from within, operate under union contracts, or offer low wages, which makes recruiting and keeping employees difficult or subject to outside influence and restrictions.
- There are legal guidelines that surround hiring practices. The Canadian Human Rights Act requires that employers provide equal employment opportunities. For example, a human rights complaint could be made if an employer said

that he would not hire a woman or a visible minority for a particular job, regardless of that person's competency. The Canadian Human Rights Act protects those that work for federally regulated organizations or service providers (e.g., chartered banks and airlines). The rest of employees are protected by provincial or territorial jurisdiction.

- The emphasis on corporate culture, teamwork, and participative management makes it important to hire people who not only are skilled but also fit in with the culture and leadership style of the organization.[11]
- Sometimes people with the necessary skills are not available; in this case, workers must be hired and then trained internally.[12]

Human resource managers turn to many sources for assistance. Figure 12.3 highlights examples of sources used by organizations. *Internal sources* include employees who are already within the firm (and may be transferred or promoted) and employees who can recommend others to hire. Using internal sources is less expensive than recruiting outside the company. The greatest advantage of hiring from within is that it helps maintain employee morale. It is not always possible to find qualified workers within the company, however, so human resource managers must use *external sources* such as advertisements, public and private employment agencies, school placement offices, management consultants, professional organizations, referrals, and online and walk-in applications. While most external sources are straightforward, some may involve difficult decisions.

Recruiting qualified workers may be particularly difficult for small businesses with few staff members and less-than-competitive compensation. Some popular recruiting Internet sites include Workopolis <*www.workopolis.com*> and Monster <*www.monster.ca*>. The Spotlight on Small Business box outlines some ways in which small businesses can address their recruitment needs.

Passion Inc. was founded by brothers Mark and Nathan Laurie from their student residence with $500 in savings and the dream of graduating from Dalhousie University debt free. Today, one of the company's three divisions is the magazine *jobpostings* <*jobpostings.ca*>, which helps students find jobs through print and online media. Have you seen this magazine on campus?

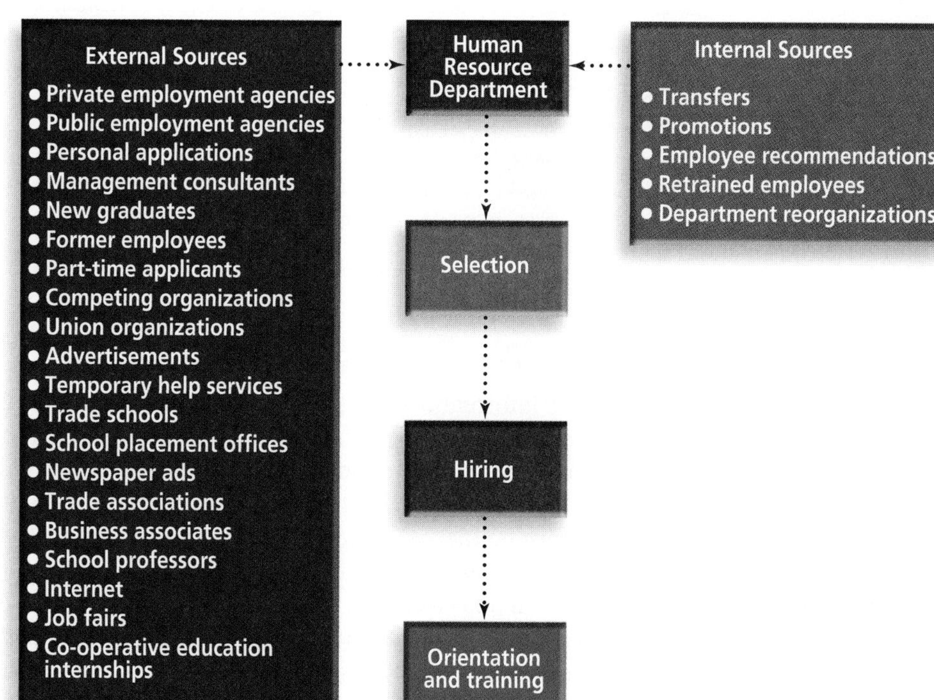

Figure 12.3

Employee Sources

Internal sources are often given first consideration. So it is useful to get a recommendation from a current employee of the firm for which you want to work. School placement offices are also an important source. Be sure to learn about their services early so that you can plan an employment strategy throughout your academic career.

SPOTLIGHT ON SMALL BUSINESS

It's Not Easy Being Small

To survive, it is critical for small businesses to recruit and retain qualified workers. However, competing for top talent is difficult when you cannot afford corporate-level benefits or expensive recruiters to hunt down the best people. Despite these hurdles, small-business management consultants say that there are many ways to lure desirable workers:

- *Transform ads into promotional tools.* Eco-print , a small print shop, brags in its advertisements about the benefits of working for this collegial company.
- *Post job openings on the Internet.* Running a 30-day job posting on an online service such as Monster.ca costs $695. A job posting (where approximately 30 to 40 words would fit within a 1.85 inch wide by 2 inch deep box) in the national Careers section of *The Globe and Mail* newspaper for three days (Wednesday, Friday, and Saturday) costs $3,903 plus HST.
- *Let your staff help select hires.* The more staff engaged in the search and interview process, the better chance to find recruits with the personality and skills to fit in.
- *Create a dynamic workplace to attract local, energetic applicants.* Sometimes word of mouth is the most effective recruiting tool.
- *Test-drive an employee.* Hiring contingent workers allows you to test candidates for a few months before deciding whether to make an offer of permanent employment.
- *Hire customers.* Loyal customers sometimes make the smartest employees. Build-A-Bear Workshop often hires customers who come into its stores and exhibit a real interest in the company and its products.
- *Check community groups and local government agencies.* Don't forget to check out provincial- or territory-run employment agencies. Many non-profit organizations serve immigrants new to a region or people in need of a job who become excellent candidates you can train.
- *Work hard for publicity in local media.* Publicity is more believable than advertising.
- *Lure candidates with a policy of promotions and raises.* Most employees want to know that they can move up in the company. Give employees an incentive for learning the business.
- *Outsource fringe benefit management to a professional employer organization (PEO).* It's tough to build a benefits program equivalent to those offered by large companies, but PEOs may be able to offer lower insurance rates for benefit programs because of greater economies of scale. Face it, any way you can close the gap may help attract qualified workers.

Sources: "Job Posting," Monster.ca, 19 June 2012, http://hiring.monster.ca/recruitment/Job-Postings.aspx; *The Globe and Mail–Classifieds Department (1-866-999-9237)*, 19 June 2012; "Why Are Your Employees Leaving?" *Nonprofit World*, 1 July 2008; "Finding, Hiring and Keeping Next-Generation Talent," Executive Quotes and Information Service, 26 May 2008; Dwayne Orrick, "Making Recruitment and Retention a Priority," *Law and Order*, 1 March 2008; and Mila Stahl, "How to Hire (or Fire) an Employee," *Wisconsin State Journal*, 1 March 2008.

selection
The process of gathering information and deciding who should be hired, under legal guidelines, to serve the best interests of the individual and the organization.

PROGRESS ASSESSMENT

- What is human resource management?
- What are the five steps in human resource planning?
- What factors make it difficult to recruit qualified employees?

Outline the five steps in selecting employees, and illustrate the use of various types of employee training and development methods.

SELECTING EMPLOYEES WHO WILL BE PRODUCTIVE

Selection is the process of gathering information and deciding who should be hired, under legal guidelines, to serve the best interests of the individual and the organization. Selecting and training employees have become extremely expensive processes in some firms. Think of what is involved: interview time, medical exams in some instances, training costs, unproductive time spent learning the job, moving expenses, and so on. Calculating the cost-per-hire can get extremely complicated and numbers vary, depending on the source. The Conference Board of Canada calculates that the average cost-per-hire as follows: Executive—$43,000; Management/Professional—$17,000; Technical—$13,300; and Clerical/Support—$3,300.[13] Keep in mind that these are average numbers and that selection expenses can vary widely depending on the position and job expectations.

What is clear is that the selection process is an important element of any human resource program. A typical selection process involves five steps:

1. *Obtaining complete application forms.* Although employment laws limit the kinds of questions that may appear on an application form, applications help reveal the applicant's educational background, work experience, career objectives, and other qualifications directly related to the requirements of the job. Canada's Wonderland <*www.canadaswonderland.com*> receives over 18,000 applications for seasonal employment each year. With only 4,000 positions to fill, a stringent screening process has been developed to select and hire candidates. All applications are individually screened and only those qualified will be granted an opportunity to move on to the interview stage of the process. Candidates who submit an application online receive an automated e-mail response that confirms that their application has been successfully transmitted.[14]

▸ Depending on the job, it is not uncommon to be involved in several interviews, one of which might include a panel interview. How would you prepare differently if this was the case?

2. *Conducting initial and follow-up interviews.* A staff member from the human resource department often screens applicants in a first interview. If the interviewer considers the applicant a potential employee, the manager who will supervise the new employee interviews the applicant as well. It is important that managers prepare adequately for the interview to avoid selection decisions they may regret.[15] This includes asking all candidates the same questions so as to be able to fairly compare answers. Always keep in mind that certain questions, no matter how innocent the intention, could later be used as evidence if that applicant files discrimination charges.[16] For example, asking an applicant about his or her family background, children, and family planning are prohibited. In the past, an employer might have asked if the applicant had children to determine whether the applicant could work shift work or on weekends. Today, the applicant would be asked if working shift work or on weekends would be a problem (without asking about children), as this is a relevant job-related question.
3. *Giving employment tests.* Organizations often use tests to measure basic competencies in specific job skills (e.g., welding or fire fighting) and to help evaluate applicants' personalities and interests.[17] In using employment tests, it is important that they be directly related to the job. Many companies test potential employees in assessment centres, where applicants perform actual job tasks. Such testing can make the selection process more efficient and will generally satisfy legal requirements.
4. *Conducting background investigations.* Most organizations now confirm a candidate's work record, school record, credit history, and references more carefully than they have in the past to help identify those most likely to succeed.[18] It is simply too costly to hire, train, and motivate people only to lose them and have to start the process over.

Be aware that more hiring managers and recruiters are visiting social networking Web sites such as Facebook and MySpace to gather background information as a way to eliminate candidates.[19] A few examples of the types of things that might cause concern and raise questions for employers can include one's recreational activities (e.g., if one appears drunk or out of control or engaged in

▸ Services such as LexisNexis <www.lexisnexis.ca> and PeopleWise <www.peoplewise.com> allow prospective employers to not only conduct speedy background checks of criminal records, driving records, and credit histories, but also to verify work experience and professional and educational credentials.

behaviour that may be considered offensive) as exhibited by photos on one's profile and friends' profiles; comments about employment situations (e.g., "I hate my boss." or "I was late again for work today. I just can't get out of bed."); or religious, political, or sexual activities or views that vary significantly from the mainstream.[20] What do you think you can do to protect yourself from embarrassment or lost employment opportunities?

5. *Establishing trial (probationary) periods.* Often, an organization will hire an employee conditionally. This enables the person to prove his or her worth on the job. After a specified probationary period (perhaps three months or a year), the firm may either permanently hire or discharge that employee on the basis of evaluations from supervisors. Although such systems make it easier to fire inefficient or problem employees, they do not eliminate the high cost of turnover.

The selection process is often long and difficult, but it is worth the effort to select new employees carefully because of the high cost of replacing workers.[21] Care helps ensure that new employees meet all requirements, including communication skills, education, technical skills, experience, and personality. Finally, where a company has a collective labour agreement (a union contract with its employees) the selection process must also follow the provisions of that agreement. This is discussed in more detail in the next chapter.

Hiring Contingent Workers

A company with employment needs that vary—from hour to hour, day to day, week to week, and season to season—may find it cost-effective to hire contingent workers. **Contingent workers** are defined as workers who do not have regular, full-time employment. Such workers include part-time workers (according to Statistics Canada, this would be anyone who works less than 30 hours per week), temporary workers (workers paid by temporary employment agencies), seasonal workers, independent contractors, interns, and co-op students.

contingent workers
Workers who do not have regular, full-time employment.

Companies may hire contingent workers when full-time employees are on some type of leave (such as maternity leave), when there is a peak demand for labour or products (like the holiday shopping season), or when quick service to customers is a priority. Companies also tend to hire more contingent workers in an uncertain economy, particularly when they are available and qualified, and when the jobs require minimum training.

Contingent workers receive few benefits; they are rarely offered health insurance, vacation time, or private pensions. They also tend to earn less than permanent workers do. On the positive side, some on temporary assignments may be offered full-time employment. The cachet of a job with the CBC (Canadian Broadcasting Corporation) <*www.cbc.ca*> is one of the reasons the Crown corporation is able to employ 30 percent of its workforce of 5,500 on contracts as freelancers, temporary workers, or casuals.[22] The voices you hear reporting from around the city and around the world often belong to stringers and freelancers hoping to make an impression and land a permanent position.[23]

MAKING ETHICAL DECISIONS

Recruiting Employees from Competitors

As the human resource director for Technocrat, Inc., it is your job to recruit the best employees. Your most recent human resource inventory indicated that Technocrat currently has an abundance of qualified designers and that several lower-level workers will soon be eligible for promotions to designer positions. Despite the surplus of qualified designers within the firm, you are considering recruiting a designer who is now with a major competitor. Your thinking is that the new employee will be a source of information about the competition's new products. What are your ethical considerations in this case? Will you lure the employee away from the competition even though you have no need for a designer? What will be the consequences of your decision?

Managers see using temporary workers as a way of weeding out poor workers and finding good hires. Because temporary workers are often told that they may, at some point, be hired as permanent workers, they are often more productive than those on the permanent payroll. Review the Making Ethical Decisions box for a dilemma that can apply to contingent workers.

Many people find that temporary work offers them a lot more flexibility than permanent employment. For example, student Daniel Butrym found that the transition from student to temp worker was not difficult. Butrym says, "You come back in town. You don't have to interview. You don't have to waste a lot of time looking for a job. The first time you walk into the temporary staffing office, they meet you, sit you down and they find out your skills. Once you're in their computer, they have all your stats, they know what you can do, and you're done. [Later] I can call from school, say 'I'm going to be home for spring break, I need some money.'" As soon as Butrym calls, he's put into the system for work assignments.

Butrym is not alone. Andy Williams of Randstad <*www.randstad.com*>, the staffing services giant, welcomes students. "A lot of the students are computer-literate, and they are familiar with many of the popular software programs that the companies use. And, they are quick to get up to speed on [any] proprietary software an employer might use. . . . Every customer is different. Some assignments are for one day. Some assignments are for weeks or for the whole summer," Williams says.[24]

In an era of rapid change and economic uncertainty, some contingent workers have even found that temping can be more secure than full-time employment.

TRAINING AND DEVELOPING EMPLOYEES FOR OPTIMUM PERFORMANCE

Because employees need to learn how to work with new equipment—such as word processors, computers, and robots—companies are finding that they must offer training programs that often are quite sophisticated. Employers find that spending money on training is usually money well spent. A quality training program could lead to higher retention rates, increased productivity, and greater job satisfaction among employees.[25] **Training and development** includes all attempts to improve productivity by increasing an employee's ability to perform. Training focuses on short-term skills, whereas development focuses on long-term abilities. But both training and development programs include three steps: (1) assessing the needs of the organization and the skills of the employees to determine training needs; (2) designing training activities to meet the identified needs; and (3) evaluating the effectiveness of the training. Some common training and development activities are employee orientation, on-the-job training, apprentice programs, off-the-job training, online training, vestibule training, and job simulation. Management development will be discussed in a separate section.

training and development All attempts to improve productivity by increasing an employee's ability to perform. Training focuses on short-term skills, whereas development focuses on long-term abilities.

employee orientation
The activity that introduces new employees to the organization; to fellow employees; to their immediate supervisors; and to the policies, practices, values, and objectives of the firm.

Employee orientation is the activity that initiates new employees to the organization, to fellow employees, to their immediate supervisors, and to the policies, practices, values, and objectives of the firm. Orientation programs include everything from informal talks to formal activities that last a day or more. They may involve such activities as scheduled visits to various departments and required reading of handbooks.[26] For example, all new Canadian Tire Financial Services (CTFS) employees attend Canadian Tire University, Niagara campus. During their orientation employees learn about the company; they are introduced to the differences between the Canadian Tire Corporation divisions, and to what CTFS does. This includes CTFS's structure, vision, purpose, and team values.

on-the-job training
Training in which the employee immediately begins his or her tasks and learns by doing, or watches others for a while and then imitates them, all right at the workplace.

On-the-job training is the most fundamental type of training. The employee being trained on the job immediately begins his or her tasks and learns by doing, or watches others for a while and then imitates them, right at the workplace. Salespeople, for example, are often trained by watching experienced salespeople perform (often called *shadowing*). Naturally, this can be either quite effective or disastrous, depending on the skills and habits of the person being watched. On-the-job training is obviously the easiest kind of training to implement when the job is relatively simple (such as clerking in a store) or repetitive (such as collecting refuse, cleaning carpets, or mowing lawns). More demanding or intricate jobs require a more intense training effort. Intranets and other new forms of technology are leading to cost-effective on-the-job training programs available 24 hours a day, all year long. Computer systems can monitor workers' input and give them instructions if they become confused about what to do next.

apprentice programs
Training programs involving a period during which a learner works alongside an experienced employee to master the skills and procedures of a craft.

Apprentice programs involve a period during which a learner works alongside an experienced employee to master the skills and procedures of a craft. Some apprenticeship programs also involve classroom training. Many skilled crafts, such as bricklaying and plumbing, require a new worker to serve as an apprentice for several years. Trade unions often require new workers to serve apprenticeships to ensure excellence among their members as well as to limit entry to the union. Workers who successfully complete an apprenticeship earn the classification of *journeyman*. In the future, there are likely to be more but shorter apprenticeship programs to prepare people for skilled jobs in changing industries. For example, auto repair will require more intense training as new automobile models include advanced computers and other electronic devices.[27]

▸ Training and development can include a combination of activities such as off-the-job training and online training.

Off-the-job training occurs away from the workplace and consists of internal or external programs to develop any of a variety of skills or to foster personal development. Training is becoming more sophisticated as jobs become more sophisticated. Furthermore, training is expanding to include education (e.g., an MBA) and personal development. Subjects may include time management, stress management, health and wellness, physical education, nutrition, and even art and languages.

Online training offers an example of how technology is improving the efficiency of many off-the-job training programs. In such training, employees "attend" classes via the Internet. These can be courses that have been created in-house or *distance learning* courses (because the students are separated by distance from the instructor or content source) that are offered by colleges and universities. Online training gives employers the ability to provide consistent content that is tailored to specific employee training needs, at convenient times, to a large number of employees.

Vestibule training (near-the-job training) is done in classrooms where employees are taught on equipment similar to that used on the job. Such classrooms enable employees to learn proper methods and safety procedures before assuming a specific job assignment in an organization. Computer and robotics training is often completed in a vestibule classroom.

Job simulation is the use of equipment that duplicates job conditions and tasks so that trainees can learn skills before attempting them on the job. Job simulation differs from vestibule training in that the simulation attempts to duplicate the exact combination of conditions that occur on the job. Such training simulations are used because the potential cost of real-world mistakes is huge. This is the kind of training given to astronauts, airline pilots, operators, ship captains, and others who must learn difficult procedures off the job.

off-the-job training
Training that occurs away from the workplace and consists of internal or external programs to develop any of a variety of skills or to foster personal development.

online training
Training programs in which employees "attend" classes via the Internet.

vestibule training
Training done in schools where employees are taught on equipment similar to that used on the job.

job simulation
The use of equipment that duplicates job conditions and tasks so that trainees can learn skills before attempting them on the job.

management development
The process of training and educating employees to become good managers and then monitoring the progress of their managerial skills over time.

Management Development

Managers need special training. To be good communicators, they especially need to learn listening skills and empathy. They also need time management, planning, and human relations skills.

Management development, then, is the process of training and educating employees to become good managers and then monitoring the progress of their managerial skills over time. Management development programs have sprung up everywhere, especially at colleges, universities, and private management development firms. Managers participate in role-playing exercises, solve various management cases, view films, and attend lectures.

Management development is increasingly being used as a tool to accomplish business objectives. Most management training programs also include several of the following:

- *On-the-job coaching.* A senior manager will assist a lower-level manager by teaching him or her needed skills and generally providing direction, advice, and helpful feedback.
- *Understudy positions.* Job titles such as undersecretary and assistant are part of a relatively successful way of developing managers. Selected employees work as assistants to higher-level managers and participate in planning and other managerial functions until they are ready to assume such positions themselves.
- *Job rotation.* So that they can learn about different functions of the organization, managers are often given assignments in a variety of departments. Through job rotation, top managers gain the broad picture of the organization necessary to their success.
- *Off-the-job courses and training.* Managers periodically go to schools or seminars for a week or more to hone their technical and human relations skills. For example, McDonald's Corporation has its own Hamburger University. Managers and potential franchisees attend six days of classes and complete a course of study equivalent to 36 hours of business-school credit.[28]

On a final note, both training and development budgets and initiatives need to be reviewed regularly to ensure that maximum impact is being achieved and that organizations of all sizes are getting the best return on their investments.

▸ Management development can include on-the-job and off-the-job training. The activities will vary depending on the person being developed and the purpose of the program.

Empowering Workers

Historically, many managers gave explicit instructions to workers, telling them what to do to meet the goals and objectives of the organization. The term for such an approach is *directing*. In traditional organizations, directing involves giving assignments, explaining routines, clarifying policies, and providing feedback on performance. Many organizations still follow this model, especially in firms such as fast-food restaurants and small retail establishments where the employees do not have the skills and experience needed to work on their own, at least at first.

Progressive managers, such as those in many high-tech firms and Internet companies, are less likely than traditional managers to give specific instructions to employees. Rather, they are more likely to empower employees to make decisions on their own. Empowerment means giving employees the *authority* (the right to make a decision without consulting the manager) and *responsibility* (the requirement to accept the consequences of one's actions) to respond quickly to customer requests. Managers are often reluctant to give up the power they have to make such decisions; thus, empowerment is often resisted. In those firms that are able to implement the concept, the manager's role is becoming less that of a boss and director and more that of a coach, assistant, counsellor, or team member.

enabling
Giving workers the education and tools they need to make decisions.

networking
The process of establishing and maintaining contacts with key managers in one's own organization and other organizations and using those contacts to weave strong relationships that serve as informal development systems.

mentor
An experienced employee who supervises, coaches, and guides lower-level employees by introducing them to the right people and generally being their organizational sponsor.

Enabling is the term used to describe giving workers the education and tools they need to make decisions. Clearly, enabling is the key to the success of empowerment. Without the right education, training, coaching, and tools, workers cannot assume the responsibilities and decision-making roles that make empowerment work. At WestJet, employees are encouraged through regular training sessions to resolve issues with WestJet customers. "From handing out flight credits to sending out for hamburgers to feed stranded passengers, they take care of things up front," says Don Bell, co-founder. "That kind of commitment comes from hiring the right people, aligning their interests to the company, and hooking the success of the business to their pocketbooks."[29]

Networking

Networking is the process of establishing and maintaining contacts with key managers in one's own organization and in other organizations and using those contacts to weave strong relationships that serve as informal development systems. Of equal or greater importance is a **mentor**, a corporate manager who supervises, coaches, and guides selected lower-level employees by introducing them to the right people and generally being their organizational sponsor. In most organizations, informal mentoring occurs as experienced employees assist less experienced workers.[30] However, many organizations formally assign mentors to employees considered to have strong potential.

Networking is important at all levels of an organization and also through professional associations and organizations. Vancouver-based Absolute Software Corporation <*www.absolute.com*> is a small company that used its senior executives to talk to top executives at Apple Computer by attending the National Education Conference in Philadelphia. John Livingston, CEO of Absolute Software, sees great value in networking: "Industry functions provide an opportunity to make contacts, but . . . networking works only when you have something to say that's of interest."[31]

Networking and mentoring can go beyond the business environment. For example, school is a perfect place to begin networking. Associations you nurture with instructors, with business people through internships, and especially with your classmates might provide you with a valuable network you can turn to for the rest of your career.

▸ Informal networking gatherings like this one are sponsored by Likemind <*likemind.us*>, an association of creative professionals who meet weekly in 55 cities worldwide. "We just show up over coffee and talk," said one participant. Why do you think younger workers might prefer such informal gatherings?

Diversity in Management Development

As women moved into management, they also learned the importance of networking and of having mentors. Unfortunately, women often have more difficulty than men in networking or finding mentors, since most senior managers are male. More women are now entering established networking systems or, in some instances, creating their own.[32] Some examples of organizations include the Canadian Women's Business Network <*www.cdnbizwomen.com*>, Women's Enterprise Centre <*www.womensenterprise.ca*>, and Canadian Association of Women Executives & Entrepreneurs <*www.cawee.net*>.

Ethnic groups are networking as well. For example, Mark Shir, a financial and computer specialist from Taiwan, felt that he would never get ahead in the companies he had worked in for ten years. When he joined Monte Jade <*www.montejade.org*>, an association that helps Taiwanese and Chinese assimilate in American business, he met people who helped him start his own successful hardware-packaging company.[33]

Companies that take the initiative to develop female and minority managers understand three crucial principles: (1) grooming women and minorities for management positions is not about legality or morality; it is about bringing more talent in the door—the key to long-term profitability; (2) the best women and minorities will become harder to attract and retain, so the companies that start now will have an edge later; and (3) having more women and minorities at all levels means that businesses can serve their female and minority customers better. If you do not have a diverse workforce, how are you going to satisfy your diverse customers?

PROGRESS ASSESSMENT

- What are the five steps in the selection process?
- What are contingent workers? Why do companies hire such workers?
- Can you name and describe four training and development techniques?

APPRAISING EMPLOYEE PERFORMANCE TO GET OPTIMUM RESULTS

Trace the six steps in appraising employee performance, and summarize the objectives of employee compensation programs.

Managers must be able to determine whether their workers are doing an effective and efficient job. This is critical if an organization is to achieve its goals. Managers determine this by using performance appraisals. A **performance appraisal** is an evaluation in which the performance level of employees is measured against established standards to make decisions about promotions, compensation, additional training, or firing. One way to look at the performance-appraisal process is to consider these six steps:

performance appraisal
An evaluation in which the performance level of employees is measured against established standards to make decisions about promotions, compensation, additional training, or firing.

1. *Establishing Performance Standards.* This is a crucial step. Standards must be understandable, subject to measurement, and reasonable. They must be accepted by both the manager and the subordinate.
2. *Communicating Standards.* Often managers assume that employees know what is expected of them, but such assumptions are dangerous at best. Employees must be told clearly and precisely what the standards and expectations are and how they are to be met.
3. *Evaluating Performance.* If the first two steps are done correctly, performance evaluation is relatively easy. It is a matter of evaluating the employee's behaviour to see if it matches standards.
4. *Discussing Results.* Some people will make mistakes and fail to meet expectations at first. It takes time to learn a new job and do it well. Discussing an employee's

Figure 12.4

Conducting Effective Appraisals and Reviews

1. **DON'T** attack the employee personally. Critically evaluate his or her work.
2. **DO** allow sufficient time, without distractions, for appraisal. (Direct your phone messages to your answering machine and close the office door.)
3. **DON'T** make the employee feel uncomfortable or uneasy. Never conduct an appraisal where other employees are present (such as on the shop floor).
4. **DO** include the employee in the process as much as possible. (For example, let the employee prepare a self-improvement program.)
5. **DON'T** wait until the appraisal to address problems with the employee's work that have been developing for some time.
6. **DO** end the appraisal with positive suggestions for employee improvement.

successes and areas that need improvement can provide managers with an opportunity to be understanding and helpful and to guide the employee to better performance. Additionally, the performance appraisal can be a good source of employee suggestions on how a particular task could be better performed.

5. *Taking Corrective Action.* As an appropriate part of the performance appraisal, a manager can take corrective action or provide corrective feedback to help the employee perform his or her job better. Remember, the key word is performance. The primary purpose of conducting this type of appraisal is to improve employee performance if possible.
6. *Using the Results to Make Decisions.* Decisions about promotions, compensation, additional training, or firing are most often based on performance evaluations. (Be aware that sometimes new hires and promotions are also influenced by other factors such as a family connection or whether the employee is particularly liked by his or her supervisor. You may have heard the phrase that "it's who you know.") An effective performance-appraisal system is also a way of satisfying legal requirements about such decisions.

Managing effectively means getting results through top performance. That is what performance appraisals are for at all levels of the organization, including at the top where managers benefit from performance reviews by their subordinates. In the *360-degree review,* for example, management gathers opinions from all around the employee, including those under, above, and on the same level, to get an accurate, comprehensive idea of the worker's abilities.[34] Figure 12.4 illustrates how managers can make performance appraisals more meaningful.

PROGRESS ASSESSMENT

- What is the primary purpose of a performance appraisal?
- What are the six steps in a performance appraisal?
- Why do employers and employees find the appraisal process so difficult?

COMPENSATING EMPLOYEES: ATTRACTING AND KEEPING THE BEST

Companies do not just compete for customers; they also compete for employees. Compensation is one of the main tools that companies use to attract (and retain) qualified employees, and one of their largest operating costs. The long-term success of a firm—perhaps even its survival—may depend on how well it can control employee costs and optimize employee efficiency. Service organizations like hospitals and airlines struggle with high employee costs since these firms are *labour intensive* (the primary cost of operations is the cost of labour). Manufacturing firms in the auto and steel industries have asked employees to take reductions in wages (called give-backs) to make the firms more competitive. (For example, this was the case during the restructuring of Air Canada.) Those are just a few reasons compensation and benefit packages are being given special attention. In fact, some experts believe that determining how best to compensate employees is today's greatest human resource challenge.

A carefully managed and competitive compensation and benefits program can accomplish several objectives:

- Attract the kinds of people the organization needs, and in sufficient numbers.
- Provide employees with the incentive to work efficiently and productively.
- Keep valued employees from leaving and going to competitors, or starting competing firms.
- Maintain a competitive position in the marketplace by paying competitively and by keeping costs low through high productivity from a satisfied workforce.
- Provide employees with some sense of financial security through fringe benefits such as insurance and retirement benefits.

Pay Equity[35]

pay equity
Equal pay for work of equal value.

Pay equity refers to equal pay for work of equal value. It compares the value of male and female jobs by objectively evaluating the jobs in terms of four neutral factors: skill, effort, responsibility, and working conditions. If a female job is approximately equal in value to a higher-paying job done mainly by men, the female job gets the same wages as the male job.

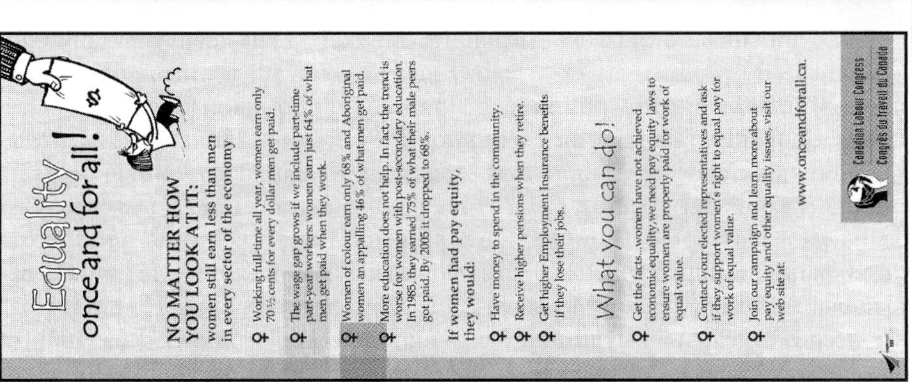

▸ When evaluating pay equity, studies have shown that women's jobs with the same value as men's work are underpaid. To get the conversation started, the Canadian Labour Congress produced this pay equity sales coupon. How receptive do you think an employer would be to this topic if presented with this coupon?

gender wage gap The difference between wages earned by men and wages earned by women

The **gender wage gap** is the difference between wages earned by men and wages earned by women. On average, Canadian women earn less than men. The persistent wage gap that women face, combined with fewer hours of work (twice as many women work part-time as men), make for a significant earnings gap. Women continue to earn between 71 percent and 75 percent of men's earnings, with the same level of education. Historical factors that have contributed to the gender wage gap include the following:

- Women choosing or needing to leave and re-enter the workforce to meet family care-giving responsibilities, resulting in a loss of seniority, advancement opportunities, and wages.
- Occupational segregation in historically undervalued and low-paying jobs, such as child care and clerical work.
- Traditionally lower levels of education (although this is becoming less of a factor as more and more women graduate from all levels of education).
- Less unionization among female workers.
- Discrimination in hiring, promotion, and compensation practices in the workplace, which is estimated to represent as much as 10 to 15 percent of the gender wage gap.

Today, women are more educated, they are working in greater numbers and for longer hours, they are having fewer children, and they are taking less time away from work. Despite these changes, women's hourly wages continue to fall below men's wages at all levels of education. Generally speaking, the wage gap between men and women has been narrowing as education level rises.

Canada has a variety of pay equity laws and policies, depending on where one works. If one works in a federally regulated industry (e.g., banking, telecommunications, transportation, or the federal government), one is covered by federal labour and human rights laws. Ontario and Quebec have proactive pay equity laws that cover both the public and private sectors. Other provinces enacted pay equity legislation that covered only the public sector. Still other jurisdictions, including the Territories, have provisions in their human rights laws that depend on an individual filing an official complaint against her employer.

For some organizations, legislation has been difficult to implement. First, how do you define equal (or comparable) value? For example, which job has more value, that of a nurse or that of a trash collector? As well, officials cite budget cutbacks and the huge costs of making up for past inequitable compensation to female employees as the reasons for delaying the implementation of this legislation. After 14 years in court and millions of dollars in lawyers, Bell Canada Enterprises (BCE) <*www.bell.ca*> agreed in 2006 to pay up to $100 million to almost 5,000 mostly female employees who worked for the company during the 1990s. As you can see, this is not an issue that can easily be resolved.

Pay Systems

The way an organization chooses to pay its employees can have a dramatic effect on efficiency and productivity. Managers thus look for a system that compensates employees fairly. Figure 12.5 outlines some of the most common pay systems.

Many companies still use the pay system known as the Hay system, devised by Edward Hay. This compensation plan is based on job tiers, each of which has a strict pay range. The system is set up on a point basis with three key factors considered: know-how, problem solving, and accountability.

John Whitney, author of *The Trust Factor,* believes that companies should begin with some base pay and give all employees the same percentage merit raise. Doing so, he says, sends out the message that everyone in the company is important. Fairness remains the issue. What do you think is the fairest pay system?

- **Salary:** Fixed compensation computed on weekly, bi-weekly, or monthly pay periods (e.g., $400 per week or $1,500 per month). Salaried employees do not receive additional pay for any extra hours worked.
- **Hourly Wage or Daywork:** Wage based on number of hours or days worked, used for most blue-collar and clerical workers. Often employees must punch a time clock when they arrive at work and when they leave. Hourly wages vary greatly. This does not include benefits such as retirement systems, which may add 30 percent or more to the total package.
- **Piecework System:** Wage based on the number of items produced rather than by the hour or day. This type of system creates powerful incentives to work efficiently and productively.
- **Commission Plans:** Pay based on some percentage of sales. Often used to compensate salespeople, commission plans resemble piecework systems.
- **Bonus Plans:** Extra pay for accomplishing or surpassing certain objectives. There are two types of bonuses: monetary and cashless. Money is always a welcome bonus. Cashless rewards include written thank-you notes, appreciation notes sent to the employee's family, movie tickets, flowers, time off, gift certificates, shopping sprees, and other types of recognition.
- **Profit-Sharing Plans:** Annual bonuses paid to employees based on the company's profits. The amount paid to each employee is based on a predetermined percentage. Profit-sharing is one of the most common forms of performance-based pay.
- **Gain-Sharing Plans:** Annual bonuses paid to employees based on achieving specific goals such as quality measures, customer satisfaction measures, and production targets.
- **Cost-of-Living Allowances (COLAs):** Annual increases in wages based on increases in the Consumer Price Index. This is usually found in union contracts.
- **Stock Options:** Right to purchase stock in the company at a specific price over a specific period of time. Often this gives employees the right to buy stock cheaply despite huge increases in the price of the stock. For example, if over the course of his employment a worker received options to buy 10,000 shares of the company stock at $10 each and the price of the stock eventually grows to $100, he can use those options to buy the 10,000 shares (now worth $1 million) for $100,000.

Figure 12.5

Pay Systems

Compensating Teams

Thus far we have talked about compensating individuals. What about teams? Since you want your teams to be more than simply a group of individuals, would you compensate them as you would individuals? If you cannot answer that question immediately, you are not alone. Most managers believe in using teams, but fewer are sure about how to pay them. Team-based pay programs are not as effective or as fully developed as managers would hope. Measuring and rewarding individual performance on teams, while at the same time rewarding team performance, is tricky—but it can be done. Football players are rewarded as a team when they go to the playoffs and to the Super Bowl, but they are paid individually as well. Companies are now experimenting with and developing similar incentive systems.

Jim Fox, founder and senior partner of compensation and human resource specialist firm Fox Lawson & Associates <*www.foxlawson.com*>, insists that setting up the team right in the first place is the key element to designing an appropriate team compensation plan. He believes the pay model to enhance performance will be a natural outcome of the team's development process.[36]

Jay Schuster, co-author of a study of team pay, found that when pay is based strictly on individual performance, it erodes team cohesiveness and makes it less likely that the team will meet its goals as a collaborative effort. Workplace studies indicate over 50 percent of team compensation plans are based on team goals. Skill-based pay and profit-sharing are the two most common compensation methods for teams.

Skill-based pay (also known as "pay for knowledge") rewards the growth of both the individual and the team. Base pay is raised when team members learn and apply new skills. Eastman Chemical Company <*www.eastman.com*> rewards its teams for proficiency in technical, social, and business knowledge skills. A cross-functional compensation policy team defines the skills. The drawbacks of the skills-based pay system are threefold: the system is complex, training costs can be high, and it is difficult to relate the acquisition of skills to profit gains.

Most *gain-sharing systems* base bonuses on improvements over previous performance. For example, steel producer Nucor Steel <*www.nucor.com*> calculates bonuses on quality—tonnes of steel that go out the door with no defects. There are no limits on bonuses a team can earn; they general run from 100 to 220 percent of base salary. With bonuses, the typical Nucor steel mill worker can earn over $70,000 per year.[37]

It is important to reward individual team players also. Outstanding team players—who go beyond what is required and make an outstanding individual contribution to the firm—should be separately recognized, with cash or non-cash rewards. A good way to compensate for uneven team participation is to let the team decide which members get what type of individual award. After all, if you really support the team process, you need to give teams the freedom to reward themselves.

Fringe Benefits

fringe benefits
Benefits such as sick-leave pay, vacation pay, pension plans, and health plans that represent additional compensation to employees beyond base wages.

Fringe benefits are benefits that provide additional compensation to employees beyond base wages. They may be divided into three categories. One group derives from federal or provincial legislation (which varies somewhat from province to province) and requires compulsory deductions from employees' pay cheques, employer contributions, or both. These include the Canada/Quebec Pension Plan, employment insurance, and income tax. You have probably seen some of these deductions on your pay stub. The second group consists of legally required benefits, including vacation pay, holiday pay, time and a half or double time for overtime, and unpaid maternity leave with job protection. The third category includes all other benefits and stems from voluntary employer programs or from employer–union contracts. Some are paid by the employer alone and others are jointly paid by the employer and employee. Among the most common are bonuses, company pension plans, group insurance, sick leave, termination pay, and paid rest periods.

Fringe benefits can include everything from paid vacations to health care programs, pension plans, recreation facilities, company cars, country club memberships, discounted massages, special home-mortgage rates, paid and unpaid sabbaticals, day-care services, and executive dining rooms.[38] Employees want packages to include dental care, mental health care, elder care, legal counselling, eye care, and short workweeks. It is important to note that some firms offer very little in the way of benefits, especially small firms. Research reveals that in Canada benefits seldom rank among the top five factors in an employee's decision of whether or not to stay with an organization. Exceptions are employees with disabilities, if benefits do not meet employees' needs, or if employees do not understand what the program consists of or how it works. Very simply, benefit plans can *prevent* employee engagement.[39]

▸ Some companies encourage employees to take short naps during the workday so that they replenish their energy and creativity. These EnergyPods block noise and light and are in use at some firms including Google and Procter & Gamble. Is napping a job benefit that appeals to you?

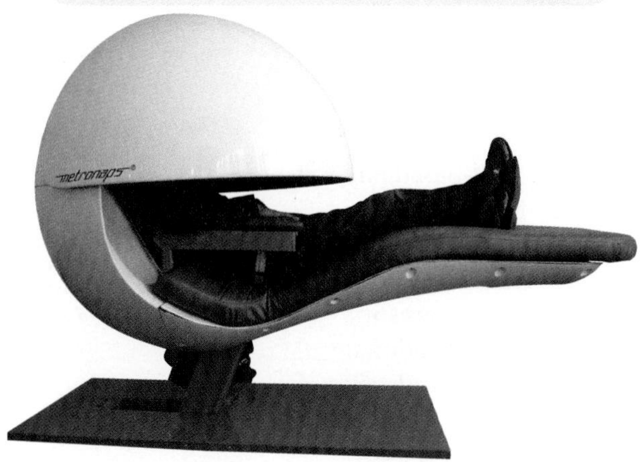

Benefits plans have become a bigger expense in the last decade, with costs increasing two to three times faster than the rate of inflation. Health-care costs—particularly drug and dental-care costs—are expected to continue to rise. Our population is aging, and as employees age, they spend more on health care. The government, which already spends a large percentage of its revenue on health care, will likely continue to shift costs to private plans by limiting and eliminating health services. Practitioners are increasingly recommending more expensive procedures, and patients are also asking for and receiving them.[40] Such outlays are a major and growing cost of doing business, and if this trend continues, total benefits and services could amount to over one-half of most firms' payroll costs in the near future.[41] As a result, employers are trying to control costs in various ways and are making cuts where possible. "Traditionally, you had post-retirement benefits, but employers are trying to get out of these. BCE, for example, announced that it would be phasing out all post-retirement benefits by 2012 for retirees over the age of 55 and it would eliminate all post-retirement benefits for those retiring post-2017."[42]

Understanding that it takes many attractions to retain the best employees, companies offer soft benefits. *Soft benefits* help workers maintain the balance between work and family life that is as important to hardworking employees as the nature of the job itself. These perks include things such as on-site haircuts and shoe repair, concierge services, and free breakfasts.[43] Freeing employees from spending time on errands and chores gives them more time for family—and work. Biotechnology firm Genetech <*www.gene.com*> even offers doggie day care and an on-site farmer's market.[44]

▶ Published annually, *Canada's Top 100 Employers* <*www.canadastop100.com*> highlights employers that lead their industries in providing the best benefits and working conditions. You can also read about Canada's top employers for young people <*www.canadastop100.com/young_people/*>. Would you consider this resource when looking for a job?

At one time, most employees sought benefits that were similar. Today, however, some may seek child-care benefits while others prefer attractive pension plans. To address such growing demands, **cafeteria-style benefits plans** (also known as **flexible benefits plans**), in which employees can choose the benefits they want up to a certain dollar amount, continue to grow in popularity. Rather than giving all employees identical benefits, managers can equitably and cost-effectively meet employees' individual needs by allowing employees some choice.[45]

As the cost of administering benefits programs has accelerated, many companies have chosen to outsource this function. Insperity <*www.insperity.com*> and Workforce Solutions Inc. <*wrksolutions.com*> both handle employee benefits administration for firms with up to 2,500 employees. Culpepper Compensation & Benefits Surveys <*www.culpepper.com*> estimates that over 50 percent of all companies outsource some portion of their human resource tasks.[46] Managing benefits can be especially complicated when employees are located in other countries. The Reaching Beyond Our Borders box at the end of this text part discusses the human resource challenges faced by global businesses. To put it simply, benefits are often as important to recruiting top talent as salary and may even become more important in the future.

cafeteria-style benefits (flexible benefits) plans
Benefit plans that allow employees to choose which benefits they want up to a certain dollar amount.

SCHEDULING EMPLOYEES TO MEET ORGANIZATIONAL AND EMPLOYEE NEEDS

Workplace trends and the increasing costs of transportation have led employees to look for scheduling flexibility. Alternative work arrangements such as flextime, telework, and job sharing are becoming important benefits employees seek.

flextime plan
Work schedule that gives employees some freedom to choose when to work, as long as they work the required number of hours.

Flextime Plans

A **flextime plan** gives employees some freedom to choose when to work, as long as they work the required number of hours. The most popular plans allow employees to come to work between 7 and 9 a.m. and leave between 4 and 6 p.m. Flextime plans generally incorporate core time. **Core time** refers to the period when all employees are expected to

core time
In a flextime plan, the period when all employees are expected to be at their job stations.

be at their job stations. For example, an organization may designate core time as between 9:30 and 11:00 a.m. and between 2:00 and 3:00 p.m. During these hours, all employees are required to be at work, as highlighted in Figure 12.6.

Flextime plans are designed to allow employees to adjust to work/life demands. Two-income families find them especially helpful.[47] For example, the stress of juggling work and family usually falls more heavily on women, says Sonya Kunkel, director for Catalyst Canada <*www.catalyst.org*>, a North American research and advisory group working to advance women in business. Catalyst has completed two studies on work-life balance in Canadian law firms, underwritten by several large firms. Kunkel says that there is a clear business case for being more accommodating of lawyers' personal lives generally, even beyond child-rearing concerns. "When associates are evaluating a workplace, work-life balance is a key issue," she says of the results of the Catalyst studies. "The younger generation of workers [has] a greater appetite around greater options and flexibility." Losing lawyers also hits the bottom line. Catalyst studies show an associate's departure costs a firm about $315,000 in recruiting, training, salaries, overhead, severance, and outplacement—not including hiring a replacement.[48]

Flextime is not for all organizations. It does not suit shift work like fast-food or assembly processes like manufacturing, where everyone on a given shift must be at work at the same time. Another disadvantage is that managers often have to work longer days to assist and supervise in organizations that may operate from 6 a.m. to 6 p.m. Flextime also makes communication more difficult since certain employees may not be there when others need to talk to them. Furthermore, if not carefully supervised, some employees could abuse the system, causing resentment among others.

compressed workweek Work schedule that allows an employee to work a full number of hours per week but in fewer days.

Another popular option is a **compressed workweek**. That means that an employee works a full number of hours in less than the standard number of days. For example, an employee may work four 10-hour days and then enjoy a long weekend instead of working five 8-hour days with a traditional weekend. There are obvious advantages of compressed workweeks, but some employees get tired working such long hours, and productivity could decline. Others find the system of great benefit, however, and are quite enthusiastic about it. Nurses often work compressed weeks.

While there are several options that employers can offer, Statistics Canada communicates what is actually happening in the Canadian marketplace:

- The most common form of alternative work arrangement is flexible hours (36.6 percent of all employees), followed by weekend work (27.9 percent).
- The incidence of flexible hours is more common among workers in the retail trade and consumer services industries (44.6 percent). About six in ten employees in these industries usually worked weekends.
- The incidence of various work arrangements is also related to the educational attainment of workers. For example, the university educated reported the greatest incidence of flexible hours (43.5 percent), but seldom had regularly scheduled weekend work (17.0 percent).

Figure 12.6

A Flextime Chart

At this company, employees can start work anytime between 6:30 and 9:30 a.m. They take a half hour for lunch anytime between 11:00 a.m. and 2:00 p.m., and can leave between 3:00 and 6:30 p.m. Everyone works an eight-hour day. The blue arrows show a typical employee's flextime day.

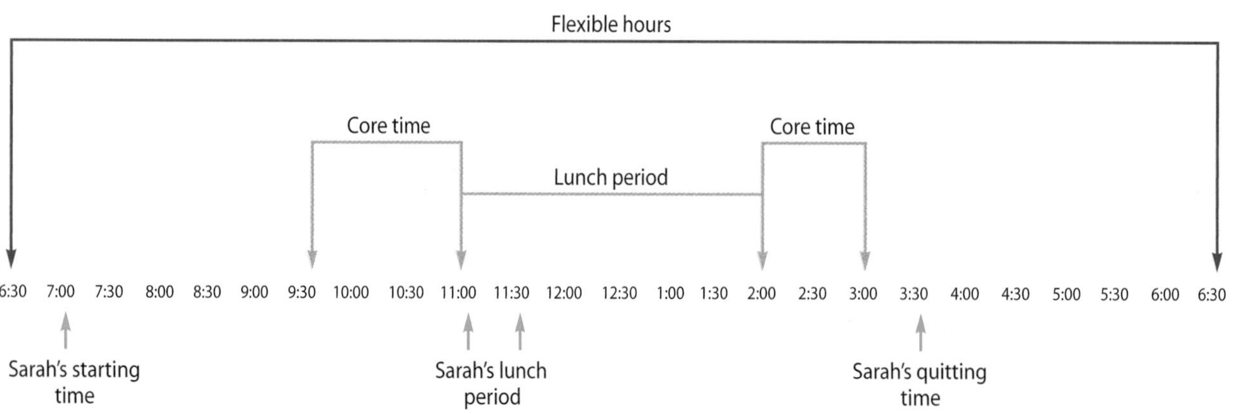

- Reduced work weeks (e.g., job sharing and work-sharing) and compressed work weeks are not widespread, with each being reported by fewer than one in ten workers. The age, occupation, and industry groups with the highest incidence of reduced work weeks were youth (19.5 percent), marketing/sales (15.5 percent), and retail trade and consumer services (13.7 percent).[49]

So, what does this mean to you? Clearly, there are different plans that employers can consider. The choice of plans will be affected by the type of job you have, your employer's needs, your age and needs, and possibly your level of education.

▸ What do you think would be your biggest challenge if you worked from home?

Telework (Telecommuting)[50]

As introduced in Appendix A, telework, also known as telecommuting, occurs when paid workers reduce their commute by carrying out all, or part, of their work away from their normal place of business. Rising gas prices, leading-edge technology, and pushes for work-life flexibility have all contributed to an increase in telework across Canada.

Home-based workers can choose their own hours, interrupt work for child care and other tasks, and take time out for various personal reasons. Working at home is not for everyone, however. It requires discipline to stay focused on the work and not be easily distracted.

Telework can also be a cost saver for employers. For example, IBM used to have a surplus of office space, maintaining more offices than it had employees. Now the company has cut back on the number of offices, with employees telecommuting, "hotelling" (being assigned to a desk through a reservations system), and "hot-desking" (sharing a desk with other employees at different times). Other companies are hiring call agents rather than using more expensive in-house operators or less-qualified offshore call centres. For example, Office Depot <*www.officedepot.ca*> says that it saves 30 or 40 percent on the cost of each call because it is not providing work space or benefits for its home-based call-centre workers. Figure 12.7 outlines the benefits and challenges of home-based work to organizations, individuals, and society.

job sharing
An arrangement whereby two part-time employees share one full-time job.

▸ Some young new moms, whose careers are not as established, are choosing to stay home because day care is expensive. (We are also seeing more dads staying home.) If more companies offered alternative work arrangements, do you think that this might change?

Job-Sharing Plans

Job sharing lets two or more part-time employees share one full-time job. Students and parents with small children, for instance, may work only during school hours, and older workers can work part-time before fully retiring or after retiring. Benefits of job sharing include:

- Employment opportunities for those who cannot or prefer not to work full-time.
- An enthusiastic and productive workforce.
- Reduced absenteeism and tardiness.
- Ability to schedule part-time workers into peak demand periods (e.g., banks on payday).
- Retention of experienced employees who might otherwise have left.

	Benefits	Challenges
To Organization	• Increases productivity due to fewer sick days, fewer absences, higher job satisfaction, and higher work performance ratings • Broadens available talent pool • Reduces costs of providing on-site office space	• Makes it more difficult to appraise job performance • Can negatively affect the social network of the workplace and can make it difficult to promote team cohesiveness • Complicates distribution of tasks (e.g., Should office files, contact lists, and such be allowed to leave the office?)
To Individual	• Makes more time available for work and family by reducing or eliminating commute time • Reduces expenses of buying and maintaining office clothes • Avoids office politics • Helps balance work and family • Expands employment opportunities for disabled individuals	• Can cause feeling of isolation from social network • Can raise concerns regarding promotions and other rewards due to being out of sight, out of mind • May diminish individual's influence within company due to limited opportunity to learn the corporate culture
To Society	• Decreases traffic congestion • Discourages community crime that might otherwise occur in bedroom communities • Increases time available to build community ties	• Increases need to resolve zoning regulations forbidding business deliveries in residential neighbourhoods • May reduce ability to interact with other people in a personal, intimate manner

Figure 12.7

Benefits and Challenges of Telework

Disadvantages include having to hire, train, motivate, and supervise twice as many people and perhaps having to prorate some fringe benefits. But firms are finding that the benefits outweigh the disadvantages.

PROGRESS ASSESSMENT

- Can you name and describe five alternative compensation systems?
- What advantages do compensation plans such as profit-sharing offer an organization?
- What are the benefits and challenges of flextime? Telework? Job sharing?

Describe the ways in which employees can move through a company: promotion, reassignment, termination, and retirement.

CAREER MANAGEMENT: UP, OVER, AND OUT

Employees do not always stay in the position they were initially hired to fill. They may excel and move up the corporate ladder or fail and move out the front door. In addition to being moved through promotion and termination, employees can be moved by reassignment and retirement. Of course, employees can choose to move themselves by quitting and going to another company.

Promoting and Reassigning Employees

Many companies find that promotion from within the company improves employee morale. Promotions are also cost-effective in that the promoted employees are already familiar with the corporate culture and procedures and do not need to spend valuable time on basic orientation.

In the new, flatter corporate structures, there are fewer levels for employees to reach now than there were in the past. Therefore, it is more common today for workers to move *over* to a new position than to move *up* to one. Such transfers allow employees to develop and display new skills and to learn more about the company overall. This is one way of motivating experienced employees to remain in a company with few upward advancement opportunities.

▸ When there is a downturn in the economy, managers sometimes terminate employees. Do you think they will rehire full-time employees when the economy recovers? Why or why not? What alternatives do they have?

Terminating Employees

The relentless pressure of global competition, shifts in technology, increasing customer demands for greater value, and uncertain economic conditions have seen human resource managers struggling to manage layoffs and firings. In the case of layoffs, older employees are often offered early retirement packages (to be discussed soon). Companies may counsel other laid-off employees to enable them to better cope with the loss of their jobs and to help them find new jobs. Some set up in-house outplacement facilities so that employees can get counselling on how to obtain a new job. For senior managers, companies usually pay for private-agency career counselling.

For those that remain, the job losses and the threat of future job losses introduce strong feelings that may include fear, insecurity, and uncertainty; frustration, resentment, and anger; sadness, depression, and guilt; and unfairness, betrayal, and distrust.[51] Insecurity undermines motivation, so HRM must deal with this issue. According to Wayne Cascio, author of numerous books on organizational restructuring and the economic impact of HR activities, "They're very worried about their own future: 'What is this going to mean for me?' So, they don't want to stick their necks out and take risks." Yet companies need to engage in risk-taking to generate new products, markets, and customers, he says. Cascio adds, "Taking the same amount of work and just loading it onto fewer workers has long-term effects in terms of stress." This stress, he says, often intensifies four to six months after the downsizing, resulting in increased absenteeism and higher turnover.[52] Keeping employees fully informed and having a clear policy on termination pay helps to remove some insecurity.

Even companies that regain financial strength, however, are hesitant to rehire new full-time employees. Why? One reason is that the cost of terminating employees is prohibitively high. The cost of firing comes from lost training costs as well as damages and legal fees paid in wrongful discharge suits. (This is why is it critical to have a good system of verbal and written notices, and record keeping, to deal with poorly-performing employees.) To save money, many companies are either using contingent workers (one company example was highlighted in the chapter profile) or outsourcing certain functions.

Retiring Employees

In addition to layoffs, another tool used to downsize companies is to offer early retirement benefits to entice older (and more expensive) workers to retire. Such benefits usually involve financial incentives such as one-time cash payments, known in some companies as *golden handshakes.* The advantage early retirement benefits have over layoffs or firing is the increased morale of surviving employees. Retiring senior workers earlier also increases promotion opportunities for more junior employees.

Losing Valued Employees

In spite of a company's efforts to retain them, some talented employees will choose to pursue opportunities elsewhere. Knowing their reasons for leaving can be invaluable in preventing the loss of other good people in the future. One way to learn the reasons is to have an outside expert conduct an *exit interview.* Outsiders can provide confidentiality and anonymity that earns more honest feedback than employees are comfortable giving in face-to-face interviews with their supervisors. Web-based systems can capture, track, and statistically analyze employee exit interview data to generate reports that identify trouble areas. Such programs can also coordinate exit interview data with employee satisfaction surveys to predict which departments should expect turnover to occur.[53] The **turnover rate** measures the percentage of employees that leave the firm each year. The most reliable way to use turnover rates is to compare an organization against itself over time as well as to the industry average.[54]

turnover rate
A measure of the percentage of employees that leave a firm each year.

Illustrate the effects of legislation on human resource management.

LAWS AFFECTING HUMAN RESOURCE MANAGEMENT[55]

The Charter of Rights and Freedoms, which is part of the Constitution, guarantees equality before the law for every Canadian. The Human Rights Act seeks to provide equal employment opportunities without regard to people's race, national or ethnic origin, colour, religion, age, sex, sexual orientation, marital status, family status, disability, or conviction for an offense for which a pardon has been granted. Human rights legislation requires that every employer ensure equal opportunities and that there is no discrimination. This legislation affects nearly every human resource function (which includes planning, recruiting, selection, training, and compensation) and it has made managing these activities more complicated. This is true in both a non-union environment, which is governed by these laws and regulations, and a union environment, which must also reflect the conditions outlined in the labour contract (to be discussed in Chapter 13).

Since Canada is a confederation of provinces and territories, jurisdiction over many aspects of our lives is divided between the federal and provincial governments. The federal government legislates on national issues such as employment insurance. The federal government also has jurisdiction over certain types of businesses that are deemed to be of a national nature. Banks, insurance companies, airlines, railways, shipping companies, telephone, radio, TV, cable companies, and others are subject to federal law, as are all federal employees. However, fewer than 10 percent of all Canadian employees are subject to federal legislation.

The provinces have jurisdiction over most provincial matters. This includes employment standards in areas such as minimum wage, hours of work, overtime, statutory holidays, parental leave, employment of people under 18 years of age, and, as noted earlier in this chapter, discrimination in the workplace.

What all of this means is that there are literally hundreds of laws and regulations, federal and provincial, which apply to all aspects of HRM. Furthermore, these laws are constantly being revised because of the changing social and political economy, as well as rulings by human rights commissions and courts. One of the most regulated areas involves discrimination.

Employment Equity

A well-known 1980s case of discrimination highlights a major problem and how it was solved. A group of women accused the Canadian National Railway (CNR) of not hiring them because they were women. The CNR, like many other companies, did not hire women for jobs that were thought to be traditional men's jobs, those for which heavy physical labour was required. In this case, the jobs involved maintenance and repairs of the tracks. The Canadian Human Rights Commission ruled in favour of the women.

The CNR appealed and the courts ruled against it all the way to the Supreme Court of Canada.

Employment equity refers to employment activities designed to increase employment opportunities for certain groups, given past discrimination toward these groups. As a result, the Employment Equity Act was introduced in 1986 to ensure that federally regulated employers with 100 or more employees "achieve equality in the workplace so that no person shall be denied employment opportunities or benefits for reasons unrelated to ability and, in the fulfillment of that goal, to correct the conditions of disadvantage in employment experienced by women, aboriginal peoples, persons with disabilities and members of visible minorities by giving effect to the principle that employment equity means more than treating persons in the same way but also requires special measures and the accommodation of differences."[56] This means that in the CNR example, CNR had to develop a plan that would result in more women than men being hired for such jobs until the balance was more even. The result is that when a man and a woman are equally qualified, the woman must be given preference. This would occur for a period of time until the balance of male and female workers was adjusted more equally.

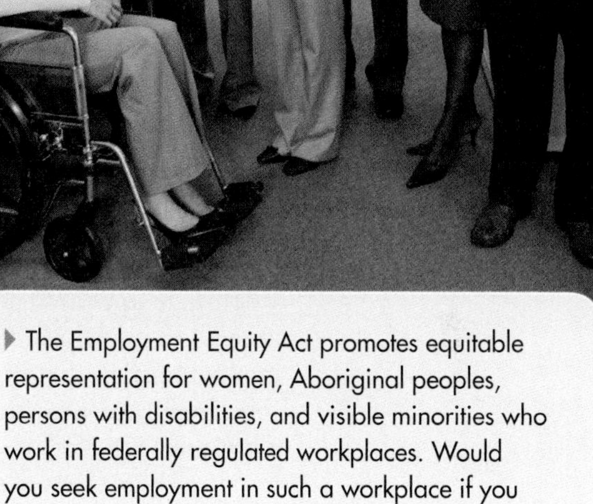

The Employment Equity Act promotes equitable representation for women, Aboriginal peoples, persons with disabilities, and visible minorities who work in federally regulated workplaces. Would you seek employment in such a workplace if you belonged to one of these groups?

Interpretation of the employment equity law eventually led employers to actively recruit and give preference to women and minority group members. Employment equity, for many employers, has become mostly a reporting function. They keep track of the numbers of employees that belong to these groups, and they try to remove any discrimination from hiring procedures, including trying to advertise positions more widely. As you might expect, interpretation of the law is often controversial and enforcement is difficult. Questions persist about the effect the program could have in creating a sort of reverse discrimination in the workplace.

employment equity
Employment activities designed to "right past wrongs" by increasing opportunities for minorities and women.

Reverse discrimination refers to the unfairness that unprotected groups (say, whites or males) may perceive when protected groups receive preference in hiring and promotion. Charges of reverse discrimination have occurred when companies have been perceived as unfairly giving preference to women or minority group members in hiring and promoting. The Canadian Charter of Rights and Freedoms specifically allows for employment equity as a method to overcome long-standing discrimination against specific groups. Therefore, the courts accept it as being non-discriminatory in the legal sense. Be aware that this continues to be a controversial issue today.

reverse discrimination
The unfairness that unprotected groups (say, whites or males) may perceive when protected groups receive preference in hiring and promotion.

Laws That Protect the Disabled

Legislation protects people with disabilities. Businesses cannot discriminate against people on the basis of any physical or mental disability. Employers are required to give disabled applicants the same consideration for employment as people without disabilities. It also requires that businesses make "reasonable accommodations" for people with disabilities. Accommodation may include modifying equipment or widening doorways. Reasonable accommodations are not always expensive. For example, a company can provide an inexpensive headset that allows someone with cerebral palsy to talk on the phone and write at the same time. Equal opportunity for people with disabilities promises to be a continuing issue into the next decade.

Laws That Protect Older Employees

In the years to come, labour shortages are forecast due to the retirement of aging baby boomers. While there is no law in Canada that requires retirement at age 65 (Nova Scotia was the last province to eliminate mandatory retirement, effective 2009), some workplaces may mandate it. For example, the Supreme Court of Canada ruled against a New Brunswick miner who challenged his company's right to compel him to retire at age 65 as a requirement of his employee pension plan. While the province's act prohibits mandatory retirement, it includes a provision allowing companies to enforce mandatory retirement under the terms or conditions of any retirement or pension plan. The Supreme Court of Canada has stated that unless there is evidence that the pension plan as a whole is not legitimate, it will be protected by the province's Human Rights Act "from the conclusion that a particular provision compelling retirement at a certain age constitutes age discrimination."[57]

Generally speaking, employees are guaranteed protection against age discrimination in the workplace. Courts have ruled against firms in unlawful-discharge suits where age appeared to be the major factor in dismissal. (An exception was noted above.) In addition, the federal government and the provinces protect over-65 workers in their labour or human rights legislation. Changes to the ban on mandatory retirement age provide opportunities for companies to retain workers who wish to work past age 65.[58]

PROGRESS ASSESSMENT

- Name three areas of HRM responsibility that are affected by government legislation.
- Explain what employment equity is and give one example of it.
- Why should HRM be concerned about legislation or court rulings when terminating employees?

Effects of Legislation

Clearly, laws and regulations affect all areas of HRM. It should be apparent that a career in HRM offers a challenge to anyone willing to put forth the effort. Figure 12.8 lists some sites that you may consult to learn about some of the topics discussed in this chapter. In summary:

- Employers must know and act in accordance with the legal rights of their employees or risk costly court cases.
- Legislation affects all areas of HRM, from hiring and training to compensating employees.
- Managers must be sensitive not only to legal requirements, but also to union contracts and social standards and expectations, which can be even more demanding.
- Court cases have made it clear that it is sometimes legal to go beyond providing equal rights for minorities and women to provide special employment (employment equity) and training to correct past discrimination.
- New court cases and legislation change HRM almost daily. The only way to keep current is to read business literature and become familiar with the issues.

Organization	URL
Benefits Canada	www.benefitscanada.com
Canadian Council of Human Resources Associations	www.cchra.ca
Canadian HR Reporter	www.canadianhrreporter.com
Canadian Human Rights Commission	www.chrc-ccdp.ca
Canadian Human Rights Reporter	www.cdn-hr-reporter.ca
The Conference Board of Canada	www.conferenceboard.ca
Government of Canada	www.canada.gc.ca
HR Council for the Nonprofit Sector	www.hrcouncil.ca
The Pay Equity Commission	www.payequity.gov.on.ca
Provincial and Territorial Government Sites	www.canada.gc.ca/othergov-autregouv/prov-eng.html
Statistics Canada	www.statcan.gc.ca

Figure 12.8

Human Resource Information Sites

SUMMARY

Explain the importance of human resource management as a strategic contributor to organizational success, and summarize the five steps in human resource planning.

Human resource management is the process of evaluating human resource needs, finding people to fill those needs, and getting the best work from each employee by providing the right incentives and job environment, all with the goal of meeting organizational objectives. Like all other types of management, human resource management begins with planning.

What are the steps in human resource planning?

The five steps are (1) preparing a human resource inventory of the organization's employees; (2) preparing a job analysis; (3) assessing future demand; (4) assessing future supply; and (5) establishing a strategic plan for recruitment, selection, training and development, evaluation, compensation, scheduling, and career management for the labour force.

Describe methods that companies use to recruit new employees, and explain some of the issues that make recruitment challenging.

Recruitment is the set of activities used to obtain a sufficient number of the right people at the right time.

What methods do human resource managers use to recruit new employees?

Recruiting sources are classified as either internal or external. Internal sources include hiring from within the firm (e.g., transfers and promotions) and employees who recommend others to hire. External recruitment sources include advertisements, public and private employment agencies, school placement offices, management consultants, professional organizations, referrals, walk-in applications, and the Internet.

Why has recruitment become more difficult?
Legal restrictions complicate hiring practices. Finding suitable employees can also be made more difficult if companies are considered unattractive workplaces.

Outline the five steps in selecting employees, and illustrate the use of various types of employee training and development methods.

Selection is the process of gathering and interpreting information to decide which applicants should be hired.

What are the five steps in the selection process?
The steps are (1) obtaining complete application forms; (2) conducting initial and follow-up interviews; (3) giving employment tests; (4) conduct background investigations; and (5) establishing a trial period of employment.

What are some of the activities used for training?
After assessing the needs of the organization and the skills of the employees, training programs are designed that may include the following activities: employee orientation, on-the-job training, apprenticeship programs, off-the-job training, online training, vestibule training, and job simulation. The effectiveness of the training is evaluated at the conclusion of the activities.

What methods are used to develop managerial skills?
Management development methods include on-the-job coaching, understudy positions, job rotation, and off-the-job courses and training.

How does networking fit in this process?
Networking is the process of establishing contacts with key managers within and outside the organization to get additional development assistance.

Trace the six steps in appraising employee performance, and summarize the objectives of employee compensation programs.

A performance appraisal is an evaluation of the performance level of employees against established standards to make decisions about promotions, compensation, additional training, or firing.

How is performance evaluated?
The steps are (1) establish performance standards; (2) communicate those standards; (3) evaluate performance; (4) discuss results; (5) take corrective action when needed; and (6) use the results for decisions about promotions, compensation, additional training, or firing.

What kinds of compensation systems are used?
Compensation systems include salary systems, hourly wages, piecework, commission plans, bonus plans, profit-sharing plans, and stock options.

What types of compensation systems are appropriate for teams?
The most common are profit-sharing and skill-based compensation programs. It is also important to reward outstanding individual performance within teams.

What are fringe benefits?

Fringe benefits include such items as sick leave, vacation pay, pension plans, and health plans that provide additional compensation to employees beyond base wages. Many firms offer cafeteria-style fringe benefits plans, in which employees can choose the benefits they want, up to a certain dollar amount.

Describe the ways in which employees can move through a company: promotion, reassignment, termination, and retirement.

Employees often move from their original positions in a company.

How can employees move within a company?

Employees can be moved up (promotion), over (reassignment), or out (termination or retirement) of a company. Employees can also choose to leave a company to pursue opportunities elsewhere.

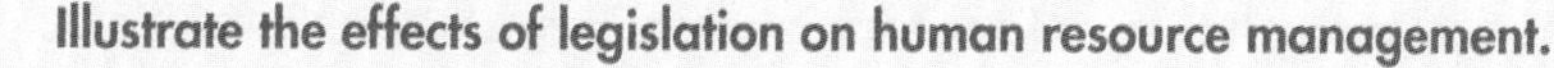

Illustrate the effects of legislation on human resource management.

There are many laws that affect human resource planning.

What are those laws?

Some important areas discussed include employment equity, laws that protect the disabled, as well as laws that protect older employees. This is an important subject for future managers to study.

KEY TERMS

apprentice programs
cafeteria-style benefits (flexible benefits)
compressed workweek
contingent workers
core time
employee orientation
employment equity
enabling
flextime plan
fringe benefits
gender wage gap
human resource management (HRM)
job analysis
job description
job sharing
job simulation
job specifications
management development
mentor
networking
off-the-job training
online training
on-the-job training
pay equity
performance appraisal
recruitment
reverse discrimination
selection
training and development
turnover rate
vestibule training

CRITICAL THINKING

1. Does human resource management interest you as a career? What are your experiences working with human resource professionals?
2. Why should you be interested in the subject matter of human resource management, even if you are not majoring in this field?
3. What effects have dual-career families had on the human resource function? How about single-parent families? Are there any similarities?
4. Do you think that most vacancies in firms are filled through a competitive process?

5. Performance appraisals are often done poorly for different reasons. For example, people may not like to complete them or have them done to them. The company's perspective also affects the effectiveness of this process. Is the appraisal conducted so employees can be assessed and corrected (some might say punished) or so that the collective can do better? What can a company do to ensure that appraisals are effectively conducted?

6. Imagine that you must fire an employee. What effect might the dismissal have on remaining employees? Explain how you would tell the employee and your remaining subordinates.

DEVELOPING WORKPLACE SKILLS

1. Look through the classified ads in your local newspaper or on the Internet and find at least two positions that you might like to have when you graduate. List the qualifications specified in each of the ads. Identify methods that the companies might use to determine how well applicants meet each of those qualifications.

2. Secure a blank performance-appraisal form from any company and for any category of entry-level employment. State specifically what dimensions of work performance are being measured and how the dimensions are measured.

3. Consider these occupations: car salesperson, computer software developer, teacher, and assembly-line worker. Identify the method of compensation that you think is appropriate for determining the wages for each of these workers. Explain your answer.

4. Imagine that you are the human resource manager at your company. You get a call from a company doing a reference check for a former employee. This former employee is being considered for a position. During the call, you are asked to provide information on the employee's medical history and his marital status. You have recently reviewed changes to the privacy laws for your province/territory through the Office of the Privacy Commissioner of Canada <*www.privcom.gc.ca*>. What do you tell this person on the phone?

5. List the three groups of fringe benefits and include benefits under each group. Speak with a local HR professional and find out what the employee and employer cost is for each benefit, on a monthly basis, for an entry-level position that a graduate might consider.

ANALYZING MANAGEMENT DECISIONS

Dual-Career Planning

Carey Moler is a 32-year-old account executive for a communications company. She is married to Mitchell Moler, a lawyer. Carey and Mitchell did not make any definite plans about how to juggle their careers and family life until Carey reached age 30. Then they decided to have a baby, and career planning took on a whole new dimension. A company named Catalyst talked to 815 dual-career couples and found that most of them, like the Molers, had not made any long-range career decisions regarding family lifestyle.

From the business perspective, such dual-career families create real concerns. There are problems with relocation, with child care, and so on that affect recruiting, productivity, morale, and promotion policies.

For a couple such as the Molers, having both career and family responsibilities is exhausting. But that is just one problem. If Carey is moving up in her firm, what happens if Mitchell gets a terrific job offer a thousand kilometres away? What if Carey gets such an offer? Who is going to care for the baby? What happens if the baby becomes ill? How do they plan their vacations when there are three schedules to balance? Who will do the housework? Dual careers require careful planning and discussion, and those plans need to be reviewed over time. A couple that decides at age 22 to do certain things may change their minds at age 30. Whether or not to have children, where to locate, how to manage the household—all such issues and more can become major problems if not carefully planned.

The same is true for corporations. They too must plan for dual-career families. They must give attention to job sharing, flextime, parental leave policies, transfer policies, nepotism rules (i.e., rules about hiring family members), and more.

Discussion Questions

1. In addition to the examples stated above, what other issues can you see developing because of dual-career families? How is this affecting children in such families?
2. What kind of corporate policies need changing to adapt to these new realities?
3. What are the advantages of dual careers? What are the disadvantages? What can newlywed couples do to minimize the problems of dual careers? How can a couple reap the rewards?

Practise and learn online with Connect.

CHAPTER

13

UNDERSTANDING EMPLOYEE–MANAGEMENT ISSUES AND RELATIONS

LEARNING OBJECTIVES

After you have read and studied this chapter, you should be able to:

LO 1 Trace the history of organized labour in Canada.

LO 2 Discuss the major legislation affecting labour unions.

LO 3 Describe the collective bargaining process.

LO 4 Outline the objectives of labour unions.

LO 5 Describe the negotiation tactics used by labour and management during conflicts.

LO 6 Explain some of today's employee–management issues.

PROFILE

GETTING TO KNOW GERRY VARRICCHIO, REGIONAL ORGANIZING COORDINATOR FOR CENTRAL AND EASTERN CANADA, LABORERS' INTERNATIONAL UNION OF NORTH AMERICA (LIUNA)

Gerry Varricchio is a labour organizer and first contract negotiator. He specializes in the construction industry in the Province of Ontario, though he regularly runs campaigns in the industrial sector and negotiates the first collective agreements in both sectors. As the Regional Organizing Coordinator for Central and Eastern Canada for the Laborers' International Union of North America (LIUNA) <*www.liuna.org*>, Varricchio works for the international office, and reports directly to Joseph S. Mancinelli, International Vice-President for Central and Eastern Canada.

Varricchio runs the Central and Eastern Canada Organizing Fund (CECOF), and has over 70 regional organizers reporting directly to him. (Contrast this to 1993 when he was the sole regional organizer.) This is a highly motivated and powerful unit dedicated to organizing the unorganized and to preserving work for its members, while keeping management competitive. To achieve this goal, Varricchio's vision encompasses a joint co-operative effort between labour and management. As a result of LIUNA's organizing initiatives through CECOF and Varricchio's efforts, LIUNA has the distinct honour of being the most prolific union organizer in Ontario.

Varricchio started his working life on the tools, first as a carpenter, and then as a member of LIUNA Local 1089 in his hometown of Sarnia, working in "Chemical Valley." He was elected to the LIUNA Local 1089 Executive board and as a delegate to the LIUNA Ontario Provincial District Council in 1985, and re-elected every four years subsequently. Experiencing his own health issues as a result of chemical spills in the workplace, Varricchio was very aware of the difficulties faced in the work environment, including health and safety issues. He recognized early on that some of the major protections for workers are accessible only thorough unionization. Consequently, when offered a job in 1987 by the LIUNA Ontario Provincial District Council as an organizer, Varricchio jumped at the chance.

In addition to his organizing duties on behalf of LIUNA, Varricchio also serves as a Trustee on the Local 1089 Training and Rehabilitation Trust Fund and on the Benefits Trust Fund. One accomplishment is that he pioneered the first union benefit plan that integrates a registered educational scholarship plan for members and their children into a union benefit trust plan as part of the standard benefit package.

In the past twenty-five years, Varricchio has adapted to the demands of the workplace. He was at the forefront in introducing the process of "top-down" organizing, a system of engaging the employer in the initial stages of organizing, with the intent of levelling the playing field for all of the employers in the industry. This reassures individual employers who believe that the presence of a union in the workplace will lead to inequalities in terms of bid power and limit their access to future contracts. Varricchio has expressed this as follows: "Unions have a dual responsibility—to ensure that their members are getting the best wage and benefit packages and working conditions available in the marketplace, and equally as important, to ensure that their contractual employers not only remain competitive, but have a labour partner that can assist them in expanding their business and market share."

Managers in both profit-seeking and non-profit organizations address labour-relations challenges every day. This chapter discusses some of these employee–management relations and issues. When asked what his thoughts are for the future of labour-management relations, Varricchio points out that the labour-management community is at the mercy of the political climate, both federally and provincially. It is important for labour and management to partner together to achieve common goals and look out for each other's interests. "Perhaps in spite of the adversarial beginnings between unions and employers and the prejudices that evolved over time," says Varricchio, "the true business value of unions will be recognized and utilized when it is most needed."

Source: Gerry Varricchio, Regional Organizing Coordinator for Central and Eastern Canada, The Laborers' International Union of North America, interviews, 26 June 2012 and 16 February 2009, Hamilton.

EMPLOYEE–MANAGEMENT ISSUES

union
An employee organization that has the main goal of representing members in employee–management bargaining over job-related issues; also known as a *labour union*.

The relationship between management (representing owners or shareholders) and employees is not always smooth. Management's responsibility to produce a profit by maximizing productivity sometimes necessitates hard decisions, which limits manager's chances to win popularity contests. Labour (the collective term for non-management workers) is interested in fair and competent management, human dignity, decent working conditions, a reasonable share in the wealth that its work generates, and assurance that the conditions of the contract and government labour laws will not be ignored. (One could argue that management is also interested in these same ideals.)

Like other managerial challenges, employee–management issues must be worked out through open discussion, goodwill, and compromise. How management and labour adapt to the changing business environment will determine our economic and political well-being in the years ahead. To make a reasoned decision, it is important to know both sides of an issue.

A good starting point in discussing employee–management relations in Canada is a discussion of unions. A **union** (known as a *labour union* in Canadian English or a *trade union* in British English) is an employee organization that has the main goal of representing members in employee–management bargaining over job-related issues.[1] Workers originally formed unions to protect themselves from intolerable work conditions and unfair treatment. They also united to secure some say in the operation of their jobs. As the number of union members grew, workers gained more negotiating power with managers and more political power as well.

Historically, employees turned to unions for assistance in gaining specific workplace rights and benefits. Labour unions were largely responsible for the establishment of minimum-wage laws, overtime rules, workers' compensation, severance pay, child-labour laws, job safety regulations, and more. In recent decades, however, union strength has waned as unions have failed to retain the economic and political power they once had. Economists suggest that increased global competition, shifts from manufacturing to service and high-tech industries that are less heavily unionized, growth in part-time work, and changes in management philosophies are some of the reasons for labour's decline.[2] Others contend the decline is the result of labour's success in seeing the issues it championed become law.

Some labour analysts forecast that unions will regain strength as companies engage in more unpopular practices such as outsourcing; others insist that unions have seen their brightest days. Few doubt that the role and influence of unions—particularly in selected regions—will continue to arouse emotions and opinions that contrast considerably. Let's briefly look at labour unions and then analyze other key issues affecting employee–management relations.

▸ In the late 2000s it seemed like almost every week another plant shut its doors, filed for bankruptcy, or announced its intention to move its operations out of Canada. As part of its campaign to stop this trend, the Canadian Auto Workers union called on all levels of government to adopt Buy Canadian policies for all public purchases. Do you think that such policies save jobs and build stronger communities?

LABOUR UNIONS FROM DIFFERENT PERSPECTIVES

Are labour unions essential in the Canadian economy today? This is a very political subject with strongly-held opposing positions. An electrician carrying a picket sign in Sudbury would say yes and elaborate on the dangers to a free society if employers continue to try to bust, or break apart unions. A small manufacturer would disagree, and complain about being restricted by union wage and benefit obligations in an increasingly competitive global economy.

Historians generally agree that today's unions are an outgrowth of the economic transition caused by the Industrial Revolution of the nineteenth and early twentieth centuries. Workers who once toiled in the fields, dependent on the mercies of nature for survival, suddenly became dependent on the continuous roll of the factory presses and assembly lines for their living. Making the transition from an agricultural economy to an industrial economy was quite difficult.[3] Over time, workers learned that strength through unity (unions) could lead to improved job conditions, better wages, and job security.

▶ While the technological achievements of the Industrial Revolution brought countless new products to market and reduced the need for physical labour in many industries, they also put pressure on workers to achieve higher productivity in factory jobs that called for long hours and low pay. Can you see how these conditions made it possible for labour unions to take hold by the turn of the twentieth century?

Varricchio believes the following: "In a perfect world, labour and management partner together to achieve common goals and look out for each other's interests. Unfortunately, human nature being what it is, greed, incompetence, and self-serving interests of players from one side or the other, or both, can supersede the common good thereby creating conflict and negative perceptions about unions. In any market, competing on a level playing field is extremely important to the success and future growth of a business. The most effective vehicle for competing businesses to utilize in creating and sustaining a level playing field, in their respective markets, is a union. Through the union structure and the collective bargaining process, employers can level off labour costs across entire markets and create optimum standards in training and health and safety practices that can be properly enforced through their collective agreements."[4] He also believes that because of the adversarial beginnings between unions and employers, and the subsequent prejudices that have evolved over time, the true business value of unions remains largely untapped.[5]

Today's critics of organized labour maintain that few of the inhumane conditions once dominant in Canadian industry still exist in the modern workplace.[6] They charge that organized labour has in fact become a large industrial entity in itself and that the real issue of protecting workers has become secondary. That is, unions can be bureaucratic, resistant to change, and political, whereby some union leaders may be self-serving and act counter to a union's best interests. Critics also maintain that the current legal system and changing management philosophies minimize the chances that the sweatshops (workplaces of the late nineteenth and early twentieth centuries with unsatisfactory, unsafe, or oppressive labour conditions) will reappear in Canada. Let's look at some of the history of labour unions.

The Early History of Organized Labour

Trace the history of organized labour in Canada.

The presence of formal labour organizations in Canada dates back to the 1800s. Early unions on the wharves of Halifax, St. John's, and Quebec during the War of 1812 existed to profit from labour scarcity. Others, such as the Montreal shoemakers

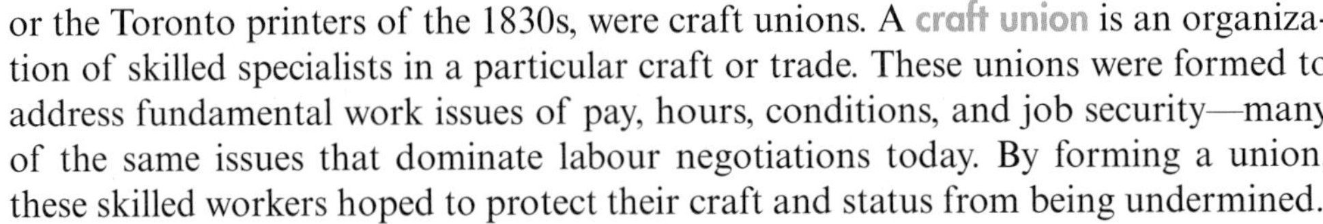

craft union
An organization of skilled specialists in a particular craft or trade.

or the Toronto printers of the 1830s, were craft unions. A **craft union** is an organization of skilled specialists in a particular craft or trade. These unions were formed to address fundamental work issues of pay, hours, conditions, and job security—many of the same issues that dominate labour negotiations today. By forming a union, these skilled workers hoped to protect their craft and status from being undermined.

Many of the early labour organizations were local or regional in membership. Also, most were established to achieve some short-range goal (e.g., a pay increase) and disbanded after attaining a specific objective. This situation changed dramatically in the late nineteenth century with the expansion of the Industrial Revolution and the emergence of modern industrial capitalism. The system of producing the necessities of society in small, home-based workplaces gave way to production in large factories driven by steam and later electricity. Enormous productivity increases were gained through mass production and job specialization. However, this brought problems for workers in terms of productivity expectations, hours of work, wages, and unemployment.

industrial union
Consists of unskilled and semi-skilled workers in mass-production industries such as automobile manufacturing and mining.

Workers were faced with the reality that production was vital. Those who failed to produce, or stayed home because they were ill or had family problems, lost their jobs. Over time, the increased emphasis on production led firms to expand the hours of work. The length of the average workweek in 1900 was 60 hours, compared to 40 hours today, but an 80-hour workweek was not uncommon for some industries.[7] Wages were low and the use of child labour was widespread. For example, small boys worked long hours in mines, in areas that were inaccessible to adults, for a few cents an hour. Minimum-wage laws and unemployment benefits were non-existent, which meant that periods of unemployment were hard on families who earned subsistence wages. As you can sense, these were not short-term issues that would easily go away. The workplace was ripe for the emergence of labour organizations.

The struggle for more humane working conditions and wages was not an easy one, because before 1872 it was illegal to attempt to form a union in Canada. The pioneers in the early struggles were treated as common criminals. They were arrested, beaten, and often shot. In 1919, for example, two protesting strikers were shot and killed by police during the Winnipeg General Strike. This was followed by 428 strikes across the country.[8]

As the years progressed, more unions were formed and more employees joined them. Other union types—such as industrial unions—were created to represent certain workers. An **industrial union** is one that consists of unskilled and semi-skilled workers in mass-production industries such as automobile manufacturing and mining.

▸ A legal holiday since 1894, Labour Day is a celebration of workers and their families. It was inspired by the first significant workers's demonstration in 1872, where, accompanied by four bands, unionists marched through the streets of Toronto. Leaders demanded better conditions for all workers, as well as the release of 24 union members who were imprisoned for going on strike. About 10,000 Torontonians turned out to see the parade and listen to the speeches.

Long after it was no longer illegal, the idea of workers forming unions to protect their interests was still regarded with suspicion by employers and governments in Canada. Democratic rights for all was still a weak concept, and the idea of people getting together to fight for their rights was not accepted as it is today. The union movement was greatly influenced by immigrants from Europe (especially Britain), who brought with them the ideas and experiences of a more advanced and often more radical background. The growing union movement in the United States also influenced Canada. Many Canadian unions started as locals of American unions, and this relationship persists today. As democracy gradually gained strength, the union movement grew with it. Its participation, in turn, helped democracy sink deeper, wider roots in Canada.

THE STRUCTURE AND SIZE OF LABOUR UNIONS IN CANADA

The organizational structure of unions in Canada is quite complex. The most basic unit is the *union local* (also called a *local* or *local union*). One local usually represents one school, government office, or a specific factory or office of a company. However, that local can also cover several small companies or other work units.

While a local can be an independent organization within a specific geographic area, it is usually part of a larger structure, namely one that is provincial or regional in focus, or a *national* (a union that charters locals in only one country) or *international body*. For example, a local of the Ford plant in Windsor, Ontario, is part of the Canadian Auto Workers (CAW) union <*www.caw.ca*>, which is a national body. A local of the U.S. Steel Canada plant in Hamilton is part of the United Steel Workers (USW) union <*www.usw.ca*>, which is an international body based in the United States.

In addition, union locals typically belong to *union centrals*. The main functions of these union centrals has been to coordinate the activities of member unions when representing the interests of labour to local, provincial, and federal governments as well as to organized labour on the world scene.[9] As a rule, union centrals in Canada have had limited authority over their affiliates, except in jurisdictional matters.[10] Some of the larger bodies in Canada include the Canadian Labour Congress (CLC) <*canadianlabour.ca*> and the Quebec-based Confédération des Syndicats Nationaux/Confederation of National Trade Unions (CSN/CNTU) <*www.csn.qc.ca*>.

The CLC is the largest union central in Canada and it promotes itself as "bringing together the majority of unions in Canada in a unified, national voice." Through its 3.3 million worker members, the CLC represents Canada's national and international unions, the provincial and territorial federations of labour, and 130 district labour councils.[11] Among other issues, the CLC promotes decent wages and working conditions and improved health and safety laws. It lobbies the government on a wide range of topics including improving Canada's Employment Insurance program, better enforcing our existing health and safety legislation, fair taxes, and strong social programs, including child care, medicare, and pensions.

Figure 13.1 charts the structure of LIUNA. It is structured under a governing constitution, which is reviewed and amended every five years at a constitutional convention, bringing together elected delegates from every local union and district council in North America. Along with constitutional resolutions, the convention also elects the

▸ The Canadian Labour Congress lobbies the different levels of government on social and economic, environmental, workplace, and international issues. For example, to make lasting changes, the CLC recognizes that it needs to affect government policies in areas such as budget analysis, labour and migration, child care, health care and medicare, pensions and retirement, and jobs and the economy.[12]

Figure 13.1

The Structure of the Laborers' International Union of North America (LIUNA)

Elections are extremely democratic at LIUNA, as members vote for representation at each level of the union's structure. Members at the union local elect their local's executive board and officers. Each local then elects a district council delegate. These delegates elect the district council's executive board. Local union members also elect the international vice-president and regional managers for their regional office. At the international union, each local member elects the general president of the union (the equivalent of a CEO) and the general secretary treasurer (the equivalent of a CFO).

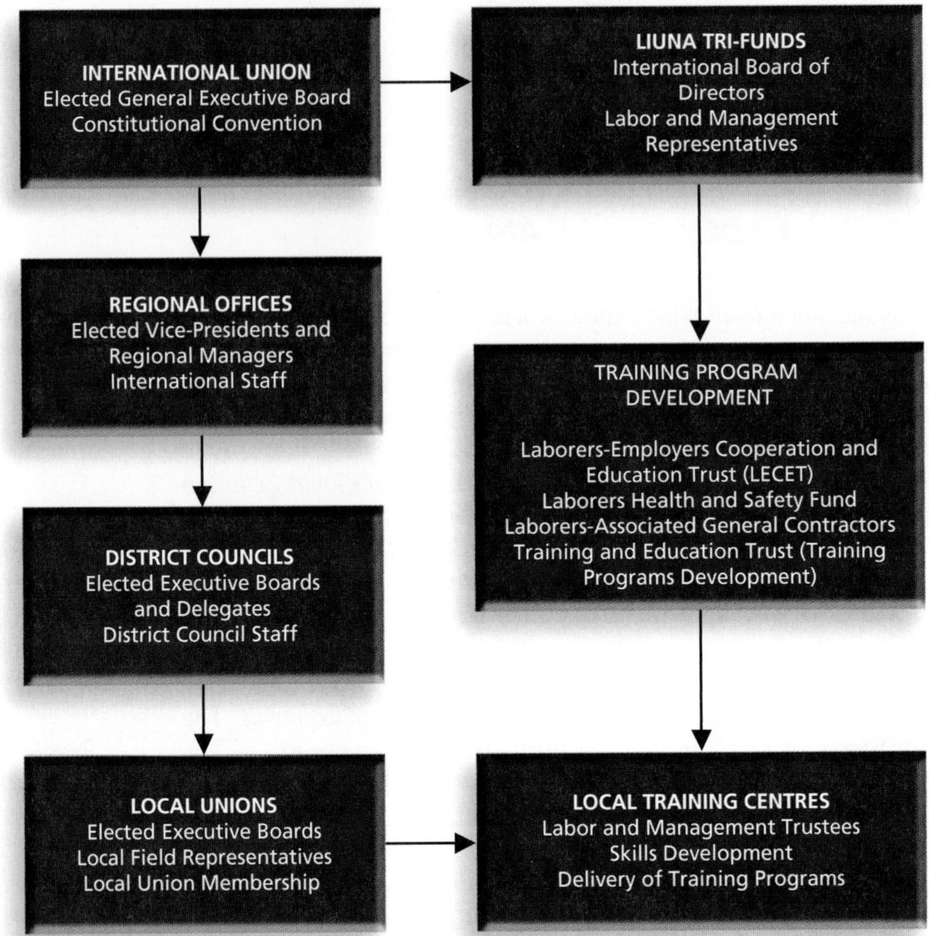

General Executive Board, composed of the general president, general secretary treasurer, and ten regional vice-presidents. The international union issues and holds the charters of all local unions and district councils that operate under the rule of the LIUNA Constitution. District councils are composed of elected delegates from local unions within a state, states, province, or provinces. These councils are responsible for collective bargaining and are the holders of "bargaining rights" on behalf of their members. LIUNA also has established national labour-management funds that are responsible for training, health and safety, and promotion of unionized construction. The funds are referred to as the Tri-Funds. These unique funds, which are supported by joint contributions, provide a broad range of services to both labour and management.

Size of Labour Unions in Canada

union density
A measure of the percentage of workers who belong to unions.

Union density measures the percentage of workers who belong to unions. In 2011, unions represented almost 30 percent (approximately 4.3 million) of all workers.[13] To contrast, when unions were most powerful in 1984, they represented almost 42 percent of workers.[14] While union membership has been increasing (i.e., the number of workers that belong to a union), this has not always been reflected in an increase in union density (i.e., the percentage of workers that belong to a union). Why do you think that this is so? Figure 13.2 summarizes union coverage by selected characteristics.

Before we discuss labour legislation, let us briefly look at two unions that are often in the news.

Factor	Percentage	Factor	Percentage
Public sector	74.7	Workplace size: under 20 employees	14.5
Private sector	17.5	Workplace size: over 500 employees	56.0
Aged 15 to 24	16.4	Nursing	81.0
Aged 25 to 54	34.3	Retail	12.0
Full-time	33.3	Business, finance, and administrative	26.4
Part-time	25.1	Newfoundland and Labrador	39.9
High school graduation	26.3	Alberta	23.9
University degree	36.5		

Source: Sharanjit Uppal, "Unionization 2011," Statistics Canada, 26 October 2011, http://www.statcan.gc.ca/pub/75-001-x/2011004/article/11579-eng.pdf, 3–7.

Figure 13.2

Union Coverage by Selected Characteristics, 2011

Coverage represents union members and persons who are not union members but are covered by collective agreements (e.g., some religious groups). Newfoundland and Labrador is the most unionized province while Alberta is the least unionized province.

The Canadian Union of Public Employees (CUPE)[15]

Formed in 1963, CUPE is Canada's largest union, with around 618,000 members and more than 70 offices across Canada. The union represents workers in health care, education, municipalities, libraries, universities, social services, public utilities, transportation, emergency services, and airlines. CUPE members are service providers, white-collar workers, technicians, labourers, skilled tradespeople, and professionals. More than half are women, and about one-third work part time.

CUPE, like other unions, lobbies the government on a number of issues. For example, the Green Box highlights some of CUPE's suggestions on what the federal government should do to protect the environment.

▸ LIUNA is the most progressive and fastest-growing union of construction workers. Its members, a half million strong, work in the construction industry.

The Canadian Auto Workers (CAW)[16]

The CAW was founded in 1985 after the Canadian members of the U.S.-based United Auto Workers (UAW) <*uaw.org*> decided to form their own Canadian-controlled union. As a result of constant organizing and mergers with 43 other unions the CAW is one of the largest private-sector unions in Canada. It represents approximately 195,000 members in all major sectors of the economy, as noted in Figure 13.3. Just over 40 percent of its members work in manufacturing, 34 percent in services, 20 percent in transportation, and 5 percent in primary industries. Auto assembly and parts represents the largest single industry in the union with 24 percent of the membership. Overall membership has been impacted by the loss of manufacturing sector jobs in Canada (249,000 lost jobs since June 2008). The auto industry alone shed 26,000 jobs.

CAW members are organized into 231 local unions in 1,550 active bargaining units. Every year, more than 500 collective agreements (to be discussed shortly) are negotiated, and more than 4,000 members (on average) are organized.

At the time this chapter was written, the Communications, Energy and Paperworkers Union of Canada voted to merge with the CAW. Once approved, this new union will become Canada's largest public-sector union with more than 300,000 members across roughly 20 sectors of the economy. Did this merger go through? What does the new union look like today?

GREENBOX

Protect the Environment

According to the Climate Change Performance Index 2008, Canada ranked 53rd out of 56 countries. CUPE feels that the federal Conservative government is to blame for this global ranking. Some of the government's actions (and inactions) that have contributed to this standing are cited as follows: (1) federal climate change programs and initiatives to help low-income Canadians increase energy efficiency and reduce energy costs were slashed; (2) Canada failed to meet its legal commitments under the Kyoto Protocol [in which Canada is no longer a participant]; (3) an effective plan to cut greenhouse gas emissions has not been developed; and (4) the Alberta oil sands developments have been allowed to grow unfettered, poisoning the air, natural landscape, and water and drinking supply of communities in the process.

Some of CUPE's suggestions for federal government action that can be taken to improve Canada's ranking are noted below:

- Develop a climate change plan that will reach emissions reduction targets in line with what is called for by the international community.
- Impose a broad-based price on carbon to prompt greenhouse gas reductions.
- Pass meaningful regulations on industry and business to cut greenhouse gases.
- End federal government subsidies to the oil sands and implement comprehensive energy conservation programs and support for clean and renewable sources of energy.
- Create an aggressive green jobs strategy to develop new types of work, supported by a fair transition program for workers displaced by an evolving green and low-carbon economy.
- Invest in green technologies and innovation.

What do you think? Does such lobbying have an impact on government policies? Do you think that the suggestions are realistic given the economic and political climate?

Source: "Protect the Environment," Canadian Union of Public Employees, 1 October 2008, http://cupe.ca/2008-federal-election/Protect-the-environm.

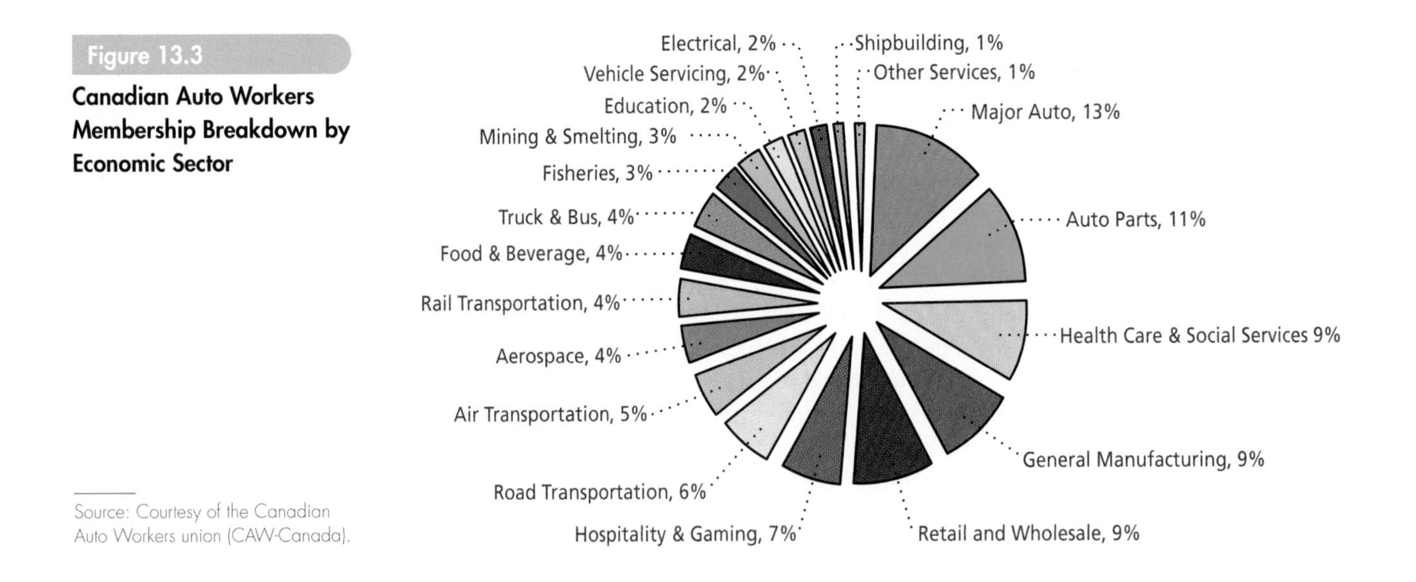

Figure 13.3

Canadian Auto Workers Membership Breakdown by Economic Sector

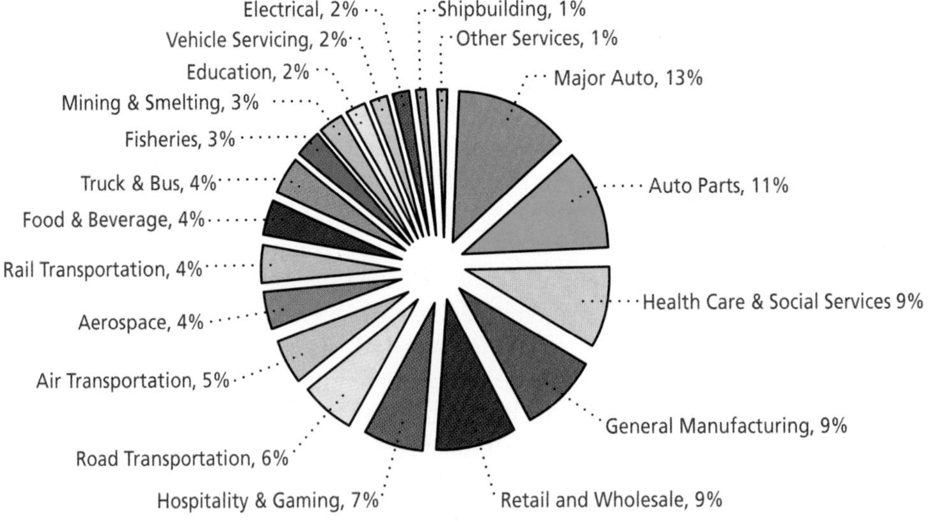

Source: Courtesy of the Canadian Auto Workers union (CAW-Canada).

PROGRESS ASSESSMENT

- Why were unions originally formed?
- List reasons why union membership has been declining.
- Describe the structure of unions. Why would a union local affiliate itself with the CLC?

LABOUR LEGISLATION

Discuss the major legislation affecting labour unions.

The growth and influence of organized labour in Canada have depended primarily on two major factors: the law and public opinion.

As with other movements for greater fairness and equity in our society—such as women's right to vote, equal rights for minorities and women, and protection for children—when support for employees' rights became widespread in Canada, laws were passed to enforce them. Today we have laws establishing minimum wage, paid minimum holidays and vacation, maximum hours, overtime pay, health and safety conditions, workers' compensation, employment insurance, the Canada/Quebec Pension Plan, and a host of other rights. It is strange to realize that at one time or another, these were all on the agenda of unions and were opposed by employers and governments for many years. They often denounced these demands as radical notions.

The effect of unions goes far beyond their numbers. Companies that want to keep unions out often provide compensation, benefits, and working conditions that match or exceed those found in union plants or offices. Thus, the levels established by unions spill over to non-union companies.

As indicated in Chapter 4, the federal government has control over specified fields of activity that are national in nature. In Chapter 12, it was mentioned that such activities apply to approximately 10 percent of Canadian workers. They work for banks, railways, airlines, telephone and cable systems, and radio and broadcasting companies. The federal government also has jurisdiction over many First Nations activities. Therefore, federal legislation applies to unions and labour–management relations in these businesses as well as to all federal Crown corporations and federal civil servants. The major legislation that governs labour–management relations for these employees is the Canada Labour Code, which is administered by Human Resources and Social Development Canada. It is also responsible for the Employment Equity Act as well as other legislation on wages and working conditions.

Provincial or territorial laws apply to the other 90 percent of the Canadian workforce. As you can imagine, these laws vary and it is the responsibility of businesses to know the rights of their workers and vice versa.

▸ Your father is sick and he needs you to take care of him. You ask for time off and your boss says no. What can you do? Could Walmart employees in Quebec have refused to search for a bomb in their store? The United Food and Commercial Workers Canada launched a "Know Your Rights" campaign to educate retail workers about their labour-law rights.

WAL-MART is correct:

Individuals *ARE* important.

In Canada, individuals have rights – and they are *FREE* to exercise them.

You have the right to be *told* your rights.

You have the right to *discuss* your rights.

You have the right to *demand* your rights.

They're your rights, eh?

LEARN 'EM!

Ask us about our FREE training sessions:

1.877.248.6483

Workplace Laws[17]

There are also various workplace laws in Canada that protect all workers. Be aware that they differ in detail in each province and territory.

One workplace law is the *right to know about workplace hazards.* By knowing about workplace hazards, workers can ensure that employers make work safer, provide protection to workers, and give training so that workers can work with the smallest possibility of injury or illness. Unfortunately, and in spite of some of the best workplace health and safety laws in the world, over 1,000 Canadian workers die each year due to an unsafe workplace. The number of people killed at work each year in Canada has risen for the past 15 years. Employers have to do more work to enforce these laws and to protect their workers if this increasing trend is going to be reversed.

Another example is the *right to refuse unsafe work,* which entitles a worker to step away from work that he or she believes

SPOTLIGHT ON SMALL BUSINESS

Helping Reduce Harassment and Violence in the Workplace

Robinson Heeney LLP <www.robinsonheeney.com>, a Toronto-based employment law firm, was founded in 2011 by lawyers Kevin Robinson and James Heeney. The firm provides advice to both employers and employees on all aspects of employment law. The firm also provides third party workplace investigations and training services.

Partner James Heeney has been named by *Canadian HR Reporter* as a leading employment lawyer in Toronto. His employer-side practice focuses on providing strategic advice and litigation support in the areas of employment agreements, policy manuals, terminations, and human rights issues. In respect of the employee side of his practice, Heeney routinely advises clients in both unionized and non-unionized issues relating to executive compensation, employment contracts, terminations, and human rights.

Why take on the challenge of starting your own business? Heeney was motivated to create a firm focused on integrity and exceptional legal advice, while still ensuring it was provided in a manner that was cost effective, timely, and practical. He wanted to influence an organization that ranked a good work environment as one of its top priorities. While he admits that running a business is not easy, there is certainly more satisfaction out of its successes. "No one wants to work long hours, but it is easier when it happens and you know it's to build your own business," says Heeney. "Many of my clients are long standing and I am so proud to be able to say that."

One area in which Heeney advises his clients is anti-harassment legislation. The courts provide anti-harassment protections throughout Canada for both complainants and respondents. Whether a province has harassment legislation or not, the courts will find employers liable where an inappropriate workplace investigation occurs or where harassment isn't addressed. An employee found to have been terminated for requesting that an employer comply with the harassment and violence provisions, for example, may be entitled to back wages and to being reinstated in his or her job. These are significant remedies which can be very costly to businesses.

Bill 168 took effect in Ontario in June 2010. It provides new protections to employees regarding workplace violence and harassment. (Similar legislation exists in Quebec, Manitoba, and Saskatchewan.) All employers, regardless of size, are required to actively adopt policies and training designed to prevent workplace harassment and violence. Employees who feel there has been a breach of the harassment and violence provisions in their workplace can file a complaint with the Ontario Labour Relations Board, and the Board has extraordinary powers when it feels a breach has occurred.

Heeney recommends the following tips on what businesses can do to limit an employer's potential liability:

1. *Take Complaints Seriously.* When complaints are filed by an employee, ensure that they are given serious consideration.
2. *Acknowledge Receipt of the Complaint.* Make sure that when complaints are filed you acknowledge to the employee that the complaint has been received and will be investigated.
3. *Perform an Unbiased Investigation.* Advise the employee alleged to have committed wrongdoing that there is a complaint. Conduct an unbiased investigation and then make the decision.
4. *Report Back With Your Findings.* Advise both sides of the findings, and in writing.
5. *Avoid Retaliation.* Always advise all parties that they will not be subjected to retaliation for participating in the investigation.

"Preparing for changes in legislation can be a lengthy and detailed process for employers," counsels Heeney, "particularly for smaller businesses with limited resources. However, the changes to the legislation are an essential step in ensuring that employers are doing their part in reducing the risk of violence and harassment in their workplaces and to avoiding possible fines and liability."

Sources: James Heeney, Partner, Robinson Heeney LLP, interview, 28 June 2012, 416-646-5169; "James Heeney, Partner," Robinson Heeney LLP, 2012, www.robinsonheeney.com/lawyers_jheeney.php; James Heeney, "Don't get blindsided by workplace harassment, violence laws," CBC News, 30 September 2011, www.cbc.ca/news/business/smallbusiness/story/2011/09/30/f-smallbiz-james-heeney.html; and James Heeney, "Is your business ready for new harassment and violence legislation?," CBC News, 28 May 2010, www.cbc.ca/money/smallbusiness/story/2010/05/28/f-james-heeney-workplace-harassment.html.

is unsafe. This right allows the worker to have the refused work investigated, and repaired if it is dangerous. During this time, the worker receives pay and is protected from an employer's possible reprisal, since it is illegal for an employer to fire or discipline a worker who refuses work that she or he believes is unsafe.

In 2006, workers at a Walmart store in St-Jean-Sur-Richelieu, Quebec, were ordered by management to help police search for a bomb, even though police recommended to company officials that the store should be completely evacuated. "This was a pretty sad message about how much value Walmart puts on the lives of its workers," said Wayne Hanley, national director of United Food and Commercial Workers (UFCW) Canada <*www.ufcw.ca*>. "It makes you wonder what kind of information Walmart gives its employees about the labour laws."

The Spotlight on Small Business box shares suggestions on what employers can do to limit potential liability in the area of workplace violence and harassment.

Labour Relations Boards[18]

A labour relations board (LRB) is a quasi-judicial body consisting of representatives from government, labour, and business. It functions more informally than a court but it has the full authority of the law.

For example, the federal government created the Canada Industrial Relations Board (CIRB) <*www.cirb-ccri.gc.ca*>. Its mandate is to contribute to and promote effective industrial relations in any work, undertaking, or business that falls within the authority of the Parliament of Canada. The CIRB plays an active role in helping parties resolve their disputes through mediation (to be discussed soon) and alternative dispute resolution approaches. It also undertakes a wide range of industrial relations activities, including the following:

- certifying labour unions
- investigating complaints of unfair labour practices
- issuing cease and desist orders in cases of unlawful strikes and lockouts
- rendering decisions on jurisdictional issues

The provincial governments have their own boards that oversee their specific legislation. The laws, regulations, and procedures vary from province to province.

THE COLLECTIVE BARGAINING PROCESS

Describe the collective bargaining process.

The LRB oversees **collective bargaining**, which is the entire process whereby union and management representatives negotiate a contract for workers. Collective bargaining includes more than the contract itself. Collective bargaining determines how unions are selected, actions that are allowed during the period prior to certification, certification, and ongoing contract negotiations. Collective bargaining also determines behaviour while a contract is in force and during a breakdown in negotiations for a contract renewal, as well as decertification. **Certification** is a formal process whereby a union is recognized by the LRB as the bargaining agent for a group of employees. **Decertification** is the process by which workers can take away a union's right to represent them.

collective bargaining
The process whereby union and management representatives negotiate a contract for workers.

certification
Formal process whereby a union is recognized by the Labour Relations Board (LRB) as the bargaining agent for a group of employees.

decertification
Process by which workers can take away a union's right to represent them.

The whole bargaining process and the important certification procedure are shown in detail in Figure 13.4. As you can see, the process is quite regulated and controlled. Employers and employees as well as unions have to follow a strict procedure to ensure that everybody is playing by the rules. For example, did you know that it is illegal for employers to fire employees for union activities? This process is also democratic and, as in any election, the minority has to accept the majority's decision.

The actual contract is quite complex, covering a wide range of topics. We will look at some of the major ones shortly.

Objectives of Organized Labour

Outline the objectives of labour unions.

The objectives of unions frequently change because of shifts in social and economic trends. For example, in the 1970s the primary objective of unions was to obtain additional pay and benefits for their members. Throughout the 1980s, objectives shifted toward issues related to job security and union recognition. In the 1990s and 2000s, unions again focused on job security, but the issue of global competition and its effects often took centre stage. Unions were a major opponent of NAFTA, passed by

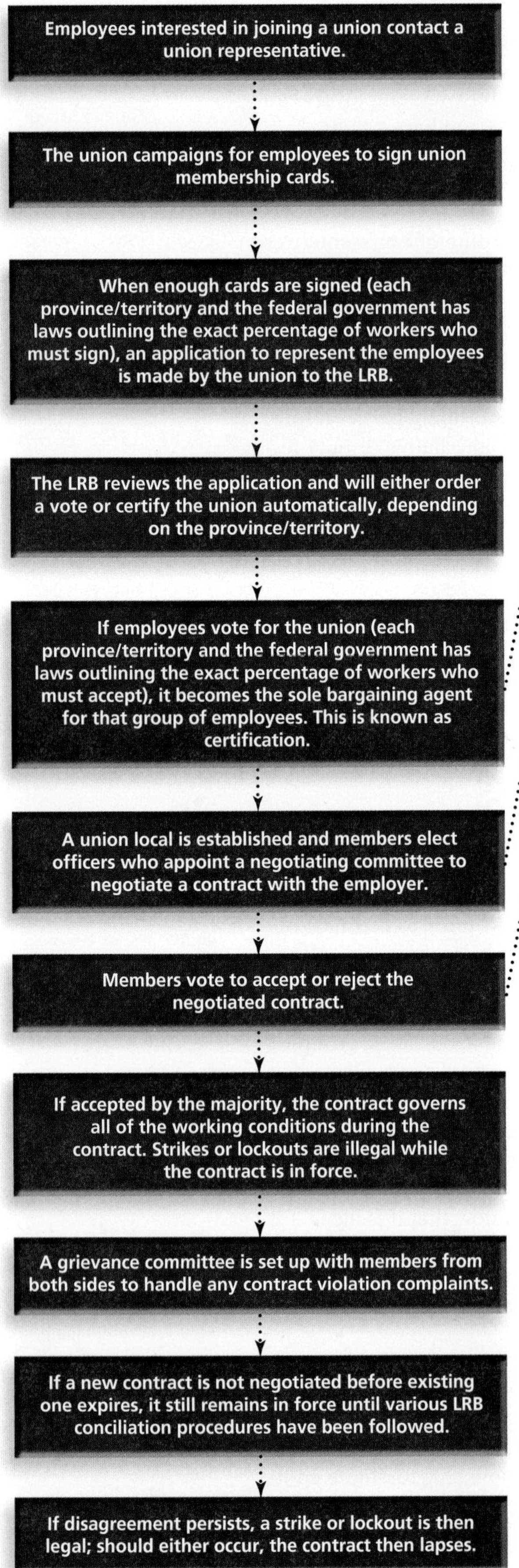

Figure 13.4

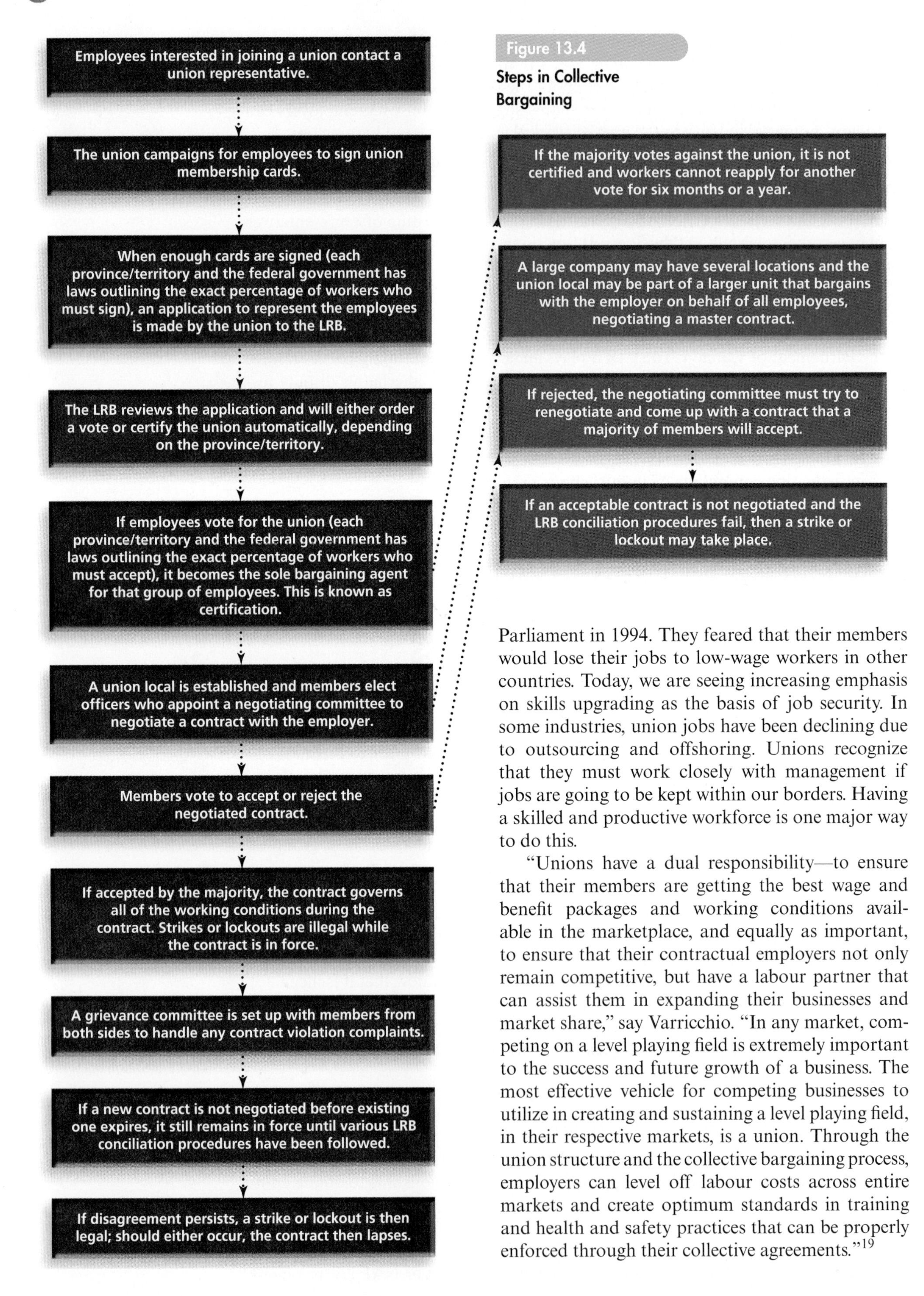

Steps in Collective Bargaining

Parliament in 1994. They feared that their members would lose their jobs to low-wage workers in other countries. Today, we are seeing increasing emphasis on skills upgrading as the basis of job security. In some industries, union jobs have been declining due to outsourcing and offshoring. Unions recognize that they must work closely with management if jobs are going to be kept within our borders. Having a skilled and productive workforce is one major way to do this.

"Unions have a dual responsibility—to ensure that their members are getting the best wage and benefit packages and working conditions available in the marketplace, and equally as important, to ensure that their contractual employers not only remain competitive, but have a labour partner that can assist them in expanding their businesses and market share," say Varricchio. "In any market, competing on a level playing field is extremely important to the success and future growth of a business. The most effective vehicle for competing businesses to utilize in creating and sustaining a level playing field, in their respective markets, is a union. Through the union structure and the collective bargaining process, employers can level off labour costs across entire markets and create optimum standards in training and health and safety practices that can be properly enforced through their collective agreements."[19]

1. Management rights
2. Union recognition
3. Union security clause
4. Strikes and lockouts
5. Union activities and responsibilities
   a. Dues checkoff
   b. Union notices
   c. Shop stewards on the floor
6. Wages
   a. Wage structure
   b. Shift differentials
   c. Wage incentives
   d. Bonuses
   e. Piecework conditions
   f. Tiered wage structures
7. Hours of work and time-off policies
   a. Regular hours of work
   b. Holidays
   c. Vacation policies
   d. Overtime regulations
   e. Leaves of absence
   f. Break periods
   g. Flextime
   h. Mealtime allotments
8. Job rights and seniority principles
   a. Seniority regulations
   b. Transfer policies and bumping
   c. Promotions
   d. Layoffs and recall procedures
   e. Job bidding and posting
9. Discharge and discipline
   a. Suspension
   b. Conditions for discharge
10. Grievance procedures
   a. Arbitration agreement
   b. Mediation procedures
11. Employee benefits, health, and welfare

Figure 13.5

Issues in a Negotiated Labour–Management Agreement

Labour and management often meet to discuss and clarify the terms that specify employees' functions within the company. The topics listed in this figure are typically discussed during these meetings.

The **negotiated labour–management agreement**, more informally referred to as the **labour contract**, clarifies the terms and conditions and sets the tone under which management and organized labour will function over a specific period. "Common sense and good business practice dictates the importance of having a binding written contract between parties engaged in a business transaction, thereby protecting the interests of all parties involved," says Varricchio. "Such a contract spells out the responsibilities and obligations of both parties, itemizes the compensation package agreed to for services rendered or products purchased, and identifies a mechanism to be employed to settle differences in the event either party violates the terms of the mutually agreed to contract. How much more important then is it to have such a contract between an employer and his/her employees that protects the interests of everyone, especially in an environment where the interaction between personalities could negatively impact the productivity of the workforce and the business?"[20] Figure 13.5 provides an abbreviated list of topics commonly negotiated by labour and management during contract talks, which often take a long time to complete. Let us briefly consider three areas: union security, checkoff, and discharge and discipline.

Labour unions generally insist that contracts contain a **union security clause**, which stipulates that employees who benefit from a union must either officially join or at least pay dues to the union. There are basically four types of clauses:

1. The clause favoured by unions is called a **closed shop**, which means that all new hires must be union members. In effect, hiring is done through the union. Unemployed members of the union register for employment or show up daily at a union hiring hall.
2. One step down is a union shop. In a **union shop**, the employer is free to hire anybody but the recruit must then join the union within a short period, perhaps a month.

negotiated labour–management agreement (labour contract)
Agreement that clarifies the terms and conditions and sets the tone under which management and labour agree to function over a period of time.

union security clause
Provision in a negotiated labour–management agreement that stipulates that employees who benefit from a union must either officially join or at least pay dues to the union.

closed shop
A workplace in which all new hires must already be union members.

union shop
A workplace in which the employer is free to hire anybody, but the recruit must then join the union within a short period, perhaps a month.

agency shop (Rand formula)
A workplace in which a new employee is not required to join the union but must pay union dues.

3. One of the most common conditions is an **agency shop**, which is based on the **Rand formula** that was devised by Supreme Court Justice Rand in 1946. The new employee is not required to join the union but must pay union dues. The argument for this requirement is that all employees who benefit from a contract signed by the union should help pay for the costs of maintaining that union—its officers, union expenses, negotiating committee, shop stewards, and so forth.
4. The hiring condition least popular with unions and the one favoured by employers is the **open shop**, where employees are free to join or not join the union and to pay or not pay union dues.

open shop
A workplace in which employees are free to join or not join the union and to pay or not pay union dues.

checkoff
A contract clause requiring the employer to deduct union dues from employees' pay and remit them to a union.

Regardless of which hiring condition prevails, the contract usually contains check-off as a standard clause. **Checkoff** requires the employer to deduct union dues from employees and to pay and remit them to the union (except for non-members in an open shop). It would obviously be a lot harder to collect union dues individually.

"A collective agreement provides protection if an employer wishes to discharge an employee. In the absence of a collective agreement, employers can fire non-union employees for almost any reason so long as the employees are given reasonable notice, or payment in lieu of notice. In a union environment," adds Aaron Rousseau, a Toronto-based employment lawyer with the law firm Whitten & Lublin, "the employer needs to prove misconduct on the part of the employee before he or she can be fired."[21]

In the future, the focus of union negotiations will most likely shift as issues such as child and elder care, worker retraining, two-tiered wage plans, outsourcing, employee empowerment, and even integrity and honesty testing further challenge union members' rights in the workplace. Unions also intend to carefully monitor immigration policies and global agreements to ensure that Canadian jobs are not lost. Before you move on, review Figure 13.6 for some of the advantages and disadvantages of joining a union.

Resolving Labour–Management Disputes

grievance
A formal protest by an individual employee, with the support of the union, when they believe that management is not abiding by or fulfilling the terms of a labour contract.

The rights of labour and management are outlined in the negotiated labour–management agreement. Upon acceptance by both sides, the agreement becomes a guide to work relations between union members and managers. However, signing the agreement does not necessarily end the employee–management negotiations. There are sometimes differences concerning interpretations of the labour–management agreement. For example, managers may interpret a certain clause in the agreement to mean that they are free to select who works overtime. Union members may interpret the same clause to mean that managers must select employees for overtime on the basis of *employee seniority*. If disagreements such as this cannot be resolved between the two parties, employees may file a grievance.

A **grievance** is a formal protest by an individual employee, with the support of the union, when they believe that management is not abiding by or fulfilling the terms of a

Figure 13.6

Some Advantaged and Disadvantages of Joining a Union

Union Advantages	Union Disadvantages
Members are generally better protected when disputes arise	Promotion and pay may be determined by seniority
Usually receive higher wages* and better benefit coverage (e.g., pension plan, supplemental health care, and dental plan)	Negotiated compensation usually leads to higher production costs
Better negotiating power as a group rather than as an individual	You may not be agree with all of the union's decisions (e.g., to go on strike)

*Employees who are members of a union and employees that are covered by a collective agreement or a union contract receive an average hourly wage of $26.97. Compare this to an average hourly wage of $21.96 in a non-union environment.

Sources: "Average hourly wages of employees by selected characteristics and profession, unadjusted data, by province (monthly)," Statistics Canada, 8 June 2012, www.statcan.gc.ca/tables-tableaux/sum-som/l01/cst01/labr69a-eng.htm; and "Joining a union in Canada," Working in Canada, [n.d.], www.workingin-canada.com/jobs/job-tools/joining-a-union.

labour contract. Companies in which relations between management and union are poor or deteriorating usually have a backlog of unresolved grievances. This is not good for the morale of the employees and, if allowed to continue for any length of time, will ultimately result in lower productivity. Where relations are good, there are few grievances and those that arise are quickly settled. Overtime rules, promotions, layoffs, transfers, job assignments, and so forth are generally sources of employee grievances.

Handling such grievances demands a good deal of contact between union officials and managers. Grievances, however, do not imply that the company has broken the law or the labour agreement. In fact, the vast majority of grievances are negotiated and resolved by **shop stewards** (union officials who work permanently in an organization and represent employee interests on a daily basis) and supervisory-level managers. However, if a grievance is not settled at this level, formal grievance procedures will begin.

shop stewards
Union officials who work permanently in an organization and represent employee interests on a daily basis.

Figure 13.7 indicates all steps, specified by the contract for a plant, in the processing of a grievance. Typically there are five or six levels in this procedure. If the grievance cannot be settled at one level, it moves up to the next level. The final step is an outside arbitrator or arbitration board (arbitration will be discussed after mediation). In practice, this is quite rare. Many complaints are settled informally and never put in writing.

Conciliation, Mediation, and Arbitration

During the negotiation process, there is generally what is called a **bargaining zone**, which is a range of options between the initial and final offer that each party will consider in reaching an agreement through collective bargaining. If labour–management negotiators are not able to agree on alternatives within this bargaining zone, and negotiations dissolve or reach an impasse, conciliation is the next necessary step.

bargaining zone
Range of options between the initial and final offer that each party will consider before negotiations dissolve or reach an impasse.

Conciliation is a process by which a labour union or an employer must use the government's services (via the Ministry of Labour) for help in resolving their differences so that they can reach a collective agreement.[22] If conciliation fails and both parties cannot reach an agreement, the Minister of Labour would then issue a "*no board,*" which is a notice informing both parties that the Minister "does not consider it advisable to appoint a conciliation board." Conciliation boards are exceedingly rare and have not been appointed since the 1960s.[23] Once conciliation fails, the union is then in a legal position to strike and the employer is also free to declare a lockout (both will be discussed soon). After a "no board" is issued, the Ministry will also suggest mediation and offer to provide this service.

conciliation
A process by which a labour union or an employer must use the government's services (via the Ministry of Labour) for help in resolving their differences so that they can reach a collective agreement.

Mediation is the use of a third party, called a *mediator,* who encourages both sides in a dispute to consider negotiating and often makes suggestions for resolving the dispute. However, it is important to remember that mediators evaluate facts in the dispute and then make suggestions, not decisions.[24] Elected officials (current and past), attorneys, and professors are often called on to serve as mediators in labour disputes. For example, the Northwest Territories Power Corporation <*www.ntpc.com*> and its employees had been without a collective agreement for more than a year and,

mediation
The use of a third party, called a mediator, who encourages both sides in a dispute to continue negotiating and often makes suggestions for resolving the dispute.

Figure 13.7

Stages in Processing Grievances

	Management	Union
Stage 1	First-level supervisor	Shop steward
Stage 2	Second-level supervisor	Chief steward
Stage 3	Plant manager	Chief grievance officer
Stage 4	Director of industrial relations	National or international union official
Stage 5	CEO or President	President of union or central labour body
Stage 6	Dispute goes to arbitration (quite rare)	

▸ After months of negotiations, Air Canada flight attendants rejected a tentative agreement and voted overwhelmingly—with 98 percent in favour—for a strike mandate. After a decade of concessions, flight attendants were negotiating for a better contract.[28] CUPE developed this ad as support for its members during this dispute.

among other issues, the union wanted employees to receive the same salary as people who do similar work for the Northwest Territories government. The two parties required mediation to settle the contract.[25]

A more extreme approach used to resolve conflict is arbitration. **Arbitration** is an agreement to bring in an impartial third party (a single arbitrator or a panel of arbitrators) to render a binding decision in a labour dispute. Arbitration may be *voluntary;* both sides decide to submit their case to an arbitrator. Arbitration may also be *compulsory* where a decision is imposed by the government or by Parliament or a provincial legislature. Compulsory arbitration usually occurs in a major or prolonged strike with serious consequences for the public. Usually, non-grievance arbitration (say, for contract disputes) is voluntary and grievance arbitration is compulsory. Employees who are designated as having essential positions (e.g., police, firefighters, and hospital employees) do not have the right to strike as stated in their collective agreements and their disputes must be settled through binding arbitration.[26]

While binding arbitration may result in a new collective agreement, it can leave contentious issues unresolved. Under threat of back-to-work legislation and two unwarranted referrals to the Canada Industrial Relations Board by the Federal Labour Minister, CUPE agreed to binding arbitration with Air Canada. "Awarding flight attendants an agreement they rejected a month ago does not in any way address serious workplace issues and flight attendants are rightfully disappointed and angry," said Paul Moist, National President of CUPE. "If Air Canada is truly interested in running a professional and efficient company they must invest in their work force. This agreement will leave flight attendants exhausted, frustrated, and underpaid."[27]

PROGRESS ASSESSMENT

- How do labour relations boards regulate labour–management relations?
- In the collective bargaining process, what happens after certification?
- What are the differences between conciliation, mediation, and arbitration?

Both mediation and arbitration can be difficult, lengthy, and costly procedures, especially when both sides are locked into rigid positions. That is why negotiators from both sides usually try to settle their differences before resorting to these steps.

LO 5 Describe the negotiation tactics used by labour and management during conflicts.

NEGOTIATION TACTICS

If labour and management cannot reach an agreement through collective bargaining and negotiations break down, either side or both sides may use specific tactics to enhance their negotiating position and perhaps sway public opinion. Keep in mind that today the great majority of labour negotiations end successfully without the disruption of a strike or lockout. Remember that mediation and arbitration are always available to the parties in dispute. They may take advantage of these procedures before, during, or after any of these tactics are exercised. Let us look at some examples next.

arbitration
An agreement to bring in an impartial third party (a single arbitrator or a panel of arbitrators) to render a binding decision in a labour dispute.

Union Tactics

The primary tactics used by organized labour are strikes and boycotts. Unions might also use picketing and work slowdowns to get desired changes.

Strikes

Strikes have historically been the most potent tactic that unions use to achieve their objectives in labour disputes. A **strike** occurs when workers collectively refuse to go to work. Strikes can attract public attention to a labour dispute and at times cause operations in a company to slow down or totally cease. Employer attempts to restructure pension plans are at the root of a good percentage of strikes over the past decade.[29]

strike
A union strategy in which workers refuse to go to work.

Prior to the actual strike, union leaders call for a *strike vote,* which is a secret ballot authorizing the union leadership to call a strike. This democratic vote is necessary if a potential strike is to be considered legal. If the union gets a strong mandate—say, more than 80 percent in favour of a strike—it can use this as a lever to convince management to accept its demands without actually going on strike.

Union tactics include rotating strikes—on and off or alternating among different plants or cities—rather than a full-fledged strike in which all employees are off the job for the duration. With rotating strikes, employees still get some pay, which is not the case in an all-out strike. Many unions build up a strike fund from union dues and use it to give their members strike pay, but that is usually a fraction of their normal wages. Sometimes, in important or long-lasting strikes, other unions will give moral or financial aid.

Strikes sometimes lead to the resolution of a labour dispute; however, they also have generated violence and extended bitterness. Often after a strike is finally settled both labour and management remain openly hostile toward each other and mutual complaints of violations of the negotiated labour–management agreement continue.

A **wildcat strike** is an unauthorized (by the union) work stoppage while a labour contract is still in effect.[30] An example of this occurred as the result of increasing tension between Toronto Transit Commission (TTC) <*www.ttc.ca*> workers and the TTC. Maintenance workers, angered at being forced into permanent overnight shifts, were quickly joined by drivers, who had their own safety concerns, for a one-day wildcat strike. Eric Lascelles, a strategist at Toronto-Dominion Bank, estimated that the strike could cost the local economy roughly $10 million in lost productivity as 800,000 commuters were forced to find alternate modes of transportation. The Ontario Labour Relations Board issued a cease and desist order to force employees back to work. Bob Kinnear, president of the Amalgamated Transit Union, warned that the relationship between union and management could get worse and "the problems have not gone away."[31]

wildcat strike
An unauthorized (by the union) work stoppage while a labour contract is still in effect.

Boycotts

Unions can use boycotts as a means to obtain their objectives in a labour dispute. A **primary boycott** occurs when organized labour encourages both its members and the general public not to buy the products or services of a firm involved in a labour dispute. Such was the case when striking employees at the Browning Harvey Ltd. <*www.browningharvey.nf.ca*> bottling plant in St. John's took their pickets to retail stores, encouraging consumers not to buy Pepsi products for as long as the dispute lasted.[32] A **secondary boycott** is an attempt by labour to convince others to stop doing business with a firm that is the subject of a primary boycott. For example, a union can initiate a secondary boycott against a supermarket chain because the chain carries goods produced by a company that is the target of a primary boycott.

primary boycott
When a union encourages both its members and the general public not to buy the products of a firm involved in a labour dispute.

secondary boycott
An attempt by labour to convince others to stop doing business with a firm that is the subject of a primary boycott.

▸ Two months after the start of the strike, and as part of its international campaign, the Public Service Alliance of Canada ran this ad in the *New York Times* and the *Wall Street Journal*. Consumers were being asked to not buy "Dirty Diamonds." Would such an ad affect your buying behaviour?

Picketing

Strikers may also picket the company, which means that they walk around the outside of the organization carrying signs and talking with the public and the media about issues in the labour dispute. Picket obstruction is illegal, but by slowing down anyone or anything from entering or leaving, strikers ensure that things are not "business as usual" for the company, with the hope that negotiations will continue. Unions also use picketing as an informational tool before going on strike. The purpose is to alert the public to an issue that is stirring labour unrest, even though no strike has been voted.

Other Tactics[33]

Sabotage, where workers damage their machines; *sit-ins,* where they occupy the workplace and refuse to move; or *work-to-rule,* where they follow the operating rules of the workplace in every detail to slow down the work, are other tactics that have been used by union members. About 15,000 unionized employees at TELUS, after having been without a contract for nearly five years, began a work-to-rule campaign. Among other suggestions by the union executive, employees were encouraged to plan the safest route to their next job site (which may not have been the shortest route), to take all scheduled breaks, and to provide "super service" by making sure that customer needs were fully met and that TELUS workers took the time to explain all options to customers. What would the implications be to the company as a result of these suggestions?

Management Tactics

Like labour, management also uses specific tactics to achieve its workplace goals. Management may announce layoffs or a shortened workweek and blame it on declining business. It may say the company is having trouble competing due to high labour costs. Quite often, management may continue to work and try to do some of the tasks formerly done by the striking workforce. Let us look briefly at how management also considers the use of lockouts, injunctions, and strikebreakers.

Lockouts

lockout
An attempt by management to put pressure on unions by temporarily closing the business.

A **lockout** is an attempt by managers to put pressure on union workers by temporarily closing the business. It may seem less costly to close down and cease paying wages than to put up with slowdowns, rotating strikes, or work-to-rule union tactics, all of which can be very disruptive. This tactic may force the union to reduce its demands if individual members cannot do without an income for very long or if there is a weak strike-vote majority.

The 2011 National Basketball Association <*www.nba.com*> delayed the season the start of the season and it reduced the regular season from 82 to 66 games. The main issues dividing the owners and the players were the division of revenue and the structure of the salary cap and luxury tax.[34] But not all lockouts result in employees going back to work. Review the Analyzing Management Decisions case at the end of the chapter for an example.

Clearly, a strike is a weapon of last resort for unions, to be used when all else fails. Similarly, management is reluctant to lock out its employees and call a halt to operations. Without products and services, there are no profits.

Injunctions

injunction
A court order directing someone to do something or to refrain from doing something.

An **injunction** is a court order directing someone to do something or to refrain from doing something. Management has sought injunctions to order striking workers back to work, limit the number of pickets that can be used during a strike, or otherwise deal with actions that could be detrimental to the public welfare. For a court to issue an injunction, management must show a "just cause," such as the possibility of violence or the destruction of property. The use of strikebreakers has been a particular source of hostility and violence in labour relations.

Strikebreakers

Sometimes, a company may try to bring in replacement workers. These workers, also known as **strikebreakers** (called *scabs* by unions), are workers who are hired to do the jobs of striking employees until the labour dispute is resolved. This often leads to violence. Picketers mass in large numbers to block buses carrying these strikebreakers, threats are uttered, articles are thrown, vehicles may be attacked, and so on.

British Columbia and Quebec have legislation banning the use of replacement workers in their provinces. At the time this chapter was written, there was no federal legislation that would put an end to the use of replacement workers during strikes and lockouts in workplaces covered by the Canada Labour Code. Supporters of such legislation cite fewer days lost due to strikes and lockouts and a quick and peaceful settlement of disputes as benefits if such legislation were to be passed.[35] Be sure to read the Making Ethical Decisions box on this issue for further insight.

▸ TELUS workers staged a walkout to protest an attempt by the company to eliminate many restrictions on the contracting out of work in its contract. TELUS immediately locked out the 12,500 workers, retained the services of professional strikebreakers, and sought injunctions to limit picketing. The lockout lasted for almost three months.

Battle for Public Support

In major cases where the public is affected—the postal service, nurses, doctors, teachers, transportation, telecommunication, and civil servants at all levels—each side plays a propaganda game to win the public to its side. It can be difficult for those not directly involved to sort out the issues. Sometimes management, if it thinks that the public is on its side and the union is perhaps not well organized or lacks strong support, will provoke the union into an unsuccessful strike, weakening the union's bargaining position.

Legislation

Essential services have traditionally been those provided 24 hours a day, 7 days a week, 365 days a year, such as health care, police officers, and firefighters.[36] Under the Labour Relations Code, essential services legislation restricts the right to strike of various levels of civil servants and quasi-government employees such as hospital workers and electric and telephone utility workers. The provinces and the federal government forbid some employees under their jurisdiction from striking. In other cases, certain minimum levels of service must be provided.

Federal or provincial governments have the power to end a particular strike by passing back-to-work legislation. **Back-to-work legislation** orders an end to a labour–management dispute that has escalated to a strike or lockout, in an industry that the government decides is essential to the operation of the economy.[37] Such legislation has been used to end strikes by teachers, nurses, postal workers, bus drivers, and others. Governments pass back-to-work legislation when they believe they have enough support among the population for such action because of serious hardship to businesses or individuals. Such was the case when the Ontario legislature passed back-to-work legislation in early 2009 mandating that the almost 3,300 contract professors and teaching, graduate, and research assistants at York University <*www.yorku.ca*> (who had been bargaining for improved job security for contract staff, and more funding for graduate students, among other issues) return to work.[38] For three months about 45,000 students had been out of class and mediation had failed to resolve the issues.[39]

strikebreakers
Replacement workers hired to do the jobs of striking employees until the labour dispute is resolved.

back-to-work legislation
Legislation that orders an end to a labour–management dispute that has escalated to a strike or lockout, in an industry that the government decides is essential to the operation of the economy.

MAKING ETHICAL DECISIONS

Crossing the Line or Double-Crossing?

Assume that you read over the weekend that More-4-Less, a grocery chain in your town, is seeking workers to replace members of the Commercial Food Workers Union who are currently on strike against the company. Some of the students at your school are employed at More-4-Less and are supporting the strike, as are several people employed by the company in your neighbourhood. More-4-Less argues that its management has made a fair offer to the union and that the demands of the workers are clearly excessive and could ruin the company. More-4-Less is offering an attractive wage rate and flexible schedules to workers willing to cross the picket line and work during the strike. As a student, you could certainly use the job and the extra money for tuition and expenses. What would you do? What will be the consequences of your decision? Is your choice ethical? What are the ethical dilemmas faced by unions? Give some examples. How do these differ from those faced by management?

▶ Do you recall reading about the York University strike? Would this have impacted your decision to apply to York University if you had been considering this school?

Union supporters believe that back-to-work legislation is a denial of the legal right to strike, therefore to a certain extent it is a restriction of the democratic rights of individuals. Consequently, there is often much controversy about such legislation. It is rarely used to deal with strikes against private businesses. If union members remain on strike after they have been legislated back to work, they are engaging in an illegal strike and are subject to punishment (e.g., substantial fines), as are all lawbreakers.

THE FUTURE OF UNIONS AND LABOUR–MANAGEMENT RELATIONS

New issues that affect labour-management relations include increased global competition, advancing technology, outsourcing, and the changing nature of work.[40] To save jobs, many unions have granted management concessions, or **givebacks**, of previous gains. For example, since Air Canada restructured in 2004, its five unions agreed to give back previous wage and benefit gains to improve the airline's financial stability.[41] Years later, Air Canada's unionized employees continue to face challenges in negotiating collective agreements. Review the Analyzing Management Decisions discussion near the end of the chapter for more discussion on this topic.

givebacks
Concessions made by union members to management; previous gains from labour negotiations are given up to help employers remain competitive and thereby save jobs.

Unions in the future will be quite different from those in the past. Union members understand that companies must remain competitive with foreign firms, and labour must do its best to maintain competitiveness. (So too, must businesses.) Many unions have taken on a new role in assisting management in training workers, redesigning jobs, and assimilating the changing workforce. They help recruit and train foreign workers, unskilled workers, and others who need special help in adapting to the job requirements of the new service and knowledge-work economy.

▸ LIUNA's employee–employer relationships embrace new technologies that advance the industry and provide a trained workforce for an ever-changing construction market.

Unions seek improved job security, profit sharing, and sometimes increased wages. Management looks for a productive, dedicated workforce capable of handling the challenges of global competition. Joseph S. Mancinelli, International Vice-President for Central and Eastern Canada of LIUNA, understands these challenges and opportunities. According to Mancinelli, "Pensions, level of skills, quality of work, productivity, and safety in the workplace have become our new challenges. These challenges cannot be met through adversarial conflict, but in a new era of unionism, through good relations with our employer partners. Good relations are paramount in ensuring such progress and evolution. Working closely with our employer partners can produce more benefits for our members, our employers, and the entire construction industry. In recognition of this fact, LIUNA has established a labour–employer co-operation trust specifically set up for both parties to work together, outside of the bargaining table, every day of the year to find creative and innovative solutions and initiatives that result in an ongoing win–win scenario for both labour and management. Concurrently, LIUNA has actively pursued public-private partnerships. Through the Labourers' Pension Fund of Central and Eastern Canada, sound, financially viable partnerships have evolved resulting in a doubly viable result: excellent returns on pension fund dollars and employment opportunities for our members across the country. An example of this relationship is LIUNA joining numerous construction companies to build several hospitals throughout the province of Ontario."[42]

How organized labour and management handle such challenges may well define the future of labour unions. After the Progress Assessment, we will look at other issues facing employees and managers in the twenty-first century.

- Why do the objectives of unions change over time?
- What are the major tactics used by unions and by management to assert their power in contract negotiations?
- When is back-to-work legislation used?

CURRENT EMPLOYEE–MANAGEMENT TOPICS

Explain some of today's employee–management issues.

This is an interesting time in the history of employee–management relations. Organizations are active in global expansion, outsourcing, and technology changes. The government has eliminated some social benefits to workers. For example, employment insurance eligibility requirements overall are stricter today than they were ten years ago. In other instances the government is taking a more active role in mandating what benefits and assurances businesses must provide to workers. The extension of maternity leave benefits from six months to one year in 2001 and the implementation of a new compassionate care program in 2004 are just two such instances.

▶ The Canadian Human Rights Commission is empowered to investigate and try to settle complaints of discrimination in employment and in the provision of services within federal jurisdiction. The Commission is also mandated to develop and conduct information and discrimination prevention programs.

It is important to note that all employees are protected under the Employment Standards Act. This Act covers issues such as minimum wage, holiday pay, and so on. In a non-union environment, if an employer violates the Act, it is up to the employee to file a complaint. An employee may seek advice and assistance from an officer of the Ministry of Labour in the province where he or she works. The employee can also contact the Canadian Human Rights Commission <*www.chrc-ccdp.ca*> or a Human Resources and Skills Development Canada <*www.hrsdc.gc.ca*> office, where he or she can talk to a federal government labour affairs officer.

Union supporters point out that a labour contract would further protect workers, as the union would represent the employee if there were a breach of the Act or the labour contract. Keep in mind that official legal protection is not very meaningful without effective enforcement.

Employees today are raising questions about fairness and workplace benefits. They are looking increasingly at company policies as they apply to workplace discrimination (e.g., wages and sexual orientation), sexual harassment, and mandatory testing (e.g., drug testing). Three other areas that are increasingly in the news are executive compensation, child care, and elder care. Let us briefly look at each of these areas.

Executive Compensation

Is it out of line for some of Canada's top executives to make tens of millions of dollars in annual compensation? Consider the total compensation received by Canada's two highest-paid executives in 2011. Gerry Schwartz (Founder, Chairman of the Board, President, and CEO of Onex Corp. <*www.onex.com*>) received US$14.3 million in base salary and bonus and Frank Stronach (Founder, Director, and Honorary Chairman of Magna International Inc.) earned US$41 million, mostly in the form of profit sharing and consulting fees.[43]

Chapter 2 explained that the free-market system is built on incentives that allow top executives to make such large amounts—or more. Today, however, the government, boards of directors, shareholders, unions, and employees are challenging this principle and arguing that executive compensation has gotten out of line. In fact, way out of line.

In the past, CEO compensation and bonuses were determined by the firm's profitability or an increase in its stock price. The logic of this assumption was that as the fortunes of a company and its shareholders grew, so would the rewards of the CEO. Today, however, executives generally receive *stock options* (the ability to buy company stock at a set price at a later date) and *restricted stock* (stock issued directly to the CEO that cannot be sold for usually three or four years) as part of their compensation. Many believe that a problem arises when executives are so compensated even when the company does not meet expectations. There are some exceptions. For example, Loblaw Cos. Ltd. chairman Galen Weston and then-president John Lederer declined to accept bonuses for 2005 after the Canadian supermarket chain's profit fell for the first time in 13 years.[44] What is even more frustrating to some people, however, is when a CEO whose poor performance forced him or her to resign walks away with a large compensation.[45] Many CEOs are also awarded fat retainers, consulting contracts, and lavish perks when they retire.

The late management consultant Peter Drucker criticized executive pay levels and he suggested that CEOs should not earn more than 20 times the salary of the company's lowest-paid employee. Not many companies, however, have placed such limits on executive compensation.[46] According to research conducted by the Canadian Centre for Policy Alternatives, by the end of 2010, Canada's Elite 100 CEOs made 189 times more than Canadians earning the average wage.[47]

As global competition intensifies, executive paycheques in Europe have increased, too, but European CEOs typically earn only about 40 percent what U.S. CEOs make.[48] In some European countries, such as Germany, workers account for 50 percent of the seats on the board of directors of major firms according to a process called *co-determination* (co-operation between management and workers in decision making). Since boards set executive pay, this could be a reason why the imbalance in pay is less in Europe.

Many executives are responsible for multi-billion-dollar corporations, work 70-plus hours a week, and often travel. Many have made decisions that turned potential problems into successes and reaped huge compensation for employees and shareholders as well as themselves. Furthermore, there are few seasoned, skilled professionals who can manage large companies, especially troubled companies looking for the right CEO to accomplish a turnaround. There's no easy answer to the question of what constitutes fair compensation for executives, but it is a safe bet that the controversy will not go away.[49]

Child Care

Child care became an increasingly important workplace issue as questions involving responsibilities for child-care subsidies, child-care programs, and even parental leave spurred debate in the private and public sectors of the economy. Many workers strongly question workplace benefits for parents, and argue that single workers and single-income families should not subsidize child care for dual-income families. Although men are increasingly shouldering child-care responsibility, most of that responsibility still falls on women. This often leads to greater stress and absenteeism in the workplace. Employers are increasingly concerned as businesses lose millions annually in lost productivity. Employee child care also raises the controversial workplace question of who should pay for child-care services.

The number of companies that offer child care as an employee benefit is growing. *Working Mother* magazine highlighted companies such as Colgate-Palmolive,

▸ On-site day care is still a relatively uncommon employee benefit today. Although it is often expensive to operate, it can pay big dividends in employee satisfaction and productivity. Who should pay for employee benefits like child care and elder care? Should it be the employee or the company?

IBM, and General Mills <*www.generalmills.com*> as being particularly sympathetic to working mothers.[50] Other large firms that offer extensive child-care programs include Johnson & Johnson, American Express <*www.americanexpress.com*>, and Campbell Soup. A few companies even provide emergency child-care services for employees whose children are ill or whose regular child-care arrangements are disrupted.

As the number of single-parent and two-income households continues to grow in the twenty-first century, child care is certain to remain a hotly debated employee–management issue. However, a new workplace storm is brewing over an issue employees and managers have not faced in times past: elder care. Let's look at this next.

Elder Care

The workforce in Canada is aging. While baby boomers will not have to concern themselves with finding child care for their children, they will confront another problem: how to care for older parents and other relatives. In the future, more workers are expected to be involved in the time-consuming and stressful task of caring for an aging relative. Current estimates suggest that companies are seeing reduced productivity, and increased absenteeism and turnover from employees who are responsible for aging relatives.[51] Denise Talbot-White, a gerontology specialist for MetLife Mature Market Institute <*www.metlife.com/mmi*>, suggests that elder care is the child care of the new millennium.

Employees with elder-care responsibilities need information on medical, legal, and insurance issues, as well as the full support of their supervisors and company. This issue may require some employees to switch to flextime, telecommuting, part-time employment, or job sharing.[52] Some firms have reacted to the effect of elder care on their workforce. At Boeing and AT&T <*www.att.com*>, employees are offered elder-care programs that include telephone hotlines that workers can call to seek help or counselling for older relatives. Unfortunately, few companies (large, medium, or small) now provide any type of elder-care programs or benefits.

As more experienced and high-ranking employees begin caring for older parents and relatives, the costs to companies will rise even higher. These arguments make sense, since older workers often hold jobs more critical to the company than those held by younger workers (who are most affected by child-care problems). Many firms now realize that transfers and promotions are sometimes out of the question for employees whose elderly parents need ongoing care. Unfortunately, as Canadians age, the elder-care situation will grow considerably worse. With an aging workforce, this employee–management issue promises to persist well into the twenty-first century.

YOU AND UNIONS

Do you think that unions are still necessary? We are fortunate to be living in a democratic country where free and private enterprise is the vital feature of our economic system. We believe that all citizens have the right to do what they can, within legal and ethical limits, to better themselves. Improving your financial situation is an admired goal, and those who do so are usually seen as good examples.

If you select the entrepreneurial route, you will try to build a successful company by providing a necessary service or product in a manner that your customers appreciate. If you are successful, you will ultimately accumulate profits and personal wealth and financial security for yourself and your family. One of the costs of doing business that you will be keeping an eye on is wages, salaries, and benefits paid to employees. Will you consider unions nothing but a hindrance?

Suppose that you do not see yourself as an entrepreneur and instead go the employee route. Imagine yourself ten years down the road: you have a partner and two children and are now a computer specialist working for a large company in a non-managerial role. Will you seek the best salary you can possibly get? How about working hours? Your partner also works and you need flexible arrangements to be able to spend time with your children and deliver them to school and various other activities. How about overtime demands on the job that cut into time with your children? Will you have adequate, affordable child care?

These are just ideas to consider. Firms that have healthy employee–management relations have a better chance to prosper than those that do not. As managers, taking a proactive approach is the best way to ensure workable employee–management environments. The proactive manager anticipates potential problems and works toward resolving those issues before they get out of hand—a good lesson to remember.

PROGRESS ASSESSMENT

- How does top-executive pay in Canada compare with top-executive pay in other countries?
- What are some of the issues related to child care and elder care, and how are companies addressing those issues?

SUMMARY

Trace the history of organized labour in Canada.

Organized labour in Canada dates back to the 1800s. Early unions on the wharves of Halifax, St. John's, and Quebec existed during the War of 1812 to profit from labour scarcity. Craft unions represented shoemakers and printers. Many of the early labour organizations were local or regional in nature.

Describe some of the main objectives of labour and whether they were achieved.

Unions hoped to improve workers' poor conditions and wages by forming unions that would fight for workers' rights. This has largely been achieved, and many early demands are now entrenched in law.

Describe some of the unions in existence today.

The Canadian Union of Public Employees (CUPE) and the Canadian Auto Workers (CAW) are two of the largest unions in Canada. They represent workers from different sectors in the economy. Many unions in Canada are national in nature. Many also belong to international organizations. The Canadian Labour Congress, which represents 3.3 million unionized workers, is the national voice of the labour movement in Canada.

Discuss the major legislation affecting labour unions.

Much labour legislation has been passed by federal and provincial governments.

What is the major piece of labour legislation?

The Canada Labour Code outlines labour legislation as it applies to federal government employees, who represent approximately 10 percent of all workers in Canada. Each provincial jurisdiction in Canada has its own labour legislation and employment standards that apply to workers within its borders.

Describe the collective bargaining process.

Collective bargaining is the process by which a union represents employees in relations with their employer.

What is included in collective bargaining?
Collective bargaining includes how unions are selected, the period prior to a vote, certification, ongoing contract negotiations, and behaviour while a contract is in force.

What are the steps in the collective bargaining process?
Refer to Figure 13.4 for the steps in the collective bargaining process.

Outline the objectives of labour unions.

The objectives of labour unions shift in response to changes in social and economic trends.

What topics typically appear in labour–management agreements?
Labour–management agreements may include issues such as management rights, union security clauses, hours of work, vacation policies, job rights and seniority principles, and employee benefits. See Figure 13.5 for a more exhaustive list.

Describe the negotiation tactics used by labour and management during conflicts.

If negotiations between labour and management break down, either or both sides may use certain tactics to enhance their position or sway public opinion.

What are the tactics used by unions in conflicts?
Unions can use strikes, boycotts, and picketing.

What are the tactics used by management in conflicts?
Management can use lockouts, injunctions, and strikebreakers.

Explain some of today's employee–management issues.

Some employee–management issues are executive compensation, child care, and elder care.

What is a fair wage for managers?
The market and the businesses in it set managers' salaries. What is fair is open to debate.

How are some companies addressing the child-care issue?
Responsive companies are providing child care on their premises, discounts with child-care chains, vouchers to be used at the employee's chosen care centres, and referral services.

What is elder care, and what problems do companies face with regard to this growing problem?
Workers with older parents or other relatives often need to find some way to care for them. Elder care is becoming a problem that will perhaps outpace the need for child care. Workers who need to care for dependent parents are generally more experienced and vital to the mission of the organization than younger workers are. The cost to business is very large and growing.

KEY TERMS

agency shop (Rand formula)
arbitration
back-to-work legislation
bargaining zone
certification
checkoff
closed shop
collective bargaining
conciliation
craft union
decertification
givebacks
grievance
industrial union
injunction
lockout
mediation
negotiated labour–management agreement (labour contract)
open shop
primary boycott
secondary boycott
shop stewards
strike
strikebreakers
union
union density
union security clause
union shop
wildcat strike

CRITICAL THINKING

1. In the last few years, thousands of government employees have lost their jobs due to budget cuts. What are the political implications of such actions?
2. Why are unionization rates much higher in the public sector than in the private sector?
3. Do businesses and government agencies have a duty to provide additional benefits to employees beyond fair pay and good working conditions? Does providing benefits such as child care and elder care to some employees discriminate against those who do not require such assistance? Propose a benefits system that you consider fair and workable for both employees and employers.
4. Do you agree that back-to-work legislation is a denial of the legal right to strike, therefore to a certain extent it is a restriction of the democratic rights of individuals? Factor in the rights of employers in your answer.

DEVELOPING WORKPLACE SKILLS

1. Debate the following statement with several classmates: Non-union firms are better managed (or perform better) than unionized firms. To get a better feeling for the other side's point of view, take the opposite side of this issue from the one you normally would. Include information from outside sources to support your position.
2. Top executives' high pay creates tremendous incentives for lower-level executives to work hard to get those jobs. Their high pay also creates resentment among workers, shareholders, and members of the general public. Debate the following in class: Business executives receive a total compensation package that is far beyond their value. They should not earn more than twenty times the compensation of the lowest-paid worker at the firm. Take the opposite side of the issue from your normal stance to get a better feel for the other point of view.
3. Find the latest information on federal and provincial legislation related to child care, parental leave, and elder-care benefits for employees. In what direction are the trends pointing? What will be the cost to businesses for these new initiatives? Do you favour such advancements in workplace legislation? Why or why not?
4. Examine an actual collective agreement and identify the constraints set upon workers and management by its provisions.

ANALYZING MANAGEMENT DECISIONS

Plant Closings, Unions, and Concessions

Over the past decade, the Canadian economy has witnessed a series of plant closing or lockout actions taken by foreign companies against employees in Canada. As well, Canada has experienced a fragile recovery from the recession, the rising value of the Canadian dollar, and a perception that workers are in a weak position. Plants and offices have laid off thousands of people or closed because of bankruptcy, consolidation, or transfer of operations to other lower-wage countries. In some cases, management advised unions that the only way that they could avoid closing would be substantial concessions in wages and other changes in existing contracts.

American-based heavy equipment maker Caterpillar Inc. <*www.cat.com*> ended a one-month standoff with locked-out workers by closing its 62-year-old Electro-Motive plant in London, Ontario, eliminating about 450 manufacturing jobs that mostly paid twice the rate of a U.S. counterpart. Caterpillar spokesman Rusty Dunn summed up the reasoning as follows: "All facilities must achieve competitive costs, quality, and operating flexibility to remain viable in the global marketplace. Expectations at the London plant were no different." These jobs are expected to be transferred to Muncie, Indiana, where Caterpillar had opened a locomotive plant and was trying to fill positions at about half the pay of the workers in Ontario.

The closing angered CAW president Ken Lewenza. Caterpillar had demanded pay cuts of 50 percent in many job categories, elimination of a defined-benefit pension plan, reductions in dental and other benefits, and the end of a cost-of-living adjustment. "I've never had a situation where I've dealt with such an unethical, immoral, disrespectful, highly profitable company like Caterpillar," said Lewenza. He said that during bargaining he told the company's negotiators: "If it's in your business plan to close us, don't punish us, let's work out a closure agreement. They said: 'We have no intention of closing the facility.'"

The situation was different in another industry, but the concessions were hard ones. Workers at international mining giant Vale <*www.vale.com*> in Ontario approved a new labour agreement, ending a year-long strike in 2010. Vale said it needed to cut labour costs to keep its operations competitive, but workers argued the Brazilian company made billions of dollars a year and did not need concessions from workers. The strike was bitter at times, with the union accusing Vale of bad faith bargaining and the company taking the union to court over a variety of alleged incidents on the picket lines. The output from the Canadian operations—which account for more than 10 percent of the world's nickel supply—was significantly decreased during the strike. The agreement resulted in more than 3,000 workers receiving a raise and a big signing bonus. However, it also saw new employees placed on a defined-contribution pension plan, as opposed to the existing defined-benefit plan. Defined-contribution plans depend on market returns and do not guarantee a steady income, unlike defined-benefit plans.

Givebacks are not being asked just by foreign-owned companies. For example, since Air Canada came out of bankruptcy protection in 2004, it has received concessions from its unions as part of its restructuring conditions. This has included concessions in the area of wages, jobs (e.g., since the end of 2000, Air Canada has reduced its total full-time equivalent staff by 47 percent, resulting in a loss of over 20,000 jobs), and pensions. Eight years later in 2012, union members grew tired of givebacks and voted to go on strike. The federal government stepped in and threatened the unions with back-to-work legislation before imposing binding arbitration in some instances.

Keep in mind that non-unionized employees also saw tens of thousands of jobs eliminated. At the start of 2001, Nortel Networks Corporation had more than 90,000 employees worldwide. By 2006, the company had cut its workforce by two-thirds as it restructured several times in an attempt to regain profitability. In the first two months of 2009, an additional 5,000 jobs were eliminated as the company filed for bankruptcy protection. In late November of that year, Nortel's union and former employees failed to persuade an Ontario appeals court they were entitled to retirement and severance payments. On July 1, 2011, Nortel reached a deal to sell the last of its assets. No employees are safe as companies try to remain competitive in the marketplace.

Union leaders and their members are in a quandary when faced with such decisions. Sometimes they think management is bluffing. Sometimes they are reluctant to give up contract conditions they fought long and hard for.

Accepting wage cuts or benefit reductions when the cost of living continues to rise is not easy. Agreeing to staff reductions to save other jobs is also a tough decision. Unions worry about where these concessions will end. Will there be another round of layoffs or even worse in a few months?

These examples highlight some of the dilemmas facing unions and employers. The business environment demands that companies become more efficient and productive. However, this will not happen unless there is mutual respect between management and labour.

Sources: James R. Hagerty, "Caterpillar Closes Plant in Canada After Lockout," *The Wall Street Journal*, 4 February 2012, http://online.wsj.com/article/SB10001424052970203889904577200953014575964.html; Greg Keenan, "Caterpillar pulls plug on London plant," *The Globe and Mail*, 3 February 2012, www.theglobeandmail.com/globe-investor/caterpillar-pulls-plug-on-london-plant/article544321/; "Timeline: Nortel - The rise and fall of a telecom giant," Global News, 18 January 2012, www.globalnews.ca/timeline+nortel+-+the+rise+and+fall+of+a+telecom+giant/6442560329/story.html; "Ont. Vale workers vote to approve new contract," The Canadian Press, 13 January 2010, www.ctvnews.ca/ont-vale-workers-vote-to-approve-new-contract-1.530694; Brent Jang, "Air Canada, Union at Odds Over Proposed Moratorium on Pension Payments," *The Globe and Mail*, 5 May 2009, www.theglobeandmail.com/servlet/story/LAC.20090505.RAIR CANADA05ART1908/TPStory/Business; "Study: The Year in Review in Manufacturing," Statistics Canada, 29 April 2009, www.statcan.gc.ca/daily-quotidien/090429/dq090429b-eng.htm; Paul Kunert, "Nortel Networks Lays off 3,200 Staff," *Computer Weekly*, 26 February 2009, www.computerweekly.com/Articles/2009/02/26/235029/nortel-networks-lays-off-3200-staff.htm; "Air Canada: Fly it Right!," Canadian Auto Workers Union, 2009, www.caw.ca/en/7423.htm; and "Nortel Rebuilding and Hiring Again: CEO," CBC News, 29 September 2006, www.cbc.ca/money/story/2006/09/29/zafirovski-nortel.html.

Discussion Questions

1. What would you recommend to union workers whose employer is threatening to close down unless they agree to wage decreases or other concessions?
2. Is there some alternative to cutting wages or closing down? What is it?
3. Union workers often feel that the company is bluffing when it threatens to close. How can such doubts be settled so that more open negotiations can take place?
4. Does government have a right to interfere with organizations (i.e., union and employer) that have already negotiated a collective agreement and force them to renegotiate?

PART 4 ENDS WITH:

DEALING WITH CHANGE

Replacing the Old Guard

Wine connoisseurs believe that most great wines get better with age. Unfortunately, the decision makers of most industrialized countries don't see it that way when evaluating people. It is anticipated that one in three Canadians will be 55 and over by 2021. By 2050, the average age of the world's population is expected to rise from 26 to 36. This aging of the population presents huge economic implications. Who will do the work in geriatric societies? Who will support the increasing number of pensioners? What will happen to economic growth with a declining labour force?

Eliminating age, gender, and cultural barriers could add 1.6 million Canadians to the workforce and increase personal incomes by $174 billion, according to a report from RBC Economics titled *The Diversity Advantage: A Case for Canada's 21st Century Economy.* The report's recommendations range from tax and policy reform, increased immigration levels, and ways in which the country should capitalize on cultural, gender, and age diversity. "With an aging population, fertility rates well below the 2.1 rate that is necessary to sustain population levels, and one in five manufacturers unable to find skilled labour, Canada needs to have an effective long-range economic strategy to ensure a successful twenty-first century economy and society," said Derek Holt, assistant chief economist at RBC. "Without a talented workforce, Canadian businesses will be unable to achieve corporate strategies for innovation and growth."

The report suggests that immigrants, women, and baby boomers approaching retirement will need to play more significant roles in the country's workforce, as Canada needs to capitalize on the broader economic benefits that a more diverse population has to offer. "To replace retiring baby boomers and maintain our current economic performance, Canada will need an additional 2.75 million workers over the next 20 years... If immigrants and women were employed at their level of education and skills training, and earning equal pay to men born in Canada, personal incomes in Canada would increase by 21 percent, or $174 billion, and 1.6 million more working-age Canadians would be employed."

As critical as the impending labour shortage is, most companies seem more concerned about the brain drain caused by experienced, knowledgeable workers taking their irreplaceable knowledge with them as they retire. Mentoring is one way that companies are working to transfer knowledge. Other companies, such as Hewlett-Packard (HP), use online communities of different professional groups, such as sales and software engineering. "They're online knowledge repositories for people who do the same kind of work. They post how they do things, solutions, and experience," explains James R. Malanson, an HP human resource executive.

Many industries and businesses are trying to keep potential retirees for as long as possible by offering consultant positions, flexible work schedules, job sharing, and gradual retirement. The challenge is to keep mature workers on the job—at least until they have shared their knowledge with their younger colleagues.

Sources: Susannah Patton, "Beating the Boomer Brain Drain Blues," *CIO,* 15 January 2006; Derek Holt, "Capitalizing on Canada's Diversity Is Key to Nation's Future Prosperity," Canada NewsWire, 20 October 2005, http://global.factiva.com/ha/default.aspx; Kathryn Tyler, "Training Revs Up," *HRMagazine,* 1 April 2005; Statistics Canada, "The Canadian Labour Market at a Glance," 2005, www.statcan.ca/english/freepub/71-222-XIE/71-222-XIE2006001.pdf;. Anne Fisher, "How to Battle the Coming Brain Drain," *Fortune,* 21 March 2005; and Marguerite Smith, "Aging Workers: Overlooked No More?" *Public Management,* 1 January 2005; and www.chrc-ccdp.ca/publications/diversity-en.asp.

REACHING BEYOND OUR BORDERS

Working Worldwide

Human resource management of a global workforce begins with the understanding of the customs, laws, and local business needs of every country in which the organization operates. Country-specific cultural and legal standards can affect a variety of human resource functions:

- *Compensation.* Salaries must be converted to and from foreign currencies. Often employees with international assignments receive special allowances for relocation, children's education, housing, travel, or other business-related expenses.
- *Health and Pension Standards.* There are different social contexts for benefits in other countries. For example, in the Netherlands, the government provides retirement income and health care.
- *Paid Time Off.* Four weeks of paid vacation is the standard of many European employers. But many other countries lack the short-term and long-term absence policies offered in Canada, including sick leave, personal leave, family leave, and medical leave. Global companies need a standard definition of *time off.*
- *Taxation.* Different countries have varying taxation rules, and the payroll department is an important player in managing immigration information.
- *Communication.* When employees leave to work in another country, they often feel disconnected from their home country. Wise companies use their intranet and the Internet to help these faraway employees keep in direct contact.

Human resource policies at home are influenced more and more by conditions and practices in other countries and cultures. Human resource managers need to sensitize themselves and their organizations to the cultural and business practices of other nations.

Sources: "Mercer Survey Reveals New Challenges and Solutions as HR Takes on Expanded Global Role," Business Wire, 26 September 2008; and Charles E. Carraher, Sarah C. Carraher, Shawn M. Carraher, Gerald R. Ferris, and Ronald M. Buckley, "Human Resource Issues in Global Entrepreneurial High Technology Firms: Do They Differ?" *Journal of Applied Management and Entrepreneurship,* 1 January 2008.

RUNNING CASE

Human Resources at Fox 40 International Inc.

For successful Canadian entrepreneur and inventor Ron Foxcroft, it all started in 1982 when he purchased Fluke Transport, a Southern Ontario trucking business. The company slogan—If It's On Time . . . It's A "FLUKE"—was soon recognized throughout North America. Over the years, Ron diversified into new ventures and the Foxcroft Group of Companies now includes Fluke Transportation Group, Fluke Warehousing Inc., Foxcroft Capital Group, and Fox 40 International Inc.

The formation of Fox 40 International Inc. (Fox 40) is the result of a dream for a pealess whistle. When developing his first Whistle, Ron was motivated by his knowledge and experience as an international basketball referee. Frustrated with faulty pea whistles, he spent three years of development with design consultant Chuck Shepherd, resulting in the creation of the Fox 40® Classic Whistle. Fast forward twenty-five years and Fox 40 dominates the global whistle industry.

Fox 40 is a privately held, family-run organization with Ron as the Chief Executive Officer and son, Dave, as the President and Chief Operating Officer. The company employs 35 individuals, and as many as 45 during peak seasons. You may be surprised to learn that there is no formal human resource department in this company. In fact, there are no layers of management. Among other reasons, this is to empower employees, regardless of position, to develop solutions to problems, with the goal of satisfying customers.

It is important to create a good working environment. Open communication is encouraged throughout the organization. There is an open-door policy within the three teams—Corporate, Product and Marketing, and Sales and Customer Service—and across the teams. Senior management is directly accessible by both employees and customers. The lack of internal titles is another signal that the owners do not stand on ceremony. Outside of the organization, however, employees have titles as this is expected by external stakeholders.

Hiring the right people is critical. According to Ron, "Managers hire people that are dumber than them, but owners hire people that are smarter than them." With this in mind, new hires are expected to contribute to the organization. There is a focus on hiring self-starters who require minimum supervision. Chemistry with current employees (i.e., organizational fit), strong communication skills, a customer-focus, enthusiasm, and honesty are required qualities. Initiative is expected and employees should have the courage to go to Ron or Dave with suggestions on how to make the company better. Examples can include improving processes, developing new products, or improving the customer experience.

For example, Dave and his team approached Ron with the idea to develop a new variation of the Fox 40 Classic. Ron struggled with this as the Fox 40 Classic was his first whistle and he was not convinced that this was the right direction. The team believed that there were some untapped opportunities. One advantage would be that a new whistle could be registered for an 18-year patent and trademark. Ron agreed and the Fox 40 Classic Eclipse was created. This whistle was re-engineered for maximum performance and style. The Fox 40 Classic Eclipse was also the first whistle to be developed using exclusive SpectraBurst™ glow-in-the dark colours that would last up to ten hours. Since its introduction in the marketplace, feedback has been tremendous.

At Fox 40 International, new hires start at the bottom. They should be prepared to do any job (except take out the garbage; this is the CEO's job). Orientation includes on-the-job training. As Dave says, "The best way to learn is by doing." Employees are assigned tasks with a timeline and their performance is monitored. During a performance review, discussions centre on finding opportunities that will tap into each employee's strengths while also discussing how to improve on any weaknesses.

Fox 40 is a non-unionized work environment. "We pay our employees fairly," says Ron. For the production staff, manufacturing output is tracked. Those that exceed their targets are also compensated with money and gift certificates that can be redeemed at local retailers.

Source: Ron Foxcroft, Founder and CEO, and Dave Foxcroft, President and COO, Fox 40 International Inc., in-person interviews, 25 June 2012, Hamilton, 905-561-4040.

Discussion Questions

1. Considering Douglas McGregor's research on managers' attitudes toward their workers. How would you categorize the management style described at Fox 40?
2. What pay systems does Fox 40 use for its production staff? (Hint: Review Figure 12.5 for some examples.)
3. What are some company advantages in not having a unionized workforce? What are some employee advantages in not belonging to a labour union?

PART 5

CHAPTER 14

MARKETING: BUILDING CUSTOMER AND STAKEHOLDER RELATIONSHIPS

LEARNING OBJECTIVES

After you have read and studied this chapter, you should be able to:

LO 1 Define marketing and explain how the marketing concept applies to both for-profit and non-profit organizations.

LO 2 List and describe the four Ps of marketing.

LO 3 Describe the marketing research process, and explain how marketers use environmental scanning to learn about the changing marketing environment.

LO 4 Explain how marketers meet the needs of the consumer market through market segmentation, relationship marketing, and the study of consumer behaviour.

LO 5 List ways in which the business-to-business market differs from the consumer market.

PROFILE

GETTING TO KNOW SOFIA COLUCCI, SENIOR MARKETING MANAGER—QUAKER FOODS AND SNACKS, PEPSICO AMERICA

Celestica. Maple Leaf Foods. PepsiCo Beverages Canada. What do these seemingly different companies have in common? They were all stepping stones to Sofia Colucci's current role as the Senior Marketing Manager of Quaker Foods and Snacks for PepsiCo America. PepsiCo is a global food and beverage leader with net revenues of more than $65 billion and a product portfolio that includes 22 brands that generate more than $1 billion each in annual retail sales. Its main businesses—Quaker, Tropicana, Gatorade, Frito-Lay and Pepsi-Cola—cover hundreds of products that are purchased throughout the world.

Colucci is new in this role, having recently transferred to Chicago from her last role as Marketing Manager—Aquafina & O.N.E. Coconut Water at PepsiCo Beverages Canada. As a Senior Marketing Manager, Colucci has two direct reports: an Associate Marketing Manager and an MBA intern. Colucci ultimately needs to grow top-line sales of her brands. This requires the development and execution of a marketing plan. No day is the same as she works with different cross-functional partners to achieve targets. Examples include partnering with Sales to launch successful products to customers, collaborating with the Consumer Insights team to develop creative concepts, and analyzing the numbers with Finance.

"Get as involved as possible in extra-curricular activities to get more exposure," Colucci advises students. "Competition is so strong that you need to do more than just go to class. Businesses want to see that you have demonstrated leadership outside of the classroom." While a student at the DeGroote School of Business, McMaster University, she participated in a six-month international student exchange to Mexico, a sixteen-month internship as a Supply Chain Analyst at Celestica, and she held a teaching assistant role in the Marketing area.

Colucci credits these undergraduate experiences with landing her first post-graduation job in the Maple Leaf Foods Management Trainee Program. This three-year rotational program gave her exposure to three different functional roles in product management, finance, and marketing. In subsequent years, she held two marketing manager roles (one in Innovation and the second in the Bacon Category) at Maple Leaf Foods before moving to PepsiCo Beverages Canada.

Colucci links much of her success at PepsiCo to the invaluable general business management training she gained at Maple Leaf Foods. As business increasingly becomes more global and competitive it is critical to not only think as a marketer, but also as a business manager, collaborating with partners across all functions. The other key success factor that Colucci stresses is the desire to make a difference. "Get visibly passionate about your work—know your business cold, be curious about the world around you, and come to the table with creative solutions."

In this chapter, you will be introduced to the importance of marketing. All companies must conduct an environmental scan to discover opportunities and threats in their industry. Customers demand a four-P marketing mix (product, price, place, and promotion) that will meet their expectations. With a greater customer-relationship management (CRM) focus today, marketers need to reach their customers wherever they may be.

Source: Sofia Colucci, Senior Marketing Manager—Quaker Foods and Snacks—PepsiCo America, interview, 27 June 2012; and "Pepsi And Billboard Join Forces To Produce First-Ever Summer Beats Concert Series," PepsiCo Inc., 20 June 2012, www.pepsico.com/PressRelease/Pepsi-And-Billboard-Join-Forces-To-Produce-First-Ever-Summer-Beats-Concert-Serie06202012.html.

Define marketing and explain how the marketing concept applies to both for-profit and non-profit organizations.

marketing
A set of business practices designed to plan for and present an organization's products or services in ways that build effective customer relationships.

WHAT IS MARKETING?

The term marketing means different things to different people. Many think of marketing as simply "selling" or "advertising." Yes, selling and advertising are part of marketing, but it is much more. The Canadian Marketing Association defines **marketing** as a set of business practices designed to plan for and present an organization's products or services in ways that build effective customer relationships.[1] We can also think of marketing, more simply, as the activities buyers and sellers perform to facilitate mutually satisfying exchanges.[2] A market (note that this is the core word in *marketing*) is defined as a group of people with unsatisfied wants and needs who have the resources and the willingness to buy. A market is, therefore, created as a result of this demand for goods and services. What marketers do at any particular time will depend on what needs to be done to fill customers' needs. This "find a need and fill it" concept is core to marketing.

In the past marketing focused almost entirely on helping the seller sell. That is why many people still think of it as mostly selling, advertising, and distribution *from the seller to the buyer.* Today, much of marketing is instead about *helping the buyer buy.* Let's examine a couple of examples.

When people want to buy a new or used car, they often turn to the Internet first.[3] They go to Web sites to search for the vehicles they want and even take virtual rides. At other Web sites they compare prices and features. By the time they go to the dealer, they may know exactly which car they want and the best price available. The Web sites have *helped the buyer buy.* Not only are customers spared searching one dealership after another to find the best price, but manufacturers and dealers are eager to participate so that they do not lose customers. The future of marketing is doing everything you can to help the buyer buy.[4]

Let's look at another case. In the past, one of the few ways students and parents could find the school with the right "fit" was to travel from campus to campus, a time-consuming and potentially expensive process. Today, schools use podcasts, virtual tours, live chats, and other interactive technologies to make on-campus visits less necessary.[5] Such virtual tours help students and their parents buy.

These are only a few examples of the marketing trend toward helping buyers buy. Consumers today spend hours searching the Internet for good deals. Wise marketers provide a wealth of information online and even cultivate customer relationships using blogs and social networking sites such as Facebook and MySpace.[6] Online communities provide an opportunity to observe people (customers and others) interacting with one another, expressing their own opinions, forming relationships, and commenting on various goods and services. It is important for marketers to track what relevant bloggers are writing by doing blog searches using key terms that define their market. Vendors who have text-mining tools can help organizations measure conversations about their products and their personnel. Much of the future of marketing lies in mining such online conversations and responding appropriately.[7]

Retailers and other marketers who rely solely on *traditional* advertising and selling are losing out to

▶ Many successful Canadian entrepreneurs suggest that their success was based on the "find a need and fill it" concept. This was the case for Brenda Carriere when she purchased a Curves International <*www.curves.com*> franchise in Saint John, New Brunswick. Curves, targeted to mostly overweight women 30 years and older, many using a gym for the first time, provides a no-frills approach to exercise: there are no showers, therapeutic massages, or fresh-fruit smoothies. Facilities are 1,200 to 1,500 square feet and can be profitable with as few as 200 members.

the new ways of marketing.[8] Let's take a brief look at how changes have influenced the evolution of marketing and how we arrived at where we are today, the social media marketing era.

The Evolution of Marketing

The evolution of marketing includes five eras, also known as orientations: (1) production, (2) sales, (3) marketing concept, (4) market orientation, and (5) social media marketing. Figure 14.1 highlights the timeline for these eras.

The Production Era

From the time the first European settlers arrived in Canada until the start of the 1900s, the general philosophy of business was to produce as much as possible. Given the limited production capabilities and the vast demand for products in those days, such a production orientation was both logical and profitable, as demand exceeded supply. Business owners were mostly farmers, carpenters, and trade workers. They needed to produce more and more, so their goals centred on *production.*

You can see this same process occurring in the oil industry today, where producers can often sell as much oil as they can produce. The greatest marketing need for this industry is for production and less expensive distribution and storage.

The Sales Era

By the 1920s, businesses had developed mass production techniques (such as automobile assembly lines), and production capacity often exceeded the immediate market demand. Therefore, the business philosophy turned from producing to *selling.* Most companies emphasized selling and advertising in an effort to persuade customers to buy existing products. Few offered extensive service after the sale.

The history of the Ford Motor Company is written in ever-increasing motoring values. The Mercury 8, an entirely new car, is a new chapter in that history. Priced between the Ford V-8 and the Lincoln-Zephyr V-12, the Mercury brings to its price field many advantages of both these Ford-built cars . . . advantages that are best expressed in the phrase "top value."

The size of the Mercury is not an illusion. This is a big, wide car, exceptionally roomy, with large luggage compartment. Note these generous dimensions—wheelbase 116 inches; over-all length 16 feet, 2 inches. The front compartment in sedan body types is 54 inches wide, and the rear compartment measures 56 inches from side to side. A new 95-horsepower V-type 8-cylinder engine assures brilliant, economical performance. • Mercury interiors combine convenience and comfort with luxury. Brakes are hydraulic. • See, drive this new quality car.

A REMARKABLY QUIET, RESTFUL CAR

The Mercury 8 offers you remarkable freedom from noise and vibration—thanks to thorough soundproofing. All the resources of modern technology have been used by Ford research engineers to track down and eliminate engine, body and chassis noises. New materials and many rubber mountings also contribute to making the Mercury "silent as the night," restful and relaxing.

FORD-BUILT MEANS TOP VALUE

FORD MOTOR COMPANY NOW OFFERS FORD, MERCURY, LINCOLN-ZEPHYR AND LINCOLN MOTOR CARS

During the sale era, the focus of marketing was on selling, with little service afterward and less customization. What economic and social factors made this approach appropriate for the times?

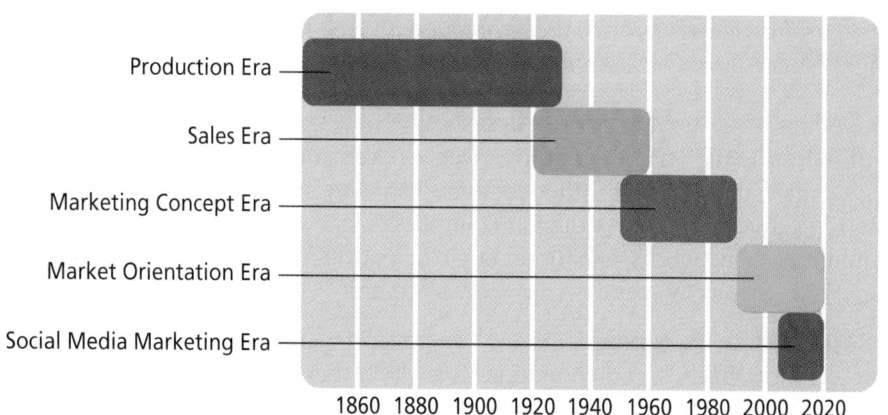

Figure 14.1

Marketing Eras

There are five different marketing eras in the history of North American business.

The Marketing Concept Era

After World War II ended in 1945, returning soldiers starting new careers and beginning families sparked a tremendous demand for goods and services. The postwar years launched the sudden increase in the birth rate that we now call the baby boom, and also a boom in consumer spending. Competition for the customer's dollar was fierce. Businesses recognized that they needed to be responsive to customers if they wanted to get their business, and a philosophy called the marketing concept emerged in the 1950s.

marketing concept
A three-part business philosophy: (1) a customer orientation, (2) a service orientation, and (3) a profit orientation.

The **marketing concept** had three parts:

1. *A customer orientation.* Find out what consumers want and provide it for them.[9] That is exactly what Cassandra Rush, founder of Sassy Cassy's Boots Inc. <*www.sassycassys.com*> did when she started her company, which specializes in boots with varying calf sizes; "Every other boot company only does standard sizing for calves, which is about 15 inches around the calf of the leg," she said. "The market calls for bigger sizes because a lot of women can't zip up regular boots. My product is different because I offer different calf sizing so the boots are better customized to the woman's leg."[10] (Note the emphasis on meeting customer needs rather than on promotion or sales.)
2. *A service orientation.* Make sure that everyone in the organization has the same objective: customer satisfaction. This should be a total and integrated organizational effort.[11] That is, everyone from the president of the firm to the delivery people should be customer oriented. Does this seem to be the norm today?
3. *A profit orientation.* Focus on those goods and services that will earn the most profit and enable the organization to survive and expand to serve more customers' wants and needs.

It took a while for businesses to implement the marketing concept. That process went slowly during the 1960s and 1970s. During the 1980s, businesses began to apply the marketing concept more aggressively than they had done over the preceding 30 years.

market orientation
Focusing efforts on (1) continuously collecting information about customers' needs and competitors' capabilities, (2) sharing this information throughout the organization, and (3) using the information to create value, ensure customer satisfaction, and develop customer relationships.

customer-relationship management (CRM)
The process of building long-term relationships with customers by delivering customer value and satisfaction.

The Market Orientation Era[12]

Many organizations transitioned from the marketing concept era to the market orientation era. Firms with a **market orientation** focus their efforts on (1) continuously collecting information about customers' needs and competitors' capabilities, (2) sharing this information throughout the organization, and (3) using the information to create value, ensure customer satisfaction, and develop customer relationships.

It is not surprising that organizations with a market orientation actually engage in **customer-relationship management (CRM)**—the process of building long-term relationships with customers by delivering customer value and satisfaction. Retaining customers over time, or managing the entire customer life cycle, is a cost-effective way for firms to grow in competitive markets. The idea is to enhance customer satisfaction and stimulate long-term customer loyalty. For example, most airlines offer frequent-flier programs that reward loyal customers with free flights. The Spotlight on Small Business shares how Chris Zane incorporates CRM in his business.

social media
The term commonly given to Web sites and online tools that allow users to interact with each other in some way—by sharing information, opinions, knowledge, and interests.

social media marketing
Consumer-generated online-marketing efforts to promote brands and companies for which they are fans (or conversely, negatively promoting brands and companies for which they are non-fans), and the use by marketers of online tools and platforms to promote their brands or organizations.

The Social Media Marketing Era[13]

Social media is the term commonly given to Web sites and online tools that allow users to interact with each other in some way—by sharing information, opinions, knowledge, and interests. As the name implies, social media involves the building of communities or networks, encouraging participation and engagement. There are two distinct dimensions to **social media marketing** era:

1. Social media marketing is about consumer-generated online-marketing efforts to promote brands and companies for which they are fans (or conversely, negatively promoting brands and companies for which they are non-fans).

SPOTLIGHT ON SMALL BUSINESS

Marketing Helps Small Firms Compete

Putting into practice old marketing techniques has enabled small retailers to compete with the giants such as Canadian Tire and Walmart. Zane's Cycles <*zanes.com*> is a good example. Chris Zane, the owner, began the shop when he was still a teenager. Early on, he learned that to keep customers a store has to offer outstanding service and more. The principle behind such service is a concept now called customer-relationship management (CRM). Long before such a concept emerged, however, small stores knew that the secret to long-term success against giant competitors is to provide superior service.

Most large stores focus on making the sale and give follow-up service little thought. Their goal is to make the transaction, and that is the end of it; thus, such an approach is called *transactional marketing*.

With CRM, in contrast, the goal is to keep a customer for life. Zane's Cycles attracts customers by setting competitive prices (and providing free coffee). Chris Zane keeps customers by giving them free lifetime service on their bicycles. He also sells helmets at cost to young people to encourage safety.

Zane keeps a database on customers so that he knows what they need and when they will need it. For example, if he sells a bicycle with a child's seat, he knows that soon the customer who purchased that bike may be buying a regular bicycle for the child—and he can send out an appropriate brochure at just the right time. Zane encourages customers to give him their names, addresses, and other such information by offering to make exchanges without receipts for those whose transaction information is in the database.

Zane also establishes close community relationships by providing scholarships for local students. Because of Zane's competitive prices, great service, and community involvement, his customers recommend his shop to others. No large store can compete with Zane's in the areas of friendly service and personal attention to each customer. That is what the new style of marketing is all about.

Are there stores in your area that offer such great service and that can compete successfully with giant department stores and national chains?

2. Social media marketing is the use by marketers of online tools and platforms to promote their brands or organizations. The most common tools or platforms used by both consumers and organizations are social networking sites (e.g., Facebook, MySpace, LinkedIn, and Twitter), blogs, wikis, podcasts, and other shared media sites such as YouTube.

It is the former dimension of social media marketing that is changing the rules of marketing and ushering in a new era of business. Social media creates a platform that empowers customers and provides them with an opportunity to communicate with an organization and with other customers. In fact, one author, Erik Qualman, suggests social media marketing is creating a new form of economy called *socialnomics* where consumers will no longer search for products or services, but rather will find them via social media. He suggests that social media is transforming the way we live and the way organizations do business. He argues that social media platforms such as Facebook connect hundreds of millions of people to each other via instant communication and that this is creating a socio-economic shift where online communities can build or destroy brands and can make traditional marketing obsolete. When you consider online activity, it is staggering. Based on population, if Facebook were a country, it would be the world's third largest. A new member joins LinkedIn every second.

To survive in this new social media world, Qualman suggests that organizations must understand, navigate, and adapt to this new landscape. Others, however, suggest that social media marketing is not necessarily a major structural shift in the marketing era but that organizations must be capable of taking advantage of social media to increase sales, cut marketing costs, and communicate more directly with their customers.

Some organizations are heeding this advice. As was mentioned in Chapter 1 (when the topic of social media was briefly introduced), 25 percent of businesses,

Based on his book, author Erik Qualman's work has captured the attention of marketers. Visit YouTube and input "Social Media Revolution" or "Socialnomics" for the most up-to-date video on why this topic is important. Were you surprised by what you learned?

▶ Advertising Standards Canada (ASC) <www.adstandards.com>, a non-profit organization, is committed to ensuring the integrity and viability of advertising in Canada through responsible industry self-regulation. Would you complain to ASC if you saw an ad that you thought was untrue or unacceptable?

in particular small businesses and entrepreneurs, are leveraging social media as a way to connect and communicate with current and potential customers. Such was the case when Lindsay Goertzen and her brother started Kelowna-based Aura Beauty <*www.aurabeauty.ca*>, a company that offers a "mobile spa" for groups such as bachelorette parties, corporate events, and home parties. "We wouldn't be here if it wasn't for social media," says Goertzen. "Our events and promotions are run 100 percent through social media and it works for us." Do not think, however, that social media is being leveraged only by small businesses; the Ford Explorer launch on Facebook generated more traffic than a Super Bowl advertisement.

Non-Profit Organizations Prosper from Marketing

Even though the marketing concept emphasizes a profit orientation, marketing is a critical part of all organizations, whether for-profit or non-profit. Charities use marketing to raise funds for combating world hunger, for instance, or to obtain other resources. For example, when Canadian Blood Services was faced with the challenge of recruiting 80,000 new blood donors to meet the ongoing need for blood for patients in Canada, it turned to marketing. A direct-response television campaign was developed to promote the emotional benefit of donating blood, coupled with a very strong call to action to the organization's national call centre and to its Web site. According to Steve Harding, Executive Director of Marketing and External Communications, "The not-for-profit category is one of the most competitive segments in the Canadian marketplace. It is of paramount importance that non-profit organizations utilize the key brand building and customer management strategies to break through and succeed. The stakes are so much greater when lives are at stake!"[14]

Environmental groups use marketing to try to cut carbon emissions.[15] Churches use marketing to attract new members and to raise funds. Politicians use marketing to get votes. Provinces use marketing to attract new businesses and tourists. Some provinces, for example, have competed to get automobile companies from other countries to locate plants in their area. Schools use marketing to attract new students. Other organizations, such as arts groups, unions, and social groups, also use marketing.

Organizations use marketing, in fact, to promote everything from environmentalism and crime prevention ("Take A Bite Out of Crime") to social issues ("Don't Drink and Drive").

List and describe the four Ps of marketing.

THE MARKETING MIX

Pleasing customers has become a priority for marketers. Much of what marketing people do has been conveniently divided into four factors, called "the four Ps" to make them easy to remember and implement. They are:

1. Product
2. Price
3. Place
4. Promotion

marketing mix
The ingredients that go into a marketing program: product, price, place, and promotion.

Managing the controllable parts of the marketing process, then, involves (1) designing a want-satisfying *product,* (2) setting a *price* for the product, (3) getting the product in a *place* where people will buy it, and (4) *promoting* the product. These four factors are called the **marketing mix** because they are blended together in a marketing program.

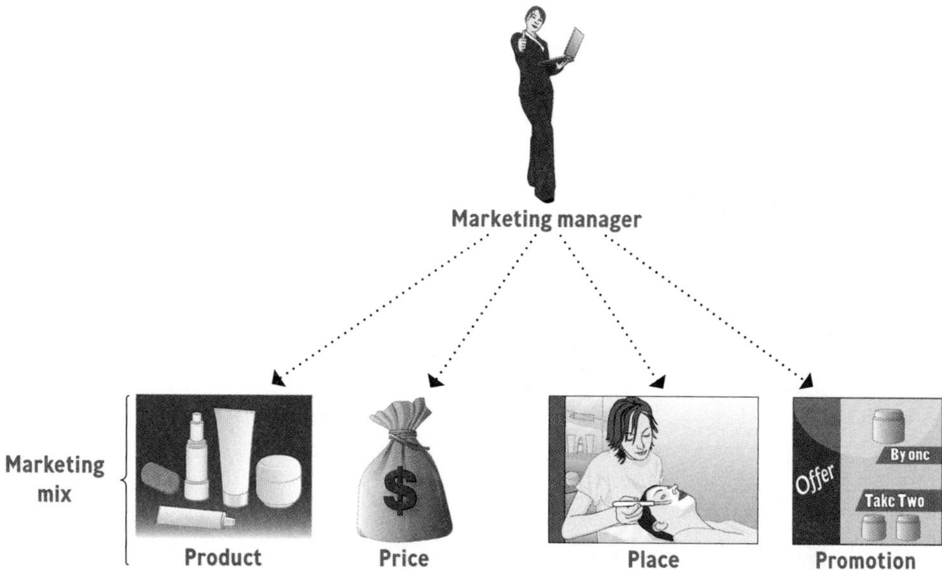

Figure 14.2

Marketing Managers and the Marketing Mix

Marketing managers must choose how to implement the four Ps of the marketing mix: product, price, place, and promotion. The goals are to please customers and make a profit.

A marketing manager, such as Sofia Colucci (the focus of this chapter's opening profile), then designs a marketing program that effectively combines the ingredients of the marketing mix (as highlighted in Figure 14.2).

The customer drives the marketing mix. The features and benefits of the product should meet, if not exceed, customer expectations. The price, place, and promotion is also driven by a desire to communicate with the customer in such a meaningful way that he or she seeks out the product (i.e., place) and is willing to purchase the product at the set price. These marketing decisions also need to achieve the organization's goals and objectives. "As business increasingly becomes more global and competitive, it is critical to not only think as a marketer," says Colucci, "but also as a business manager, collaborating with partners across all functions."

Applying the Marketing Process

The four Ps are a convenient way to remember the basics of marketing, but they do not include everything that goes into the marketing process for all products. One of the best ways to understand the entire marketing process is to take a product and follow the process that led to its development and sale. Figure 14.3 outlines some of these steps. In Chapter 15, we will investigate each of the four Ps in more detail.

Imagine, for example, that you and your friends want to start a money-making business near your school. You have noticed that there are a lot of vegetarians among your friends. You do a quick survey in a couple of dorms and other campus clubs and find that there are many vegetarians—and other students who like to eat vegetarian meals once in a while.[16] Your preliminary research indicates that there may be some demand for a vegetarian restaurant nearby. You check the fast-food stores in the area and find none offer more than one or two vegetarian meals. In fact, most do not have any vegetarian options except salads and some soups.

Further research indicates that there are a number of different kinds of vegetarians. Lacto-ovo vegetarians eat dairy products and eggs. Lacto-vegetarians eat dairy products, but no eggs. Fruitarians eat mostly raw fruits, grains, and nuts. Vegans eat neither eggs nor dairy products nor meats. Your research identifies vegan farmers who do not use any synthetic chemical fertilizers, pesticides, herbicides, or genetically modified ingredients.[17] You also find that KFC Canada offers a vegan version of its chicken sandwich in 500 of its 750 outlets.[18] Is the Colonel on to something? He may be, since there are successful vegetarian restaurants even in Argentina, where

Figure 14.3

The Marketing Process with the Four Ps

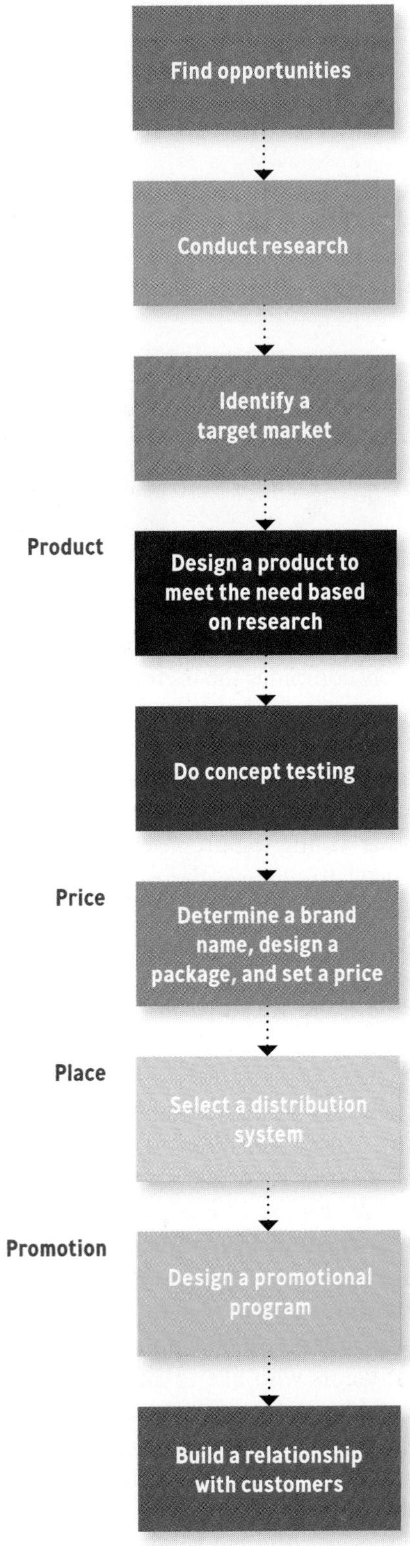

the per-capita consumption of beef is the highest in the world.[19] You conclude that a vegetarian restaurant would have to appeal to all kinds of vegetarians to be a success.

You have just performed the first few steps in the marketing process. You noticed an opportunity (a need for vegetarian food near campus). You conducted some preliminary research to see whether your idea had any merit. And then you identified groups of people who might be interested in your product. They will be your *target market* (the people you will try to persuade to come to your restaurant).

Designing a Product to Meet Customer Needs

Once you have researched customer needs and found a target market for your product, the four Ps of marketing come into play. You start by developing a product or products. A **product** is any physical good, service, or idea that satisfies a want or need plus anything that would enhance the product in the eyes of consumers, such as the brand name. In this case, your proposed product is a restaurant that would serve different kinds of vegetarian meals.

product
Any physical good, service, or idea that satisfies a want or need.

Many products today are not pure goods or pure services. Figure 14.4 illustrates the service continuum, which is a range from the tangible to the intangible or good-dominant to service-dominant offerings.[20] The service sector generates nine out of ten new jobs in Canada. At this rate, experts predict that almost all Canadians will be working in services by 2025.[21] While this text briefly introduces you to the concepts of marketing, services marketing is an area that warrants more attention as you pursue your studies in this discipline.

It is a good idea at this point to do *concept testing*. That is, you develop an accurate description of your restaurant and ask people, in person or online, whether the idea of the restaurant and the kind of meals you intend to offer appeals to them. If it does, you might go to a supplier, like Amy's Kitchen <*www.amys.com*>, that makes vegetarian meals, to get samples you can take to consumers to test their reactions. The process of testing products among potential users is called **test marketing**.

test marketing
The process of testing products among potential users.

If consumers like the product and agree that they would buy it, you have the information you need to find investors and a convenient location to open a restaurant.

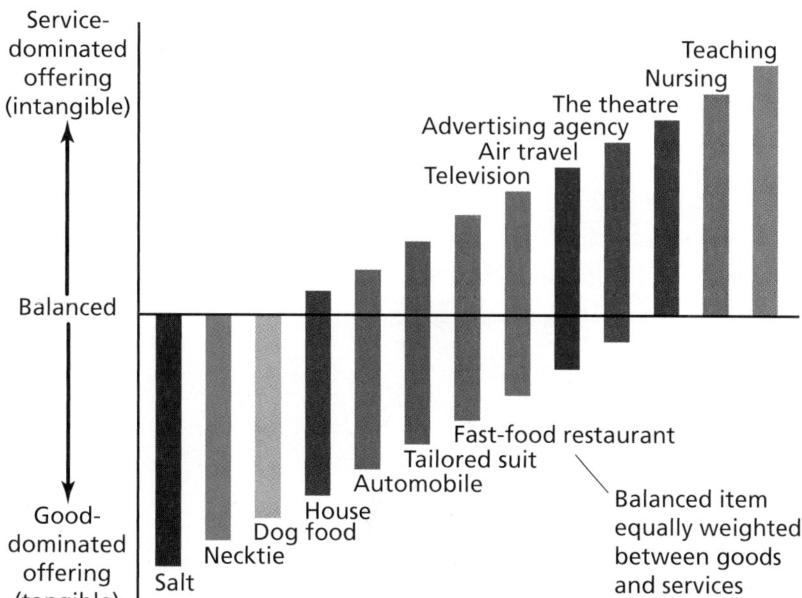

Figure 14.4

The Service Continuum Products and services range from the tangible to the intangible.

You will have to think of a catchy name for the restaurant. (For practice, stop for a minute and try to think of one.) We'll use Very Vegetarian in this text. Let's continue with the discussion of product development.

You may want to offer some well-known brand names to attract people right away. A **brand name** is a word, letter, or group of words or letters that differentiates one seller's goods or services from those of competitors.[22] Brand names of vegetarian meals include, for example, Tofurky Feast, Mori-Nu Silken Soft Tofu, and Yves Veggie Cuisine. In the next chapter, we will follow the vegetarian restaurant and products to show you how all marketing and other business decisions tie together. For now, we are simply sketching the marketing process to give you an idea of the overall picture. So far, we have covered the first P of the marketing mix: product. Let us consider price next.

brand name
A word, letter, or group of words or letters that differentiates one seller's goods or services from those of competitors.

price
The money or other consideration (including other goods and services) exchanged for the ownership or use of a good or service.

Setting an Appropriate Price

After you have decided what products and services you want to offer, you have to set appropriate prices. From a marketing viewpoint, **price** is the money or other consideration (including other goods and services) exchanged for the ownership or use of a good or service.[23] The price depends on a number of factors. In the restaurant business, the price could be close to what other restaurants charge to stay competitive. Or you might charge less to attract business, especially at the beginning.[24] Or, you may charge more and offer high-quality products for which customers are willing to pay a little more (as Starbucks does).[25] You also have to consider the costs of producing, distributing, and promoting the product, which all influence your price.

▸ A vegetarian restaurant might fill a need in the neighbourhood of many school campuses today. Is there one near your school? What can you tell about its manager's application of the four Ps of marketing – product, price, place, and promotion?

Getting the Product to the Right Place

There are several ways you can serve the market for vegetarian meals. You can have people come in, sit down, and eat at the restaurant, but that is not the only

▸ Marketers try to develop promotional campaigns that are eye-catching and memorable. Seeing this advertisement, would you be interested in visiting this retailer? What is the message being communicated?

alternative. Think of pizza. You could deliver the food to customers' dorms, apartments, and student unions. You may want to sell your products in supermarkets or health-food stores, or through organizations that specialize in distributing food products. Such *intermediaries* are the middle links in a series of organizations that distribute goods from producers to consumers. (The more traditional word for them is *middlemen.*) Getting the product to consumers when and where they want it is critical to market success. Do not forget to consider the Internet as a way to reach consumers.[26]

Developing an Effective Promotional Strategy

promotion
All of the techniques sellers use to motivate customers to buy their products.

The last of the four Ps of marketing is promotion. **Promotion** consists of all of the techniques sellers use to inform people and motivate them to buy their goods or services. They include advertising, personal selling, public relations, direct marketing, and sales promotion (such as coupons, rebates, and samples).

Promotion often includes relationship building with customers.[27] Among other activities that means responding to suggestions customers make to improve the products or their marketing, including price and packaging. For Very Vegetarian, post-purchase (or after-sale) service may include refusing payment for meals that were not satisfactory and stocking additional vegetarian products customers say they would like. Listening to customers and responding to their needs is the key to the ongoing process that is marketing.[28]

PROGRESS ASSESSMENT

- What does it mean to "help the buyer buy"?
- State each marketing era and the emphasis for each.
- What are the three parts of the marketing concept?
- What are the four Ps of the marketing mix?

PROVIDING MARKETERS WITH INFORMATION

Describe the marketing research process, and explain how marketers use environmental scanning to learn about the changing marketing environment.

Every decision in the marketing process depends on information. When they conduct marketing research, marketers analyze markets to determine opportunities and challenges, and to find information they need to make good decisions.

Marketing research helps identify what products customers have purchased in the past, and what changes have occurred to alter what they want now and what they are likely to want in the future. The latter can be to both create customer needs as well as to meet needs. Marketers also conduct research on business trends, the ecological impact of their decisions, global trends, and more. Businesses need information to compete effectively, and marketing research is the activity that gathers that information. Besides listening to customers, marketing researchers also pay attention to what employees, shareholders, dealers, consumer advocates, media representatives, and other stakeholders have to say. As noted earlier, some of that research is now being gathered online through blogs and social networks.[29]

marketing research
The analysis of markets to determine opportunities and challenges, and to find the information needed to make good decisions.

The Marketing Research Process

A simplified marketing research process consists of at least four key steps:

1. Defining the question (the problem or opportunity) and determining the present situation
2. Collecting research data
3. Analyzing the research data
4. Choosing the best solution and implementing it

The following sections look at each of these steps.

Step 1: Defining the Question and Determining the Present Situation

Marketing researchers need the freedom to discover what the present situation is, what the problems or opportunities are, what the alternatives are, what information they need, and how to go about gathering and analyzing data.

Step 2: Collecting Data

Usable information is vital to the marketing research process. Research can become quite expensive, however, so marketers must often make a trade-off between the need for information and the cost of obtaining it. Normally the least expensive method is to gather information that has already been compiled by others and published in journals and books or made available online.

Such existing data are called secondary data since you are not the first one to gather them. Figure 14.5 lists the principal sources of secondary marketing research information. Despite its name, *secondary* data is what marketers should gather *first* to avoid incurring unnecessary expense. To start your secondary data search about vegetarians, go to the Web site for *Vegetarian Times* <*www.vegetariantimes.com*> or search other Web sites on vegetarians.

secondary data
Information that has already been compiled by others and published in journals and books or made available online.

Often, secondary data do not provide all of the information managers need to make important decisions. To gather additional, in-depth information, marketers must do their own research. The results of such *new* studies are called primary data. Primary data are facts, figures, and opinions that you have gathered yourself (not from secondary sources such as books, journals, and newspapers). Four sources of primary data are surveys (also known as questionnaires), personal interviews, focus groups, and observation.

primary data
Data that you gather yourself (not from secondary sources such as books, journals, and newspapers).

Primary data can be gathered by developing a list of questions and conducting a survey. Telephone surveys, mail surveys, and online surveys are some examples.

Figure 14.5

Selected Sources of Primary and Secondary Information

Primary Sources	
Survey (e.g., phone, online, and mail) Personal interview	Focus group Observation
Secondary Sources	
Statistics Canada Publications *Canada Year Book* *Canadian Economic Observer* *Survey of Household Spending* *The Daily* **Newspapers** *The Globe and Mail* *The National Post* Local newspapers (e.g., *Calgary Herald*) **Internal Sources** Company records Balance sheets Income statements Prior research reports **Indexes and Directories** *Scott's Directories* Canadian Business Database Canadian Key Business Directory **General Internet Sites** Industry Canada—*www.ic.gc.ca* Statistics Canada—*www.statcan.gc.ca* Market news, annual reports, etc.	**Trade Sources** A.C. Nielsen Conference Board of Canada Dun & Bradstreet Canada Direct Marketing Association Retail Council of Canada **Periodicals** *Marketing Magazine* *Journal of Marketing* *Advertising Age* *Maclean's* *Canadian Business* *PROFIT* **Databases** ABI/Inform CANSIM (Statistics Canada) Canadian Business and Current Affairs Factiva LexisNexis Academic

Surveys are best carried out by independent third parties so that the information gathered and the results reported can be as objective as possible. You can use the information to understand behaviours, perceptions, preferences, and opinions. While the information gathered is useful, there are some disadvantages to this method. Not everyone who is approached may be willing to answer your questions, respondents may not be truthful, and (for written surveys) not everyone can read and write. What do you think would be the best way to survey students about your potential new restaurant? Would you conduct a different kind of survey after you have been open a few months? How could you help vegetarians find your restaurant? That is, how could you help your buyers buy? One question that researchers pay close attention to is this: Would you recommend this product to a friend?

To increase the response and accuracy rate, marketers use personal interviews. *Personal interviews* are a face-to-face opportunity to ask consumers prepared questions. While this research method can be more expensive than surveys, the interviewer has the opportunity to observe reactions and to dig a little deeper with the questions if the respondent wishes to add more information.

▸ The authors of this text benefit from focus group research data. Faculty and students come to these meetings and tell us how to improve this book. We listen carefully and make as many changes as we can in response. Suggestions have included adding more descriptive captions to the photos and making the book as user-friendly as possible. How are we doing so far?

A **focus group** is a small group of people (8 to 14 individuals, for example) who meet under the direction of a discussion leader to communicate their opinions about an organization, its products, or other issues. These questions should be free of bias and participants should be encouraged to answer questions honestly without being influenced by the responses of others in the focus group. This textbook is updated periodically using many focus groups made up of faculty and students. They tell us, the authors, what subjects and examples they like and dislike, and the authors consider their suggestions when making changes.

focus group
A small group of people who meet under the direction of a discussion leader to communicate their opinions about an organization, its products, or other issues.

Observation involves watching, either mechanically or in person, how people behave.[30] Observation may provide insight into behaviours that consumers do not even know they exhibit while shopping. For example, companies have followed customers into supermarkets to record their purchasing behaviours for products such as meat, bread, and laundry detergent. These marketers may observe that consumers do not bend to look at products, that they compare prices, and that they handle products to assess their weight. In some circumstances, the speed of events or the number of events being observed make mechanical or electronic observation more appropriate than personal observation; retailers, for example, can use electronic cameras to count the number of customers entering or leaving a store.[31]

observation
Involves watching, either mechanically or in person, how people behave.

It is up to each organization to determine its research data collection approach. The following highlights some examples of how primary research is gathered at lululemon athletica inc.:

> When it comes to making decisions, lululemon doesn't use focus groups, Web site visits, or the industry staple, customer-relationship management software, which tracks purchases. Instead, CEO Christine Day spends hours each week in stores observing how customers shop, listening to their complaints, and then using the feedback to tweak product and stores. "Big data gives you a false sense of security," says Day. During one store visit, Day noticed that women trying on a certain knit sweater found the sleeves too tight. After asking store associates if they had heard similar complaints, she cancelled future orders. The company also trains its workers to eavesdrop, placing the clothes-folding tables on the sales floor near the fitting rooms rather than in a back room so that workers can overhear complaints. Nearby, a large chalkboard lets customers write suggestions or complaints that are sent back to headquarters.[32]

Marketers gather both secondary and primary data online. The authors of this text, for example, do much research online. They also gather data from books, articles, databases, and other sources.

Step 3: Analyzing the Research Data

Marketers must turn the data collected in the research process into useful information. Careful, honest interpretation of the data collected can help a company find useful alternatives to specific marketing challenges. For example, by conducting primary research, Fresh Italy, a small Italian pizzeria, found that its pizza's taste was rated superior to that of the larger pizza chains. However, the company's sales lagged behind the competition. Secondary research on the industry revealed that free delivery (which Fresh Italy did not offer) was more important to customers than taste. Fresh Italy now delivers—and it has increased its market share.

Step 4: Choosing the Best Solution and Implementing It

After collecting and analyzing the data, market researchers determine alternative strategies and make recommendations as to which strategy may be best and why. This final step in a research effort also involves following up on the actions taken to see if the results were what was expected. If not, the company can take corrective action and conduct new studies in its ongoing attempt to provide consumer satisfaction at the lowest cost. You can see, then, that marketing research is a continuous process of responding to changes in the marketplace and in consumer preferences.[33]

In today's customer-driven market, ethics is important in every aspect of marketing. Ideally, companies should therefore do what is right as well as what is profitable. This step could add greatly to the social benefits of marketing decisions. See the Making Ethical Decisions box for such an example.

Environmental Scanning

environmental scanning The process of identifying the factors that can affect marketing success.

Marketing managers must be aware of the surrounding environment when making marketing mix decisions. **Environmental scanning** is the process of identifying the factors that can affect marketing success. Figure 14.6 should look familiar; it is a

Figure 14.6

Environmental Scanning of the Dynamic Business Environment

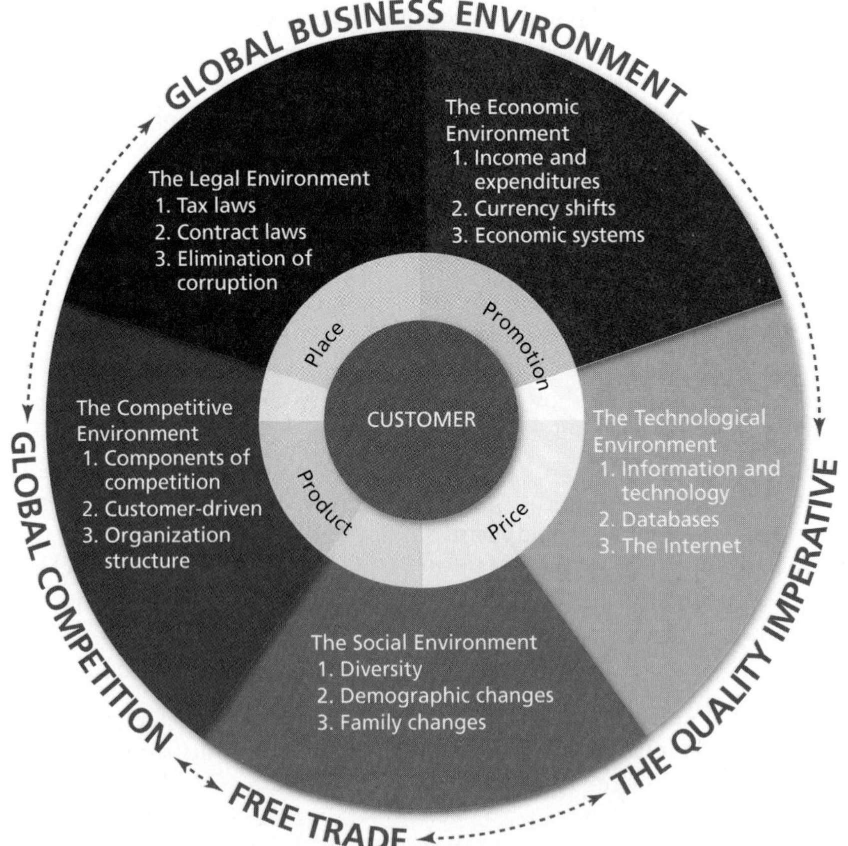

MAKING ETHICAL DECISIONS

No Kidding

Marketers have long recognized that children can be an important influence on their parents' buying decisions. In fact, many direct appeals for products are focused on children. Let's say that you have experienced a great response to a new high-fibre, high-protein cereal among health-conscious consumers. The one important group you have not been able to attract is children. Therefore, the product development team is considering introducing a child-oriented brand to expand the product line.

The new children's cereal may have strong market potential if you follow two recommendations of the research department. First, coat the flakes generously with sugar (significantly changing the cereal's nutritional benefits). Second, promote the product exclusively on children's TV programs. Such a promotional strategy should create a strong demand for the product, especially if you offer a premium (a toy or other "surprise") in each box. The consensus among the research department is that kids will love the new taste and parents will agree to buy the product because of their positive impression of your best-selling brand. The research director commented, "The chance of a parent actually reading our label and noting the addition of sugar is nil."

Would you introduce the children's cereal following the recommendations of your research department? What are the benefits of doing so? What are the risks involved in following these recommendations? What would you do if you were the marketing manager for this product?

duplication of Figure 1.3. As introduced in Chapter 1, the business environment consists of six elements—global, technological, social, competitive, economic, and legal—that either help or hinder the development of businesses. It is helpful to review them strictly from a marketing perspective.

Global Environment

Using the Internet, businesses can reach many of the world's customers relatively easily and carry on a dialogue with them about the goods and services they want. By 2018, half of all small businesses will be engaged in global trade.[34]

This globalization of marketing puts more pressure on those whose responsibility it is to deliver products. Many marketers outsource that function to companies such as Purolator <*www.purolator.com*>, which has a good reputation for delivering goods quickly. Are there any food delivery firms in your area that you could use to distribute your vegetarian products and meals?

Technological Environment

The most important technological changes also relate to the Internet. Using customer databases, blogs, social networking and the like, firms can develop products and services that closely match customers' needs.[35] Firms can now produce customized goods and services for about the same price as mass-produced goods. Thus, flexible manufacturing and mass customization are also major influences on marketers. You can imagine, for example, using databases to help you devise custom-made fruit mixes and various salads for your customers at Very Vegetarian.

Since 1984, TLN Telelatino Network has been providing programming in Italian, Spanish, and English to 6 million Canadian homes coast to coast. Are you aware of any stations that target ethnic communities?

Social Environment

Marketers must monitor social trends to maintain their close relationship with customers since population growth and changing demographics can have an effect on sales. The fastest-growing segment of the Canadian population is baby boomers. By 2031, one in four Canadians will be 65 years or older, and as this segment ages there will be growing demand for recreation, travel, continuing education, health care, and nursing homes.[36] As well, opportunities exist for firms that target Canada's 2.5 million "tweens" (ages 9 to 14). According to the YTV Tween Report, in addition to spending $2.9 billion of their own money on food, entertainment, and clothing each year, tweens also influence another $20 billion in household purchases.[37]

Other shifts in the Canadian population are creating new opportunities for marketers as they adjust their products to meet the tastes and preferences of growing ethnic groups. To appeal to diverse groups, marketers must listen better and be more responsive to unique ethnic needs. What might you do to appeal to specific ethnic groups with Very Vegetarian?

Competitive Environment

Of course, marketers must pay attention to the dynamic competitive environment. Many brick-and-mortar companies must be aware of new competition on the Internet, including companies that sell automobiles, insurance, music videos, and clothes. In the book business, Indigo is competing with Amazon.ca's huge selection of books at good prices. Now that consumers can literally search the world for the best buys through the Internet, marketers must adjust their pricing policies accordingly. Similarly, they have to adjust to competitors who can deliver products quickly or provide excellent service. Can you see any opportunities to sell vegetarian food over the Internet?

Economic Environment

As we began the new millennium, Canada was experiencing unparalleled growth and customers were eager to buy expensive automobiles, watches, and vacations. But as the economy slowed, marketers had to adapt by offering products that were less expensive and more tailored to customers with modest incomes. You can see, therefore, that environmental scanning is critical to a company's success during rapidly changing economic times. What economic changes are occurring around your school that might affect a new restaurant?

Legal Environment[38]

Governments enact laws to protect consumers and businesses. Businesses must be aware of how these may impact their practices. For example, the Supreme Court of Canada dismissed Great Glasses founder Bruce Bergez's two applications to appeal a

▸ Legislation not only needs to be in place to protect consumers and businesses, but it must also be enforced. What can be done to force companies to stop illegal activities immediately? Is this realistic?

contempt ruling and more than $46 million in fines. Bergez had been fined $1 million in 2006—the largest fine for a civil contempt case in Canadian history—and a further $50,000 a day for every day since that he had not been in compliance with Ontario legislation. Legislation requires that eyeglasses and contact lenses be dispensed by a registered optician based on a prescription supplied either by an optometrist or a physician. Great Glasses was dispensing glasses based on eye tests conducted on a computerized machine without a proper prescription. On top of this, the Supreme Court also ordered Bergez to pay unspecified costs to Ontario's College of Optometrists.

A change in one environment can have an impact on another environment, or more. This is why marketers *continuously* scan the business environment to understand the impact of changes on their businesses. For example, a change in legislation (i.e., as evidenced in the legal environment) that will encourage the entry of more businesses will create a more competitive marketplace (i.e., as reflected in the competitive environment). If increased competition leads to lower prices, then this would be reflected in lower consumer spending for this product or service category (i.e., as measured in the economic environment).

Let us consider how a change in legislation might apply to this scenario. The Canadian Radio-television and Telecommunications Commission (CRTC) is opening Canada's North to local telephone competition. As of May 2012, residents in many parts of the Yukon, Northwest Territories, and Nunavut will have the option to choose from competing telephone service providers for the first time. Says Leonard Katz, the CRTC's vice-chairman of telecommunications, "Competition will be introduced as soon as possible to bring choice and innovative options to Canada's North." The CRTC will closely monitor the situation in the North during the next two years as local competition is implemented. Do you know if prices fell as a result of increased competition?

Two Different Markets: Consumer And Business-To-Business

Marketers must know as much as possible about the market they wish to serve. There are two major markets in business: the consumer market and the business-to-business market. The **consumer market** consists of all individuals or households that want goods and services for personal consumption or use and have the resources to buy

consumer market
All individuals or households that want goods and services for personal consumption or use.

▸ Many goods could be classified as consumer goods or business-to-business (B2B) goods, based on their uses. For example, a computer that a person uses at home for personal use would clearly be a consumer good. But that same computer used in a commercial setting, such as an accounting firm or a manufacturing plant, would be classified as a B2B good. What difference does it make how a good is classified?

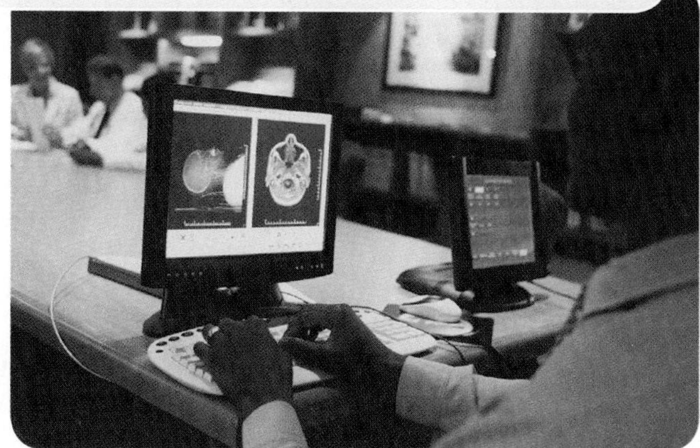

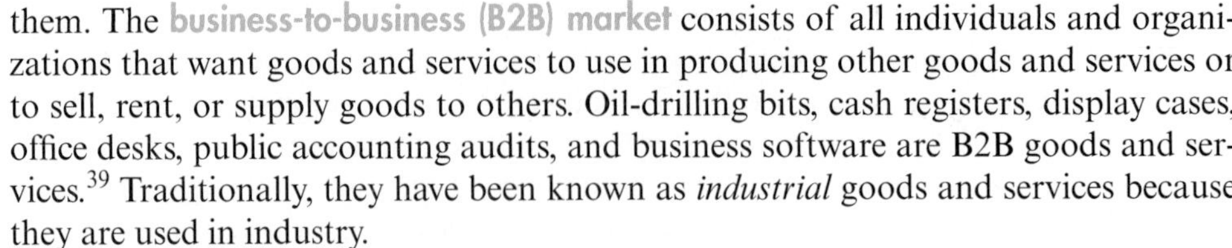

them. The **business-to-business (B2B) market** consists of all individuals and organizations that want goods and services to use in producing other goods and services or to sell, rent, or supply goods to others. Oil-drilling bits, cash registers, display cases, office desks, public accounting audits, and business software are B2B goods and services.[39] Traditionally, they have been known as *industrial* goods and services because they are used in industry.

business-to-business (B2B) market
All individuals and organizations that want goods and services to use in producing other goods and services or to sell, rent, or supply goods to others.

The important thing to remember is that the buyer's reason for buying—that is, the end use of the product—determines whether a product is considered a consumer product or a B2B product. A cup of yogurt that a student buys for breakfast is a consumer product. However, when Very Vegetarian purchases the same cup of yogurt from a manufacturer, this yogurt would be a B2B product. The following sections outline consumer and B2B markets.

market segmentation
The process of dividing the total market into groups whose members have similar characteristics.

target marketing
Marketing directed toward those groups (market segments) an organization decides it can serve profitably.

PROGRESS ASSESSMENT

- What are the four steps in the marketing research process?
- What is environmental scanning? What factors do you consider in environmental scanning?
- Can you define the terms consumer market and business-to-business market?

Explain how marketers meet the needs of the consumer market through market segmentation, relationship marketing, and the study of consumer behaviour.

THE CONSUMER MARKET

The total potential global consumer market consists of more than 7 billion people.[40] Because consumer groups differ greatly in age, education level, income, and taste, a business usually cannot fill the needs of every group. It must decide which groups to serve, and then develop products and services specially tailored to their needs.

Take the Campbell Soup Company, for example. You know Campbell for its traditional soups such as chicken noodle and tomato. Campbell has expanded its product line to appeal to a number of different tastes. In Texas and California, where people like their food with a bit of kick, Campbell makes its nacho cheese soup spicier than in other markets. Recent Canadian launches include Campbell's® Créations, a made-in-Canada line of six reduced-sodium soups; a no-salt added chicken broth; a Cream of Mushroom soup that is rich in Vitamin D; and Nourish, a nutritionally-dense meal-in-a-can created in partnership with Food Banks Canada to help fight hunger.[41] This is just one company that has had some success studying the consumer market, breaking it down into categories, and developing products for separate groups.

▸ Created to help address the growing issue of hunger in Canada and abroad, Nourish is a complete meal that delivers vegetables, fibre, and 18 grams of protein thanks to a uniquely Canadian grain innovation. Nourish is a first-of-its kind product designed to be a reliable and appealing food source for those who prosper, those in need at food banks, and those impacted by disaster situations abroad.[42]

The process of dividing the total market into several groups whose members have similar characteristics is called **market segmentation**. Selecting which groups or segments an organization can serve profitably is called **target marketing**. For example, a shoe store may choose to sell only women's shoes, only children's shoes (e.g., Kiddie Kobbler <*www.kiddiekobbler.ca*>), or only athletic shoes. The issue is finding the right *target market*—the most profitable segment—to serve.

The B.C. Lions, a Vancouver-based football team, is the first Canadian professional sports franchise to have its own beer brand—B.C. Lions Lager—as a result of its partnership with the Russell Brewing Company <*russellbeer.com*>.[43]

Main Dimension	Sample Variables	Possible Segments
Geographic Segmentation	Region	British Columbia, Prairies, Nunavut, Eastern Quebec, Sydney, St. John's
	City or Country Size	under 5,000; 5,000–20,000; 20,001–50,000; 50,001–100,000; 100,001–250,000; 250,001–500,000; 500,001–1,000,000; 1,000,000+
	Density	urban; suburban; rural
Demographic Segmentation	Gender	male; female
	Marital Status	single; married; widowed; divorced
	Age	0–5; 6–11; 12–17; 18–24; 25–34; 35–49; 50–64; 65+
	Education Attainment	some education; high school graduation certificate; trades certificate or diploma; college certificate or diploma; university certificate or diploma below bachelor level; bachelor's degree; university certificate or diploma above bachelor level; medical degree; master's degree; earned doctorate
	Ethnic Origin	Canadian; English; French; Scottish; Irish; German; Italian; Chinese; Ukrainian; North American Indian; Dutch; Polish; East Indian; Jewish; Russian; American; Jamaican; Vietnamese; other
	Occupation	professional; technical; clerical; sales supervisor; farmer; homemaker; self-employed; student; unemployed; retired; other
	Religion	Catholic; Protestant; Christian Orthodox; other Christian; Muslim; Jewish; Buddhist; Hindu; Sikh; Eastern religions; other; no affiliation
Psychographic Segmentation	Personality	gregarious; compulsive; extroverted; aggressive; ambitious
	Social Class	lower lowers; upper lowers; working class; middle class; upper middles; lower uppers; upper uppers
	Values	actualizers, fulfillers, achievers, experiencers, believers, strivers, makers, strugglers
Behavioural Segmentation	Benefits Sought	quality; service; low price; luxury; safety; status
	Usage Rate	light user; medium user; heavy user
	User Status	non-user; ex-user; prospect; first-time user; regular user
	Loyalty Status	none; medium; strong

Figure 14.7

Market Segmentation

This table shows some of the dimensions and variables that marketers use to select their markets. The aim of segmentation is to break the market into smaller units.

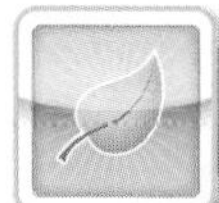

GREENBOX

When Green Is Not Really Green

Concerns about the environment and global warming are in the public's mind as never before, and companies are responding to this in a variety of ways. *Green marketing* refers to marketing efforts to produce, promote, and reclaim environmentally-sensitive products. As an alternative to plastic water bottles that are hazardous to the environment, Onebottle developed a reusable and recyclable stainless steel water container. One dollar from every Onebottle sold was donated to World Wildlife Fund Canada's conservation efforts.

Advertisements that include environmental claims are becoming more prevalent. In their desire to convince consumers that a product causes no harm and may even benefit the environment, making claims that do not exaggerate a product's benefit or minimize its negative impact must seem to many advertisers to be like a high-wire act without a safety net.

Advertising Standards Canada (ASC) has created an Advisory that is intended to provide guidance to advertisers and the public about circumstances in which "green" advertising claims may raise issues under the Canadian Code of Advertising Standards. While ASC has only recently been hearing complaints from consumers about advertisements they believe make misleading environmental claims, this issue is not new.

In most cases, allegedly misleading environmental claims are evaluated under Clause 1 (Accuracy and Clarity) of the Canadian Code of Advertising Standards. Whether any particular "green" claim actually raises an issue under Clause 1 depends on various factors. These include:

1. Does the environmental benefit claimed for the product appear to be supported by science-based evidence?
2. Is the scientific evidence that is being used to substantiate the claim generally well-recognized and accepted by authorities on the subject?
3. Is the advertisement unbalanced by singling out one environmentally positive attribute of the product while ignoring other characteristics or issues that may be harmful to the environment?
4. Does the advertisement make absolute and unqualified claims, such as "environmentally friendly" or "not harmful to the environment"? Or does the advertiser qualify its claims by appropriately communicating a product's limitations?

Consumers have a difficult time finding reliable information on which to base buying decisions about products that make claims about environmental benefits. "Green" advertising is a useful way to communicate important information to consumers who want to make responsible and environmentally conscious choices between competing products that claim to respect the environment. To this end, advertisers must make "green" claims that are truthful, fair, accurate and in compliance with the Code.

Sources: © Advertising Standards Canada; Mike Wood, "Helping The Environment One Bottle At A Time," NowPublic.com, 22 May 2008, www.nowpublic.com/environment/helping-environment-one-bottle-time; and Susan Ward, "Green Marketing," http://sbinfocanada.about.com/od/marketing/g/greenmarketing.htm.

▸ Canadian television personalities Brad Pattison and Gail Vaz-Oxlade both host popular TV shows, namely *At the End of My Leash* and *Til Debt Do Us Part*. When considering viewers for these shows, what segmentation variables are being applied? Have you seen these shows? If so, do you think that you are part of the primary target market?

total market (everyone). Or it may mean going after ever-smaller segments. We'll discuss that strategy after this next example of how a firm uses a combination of segmentation variables.

Shoppers Drug Mart uses multiple variables when it offers a selection of seasonal goods that cater to local ethnic populations. At holiday time, some stores stock Hanukkah items along with Christmas items. This combination of geographic and demographic segmentation is an attempt to steal business from grocery chains, discounters, and department stores.[47]

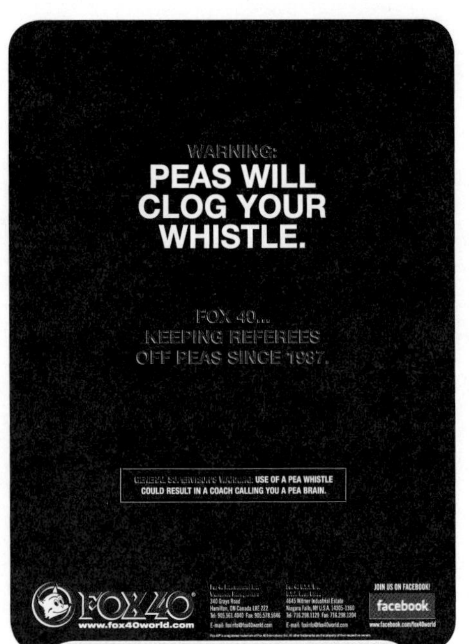

▶ A clever and comical spin off of the Surgeon General's warning reinforces to referees the benefits of using a pealess whistle. With the Fox 40 Whistle brand, there is nothing to obstruct sound, nothing to stick or fail. Faultless performance every time! Take some time to read the running case at the end of each text part to learn more about Fox 40 International Inc.

Reaching Smaller Market Segments

Niche marketing is identifying small but profitable market segments and designing or finding products for them. *Vita* magazine, for example, is sold in Quebec and it includes content that is relevant to French-Canadian women in their forties.[48] Because it so easily offers an unlimited choice of goods, the Internet is transforming a consumer culture once based on big hits and bestsellers into one that supports more specialized niche products.[49] The *long tail* is a phrase coined by Chris Anderson, editor-in-chief of *Wired* magazine, in an article explaining how companies selling more products with lower demand can easily compete with (or even surpass) those solely dependent on big sellers.[50] Just how small such a segment can be is illustrated by *FridgeDoor.com* <*www.fridgedoor.com*>. This company sells refrigerator magnets on the Internet. It keeps some 1,500 different magnets in stock and sells as many as 400 a week.

One-to-one marketing means developing a unique mix of goods and services for each *individual customer.* Travel agencies often develop such packages, including airline reservations, hotel reservations, rental cars, restaurants, and admission to museums and other attractions for individual customers. In another example, Dell can produce a unique computer system for each customer. Can you envision designing special Very Vegetarian menu items for individual customers?

niche marketing
The process of finding small but profitable market segments and designing or finding products for them.

one-to-one marketing
Developing a unique mix of goods and services for each individual customer.

mass marketing
Developing products and promotions to please large groups of people.

relationship marketing
Marketing strategy with the goal of keeping individual customers over time by offering them products that exactly meet their requirements.

Moving Toward Relationship Marketing

In the world of mass production following the Industrial Revolution, marketers responded by practising mass marketing. **Mass marketing** means developing products and promotions to please large groups of people. That is, there is little segmentation. The mass marketer tries to sell products to as many people as possible. That means using mass media, such as TV, radio, and newspapers to reach them. Although mass marketing led many firms to success, marketing managers often got so caught up with their products and competition that they became less responsive to the market.

Relationship marketing tends to lead away from mass production and toward custom-made goods and services. The goal is to keep individual customers over time by offering them new products that exactly meet their requirements. The latest in technology enables sellers to work with individual buyers to determine their wants and needs and to develop goods and services specifically designed for them, like hand-tailored shirts and unique vacations. G Adventures <*www.gadventures.com*>, a leading small-group adventure tour operator, has been chosen as Canada's favourite adventure tour operator for several years in Baxter Travel Media's Agents' Choice Awards.[51] "Twitter has revolutionized our business," says founder Bruce Poon Tip. "Facebook has done the same thing. We have the ability to deliver our culture anywhere in the world now."[52]

Understanding consumers is so important to marketing that a whole area of marketing emerged called consumer behaviour. We explore that area next.

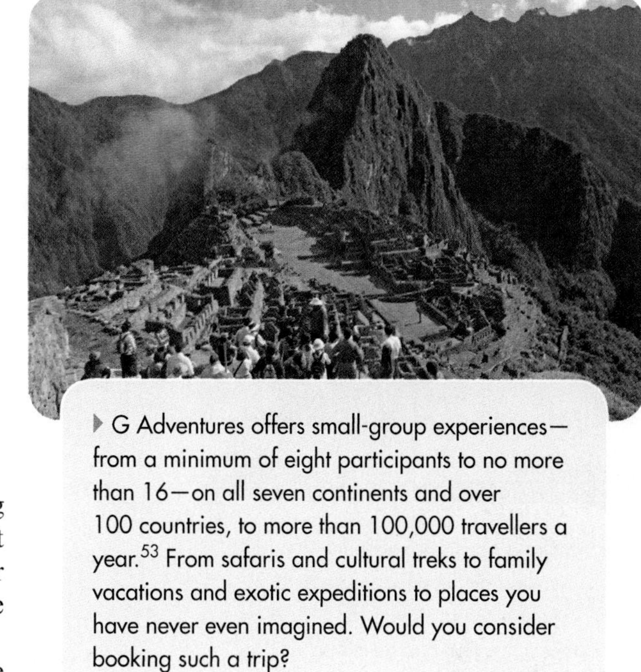

G Adventures offers small-group experiences—from a minimum of eight participants to no more than 16—on all seven continents and over 100 countries, to more than 100,000 travellers a year.[53] From safaris and cultural treks to family vacations and exotic expeditions to places you have never even imagined. Would you consider booking such a trip?

The Consumer Decision-Making Process

Figure 14.8 shows the consumer decision-making process and some of the outside factors that influence it. The five steps in the process are often studied in courses on consumer behaviour.

The first step is problem recognition, which may occur when your washing machine breaks down and you realize you need a new one or it needs to be repaired. Let's assume you decide that you will purchase a new one. This leads to an information search—you look for ads about washing machines and read brochures about them. You may consult a secondary data source such as *Consumer Reports* or other information, perhaps online. And you will likely seek advice from other people who have purchased washing machines.

After compiling all this information, you evaluate alternatives and make a purchase decision. But your buying decision does not end here. After the purchase, you may ask the people you spoke to previously how their machines perform and then do other comparisons to your new washer.

Cognitive dissonance is a type of psychological conflict that can occur after a purchase. Consumers who make a major purchase (i.e., washing machines) may have doubts about whether they got the best product at the best price. Marketers must

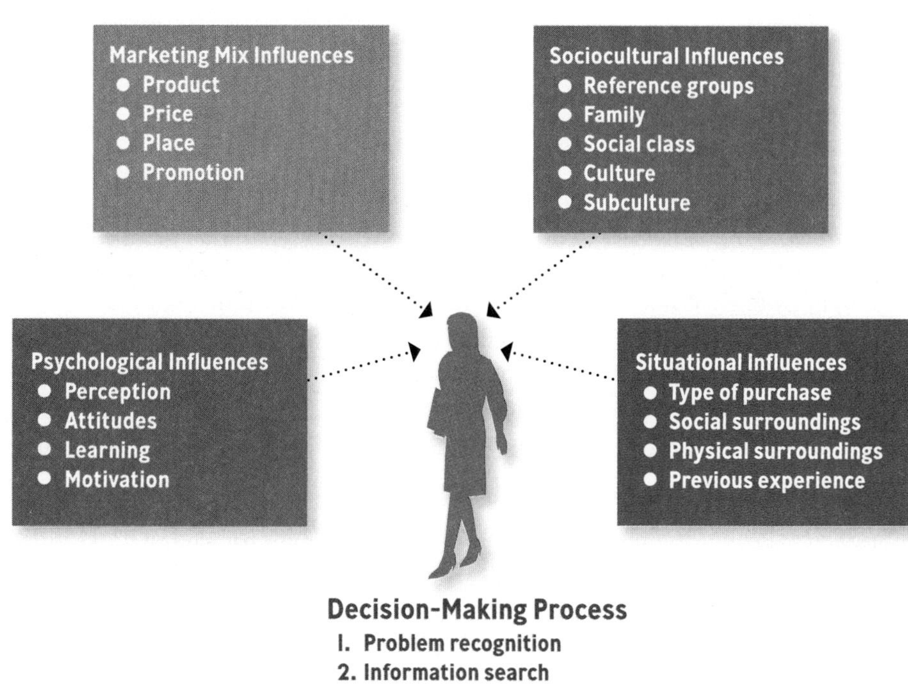

Figure 14.8

The Consumer Decision-Making Process and Outside Influences

There are many influences on consumers as they decide which goods and services to buy. Marketers have some influence, but it is not usually as strong as sociocultural influences. Helping consumers in their information search and their evaluation of alternatives is a major function of marketing.

Canadians are becoming increasingly health-conscious, creating opportunities for marketers that can develop products to address this change in buying behaviour. Do you think that baby boomers are driving this demand, or is it being driven by people of all ages?

reassure such consumers after the sale that they made a good decision. An auto dealer, for example, may send the customer positive press articles about the particular car purchased, offer product guarantees, and provide certain free services.

Marketing researchers investigate these consumer-thought processes and behaviour at each stage in a purchase to determine the best way to help the buyer buy. This area is called *consumer behaviour.*

Consumer behaviour researchers also study the various influences that affect consumer behaviour. Figure 14.8 shows several such influences: marketing mix variables (the four Ps); psychological influences, such as perception and attitudes; situational influences, such as the type of purchase and the physical surroundings; and sociocultural influences, such as reference groups and culture. Other important factors include these:

- *Learning* creates changes in an individual's behaviour resulting from previous experiences and information. If you have tried a particular brand of shampoo and you do not like it, you have learned not to buy it again.
- *Reference group* is the group an individual uses as a reference point in forming beliefs, attitudes, values, or behaviour. A student who carries a briefcase instead of a backpack may see business people as his or her reference group.
- *Culture* is the set of values, ideas, and attitudes that are learned and shared among the members of a group.[54] These are transmitted from one generation to another. Attitudes toward work, lifestyles, and consumption are evolving and examples include the following: more women are working outside the home, contributing to *time poverty* (the increasing need for convenient products due to having less time); Canadians are changing their attitudes toward health and as a result, fitness activity and sports participation are on the rise; and there is a trend toward *value-consciousness* (the concern for obtaining the best quality, features, and performance of a product or service for a given price).[55] Consider how Very Vegetarian can profit from healthy takeout food that is quickly prepared.
- *Subculture* is the set of values, attitudes, and ways of doing things that results from belonging to a certain ethnic group, religious group, or other group with which one closely identifies. Subcultures can be identified by age (e.g., teenagers), geography (e.g., Western Canada), and ethnicity (e.g., French-Canadians).[56]

Consumer behaviour is a long-standing part of a marketing curriculum. Many schools have expanded the curriculum to include courses in business-to-business marketing. As you will learn next, that market is huge.

LO 5

List ways in which the business-to-business market differs from the consumer market.

THE BUSINESS-TO-BUSINESS MARKET

B2B marketers include manufacturers; intermediaries such as retailers; institutions like hospitals, schools, and charities; and the government. The B2B market is larger than the consumer market because items are often sold and resold several times in the B2B process before they are sold to the final consumer. B2B marketing strategies also differ from consumer marketing because business buyers have their own decision-making process.[57] Several factors make B2B marketing different, including these:

1. *Customers in the B2B market are relatively few.* There are far fewer construction firms or mining operations compared to the more than 34 million potential customers in the Canadian consumer market.

2. *The size of business customers is relatively large.* That is, big organizations account for most of the employment and production of various goods and services. Nonetheless, there are many small to medium-sized firms in Canada that together make an attractive market.
3. *B2B markets tend to be geographically concentrated.* For example, diamonds tend to be concentrated in Canada's Northwest Territories. Consequently, marketing efforts may be concentrated in a particular geographic area and distribution problems can be minimized by locating warehouses near industrial centres.
4. *Business buyers are generally more rational and less emotional than ultimate consumers.* They use product specifications to guide buying choices and often more carefully weigh the total product offer, including quality, price, and service.
5. *B2B sales tend to be direct, but not always.* Tire manufacturers sell directly to auto manufacturers but use intermediaries, such as wholesalers and retailers, to sell to ultimate consumers.
6. *There is much more emphasis on personal selling in B2B markets than in consumer markets.* Whereas consumer promotions are based on *advertising,* B2B sales are based on *selling.* There are fewer customers and they usually demand more personal service. As well, the quantities being purchased justify the expense of a sales force.

As with consumers, B2B buyers use the Internet to make purchases.[58] BtoB Online reports that B2B marketers are also embracing social media marketing with more than nine out of ten B2B marketers engaged to some extent in social media marketing. LinkedIn was cited as their most important social channel, followed by Facebook (20 percent), blogging (19 percent), customer communities (14 percent), and YouTube (7 percent). Respondents said social sites are useful overall in supporting branding efforts, although different channels are considered to have their own unique strengths. LinkedIn, for example, was cited primarily for supporting lead generation, Facebook was considered strong in promoting products and events, and Twitter was noted for its Web site traffic-building qualities.[59] Figure 14.9 shows some of the differences between buying behaviour in the B2B market and the consumer market.

Figure 14.9

Comparing Business-to-Business and Consumer Buying Behaviour

	Business-To-Business Market	Consumer Market
Market structure	Relatively few potential customers Larger purchases Geographically concentrated	Many potential customers Smaller purchases Geographically dispersed
Products and Services	Require technical, complex products Frequently require customization Frequently require technical advice, delivery, and after-sale service	Require less technical products Sometimes require customization Sometimes require technical advice, delivery, and after-sale service
Buying procedures	Buyers are trained Negotiate details of most purchases Follow objective standards Formal process involving specific employees Closer relationships between marketers and buyers Buy from pre-approved suppliers	No special buyers' training Accept standard terms for most purchases Use personal judgment Informal process involving household members Impersonal relationships between marketers and consumers Buy from multiple sources

PROGRESS ASSESSMENT

- Can you define the terms consumer market and business-to-business market?
- Can you name and describe four ways to segment the consumer market?
- What is niche marketing and how does it differ from one-to-one marketing?
- List the five steps in the decision-making process.
- What are four key factors that make the business-to-business market different from the consumer market?

YOUR PROSPECTS IN MARKETING

There is a wider variety of careers in marketing than in most business disciplines. If you major in marketing an array of career options will be available to you. You could conduct marketing research or get involved in product management. You could become a manager in a retail store. You could work in transportation, storage, or international distribution. You could go into selling, advertising, sales promotion, or public relations. You could design interactive Web sites to implement CRM. These are just a few of the possibilities. As you read Chapter 15, consider whether a marketing career would interest you.

SUMMARY

Define marketing and explain how the marketing concept applies to both for-profit and non-profit organizations.

Marketing is the process of determining customer wants and needs and then providing customers with goods and services that meet or exceed these expectations.

How has marketing changed over time?

During the *production era,* marketing was largely a distribution function. Emphasis was on producing as many goods as possible and getting them to markets. By the early 1920s, during the *sales era,* the emphasis turned to selling and advertising to persuade customers to buy the existing goods produced by mass production. After the Second World War, the tremendous demand for goods and services led to the *marketing concept era,* during which businesses recognized the need to be responsive to customers' needs.

Many organizations transitioned from the marketing concept era to the market orientation era. Firms with a *market orientation* focus their efforts on (1) continuously collecting information about customers' needs and competitors' capabilities, (2) sharing this information throughout the organization, and (3) using the information to create value, ensure customer satisfaction, and develop customer relationships. Organizations with a market orientation actually engage in customer-relationship management (CRM), the process of building long-term relationships with customers by delivering customer value and satisfaction. Retaining customers over time, or managing the entire customer life cycle, is a cost-effective way for firms to grow in competitive markets.

The *social media marketing era* is where we now see firms using social media (e.g., blogs) to build communities and networks with a focus on encouraging customer participation and engagement.

What are the three parts of the marketing concept?
The three parts of the marketing concept are (1) a customer orientation, (2) a service orientation, and (3) a profit orientation (that is, market goods and services that will earn the firm a profit and enable it to survive and expand to serve more customer wants and needs).

What kinds of organizations are involved in marketing?
All kinds of organizations use marketing, both for-profit and non-profit organizations. Examples of non-profit organizations include the provinces and other government agencies, charities (e.g., churches), politicians, and schools.

List and describe the four Ps of marketing.

The marketing mix consists of the four Ps of marketing: product, price, place, and promotion.

How do marketers implement the four Ps?
The idea is to design a product that people want, price it competitively, get it in a location where consumers can find it easily, and promote it so that consumers know it exists. While this chapter briefly outlined these four Ps, they will be discussed in more detail in Chapter 15.

Describe the marketing research process, and explain how marketers use environmental scanning to learn about the changing marketing environment.

Marketing research is the analysis of markets to determine opportunities and challenges and to find the information needed to make good decisions.

What are the steps to follow when conducting marketing research?
The four steps are as follows: (1) define the problem or opportunity and determine the present situation, (2) collect data, (3) analyze the research data, and (4) choose the best solution and implement it.

What are different methods used to gather research?
Research can be gathered through secondary data (information that has already be compiled by others) and published in sources such as journals, newspapers, directories, databases, and internal sources. Primary data (data that you gather yourself) includes observation, surveys, interviews, and focus groups.

What is environmental scanning?
Environmental scanning is the process of identifying the factors that can affect marketing success. Marketers pay attention to all environmental factors that create opportunities and threats.

What are some of the more important environmental trends in marketing?
The most important global and technological change is probably the growth of the Internet. Another is the growth of customer databases, with which companies can develop products and services that closely match the needs of customers. Marketers must also monitor social trends like population growth and shifts to maintain their close relationship with customers. Of course, marketers must also monitor the dynamic competitive environment and pay attention to the economic environment. Changes in laws can create opportunities and threats for business activities; thus, this is another important environment to scan.

Explain how marketers meet the needs of the consumer market through market segmentation, relationship marketing, and the study of consumer behaviour.

The process of dividing the total market into several groups whose members have similar characteristics is called market segmentation.

What are some of the ways that marketers segment the consumer market?

Geographic segmentation means dividing the market into different regions. Segmentation by age, income, and education level are methods of demographic segmentation. We study a group's values, attitudes, and interests using psychographic segmentation. Behavioural segmentation divides the market based on behaviour with or toward a product. Different variables of behavioural segmentation include benefits sought, usage rate, and user status. The best segmentation strategy is to use as many of these segmentation bases as possible to come up with a target market that is sizable, reachable, and profitable.

What is the difference between mass marketing and relationship marketing?

Mass marketing means developing products and promotions to please large groups of people. Relationship marketing tends to lead away from mass production and toward custom-made goods and services. Its goal is to keep individual customers over time by offering them goods or services that meet their needs.

What are some of the factors that influence the consumer decision-making process?

See Figure 14.8 for some of the major influences on consumer decision making. Some other factors in the process are learning, reference group, culture, and subculture.

List ways in which the business-to-business market differs from the consumer market.

The B2B market consists of manufacturers, intermediaries such as retailers, institutions (e.g., hospitals, schools, and charities), and the government.

What makes the business-to-business market different from the consumer market?

The number of customers in the B2B market is relatively small, and the size of business customers is relatively large. B2B markets tend to be geographically concentrated, and industrial buyers generally are more rational than ultimate consumers in their selection of goods and services. B2B sales tend to be direct, and there is much more emphasis on personal selling in B2B markets than in consumer markets.

KEY TERMS

behavioural segmentation
brand name
business-to-business (B2B) market
consumer market
customer-relationship management (CRM)
demographic segmentation
environmental scanning
focus group
geographic segmentation
market orientation
market segmentation
marketing
marketing concept
marketing mix
marketing research
mass marketing
niche marketing
observation
one-to-one marketing
price

primary data
product
promotion
psychographic segmentation
relationship marketing
secondary data
social media
social media marketing
target marketing
test marketing

CRITICAL THINKING

1. Do you agree that individual consumers are not rational decision makers? Are you aware of marketers' efforts, and in some cases success, in targeting you for goods and services?
2. When businesses buy goods and services from other businesses, they usually buy in large volumes. Salespeople in the B2B area usually are paid on a commission basis. Do you agree that it is more professionally rewarding for employees to be engaged in B2B marketing/sales?
3. Retailers such as the Hudson's Bay Company (HBC Rewards) and Canadian Tire Corporation (Canadian Tire money) offer loyalty programs. Are you encouraged to visit these retailers more often as a result of such programs? Do you buy more products as a result of such programs? Many retailers also offer incentives to use their credit cards. For example, you may get 10 percent off your purchase if you open an HBC credit card account. Points that you accumulate on your Canadian Tire Options® MasterCard® can be redeemed for Canadian Tire merchandise, auto parts, or auto labour. Do you feel that companies are trying to bribe you to support their businesses, or do you think that these are good business practices? How effective is social networking in building loyalty? Explain.
4. Marketers must adapt as new technologies emerge. For example, younger consumers now watch programs on the Internet and/or PVR, rather than during their scheduled television slots. What does this mean for traditional television advertisements (i.e., commercials)? How should marketers evaluate and plan a move to marketing on the Web?

DEVELOPING WORKPLACE SKILLS

1. Think of an effective marketing mix for one of the following products: a new electric car, an easy-to-use digital camera, or a car wash for your neighbourhood. Be prepared to discuss your ideas in class.
2. Working in teams of five (or on your own if class size is a problem), think of a product that your friends want but cannot get on or near campus. You might ask your friends at other schools what is available there. What kind of product would fill that need? Discuss your results in class and determine how you might go about marketing that new product.
3. Relationship marketing efforts include frequent-flier deals at airlines, special discounts for members at certain supermarkets (e.g., Sobeys), and Web sites that remember your name and what you have purchased in the past and recommend new products that you may like (e.g., Amazon.ca). Evaluate any one of these programs. (If you have no personal experience with them, look up such programs on the Internet.) What might they do to increase your satisfaction and loyalty? Be prepared to discuss these programs in class.
4. Working in teams of four or five, list as many brand names of pizza as you can. Merge your list with those from other groups. Then try to identify the "target market" for each brand. Do they all seem to be after the same market, or are there different brands for different markets? What are the separate appeals?
5. Take a little time to review the concepts in this chapter as they apply to Very Vegetarian, the restaurant we used as an example throughout. Have an open discussion in class about (a) a different name for the restaurant, (b) a location for the restaurant, (c) a promotional program (including social media initiatives), and (d) a way to establish a long-term relationship with customers.

ANALYZING MANAGEMENT DECISIONS

Applying Customer-Oriented Marketing Concepts at Thermos

Thermos <*www.thermos.com*> is the company made famous by its Thermos bottles and lunch boxes. Thermos also manufactures cookout grills. Its competitors include Sunbeam <*www.sunbeam.com*> and Weber <*www.weber.com*>. To become a world-class competitor, Thermos completely reinvented the way it conducted its marketing operations. By reviewing what Thermos did, you can see how new marketing concepts affect organizations.

First, Thermos modified its corporate culture. It had become a bureaucratic firm organized by function: design, engineering, manufacturing, marketing, and so on. That organizational structure was replaced by flexible, cross-functional, self-managed teams. The idea was to focus on a customer group—for example, buyers of outdoor grills—and build a product development team to create a product for that market.

The product development team for grills consisted of six middle managers from various disciplines, including engineering, manufacturing, finance, and marketing. They called themselves the Lifestyle Team because their job was to study grill users to see how they lived and what they were looking for in an outdoor grill. To get a fresh perspective, the company hired Fitch, Inc. <*www.fitch.com*>, an outside consulting firm, to help with design and marketing research. Team leadership was rotated based on needs of the moment. For example, the marketing person took the lead in doing field research, but the R&D person took over when technical developments became the issue.

The team's first step was to analyze the market. Together, team members spent about a month on the road talking with people, videotaping barbecues, conducting focus groups, and learning what people wanted in an outdoor grill. The company found that people wanted a nice-looking grill that did not pollute the air and was easy to use. It also had to be safe enough for apartment dwellers, which meant that it had to be electric.

As the research results came in, engineering began playing with ways to improve electric grills. Manufacturing kept in touch to ensure that any new ideas could be produced economically. Design people were already building models of the new product. R&D people relied heavily on Thermos's strengths. The company's core strength was the vacuum technology it had developed to keep hot things hot and cold things cold in Thermos bottles. Drawing on that strength, the engineers developed a domed lid that contained the heat inside the grill.

Once a prototype was developed, the company showed the model to potential customers, who suggested several changes. Employees also took sample grills home and tried to find weaknesses. Using the input from potential customers and employees, the company used continuous improvement to manufacture what became a world-class outdoor grill.

No product can become a success without communicating with the market. The team took the grill on the road, showing it at trade shows and in retail stores. The product was such a success that Thermos is now using self-managed customer-oriented teams to develop all of its product lines.

Discussion Questions

1. How could the growth of self-managed cross-functional teams affect marketing departments in other companies? Do you believe that would be a good change or not? Explain.
2. How can Thermos now build a closer relationship with its customers using the Internet?
3. What other products might Thermos develop that would appeal to the same market segment that uses outdoor grills?

Practise and learn online with Connect.

CHAPTER

15

MANAGING THE MARKETING MIX: PRODUCT, PRICE, PLACE, AND PROMOTION

LEARNING OBJECTIVES

After you have read and studied this chapter, you should be able to:

LO 1 Explain the concept of a total product offer and summarize the functions of packaging.

LO 2 Contrast *brand, brand name, and trademark,* and discuss the concept of brand equity.

LO 3 Describe the product life cycle.

LO 4 Identify various pricing objectives and strategies, and explain why non-pricing strategies are growing in importance.

LO 5 Explain the concept of marketing channels and the value of marketing intermediaries.

LO 6 Discuss retailing and explain the various kinds of non-store retailing.

LO 7 Define promotion and list the five traditional tools that make up the promotion mix.

PROFILE

GETTING TO KNOW HEATHER REISMAN OF INDIGO BOOKS & MUSIC INC.

Heather Reisman is the founder and CEO of Indigo Books & Music Inc. (Indigo) <*www.chapters.indigo.ca*>, Canada's largest book and specialty retailer. She was born in Montreal and educated at McGill University. For the first sixteen years of her career she was Managing Director of Paradigm Consulting, the strategy and change management firm she co-founded in 1979. Paradigm was the world's first strategic change consultancy and pioneered many organizational change strategies still in use today.

Reisman left Paradigm in 1992 to become President of Cott Corporation <*www.cott.com*>. During her tenure as President, Cott grew from a Canadian-based regional bottler to the world's largest retailer-branded beverage supplier. Harvard Business School wrote two case studies focusing on the company's growth and development under her leadership.

In 1996, Reisman launched Indigo. She wanted to create a book-lover's cultural department store. With big box stores booming, Indigo became the go-to place for literary goods, eventually acquiring rival Chapters in 2001 to form the largest book retailer in Canada.

Today, Indigo operates 244 stores, including 97 large-format stores under the banners Indigo, Chapters, and the World's Biggest Bookstore, and 147 small-format stores under the banners Coles, Indigo, IndigoSpirit, SmithBooks, and The Book Company. It also operates *indigo.ca*, a popular online destination offering millions of products including books, eBooks, toys, stationery, home décor, gourmet confections, CDs, DVDs, and more.

Indigo's membership rewards programs include the Plum Rewards and irewards programs. Plum Rewards is a free program offering points on almost everything purchased in store and preferred pricing online at *indigo.ca*. The Plum Rewards program was created to provide Indigo customers with personalized and inspirational book and product recommendations, promotional offers and VIP experiences. Indigo's irewards program—for an annual fee of \$35—offers a 10 percent discount on books and a 5 percent discount on most non-book products.

Indigo is committed to reading, regardless of the format, and it created and launched the global eReading service, Kobo. With one of the largest eReading catalogues in the world, Kobo has since driven its membership to over 6 million readers in 100 countries. In November 2011, Indigo agreed to the sale of Kobo to Rakuten Inc., one of the world's leading Internet service companies, for US\$315 million.

Reisman's goal is to build the organization into the most valued retailer in the world for booklovers and their friends. Connecting with customers is important to Indigo and its successful online community boasts more than 275,000 members sharing their passion for books, authors, and reading at *indigo.ca*. Indigo's Facebook fan base has grown to more than 240,000.

Reisman clearly recognizes that there will continue to be hurdles moving forward. "Starting Indigo was the single most challenging thing I've ever done," says Reisman. "I am at an equally challenging moment now. While sustaining the book business for all people who care about it, we also have to transform it to deal with the reality that 30 or 40 percent of books will be bought digitally. That means 30 percent of my business that needs to be replaced. That's a big transformation." Adapting her bookstores to the current consumer need has Reisman reinstalling inviting armchairs, working on an expanded role for Starbucks, enhancing Indigo's housewares offerings, and embracing the new demand for digital books.

Marketing begins with watching people to understand their needs. It then involves developing products and services that customers might want. Those products and services need to be perfected and tested in the marketplace. Then one must decide how to distribute and sell those products. Should they be sold through large retailers, on the Internet, or a combination of these options? This profile has briefly introduced you to some of the retailing options that Indigo offers its customers. How should we inform our stakeholders about the goods and services? One must develop a marketing mix that will resonate with the target market. Making such decisions is challenging, but if you are successful, you can make a lot of customers very happy. This is what marketing is all about.

Sources: "Our Company," Indigo Books & Music Inc., 2012, www.chapters.indigo.ca/our-company/management/and www.chapters.indigo.ca/our-company/fast-facts/; Dawn Calleja, "LEGENDS OF THE SMALL," *Report on Small Business–The Globe and Mail*, June 2012, 12; and Carolyn Patricia Grisold, "Founder & CEO, Indigo Books & Music Inc.," Women of Influence, 2011, www.womenofinfluence.ca/heather-reisman-2/.

LO 1

Explain the concept of a total product offer and summarize the functions of packaging.

value
Good quality at a fair price. When consumers calculate the value of a product, they look at the benefits and then subtract the cost to see if the benefits exceed the costs.

PRODUCT DEVELOPMENT AND THE TOTAL PRODUCT OFFER

The only way to compete today is to design and promote better products, meaning products that are perceived to have the best **value**—good quality at a fair price.[1] When consumers calculate the value of a product, they look at the benefits and then subtract its cost (price) to see whether the benefits exceed the cost, including the cost of driving to the store (or shipping fees if they buy the product online). The Spotlight on Small Business box shares how one company tries to add value.

Whether consumers perceive a product as the best value depends on many factors, including the benefits they seek and the service they receive. To satisfy consumers, marketers must learn to listen better and constantly adapt to changing market demands.[2] For example, traditional phone companies must adapt to Voice Over Internet Protocol (VoIP)—a system that allows people to make inexpensive phone calls through the Internet.[3] Sometimes customers develop their own uses for the original products and services. Examples include the following:[4]

- Play-Doh was first produced as a wallpaper cleaner in the 1930s. By the 1950s, it had been reworked and remarketed to children in toy stores after children in a nursery school began using the product to make Christmas ornaments
- Text messages were originally developed by cell carriers to let customers know about problems with their networks. The unintended use of texting caught on so quickly that most carriers did not initially have a system in place to charge their customers.

SPOTLIGHT ON SMALL BUSINESS

Home Cooking in Half the Time

Men and women today are often very busy with work and do not have much time to make home-cooked meals. Nonetheless, they would like to offer their families good meals. Such meals create more family time and are often more nutritious than restaurant fare. What can marketers do to help working families prepare meals? One answer is a company called Let's Dish <*www.letsdish.com*>. Let's Dish does the planning, shopping, and chopping for you. All you have to do is combine the ingredients, then cook at home whenever you're ready.

The idea behind Let's Dish is popular. (Competitors Dream Dinners <*dreamdinners.com*> and SupperWorks <*www.supperworks.com*> rely on a similar concept.) It's like a community kitchen where adults can whip up a couple of weeks' worth of meals in just one or two hours. Here's how it works. Customers go to a Web site to pick a time and date and the meals they would like to prepare, like herb-crusted flank steak. When they arrive at Dream Dinners the ingredients are ready. Customers mix and package them and bring them home, uncooked. They put the meals in the refrigerator until needed. No shopping for groceries. No looking for recipes. Just meals, ready to go. Sound good?

What does such a company offer as its "product"? First, it provides a place to meet others and have a good time preparing meals. Second, it saves time for people too busy to shop for groceries and prepare meals at home every night. Third, it saves a lot of stress and mess. Finally, the company saves people money, because they do not have to buy big supplies of condiments they will use only sparingly. Perhaps most important, the company offers a quick and easy way to create healthy and satisfying meals for the whole family. What else might such a company add to its product offer?

Sources: "How It Works," Dream Dinners, 2012, www.dreamdinners.com; "How It Works," Simply Cook It, 2009, www.simplycookit.net; and "Get Dish-ing," an advertising supplement to the *Gaithersburg Gazette*, March 2008.

How would you like a beer or glass of wine with your Big Mac? You can get both at this McDonald's in Paris (shown left). Around the world, McDonald's adapts its architectural scheme, menus, and interior design to fit the tastes and cultural demands of each country.

Marketers have learned that adapting products to new competition and new markets is an ongoing need. We are sure that you have noticed menu changes at your local fast-food restaurant over time. An organization cannot do a one-time survey of consumer wants and needs, design a group of products to meet those needs, put them in the stores, and then just relax. It must constantly monitor changing consumer wants and needs, and adapt products and policies accordingly.

Product development, then, is a key activity in any modern business, anywhere in the world. There's a lot more to new-product development than merely introducing goods and services, however. What marketers do to create excitement for those products is as important as the products themselves.

Developing a Total Product Offer

From a strategic marketing viewpoint, a total product offer is more than just the physical good or service. A **total product offer** consists of everything that consumers evaluate when deciding whether to buy something. Thus, the basic good or service may be a washing machine, an insurance policy, or a beer, but the total product offer includes some or all of the value enhancers in Figure 15.1. You may hear some people call the basic product the "core product" and the total product offer the "augmented product."[5]

total product offer Everything that consumers evaluate when deciding whether to buy something.

When people buy a product, they may evaluate and compare total product offers on many dimensions.[6] Some are tangible (the product itself and its package); others are intangible (the producer's reputation and the image created by advertising). A successful marketer must begin to think like a customer and evaluate the total product offer as a collection of impressions created by all of the factors listed in Figure 15.1. It is wise to talk with customers to learn which features and benefits are most important to them and which value enhancers they want in the final offerings.[7]

What questions might you ask consumers when developing the total product offer for your Very Vegetarian restaurant? (Recall the business idea introduced in Chapter 14.) Remember, store surroundings are important in the restaurant business, as are the parking lot and the condition of the bathrooms.

Figure 15.1

Potential Components of a Total Product Offer

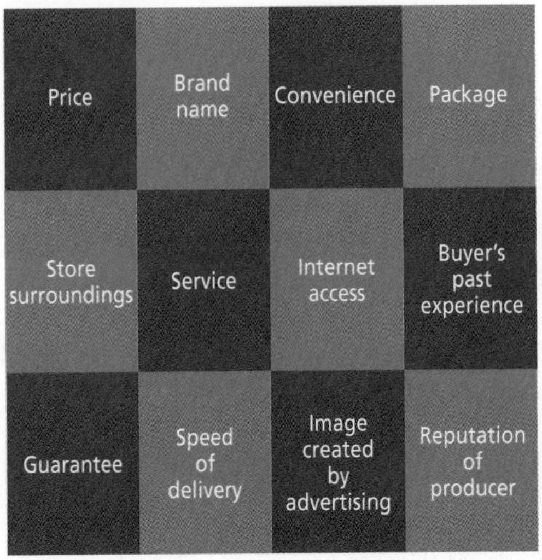

Price	Brand name	Convenience	Package
Store surroundings	Service	Internet access	Buyer's past experience
Guarantee	Speed of delivery	Image created by advertising	Reputation of producer

Sometimes an organization can use low prices to create an attractive total product offer. For example, outlet stores offer brand-name goods for less. Shoppers like getting high-quality goods at low prices, but they must be careful. Outlets also carry lower-quality products with similar but not exactly the same features as goods carried in regular stores. Different consumers may want different total product offers, so a company must develop a variety of offerings.

Product Lines and the Product Mix

product line
A group of products that are physically similar or are intended for a similar market.

product mix
The combination of product lines offered by an organization.

Companies usually do not sell just one product. A **product line** is a group of products that are physically similar or are intended for a similar market. They usually face similar competition. Procter & Gamble's (P&G) <*www.pg.com*> product lines include hair care, oral care, and household cleaners. In one product line, there may be several competing brands. For example, P&G has many brands in its laundry and fabric care product line, which includes the Cheer, Tide, and Ivory brands. All of P&G's product lines make up its **product mix**, the combination of product lines offered by this manufacturer.

Service providers have product lines and product mixes as well. Financial services firms such as banks and credit unions may offer a variety of services. The product mix may include savings products (such as savings accounts and term deposits), credit products (including loans, mortgages, and credit cards), and a variety of other services (such as safety deposit boxes).

Companies must decide what mix is best. The mix may include both goods and services to ensure that all of the customer's needs are being met. As well, a diversified mix would minimize the risks associated with focusing all of a firm's resources on only one target market.

Product Differentiation

product differentiation
The creation of real or perceived product differences.

Product differentiation is the creation of real or perceived product differences. Actual product differences are sometimes quite small, so marketers must use a creative mix of pricing, advertising, and packaging (value enhancers) to create a unique, attractive image. Various bottled water companies, for example, have successfully attempted product differentiation. These companies made their bottled waters so attractive through pricing and promotion that some restaurant customers order water by brand name (e.g., Perrier).

There's no reason why you could not create an attractive image for Very Vegetarian, your vegetarian restaurant. It would be easy to differentiate such a restaurant from the typical burger joint. Small businesses can often win market share with creative product differentiation. Yearbook photographer Charlie Clark competes by offering multiple clothing changes, backgrounds, and poses along with special allowances, discounts, and guarantees. His small business has the advantage of being more flexible in adapting to customer needs and wants, and he is able to offer attractive product options. Clark has been so successful that companies use him as a speaker at photography conventions. How would you respond creatively to the consumer wants of vegetarians?

▸ The product mix for Fox 40® International Inc. includes the following product lines: whistles, pro coaching boards, mouth guards, and a marine line. The entire pealess whistle product line is shown here. How does the company differentiate its whistles? Fox 40® pealess whistles cannot be overblown and they never fail—the harder you blow, the louder the sound! They are faultless, reliable, and trusted. Have you tried a Fox 40® whistle?

Packaging Changes the Product

Consumers evaluate many aspects of the total product offer, including the brand. It is surprising how important packaging can be in such evaluations. Many companies have used packaging to change and improve their basic product. Thus, we have squeezable ketchup bottles that stand upside down on their caps for easier pouring, square paint cans with screw tops and integrated handles; plastic bottles for motor oil that eliminate the need for funnels; toothpaste pumps; single-use packets of spices; and so forth.[8] In each case, the package changed the product in the minds of consumers and opened large markets.

Packages must perform the following functions:

1. Attract the buyer's attention.
2. Protect the goods inside, stand up under handling and storage, be tamperproof, and deter theft.
3. Be easy to open and use.
4. Describe and give information about the contents.
5. Explain the benefits of the good inside.
6. Provide information on warranties, warnings, and other consumer matters.
7. Give some indication of price, value, and uses.

Packaging can also make a product more attractive to retailers. For example, the universal product codes (UPCs) on many packages help stores control inventory. They combine a bar code (black and white lines) and a preset number that gives the retailer information about the product's price, size, colour, and other attributes. In short, packaging changes the product by changing its visibility, usefulness, or attractiveness.

One relatively new packaging technology for tracking products is the radio frequency identification (RFID) chip, especially the ones made with nanoparticle powder.[9] When attached to a product, the chip sends out signals telling a company where the product is at all times. RFID chips carry more information than bar codes, do not have to be read one at a time (whole pallets can be read in an instant), and can be read at a distance.

The Growing Importance of Packaging

Today, packaging carries more of the promotional burden than in the past. Many products once sold by salespeople are now being sold in self-service outlets, and the package has acquired more sales responsibility.

Packaging may make use of a strategy called bundling, which combines goods and/or services for a single price. Virgin <*www.virgin.com*> has bundled door-to-door limousine service and in-flight massages in its total product offer. Financial institutions are offering everything from financial advice to help in purchasing insurance, stocks, bonds, mutual funds, and more. When combining goods or services into one package, marketers must not include so much that the price becomes too high. It is best to work with customers to develop value enhancers that meet their individual needs.

brand
A name, symbol, or design (or combination thereof) that identifies the goods or services of one seller or group of sellers and distinguishes them from the goods and services of competitors.

brand equity
The value of the brand name and associated symbols.

PROGRESS ASSESSMENT

- What's the difference between a product line and a product mix?
- What functions does packaging now perform?
- What value enhancers may be included in a total product offer?

Contrast brand, brand name, and trademark, and discuss the concept of brand equity.

BRANDING AND BRAND EQUITY

A **brand** is a name, symbol, or design (or combination thereof) that identifies the goods or services of one seller or group of sellers and distinguishes them from the goods and services of competitors. The word *brand* includes practically all means of identifying a product. As we noted in Chapter 14, a *brand name* consists of a word, letter, or group of words or letters that differentiates one seller's goods and services from those of competitors.[10] Brand names you may be familiar with include Air Canada, Roots, President's Choice, and Google.

Brand names give products a distinction that tends to make them attractive to customers. For the buyer, a brand name assures quality, reduces search time, and adds prestige to purchases. For the seller, brand names facilitate new-product introductions, help promotional efforts, add to repeat purchases, and differentiate products so that prices can be set higher.

brand loyalty
The degree to which customers are satisfied, enjoy the brand, and are committed to further purchase.

As mentioned in Appendix B, a *trademark* is a brand that has exclusive legal protection for both its brand name and its design. Trademarks such as the Quebec Winter Carnival's Bonhomme Carnaval mascot, the National Hockey League's Stanley Cup, and McDonald's golden arches are widely recognized. Trademarks need to be protected from other companies that may want to trade on the trademark holder's reputation and image. Companies often sue other companies for too closely matching brand names. This was the case when Mattel, Inc. <*www.mattel.com*>, owner of the Barbie doll registered trademark, tried to stop Barbie's, a small chain of Montreal restaurants, from registering the word "Barbie's" as a trademark for use with restaurant services. However, the Supreme Court of Canada ruled in favour of the restaurant chain as "there was no evidence that adult consumers would consider a doll manufacturer to be a source of good food."[11]

▸ The Victoria School of Business and Technology (VSBT) received a cease and desist letter from Apple Inc. claiming that the school's logo "reproduces, without authority, our client's Apple design logo which it widely uses. By doing so, you are infringing Apple's rights, and further, falsely suggesting that Apple has authorized your activities."[12] Do you agree with this position?

Generating Brand Equity and Loyalty

A major goal of marketers in the future will be to re-establish the notion of brand equity. **Brand equity** is the value of the brand name and associated symbols. Usually the company cannot know the value of its brand until it sells it to another company.[13] Brand names with high reported brand equity ratings include Reynolds Wrap aluminum foil and Ziploc food bags. In the past, companies tried to boost their short-term performance by offering coupons and price discounts to move goods quickly. This eroded consumers' commitment to brand names, especially of grocery products. Now companies realize the value of brand equity, and are trying harder to measure the earning power of strong brand names.[14]

The core of brand equity is brand loyalty. **Brand loyalty** is the degree to which customers are satisfied, enjoy the brand, and are committed to further purchases. A loyal group of customers represents substantial value to a firm, and that value

GREENBOX

Couldn't You Make a Smaller Footprint?

To help consumers make "green" choices, companies are putting carbon labels on products. Timberland shoes, for example, places a card in each shoebox that provides a carbon rating of 0 to 10. A 0 rating means less than 2.5 kilograms of carbon and other greenhouse gases were emitted when the shoes were produced and shipped. If a shoe gets a 10 rating, its manufacture created as much carbon output as a car driven 240 miles (or approximately 386 kilometres).

The British-based grocery chain Tesco <*www.tesco.com*> is in the process of putting carbon labels on all its products—from bags of parsley to flat-panel TVs. Boots <*www.boots.com*>, Britain's largest pharmaceutical chain, put up signs in the store explaining the carbon output from making its Botanics shampoo. Many other marketers are taking advantage of environmental awareness to help promote their products. Meanwhile, China continues to build coal-powered plants, and India is building roads that will eventually allow millions of additional cars to go from city to city. Clearly, the focus on climate change varies greatly from country to country.

Do you pay attention to your carbon footprint? Are you doing anything to lower it? How do you feel about marketers using concern about climate change as a promotional device?

Sources: Kenneth T. Walsh, "Changing America's Energy Ways," *U.S. News & World Report*, April 2009; George Anders, "Carbon-Market Concept Moves to Mainstream," *The Wall Street Journal*, 14 May 2008; Edward Taylor, "Start-Ups Race to Produce 'Green' Cars," *The Wall Street Journal*, 6 May 2008; and Heather Green and Kerry Capell, "Carbon Confusion," *BusinessWeek*, 17 March 2008.

can be calculated. Retailer Canadian Tire Corp. is starting a driving school—the Canadian Tire Drivers Academy—as part of a strategy to strengthen its presence in the automotive market by fending off competition and improving customer loyalty: "Our aspirations are to continue to be Canada's automotive authority," said Allan MacDonald, Senior Vice President of Automotive at Canadian Tire.[15] Canadian brand names with the highest brand values—that is, how much profit the brands are likely to generate for their owners—and their corresponding brand values are as follows: the Royal Bank of Canada ($8.7 billion), the Toronto-Dominion Bank ($8.5 billion), and Scotiabank ($5.7 billion).[16] One way manufacturers are trying to create more brand loyalty is by highlighting the carbon footprint of their products.[17] The Green Box shares some examples.

Brand awareness refers to how quickly or easily a given brand name comes to mind when a product category is mentioned. Advertising helps build strong brand awareness. Established brands such as Coca-Cola and Pepsi are usually among the highest in brand awareness. Event sponsorship, such as the Rogers Cup tennis tournament and the RONA MS Bike Tour, helps improve brand awareness. Simply being there over and over again also increases brand awareness. That is one way Google became such a popular brand.[20]

▸ Greenpeace's report, *Dirty Laundry*, alleged that clothing from top brands such as Calvin Klein, H&M, Abercrombie & Fitch, Converse, and Ralph Lauren are tainted with various hazardous chemicals.[18] As part of Greenpeace's Detox Campaign, Puma was the first to promise a toxin-free product and also to eliminate toxins from its entire supply chain and life cycle by 2020; Nike and Adidas followed with their own initiatives.[19] Do you seek out products that are sold by companies that support corporate social responsibility?

Brand Management

A **brand manager** (known as a *product manager* in some firms) has direct responsibility for one brand or product line. This individual also manages all the elements of the marketing mix—product, price, place, and promotion—throughout the life cycle of each product and service. Thus, you might think of the brand manager as the president of a one-product firm.

brand awareness
How quickly or easily a given brand name comes to mind when a product category is mentioned.

brand manager
A manager who has direct responsibility for one brand or one product line; called a product manager in some firms.

One reason many large consumer product companies created this position was to have greater control over new-product development and product promotion. Some companies have brand management *teams* to bolster the overall effort. In B2B companies, brand managers are often known as product managers.

For example, what do you do with a product that has a well-known brand name but fading sales? One solution may be to reinvent the product to satisfy the needs of loyal customers in the form of a new and improved version of the original product. Companies also need to introduce new products and services to satisfy customers' needs or risk having competitors steal their business. In other instances, the decision may be made to abandon the product or service and focus on other areas. This was the case when IBM sold its personal computer unit in favour of focusing on offering technology and consulting services.[21] Let us review the stages of a product's life cycle next.

Describe the product life cycle.

THE PRODUCT LIFE CYCLE

product life cycle
A theoretical model of what happens to sales and profits for a product class over time; the four stages of the cycle are introduction, growth, maturity, and decline.

Once a product has been developed and tested, it goes to market. There it may pass through a **product life cycle** of four stages: introduction, growth, maturity, and decline (as noted in Figure 15.2). This cycle is a *theoretical* model of what happens to sales and profits for a *product class* over time. However, not all individual products follow this life-cycle shape, and particular brands may act differently. Some product classes, such as microwave ovens, stay in the introductory stage for years. Other products, like ketchup, become classics and never experience decline. Fad products (think Beanie Babies and mood rings) may go through the entire cycle in a few months. Still others may be withdrawn from the market altogether. Nonetheless, the product life cycle may provide some basis for anticipating future market developments and for planning marketing strategies.

Example of the Product Life Cycle

The product life cycle can give marketers valuable clues to successfully promoting a product over time. Some products, like crayons and sidewalk chalk, have very long product life cycles, change very little, and never seem to go into decline. Crayola's <*www.crayola.com*> crayons have been popular for 100 years!

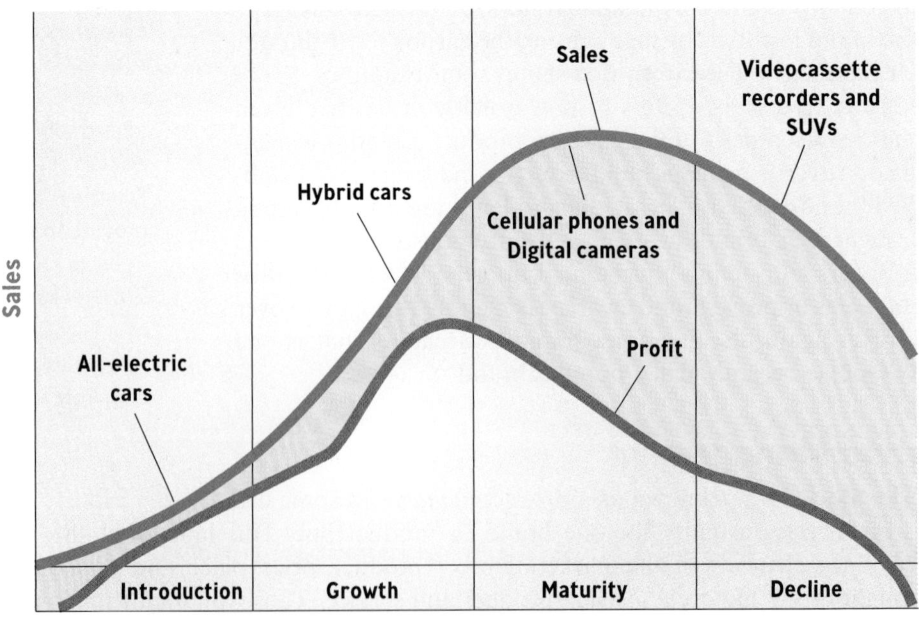

Figure 15.2

Sales and Profits During the Product Life Cycle
Profit levels start to fall *before* sales reach their peak. This is due to increasing price competition. When profits and sales start to decline, it is time to come out with a new product or to remodel the old one to maintain interest and profits.

You can see how the theory works by looking at the product life cycle of instant coffee. When it was introduced, most people did not like it as well as "regular" coffee, and it took several years for instant coffee to gain general acceptance (introduction stage). At one point, though, instant coffee grew rapidly in popularity, and many brands were introduced (growth stage). After a while, people became attached to one brand and sales levelled off (maturity stage). Sales then went into a slight decline when freeze-dried coffees were introduced (decline stage). Now freeze-dried coffee is, in turn, in the decline stage as consumers are buying fresh specialty beans from companies such as Second Cup and grinding them at home. It is extremely important for marketers to recognize what stage a product is in so that they can make intelligent and efficient marketing decisions about it.

Using the Product Life Cycle

Different stages in the product life cycle call for different marketing strategies. Figure 15.3 outlines the marketing mix decisions you might make. As you go through the figure, you will see that each stage calls for multiple marketing mix changes. These concepts are largely theoretical and you should use them only as guidelines. (We'll discuss the price strategies mentioned in the figure later in this chapter.)

Note that at the maturity stage, the product may reach the top in sales growth while profit is decreasing. At that stage, a marketing manager may decide to create a new image for the product to start a new growth cycle. You may have noticed how Arm & Hammer baking soda gets a new image every few years to generate new sales. One year it is positioned as a deodorant for refrigerators and the next as a substitute for harsh chemicals in swimming pools. Knowing what stage in the cycle a product has reached helps marketing managers decide when such strategic changes in the marketing mix are needed.

PROGRESS ASSESSMENT

- What's the difference between a brand name and a trademark?
- What are the key components of brand equity?
- Explain the role of brand managers.
- What is the theory of the product life cycle?

Figure 15.3

Sample Marketing Mix Strategies Followed During the Product Life Cycle

	Marketing Mix Elements			
Life Cycle Stage	Product	Price	Place	Promotion
Introduction	Offer market-tested product; keep mix small	Go after innovators with high introductory price (skimming strategy) or a low introductory price (penetration pricing)	Use wholesalers, selective distribution	Dealer promotion and heavy investment in advertising and sales promotion to get stores to carry the product and consumers to try it
Growth	Improve product; keep product mix limited	Adjust price to meet competition	Increase distribution	Heavy competitive advertising
Maturity	Differentiate product to satisfy different market segments	Further reduce price	Take over wholesaling function and intensify distribution	Emphasize brand name as well as product benefits and differences
Decline	Cut product mix; develop new-product ideas	Adjust price to remain profitable	Consolidate distribution; drop some outlets	Reduce advertising to only loyal customers

Identify various pricing objectives and strategies, and explain why non-pricing strategies are growing in importance.

COMPETITIVE PRICING

Pricing is so important to marketing and the development of total product offers that it has been singled out as one of the four Ps in the marketing mix. It is one of the most difficult of the four Ps for a manager to control, however, because price is such a critical ingredient in consumer evaluations of the product. In this section, we'll explore price both as an ingredient of the total product offer and as a strategic marketing tool.

Pricing Objectives

A firm may have several objectives in mind when setting a pricing strategy. When pricing a new vegetarian offering, we may want to promote the product's image. If we price it *high* and use the right promotion, maybe we can make it the Evian of vegetarian meals. We also might price it high to achieve a certain profit objective or return on investment. We could also price our product *lower* than its competitors, because we want low-income people to afford this healthy meal. That is, we could have some social or ethical goal in mind. Low pricing may also discourage competition because it reduces the profit potential. It may also help us capture a larger share of the market.

Thus, a firm may have several pricing objectives over time, and it must formulate these objectives clearly before developing an overall pricing strategy. Popular objectives include the following:

1. *Achieving a target return on investment or profit.* Ultimately, the goal of marketing is to make a profit by providing goods and services to others. Naturally, one long-run pricing objective of almost all firms is to optimize profit.
2. *Building traffic.* Supermarkets often advertise certain products at or below cost to attract people to the store. These products are called *loss leaders.* The long-run objective is to make profits by following the short-run objective of building a customer base. The Internet portal, Yahoo, once provided a free auction service to compete with eBay. Why give such a service away? To increase advertising revenue on the Yahoo site and attract more people to Yahoo's other services.
3. *Achieving greater market share.* One way to capture a larger part of the market is to offer lower prices, low finance rates (like 0 percent financing), low lease rates, or rebates.
4. *Creating an image.* Certain watches (e.g., Rolex), perfumes, and other socially visible products are priced high to give them an image of exclusivity and status.
5. *Furthering social objectives.* A firm may want to price a product low so that people with little money can afford it. The government often subsidizes the price of farm products to keep basic necessities like milk and bread easily affordable.

▶ Some products are priced high to create a high-status image of exclusivity and desirability. Patek Philippe <*www.patek.com*> watches fall into this category. What is the total product offer for a product like this?

A firm may have short-run objectives that differ greatly from its long-run objectives. Managers should understand both types of objectives from the start and put both into their strategic marketing plan. They should also set pricing objectives in the context of other marketing decisions about product design, packaging, branding, distribution, and promotion. All these marketing decisions are interrelated.

Intuition tells us the price charged for a product must bear some relationship to the cost of producing it. Prices usually *are* set somewhere above cost. But as we'll see, price and cost are not always related. In fact, there are three major approaches to pricing strategy: cost-based, demand-based (target costing), and competition-based.

▶ Bundle pricing, an example of demand-based pricing, groups two or more products together and prices them as a unit. It is based on the idea that consumers value the package more than the individual items. Can you think of other examples of bundle pricing?

Cost-Based Pricing

Producers often use cost as a primary basis for setting price. They develop elaborate cost accounting systems to measure production costs (including materials, labour, and overhead), add in some margin of profit, and come up with a price. Picture the process in terms of producing a car. You add up all the various components—engine parts, body, tires, radio, door locks, windows, paint, and labour—add a profit margin, and come up with a price. The question is whether the price will be satisfactory to the market as well. As discussed in Chapter 2, in the long run the market—not the producer—determines what the price will be. Pricing should take into account costs, but it should also include the expected costs of product updates, the marketing objectives for each product, and competitor prices.

Demand-Based Pricing

Unlike cost-based pricing, **target costing** is demand-based. That means we design a product so it not only satisfies customers but also meets profit margins we set. Target costing makes the final price an *input* to the product development process, not an outcome of it. You first estimate the selling price people would be willing to pay for a product and then subtract your desired profit margin. The result is your target cost of production, or what you can spend to profitably produce the item. Imagine how you would use this process to make custom-made jewellery.

Competition-Based Pricing

Competition-based pricing is a strategy based on what all the other competitors are doing. The price can be at, above, or below competitors' prices. Pricing depends on customer loyalty, perceived differences, and the competitive climate. **Price leadership** is evident when one or more dominant firms set the pricing practices that all competitors in an industry follow. You may have noticed this practice among oil and gas companies.

Break-Even Analysis

Before you begin selling a new vegetarian sandwich, it may be wise to determine how many sandwiches you would have to sell before making a profit. You would then determine whether you could reach such a sales goal. **Break-even analysis** is the process used to determine profitability at various levels of sales. The break-even point is the point where revenue from sales equals all costs. The formula for calculating the break-even point is as follows:

$$\text{Break-even point (BEP)} = \frac{\text{Total fixed cost (FC)}}{\text{(Price of one unit (P)} - \text{Variable cost (VC) of one unit)}}$$

Total fixed costs are all expenses that remain the same no matter how many products are made or sold. Among the expenses that make up fixed costs are the amount paid to own or rent a factory or warehouse and the amount paid for business insurance. **Variable costs** change according to the level of production. Included are the expenses for the materials used in making products and the direct costs of labour used to make those goods.

To produce a specific product, let's say you have a fixed cost of \$200,000 (for mortgage interest, real estate taxes, equipment, and so on). Your variable cost (e.g., labour and materials) per item is \$2. If you sold the product for \$4 each, the break-even

target costing
Designing a product so that it satisfies customers and meets the profit margins desired by the firm.

competition-based pricing
A pricing strategy based on what all the other competitors are doing. The price can be set at, above, or below competitors' prices.

price leadership
The procedure by which one or more dominant firms set the pricing practices that all competitors in an industry follow.

break-even analysis
The process used to determine profitability at various levels of sales.

total fixed costs
All expenses that remain the same no matter how many products are made or sold.

variable costs
Costs that change according to the level of production.

point would be 100,000 items. In other words, you would not make any money selling this product unless you sold more than 100,000 of them:

$$\text{BEP} = \frac{\text{FC}}{(\text{P} - \text{VC})} = \frac{\$200{,}000}{(\$4.00 - \$2.00)} = \frac{\$200{,}000}{\$2.00} = 100{,}000 \text{ items}$$

Air Canada reduced aircraft weight in an attempt to save fuel; measures included tightening weight limits on the checked-luggage allowance, only partly filling water tanks, disposing of empty wine bottles at the arrival city instead of flying them back to the departure site, and replacing glass wine bottles with Tetra Paks.[22] Would these measures be targeted at decreasing fixed costs or variable costs?

Pricing Strategies for New Products

skimming price strategy
A strategy in which a new product is priced high to make optimum profit while there's little competition.

penetration price strategy
A strategy in which the product is priced low to attract many customers and discourage competitors.

Let's say that a firm has just developed a new line of products, such as Blu-ray players. The firm has to decide how to price these sets at the introductory stage of the product life cycle. A **skimming price strategy** prices a new product high, to recover research and development costs and to make as much profit as possible while there's little competition. Of course, those large profits will eventually attract competitors.

A second strategy would be to price the new players low. Low prices will attract more buyers and discourage other companies from making sets because profits are slim. This **penetration price strategy** enables the firm to penetrate or capture a large share of the market quickly. For example, Nintendo <*www.nintendo.com*> consciously chose a penetration strategy when it originally introduced its GameCube video game console (predecessor to Nintendo's Wii) by choosing a price substantially lower than Microsoft's Xbox and Sony's PlayStation consoles.[23] What are disadvantages of such a strategy?

Retailer Pricing Strategies

everyday low pricing (EDLP)
Setting prices lower than competitors and then not having any special sales.

high–low pricing strategy
Set prices that are higher than EDLP stores, but have many special sales where the prices are lower than competitors.

Retailers use several pricing strategies. **Everyday low pricing (EDLP)** is the choice of Home Depot and Walmart. They set prices lower than competitors and do not usually have many special sales. The idea is to bring customers to the store whenever they want a bargain rather than waiting until there is a sale.

Department stores and some other retailers most often use a **high–low pricing strategy**. Regular prices are higher than at stores using EDLP, but during special sales they are lower. The problem with such pricing is that it encourages customers to wait for sales, thus cutting into profits. As online shopping continues to grow, you may see fewer stores with a high–low strategy because customers will be able to find better prices on the Internet.

▸ Shoppers around the world look for bargains, as these consumers in Seoul, South Korea, are doing. How many different ways can marketers appeal to shoppers' desire to find the lowest price? Do online retailers adopt different pricing strategies?

Retailers can use price as a major determinant of the goods they carry. Some promote goods that sell for only $1 (e.g., Dollarama), or only $10. Some of these dollar stores have raised some of their prices to over one dollar because of rising costs.[24]

Psychological pricing means pricing goods and services at price points that make the product appear less expensive than it is. A house might be priced at $299,000 because that sounds like a lot less than $300,000.[25] Gas stations almost always use psychological pricing.[26]

psychological pricing
Pricing goods and services at price points that make the product appear less expensive than it is.

How Market Forces Affect Pricing

Recognizing that different consumers may be willing to pay different prices, marketers sometimes price on the basis of consumer demand rather than cost or some other calculation. That is called *demand-oriented pricing* and it is reflected by movie theatres (i.e., Cineplex) with lower rates on Tuesdays and by retailers, such as Shoppers Drug Mart, that offer discounts to senior citizens if they shop there on certain days.

Marketers are facing a new pricing problem: customers can now compare prices of many goods and services on the Internet. For example, you may want to check out deals on sites such as *Travelocity.ca* or *Hotels.ca*. *Priceline.com* introduced consumers to a "demand collection system," in which buyers post the price they are willing to pay and invite sellers to either accept or decline the price. Consumers can get great prices on airlines, hotels, and other products by naming their price. They can also buy used goods online. Have you or any of your friends bought or sold anything on *eBay.ca*, *Kijiji.ca*, or *Craigslist.ca*? Clearly, price competition is going to heat up as consumers have more access to price information from around the world. As a result, non-price competition is likely to increase.

▸ The Home Depot offers free Know-How Workshops on everything from laying tile to installing a toilet to how to save money on your energy bills. What other retailers use non-price competition?

NON-PRICE COMPETITION

Marketers often compete on product attributes other than price. You may have noted that price differences are small with products such as gasoline, candy bars, and even major products such as compact cars. You will not typically see price as a major promotional appeal on television. Instead, marketers tend to stress product images and consumer benefits such as comfort, style, convenience, and durability.

Often marketers emphasize non-price differences because prices are so easy to match. Many small organizations promote the services that accompany basic products rather than price in order to compete with bigger firms. Good service will enhance a relatively homogeneous product. However, few competitors can match the image of a friendly, responsive, customer-oriented company. Other strategies to avoid price wars include adding value (e.g., home delivery from a drugstore), educating consumers on how to use the product, and establishing relationships. Customers will pay extra for goods and services when they have a friendly relationship with the seller. The services are not always less expensive, but they offer more value.

PROGRESS ASSESSMENT

- Can you list two short-term and two long-term pricing objectives? Can the two be compatible?
- What's a disadvantage of using a cost-based pricing strategy?
- Can you calculate a product's break-even point if producing it costs $10,000 and revenue from the sale is $20?
- Why is increasing focus being placed on non-price competition?

Explain the concept of marketing channels and the value of marketing intermediaries.

marketing intermediaries
Organizations that assist in moving goods and services from producers to business and consumer users.

channel of distribution
A set of marketing intermediaries, such as agents, brokers, wholesalers, and retailers, that join together to transport and store goods in their path (or channel) from producers to consumers.

agents/brokers
Marketing intermediaries that bring buyers and sellers together and assist in negotiating an exchange but do not take title to the goods.

wholesaler
A marketing intermediary that sells to other organizations.

retailer
An organization that sells to ultimate consumers.

THE IMPORTANCE OF CHANNELS OF DISTRIBUTION

Marketing intermediaries are organizations that assist in moving goods and services from producers to businesses (B2B) and from businesses to consumers (B2C). They are called intermediaries because they are in the middle of a series of organizations that join together to help distribute goods from producers to consumers. A **channel of distribution** consists of a whole set of marketing intermediaries, such as agents, brokers, wholesalers, and retailers, that join together to transport and store goods in their path (or channel) from producers to consumers.

Agents/brokers are marketing intermediaries who bring buyers and sellers together and assist in negotiating an exchange, but do not take title to the goods. That is, at no point do they own the goods. Think of real estate agents as an example.

A **wholesaler** is a marketing intermediary that sells to other organizations, such as retailers and institutions (e.g., hospitals). Wholesalers are part of the B2B system. Walmart has been trying to eliminate independent wholesalers from its system and do the job itself.[27] That is, Walmart provides its own warehouses and has its own trucks.

A **retailer** is an organization that sells to ultimate consumers (that is, people like you and me) who buy for their own use. For consumers to receive the maximum benefit from marketing intermediaries, the various organizations must work together to ensure a smooth flow of goods and services to the customer.

Channels of distribution help ensure communication flows *and* the flow of money and title to goods. They also help ensure that the right quantity and assortment of goods will be available when and where needed. Figure 15.4 shows selected channels of distribution for both consumer and industrial goods.

How Intermediaries Create Exchange Efficiency

Manufacturers do not always need marketing intermediaries to sell their goods to consumer and business buyers.[28] Figure 15.4 shows that some manufacturers sell directly to buyers, known as a *direct channel*. So why have marketing intermediaries at all? The answer is that intermediaries perform certain marketing tasks—such as transporting, storing, selling, advertising, and relationship building—faster and cheaper than most manufacturers could.[29] A simple analogy is this: You could deliver packages in person to people anywhere in the world, but usually you do not. Why not? Because it is usually cheaper and faster to have them delivered by Canada Post or a private firm such as Purolator.

Similarly, you could sell your home by yourself, or buy stock directly from other people, but you probably would not do so. Why? Again, because there are specialists (agents and brokers) who make the process more efficient and easier than it would be otherwise. Agents and brokers are marketing intermediaries. They facilitate the exchange process.

Here is a way to see the benefits of using marketing intermediaries, known as an *indirect channel*. Suppose five manufacturers of various food products each tried to sell directly to five retailers. The number of exchange relationships that would have to be established is 5 times 5, or 25. But picture what happens when a wholesaler enters the system. The five manufacturers would contact one wholesaler to establish five exchange relationships. The wholesaler would have to establish contact with the five retailers. That would also mean five exchange relationships. Note that the number of exchanges is reduced from 25 to only 10 by the addition of a wholesaler. Figure 15.5 shows this process.

Some economists have said that intermediaries add costs and need to be eliminated. Marketers say that intermediaries add value and that the *value greatly exceeds*

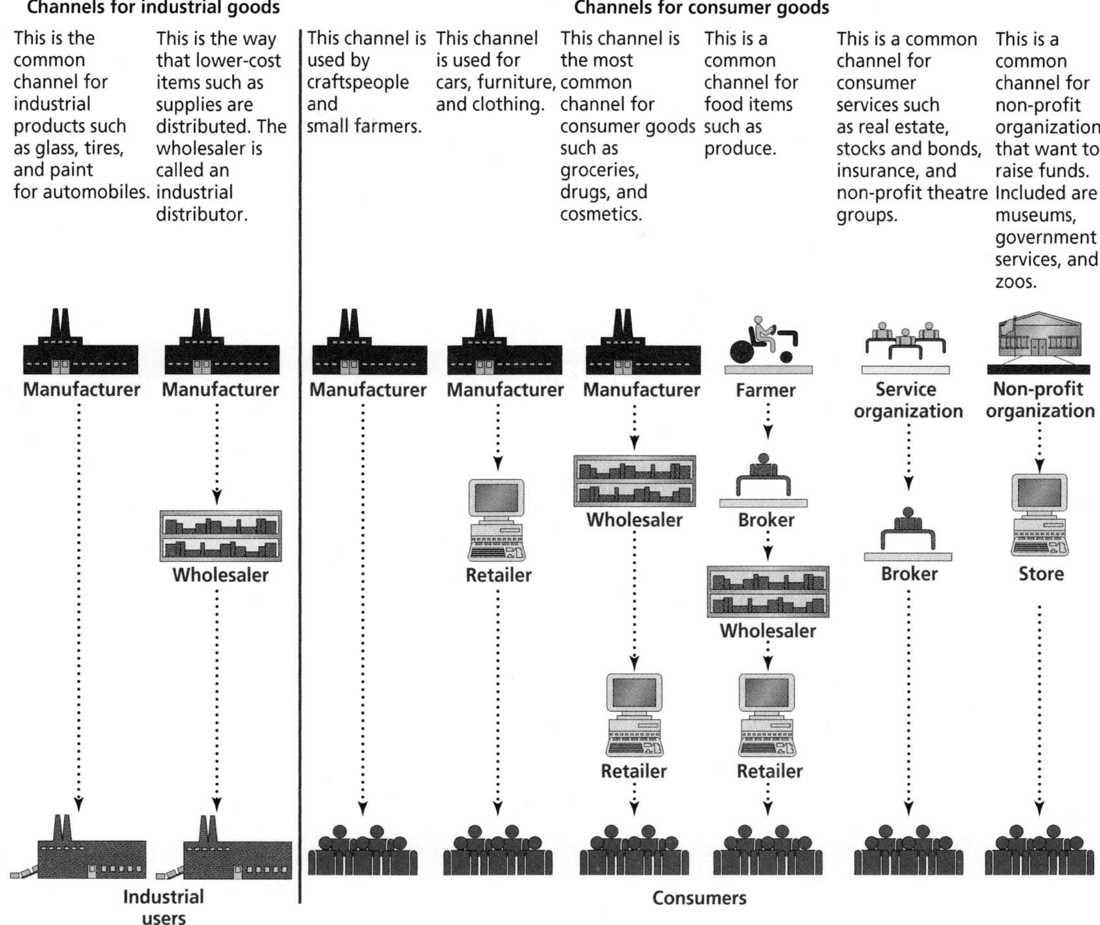

Figure 15.4

Selected Channels of Distribution for Industrial and Consumer Goods and Services

the cost. While marketing intermediaries can be eliminated, their activities cannot if consumers are to have access to products and services. Intermediary organizations have survived because they have performed marketing functions faster and cheaper than others could.

PROGRESS ASSESSMENT

- What is a channel of distribution, and what intermediaries are involved?
- Why do we need intermediaries?
- Can you illustrate how intermediaries create exchange efficiency?

RETAIL INTERMEDIARIES

Discuss retailing and explain the various kinds of non-store retailing.

Perhaps the most useful marketing intermediaries, as far as you are concerned, are retailers. Remember that retailers sell to ultimate consumers. They are the ones who bring goods and services to your neighbourhood and make them available day and night. Retailing is important to our economy. In 2011, retail trade generated approximately $456.4 billion and employed almost 1.9 million Canadians.[30] These numbers do not include sales generated via the Internet.

Figure 15.6 lists, describes, and gives examples of various kinds of retailers. Have you shopped in each kind of store? What seems to be the advantage of each?

Figure 15.5

How Intermediaries Create Exchange Efficiency

This figure shows that adding a wholesaler to the channel of distribution cuts the number of contacts from 25 to 10. This improves the efficiency of distribution.

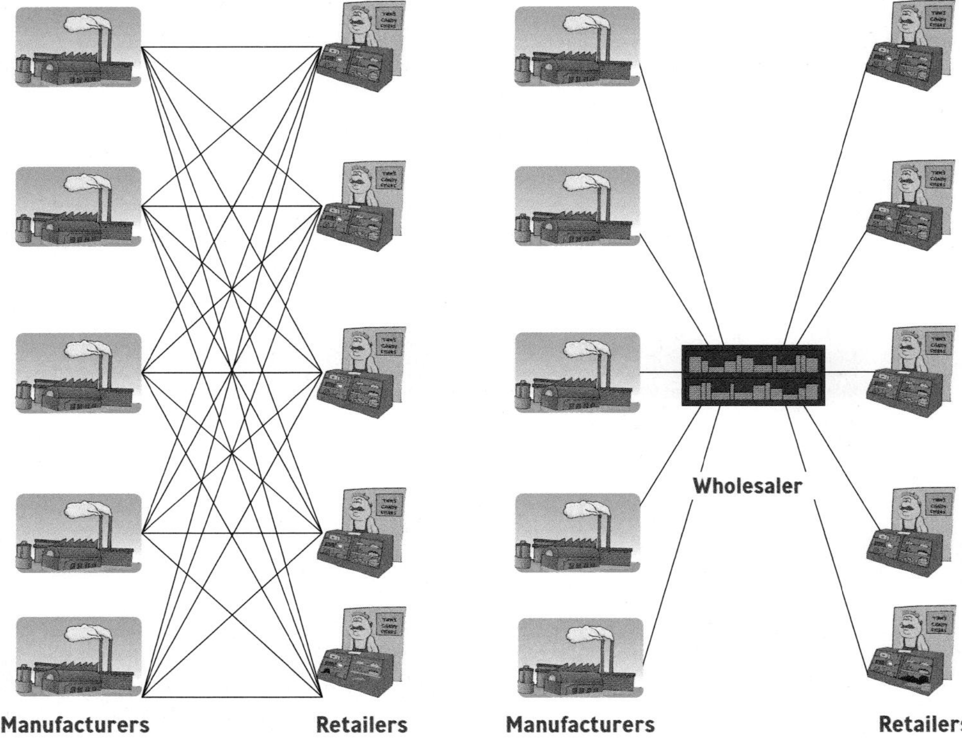

Figure 15.6

Types of Retail Stores

Type	Description	Example
Department store	Sells a wide variety of products (clothes, furniture, and housewares) in separate departments	Sears, The Bay
Discount store	Sells many different products at prices generally below those of department stores	Giant Tiger, Dollar Store
Supermarket	Sells mostly food with other non-food products such as detergent and paper products	Metro, Sobeys, Provigo
Warehouse club	Sells food and general merchandise in facilities that are usually larger than supermarkets and offers discount prices; membership may be required	Costco Wholesale, Real Canadian Wholesale Club
Convenience store	Sells food and other often-needed items at convenient locations; may stay open all night	Mac's, 7-Eleven
Category killer	Sells a huge variety of one type of product to dominate that category of goods	Indigo Books & Music, Sleep Country Canada, Staples
Outlet store	Sells general merchandise directly from the manufacturer at a discount; items may be discontinued or have flaws ("seconds")	Nike, Rockport, Liz Claiborne
Specialty store	Sells a wide selection of goods in one category	Jewellery stores, shoe stores, bicycle shops
Supercentre	Sells food and general merchandise at discount prices; no membership required	Loblaws (some locations), Walmart (some locations)

Retail Distribution Strategy

A major decision that marketers must make is selecting the right retailers to sell their products. Different products call for different retail distribution strategies.

Intensive distribution puts products into as many retail outlets as possible, including vending machines. Products that need intensive distribution include candy, gum, and popular magazines.

Selective distribution uses only a preferred group of the available retailers in an area. Such selection helps assure producers of quality sales and service. Manufacturers of appliances, furniture, and clothing use selective distribution.

Exclusive distribution is the use of only one retail outlet in a given geographic area. The retailer has exclusive rights to sell the product and is therefore likely to carry a large inventory, give exceptional service, and pay more attention to this brand than to others. Auto manufacturers usually use exclusive distribution, as do producers of specialty goods such as skydiving equipment or fly-fishing products.

intensive distribution
Distribution that puts products into as many retail outlets as possible.

selective distribution
Distribution that sends products to only a preferred group of retailers in an area.

exclusive distribution
Distribution that sends products to only one retail outlet in a given geographic area.

electronic retailing
Selling goods and services to ultimate customers (e.g., you and me) over the Internet.

telemarketing
The sale of goods and services by telephone.

Non-Store Retailing

Nothing else in retailing has received more attention recently than electronic retailing. This is just one form of non-store retailing. Other categories include telemarketing; vending machines, kiosks, and carts; and direct selling. Small businesses can use non-store retailing to open up new channels of distribution for their products.

Electronic Retailing

Electronic retailing consists of selling products to ultimate consumers (e.g., you and me) over the Internet. But getting customers is only half the battle. The other half is delivering the goods, providing helpful service, and keeping your customers. When electronic retailers fail to have sufficient inventory or fail to deliver goods on time (especially during holidays and other busy periods), customers give up and go back to brick-and-mortar stores.

Most Internet retailers now offer e-mail confirmation. But sometimes electronic retailers are not as strong at handling complaints, accepting returns, and providing personal help. Some are improving customer service by adding help buttons that lead customers to real-time assistance from a human employee.

Brick-and-mortar stores that add online outlets are also called brick-and-click stores. They allow customers to choose which shopping technique suits them best. Most companies that want to compete in the future will probably need both a real store and an online presence to provide customers with all the options they want.

Telemarketing

Telemarketing is the sale of goods and services by telephone. Telemarketing is used to supplement or replace in-store selling and to complement online selling. Many telemarketers send a catalogue to consumers and let them order by calling a toll-free number. As we noted, many electronic retailers provide a help feature online that serves the same function. Telemarketing is a $4 billion industry in Canada.[32] If you wish to reduce the number of telemarketing calls you receive, you may register your residential, wireless, fax, or VoIP telephone number(s) on the National Do Not Call List, which includes about 10.6 million registered phone and fax numbers.[33]

▸ Registration on the Do Not Call List will not eliminate all telemarketing calls as there are some exemptions. Examples include calls on behalf of Canadian registered charities and persons collecting information for a survey of members of the public.

Carts are convenient and easy for customers to use. They also have lower overhead than stores do. What do stores provide that kiosks and vending machines do not?

Vending Machines, Kiosks, and Carts

Vending machines dispense convenience goods when customers deposit sufficient money in the machine. These machines carry the benefit of location—they are found in airports, schools, office buildings, service stations, and other areas where people want convenience items. In Japan, they sell everything from bandages and face cloths to salads and spiced seafood. North American vending machines are already selling iPods, headphones, sneakers, digital cameras, and DVD movies.

Kiosks and carts have lower overhead costs than stores do, so they can offer lower prices on items such as T-shirts, purses, watches, and cell phones.[34] You often see vending carts outside stores on the sidewalk or along walkways in malls. Many mall owners love them because they are colourful and create a marketplace atmosphere.

Kiosk workers often dispense coupons and provide all kinds of helpful product information. You may have noticed airlines using kiosks to speed the process of getting on the plane. Most provide a boarding pass and allow you to change your seat. Many kiosks serve as a gateway to the Internet, so in one place customers can shop at a store and still have access to all of the products available on the Internet. Samsung Electronics Canada plans to open special Samsung-branded "Experience Zones" and "store-within-a-store" kiosks inside certain electronics and partner stores that will feature the company's products, including televisions, mobile phones, tablets, and appliances.[35] "We want to give consumers the opportunity to experience the brand and the products in a way that they've never seen before, that really takes that experience up," says Samsung Electronics President, James Politeski.[36]

direct selling
Selling to consumers in their homes or where they work.

Direct Selling

Direct selling reaches customers in their homes or workplaces. Because so many men and women work outside the home and are not in during the day, companies that use direct selling are sponsoring parties at workplaces or during evenings and weekends. Major users of this category include cosmetics producers and vacuum cleaner manufacturers. Trying to copy their success, other businesses are venturing into direct selling with lingerie, artwork, and candles sold at house parties they sponsor.

Cupcake Diner <*www.cupcakediner.ca*> is Canada's first mobile cupcake shop. Visit the company's site for a schedule of where you can find the 1950s diner-inspired mobile cupcake shop on any day. In addition to curbside service, Cupcake Diner caters to social events, corporate events, and weddings. Do you find this concept appealing?

Choosing the Right Distribution Mode

A *supply chain* is longer than a channel of distribution because it includes links from suppliers that provide raw materials to manufacturers, whereas the channel of distribution begins with manufacturers. Channels of distribution are part of the overall supply chain. A primary concern of supply-chain managers is selecting a transportation mode that will minimize costs and ensure a certain level of service. (*Modes,* in the language of distribution, are the various means used to transport goods, such as by truck, train, plane, ship, and pipeline.) Generally speaking, the faster the mode of transportation, the higher the cost.

Mode	Cost	Speed	On-Time Dependability	Flexibility Handling Products	Frequency of Shipments	Reach
Railroad	Medium	Slow	Medium	High	Low	High
Trucks	High	Fast	High	Medium	High	Most
Pipeline	Low	Medium	Highest	Lowest	Highest	Lowest
Ships (water)	Lowest	Slowest	Lowest	Highest	Lowest	Low
Airplane	Highest	Fastest	Low	Low	Medium	Medium

Figure 15.7

Comparing Transportation Modes

Combining trucks with railroads lowers cost and increases the number of locations reached. The same is true when combining trucks with ships. Combining trucks with airlines speeds goods long distances and gets them to almost any location.

Today, supply chains involve more than simply moving products from place to place; they involve all kinds of activities such as processing orders and taking inventory of products. In other words, logistics systems involve whatever it takes to see that the right products are sent to the right place quickly and efficiently.

The job of the supply-chain manager is to find the most efficient combination of these forms of transportation. Figure 15.7 shows the advantages and disadvantages of each mode.

PROGRESS ASSESSMENT

- What are some of the ways in which retailers compete?
- What kinds of products would call for each of the different distribution strategies: intensive, selective, and exclusive?
- Give examples of non-store retailing and describe each.
- Which transportation mode is fastest, which is cheapest, and which is most flexible?

PROMOTION AND THE PROMOTION MIX

Define promotion and list the five traditional tools that make up the promotion mix.

Recall from Chapter 14 that *promotion* consists of all techniques that sellers use to motivate customers to buy their products. Marketers use many different tools to promote their products and services. Traditionally, as shown in Figure 15.8, those tools include advertising, personal selling, public relations, sales promotion, and direct marketing. The combination of promotional tools an organization uses is called its **promotion mix**. The product is shown in the middle of the figure to illustrate the fact that the product itself can be a promotional tool such as when marketers give away free samples.

Each target group calls for a separate promotion mix. For example, large homogeneous groups of consumers (i.e., groups whose members share specific similar traits) are usually most efficiently reached through advertising. Large organizations are best reached through personal selling.

Integrated marketing communication (IMC) combines all promotional tools into one comprehensive and unified promotional strategy. The idea is to use all promotional tools and company resources to create a positive brand image and to meet the strategic marketing and promotional goals of the firm.[37] An ongoing challenge for marketers is to develop a mix that will break through the clutter of the over 3,000 daily marketing messages that consumers receive.[38] Let us briefly explore each of the promotional tools.

Figure 15.8

The Traditional Promotion Mix

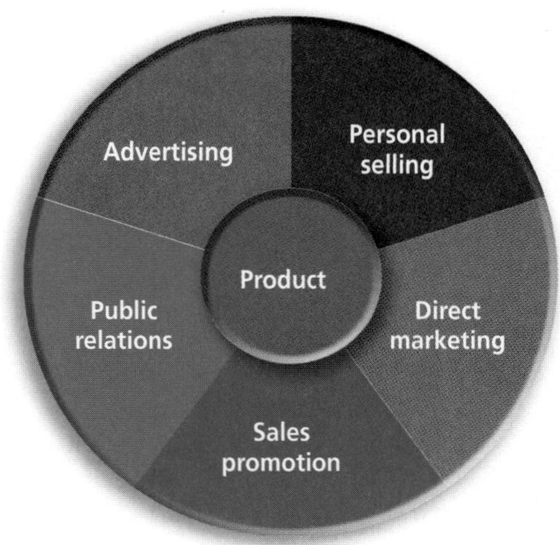

promotion mix
The combination of promotional tools an organization uses.

integrated marketing communication (IMC)
A technique that combines all promotional tools into one comprehensive and unified promotional strategy.

advertising
Paid, non-personal communication through various media by organizations and individuals who are in some way identified in the advertising message.

Advertising: Informing, Persuading, and Reminding

Advertising is paid, non-personal communication through various media by organizations and individuals who are in some way *identified in the message.* There are various categories of advertising, including retail advertising, product advertising, and online advertising.

According to GroupM <*www.groupm.com*>, total media ad spend in 2012 is expected to climb 3.9 percent from 2011 to reach approximately $13.4 billion. This reflects forecasted ad spend increases in digital advertising, TV, newspapers, and consumer magazines. The report notes that radio continues to be a strong medium in major Canadian markets. P&G reigns as Canada's biggest advertiser, spending $200 million in 2011, followed by GM ($143 million), Rogers Communications ($125 million), and the Government of Canada ($109 million).[39] Review the latest report. What has changed since this information was published?

How do we, as consumers, benefit from advertising expenditures? First, ads are informative. Direct mail is full of information about products, prices, features, store policies, and more. So is newspaper advertising. Second, not only does advertising inform us, but the money advertisers spend for commercial time pays the production costs of TV and radio programs. Advertising also covers the major costs of producing newspapers and magazines. Subscription and newsstand revenues cover only mailing and promotional costs. Figure 15.9 discusses the advantages and disadvantages of various advertising media to the advertiser. Notice that newspapers, radio, and the Yellow Pages are especially attractive to local advertisers.

Marketers must choose which media can best be used to reach the audience they desire. Radio advertising, for example, is less expensive than TV advertising and often reaches people when they have few other distractions, such as while they are driving. Radio is thus especially effective at selling services people do not usually read about

Figure 15.9

Advantages and Disadvantages of Various Advertising Media

The most effective media are often very expensive. The inexpensive media may not reach your market. The goal is to use the medium that can reach your desired market most efficiently.

Medium	Advantages	Disadvantages
Newspapers	Good coverage of local markets; ads can be placed quickly; high consumer acceptance; ads can be clipped and saved	Ads compete with other features in paper; poor colour; ads get thrown away with paper (short lifespan)
Television	Uses sight, sound, and motion; reaches all audiences; high attention with no competition from other material	High cost; short exposure time; takes time to prepare ads; digital video recorders skip over ads
Radio	Low cost; can target specific audiences; very flexible; good for local marketing	People may not listen to ad; depends on one sense (hearing); short exposure time; audience can't keep ad
Magazines	Can target specific audiences; good use of colour; long life of ad; ads can be clipped and saved	Inflexible; ads often must be placed weeks before publication; cost is relatively high
Outdoor	High visibility and repeat exposures; low cost; local market focus	Limited message; low selectivity of audience
Direct mail	Best for targeting specific markets; very flexible; ad can be saved	High cost; consumers may reject ad as junk mail; must conform to post office regulations
Yellow Pages–type advertising	Great coverage of local markets; widely used by consumers; available at point of purchase	Competition with other ads; cost may be high for very small businesses
Internet	Inexpensive global coverage; available at any time; interactive	Customers can leave the site before buying
Mobile advertising	Great reach among younger shoppers	Easy to ignore and avoid

in print media—services such as banking, mortgages, and continuing education, to name a few. On the other hand, radio has become so commercial-ridden that some people are switching to commercial-free satellite radio. Marketers also search for other places to put advertising, such as on video screens mounted in elevators.[40] Have you noticed ads on park benches and grocery carts?[41] You have certainly seen them on Web sites you visit.

Mobile marketing via cell phones started out mostly as text messages, but now Starbucks <*www.starbucks.ca*> can send signals to your phone as you approach the store, reminding you to stop in for a latte. Kraft Foods <*www.kraftfoodscompany.com*> developed the iPhone Assistant, an iPhone application that serves up recipes for users—recipes made with Kraft products.[42] Other retailers use e-mail advertisements to build brand awareness and drive people to their stores or Web sites.[43]

Another way to get more impact from advertising is to appeal to the interest in green marketing among consumers and businesses. A brief glance through magazines and the business press reveals all kinds of appeals that refer to sustainability and carbon-cutting.

Advocacy advertising, also known as cause advertising, is advertising that supports a particular view of an issue. The Media Foundation produces *Adbusters* <*www.adbusters.org/magazine*>, a non-profit "ecological magazine that is dedicated to examining the relationship between human beings and their physical and mental environment." What is the message being communicated in this ad?

Global Advertising

Global advertising involves developing a product and promotional strategy that can be implemented worldwide. Certainly, global advertising that is the same everywhere can save companies money in research and design. In some cases, however, promotions tailored to specific countries or regions may be much more successful since each country or region has its own culture, language, and buying habits.

Some problems do arise when marketers use one campaign in all countries. When a Japanese company tried to use English words to name a popular drink, it came up with Pocari Sweat, not a good image for most English-speaking people. Canadians may have difficulty with Krapp toilet paper from Sweden. Clairol introduced its curling iron, the Mist Stick, to the German market, not realizing that mist in German can mean "manure." As you can see, getting the words right in international advertising is tricky and critical, which calls for researching each country, designing appropriate ads, and testing them.

Even in Canada we have regional differences that are important enough to constitute separate market segments. Each province has its own history and culture. The large metropolitan areas such as Vancouver, Toronto, and Montreal are different from the rest of the provinces in which they are located. All require their own promotions and advertising.

Many marketers today are moving from globalism (one ad for everyone in the world) to regionalism (specific ads for each country or for specific groups within a country). In the future, marketers will prepare more custom-designed promotions to reach smaller audiences—audiences as small as one person.

Personal Selling: Providing Personal Attention

Personal selling is the face-to-face presentation and promotion of goods and services. It also involves the search for new prospects and follow-up service after the sale. Effective selling is not simply a matter of persuading others to buy. In fact, it

personal selling
The face-to-face presentation and promotion of goods and services.

"Beer and football are pretty synonymous. They've got the same demographics," said Brian Harris, CEO of the small Surrey, B.C.-based microbrewery, adding the target market for the brewery and the football team is males, aged 25–40.[44]

Segmenting the Consumer Market

There are several ways a firm can segment the consumer market, as outlined in Figure 14.7. For example, rather than trying to sell a product throughout Canada, you might try to focus on just one or two regions of the country where you might be most successful. Dividing the market by geographic area (i.e., cities, counties, provinces, etc.) is called **geographic segmentation**. A few years ago, HSBC Bank Canada <*www.hsbc.ca*> pursued an expansion strategy in Canada by building branches in growing suburban communities, as this is where HSBC's target customers live. Lindsay Gordon, CEO of HSBC Bank Canada, is a big believer in the "bricks and clicks" strategy: "With more customers doing their banking online, branches are becoming a destination for financial services and advice, rather than basic transactions."[45]

geographic segmentation Dividing the market by geographic area.

Alternatively, you could aim your product's promotions toward people aged 25 to 45 who have some post-secondary training and have above-average incomes. Automobiles such as Lexus are often targeted to this audience. Segmentation by age, income, and education level are ways of **demographic segmentation**. So are religion, ethnic origin, and profession. Demographics are the most widely used segmentation variable, but not necessarily the best.

demographic segmentation Dividing the market by age, income, and education level.

You may want your ads to portray a target group's lifestyle. To do that, you would study the group's values, attitudes, and interests in a strategy called **psychographic segmentation**. If you decide to target teenagers, you would do an in-depth study of their values and interests, like which TV shows they watch and which personalities they like the best. With that information you would develop advertisements for those TV shows using those stars.

psychographic segmentation Dividing the market using the group's values, attitudes, and interests.

When marketers use consumers' behaviour with or toward a product to segment the market, they are using **behavioural segmentation**.[46] Let us examine questions that you might ask while considering different variables of this segmentation strategy as it applies to Very Vegetarian:

behavioural segmentation Dividing the market based on behaviour with or toward a product.

- *Benefits Sought*—What benefits of vegetarianism and your food might you discuss? Should you emphasize freshness, heart-healthiness, taste, or something else? The Green Box highlights some concerns that consumers have raised about "green" advertising claims.
- *Usage Rate*—In marketing, the 80/20 rule says that 80 percent of your business is likely to come from just 20 percent of your customers. Determine who the big eaters are of vegetarian food. Does your restaurant attract more men or more women? More students or more faculty and staff members?
- *User Status*—Are your repeat customers from the local community or are they commuters? Once you know who your customer base is, you can design your promotions to better appeal to that specific group.

The best segmentation strategy is to use a combination of these variables to come up with a consumer profile that represents a *sizable, reachable,* and *profitable* target market. That may mean not segmenting the market at all and instead going after the is more accurately described today as helping others satisfy their wants and needs (again, helping the buyer buy).[44]

Given that perspective, you can see why salespeople use the Internet, laptop computers, paging devices, fax machines, and other technology to help customers search for information, design custom-made products, look over prices, and generally do everything it takes to complete the order. The benefit of personal selling is that there is a person to help you complete a transaction. The salesperson can listen to your needs, help you reach a solution, and do everything possible to make accomplishing it smoother and easier.

It is costly for firms to provide customers with personal attention, so those companies that retain salespeople must train them to be especially effective, efficient, and helpful. To attract new salespeople, companies are paying them quite well. The average cost of a single sales call to a potential business-to-business (B2B) buyer is about $400. Surely no firm would pay that much to send anyone but a skillful and highly trained professional salesperson and consultant.

The Business-to-Consumer (B2C) Sales Process

Most sales to consumers take place in retail stores where knowing the product comes first. However, it is important to understand as much as possible about the type of people who shop at a given store. One thing is certain, though: a salesperson needs to focus on the customer and refrain from talking to fellow salespeople—or, worse, talking on the phone to friends—while customers are around.

The first formal step in the B2C sales process, then, is the *approach.* Too many salespeople begin with a line like "May I help you?" but the answer too often is "No." A better approach is "How can I help you?" or simply "Welcome to our store." The idea is to show the customer that you are there to help and that you are friendly and knowledgeable.

Discover what the customer wants first, and then make *a presentation.* Show customers how your products meet their needs and answer questions that help them choose the right products for them.

public relations (PR)
The management function that evaluates public attitudes, changes policies and procedures in response to the public's requests, and executes a program of action and information to earn public understanding and acceptance.

Next comes the *trial close.* "Would you like me to put that on hold?" or "Will you be paying for that with your store credit card?" are two such efforts. Selling is an art, and a salesperson must learn how to walk the fine line between being helpful and being pushy. Often individual buyers need some time alone to think about the purchase. The salesperson must respect that need but still be clearly available when needed.

After-sale follow-up is an important but often neglected step. If the product is to be delivered, the salesperson should follow up to be sure it is delivered on time. The same is true if the product has to be installed. There is often a chance to sell more merchandise when a salesperson follows up on a sale. Figure 15.10 shows the B2C selling process.

Figure 15.10

Steps in the Business-to-Consumer (B2C) Selling Process

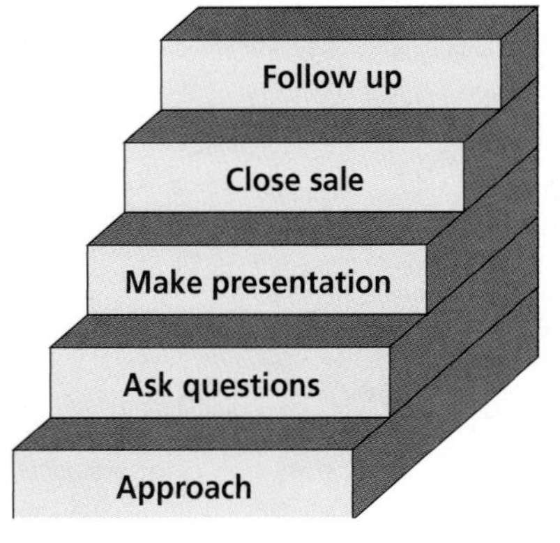

PROGRESS ASSESSMENT

- What are the five traditional elements of the promotion mix?
- Define integrated marking communication and explain why it is important.
- Define advertising and explain why advertising today is moving from globalism to regionalism.
- What are the five steps in the B2C selling process?

Public Relations: Building Relationships

Public relations (PR) is the management function that evaluates public attitudes, changes policies and procedures in response to the public's requests, and executes a program of action and information to earn public

MAKING ETHICAL DECISIONS

Is the Ad as Honest as the Product?

You are producing a high-fibre, nutritious cereal called Fiberrific and are having a modest degree of success. Research shows that your number of customers, or market segment, is growing but is still a relatively small percentage of breakfast cereal buyers. Generally, Fiberrific appeals mostly to health-conscious people aged 25 to 60. You are trying to broaden the appeal of your cereal to the under-25 and over-60 age groups. You know that Fiberrific is a tasty and healthy product that is good for customers. Joan, one of your managers, suggests that you stretch the truth a bit in your advertising and publicity material so that it will attract more consumers in the age groups you are targeting. After all, your product can't hurt anybody and is actually good for them.

Joan's idea is to develop two ads, each with two segments. The first segment of one ad would show a young woman on a tennis court holding a racquet and talking across the net to a young man. She is complaining that she seems to tire easily. The next segment would show the same two people, with the woman looking lively and saying that she tried this new breakfast cereal, Fiberrific, for two weeks and feels so energized, like a new person. A similar ad would be used to show two senior citizens walking uphill and talking. The first segment would show the man wondering why he tires so easily and the second one would show the same scene, with one man now a little ahead of the other, looking lively and stating that he is amazed at the improvement in his energy and endurance after eating Fiberrific for only two weeks. Would you go along with Joan's suggestion? What is your decision based on? Explain.

understanding and acceptance. The PR department maintains close ties with company stakeholders (e.g., customers, media, community leaders, and government officials). The idea is to establish and maintain a dialogue with all stakeholders so that the company can quickly respond to inquiries, complaints, and suggestions.[45]

Public relations is a good alternative to advertising. As newspapers cut back on their reporting staff, they are looking for other sources of news information, including publicity releases.[46] Linking up with bloggers has also become an important way to keep company names in the news.[47]

Publicity: The Talking Arm of PR

Publicity is the talking arm of public relations. **Publicity** is any information about an individual, product, or organization that is distributed to the public through the media and that is not paid for, or controlled, by the seller.

publicity
Any information about an individual, product, or organization that is distributed to the public through the media and that is not paid for or controlled by the seller.

Much skill is involved in writing such releases so that the media will want to publish them. You may need to write different stories for different media. One may introduce the new owners. Another may talk about the unusual product offerings. If the stories are published, news about your store will reach many potential consumers (and investors, distributors, and dealers), and you may be on your way to becoming a successful marketer. Publicity works only if the media find the material interesting or newsworthy. The idea, then, is to write publicity that meets those criteria.

Besides being free, publicity has several further advantages over other promotional tools, such as advertising. It may reach people who would not read an ad. It may appear on the front page of a newspaper or in some other prominent position, or be given air time on a television news show. Perhaps the greatest advantage of publicity is its believability. When a newspaper or magazine publishes a story as news, the reader treats that story as news—and news is more believable than advertising. Review the Making Ethical Decisions box for a dilemma that you might face as a marketer when you consider publicity.

Publicity has several disadvantages as well. For example, marketers have no control over whether, how, and when, the media will use the story. The media are not obligated to use a publicity release, and most are thrown away. Furthermore, the story may be altered so that it is not so positive. Also, once a story has run, it is not likely to be repeated. Advertising, in contrast, can be repeated as often as needed. One way to see that publicity is handled well by the media is to establish a friendly relationship with media representatives and being responsive with them when they seek information. Then, when you want their support, they are more likely to co-operate.

You might prepare a publicity release describing Very Vegetarian and the research results showing that consumers love it, and send it to the various media. What might your vegetarian restaurant do to help the community and thus create more publicity?

PROGRESS ASSESSMENT

- What is the responsibility of the public relations department?
- What are the advantages and disadvantages of publicity versus advertising?

Sales Promotion: Giving Buyers Incentives

sales promotion
The promotional tool that stimulates consumer purchasing and dealer interest by means of short-term activities.

Sales promotion is the promotional tool that stimulates consumer purchasing and dealer interest by means of short-term activities. Sales promotion programs are designed to supplement personal selling, advertising, and PR efforts by creating enthusiasm for the overall promotional program. See Figure 15.11 for a list of sales promotion techniques.

Sales promotion can take place both within and outside the company. Often it is just as important to generate employee enthusiasm about a product as it is to attract potential customers. The most important internal sales promotion efforts are directed at salespeople and other customer-contact people, such as customer-service representatives and clerks. Internal sales promotion efforts include (1) sales training; (2) the development of sales aids such as flip charts, portable audiovisual displays, and videotapes; and (3) participation in trade shows where salespeople can get leads.

After generating enthusiasm internally, marketers may want to make distributors and dealers eager to help promote the product. Trade shows allow marketing intermediaries to see products from many different sellers and make comparisons among them. Today, virtual trade shows on the Internet, called Webinars, enable buyers to see many products without leaving the office. Such promotions are usually interactive, so buyers can ask questions, and the information is available 24/7 (i.e., 24 hours a day, seven days a week).[48]

After the company's employees and intermediaries have been motivated with sales promotion efforts, the next step is to promote to final consumers using samples,

Figure 15.11

Business-to-Business and Consumer Sales Promotion Techniques

Business-to-Business	
Trade shows	Catalogues
Portfolios for salespeople	Conventions
Deals (price reductions)	Event sponsorship
Consumer Sales	
Coupons	Bonuses (buy one, get one free)
Cents-off promotions	Catalogues
Sampling	Demonstrations
Premiums	Special events
Sweepstakes	Lotteries
Contests	In-store displays

coupons, store demonstrations, rebates, displays, and so on. Sales promotion is an ongoing effort to maintain enthusiasm, so sellers use different strategies over time to keep the ideas fresh. You could put food displays in your Very Vegetarian restaurant to show customers how attractive the products look. You could also sponsor in-store cooking demonstrations to attract new vegetarians.

One popular sales promotion tool is sampling—letting consumers have a small sample of the product for no charge. Because many consumers will not buy a new product unless they have had a chance to see it or try it, grocery stores often have people handing out small portions of food and beverage products in the aisles. Sampling is a quick, effective way of demonstrating a product's superiority at a time when consumers are making a purchase decision. Standing outside Very Vegetarian and giving out samples would surely attract attention.

▸ Everyone likes a free sample. Sampling is a promotional strategy that lets people try a new product, often in a situation when they can buy it right away if they like it. What are some advantages of sampling food products that advertising can't duplicate?

Direct Marketing[49]

Direct marketing uses direct communication with consumers to generate a response in the form of an order, a request for further information, or a visit to a retail outlet. The communication can take many forms including face-to-face selling, direct mail, catalogues, telephone solicitation (e.g., telemarketing), and direct response advertising on television, radio, print, e-mail, social media, or over mobile communications devices. The Reaching Beyond Our Borders box at the end of this text part showcases a company that chooses to not produce catalogues as its products change frequently.

Like personal selling, direct marketing often consists of interactive communication. It also has the advantage of being customized to match the needs of specific target markets. Messages can be developed and adapted quickly to facilitate one-to-one relationships with customers.

While direct marketing has been one of the fastest-growing forms of promotion, it has several disadvantages. First, most forms of direct marketing require a comprehensive and up-to-date database with information about the target market. Developing and maintaining the database can be expensive and time-consuming. In addition, growing concern about privacy has led to a decline in response rates among some customer groups. The Dealing with Change box at the end of this text part highlights a piece of legislation that was enacted to protect consumer privacy. Companies with successful direct marketing programs are sensitive to these issues and often use a combination of direct marketing alternatives together, or direct marketing combined with other promotional tools, to increase value for customers.

sampling
A promotional tool in which a company lets consumers have a small sample of a product for no charge.

direct marketing
Uses direct communication with consumers to generate a response in the form of an order, a request for further information, or a visit to a retail outlet.

WORD OF MOUTH AND OTHER PROMOTIONAL TOOLS[50]

Although word of mouth was not traditionally listed as one of the major promotional efforts (it was not considered to be manageable), it is now one of the most effective, especially on the Internet. In word-of-mouth promotion, people tell other people about products they have purchased.

When James and Ann Scaggs started a company that repairs iPods, customers were hesitant to part with their units without assurance they would be fixed properly. The Scaggs implemented a Web 2.0 system for collecting and displaying word

word-of-mouth promotion
A promotional tool that involves people telling other people about products they have purchased.

buzz marketing
Popularity created by consumer word of mouth.

blog
An online diary (Web log) that looks like a Web page but is easier to create and update by posting text, photos, or links to other sites.

podcasting
A means of distributing audio and video programs via the Internet that lets users subscribe to a number of files, also known as feeds, and then hear or view the material at the time they choose.

of mouth in the form of customer feedback on their Web site. Sales immediately went up. Anything that encourages people to talk favourably about an organization can be effective word of mouth. Notice, for example, how stores use clowns, banners, music, fairs, and other attention-getting devices to create word of mouth. Clever commercials can also generate word of mouth. The more that people talk about your products and your brand name, the more easily customers remember them when they shop. You might enjoy brainstorming strategies for creating word of mouth about Very Vegetarian.

Increasingly, companies are working hard to stimulate positive word of mouth about their goods and services. Have you recently heard about a new product, movie, Web site, book, or restaurant from someone you know, or a complete stranger? If so, you may have had a buzz experience. **Buzz marketing** is popularity created by consumer word of mouth.

The electronic or online version of word of mouth is called *viral marketing.* This involves the use of messages "infectious" enough that consumers wish to pass them along to others through online forums, social networks, chat rooms, bulletin boards, blogs, message boards threads, instant messages, and e-mails. People who agree to promote products in this way may get what the industry calls *swag*—free tickets, backstage passes, T-shirts, and other such merchandise. What do you think of the ethics of rewarding people to promote goods and services?

Word of mouth is so powerful that negative word of mouth can hurt a firm. Criticism of a product or company can spread through online forums, chat rooms, bulletin boards, and Web sites. Addressing consumer complaints quickly and effectively is one of the best ways to reduce the effects of negative word of mouth.

Blogging

A **blog**—short for Web log—is an online diary that looks like a Web page but is easier to create and update by posting text, photos, or links to other sites. There are millions of blogs on the Internet, and thousands of new ones are added each day.[51] How do blogs affect marketing? When a book called *Freakonomics* was about to be released, the publisher sent advance copies to 100 bloggers. These bloggers sent reviews to other bloggers (word of mouth), and soon *Freakonomics* was number three on *Amazon.com*'s list of most-ordered books. You can imagine what blogging can do to promote movies, TV shows, and more.

Podcasting

Podcasting is a means of distributing audio and video programs via the Internet. It lets users subscribe to a number of files, also known as feeds, and then hear or view the material when they choose. Podcasting allows you to become your own newscaster, since—besides giving broadcast radio and TV a new distribution medium—it enables independent producers to create self-published, syndicated "radio shows." Many companies have also found success in creating videos for YouTube.

Mobile Media

With mobile media, marketers make use of the cell phone, using text messaging to promote sweepstakes, send customers news or sports alerts, and give them company information.[52] Companies can now determine where you are and send you messages about restaurants and other services in your vicinity.[53] Despite some technological glitches to work through, mobile marketing is catching on.

▸ Mobile media allow marketers to reach customers through text messaging. Have you received such promotional messages? For which products are they most effective?

Are you getting the idea that traditional promotional methods are slowly but surely being replaced by new technology? If so, you are getting the right idea. By keeping up with the latest trends, you may be able to grab a good job in promotion while traditionalists are still wondering what happened.

push strategy
Promotional strategy in which the producer uses advertising, personal selling, sales promotion, and all other promotional tools to convince wholesalers and retailers to stock and sell merchandise.

pull strategy
Promotional strategy in which heavy advertising and sales promotion efforts are directed toward consumers so that they will request the products from retailers.

MANAGING THE PROMOTION MIX: PUTTING IT ALL TOGETHER

Each target group calls for a separate promotion mix. Advertising is most efficient for reaching large groups of consumers whose members share similar traits. Personal selling is best for selling to large organizations. To motivate people to buy now rather than later, marketers use sales promotions like sampling, coupons, discounts, special displays, and premiums. Publicity supports other efforts and can create a good impression among all consumers. Word of mouth is often the most powerful promotional tool. Generate it by listening, being responsive, and creating an impression worth passing on to others that you spread through blogging and podcasting.

Push and Pull Strategies

How do producers move products to consumers? In a **push strategy**, the producer uses advertising, personal selling, sales promotion, and all other promotional tools to convince wholesalers and retailers to stock and sell merchandise, *pushing* products through the distribution system to the stores. If the push strategy works, consumers will walk into a store, see the product, and buy it.

A **pull strategy** directs heavy advertising and sales promotion efforts toward *consumers.* If the pull strategy works, consumers will go to the store and ask for the products. The store owner will order them from the wholesaler, who in turn will order them from the producer. Products are thus *pulled* through the distribution system.

Dr Pepper <*www.drpepper.com*> has used TV advertising in a pull strategy to increase distribution. Tripledge, a maker of windshield wipers, also tried to capture the interest of retail stores through a pull strategy. Of course, a company could use both strategies in a major promotional effort. The latest pull and push strategies are being conducted on the Internet, with companies sending messages to both consumers and businesses.

It has been important to make promotion part of a total systems approach to marketing. The idea is to develop a total product offer that would appeal to everyone: manufacturers, distributors, retailers, and consumers.

▸ Fox 40 International Inc. is a family run and operated business. This ad promotes the evolution of the pealess whistle products. It also depicts a new generation of referees from the Foxcroft family as founder Ron Foxcroft's son, Ronnie, can be seen here in action. Is this ad an example of a push strategy or a pull strategy? To learn more about this new product, read the running case part near the end of this chapter.

PROGRESS ASSESSMENT

- What are the sales promotion techniques used to reach consumers and businesses?
- Why has direct marketing become popular?
- Describe word-of-mouth promotion and list three other promotional tools.
- How does a push strategy differ from a pull strategy?

SUMMARY

Explain the concept of a total product offer and summarize the functions of packaging.

A total product offer consists of everything that consumers evaluate when deciding whether to buy something.

What's included in a total product offer?

A total product offer includes price, brand name, satisfaction in use, and more.

What's the difference between a product line and a product mix?

A product line is a group of physically similar products with similar competitors. A product line of gum may include bubble gum and sugarless gum. A product mix is a company's combination of product lines. A manufacturer may offer lines of gum, candy bars, and so on.

What are the functions of packaging?

The functions of packaging include the following: (1) attract the buyer's attention; (2) protect the goods inside, stand up under handling and storage, be tamperproof, and deter theft; (3) be easy to open and use; (4) describe the contents; (5) explain the benefits of the good inside; (6) provide information about warranties, warnings, and other consumer matters; and (7) indicate price, value, and uses.

Contrast *brand, brand name, and trademark,* and discuss the concept of brand equity.

A *brand* is a name, symbol, or design (or combination thereof) that identifies the goods or services of one seller or group of sellers and distinguishes them from the goods and services of competitors. The word *brand* includes all means of identifying a product. A *brand name* consists of a word, letter, or group of words or letters that differentiates one seller's goods and services from those of competitors. A *trademark* is a brand that has exclusive legal protection for both its brand name and design.

What is brand equity and brand loyalty?

Brand equity is the value of a brand name and associated symbols. The core of brand equity is brand loyalty, which is the degree to which customers are satisfied, like the brand, and are committed to further purchases.

Describe the product life cycle.

The product life cycle is a theoretical model of what happens to sales and profits for a product class over time.

What are the four stages in the product life cycle?

The four product life cycle stages are introduction, growth, maturity, and decline.

List the various pricing objectives and strategies, and explain why non-pricing strategies are growing in importance.

Pricing is one of the four Ps of marketing.

What are pricing objectives?

Objectives include achieving a target profit, building traffic, increasing market share, creating an image, and meeting social goals.

What's the break-even point?

At the break-even point, total cost equals total revenue. Sales beyond that point are profitable. An example is

$$\text{BEP} = \frac{\text{FC}}{\text{P} - \text{VC}} = \frac{\$200{,}000}{\$4.00 - \$2.00} = \frac{\$200{,}000}{\$2.00} = 100{,}000 \text{ items}$$

What strategies can marketers use to determine a product's price?

For new products, a skimming price strategy is one in which the product is priced high to make optimum profit while there's little competition, whereas a penetration strategy is one in which a product is priced low to attract more customers and discourage competitors. Cost-oriented pricing occurs when producers often use cost as a primary basis for setting price. Demand-oriented pricing is based on consumer demand rather than cost. Competition-oriented pricing is a strategy based on all competitors' prices. Price leadership occurs when all follow the pricing practice of one or more dominant companies.

Why do companies use non-price strategies?

Pricing is one of the easiest marketing strategies to copy. Therefore, often it is not a good long-run competitive tool. Instead, marketers may compete using non-price strategies that are less easy to copy, including offering great service, educating consumers, and establishing long-term relationships with customers.

Explain the concept of marketing channels and the value of marketing intermediaries.

A channel of distribution consists of a set of marketing intermediaries, such as agents, brokers, wholesalers, and retailers, that join together to transport and store goods in their path (or channel) from producers to consumers.

How do marketing intermediaries add value?

Intermediaries perform certain marketing tasks—such as transporting, storing, selling, advertising, and relationship building—faster and cheaper than most manufacturers could. Channels of distribution ensure communication flows and the flow of money and title to goods. They also help ensure that the right quantity and assortment of goods will be available when and where needed.

What are the principles behind the use of such intermediaries?

Marketing intermediaries can be eliminated, but their activities cannot. Intermediary organizations have survived in the past because they have performed marketing functions faster and more cheaply than others could. Intermediaries add costs to products, but these costs are usually more than offset by the value they create.

Discuss retailing and explain the various kinds of non-store retailing.

A retailer is an organization that sells to ultimate consumers.

What are three distribution strategies that marketers use?

Marketers use three basic distribution strategies: intensive (putting products in as many places as possible), selective (choosing only a few stores in a chosen market), and exclusive (using only one store in each market area).

What is non-store retailing?

Non-store retailing is retailing done outside a traditional store. Non-store retailing includes electronic retailing; telemarketing (marketing by phone); vending machines, kiosks, and carts (marketing by putting products in convenient locations, such as in the halls of shopping centres); and direct selling (marketing by approaching consumers in their homes or places of work). Telemarketing can also be used as part of direct marketing, which is a promotional tool.

Define promotion and list the five traditional tools that make up the promotion mix.

Promotion is an effort by marketers to inform and remind people in the target market about products and to persuade them to participate in an exchange.

What are the five traditional promotional tools that make up the promotional mix?

The five traditional promotional tools are advertising, personal selling, public relations, sales promotion, and direct marketing.

How are sales promotion activities used both within and outside the organization?

Internal sales promotion efforts are directed at salespeople and other customer-contact people to keep them enthusiastic about the company. Internal sales promotion activities include sales training, sales aids, audiovisual displays, and trade shows. External sales promotion (promotion to consumers) involves using samples, coupons, cents-off deals, displays, store demonstrators, premiums, and other such incentives.

What are examples of other promotional tools?

In word-of-mouth promotion, people tell other people about products they have purchased. Examples of word-of-mouth promotion include buzz marketing and viral marketing. Other promotional tools include blogging, podcasting, and mobile media.

What is the difference between a push strategy and a pull strategy?

In a push strategy, the producer uses advertising, personal selling, sales promotion, and all other promotional tools to convince wholesalers and retailers to stock and sell merchandise, *pushing* it through the distribution system to the stores. A pull strategy directs heavy advertising and sales promotion efforts toward *consumers.* If the pull strategy works, consumers will go to the store and ask for the products. The store owner will order them from the wholesaler, who in turn will order them from the producer. Products are thus *pulled* through the distribution system.

KEY TERMS

advertising
agents/brokers
blog
brand
brand awareness
brand equity
brand loyalty
brand manager
break-even analysis
buzz marketing
channel of distribution
competition-based pricing
direct marketing
direct selling
electronic retailing
everyday low pricing (EDLP)
exclusive distribution
high–low pricing strategy
integrated marketing communication (IMC)
intensive distribution
marketing intermediaries
penetration price strategy
personal selling
podcasting
price leadership
product differentiation
product life cycle
product line
product mix
promotion mix
psychological pricing
public relations (PR)
publicity
pull strategy
push strategy
retailer
sales promotion
sampling
selective distribution
skimming price strategy
target costing
telemarketing
total fixed costs
total product offer
value
variable costs
wholesaler
word of mouth promotion

CRITICAL THINKING

1. What value enhancers affected your choice of the school you attend? Did you consider size, location, price, reputation, library services, sports, placement, and selection of courses offered? What factors were most important? Why?
2. Which intermediary do you think is most important and why? If intermediaries were eliminated, would financial returns to the producers go up or down? Why?
3. What kind of products do you think you would enjoy selling? Think of the customers for that product. Can you imagine yourself going through the selling process with them? Which steps would be the hardest? Which would be the easiest? Can you picture yourself going through most of the sales process on the phone (telemarketing)?
4. As interactive communications between companies and customers grow, do you think traditional advertising will grow or decline? What will be the effect of growth or decline on the price we pay for TV programs, newspapers, and magazines?
5. How have blogging and podcasting affected other media you use, like news sites, newspapers, or television? Do you think blogging is an influential word-of-mouth promotional tool?

DEVELOPING WORKPLACE SKILLS

1. Look around your classroom and notice the different types of shoes students are wearing. Ask what product qualities were they looking for when they chose their shoes? How important were price, style, brand name, and colour? Describe the product offerings you would feature in a new shoe store designed to appeal to students.
2. How important is price to you when buying the following products: shoes, milk, computers, haircuts, and transportation (e.g., airline)? What non-price factors are more important, if at all, in making these choices? How much time does it take to evaluate factors other than price when making such purchases?

3. Imagine that you are involved in a money-raising activity for your school. You decide to sell large pizzas for $12 each. You buy a used pizza oven for $12,000. That is the only fixed cost. The variable cost per unit is $6. Calculate the break-even point and decide whether you should go ahead with the project. That is, do you think you could sell enough pizzas to make a sizable profit?
4. List at least four products that you've seen or purchased that are clearly "green" products. How much influence do green promotions have on your purchasing decisions? What can businesses do to be proactive in today's (more) environmentally conscious society?
5. In small groups, make a list of five products (goods and services) that most students own or use and then discuss which promotional techniques (advertising, personal selling, public relations, sales promotions, and direct marketing) prompted them to buy these goods and services. Which tool seems to be most effective for your group? Why do you suppose that is?

ANALYZING MANAGEMENT DECISIONS

Measuring Marketing Effectiveness

One of the major issues facing marketers today is measuring the effectiveness of various marketing campaigns. In the past, marketers set a budget for advertising, personal selling, and the like based on past sales or the need to push future sales. Measuring results has always been difficult and was given less attention. Now, however, marketers are demanding more accountability from their advertising agencies, their sales forces, and their Web site activities. They want to know who is receiving their messages and what the results are.

Many companies do not know how to establish such *metrics,* or measures of effectiveness. Digital media have more accurate metrics, and these are forcing marketers to find more reliable statistics for traditional marketing methods like TV advertising. Some companies have turned to the finance department to help develop metrics. The question often comes down to whether the measure should be of sales or of consumer attitudes. Some 60 percent of marketers measure consumer attitudes as a result of marketing campaigns, but fewer than 40 percent use the data for preparing their marketing budgets, preferring instead to rely on their own instincts.

Discussion Questions

1. You are planning a marketing campaign for Very Vegetarian. How might you go about measuring the effectiveness of your advertising?
2. What would your reaction be if you found potential customers had heard about your restaurant but had not yet acted on that information and come in to buy?
3. Using your own reactions, discuss what marketing tools are most effective in reaching students and others. Talk with fellow students from different ethnic and age groups to determine whether their answers are different from yours and how.

PART 5 ENDS WITH:

DEALING WITH CHANGE

The Personal Information Protection and Electronic Documents Act (PIPEDA)

The use of personal information in Canadian commercial activities is protected by federal legislation under the Personal Information Protection and Electronic Documents Act (PIPEDA), or by provincial legislation that is "substantially similar" to the federal legislation. PIPEDA applies to both traditional, paper-based business as well as online commercial activities. PIPEDA was enacted to alleviate consumer concerns about privacy and to allow Canada's business community to compete in the global digital economy. Organizations that make changes to their business practices as a result of this legislation demonstrate their respect for, and protection of, personal information. They will gain a cutting edge on the competition, and complying with PIPEDA will build trust in the digital marketplace and create opportunities for Canadian businesses.

As a result of this legislation, Canadian organizations need to develop and implement privacy policies. There are a set of ten principles that organizations must follow when collecting, using and disclosing personal information in the course of commercial activity. The principles include:

- *Accountability*—An organization is responsible for personal information under its control and shall designate an individual or individuals who are accountable for the organization's compliance with the principles of the Act.
- *Identifying Purposes*—The purposes for which personal information is collected shall be identified by the organization at or before the time the information is collected.
- *Consent*—The knowledge and consent of the individual are required for the collection, use, or disclosure of personal information, except where inappropriate.
- *Limiting Use, Disclosure, and Retention*—Personal information shall not be used or disclosed for purposes other than those for which it was collected, except with the consent of the individual or as required by law. Personal information shall be retained only as long as necessary for the fulfillment of those purposes.

PIPEDA defines personal information as "information about an identifiable individual" that includes any personal information, recorded or not, in any form, including digital or paper format. For example, the following would be considered personal information: your name, address, telephone number, and gender; identification numbers, income, or blood type; and credit records, loan records, existence of a dispute between a consumer and a merchant, and intentions to acquire goods or services. The legislation also protects personal information of a sensitive nature, which may include health or medical history, racial or ethnic origin, political opinions, religious beliefs, trade union membership, and sexual orientation.

Let us consider one investigation conducted under PIPEDA. The Canadian Internet Policy and Public Interest Clinic, a public advocacy group, filed a complaint with the Office of the Privacy Commissioner of Canada against Facebook. Issues of concerns included the following: sharing of personal information with third-party developers creating Facebook applications such as games and quizzes; privacy settings not being transparent and accessible enough to users; and how Facebook presented information related to date of birth, account deactivation and deletion, advertising, and personal information of non-users. As a result of Facebook's undertakings in response to the Office's findings, the issues were resolved and this investigation was officially closed.

The Office has since received further complaints about issues that were not part of the initial investigation. It is now examining Facebook's invitation feature (the process by which Facebook suggests friends to new users), and Facebook social plug-ins (the Facebook "Like" buttons that other Web sites can add to their sites). Do you see the need for such oversight?

Source: "Facebook investigation follow-up complete," Office of the Privacy Commissioner of Canada, 22 September 2010, www.priv.gc.ca/media/nr-c/2010/bg_100922_e.asp; "The Digital Economy in Canada," Industry Canada, 19 December 2008, www.ic.gc.ca/eic/site/ecic-ceac.nsf/eng/h_gv00464.html; and the Personal Information Protection and Electronic Documents Act (PIPEDA), http://laws-lois.justice.gc.ca/eng/acts/P-8.6/index.html.

REACHING BEYOND OUR BORDERS

Reach High with lululemon athletica

After 20 years in the surf, skate, and snowboard business, founder Chip Wilson took his first commercial yoga class in Vancouver and found the result exhilarating. The post-yoga feeling was so close to surfing and snowboarding that he began to build a business with a yoga focus. At the time, cotton clothing was being used for sweaty, stretchy power yoga and seemed completely inappropriate to Wilson, whose passion lay in technical athletic fabrics. From this, a design studio was born that became a yoga studio at night to pay the rent. Clothing was offered for sale and an underground yoga clothing movement was born.

Founded in 1998, lululemon athletica <*www.lululemon.com*> is a yoga-inspired athletic apparel company for both women and men. By producing products that help keep people active and stress free, lululemon believes that the world will be a better place. Setting the bar in technical fabrics and functional designs, lululemon works with yogis and athletes in local communities for continuous research and product feedback.

The company's first real store opened in the beach area of Vancouver, called Kitsilano, in November of 2000. The idea was to have the store be a community hub where people could learn and discuss the physical aspects of healthy living from yoga and diet to running and cycling as well as the mental aspects of living a powerful life of possibilities. Unfortunately for this concept, the store became so busy that it was impossible to help the customer in this way in addition to selling the product. So the focus of training shifted solely to the lululemon educator or staff person.

Styles and colours are constantly updated within each season. Photos and information on the company's newest products can be reviewed and purchased on the company's online Web site. Customers can interact with staff at lululemon athletica and learn about the full benefits and technical features of the products. lululemon is also available via wholesale partners in yoga, Pilates, and fitness studios.

lululemon has gone from a niche Vancouver start-up specializing in yoga gear to an international lifestyle brand worth nearly $5 billion. The company has grown to more than 150 stores and has launched dance, swimming, cycling, hiking, and casual wear lines. Work is done with factories in Canada, the United States, China, Taiwan, South Korea, Peru, Israel, Cambodia, Thailand, and Vietnam that share the company's commitment to quality and ethics. It is vital for lululemon to keep a manufacturing base in Vancouver for security and speed-to-market of its core designs.

Sources: "lululemon athletica inc. announces fourth quarter and full year fiscal 2011 results," lululemon athletic inc., 22 March 2012, www.lululemon.com/media/index.php?id=219; "lululemon's Christine Day named CEO of the year," CANOE Inc., 23 November 2011, http://cnews.canoe.ca/CNEWS/Canada/2011/11/23/19008561.html; and Timothy Taylor, "CEO of the Year: Christine Day of lululemon," *The Globe and Mail*, 24 November 2011, www.theglobeandmail.com/report-on-business/rob-magazine/ceo-of-the-year-christine-day-of-lululemon/article4252293/.

RUNNING CASE

Marketing: The Fox 40® Sonik Blast Whistle: Breaking the Sound Barrier!

The formation of Fox 40 International Inc. (Fox 40) is the result of a dream for a pealess whistle. When successful Canadian entrepreneur Ron Foxcroft began developing his first whistle, he was motivated by his knowledge and experience as an international basketball referee. Frustrated with faulty pea whistles, he spent three years of development with design consultant Chuck Shepherd. They had about 25 prototypes but narrowed them down after two years to 14 prototypes, and then down to two prototype whistles that worked.

First introduced in 1987, the Fox 40® Classic Whistle is a finely tuned precision instrument does not use a pea to generate sound. In fact, there are no moving parts. The patented design moves the air blast through three tuned chambers. This whistle, and all the subsequent whistles that have since been introduced, is 100 percent constructed of high-impact ABS plastic so it is impervious to moisture. Wet or dry, Fox 40® Pealess Whistles cannot be overblown and never fail—the harder you blow, the louder the sound! They can be heard for miles and work in all conditions. They are faultless, reliable, and trusted.

How did Ron tackle the $150,000 debt that he had incurred in developing the Fox 40® Classic Whistle? The answer is marketing. "I took the two whistles to the Pan Am Games in August 1987. I went upstairs in the dorm where the referees were living, and at 2 a.m., I blew the Whistle. Hundreds of referees opened the doors, standing there in their underwear, wondering what kind of whistle they heard. The next day, I got orders for 20,000 Whistles at $6.00 each in U.S. funds. That was $8.00 per Whistle in Canadian funds. My $150,000 debt was covered."

Over the years, Fox 40® has continued to introduce new whistles in its Whistle product line. One such example is the Fox 40® Sonik Blast. This Whistle was in response to referee requests for a louder whistle in large stadiums. Let us consider how the four Ps of marketing were applied to this product.

Product: Introduced in 2010, the Fox 40® Sonik Blast is a two-chamber Whistle that exceeds 120 decibels of sound. (This is louder than the Fox 40® Classic Whistle's 115 decibels of power.) It also has no down side, which means that it does not matter which side you put in your mouth as both sides are up. As a result, a referee (or anyone else that uses the Whistle) does not have to think about which side of the Whistle needs to go "up" before blowing it. To slow down counterfeiters, the cushioned mouth guard (CMG) feature became available at the same time. The CMG is a cushioned mouthgrip for better grip, better control, and a softer feel on one's teeth.

In support of its GREEN PLAN the company has changed its packaging. The packaging is made from recycled water and pop bottles that use virgin Polyethylene Terephthalate (PET). The switch to PET plastic for the blister is more environmentally friendly. There has also been a movement away from clam packaging. This has been replaced with a packaging system that uses Radio Frequency (RF) and Heat, known as RF/Heat Packaging, to seal the blister within two cards. The blister and cards can be separated and added to Blue Box recycling. An added benefit is that the packaging is tamper proof. Included in each package is print material that contains recyclable and/or recycled post-consumer waste material. This colourful cardboard communicates the product's brand name and benefits, head office location, and contact information.

According to Dave Foxcroft, President and COO, one advantage that the company has in manufacturing the Whistles in Canada is that they can build to order products and different packages, given the market. Since different markets require different packages, the actual package will vary depending on the marketing channel. For example, the package and label for a Fox 40® Whistle sold in a Canadian Tire store may be different for a Whistle that is targeted to referees in the sports aisle versus a Whistle that is placed in the marine area. Lately, Dave has noticed that more distributors are moving away from these private labels (whereby Fox 40® manufactures the product with the distributor's name on it) and requesting that the Whistles focus on the Fox 40® brand. These distributors were noticing that they were losing sales as customers were looking specifically for the Fox 40 brand and did not realize that the private labels were also Fox 40® Whistles.

The total product offer also includes the high level of service that employees provide to customers. "We stand out," states Ron. "When you call the company, you get a live person. You don't need to go through layers of management to get an answer. The employee can answer a question or find someone right away to answer the question. Customers will not get unanswered questions."

Price: Similar to the other Whistles, the Fox 40® Sonik Blast is a premium-priced whistle. This is justified by the product's features, benefits, and high quality. When the Whistle was first introduced, an introductory promotional price was offered to the company's distributors, including trade show specials. The price Fox 40® charges to its distributors varies depending on several factors: the target market (e.g., sports or marine); the geographic market; and the volume purchased. For example, some global markets are driven by price versus quality. While the suggested retail price is $8.95, it is the distributors that ultimately set the price in their markets. According to Dave, "These distributors own their markets and they know the best price to charge in their specific area. Fox 40® provides its customers with the best products and the goal is that all of the channel members in the distribution channel are financially successful along the way."

Pricing decisions are influenced by many factors that impact costs. For example, Dave cites the ever-changing government regulations around the world in reference to colour, plastics, chemicals, etc. As a result, the Whistle is not the same today as it was 20 years ago due to product restrictions. According to Juliana Child, Manager, Marketing & Events, the company also considers the cost of new imprinting techniques that produce better quality logos. Given such changes, the costs and price are revised annually for imprinted products.

Place: The majority of sales are generated through an indirect channel of distribution. Fox 40® follows a B2B marketing channel structure that incorporates distributors between the company and its ultimate users. These distributors perform a variety of marketing channel functions including selling, stocking, and delivering the Fox 40 products.

Customers interested in buying Fox 40® products can do so directly from established distributors and retail partners or through electronic marketing channels such as *www.fox40shop.com*. If a customer chooses to purchase a product through this direct online site, a commission is paid to the local distributor or retail partner.

The commission can be used toward future purchases. This unique arrangement is in recognition of the importance of this business-to-business relationship and the company's commitment to support its channel members. For those channel members that choose to join the site, Fox 40 communicates their information (e.g., name and location) in the package that includes the ordered product. This way, customers are made aware of local channel members for future purchases. Information is also sent to channel members about products that are being ordered by customers in their local area so that they can review products that they carry.

Promotion: The overall promotion budget is 12 percent of the previous year's sales. Money is directed primarily in the areas of advertising and sales. This budget is broken down as follows:

- 65 percent is allocated to direct sales (45 percent is for awareness and 25 percent includes online social media activities, support of the *www.fox40shop.com* site, etc.)
- 9 percent is allocated to research and development
- 6 percent is allocated to public relations (which includes community social responsibility initiatives)
- 20 percent is allocated to trade shows and customer visits

When the Fox 40® Sonik Blast was introduced, *public relations* activities included media releases that highlighted the features and benefits of the new product. Web blasts were sent to channel members in the different segments (i.e., marine, safety, etc.) via e-mail marketing tool, Constant Contact. Fox 40 also has a B2B online site where channel members can access information such as catalogues, product images, etc. While the paper catalogue continues to be available as it remains the company's best sales tool, the online site supports channel members.

Advertising is a large part of the promotional budget. While on occasion there may be ads that highlight only one Whistle, the majority of ads highlight the family of Fox 40® Whistles. Advertising in trade magazines that target the company's different markets, such as *REFEREE Magazine,* occurred to promote the Fox 40® Sonik Blast. Social media initiatives were also created to introduce the new product. This included banner ads and Facebook advertising.

Product seeding was *a trade sales promotion* strategy that was targeted to channel members. This form of sampling meant getting the product into the hands of those that would actually use the Whistle. For example, free Fox 40® Sonik Blast Whistles, with the distributor's contact information printed on them, were sent to approved distributors. These distributors were then encouraged to hand out the free Whistles to users in their markets.

When you consider *personal selling* efforts, company representatives attend approximately 20 trade shows per year. The product was promoted at trade shows that target the sport, safety, outdoor, pet, and marine markets. Occasionally, a show promotion was offered but it was primarily the distributor that would offer the promotion. Distributor site visits around the world are also an ongoing aspect of the personal selling element of the promotion mix. These efforts are used to maintain and build long-term and profitable relationships with global distributors.

Increasingly, company attention is focusing on *direct marketing.* Information from current customers and prospects that is generated at trade shows is updated in the company's database. Personalized communications (i.e., e-blasts, letters, etc.) are created and sent out. This is followed by personal communication to confirm if a sale could be generated. There is a particular focus on current customers. As Ron states, "The best increase in sales is from within the company."

Fox 40 also runs a promotional products division. Approximately 65 percent of all Whistles sold have another organization's logo on them. According to Juliana, since the Fox 40® brand is so well established, it can effectively be directed to promotional sales. This co-branding is another opportunity to link the Fox 40® brand with a company brand that is meaningful to the receiver of the Whistle. Given the different package and imprint capabilities, the company can quickly fill personalized orders. Dave believes that this number will increase to 70 percent by mid-2013 as safety awareness is growing. "Organizations recognize the increasing importance of safety," says Dave. "These organizations want to associate themselves with a superior performing safety brand like Fox 40®."

Sources: Ron Foxcroft, Founder and CEO, and Dave Foxcroft, President and COO, Fox 40 International Inc., in-person interviews, 25 June 2012, Hamilton; "The Fox 40 pea-less whistle story," Canada.com, 4 April 2012, www.canada.com/sports/football/less+whistle+story/6410154/story.html; Kelley Horton, Vice President Sales, Fox 40 International Inc., interview, 24 June 2008; Juliana Child, Manager, Marketing & Events, Fox 40 International Inc., interview, 24 June 2008; and "Not An Inadvertent Whistle," *REFEREE,* July 2007, 45–47

Discussion Questions

1. What new-product pricing strategy did Fox 40 International Inc. use for the Fox 40® Sonik Blast?
2. What retail distribution strategy do you think is used for the Fox 40® Sonik Blast? Justify your answer.
3. Which promotional strategy is the most effective when selling the Fox 40® Sonik Blast? Explain.

PART 6

CHAPTER 16

UNDERSTANDING ACCOUNTING AND FINANCIAL INFORMATION

LEARNING OBJECTIVES

After you have read and studied this chapter, you should be able to:

LO 1 Describe the role that accounting and financial information play for a business and for its stakeholders.

LO 2 Identify the different disciplines within the accounting profession.

LO 3 List the steps in the accounting cycle, distinguish between accounting and bookkeeping, and explain how computers are used in accounting.

LO 4 Explain how the major financial statements differ.

LO 5 Describe the role of accounting rules and principles in reporting financial information.

LO 6 Demonstrate the application of ratio analysis with financial information.

PROFILE

GETTING TO KNOW DEBORAH WATT OF LOCKHEED MARTIN CANADA INC.

Lockheed Martin Corporation has been a valued partner to the Canadian military since 1937, when it first established a business presence. Today, more than 500 professionals work in locations across the country in support of all branches of the Canadian Forces.

Lockheed Martin Canada *<www.lockheedmartin.com/ca.html>* is the prime contractor for the modernization of the combat systems on board the HALIFAX Class frigates. Awarded the contract in 2008, today the company is working in partnership with the navy and shipyards on both West and East Coasts to replace major critical sensors and command and control systems, modernize operations rooms, and deliver a suite of related simulation/training systems.

Additionally, Lockheed Martin Canada is a key provider of information management/information technology systems for both military and civil government departments including the Canadian Forces Health Information System, the Canadian Forces Command System, the Air Force Command Information System, and the Defence Information Services Broker.

The company delivered mission critical software to Statistics Canada for the past two censuses that allowed the country to be the first in the world to conduct an online census.

Lockheed Martin Canada has a rich history in providing electronic products and systems to all branches of the Forces. In-service support is a critical element of the company's business and it currently supports various elements of Canada's fleet of CP-140, CF-18, and CC-130J aircraft as well as coastal radar systems located on Vancouver Island and Newfoundland.

Taking into account its historic relationships with the Canadian forces and future plans and commitments, Lockheed Martin will have over a century of commitment to Canada and the development of a North American defence industrial base. Beyond their defence partnerships, Lockheed Martin Corporation stands ready to continue and grow their support to Canada's Census, health care management, information technology, as well as infrastructure and border security to ensure the safe, secure, and efficient transit of people, goods, and services between Canada and the United States.

Debbie Watt is the Controller at Lockheed Martin Canada Inc. in Ottawa, Ontario. With over 25 years experience in accounting and auditing, Debbie manages the accounting operations, internal controls, financial reporting, and cash management for this defence and security company that operates in six provinces across Canada. Lockheed Martin Canada Inc. is a wholly-owned subsidiary of Lockheed Martin Corporation, which is headquartered in Bethesda, Maryland, USA, and has over 123,000 employees worldwide. Its core business areas include aeronautics, electronic systems, information systems and global solutions, and space systems. Debbie enjoys working in a large company that focuses on leadership development and is committed to the highest standards of ethical conduct in all aspects of the business.

Prior to joining Lockheed Martin Debbie worked closely with the owners of Trillium Converting Corporation, a paper converting company servicing Domtar Paper *<www.domtar.com>*, to obtain financing to purchase several large paper converting machines to triple production at the Ottawa production facility and expand business into Montreal. Within her first five years as Controller she developed and implemented a profit sharing plan to motivate employees.

Debbie worked her way up from a Waterloo Co-op position to Audit Manager at Ginsberg, Gluzman, Fage & Levitz, Chartered Accountants *<www.ggfl.ca>* in Ottawa, Ontario. She obtained her Chartered Accountant designation and her Certified Financial Planner designation after graduating from the University of Waterloo with a Bachelor of Math, CA Option.

In addition to her busy family life with her supportive husband and two energetic teenage daughters, Debbie is actively involved in her community. She prepares financial statements and charity returns as a board member for three charities: Suzart Productions Inc., Diamond United Cemetery, and the Arnprior and District Breast Cancer Support Group. She is also involved as the Scenic Artist at Suzart Productions where she explores her creative side painting sets for musical theatre productions.

Controlling costs, managing cash flows, understanding profit margins and taxes, and reporting financial results accurately are keys to survival for both profit-seeking and non-profit organizations. This chapter will introduce you to the accounting fundamentals and financial information informing business success. The chapter also briefly explores the financial ratios that are essential in measuring business performance.

Source: Information provided by Lockheed Martin Canada Communications Department, June 2012

Describe the role that accounting and financial information play for a business and for its stakeholders.

THE ROLE OF ACCOUNTING INFORMATION

Small and sometimes large businesses often survive or fail according to how well they handle financial procedures. Financial information is the heartbeat of competitive businesses, and accounting information keeps the heartbeat stable.

Accounting reports and financial statements reveal as much about a business's health as pulse and blood pressure readings tell us about a person's health. Thus, you have to know something about accounting if you want to succeed in business. It is almost impossible to understand business operations without being able to read, understand, and analyze accounting reports and financial statements.[1]

By the end of this chapter, you should have a good idea of what accounting is, how it works, and the value it offers. You should also know some accounting terms and understand the purpose of accounting statements. Your new understanding will pay off as you become more active in business or simply in understanding what is going on in the world of business and finance.

What Is Accounting?

accounting
The recording, classifying, summarizing, and interpreting of financial events to provide management and other interested parties the financial information they need to make good decisions.

Accounting is the recording, classifying, summarizing, and interpreting of financial events to provide management and other interested parties with the financial information they need to make good decisions. Financial transactions include buying and selling goods and services, acquiring insurance, paying employees, and using supplies. Once the business's transactions have been recorded, they are usually classified into groups that have common characteristics. For example, all purchases are grouped together, as are all sales transactions. The method used to record and summarize accounting data into reports is called an *accounting system* (see Figure 16.1).

A major purpose of accounting is to help managers make well-informed decisions. Another is to report financial information about the firm to interested stakeholders, such as employees, owners, creditors, suppliers, unions, community activists, investors, and the government (for tax purposes) (see Figure 16.2). Accounting is divided into several major disciplines. Let's look at those areas next.

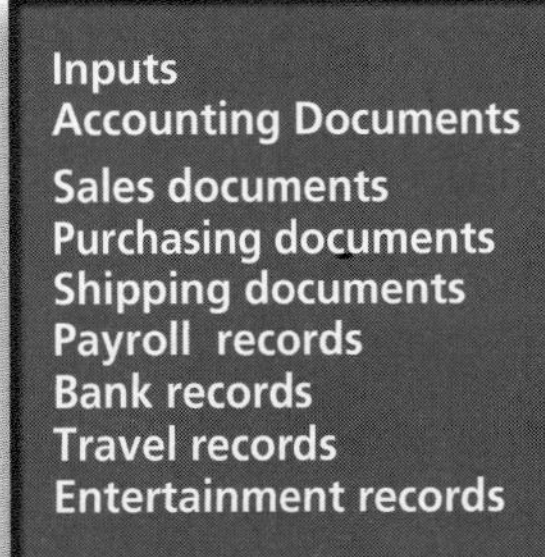

Inputs
Accounting Documents
Sales documents
Purchasing documents
Shipping documents
Payroll records
Bank records
Travel records
Entertainment records

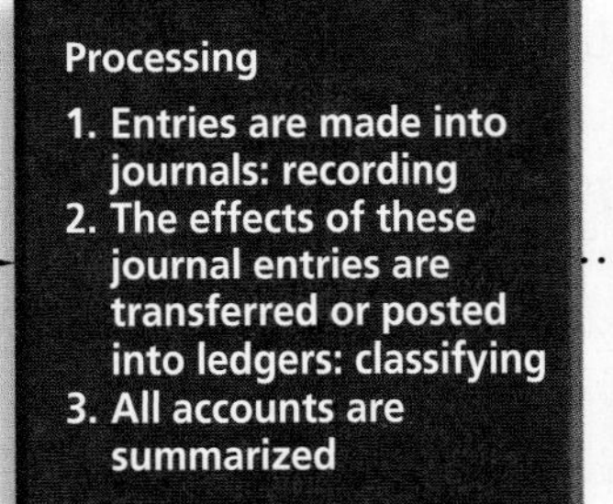

Processing
1. Entries are made into journals: recording
2. The effects of these journal entries are transferred or posted into ledgers: classifying
3. All accounts are summarized

Outputs
Financial Statements
Balance sheet
Income statement
Cash flow statement
Other reports
(e.g., annual reports)

Figure 16.1
The Accounting System
The inputs to an accounting system include sales documents and other records. The data are recorded, classified, and summarized. They are then put into summary financial statements such as the income statement and balance sheet.

Users	Type of Report
Government taxing authorities (e.g., Canada Revenue Agency)	Tax returns
Government regulatory agencies	Required reports
People interested in the organization's income and financial position (e.g., owners, creditors, financial analysts, suppliers)	Financial statements found in annual reports (e.g., income statement, balance sheet, cash flow statement)
Managers of the firm	Financial statements and various internally distributed financial reports

Figure 16.2
Users of Accounting Information and the Required Reports
Many types of organizations use accounting information to make business decisions. The reports needed vary according to the information each user requires. An accountant must prepare the appropriate forms.

ACCOUNTING DISCIPLINES

Identify the different disciplines within the accounting profession.

You may think that accounting is only for profit-seeking firms. Accounting, also called the language of business, allows for the reporting of financial information about non-profit organizations such as churches, schools, hospitals, and government agencies. The accounting profession is divided into five key working areas: managerial accounting, financial accounting, compliance (auditing), tax accounting, and governmental and not-for-profit accounting. All five areas are important, and all create career opportunities. Let's explore each.

Managerial Accounting

managerial accounting Accounting used to provide information and analyses to managers inside the organization to assist them in decision making.

Managerial accounting provides information and analyses to managers *inside* the organization to assist them in decision making. Management accounting is concerned with measuring and reporting costs of production, marketing, and other functions; preparing budgets (planning); checking whether or not units are staying within their budgets (controlling); and designing strategies to minimize taxes.[2]

Analysis of the accounts receivable will help in evaluating the credit policies of a company. Monitoring profit margins, unit sales, travel expenses, cash flow, inventory turnover, and other such data is critical to the success of a firm. Management decision making is based on such data.

Some of the questions that managerial accounting reports are designed to answer include:

- What goods and services are selling the most and what promotional tools are working best?
- How quickly is the firm selling what it buys?
- What is the appropriate allocation of expenses between products?
- Which expenses change with changes in revenue?
- How much tax is the firm paying, and how can it minimize that amount?
- Will the firm have enough cash to pay its bills? If not, has it made arrangements to borrow that money?

Assembling a marine diesel engine involves many tools, parts, raw materials, and other components as well as labour costs. Keeping these costs at a minimum and setting realistic production schedules is critical to a business's survival. What other internal departments must management accountants team with to ensure company competitiveness?

Data within a company is often compared over a period of time to identify trends or it is compared to other companies operating in the same industry when benchmarking a company's performance. Another aspect of managerial accounting concerns sustainability practices employed by business organizations. See the Green Box for a discussion on what one company is including in this type of reporting. With growing emphasis on global competition, outsourcing, and organizational cost-cutting, managerial accounting is an area of importance in terms of anyone's career.

Financial Accounting

financial accounting Accounting information and analyses prepared for people outside the organization.

annual report A yearly statement of the financial condition, progress, and expectations of an organization.

Financial accounting differs from managerial accounting in that the information and analyses it generates are for people primarily *outside* the organization. The information goes not only to company owners, managers, and employees but also to creditors and lenders, employee unions, customers, suppliers, government agencies, and the general public. External users are interested in questions like: Is the organization's profitable? Is it able to pay its bills? How much debt does it owe? These questions and others are often answered in the company's **annual report**, a yearly statement of the financial condition, progress, and expectations of an organization. As pressure from stakeholders for detailed financial information has grown, companies have poured more information than ever into their annual reports.

▶ Every public company is required to provide financial information. Users can access this information either from the company's Web site or from a service provided from sites like *www.sedar.com*. This information varies from a quarterly set of financial statements, with accompanying notes, to annual reports with a breadth of financial information.

GREENBOX

Annual Accountability Report

More and more companies are committing to reporting of their "green" initiatives. Mountain Equipment Co-op's (MEC, <*www.mec.ca*>) third comprehensive sustainability report includes information on their targets and performance in eight areas: design, manufacturing, operations, employees, members, the community, economics, and governance. The results are subject to independent assurance or external review.

They source or require organically grown cotton in the clothing they sell along with the growing use of re-cycled polyester. They have reduced the amount of materials used in their packaging. They require all the factories they use to sign a Supplier Code of Conduct related to worker health and safety. More importantly, they follow up with rotational audits, categorizing non-compliance issues up to a level of zero tolerance (for example, in terms of child labour); and then working on the reduction of these issues.

Operationally they report on the reduction of energy usage and are working toward a goal of zero operational waste, which means diverting all material waste from landfills. Currently, they are averaging about 90% diversion. Categories of energy usage include product transportation, employee commuting, facility emissions, and corporate business travel. In terms of employees they report on training and support, hourly compensation rates, health and safety, turnover rates, and employee diversity (including numbers of female and visible minorities employed). Employee surveys are used to obtain some of the data.

They also survey members on issues including product quality, functionality, and form; satisfaction; and product availability and advice provided. They report on their promotion of recreation and leisure activity in Canada and their multimillion dollar contributions supporting community-based conservation. And finally, they comment on their own economic viability using accounting data, which we will talk about in this chapter.

MEC take issues surrounding sustainability very seriously, "they walk the talk." Why do you think companies like MEC are committing significant time and resources to these types of activities?

Source: Courtesy of Mountain Equipment Co-op.

Financial accounting reports provide the information that allows readers to answer questions such as:

- Has the company's income been satisfactory? Should we invest in this company?
- Should we lend money to this company? Will it be able to pay it back?
- Are the company's costs getting out of control?
- Is the company financially strong enough to stay in business to honour product warranties?
- Should we sell to this company? Will it be able to pay its bills?

Compliance

Reviewing and evaluating the records used to prepare a company's financial statements is referred to as **compliance**. Private accountants within the organization often perform internal audits to ensure that is carrying out proper accounting procedures and financial reporting. Public accountants also conduct independent audits of accounting and related records. An **independent audit** is an evaluation and unbiased opinion about the accuracy of a company's financial statements.

All stakeholders, including the public, governments, financial institutions, and shareholders (owners) are interested in the results of these audits. This audit is required for all public corporations in Canada whose shares are traded in a public stock exchange.

A relatively new area of accounting that focuses its attention on fraudulent activity is **forensic accounting**. This field of accounting gathers evidence for presentation in a court of law. This evidence comes from a review of financial and other records.

compliance
The job of reviewing and evaluating the records used to prepare a company's financial statements.

independent audit
An evaluation and unbiased opinion about the accuracy of a company's financial statements.

forensic accounting
A relatively new area of accounting that focuses its attention on fraudulent activity.

Tax Accounting

tax accountant
An accountant trained in tax law and responsible for preparing tax returns or developing tax strategies.

Taxes enable governments to pay for roads, parks, schools, police protection, the military, and other functions. Federal and provincial governments require submission of tax returns that must be filed at specific times and in a precise format. A **tax accountant** is trained in tax law and is responsible for preparing tax returns or developing tax strategies. Since governments often change tax policies according to specific needs or objectives, the job of the tax accountant is certainly challenging. Also, as the burden of taxes grows in the economy, the role of the tax accountant becomes increasingly important to the organization or entrepreneur.

Governmental and Not-for-Profit Accounting

Governmental and not-for-profit accounting supports organizations whose purpose is not generating a profit but rather serving ratepayers, taxpayers, and others according to a duly approved budget. The different levels of government require an accounting system that helps citizens, special interest groups, legislative bodies, and donors ensure that the government and not-for-profit organizations are fulfilling their obligations and marking proper use of the funding with which they have been provided. Canada's auditor general regularly audits the federal government. Charities (such as the Canadian Cancer Society <*www.cancer.ca*> and the United Way of Canada <*www.unitedway.ca*>), universities and colleges, hospitals, and trade unions all hire accountants to show how the funds they raise are being spent. Some charities are having a particularly hard time because of the losses they suffered from the illegal activities of Bernard Madoff and others like him. The ongoing financial crisis is also having a negative effect, causing some individuals cut back on donations, and accounting for every dollar became even more important.[3]

As you can see, managerial and financial accounting, compliance, tax accounting, and governmental and not-for-profit accounting each require specific training and skill. Before we leave this section let's look at the difference between private and public accountants; and Canadian accounting designations.

Private and Public Accountants

private accountant
An accountant who works for a single firm, government agency, or non-profit organization.

public accountant
An accountant who provides his or her accounting services to individuals or businesses on a fee basis.

It is critical to keep accurate financial information. Therefore many organizations employ **private accountants**, who work for a single firm, government agency, or non-profit organization. However, not all organizations want or need a full-time accountant. Therefore, they hire independent public accounting firms to maintain their financial records.

For a fee, a **public accountant** will provide accounting services to individuals or businesses that include designing an accounting system, helping select the correct computer system and software to run the system, analyzing the financial strength of an organization, providing consulting services (including operational effectiveness and efficiencies), and compliance.[4] Large accounting and auditing firms operate internationally to serve large transnational companies.

It is vital for the accounting profession to assure users of financial information that the information provided is accurate. Accountants must follow a set of generally accepted accounting principles (GAAP).[5] If financial reports are prepared in accordance with GAAP, users can expect that the information is reported according to standards agreed upon by accounting professionals.[6] We will discuss GAAP later in this chapter. In the early 2000s, the accounting profession suffered through perhaps the darkest period in its history.[7] Accounting scandals involving high-profile companies such as Enron, WorldCom, and Tyco raised public suspicions of the profession and of corporate integrity in general.[8] Arthur Anderson, one of the world's leading

▸ The Canadian Institute of Chartered Accountants, together with the CA institutes/ordre, represents over 80,000 CAs and 10,000 students in Canada and Bermuda. The CICA conducts research into current business issues and supports the setting of accounting, auditing, and assurance standards for business, not-for-profit organizations, and government.

accounting firms, went out of business after being convicted of obstruction of justice for shredding records in the Enron case (the conviction was later overturned by the U.S. Supreme Court). Canadian companies are not immune either; Nortel (no longer in business) has been investigated for their accounting practices related to large bonuses paid to senior management.

Based on the above-mentioned breadth of services provided by public accountants, they could easily find themselves in a conflict of interest when providing both consulting advice and also compliance activities to the same firm. Scrutiny of the accounting industry intensified and culminated with the U.S. Congress's passage of the Sarbanes-Oxley Act.[9] This legislation created new government reporting standards for publicly-traded companies.[10] Figure 16.3 lists a few of the major provisions of Sarbanes-Oxley. This Act also applies to any Canadian public company wishing to have their shares traded on an American stock exchange. In Canada, the Ontario Securities Commission introduced Bill 198. CEOs and CFOs of public companies are now required to certify reports. Auditors are now also required to be part of the Canadian Public Accountability Board Oversight Program, which reviews the audited financial statements of public companies. In addition, standards for the independence and education experience of Audit Committees were defined.

Accounting Designations

In Canada there are currently three different professional accounting designations. Typically considered the most prestigious is chartered accountant. A **chartered accountant (CA)** is an accountant who has met the examination, education, and experience requirements of the Canadian Institute of Chartered Accountants (CICA <*www.cica.ca*>), which includes the Uniform Evaluation (UFE), widely recognized as one of the most rigorous professional examinations in the world. CAs are widely recognized as the leading financial and accounting professionals in Canada.

chartered accountant (CA) An accountant who has met the examination, education, and experience requirements of the Canadian Institute of Chartered Accountants.

- Prohibits accounting firms from providing certain non-auditing work (such as consulting services) to companies they audit.
- Strengthens the protection for whistleblowers who report wrongful actions of company officers.
- Requires company CEOs and CFOs to certify the accuracy of financial reports and imparts strict penalties for any violation of securities reporting (e.g., earnings misstatements).
- Prohibits corporate loans to directors and executives of the company.
- Establishes the five-member Public Company Accounting Oversight Board under the Securities and Exchange Commission (SEC) to oversee the accounting industry.
- Stipulates that altering or destroying key audit documents will result in felony charges and significant criminal penalties.

Figure 16.3

Key Provisions of the Sarbanes-Oxley Act

certified management accountant (CMA)
An accountant who has met the examination, education, and experience requirements of the Society of Management Accountants of Canada.

certified general accountant (CGA)
An accountant who has met the examination, education, and experience requirements of the Certified General Accountants Association of Canada.

accounting cycle
A six-step procedure that results in the preparation and analysis of the major financial statements.

bookkeeping
The recording of business transactions.

A certified management accountant (CMA) is a professional accountant who has met certain educational and experience requirements, passed a qualifying exam in the field, participated in a two-year professional development program, and been certified by the Society of Management Accountants of Canada (CMA Canada <*www.cma-canada.org*>).

The Certified General Accountants Association of Canada (CGA-Canada <*www.cga-canada.org*>) also trains and certifies accountants. Certified general accountants (CGAs) are those who have met the examination, education, and experience requirements of CGA-Canada. CGAs offer expertise in taxation, finance, information technology, and strategic business management.[11]

Accountants with any of these designations work in all areas of business. One third of CAs work in industry; another third are in public practice, and the rest primarily work in government and education. Managerial accountants primarily work in industry but recently have been given the legal right to work in public practice. Many CGAs are employed by different levels of government, while others are in public practice. See the discussion in the Dealing with Change box at the end of this Part for information on the latest attempt to deal with the apparent confusion caused by the multiple professional designations.

After the Progress Assessment, we will clarify the difference between accounting and bookkeeping.

PROGRESS ASSESSMENT

- Could you define accounting to a friend so that he or she would clearly understand what is involved?
- What is the key difference between managerial and financial accounting?
- How is the job of a private accountant different from that of a public accountant?
- Describe the three accounting designations.

List the steps in the accounting cycle, distinguish between accounting and bookkeeping, and explain how computers are used in accounting.

THE ACCOUNTING CYCLE

The accounting cycle is a six-step procedure that results in the preparation and analysis of the major financial statements (see Figure 16.4). It relies on the work of both the bookkeeper and the accountant. Bookkeeping, the recording of business transactions, is a basic part of financial reporting. Accounting, however, goes far beyond the mere recording of financial information. Accountants classify and summarize financial data provided by bookkeepers and then interpret the data and report the information to management. They also suggest strategies for improving the financial condition and prepare financial analysis and income tax returns.

A bookkeeper's first task is to divide all of the firm's transactions into meaningful categories such as sales documents, purchasing receipts, and shipping documents,

Figure 16.4
Steps in the Accounting Cycle

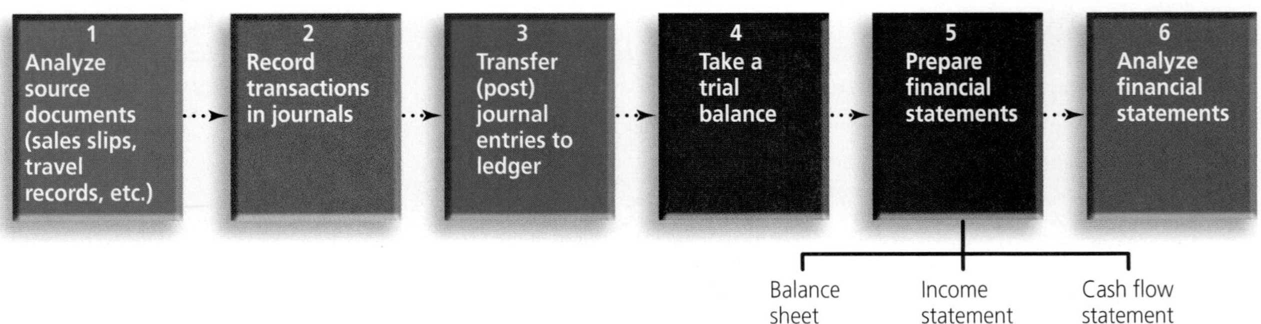

being very careful to keep the information organized and manageable. Bookkeepers then record financial data from the original transaction documents (sales slips and so forth) into a record book (either manually or using accounting software) called a journal. The word *journal* comes from the French word *jour,* which means "day." Therefore, a **journal** is where the day's transactions are kept.

journal The record book where accounting data are first entered.

double-entry bookkeeping The concept of every business transaction affecting at least two accounts.

accounts Different types of assets, liabilities, and owners' equity

fundamental accounting equation Assets are equal to liabilities plus owners' equity; this is the basis for the balance sheet.

ledger A specialized accounting book in which information from accounting journals is accumulated into accounts and posted so that managers can find all of the information about a specific account in one place.

trial balance A summary of all of the data in the account ledgers to show whether the figures are correct and balanced.

The Fundamental Accounting Equation

The practice of having every transaction affect at least two accounts is called **double-entry bookkeeping**. **Accounts** are different types of assets, liabilities, and owners' equity (which will be discussed later). This practice is consistent with the **fundamental accounting equation**: Assets = Liabilities + Owners' equity.

In accounting, this equation must always be balanced. For example, suppose that you have $50,000 in cash and decide to use that money to open a small coffee shop. Your business has assets of $50,000 and no debts. The accounting equation would be:

Assets	=	Liabilities	+	Owners' equity
$50,000	=	$0	+	$50,000

Remember, each business transaction impacts at least two accounts. Each entry has at least one debit and credit. Debits or credits on their own are neither good nor bad, simply a mechanism for maintaining the balance of the accounting equation.

Referring back to our example, your business has $50,000 cash and $50,000 owners' equity (the amount of your investment in the business—sometimes referred to as net worth). However, before opening the business, you borrow $30,000 from a local bank; the equation now changes. You have $30,000 of additional cash, but you also have a debt (liability) of $30,000.

Your financial position within the business has changed. The equation is still balanced but is changed to reflect the transaction:

Assets	=	Liabilities	+	Owners' equity
$80,000	=	$30,000	+	$50,000

One more bookkeeping tool is used. Suppose a business wanted to determine how much it paid for office supplies in the first quarter of the year. Even with accurate accounting journals, you have to review all journal entries and summarize those that included office supplies. Therefore, bookkeepers use of a specialized accounting book called a **ledger**. In the ledger they transfer (or post) information from accounting journals into specific accounts so managers can find all of the information about a specific account, like office supplies, in one place.

The next step is to prepare a **trial balance**, a summary of all of the financial data in the accounts ledger that ensures the figures are balanced. If the information in the accounts is not accurate, it must be corrected before the firm's financial statements are prepared. The accountant then prepares the financial statements, including a balance sheet, income statement, and cash flow statement according to GAAP. Using information in the financial statements, the accountant analyzes and evaluates the financial condition of the firm.

▶ The integrity of a firm's financial statements is vital. Accounting irregularities that occurred at firms like Livent, Nortel, and Parmalat made the companies look stronger than they actually were. Accountants are now committed to regaining the trust and respect their profession enjoyed in the past. What part should the government play in overseeing the accounting industry?

"I'LL TELL YOU HARRIS, THEY DON'T MAKE ACCOUNTANTS LIKE THEY USED TO. THOSE I HAD IN THE 1990'S NEVER BROUGHT ME FIGURES LIKE THESE."

Accounting Technology

Computers and accounting software have considerably simplified the accounting process. Computerized accounting programs post information from journals instantaneously, even from remote locations, so that financial information is readily available whenever the organization needs it. That frees accountants for more important tasks such as financial analysis.[12] Computerized accounting programs are particularly helpful to small-business owners who often lack the strong accounting support within their companies that larger firms enjoy. Accounting software—such as Simply Accounting and Quicken—addresses the specific needs of small business, which are often significantly different from the needs of a major corporation. Business owners should, however, understand exactly which computer system and programs are best suited for their particular needs.[13] That is one reason entrepreneurs planning to start a company should hire or consult with an accountant to identify the particular accounting needs of their firm. Then, a specific computer system and software can be chosen.

A computer is a wonderful tool for business people and helps ease the monotony of bookkeeping and accounting work, but no computer has yet been programmed to make good financial decisions by itself.[14] The work of an accountant requires training and very specific competencies. After the Progress Assessment, we'll look at the balance sheet, income statement, and cash flow statement—and the important financial information that each provides.

PROGRESS ASSESSMENT

- How is the job of the bookkeeper different from an accountant?
- What's the purpose of accounting journals and a ledger?
- Why does a bookkeeper prepare a trial balance?
- What advantages do computers provide businesses in maintaining and compiling accounting information?

Explain how the major financial statements differ.

UNDERSTANDING KEY FINANCIAL STATEMENTS

financial statement
A summary of all of the transactions that have occurred over a particular period.

A **financial statement** is a summary of all of the transactions that have occurred over a particular period. Financial statements indicate a firm's financial health and stability and are key factors in management decision making. That is why shareholders (the owners of the firm), bondholders and banks (people and institutions that lend money to the firm), labour unions, employees, and the Canada Revenue Agency are all interested in a firm's financial statements. The key financial statements of a business are:

1. The *balance sheet,* which reports the firm's financial position *on a specific date,* normally, at the end of a period.
2. The *income statement,* which summarizes revenues, cost of goods, and expenses (including taxes) for a specific period of time and highlights the total profit or loss the firm experienced *during that period.*
3. The *cash flow statement,* which provides a summary of money coming into and going out of the firm *during a period.*

The differences among the financial statements can be summarized this way: The balance sheet details what the company owns and owes on a certain day; the income statement shows the revenue a firm earned selling its products compared to its selling costs (profit or loss) over a specific period of time; and the cash flow statement highlights the difference between cash coming in and cash going out over a specific period of time. To fully understand this important financial information, you need to know the purpose of an organization's financial statements. To help you with this task, we'll explain each statement in more detail.

VERY VEGETARIAN Balance Sheet December 31, 2012			
Assets			
① Current assets			
Cash		$ 15,000	
Accounts receivable		200,000	
Notes receivable		50,000	
Inventory		335,000	
Total current assets			$600,000
② Capital assets			
Land		$ 40,000	
Building and improvements	$200,000		
Less: Accumulated amortization	−90,000		
		110,000	
Equipment and vehicles	$120,000		
Less: Accumulated amortization	−80,000		
		40,000	
Furniture and fixtures	$26,000		
Less: Accumulated amortization	−10,000		
		16,000	
Total fixed assets			206,000
③ Intangible assets			
Goodwill		$ 20,000	
Total intangible assets			20,000
Total assets			$826,000
Liabilities and Owners' or Shareholders' Equity Liabilities			
④ Current liabilities			
Accounts payable		$ 40,000	
Notes payable (due June 2013)		8,000	
Accrued taxes		150,000	
Accrued salaries		90,000	
Total current liabilities			$288,000
⑤ Long-term liabilities			
Notes payable (due Mar. 2015)		$ 35,000	
Bonds payable (due Dec. 2020)		290,000	
Total long-term liabilities			325,000
Total liabilities			$613,000
⑥ Shareholders' equity			
Common stock (1,000,000 shares)		$100,000	
Retained earnings		113,000	
Total shareholders' equity			213,000
Total liabilities & shareholders' equity			$826,000

Figure 16.5

Sample Very Vegetarian Balance Sheet

① Current assets: Items that can be converted to cash within one year.
② Capital assets: Items such as land, buildings, and equipment that are relatively permanent.
③ Intangible assets: Items of value such as patents and copyrights that do not have a physical form.
④ Current liabilities: Payments that are due in one year or less.
⑤ Long-term liabilities: Payments not due for one year or longer.
⑥ Shareholders' equity: The value of what shareholders own in a firm (also called owners' equity).

The Balance Sheet

A balance sheet is the financial statement that reports a firm's financial condition at a specific time. As highlighted in the sample balance sheet in Figure 16.5 (for our hypothetical vegetarian restaurant Very Vegetarian introduced in Chapter 14), assets are listed first, followed by liabilities and owners' (or shareholders') equity. The assets are

balance sheet
The financial statement that reports a firm's financial condition at a specific time and is composed of three major types of accounts: assets, liabilities, and owners' equity.

equal to or are balanced with the liabilities and owners' (or shareholders') equity. The balance is that simple. Since it is critical that business people understand the financial information in the balance sheet, let's take a closer look at what are the asset accounts and what are the liabilities and owners' equity accounts.

Let's say that you want to know what your financial condition is at a given time. Maybe you want to buy a house or car and therefore need to calculate your available resources. One of the best measuring sticks is your balance sheet. First, you would add up everything you own—cash, property, and money owed you. These are your assets. Subtract from that the money you owe others—credit card debt, IOUs, car loan, and student loan. These are your liabilities. The resulting figure is your net worth or equity. This is fundamentally what companies do in preparing a balance sheet: follow the procedures set in the fundamental accounting equation. In that preparation it is important to follow generally accepted accounting principles (GAAP).

Assets

assets
Economic resources (things of value) owned by a firm.

Assets are economic resources (things of value) owned by a firm. Assets include productive, tangible items such as equipment, buildings, land, furniture, fixtures, and motor vehicles that help generate income, as well as intangibles with value like patents, trademarks, copyrights, or goodwill. Think, for example, of the value of brand names such as Roots, WestJet, and Canadian Tire. Intangibles such as brand names can be among the firm's most valuable assets.[15] Goodwill is the value that can be attributed to factors such as reputation, location, and superior products.[16] It is included on the balance sheet when a firm acquiring another firm pays more than the value of that firm's tangible assets. Not all companies, however, have intangible assets.

liquidity
How fast an asset can be converted into cash.

current assets
Items that can or will be converted into cash within one year.

capital assets
Assets that are relatively permanent, such as land, buildings, and equipment.

intangible assets
Long-term assets (e.g., patents, trademarks, copyrights) that have no real physical form but do have value.

Assets are listed on the firm's balance sheet according to their liquidity. **Liquidity** refers to how fast an asset is expected to be converted into cash. Speedier conversion means higher liquidity. For example, an *account receivable* is an amount of money owed to the firm that it expects to receive within one year. It is considered a liquid asset because it can be quickly converted to cash. However, the longer a firm takes to collect its receivables, the less collectible they become. Land, however, is typically owned for many years; thus, land is a long-term asset (an asset expected to last more than one year) and not considered liquid. Thus, assets are divided into three categories according to how quickly they can be turned into cash:

1. **Current assets** are items that can or will be converted into cash within one year. Current assets include cash, accounts receivable, and inventory.
2. **Capital assets** are items that are relatively permanent goods, such as land and buildings, acquired to produce products for a business. They are not bought to be sold but to generate revenue. (On a balance sheet they are also referred to as fixed assets or property, plant, and equipment.)
3. **Intangible assets** are long-term assets that have no real physical form but do have value. Patents, trademarks, copyrights, and goodwill are examples of intangible assets.

Liabilities and Owners' (Shareholders') Equity Accounts

liabilities
What the business owes to others (debts).

accounts payable
Current liabilities are bills a company owes to others for merchandise or services purchased on credit but not yet paid for.

notes payable
Short-term or long-term liabilities that a business promises to repay by a certain date.

Liabilities are what the business owes to others—its debts. *Current liabilities* are debts due in one year or less. *Long-term liabilities* are debts not due for one year or longer. The following are common liability accounts recorded on a balance sheet (refer to Figure 16.5):

1. **Accounts payable** are current liabilities or bills a company owes others for merchandise or services purchased on credit but not yet paid. The longer you take to pay, the greater the risk that a supplier will no longer grant you credit.
2. **Notes payable** can be short-term or long-term liabilities (e.g., loans from banks) that a business promises to repay by a certain date.

3. **Bonds payable** are long-term liabilities; money lent to the firm that must be paid back. (We will discuss bonds in depth in Chapters 17 and 18.)
4. **Taxes payable** include sales taxes and GST or HST collected, and income tax payable.

bonds payable
Long-term liabilities that represent money lent to a firm that must be paid back.

taxes payable
Sales taxes and GST or HST collected, and income tax payable.

As the fundamental accounting equation highlighted earlier, the value of things you own (assets) minus the amount of money you owe others (liabilities) is called *equity*. The value of what shareholders own in a firm (minus liabilities) is called *shareholders' equity* (or *stockholders' equity*).

The **owners' equity** in a company consists of all that the owners have invested in the company plus all profits that have accumulated since the business commenced but that have not yet been paid out to them. This figure always equals the book value of the assets minus the liabilities of the company.

owners' equity
The amount of the business that belongs to the owners minus any liabilities owed by the business.

In a partnership, owners' equity is called partners' equity or capital. In a sole proprietorship, it is called owner's or proprietor's equity or capital. In a corporation, it is called shareholders' equity and is shown in two separate accounts. The amount the owners (shareholders) invest is shown in one account, called common stock. The accumulated earnings from a firm's profitable operations that remains in the business and not paid out to shareholders as dividends is shown in an account called **retained earnings**. We will discuss dividends in Chapter 17. Take a few moments to review Figure 16.5 and see what facts you can determine about Very Vegetarian from its balance sheet.

retained earnings
The accumulated earnings from a firm's profitable operations that remains in the business and not paid out to shareholders as dividends.

PROGRESS ASSESSMENT

- What is the formula for the balance sheet? What do we call this formula?
- What does it mean to list various assets according to liquidity?
- What is included in the liabilities accounts in the balance sheet?
- What is owners' equity and how is it determined?

The Income Statement

The financial statement that shows a firm's bottom line—that is, its profit after costs, expenses, and taxes—is the **income statement**. The income statement summarizes all of the resources (called revenue) that have been earned by the firm from operating activities, resources that were used up, expenses incurred in doing business, and the resources left after all costs and expenses, including taxes, were incurred. The resources (revenue) left over are referred to as **net income or net loss** (see Figure 16.6).

income statement
The financial statement that shows a firm's profit after costs, expenses, and taxes; it summarizes all of the resources (called revenue) that have been earned, all of the resources that were used up, and the resulting net income.

The income statement reports the firm's financial operations over a particular period of time, usually a year, a quarter of a year, or a month. It is the financial statement that reveals whether the business is actually earning a profit or not. The income statement includes valuable financial information for shareholders, lenders, investors (or potential investors), employees, and of course the government. Because it is so valuable, let's take a quick look at how to compile the income statement according to generally accepted accounting principles (GAAP), which we will discuss later in the chapter:

net income or net loss
Revenue left over after all costs and expenses, including taxes, are paid.

Revenue
− Cost of goods sold

= Gross profit (gross margin)
− Operating expenses

= Net income before taxes
− Taxes

= Net income or loss

Figure 16.6

Sample Very Vegetarian Income Statement

① Revenues: Value of what is received from goods sold, services rendered, and other financial sources.
② Cost of goods sold: Cost of merchandise sold or cost of raw materials or parts used for producing items for resale.
③ Gross profit: How much the firm earned by buying or selling merchandise.
④ Operating expenses: Cost incurred in operating a business.
⑤ Net income after taxes: Profit or loss over a specific period after subtracting all costs and expenses including taxes.

VERY VEGETARIAN Income Statement For the Year Ended December 31, 2012			
① Revenues			
Gross sales		$720,000	
Less: Sales returns and allowances	$ 12,000		
Sales discounts	8,000	−20,000	
Net sales			$700,000
② Cost of goods sold			
Beginning inventory, Jan. 1		$200,000	
Merchandise purchases	$400,000		
Freight	40,000		
Net purchases		440,000	
Cost of goods available for sale		$640,000	
Less ending inventory, Dec. 31		−230,000	
Cost of goods sold			−410,000
③ Gross profit			$290,000
④ Operating expenses			
Selling expenses			
Salaries for salespeople	$ 90,000		
Advertising	18,000		
Supplies	2,000		
Total selling expenses		$110,000	
General expenses			
Office salaries	$ 67,000		
Amortization	1,500		
Insurance	1,500		
Rent	28,000		
Light, heat, and power	12,000		
Miscellaneous	2,000		
		112,000	
Total operating expenses			222,000
Net income before taxes			$ 68,000
Less: Income tax expense			19,000
⑤ Net income after taxes			$ 49,000

Revenue

As defined in Chapter 1, revenue is the monetary value received for goods sold, services rendered, and other financial sources. Note that there is a difference between revenue and sales. Most revenue comes from sales, but there could be other sources of revenue that are included in reporting revenue, such as rents received, money paid to the firm for use of its patents, and interest earned. Be careful not to confuse the terms *revenue* and *sales,* or to use them as if they were synonymous. Also, a quick glance at the income statement shows you that gross sales are the total of all sales the firm completed. *Net sales* are gross sales minus returns, discounts, and allowances.

cost of goods sold (or cost of goods manufactured) A measure of the cost of merchandise sold or cost of raw materials and supplies used for producing items for resale.

Cost of Goods Sold (Cost of Goods Manufactured)

The **cost of goods sold** (or **cost of goods manufactured**) measures the cost of merchandise sold or cost of raw materials and supplies used in producing items for resale.

It makes sense to compare how much a business earned by selling merchandise over the period being evaluated, compared to how much it spent to buy, or produce, the merchandise. The cost of goods sold includes the purchase price plus any freight charges paid to transport goods (or all the costs associated with producing the merchandise). In other words, all of the costs of buying (making) are included in the cost of goods sold. It is critical that companies accurately report and manage this important income statement item.

When we subtract the cost of goods sold from net sales, we get gross profit or gross margin. **Gross profit (or gross margin)** is how much a firm earned by buying (or making) and selling merchandise. In a service firm there is no cost of goods sold; therefore, net revenue equals gross profit. Gross profit does not tell you everything you need to know about the firm's financial performance. To get that, you must subtract the business's expenses.

gross profit (or gross margin)
How much a firm earned by buying (or making) and selling merchandise.

Operating Expenses

In selling goods or services, a business incurs certain **operating expenses** such as rent, salaries, supplies, utilities, insurance, research, and even amortization of equipment. (We will look at amortization a little later.) Operating expenses can generally be classified into two categories: selling expenses and general expenses. *Selling expenses* are expenses related to the marketing and distribution of the firm's goods or services (such as salaries for salespeople, advertising, and supplies). *General expenses* are administrative expenses of the firm (such as office salaries, amortization, insurance, and rent). Accountants are trained to help you record all applicable expenses and find other relevant expenses you need to deduct as part of doing business.

operating expenses
Costs involved in operating a business, such as rent, utilities, and salaries.

Net Profit or Loss

After deducting all expenses, we can determine the firm's net income before taxes, also referred to as net earnings or net profit (refer to Figure 16.6). After allocating for taxes, we get to the *bottom line,* which is the net income (or perhaps net loss) the firm incurred from revenue minus sales returns, costs, expenses, and taxes over a period of time. We can now answer the question "Did the business earn or lose money in the reporting period?"

The basic principles of the balance sheet and income statement are somewhat familiar to you. You know how to keep track of costs and expenses when you prepare your own budget. If your rent and utilities exceed your revenues (how much you earn), you know you are in trouble. If you need more money (revenue), you may need to sell some of the things you own to pay your expenses. The same is true in business. Companies need to keep track of how much money they earn and spend, how much cash they have on hand. The only difference is that companies tend to have more complex problems and a good deal more information to record than you do.

Users of financial statements are interested in how a firm handles the flow of cash coming in and flowing out. Some very profitable businesses have experienced serious cash flow problems. Keep this in mind as we look at the cash flow statement next.

The Cash Flow Statement

The **cash flow statement** reports cash receipts and disbursements related to the three major activities of a firm:

- operations: cash transactions associated with running the business
- investing: cash used in or provided by the firm's investing activities (normally including capital assets)
- financing: cash raised from the issuance of new debt or equity capital or cash used to repay loans or company dividends. We will discuss these terms in Chapter 17.

cash flow statement
A financial statement that reports cash receipts and disbursements related to a firm's three major activities: operations, investing, and financing.

Accountants analyze all of the cash changes that have occurred from operating, investing, and financing and determine the firm's net cash position. The cash flow statement also gives the firm some insight into how to handle cash better so that no cash flow problems (e.g., having no cash on hand) occur.

Figure 16.7 shows a cash flow statement, again using the example of Very Vegetarian. As you can see, this financial statement answers such questions as: How much cash came into the business from current operation such as buying and selling goods and services? Did the firm use cash to buy stocks, bonds, or capital assets? Did it sell some investments that brought in cash? How much money came into the firm from issuing stock?

We analyze these and other financial transactions to see their effect on the firm's cash position. Managing cash flow can mean the success or failure of any business, which is why we analyze it in more depth in the next section.

The Importance of Cash Flow Analysis

Cash flow, if not properly managed, can cause a business much concern. Cash flow analysis is really rather simple to comprehend.[17] Let's say that you borrow $100 from a friend to buy a used bike and agree to pay your friend back at the end of the week. You then sell the bike for $150 to someone else, who also agrees to pay you by the end of the week. Unfortunately, by the weekend, your buyer does not have the money as promised and says he will have to pay you next month. Meanwhile, your friend wants the $100 you agreed to pay her by the end of the week!

What seemed like a great opportunity to make an easy $50 profit is now a cause for concern. You owe $100 and have no cash. What do you do? If you were a business, you might default on the loan and possibly go bankrupt, even though you had profits.

cash flow
The difference between cash coming in and cash going out of a business.

It is possible for a business to increase sales and profit yet still suffer cash flow problems. **Cash flow** is simply the difference between cash coming in and cash going

Figure 16.7

Sample Very Vegetarian Cash Flow Statement

① Cash receipts from sales, commissions, fees, interest, and dividends. Cash payments for salaries, inventories, operating expenses, interest, and taxes.

② Includes cash flows that are generated through a company's purchase or sale of long-term operational assets, investments in other companies, and its lending activities.

③ Cash inflows and outflows associated with the company's own equity transactions or its borrowing activities.

VERY VEGETARIAN Cash Flow Statement For the Year Ended December 31, 2012		
① Cash flows from operating activities		
Cash received from customers	$150,000	
Cash paid to suppliers and employees	(90,000)	
Interest paid	(5,000)	
Income tax paid	(4,500)	
Interest and dividends received	1,500	
Net cash provided by operating activities		$52,000
② Cash flows from investing activities		
Proceeds from sale of plant assets	$ 4,000	
Payments for purchase of equipment	(10,000)	
Net cash provided by investing activities		(6,000)
③ Cash flows from financing activities		
Proceeds from issuance of short-term debt	$ 3,000	
Payment of long-term debt	(7,000)	
Payment of dividends	(15,000)	
Net cash inflow from financing activities		(19,000)
Net change in cash and equivalents		$27,000
Cash balance (beginning of year)		(2,000)
Cash balance (end of year)		$25,000

MAKING ETHICAL DECISIONS

On the Accounting Hot Seat

You are the only accountant employed by a small manufacturing firm. You are in charge of keeping the books for the company, which has been suffering from an economic downturn that shows no signs of lightening in the near future.

You know that your employer is going to ask the bank for an additional loan so the company can continue to pay its bills. Unfortunately, the financial statements for the year will not show good results, and your best guess is that the bank will not approve a loan increase on the basis of the financial information you will present.

Your boss approaches you in early January before you have closed the books for the preceding year and suggests that perhaps the statements can be "improved" by treating the sales that were made at the beginning of January as if they were made in December. He also asks you to do a number of other things that will cover up the trail so that the auditors will not discover the padding of the year's sales.

You know that these results go against the professional rules, and you argue with your boss. Your boss tells you that, if the company does not get the additional bank loan, there's a very good chance the business will close. That means you and everyone else in the firm will be out of a job. You believe your boss is probably right and you know that, with the current economic downturn, finding a job will be tough for you and almost impossible for others in the company. What are your alternatives? What are the likely consequences of each alternative? How will jobs be affected? What will you do?

out of a business. A common mistake among start-ups is to focus on the product and not the running of the business, explained Blair Davidson, KPMG partner in the Financial Advisory Services Group, at a recent York Technology Association and Canadian Technology Network breakfast speech. "Business can be viewed as a triangle of operations: making, selling, and scorekeeping. If you devote yourself only to production and neglect the other sides, the imbalance will show up in the bottom line and shake the confidence of potential investors in the future," he said.[18]

Cash flow is a constant challenge for businesses of all sizes. Consider how critical this is for seasonal businesses (such as ski resorts) in which the flow of cash into the business is sporadic. Accountants sometimes face tough ethical challenges in reporting the flow of funds into a business. Read the Making Ethical Decisions box to see how such an ethical dilemma (remember the discussion in Chapter 5) can arise.

How do cash flow problems start? Often, to meet the demands of customers, a business buys more and more goods on credit (no cash is involved). Similarly, more and more goods are sold on credit (no cash is involved). If their customers delay in paying, all of the credit it has with its lenders will get used. When the firm requests more money from its bank to pay a crucial bill, the bank refuses the loan because the credit limit has been reached. All other credit sources refuse funds as well. The problem could, unfortunately, force the firm into bankruptcy—even though sales may be strong—because no cash was available when needed.

Cash flow analysis shows that a business's relationship with its banker(s) is critical to preventing cash flow problems. Accountants provide valuable insight and advice to businesses in managing cash flow, suggesting whether they need cash and how much.[19]

APPLYING ACCOUNTING KNOWLEDGE IN BUSINESS

Describe the role of accounting rules and principles in reporting financial information.

If accounting consisted of nothing more than repetitive functions of gathering and recording transactions and preparing financial statements, the tasks could be assigned solely to computers. In fact, most medium and large firms as well as growing numbers of small businesses have done just that. The Internet has initiated a new way of managing a firm's finances: online accounting. But the truth is that how you record and report financial data is also critically important.

Generally Accepted Accounting Principles

Business transactions require certain guidelines that help accountants make proper and consistent decisions. These guidelines were originally developed on a country to country basis and were called generally accepted accounting principles (GAAP). In Canada they were published in the handbook of the Canadian Institute of Chartered Accountants, along with many other important guidelines. This handbook was the ultimate authority of the accounting profession. Bankers, financial analysts, and others referred to these rules to understand how certain financial events should be reflected in the financial statements. From time to time (and after much discussion) it was updated or modified.

There used to be about a dozen important accounting principles, which provided options for how certain financial events were recorded. Every audited set of financial statements included a series of notes explaining how these principles had been applied, as well as a report by the auditors that GAAP had been used. This makes it possible for financial statements to be compared from one year to the next as well as from one company to another.

For years multi-nationals adapted their accounting reporting to the rules of multiple countries, since no global set of accounting guidelines existed. However, that situation is changing. As a growing number of countries have adopted the International Financial Reporting Standards (IFRS), the International Accounting Standards Board (IASB, <*www.ifrs.org*>) has pushed to make them the clear accounting authority worldwide.

The European Union, Australia, and New Zealand were the first areas to adopt these standards. Canada, China, Japan, India, and South Korea have recently implemented these standards. In total, over 100 countries are in the process of adopting the IFRS. Since January of 2011, Canadian Crown and public organizations are required to use IFRS. Other types of companies are free to choose which set of rules and principles to use. Converting to the IFRS takes up to two years for well-established, large organizations. On the other hand the United States has yet to agree to implementing IFRS. There, debate is ongoing as to how these new standards will impact the quality of reporting. Regardless of if or when the United States changes, the adoption of these new standards is having a big impact on accounting globally. In Canada, subsidiaries of U.S. companies can still continue to report using one set of rules while Canadian-owned companies operating in the same industry are subject to another set of rules. Some of the differences in the rules results in significant differences in amounts appearing in the financial statements.[20]

The accounting profession still needs to resolve some questions: Do international standards produce the same quality of reporting as country based GAAP? Would application and enforcement of international standards in the United States be as rigorous as they have been for GAAP? Canadian accounting exams and textbooks now include information on two sets of rules that can be used. This has resulted in another level of complication with financial statements for some companies operating in Canada.

Amortization, LIFO, and FIFO

Take a look at Figures 16.5 and 16.6 again. Note that in Figure 16.5, Very Vegetarian lists accumulated amortization on its property, plant, and equipment, and in Figure 16.6, Very Vegetarian lists amortization as a general expense. What exactly does this mean, and how does it affect the company's financial position? **Amortization** is the systematic writeoff of the cost of a tangible asset over its estimated useful life. These assets, including buildings, equipment, and furniture and fixtures, are used for a number of years to help a business earn revenues. Therefore, their cost needs to be *matched* against the revenues earned from using these assets, over this time period, to properly determine the profits. The **matching principle** states that revenues are recorded when earned and expenses recorded when incurred.

amortization
The systematic writeoff of the cost of a tangible asset over its estimated useful life.

matching principle
Revenues are recorded with earned and expenses are recorded when incurred.

SPOTLIGHT ON SMALL BUSINESS

Accounting for What's Coming and Going in a Small Business

A bookstore maintains stock in a certain introductory-level textbook all year. In late December, when the bookstore orders 50 additional copies of a text to sell for the coming term, the publisher's price has increased from $70 to $80 a copy due to inflation and other costs. The bookstore now has in its inventory 100 copies of the same textbook from different purchase cycles. If it sells 50 copies to students at $100 each at the beginning of the new term, what is the bookstore's cost of the book for accounting purposes? It depends.

The books are identical, but the accounting treatment is different. If the bookstore uses a method called first in, first out (FIFO), the cost of goods sold is $70 for each textbook, because the textbook the store bought first—the first in—cost $70. The bookstore could use another method, however. Under last in, first out (LIFO), its last purchase of the textbooks, at $80 each, determines the cost of each of the 50 textbooks sold. If the book sells for $100, what is the difference in gross margin between using FIFO and using LIFO? Eventually, when all 100 copies are sold the cumulative net income will be the same regardless of whether FIFO or LIFO is used. The choice between the two methods solely affects the timing of when the net income is realized.

Subject to certain technical accounting rules (set by GAAP, IFRS, and the Canada Revenue Agency) that are beyond the scope of this chapter, a firm may use one of several different techniques for calculating amortization. The key thing to understand right now is that different amortization techniques could result in a different net income for a firm. Accountants are able to offer financial advice and recommend ways of legally handling questions regarding amortization, as well as other accounts such as inventory, where different valuation methods can affect a firm's financial performance. Let's look briefly at how accountants can value inventory.

The valuation of a firm's inventory presents an interesting accounting application. Inventories are a key part of many companies' financial statements and are important in determining a firm's cost of goods sold (or manufactured) on the income statement. Look again at Very Vegetarian's income statement in Figure 16.6. When a firm sells merchandise from its inventory, it can calculate the cost of that item in different ways. In financial reporting regardless of when a particular item was actually placed in a firm's inventory, a different cost can be transferred to the income statement when the item is sold. The two most divergent accounting treatments are **first in, first out (FIFO)** and **last in, first out (LIFO)**. Sound a bit confusing? See the Spotlight on Small Business box for an example of how different inventory valuation methods can affect the numbers in an income statement.

first in, first out (FIFO)
An accounting method for calculating cost of inventory; it assumes that the first goods to come in are the first to go out.

last in, first out (LIFO)
An accounting method for calculating cost of inventory; it assumes that the last goods to come in are the first to go out (this method is not allowed in tax accounting by governments).

What is important to understand about amortization and inventory valuation is that both GAAP and IFRS can permit an accountant to use different methods of amortizing a firm's long-term assets and valuing a firm's inventory. That is why companies provide readers of their financial statements with complete information concerning their financial operations.[21]

PROGRESS ASSESSMENT

- What are the key steps in preparing an income statement?
- What is the difference between revenue and income on the income statement?
- What is the connection between the income statement and the balance sheet?
- Why is the cash flow statement important in evaluating a firm's operations?
- What is the difference between LIFO and FIFO inventory valuation? How could the use of these methods change financial results?

Demonstrate the application of ratio analysis with financial information.

ratio analysis The assessment of a firm's financial condition and performance through calculations and interpretations of financial ratios developed from the firm's financial statements.

ANALYZING FINANCIAL STATEMENTS: RATIO ANALYSIS

A firm's financial statements—its balance sheet, income statement, and cash flow statement—provide the information for financial analyses. **Ratio analysis** is the assessment of a firm's financial condition, using financial ratios calculated from the firm's financial statements. Financial ratios are especially useful in analyzing the actual performance of a company compared to its past performance, current financial objectives, and to other firms within its industry.[22] You are probably already familiar with the use of ratios. For example, in basketball, the number of shots made from the foul line is expressed by a ratio: shots made to shots attempted. A player who shoots 85 percent from the foul line is considered an outstanding foul shooter, and suggestions are to not foul him or her in a close game.

Whether ratios measure an athlete's performance or the financial health of a business, they provide a good deal of valuable information. Financial ratios provide key insights on changes in a firm's performance over time and how a firm compares to other firms in its industry in the important areas of liquidity, amount of debt, profitability, and overall business activity. Understanding and interpreting business ratios is a key to sound financial analysis. Let's look briefly at four types of ratios businesses use to measure financial performance.

Liquidity Ratios

Liquidity refers to how fast an asset can be converted to cash. Liquidity ratios measure a company's ability to turn some assets into cash to pay its short-term debts (liabilities that must be repaid within one year).[23] These short-term debts are of particular importance to creditors/lenders of the firm, who expect to be paid on time. Two key liquidity ratios are the current ratio and the acid-test ratio.

The *current ratio* is the ratio of a firm's current assets to its current liabilities. The numbers used to calculate this ratio can be found on the firm's balance sheet. Look back at Figure 16.5, Very Vegetarian's balance sheet. Very Vegetarian lists current assets of \$600,000 and current liabilities of \$288,000. The firm therefore has a current ratio of 2.08, which means Very Vegetarian has \$2.08 of current assets for every \$1 of current liabilities. See the following calculation:

$$\text{Current ratio} = \frac{\text{Current assets}}{\text{Current liabilities}} = \frac{\$600{,}000}{\$288{,}000} = 2.08$$

Given this figure, is Very Vegetarian financially secure for the short term (less than one year)? It depends! Usually a company with a current ratio of 2 or better is considered a safe risk for creditors/lenders granting short-term credit, since it has over two times more current assets available to pay their current liabilities. However, creditors/lenders will also compare Very Vegetarian's current ratio to that of competing firms in its industry and to its current ratio from the previous year investigating any significant changes.

Another key liquidity ratio, called the *acid-test* or *quick ratio,* measures the cash, marketable securities (such as stocks and bonds), and receivables of a firm, compared to its current liabilities:

$$\text{Acid test ratio} = \frac{\text{Cash} + \text{Accounts receivable} + \text{Marketable securities}}{\text{Current liabilities}}$$

$$= \frac{\$265{,}000}{\$288{,}000} = .92$$

This ratio is particularly important to firms with relatively large inventory, which can take longer than other current assets to convert into cash. It helps answer such questions as: What if sales drop off and we cannot sell our inventory? Can we still pay our short-term debt? Though ratios vary among industries, an acid-test ratio over 1.0 is usually considered satisfactory, but a ratio under 1.0 could be a hint of some cash flow problems. Therefore, Very Vegetarian's acid-test ratio of .92 could raise concerns that perhaps the firm may not meet its short-term debt obligations and may therefore have to go to a high-cost lender for financial assistance.

Leverage (Debt) Ratios

Leverage (debt) ratios measure the degree to which a firm relies on borrowed funds in its operations. A firm that takes on too much debt could experience problems repaying lenders or meeting promises made to shareholders. The *debt to owners' equity ratio* measures the degree to which the company is financed by borrowed funds that must be repaid. Again, we can use data from Figure 16.5 to measure Very Vegetarian's level of debt:

$$\text{Debt to owner's equity} = \frac{\text{Total liabilities}}{\text{Owner's equity}} = \frac{\$613{,}000}{\$213{,}000} = 287\%$$

Any number above 100 percent shows that a firm has more debt than equity. With a ratio of 287 percent, Very Vegetarian has a rather high degree of debt compared to its equity, which implies that lenders and investors may perceive the firm to be quite risky. However, it is always important to compare a firm's debt ratios to those of other firms in its industry because debt financing is more acceptable in some industries than it is in others. Comparisons with the same firm's past debt ratios can also identify trends within the firm.

Profitability (Performance) Ratios

Profitability (performance) ratios measure how effectively a firm is using its various resources to achieve profits. Company management's performance is often measured by the firm's profitability ratios. Three of the more important ratios are earnings per share (EPS), return on sales, and return on equity.

EPS is a revealing ratio because earnings help stimulate a firm's growth and provide for shareholder dividends.[24] Companies report their quarterly EPS in two ways: basic and diluted. The *basic earnings per share* (*basic EPS*) *ratio* helps determine the amount of profit a company earned for each share of outstanding common stock. The *diluted earnings per share* (*diluted EPS*) *ratio* measures the amount of profit earned for each share of outstanding common stock, but also considers stock options, warrants, preferred stock, and convertible debt securities, which can be converted into common stock. For simplicity's sake, we will compute only the basic EPS for Very Vegetarian.

$$\text{Basic earnings per share} = \frac{\text{Net income after taxes}}{\text{Average number of common shares outstanding}}$$

$$= \frac{\$49{,}000}{1{,}000{,}000} = \$.049 \text{ per share}$$

Another reliable indicator of performance is *return on sales,* which tells us how well a company is doing is generating income from sales in comparison to past performance and their competitors. Very Vegetarian's return on sales is 7 percent, a figure that must be measured against past performance and competing firms in its industry to judge its performance.

$$\text{Return on sales} = \frac{\text{Net income}}{\text{Net sales}} = \frac{\$49{,}000}{\$700{,}000} = 7\% \text{ (return on sales)}$$

The higher the risk involved in an industry, the higher the return investors expect on their investment. Therefore, the level of risk involved in an industry (which the debt ratio measures) the higher the return investors expect on their investment. *Return on equity* measures how much was earned for each dollar invested by owners. Very Vegetarian's return on equity looks reasonably sound given its debt to equity ratio:

$$\text{Return on equity} = \frac{\text{Net income}}{\text{Average total owner's equity}} = \frac{\$49{,}000}{\$213{,}000} = 23\% \text{ (return on equity)}$$

Remember that profits help companies like Very Vegetarian grow. That is why profitability ratios are such closely watched measurements of company growth and management performance.

When calculating profitability ratios you need to take into consideration the time periods involved. The EPS and return on equity ratios compare the income earned over a period of time with the number of shares outstanding and owners' equity, respectively. The latter two amounts come from the balance sheet, which provides amounts at a point of time. To deal with these timing differences, each ratio uses an average of the balance sheet amounts using balance sheets at the beginning and end of the period covered by the net income. For the above calculations, only one set of balance sheet figures is all the information we were given in Figure 16.5. You will see this approach repeated in the discussion of activity ratios.

Activity Ratios

Converting the firm's inventory to profits is a key function of management. Activity ratios tell us how effectively management is turning over inventory.

▶ Inventory turnover is critical to just about any business, particularly restaurants that serve perishable items and that must turn over tables to keep the flow of food moving and profits up. (They are limited in their earnings potential by the number of seats they have.) Can you think of other businesses that need to watch their inventory turnover closely?

Inventory turnover ratio measures the speed with which inventory moves through a firm and gets converted into sales. Idle inventory sitting in a warehouse earns nothing and costs money.[25] The more efficiently a firm sells or turns inventory, the higher its revenue. Very Vegetarian's inventory turnover is:

$$\text{Inventory turnover} = \frac{\text{Cost of goods sold}}{\text{Average inventory}} = \frac{\$410{,}000}{\$215{,}000} = 1.9 \text{ times}$$

Note that the average inventory is calculated by adding the beginning and ending inventories and dividing by two.

A lower-than-average inventory turnover ratio often indicates obsolete merchandise on hand or poor buying practices. A higher-than-average ratio may signal lost sales because of inadequate stock. Rates of inventory turnover vary from industry to industry.

Managers need to be aware of proper inventory control and expected inventory turnover to ensure proper performance. Have you ever worked as a food server in a restaurant? How many times did your employer expect you to turn over a table (keep changing customers at the table) in an evening? The more times a table turns, the higher the return to the owner.

Accountants and other finance professionals use several other specific ratios, in addition to the ones we have discussed, to learn more about a firm's financial condition. The key purpose here is to acquaint you with what financial ratios are, the relationship they have with the firm's financial statements, and how business people—including investors, creditors, lenders, and managers—use them. To review where the accounting information in ratio analysis comes from, see Figure 16.8 for a quick reference. Remember, financial analysis begins where the accounting statements end.

We hope that you can see from this chapter that there is more to accounting than meets the eye. It can be fascinating and is critical to the firm's operations. It is worth saying one more time that, as the language of business, accounting is a worthwhile language to learn.

PROGRESS ASSESSMENT

- What is the primary purpose of performing ratio analysis using a firm's financial statements?
- What are the four main categories of financial ratios?

Figure 16.8

Accounts in the Balance Sheet and Income Statement

BALANCE SHEET ACCOUNTS		
Assets	**Owners' Liabilities**	**Shareholders' Equity**
Cash	Accounts payable	Capital stock
Accounts receivable	Notes payable	Retained earnings
Inventory	Bonds payable	Common stock
Investments	Taxes payable	
Equipment		
Land		
Buildings		
Motor vehicles		
Goodwill		

INCOME STATEMENT ACCOUNTS			
Revenues	**Cost of Goods Sold**	**Expenses**	
Sales revenue	Cost of buying goods	Wages	Interest
Rental revenue	Cost of storing goods	Rent	Donations
Commissions revenue		Repairs	Licences
Royalty revenue		Travel	Fees
		Insurance	Supplies
		Utilities	Advertising
		Entertainment	Taxes
		Storage	Research

SUMMARY

Describe the role that accounting and financial information play for a business and for its stakeholders.

Financial information is critical to the growth and development of an organization. Accounting provides the information to measure a firm's financial condition in support of managing a business.

What is accounting?

Accounting is the recording, classifying, summarizing, and interpreting of financial events that affect an organization. The methods used to record and summarize accounting data into reports are called an accounting system.

Identify the different disciplines within the accounting profession.

The accounting profession covers five major areas: managerial accounting, financial accounting, compliance, tax accounting, and governmental and not-for-profit accounting.

How does managerial accounting differ from financial accounting?

Managerial accounting provides information (often of segments of a business) for planning and control purposes to managers within the firm to assist them in decision making. Financial accounting provides information in the form of the three basic financial statements to managers and external users of data such as creditors and lenders.

What is the job of an auditor?

Auditors review and evaluate the standards used to prepare a company's financial statements. An independent audit is conducted by a public accountant and is an evaluation and unbiased opinion about the accuracy of a company's financial statements.

What is the difference between a private accountant and a public accountant?

A public accountant provides services for a fee to a variety of companies, whereas a private accountant works for a single company. Private and public accountants do essentially the same things, with the exception of independent audits. Private accountants do perform internal audits, but only public accountants supply independent audits.

List the steps in the accounting cycle, distinguish between accounting and bookkeeping, and explain how computers are used in accounting.

Many people confuse bookkeeping and accounting.

What are the six steps of the accounting cycle?

The six steps of the accounting cycle are (1) analyzing documents; (2) recording information into journals; (3) posting that information into ledgers; (4) developing a trial balance; (5) preparing financial statements (the balance sheet, income statement, and cash flow statement); and (6) analyzing financial statements.

What is the difference between bookkeeping and accounting?

Bookkeeping is part of accounting and includes the mechanical part of recording data. Accounting also includes classifying, summarizing, interpreting, and reporting data to management.

What are journals and ledgers?

Journals are the first place bookkeepers record transactions. Bookkeepers than summarize journal entries by posting them to ledgers. Ledgers are specialized accounting books that arrange the transactions by homogeneous groups (accounts).

How can computers help accountants?

Computers can record and analyze data and provide financial reports. Software can ensure that the accounting equation is always in balance when recording each transaction. Computers can help decision making by providing appropriate information, but they cannot make good financial decisions independently. Accounting applications and creativity are still human traits.

Explain how the major financial statements differ.

Financial statements are a critical part of the firm's financial results/position.

What is a balance sheet?

A balance sheet reports the financial position of a firm on a particular day. The fundamental accounting equation used to prepare the balance sheet is Assets = Liabilities + Owners' equity.

What are the major accounts of the balance sheet?

Assets are economic resources owned by the firm, such as buildings and machinery. Liabilities are amounts owed by the firm to creditors, bondholders, and others. Owners' equity is the value of everything the firm owns—its assets—minus any liabilities; thus, Owners' equity = Assets − Liabilities.

What is an income statement?

An income statement reports revenues, costs, and expenses for a specific period of time (e.g., for the year ended December 31, 2012). The formulas used in preparing the income statement are:

Revenue − Cost of goods sold = Gross margin
Gross margin − Operating expenses = Net income before taxes
Net income before taxes − Taxes = Net income (or net loss)

Net income or loss is also called the bottom line.

What is a cash flow statement?

Cash flow is the difference between cash receipts (money coming in) and cash disbursements (money going out). The cash flow statement reports cash receipts and disbursements related to the firm's major activities: operations, investing, and financing.

Describe the role of accounting rules and principles in reporting financial information.

Various accounting rules make the reporting and analysis of data a challenge. Amortization is a key account that accountants evaluate. Two accounting techniques for valuing inventory are known as LIFO and FIFO.

What has happened to the nature of rules used to record business transactions?

For many years each country had their own set of rules. Each set of rules could result in differing amounts appearing in a set of financial statements based on the same set of transactions. To eliminate this issue, more and more countries are agreeing to use one set of rules, IFRS.

What is amortization?

Amortization, an application of the matching principle, is the transfer of the cost of a tangible asset to the income statement (writeoff) over its estimated useful life as an offset against the revenue earned from the use of this asset. Amortization is reflected in both the balance sheet and the income statement.

What are LIFO and FIFO?

LIFO and FIFO are methods of transferring a cost of inventory sold to the income statement. FIFO means first in, first out; LIFO means last in, first out. The method an accountant to value the transfer, FIFO or LIFO, can affect a firm's net income.

Demonstrate the application of ratio analysis with financial information.

Financial ratios are a key part of analyzing financial information.

What are the four key categories of ratios?

There are four key categories of ratios: liquidity ratios, leverage (debt) ratios, profitability (performance) ratios, and activity ratios.

What is the major value of ratio analysis to the firm?

Ratio analysis provides the firm with information about its financial position in key areas for comparison to similar firms in its industry and its past performance.

KEY TERMS

accounting
accounting cycle
accounts
accounts payable
amortization
annual report
assets
balance sheet
bonds payable
bookkeeping
capital assets
cash flow
cash flow statement
certified general accountant (CGA)
certified management accountant (CMA)
chartered accountant (CA)
compliance
cost of goods sold (cost of goods manufactured)
current assets
double-entry bookkeeping
financial accounting
financial statement
first in, first out (FIFO)
forensic accounting
fundamental accounting equation
gross profit (gross margin)
income statement
independent audit
intangible assets
journal
last in, first out (LIFO)
ledger
liabilities
liquidity
managerial accounting
matching principle
net income or net loss
notes payable
operating expenses
owners' equity
private accountant
public accountant
ratio analysis
retained earnings
tax accountant
taxes payable
trial balance

CRITICAL THINKING

1. In business, hundreds of documents are received or created every day, so you can appreciate the valuable role an accountant plays. Can you see why most businesses have to hire people to do this work? Would it be worth the owners' time to do all the paperwork? Can you understand why most accountants find it easier to do this work on a computer?
2. As a potential investor in a firm or perhaps the buyer of a business, would you be interested in evaluating the company's financial statements? Why or why not? What key information you would seek from a firm's financial statements?
3. Why should information on the rules and principles followed in preparing a set of financial statements be disclosed? Would it be advisable to allow businesses some flexibility or creativity in preparing financial statements?
4. What value do financial ratios offer investors in reviewing the financial performance of a company? Why is it important to remember financial ratios can differ from industry to industry?

DEVELOPING WORKPLACE SKILLS

1. Visit, telephone, or e-mail a professional accountant from a local company in your area, or talk with one in your school's business department. Ask what challenges, changes, and opportunities he or she foresees in the accounting profession in the next five years. List the forecasts on a sheet of paper and then compare them with the information in this chapter.
2. Place yourself in the role of a small-business consultant. One of your clients, Be Pretty Fashions, is considering opening two new stores. Their industry experiences continuous style changes that occur in the fashion industry. Prepare a formal draft memo to Be Pretty Fashions explaining the difficulties a firm experiences when it encounters the cash flow problems that typically occur in this industry. Think of a business option that Be Pretty Fashions could try to avoid cash flow problems.
3. Suppose you are a new board member for an emerging not-for-profit organization hoping to attract new donors. Contributors large and small want to know how efficiently not-for-profit organizations use their donations. Unfortunately, your fellow board members see little value in financial reporting and analysis and believe the good works of the organization speak for themselves. Prepare a fact sheet convincing the board of the need for effective financial reporting with arguments about why it helps the organization's fund-raising goals.
4. Obtain the most recent annual report for a Canadian company of your choice. (*The Globe and Mail* has a free annual reports service; order a report at http://globeinvestor.ar.wilink.com/v5/index.asp?cp_code=%20A169&.) Using data from the annual report, try your hand at computing financial ratios. Compute the current ratio, debt to owners' equity ratio, and return on sales for the firm. Next, obtain an annual report of one of the company's competitors and compute the same ratios for that company; then compare the ratios.

ANALYZING MANAGEMENT DECISIONS

Getting Through the Hard Times at Hard Rock

In the mid-1990s, the theme-dining business seemed like a path lined with gold. With regularity, celebrity stargazers, enthusiastic press from around the globe, and hungry customers gathered at the openings of theme restaurants such as Planet Hollywood and Motown Cafe. Unfortunately, the situation changed. In the late 1990s and early 2000s, Planet Hollywood filed for bankruptcy protection and Motown Cafe closed units across the country. Consumer boredom, a slowing economy, and a saturated market were blamed.

The changing "entertainment" market raised eyebrows at the granddaddy of theme restaurants, the Hard Rock Cafe (HRC <*www.hardrock.com*>). HRC knew that its market position was shaky due to increased competition and shifting consumer attitudes. The company also felt growing financial pressures and speculated that a change in financial management might be needed. HRC had operated with a traditional, competent accounting department that ensured that the company paid its bills, had money left at the end of the day, and could state how much it was earning. The problem was that HRC lacked the ability to analyze its financial information fully and use it to improve operations. To address these concerns, the company recruited a new CFO and dedicated itself to changing the financial reporting and information structure at the company.

Hard Rock Cafe believed that it had a tremendous undervalued asset—a premium global brand. The company dedicated itself to protecting and expanding that asset. However, it was evident that, without revenue, brand loyalty did not matter. Hard Rock's CFO was astonished to find that HRC sold $180 million per year in merchandise (primarily its well-known T-shirts) in addition to food, yet could not explain exactly how these individual items contributed to the firm's profit. It was then that the company realized that Hard Rock Cafe's accounting and financial management had to change.

To begin, the company piloted a food and beverage management system to track usage and item profitability. This system included information such as daily and seasonal buying patterns, profitability of one menu versus another, average weekly guest counts per restaurant, and specific cost of sales and profit margins per item. The company then shifted the responsibility of the firm's accountants. Instead of being responsible for profit-and-loss statements for a certain number of restaurants, company accountants now were responsible for one major financial category only, such as cost of goods sold, for all of the company's operations. The objective was to compile companywide information for sound financial decision making.

Hard Rock Cafe also broke down the barriers that existed between the finance and accounting departments and operations, merchandising, and marketing. Today, financial information is shared directly with managers who can execute the recommendations at the restaurant level. Still, the company realized that this was not going to be a quick fix but rather an ongoing challenge. There are now 139 Hard Rock Cafe locations and 16 Hotels/Casinos located in 53 countries around the world. Even so, competitors such as Rainforest Cafe promise to make the fight for entertainment customers an interesting one.

Sources: "Hard Rock History," http://www.hardrock.com/corporate/history.aspx, 4 September 2012; Larry Bleiberg. "Cafe Quest Has Retiree on a Roll," *Dallas Morning News*, 15 March 2000, 12G; "Rank Is Betting on Another Good Year," *Birmingham (UK) Post*, 1 March 2003, 15; and Jon Griffin, "Rank Is Backing a Winner," *Evening Mail (UK)*, 28 February 2003, 26.

Discussion Questions

1. Why is it important for Hard Rock Cafe to know how different products contribute financially to overall company profits?
2. Do you think that Hard Rock Cafe's focus on improved financial reporting helped its company planning capabilities? How?
3. In terms of accounting principles, what would you need to remember when analyzing the financial performance of the Hard Rock Cafe, a U.S. business, to the Keg Steakhouse and Bar, a Canadian business?

Practise and learn online with Connect.

CHAPTER 17

FINANCIAL MANAGEMENT

LEARNING OBJECTIVES

After you have read and studied this chapter, you should be able to:

LO 1 Explain the role and responsibilities of financial managers.

LO 2 Outline the financial planning process, and explain the three key budgets in the financial plan.

LO 3 Explain why firms need funds.

LO 4 Identify and describe different sources of short-term financing.

LO 5 Identify and describe different sources of long-term financing.

PROFILE

GETTING TO KNOW STEVE GLOVER OF CLEARVIEW RESOURCES LTD. AND WESTERN PLAINS PETROLEUM LTD.

Clearview Resources Ltd. is a conventional oil and gas company that was reorganized and recapitalized in 2010. Since that time three producing oil and gas properties have been purchased, giving the company estimated oil and gas reserves of 2.0 million barrels of liquids (oil and other natural gas liquids) and 4.2 million mcf of natural gas. The company raised $23 million in equity and arranged bank credit facilities totalling $19.0 million. Going forward, Clearview expects its cash flows from future oil and natural gas production to fund capital expenditures and dividends.

Western Plains Petroleum Ltd. <*www.westernplainspetroleum.com*>, a heavy oil producer, was founded in Lloydminster, Alberta, in 2004 and listed on the TSX Venture Exchange. This junior oil and gas company is involved in the acquisition, exploration, and development of conventional heavy oil.

The company currently operates oil properties in close proximity to each other in eastern Alberta and western Saskatchewan. Revenue fluctuated between $800 thousand and $1,200 thousand for the quarters ended December 31, 2011, and March 31, 2012. This fluctuation was due in part to shutting down some production in the most recent quarter for some significant repairs at well sites.

Funding comes from both debt and equity financing, which will be discussed in this chapter. Recently the company violated their bank loan agreement in terms of the relationship between their current assets and liabilities. This situation is one of the risks associated with the use of debt to finance a business.

Both of these public companies have risks associated with operations in the context of finding and developing oil and gas reserves, safety and environmental concerns, and financial risks with respect to commodity prices, interest rates, and exchange rates. One of the ways to manage the financial risks is through hedging oil prices by entering future contracts for the sale of oil based on a fixed price.

Steve Glover is the Chief Financial Officer for both of these public companies. He is also on the Board of Directors, as Chair of the Audit Committee, of Genesis Land Development Corporation <*www.genesisland.com*>; a land development company that has been involved in residential, commercial, and light industrial properties since 1997. This company's main focus is in and around Calgary. For the three months ended March 31, 2012, revenues were over $22 million, and as at March 31, 2012, the balance sheet had assets of $370 million. He is also on the board of Travel Alberta <*travelalberta.com*>, a relatively new Crown corporation of the Province of Alberta, with a current annual budget of $50 million per year. The mandate of this organization is to promote tourism in the province. As the Chair of the Audit Committee, Steve draws on his strong financial skill set in supporting this not-for-profit's important mandate and meeting its requirement to be publicly accountable.

Steve received his undergraduate degree in 1975, became a professional accountant in 1976, and subsequently completed his MBA in 1986. He was also employed in two other oil and gas companies as their Vice President, Finance, and Chief Financial Officer. Before assuming these senior positions in for the for-profit sector, Steve worked for over 25 years for the Institute of Chartered Accountants of Alberta.

For a great portion of his career Steve has served in a number of volunteer positions, including his current role as Treasurer for the Yellowstone to Yukon Conservation Initiative <*y2y.net*>. This initiative is a joint Canada–United States not-for-profit organization that seeks to preserve and maintain the wildlife, native plants, wilderness, and natural processes of the mountainous region from Yellowstone Park to the Yukon territory. Cross-border restrictions and land conservation goals create unique governance, operational, tax, and financial management issues for which high-order business and financial skills are critical.

Starting his career with a primary focus on accounting, Steve's experience has led him to senior financial positions in multiple organizations where financial expertise is required to ensure their long-term viability. Steve exemplifies the importance of a sound understanding of the complementary relationship of accounting and finance, which will be discussed in this chapter.

Source: MD & A, Western Plains Petroleum for the Year-ended December 31, 2011; MD & A, Western Plains Petroleum for the 3 months ended March 31, 2012; MD & A for Clearview Resources for the 3 months ending March 31, 2012; MD & A, Genesis Land Development Corporation for the 3 months ending March 31, 2012; resume provided by Steve Glover, June 2012.

Explain the role and responsibilities of financial managers.

finance
The function in a business that acquires funds for the firm and manages them within the firm.

financial management
The job of managing a firm's resources to meet its goals and objectives.

financial managers
Managers who examine the financial data prepared by accountants and recommend strategies for improving the financial performance of the firm.

THE ROLE OF FINANCE AND FINANCIAL MANAGERS

The goal of this chapter is to answer two major questions: "What is finance?" and "What do financial managers do?" **Finance** is the function in a business that acquires funds for the firm and manages them within the firm. Finance activities include preparing budgets; doing cash flow analysis; and planning for the expenditure of funds on such assets as plant, equipment, and machinery. **Financial management** is the job of managing a firm's resources to meet its goals and objectives. Without a carefully calculated financial plan, the firm has little chance for survival, regardless of its product or marketing effectiveness. Let's briefly review the roles of accountants and financial managers.

We can compare an accountant to a skilled laboratory technician who takes blood samples and other measures of a person's health and writes the findings on a health report (in business, the process is the preparation of financial statements). A financial manager is like the doctor who interprets the report and makes recommendations that will improve the patient's health. In short, **financial managers** examine the financial data prepared by accountants and recommend strategies for improving the financial performance of the firm.

Clearly financial managers can make sound financial decisions only if they understand accounting information. That is why we examined accounting in Chapter 16. Similarly, a good accountant needs to understand finance. Accounting and finance go together like peanut butter and jelly. In large and medium-sized organizations, both the accounting and the finance functions are generally under the control of a chief financial officer, treasurer, or a vice president of finance.[1]

Figure 17.1 highlights a financial manager's tasks. As you can see, two key responsibilities are to obtain funds and to effectively control the use of those funds.[2] Finance is a critical activity in both profit-seeking and non-profit organizations. The role of advising top management on financial matters has become even more important in recent years as risk has increased. Appendix D, immediately following this chapter, is devoted to the subject of financial risk.

Finance is important regardless of a firm's size. As you may remember from Chapter 7, financing a small business is essential if a firm expects to survive its important first five years. But the need for careful financial management remains a challenge that a business, large or small, must face throughout its existence. In 2009 and 2010 the Canadian divisions of General Motors and Chrysler required significant loans from both the federal and Ontario governments because of severe financial problems.[3]

Figure 17.1

What Financial Managers Do

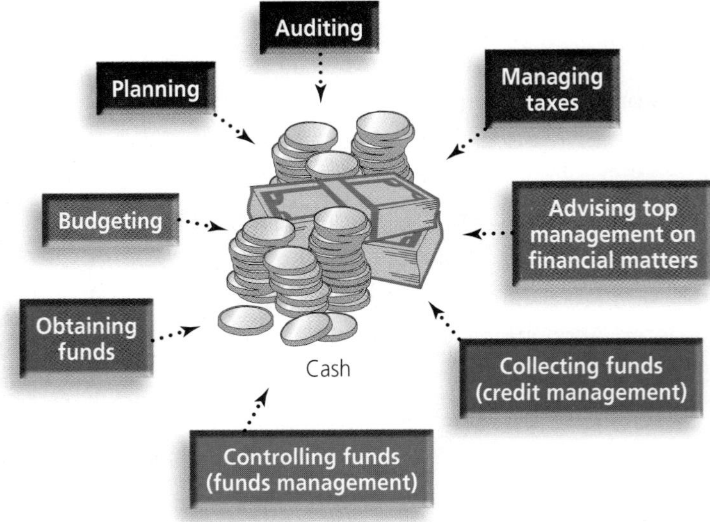

The Value of Understanding Finance

Three of the most common reasons a firm fails financially are:

1. Undercapitalization (insufficient funds to start a business)
2. Poor control over cash flow
3. Inadequate expense control

You can see all three in the following story.

Two friends, Elizabeth Bertani and Pat Sherwood, started a company called Parsley Patch on what can best be described as a shoestring budget. It began when Bertani prepared salt-free seasonings for her husband, who was on a no-salt diet. Her friend Sherwood thought the seasonings were good enough to sell. Bertani agreed, and Parsley Patch Inc. was born. The business began with an investment of $5,000, rapidly depleted on a logo and label design. Bertani and Sherwood quickly learned the importance of capital in getting a business going. Eventually, they invested more than $100,000 of their own money to keep the business from being undercapitalized.

Everything started well, and hundreds of gourmet shops adopted the product line. But when sales failed to meet expectations, the women decided the health-food market offered more potential because salt-free seasonings were a natural for people with restricted diets. The choice was a good one. Sales soared, approaching $30,000 a month. Still, the company earned no profits.

Bertani and Sherwood were not trained in monitoring cash flow or in controlling expenses. In fact, they had been told not to worry about costs, and they hadn't. They eventually hired a chartered accountant (CA) and an experienced financial manager, who taught them how to compute the costs of their products, and how to control expenses as well as cash moving in and out of the company (cash flow). Soon Parsley Patch was earning a comfortable margin on operations that ran close to $1 million a year. Luckily, the owners were able to turn things around before it was too late. Eventually, they sold the firm to spice and seasonings giant McCormick.

If Bertani and Sherwood had understood finance before starting their business, they may have been able to avoid the problems they encountered. The key word here is *understood.* You do not have to pursue finance as a career to understand it. Understanding finance is important to anyone who wants to start a small business, invest in stocks and bonds, or plan a retirement fund.[4]

In short, finance and accounting are two areas everyone involved in business should study. Since we discussed accounting in Chapter 16, let's look more closely at what financial management is all about.

What Is Financial Management?

Financial managers are responsible for paying a company's bills at the appropriate time and for collecting overdue payments to make sure the company does not lose too much money to bad debts (people or firms that do not pay their bills). Therefore, finance functions such as buying merchandise on credit (accounts payable) and collecting payments from customers (accounts receivable) are key components of the financial manager's job (see Figure 17.1). While these functions are vital to all types of businesses, they are critical to small and medium-sized businesses, which typically have smaller cash or credit cushions than large corporations.[5]

▸ Most businesses have predictable day-to-day needs, like the need to buy supplies, pay for fuel and utilities, and pay employees. Financial management is the function that helps ensure firms have the funds they need when they need them. What would happen to the company providing the work in this photo if it couldn't buy gas for its truck and tools for its employees?

It is essential that financial managers stay abreast of changes in tax law, since taxes represent an outflow of cash from a business.[6] Financial managers must also analyze the tax implications of managerial decisions to minimize the taxes the business must pay. Usually a member of a firm's finance department, the internal auditor, also checks the journals, ledgers, and financial statements the accounting department prepares, to make sure all transactions are in accordance with generally accepted accounting principles.[7] Without such audits, accounting statements would be less reliable. Therefore, it is important that internal auditors be objective and critical of any improprieties or deficiencies noted in their evaluation. Another purpose of an internal audit is to safeguard assets, including cash. Thorough internal audits assist the firm in financial planning, which we'll look at next.

Outline the financial planning process, and explain the three key budgets in the financial plan.

FINANCIAL PLANNING

Financial planning means analyzing short-term and long-term money flows to and from a firm. Its overall objective is to optimize the firm's profitability and make the best use of its money.[8] It has three steps: (1) forecasting a firm's short-term and long-term financial needs, (2) developing budgets to meet those needs, and (3) establishing financial control to see whether the company is achieving its goals (see Figure 17.2). Let's look at each step and the role it plays in improving the organization's financial health.

short-term forecast
Forecast that predicts revenues, costs, and expenses for a period of one year or less.

cash flow forecast
Forecast that predicts the cash inflows and outflows in future periods, usually months or quarters.

Forecasting Financial Needs

Forecasting is an important part of any firm's financial plan. A **short-term forecast** predicts revenues, costs, and expenses for a period of one year or less. Part of the short-term forecast may be in the form of a **cash flow forecast**, which predicts the cash inflows and outflows in future periods, usually months or quarters. The inflows

Figure 17.2

Financial Planning

Note the close link between financial planning and budgeting.

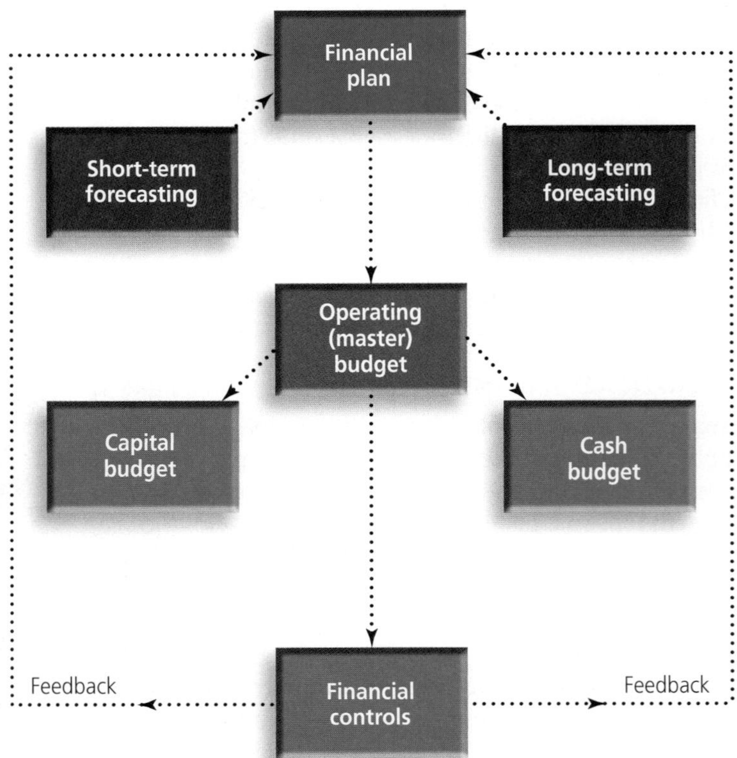

and outflows of cash recorded in the cash flow forecast are based on expected sales revenues and on various costs and expenses incurred, as well as when they are due for payment.[9] The company's sales forecast estimates the firm's projected sales for a particular period. A business often uses its past financial statements as a basis for projecting expected sales and various costs and expenses.[10]

A **long-term forecast** predicts revenues, costs, and expenses for a period longer than one year, and sometimes as long as five or ten years. This forecast plays a crucial part in the company's long-term strategic plan, which asks questions such as these: What business are we in? Should we be in it five years from now? How much money should we invest in technology and new plant and equipment over the next decade? Will there be cash available to meet long-term obligations? Innovations in Web-based software help financial managers address these long-term forecasting questions.

The long-term financial forecast gives top management, as well as operations managers, some sense of the income or profit of different strategic plans. It also helps in preparing company budgets.

long-term forecast
Forecast that predicts revenues, costs, and expenses for a period longer than one year, and sometimes as far as five or ten years into the future.

budget
A financial plan that sets forth management's expectations, and, on the basis of those expectations, allocates the use of specific resources throughout the firm.

operating (master) budget
The budget that ties together all of a firm's other budgets and summarizes the business's proposed financial activities.

capital budget
A budget that highlights a firm's spending plans for major asset purchases that often require large sums of money, like property, buildings, and equipment.

cash budget
A budget that estimates a firm's cash inflows and outflows during a particular period (e.g. monthly, quarterly).

Working with the Budget Process

A **budget** sets forth management's expectations for revenues and, on the basis of those expectations, allocates the use of specific resources throughout the firm. As a financial plan, it depends heavily on the accuracy of a firm's balance sheet, income statement, the cash flow statement, and short-term and long-term financial forecasts, all of which need to be as accurate as possible. To prepare budgets, financial managers must therefore take their forecasting responsibilities seriously.[11] A budget becomes the primary guide for the firm's financial operations and financial needs.

There are usually several types of budgets established in a firm's financial plan:

- An operating (master) budget
- A capital budget
- A cash budget

The **operating (master) budget** ties together all of the firm's other budgets and summarizes the business's proposed financial activities. More formally it estimates costs and expenses needed to run a business, given projected revenues.[12] A firm's spending on supplies, travel, rent, advertising, research, salaries, and so forth is determined in the operating (master) budget. This budget is generally the most detailed (firms will prepare this budget for each of their divisions/departments) and most used budget that a firm prepares (see the following discussion on financial controls). Most firms will prepare 12 monthly operating budgets for the next year. Typically, those responsible for the activities reflected within the operating budget(s) are involved in its preparation. Ultimately the firm's board of directors is responsible for approving all budgets. Often the entire budget process can take months and involve a significant amount of time.

A **capital budget** highlights a firm's spending plans for major asset purchases that often require large sums of money, like property, buildings, and equipment.

A **cash budget** estimates cash inflows and outflows during a particular period (e.g., monthly, quarterly). It helps managers anticipate borrowing needs, debt repayment, operating expenses, and short-term investments,

▸ Special processing equipment turns an average potato into the chips and fries we consume. The firm's capital budget is the financial tool that controls business spending for expensive assets such as this processing equipment. Such major assets are referred to as capital assets or property, plant, and equipment. What items would be in your school's capital budget?

Figure 17.3

A Sample Cash Budget for Very Vegetarian

VERY VEGETARIAN Monthly Cash Budget			
	January	*February*	*March*
Sales forecast	$50,000	$45,000	$40,000
Collections			
Cash sales (20%)		$9,000	$8,000
Credit sales (80% of past month)		$40,000	$36,000
Monthly cash collection		$49,000	$44,000
Payments schedule			
Supplies and material		$11,000	$10,000
Salaries		12,000	12,000
Direct labour		9,000	9,000
Taxes		3,000	3,000
Other expenses		7,000	6,000
Monthly cash payments		$42,000	$40,000
Cash budget			
Cash flow		$7,000	$5,000
Beginning cash		−1,000	6,000
Total cash		$6,000	$11,000
Less minimum cash balance		−6,000	−6,000
Excess cash to market securities		$0	$5,000
Loans needed for minimum balance		0	0

and is often the last budget prepared.[13] A sample cash budget for our example company, Very Vegetarian, is provided in Figure 17.3. When looking at the collection of sales in Figure 17.3, notice that collections are divided into cash and credit sales. Typically collections of sales occur over more than the month when the sale is made. Sales, especially made in the latter part of a given month, will not be collected until the following month. In Figure 17.3, amounts representing the monthly cash collections are based on collecting 20 percent of the current month's sales and 80 percent of the prior month's sales.

When forecasting the cash budget, not only do you want to identify the projected increase or decrease in cash for the month, but you also want to ensure that you maintain a minimum cash balance (a safety level). For planning purposes, you need to know when your projected cash balance may fall below the minimum, so that you can change how you will manage either your cash collections or your cash payments.

For example, when putting together the monthly cash budget in Figure 17.3, if the original payments schedule had projected salaries of $15,000, then February's cash budget would have ended up with total cash of $3,000. As such, after subtracting the minimum cash balance the excess cash would have had a balance of −$3,000. This amount would not be acceptable and therefore changes would have to be made to some of the assumptions. The other option would be to arrange for short-term financing to cover the expected shortfall.

Conversely, you should manage cash surpluses by planning for short-term investments (as illustrated in March in Figure 17.3) given the time value of money (which we will discuss later in this chapter). Regardless of how comfortable you are with your planning, investing your excess cash with fraudulent financiers like Bernie Madoff can have a devastating impact on your ability to carry on your business.

Clearly, financial planning plays an important role in a firm's operations and often determines what long-term investments it makes, when it will need specific funds, and how it will generate them. Once a company forecasts its short-term and long-term financial needs and compiles budgets to show how it will allocate funds, the final step in financial planning is to establish financial controls. We will discuss this topic in a moment. But first, the Spotlight on Small Business box on the next page challenges you to check your personal financial planning skill by developing a monthly budget for "You, Incorporated."

Establishing Financial Controls

Financial control is a process in which a firm periodically compares its actual revenues, costs, and expenses with its budget. Most companies hold at least monthly financial reviews as a way to ensure financial control. Such control procedures help managers identify variances to the financial plan and allow them to take corrective action if necessary. Financial controls also provide feedback to help reveal which accounts, which departments, and which people are varying from the financial plans. Finance managers can judge if these variances may or may not be justified, allowing them to make some financial adjustments to the plan when needed. The rapid spike and equally rapid fall in oil prices in 2008 caused many companies to adjust their financial plans.[14] The credit crisis that year also forced many companies to alter their long-term financing plans. The Making Ethical Decisions box details a management situation related to financial control. After the Progress Assessment, we will see why firms need readily available funds.

financial control
A process in which a firm periodically compares its actual revenues, costs, and expenses with its projected ones.

PROGRESS ASSESSMENT

- Name three finance functions important to the firm's overall operations and performance.
- What are the three primary financial problems that cause firms to fail?
- How do short-term and long-term financial forecasts differ?
- What is the purpose of preparing budgets in an organization? Can you identify three different types of budgets?

MAKING ETHICAL DECISIONS

Sail Smoothly or Rock the Boat?

Assume you have recently taken a new job as financial manager at a mid-sized pharmaceutical company. After working there just a few months, you sense the attitude of most employees at the company is "Who cares?" Salespeople do not turn in detailed expense reports for their travel, nor do they provide receipts to receive reimbursement for meals and other expenses, through the company operations manual say such documentation is required. You also notice employees readily help themselves to office supplies like pens, paper, printer cartridges, and staplers, with no questions asked.

As a meeting of the firm's executive committee you cite the many financial control flaws you have noted and suggest that the company toughen up on lax employee behaviour. The CEO says, "My dad started this company twenty-eight years ago and frankly this is the way it's always been. Probably the best thing we can do is not rock the boat." What will you do? What could result from your decision?

SPOTLIGHT ON SMALL BUSINESS

You, Incorporated, Monthly Budget

Let's develop a monthly budget for You, Inc. Be honest and think of everything that needs to be included for an accurate monthly budget for You! Much like a small business, when putting the monthly budget together, remember that the norm is to overestimate income and underestimate expenses. Often you need to revisit the budget a number of times before finalizing the numbers as you try to balance the income with the expenses to hopefully eliminate cash deficits.

	Expected	Actual	Difference
Monthly income:			
Wages (net pay after taxes)	______	______	______
Savings account withdrawal	______	______	______
Family support	______	______	______
Other sources	______	______	______
Total monthly income	______	______	______
Monthly expenses:			
Fixed expenses			
Rent or mortgage	______	______	______
Car payment	______	______	______
Life insurance	______	______	______
Tuition or fees	______	______	______
Other fixed expenses	______	______	______
Subtotal of fixed expenses	______	______	______
Variable expenses			
Food	______	______	______
Clothing	______	______	______
Entertainment	______	______	______
Transportation	______	______	______
Phone	______	______	______
Utilities	______	______	______
Publications	______	______	______
Internet connection	______	______	______
Cable television	______	______	______
Other expenses	______	______	______
Subtotal of variable expenses	______	______	______
Total expenses	______	______	______
Total income − Total expenses = Cash on hand/(Cash deficit)	______	______	______

THE NEED FOR FUNDS

Explain why firms need funds.

In business, the need for funds never seems to cease. That is why sound financial management is essential to all businesses. Like our personal financial needs, those of a business change over time. Remember the example of Parsley Patch to see why a small business's financial requirements can shift considerably. The same is true for large corporations such as Barrick Gold Corporation <*www.barrick.com*>, Irving Oil, and McCain Foods when they venture into new product areas or markets. Virtually all organizations have needs for which funds must be available. Key areas include:

- Managing day-to-day needs of the business;
- Controlling credit operations;
- Acquiring needed inventory; and
- Making capital expenditures.

Let's look at these financial needs, which affect both the smallest and the largest of businesses.

Managing Day-to-Day Needs of a Business

If workers expect to be paid on Friday, they do not want to have to wait until Monday for their paycheques. If tax payments are due on the fifteenth of the month, the government expects the money on time. If the payment on a business loan is due on the thirtieth, the lender does not mean the first of the next month. Refer to the Green Box for a discussion of funding needs associated with an environmental issue. As you can see, funds have to be available to meet the daily operational costs of a business.

Financial managers must ensure that funds are available to meet daily cash needs without compromising the firm's opportunities to invest money for its future. Money has *time value.*[15] In other words, if someone offered to give you $200 today or one year from today, you would benefit by taking the $200 today. Why? It is very simple. You could invest the $200 you receive today, start collecting interest, and over a year's time it would grow. The same thing is true in business; the interest a firm gains on its investments is important in maximizing the profit it will gain. That is why financial managers often try to minimize cash expenditures to free up funds for investment in interest-bearing accounts.[16] They suggest the company pay its bills as late as possible (unless a cash discount is available for early payment). They also advise companies to try to collect what is owed to them as fast as possible, to maximize the investment potential of the firm's funds. Efficient cash management is particularly important to small firms since their access to capital is much more limited than that of larger businesses.[17]

▸ It's difficult to think of a business that doesn't make credit available to its customers. Collecting accounts receivable from some customers can be time-consuming and costly. Accepting credit cards like Visa, MasterCard, or American Express simplifies transactions, guarantees payment, and provides convenience for both customers and businesses at minimal cost. For what sort of purchases do you regularly use a credit card?

Controlling Credit Operations

Financial managers know that making credit available helps keep current customers happy and attracts new ones, especially in today's highly competitive business environment. Credit for customers was especially important during the financial crisis of 2008 since banks were hesitant to make loans.

GREENBOX

Environmental Credits, Cap and Trade

Carbon credits are meant to reduce greenhouse gas emissions and fight climate change through the use of carbon offsets. In the past few years, environmentalists and green-minded civilians have been jumping on board the carbon credit bandwagon, calculating their personal emissions and purchasing credits to neutralize the pollution they contribute to the atmosphere by the simple act of driving to work or running the dishwasher.

Carbon credits correspond to a determined tradable quantity of greenhouse gas (GHG) emissions. They are normally quoted in metric tonnes of carbon dioxide equivalent, and are used to offset emissions from the combustion of fossil fuels in any process that uses energy that emits GHGs, whether in industry, transportation, or the household.

In August of 2008, the province of British Columbia was the first Canadian jurisdiction to pass legislation dealing with climate change. They passed the Western Climate Initiative, which requires B.C. businesses to begin reducing their GHG emissions to 33 percent below their 2005 levels. If these greenhouse gases cannot be reduced, companies will be required to offset their pollution via a new form of environmental currency, the carbon credit.

Companies (such as Planetair <*planetair.ca*>, a not-for-profit service offered by the Unisféra International Centre <*unisfera.org*>) have been created to help individuals, corporations, and institutions reduce their climate footprint by raising awareness of how day-to-day activities impact global climate and supporting initiatives like the trading of carbon credits.

In 2009 the trading of carbon credits globally amounted to over $100 billion. Many organizations now have to provide funds specifically for the purchase of these credits.

There's no shortage of carbon-neutral suppliers to choose from, but prices can vary. While some companies charge as little as US$5.50 per metric tonne of carbon dioxide, the price can go as high as US$13.00 per tonne.

Sources: Planetair Home Page, http://planetair.ca; and wikipedia.org/wiki/Carbon_offset.

The problem with selling on credit is that a large percentage of a non-retailer's business assets could be tied up in its credit accounts (accounts receivable). This forces the firm to use its own funds to pay for goods or services sold to customers who bought on credit. Financial managers in such firms often develop efficient collection procedures like offering cash or quantity discounts to buyers who pay their accounts by a certain time. They also scrutinize old and new credit customers to see whether they have a history of meeting their credit obligations on time.[18]

One convenient way to decrease the time and expense of collecting accounts receivable is to accept bank credit cards such as MasterCard or Visa.[19] The banks that issue these cards have already established the customer's creditworthiness, which reduces the business's risk. Businesses must pay a fee to accept credit cards, but the fees are usually offset by the benefits.

Acquiring Needed Inventory

As we noted earlier in the text, effective marketing requires focusing on the customer and providing high-quality service and readily available goods. A carefully constructed inventory policy helps manage the firm's available funds and maximize profitability. For example, Take-a-Dip, a neighbourhood ice cream parlour, ties up more funds in inventory (ice cream) in the summer than in the winter. It is obvious why. Demand for ice cream goes up in the summer.

Just-in-time inventory control (discussed in Chapter 10) and other such methods reduce the funds a firm must tie up in inventory. Carefully evaluating its inventory turnover ratio (discussed in Chapter 16), can also help a firm control outflow of cash for inventory. A business of any size must understand that poorly managed inventory can seriously affect cash flow and drain its finances dry.

Making Capital Expenditures

Capital expenditures are major investments in either tangible long-term assets such as land, buildings, and equipment, or intangible assets such as patents, trademarks, and copyrights. In many organizations the purchase of major assets—such as land for future expansion, manufacturing plants to increase production capabilities, research to develop new product ideas, and equipment to maintain or exceed current levels of output—is essential. Expanding into new markets can be expensive with no guarantee of success. Therefore, it is critical that companies weigh all possible options before committing a large portion of available resources.

capital expenditures
Major investments in either tangible long-term assets such as land, buildings, and equipment, or intangible assets such as patents, trademarks, and copyrights.

Consider a firm that needs to expand its production capabilities due to increased customer demand. It could buy land and build a new plant, purchase an existing plant, or rent space. Can you think of financial and accounting considerations at play in this decision?

The need for operating funds raises several questions for financial managers: How does the firm obtain funds to finance operations and other business needs? Will it require specific funds in the long term or short term? How much will it cost to obtain these funds? Will they come from internal or external sources? We address these questions next.

Alternative Sources of Funds

We described finance earlier as the function in a business responsible for acquiring and managing funds. Sound financial management determines the amount of money needed and the most appropriate sources from which to obtain it. A firm can raise needed capital by borrowing money (debt), selling ownership (equity), or earning profits (retained earnings). **Equity financing** is money raised from within the firm (from operations) or through the sale of ownership in the firm (stock). **Debt financing** refers to funds raised through various forms of borrowing that must be repaid. Firms can borrow funds either short-term or long-term. **Short-term financing** refers to funds needed for one year or less. **Long-term financing** refers to funds needed for more than one year (usually two to ten years).[20] Figure 17.4 highlights why firms may need short-term and long-term funds.

We'll explore the different sources of short-term and long-term financing next. Let's first pause to check your understanding by doing the Progress Assessment.

equity financing
Funds raised from operations within the firm or through the sale of ownership in the firm.

debt financing
Funds raised through various forms of borrowing that must be repaid.

short-term financing
Borrowed funds that are needed for one year or less.

long-term financing
Borrowed funds that are needed for a period more than one year.

PROGRESS ASSESSMENT

- Money has time value. What does this mean?
- Why is accounts receivable a financial concern to a firm?
- What's the primary reason an organization spends a good deal of its available funds on inventory and capital expenditures?
- What is the difference between debt and equity financing?

Short-Term Funds	Long-Term Funds
Monthly expenses	New-product development
Unanticipated emergencies	Replacement of capital equipment
Cash flow problems	Mergers or acquisitions
Expansion of current inventory	Expansion into new markets (domestic or global)
Temporary promotional programs	New facilities

Figure 17.4
Why Firms Need Funds

LO 4

Identify and describe different sources of short-term financing

OBTAINING SHORT-TERM FINANCING

The bulk of a finance manager's job does not involve obtaining long-term funds.[21] In small businesses, for example, long-term financing is often out of the question. Instead, day-to-day operations call for the careful management of *short-term* financial needs. Firms may need to borrow short-term funds to purchase additional inventory or to pay unexpected bills. Like an individual, a business, especially a small business, sometimes needs to secure short-term funds if its cash reserves are low. Let's see how it does so.

Most small businesses are primarily concerned with just staying afloat until they are able to build capital and creditworthiness. Until a small business gets to that point, normally a lender will require some form of security for a loan. The security would typically be in the form of collateral (to be discussed later), or a personal guarantee. Firms can obtain short-term financing in several different ways. Let's look at the major forms of short-term financing and what is meant by secured and unsecured financing with regard to different ways of obtaining needed funds.

Trade Credit

trade credit
The practice of buying goods and services now and paying for them later.

Trade credit is the practice of buying goods or services now and paying for them later. It is the most widely used source of short-term funding, the least expensive, and the most convenient. Small businesses rely heavily on trade credit from firms such as United Parcel Service, as do large firms such as the Bay. When a firm buys merchandise, it receives an invoice (a bill) much like the one you receive when you buy something with a credit card. As you will see, however, the terms businesses receive are often different than those on your monthly statement.

Business invoices usually contain terms such as *2/10, net 30.* This means the buyer can take a 2 percent discount for paying the invoice within 10 days. Otherwise the total bill (net) is due in 30 days. Finance managers pay close attention to such discounts because they create opportunities to reduce the firm's costs. Think about it for a moment: If terms are 2/10, net 30, the customer will pay 2 percent more by waiting an extra 20 days to pay the invoice. If the firm *can* pay its bill within 10 days, it is needlessly increasing its costs by waiting.

Some suppliers hesitate to give trade credit to an organization with a poor credit rating, no credit history, or a history of slow payment. They may insist the customer sign a **promissory note**, a written contract with a promise to pay a supplier a specific sum of money at a definite time. Promissory notes are negotiable. The supplier can sell them to a bank at a discount (the amount of the note less a fee for the bank's services in collecting the amount due).

promissory note
A written contract with a promise to pay.

Family and Friends

Many small firms obtain short-term funds by borrowing money from family and friends. Such loans can create problems, however, if both the lender and borrower do not understand cash flow.[22] It is sometimes better to go to a commercial bank that fully understands the business's risk and can help analyze its future financial needs rather than borrow from friends or relatives.

Entrepreneurs appear to be listening to this advice. According to the National Federation of Independent Business, entrepreneurs today are relying less on family and friends as a source of borrowed funds than they have in the past.[23] If an entrepreneur decides to ask family or friends for financial assistance, it is important that both parties (1) agree on specific loan terms, (2) put the agreement in writing, and (3) arrange for repayment in the same way they would for a bank loan. Such actions help keep family relationships and friendships intact.[24]

▸ Did you ever wonder how retailers get the money to buy all of the items available during the holiday season? Department stores and other large retailers make extensive use of commercial banks and other lenders to borrow the money needed to buy merchandise to stock their shelves. How do stores benefit from using this type of financing?

Commercial Banks

Banks, being sensitive to risk, generally prefer to lend short-term money to larger, established business. Imagine the different types of business people who go to banks for a loan, and you will get a better idea of the requests bankers evaluate. Picture, for example, a farmer going to the bank in spring to borrow funds for seed, fertilizer, supplies, and other needs that will be repaid after the fall harvest. Or consider a local toy store buying merchandise for holiday-season sales. The store borrows the money for such purchases in the summer and plans to pay it back after the holidays. Restaurants often borrow funds at the beginning of the month and repay by the end of the month.

How much a business borrows and for how long depends on the kind of business it is and how quickly it can resell the merchandise it purchases with a bank loan or use it to generate funds. In a large business, specialists in a company's finance and accounting departments do a cash flow forecast. Small-business owners generally lack such specialists and monitor cash flow themselves.

Nonetheless, a promising and well-organized small business may be able to get a bank loan. In fact, commercial banks provide almost half of small business financing today. If a small firm gets a bank loan, the owner or person in charge of finance should keep in close touch with the bank and send regular financial statements to keep the bank up-to-date on its operations. The bank may spot cash flow problems early or be more willing to lend money in a crisis if a business has established a strong relationship built on trust and sound management.

Different Forms of Short-Term Loans

Banks and other financial institutions offer different types of loans. A **secured loan** is backed by *collateral,* something valuable such as property. If the borrower fails to pay the loan, the lender may take possession of the collateral. An automobile loan is a secured loan. If the borrower does not repay it, the lender will repossess (take back) the car. Inventory of raw materials like coal and steel often serves as collateral for business loans. Collateral removes some of the bank's risk in lending money.

secured loan
A loan backed by collateral, something valuable such as property.

Accounts receivable are company assets often used as collateral for a loan; the process is called *pledging* and works as follows: a percentage of the value of a firm's

A secured loan is backed by collateral, a tangible item of value. A car loan, for instance, is a secured loan in which the car itself is the collateral. What is the collateral in a mortgage loan?

accounts receivable pledged (usually about 75 percent) is advanced to the borrowing firm. As customers pay off their accounts, the funds received are forwarded to the lender in repayment of the funds that were advanced.[25]

unsecured loan
A loan that does not require any collateral.

An **unsecured loan** is more difficult to obtain because it does not require any collateral. Normally, lenders give unsecured loans only to highly regarded customers—long-standing businesses considered financially stable.

line of credit
A given amount of unsecured funds a bank will lend to a business.

If a business develops a good relationship with a bank, the bank may open a **line of credit** for the firm, a given amount of unsecured short-term funds a bank will lend to a business, provided the funds are available. A line of credit is *not* guaranteed to a business. However it speeds up the borrowing process since a firm does not have to apply for a new loan every time it needs funds. As businesses mature and become more financially secure, banks will often increase their line of credit, much like the credit limit on your credit card. Some even offer a **revolving credit agreement**, a line of credit that is guaranteed but usually comes with a fee. Both lines of credit and revolving credit agreements are particularly good sources of funds for unexpected cash needs.

revolving credit agreement
A line of credit that is guaranteed but usually comes with a fee.

If a business is unable to secure a short-term loan from a bank, the financial manager may seek short-term funds from **commercial finance companies**. These non-deposit-type organizations make short-term loans to borrowers who offer tangible assets (e.g., property, plant, and equipment) as collateral.[26] Commercial finance companies often make loans to individuals and businesses that cannot get funds elsewhere (e.g., General Electric loaned money to Air Canada as the airline restructured its business). Since commercial finance companies assume higher degrees of risk than banks, they usually charge higher interest rates.

commercial finance companies
Organizations that make short-term loans to borrowers who offer tangible assets as collateral.

Factoring Accounts Receivable

factoring
The process of selling accounts receivable for cash.

One relatively expensive source of short-term funds for a firm is **factoring**, the process of selling accounts receivable for cash. Factoring dates as far back as 4,000 years, during the days of ancient Babylon. Here is how it works: let's say a firm sells many of its products on credit to consumers and other businesses, creating a number of accounts receivable. Some buyers may be slow in paying their bills, so a large amount of money due to a firm. A *factor* is a market intermediary (usually a financial institution such as a commercial bank or commercial finance company) that agrees to buy the firm's accounts receivable, at a discount, for cash.[27] The discount depends on the age of the accounts receivable, the nature of the business, and the condition of the economy. When it collects the accounts receivable that were originally owed to the firm, the factor keeps them.

While factors charge more than bank's loan rates, remember many small businesses cannot qualify for a loan.[28] So even though factoring is an expensive way of raising short-term funds, it is popular among small businesses.[29] A company can often reduce its factoring cost if it agrees to reimburse the factor for slow-paying accounts, or to assume the risk for customers who do not pay at all. Remember factoring is not a loan; it is the sale of a firm's asset (accounts receivable).[30] Factoring is common in the clothing and furniture businesses, and in growing numbers of global trade ventures.

Commercial Paper

Often a corporation needs funds for just a few months and prefers not to have to negotiate with a bank. One strategy available to large firms is to sell commercial paper. **Commercial paper** consists of *unsecured* promissory notes, in amounts of $100,000 and up, that mature (come due) in 365 days (366 days in a leap year) or less. Commercial paper states a fixed amount of money the business agrees to repay to the lender (investor) on a specific date at a specific rate of interest. The interest rate for commercial paper is stated in the agreement.

commercial paper
Unsecured promissory notes of $100,000 and up that mature (come due) in 365 days or less.

Because commercial paper is unsecured, only financially stable firms (mainly large corporations with excellent credit reputations) are able to sell it.[31] For these companies it is a quick path to short-term funds for less interest than charged by commercial banks. Since most commercial paper matures in 30 to 90 days, it is an investment opportunity for buyers who can afford to put up cash for short periods to earn some interest on their money. However, in late 2008 and into 2009, the ability for any large credit-worthy corporation to sell commercial paper was significantly curtailed by the world-wide credit crunch.

Credit Cards

Letitia Mulzac seemed to have things going her way as she planned to open an imported gift and furniture shop. She had a great location and reliable business contacts lined up in India, Indonesia, and Morocco. Unfortunately, she did not have enough money in her savings to start the business.[32] She did, however, have a Small Business Visa card with a high credit limit. Letitia was able to use her credit card to pay for the stock to start her business. Credit cards provide a readily available line of credit to a business that can save time and the likely embarrassment of being rejected for a bank loan. Of course, in contrast to the convenience that credit cards offer, they are extremely risky and costly. Interest rates can be exorbitant, and there are considerable penalties if users fail to make their payments on time. Credit cards are an expensive way to borrow money and are probably best used as a last resort. The recent credit problems were attributed in part to the excessive use of credit cards and the resulting inability of borrowers to make even the minimum monthly payments.

After checking your progress below, we'll look into long-term financing.

PROGRESS ASSESSMENT

- What does an invoice containing the terms "2/10, net 30" mean?
- What's the difference between trade credit and a line of credit?
- What's the key difference between a secured loan and an unsecured loan?
- What is factoring? What are some of the considerations involved in establishing the discount rate?

Identify and describe different sources of long-term financing.

OBTAINING LONG-TERM FINANCING

In a financial plan, forecasting determines the amount of funding the firm will need over various periods and the most appropriate sources for obtaining those funds. In setting long-term financing objectives, financial managers generally ask three major questions:

1. What are the organization's long-term goals and objectives?
2. What funds do we need to achieve the firm's long-term goals and objectives?
3. What sources of long-term funding (capital) are available, and which will best fit our needs?

Firms need long-term capital to purchase expensive assets such as plant and equipment, to develop new products, and perhaps finance their expansion. In major corporations, the board of directors and top management usually make decisions about long-term financing, along with finance and accounting executives. Pfizer, the world's largest research-based biomedical and pharmaceutical company, spends more than $8 billion a year researching and developing new products.[33] The development of a single new drug could take 10 years and cost close to $1 billion before it brings in any profit. It is easy to see why high-level managers make the long-term financing decisions at Pfizer. Owners of small and medium-sized businesses are almost always actively engaged in analyzing long-term financing decisions.

As we noted earlier, long-term funding comes from two major sources: debt financing and equity financing. Let's look at these sources next.

Debt Financing

Debt financing is borrowing money a company has a legal obligation to repay. Firms can borrow either by getting a loan from a lending institution or by issuing bonds.

Debt Financing by Borrowing Money from Lending Institutions

Long-term loans are usually due within 3 to 7 years but may extend to 15 or 20 years. A **term-loan agreement** is a promissory note that requires the borrower to repay the loan with interest in specified monthly or annual instalments. A major advantage is that the interest paid is tax deductible.

term-loan agreement
A promissory note that requires the borrower to repay the loan in specified instalments.

Long-term loans are both larger and more expensive to the firm than short-term loans. Since the repayment period can be quite long, lenders assume more risk and usually require collateral, which may be real estate, machinery, equipment, stock, or other items of value. The interest rate is based on the adequacy of collateral, the firm's credit rating, and the general level of market interest rates. The greater the risk a lender takes in making a loan, the higher the rate of interest. This principle is known as the **risk/return trade-off**. Lenders may also often require certain restrictions on a firm's operations to force the firm to act responsibly in its business practices.

risk/return trade-off
The principle that the greater the risk a lender takes in making a loan, the higher the interest rate required.

Debt Financing by Issuing Bonds

If an organization is unable to obtain its long-term financing needs by getting a loan from a lending institution, it may try to issue bonds. A **bond** is a long-term legal obligation of a corporation or government to make regular interest payments and to repay the entire bond principal amount at a prescribed time, called the maturity date.

bond
A long-term legal obligation of a corporation or government to make regular interest payments during the term of the bond and to repay the entire bond principal at a prescribed date. Bonds can be issued by large organizations including different levels of government, government agencies, corporations, and foreign governments and corporations.

Maybe your community is building a new stadium or cultural centre and is selling bonds to finance the project. Potential investors (individuals and institutions) measure the risk of purchasing a bond against the return (interest) the bond promises to pay and the issuer's ability to repay when promised.

Like long-term loans, the interest rate paid on a bond varies according to factors such as the general level of market rates, the reputation of the company issuing the bond, and the going interest rate for government bonds or bonds of similar companies. Once an interest rate is set for a corporate bond issue (except in the case of what is called a floating-rate bond), it cannot be changed.

Bonds of all types are evaluated (rated) in terms of their risk to investors by independent rating firms such as Dominion Bond Rating Service <*www.dbrs.com*> and Standard & Poor's <*www.standardandpoors.com*>. Bond ratings can range from high quality to bonds considered junk. Naturally, the higher the risk associated with the bond issue, the higher the interest rate the organization must offer investors. Investors should not assume high levels of risk if they do not feel that the potential return is worth it. The European debt crisis is discussed in Reaching Beyond our Borders at the end of this part. Many European governments are facing significant interest costs on the debt they are issuing because lenders believe the risk is high.

Bonds are issued with a denomination, which is the amount of debt represented by one bond. (Bonds are almost always issued in multiples of $1,000.) The principal is the face value of a bond. The issuing company is legally bound to repay the bond principal to the bondholder in full on the **maturity date**. For example, if Very Vegetarian issues a $1,000 bond with an interest rate of 5 percent and a maturity date of 2025, the company is agreeing to pay a bondholder a total of $50 in interest each year until a specified date in 2025, when the full $1,000 must be repaid. Though bond interest is quoted for an entire year, it is usually paid in two instalments (semi-annually). Maturity dates for bonds can vary. For example, firms such as Disney and Coca-Cola have issued bonds with 50-year maturity dates.

maturity date
The exact date the issuer of a bond must pay the principal to the bondholder.

Advantages and Disadvantages of Issuing Bonds Bonds offer several long-term financing advantages to an organization. The decision to issue bonds is often based on advantages such as the following:

- Bondholders are creditors, not owners, of the firm and seldom have a vote on corporate matters; thus, management maintains control over the firm's operations.
- Interest paid on bonds is tax deductible to the firm issuing the bond.
- When bonds are repaid the debt obligation is eliminated.
- Bonds can be repaid before the maturity date if they contain a call provision. Some may also be converted to common shares (which is discussed later in this chapter).

But bonds also have their drawbacks:

- Bonds increase debt (long-term liabilities, an additional risk) and may adversely affect the market's perception of the firm.
- Paying interest on bonds is a legal obligation. If interest is not paid, bondholders can take legal action to force payment.
- The face value (denomination) of bonds must be repaid on the maturity date. Without careful planning, this repayment can cause cash flow problems when the bonds come due.

Different Classes of Bonds Like other forms of long-term debt, bonds can be secured or unsecured. The first class of bonds is *secured bonds,* which are backed by some tangible asset (collateral) that is pledged to the bondholder if bond interest or the principal is not paid back when promised. For example, a mortgage bond is a bond secured by a company's land and buildings.

The second class is unsecured bonds, which are not backed by any collateral (such as equipment). These bonds are usually referred to as **debenture bonds**. Generally, only well-respected firms with excellent credit ratings can issue debenture bonds, since the only security the bondholder has is the reputation and credit history of the company.

debenture bonds
Bonds that are unsecured (i.e., not backed by any collateral such as equipment).

In issuing bonds, a company can choose to include different features in the various bond issues. Let's look at some possible special bond features.

sinking fund
A reserve account in which the issuer of a bond periodically sets aside some part of the bond principal prior to maturity so that enough capital will be accumulated by the maturity date to pay off the bond.

Special Bond Features By now you should understand that bonds are issued with an interest rate, are unsecured or secured by some type of collateral, and must be repaid at their maturity date. This repayment requirement often leads companies to establish a reserve account called a **sinking fund**, whose primary purpose is to ensure that enough money will be available to repay bondholders on the bond's maturity date. Firms issuing sinking-fund bonds periodically set aside some part of the bond principal prior to maturity so that enough capital will be accumulated by the maturity date to pay off the bond. Sinking funds can be attractive to issuing firms and potential investors for several reasons:

- They provide for an orderly retirement (repayment) of a bond issue
- They reduce the risk the bond will not be repaid
- The market price of the bond is supported because the risk of the firm not repaying the principal on the maturity date is reduced

Another special feature that can be included in a bond issue is a call provision. A *callable bond* permits the bond issuer to pay off the bond's principal (i.e., call the bond) prior to its maturity date. Call provisions must be included when a bond is issued, and bondholders should be aware of whether a bond is callable. Callable bonds give companies some discretion in their long-term forecasting. For example, suppose that Very Vegetarian issued $50 million in 20-year bonds in 2012 with an interest rate of 5 percent. The yearly interest expense would be $2.5 million ($50 million times 5 percent). If market conditions change in 2014, and bonds issued of the same quality are only paying 3 percent, Very Vegetarian would be paying excess interest. Obviously, Very Vegetarian could benefit if it could call in (pay off) the old bonds and issue new bonds at the lower interest rate.

Another feature sometimes included in bonds is convertibility. A *convertible bond* is a bond that can be converted into common shares in the issuing company.[34] This feature is often an incentive for an investor to buy a bond. Why, you may ask, would bond investors want to convert their investment to shares? That's easy. If the value of the firm's common shares grows sizably over time, bondholders can compare the value of continued bond interest with the possible sizable profit they could gain by converting to a specified number of common shares. When we discuss common shares in the next section, this advantage will become more evident to you.

PROGRESS ASSESSMENT

- What are the major forms of debt financing available to a firm?
- What role do bond rating services play in the bond market?
- What does it mean when a firm states that it is issuing a 9 percent debenture bond due in 2025?
- What are advantages and disadvantages of bonds?
- Why do companies like callable bonds? Why might investors dislike them?
- Why are convertible bonds attractive to investors?

Equity Financing

Rather than obtaining a long-term loan from a lending institution or selling bonds to investors, a firm may look at equity financing. Equity financing makes funds available when the owners of the firm sell shares of ownership (including selling shares to venture capitalists) or when they reinvest earnings. Figure 17.5 compares debt to equity financing options.

	Type of Financing	
	Debt	Equity
Management influence	There's usually none unless special conditions have been agreed on.	Common shareholders have voting rights.
Repayment	Debt has a maturity date. Principal must be repaid.	Stock has no maturity date. The company is never required to repay equity.
Yearly obligations	Payment of interest is a contractual obligation.	The firm is not usually legally liable to pay dividends.
Tax issues	Interest is tax deductible.	Dividends are paid from after-tax income and are not deductible.

Figure 17.5

Differences Between Debt and Equity Financing

Equity Financing by Selling Stock

Stocks represent ownership in a company. Both common and preferred shares (to be discussed soon) form the company's capital stock, also known as equity capital.[36]

The key thing to remember about stock is stockholders (also known as shareholders) become owners in the organization. Generally, the corporation's board of directors decides the number of shares of stock that will be offered to investors for purchase. The first time a corporation offers to sell new stock to the general public is called an initial public offering (IPO).

A stock certificate is evidence of stock ownership that specifies the name of the company, the number of shares it represents, and the type of stock being issued (see Figure 17.6). Today, stock certificates are generally held electronically for the owners of the stock. Certificates sometimes indicate a stock's *par value,* which is a dollar amount assigned to each share of stock by the corporation's charter. Since par values do not reflect the market value of the stock, most companies issue "no-par" stock. Dividends are part of a firm's profits that may be distributed to shareholders as either cash payments or additional shares of stock. Dividends are declared by a corporation's board of directors and are generally paid quarterly. Although it is a legal obligation for companies that issue bonds to pay interest, companies that issue stock are not usually required to pay dividends.[37]

stocks
Shares of ownership in a company.

initial public offering (IPO)
The first public offering of a corporation's stock.

stock certificate
Evidence of stock ownership that specifies the name of the company, the number of shares it represents, and the type of stock being issued.

dividends
Part of a firm's profits that may be distributed to shareholders as either cash payments or additional shares of stock.

Figure 17.6

Stock Certificate for Pet Inc.

Examine this certificate for key information about this stock.

Advantages and Disadvantages of Issuing Stock The following are some advantages to the firm of issuing stock:

- As owners of the business, shareholders never have to be repaid.
- There's usually no legal obligation to pay dividends to shareholders; therefore, income (retained earnings) can be reinvested in the firm for future financing needs.
- Selling stock has no risk since issuing stock creates no debt. (A corporation may also buy back its stock to improve its balance sheet and make the company appear stronger financially.)

Disadvantages of issuing stock include the following:

- As owners, shareholders (usually only common shareholders) have the right to vote for the company's board of directors. Typically one vote is granted for each share of stock. Hence, the direction and control of the firm can be altered by the sale of additional shares of stock.
- Dividends are paid out of profit after taxes and thus are not tax deductible.[38]
- Management's decisions can be affected by the need to keep shareholders happy.

Companies can issue two classes of shares: common and preferred. Let's see how these two forms of equity financing differ.

common shares
The most basic form of ownership in a firm; it confers voting rights and the right to share in the firm's profits through dividends, if offered by the firm's board of directors.

Issuing Common Shares Common shares are the most basic form of ownership in a firm. In fact, if a company issues only one type of stock, it must be common. Holders of common stock have the right (1) to vote for company board directors and important issues affecting the company, and (2) to share in the firm's profits through dividends, if approved by the firm's board of directors. Having voting rights in a corporation allows common shareholders to influence corporate policy since the elected board chooses the firm's top management and makes major policy decisions. Common shareholders also have what is called a pre-emptive right, which is the first right to purchase any new common shares the firm decides to issue. This right allows common shareholders to maintain a proportional share of ownership in the company.

preferred shares
Stock that gives its owners preference in the payment of dividends and an earlier claim on assets than common shareholders if the company is forced out of business and its assets are sold.

Issuing Preferred Shares Owners of preferred shares enjoy a preference (hence the term *preferred*) in the payment of dividends; they also have a prior claim on company assets if the firm is forced out of business and its assets are sold. Normally, however, preferred shares do not include voting rights in the firm. Preferred shares are frequently referred to as a hybrid investment because they have characteristics of both bonds and stocks. To illustrate this, consider the treatment of preferred share dividends.

Preferred share dividends differ from common share dividends in several ways. Preferred shares are generally issued with a par value that becomes the base for the dividend the firm is willing to pay. For example, if a preferred share's par value is $100 a share and its dividend rate is 4 percent, the firm is committing to a $4 dividend for each share of preferred stock the investor owns (4 percent of $100 = $4). An owner of 100 shares of this preferred stock is promised a fixed yearly dividend of $400. In addition, the preferred shareholder is also assured that this dividend must be paid in full before any common share dividends can be distributed.[39]

Preferred shares are therefore quite similar to bonds; both have a face (or par) value and both have a fixed rate of return. Also, like bonds, rating services rate preferred shares according to risk. So how do bonds and preferred shares differ? Remember that companies are legally bound to pay bond interest and to repay the face value (denomination) of the bond on its maturity date. In contrast, even though preferred share dividends are generally fixed, they do not legally have to be paid; also shares (preferred or common) never have to be repurchased. Though both bonds and stock can increase in market value, the price of stock generally increases at a higher percentage than bonds. Of course, the market value of both could also go down. Figure 17.7 compares features of bonds and stock.

	Bonds	Common Share	Preferred Share
Interest or Dividends			
Must be paid	Yes	No	Depends
Pays a fixed rate	Yes	No	Usually
Deductible from payor's income tax	Yes	No	No
Canadian payee is taxed at reduced rate		(if payor company is Canadian)	
	No	Yes	Yes
Stock or Bond			
Has voting rights	No	Yes	Not normally
May be traded on the stock exchange	Yes	Yes	Yes
Can be held indefinitely	No	Yes	Depends
Is convertible to common shares	Maybe	No	Maybe

Figure 17.7

Comparison of Bonds and Stock of Public Companies

The different features help both the issuer and the investor decide which vehicle is right for each of them at a particular time.

Special Features of Preferred Shares Preferred shares can have special features that do not apply to common shares. For example, like bonds, preferred shares can be callable. This means that preferred shareholders could be required to sell back their shares to the corporation. Preferred shares can also be convertible to common shares. Another important feature of preferred shares is that they can often be cumulative. That is, if one or more dividends are not paid when promised, the missed dividends will be accumulated and paid later to a cumulative preferred shareholder. This means that all dividends, including any back dividends, must be paid in full before any common share dividends can be distributed. Figure 17.8 lists some optional features of preferred shares.

Equity Financing from Venture Capital

The hardest time for a business to raise money is when it is just starting up or just beginning to expand. A start-up business typically has few assets and no market track record, so the chances of borrowing significant amounts of money from a bank are slim.

Preferred Share Feature	Description
Convertible	The shares may be exchanged after a stated number of years for common shares at a preset rate, at the option of the shareholder.
Cumulative	If the dividend is not paid in full in any year, the balance is carried forward (accumulates). The cumulative unpaid balance must be paid before any dividends are paid to common shareholders.
Callable	The company that issued the shares has the right after a stated number of years to call them back by repaying the shareholders their original investment.*
Redeemable	After a stated number of years, the investor may return the stock and ask for repayment of his or her investment.*

*If the shares are also cumulative, all dividend arrears must be paid as well.

Figure 17.8

Optional Features Available with Preferred Shares

Each feature holds some attraction for the potential investor.

▸ When credit grew tight in the recent financial crisis, John Mickey, who makes promotional items with corporate logos, tapped his retirement funds to obtain start-up money for his new venture. Why is this financing strategy considered risky?

venture capital Money that is invested in new or emerging companies that are perceived as having great profit potential

Recall from Chapter 7 that venture capitalists are a potential source of funds. **Venture capital** is money that is invested in new or emerging companies that some investors—venture capitalists—believe have great profit potential. Venture capitalists invest in a business in return for part ownership of the business. They expect higher-than-average returns and competent management performance in the firms they invest in. Venture capital helped firms like Intel <*www.intel.com*>, Apple, and Cisco Systems <*www.cisco.com*> get started and let Facebook and Google expand and grow.[35]

Equity Financing from Retained Earnings

You probably remember from Chapter 16 that the profits the company keeps and reinvests in the firm are called *retained earnings.* Retained earnings are often a major source of long-term funds, especially for small businesses. They often have fewer financing alternatives, such as selling bonds or stock, than large businesses do. However, large corporations also depend on retained earnings for long-term funding. In fact, retained earnings are usually the most favoured source of meeting long-term capital needs. A company that uses them saves interest payments, dividends (payments for investing in stock), and any possible underwriting fees for issuing bonds or stock. Retained earnings also create no new ownership in the firm, as stock does.

Suppose you want to buy an expensive personal asset such as a new car. Ideally you would go to your personal savings account and take out the necessary cash. No hassle! No interest! Unfortunately, few people have such large amounts of cash available. Most businesses are no different. Even though they would like to finance long-term needs from operations, few have the resources available to accomplish this.

Choosing Between Debt and Equity Financing

leverage Raising needed funds through borrowing to increase a firm's rate of return.

Raising funds through borrowing to increase the firm's rate of return is referred to as **leverage**. Although debt increases risk because it creates a financial obligation that must be repaid, it also enhances a firm's ability to increase profits. Recall that two key jobs of the financial manager or CFO are forecasting the firm's need for borrowed funds and planning how to manage these funds once they are obtained.

If the firm's earning are larger than the interest payments on borrowed funds, business owners can realize a higher rate of return than if they had used equity financing. Figure 17.9 shows an example, again involving our vegetarian restaurant, Very Vegetarian. If Very Vegetarian needed $200,000 in new financing, it could consider debt by selling bonds or equity through offering stock. Comparing the two options in this situation, you can see that Very Vegetarian would benefit by selling bonds because the company's increase in earnings would be greater than the interest paid on borrowed funds (bonds). However, if the firm's increase in earnings were less than the interest paid on borrowed funds (bonds), Very Vegetarian would be worse off using borrowed funds. It is also important to remember that bonds, like all debt, have to be repaid at a specific time.

Individual firms must determine exactly how to balance debt and equity financing by comparing the costs and benefits of each. Leverage ratios (discussed in Chapter 16) can also give companies an industry standard for this balance, to which they can compare themselves. CanWest Global Communications relied so heavily on debt financing that when their revenues fell they were forced out of business because they could not repay their debt. In contrast, Apple, at the other extreme, has close to $100 billion in cash available. According to Standard & Poor's and Moody's Investors Services <*www.moodys.com*> (firms that provide corporate and financial research as well as the bond rating services mentioned above), the debt of a large industrial corporation typically ranges between 33 and 40 percent of its total assets. The amount of small-business debt varies considerably from firm to firm.

Financial Management in Trying Times

The collapse of financial markets in 2008 put the spotlight directly on the failure of financial managers to do their job effectively. Poor investment decisions and risky financial dealings (especially in areas such as real estate, although financial dealings in Canada were far less risky than the United States) caused financial markets to suffer their worst fall since the 1920s and 1930s. As the requirements of financial institutions became more stringent following the financial crisis, the job of the financial manager has become more challenging. Investors who watched long-standing

Figure 17.9

Using Leverage (Debt) Versus Equity Financing

Very Vegetarian wants to raise $200,000 in new capital. Compare the firm's debt and equity options.

Additional Debt		Additional Equity	
Shareholders' equity	$500,000	Shareholders' equity	$500,000
Additional equity	–	Additional equity	$200,000
Total equity	$500,000	Total equity	$700,000
Bond (interest $16,000)	$16,000	Bond interest	–
	Year-End Earnings		
Gross Profit ($80,000 + $20,000 in additional earnings)	$100,000	Gross Profit ($80,000 + $20,000 in additional earnings)	$100,000
Less bond interest	–16,000	Less interest	–
Operating Profit	$84,000	Operating Profit	$100,000
Return on equity ($84,000 – $500,000 = 16.6%)	16.6%	Return on equity ($100,000 ÷ $700,000 = 14.2%)	14.2%

financial firms such as Lehman Brothers close their doors not only saw respected businesses disappear but also saw their invested funds disappear with them. Financial managers have long road back to earning the trust of the public.

PROGRESS ASSESSMENT

- What are the major forms of equity financing available to a firm?
- Name at least two advantages and two disadvantages of issuing stock as a form of equity financing.
- What are the major differences between common shares and preferred shares?
- In what ways are preferred shares similar to bonds? How are they different?

SUMMARY

Explain the role and responsibilities of financial managers.

Finance comprises those functions in a business responsible for acquiring funds for the firm, managing funds within the firm (e.g., preparing budgets and doing cash flow analysis), and planning for the expenditure of funds on various assets.

What are the most common ways in which firms fail financially?
The most common financial problems are (1) undercapitalization, (2) poor control over cash flow, and (3) inadequate expense control.

What do financial managers do?
Financial managers plan, budget, control funds, obtain funds, collect funds, audit, manage taxes, and advise top management on financial matters.

Outline the financial planning process, and explain the three key budgets in the financial plan.

Financial planning involves forecasting short-term and long-term needs, budgeting, and establishing financial controls.

What are the three budgets in a financial plan?
The operating (master) budget summarizes the information in the other two budgets; it projects dollar allocations to various costs and expenses given various revenues. The capital budget is the spending plan for expensive assets, such as property, plant, and equipment. The cash budget is the projected cash inflows and outflows for a period and the balance at the end of a given period.

Explain why firms need funds.

During the course of a business's life, its financial needs shift considerably.

What are firms' major financial needs?
Businesses need financing for four major tasks: (1) managing day-to-day needs of the business, (2) controlling credit operations, (3) acquiring needed inventory, and (4) making capital expenditures.

are sacrificed for future uncertain returns? Problems can arise when risk factors suddenly begin to act together.[5] Risk management is all about minimizing the losses from unexpected events.

How Rapid Change Affects Risk Management

Risk goes beyond the obvious dangers of fire, theft, or accident. It is inherent in every decision a manager makes, and the prudent company assesses its exposure in all of them. Risk managers are expanding their expertise into human resources, IT, security, law, site construction, and more.[6] Changes are occurring so fast in the business world that it is difficult to identify new risks until they are upon us. Who can evaluate the risks of buying or selling products through the Internet? How will currencies fluctuate in a financial crisis, and how will their daily ups and downs affect the profits of global trade? How will climate change affect farms and raising cattle and the price of food? What would happen to the economy if there were a new terrorist attack or a larger swine flu epidemic? What can we do to manage the risks of financial failure at home and social unrest abroad?[7]

Let's explore how companies go about managing risk. We'll begin by going over a few key terms.

MANAGING RISK

Explain the four ways of managing risk, and distinguish between insurable and uninsurable risk.

Risk is the chance of loss, the degree of probability of loss, and the amount of possible loss. There are two different kinds of risk:

- **Speculative risk** can result in *either* profit or loss. A firm takes on speculative risk by buying new machinery, acquiring more inventory, and making other potentially profitable decisions in which the probability of loss may low and the amount of loss is known.[8] An entrepreneur's chance to make a profit is a speculative risk.[9] Banks that bought mortgage-backed securities were taking a speculative risk.
- **Pure risk** is the threat of loss with *no* chance for profit, such as the threat of fire, accident, or theft. If such events occur, a company loses money; but if they do not, the company gains nothing.[10]

risk
The chance of loss, the degree of probability of loss, and the amount of possible loss.

speculative risk
A chance of either profit or loss.

pure risk
The threat of loss with no chance for profit.

The risk that most concerns business people is pure risk. It threatens the very existence of some firms. Once they identify pure risks, firms have several options:

1. Reduce the risk
2. Avoid the risk
3. Self-insure against the risk
4. Buy insurance against the risk

We'll discuss the option of buying insurance in detail later. First, we will discuss each of the other alternatives for managing risk, which reduce the need for outside insurance.

Reducing Risk

A firm can reduce risk by establishing loss-prevention programs such as fire drills, health education, safety inspections, equipment maintenance, accident prevention programs, and so on. Many retail stores use mirrors, video cameras, and other devices to prevent shoplifting. Water sprinklers and smoke detectors minimize fire loss. Most industrial machines have safety devices to protect workers' fingers, eyes, and so on. After a terrorist attack in Mumbai, India, one hotel owner added luggage scanners, metal detectors, and more security cameras to his 20 hotels in India.[11]

When an estimated 400 deaths in traffic accidents were blamed on faulty tires a few years ago, Firestone <*www.firestone.com*> and Ford recalled thousands of tires before more people could be killed or hurt. Quick response to such threats is critical to risk management.[12] As mentioned already, the listeriosis outbreak resulted in Maple Leaf Foods recalling all its production from their Toronto facility.[13]

Employees as well as managers can reduce risk. Truck drivers can wear seat belts to minimize injuries from accidents, operators of loud machinery can wear earplugs to reduce the chance of hearing loss, and those who lift heavy objects can wear back braces. The beginning of an effective risk management strategy is a good loss-prevention program. However, high insurance rates have forced some firms to go beyond merely preventing risks to avoiding them, in extreme cases by going out of business.

Avoiding Risk

self-insurance
The practice of setting aside money to cover routine claims and buying only "catastrophe" policies to cover big losses.

We cannot avoid every risk. There is always the chance of fire, theft, accident, or injury. But some companies are avoiding risk by not accepting hazardous jobs and by outsourcing shipping and other functions.[14] The threat of lawsuits has driven some drug companies to stop manufacturing vaccines, and some consulting engineers refuse to work on hazardous sites. Some companies are losing outside members of their boards of directors who do not have liability coverage protecting them from legal action against the firms they represent. Many companies have cut back on their investments to avoid the risk of financial losses, especially since the market fall of 2008–09.

Self-Insuring

Self-insurance is the practice of setting aside money to cover routine claims and buying only "catastrophe" insurance policies to cover big losses. It is most appropriate when a firm has several widely distributed facilities or when a group of similar organizations, like universities, with similar risks, self-insure as a group. Firms with a single huge facility, in which a major fire or earthquake could destroy the entire operation, usually turn to insurance companies to cover the risk of loss.

▶ Businesses cannot accurately estimate damage from natural disasters like hurricanes beforehand. That's the reason for having insurance. But what happens if the insurance company says that hurricane damage to your store was from water, not the winds of the hurricane, and thus your loss isn't covered?

Buying Insurance to Cover Risk

Although well-designed and enforced risk-prevention programs reduce the probability of claims, accidents do happen. Insurance is the armour individuals, businesses, and non-profit organizations use to protect themselves from various financial risks. Together they spend about 10 percent of gross domestic product (GDP) on insurance premiums. Some insurance protection is provided by governments (see Figure D.1), but individuals and businesses must cover most on their own.[15] To reduce the cost of insurance, some companies buy a business ownership policy (BOP), a package that includes property and liability insurance. We

Type of Insurance	What It Does
Canadian Public Health Care	Provides all Canadians with free basic health care, free doctor visits, free hospital ward care, free surgery, and free drugs and medicine while in hospital.
Employment Insurance	Provides financial benefits, job counselling, and placement services for unemployed workers.
Old Age Security /Canada Pension Plan	Provides retirement benefits and life insurance.
Canada Mortgage Housing Corporation (CMHC)	Provides mortgage insurance to lenders to protect against default by home buyers.
Canada Deposit Insurance Corporation	Provides re-imbursement of up to $100,000 for funds held in banks, trusts, and loan companies that fail.
Provincial Auto Insurance (Manitoba, Saskatchewan, British Columbia)	Provides all citizens in these provinces with standard automobile insurance including collision, liability, and accident benefits.

Figure D.1

Public Insurance
Provincial or federal government agencies that provide insurance protection.

will continue our discussion of insurance by identifying the types of risks that are uninsurable and insurable.

What Risks Are Uninsurable?

Not all risks are insurable. An **uninsurable risk** is one that no insurance company will cover. Examples of things that you cannot insure include market risks (e.g., losses that occur because of price changes, style changes, or new products that make your product obsolete); political risks (e.g., losses from war or government restrictions on trade); some personal risks (such as loss of a job); and some risks of operation (e.g., strikes or inefficient machinery).

uninsurable risk
A risk that no insurance company will cover.

What Risks Are Insurable?

An **insurable risk** is one that the typical insurance company will cover using the following guidelines:

1. The policyholder must have an **insurable interest**, which means that the policyholder is the one at risk to suffer a loss. You cannot, for example, buy fire insurance on your neighbour's house and collect if it burns down.
2. The loss must be measurable.
3. The chance of loss must be measurable.
4. The loss should be accidental.
5. The risk should be dispersed; that is, spread among different geographical areas so that a flood or other natural disaster in one area would not bankrupt the insurance company.
6. The insurance company must be able to set standards for accepting the risk.

insurable risk
A risk that the typical insurance company will cover.

insurable interest
The possibility of the policyholder to suffer a loss.

PROGRESS ASSESSMENT

- Why are companies more aware now of the need to manage risk?
- What is the difference between pure risk and speculative risk?
- What are the four major options for handling risk?
- What are some examples of uninsurable risk?

Define insurance policies, and explain the law of large numbers and the rule of indemnity.

UNDERSTANDING INSURANCE POLICIES

An insurance policy is a written contract between the insured, whether an individual or organization, and an insurance company that promises to pay for all or part of a loss by the insured. A premium is the fee the insurance company charges, the cost of the policy to the ensured. A claim is a statement of loss that the insured sends to the insurance company to request payment.

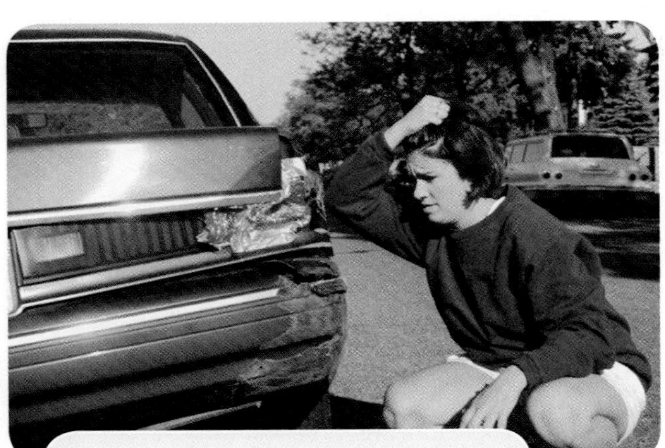

▸ Almost everyone who drives is exposed to the risk of having an accident at some point. Insurance companies use the law of large numbers to predict the losses such accidents will cause and set their policy premiums high enough to cover the losses while earning a profit. How much do you pay for your auto policy?

Like all private businesses, insurance companies are designed to make a profit. They therefore gather data to determine the extent of various risks. What makes it possible for insurance companies to accept risk is the law of large numbers.

The law of large numbers says that if a large number of people or organizations are exposed to the same risk, a predictable number of losses will occur during a given period of time. Once the insurance company predicts the number of losses likely to occur, it can determine the appropriate premiums for each policy it issues against the loss. The premium will be high enough to cover expected losses and yet earn a profit for the firm and its shareholders. Today, many insurance companies are charging high premiums not for expected losses but for the costs they anticipate from the increasing number of court cases and high damage awards.

Insurance companies can also earn revenue from investing the premiums they collect. Premiums are usually collected at the beginning of a policy period. Until policy claims need to be paid out, premiums can be placed in very secure, interest-paying investments.

Rule of Indemnity

The rule of indemnity says that an insured person or organization cannot collect more than the actual loss from an insurable risk. Nor can you buy two insurance policies, even from two insurance companies, and collect from both for the same loss. You cannot gain from risk management; you can only minimize losses.

Types of Insurance Companies

There are two major types of insurance companies. A stock insurance company is owned by shareholders, just like any other investor-owned company. A mutual insurance company is owned by its policyholders. It is a non-profit organization, and any excess funds (over losses, expenses, and growth costs) go to the policyholders in the form of dividends or premium reductions.

PROGRESS ASSESSMENT

- What is the law of large numbers?
- What is the rule of indemnity?

insurance policy
A written contract between the insured and an insurance company that promises to pay for all or part of a loss.

premium
The fee charged by an insurance company for an insurance policy.

claim
A statement of a loss that the insured sends to the insurance company to request payment.

law of large numbers
Principle that if a large number of people are exposed to the same risk, a predictable number of losses will occur during a given period of time.

INSURANCE COVERAGE FOR VARIOUS KINDS OF RISK

Discuss the various types of insurance businesses can buy to manage risk.

There are many types of insurance that cover various losses: property and liability insurance, health insurance, and life insurance. Property losses result from fires, accidents, theft, or other perils. Liability losses result from property damage or injuries suffered by others for which the policyholder is held responsible. Figure D.2 lists the types of insurance available. Let's begin our exploration of insurance by looking at health insurance.

rule of indemnity
Rule saying that an insured person or organization cannot collect more than the actual loss from an insurable risk.

stock insurance company
A type of insurance company owned by shareholders.

mutual insurance company
A type of insurance company owned by its policyholders.

Health Insurance

Canada provides universal health care for every citizen. The description of the coverage provided is found in Figure D.1. Above and beyond this insurance, individuals can be covered by benefit plans usually provided through their employer or a group the individual is affiliated with. Coverage typically includes dental, extended health care, survivors' benefits, worldwide travel benefits, income continuance, and pensions.

Dental coverage can vary from basic preventative care through to major procedures (e.g., dentures). Extended health care can cover prescription drugs, a number of paramedical services (e.g., massage), vision care, and upgraded hospital accommodation, normally up to a semi-private room. Worldwide travel benefits cover expenses that are the result of an accident or unexpected illness incurred while on business or vacation in a foreign country. Eligible expenses may include hospital accommodation and private duty nursing. Survivor benefits can include a death benefit (lump sum payment) for a spouse and dependent children, as well as a pension. Income continuance provides for both short- and long-term disability. Pensions provide monthly income for a retired employee.

Over the past few years, the cost of benefit plans has increased significantly. As a result, coverage limits have been reduced, and a greater share of the cost has become the responsibility of the insured.

Disability Insurance

Disability insurance replaces part of your income—usually 50 to 70 percent—if you become disabled and thus unable to work. You must usually be disabled for a certain period, such as 60 days, before you can begin collecting. Insurance experts recommend getting disability insurance if your employer does not offer it, because the chances of becoming disabled by a disease or accident when young are much higher than the chance of dying. The premiums for such insurance vary according to age, occupation, and income.

Workplace Safety and Insurance

Provincial workplace safety and insurance boards guarantee payment of wages, medical care, and rehabilitation services (e.g., retraining) for employees who are injured on the job. Employers in all provinces and territories are required to provide this insurance. It also pays benefits to the survivors of those who die as a result of work-related injuries. The cost of insurance varies in relation to the company's safety record, the size of its payroll, and the types of hazards its workers face. It costs more to insure a steelworker than an accountant because the risk of injury is greater.

Figure D.2
Private Insurance

Types of Insurance	What It Does
Property and Liability Insurance	
Fire	Covers losses to buildings and their contents from fire.
Automobile	Covers property damage, bodily injury, collision, fire, theft, vandalism, and other related vehicle losses.
Homeowners	Covers the home, other structures on the premises, home contents, expenses if forced from the home because of an insured peril, third-party liability, and medical payments to others.
Computer coverage	Covers loss of equipment from fire, theft, sometimes spills, power surges, and accidents.
Professional liability	Covers court-awarded losses stemming from mistakes made or bad advice given in a professional context.
Business interruption	Provides compensation for loss due to fire, theft, or similar disasters that close a business. Covers lost income, continuing expenses, and utility expenses.
Non-performance loss protection	Protects from failure of a contractor, supplier, or other person to fulfill an obligation.
Criminal loss protection	Protects from loss due to theft, burglary, or robbery.
Commercial credit insurance	Protects manufacturers and wholesalers from credit losses due to insolvency or default.
Public liability insurance	Provides protection for businesses and individuals against losses resulting from personal injuries or damage to the property of others for which the insured is responsible.
Extended product liability insurance	Covers potentially toxic substances in products; environmental liability; and, for corporations, director and officer liability.
Fidelity bond	Protects businesses from employee dishonesty.
Surety bond	Covers losses resulting from a second party's failure to fulfill a contract.
Title insurance	Protects buyers from losses resulting from errors in title to property.
Health Insurance	
Extended health care	Pays a percentage of prescription drug costs, dental care, vision care, and paramedical services.
Disability income insurance	Pays income while the insured is disabled as a result of accident or illness.
Life Insurance	
Group life insurance	Covers all the employees of a firm or members of a group.
Owner or key executive insurance	Enables businesses of sole proprietors or partnerships to pay bills and continue operating, saving employee jobs if the owner or a key executive dies. Enables corporations to hire and train or relocate another manager with no loss to the firm.
Retirement and pension plans	Provides employees with supplemental retirement and pension plans.
Credit life insurance	Pays the amount due on outstanding credit (e.g., loan, line of credit, etc.) if the debtor dies.

Liability Insurance

Professional liability insurance covers people who are found liable for professional negligence. If a lawyer gives advice carelessly and the client loses money, the client may sue the lawyer for an amount equal to that lost, and liability insurance would cover the lawyer's loss. Professional liability insurance is also known as *malpractice insurance.* That term may bring doctors and dentists to mind, but many other professionals, including accountants, are buying professional liability insurance because of large lawsuits their colleagues have faced.

Product liability insurance covers liability arising out of products sold. (You may recall the product liability discussion in Appendix B.) A person who is injured by, say, a ladder or some other household good may sue the manufacturer for damages. Insurance usually covers such losses.

Personal liability insurance covers liability of any individual through a negligent act either at work or at home.

Premises liability insurance would cover claims resulting from an accident occurring either at a place of work or personal residence.

Key Employee Insurance

Regardless of how careful we are, we all face the prospect of death. To ensure that those left behind will be able to continue the business, entrepreneurs often buy life insurance that will pay partners and others what they need to keep the firm going. The same risk for businesses relates to the loss of a key employee. The best kind of insurance to cover executives in the firm is term insurance, but dozens of new policies with interesting features are now available.

Insurance Coverage for Home-Based Businesses

Homeowner's policies usually do not have adequate protection for a home-based business. For example, they may have a limit of $2,500 for business equipment. For more coverage, you may need to add an *endorsement* ,sometimes called a *rider,* to your homeowners policy.[16] For about $25 a year you can increase the coverage to $10,000. If clients visit your office or if you receive deliveries regularly, you may need home-office insurance. It costs around $150 a year, but it protects you from slip-and-fall lawsuits and other risks associated with visitors. For more elaborate businesses, such as custom cabinetry shops and other types of manufacturing or inventory-keeping businesses, you may need a business-owner policy for about $300 a year or more. Unless you are an expert on insurance, you will need to consult an insurance agent about the best insurance for your home-business needs.

The Risk of Damaging the Environment

Due to high safety standards, Ontario nuclear power plants are closely watched for safety violations. Yet since coal-fired power plants are said to cause acid rain (and global warming), and other inexpensive fuel sources have not been fully developed, nuclear power plants are still considered by some to be a necessity. However nuclear power plants also pose environment concerns.

Clearly, risk management now goes far beyond the protection of individuals, businesses, and non-profit organizations from known risks. It means the evaluation of worldwide risks, with many unknowns, such as climate change.[17] It also means prioritizing these risks so that international funds can be spent where they can do the most good. No insurance company can protect humanity from such risks. These risks are the concern of businesses and governments throughout the world, with the assistance of the international scientific community.[18] They should also be your concern as you study risk management in all its dimensions.

The benefits of adopting a global environmental outlook in risk management are becoming more obvious. According to Green Marketing International Inc., a recent survey found that 94 percent of all consumers prefer to do business with companies that demonstrate that they care about the environment. About 80 percent said they would pay more for environmentally friendly products.[19]

PROGRESS ASSESSMENT

- Why should someone buy disability insurance?
- How many different kinds of private insurance can you name?

SUMMARY

Identify the environmental changes that have made risk management important.

Risk management is becoming a critical part of management in most firms.

What changes have made risk management more important?
Hurricanes, floods, terrorist threats, identity theft, and an unstable economy have all contributed to additional risk and the need for more risk management.

Explain the four ways of managing risk, and distinguish between insurable and uninsurable risk.

There are several ways of handling risk. Some risks are insurable and others are not.

What are the four major ways of managing risk?
The major ways of managing risk are: (1) reduce risk, (2) avoid risk, (3) self-insure, and (4) buy insurance.

What's the difference between insurable and uninsurable risk?
Uninsurable risk is risk that no insurance company will cover. Examples of things that you cannot insure include market risks, political risks, some personal risks (such as loss of a job); and some risks of operation (e.g., strikes or inefficient machinery).

An insurable risk is one that the typical insurance company will cover. Generally, insurance companies use the following guidelines when evaluating whether or not a risk is insurable: (1) the policyholder must have an insurable interest, (2) the loss should be measurable, (3) the chance of loss should be measurable, (4) the loss should be accidental, (5) the risk should be dispersed, and (6) the insurance company can set standards for accepting risks.

Define insurance policies, and explain the law of large numbers and the rule of indemnity.

There are some things one should know about insurance company rules.

What is the rule of indemnity?
The rule of indemnity says that an insured person or organization cannot collect more than the actual loss from an insurable risk.

What are the two kinds of insurance companies?

A stock insurance company is owned by shareholders, just like any other investor-owned company. A mutual insurance company is owned by its policyholders.

Discuss the various types of insurance businesses can buy to manage risk.

There are insurance policies to cover all different kinds of risk.

What kind of policy covers health risks?

Individuals can obtain benefit plans that cover dental care, extended health care, survivors' benefits, income continuance, and pensions. These coverages are over and above the universal health care system that operates in Canada. The cost of benefit plans has increased significantly in recent years. To manage these costs, coverage limits have been reduced and deductibles have been raised.

What kinds of insurance do most businesses have?

Workers' compensation insurance guarantees payment of wages, medical care, and rehabilitation services (e.g., retraining) for employees who are injured on the job. Employers in all provinces and territories are required to provide this insurance. Professional liability insurance covers people who are found liable for professional negligence. Product liability insurance provides coverage against liability arising out of products sold. If a person is injured by a ladder or some other household good, he or she may sue the manufacturer for damages. Personal and premises liability insurance provides coverage for individuals based on their negligent acts or an accident occurring. Most businesses also have some kind of life insurance for their executives. If you conduct business from home, you should also have some form of home-office insurance to cover certain risks.

What are businesses doing to cover the risks of harming the environment?

Many businesses are doing what they can to minimize damage to the environment. Such risks, however, are often beyond what businesses can manage. They are the concern of governments around the world.

KEY TERMS

claim
insurable interest
insurable risk
insurance policy
law of large numbers
mutual insurance company
premium
pure risk
risk
rule of indemnity
self-insurance
speculative risk
stock insurance company
uninsurable risk

CRITICAL THINKING

1. Are you self-insuring your apartment (or where you live) and your assets? What have you done to reduce the risk? Have you done anything to avoid risk? How much would it cost to buy insurance for your dwelling and the contents?
2. What risks do you take that insurance cannot cover?
3. What actions have you taken to avoid risk?
4. What can you do to lower your personal risk of loss from natural disasters such as floods, hurricanes, and tornadoes?

DEVELOPING WORKPLACE SKILLS

1. Write a one-page paper about ways you could reduce risk in your life (e.g., such as not driving above the speed limit). Form into small groups and share what you have written. Which of your classmates' suggestions can you adopt in your life?
2. You cannot insure yourself against speculative risk. However, you can minimize the risks you take when investing. Compare and contrast the risks of investing in stocks versus bonds for the long term. Has your attitude toward investing changed since the fall of the stock market in 2008–09?
3. Much of risk management consists of reducing risky behaviour. What kind of risky behaviour have you observed among fellow students? How can students learn about and minimize these risks? Are you doing so? Discuss the merits of having a risk manager for education facilities.
4. Form into small groups and discuss liability insurance, automobile insurance, renter's insurance, life insurance, and disability insurance. Develop a list of questions to discuss openly in class so that everyone is more informed about these issues. Do your fellow students understand all of these types of insurance?
5. Write a two-page essay on the risks of a terrorist attack, a natural disaster, global warming, or a major health disaster such as swine flu. Which risk do you perceive as most likely? Most dangerous? Discuss what you could do to warn others of such risks and motivate them to do something about them.

Practise and learn online with Connect.

CHAPTER 18

THE FINANCIAL SERVICES INDUSTRY IN CANADA

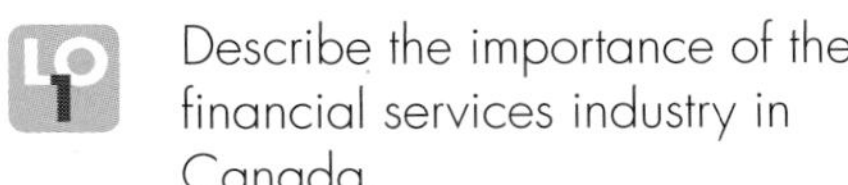

After you have read and studied this chapter, you should be able to:

- LO 1 Describe the importance of the financial services industry in Canada.
- LO 2 Explain what money is, what makes it useful, and how is it controlled.
- LO 3 Discuss the role that banks play in providing financial services.
- LO 4 Describe the role of the securities market.
- LO 5 Explain the different options for investing in securities.

PROFILE

GETTING TO KNOW ANISH CHOPRA OF TD ASSET MANAGEMENT

Anish Chopra graduated from the University of Waterloo with a Masters Degree in Accounting (Gold Medallist). After attaining his professional accounting designation he focused his career in the financial services industry. First he obtained his Chartered Financial Analyst designation. He also holds the Chartered Alternative Investment Analyst designation and is a Chartered Business Valuator (Canadian Gold Medallist).

Anish joined TD Asset Management (TDAM) in 1998. He has lead management responsibilities on the Canadian Value and Target Return strategies for both TD Mutual Funds and TD Waterhouse Private Investment Counsel. He is also the lead manager for several institutional hedge fund strategies. In addition, he is a part of the management team supporting the TD Pension Fund and a member of the TD Wealth Asset Allocation Committee. Anish has won numerous awards including being the inaugural recipient of the Canadian Institute of Chartered Business Valuators (CICBV) Top Chartered Business Valuator Under 40 Award.

Anish has over 11 years' experience managing proprietary funds within TDAM, with knowledge in Canadian, U.S., and global equities as well as numerous absolute return strategies. Prior to joining TDAM, Anish worked as a member of TD Securities' mergers and acquisitions group.

Anish appears regularly on television as well as in print media discussing business and investment issues. He has presented at numerous investment industry conferences across North America. For over a decade, Anish also served as a Course Leader and Course Co-Author for several finance courses with the CICBV. He has served as an instructor for the Institute of Chartered Accountants of Ontario. In addition, Anish has been a guest lecturer at many business schools including the Schulich School of Business (York University) and the John Molson School of Business (Concordia University).

Anish is also very involved in the community. At the University of Waterloo, he serves as the Chair of the Advisory Board for the Student Investment Fund. He is the Vice Chair of the User Advisory Council of the Canadian Institute of Chartered Accountants, serves as a member of the Ontario Judicial Council, and is a Chapter Executive with the Chartered Alternative Investment Analyst (CAIA) Association in Toronto. He also held numerous positions on the Board of Directors of the Canadian Cancer Society (Central Toronto Unit) where, as Chairperson of the Fundraising Committee, he led the unit in receiving the Toronto Regional Fundraising Award.

TD Asset Management is a North American investment manager offering progressive investment solutions to both institutional and individual investors. For over two decades, TDAM has established competitive market positions in active, quantitative, and passive portfolio management. During this time, TDAM has expanded its offering to include alternative investments and customized portfolio integration services. Assets under management at TDAM were over C$192 billion as of December 31, 2011.

TD Asset Management operates in the United States as TDAM USA Inc. and in Canada as TD Asset Management Inc. Both firms are wholly-owned subsidiaries of the Toronto-Dominion Bank ("TD Bank"), one of North America's strongest banks, and one of only two banks in North America that retains a rating of Aaa for credit risk by Moody's Investors Service, Inc.

As we see in the discussion of the financial services industry in Canada, the past 10 years have witnessed a dramatic growth in terms of the dollar value of investments and complexity of investment products. Governments, corporations, and individuals are looking more and more to this industry for their financial security. The story of TD Asset Management and the skill set provided by professionals like Anish Chopra are a prime example of this trend.

Sources: www.tdassetmanagement.com; Anish Chopra's profile provided by the School of Accounting and Finance of the University of Waterloo, June 2012; and www.morningstar.ca/globalhome/industry/managermonitor.asp?reportid=365955.

How the Financial Services Industry Is Regulated[6]

Because of its important role in the economy, the financial industry is one of the most regulated sectors in the country. Regulation is designed to ensure the integrity, safety, and soundness of financial institutions and markets. Legislative, self-regulatory, and other initiatives help minimize crises and company failures. In addition, they protect investors, depositors, and policyholders. These detailed and varied compliance requirements take a considerable amount of time and money for companies in this industry to complete.

In Canada, there is no single body that regulates the entire industry. It is a responsibility shared among different organizations and levels of government. To start with, financial institutions may be regulated at either the federal or the provincial level, or jointly. For example, banks are federally regulated. Securities dealers, credit unions, and caisses populaires are provincially regulated. Insurance providers, trust and loan companies, and co-operative credit associations may be federally and/or provincially regulated, depending on the jurisdiction under which the company is incorporated or registered.

For institutions under federal responsibility, the Department of Finance is charged with overseeing their overall powers—in other words, what they can and cannot do. The Department of Finance relies on three federal agencies to supervise the ongoing operations of these institutions and their compliance with legislation:

- The Office of the Superintendent of Financial Institutions monitors the day-to-day operations of institutions with respect to their financial soundness.
- Overseeing the deposit insurance system is the Canada Deposit Insurance Corporation (CDIC) <*www.cdic.ca*>, which protects deposits that Canadians have in their federal financial institutions. CDIC will be discussed below.
- The Financial Consumer Agency of Canada monitors financial institutions to ensure that they comply with federal consumer protection measures, which range from disclosure requirements to complaint-handling procedures.

For institutions under provincial jurisdiction, the province(s) in which a company is incorporated or registered is (are) responsible for regulating the company's overall powers. As at the federal level, provinces are supported by agencies and organizations that supervise the ongoing operations of these institutions.

The Canada Deposit Insurance Corporation[7]

The Canada Deposit Insurance Corporation is a federal Crown corporation that was created in 1967 to provide deposit insurance and contribute to the stability of Canada's financial system. CDIC insures eligible deposits at member institutions (e.g., banks and trust companies) against these institutions' failure or collapse. CDIC guarantees deposits up to $100,000 (principal and interest) in each member institution. It is funded primarily by premiums paid by banks and trust companies that belong to this program.

Keep in mind that CDIC does not cover all types of deposits. For example, foreign-currency accounts, term deposits with a maturity of greater than five years, and investments in mortgages, stocks, and mutual funds are not covered.

To date, CDIC has provided protection to depositors in 43 member institution failures. As of April 2010, CDIC had insured some $604 billion in deposits.

PROGRESS ASSESSMENT

- What components of the financial services industry were known as the four pillars?
- Describe some changes to the industry as a result of Bill C-8.
- Contrast credit unions and caisses populaires, and list some non-bank competitors.
- Describe the responsibilities of three federal agencies that oversee financial institutions.
- What deposits are not secured by CDIC?

WHY MONEY IS IMPORTANT

Explain what money is, what makes it useful, and how it is controlled.

The Canadian economy depends heavily on money: its availability and its value relative to other currencies. Economic growth and the creation of jobs depend on ready availability of money. Money is so important to the economy that many institutions have evolved to manage it and make it available when you need it. Today, you can get cash from an ATM almost anywhere in the world, and most organizations will accept a cheque, credit card, debit card, or smart card for purchases.[8] Behind the scenes is a complex system of banking that makes the free flow of money possible. Each day, more than $1.9 *trillion* is exchanged in the world's currency markets. Therefore, what happens to any major country's economy has an effect on the Canadian economy and vice versa.

The Bank of Canada (introduced in Chapter 4) is the organization in charge of money in Canada. You regularly hear a lot about it and its head, the Governor. The banking crisis and the moves being made globally by the Bank of Canada and other banks to halt a global financial crisis are too complex to discuss in detail here.[9] However, looking back on the fall of 2008 and through 2012, it is clear that the global interconnectivity of banking systems resulted in a widespread liquidity crisis, which led to major government interventions. There's no way to understand the Canadian economy without understanding global money exchanges and the institutions involved in the creation and management of money. Let's start at the beginning by discussing exactly what the word *money* means and how the supply of money affects the prices you pay for goods and services.

What Is Money?

money
Anything that people generally accept as payment for goods and services.

barter
The trading of goods and services for other goods and services directly.

Money is anything that people generally accept as payment for goods and services. In the past, objects as diverse as salt, feathers, stones, rare shells, tea, and horses have been used as money. In fact, until the 1880s, cowrie shells were one of the world's most popular currencies.

Barter is the direct trading of goods or services for other goods and services. Though barter may sound like something from the past, many people have discovered the benefits of bartering online. Others barter goods and services the old-fashioned way—face to face. In Siberia people have bought movie tickets with two eggs, and in Ukraine people have paid their energy bills with sausages and milk. Today you can go to a barter exchange where you can put goods or services into the system and get trade credits for other goods and services that you need. The barter exchange makes it easier to barter because you do not have to find people with who to barter. The exchange does that for you.

The problem with traditional barter is that eggs and milk are difficult to carry around. Most people need some object that is portable, divisible, durable, and stable so that they can trade goods and services without carrying the actual goods around with them. One solution is coins and paper bills. The five standards for a useful form of money are:

- *Portability.* Coins are a lot easier to take to market than are pigs or other heavy products.
- *Divisibility.* Different-sized coins and bills can represent different values. Because silver is now too expensive, today's coins are made of other metals, but the accepted values remain.
- *Stability.* When everybody agrees on the value of coins, the value of money is relatively stable. In fact, U.S. money has become so stable that much of the world's currencies have a value in relation to the U.S. dollar.
- *Durability.* Coins last for thousands of years, even when they have sunk to the bottom of the ocean, as you have seen when divers find old coins in sunken ships.

▶ A new series of polymer notes is being released. The most popular note is the $20 note seen above. Its security features include: raised ink, transparency, metallic portraits, display of small numbers, use of hidden numbers, maple leaf boarder, and a "window." See the Bank of Canada site <www.bankofcanda.ca/banknotes> for a more detailed description. If you owned a store, would you teach your employees how to recognize a counterfeit bill?

- *Uniqueness.* It is hard to counterfeit, or copy, elaborately designed and minted coins. With the latest colour copiers, people are able to duplicate the look of paper money relatively easily. Thus, the government has had to go to extra lengths to ensure that *real* dollars are readily identifiable. That is why some denominations have raised print or raised ink, watermarks, and fine-line patterns.[10]

Coins and paper money simplify exchanges. Most countries have their own currencies, and they are all about equally portable, divisible, and durable. However, they are not always equally stable.

Electronic cash (e-cash) is the latest form of money.[11] You can use online payments using Quicken or Microsoft Money, and you can e-mail e-cash using PayPal. Recipients can choose automatic deposit to their bank, e-dollars for spending online, or a traditional cheque in the mail.

What Is the Money Supply?

The Bank of Canada is in control of the Canadian money supply. The **money supply** is the amount of money the Bank of Canada makes available for people to buy goods and services. The money supply is referred to in a number of different ways. Some of these different measures, called monetary aggregates, are described in Figure 18.2.

money supply
The amount of money the Bank of Canada makes available for people to buy goods and services.

M1++ represents money that can be accessed quickly and easily. M2, M3, M2+, and M2++ are even broader measures of the money supply. Before we consider how the Bank of Canada controls the money supply, let us first consider why the money supply needs to be controlled and its impact on the global exchange of money.

Figure 18.2

Measures of Money—Canada's Money Supply

Measures of Money (Monetary Aggregates)	Definition of the Monetary Aggregates
M1++	The currency (bank notes and coins) in circulation plus chequable and non-chequable deposits (other than fixed-term deposits) at banks, trust and mortgage loan companies, credit unions, and caisses populaires.
M2	M1++ plus bank personal deposits, bank non-personal demand and notice deposits.
M3	M2 plus bank non-personal term deposits and foreign-currency deposits of residents.
M2+	M2 plus deposits at trust and mortgage loan companies and at government savings institutions; deposits and shares at credit union and caisses populaires; life insurance company individual annuities; and money market mutual funds.
M2++	M2+ plus Canada Savings bonds and other retail debt instruments; plus non-money market mutual funds.

Source: Bank of Canada, "Canada's Money Supply," October 2011, www.bankofcanada.ca/wp-content/uploads/2010/11/canada_money_supply.pdf.

Why Does the Money Supply Need to Be Controlled?

Imagine what would happen if governments or non-governmental organizations were to generate twice as much money as exists now. There would be twice as much money available, but still the same amount of goods and services. What would happen to prices? (Hint: Remember the laws of supply and demand from Chapter 2.) Prices would go up, because more people would try to buy goods and services with their money and would bid up the price to get what they wanted. This rise in price is called inflation, which some people call "too much money chasing too few goods."[12]

Now think about the opposite: What would happen if the Bank of Canada took money out of the economy? What would happen to prices? Prices would go down because there would be an oversupply of goods and services compared to the money available to buy them; this decrease in prices is called deflation.[13] If too much money is taken out of the economy, a recession might occur. That is, people would lose jobs and the economy would stop growing.

Now we come to a second question about the money supply: Why does it need to be controlled? The reason is that doing so allows us to manage, somewhat, the prices of goods and services. And controlling the money supply affects employment and economic growth or decline.

The Global Exchange of Money

A *falling dollar value* means that the amount of goods and services you can buy with a dollar decreases.[14] A *rising dollar value* means that the amount of goods and services you can buy with a dollar goes up. Thus, the price in U.S. dollars you pay for that cool pair of jeans you buy at an outlet mall in the United States will be lower if the Canadian dollar rises relative to the U.S. dollar, and vice versa.

What makes the dollar weak (falling dollar value) or strong (rising dollar value) is the position of the Canadian economy relative to other economies. When the economy is strong, the demand for dollars is high, and the value of the dollar rises. As commodity prices rose from 2007 through 2008, the value of the Canadian dollar rose dramatically. After years of the exchange rate of a Canadian dollar being below par compared to a U.S. dollar, the exchange rate rose above parity. When the economy is perceived as weakening, however, the demand for dollars declines, and the value of the dollar falls. The value of the dollar thus depends on a relatively strong economy. Clearly, control over the money supply is important. In the following section, we'll discuss briefly how the money supply is controlled.

Control of the Money Supply[15]

You already know that money plays a huge role in a nation's and in the world's economies. Therefore, it is important for a country to have an organization that controls the money supply to try to keep the economy from growing too fast or too slow. Theoretically, with the proper monetary policy in place to control the money supply, one can keep the economy growing without causing inflation. As mentioned in Chapter 4, in Canada the organization in charge of monetary policy is the Bank of Canada.

The Bank of Canada monitors the money supply. Indicators such as changes in M1++ provide useful information about changes that are occurring in the economy. The availability of money and credit must expand over time, and the Bank of Canada is responsible for ensuring that the rate at which more money is introduced into the economy is consistent with long-term stable growth.

The Bank's economic research indicates that the growth of M1++ provides useful information about the future level of production in the economy. The growth of the broader monetary aggregates is a good leading indicator of the rate of inflation.

The objective of the Bank of Canada's monetary policy is to support a level of spending by Canadians that is consistent with the Bank's goal of price stability. This is defined as keeping inflation within the inflation-control target range (of 1 to 3 percent). By influencing the rate at which the supply of money and credit is growing, total spending on goods and services in the economy can be stabilized.

The Bank of Canada manages the rate of money growth indirectly through the influence it exercises over short-term interest rates. When these rates change, they carry other interest rates—such as those paid by consumers for loans from commercial banks—along with them. When interest rates rise, consumers and businesses are apt to hold less money, to borrow less, and to pay back existing loans. The result is a slowing in the growth of M1++ and the other broader monetary aggregates.[16]

The Bank of Canada has an influence on very short-term interest rates through changes in its target for the overnight rate. The target for the overnight rate is the main tool used by the Bank of Canada to conduct monetary policy. It tells major financial institutions the average interest rate the Bank of Canada wants to see in the marketplace where they lend each other money for one day, or "overnight." When the Bank changes the target for the overnight rate, this change usually affects other interest rates charged by commercial banks.

When the Bank changes the target for the overnight rate, this sends a clear signal about the direction in which it wants short-term interest rates to go. These changes usually lead to moves in the prime rate at commercial banks. The **prime rate** is the interest rate that banks charge their most creditworthy customers. The prime rate serves as a benchmark for many of their loans. These changes can also indirectly affect mortgage rates and the interest paid to consumers on bank accounts, term deposits, and other savings.

prime rate
The interest rate that banks charge their most creditworthy customers.

When interest rates go down, people and businesses are encouraged to borrow and spend more, boosting the economy. But if the economy grows too fast, it can lead to inflation. The Bank may then raise interest rates to slow down borrowing and spending, putting a brake on inflation.

In choosing a target for the overnight rate, the Bank of Canada picks a level that it feels will keep future inflation low, stable, and predictable. Keeping inflation low and stable helps provide a good climate for sustainable economic growth, investment, and job creation.[17]

PROGRESS ASSESSMENT

- What are the characteristics of useful money?
- What is the money supply and why is it important?
- What are the various ways in which the Bank of Canada controls the money supply?

Discuss the role that banks play in providing financial services.

THE BANKING INDUSTRY

Following legislative changes in 1992, banks were allowed to own insurance, trust, and securities subsidiaries. Today, most of Canada's large banks have subsidiaries in these areas. As major players in Canada's financial industry, the banks serve millions of customers. They include individuals, small and medium-sized businesses, large corporations, governments, institutional investors, and non-profit organizations. The major banks offer a full range of banking, investment, and financial services. They have extensive nationwide distribution networks and also are active in the United States, Latin America, the Caribbean, Asia, and other parts of the world. Close to half of their earnings are generated outside of Canada.

Figure 18.3
Canada's Six Largest Banks

Bank Name	Total Assets	Total Loans	Net Income for Fiscal Year Ended October 31, 2011
	($ millions)		
RBC Financial Group	751,702	381,209	4,852
Scotiabank	575,256	325,004	5,175
TD Bank Financial Group	686,360	357,095	5,889
BMO Financial Group	477,423	237,275	3,266
CIBC	353,649	212,859	3,079
National Bank of Canada	156,297	73,209	1,213
Total 6 Banks	3,000,687	1,586,651	23,474

Source: Courtesy of Canadian Bankers Association.

Figure 18.3 outlines Canada's six largest banks. Strong players in the Canadian economy, Canada's banks are for the most part extremely profitable but have seen their profits fall during difficult economic times. These financial results have garnered criticism by some who believe that the banks are taking advantage of customers by charging high service charges. The reality is that the majority of their earnings come from their lending activities along with the following value-added services: trading of securities, assisting companies to issue new equity financing, commissions on securities, and wealth management. As well, banks distribute a good portion of their net income to their shareholders. Most Canadians own bank shares, whether they know it or not; bank shares form a large part of many major mutual funds (to be discussed later in this chapter) and pension funds.[18] In 2011, Canada's banks distributed 36 percent of their net income as dividends to their shareholders.[19]

commercial bank
A profit-seeking organization that receives deposits from individuals and corporations in the form of chequing and savings accounts and then uses some of these funds to make loans.

Some of the major banks have been trying to merge for several years. They believe that if they were permitted to merge, they would be able to take advantage of economies of scale and be more efficient. They argue that they are not big players globally (see Figure 18.4), and that they are increasingly being forced to look outside Canada for more opportunities due to the laws and regulations that control their domestic activities. Shareholders continue to demand good returns, and the banks are under more pressure to continue to deliver, year after year. This is an issue that will not go away in the years to come. However, all the aggressive growth over the past few years has been stalled by the banking crisis that started at the end of 2008. The Reaching Beyond Our Borders box, at the end of this part of the text, talks about the global nature of this banking crisis.

Figure 18.4
Worldwide Bank Rankings, 2008

Rank	Bank	Assets (Cad$ Billions)
1	BNP Paribas (France)	2,657
36	Royal Bank of Canada	709
38	Toronto-Dominion Bank	605
43	Scotiabank	514
57	Bank of Montreal	402
62	CIBC	344
105	Desjardins Group	171
125	National Bank of Canada	142

Source: Courtesy of Canadian Bankers Association.

Commercial Banks

A commercial bank is a profit-seeking organization that receives deposits from individuals and corporations in the form of chequing and savings accounts and then uses some of these funds to make loans. It has two types of customers, depositors and borrowers, and is equally responsible to both. A commercial bank makes a profit by efficiently using customer deposits as inputs (on which it pays interest) to invest in interest-bearing loans to other customers. If the revenue generated by loans exceeds the interest paid to depositors plus all other operating expenses, the bank makes a profit.

demand deposit
The technical name for a chequing account; the money in a demand deposit can be withdrawn anytime on demand from the depositor.

time deposit
The technical name for a savings account; the bank can require prior notice before the owner withdraws money from a time deposit.

certificate of deposit
A time-deposit (savings) account that earns interest to be delivered at the end of the certificate's maturity date.

Some Services Provided by Banks

Individuals and corporations that deposit money in a *chequing account* can write personal cheques to pay for almost any purchase or transaction. The technical name for a chequing account is a **demand deposit** because the money is available on demand from the depositor. Typically, banks impose a service charge for cheque-writing privileges or demand a minimum deposit. They might also charge a small handling fee for each cheque written. For business depositors, the amount of the service charge depends on the average daily balance in the chequing account, the number of cheques written, and the firm's credit rating and credit history.

In the past, chequing accounts paid no interest to depositors, but interest-bearing chequing accounts have experienced phenomenal growth in recent years. Commercial banks also offer a variety of savings account options. A savings account is technically a **time deposit** because the bank can require a prior notice before you make a withdrawal.

A **certificate of deposit** is a time-deposit (savings) account that earns interest, to be delivered on the certificate's maturity date. The depositor agrees not to withdraw any of the funds in the account until then. The longer the term deposit is to be held by the bank, the higher the interest rate. The interest rates also depend on economic conditions.

Banks also offer a variety of other products. Some examples of credit products for creditworthy customers include credit cards, lines of credit, loans, mortgages, and overdraft protection on chequing accounts. Additional products are access to automated teller machines (ATMs), life insurance coverage on credit products, brokerage services, financial counselling, telephone and Internet bill payment options, safe-deposit boxes, registered retirement accounts, and traveller's cheques. Visit a local bank branch to find out the details for all of these types of products. It is up to each individual to compare the different features on each type of account or service as they vary from institution to institution. Features and rates are competitive. Compare online and neighbourhood banks to find where your money can earn the most interest.

ATMs give customers the convenience of 24-hour banking at a variety of outlets such as supermarkets, department stores, and drugstores, in addition to the bank's regular branches. Depositors can—almost anywhere in the world—transfer funds, make deposits, and get cash at their own discretion with the use of a computer-coded personalized plastic access card. Beyond all that, today's ATMs are doing even more. New ATMs can dispense maps and directions, phone cards, and

▸ The Canadian Bankers Association provides a series of online resources for both consumers and small businesses. For consumers some topics include: banking basics, saving and investing, and safeguarding of your money. For small businesses some topics include: getting started in small business, small-business financing, and business credit availability program. For more details, visit the Web site at *www.cba.ca* and click on "Consumer Information."

SPOTLIGHT ON SMALL BUSINESS

How the Banking Crisis Continues to Affect Small Business

One of the consequences of the banking crisis of 2008–09 was that it became more difficult to get a loan from a bank, especially if you ran a small business. It used to be that small businesses could get an "air-ball loan," that is, a loan based more on the borrower's personal relationship with the banker than on his or her assets. Today, however, banks are more reluctant to give out loans. Sometimes the bank will demand that the borrower make a "substantial" deposit—up to half the loan amount—to get a loan. Some banks have even cut lending to new customers to conserve available funds for existing customers. While the scope of the crisis has not been quite as severe in Canada compared to the United States, small business has found it more and more difficult to borrow from banks. Because borrowing from a bank has become so difficult, you might have to look to alternative sources of funds. For example, if you are buying equipment, you might ask the vendor for financing.

In Canada, banks have wanted to reduce their risk, so they have been advocating for more government guarantees for small-business loans or have simply become more risk averse in their lending practices. Back in 2008 the federal government granted the Export Development Canada domestic lending powers. For instance, it financed aircraft purchases of Porter Airlines from Bombardier Inc. This short-term measure has been extended twice, most recently in 2012 for another year.

Some small businesses use credit cards to get started, but the fees can be extremely high if the bills are not paid promptly. Many small-business owners turn to friends and family for loans, but that too can be dicey if the business does not do well. What other sources of funds are available? Angel investors are wealthy individuals who use their own money to fund start-up companies at the early stages of their development. They usually seek out high-growth companies in fields like technology and biotech that might issue stock or get profitably bought out in a few years. Local companies like restaurants, roofers, and deck cleaners usually cannot get a hearing, much less a loan. In short, banks and non-banks are often reluctant to loan money to small businesses. Small business has to be far more diligent in searching out sources of funding as they try to expand their operations.

Sources: Barrie McKenna, "Ottawa to Prolong EDC's Domestic Lending Role," *The Globe and Mail,* 13 March 2012; Norm Brodsky, "What the Financial Crisis Means to You," *Inc.,* November 2008; Binyamin Appelbaum and David Cho, "Small Banks, Tight Credit," *The Washington Post,* 27 August 2008; C. J. Prince, "Something to Bank On," *Entrepreneur,* August 2008; and Bob Seiwert, "Borrowing Trouble," *Black Enterprise,* January 2009.

postage stamps. They can sell tickets to movies, concerts, and sporting events and show movie trailers, news tickers, and video ads. Some can take orders for flowers and DVDs, and can download music and games.

Services to Borrowers

Banks offer a variety of services to individuals and corporations in need of a loan, as do other financial services firms and government agencies (such as the Business Development Bank of Canada). Generally, loans are given on the basis of the recipient's creditworthiness, although the real estate collapse of 2008–09 in the United States was largely due to banks ignoring that rule. Banks want to manage their funds effectively and are supposed to screen loan applicants carefully to ensure that the loan plus interest will be paid back on time. Small businesses historically have looked to banks for their financing needs. The Spotlight on Small Business box discusses the new relationship between small businesses and banks after the 2008–09 banking crisis.

▸ Many consumers, especially first-time credit card owners, are unable to properly manage their money and often end up with severely damaged credit ratings—or worse, in bankruptcy. That's why it may be a good idea for you to pass up the free T-shirt or other offer made by credit card companies.

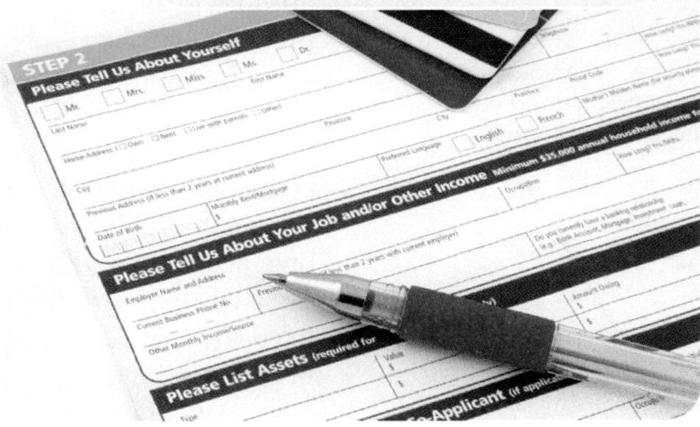

Managing Your Personal Finances

A major reason for studying business is that it prepares you for finding and keeping a good job. You already know that one of the secrets to finding a well-paying job is to have a good education. With your earnings, you can take vacations, raise a family, make investments, buy the products you want, and give generously to others.

Money management, however, is not easy. You have to earn the money in the first place. Then you have to learn how to save money, spend money wisely, and insure yourself against any financial and health risks. While these topics are important from a personal perspective, they are outside the scope of this chapter.

Online Banking

All top Canadian retail banks allow customers to have access to their accounts online, and most have bill-paying capacity. Thus, you can complete all your financial transactions from home, using your telephone or your computer to transfer funds from one account to another, pay your bills, and check the balance in each of your accounts.[20] You can apply for a loan or mortgage and get a response while you wait. Buying and selling stocks and bonds is equally easy.

Internet banks (such as ING) have been created that offer branchless banking. Such banks can offer high interest rates and low fees because they do not have the overhead costs that traditional banks have. While many consumers are pleased with the savings and convenience, not all are happy with the service. Why? Some are nervous about security. People fear putting their financial information into cyberspace, where others may see it despite all of the assurances of privacy. Further, some people want to be able to talk to a knowledgeable person one on one when they have banking problems.

The future seems to be with traditional banks that offer both online services and brick-and-mortar facilities.[21]

PROGRESS ASSESSMENT

- Why are banks interested in merging?
- List some services provided by commercial banks.
- What are some benefits of electronic banking to users?

Describe the role of the securities market.

THE CANADIAN SECURITIES INDUSTRY[22]

Almost 100 years ago the Investment Dealers Association of Canada was formed. Today two organizations exist, the Investment Industry Association of Canada <*www.iiac.ca*>, which is an independent industry association, and the Investment Industry Regulatory Organization of Canada <*www.iiroc.ca*>, a self-regulatory organization that oversees all investment dealers and trading activity on debt and equity markets.

securities dealer
A firm that trades securities for its clients and offers investment services.

Growth in this industry has dramatically increased over the last 10 years. There are now over 200 investment dealer firms and the number of registered investment professionals has grown by 30 percent to over 30,000. A **securities dealer** (also known as an investment dealer or brokerage house) is a firm that trades securities for its clients and offers investment services. This industry is involved with the following: providing financial advice to investors and executing trades on their behalf, raising all forms of capital for new and expanding businesses, underwriting and acting as primary distributor for government debt, and creating markets by trading on their own accounts.

Two main groups of products are traded in this industry, equities and debt or fixed-income securities. Equities are traded on stock exchanges while fixed-income products (bonds and money market instruments such as treasury bills, commercial paper, and bankers' acceptances), are traded over the dealing desks of investment dealer firms. Mutual funds are also offered by these firms. Firms themselves trade more sophisticated instruments such as options, futures, or other risk-management products. A significant contributor to the financial crisis starting in late 2008 related to poor risk assessment of these sophisticated risk products.

Over the 10 year period ending in 2009 the value of this business was:

- $450 billion in new equity including 2,700 initial public offerings;
- $630 billion in corporate debt raised; and
- $1.1 trillion in government debt raised.

In 2010 alone $130 billion in debt and equity was raised for companies and governments, which is double the levels from 10 years ago.

In terms of individuals, in 2010 investment dealers managed $950 billion (double the level from 10 years ago), which represented 40 percent of all uncommitted funds for half of all working Canadians. Of this amount $250 billion was invested in Registered Retirement Savings Plans, $60 billion in Registered Retirement Income Funds, and $4 billion in Registered Education Savings Plans. This increase in invested funds is the result of more Canadians turning to the securities industry to ensure their financial security. Companies and government agencies are also investing more and more in the securities market. Insurance companies will invest all of the excess of premiums they collect at the beginning of a policy year, over operating and claim costs. Pension plans, including the Canada Pension Plan <*www.servicecanada.gc.ca/eng/isp/cpp/cpptoc.shtml*>, are investing a greater portion of their reserves. In all cases, investors want to increase their returns, but this also comes with increased risks. To place these figures in context, however, the Canadian securities market is less than 3 percent of total world markets.

Securities Regulations[23]

As mentioned earlier in the textbook, one of the reasons why private corporations become public corporations is to raise capital to expand their existing operations. In recent times, companies such as Tim Hortons, Sleep Country Canada, and The Brick <*www.thebrick.com*> became publicly traded companies following the successful completion of their **initial public offering (IPO)**.

Companies seeking public financing must issue a prospectus. A **prospectus** is a condensed version of economic and financial information that a company must make available to investors before they purchase the security. The prospectus must be approved by the securities commission in the province where the public funding is being sought. The **securities commission** is a government agency that administers provincial securities legislation.[24] The mandate of the Ontario Securities Commission is to "protect investors from unfair improper and fraudulent practices, foster fair and efficient capital markets, and maintain public and investor confidence in the integrity of those markets." Violators of the legislation can be imprisoned and fined. In 2008, stock promoter Stevens Demers was found guilty of multiple counts of securities violations under the Quebec Securities Act. Charges were laid by Autorité des marchés financiers, the securities commission in Quebec.[25]

Canada's ten provinces and three territories are responsible for the securities regulations within their respective borders. The Canadian Securities Administrators (CSA) <*www.securities-administrators.ca*> is a forum for these securities regulators to coordinate and harmonize regulation of the Canadian capital markets. The CSA brings provincial and territorial securities regulators together. The focus of these meetings is to share ideas, work at designing policies and regulations that are consistent across the country, and ensure the smooth operation of Canada's securities industry. By collaborating on rules, regulations, and other programs, the CSA helps

initial public offering (IPO)
The first public offering of a corporation's stock.

prospectus
A condensed version of economic and financial information that a company must make available to investors before they purchase a security.

securities commission
A government agency that administers provincial securities legislation.

avoid duplication of work and streamlines the regulatory process for companies seeking to raise investment capital and others working in the investment industry. However, perceptions exist in capital markets that the level of enforcement of regulations varies from one jurisdiction to another.

Canada's regulatory framework has been reviewed over the past number of years. Successive Ministers of Finance have continued to encourage a solution that would address the problems of a costly, cumbersome regulatory framework. Most recently the Minister of Finance, Jim Flaherty, has championed an approach where the provinces outsource the administration of securities regulations to Ottawa while leaving the responsibility for securities legislation with the provinces as per their constitutional rights.[26]

THE FUNCTION OF SECURITIES MARKETS

stock exchange
An organization whose members can buy and sell (exchange) securities for companies and investors.

A **stock exchange** is an organization whose members can buy and sell (exchange) securities for companies and investors. A security is a transferable certificate of ownership of an investment product such as a stock or bond.[27] The Toronto Stock Exchange <*www.tmx.com*> and the Montréal Exchange <*www.m-x.ca/accueil_en.php*> are just two examples of securities markets in Canada. These institutions serve two major functions. First, they assist businesses in finding long-term funding to finance capital needs, such as beginning operations, expanding their businesses, or buying major goods and services. Second, they provide private investors with a place to buy and sell securities (investments), such as stocks, bonds, and mutual funds that can help them build their financial future.

▸ The Toronto Stock Exchange and the TSX Venture Exchange are not the only fish in the stock exchange sea. Exchanges like the London Stock Exchange <*www.londonstockexchange.com*> (pictured here) are located throughout the world, even in former communist-bloc countries like Poland and Hungary. If you think a foreign company is destined to be the next Magna or Bombardier, call a broker and get in on the opportunity.

Securities markets are divided into primary and secondary markets. *Primary markets* handle the sale of *new* securities. This is an important point to understand. Corporations make money on the sale of their securities only once—when they are first sold on the primary market through an IPO.[28] After that, the *secondary market* handles the trading of securities between investors, with the proceeds of a sale going to the investor selling the stock, not to the corporation whose stocks are sold. For example, imagine your vegetarian restaurant, Very Vegetarian, had grown into a chain and your products are available in many retail stores throughout the country. You want to raise additional funds to expand further. If you offer 1 million shares of stock in your company at $10 a share, you can raise $10 million at this initial offering. However; after the initial sale, if Shareholder Jones decides to sell 100 shares of her Very Vegetarian stock to Investor Smith, Very Vegetarian collects nothing from this transaction. Smith bought the stock from Jones, not from Very Vegetarian. It is possible, however, for companies like Very Vegetarian to offer additional shares of stock for sale to raise additional capital.

We cannot overemphasize the importance to business of normally meeting their long-term financial needs by using retained earnings or by borrowing from a lending institution (e.g., bank, pension fund, or insurance company). However, if long-term funds are not available from retained earnings or a lender, a company may be able to raise funds by issuing corporate stock or bonds. Recall from Chapter 17 that issuing corporate bonds is a form of debt financing and selling stock in the corporation is a form of equity financing. These forms of debt financing or equity financing are not available to all companies, especially small businesses. However, many firms use such financing options to meet long-term financial needs.

PROGRESS ASSESSMENT

- Describe the Canadian securities industry. Why are more Canadians turning to this industry?
- What is the role of the Canadian Securities Administrators?
- What is the primary purpose of a stock exchange? Can you name a stock exchange in Canada?

HOW INVESTORS BUY SECURITIES

Explain the different options for investing in securities.

stockbroker
A registered representative who works as a market intermediary to buy and sell securities for clients.

Investing in bonds, stocks, or other securities is not very difficult. First, you decide what bond or stock you want to buy. After that, you find a registered representative authorized to trade securities to execute your order. A **stockbroker** is a registered representative who works as a market intermediary to buy and sell securities for clients. Brokers prefer to make stock purchases in *round lots* of 100 shares at a time. Investors, however, usually cannot afford to buy 100 shares, which could see for well over $100 each, and therefore often buy in *odd lots;* of fewer than 100 shares at a time. Stockbrokers place an order where the bond or stock is traded and negotiates a price. After the transaction is completed, the trade is reported to your broker, who notifies you. Large brokerage firms maintain automated order systems that allow brokers to enter your order the instant you make it. The order can be confirmed in seconds.

A broker can also be a source of information about what stocks or bonds would best meet your financial objectives, but it is still important to learn about stocks and bonds on your own. Investment analysts' advice may not always meet your specific expectations and needs.[29]

Investing Through Online Brokers

Instead of using traditional brokerage services, investors today can choose from multiple online trading services to buy and sell stocks and bonds.[30] BMO Investorline <*www.bmoinvestorline.com*>, TD Waterhouse, and iTrade Canada <*www.scotiaitrade.com*> are a few of the leading providers of this service. Their investors are generally willing to do their own research and make investment decisions without the direct assistance of a broker, so the commissions these services charge are low. The leading online services do provide important market information, such as company financial data, price histories of a stock, and analysts' reports. Often the level of information services you can get depends on the size of your account and your level of trading.

Whether you decide to use an online broker or to invest through a traditional stockbroker, remember that investing means committing your money with the hope of making a profit.[31] As the market downturn in the fall of 2008 highlighted, investing is often a risky business. Therefore, the first step in any investment program is to determine your level of risk tolerance. Other factors to consider include your desired income, cash requirements, and need to hedge against inflation, along with the investment's growth prospects.

You are never too young or too old to invest, but you should first ask questions and consider alternatives. Let's take a look.

Choosing the Right Investment Strategy

Investment objectives change over the course of a person's life. A young person can better afford to invest in high-risk investment options such as stocks than a person nearing retirement. Younger investors generally look for significant growth in the value of their investments over time. If stocks go into a tailspin and decrease in value, as they did in 2008, a younger person has time to wait for stocks to rise again. Older people, perhaps on a fixed income, lack the luxury of waiting and may be more inclined to invest in bonds that offer a steady return as a protection against inflation.

Consider five key criteria when selecting investment options:

1. *Investment risk*—the chance that an investment will be worth less at some future time than it is worth now.
2. *Yield*—the expected rate of return on an investment, such as interest or dividends, usually over a period of one year.
3. *Duration*—the length of time your money is committed to an investment.
4. *Liquidity*—how quickly you can get back your invested funds if you want or need them.
5. *Tax consequences*—how the investment will affect your tax situation.

What is important in any investment strategy is the risk/return trade-off. Setting investment objectives such as *growth* (choosing stocks you believe will increase in price) or income (choosing stocks that pay consistent dividends) should set the tone for your investment strategy. Bonds, stocks, and mutual funds all offer opportunities for investors to enhance their financial future. We will look first at the potential of bonds as an investment, then move on to stocks and mutual funds.

INVESTING IN BONDS

Investors looking for guaranteed income and limited risk often turn to government bonds as a secure investment. These bonds have the financial backing and full faith and credit of the government. In recent history no government bond issue in Canada has been defaulted on. Corporate bonds are a bit more risky and challenging. Taxes are another consideration. Bond interest is fully taxable in the hands of the bond holder, while dividend income qualifies for tax credits.

First-time corporate bond investors often ask two questions. The first is, "If I purchase a corporate bond, do I have to hold it until the maturity date?" No, you do not. Bonds are bought and sold daily on major securities exchanges (the secondary market we discussed earlier). However, if you decide to sell your bond to another investor before its maturity date, you may not get its face value (usually $1,000). If your bond does not have features that make it attractive to other investors, like a relatively high interest rate or early maturity, you may have to sell at a *discount*; that is, a price less than the bond's face value. But if other investors highly value it, you may be able to sell your bond at a *premium*; a price above its face value. Bond prices generally fluctuate inversely with current market interest rates. *As interest rates go up, bond prices fall, and vice versa.* Like all investments, bonds have a degree of risk.

The second question is, "How can I assess the investment risk of a particular bond issue?" Standard & Poor's and Moody's Investors Service rate the risk of many corporate and government bonds. And recall the risk/return trade-off: The higher the risk of a bond, the higher the interest rate the issuer must offer. Investors will invest in a bond that is considered risky only if the potential return is high enough.[32] It is important to remember that investors have many investment options besides bonds. One such option is to buy stock.

INVESTING IN STOCKS

Buying stock makes investors part owners of a company who participate in its success. Shareholders can also lose money if a company does not do well or if the overall stock market declines. The market freefall of 2008–09 was proof of that.

Stock investors are often called bulls or bears according to their perceptions of the market.[33] *Bulls* believe that stock prices are going to rise; they buy stock in anticipation of the increase. A bull market is when overall stock prices are rising. *Bears* expect stock prices to decline and sell their stocks in anticipation of falling prices.[34] When the prices of stocks decline steadily, the market is called a bear market.[35]

The market price and growth potential of most stocks depends heavily on how well the corporation meets its business objectives. A company that achieves its objectives offers great potential for **capital gains**, the positive difference between the price at which you bought a stock and what you sell it for.[36] For example, an investment of $2,250 in 100 shares of McDonald's when it first went public in 1965 would have grown to 74,360 shares (after the company's 12 stock splits) worth approximately $7.5 million as of year-end market close in December 31, 2011. Stocks can be subject to a high degree of risk, however. While the late 1990s and early 2000s witnessed significant drops in the stock market, from 2004 to 2008 the Canadian stock market rose significantly as a result of the worldwide escalating demand for all types of natural resources. However, a financial crisis starting in the fall of 2008 drove markets down by close to 50 percent.

Crystal Hanlan started with Home Depot as a cashier several years ago. She began buying shares in the company as part of an employee ownership plan and is now worth over a million dollars. There are over a million other employees who got to be millionaires the same way. Are you getting the idea that it is a good idea to participate in such ownership programs and to put the maximum you can into such accounts?

capital gains
The positive difference between the purchase price of a stock and its sale price.

Investors may select stocks depending on their investment strategy. Stocks issued by higher-quality companies such as the Royal Bank and CN Rail are referred to as *blue-chip stocks;* they pay regular dividends and generally experience consistent stock price appreciation.

Stocks in corporations in emerging fields such as technology, biotechnology, or Internet-related firms, whose earnings are expected to grow at a faster rate than other stocks, are referred to as *growth stocks.* While a little riskier, growth stocks offer the potential for high returns. Stocks of public utilities are considered *income stocks* because they usually offer investors a higher dividend yield that generally keep pace with inflation.

There are even *penny stocks,* representing ownership in companies that compete in high-risk industries like oil exploration. Penny stocks sell for less that $2 (some analysts say less than $5) and are considered risky investments.

Stock investors have choices when placing buy orders. A *market order* tells a broker to buy or to sell a stock immediately at the best price available. A *limit order* tells the broker to buy or sell a stock at a specific price, if that price becomes available. Let's say a stock is selling for $40 a share. You believe the price will eventually go higher but could drop to $36 first. You can place a limit order at $36, so your broker will buy the stock at $36 if it drops to that price. If the stock never falls to $36, the broker will not purchase it for you. See the Making Ethical Decisions box about a story concerning a famous personality and limit orders.

Stock Indexes

Stock indexes measure the trend of different stock exchanges. Every country with a stock exchange has such indexes. In Canada, there are several thousand companies listed, and the prices of their shares fluctuate constantly. Some may be rising over a

MAKING ETHICAL DECISIONS

Was It a Limit Order?

In a case involving a famous personality, Martha Stewart was convicted of perjury and collusion for selling of shares in a drug company, ImClone <*www.imclone.com*>, bcsed on information she received from her broker, who was the same broker for the company's CEO. The CEO ordered his broker to sell his shares in the company after he became aware that a new drug (in which the company had invested heavily in research and development) did not receive approval from the Food and Drug Administration for sale. Martha maintains she had an outstanding limit order in place for this company's stock.

What is insider trading? Was the CEO involved in insider trading? What obligation does a shareholder in a company have to inform other shareholders, if they become aware of insider information?

certain period and others may be falling. Various indexes have been developed to give interested parties useful information about significant trends, and more and more indexes are being developed. Another use of an index is as an investment vehicle. Investors who do not have the time or expertise to actively manage their investments are choosing to be passive investors by investing in index funds.

In Canada, the largest index is the S&P/TSX Composite Index. There is no requirement for the index to hold a certain number of companies. The number of stocks that make up the index will vary over time and stocks will be included in the index if they qualify (based on size and liquidity) after quarterly reviews.[37]

Staying abreast of what is happening in the market will help you decide what investments seem most appropriate to your needs and objectives. However, it is important to remember two key investment realities: (1) your personal financial objectives will change over time, and (2) markets can be volatile.

Buying on Margin

buying on margin
Purchasing securities by borrowing some of the cost from the broker.

Buying on margin means borrowing some of the stock's purchase cost from the brokerage firm. The margin is the portion of the stocks' purchase price that the investors must pay with their own money. Provincial regulatory agencies, such as the Ontario Securities Commission, set *margin rates.* Briefly, if the margin rate is 50 percent, an investor who qualifies for a margin account may borrow up to 50 percent of the stock's purchase price from the broker.

Although buying on margin sounds like an easy way to buy more stocks, the downside is that investors must repay the credit extended by the broker, plus interest. If the investor's account goes down in value, the broker may issue a margin call, requiring the investor to come up with more money to cover the losses the account has suffered.[38] If the investor in unable to fulfill the margin call, the broker can legally sell off shares of the investor's stock to reduce the broker's chance of loss. Margin calls can force an investor to repay a significant portion of his or her account's loss within days or even hours. Buying on margin is thus a risky way to invest in stocks

Stock Splits

stock splits
An action by a company that gives shareholders two or more shares of stock for each one they own.

High per-share prices often induce companies to declare **stock splits**, in which they issue two or more shares for every one that is outstanding.[39] If Very Vegetarian stock were selling for $100 a share, the firm could declare a two-for-one stock split. Investors who owned one share of Very Vegetarian would now own two, each worth only $50 (half as much as before the split).

Stock splits cause no change in the firm's ownership structure and no immediate change in the investment's value. Investors generally approve of stock splits, however,

Figure 18.5

Understanding Stock Quotations

because demand for a stock may be greater at $50 than $100, and the price may then go up in the near future. A company cannot be forced to split its stock. Warren Buffett's firm, Berkshire Hathaway, has never split its Class A stock even when its per-share price surpassed $150,000.

Understanding Stock Quotations

Publications like the *Globe and Mail* and the *Financial Post* carry a wealth of information concerning stocks and other investments. Your local newspaper may carry similar information as well. Financial Web sites like Yahoo! Finance Canada carry up-to-the-minute information about companies that is much more detailed and only a click away. Take a look at Figure 18.5 to see an example of a stock quote from MSN Money for Microsoft. Microsoft trades on the NASDAQ exchange under the symbol MSFT. Preferred stock is identified by the letters *pf* following the company symbol. Remember, corporations can have several different preferred stock issues.

Information provided in the quote includes the highest and lowest price the stock traded for that day, the stock's high and low over the past 52 weeks, the dividend paid (if any), the stock's dividend yield (annual dividend as a percentage of the price per share), and important ratios like the price/earnings (P/E) ratio (the price of the stock divided by the firm's per share earnings). Investors can also see the total market capitalization of the firm. More technical features, such as the stock's beta (which measures degree of risk), may also appear. Figure 18.5 illustrates the stock's intraday trading (trading throughout the current day), but you can also click to see charts for different time periods. Similar information about bonds, mutual funds, and other investments is available online.

PROGRESS ASSESSMENT

- What is the key advantage to online investing? What do investors need to remember if they decide to do their investing online?
- What is a stock split? Why do companies sometimes split their stock?
- What is meant by buying on margin?

INVESTING IN MUTUAL FUNDS

A **mutual fund** buys stocks and bonds and then sells shares in those securities to the public. A mutual fund is like an investment company that pools investors' money and then buys stocks or bonds in many companies in accordance with the fund's specific

mutual fund
A fund that buys stocks and bonds and then sells shares in those securities to the public.

GREENBOX

Socially Responsible Investing

Also known as sustainable investing, Socially Responsible Investing (SRI) is an investment strategy that seeks to achieve both financial return and social good. One of the focuses for SRI is environmental stewardship, including sustainability with a focus on renewable energy. Specifically, investment should be channelled away from companies that are perceived to negatively impact climate change.

Through the financial crisis in 2008–09 the total SRI funds held steady and have grown to 1/5 of the assets under management in the financial industry. As of June 2010 total funds invested in these type of funds was $531 billion, of which over 80 percent were from pensions. Pension funds are more focused than other sources of investment funds on environmental, social, and governance issues.

A growing array of options exist for SRI. SRI is becoming more of a mainstream tool for value enhancement, risk management, and realization of social and environmental goals.

Source: "Socially-Responsible Investing," http://en.wikipedia.org/wiki/Socially_responsible_investing; and "Canadian Socially Responsible Investment Review 2010," May 2011, www.socialinvestment.ca/publications.htm.

purpose. Mutual fund managers are specialists who pick what they consider to be the best stocks and bonds available.

Investors can buy shares of the mutual funds and thus take part in the ownership of many different companies that they could not afford to invest in individually. Thus, for a fee, mutual funds provide professional investment management and help investors diversify. Funds range from very conservative funds that invest only in government securities or secure corporate bonds to others that specialize in emerging high-tech firms, Internet companies, foreign companies, precious metals, and other investments with greater risk. A number of mutual funds invest only in indexes (refer to the earlier discussion on stock indexes). Some mutual funds even invest exclusively in socially responsible companies. See the Green Box for a discussion of socially responsible investing.

In Canada, mutual fund companies fall under the jurisdiction of the provincial securities commissions. Some examples of companies that manage mutual fund assets include Investors Group <*www.investorsgroup.com*>, Mackenzie Financial <*www.mackenziefinancial.com*>, and TD Asset Management. According to the Investment Funds Institute of Canada <*www.ific.ca*>, total assets under administration were just less than $810 billion at the end of April 2012.[40]

diversification
Buying several different investment alternatives to spread the risk of investing.

With mutual funds, investors benefit from diversification. **Diversification** involves buying several different investment alternatives to spread the risk of investing. Consequently, a mutual fund investor is not 100 percent invested in only one company. So, if one company's shares decrease, hopefully there will be increases in the value of other companies' shares. This is also applicable if a mutual fund holds bonds.

One key advantage of mutual funds is that you can buy some funds directly and save any fees or commissions. The Internet has made access in and out of mutual funds easier than ever. A true *no-load fund* is one that charges no commission to investors to either buy or sell its shares. A load fund would charge a commission to investors to buy shares in the fund or would charge a commission when investors sell shares in the fund. It is important to check the costs involved in a mutual fund, such as fees and charges imposed in the managing of a fund, because these can differ significantly. It is also important to check the long-term performance record of the fund's management.[41] Some funds, called *open-end funds,* will accept the investments of any interested investors. *Closed-end funds* limit the number of

Investment	Degree of Risk	Expected Income	Possible Growth (Capital Gain)
Bonds	Low	Secure	Little
Preferred shares	Medium	Steady	Little
Common shares	High	Variable	Good
Mutual funds	Medium	Variable	Good

Figure 18.6

Comparing Investments

shares; once the fund reaches its target number, no new investors can buy into the fund.

Most financial advisers put mutual funds high on the list of recommended investments for small or beginning investors. Figure 18.6 evaluates bonds, stocks, and mutual funds according to risk, income, and possible investment growth (capital gain).

We hope you have enjoyed the discussion of investing in this chapter. It is critical for you to know that there's no such thing as easy money or a sure thing. Investing is a challenging and interesting field that is always changing.

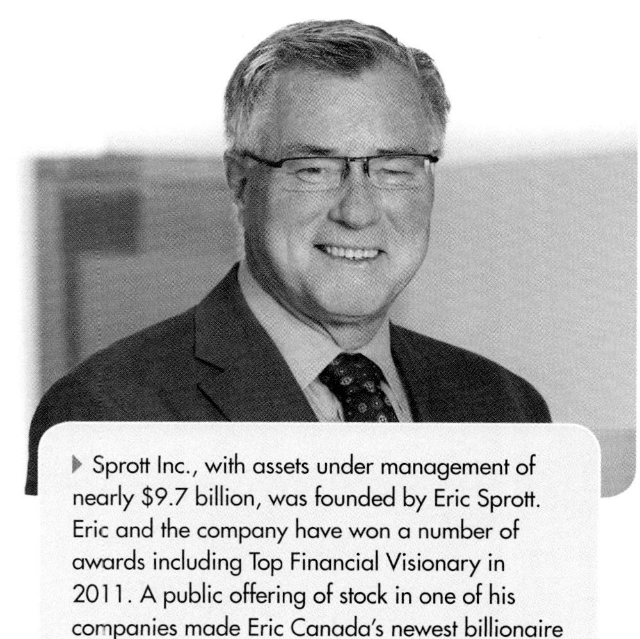

▶ Sprott Inc., with assets under management of nearly $9.7 billion, was founded by Eric Sprott. Eric and the company have won a number of awards including Top Financial Visionary in 2011. A public offering of stock in one of his companies made Eric Canada's newest billionaire in 2008.

PROGRESS ASSESSMENT

- What is a mutual fund and what is the role of mutual fund managers?
- How do mutual funds benefit small investors?
- Describe the degree of risk, expected income, and possible growth one can expect with mutual funds.

SUMMARY

Describe the importance of the financial services industry in Canada.

Figure 18.1 briefly lists the variety of financial organizations that comprise this industry.

Why is this industry important to Canada?

The financial services industry employs more than 1.12 million Canadians, directly or indirectly. Its activities represent $81.5 billion of Canada's GDP. Because of its important role in the economy, the financial industry is one of the most regulated sectors in the country. Regulation is designed to ensure the integrity, safety, and soundness of financial institutions and markets. Canada's banking system is ranked as the soundest in the world.

Explain what money is, what makes it useful, and how it is controlled.

Money is anything that people generally accept as payment for goods and services.

How is the value of money determined?
The value of money depends on the money supply; that is, how much money is available to buy goods and services. Too much money in circulation causes inflation. Too little money causes deflation, recession, and unemployment.

Discuss the role that banks play in providing financial services.

As major players in Canada's financial industry, banks serve millions of customers.

Who benefits from the services offered by banks?
Bank customers include individuals, small and medium-sized businesses, large corporations, governments, institutional investors, and non-profit organizations. The major banks offer a full range of banking, investment, and financial services.

Describe the role of the securities market

Growth of the Canadian securities industry has been significant over the past 10 years.

What is driving this growth in investing in the securities market?
Individuals, especially baby boomers, want to financially secure their future as they move into retirement. Companies and government agencies, including the Canada Pension Plan, are earning very low interest given the current climate of historically low interest rates.

Explain the different options for investing in securities.

The basic options for investing include bonds, stocks, and mutual funds.

What are the key criteria when selecting investment options?
Five key criteria are investment risk (the chance that an investment will be worth less at some future time than it is worth now); yield (the expected rate of return on an investment over a period of time); duration (the length of time your investment is committed to an investment); liquidity (how quickly you can get your money back if you need it); and tax consequences (how the investment will affect your tax situation).

KEY TERMS

barter
buying on margin
capital gains
certificate of deposit
commercial bank
credit unions
demand deposit
diversification
initial public offering (IPO)
money
money supply
mutual fund
non-banks
pension funds
prime rate
prospectus
securities commission
securities dealer
stock exchange
stock splits
stockbroker
time deposit
trust company

CRITICAL THINKING

1. Imagine that you have just inherited $100,000 and you want to invest it to meet two financial goals: to save for your wedding, which you plan to have in two years, and to save for your retirement, 30 to 35 years from now. How would you invest the money? Explain your answer.

2. The overnight bank rate, set by the B is currently very low. What circumsta the Governor of the Bank of Canad raise this rate? What impact would this rise have on individuals with debt? In a worst-case scenario what impact would this rise have?

DEVELOPING WORKPLACE SKILLS

1. In a small group, discuss the following: What services do you use from banks? Does anyone use Internet banking? What seem to be the pros and cons of online banking? Use this opportunity to compare the rates and services of various local banks.

2. Poll the class to see who uses banks and who uses a credit union or caisse populaire. Have class members compare the services at each (interest rates given on accounts, the services available, and the loan rates). If anyone uses an online service, see how those rates compare. If no one uses a credit union or online bank, discuss the reasons.

3. Break up into small groups and discuss when and where you use cheques versus credit cards and cash. Do you often write cheques for small amounts? Would you stop doing that if you calculated how much it costs to process such cheques? Discuss your findings with others in the class.

ANALYZING MANAGEMENT DECISIONS

Financial Crisis—Banking Disaster

2011 was characterized as a year with a sluggish economy and high unemployment, when millions of Americans lost their homes and businesses closed. How did we get there? Back in 2008 we had a global banking crisis that was the worst since the Great Depression of the 1930s. Several major American investment banks went bankrupt, markets plummeted around the world, and we experienced a global recession. The causes of the crisis included failures in financial regulations, reckless behaviour by financial firms, excessive borrowing by households and investment banks, and a lack of accountability and ethics at many levels.

Back even further, in 2000, the tech bubble burst. Share prices in high-tech companies fell dramatically and major financial frauds were discovered, including Worldcom, Enron, and Global Crossings. Governments wanted to keep consumers spending to head off an economic slowdown, so they chose to dramatically cut interest rates by over 5 percent, down to near 1 percent. Given this historic low cost of credit, consumers borrowed money, lots of it. By far the most significant borrowing related to home loans, that is, mortgages. By 2007, household debt rose to 127 percent of disposable income in the United States and Canadian household debt was climbing also. Home mortgages resulting from the housing boom became the biggest financial bubble in history. As more and more homes were purchased housing costs rose rapidly.

While everyone wants a home, the reality is that not everyone can afford the cost of buying one. But with relatively cheap mortgage interest everyone was buying a home, from first-time homeowners to long-time homeowners who wanted a bigger and fancier house. And banks were writing up mortgages for people who would not normally qualify. Banks typically look at the income of the borrower and assess the ability of the borrower to make the mortgage payments. But this criterion was overlooked more and more because the banks and everyone else believed that the price of houses would continue to rise. These mortgages were called sub-prime mortgages. In 2004, sub-prime mortgages made up 10 percent of all mortgages. By 2006, this percentage doubled.

These bad mortgages became an international problem. After mortgages were written, the banks sold them to investment banks. The investment banks in turn bundled these mortgages into securities, selling them in the open market to investors. They were called mortgage backed securities, or ("MBSs").

MBSs had been traded since the 1980s as a safe investment, as only low-risk conventional mortgages were bundled. With the rapid increase in mortgages being written, more and more MBSs appeared and investors liked the increasing return that was promised, given the higher and higher percentage of sub-prime mortgages that made up the newer MBSs. And bank lenders wrote riskier and riskier mortgages because investment banks demanded them and the banks were passing on the risk to investment banks and investors. Given the involvement of banks, investment banks, and investors it was very difficult to know where the risk was. Investors relied on ratings agencies, specifically Moody's and Standard and Poor's, for advice on safe investments. And these agencies were more than willing to oblige. Between 2000 and 2006 the number of AAA ratings exploded. MBSs were rated as AAA even though they consisted of a higher percentage of sub-prime mortgages.

The potential return from MBSs convinced the investment banks to request that the limits on the amount of money they could borrow to buy these securities be raised. In 2004 the SEC relaxed limits on leverage and these banks were allowed to take on as much risk as they liked. By 2007 the five largest investment banks increased their leverage significantly—they believed that housing prices would continue to go up and that MBSs were a good source of income.

In 2007 the real estate bubble burst and the growing recession left many homeowners unable to pay their mortgages, especially sub-prime mortgages. The number of foreclosures jumped 79 percent. As housing prices fell, many homeowners found themselves underwater, with mortgages higher than the value of their home. The financial incentive to pay their mortgages was gone, so they defaulted. The value of MBSs plummeted, leaving both investment banks and investors with hundreds of billions of dollars of defaulted mortgages with little chance of recouping the value of the mortgages. All the major investment banks were impacted; some consolidated, while others failed.

Many countries and international companies, including Canadian banks and investors, had invested in the U.S. housing market through MBSs. They were all affected. Foreign markets collapsed, the crisis went global.

As we look back on this time period, we realize that this financial crisis was the largest the world had ever experienced. Not since the Great Depression of the 1930s have we seen, on a global basis, rising unemployment, many failed businesses, plummeting consumer wealth, declining international trade, and the near-collapse of many foreign governments, especially in Europe. At the writing of this book we still do not fully comprehend the long-term impact of this crisis.

Discussion Questions

1. What does "household debt increasing to 127 percent of disposable income" mean and what is the implication for homeowners?
2. How is a sub-prime mortgage different from a conventional mortgage and why were banks apparently so willing to approve this type of mortgage?
3. Why did the returns from MBSs continue to rise?
4. Why did the housing bubble burst?

Practise and learn online with Connect.

PART 6 ENDS WITH:

DEALING WITH CHANGE

All Accountants May Soon Be the Same

For many years now, as discussed in Chapter 16, three different accounting designations have existed in Canada. In recent years the scope of accounting work performed by each of these three bodies has become more and more similar, creating confusion in the minds of the public in terms of the difference between Chartered Accountants, Certified Management Accountants, and Certified General Accountants. They each require a university degree and all three promote their members as trusted business advisers rather than simply "bean counters." You can find all three types of accountants working in industry, in education, and in governments as private accountants. You can also find all three working in public practice. Most other professions have only one type of professional accreditation.

In 2011, these three bodies again began negotiations aimed at setting aside decades of rivalry. Their plan is to merge and adopt a single super-designation; the Chartered Professional Accountant (CPA). The largest group, the CAs, have close to 80,000 members and view themselves as the profession's aristocracy. The CMAs have close to 40,000 members, while the CGAs have close to 75,000 members. As each of the professions is subject to provincial government regulations, between the three bodies and their respective federal and provincial arms 39 separate organizations are involved in the negotiations.

Attempts to merge two or more of these groups has occurred roughly once every 10 years for the past 90 years. However, ct this point each group is concerned about their relevance amid global integration of the accounting profession. There are currently twice as many CPAs in the world as there are CAs and all three groups want to be associated with the global brand of choice. In addition, the Province of Quebec has already moved ahead with legislation combining the province's three groups and creating the new CPA designation.

However, as negotiations continued through 2012, some provincial and federal arms of all three groups have opted out of the merger while the remaining groups continue to work on the merger. An expectation exists that if a merger happens in other areas of Canada, over time all the arms of every group will merge.

What could be a reason why certain arms of each group may initially not be in support of the merger? If the merger does not happen outside of Quebec, what would be impact of having four accounting designations in Canada?

Sources: Matthew McClearn, "The Settling of Accounts," *Canadian Business*, 24 January 2012.

REACHING BEYOND OUR BORDERS

European Debt Crisis

For the past several years, the world financial markets have been dominated by the sovereign (government) debt crisis of many European countries. When the decision was made to utilize a common currency, the euro, many government leaders throughout Europe believed that this one monetary decision was the key to future wealth and prosperity for every country in the EU, whose combined population and economic output rivalled every other country or trading pact in the world. Such was not the case. From 2002 through 2008 trade imbalances continued to grow between those member countries with strong economies, especially Germany, and those with weaker economies, such as Greece, Ireland, Italy, and Spain. With easy credit conditions throughout all member countries, the level of sovereign debt grew and grew to levels approaching $9 trillion euros in 2012.

These levels of debt were and are unsustainable. Slow global economic growth in 2008 and 2009 contributed to the growing crisis. European financial institutions held large amounts of European government debt and depressed real estate assets worth hundreds of billions of euros as collateral for the loans they had made. Investor confidence in the economies of the weaker European countries continued to fall. Many of these countries needed to sell billions of dollars of government bonds to re-finance their existing debt and cover their current account deficits. The falling confidence led to higher and higher interest demanded by those investors who were still willing to lend.

Governments in the better off economies, Germany and France, are only willing to support the economies of weaker countries through the provision of new or replacement debt if the governments of the weaker economies undergo additional belt tightening through fiscal discipline. Such an approach may well push the weaker economies further into recession, where unemployment rates for some sectors of the workforce is already over 25 percent.

How will the European banks be affected if a significant number of their loans are at risk? How would this situation impact the Canadian economy?

Source: "European Sovereign Debt Crisis: Overview, Analysis and Timeline of Major Events", *CFA Institute—Enterprising Investor,* 21 November, 2011; "European Debt Crisis", *The New York Times,* 8 April 2012; and Daniel Minihan, "The Definitive Summary of the European Debt Crisis", 14 February 2012, *The Hyperion Effect,* www.thehyperioneffect.com/?p=1984.

RUNNING CASE

Accounting, Financial Management, and Risk Management at Fox 40 International Inc.

Here are some facts to help get a perspective on the nature of Fox 40's financial statements and the scope of their business. The company has close to 200 accounts in their general ledger, of which 70 are expense accounts. They have over 3000 products grouped into 12 product lines. The product lines are then grouped in the income statement into three markets: Domestic, Export USA, and Export International. Expenses are grouped into three departments: sales and marketing, production and distribution, and general management administration. When comparing these statistics to the financial statements of Very Vegetarian you should appreciate the increased complexity of Fox 40's operations. Even with this level of complexity Fox 40 prepares monthly financial statements by the 12th to the 15th of the following month. For Ron Foxcroft, the CEO, with all the financial data available, he first looks at the bottom line, the net profit as reflected in the income statement.

Ron is also concerned with profitability by product, which is reflected in a product's gross margin. There is an expected range in gross margins between 40 percent to 60 percent. Fox 40 is also concerned with how well their receivables and inventory are managed. They expect their accounts receivable turnover to be 8, which translates into average days credit sales in receivables of 45. Meanwhile, inventory turnover will range from 1 to 12 depending on the product, which translates into their average inventory by product being sold between 30 days to 1 year.

The company's lenders closely monitor the debt to equity ratio and debt service coverage. The latter ratio compares the cash flow to the principal and interest payments on bank loans.

Financial planning is managed through a set of monthly budgeted financial statements for their fiscal year, which starts July 1. When comparing actual to budgeted performance any variance of more than 3 percent on a product line and any negative variance on expense items is investigated. Sales meetings are held every other week and current monthly sales are always discussed.

Bank balances are managed daily, and transfers can be made between any of the associated company bank accounts to ensure that sufficient funds are available to cover operating requirements and properly manage their various operating lines.

Fox 40 has approximately 200 Canadian credit customers, the majority of their customers, with terms ranging from 15 to 90 days. New international customers are required to pay in advance for their purchases until Fox 40 has experience in dealing with a particular customer. After a good relationship has been established about 25 percent of these customers are given credit. However, the Export Development Corporation (remember from the discussion in Chapter 4) insures these credit sales.

Operating lines are in place and inventory and receivables are pledged as collateral. These lines are set up with their bank, who they have been dealing with for 20 years. In fact, during this time they have been dealing with the same bank manager. They also have long-term financing arranged through the same bank for certain capital assets: moulds and dies used to manufacture many of their products and leasehold improvements for office and assembly space in their buildings. In addition they have a relatively small amount of long-term leasing arrangements. In addition, the company's financing needs are met in part through investments by the shareholders.

Risks are twofold in nature. One risk relates to major receivables defaulting, which occurs when a credit customer goes bankrupt. The second risk relates to the economy in general, when a downturn occurs. They manage the former through the rigour they employ from the decision to first grant a customer credit to regularly reviewing each credit customer's account. According to Ron Foxcroft, since this last happened in 2008 and 2009, "our company has to be able to 'turn-on-a-dime'." In terms of the second risk, Fox 40 frequently monitors sales and quickly makes decisions on controlling costs when they see sales contracting.

Sources: Used with the permission of Ron Foxcroft, founder and CEO, Fox 40 International Inc.

Discussion Questions

1. A ratio mentioned above is the debt service coverage, which is not covered in Chapter 16. Based on the definition provided, why would a lender be interested in this ratio and would they be looking for the cash flow to be more than, equal to, or less than interest payments?
2. Why are the financial controls for expenses so tight that every negative dollar variance needs to be investigated while on sales there is a leeway of 3 percent?
3. When compared to domestic credit customers, why are international credit customers less creditworthy, given the limited number of international credit customers and the fact that EDC insures credit sales to international customers?
4. What does it mean for Fox40 to be able to "turn-on-a-dime" if the economy experiences a downturn and what would be an example of a decision they could make in such a situation?

VIDEO CASES

CHAPTER 1 No Clowning Around—Cirque du Soleil

Several themes were introduced in this first chapter, including the importance of entrepreneurship to the success of the overall economy, the need for entrepreneurs to take risks (and the greater the risk, the higher the profit may be), and the dynamic business environment and the challenges it presents. Few organizations in today's society are more indicative of the new challenges than Cirque du Soleil.

First, Guy Laliberté took a huge risk by challenging the established circus tradition. The elaborate shows are expensive to start, and the talent must be the best in the world. But the risk pays off big time with sales of almost a billion dollars per year. Cirque du Soleil creates thousands of new jobs and contributes greatly to the communities it serves. It does this not only through the taxes it pays, but also through community outreach programs. Because of its entertainment value, Cirque contributes to both standard of living (through the taxes it pays) and quality them (the fun it provides for citizens of all ages).

Like all organizations, Cirque du Soleil has many stakeholders. They include the owners, the employees, and the local community. The organization is especially focused on the stakeholder group called customers. It wants to put on the best show possible, and that means providing the best talent in the best locations. To reach as many people as possible, many of the shows go on the road. You can even watch some of the shows on TV.

The business environment presents many challenges for Cirque du Soleil, as it does for all businesses. The economic and legal environment of Canada greatly supports entrepreneurs like Laliberté. The technological environment in Canada and the United States is also supportive of new business ventures. No circus in the past came close to the elaborate technological devices used by Cirque du Soleil. The stage for one of the Cirque productions in Las Vegas, for example, is a huge pool that delights the audience with its ability to change from a place where the actors can seem to walk on water to one where they can dive from many feet above it.

The social environment is also conducive to new businesses. The variety of the Canadian population has contributed greatly to the ability of the circus to find diverse acts and to recruit acts from around the world. The ability of the organization to adapt to many cultures is shown by its success in various cities throughout the world.

Of course, success is likely to breed much competition, and Cirque has its share. Even traditional circuses are tending to offer more exciting programs that reflect what Cirque has been doing for years. Competition is good for business, as it prompts all businesses to offer the best products possible.

One of the best things about this video is that it allows you to see part of Cirque du Soleil in action. If you have never seen a Cirque show, search one out—if only on TV. It is exciting and fun, and it shows that entrepreneurship is alive and well and providing wonderful new services. The result is profits for the owners and a better quality of life for us.

Discussion Questions

1. Guy Laliberté is an example of an entrepreneur that found an opportunity within a changing business environment. What are other lessons that you can take from this video that might result in an entrepreneur's success?

2. What are some of the challenges and opportunities you can identify for Cirque du Soleil in today's dynamic business environment?

3. How would you compare the excitement and fun of working for a new entrepreneurial venture like Cirque du Soleil with working for a large, traditional business? What are the risks? The rewards? The challenges?

CHAPTER 2 The Bank of Canada: Count on Us

The Bank of Canada contributes to the well-being of the Canadian economy through the implementation of monetary policy, its role in the Canadian financial system, and its management of Canada's bank notes. Located in Ottawa, Ontario, the Bank of Canada is our country's central bank. It is not a commercial bank and it does not offer banking services to the public. Its principal role, as defined in the Bank of Canada Act, is "to promote the economic and financial welfare of Canada." The Bank was founded in 1934 as a privately owned corporation. In 1938, it became a Crown corporation belonging to the federal government. (Crown corporations are discussed in Chapter 4.)

Take a second and think of your bank balance. What makes that money valuable? According to the Bank of Canada's Governor, Mark Carney, you don't have to worry about your money or the financial system in Canada due to the work of the Bank of Canada.

The Bank of Canada's main job is to direct monetary policy, which involves setting the interest rates that people and businesses pay when they borrow money. The Bank's objective is to influence interest rates so that the economy can remain healthy and create jobs. A healthy and stable economy helps families and businesses adapt to the changing conditions in the world economy.

As long as inflation is low, stable, and predictable we can remain confident in the future value of our money. The Bank of Canada and the Government of Canada aim for an annual inflation rate of 2 percent. This is known as the inflation target. The Bank of Canada sets the policy interest rate, which influences commercial interest rates. For consumers, low interest rates mean that it costs less to borrow money. For businesses, low-cost loans help them buy new equipment and expand their operations. All of this economic activity helps to push rates up. On the reverse, when everyone spends less due to higher interest rates, inflation tends to come down.

From buyers to sellers, from sellers to banks, and from banks back to businesses and consumers, it is easy to take all of these millions of transfers for granted. Money moves through a financial system. The Bank of Canada oversees these large complex systems that are used for making these daily financial transfers.

Since Canada is an open economy (i.e., we depend more on international trade and capital flows than many other countries), it is important to understand the global economic environment as well. To this end, the Bank of Canada works to ensure that the financial system stays strong and secure by working with the G20 (the 20 largest countries in the world), the IMF (International Monetary Fund), and the BIS (Bank of International Systems) to raise the standard of regulation and also ensure that other countries are applying these regulations and supervision through their banks, insurance companies, and financial systems so that Canada is not impacted by shocks from abroad.

When the Bank of Canada was established, it was given the sole authority to issue bank notes in Canada and to preserve the value of money. Bank notes are designed to be attractive, easy to use, durable, and difficult to counterfeit. If it was hard to tell a real Canadian bank note from a fake, confidence in our currency would disappear. All of our bank notes have security features that are easy to check.

Discussion Questions

1. The Bank of Canada has the mandate to contribute and enhance the well-being of Canadians. What three areas are targeted by the Bank of Canada as a way to do this?
2. How does the Bank of Canada try to keep the inflation in check?
3. What is the impact of high interest rates for consumers and businesses? How about low interest rates?

CHAPTER 3 The Mouse That Doesn't Come with a Computer

Who has not heard of Mickey Mouse? M I C, K E Y, M O U S E! How would you say that in French or Chinese or Spanish? Would it have the same meaning or the same appeal? Those are the questions Disney faced when planning to take the Disneyland experience overseas. Would the "Happiest Place on Earth" be equally happy for people who hadn't been exposed since birth to Mickey Mouse, Donald Duck, and the other Disney characters?

Walt Disney Imagineering is the creative arm of the Walt Disney Company <*thewaltdisneycompany.com*>.

The people in Imagineering come up with solutions to the questions posed above. The problem may be easier to solve than you imagine, because people all over the world have similar likes, fears, and imaginations. Just because they come from a different culture and speak a different language doesn't mean that they won't be equally enchanted by Cinderella, Snow White, and Mickey Mouse. On the other hand, there may be huge differences in the way people react.

So, what can you do to minimize the potential for disharmony? One answer is to hire local people to help in every phase of the project. They know the culture. They know the language. And they know what people like and dislike—in each specific country or town or village.

Taking Disney to China would have many positive benefits for both countries. It would create jobs in China and bring new entertainment to the people there. A Chinese Disneyland would create a more favourable balance of trade for the United States and possibly lead the way to more trade with China. Chinese labour is less expensive than U.S. labour, so a Disney park could perhaps be built for less—if local architects, engineers, and set designers were used. Everything would have to be planned with a Chinese audience in mind.

The same would be true in other countries. For example, in Japan, people like to shop for gifts, so the gift shop might be bigger and have more clerks. In France, people may prefer to drink wine instead of Coke. Local laws and local tastes must be considered. In short, taking a business overseas is a real challenge. It means listening to what locals have to say and then adapting your offerings accordingly.

Many questions need to be answered. For example, would people in other countries be willing to spend the same amount of money to enter the parks? Are there alternative ways to charge for the experience? Which of the Disney characters would appeal the most to people from China? How would you find the answers to such questions?

Discussion Questions

1. Working in another country can be a fun and challenging experience. If you had to choose one country to live in other than Canada, what would it be? Explain why. What Canadian companies are located there?
2. What products have you bought lately that were made in a different country? What countries produced them? Did you have any difficulty accepting the fact that the product came from there? Did you have any difficulty with the directions or the follow-up service? What does that tell you about global marketing and global business?
3. Imagine yourself trying to sell someone from France on the idea of visiting the Disney park. What issue might you expect to encounter? What issues may you encounter when trying to get someone visiting from France to go to the original Disneyland park in the United States?

CHAPTER 4 Creating a Buzz: Red Bull

In this chapter, you were introduced to the ways in which government activities can affect businesses. Let us consider how the creation of laws and regulations, one of the six government activities discussed, can create an opportunity for the sale of a product that some believe is dangerous to one's health.

Developed in Austria, Red Bull <*www.redbull.com*> is an energy drink with high caffeine content. It is creating quite a buzz, literally. It is promoted to people who need an energy boost.

Health Canada <*www.hc-sc.gc.ca*> is the federal department responsible for helping Canadians maintain and improve their health while respecting individual choices and circumstances. Health Canada oversees legislation for health products, regulating everything from vitamins to herbal remedies. Under this legislation, Red Bull was approved as a health product, with many warnings. These warnings include the following: Red Bull is not recommended for children, for pregnant women or those who are breastfeeding, or for caffeine-sensitive persons; it is not to be mixed with alcohol; and people should not consume more than 500 mL per day.

Some believe that Red Bull should not have been approved for sale in Canada as a health product. Too much consumption of Red Bull can be dehydrating. Despite allegations to the contrary, there was no evidence at the time of this video supporting the claim that Red Bull negatively affects people's hearts. There was no long-term research on how the combination of ingredients in this product interacts with the body. Regardless, some countries—Norway, Denmark, and

France—were so concerned that they banned Red Bull. The governments in Sweden and Iceland have also voiced concerns.

In addition to other marketing activities, Red Bull sponsors extreme sporting events. The product can be purchased in a variety of locations across Canada, including bars and local variety stores. It is a number-one seller in 7-Eleven variety stores, which are easily accessible to children. The video shows how Red Bull representatives are promoting their product throughout Canada and encouraging participants to try it. From the footage shown, it does not appear that they are consistently communicating the warnings on the label, including that Red Bull should not be mixed with alcohol.

Have you tasted Red Bull? If so, did you like it? If not, are you curious to try it?

Discussion Questions

1. What ingredients are found in Red Bull? What is the controversy surrounding these ingredients?
2. Why did Health Canada approve the sale of Red Bull when other countries have banned the sale of this product?
3. Do you agree that people must take responsibility for their own health, including reading labels and following instructions? In your opinion, should Health Canada be doing more? Explain.

CHAPTER 5 If It Isn't Ethical, It Isn't Right

Cancer affects the lives of millions of people each year. While significant progress has been made toward fighting the disease, finding a cure is considered by many to be the "holy grail" of medicine. For most of the twentieth century, cancer-fighting drugs were like bombers in the Second World War. They'd drop thousands of bombs, hoping that a few would get lucky and hit the target. Since the drugs couldn't tell the difference between a cancer cell and a healthy cell, they killed them both. But new generations of drugs are more precise and target individual disease cells, leaving healthy cells unharmed.

Unfortunately, developing effective new treatments for cancer is a lengthy and costly process. Every step in the process of developing a new drug calls for ethical decision making. The temptation may be to rush the process and cut corners to minimize costs and maximize profits. Does the drug violate a patent that already exists? How far should a company go in testing the effectiveness and the side effects of the new product? Should the drug be tested on animals? Should it be tested on humans? How much should a company charge for the drug? What should the company say in its promotions?

Jennie Mather founded a company called Raven Biotechnologies to develop solutions to the most serious cancer illnesses. She understood from the beginning that ethical decisions are based on ethical management. She used the latest monoclonal technology because it enabled her company to target and attack a single disease cell such as a cancer cell. This is a much safer and ethical way of solving the problem because it dramatically reduces the serious side effects caused by "shotgun" treatments. Because of these precautions, such drugs tend to make it through the government screening process faster and easier.

Mather hires employees who have the same ethical approach to business and the same kind of scientific approach that she has. She knows that management sets the ethical parameters, but that employees must maintain those standards. Business people today are conscious of the fact that the public is very sensitive to ethical practices because of companies, such as Enron, that violated ethical principles. The public is particularly sensitive to issues surrounding pharmaceutical companies. One popular movie focused on the ethics of product testing. Should drugs be tested on humans? If so, how should people taking the test drugs be treated? Is it right to give some people the test medicine and others a placebo (a fake medicine)?

Another fundamental issue is price. It costs a lot of money to develop a new drug, and companies cannot come up with new solutions to illnesses without recouping those huge costs. On the other hand, people without health insurance and people in developing countries simply cannot afford high prices for drugs. Who should bear the cost of providing life-saving drugs to those people?

Mather and her employees take an ethical approach to everything they do. Everyone looks forward to the day when there are effective drugs for pancreatic cancer, colorectal cancer, and other serious illnesses. We look to science to solve those problems, and we look to ethical managers to apply the science in the right way.

Discussion Questions

1. What ethical issues concern you most about the development and sale of pharmaceutical drugs? Does Raven Biotechnologies address all of your concerns?
2. One of the major issues involving pharmaceutical drugs is their high cost. Why do drug companies have to charge such high prices? Should they charge lower prices in countries where the people cannot afford expensive drugs?
3. Is the need for high ethical standards more or less important in the pharmaceutical industry? Why? What could be done to assure the public that the highest standards are being used?

CHAPTER 6 Java Nook

Annette Lavigne, mother of six, is starting a business selling coffee with her new life and business partner, John Welter. Apart from a few jobs at minimum wage, Lavigne has spent the last twenty years at home with her children. Armed with a high school "how-to course" in business, Lavigne is turning first-time entrepreneur in one of the riskiest service businesses; as many as 40 percent of new restaurants close within two years.

The partners found a low-rent location for their small café and are hoping for sales of $400 a day to start when they open. We learn of some of the challenges that they face as their opening date keeps getting pushed back. Starting the venture with $20,000 that Lavigne received in an accident settlement, they soon realize that they have underestimated both the amount of money and time needed to commercialize their business. The money is soon gone and the bills keep piling in. Lavigne is approved for $30,000 from a second mortgage on her house to continue with this dream of a lifetime.

One week from opening, they still have a lot to do. Among other tasks, they are deciding what food to serve, where to place it, and how to run the espresso machine. With less than twenty hours to go, the carpenter is still putting up walls.

The first week of the Java Nook's opening was a great success. So much so, in fact, that the carpenter became a full partner. With less than two weeks under their belt, Lavigne and Welter decide to expand. They lease the space next door and plan to sell local art. They're going for broke if they don't go broke. "If it doesn't succeed," says Lavigne, "we know that we will have done our best and at least we will have the Java Nook."

Discussion Questions

1. What are the advantages and disadvantages of starting a partnership?
2. Do Annette and John have the backgrounds needed to succeed in business? Explain.
3. If you were seeking to open a similar business, would you prefer to do it on your own or to purchase a franchise? What are some of the advantages and disadvantages of purchasing a franchise?

CHAPTER 7 dougieDOG in the *Dragons' Den*

Aspiring entrepreneurs enter the *Dragons' Den* and pitch their business concepts and products to a panel of Canadian business people who have the cash and the knowledge to make their dreams happen. But it takes more than passion to convince these investors, as it is their money that is on the line.

In this segment, we meet Dougie Luv, a Vancouver entrepreneur with a gourmet take on a campfire classic. President of dougieDOG Hot Dogs <*dougiedog.com*>, he is seeking $200,000 for 25 percent of his company. Two and a half years ago, Luv decided to research the hot dog, a comfort food. He drove to Los Angeles and spent eight weeks on the road, eating hot dogs. Returning to Vancouver, he opened British Columbia's first hot dog restaurant.

The hot dogs are all natural, free of hormones, preservatives, and chemical additives. His restaurant serves more than 26 varieties of this all-natural hot dog. Costing $7 each, the price is more than double the price of a hot dog that is purchased from a street vendor (also known as street meat).

The operation is 650 square feet with monthly sales between $25,000 to $30,000. While the operation lost $10,000 in its first year, Luv has since adjusted the food costs and wages. It is in a great location, Vancouver's entertainment district. A lot of his business occurs after 10:00 p.m. when people leave the bars and clubs in the area.

Luv is passionate about his company and he is convinced that it is going to make money on this exclusive brand of hot dog. In fact, he is legally ready to franchise his business. "This is what being an entrepreneur is about," says Luv. "Believing in your product, doing it, and making it work."

Unfortunately, Luv is not successful in convincing the Dragons to give him the money. Watch the video to learn why believing in your product and making it work is not always enough.

Discussion Questions

1. According to Jim Treliving, one of the Dragons, how much does a business between 600 to 800 square feet have to make to break even in a year? How close is this business, as it now stands, to this point?
2. What are the reasons given by the Dragons as to why they will not invest in dougieDOG? Do they make valid points?
3. Would you invest in adougieDOG franchise based on what you learned in this video? Explain.

CHAPTER 8 How Bad Is Your Boss?

No matter where you work, no matter how important you think you are, you can't escape the boss. Some are demanding, some are out of touch, and they are creating stress in the workplace.

Shaun Belding, author of *Winning with Bosses from Hell*, shares the seven deadly sins of bosses. You will hear from former employees examples of bad boss behaviour that contributed to a negative work environment. In many instances, employees quit their jobs as a result of poor management styles.

Business people who have risen through the ranks share some of their insights based on years of experience. In one instance, you will hear how treating workers well can boost the bottom line: good management is important for the health of an organization and the individual, while poor management makes organizations and people unhealthy. One former executive believes that employees are asking for reality, clarity, and opportunity in the workplace, and that this is what executives need to deliver.

In this chapter you read about changes occurring in the areas of management and leadership. Most managers today are flexible and open to new ideas. They tend to give their workers more responsibility and authority and act more like leaders than bosses who tell their workers what to do. Robert Lemieux is a young executive at the Delta Chelsea in Toronto, Canada's biggest hotel. He is the director of sales, with a staff of 50. In order to become president or vice-president, he knows that he has to become a great boss. To help him avoid becoming a bad boss, he agrees to work with Lindsay Sukornyk, founder of North Star Coaches <*www.northstarcoaches.com*>, an executive coaching firm. As part of the process, she helps identify those things he does well as a boss and those things he needs to do better. The result is that in addition to his positive traits, Lemieux learns that there is a perception that he over-promises and under-delivers with his employees as he becomes too involved in projects. In a discussion with his employees, he shares this feedback and solicits their advice on how he can change his approach to become a better supervisor. Such open communication is reflective of his strong leadership and the care that he demonstrates for his employees.

When you consider your answers to the seven questions posed in the video, it is important to recognize that not everyone can be perfect all of the time. However, if you said yes to between three and six questions, you have (or have had) a bad boss. If you are in this situation now, you may need to take action to change the situation, but be careful if you confront your boss. After all, you are the subordinate and such a discussion would require a high degree of tact.

If you have limited work experience, this video is still of value to you. One day you likely will hold a management position, and hopefully you will remember some of these points as you move up the corporate ladder.

Discussion Questions

1. What are the seven deadly sins of bosses?
2. Do you believe that people can be coached to be better managers? Explain.
3. What leadership style should Robert Lemieux use to be considered more effective by his staff?
4. What can workers do to protect themselves from a bad boss?

CHAPTER 9 One Smooth Stone

David slew Goliath with a single smooth stone, and thus was born the name of the company One Smooth Stone (OSS). It's an unusual name for an unusually interesting company. OSS is in the business of providing materials for big corporate events: sales meetings, client meetings, and product presentations. Most people in industry have attended many such meetings, so keeping them entertained is a major challenge. And that's where OSS comes in: It uses project teams to come up with original and captivating presentations for its customers.

You read about the history of organizational design in this chapter. You learned, for example, about Fayol and his principles of organization. The first principle is unity of command (every worker is to report to one, and only one, boss). Other principles include order, equity, and esprit de corps. This video shows that OSS understands the importance of esprit de corps. It is a fun and interesting place to work, and employee turnover is very low. The company does not follow many of Weber's principles dealing with written rules and consistent procedures. Quite the contrary: OSS is structured to be flexible and responsive to its clients. There are no set rules, and the company is certainly not consistent with its projects. Everything is custom-made to the needs of each client.

OSS uses a flat organization structure. There are a few project managers, who have workers under them, but they don't look over the employees' shoulders telling them what to do or how to do it. That means there is decentralized authority. Whereas many companies are structured by department—design, engineering, marketing, finance, accounting, and so forth—OSS is structured using project teams. Each team is structured to meet the needs of an individual client. For example, the company hires people with specific skills as they are needed. The term for this is outsourcing, and OSS outsources many of its tasks to freelance professionals. Together, these professionals work as self-managed teams. The teams focus on client needs. There are some staff workers to help with personnel, legal, and other such services.

The company is not keen on making strategic plans because its environment changes so rapidly that such plans are obsolete as soon as they are made. Therefore, the company engages in "strategic improvising." Although OSS sounds less structured and more informal than most companies, it still focuses on total quality and practises continuous improvement.

In addition, the company is particularly concerned about its corporate culture. It has three values: smart, fast, and kind. It works smart, responds quickly, and is always kind to others, including its own workers. Because of its culture and responsiveness, the company has been able to capture big accounts such as Motorola, Sun Microsystems, and International Truck and Engine.

The long-run success of the firm, however, is based on its project management teams. They carefully listen to what clients are trying to accomplish and then come up with solutions to their problems. You can see their creativity in this video. Clearly, OSS has been able to impress the Goliaths of big business with its presentations.

Discussion Questions

1. What have you learned from this video about the use of teams as an organizational tool versus the traditional line or line-and-staff forms of organization?
2. Does working at OSS look like more or less fun than working for a company with a more traditional approach to organizational structure and operations? Why?
3. From what you saw in the video, what do you think the core competencies of the company might be?

CHAPTER 10 Reality on Request: Digital Domain

As chairman and CEO of Digital Domain <*digitaldomain.com*>, Scott Ross runs one of the largest digital production studios in the world. His studio won an Academy Award for simulating the sinking of the *Titanic* in the movie of the same name. It also created the digital waves that wiped out the horsemen in *The Lord of the Rings*.

Operations management is unique at Digital Domain because no two projects are ever the same. One day the company may be making a digital cow

(*O Brother, Where Art Thou?*), on another a digital spaceship (*Apollo 13*), and on still another digital waves (*Titanic*). Digital Domain is both a production and a service provider. How so? In addition to producing digital scenes for movies, the company advises movie producers as to what is possible to accomplish digitally. Still, certain activities, such as facility location and facility layout, are common to both service organizations and production firms.

Since many movies are made in Los Angeles, it's important for Digital Domain to be close to the city. Actors are often chosen from that area, as are workers and specialists at Digital. The company believes that its most important resource is its workers. Thus, facilities layout is designed to make workers' jobs easier yet efficient. For example, there's a combination conference room and cafeteria. Given the company's passion for quality, everything is designed to be clean and logical. Facility layout assists workers in developing the highest-quality product possible given time and money constraints.

Materialsrequirementplanning(MRP)isacomputer-based operations management system that uses sales forecasts to make needed parts and materials available at the right time and place. Since Digital's primary resource is people, the company lists 54 key disciplines in its database, so it's easy to find the right person for the right job. For example, a project may come up on Wednesday that demands resources be available the next Monday. People have to be contacted and hired just in time to keep the project on time and within budget.

The company does much of its purchasing on the Internet. It also uses flexible manufacturing. To keep costs down, Digital also uses lean manufacturing, the production of goods using less of everything: less human effort, less manufacturing space, less investment in tools, and less engineering time for a given project. To keep costs down, the company does a lot of previsualizing—simulating projects to determine the best way to proceed.

Of course, mass customization is basically what Digital Domain is all about: creating new and different scenes that cannot be duplicated. However, once the company learns to create artificial waves or some other image, it is easier to duplicate a similar image next time. Since film is very expensive, many ideas are created using pen and pencil first. From such "primitive" tools, the company goes on to use computer-aided design.

Making movies is expensive. Everything needs to be done as planned. Scott Ross knows it's show business, and that making a profit is vital. For this reason, getting things done right and on time is the hallmark at Digital Domain.

Discussion Questions

1. Do you have an appreciation for operations management now that you've seen how exciting such a job can be at a company like Digital Domain?
2. Mass customization is critical in the production of movies and special effects. As a consumer, what benefits do you see in being able to buy custom-made shoes, clothes, automobiles, and more?
3. What lessons did you learn from this video that you could apply at any job you might get?
4. This video points out that certain workers are very focused on quality, and that there comes a time when you have to stop improving things because time has a cost. Have you had to make a trade-off between perfection and "good enough"? What were the consequences?

CHAPTER 11 Motivation Is a Hot Topic

We all have witnessed retail employees who seem at best indifferent to customer satisfaction. They are as likely to be talking to one another as to customers—sometimes on the phone. It doesn't take a retailing expert to know that such employees do not contribute to the success of the firm. So, how do firms get retail employees to be passionate about their work? To answer that question, consider Hot Topic Incorporated <*www.hottopic.com*>.

Hot Topic stores sell clothing and accessories that appeal to the alternative culture. Emphasis is on the latest music trends and the fashions that accompany them. Employees, therefore, need to be familiar with the newest bands and the latest music. That means going to concerts and observing what people wear and becoming very familiar with the cultural trends within those groups.

Torrid <*www.torrid.com*> is another store run by the same company. It caters to an entirely different audience: more mature women who are looking for fashionable plus sizes. Hot Topic Incorporated runs both stores. The CEO of the company is Betsy

McLaughlin. She has learned how to motivate the employees at both stores using well-established managerial techniques outlined in this chapter.

There is much emphasis in this text on employee empowerment. At Hot Topic, that means that employees are paid to attend music concerts where they not only have a good time, but also learn more about the culture of the people they will be serving. Since promotions come from within, that culture carries over into headquarters. There are none of the usual offices that designate hierarchy. Instead, all employees are encouraged to make decisions on their own, within reason, and to be responsive to customer needs. As you read in this chapter, Herzberg says that employees have certain needs that are not motivating but result in dissatisfaction (and possible poor performance) if not present. They include salary and other benefits. Thus, the salary and benefits at both stores have to be competitive.

Employees feel good about their work when they are empowered to do what it takes to please customers. Empowerment often demands some in-house training to teach employees the skills they need to be responsive to customer demands. All of this falls under the concepts of Theory Y, which states that people are willing to work hard if given the freedom and opportunity to do so. Such freedom is what Hot Topic Incorporated is all about.

Discussion Questions

1. What motivators identified by Herzberg are used at Hot Topic?
2. How do you think Hot Topic employees would react if the company gave them each a small raise, but stopped paying them to attend music concerts? Would they be more or less motivated to please customers? Why?
3. How well would a Theory X manager perform at Hot Topic? Why?

CHAPTER 12 Surf's Up at Patagonia!

Human resource management (HRM) can be one of the most exciting and enjoyable parts of a firm, depending on management's commitment to workers' needs. No company reflects this commitment better than Patagonia. Patagonia's HRM doesn't have to worry about where it's going to get its next worker, as people are lined up to get a job with the company. Why? Because this is a firm with passion—passion for making the best products possible, passion for making its employees happy, and passion about the environment.

Patagonia believes that a great business begins with great products. Who could argue with that? Great products meet the needs of customers. In this case, that means that they will be long-lasting and are backed by a full guarantee. But great products do more than satisfy consumers; they also have a minimal impact on the environment.

Workers at Patagonia are pleased that the company's commitment to the environment is not just a slogan. Ten percent of its pre-tax profit goes to environmental groups of all kinds. Employees are encouraged to get to know these groups and to participate in selecting the groups that receive the company's donations. If an environmental group is not familiar with best business practices, such as writing a business plan, Patagonia will give it that training.

Given that thousands of people are willing to work for Patagonia, how does the HRM department choose which ones to hire? They are looking for people who are as passionate as they are. What kind of passion do they require? Any kind: a passion for cooking, for cleaning, for life. When employees have passion, they will stick with an employer. That's why the turnover rate at Patagonia is a low 4 percent per year. Some businesses have a turnover rate approaching 100 percent per year. These businesses have to train and retrain their employees constantly. Patagonia can put all of that effort into satisfying the needs of employees who want to stay.

What does the company do for its employees that makes it stand out from other companies? For one thing, Patagonia knows that parents often feel uncomfortable leaving their children with child-care centres. Patagonia provides onsite daycare—and they did so long before other companies even dreamed about offering such a benefit. Children thus become part of the company's atmosphere. There are children everywhere, and the parents feel comfortable having them nearby.

All employees experience days when the sun is shining and nature is calling. You simply can't get your work done because you are dreaming about fishing or golfing or mountain climbing or whatever. How would you like it if your manager said, "Go ahead, take off. Have fun!" How can a company do that? One way is to have a flexible work schedule. With such a schedule, workers can take off early or come in late when the "surf's up"—that is, when recreation calls. Patagonia's top managers have a passion for sports and sports equipment—the kind that Patagonia sells. Since they expect their employees to have the same passion, that means letting them go when they need to go. That employee passion is communicated to customers, who buy more. It's a win–win deal for the company. Employees are happy with the freedom they have, and the company is happy with the productivity that such freedom creates.

What other company offers surfing lessons to its employees? Few companies let their employees leave when the surf's up, but many other companies offer employees flexible work schedules and other incentives that allow them to balance their work and personal lives. These companies also have workers who are passionate about the company and their work. Who organizes all of these activities for workers? HRM!

Discussion Questions

1. Patagonia stresses the importance of hiring employees with passion—a passion for anything, not just sports. Why does it place such importance on passion? Why would it think that someone with a passion for something unrelated to sports (e.g., cooking) might be an excellent employee?
2. What effect do Patagonia's practices of providing child care and donating to environmental groups have on employee productivity and retention? Why?
3. Can you see the potential for possible abuses of a flextime program? What could a company do to prevent such abuses before they occur?

CHAPTER 13 United We Stand

After reading this chapter, you are familiar with the history of labour unions. You have learned the tactics that labour uses to get new benefits from management, and you have learned the tactics that management uses to respond to labour demands. What should be evident is that labour unions are still important today and they continue to seek fair treatment for the employees that they represent.

We are so accustomed to thinking about labour unions in the auto, steel, and other related industries that we tend to overlook other key industries where labour unions are very important. Have you heard of the Screen Actors Guild (SAG), the American Federation of TV and Radio Artists (AFTRA), and the Writers Guild of America (WGA) <*www.wga.org*>? Do you have any idea what issues the membership faces in such unions? Are they the same issues that unions have always faced: seniority, pay, benefits, and such? Or are they different somehow?

Some young people dream of becoming movie stars. They see the glamour, the excitement, the adulation of the fans, and the huge paycheques. What they don't see behind the scenes is the constant fight going on to win and keep certain privileges that past actors have won. Back in the 1930s, actors worked unrestricted hours, had no required meal breaks, and had unbreakable seven-year contracts. The producers tried to control who you could marry, what political views you could express, and what your morals were. The SAG won some concessions for the actors in 1937, but the studios pretty much still "owned" their stars. Eventually the stars won the right to better contracts—to the point where independent studios were formed and actors could control their own careers, even demanding a percentage of gross for their pay (e.g., Jimmy Stewart in 1950).

Other issues concerned residuals for films shown on TV and in reruns. Other contracts had to do with commercials and how the actors would be paid for them. Today's contracts deal with issues like diversity, salary and work conditions, financial assurances, safety considerations, and so on. Things are constantly changing for actors. For example, independent film producers around the world have different rules and requirements. TV commercials now appear on cell phones. SAG keeps up with such changes to assure fair treatment of its members.

While SAG is for movie actors, AFTRA is a performer's union for actors, radio and TV announcers and newspersons, singers, and others who perform on radio and TV. It negotiates wages and working conditions much like the SAG, including health care and pensions. You can imagine negotiating an issue like equal pay for equal work when dealing with highly paid actors and actresses with huge egos.

The WGA represents writers in the motion picture, broadcast, and new media industries. (The Writers Guild of Canada represents Canadian writers.) Like actors, writers have issues dealing with pay, benefits, retirement, and so forth. The more you think about it, the more it will become clear to you that actors and others in the entertainment industry need unions or some other kind of organization to protect them from unfair practices. You can only imagine what treatment actors and others get from independent companies in other countries if they don't have representation.

Discussion Questions

1. Imagine what it would be like to try to get a job as an actor in Hollywood. What role might a union play in helping you find a job, negotiate a contract, and otherwise look out for your interests? You might look on the SAG-AFTRA <*www.sagaftra.org*> and WGA Web sites for more information (as an update to the video, SAG and AFTRA merged in March 2012).
2. What issues might actors, performers, and writers have that other workers may not have?
3. What is the general attitude in your class toward labour unions? Are there many union workers in your city? Where do you see labour unions gaining strength in the future?

CHAPTER 14 Going for the Green Market

You can't go to a grocery store or hardware store these days without noticing how many products are being promoted as "green" products. They are called "eco-friendly" or "natural" or simply "green." There is "green" paint with no smell, "green" cars that use less gas, and "green" environmental paper products.

This video features several green products including Green Works from The Clorox Company <*www.thecloroxcompany.com*>. Clorox considered making such products for five years before deciding that the market was ready for them. Using the concept of "Find a need and fill it," the company used focus groups to find out what customers wanted in cleaning products. Consumers indicated that they wanted to go green, but didn't want to change their behaviour radically. The company responded accordingly, and did not create a niche product but one that would appeal to everybody.

Clorox believes its product is truly green. It contains coconuts, lemon, and corn ethanol. It is Clorox's first new brand in twenty years, so they wanted to make it right. In fact, the Sierra Club <*www.sierraclub.org*>, an environmental organization, has gone so far as to endorse the product. Some people have questioned whether or not the Sierra Club should be endorsing any products from companies like Clorox that make other products, such as bleach, that many say harm the environment. Clorox contends that Clorox bleach becomes nothing more than salt and water after use and is environmentally safe. In fact, bleach has saved lots of lives because of its ability to kill germs.

The validity of the Sierra Club endorsement was criticized by others because the organization gets money from Clorox—a fact that puts some doubt in people's minds about the ethics of the whole process. The Sierra Club calls it "cause-related marketing" and finds nothing wrong with the fact that it receives money from Clorox.

The question for all of us is, "How do we know which products are truly green and which are not?" Are the companies helping to save the world or are they simply practicing good marketing? The answer, the video points out, is that we really don't know which products are "good" for the environment. In fact, there is a call for strict government guidelines as to which products should be able to use the words "green" and "sustainable."

Another company featured in the video is Home Depot. It offers green paint, green light bulbs, and other green products. It uses Scientific Certification Systems <*www.scscertified.com*> to test its products and does its own testing as well. Nonetheless, there is a call for better labelling of green products, including the ingredients. If a product doesn't list all the ingredients, the video suggests you not buy them.

Pretending a product is green when it really is not is called "green washing" and confuses the consumer. Many people believe that almost all products in the future will be greener than ones on the shelf now. On the other hand, others contend that the "green revolution" may not last for more than a few years. Whether or not green products are here to stay is up to consumers like you.

Discussion Questions

1. List at least four products that you've seen or purchased that are clearly green products. How much influence do green promotions have on your purchasing decisions? Discuss.
2. There was some discussion in the video about the future of green products. Do you believe that green products are here to stay?
3. Would you like to see more green labelling, including the listing of ingredients? Do you believe that the use of such products will make a significant difference in the sustainability of the planet? Why or why not?

CHAPTER 15 Promotion Gets a Big Push

Students today are witnessing a major revolution in promotion. They have seen radio change from standard broadcasting to commercial-free satellite radio. They have watched families blank out TV commercials with TiVo and other digital video recording devices. Students spend less time reading newspapers and magazines and more time talking on the phone, playing video games, and listening to their iPods. More entertainment options are available today and there are more distractions from traditional promotional tools.

Today's students also have a wonderful opportunity to reinvent promotion, changing it from a one-way stream of sales pitches to an interactive dialogue among promoters and consumers. Traditional promotional tools—selling, advertising, public relations, and sales promotion—have always provided fun and interesting careers. The challenge today is to create promotions for the new realities of the marketplace. That means, for one thing, creating advertising and other promotions on the Internet. One of the cutting-edge advertising agencies in this regard is Night Agency <*www.nightagency.org*>, which has become an integral part of the marketing process for the firms it serves. It does everything from helping in the design of the product to working with the company to develop a winning brand name, effective packaging, and fast distribution.

A company like Night Agency has to promote itself to other businesses. Like most firms, Night Agency relies heavily on word of mouth to spread its name. Publicity in the form of articles written about the company is another powerful promotional tool. Night Agency teaches other firms how to use public relations and publicity to educate the public about the good things the firms do and to give the firm's side of the story during controversies. Think of the public relations challenge that oil companies have had over high gas prices at the pump.

Often, promotional efforts begin inside a company. Salespeople, clerks, and other customer-contact people (and that means almost everyone in the firm, because all workers contact other people) often don't understand everything they need to know about the products they make and sell. That means using internal promotions to keep employees informed. That may take the form of videos, brochures, meetings, charts, and more. Full-function advertising agencies get involved in such internal promotions as well as the more traditional external promotions that you are more used to seeing.

One of the more innovative products from Night Agency is interactive web games and demonstrations. Such promotions get potential customers more deeply involved in promotions than they have been in the past. However, such promotions need to be measured like any other promotional tool to ensure that they are seen, remembered, and followed. One of the more memorable of Night Agency's efforts was the Darfur Digital Activist Contest, which was designed to increase awareness of the desperate need for aid among the people in Darfur, Sudan. It is exciting and rewarding to use promotional tools to make a difference in the world, and doing what you can to end world hunger, poverty, disease, and war is part of that challenge.

Discussion Questions

1. What kinds of promotions have led you to buy the items you have purchased recently? These items include the school you attend (what prompted you to go there?), the clothes you wear, the music you listen to, the restaurants you go to, and so on.
2. What differences, if any, did you notice between what Night Agency does and what you are used to seeing in promotions?
3. What has been your reaction thus far to Internet promotions? Do you pay any attention to them? Are they getting better? If so, in what way?

CHAPTER 16 Goodwill Industries

Goodwill Industries <*www.goodwill.org*> is a major charitable organization that relies primarily on financial and non-financial donations and grants. It has retail operations that help sustain its financial operations so as to fulfill its mission to help train, support, and employ disadvantaged individuals and those with disabilities.

The video introduces the accounting function and the specific steps involved in the accounting cycle. The similarities and differences between for-profit and not-for-profit entities are discussed in detail. The importance of accounting in providing financial information and analysis is featured. Emphasis is placed on financial statements as well as ratio analysis in helping gauge the financial health of the organization.

Accounting is crucial for all organizations, whether they are a small business, large corporation, or a governmental or not-for-profit organization. The different types of accounting are discussed, including managerial, financial, tax, auditing, governmental, and not-for-profit. Balance sheets, income statements, and statements of cash flows provide important information for managers and others in the organization and help to demonstrate whether the organization is on budget or whether there are variances between projected and actual revenues. Costs and expenses have to be kept in line and are carefully monitored and analyzed by the accounting function.

Sufficient cash flow is critical to the sustainability of any organization, particularly the not-for-profit organization; in this case, Goodwill. Not-for-profit organizations utilize performance ratio analysis to gauge their overall financial performance. The results of these analyses help management assess the organization's performance against its plan or budget. They also help to develop strategic plans for the future as well as to benchmark against other similar companies.

Discussion Questions

1. Discuss the implications of long-term viability for not-for-profit businesses.
2. Discuss how Goodwill Industries applies the elements of the accounting cycle in the running of their business.
3. Compare the nature of the three basic financial statements for Goodwill Industries versus a for-profit business.
4. Which financial ratios does Goodwill Industries use and how do they use each of them?

CHAPTER 17 It's My Money

Entrepreneurs tend to be an independent bunch of people, but few are as independently minded as Todd McFarlane. He started out working for others as a cartoonist and eventually started his own firm. Now he focuses more on making toys; that is, collectibles of sports personalities, musicians, movie heroes, and the like. You can see in the video that McFarlane takes a rather casual approach to business. That doesn't mean, however, that he is not constantly aware of his need for financing. Nor does it mean that he doesn't know everything he needs to know about financing options.

Of course, the number-one financing option is to put up your own money. The advantage of doing that is that no one can tell you what to do. And that means a lot to McFarlane. But usually your own money won't pay for everything that you need. In that case, you have to go to the banks and other sources to get funding. It helps to have a financial expert on board to determine what funds are needed, to budget those funds, and to keep track of spending. Steve Peterson is that guy for McFarlane. Nonetheless, McFarlane has trained himself to be able to read reports and keep track of everything that's going on in the finance area. All entrepreneurs could learn from his example.

McFarlane knows that it is easy to spend too much money on something—and to lose a lot of money in the bargain. That means being wise in both long-term and short-term financing. Usually, McFarlane stays away from investors, but that isn't possible when funding a major project such as a movie. Furthermore, when you get into ownership financing, you also lose some control over the project. Normally, McFarlane doesn't like to lose such control, but in some cases, such as making an animated movie, it's necessary.

One way to keep loan costs down is to be a good customer of the bank. If you repay your loans in time, you can get lower interest rates on future loans. McFarlane also knows the benefit of having a budget and sticking to it. That's as true in your personal finances as it is in business. If you make $25,000, you need to spend less than $25,000. And if you make $1 million, you have to spend less than $1 million. It's the same principle.

Sometimes people spend money on a passion. In McFarlane's case, that means baseball. He once paid several million dollars for a home-run ball hit by one of the home-run leaders. The problem was that the player didn't remain the leader very long, and soon the ball was not worth nearly as much money. So? The publicity that McFarlane received for buying the ball—and losing millions—made up for the loss. It earned him licensing agreements with many ball clubs, and the right to make the images he sells. He expects to make millions from the investment in the long run.

So, what do you do with your money when you have millions more than you need? For McFarlane, it means giving money to the ALS Association, which fights Lou Gehrig's disease. Again, the publicity that McFarlane receives attracts more donors to the cause.

So, what can we learn from this video? Every entrepreneur needs to understand finance to be successful in the long run. You can be as casual as you want about business, but when it comes to finance, you had better know what you're doing. And the money you make is yours to spend. You can have a good time buying what you want, but you can also make a difference in the world by helping a favourite cause to raise money.

Discussion Questions

1. Why do you suppose a free thinker like McFarlane tries to avoid getting other investors involved in his business? What is the advantage, in this instance, of debt financing?
2. What is the advantage of having a line of credit at the bank? What can a business do to keep loan charges at a minimum?
3. Do business people have a special obligation to give some of their money to charity? What famous business people have been in the news because of their giving? Should others follow their example?

CHAPTER 18 Would You Like Banking with That Insurance?

It's not unusual to hear employees at a fast-food restaurant ask, "Would you like fries with that?" But you don't expect your banker to ask, "Would you like insurance while we are taking care of your banking needs?" Nonetheless, that's exactly what is happening at the major banks in Canada. This chapter is all about money and banking, and the latest trends in banking. One of those trends is to combine banking with insurance, as you will see in this video.

Recent changes in legislation have allowed banks to start selling insurance, either directly or through an insurance company they own (the Toronto Dominion bank owns Meloche, Monnex). In the United States, an example of these combined services is State Farm Insurance <*www.statefarm.com*>. State Farm also operates a virtual bank; that is, an online bank in the United States. At State Farm Bank, you can get regular banking services such as chequing accounts, loans, short-term investments, and more.

So, how does State Farm offer such services? State Farm Insurance agents will handle any of your banking needs. But, like most online banks, you can do most of your banking online via the Internet. Customer service is available 24 hours a day. Any remaining questions can be directed to a State Farm agent.

This chapter talked about banks. State Farm has its deposits, insured much like we have deposits insured in Canada, through the Canadian Deposit Insurance Corporation. State Farm, however, does not have strategic partnerships with car dealerships or other firms like General Motors Acceptance Corporation does.

Because it is in the health and banking business, State Farm offers products such as health insurance plans that are low in cost and that have a high deductible. Although State Farm's insurance and banking operations have been integrated, that integration was not as easy as might be imagined. Two different corporate cultures had to be merged, but that merger has gone relatively smoothly. Now, when a customer suffers a major loss because of a flood, hurricane, or something similar, the bank can easily respond and adjust insurance payments and house payments accordingly.

Like all corporations, State Farm has ethical issues to confront. For example, agents ensure that customers understand that they can buy insurance and not get involved in banking, and vice versa. The whole idea is to listen to customers to determine their wants and needs. If they want to buy a new car, financing can be made available—and insurance, too. Because of their good products and good service, State Farm mostly relies on word of mouth to promote its products. Of course, there are highly trained salespeople to help customers as well.

Discussion Questions

1. What advantages and disadvantages do you see with doing both insurance and banking with the same company?
2. Are you as comfortable banking online as you are with a clerk in a brick-and-mortar bank? Would it help to be able to work with your insurance agent instead of a banking clerk?
3. What kind of services do you get from a brick-and-mortar bank (such as ATMs) that you might not get as easily from an online bank?

ENDNOTES

Chapter 1

1. Tennile M. Robinson, "Borrowing Trouble," *Black Enterprise*, January, 2009.
2. Jim McElhatton, "Community Colleges Seen as Essential," *The Washington Times*, 14 April 2008.
3. Heron Marquez Estrada, "EdCampus Aims to Transform Higher Education," *The Washington Times*, 31 March 2008.
4. "Key Small Business Statistics," Industry Canada, July 2010, www.ic.gc.ca/eic/site/sbrp-rppe.nsf/vwapj/KSBS-PSRPE_July-Juillet2010_eng.pdf/$FILE/KSBS-PSRPE_July-Juillet2010_eng.pdf.
5. Small Business Quarterly, "Business Insolvencies," Industry Canada, May 2008, www.ic.gc.ca/epic/site/sbrp-rppe.nsf/vwapj/SBQ_May2008_Eng.pdf/$FILE/SBQ_May2008_Eng.pdf.
6. Fareed Zakaria, "Switched-On Highways," *Newsweek*, 19 January 2009.
7. "Research In Motion Reports Third Quarter Fiscal 2012 Results," Research In Motion Ltd., 15 December 2011, www.rim.com/investors/documents/pdf/financial/2012/Q3_FY2012_Financial_Information.pdf; "Mike Lazaridus," Wikipedia, 30 December 2011, http://en.wikipedia.org/wiki/Mike_Lazaridis.
8. "Cost of Living Comparison Between Canada and Japan," Numbeo.com, December 2011, www.numbeo.com/cost-of-living/compare_countries_result.jsp?country1=Canada&country2=Japan.
9. Jonathan Clements, "Down the Tube: The Sad Stats on Happiness, Money and TV," *The Wall Street Journal*, 2 April 2008.
10. Pete Engardio, "The Future of Outsourcing," *BusinessWeek*, 30 January 2006, 50–58.
11. John R. Baldwin and Wulong Gu, "Outsourcing and Offshoring in Canada," Statistics Canada, May 2008, www.statcan.ca/english/research/11F0027MIE/11F0027MIE2008055.pdf.
12. Erin White, "Smaller Companies Join the Outsourcing Trend," *The Wall Street Journal*, 8 May 2006, B3.
13. Baldwin and Gu, "Outsourcing and Offshoring in Canada."
14. Pete Engardio and Bruce Einhorn, "Outsourcing Innovation," *BusinessWeek*, 21 March 2005, 84–94.
15. Ibid.
16. Steve Hamm, "When the Bottom Line Is Ending Poverty," *BusinessWeek*, 10 March, 2008.
17. "Welcome to CharityVillage.com," Charity Village, 30 December 2011, www.charityvillage.com/.
18. "Corporate Profile," Tim Hortons, 30 December 2011, www.timhortons.com/en/about/profile.html.
19. Frederick G. Crane et al., *Marketing*, 8th Canadian ed.,(Canada: McGraw-Hill Ryerson, 2011), 92.
20. Ibid.
21. Amir Efrati, "Scope of Alleged Fraud Is Still Being Assessed," *The Wall Street Journal*, 18 December , 2008.
22. Annys Shin, "Economic Picture Bleak in Fed Report," *The Washington Post*, 15 January 2009.
23. "'Sense of Urgency,' as Premiers Meet with Central Banker," CBC News, 18 July 2008, www.cbc.ca/canada/saskatchewan/story/2008/07/18/premiers-economy.html.
24. Spencer E. Ante and Catherine Holahan, "Generation MySpace Is Getting Fed Up," *BusinessWeek*, 18 February 2008.
25. Frederick G. Crane et al., *Marketing*, 8th Canadian ed., (Toronto: McGraw-Hill Ryerson Ltd., 2011), 86.
26. "E-Commerce: Shopping on the Internet," Statistics Canada, 5 July 2011, www.statcan.gc.ca/daily-quotidien/100927/dq100927a-eng.htm; and "Individual Internet use and E-commerce," Statistics Canada, 12 October 2011, www.statcan.gc.ca/daily-quotidien/111012/dq111012a-eng.htm.
27. "Talent Technology Corp.," PROFIT 100—Canada's Fastest Growing Companies, 2008 http://list.canadianbusiness.com/rankings/profit100/2008/DisplayProfile.aspx?profile=17.
28. Kara Rowland, "Man without a Plan," *The Washington Times*, 29 February 2008.
29. Marcia Layton Turner, "Get Sold on eBay," *Entrepreneur*, March 2008.
30. "Numbers," *Time*, 5 May 2008.
31. "E-BUSINESS," Webster's Online Dictionary, 2009, www.websters-online-dictionary.org/definition/e-business.
32. "Introduction to e-Business," Kioskea.net, 16 October 2008, http://en.kioskea.net/contents/entreprise/e-business.php3.
33. Jena McGregor, "Customer Service Champs," *Business-Week*, 3 March 2008.
34. "Privacy Legislation in Canada," Office of the Privacy Commissioner of Canada, 5 December 2008, www.priv.gc.ca/fs-fi/02_05_d_15_e.cfm.
35. Crane et al., *Marketing*, 18.
36. Ibid., 90.
37. David Foot with Daniel Stoffman, *Boom Bust & Echo 2000* (Toronto: Macfarlane Walter & Ross, 1998), 24–31.
38. "Boom, Bust & Echo, Profiting from the Demographic Shift in the 21st Century," Footwork Consulting Inc., 2008, www.footwork.com/21c.asp.
39. "Facts and figures 2010 – Immigration overview: Permanent and temporary residents," Citizenship and Immigration Canada, 30 August 2011, www.cic.gc.ca/english/resources/statistics/facts2010/permanent/01.asp; "Census Snapshot – Immigration in Canada: A Portrait of the Foreign-born Population, 2006 Census," Statistics Canada, 21 November 2008, www.statcan.gc.ca/pub/11-008-x/2008001/article/10556-eng.htm#1.
40. "About Us—Careers," NAV CANADA, 2008, www.navcanada.ca/NavCanada.asp?Language=en&Content=ContentDefinitionFiles\AboutUs\Careers\ValuingDiversity\default.xml.
41. Diane Francis, "Is Canada headed for demographic disaster?" *Financial Post*, 21 September, 2012, http://opinion.financialpost.com/2012/09/21/is-canada-headed-for-demographic-disaster/; Tasha Kheiriddin, "Tasha Kheiriddin on the census: The family road less travelled," *National Post*, 20 September 2012, http://fullcomment.nationalpost.com/2012/09/20/tasha-kheiriddin-on-the-census-the-family-road-less-travelled/; "2011 Census of Population: Families, households, marital status, structural type of dwelling, collectives," Statistics Canada, 19 September 2012, www.statcan.gc.ca/daily-quotidien/120919/dq120919a-eng.htm; "More Canadian single dads head rise in lone-parent families," The Canadian Press, 19 September 2012, www.cbc.ca/news/canada/story/2012/09/19/census-single-parent-families.html; Bill Curry, "Canadian families shrinking, couples in decline: Census," *The Globe and Mail*, 19 September 2012, www.theglobeandmail.com/news/politics/canadian-families-shrinking-married-couples-in-decline-census/article4553124/; and Joe O'Connor, "Joe O'Connor: Trend of couples not having children just plain selfish," 19 September 2012, *National Post*, http://fullcomment.nationalpost.com/2012/09/19/joe-oconnor-selfishness-behind-growing-trend-for-couples-to-not-have-children/.
42. Andrea Cooper, "The Influencers," *Entrepreneur*, March 2008.
43. Gross domestic product at basic prices, manufacturing and construction industries," Statistics Canada, 23 December 2011, www40.statcan.gc.ca/l01/cst01/manuf10-eng.htm.
44. "Manufacturing and exporting matter," Canadian Manufacturers & Exporters, [2011?], www.cme-mec.ca/?action=show&lid=4C5YW-NTFVK-B7S35.
45. Joanna Pachner, "Born to run—really fast," PROFIT200, 1 June 2011, www.profitguide.com/article/28250--born-to-run-really-fast.

Appendix A

1. Nick Wingfield and Don Clark, "Internet-Ready TVs Usher Web into Living Room," *The Wall Street Journal*, 5 January 2009.
2. Daniel McGinn, "Movies on the Move," *Newsweek*, 17 October 2005, E4; Michael Hastings, "A Click Away: Internet TV," *Newsweek*, 31 January 2005, E10; Rana Foroohar, "Hi! The Net Is Calling," *Newsweek*, 31 January 2005, E4; Steven Levy, "Life Isn't Just as You Want It? Remix It!" *Newsweek*,

28 March 2005, 17; Karen Breslau and Daniel McGinn, "A Movie Classic for a New Age," *Newsweek*, 17 October 2005, E6–E10; and "Google Enters Video-on-Demand Domain," *Screen Digest*, 1 January 2006.

3. Jon Fortt, "Netbooks Could Be the Next Hit Cell Phones," *Fortune*, 28 January 2009.
4. Meridith Levinson, "The Brain Behind the Big, Bad Burger," *CIO*, 15 March 2005, 49–58; and Meridith Levinson, "Business Intelligence: Not Just for Bosses Anymore," *CIO*, 15 January 2006.
5. "Operational BI Comes of Age," *Businessweek*, 23 May 2005, S2–S10; and Jennifer McAdams and Heather Havenstein, "WHAT'S NEXT: Business Intelligence," *Computerworld*, 2 January 2006.
6. Glover Ferguson, Sanjay Mathur, and Baiju Shah, "Evolving from Information to Insight," *MIT Sloan Management Review*, Winter 2005, 51–58.
7. Grant Buckler, "It's About Time," *tq Magazine*, Spring 2008, 9.
8. Ibid.
9. Michelle V. Rafter, "Document This: How to Organize Computer Data," www.technology.inc.com, accessed 12 February 2009; Christopher F. Chabris, "You Have Too Much Mail," *The Wall Street Journal*, 14 December 2008; and Elizabeth Wasserman, "TechTalk: E-mail Storage Sails for Boat Supplier," www.technology.inc.com, accessed 12 February 2009.
10. Darren Dahl, "Trust Me: You're Gonna Love This," *Inc.*, November 2008.
11. Terence Belford, "How the Mailman Pushed the Envelope," *tq Magazine*, Spring 2006, 16–17.
12. Robert D. Hof, "The Future of Tech," *BusinessWeek*, 20 June 2005, 73–82; Steven Levy, "Ma Bell's Kids Will Live on the Net," *Newsweek*, 28 February 2005, 14; and Richard Waters, "It's the Internet, But Not as We Know It," *Financial Times*, 30 April 2005, 1.
13. "Canadian Internet Use Survey," Statistics Canada, 25 March 2011, www.statcan.gc.ca/daily-quotidien/110525/dq110525b-eng.htm.
14. Ibid.
15. Rochester Institute of Technology, "The Next Step in Health Care: Telemedicine Researchers Broadcast Live Surgery Using Internet2," *Ascribe Higher Education News Service*, 12 November, 2008.
16. "About Us," Internet2, 2008, www.internet2.edu/membership/index.cfm.
17. Brent Leary, "Social Media's Good, Bad, Ugly and Unexpected," *Inc.*, January 2009.
18. "Social Networking: Brave New World or Revolution from Hell?" *ZDNet White Papers*, January 2008.
19. Salvatore Parise, Patricia J. Guinan, and Bruce D. Weinberg, "The Secrets of Marketing in a Web 2.0 World," *The Wall Street Journal*, 1 January 2009.
20. Jessi Hempel, "Web 2.0 Is So Over. Welcome to Web 3.0," *Fortune*, 8 January 2009.
21. Amol Sharma and Jessica E. Vascellaro, "Companies Eye Location-Services Market," *The Wall Street Journal*, 28 November 2009.
22. Jon Fortt, "Goodbye, PC (and Mac). Hello, Services," *Fortune*, 4 February 2009.
23. Ian Harvey, "Talkin' 'Bout A Revolution," *tq Magazine*, Spring 2008, 16.
24. Mary O. Foley, "10 Hot Technologies for 2009," *Inc.*, December 2008.
25. Rachael King, "The Coming Desktop Revolution?" *BusinessWeek*, 5 January 2008.
26. Rob Preston, "Will Cloud Computing Rain on IT's Parade?" *InformationWeek*, 18 February 2008; and Jason Hiner, "Four Reasons Why 2009 Will Be a Watershed Year in Technology," *TechRepublic*, 9 February 2009.
27. Ryan Underwood, "Save the Planet—and Save the Company a Lot of Power and Paper," *Inc.*, June 2008.
28. Don Tapscott, "How to Teach and Manage 'Generation Net'," *BusinessWeek*, 30 November 2008.
29. Mike Richman, "The Quest for Zero Defects," *Quality Digest*, April 2005, 40–43; and Ted Kritsonis, "They Used to Attack Your Computer System Just for the Thrill of It. Now the Thieves Are After Your Money," *tq Magazine*, Summer 2006, 21.
30. Michelle V. Rafter, "2009 Tech Security Forecast," www.technology.inc.com, accessed 13 February 2009.
31. Minda Zetlin, "Would Your Network Survive a Targeted Attack?" www.technology.inc.com, accessed 9 February 2009.
32. Michael Sivy, Pat Regnier, and Carolyn Bigda, "What No One Is Telling You about Identity Theft," *Money*, July 2005, 95–99; and Julie Tripp, "Stolen Pins Expose Debit Cards to Fraud; Hundreds of Thousands Were Taken, Unlocking Access to Victims' Bank Accounts," *The Post-Standard*, 23 March 2006.
33. Kritsonis, "They Used to Attack Your Computer System Just for the Thrill of It," 20.
34. Treena Hein, "Barbarians Inside the Gates," *tq Magazine*, Summer 2006, 28.
35. Ibid.

Chapter 2

1. William H. Peterson, "Indexing Freedom," *The Washington Times*, 26 February 2008.
2. Justin Gillis, "Old Laws, New Fish," *Washington Post*, 15 January 2003, E1.
3. "Transportation," Burnaby: Ballard Power Systems, 2004, www.ballard.com/tC.asp?pgid_44.
4. Anne Underwood, "Designing the Future," *Newsweek*, 16 May 2005, 40–45.
5. Kristin Ohlson, "Burst of Energy," *Entrepreneur*, February 2006, 46–47.
6. "Net Is Cast for Fish Farms," *Washington Times*, 4 April 2005, A8.
7. Justin Lahart, Patrick Barta, and Andrew Batson, "New Limits to Growth Revive Malthusian Fears," *The Wall Street Journal*, 24 March 2008.
8. William R. Easterly, "Why Bill Gates Hates My Book," *The Wall Street Journal*, 7 February 2008.
9. "Quirky Causes," *Forbes*, 28 March 2005, 172.
10. Jack Welch and Suzy Welch, "Resolutions for the Recession," *BusinessWeek*, 12 January, 2009.
11. Romano Prodi, "To Avoid a Food Disaster," *The Washington Times*, 27 April 2008.
12. Frederick G. Crane et al. *Marketing*, 8th Canadian ed. (Toronto: McGraw-Hill Ryerson Limited, 2011), 90.
13. "Bill Gates No Longer Tops World's-Richest List," *The Chronicle of Philanthropy*, 6 March 2008, http://philanthropy.com/news/philanthropytoday/4105/bill-gates-no-longer-tops-worlds-richest-list.
14. "Community Relations," Cirque du Soleil, [2012?], www.cirquedusoleil.com/en/about/global-citizenship/community.aspx.
15. Richard Rahn, "Weapons of Mass Disinformation," *Washington Times*, 21 March 2005, A15.
16. Marjory Abrams, "The Economy in a Nutshell," *Bottom Line Personal*, 1 May 2008.
17. Brian M. Carney, "Europe Hasn't Outgrown 'That '70s Show,'" *The Wall Street Journal*, 9 May 2005, A23.
18. Steve Chapman, "A Comeback for Communism," *The Washington Times*, 28 November 2007.
19. Laura D'Andrea Tyson, "How Europe Is Revving Its Engine," *BusinessWeek*, 21 February 2005, 24.
20. Eric J. Savitz, "Look Who's Storming the Net," *Smart Money*, June 2005, 40–48.
21. "Latest Indicators, Population Estimate (April 2012)," Statistics Canada, 31 August 2012, www.statcan.gc.ca/start-debut-eng.html.
22. Matthew Coutts, "Complacency Hurts Nation: Think-Tank; Quality of Life Declining, Report Warns," *National Post*, 30 June 2008, A4.
23. Ibid.
24. "Economic Concepts—Unemployment Rate," Government of Canada, 4 May 2007, http://canadianeconomy.gc.ca/english/economy/unemployment2.html.
25. Ibid.
26. "Classification of Labour Status," Statistics Canada, 21 July 2011, www.statcan.gc.ca/concepts/definitions/labour-travail-class01a-eng.htm.
27. David Pilling, "Japan Still in Grip of Deflation as Prices Fall," *Financial Times*, 27 April 2005, 7.
28. E. S. Browning, "Stagflation Fear Puts a Chill into Blue Chips," *The Wall Street Journal*, 29 April 2005, C1 and C4.
29. "Consumer Price Index," Statistics Canada, 17 February 2012, www.statcan.gc.ca/daily-quotidien/120217/dq120217a-eng.htm.
30. Victor Zarnowitz and Dara Lee, "Can U.S. Business Cycles Still Be Dated by Monthly Coincident Indicators Alone?" *Business Cycle Indicator*, March 2005, 3–4.
31. "Business Cycle," Wikimedia Foundation Inc., 18 August 2008, http://en.wikipedia.org/wiki/Business_cycle.

Chapter 3

1. Sattar Bawany, "Transition Coaching Helps Ensure Success for Global Assignments," *Today's Manager*, 1 December, 2008.
2. "Current World Population," Worldometers, 2012, www.worldometers.info/world-population/; "Latest Indicators, Population Estimate (April 2012)," Statistics Canada, 31 August 2012, www.statcan.gc.ca/start-debut-eng.html.
3. "World Population by Estimates," One World - Nations Online, 24 September 2011, www.nationsonline.org/oneworld/.
4. "Profile," Bombardier Inc., 2012, http://ir.bombardier.com/en/profile.

5. Ibid.
6. "Our Story," LIJA Style Inc., 2012, www.lijastyle.com/about; "Canada's Fastest-Growing Companies - LIJA," *Profit*, June 2008, 50–51.
7. Ibid.
8. "Hargrove calls for help from feds after another round of Chrysler cuts," CBC News, 24 July 2008, www.cbc.ca/canada/story/ 2008/07/24/chrysler-caw.html; Nicolas Van Praet, "Polywheels grinds to halt in Oakville," *Financial Post*, 10 July 2008, http://network.nationalpost.com/np/blogs/fpposted/archive/2008/07/10/polywheels-grinds-to-halt-in-oakville.aspx; "2,000 jobs lost as auto-parts plants close," The Canadian Press, 3 July 2008, www.cbc.ca/canada/toronto/story/2008/07/03/plant-closure.html.
9. Frank Vargo, "U.S. Trade Policy: Free Trade Agreements Level the Playing Field for Everyone," *Rubber & Plastics News*, 2 May 2005; "Free Trade Winds in the Mideast," *The Wall Street Journal*, 11 January 2006.
10. "Canada: A Diamond-Producing Nation," Natural Resources Canada, 30 June 2011, www.nrcan.gc.ca/minerals-metals/business-market/3630.
11. "The Fragility of Perfection," *The Economist*, 3 May, 2008.
12. "Key Small Business Statistics," Industry Canada, July 2008, www.ic.gc.ca/epic/site/sbrp-rppe.nsf/vwapj/KSBS_July2008_Eng.pdf/$FILE/KSBS_July2008_Eng.pdf; "Canada's State of Trade—Trade and Investment Update 2008, Export Establishments by Employee Size," Foreign Affairs and International Trade Canada, 8 May 2008, www.international.gc.ca/eet/trade/sot_2008/sot-2008-en.asp.
13. "Canada's State of Trade 2011," Foreign Affairs and International Trade Canada, 2011, www.international.gc.ca/economist-economiste/assets/pdfs/SoT_2011_e.pdf; "Importing into Canada," Foreign Affairs and International Trade Canada, 26 May 2010, www.international.gc.ca/controls-controles/about-a_propos/impor/canada.aspx?menu_id=1&view=d; "Canada's Merchandise and Service Trade, 2007," adapted from Statistics Canada Web site "Exports of Goods on a Balance-of-Payments Basis, by Product," Statistics Canada, 13 August 2008, www40.statcan.ca/l01/cst01/gblec04.htm; "Imports of Goods on a Balance-of-Payments Basis, by Product," Statistics Canada, 13 August 2008, www40.statcan.ca/l01/cst01/gblec05.htm; and "Canada's Balance of International Payments," Statistics Canada, 29 May 2008, www40.statcan.ca.libaccess.lib.mcmaster.ca/l01/cst01/econ01a.htm?sdi=services.
14. Canada's State of Trade: Trade and Investment Update 2012 - Table 2-1 World Merchandise Trade By Region and Selected Countries (US$ billions and %)," Foreign Affairs and International Trade Canada, 13 September 2012, http://www.international.gc.ca/economist-economiste/assets/pdfs/performance/SoT_2012/SoT_2012_Eng.pdf, 16 and 23; and "Canada's State of Trade 2011," 35.
15. "Canada's State of Trade: Trade and Investment Update 2012," 16; and "Canada's State of Trade 2011," 20.
16. Ibid., 20.
17. "Less dependent on Uncle Sam," *The Globe and Mail*, 6 February 2012, B10.
18. "Canada's State of Trade: Trade and Investment Update—2009," Foreign Affairs and International Trade Canada, 2009, www.international.gc.ca/economist-economiste/assets/pdfs/DFAIT_SoT_2009_en.pdf; "Seizing Global Advantage: A Global Commerce Strategy for Securing Canada's Growth & Prosperity," Foreign Affairs and International Trade Canada, 2008, www.international.gc.ca/commerce/assets/pdfs/GCS-en.pdf; "A Global Commerce Strategy for Securing Canada's Growth and Prosperity, A Message from the Minister," Foreign Affairs and International Trade Canada, 12 August 2008, www.international.gc.ca/commerce/strategy-strategie/minister-ministre.aspx; Jim Middlemiss, "Canada Readying to Ride the Tiger," *Financial Post*, 28 May 2008, www.financialpost.com/reports/legal/story.html?id=546037; "International Science and Technology Partnerships Program—ISTPP," Foreign Affairs and International Trade Canada, 5 June 2007, www.infoexport.gc.ca/science/istpp-en.htm.
19. "Tokyo Disney Parks Operator Sees Sales, Profit Fall," *Kyodo World News Service*, 9 May 2005.
20. Ryan Nakashima, "Hollywood Hopes Theme Parks, Superheroes Fly in Middle East," AP Worldstream, 19 April 2008.
21. "About Us," Yogen Fruz, 2012, www.yogenfruz.com/home/en/about-us.
22. "About Us," BeaverTails Pastry, 2012, www.beavertailsinc.com.
23. "Workers in Contract Factories," Nike, 2007, www.nike.com/nikebiz/nikeresponsibility/pdfs/color/3_Nike_CRR_Workers_C.pdf.
24. "FouFou Dog," *PROFIT*, 2009, http://list.canadianbusiness.com/rankings/hot50/2008/DisplayProfile.aspx?profile=32; Jerry Langton, "Canine Couture," *Toronto Star*, 17 November 2008, www.thestar.com/Business/SmallBusiness/article/538014; "About Us," FouFou Dog, 2009, www.foufoudog.com/about.html.
25. Orit Gadiesh and Till Vestring, "The Consequences of China's Rising Global Heavyweights," *MIT Sloan Management Review*, Spring 2008.
26. "About Us," Nestlé Company, 2012, www.corporate.nestle.ca/en/aboutus/Pages/aboutus.aspx.
27. Michael Mandel, "Multinationals: Are They Good for America?" *BusinessWeek*, 10 March 2008.
28. Godwin Maidment, "The Globe's New Stars," *Forbes*, 24 March 2008.
29. Mark Srite, "Levels of Culture and Individual Behavior: An Integrative Perspective," *Journal of Global Information Management*, 1 April 2005.
30. Michelle Higgins, "The Greenback Is Losing Universal Appeal," *The New York Times*, 10 February 2008.
31. Steve H. Hanke, "The Strong Dollar Charade," *Forbes*, 3 February 2003, 122.
32. Ed Zwirn, "Dollar Doldrums," *CFO*, May 2005, 35–38.
33. Matt Krantz, "Regulators Look Closely at Bartering," *USA Today*, 21 May 2002, 35.
34. Alan O. Sykes, "New Directions in Law and Economics," *American Economist*, 1 April 2002, 10.
35. Martin Crutsinger, "U.S. Wins Victory over China Imports," AP Online, 21 June, 2008.
36. Alma Olaechea, "Globalization Is Best for All," *University Wire*, 13 February 2002.
37. "Washington to Fight New Tariffs on U.S. Corn," CBC News, 6 December 2005, www.cbc.ca/story/business/national/ 2005/12/16/corn-051216.html.
38. "Controlled Products," Foreign Affairs and International Trade Canada, 2 February 2012, www.international.gc.ca/controls-controles/prod/index.aspx?menu_id=1&view=d.
39. "Exporting," Foreign Affairs and International Trade Canada, 2 February 2012, www.international.gc.ca/controls-controles/about-a_propos/expor/before-avant.aspx?lang=eng&view=d.
40. "Important Information Related to Canada's Sanctions Against Burma," Foreign Affairs and International Trade Canada, 7 July 2008, www.international.gc.ca/international/Sanctions_Burma-Birmanie.aspx.
41. John Zarocostas, "WTO to Focus on Barriers," *Footwear News*, 10 January 2005; Evan Ramstad, "Tech Companies Push for Tariff Overhauls as Products Converge," *The Wall Street Journal*, 15 December 2005.
42. "Mad Cow in Canada: The Science and the Story," CBC.ca, 13 March 2006, www.cbc.ca/news/background/madcow/.
43. "Members and Observers," World Trade Organization, 23 July 2008, www.wto.org/english/thewto_e/whatis_e/tif_e/org6_e.htm; Elizabeth Wasserman, "Happy Birthday WTO," *Inc.*, January 2005, 21–23; Julian Morris, "The Future of World Trade," *The Wall Street Journal*, 20 December 2005.
44. The Doha Dilemma," *The Economist*, 31 May 2008.
45. Peter Coy, "Free Trade after Doha's Collapse," *BusinessWeek*, 31 July 2008; and "WTO Chief Lamy Only Candidate for Next Term," AP Online, 5 January 2009.
46. "North American Free Trade Agreement," Wikimedia Foundation, Inc., 21 February 2012, http://en.wikipedia.org/wiki/NAFTA.
47. "European Union," Wikimedia Foundation, Inc., 20 February 2012, http://en.wikipedia.org/wiki/European_union.
48. Eric Lam, "Canada moves to lower U.S. dependence," *Financial Post*, 2 February 2012, FP6.
49. "EU Ready to Negotiate New Trade Deal with Canada," CBC News, 27 April 2009, www.cbc.ca/world/story/2009/04/27/eu-trade.html.
50. "Euro," Wikimedia Foundation, Inc., 20 February 2012, http://en.wikipedia.org/wiki/Euro.
51. Mark Gollom, "Why Canadians should care about a euro collapse," CBC News, 1 December 2011, www.cbc.ca/news/canada/story/2011/11/30/euro-impact-canada.html; Jeremy Kinsman, "ANALYSIS | Jeremy Kinsman: Can Europe be saved?" CBC News, 28 November 2011, www.cbc.ca/news/world/story/2011/11/25/f-vp-kinsman-europe.html; and "Europe's debt woes 'dire'," CBC News, 25 November 2011, www.cbc.ca/news/business/story/2011/11/25/flaherty-economy-speech.html#socialcomments.
52. "Union of South American Nations," Wikimedia Foundation, Inc., 20 February 2012, http://en.wikipedia.org/wiki/Union_of_South_American_Nations; "Association of Southeast Nations," Wikimedia Foundation, Inc., 20 February 2012, http://en.wikipedia.org/wiki/Association_of_Southeast_Asian_Nations; Angel Perez, "Latin America/EU: Leaders Agree to Accelerate Trade Talks," International Press Service English News Wire, 19 May, 2008
53. "Canada's State of Trade: Trade and Investment Update 2012," 21.
54. Ibid.
55. William Triplett, "China, Russia Still Serious Piracy Threat," *Daily Variety*, 28 April 2008.
56. Frederik Balfour, "Fakes," *BusinessWeek*, 7 February 2005, 54–64.
57. Peter Mandelson, "India's New Leadership Role: An Economic Giant," *International Herald Tribune*, 15 January 2005; Foster Klug, "Lawmaker

Says Tour of China and India a 'Reality Check on Asia's Growing Economies,'" AP Worldstream, 6 January 2006.

58. Gaurav Baghuvanshi and Eric Bellman, "Wal-Mart Sets India Plans, Aims to Back Local Players," *The Wall Street Journal*, 21 February 2008.

59. Mary Dejevsky, "Forget the China Story, Russia Offers a Greater Prize for Western Investors," *Independent*, 22 April 2005.

60. Pete Engardio, "The Future of Outsourcing," *BusinessWeek*, 30 January 2006, 50–58.

61. Anne Fisher, "Offshoring Could Boost Your Career," *Fortune*, 24 January 2005, 36.

Chapter 4

1. Eric Lam, "Canada moves to lower U.S. dependence," *Financial Post*, 2 February 2012, FP6.

2. "Selling Crown Corporations: Should Governments Do It?" *Financial Uproar*, 21 July 2010, http://financialuproar.com/2010/07/21/selling-crown-corporations-should-governments-do-it/.

3. "Heritage Fund 2011-12 Third Quarter Update and 2011-15 Business Plan released," Government of Alberta, 4 March 2012, www.finance.alberta.ca/business/ahstf/index.html.

4. "Home," Caisse de Dépôt et Placement du Québec, 4 March 2012, www.lacaisse.com/en.

5. Andrew Willis and Boyd Erman, "Ontario ponders sale of Crown corporations to beat down deficit," *The Globe and Mail*, 15 December 2009, www.theglobeandmail.com/report-on-business/ontario-ponders-sale-of-crown-corporations-to-beat-down-deficit/article1401807/.

6. "Sources of Canadian Law," Department of Justice Canada, 24 April 2003, http://canada.justice.gc.ca/en/dept/pub/just/CSJ_page7.html.

7. Eugene A. Forsey, *How Canadians Govern Themselves*, 6th ed., Government of Canada, 2005, www.parl.gc.ca/information/library/idb/forsey/index-e.asp; "Canada Health Transfer," Department of Finance Canada, 19 December 2011, www.fin.gc.ca/fedprov/cht-eng.asp.

8. Campbell Clark and Rheal Seguin, "Ottawa Pushes for New Chapter in Free Trade with U.S.," *The Globe and Mail*, 4 June 2009, A1.

9. "Suncor (Sunoco) Energy Pleads Guilty to Price-Fixing in Belleville, Ontario," Competition Bureau Canada, 13 April 2012, www.competitionbureau.gc.ca/eic/site/cb-bc.nsf/eng/03460.html; "Kyle Kipp, "Ontario and Quebec companies plead guilty to fixing gas prices—Whistleblowers, immune to prosecution, integral to investigating private collusion," Postmedia News, 14 April 2012, www.canada.com/business/Ontario+Quebec+companies+plead+guilty+fixing+prices/6459274/story.html; and "Gasoline Companies Plead Guilty to Price-Fixing in Kingston and Brockville, Ontario," Competition Bureau Canada, 20 March 2012, www.competitionbureau.gc.ca/eic/site/cb-bc.nsf/eng/03448.html.

10. "Gasoline Companies Plead Guilty to Price-Fixing in Kingston and Brockville, Ontario," Competition Bureau Canada, 20 March 2012, www.competitionbureau.gc.ca/eic/site/cb-bc.nsf/eng/03448.html.

11. Paul Waldie, "Judge weights Wheat Board bid for injunction against, Tories," *The Globe and Mail*, 17 January 2012, www.theglobeandmail.com/news/politics/judge-weighs-wheat-board-bid-for-injunction-against-tories/article2305555/; "About Us," Canadian Wheat Board, 29 June 2009 and 7 September 2008, www.cwb.ca; "Canadian Wheat Board Gag Order Unconstitutional, Court Rules," CBC.ca, 20 June 2008, www.cbc.ca/canada/saskatchewan/story/2008/06/20/cwb-ruling.html; and "Strahl Must Defend Canadian Wheat Board and Supply Management," Liberal Party of Canada, 15 March 2006, www.liberal.ca/news_e.aspx? id=11502.

12. Eugene A. Forsey, *How Canadians Govern Themselves*, 6th ed., Government of Canada, 2005, www.parl.gc.ca/information/library/idb/forsey/index-e.asp; "P3s = Private Profits, Public Pays," Canadian Health Coalition, 2009, http://medicare.ca/main/the-facts/p3s-private-profits-public-pays; "News," The Canadian Council for Public-Private Partnerships, 2012, www.pppcouncil.ca/resources/news.html.

13. "Certified General Accountants Applaud Movement on Labour Mobility and Resolving Disputes," Certified General Accountants Association of Canada, 30 July 2008, www.cga-canada.org/en-ca/MediaCentre/CurrentMediaReleases/Pages/ca_mdr_2008-07-30.aspx; "Labour Mobility Deal Will Enhance Competitiveness; B.C.'s Campbell and Alberta's Stelmach Deserve Praise for Getting Other Premiers to Sign Up," *Vancouver Sun*, 22 July 2008, A10; "Improving Internal Trade: A Bold Approach," Certified General Accountants Association of Canada, 2008, www.cga-canada.org/en-ca/DiscussionPapers/ca_rep_internal_trade_position-paper2008.pdf; "Overview of the Agreement on Internal Trade, 2009" Internal Trade Secretariat, www.intrasec.mb.ca/index_en/ait.htm; and Paul Vieira, "Internal Barriers an Obstacle," *National Post*, 26 April 2006.

14. Forsey, *How Canadians Govern Themselves*.

15. "Research in Motion Opens Technical Support Centre in Halifax," Canadian Press, 21 April 2006, http://finance.sympatico.msn.ca/content/investing/other/P40361.asp.

16. Milagros Palacios and Niels Veldhuis, "Taxes versus the Necessities of Life: The Canadian Consumer Tax Index 2012 Edition," The Fraser Institute, April 2012, www.fraserinstitute.org/uploadedFiles/fraser-ca/Content/research-news/research/publications/canadian-consumer-tax-index-2012.pdf.

17. Elliot Ferguson, "Report distracts from problematic tax system: Prof.," *The Whig-Standard*, 27 April 2012, www.thewhig.com/ArticleDisplay.aspx?e=3545447.

18. Ibid.

19. Alan Reynolds, "Improvements . . . and Horror Replays," *Washington Times*, 12 January 2003, B8.

20. "Canada's Federal Debt," Canadian Taxpayers Federation, 3 May 2012, http://taxpayer.com/node/9473.

21. Budget Deficit in 2009–10, Flaherty Confirms," CBC News, 17 December 2008, www.cbc.ca/canada/story/2008/12/17/finance-meeting.html; "Top TD Economist Sees Lingering Canadian Deficits," Reuters, 2 June 2009, http://finance.sympatico.msn.ca/investing/news/breakingnews/article.aspx?cp-documentid=20169426.

22. "Key numbers in Canada's provincial budgets – Federal," CBC News, 24 April 2012, www.cbc.ca/news/interactives/budgets-provinces/.

23. "Quebec student loses legal bid to limit tuition protest," The Canadian Press, 30 March 2012, www.cbc.ca/news/canada/montreal/story/2012/03/30/montreal-student-protest-court.html.

24. Richard S. Dunham, "The Struggle to Sell the Economy's Sizzle," *BusinessWeek*, 23 January 2006, 43.

25. "Glossary: Vocabulary for a Financial Crisis," CBC News, 24 March 2009, www.cbc.ca/money/story/2008/10/24/f-econoglossary.html; "Canada's Banks: Admired Worldwide for their Management—and Cash," CBC News, 3 March 2009, www.cbc.ca/money/story/2009/03/03/f-canada-banks.html; "$25B Credit Backstop for Banks 'Not a Bailout': Harper," CBC News, 10 October 2008, www.cbc.ca/canada/story/2008/10/10/flaherty-banks.html; Michel Chossudovsky, "Canada's 75 Billion Dollar Bank Bailout," Global Research, 25 January 2009, www.globalresearch.ca/index.php?context=va&aid=12007; Stefan Theil, "Europe's Bank Bailout: Is It Enough?" *Newsweek*, 13 October 2008, http://blog.newsweek.com/blogs/ov/archive/ 2008/10/13/europe-bank-bailout-is-it-enough.aspx; Kimberly Amadeo, "Understanding the Subprime Mortgage Crisis," About.com, 2008, http://useconomy.about.com/od/economicindicators/tp/Subprime-Mortgage-Primer.htm; Joel Schlesinger, "Why the Bank of Canada Is Doing What It's Doing," *Winnipeg Free Press*, 31 May 2009, www.winnipegfreepress.com/business/making-the-money-move-46566862.html?viewAllComments=y; Peter Henderson, "Canadians not told about 'secret bailout' for banks: study," *The Gazette*, 30 April 2012, www.montrealgazette.com/business/Canadians+told+about+secret+bailout+banks+study/6543481/story.html; "Occupy movement," Wikimedia Foundation, Inc., 5 May 2012, http://en.wikipedia.org/wiki/Occupy_movement.

26. "Canadian Subsidy Directory," Canadian Publications, 2008, www.mgpublishing.net/grants-and-loans.htm#CSD.

27. "Nfld. Announces $18-million Aid for Crab Workers," Canadian Press Newswire, 28 June 2005, http://proquest.umi.com/pqdweb.

28. "U.S. Takes Dim View of Government Aid to Bombardier," CBC.ca, 11 August 2008, www.cbc.ca/money/story/2008/08/11/bombardier-aid.html.

29. L. Ian MacDonald, "Harper Had No Choice," *The Gazette*, 3 June 2009, www.montrealgazette.com/Business/Harper+choice/1657861/story.html.

30. "Ocean Choice Buys Polar Foods," PEI.CBC.CA 24 March 2004. Retrieved from http://pei.cbc.ca/regional/servlet/View?filename_pe_oceanbuys20040324.

31. "Equalization Program," Department of Finance Canada, 19 December 2011, www.fin.gc.ca/fedprov/eqp-eng.asp.

32. "Preparing to sell to the Government," Government of Canada, 5 May 2012, www.canadabusiness.ca/eng/page/2757/.

33. "Overview," MERX, 2012, www.merx.com/English/NonMember.asp?WCE=Show&TAB=1&PORTAL=MERX&State=6&hcode=G4neZSoJ0B3Ef%2bl2%2bfWuBQ%3d%3d.

34. "About NRC," National Research Council Canada, 7 August 2012, www.nrc-cnrc.gc.ca/eng/about/index.html.

35. "Trade and Investment at 10," Foreign Affairs and International Trade Canada, 10 July 2007, www.dfait-maeci.gc.ca/canada-magazine/issue24/06-title-en.asp.

36. Glossary of Key Terms: Minority Government," British Columbia Referendum Office, 2009, www.gov.bc.ca/referendum_info/first_past_the_post_bc_stv/glossary.html.
37. "Thousands of Forestry Workers Protest in Ottawa," CBC News, 2 June 2009, www.cbc.ca/canada/ottawa/story/2009/06/02/forestry-demonstration-ottawa002.html.

Chapter 5

1. Brent Jang, "WestJet Admits Spying," globeandmail.com, 29 May 2006, www.theglobeandmail.com/servlet/story/RTGAM.20060529.waircanada0529/BNStory/Business.
2. Ibid.
3. Laura Payton, "Conservatives deny party focus of robocalls probe," CBC News, 17 April 2012, www.cbc.ca/news/politics/story/2012/04/17/pol-robocalls-guelph-investigation-extends.html.
4. Ibid.
5. Pallavi Guniganti, "Ethics' Place in Education," *University Wire*, 16 April 2002.
6. Mark Steyn, "Conrad Black Trial," *Maclean's*, 24 December 2008, http://forums.macleans.ca/advansis/?mod=for&act=dis&eid=52&so=1&sb=1&ps=5; "Former Sponsorship Ad Exec Facing Criminal Charges," CBC News, 17 December 2008, www.cbc.ca/canada/story/2008/12/17/gosselin-charges.html; "Chicago Judges Reject Request to Reconsider Conrad Black's Appeal," CBC News, 21 August 2008, www.cbc.ca/money/story/2008/08/21/black.html; "Police Probe in Lottery Scandal not Over Yet," CBC News, 20 December 2007, www.cbc.ca/canada/toronto/story/2007/12/20/lottery-investigation.html; "Forgive and (Maybe) Forget," Canadian Business Online, 6 November 2007, www.canadianbusiness.com/columnists/john_gray/article.jsp?content=20071106_153800_5340; "Lotto 6/49 Bonus Rounds Coincided with Lottery Scandals," CBC News, 30 May 2007, www.cbc.ca/canada/toronto/story/2007/05/30/lotto649-bonus-rounds.html; "U.S. Judge Decides not to Revoke Black's Bond," CTV.ca, 26 June 2006, www.ctv.ca/servlet/ArticleNews/story/CTVNews/20060626/black_bond_060626/20060626/; Ross Marowits, "Guite Sentenced to 3 1/2 Years in Prison," Canoe Inc., 19 June 2006, http://CNRews.canoe.ca/CNREWS/Law/2006/03/29/1511103-cp.html; and "Federal Sponsorship Scandal," CBC News Online, 19 June 2006, www.cbc.ca/news/background/groupaction/.
7. Kenneth Blanchard and Norman Vincent Peale, *The Power of Ethical Management* (New York: William Morrow, 1996); Shoshana Zuboff, "A Starter Kit for Business Ethics," *Fast Company*, 1 January 2005.
8. Turn It In, www.turnitin.com; Sue R. Whittle and Deborah G. Murdoch-Eaton, "Learning about Plagiarism Using TurnItIn Detection Software," *Medical Education*, May 2008.
9. Kathy Gurchiek, "Ethics, Schmethics, U.S. Teens Say," *HR News*, 1 February 2008.
10. Jacqueline A. Burke, Ralph S. Polimeni, and Nathan S. Slavin, "Academic Dishonesty: A Crisis on Campus," *CPA Journal*, May 2007.
11. Blanchard and Peale, *The Power of Ethical Management*.
12. "Small Business Owners Doing Little to Promote Ethics," *Ascribe Newswire*, 25 June 2002.
13. Amy Johnson, "Practicing Good Ethics Gives Competitive Advantage," *St. Louis Business Journal*, 29 February 2008.
14. Bob Sullivan, "Can't Cancel That Service? Blame 'Perverse Incentives'," www.redtape.msnbc.com, 13 May 2008; and Gill Corkindale, "What the SocGen Mess Means for Your Company," *Harvard Business Online*, 30 January 2008.
15. Frank C. Bucaro, "If Good Ethics Is Good Business, What's the Problem?" *Business First*, 4 January 2008; Dave Blanchard, "How Ethical Is Your Supply Chain?" *Industry Week*, 1 January 2008; Michael Smigocki, "Complying with New Ethics Rules," *Set-Aside Alert*, 8 February 2008; and Kurt A. Powell, "More Than the Math: CFOs Should Be 'People People' Too," *HRMagazine*, 1 February 2008.
16. "A brief history of SNC-Lavalin," CBC News, 30 April 2012, www.cbc.ca/news/business/story/2012/04/30/snc-lavalin-faq.html.
17. Ibid.
18. Sean M. Connolly and David T. Hickey, "Codes of Conduct Don't Always Protect Reputation," *National Defense*, 1 January 2008.
19. Stephen Spector, "SOX and SOX North, Part 3 The Impact of SOX," Professional Development Network, www.cga-pdnet.org/Non_VerifiableProducts/ArticlePublication/SOX_E/SOX_part_3.pdf; "What is SOX?" Metso Corporation, 10 March 2006, www.metso.com/corporation/home_eng.nsf/FR?ReadForm&ATL=/corporation/articles_eng.nsf/WebWID/WTB-050704-2256F-A1200; Curtis Verschoor, "Is This the Age of Whistleblowers?" *Strategic Finance*, 1 February 2005; Guillermo Contreras, "San Antonio Whistleblower Doubly Rewarded in Exposing HealthSouth Fraud," *San Antonio Express News*, 14 January 2005; and Paul K. Mcmasters, "Inside the First Amendment: Blowing the Whistle Can Also Blow a Career," *Gannett News Service*, 16 January 2006.
20. Rob Ferguson, "ORNGE: Proposed bill would block ombudsman oversight," Queen's Park Bureau, 27 April 2012, www.thestar.com/news/canada/politics/article/1169002–ornge-proposed-bill-would-block-ombudsman-oversight; James Wood, "Alberta's lack of whistleblower law criticized," FAIR, 19 March 2012, http://fairwhistleblower.ca/content/albertas-lack-whistleblower-law-criticized; Kevin Donovan, "$25M in ORNGE money unaccounted for," *The Toronto Star*, 24 February 2012, www.thestar.com/news/canada/politics/article/1136628–25m-in-ornge-money-unaccounted-for; Kevin Donovan, "Whistleblower warned Ministry about ORNGE in 2008, Federal Accountability Initiative for Reform, 3 February 2012, http://fairwhistleblower.ca/content/ministry-was-warned-about-ornge-spending-four-years-ago-whistleblower-says; "Federal Conservatives broke their whistleblower protection and open government election promises, as the Afghan prisoner scandal makes clear," Democracy Watch, 2010?, www.dwatch.ca/camp/OpEdNov2509.html; David Hutton and Gerard Seijts, "Canada needs whistleblowers to protect stimulus package," *The Hill Times*, 16 February 2009, http://fairwhistleblower.ca/news/articles/2009-02-16_Canada_needs_whistleblowers_to_protect_stimulus_package.html; "Ontario passes whistleblower law," Canadian Press, 13 December 2006, www.thestar.com/news/article/148456--ontario-passes-whistleblower-law; and "Providing real protection for whistleblowers," Treasury Board of Canada Secretariat, 11 April 2006, www.tbs-sct.gc.ca/faa-lfi/fs-fi/16/09fs-fi-eng.asp.
21. John S. McClenahen, "Defining Social Responsibility," *Industry Week*, 1 March 2005.
22. Milton Friedman, "The Social Responsibility of Business is to Increase its Profits," *The New York Times Magazine*, 13 September 1970, www.colorado.edu/studentgroups/libertarians/issues/friedman-soc-resp-business.html.
23. "The Next Question," *The Economist*, 19 January 2008; Allen L. White, "Confessions of a CSR Champion," *Stanford Social Innovation Review*, 1 January 2009; and Pat Galagan, "Not Your Father's MBA," *T + D*, 1 January 2009.
24. Just Good Business," *The Economist*, 19 January 2008; Adrienee Fox, "Be an Insider on Social Responsibility," *HRMagazine*, 1 February 2008; "A Stitch in Time," *The Economist*, 19 January 2008; and Sheena Harrison, "Philanthropy Good for Business," *Crain's Detroit Business*, 18 February 2008.
25. "Jumpstart Launches One Million Red Balls Campaign to Help 20,000 Kids Play Sports This Summer," Canadian Tire Jumpstart, 30 April 2012, www.sacbee.com/2012/04/30/4453231/canadian-tire-jumpstart-launches.html.
26. William Damon, "Saints and Sinners in Business," *Security Management*, 1 January 2005.
27. "Our Reason for Being," Patagonia, Inc., 2012, www.patagonia.com/ca/patagonia.go?assetid=2047.
28. Xerox Awards Six Employees Social Service Leave for 2008," Business Wire, 11 February 2008.
29. Samantha Marshall, "Incorporating the Cause; Gen Y Entrepreneurs Pair Profits with Philanthropy," *Crain's New York Business*, 14 January 2008.
30. "Corporate Social Responsibility," Wikimedia Foundation, Inc., 5 June 2009, http://en.wikipedia.org/wiki/Corporate_social_responsibility.
31. Maple Leaf announces new recall, Q4 loss, *Financial Post*, 24 February 2009, www.financialpost.com/related/topics/Maple+Leaf+announces+recall+loss/1323505/story.html.
32. Don Frischmann, "Nothing Is Insignificant When It Comes to Brand Fulfillment," *Advertising Age*, 21 January 2008.
33. "Maple Leaf announces new recall, Q4 loss, *Financial Post*, 24 February 2009, www.financialpost.com/related/topics/Maple+Leaf+announces+recall+loss/1323505/story.html; and Dave Fleet, "7 Lessons From Maple Leaf Foods' Crisis Communications," davefleet.com, 25 August 2008, http://davefleet.com/2008/08/7-lessons-from-maple-leaf-foods-crisis-communications/.
34. "Earl Jones gets 11 years for $50M Ponzi scheme," *The Gazette*, 16 February 2010, www.montrealgazette.com/news/Earl+Jones+gets+years+swindling/2567329/story.html; Sidhartha Banerjee, "Disgraced Financier Lived Lavishly," The Canadian Press, 30 July 2009, www.thestar.com/news/canada/article/673888; "Trustee Sues Madoff's Wife for $45M," CBS News, 29 July 2009, www.cbsnews.com/stories/2009/07/29/business/main5196249.shtml?source=related_story&tag=related; "Nortel May

Lose NYSE Listing," CBC News, 11 December 2008,www.cbc.ca/mobile/text/story_news- technology.html?/ept/html/story/2008/12/11/nortellisting.html; Steven Skurka, "Black vs. Drabinsky: Two Trials, Two Very Different Systems," *National Post*, 4 June 2009, http://network.nationalpost.com/np/blogs/fullcomment/archive/2009/06/04/steven-skurka-on-black-vs-drabinsky-two-trials-two-very-different-systems.aspx; "Livent Sentencing Hearing Postponed," The Canadian Press, 3 June 2009, www.thestar.com/article/644834; Joe Schneider, "Livent Founders Convicted of C$500 Million Fraud (Update3)," Bloomber.com, 25 March 2009, www.bloomberg.com/apps/news?pid=20601082& sid=aBkY_Qtnf9y8&refer=Canada; Stephen Payne, "Investors Oppose SEC Proposal on Shareholder Rights," *Oil & Gas Investor*, 1 January 2008; and Robert Kuttner, "Dishonest Capitalism Won't Go Unpunished," *BusinessWeek*, 23 May 2005, 32.

35. Tara Perkins, "Andrew Rankin Gets 6 Months in Canada's 1st Stock-Tipping Conviction," CBC News, 10 April 2005, www.cbc.ca/cp/business/051027/b1027100.html; "Former RBC Dominion Securities Exec Faces Insider Trading Charges," CBC News, 5 February 2004, www.cbc.ca/stories/2004/02/04/rankin040204; Nancy Carr, "Daniel Duic to Pay $1.9M, Stop Trading in Ont., Testify at Rankin Trial: OSC," Canoe Money, 3 March 2004, http://money.canoe.ca/News/Other/2004/03/03/369029-cp.html.
36. David Saxby, "What Makes a Satisfied Employee?" *Rural Telecommunications*, 1 January 2008.
37. Cheryl Winokur Munk, "Winning Workplaces," *Community Banker*, 1 January 2008; Andrew Thomas, "Arizona Businesses Help Employees during Economic Slump," *Arizona Capitol Times*, 9 January 2009; and Melanie Scarborough, "The Rewards of Recognition: Six Strategies for Successful Employee Programs," *Community Banker*, 1 January 2009.
38. Vicki O'Brien, "Hands in Your Pocket," BC Business Online, 1 August 2007, www.bcbusinessonline.ca/bcb/top-stories/2007/08/01/hands-your-pockets.
39. Ibid.
40. Ibid.
41. Heather Green and Kerry Capell, "Carbon Confusion," *BusinessWeek*, 6 March 2008.
42. Colin Perkel, "Harris Apologizes for Government's Role in Tragedy," 18 January 2002, Canoe C-Health, www.canoe.ca/EcoliTragedy/020118_report-cp.html.
43. "First Nations take their pipeline protest to the top," *The Globe and Mail*, 9 May 2009, www.theglobeandmail.com/report-on-business/industry-news/energy-and-resources/first-nations-take-their-pipeline-protest-to-the-top/article2427947/?from=2427450; and "Northern Gateway Pipeline: First Nations protesters take to a train to share their protest," *The Star*, 8 May 2012, www.thestar.com/news/canada/article/1175292--northern-gateway-pipeline-first-nations-protestors-take-to-a-train-to-share-their-protest?bn=1.
44. Eric Pfeiffer, "BP oil spill two-year anniversary marked by somber statistics," 20 April 2012, The Sideshow, http://news.yahoo.com/blogs/sideshow/bp-oil-spill-two-anniversary-marked-somber-statistics-185242840.html; "BP oil disaster largely blamed on cement failure," The Associated Press, 14 September 2011, www.cbc.ca/news/world/story/2011/09/14/bp-offshore-oil-spill-report.html; Sylvia Pfeifer and Sheila McNulty, "BP oil spill confirmed as 'world's worst," *The Financial Times*, 3 August 2010, www.ft.com/cms/s/0/3e40d4ac-9e5d-11df-a5a4-00144feab49a.html#axzz1uZlfDvgn; Jim MacDonald, "Syncrude Charged After 500 Ducks Perished on Oilsands Pond," The Canadian Press, 9 February 2009, www.thestar.com/article/584719; "About Imagine—Who We Are," Imagine Canada, 2008, www.imagine.ca/content/about_imagine/who_we_are.asp?section=about.; "Home," Jantzi Research, 2005, www.jantziresearch.com; "Our Site Overview," Province of Nova Scotia: Sydney Tar Ponds Agency, 2004, www.gov.ns.ca/stpa; Chris Sebastian, "Canada Getting Tough on Spills," *Times Herald*, 12 May 2004, www.thetimesherald.com/news/stories/20040512/localnews/403633.html; Pat Currie, "All's Not Well in This Valley," *Lake Ontario Waterkeeper*, 3 April 2004, www.waterkeeper.ca/lok; "The Great Lakes Atlas," The United States Environmental Protection Agency, 2003, www.epa.gov/glnpo/atlas; "Tar Ponds in Sydney, Nova Scotia," PageWise Inc., 2002, http://tntn.essortment.com/tarpondssydney_rhxq.htm; and "Sydney Nova Scotia Tar Ponds Move Closer to Cleanup" Ellicott, www.dredge.com/casestudies/enviro8.htm.
45. Elizabeth Laurienzo, "Calvert Social Index Quarterly Adjustments," PR Newswire, 17 March 2005; "Corporate Social Concerns: Are They Good Citizenship, or a Rip-Off for Investors?" *The Wall Street Journal*, 6 December 2005.
46. "Triple Bottom Line," Wikipedia, 13 December 2008, http://en.wikipedia.org/wiki/Triple_bottom_line.
47. "What Is the Triple Bottom Line?" SustainAbility Ltd., www.sustainability.com/downloads_public/news/TBL.pdf.
48. Ibid.
49. "Defining Sustainability," Sustainability Reporting Program, 2000, www.sustreport.org/background/definitions.html; "Introducing Revive," Green Solutions North American, Inc., 2009, http://revive-d.com/revive_overview.cfm; and "Loblaws, Sobeys put a wrap on plastic bags," The Canadian Press, 27 November 2008, www.cbc.ca/consumer/story/ 2008/11/27/loblaw-sobeys-bags.html.
50. "Fair trade – An alternative economic model," CBC News, 23 April 2007, www.cbc.ca/news/background/fair-trade/.
51. Ibid.
52. "Fairtrade Canada," Fairtrade Canada, 11 May 2012, http://fairtrade.ca/en/about-fairtrade/fairtrade-canada.
53. Joint Initiative on Corporate Accountability and Workers' Rights, www.jo-in.org, accessed 1 August 2008.

Chapter 6

1. Alan B. Graves, "As Your Small Business Grows, It's Time to Think about Incorporating," *San Diego Business Journal*, 10 March 2008.
2. "Proprietorship," Canadian Tax and Financial Information, Taxtips.ca, 17 March 2012, www.taxtips.ca/smallbusiness/incorporate.htm.
3. Ibid.
4. Ibid.
5. Ibid.
6. "Partnership," Canadian Tax and Financial Information, Taxtips.ca, 17 March 2012, www.taxtips.ca/smallbusiness/incorporate.htm.
7. "Limited liability partnership," Wikimedia Foundation, Inc., 19 April 2012, http://en.wikipedia.org/wiki/Limited_liability_partnership#cite_note-CBA-2.
8. Jeff Opdyke, "When Business and Friendship Don't Mix," *The Wall Street Journal*, 17 March 2005; Paulette Thomas, "One Sweet Solution to a Sour Partnership," *The Wall Street Journal*, 23 March 2005.
9. "Partnership," Canadian Tax and Financial Information, Taxtips.ca, 17 March 2012, www.taxtips.ca/glossary.htm#P.
10. "Partnership," Canadian Tax and Financial Information.
11. Susan Ward, "Corporate Tax Advantages of the Canadian-Controlled Private Corporation," About.com, 2012, http://sbinfocanada.about.com/od/corporatetax/a/ccpcadvantages.htm.
12. "McCain Business Empire has Deep Roots," CBC.ca, 19 March 2004, www.cbc.ca/stories/2004/03/19/mccainbiz_040319.
13. Josh Fineman and David Scanlan," Tim Hortons Shares May Rise After Raising $671 Million in IPO," Bloomberg, 24 March 2006, www.bloomberg.com/apps/news?pid=newsarchive&sid=aq7mLjay_GVs&refer=us.
14. "The Story of Tim Hortons," Tim Hortons, 2012, www.timhortons.com/ca/en/about/index.html.
15. "The Basics of Corporate Structure," Investopedia.com, 2008, www.investopedia.com/articles/basics/03/022803.asp.
16. "Time Warner Inc. Announces Plan to Separate AOL," Time Warner Inc., 28 May 2009, www.timewarner.com/corp/newsroom/pr/0,20812,1901397,00.html; Gregory Zuckerman and Ian Mcdonald, "Time to Slice the Mergers," *The Wall Street Journal*, 10 January 2006, C; Harry Berkowitz. "Time Warner Pays $2.4B to Settle Class-Action Suit," *Newsday*, 4 August 2005; Robert Barker, "P&G's $57 Billion Bargain," *BusinessWeek*, 25 July 2005; and Shawn Tully, "The Urge to Merge," *Fortune*, 21 February 2005.
17. Sean Silcoff, "Old Dutch Buys Humpty Dumpty," *National Post*, 22 March 2006, FP1.
18. Ibid., FP3.
19. "About CARA," Cara Operations, 2012, www.cara.com/about.php.
20. Matthew Benjamin, "Deal Mania," *U.S. News & World Report*, 18 April 2005.
21. "Fast Franchise Facts," Canadian Franchise Association, 2012, www.cfa.ca/Publications_Research/FastFacts.aspx.
22. "Food Restaurants—Boston Pizza International," Canadian Franchise Association, 2006, www.cfa.ca/members/food_restaurants.html#boston_pizza_international.
23. UPS Store, www.theupsstore.com, accessed January 24, 2009.
24. Ian Mount, "New Franchise Rule: More Disclosure, Same High Risks," *Fortune Small Business*, 29 February 2008; and Courtney Dentch, "Fewer Franchises Is Chain Reaction to Bad Economy," *Deseret News (Salt Lake City)*, 8 January 2009.
25. "Kumon Franchise," Occasionfranchise.ca, 2008, http://canada.occasionfranchise.ca/brochure/43/Kumon-franchise.html.

26. "Franchise FAQ," The Keg Steakhouse & Bar, 2008, http://en.kegsteakhouse.com/franchise/faq#1.
27. "$2B Tim Hortons franchisee lawsuit deemed half-baked," CBC News, 28 February 2012, www.cbc.ca/news/business/story/2012/02/28/tim-hortons-class-action.html.
28. Ibid.
29. Julie Bennett, "A Franchiser's Path to International Success Is Often Paved with Pitfalls," *The Wall Street Journal*, 7 April 2005, D7; Anne Fisher, "Hidden Risk," *Fortune*, 26 December 2005.
30. Carmen Caruso and Brandi Van Leeuwen, "Communicating a Franchisor's Value without Crossing the Line," *Franchising World*, 1 March 2008; and Mary Beth Brody, "Addressing the Most Common Franchisee Claims," *Franchising World*, 1 May 2008.
31. "FAQS," Canadian Tire Corporation, 2011, http://corp.canadiantire.ca/EN/JoinOurTeam/RetailOwnership/Pages/FAQs.aspx.
32. "About Us," Yogen Früz, 2012, www.yogenfruz.com/home/en/about-us; "Taco Chain Heads East," *Canadian Business Franchise*, 2006, www.cgb.ca/hotnews1.html.
33. "About Co-ops in Canada," Government of Canada, 12 December 2011, www.coop.gc.ca/COOP/display-afficher.do?id=1232131333489&lang=eng; "Various Kinds of Co-operatives," Government of Canada, 16 January 2009, www.coop.gc.ca/COOP/display-afficher.do?id=1232133235546&lang=eng; "Key Benefits of Co-operatives," Government of Canada, 16 January 2009, www.coop.gc.ca/COOP/display-afficher.do?id=1232133811797&lang=eng; "Cooperatives in Canada," Coop Zone, [2008?], www.coopzone.coop/en/coopsincda; "About Cooperatives," Canadian Co-Operative Association, 2008, www.coopscanada.coop/aboutcoop/.

Chapter 7

1. "Employment by class of worker and industry (based on NAICS1) – Seasonally adjusted," Statistics Canada, , 7 September 2012, http://www5.statcan.gc.ca/cansim/pick-choisir?lang=eng&p2=33&id=2820011; "A Definition of Entrepreneurship," Internet Center for Management and Business Administration, Inc., 1999–2007, www.quickmba.com/entre/definition/.
2. "Entrepreneurship vs. Small Business," Internet Center for Management and Business Administration, Inc., 1999–2007, www.quickmba.com/entre/definition/; "Entrepreneurship vs. Small Business," Ryerson University, 2008, www.ryerson.ca/career/jobsearch/searchjob/entrepreneurship/.
3. Retrieved 16 May 2012 from the following company Web sites: www.jimpattison.com/corporate-info/about-us.aspx; http://corp.canadiantire.ca/EN/AboutUs/WhoWeAre/Pages/default.aspx and http://corp.canadiantire.ca/EN/AboutUs/Pages/FastFacts.aspx; www.leons.ca/shared/customerservice/aboutus.aspx; www.theglobeandmail.com/globe-investor/news-sources/?date=20120503&archive=ccnm&slug=201205030787243001; www.sobeyscorporate.com/en/Our-Company/At-A-glance.aspx; www.irvingoil.com/who_we_are/; www.mccain.com/newsroom/Pages/McCainannouncesDirkVandePutasPresidentCEO.aspx; http://about.roots.com/on/demandware.store/Sites-RootsCorporate-Site/default/Page-Show?cid=MSTR_OUR_ROOTS.
4. "About Us," Travel CUTS, 2008, www.travelcuts.com/en/ 01%20Home/About%20Us.asp.
5. Cindy Kibbe, "Stonyfield Institute: A Success Story," *New Hampshire Business Review*, 29 February 2008; Matthew Bandyk, "How Entrepreneurs Make Money and Lead Happy Lives," *U.S. News & World Report*, 30 May 2008.
6. "Jean Paré Has Retired," Company's Coming Publishing Limited, 1 March 2011, www.companyscoming.com/about_cc/media_news/.
7. Thomas Duening, "Nature vs. Nurture: Are Entrepreneurs Made, or Are They Born?" *Phoenix Business Journal*, 18 January 2009; "Lessons from the Leaders," *PROFIT*, June 2008, 31; Michelle Simms, "Are Entrepreneurial Characteristics Inherited or Learned?" *Bellingham Business Journal*, 1 June 2008; Sarah Pierce, "Spirit of the Entrepreneur," Entrepreneur.com, 28 February 2008; and Karen E. Klein, "Starting a Startup," *BusinessWeek*, 11 June 2008.
8. "Where Others See Problems, Entrepreneurs Recognize Opportunities," *The Washington Times*, 13 May 2008; Tennille M. Robinson, "BE Next: Fearless Young Entrepreneurs Reveal Their MVP—Most Valuable Play," *Black Enterprise*, 1 January 2009.
9. "An Idea Is Not Necessarily an Opportunity," *The Washington Times*, 13 May 2008.
10. "Key Small Business Statistics – July 2012," Industry Canada, July 2012, 38, www.ic.gc.ca/eic/site/061.nsf/vwapj/KSBS-PSRPE_July-Juillet2012_eng.pdf/$FILE/KSBS-PSRPE_July-Juillet2012_eng.pdf; and "CIBC Report Predicts Canada Will Be Home to One Million Women Entrepreneurs by 2010," Canada NewsWire, 28 June 2005, http://proquest.umi.com/pqdweb.
11. Helle Neergaard, "Networking Activities in Technology-Based Entrepreneurial Teams," *International Small Business Journal*, 16 January 2005.
12. Matthew Bandyk, "5 Things Entrepreneurs Should Know about Business Partners," *U.S. News & World Report*, 6 May 2008.
13. Industry Canada "Key Small Business Statistics," 5.
14. Ibid., 8. Total number of businesses with 1–4 employees is 615,599.
15. Dan Strempel, "UConn Mulls Stamford Tech Incubator," *Fairfield County (Connecticut) Business Journal*, 11 April 2005; Emily Le Coz, "Incubators Provide Tools for Entrepreneurs," *Northeast Mississippi Daily Journal*, 6 January 2006; and Nancy Cambria, "'Incubator' Loan Program Will Foster Small Businesses," *St. Louis Post-Dispatch*, 19 January 2006.
16. Sammi King, "Internet a Boon to Home-Based Businesses," *Arlington Heights (Illinois) Daily Herald*, 22 February 2005; Steve Jones, "Home Businesses Can Be Path to Freedom," *Myrtle Beach (South Carolina) Sun News*, 15 May 2005; and Kristen Millares Bolt, "Moms Setting Up Online Businesses," *Seattle Post-Intelligencer*, 5 February 2005.
17. "Michael Smith (chef)," Wikimedia Foundation, Inc. 9 May 2012, http://en.wikipedia.org/wiki/Michael_Smith_(chef).
18. Deb Gruver, "Small-Business Owners Face Pros, Cons of Home-Based Enterprises," *Wichita Eagle*, 3 June 2005; Deb Gruver, "Home-Based Businesses Need to Use Caution with Deductions," *Wichita Eagle*, 18 March 2005; "Parenting, Work-at-Home Experts Join to Author Book Series for Busy Moms," *PR Newswire*, 31 January 2005; and Janel Stephens, "Disciplined Commute from Bed to Home Office," *Sarasota Herald Tribune*, 17 March 2005.
19. Sean Silcoff, "What keeps online retail in Canada from clicking?" *The Globe and Mail*, 12 May 2012, www.theglobeandmail.com/report-on-business/what-keeps-online-retail-in-canada-from-clicking/article2430484/page1/.
20. "Welcome to Shop.ca," Shop.ca, 16 May 2012, www.shop.ca/shop/en/shopdotca.
21. Chuck Soder, "Got a Good Idea? Throw It Out There," *Crain's Cleveland Business*, 14 January 2008.
22. Larry Olmsted, "Nonstop Innovation: How One Company Transforms Its Employees into Entrepreneurs," *Inc.*, July 2005, 34; Alan Deutschman, "Building a Better Skunk Works," *Fast Company*, March 2005, 68–73; and Nicole Marie Richardson, "What It Takes to Be a Successful Intrapreneur," *Black Enterprise*, 1 December 2005.
23. Robert D. Ramsey, "Gaining the Edge over the Competition," *Supervision*, 1 May 2005; and Phil Bishop, "Strengthening the Innovation Chain," *Electronic Business*, 1 December 2004.
24. "Business Incubation," Canadian Association of Business Incubation 2008, www.cabi.ca/business-incubation.php; "Business Incubation FAQ?" National Incubation Association, 2009, www.nbia.org/resource_library/faq/index.php#3; "Business Incubation," Canadian Association of Business Incubation, 2006, www.cabi.ca/page_05.htm; "Business Incubation FAQ," National Incubation Association, 31 March 2006, www.nbia.org/resource_center/bus_inc_facts/index.php; "Canada Business—About Us," Government of Canada, 8 December 2005, www.cbsc.org/servlet/ContentServer?cid=1063391060815&pagename=CBSC_FE/CBSC_WebPage/CBSC_WebPage_Temp&lang=eng&c=CBSC_WebPage; "Aboriginal Business Service Network," Government of Canada, 5 August 2003, www.cbsc.org/servlet/ContentServer?cid=1091626045548&pagename=ABSN_FE%2FCBSC_WebPage%2FCBSC_WebPage_Temp&lang=en&c=CBSC_WebPage; Jean-Pierre Trudel, "Laval's Biotech City Adds Two New Biotech Development Centres to Its Complex," *LifeSciencesWorld*, 26 April 2003, www.biotecfind.com/pages/articles_eg/laval/laval.htm.
25. Industry Canada, "Key Small Business Statistics," 6–10.
26. Ibid., 3–4; Simona Covel and Raymund Flandez, "Three Strategies to Get Customers to Say 'Yes,'" *The Wall Street Journal*, 29 May 2008; and Nina Wu, "Hawaii's Small Businesses Sustain Half of Private Jobs," *Honolulu Star-Bulletin*, 24 January 2009.
27. Industry Canada, "Key Small Business Statistics," 4.
28. Thomas Duening, "Many Ingredients Are Essential for Entrepreneurial Success," *Phoenix Business Journal*, 2 May 2008.
29. "About Bullfrog Power," Bullfrog Power, 22 September 2008, www.bullfrogpower.com/about/about/cfm.
30. "History," Running Room, 2012, www.runningroom.com/hm/inside.php?lang=1&id=3036.
31. Andy Holloway, "Fill Your Shoes: Small-Business Succession," *Canadian Business*, March 27–April 9, 2006, www.canadianbusiness.com/managing/strategy/article.jsp?content=20060327_75741_75741.

32. "Canwest," Wikimedia Foundation, Inc., 30 April 2012, http://en.wikipedia.org/wiki/Canwest; Dana Flavelle and Rita Trichur, "CanWest's newspaper empire for sale," *Toronto* Star, 9 January 2010, www.thestar.com/news/canada/article/748513--canwest-s-newspaper-empire-for-sale; "Leonard Asper stepping down from Canwest," *Financial Post*, 4 March 2010, www.financialpost.com/Leonard+Asper+stepping+down+from+Canwest/2640633/story.html; "Governance for the Family Business," KPMG in Canada, 2008, www.kpmg.ca/en/services/enterprise/issuesGrowthGovernance.html; and "Succession Planning for Family Business," BDO Canada LLP, [2012?], www.bdo.ca/library/publications/familybusiness/succession/planning1.cfm.
33. Small Business Administration, www.sba.gov, accessed 27 January, 2009.
34. "BBB Tips Give Entrepreneurs the Inside Track on Small Business Start-Up," *Business Wire*, 24 August 2005; Perri Capell, "Typical Funding Mistakes That You Should Avoid," *The Wall Street Journal*, 12 April 2005.
35. "Banks and the Economy," Canadian Bankers Association, 9 March 2012, www.cba.ca/en/media-room/50-backgrounders-on-banking-issues/122-contributing-to-the-economy.
36. "Venture Capitalists Invested $4.63 Billion During the First Three Months of 2005," *Purchasing*, 19 May 2005; Amanda Fung, "Startups Find Few VC Funds," *Crain's New York Business*, 1 August 2005; and Tricia Bishop, "Fewer Venture Capital-Funded Companies Go Public in 2005," *Baltimore Sun*, 4 January 2006.
37. Christopher Farrell, "How Angel Investors Get Their Wings," *Black Enterprise*, August 2008.
38. Rick Spence, "2006 Financing Guide: Angel investors," *PROFIT*, 27 June 2006, www.profitguide.com/article/3715--2006-financing-guide-angel-investors.
39. "The Cervélo History," Cervélo Cycles, 2012, www.cervelo.com/en_us/company/history/; "The Amazing Race: Cervélo Cycles," *PROFIT*, May 2006, www.canadian business.com/entrepreneur/managing/article.jsp?content=20060404_153018_5420.
40. Christopher Hosford, "Measuring the Social," *B2B*, 8 December 2008.
41. Sean Silcoff, "What keeps online retail in Canada from clicking?" World Wide Web.

Chapter 8

1. Jack Welch and Suzy Welch, "How to Be a Good Leader," *Newsweek*, 4 April 2005, 45–48.
2. Greg Thompson, "Great Expectations, the Secret to Coaching," *CMA Magazine*, April 2008, 22–23.
3. Gary Hamel, "The Why, What, and How of Management Innovation," *Harvard Business Review*, February 2006, 72–84.
4. Peter Cappelli and Monika Hamori, "The New Road to the Top," *Harvard Business Review*, January 2005, 25–32.
5. Marcus Buckingham, "What Great Managers Do," *Harvard Business Review*, March 2005, 70–79.
6. Elizabeth Fenner, "Happiness," *Fortune*, 21 February 2005, 36.
7. Kenneth R. Brousseau, Michael J. Driver, Gary Hourihon, and Rikard Larsson. "The Seasoned Executive's Decision-Making Style," *Harvard Business Review*, February 2006, 111–121.
8. John E. West, "Listening to the Customer," *Quality Digest*, February 2006, 16.
9. Jack Welch, "It's All in the Sauce," *Fortune*, 18 April 2005, 138–144.
10. "GM posts record $7.6B profit in 2011," 16 February 2012, www.cbc.ca/news/business/story/2012/02/16/gm-record-profit.html.
11. Bill Breen, "The Clear Leader," *Fast Company*, March 2005, 65–67.
12. Janel M. Radtke, "How to Write a Mission Statement," *TCCI Magazine Online*, 2005.
13. Giovanni Gavetti and Jan W. Rivkin, "How Strategists Really Think," *Harvard Business Review*, April 2005, 54–63.
14. Michael C. Mankins and Richard Steele, "Stop Making Plans: Start Making Decisions," *Harvard Business Review*, January 2006, 76–84.
15. Robert J. Samuelson, "No Joke: CEOs Do Some Good," *Newsweek*, 18 April 2005, 49.
16. Omar el Akkad, "Retailers Slash Prices on RIM's PlayBook tablet," 26 September 2011, www.theglobeandmail.com/new/technology/tech-news/retailers-slash-prices-on-rims-playbook-tablet/article2180618/.
17. Iain Marlow, "Rim chops all PlayBook prices to $299," 3 January 2012, www.theglobeandmail.com/news/technology/tech-news/rim-chops-all-playbook-prices-to-299/article2289840/.
18. "The New Contingency Plan—Health-Related Emergencies," 27 May 2003, Toronto: Morneau Sobeco. Retrieved from www.morneausobeco.com/PDF/SARSCommuniqué_E.pdf.
19. Roma Luciw, "Is Your Company Ready for a Disaster?" *The Globe and Mail*, 21 June 2006, www.theglobeandmail.com/servlet/story/RTGAM.20060621.wdisaster0621/BNStory/Business.
20. Ibid.
21. Gary Silverman, "How May I Help You?" *Financial Times*, 4/5 February 2006, W1 and W2.
22. Paul Rogers and Marcia Blenko, "Who Has the D?" *Harvard Business Review*, January 2006, 53–61.
23. "Trends in Airline Governance, Management Structures and Mandates," 14 June 2011, www.iaaia.com/PDF/ent_trends_in_airline_governance_at_14-06-11.pdf.
24. Sunny Freeman, "Loblaw Profits Jump 20 Per Cent But Still Hit by Infrastructure Overhaul, 16 November 2011, www.canadianbusiness.com/article/57306--loblaw-profits-jump-20-per-cent-but-still-hit-by-infrastructure-overhaul.
25. Andreas Priestland and Robert Hanig, "Developing First-Level Leaders," *Harvard Business Review*, June 2005, 113–120.
26. Robert Kutz, "Skills of an Effective Administrator," *Harvard Business Review*, Sept – Oct 1974, 90–101.
27. Anthony Davis, "Sky High," *PROFIT Guide*, March 2004, www.profitguide.com/shared/print.jsp?content_20040213_171556_4580.
28. P. Fraser Johnson and Robert D. Klassen, "E-Procurement," *MIT Sloan Management Review*, Winter 2005, 7–10.
29. Mahender Singh, "Supply Chain Reality Check," *MIT Sloan Management Review*, Spring 2005, 96.
30. Murray Johannsen, "Nine Characteristics of Successful Entrepreneurs and Business Leaders," www.legacee.com/Info/Leadership/LeadershipEntrepreneurial.html.
31. Taria Grant, "Canada a Laggard in Developing Women Leaders," 3 March 2011, www.theglobeandmail.com/reprot-on-business/economy/economy-lab/daily-mix/canada-a-laggard-in-developing-women-leaders/article1928363/.
32. Bertrand Marotte, "Management Guru Assails Excessive CEO Salaries," *The Globe and Mail*, 8 May 2003, B7.
33. H. James Harrington, "Knowledge Management Takes Us from Chance to Choice," *Quality Digest*, April 2003, 14–16.
34. Laura Bogomolny, "Most Innovative Exec/Canadian Tire—Janice Wismer," *Canadian Business*, 2004, www.canadianbusiness.com/allstars/best_innovative_exec.html.

Chapter 9

1. Linda Teschler, "Is Your Company up to Speed?" *Fast Company*, June 2003, 81–111.
2. Stephen H. Wildstrom, "A Stroll through the IPhone App Store," *BusinessWeek*, 28 July 2008.
3. Fred Reichheld, "The Microeconomics of Customer Relations," *MIT Sloan Management Review*, Winter 2006, 73–78.
4. Henry Mintzberg and James Brian Quinn, *The Strategy Process: Concepts and Contexts* (New Jersey: Prentice Hall Inc., 1992).
5. Henry Mintzberg, *Managers not MBAs* (San Francisco: Berrett-Koehler Publishers, 2004).
6. Magna International, "Magna 2005 Annual Report," 2006, www.magna.com/magna/en/investors/governance/documents/pdf/Annual%20Report%20 2005.pdf.
7. Harry Maurer, "News You Need to Know," *BusinessWeek*, 6 February 2006, 32.
8. Ron Adner, "Innovation Ecosystem," *Harvard Business Review*, April 2006, 98–107.
9. Jon R. Katzenbach and Douglas K. Smith, "The Discipline of Teams," *Harvard Business Review*, July–August 2005, 162–71.
10. Jeff Weiss and Jonathan Hughes, "Want Collaboration?" *Harvard Business Review*, March 2005, 93–101.
11. Bill Fischer and Andy Boynton, "Virtuoso Teams," *Harvard Business Review*, July–August 2005, 117–21.
12. John E. (Jack) Wert, "Listening to the Customer," *Quality Digest*, February 2006, 16.
13. Philip Evans and Bob Wolf, "Collaboration Rules," *Harvard Business Review*, July–August 2005, 96–104.
14. Jerker Denrell, "Selection Bias and the Perils of Benchmarking," *Harvard Business Review*, April 2005, 114–19.
15. Jeff Sanford, "Clean and Green, Suncor Uses Sustainability Performance to Track Business," *Canadian Business*, 22 February 2006.

16. Pete Engardio, "Mom-and-Pop Multinationals," *BusinessWeek*, 14 and 21 July 2008.
17. Pip Coburn, "China's Magic Number," *Red Herring*, February 2003, 67.
18. Spencer E. Ante, "Has Facebook's Value Taken a Hit?" *BusinessWeek*, 18 August 2008.
19. "Ottawa doesn't regret GM bailout," 21 April 2010, www.cbc.ca/news/canada/windsor/story/2010/04/21/wdr-detroit-gm-government-loans-100421.html.
20. Christopher Hosford, "Optimum Results," *BtoB*, 5 May 2008.
21. Leslie Laredo, "How Older Pros Can Transition to Digital," *Advertising Age*, 24 March 2008.
22. Sandy Carter, *The New Language of Marketing 2.0* (New York: IBM Press, 2009).
23. Amy Barrett, "Man with Scalpel," *BusinessWeek*, 18 April 2005, 42.
24. David Ernst and James Bamford, "Your Alliances Are Too Stable," *Harvard Business Review*, June 2005, 133–141.
25. Lance A. Bettencourt and Anthony W. Ulwick, "The Customer-Centered Innovation Map," *Harvard Business Review*, May 2008.
26. Jean Halliday, "Ford Puts Consumers at Center of 'Rebirthing,'" *Advertising Age*, 30 January 2006, 31.
27. Keith Naughton, "Detroit Hoping for a Small Victory," *Newsweek*, 6 February 2006, 10.
28. Celestica, www.celestica.com/News/News.aspx?id=3092/.
29. Henry Mintzberg and James Brian Quinn, *The Strategy Process: Concepts and Contexts* (New Jersey: Prentice Hall Inc., 1992).
30. Steven Watters, "The Organization Woman," *Business 2.0*, April 2006, 106–110.
31. www.td.com/careers
32. "Will CEO Pain Lead to Labor Gains?" *Business Week*, 16 September 2002, 6.

Chapter 10

1. "*Innovation in Canada*," Sackville: Centre for Canadian Studies at Mount Allison University, www.mta.ca/faculty/arts/canadian_studies/english/about/innovation/.
2. Innovation Analysis Bulletin, Vol. 6, No. 1, March 2004, www.statcan.gc.ca/pub/88-003-x/88-003-x2004001-eng.pdf.
3. "Spending on research and development," 13 January 2012, www.statcan.gc.ca/daily-quotidien/120113/dg120113d-eng.htm.
4. "Federal government spending on science and technology," The *Daily*, 18 October 2011, www.statcan.gc.ca/daily-quotidien/111018/dg111018b-eng.htm.
5. "Top 100 Corporate R & D Spenders List 2011 Analysis," Research Infosource, Inc., www.researchinfosouce.com/top100.shtml.
6. "Spending on research and development," 13 January 2012, www.statcan.gc.ca/daily-quotidien/120113/dg120113d-eng.htm.
7. Canadian Manufacturers & Exporters, "State of Advanced Manufacturing: A Canadian Perspective," October 2011, www.cme-mec.ca/english/publications/cme-publications-reports.html.
8. Kathryn Jones, "The Dell Way," *Business 2.0*, February 2003, 61–66.
9. Spencer E. Ante, "The New Blue," *Business Week*, 17 March 2003, 80–88.
10. Daniel Eisenberg, "There's a New Way to Think @ Big Blue," *Time*, 20 January 2003, 49–53.
11. Pete Engardio, Aaron Bernstein, and Manjeet Kripalani, "Is Your Job Next?" *Business Week*, 3 February 2003, 50–60.
12. David Atkin, "HP Toronto Plant Aimed at Dell," *The Globe and Mail*, 14 November 2003, B1.
13. "Hoover's Profile: Gilden Activewear, Inc.," Answers.com, www.Answers.com/topic/gildan-activewear-inc.
14. Richard Wilding, "The Ghost in the Machine," *Financial Times*, 7 April 2006, p. 5 of a section called "Mastering Uncertainty."
15. Gordon Pitts, "Kodiak Comes Home," *The Globe and Mail*, 15 May 2006, B5.
16. Gary Norris, "Honda Putting New Assembly Plant in U.S.; Ontario Gets $154M Engine Factory," Canadian Business Online, 17 May 2006, www.canadianbusiness.com/markets/headline_news/article.jsp?content=b051777A.
17. David Crane, "We've Got to Use Our Brains More than Our Brawn," *Toronto Star*, D2.
18. International Association of Outsourcing Professionals, "State of Global Provider Industry: Findings from the 2010 ORN Global Service Provider Survey, www.iaop.org.
19. CORE Centre for Outsourcing Research and Education, www.core-outsourcing.org.
20. Gordon Pitts, "Small Producer Cleans Up Making Soap," *The Globe and Mail*, 28 July 2003, B1.
21. "IT Outsourcing to Canada," IMEX Systems, Inc., www.imexsystems.com/pdf/Outsourcing_USA.pdf.
22. Virginia Galt, "Take Our Business, Take Our People: BMO," *The Globe and Mail*, 19 May 2003, B1.
23. Canadian Vehicle Manufacturers Association, "The Automotive Industry in Canada," 2006, www.cvma.ca/eng/industry/industry.asp.
24. Richard Waters, "Manufacturing Glitches Dent Xbox Sales," *Financial Times*, 27 January 2006, 17.
25. Michelle Conlin, "Call Centers in the Rec Room," *BusinessWeek*, 23 January 2006, 76–77.
26. Michelle Conlin, "The Waning Days of the Road Warrior," *BusinessWeek*, 2 June 2008.
27. Janet Bealer Rodie, "Brückner, M-Tec Partner to Provide Carpet Solutions," *Textile World*, 1 May 2005.
28. Davis Balestracci, "When Processes Moonlight as Trends," *Quality Digest*, June 2005, 18.
29. "Royal Canadian Mint," September 2003, Cognos, www.cognos.com/products/applications/success.html.
30. Ibid.
31. Horst-Henning Wolf, "Making the Transition to Strategic Purchasing," *MIT Sloan Management Review*, Summer 2005, 17–24.
32. Daren Fonda, "Why the Most Profitable Cars Made in the U.S.A. are Japanese and German," *Time*, June 2003, A9–A13.
33. Centre for Research and Information on Canada, "Background," 11 May 2006, www.cric.ca/en_html/guide/border/border.html#faqs.
34. "More about NQI" and "Canada Awards for Excellence," Toronto: National Quality Institute, www.nqi.ca.
35. John E. West, "Making Products Better," *Quality Digest*, February 2008.
36. Scott M. Paton, "The Cost of Quality," *Quality Digest*, January 2006, 128.
37. "ISO Standards," International Organization for Standardization, www.iso.org/iso/iso_catalogue.htm.
38. SNC-Lavalin Group Inc., "Quality Policy," www.snclavalin.com/en/6_0/6_10.aspx.
39. "Extensive debate improves consensus on future ISO 26000 standard on social responsibility," International Organization for Standardization, 4 June 2009, www.iso.org/iso/pressrelease.htm?refid=Ref1229.
40. "Grocery Chain in Drive to Improve," *National Post*, 31 October 2001, JV3.
41. "The Juggling Act Behind the Cirque," *National Post*, 31 October 2001, JV4.
42. Gordon Pitts, "Kodiak Comes Home," *The Globe and Mail*, 15 May 2006, www.theglobeandmail.com/servlet/story/LAC.20060515.RKODIAK15/TPStory/?query=kodiak.
43. Robyn Waters, "The Secret of Feel-Good Shopping," *Kiplinger's*, January 2006, 20–22.
44. Greg Keenan, "Ford's New Maxim: Flex Manufacturing; New Oakville Plant Should Be Able to Switch Models in Days, not Weeks," *The Globe and Mail*, 10 May 2006, B3.
45. Ibid.
46. Derrell S. James, "Using Lean and Six Sigma in Project Management," *Quality Digest*, August 2005, 49–55; Bill Ritsch, "Breaking the Bottleneck," *Quality Digest*, March 2006, 41.
47. Jerry Feingold, "Lean Roots—A Quick History Lesson," *Quality Digest*, May 2008.
48. Dennis Sowards, "Lean Construction," *Quality Digest*, November 2007.
49. Thomas R. Cutler, "Bored by Lean," *Quality Digest*, May 2008.
50. Alan Henry, "Most Popular Online Custom Clothing Store: Indochino," http://lifehacker.com/5910371/most-popular-online-custom-clothing-store-indochino, accessed 23 August 2012.
51. Robyn Waters, "The Secret of Feel-Good Shopping," *Kiplinger's*," January 2006, 20–22.

Chapter 11

1. Hermann Schwind et al, *Canadian Human Resource Management, A Strategic Approach*, 8th ed. (Toronto: McGraw-Hill Ryerson, 2007), 398.
2. Ibid.
3. "How Employee Satisfaction and Motivation Are Tied to Customer Satisfaction," *Managing Training & Development*, 1 January 2005; Michael Skapinker, "Measures of Success Must Go Beyond Financial Results," *Financial Times*, 2 March 2005; and "Employee Retention and Succession Programs Lead to Higher Retention, Increased ROI, Says AberdeenGroup," *Business Wire*, 9 January 2006.
4. "What's the Real Cost of Turnover?" go2 Tourism Society, 2008, www.go2hr.ca/ForbrEmployers/Retention/StaffTurnover/WhatstheRealCostofTurnover/tabid/1624/Default.aspx.

5. Ibid.
6. Michael Wilson, "The Psychology of Motivation and Employee Retention," *Maintenance Supplies*, 1 July 2005; Jeff Kirby, "Light Their Fires: Find Out How to Improve Employee Motivation and Increase Overall Company Productivity," *Security Management*, 1 June 2005; and Michael Arndt, "Nice Work If You Can Get It," *BusinessWeek*, 9 January 2006.
7. Jane Gaboury, "Tension Invention," *Industrial Engineer*, 1 July 2005; and "Hawthorne Studies," Analytic Technologies, www.analytictech.com/mb021/handouts/bank_wiring.htm.
8. Richard DiPaolo, "Ergonomically Inclined," *Maintenance Supplies*, 1 June 2005.
9. David Montgomery, *The Fall of the House of Labor: The Workplace, the State, and American Labor Activism*, 1865–1925, (New York: Cambridge University Press, 1987); and "Frederick Winslow Taylor," Wikimedia Foundation, Inc., 15 December 2008, http://en.wikipedia.org/wiki/Frederick_Winslow_Taylor#cite_note-8.
10. Jay Velury, "Empowerment to the People," *Industrial Engineer*, 1 May 2005.
11. Horst Brand, "Working in the Digital Age," *Monthly Labor Review*, 1 January 2005.
12. Steven Bratman, "The Double-Blind Gaze," *Altadena (California) Skeptic*, 1 January 2005.
13. Mike Hofman, "The Idea That Saved My Company," *Inc.*, October 2007.
14. "Canada's Top 100 Employers," Mediacorp Canada Inc., 2012, www.canadastop100.com/national/.
15. Derek Sankey, "CP Railway Offers Best Overall Package," *Financial Post*, 22 October 2008, www.financialpost.com/working/story.html?id=899342.
16. Karl Kopen, "Al-Pac a Top 100 Canadian employer - five years running," Alberta-Pacific Forest Industries Inc., 11 October 2011, www.alpac.ca/content/files/AlPacTopEmployerFiveYearsRunning.pdf.
17. Michael Wilson, "The Psychology of Motivation and Employee Retention," *Maintenance Supplies*, 1 July 2005; Jeff D. Opdyke, "Money Can't Buy Job Happiness," *The Wall Street Journal*, 19 April 2005; and "Incentives on the Rise," *Financial & Insurance Meetings*, 1 January 2006.
18. Career Connection, "Getting Along with Your Boss?" 12 March 2003, www.canoe.ca/CareerConnectionNews/031203_flash2.html.
19. "Boosting Morale from an Employer's Perspective," Training + Development Blog, 18 November 2008, http://tdblog.typepad.com/td_blog/surveys/.
20. "Job Satisfaction," Psychology Wikia, 2008, http://psychology.wikia.com/wiki/Job_satisfaction#cite_note-5.
21. "Ergonomics Glossary: Job Enlargement," CAE Association of Canadian Ergonomists/Association canadienne d'ergonomie, 2008, www.ace-ergocanada.ca/index.php?command=buildBlock&contentid=245#[J].
22. Ibid.
23. Margaret Heffernan, "The Morale of the Story," *Fast Company*, March 2005, 79–81.
24. Patricia M. Buhler, "Managing in the New Millennium: Human Resources," *Supervision*, 1 January 2005; Jena McGregor, "The Struggle to Measure Performance," *BusinessWeek*, 9 January 2006.
25. Deena Waisberg, "Simple Steps to Super Growth: Open the Books," *PROFIT*, 2003, www.profitguide.com/profit100/2003/article.asp?ID=1265.
26. Richard A. Roberts, "Success Means Change," *Supervision*, 1 April 2005; and Dawn Sagario, "With a Plan, Delusional Office Slackers Can Be Put Back on Track," *Gannett News Service*, 30 June 2005.
27. Leonard Karakowsky and Sara L. Mann, "Setting Goals and Taking Ownership," *Journal of Leadership & Organizational Studies*, 1 February 2008.
28. Karen van Dam, "Employee Attitudes Toward Job Changes," *Journal of Occupational and Organizational Psychology*, 1 June 2005; and Goutam Challagalla, "Adapting Motivation, Control, and Compensation Research to a New Environment," *Journal of Personal Selling & Sales Management*, 22 March 2005.
29. Brian Horn, "Fast Lane," *Smart Business Detroit*, 1 March 2008.
30. David Nadler and Edward Lawler, "Motivation—A Diagnostic Approach," in *Perspectives on Behavior in Organizations* (New York: McGraw-Hill, 1977).
31. "B. F. Skinner," Wikimedia Foundation, Inc., 3 January 2009, http://en.wikipedia.org/wiki/B.F._Skinner.
32. Rebecca M. Chory-Assad, "Motivating Factors: Perceptions of Justice and Their Relationship with Managerial and Organizational Trust," *Communication Studies*, 1 March 2005; and Christine A. Henle, "Predicting Workplace Deviance from the Interaction Between Organizational Justice and Personality," *Journal of Managerial Issues*, 22 June 2005.
33. Dean B. McFarlin, "Wage Comparisons with Similar and Dissimilar Others," *Journal of Occupational and Organizational Psychology*, 1 March 2005; and Katherine Reynolds Lewis, "If You Think You're Underpaid, Think Again," *Post-Standard*, 18 January 2006.
34. Holly J. Payne, "Reconceptualizing Social Skills in Organizations: Exploring the Relationship Between Communication Competence, Job Performance, and Supervisory Roles," *Journal of Leadership & Organizational Studies*, 1 January 2005.
35. John E. Guiniven, "Making Employee Communication Work," *Journal of Employee Assistance*, 1 March 2005; Dean A. Hill, "Communication Strategy: Conquer the Hurdles That Are Inhibiting Dialogue with Your Employees," *Detroiter*, 1 January 2005; Mark Faircloth, "Eight Strategies for Building a Sales Culture," *Community Banker*, 1 August 2005; "Communications Q&A," *Pensions Management*, 1 August 2005; and Mark Henricks, "The Truth? Your Employees Can Handle It, So Just Communicate with Them, Already," *Entrepreneur*, 1 July 2005.
36. "Employer Review: Great Little Box Company Ltd., The," Eluta Inc., 2008, www.eluta.ca/top-employer-great-little-box-company.
37. Mila Stahl, "Listen Up!" *Wisconsin State Journal*, 1 April, 2008; and Ellen M. Heffes, "Communication with Staff: Morale-Lifter," *Financial Executive*, 1 January 2009.
38. Michael Nowicki and Jim Summers, "When Participative Management Leads to Garbled Communication," *Healthcare Financial Management*, 1 February 2008; and Erik Cassano, "Clear Communication," *Smart Business Indianapolis*, 1 January 2009.
39. Paula Ketter, "What's the Big Deal about Employee Engagement?" *Training and Development*, 1 January 2008.
40. Steven Cole Smith, "Copycat Auto Companies Bank on Pony Cars," *Pittsburgh Tribune-Review*, 17 May 2008.
41. "The Global Star Search," *Fortune*, 4 February 2008.
42. Joan Lloyd, "The Holy Grail of Motivation," *Minneapolis/St. Paul Business Journal*, 11 January 2008; and Melanie Scarborough, "The Rewards of Recognition: Six Strategies for Successful Employee Programs," *Community Banker*, 1 January 2009.
43. Jack Welch and Suzy Welch, "What's Hobbling the IRS," *BusinessWeek*, 15 September 2008; Kelly Spors, "Want to Retain Employees? Think Dogs and Free Lunch," *The Wall Street Journal*, 15 February 2009; Bob Nelson, "Find Simple Ways to Reward Employees to Get That Return on People," *Memphis Business Journal*, 18 January 2008; and Michelle Conlin, "Glum Chums? Call in the Happiness Police," *BusinessWeek*, 25 August 2008.
44. Paul Orfalea, "Ask *Inc.*," *Inc.*, June 2008.
45. Michael D. Hais and Morley Winograd, "The Boomers Had Their Day," *The Washington Post*, 3 February 2008; and Kathryn Tyler, "Generation Gaps," *HR Magazine*, 1 January 2008
46. David K. Foot, *Boom Bust & Echo 2000* (Toronto: Macfarlane Walter & Ross, 1998), 24–31.
47. Michael D. Hais and Morley Winograd, "The Boomers Had Their Day," *The Washington Post*, 3 February 2008; and Kathryn Tyler, "Generation Gaps," *HR Magazine*, 1 January 2008.
48. Tim Shaver, "Make the Workplace Fun to Retain Your Gen X, Y Workers," *Nashville Business Journal*, 28 March 2008; Anne Houlihan, "When Gen-X Is in Charge," *Supervision*, 1 April 2008; and Athima Chansanchai, "To Him, Gen X Still Marks the Spot," *Seattle Post-Intelligencer*, 9 April 2008.
49. Rebecca R. Hastings, "Millennials Expect a Lot from Leaders," *HR Magazine*, 1 January 2008; and "Generation Y Goes to Work," *The Economist*, 3 January 2009.
50. Colin Simpson, "A New Work Force Wave," *Bellingham Business Journal*, 1 June 2008; Kinglsey Kanu Jr. "Here's What I'm Looking For!" *Black Enterprise*, April 2008; and Kathryn Yeaton, "Recruiting and Managing the 'Why?' Generation," *CPA Journal*, 1 April 2008.
51. Robert Rodriquez, "Millennials on Board," *Fresno Bee*, 20 April 2008; and Mark Szakonyi, "Different Generations Require Different Feedback, Motivation," *Jacksonville Business Journal*, 4 January 2008.

Chapter 12

1. "Janice Wismer," *Canadian Business*, 2004, www.canadianbusiness.com/allstars/best_innovative_exec.html.
2. Deborah Aarts, "The lean growth machine," *PROFIT* Hot 50, 31 August 2012, www.profitguide.com/manage-grow/leadership/the-lean-growth-machine-30217; and Eleanor Beaton, "Built to scale," *PROFIT HOT* 50, 30 August 2011, www.profitguide.com/manage-grow/human-resources/built-to-scale-30204.
3. Deborah Aarts, "Canada's hottest startups," *PROFIT* HOT 50, 29 August 2011, www.profitguide.com/start/success-stories/canadas-hottest-startups-2-30197.
4. Erin White, "HR Departments Get New Star Power at Some Firms," *The Wall Street Journal*, 23 June 2008; and J. Bret Becton and Mike Schraeder,

"Strategic Human Resources Management: Are We There Yet?" *Journal for Quality and Participation*, 1 January 2009.

5. David Brown, "HR and the Workforce 10 Years from Now," *Canadian HR Reporter*, 20 October 2003, 2.
6. Susan Carr and Lydia Morris Brown, "People Perfect," *Business of Management*, http://learning.indiatimes.com/bm/features/books/book2.htm.
7. Matthew D. Breitfelder and Daisy Wademan Dowling, "Why Did We Ever Go into HR?" *Harvard Business Review*, July–August 2008; and Marcia A. Reed-Woodard, "The People Advantage: An HR Executive Employs a New Company Strategy," *Black Enterprise*, 1 February 2009.
8. Bill Berry, "Memo to Workers: You're on Your Own, Suckers," *Capital Times (Madison, WI)*, 10 June 2008; "Unionization Bill May Require HR to Hone Skills in Labor Relations," *Workforce Management*, 19 January 2009; Joel E. Anderson, "Help Wanted," *Arkansas Business*, 28 January 2008; Anton Troianovski, "Skilled Trades Seek Workers," *The Wall Street Journal*, 19 August 2008; Mark Anderson, "Workers Needed: Retiring Baby Boomers Will Leave Shortage of Skilled Trades People," *Wisconsin State Journal*, 3 August 2008; Gina Chen, "Faces of Fatherhood: These Dads Talk about Life as a Parent," *Post-Standard (Syracuse, NY)*, 15 June 2008; Maryann Tan, "Flexibility at Work on the Rise," *Financial Adviser*, 25 September 2008; Karen Springen, "Cutting Back Your Hours," *Newsweek*, 12 May 2008; Tara Weiss, "Layoff Lessons," *Forbes*, 9 September 2008; Joshua Zumbrun, "Help Wanted," *Forbes*, 27 March 2008; "What's New," Canadian Council of Human Resources Associations, 2008, www.cchra.ca/Web/CCHRA/content.aspx?f=29943; and Jean-Michel Caye, Andrew Dyer, Michael Leicht, Anna Minto, and Rainer Strack, Creating People Advantage: How to Address HR Challenges Worldwide Through 2015," The Boston Consulting Group, Inc. and World Federation of Personnel Management Associations, 14 April 2008, www.bcg.com/impact_expertise/publications/files/Creating_People_Advantage_Summary_May_2008.pdf.
9. Lee Froschheiser, "Business Recruitment Fundamentals: How to Onboard More 'A' Players," *Supervision Magazine*, 1 July 2008.
10. Elena Malykhina, "Supplying Labor to Meet Demand," *Informationweek*, 21 March 2005, 69–72.
11. Anthony R. Wheeler, "Post-Hire Human Resource Management Practices and Person-Organization Fit: A Study of Blue-Collar Employees," *Journal of Managerial Issues*, 22 March 2005.
12. "What to Do Now That Training Is Becoming a Major HR Force," *HR Focus*, 1 February 2005.
13. Alan Davis, "Calculating the Cost-per-Hire," CharityVillage Ltd., 14 January 2008, www.charityvillage.com/cv/research/rhr33.html
14. "Our Hiring Process," Cedar Fair Entertainment Company, 2009, www.canadaswonderland.com/jobs/jobs_benefits.cfm?et_id=1.
15. Liz Kislik, "A Hire Authority," *Catalog Age*, 1 April 2005; and "HR by Numbers: How to Hire the Right People and Then Lead Them to Success," *Prosales*, 1 January 2006.
16. Marcela Creps, "What Not to Ask Applicants at a Job Interview," *Bloomington (Indiana) Herald-Times*, 31 May 2005.
17. Tara Pepper, "Inside the Head of an Applicant," *Newsweek*, 21 February 2005; and "Personality Assessment Tests," PR Newswire, 12 April 2005.
18. David Hench, "Maine Overwhelmed as Background Checks Balloon," *Portland (Maine) Press Herald*, 18 April 2005; Carol Hymowitz, "Add Candidate's Character to Boards' Lists of Concerns," *The Wall Street Journal*, 17 March 2005; James Swann, "Guarding the Gates with Employee Background Checks," *Community Banker*, 1 August 2005; Carol Patton, "To Tell the Truth: It's an Institution's Duty to Ensure that New Hires Are Who They Say They Are," *University Business*, 1 January 2006; and Mary Jane Maytum, "Look a Little Closer: Investigators Say Employers Can Thwart Value of Background Checks; Some Should Dig Deeper," *Business First*, 27 January 2006.
19. "Reference Check: Is Your Boss Watching? Privacy and Your Facebook Profile," Office of the Information and Privacy Commissioner of Ontario, 2008, www.ipc.on.ca/images/Resources/up-facebook_refcheck.pdf.
20. Ibid.
21. Morey Stettner, "Select Top Job Candidates While Screening Out Duds," *Investors Business Daily*, 15 September 2008; and "Avoid Hiring That Bad Apple . . . ," *Credit Management*, 1 February 2009.
22. "9 Years on Contracts and No Full-Time Job in Sight," *Toronto Star*, 4 December 2008, www.thestar.com/News/GTA/article/548153.
23. Ibid.
24. Maria Mallory White, "Student Gives Temp Work 'A' Experience, Pay Found Rewarding," *Atlanta Journal and Constitution*, 14 July 2002, R1.
25. Alison Maitland, "Employers Nurse the Stress Bug," *Financial Times*, 19 April 2005, 12.
26. Robert Green, "Effective Training Programs: How to Design In-House Training on a Limited Budget," *CADalyst*, 1 March 2005; and Lynne M. Connelly, "Welcoming New Employees," *Journal of Nursing Scholarship*, 22 June 2005.
27. Patrick J. Sauer, "The Problem: Magnetech Wants to Triple Its Workforce," *Inc.*, January 2005, 38–39.
28. "Big Bite; American History," *The Economist*, 26 April 2008; and McDonald's, www.mcdonald's.com, accessed 17 February 2009.
29. Anthony Davis, "Sky High," *PROFIT Guide*, March 2004, www.profitguide.com/shared/print.jsp?content_20040213_171556_4580.
30. Julie Bird, "Proper Mentor Unlocks Mentee's Potential," *Charlotte Business Journal*, 14 March 2008; and Beth N. Carvin, "The Great Mentor Match," *T + D*, 1 January 2009.
31. John Worsley Simpson, "All Great Networkers Are Successful," *National Post*, 22 March 2006, WK5.
32. "The Puzzle of the Lost Women," *Financial Times*, 1 March 2005, 10.
33. "Networking Should Cross Ethnic Lines," *Orange County Register*, 18 August 2005; Dean Takahashi, "Ethnic Network Helps Immigrants Succeed," *The Wall Street Journal Interactive Edition*, 28 July 1999; and Benita Newton, "National Networking Event Makes Its Way to Virginia for First Time," Norfolk, (Virginia) *Virginian-Pilot*, 21 July 2005.
34. Anthony J. Kubica, "Transitioning Middle Managers," *Healthcare Executive*, 1 March 2008.
35. "Budget 2012—What Does it Mean for Women's Economic Equality?, Canadian Labour Congress, May 2012, www.canadianlabour.ca/news-room/publications/budget-2012-what-does-it-mean-women-s-economic-equality; "The Gender Wage Gap," Pay Equity Commission, 7 February 2012, www.payequity.gov.on.ca/en/about/pubs/genderwage/wagegap.php; "Women's Economic Equality Campaign," Canadian Labour Congress, 2009, www.canadianlabour.ca/en/womens_economic_equa; "Labour Force and Participation Rates by Sex and Age Group," Statistics Canada, 8 January 2009, http://www40.statcan.gc.ca/l01/cst01/labor05-eng.htm; "Status Report on Pay Equity Laws in Canada," Canadian Labour Congress, 10 November 2008, http://canadianlabour.ca/en/status-report-pay-equity-laws-canada;"Working Women: Still a Long Way from Equality," Canadian Labour Congress, 3 March 2008, http://canadianlabour.ca/sites/clc/files/updir/WorkingWomenEn.txt; "Pay Equity and Women in Canada," Canadian Feminist Alliance for International Action, 1 January 2007, www.fafia-afai.org/en/pay_equity_and_women_in_canada; and Colin Freeze, "Bell Settles Pay Equity Dispute," *The Globe and Mail*, 16 May 2006, A5.
36. Matt Botch, "Rewarding the Team: Make Sure Team-Oriented Compensation Plans Are Designed Carefully," *HR Magazine*, 1 February 2007.
37. Ibid.
38. Christine Larson, "Time Out," *U.S. News & World Report*, 28 February 2005; Lynda V. Mapes, "Two Local Companies Are Proving It Pays to Do Well by Workers," *Seattle Times*, 31 January 2005; Danielle Sacks, "Not the Retiring Sort," *Fast Company*, May 2005; and "Baby Boomer and Generation X Workers Agree When It Comes to Voluntary Benefits, Says Aon Consulting," PR Newswire, 31 January 2006.
39. Linda M. Byron, "Strategic Benefit Plan Design to Meet Demographic Change," *Canadian Benefits & Compensation Digest*, December 2008, 10.
40. Jim Pearse, "Premium Value," *Benefits Canada*, 1 May 2008, www.benefitscanada.com/benefit/health/article.jsp?content=20080529_110610_4324.
41. Hermann Schwind, Hari Das, and Terry Wagar, *Canadian Human Resource Management — A Strategic Approach*, 8th ed. (Toronto: McGraw-Hill Ryerson, 2007), 414.
42. Sarah Coles, "Canada's Crunch," *Employee Benefits*, January 2009, 28; and Brooke Smith, "Out of Reach," *Benefits Canada*, 23 May 2007, www.benefitscanada.com/benefit/health/article.jsp?content=20070523_150213_6320.
43. Michael Hayes, "Outrageous Employee Benefits," *Journal of Accountancy*, 1 May 2005.
44. Jeffrey M. O'Brien, Patricia Neering, and Christopher Tkaczyk, "100 Best Companies to Work for in 2008," *Fortune*, 4 February 2008.
45. Leah Carlson, "Businesses Decry Proposed Tax on Flex Benefits," *Employee Benefit News*, 1 May 2005.
46. Taylor Mallory, "May I Handle That for You? Companies That Will Take Payroll—and the Rest of the HR Department—Off Your Plate," *Inc.*, March 2008.
47. Colleen Diskin, "Flexible Schedules Can Pay Off for Employers, Too," *The Record (Bergen County, NJ)*, 28 May 2008.

48. Sarah Dougherty, "Flex Schedules Save Money," *Financial Post*, 3 May 2006, http://web.lexis-nexis.com/universe/.
49. "The Canadian Labour Market at a Glance: Alternative Work Arrangements," Statistics Canada, 25 November 2008, www.statcan.gc.ca/pub/71-222-x/2008001/sectionl/l-work-travail-eng.htm.
50. "Canadian Studies on Telework, etc." InnoVisions Canada, 2009, www.ivc.ca/studies/canada/index.htm; Sarah Dougherty, "Flex Schedules Save Money," *Financial Post*, 3 May 2006, http://web.lexis-nexis.com/universe/; Michelle Conlin, "Call Centers in the Rec Room," *BusinessWeek*, 23 January 2006; and InnoVisions Canada, "Telework: Recruitment, Retention and Jobs," InnoVisions Canada, 2006, www.ivc.ca/jobs/index.html.
51. Susan J. Wells, "Layoff Aftermath," *HR Magazine*, November 2008, 38.
52. Ibid.
53. "How New Style Exit Interviews Can Help You Reduce Turnover," *Human Resource Department Management Report*, 1 April 2005; Lee Conrad, "Hated Working Here? Log On and Vent," *Bank Technology News*, 1 April 2005; and Robert Half, "Enlightening Departures," *NZ Business*, 1 August 2005.
54. Uyen Vu, "What's Our Turnover Rate?" *Canadian HR Reporter*, 20 October 2003, 5.
55. Schwind, Das, and Wagar, *Canadian Human Resource Management*, 163.
56. "Employment Equity Act," Department of Justice Canada, 3 March 2006, http://laws.justice.gc.ca/en/E-5.401/238505.html#rid-238508.
57. "Top Court Rules Against N.B. Miner in Mandatory Retirement Case," CBC News, 18 July 2008, www.cbc.ca/canada/story/2008/07/18/scoc-retirement.html.
58. "Retiring Mandatory Retirement," CBC News Online, 9 December 2005, www.cbc.ca/news/background/retirement/mandatory_retirement.html.

Chapter 13

1. "Trade union," Wikipedia, 23 June 2012, http://en.wikipedia.org/wiki/Labor_union.
2. Kevin O'Marah, "The Real Threat to U.S. Manufacturing," *Forbes*, 23 April 23 2008; and Steven Greenhouse, "Union Membership Up Sharply in 2008, Report Says," *New York Times*, 29 January 2009.
3. Robert J. Samuelson, "Globalization's Achilles' Heel," *Newsweek*, 21 July 2008.
4. Gerry Varricchio, Director of Organizing for Central and Eastern Canada for the Labourers' International Union of North America (LIUNA), interview, 16 February 2009.
5. Ibid.
6. Steve Elbow, "State Responds to Report Alleging Sweatshop Contracts," *Capital Times (Madison, WI)*, 1 July 2008; and Alec MacGillis, "Troubles in Service Workers' Union May Dim Hopes for Labor," *The Washington Post*, 9 January 2009.
7. Marlon Manuel, "Warped Speed: Where Has All the Time Gone?" *Atlanta Journal and Constitution*, 12 May 2002, A1.
8. "Labour Unions," Statistics Canada, 19 March 2004, http://142.206.72.67/02/02e/02e_011_e.htm.
9. "Union Centrals, National," The Canadian Encyclopedia, 2006, www.thecanadianencyclopedia.com/index.cfm?PgNm=TCE&Params=A1ARTA0008214.
10. Ibid.
11. "5.8 unemployed workers for every job vacancy: Georgetti says government has no job creation strategy," Canadian Labour Congress, 21 June 2012, www.canadianlabour.ca/national/news/58-unemployed-workers-every-job-vacancy-georgetti-says-government-has-no-job-creation-.
12. "Social and Economic Issues," Canadian Labour Congress, 2009, www.canadianlabour.ca/issues/social-and-economic-issues.
13. Sharanjit Uppal, "Unionization 2011," Statistics Canada, 26 October 2011, www.statcan.gc.ca/pub/75-001-x/2011004/article/11579-eng.pdf.
14. D.W. Livingston and M. Raykov, "Union Influence on Worker Education and Training in Canada in Tough Times," *Just Labour*, Vol. 5 (Winter 2005), www.justlabour.yorku.ca/Livingstone_Raykov.pdf.
15. "Welcome to Canada's Largest Union," Canadian Union of Public Employees, 2012, http://cupe.ca/about/Welcome_to_Canadas_l.
16. "Merger creates largest private-sector union," The Canadian Press, 21 October 2012, http://www.ottawacitizen.com/jobs/Merger+creates+largest+privatesector+union/7423138/story.html. "About the CAW," Canadian Auto Workers, 2012, www.caw.ca/en/about-the-caw.htm; and "Facts," Canadian Auto Workers, 2012, www.caw.ca/en/media-centre-facts.htm.
17. "Over 1,000 Canadian Workers Die Each Year Due to an Unsafe Workplace," The Canadian Labour Congress, 27 April 2009, http://canadianlabour.ca/en/canadian-labour-congress-action-centre/over-1000-canadian-workers-die-each-year-due-unsafe-workplace; Speech at the National Day of Mourning Ceremony in Halifax, The Canadian Labour Congress, 28 April 2010, www.canadianlabour.ca/news-room/speeches/speech-national-day-mourning-ceremony-halifax; "Safe Workplaces: The Right to a Safe and Healthy Workplace," Workrights.ca, www.workrights.ca/Health+and+Safety/Safe+Workplaces.htm; "Workplace Dangers (Right to Know About Workplace Dangers)," Workrights.ca, www.workrights.ca/Health+and+Safety/Workplace+dangers.htm; and "Life Is Cheap at Wal-Mart: Company Orders 40 Employees to Search for a Bomb," United Food and Commercial Workers Canada., 11 July 2006, www.ufcw.ca/Default.aspx?SectionId=af80f8cf-ddd2-4b12-9f41-641ea94d4fa4&LanguageId=1&ItemId=d11797a6-5cc1-4a82-ac07-ccb922d6fa83.
18. "The Board's Role," Canada Industrial Relations Board, 23 October 2003, /www.cirb-ccri.gc.ca/about/role_e.html.
19. Varricchio, interview, 16 February 2009.
20. Ibid.
21. Emily Jackson, "FedEx delivery guy wasn't. So, what does it take to get fired?" The Star.com, 22 December 2011, www.thestar.com/business/article/1105633--fedex-delivery-guy-wasn-t-so-what-does-it-take-to-get-fired; and Aaron Rousseau, Lawyer, Whitten & Lublin, interview, 27 June 2012.
22. "What is Conciliation?" Government of Ontario, 27 September 2005, www.labour.gov.on.ca/english/lr/faq/lr_faq2.html.
23. Ibid.
24. "National Mediation Board Puts UPS Talks with IPA in Recess," Business Wire, 23 June 2005; and Paul Monies, "Settlements Offered in DHL-Teamsters Dispute," *Daily Oklahoman*, 6 January 2006.
25. "N.W.T. Power Employees Holding Strike Vote," CBC News, 6 April 2006, www.cbc.ca/north/story/nor-power-mediation.html.
26. "Arbitration award for flight attendants profoundly disappointing: Moist," Canadian Union of Public Employees, 7 November 2011, http://cupe.ca/airlines/arbitration-award-flight-attendants.
27. "Essential Services," CBC News, 6 May 2008, www.cbc.ca/news/background/strike/.
28. New ads ask Air Canada to offer a fair deal and avoid a strike," Canadian Union of Public Employees, 17 September 2011, http://cupe.ca/air-canada/ads-air-canada-offer-fair-deal-avoid.
29. David Doorey, "On Strikes, Replacement Workers, and Back-to-Work Legislation," Doorey's Workplace Law Blog, 15 June 2011, www.yorku.ca/ddoorey/lawblog/?p=3431.
30. "Definition—Wildcat Strike," WebFinance Inc., 2005, www.investorwords.com/5316/wildcat_strike.html.
31. Tavia Grant, "TTC Strike Could Cost Toronto," *The Globe and Mail*, 29 May 2006, www.theglobeandmail.com/servlet/story/RTGAM.20060529.wttceco0529/BNStory/Business/home; and "TTC Strike Is Over, but More Trouble Could Lie Ahead," CBC News, 30 May 2006, www.cbc.ca/toronto/story/toTTCstrike0060530.html.
32. "Boycott Pepsi, Strikers Tell Consumers," CBC News, 30 May 2006, www.cbc.ca/nl/story/nf-pepsi-strike-20060530.html.
33. "Strikes and Lockouts," The Canadian Encyclopedia, 2006, www.thecanadianencyclopedia.com/index.cfm?PgNm=TCE&Params=J1ARTJ0007754; and "Telus Workers Launch Work-to-Rule," CBC News, 20 June 2005, www.cbc.ca/story/business/national/2005/06/20/telus-050620.html.
34. "2011 NBA lockout," Wikipedia, 24 June 2012, http://en.wikipedia.org/wiki/2011_NBA_lockout.
35. "Essential Services Legislation Undermines Public Education," British Columbia Teachers' Federation, www.bctf.ca/bargain/rights/EssentialServices.html.
36. "Back-to-Work Legislation: When Negotiations Fail," CBC News Online, 13 October 2005, www.cbc.ca/news/background/strike/backtowork.html.
37. "CAW Reaches Pension Funding Agreement with Air Canada," Canadian Auto Workers, 19 February 2004, www.caw.ca/news/newsnow/news.asp?art10_369.
38. "Ontario Legislature Ends York University Strike," CBC News, 29 January 2009, www.cbc.ca/canada/toronto/story/2009/01/29/york-strike.html.
39. Ibid.
40. Charley Reese, "Free-Market Economies Are Killing Unions," *Columbia Daily Tribune*, 18 July 2008.
41. Allan Swift, "Storm Gathers over Sky-High Compensation for Top Air Canada Executives," *Canoe*, 16 November 2003, http://money.canoe.ca/News/Sectors/Consumer/AirCanada/2003/11/16/pdf-259744.html; Norm Brodsky, "Why the Union Can't Win," *Inc.*, March 2005, 55–56; and James Cowan, "Can Air Canada be saved?" *Canadian Business*, 27 April 2012, http://ca.finance.yahoo.com/news/air-canada-saved-160000769.html.
42. Joseph S. Mancinelli, International Vice-President for Central and Eastern Canada for the Labourers' International Union of North America (LIUNA), interview, 16 February 2009.

43. "Meet 5 of Canada's highest paid executives," *The Globe and Mail*, 8 June 2012, www.theglobeandmail.com/report-on-business/careers/management/executive-compensation/meet-5-of-canadas-highest-paid-executives/article4242570/#gallery_1752=2.
44. "Loblaw Executives Forgo 2005 Bonuses," *The Globe and Mail*, 18 March 2006, B3.
45. John Cassidy, "The C.E.O.'s New Armor," *Condé Nast Portfolio*, June 2008.
46. Carol Hymowitz, "Pay Gap Fuels Worker Woes," *The Wall Street Journal*, 28 April 2008; and Chuck Collins, "Put a Cap on Runaway CEO Pay," *The Record (Bergen County, NJ)*, 4 February 2009.
47. CEOs vs the 99%: No contest when it comes to pay," Canadian Centre for Policy Alternatives, 3 January 2012, www.policyalternatives.ca/newsroom/news-releases/ceos-vs-99-no-contest-when-it-comes-pay.
48. Pay Attention," *The Economist*, 14 June 14, 2008; and "Let the Fight Begin," *The Economist*, 14 June 2008.
49. Mark Gongloff and Craig Karmin, "Shareholders Bring the Heat on Executive Pay," *The Wall Street Journal*, 8 April 2008.
50. Ann Merrill, "General Mills Lauded for Aid to Working Mothers," *Minneapolis Star Tribune*, 24 September 2002, 1D.
51. Laura Koss-Feder, "Providing for Parents the 'Sandwich Generation' Looks for New Solutions," *Time*, 17 March 2003, G8.
52. Stephen Barr, "Elder Care Becoming Major Issue for Many Workers," *Washington Post*, 20 August 2002, B2.

Chapter 14

1. "Definition of Marketing," Canadian Marketing Association, 2012, www.the-cma.org/regulatory/code-of-ethics.
2. John Q. Quelch and Katherine E. Jocz, "Marketing, Much Like Democracy, Is Good for You (Yes, Really)," *Advertising Age*, 11 February 2008; and the American Marketing Association's Marketing Power, www.marketingpower.com, accessed February 2009.
3. Michael S. Malone, "Taking On the World," *The Wall Street Journal*, 5–6 April, 2008.
4. Karen J. Bannan, "10 Great Websites," *BtoB*, 15 September 2008.
5. Michael Rubincam, "Marketing Matriculation," *The Washington Times*, 1 May 2008.
6. Rachael King, "Go Ahead, Use Facebook," *BusinessWeek*, 1 September 2008.
7. A good place to start learning about these new tools and reading how they are applied can be found in Sandy Carter, *The New Language of Marketing 2.0* (New York: IBM Press, 2009).
8. Ian Schafer, "We Better Start Monetizing Social Media Before It's Too Late," *Advertising Age*, 5 May 2008.
9. A. G. Lafley and Ram Charan, "The Consumer Is Boss," *Fortune*, 17 March 2008.
10. Ryan Charkow, "5 young Canadian entrepreneurs reveal secrets to success," CBC News, 6 October 2011, www.cbc.ca/news/business/smallbusiness/story/2011/09/28/f-smallbiz-young-entrepreneurs.html.
11. Mark Johnson and Joe Sinfield, "Focusing on Consumer Needs Is Not Enough," *Advertising Age*, 28 April 2008.
12. Frederick G. Crane et al., *Marketing*, 8th Canadian ed. (Toronto: McGrawHill Ryerson, 2011), 15–16.
13. Ibid., 18; "Social Media Marketing Quick-Start Guide," Canadian Marketing Association, 19 July 2011, www.the-cma.org/Media/Default/Downloads/Library/2011/SocialMediaQSG.pdf; "blogYOUR TAKE/Mobile spa relies 100% on social media," CBC News, 17 October 2011, www.cbc.ca/news/business/smallbusiness/story/2011/10/17/small-business-your-take-blog-goertzen.html; "Social Media Revolution 2012, YouTube.com, 2012, www.youtube.com/watch?v=ZQzsQkMFgHE; and Erik Qualman, *Socialnomics* (New York: Wiley, 2009).
14. Steve Harding, Executive Director of Marketing and Communications, Canadian Blood Services, interview, 26 June 2006.
15. Steve Garmhausen, "Growing a Green Business," *Black Enterprise*, April 2008.
16. Emily Bryson York, "College Students Demand 'Organic' Fare," *Advertising Age*, 18 February 2008.
17. Melanie Dabovich, "Farm Fertilizers Go Green," *The Washington Times*, 20 June 2008.
18. Ali McConnon, "No Bird in This Bucket," *BusinessWeek*, 7 July 2008.
19. Paola Singer, "'Vegetarians Have a Stake in Buenos Aires," *The Washington Post*, 18 May 2008.
20. Crane et al., *Marketing*, 8th Canadian ed., 312.
21. Ibid., 309.
22. Eve Conant, "Branding for Beginners," *Newsweek*, 17 March, 2008.
23. Crane et al., *Marketing*, 8th Canadian ed., 332.
24. Jack Ewing, "Mad Dash for the Low End," *BusinessWeek*, 18 February 2008.
25. Geoff Colvin, "For Some Businesses, the Higher Price Is Right," *The Washington Post*, 10 February 2009.
26. Heather Clancy, "Web Sight Shipping 2.0," *Entrepreneur*, April 2008.
27. Mary E. Morrison, "Relationships Pay Dividends," *BtoB's Vertical Insight Guide*, 2008.
28. Maxine Clark, "Is the Customer Always Right?" *Inc.*, July 2008.
29. "Marketers Lag in Tracking Customers," *BtoB*, 9 February 2009.
30. Crane et al., *Marketing*, 8th Canadian ed., 214.
31. Ibid.
32. "Lululemon's Secret Sauce," *The Wall Street Journal*, 22 March 2012, http://online.wsj.com/article/SB10001424052702303812904577295882632723066.html.
33. Jack Neff, "Making Market Research Cool," *Advertising Age*, 28 April 2008.
34. Matthew Bandyk, "Now Even Small Firms Can Go Global," *U.S. News & World Report*, 10 March 2008.
35. Louis Jones, "What You Need to Know about Social Networks," *Kiplinger's Personal Finance*, March 2009.
36. Lynda Hurst, "How the Boomers Will Go Bust," *Toronto Star*, 23 September 2000, A20.
37. "Kidfluence," YTV Media, 2008, www.corusmedia.com/ytv/research/index.asp#TWEEN.
38. Steve Buist, "Great Glasses Appeal Dismissed by Supreme Court of Canada," *The Burlington Post*, 17 June 2009, www.burlingtonpost.com/news/article/261941; and "CRTC opens North to local phone competition," CBC News, 14 December 2011, www.cbc.ca/news/canada/north/story/2011/12/14/north-crtc-local-phone.html.
39. Steve Hamm, "An eBay for Business Software," *BusinessWeek*, 19 September 2005, 78–79.
40. "Current World Population," Worldometers, 2012, www.worldometers.info/world-population/.
41. Rebecca Harris, "HEINZ DOES IT UP," *Marketing Magazine*, 7 May 2012, 38.
42. "Campbell Canada launches Nourish in response to growing hunger issue here and abroad," CNW Group, 28 February 2011, http://smr.newswire.ca/en/campbell-company-of-canada/campbell-canada-launches-nourish.
43. Eve Lazarus, "B.C. Lions Brew Up New Brand Extension," *Marketing Magazine*, 27 August 2008, www.marketingmag.ca/english/news/marketer/article.jsp?content=20080827_145922_31268.
44. Ibid.
45. Omar El Akkad, "For HSBC, It's All About Location," *The Globe and Mail*, 6 May 2006, B3.
46. Crane et al., *Marketing*, 8th Canadian ed., 237.
47. "Shoppers Moves to Localize Merchandise, Boost Marketing," *The Globe and Mail*, 2 May 2006, B10.
48. Paul Brent, "The Best of '08 Media Players: Transcontinental Media," *Marketing Magazine*, 24 November 2008, www.marketingmag.ca/english/news/media/article.jsp?content=20081218_110059_17612.
49. Anita Elberse, "Should You Invest in the Long Tail?" *Harvard Business Review*, July–August 2008.
50. Susan Greco, "A World without Bestsellers: Creating a 'Long Tail' Product Mix," *Inc.*, September 2007.
51. "G adventures named Canada's favourite adventure travel tour operator," G Adventures, 28 Jun 2012, www.gadventures.com/press-releases/2012/Jun/28/g-adventures-named-canadas-favourite-adventure-travel-tour-operator/.
52. "LEGENDS OF THE SMALL," Report on Small Business, *The Globe and Mail*, June 2012, 17.
53. "Why Travel with G Adventures?" G Adventures, 2012, www.gadventures.com/about-us/why-travel-with-gadventures/.
54. Crane et al., *Marketing*, 8th Canadian ed., 81.
55. Ibid., 81–83.
56. Ibid., 139.
57. Richard J. Harrington and Anthony K. Tjan, "Transforming Strategy One Customer at a Time," *Harvard Business Review*, March 2008.
58. Mary E. Morrison, "Industrial Buyers Shopping Online," *BtoB*, 13 October 13, 2008.
59. "B2B study: Social marketing pervasive, LinkedIn most important," Canadian Marketing Association, 11 April 2011, www.the-cma.org/resource/newsletters/b2b/data-issues-augmented-reality-social-media.

Chapter 15

1. Emily Bryson York, "McD's Secret Sauce: It Embodies Value," *Advertising Age*, 2 February 2009.
2. A. G. Lafley and Ram Charan, "The Consumer Is Boss," *Fortune*, 17 March 2008.
3. Paul Taylor, "Can There Be Any Future for Traditional Telephony?" *Financial Times*, 22 February 2006, 1.
4. "9 Stellar Examples of the Unintended Use of Products," *Printwand*, 2012, www.printwand.com/blog/9-stellar-examples-of-the-unintended-use-of-products.
5. Richard S. Tedlow, "Leaders in Denial," *Harvard Business Review*, July–August 2008.
6. Christopher Palmeri and Nanette Byrnes, "Code and Pepsi Try Reinventing Water," *BusinessWeek*, 2 March 2009.
7. Thomas Pyzdek, "What Does Your Customer Expect?" *Quality Digest*, July 2008.
8. Jeremy Caplan, "Spice Girls," *Time*, 14 July 2008.
9. Erica Westley, "A Printed Silicon Chip," *Inc.*, February 2009.
10. Jane Stevenson, "Use Merchandising to Build Brand and Attract Consumers," *Advertising Age*, 25 February 2008.
11. Eric Swetsky, "Barbie's Rule," *Marketing Magazine*, 3 July 2006, www.marketingmag.ca/magazine/current/top_mind/article.jsp?content=20060703_68651_68651.
12. "No Apple for Vancouver Island School, Says Computer Corporation," CBC News, 6 October 2008, www.cbc.ca/technology/story/2008/10/06/bc-school-apple-logo.html.
13. Betsy D. Gelb and Partha Krishnamurthy, "Protect Your Product's Look and Feel from Imitators," *Harvard Business Review*, October 2008.
14. Keith Goldberg, "How You Can Stay in Control of Your Brand's Reputation," *Advertising Age*, 9 February 2009.
15. Hollie Shaw, "Canadian Tire starts driving school," *National Post*, 22 June 2012, FP5.
16. Daniel Tencer, "Top Canadian Brands 2012: Brand Finance Survey Shows Banking and Finance Companies Dominate," The Huffington Post Canada, 23 July 2012, http://www.huffingtonpost.ca/2012/07/22/top-canadian-brands-2012-_n_1693192.html#anyword.
17. Heather Green and Kerry Capell, "Carbon Confusion," *BusinessWeek*, 17 March 2008.
18. Akhila Vijayaraghavan, "Puma, Nike and Adidas Run Towards Toxin-Free Products With Greenpeace," Triple Pundit, com, 7 September 2011, www.triplepundit.com/2011/09/puma-nike-adidas-greenpeace/.
19. Ibid.
20. Daniel Tencer, "Top Canadian Brands 2012: Brand Finance Survey Shows Banking And Finance Companies Dominate," The Huffington Post Canada, 23 July 2012, http://www.huffingtonpost.ca/2012/07/22/top-canadian-brands-2012-_n_1693192.html#anyword.
21. "IBM to Sell PC Unit: Report," CBC News, 3 December 2004, www.cbc.ca/money/story/2004/12/03/ibm-sale041203.html.
22. Brent Jang, "Air Canada Goes Off the Bottle," *The Globe and Mail*, 20 April 2006, A6.
23. "Nintendo GameCube Set at Mass Market Price of $199.95," Encyclopedia.com, 21 May 2001, www.encyclopedia.com/doc/1G1-74824260.html; and "Dedicated Gameplay System Launches November 5, 2001, with Six First-Party Titles Prices at $49.95," Nintendo of America, *Inc.*, 21 May 2001, www.nintendoworldreport.com/newsArt.cfm?artid=5963.
24. Jennifer Hoyt, "99-Cent-Only Stores Find Wiggle Room on Pricing," *The Wall Street Journal*, 10 September 2008; and Jeoff Colvin, "Yes, You Can Raise Prices," *Fortune*, 2 March 2009.
25. Sandra Fleishman, "Maybe Not a 000-Sum Game," *The Washington Post*, 16 February 2008.
26. Jonathan Clements, "Price Fixing: In This Market, Selling a Home Requires Savvy," *The Wall Street Journal*, 27 February 2008.
27. Suzanne Kapner, "Wal-Mart Puts the Squeeze on Food Costs," *Fortune*, 9 June 2008.
28. Kyle Cattani, Hans Sebastian Heese, Wendell Gilland, and Jayashankar Swaminathan, "When Manufacturers Go Retail," *MIT Sloan Management Review*, Winter 2006, 9.
29. Daniel Nissanoff, "Futureshop," *Fast Company*, January–February 2006, 103.
30. "Retail Trade, by Industry," Statistics Canada, 21 June 2012, www.statcan.gc.ca/tables-tableaux/sum-som/l01/cst01/trad15a-eng.htm; and "Employment, Payroll Employment, by Industry (Retail Trade)," Statistics Canada, 30 March 2012, www.statcan.gc.ca/tables-tableaux/sum-som/l01/cst01/labr71a-eng.htm.
32. Sarah Schmidt, "'Do Not Call List' Has Telemarketers Worried About Hackers Eliminating Entire Phone Book, *The Vancouver Sun*, 19 March 2008, http://www.canada.com/vancouversun/news/story.html?id=5c2c11b6-6fa3-470f-8351-c4291cbf57fa.
33. "National Do Not Call List," Canadian Radio-television and Telecommunications Commission, 22 November 2008, https://www.lnnte-dncl.gc.ca/insnum-regnum-eng; and "Telemarketers to pony up cost of Do Not Call," The Canadian Press, 29 April 2012.
34. Ali McConnon, "Vending Machines Go Luxe," *Business-Week*, 28 January 2008.
35. Matt Hartley, "Samsung has big retail plans for Canada," *National Post*, 3 April 2012, FP3.
36. Ibid.
37. Leslie Laredo, "How Older Pros Can Transition to Digital," *Advertising Age*, 24 March 2008.
38. "Behind the Scenes," Rubicon Consulting, 2 March 2007, http://rubiconconsulting.com/nilofer/view/2007/03/3000-marketing-messages-per-da/.
39. "GroupM's latest Canadian and global ad spend forecast released," *Marketing Magazine*, 19 July 2012, www.marketingmag.ca/news/marketer-news/groupms-latest-canadian-and-global-ad-spend-forecast-released-57663.
40. Jeffrey F. Rayport, "Where Is Advertising Going? Into 'Stitals,'" *Harvard Business Review*, May 2008.
41. Lena H. Sun, "Captivating an Audience," *The Washington Post*, 6 April 2008.
42. "Kraft Provides Recipe for Mobile-Marketing Success," *Advertising Age*, 26 January 2009.
43. Karen J. Bannan, "E-Mail Marketing Includes Placing Ads When Needed," *BtoB's E-Mail Marketer Insight Guide*, 2008.
44. Barry Farber, "Good Connections," *Entrepreneur*, January 2009.
45. Clark S. Judge, "PR Lessons from the Pentagon," *The Wall Street Journal*, 1 April 2003, B2.
46. Sean Callahan, "Marketers Stay in the Conversation with PR," *BtoB*, 9 February 2009.
47. Paul Gillin, "New PR Reality: Link over Inc," *BtoB*, 9 March 2009.
48. Karen J. Bannan, "Objectworld Shifts from Trade Shows to Webinars," *BtoB*, 13 October 2008.
49. Frederick G. Crane et al., *Marketing*, 8th Canadian ed. (Toronto: McGraw-Hill Ryerson, 2011), 434.
50. Ibid., 135–136; and Heather Clancy, "Tell It to Me Straight," *Entrepreneurship*, June 2008.
51. Eric Tegler, "Ford Is Counting on Army of 100 Bloggers to Launch New Fiesta," *Advertising Age*, 20 April 2009.
52. Alice Z. Cuneo, "So Just What Is Mobile Marketing?" *Advertising Age*, 17 March 2008.
53. Alice Z. Cuneo, "Mobile Marketing Based on Place Is Finally Making Strides," *Advertising Age*, 31 March 2008.

Chapter 16

1. Norm Brodsky, "Our Irrational Fear of Numbers," *Inc.*, January–February 2009.
2. Clinton B. Douglas and Angella Sutthiwan, "The Conflicting Roles of Controllership and Compliance," *Strategic Finance*, 1 July, 2008.
3. Matthew Goldstein, "Stanford: Where Was the SEC?" *BusinessWeek*, 2 March 2009.
4. Michael Connor, "Accountants Group Sees Continued Role," *Reuters Business*, 20 March 2003.
5. David Henry, "The Business Week 50: Investing for Growth: Cleaning Up the Numbers," *Business Week*, 25 March 2003, 126.
6. David Henry and Robert Berner, "Finance: Accounting: Ouch! Real Numbers," *Business Week*, 24 March 2003, 72.
7. Greg Farrell, "CPAs Look for an Ad Agency to Rebuild Images," *USA Today*, 26 February 2003, 2B.
8. Elizabeth MacDonald, "Figures Don't Lie, But Liars Figure," *Forbes*, 14 March 2007; "Accountant and S.E.C. Reach Deal in Enron Case," *Reuters*, 29 January 2008; and "New York's Closer Scrutiny of CPAs," *Practical Accountant*, 1 February 2009.
9. J. Bonasia, "Deloitte Going Against the Grain in 'Mixing' Accounting, Consulting," *Investors Business Daily*, 24 February 2005, A4.
10. Steve Hamm, "Death, Taxes, & Sarbanes-Oxley," *BusinessWeek*, 17 January 2005, 28–32; and Terence O'Hara, "Excavations in Accounting; To Monitor Internal Controls, Firms Dig Ever Deeper into Their Books," *Washington Post*, 30 January 2006.

11. "Become a CGA," CGA-Canada, www.cga-canada.org/eng/designation/cga-become.htm.
12. Randy Johnston, "Management & Compliance: Accounting Software Is Morphing to Business Management Software," *CPA Technology Advisor*, 1 August 2005.
13. Richard Moroshove, "The Right FIT," *CA Magazine*, 1 March 2008.
14. Danielle Kost, "What's the Best Way to Prepare Returns: Accountant or Software?" *Boston Globe*, 16 March 2008.
15. David Whelan, "Beyond the Balance Sheet: Hot Brand Values," *Forbes*, 20 June 2005, 113–15.
16. Kenneth Dogra, "Accounting for Goodwill: Why Are Firms Willing to Pay So Much for Takeovers When the Goodwill Burden Is Onerous?" *Financial Management*, 1 May 2005; and Greg Paeth, "Scripps Weighs Sale of Channel," *Cincinnati Post*, 3 February 2006.
17. Virginia Munger Kahn, "Beating the Cash Crunch," *BusinessWeek Small Biz*, Spring 2005; Kenneth L. Parkinson, "Cash Flow Forecasting: Do It Better and Save," *Financial Executive*, 1 January 2006; and John S. McClenahen and Traci Purdum, "Cash Flow Is King," *Industry Week*, 1 February 2006.
18. "Warning! How to Tell if You Are Having Cash Flow Problems Before It's Too Late," Visa Canada, www.visa.ca/smallbusiness/article.cfm?cat_3&subcat_95&articleID_101.
19. John C. Woosley, "Deductions Can Boost Small-Biz Cash Flow," *New Mexico Business Weekly*, 27 June 2008.
20. Nadia Chlala and Andree Lavigne, "Seven Key Differences", www.camagazine.com/archives/print-edition/2009/june-july/features/camagazine19845.aspx.
21. Mike McNamee, "Finance: Annual Reports: Still Not Enough Candor," *Business Week*, 24 March 2003, 74.
22. Sativa Ross, "All in the Numbers: Does Your Income Statement and Balance Sheet Provide a Winning Combination?" *Aftermarket Business*, 1 May 2005.
23. Tom Judge, "Liquidity Ratio Can Help Spot Cash Gap," *Powersports Business*, 14 March 2005.
24. "The Investor Professor," *American Association of Individual Investors Journal*, August 2007.
25. Ellen Depasquale, "Managing Inventory for Profitability," Inc.com, 22 January 2008.

Chapter 17

1. Andre de Haan, "Time for CFOs to Lead," *CA Magazine*, 1 August 2008.
2. Louise Mawhinney, "Working with Your CFO," *Research-Technology Management*, 1 July 2007.
3. "Targeted Assistance for the Automotive Sector (Budget 2009 and Budget 2010), www.actionplan.gc.ca./initiatives/eng/index.asp?initiativeID=179&mode=3.
4. Kimberly Palmer, "Learning the Tricks of Managing Money," *U.S. News & World Report*, 19 May 2008.
5. Carol Tice, "It's Now or Never," *Entrepreneur*, August 2008; and Jessica Marquez, "A Master Financial Plan; Special Report: Pension & Retirement Benefits," *Workforce Management*, 19 January 2009.
6. Sue Asci, "Taxes on the Mind," *Investment News*, 25 August 2008.
7. John Cummings, "10 Best Practices for Co-Sourcing Internal Audit," *Business Finance*, 1 July 2008.
8. Gary McWilliams, "Dell Puts Cash Flow to Work," *The Wall Street Journal*, 25 April 2005, C3.
9. Michael Hunstad, "Better Forecasting: Know Your Cash Flows," *Financial Executive*, 1 May 2005; and Kenneth L. Parkinson, "Cash Flow Forecasting: Do It Better and Save," *Financial Executive*, 1 January 2006.
10. Patrick Kilts, "Effective Cash Flow Management Improves Investment Outlook," *Crain's Cleveland Business*, 19 September 2005; Bruce Perryman, "Grow with the Flow," *Stitches Magazine*, 1 January 2005; and Andi Gray, "The Optimum Growth Model," *Fairfield County Business Journal*, 30 January 2006.
11. Kathy Williams, "What Are Your Budget Headaches?" *Strategic Finance*, 1 January 2008; and "U.S. Bancorp Asks Managers to Trim Budgets," *Business First of Louisville*, 9 February 2009.
12. Jordan I. Shifrin, "All Boards Must Grapple with Budget Issues," *Daily Herald*, 4 June 2005.
13. Charles Mulford, "A Best Practices Approach to Cash Flow Reporting: Implications for Analysis," *Business Credit*, 1 January 2005.
14. Ellen Simon, "Oil's Climb Forced Companies to Become Leaner," AP Online, 4 September 2008.
15. Tom Grandy, "The Law of Money: Grab That Cash with Both Hands and Make a Stash," *Reeves Journal*, 1 April 2008.
16. Anne Tergesen, "Cash-Flow Hocus-Pocus," *BusinessWeek*, 16 July 2002, 130–32.
17. Paul Katzeff, "Manage Accounts Receivable Upfront Before There's a Problem," *Investors Business Daily*, 27 January 2003, A4.
18. Krissah Williams Washington, "How Stores Play Their Cards: They'll Give Discounts and Awards to Get Interest and Bigger Sales," *Washington Post*, 2 February 2003, H5.
19. Linda Stern, "Credit Card Issuers Offer Some Good Deals," *Reuters Business*, 1 March 2003.
20. "The Basics of Balance Sheets," www.inc.com, accessed 21 January, 2009.
21. Nelson Wang, "Finance Keeps Cranking Away," *CFO*, February 2009.
22. Susan C. Thompson, "Mixing Personal, Business Funds Is a Formula for Bankruptcy," *St. Louis Post-Dispatch*, 5 August 2005; and Carolyn M. Brown, "Borrowing from Dad: Financing from Relatives and Friends Has Risks and Rewards," *Black Enterprise*, 1 January 2005.
23. National Federation of Independent Businesses, www.nfib.com, accessed 24 February 2009.
24. Kate Ashford, "Lend to a Friend (Without Regret): Four Things to Do When a Pal Asks for a Loan," *Money*, 1 November 2005.
25. John M. Berry, "Low Interest Rates Are Allowing Corporations to Boost Profit," *Washington Post*, 19 April 2003, D12.
26. "CIT Group Provides Line of Credit to CHF Industries," Business Wire, 7 May 2008.
27. Donald J. Korn, "Good to Get," Black Enterprise.com, accessed March 2009.
28. C. J. Prince, "Currency New Money," *Entrepreneur*, March 2008.
29. Aliza Earnshaw, "Businesses Turn to Factoring to Counter Cash Crunch," *Portland Business Journal*, 27 June 2008.
30. Kelly K. Spors and Simona Covel, "Slow Payments Squeeze Small-Business Owners," *The Wall Street Journal*, 31 October 2008.
31. Toni Clarke and Jed Stelzer, "Merck Profit Rises on Higher Drug Sales," *Reuters Business*, 21 April 2003.
32. Jean Ende, "Card Issuers Charge After Owners," *Crain's New York Business*, 18 July 2005.
33. Amy Barrett, "Pfizer's Funk," *BusinessWeek*, 28 February 2005; and Jennifer Bayot, "Pfizer's Pain Inflamed by Weak Sales," *International Herald Tribune*, 6 April 2005.
34. The Canadian Securities Course 1993 (Toronto: The Canadian Securities Institute, 1992), 63.
35. Will Oremus, "Facebook to Move in Early 2009," *Oakland Tribune*, 5 September 2008; and Evan Hessel, "Venture's New Grail," *Forbes*, 16 February 2009.
36. Justin Fox, "Show Us the Money," *Fortune*, 3 February 2003, 76–78.
37. Walter Updegrave, "Dividend Mania, What the Bush Dividend Plan Would Really Mean for You," *Money*, 1 March 2003, 69–74.
38. "The Preferred Route to Income Preferred Stocks Offer the Most Sumptuous Dividend Payments Around," *Money*, 1 March 2003, 54B.
39. Michael Barbaro, "Primus Agrees to Sell Convertible Preferred Stock," *Washington Post*, 1 January 2003, E5.

Appendix D

1. Nitin Nohria, "Risk, Uncertainty, and Doubt," *Harvard Business Review*, February 2006, 39–40.
2. Andrew Jack, "The Bird Flu Issue Has Landed," *Financial Times*, 10 January 2006, 8.
3. Eric Schoeniger, "How to Plug the $13 Billion Leak," *BusinessWeek*, 20 March 2006, 2–5; and M. Eric Johnson, "A Broader Context for Information Security," a special section in *Financial Times* called "Mastering Risk," 16 September 2005, 1–12.
4. Charlie Ross, "Jackson Action," *The Wall Street Journal*, 15 September 2005, A21.
5. Michel Crouhy, Dan Galai, and Robert Mark, *The Essentials of Risk Management*, (New York: McGraw Hill, 2006), 1–11.
6. "Rising Trends in Risk Management," *The Wall Street Journal*, 21 April, 2009.
7. Kevin Buehler, Andrew Freeman, and Ron Hulme, "The New Arsenal of Risk Management," *Harvard Business Review*, September 2008.
8. Deborah Wince-Smith, "Innovate at Your Own Risk," *Harvard Business Review*, May 2005, 25.
9. Keith Goffin and Rick Mitchell, "The Risks of Innovation," a special section in *Financial Times* called "Managing Risk," 30 September 2005, 1–12.

10. Maggie Urry, "Business Stands By and Sees Profits Go to Blazes," *Financial Times*, 25 April 2006, 4.
11. Naazneen Karmali, "The Raja of Rooms," *Forbes*, 12 January 2009.
12. "15,000 Hens Killed in Bird-Flu Scare," *The Washington Times*, 4 June 2008.
13. Tamsyn Burgmann and Joan Bryden, "Health Officials Tie Listeria Outbreaks to Maple Leaf Meats," *The Globe and Mail*, 23 August 2008, www.theglobeandmail.com/servlet/story/RTGAM.20080823.wmapleleaf0823/BNStory/National.
14. Erin White, "Smaller Companies Join the Outsourcing Trend," *The Wall Street Journal*, 8 May 2006, B3.
15. Amy Borrus, Mike McNamee, and Howard Gleckman, "Up to His Neck in the Risk Pool," *BusinessWeek*, 6 June 2005, 109–11; Andrea Siedsma, "Insurance Well Spent," *Hispanic Business*, March 2006, 48–50.
16. Stacy Tillie, "What's Riding on Your Insurance Policy?" *AAA World*, January/February 2009.
17. Holman W. Jenkins, "A Global Warming Worksheet," *The Wall Street Journal*, 1 February 2006, A15.
18. Chip Giller and David Roberts, "Green Gets Going," *Fast Company*, March 2006, 73–78.
19. Mya Frazier, "Who's in Charge of Green?" *Advertising Age*, 9 June 2008.

Chapter 18

1. Financial Consumer Agency of Canada, "For Consumers", www.fcac-acfc.gc.ca.
2. Financial Consumer Agency of Canada, "About the Financial Services Sector—Facts & Figures," 22 February 2009, www.fcac-acfc.gc.ca/eng/media/facts/default.asp.
3. Binyamin Applebaum, "U.S. Aid Goes to Credit Unions," *The Washington Post*, 29 January 2009.
4. John J. McKechnie III, "A Credit Union May Be Better Than a Bank," *Bottom Line Personal*, 1 March 2008.
5. Canadian Bankers Association, "Competition in the Canadian Financial Services Sector," May 2012, www.cba.ca/en/media-room/50-backgrounders-on-banking-issues/121-competitition-in-the-financial-services-sector.
6. Financial Consumer Agency of Canada, "How the Industry Is Regulated," 22 February 2009, www.fcac-acfc.gc.ca/eng/industry/actsregs/default.asp.
7. The Canada Deposit Insurance Corporation, 29 January 2004, www.cdic.ca.
8. Hans F. Sennholz, "The Origins of Money," *St. Croix Review*, April 2008.
9. Evan I. Schwartz, "How You'll Pay," *Technology Review*, January 2003, 50–56.
10. Bank of Canada, "Counterfeit Detection," www.bankofcanada.ca/en/banknotes/counterfeit/security/index100b.html.
11. Catherine Siskos, "Cash in a Flash," *Kiplinger's*, October 2002, 30–31.
12. Hans F. Sennholz, "The Origins of Money," *St. Croix Review*, April 2008.
13. "Deflation Warning," *Washington Times*, 14 May 2003, A20.
14. Patrick Barta and Michelle Higgins, "Dollar's Fall Could End Many Bargains," *The Wall Street Journal*, 9 January 2003, D1, D4.
15. Bank of Canada, "Canada's Money Supply," January 2000, www.bankofcanada.ca/en/backgrounders/bg-m2.htm; and Bank of Canada, "Target for the Overnight Rate," July 2001, www.bankofcanada.ca/en/backgrounders/bg-p9.htm.
16. Bank of Canada, "Canada's Money Supply."
17. Bank of Canada, "Target for the Overnight Rate."
18. Canadian Bankers Association, "Bank Revenues and Profits," May 2012, www.cba.ca/en/media-room/50-backgrounders-on-banking-issues/119-bank-revenues-and-earnings-profits.
19. Ibid.
20. Stephanie Miles, "What's a Check?" *The Wall Street Journal*, 21 October 2002, p. R5.
21. Pallavi Gogoi, "The Hot News in Banking: Bricks and Mortar," *BusinessWeek*, 21 April 2003, 83–84.
22. Investment Industry Association of Canada, "Fact Sheet," iiac.ca/welcome-to-iiac/about-us/who-we-are.
23. Bertrand Marotte, "Regulator Assails Plan for National Stock Watchdog," *The Globe and Mail*, 22 January 2004, B6; Karen Howlett and Heather Scoffield, "Consensus Elusive over Regulator," *The Globe and Mail*, 20 January 2004, B6; and "What Is the CSA?" and "Who Are the Canadian Securities Administrators?" June 2001: Canadian Securities Administrators, www.csa-acvm.ca/html_CSA/about_who_are_csa.html and www.csa-acvm.ca/html_CSA/about.html.
24. Financial Consumer Agency of Canada, "Financial Consumer Agency of Canada Glossary—Securities Commission Definition," 26 February 2004, www.fcac-acfc.gc.ca/eng/glossary.asp.
25. "Demen Found Guilty of Securities Violations," *The Gazette*, 30 September 2008, www.canada.com/montrealgazette/news/business/story.html?id=dc8f3467-0591-490f-bf65-ea5b76b732d2.
26. Theresa Tedesco, "Ottawa Pushes for National Securities Regulator Within Year," *Financial Post*, 27 April 2012.
27. Financial Consumer Agency of Canada, "Financial Consumer Agency of Canada Glossary—Security Definition," 26 February 2004, www.fcac-acfc.gc.ca/eng/glossary.asp.
28. "The Case for Going Private: Corporate Ownership," *The Economist*, 25 January 2003, 67.
29. Ben White and Kathleen Day, "SEC Approves Wall Street Settlement; Conflict of Interest Targeted," *Washington Post*, 29 April 2003, A1.
30. Mara Der Hovanesian, "The Market's Closed—Wake Up," *BusinessWeek*, 3 March 2003, 132.
31. Ben White, "A Crisis of Trust on Wall Street," *Washington Post*, 4 May 2003, F1.
32. E. S. Browning, "Corporate Bonds Become Fund Managers' Favorite," *The Wall Street Journal*, 29 September 2008.
33. Debra Silversmith and Don Silversmith, "We're Close to a Bear Market, but Hang On for Inevitable Fix," *Denver Business Journal*, 31 March 2008.
34. Kerry Hannon, "Plotting a Withdrawal Strategy: Tapping Retirement Funds Should Be Done with Great Care," *U.S. News & World Report*, 3 November 2008; and Dave Carpenter, "After End of Bear Market Looms Uncertainty," AP Worldstream, 3 November 2008.
35. Eric Troseth, "Finding a Rally in Bearish Times," *Christian Science Monitor*, 5 May 2003, 14.
36. Amy Feldman, "Financial Planning: What Higher Taxes Could Mean," *BusinessWeek*, 16 October 2008.
37. "Hillsdale Hedge Funds Prepared for May 1st S&P/TSE Composite Index Changes," Hillsdale Investment Management, February 2002, www.hillsdaleinv.com/research/pdf/tse_change.pdf.
38. Tim Paradis, "Stocks Point Lower Open as Overseas Markets Slide," AP Online, 27 October 2008; and Renee Montagne, "Investors Fear Dreaded Margin Call," *NPR Morning Edition*, 7 November 2008.
39. "Stock Splits Help Keep Share Prices in Check," *Virginian Pilot*, 4 May 2008.
40. The Investment Funds Institute of Canada, April 2012, www.ific.ca/Home/HomePage.aspx.
41. John Rekenthaler, "When Mutual Funds Die, Companies Bury Their Mistakes, Distorting Returns," *Money*, April 2003, 49–53.

GLOSSARY

Absolute advantage The advantage that exists when a country has a monopoly on producing a specific product or is able to produce it more efficiently than all other countries.

Accounting The recording, classifying, summarizing, and interpreting of financial events to provide management and other interested parties the financial information they need to make good decisions.

Accounting cycle A six-step procedure that results in the preparation and analysis of the major financial statements.

Accounts payable Current liabilities are bills a company owes to others for merchandise or services purchased on credit but not yet paid for.

Accounts Different types of assets, liabilities, and owners' equity.

Acquisition One company's purchase of the property and obligations of another company.

Administrative agencies Federal or provincial institutions and other government organizations created by Parliament or provincial legislatures with delegated power to pass rules and regulations within their mandated area of authority.

Advertising Paid, non-personal communication through various media by organizations and individuals who are in some way identified in the advertising message.

Affiliate marketing An Internet-based marketing strategy in which a business rewards individuals or other businesses (affiliates) for each visitor or customer the affiliate sends to its Web site.

Agency shop (Rand formula) A workplace in which a new employee is not required to join the union but must pay union dues.

Agents/brokers Marketing intermediaries that bring buyers and sellers together and assist in negotiating an exchange but don't take title to the goods.

Amortization The systematic writeoff of the cost of a tangible asset over its estimated useful life.

Angel investors Private individuals who invest their own money in potentially hot new companies before they go public.

Annual report A yearly statement of the financial condition, progress, and expectations of an organization.

Apprentice programs Training programs involving a period during which a learner works alongside an experienced employee to master the skills and procedures of a craft.

Arbitration An agreement to bring in an impartial third party (a single arbitrator or a panel of arbitrators) to render a binding decision in a labour dispute.

Articles of incorporation A legal authorization from the federal or provincial/territorial government for a company to use the corporate format.

Assembly process That part of the production process that puts together components.

Assets Economic resources (things of value) owned by a firm.

Autocratic leadership Leadership style that involves making managerial decisions without consulting others.

Baby boomers A demographic group of Canadians that were born in the period from 1947 to 1966.

Baby-boom echo A demographic group of Canadians that were born in the period from 1980 to 1995; the children of the baby boomers.

Back-to-work legislation Legislation that orders an end to a labour–management dispute that has escalated to a strike or lockout, in an industry that the government decides is essential to the operation of the economy.

Balance of payments The difference between money coming into a country (from exports) and money leaving the country (for imports) plus money flows from other factors such as tourism, foreign aid, military expenditures, and foreign investment.

Balance of trade A nation's ratio of exports to imports.

Balance sheet The financial statement that reports a firm's financial condition at a specific time and is composed of three major types of accounts: assets, liabilities, and owners' equity.

Bankruptcy The legal process by which a person, business, or government entity unable to meet financial obligations is relieved of those obligations by a court that divides debtor assets among creditors, allowing creditors to get at least part of their money and freeing the debtor to begin anew.

Bargaining zone Range of options between the initial and final offer that each party will consider before negotiations dissolve or reach an impasse.

Barter The trading of goods and services for other goods and services directly.

Behavioural segmentation Dividing the market based on behaviour with or toward a product.

Benchmarking Comparing an organization's practices, processes, and products against the world's best.

Blog An online diary (Web log) that looks like a Web page but is easier to create and update by posting text, photos, or links to other sites.

Bond A long-term legal obligation of a corporation or government to make regular interest payments during the term of the bond and to repay the entire bond principal at a prescribed date. Bonds can be issued by large organizations including different levels of government, government agencies, corporations, and foreign governments and corporations.

Bonds payable Long-term liabilities that represent money lent to a firm that must be paid back.

Bookkeeping The recording of business transactions.

Brain drain The loss of educated people to other countries.

Brainstorming Coming up with as many solutions to a problem as possible in a short period of time with no censoring of ideas.

Brand A name, symbol, or design (or combination thereof) that identifies the goods or services of one seller or group of sellers and distinguishes them from the goods and services of competitors.

Brand awareness How quickly or easily a given brand name comes to mind when a product category is mentioned.

Brand equity The value of the brand name and associated symbols.

Brand loyalty The degree to which customers are satisfied, enjoy the brand, and are committed to further purchase.

Brand manager A manager who has direct responsibility for one brand or one product line; called a product manager in some firms.

Brand name A word, letter, or group of words or letters that differentiates one seller's goods or services from those of competitors.

Breach of contract When one party fails to follow the terms of a contract.

Break-even analysis The process used to determine profitability at various levels of sales.

Broadband technology Technology that offers users a continuous connection to the Internet and allows users to send and receive mammoth files that include voice, video, and data much faster than ever before.

Budget A financial plan that sets forth management's expectations, and, on the basis of those expectations, allocates the use of specific resources throughout the firm.

Bureaucracy An organization with many layers of managers who set rules and regulations and oversee all decisions.

Business Any activity that seeks to provide goods and services to others while operating at a profit.

Business cycles (economic cycles) The periodic rises and falls that occur in economies over time.

Business environment The surrounding factors that either help or hinder the development of businesses.

Business establishment Must meet at least one of the following minimum criteria: it must have at least one paid employee, it must have annual sales revenue of $30,000, or it must be incorporated and have filed a federal corporate income tax return at least once in the previous three years.

Business intelligence (BI) BI refers to a variety of software applications that analyze an organization's raw data and take useful insights from it.

Business law Rules, statutes, codes, and regulations that are established to provide a legal framework within which business must be conducted and that are enforceable by court action.

Business plan A detailed written statement that describes the nature of the business, the target market, the advantages the business will have in relation to competition, and the resources and qualifications of the owner(s).

Business-to-business (B2B) market All individuals and organizations that want goods and services to use in producing other goods and services or to sell, rent, or supply goods to others.

Buying on margin Purchasing securities by borrowing some of the cost from the broker.

Buzz marketing Popularity created by consumer word of mouth.

Cafeteria-style benefits (flexible benefits) Benefit plans that allow employees to choose which benefits they want up to a certain dollar amount.

Capital assets Assets that are relatively permanent, such as land, buildings, and equipment.

Capital budget A budget that highlights a firm's spending plans for major asset purchases that often require large sums of money, like property, buildings, and equipment.

Capital expenditures Major investments in either tangible long-term assets such as land, buildings, and equipment, or intangible assets such as patents, trademarks, and copyrights.

Capital gains The positive difference between the purchase price of a stock and its sale price.

Capitalism An economic system in which all or most of the factors of production and distribution are privately owned and operated for profit.

Cash budget A budget that estimates a firm's cash inflows and outflows during a particular period (e.g., monthly, quarterly).

Cash flow The difference between cash coming in and cash going out of a business.

Cash flow forecast Forecast that predicts the cash inflows and outflows in future periods, usually months or quarters.

Cash flow statement A financial statement that reports cash receipts and disbursements related to a firm's three major activities: operations, investing, and financing.

Centralized authority An organization structure in which decision-making authority is maintained at the top level of management at the company's headquarters.

Certificate of deposit A time-deposit (savings) account that earns interest to be delivered at the end of the certificate's maturity date.

Certification Formal process whereby a union is recognized by the Labour Relations Board (LRB) as the bargaining agent for a group of employees.

Certified General Accountant (CGA) An accountant who has met the examination, education, and experience requirements of the Certified General Accountants Association of Canada.

Certified Management Accountant (CMA) An accountant who has met the examination, education, and experience requirements of the Society of Management Accountants of Canada.

Chain of command The line of authority that moves from the top of a hierarchy to the lowest level.

Channel of distribution A set of marketing intermediaries, such as agents, brokers, wholesalers, and retailers, that join together to transport and store goods in their path (or channel) from producers to consumers.

Chartered Accountant (CA) An accountant who has met the examination, education, and experience requirements of the Canadian Institute of Chartered Accountants.

Checkoff A contract clause requiring the employer to deduct union dues from employees' pay and remit them to a union.

Civil law Legal proceedings that do not involve criminal acts.

Claim A statement of a loss that the insured sends to the insurance company to request payment.

Climate change The movement of the temperature of the planet up or down over time.

Closed shop A workplace in which all new hires must already be union members.

Cloud computing A form of virtualization in which a company's data and applications are stored at offsite data centres that are accessed over the Internet (the cloud).

Collective bargaining The process whereby union and management representatives negotiate a contract for workers.

Command economy An economy in which the government largely decides what goods and services are produced, who gets them, and how the economy will grow.

Commercial bank A profit-seeking organization that receives deposits from individuals and corporations in the form of chequing and savings accounts and then uses some of these funds to make loans.

Commercial finance companies Organizations that make short-term loans to borrowers who offer tangible assets as collateral.

Commercial paper Unsecured promissory notes of $100,000 and up that mature (come due) in 365 days or less.

Common law The body of law that comes from decisions handed down by judges; also referred to as unwritten law.

Common market (trading bloc) A regional group of countries that have a common external tariff, no internal tariffs, and a coordination of laws to facilitate exchange; also called a trading bloc.

Common shares The most basic form of ownership in a firm; it confers voting rights and the right to share in the firm's profits through dividends, if offered by the firm's board of directors.

Communism An economic and political system in which the state (the government) makes all economic decisions and owns almost all of the major factors of production.

Comparative advantage theory Theory that states that a country should sell to other countries those products that it produces most effectively and efficiently, and buy from other countries those products that it cannot produce as effectively or efficiently.

Competition-based pricing A pricing strategy based on what all the other competitors are doing. The price can be set at, above, or below competitors' prices.

Compliance The job of reviewing and evaluating the records used to prepare a company's financial statements.

Compliance-based ethics codes Ethical standards that emphasize preventing unlawful behaviour by increasing control and by penalizing wrongdoers.

Compressed workweek Work schedule that allows an employee to work a full number of hours per week but in fewer days.

Computer-Aided Design (CAD) The use of computers in the design of products.

Computer-Aided Manufacturing (CAM) The use of computers in the manufacturing of products.

Computer-Integrated Manufacturing (CIM) The uniting of computer-aided design with computer-aided manufacturing.

Conceptual skills Skills that involve the ability to picture the organization as a whole and the relationships among its various parts.

Conciliation A process by which a labour union or an employer must use the government's services (via the Ministry of Labour) for help in resolving their differences so that they can reach a collective agreement.

Conglomerate merger The joining of firms in completely unrelated industries.

Consideration Something of value; consideration is one of the requirements of a legal contract.

Consumer market All individuals or households that want goods and services for personal consumption or use.

Consumer Price Index (CPI) A monthly statistic that measures the pace of inflation or deflation.

Consumerism A social movement that seeks to increase and strengthen the rights and powers of buyers in relation to sellers.

Contingency planning The process of preparing alternative courses of action that may be used if the primary plans do not achieve the organization's objectives.

Contingent workers Workers who do not have regular, full-time employment.

Continuous improvement (CI) Constantly improving the way the organization does things so that customer needs can be better satisfied.

Continuous process A production process in which long production runs turn out finished goods over time.

Contract A legally enforceable agreement between two or more parties.

Contract law Set of laws that specify what constitutes a legally enforceable agreement.

Contract manufacturing A foreign country's production of private-label goods to which a domestic company then attaches its brand name or trademark; also called outsourcing.

Controlling A management function that involves establishing clear standards to determine whether or not an organization is progressing toward its goals and objectives, rewarding people for doing a good job, and taking corrective action if they are not.

Cookies Pieces of information, such as registration data or user preferences, sent by a Web site over the Internet to a Web browser that the browser software is expected to save and send back to the server whenever the user returns to that Web site.

Co-operative An organization that is owned by members and customers, who pay an annual membership fee and share in any profits.

Copyright A form of intellectual property that protects a creator's rights to materials such as books, articles, photos, and cartoons.

Core competencies Those functions that an organization can do as well as or better than any other organization in the world.

Core time In a flextime plan, the period when all employees are expected to be at their job stations.

Corporate governance The process and policies that determine how an organization interacts with its stakeholders, both internal and external.

Corporate philanthropy Dimension of social responsibility that includes charitable donations.

Corporate policy Dimension of social responsibility that refers to the position a firm takes on social and political issues.

Corporate responsibility Dimension of social responsibility that includes everything from hiring minority workers to making safe products.

Corporate social initiatives Dimension of social responsibility that includes enhanced forms of corporate philanthropy that are more directly related to the company's competencies.

Corporate social responsibility (CSR) A business's concern for the welfare of society.

Corporation A legal entity with authority to act and have liability separate from its owners.

Cost of goods sold (cost of goods manufactured) A measure of the cost of merchandise sold or cost of raw materials and supplies used for producing items for resale.

Countertrading A complex form of bartering in which several countries may be involved, each trading goods for goods or services for services.

Craft union An organization of skilled specialists in a particular craft or trade.

Credit unions Non-profit, member-owned financial co-operatives that offer a full variety of banking services to their members.

Criminal law Defines crimes, establishes punishments, and regulates the investigation and prosecution of people accused of committing crimes.

Crisis planning Involves reacting to sudden changes in the environment.

Critical path In a PERT network, the sequence of tasks that takes the longest time to complete.

Crown corporations Companies that are owned by the federal or provincial government.

Culture The set of values, beliefs, rules, and institutions held by a specific group of people.

Current assets Items that can or will be converted into cash within one year.

Customer Relationship Management (CRM) The process of building long-term relationships with customers by delivering customer value and satisfaction.

Damages The monetary settlement awarded to a person who is injured by a breach of contract.

Database An electronic storage file for information.

Debenture bonds Bonds that are unsecured (i.e., not backed by any collateral such as equipment).

Debt financing Funds raised through various forms of borrowing that must be repaid.

Decentralized authority An organization structure in which decision-making authority is delegated to lower-level managers more familiar with local conditions than headquarters management could be.

Decertification Process by which workers can take away a union's right to represent them.

Decision making Choosing among two or more alternatives.

Deficit Occurs when a government spends over and above the amount it gathers in taxes for a specific period of time (namely, a fiscal year).

Deflation A situation in which prices are declining.

Demand The quantity of products that people are willing to buy at different prices at a specific time.

Demand deposit The technical name for a chequing account; the money in a demand deposit can be withdrawn anytime on demand from the depositor.

Demographic segmentation Dividing the market by age, income, and education level.

Demography The statistical study of the human population with regard to its size, density, and other characteristics such as age, race, gender, and income.

Departmentalization Dividing an organization into separate units.

Depression A severe recession.

Deregulation Government withdrawal of certain laws and regulations that seem to hinder competition

Devaluation Lowering the value of a nation's currency relative to other currencies.

Direct marketing Uses direct communication with consumers to generate a response in the form of an order, a request for further information, or a visit to a retail outlet.

Direct selling Selling to consumers in their homes or where they work.

Disinflation A situation in which price increases are slowing (the inflation rate is declining).

Diversification Buying several different investment alternatives to spread the risk of investing.

Dividends Part of a firm's profits that may be distributed to shareholders as either cash payments or additional shares of stock.

Double-entry bookkeeping The concept of every business transaction affecting at least two accounts.

Dumping Selling products in a foreign country at lower prices than those charged in the producing country.

E-business Any information system or application that empowers business processes.

E-commerce The buying and selling of goods and services over the Internet.

Economics The study of how society chooses to employ resources to produce goods and services and distribute them for consumption among various competing groups and individuals.

Economies of scale The situation in which companies can reduce their production costs if they can purchase raw materials in bulk and develop specialized labour; resulting in the average cost of goods going down as production levels increase.

Electronic retailing Selling goods and services to ultimate customers (e.g., you and me) over the Internet.

Embargo A complete ban on the import or export of a certain product or the stopping of all trade with a particular country.

Employee orientation The activity that introduces new employees to the organization; to fellow employees; to their immediate supervisors; and to the policies, practices, values, and objectives of the firm.

Employer business Meets one of the business establishment criteria and usually maintains a payroll of at least one person, possibly the owner.

Employment equity Employment activities designed to "right past wrongs" by increasing opportunities for minorities and women.

Empowerment Giving front-line workers the responsibility, authority, and freedom to respond quickly to customer requests.

Enabling Giving workers the education and tools they need to make decisions.

Enterprise resource planning (ERP) A computer application that enables multiple firms to manage all of their operations (finance, requirements planning, human resources, and order fulfillment) on the basis of a single, integrated set of corporate data.

Entrepreneur A person who risks time and money to start and manage a business.

Entrepreneurial team A group of experienced people from different areas of business who join together to form a managerial team with the skills needed to develop, make, and market a new product.

Entrepreneurship Accepting the challenge of starting and running a business.

Environmental scanning The process of identifying the factors that can affect marketing success.

Equalization A federal government program for reducing fiscal disparities among provinces.

Equity financing Funds raised from operations within the firm or through the sale of ownership in the firm.

Equity theory The idea that employees try to maintain equity between inputs and outputs compared to others in similar positions.

Ethics Standards of moral behaviour; that is, behaviour that is accepted by society as right versus wrong.

Ethnocentricity An attitude that one's own culture is superior to all others.

Everyday low pricing (EDLP) Setting prices lower than competitors and then not having any special sales.

Exchange rate The value of one nation's currency relative to the currencies of other countries.

Exclusive distribution Distribution that sends products to only one retail outlet in a given geographic area.

Expectancy theory Victor Vroom's theory that the amount of effort employees exert on a specific task depends on their expectations of the outcome.

Exporting Selling products to another country.

Express warranties Specific representations by the seller that buyers rely on regarding the goods they purchase.

External customers Dealers, who buy products to sell to others, and ultimate customers (or end users), who buy products for their own personal use.

Extranet A semi-private network that uses Internet technology and allows more than one company to access the same information or allows people on different servers to collaborate.

Extrinsic reward Something given to you by someone else as recognition for good work; extrinsic rewards include pay increases, praise, and promotions.

Facility layout The physical arrangement of resources (including people) in the production process.

Facility location The process of selecting a geographic location for a company's operations.

Factoring The process of selling accounts receivable for cash.

Factors of production The resources used to create wealth: land, labour, capital goods, entrepreneurship, and knowledge.

Federal budget A comprehensive report that reveals government financial policies for the coming year.

Finance The function in a business that acquires funds for the firm and manages them within the firm.

Financial accounting Accounting information and analyses prepared for people outside the organization.

Financial control A process in which a firm periodically compares its actual revenues, costs, and expenses with its projected ones.

Financial management The job of managing a firm's resources to meet its goals and objectives.

Financial managers Managers who examine the financial data prepared by accountants and recommend strategies for improving the financial performance of the firm.

Financial statement A summary of all of the transactions that have occurred over a particular period.

First in, first out (FIFO) An accounting method for calculating cost of inventory; it assumes that the first goods to come in are the first to go out.

Fiscal policy The federal government's effort to keep the economy stable by increasing or decreasing taxes or government spending.

Flat organization structure An organization structure that has few layers of management and a broad span of control.

Flexible manufacturing Designing machines to do multiple tasks so that they can produce a variety of products.

Flextime plan Work schedule that gives employees some freedom to choose when to work, as long as they work the required number of hours.

Focus group A small group of people who meet under the direction of a discussion leader to communicate their opinions about an organization, its products, or other issues.

Foreign Direct Investment (FDI) The buying of permanent property and businesses in foreign nations.

Foreign subsidiary A company owned in a foreign country by the parent company.

Forensic accounting A relatively new area of accounting that focuses its attention on fraudulent activity.

Form utility The value added by the creation of finished goods and services.

Formal organization The structure that details lines of responsibility, authority, and position; that is, the structure shown on organization charts.

Franchise The right to use a specific business's name and sell its goods or services in a given territory.

Franchise agreement An arrangement whereby someone with a good idea for a business sells the rights to use the business name and sell its goods and services in a given territory.

Franchisee A person who buys a franchise.

Franchisor A company that develops a product concept and sells others the rights to make and sell the products.

Free trade The movement of goods and services among nations without political or economic barriers.

Free-market economy An economy in which the market largely determines what goods and services are produced, who gets them, and how the economy grows.

Free-rein (laissez-faire) leadership Leadership style that involves managers setting objectives and employees being relatively free to do whatever it takes to accomplish those objectives.

Fringe benefits Benefits such as sick-leave pay, vacation pay, pension plans, and health plans that represent additional compensation to employees beyond base wages.

Fundamental accounting equation Assets = liabilities + owners' equity; this is the basis for the balance sheet.

Gantt chart Bar graph showing production managers what projects are being worked on and what stage they are in at any given time.

Gender wage gap The difference between wages earned by men and wages earned by women

General Agreement on Tariffs and Trade (GATT) A 1948 agreement that established an international forum for negotiating mutual reductions in trade restrictions.

General partner An owner (partner) who has unlimited liability and is active in managing the firm.

General partnership A partnership in which all owners share in operating the business and in assuming liability for the business's debts.

Geographic segmentation Dividing the market by geographic area.

Givebacks Concessions made by union members to management; previous gains from labour negotiations are given up to help employers remain competitive and thereby save jobs.

Goals The broad, long-term accomplishments an organization wishes to attain.

Goal-setting theory The idea that setting ambitious but attainable goals can motivate workers and improve performance if the goals are accepted, accompanied by feedback, and facilitated by organizational conditions.

Goods Tangible products such as computers, food, clothing, cars, and appliances.

Greening The trend toward saving energy and producing products that cause less harm to the environment.

Grievance A formal protest by an individual employee, with the support of the union, when they believe that management is not abiding by or fulfilling the terms of a labour contract.

Gross Domestic Product (GDP) The total value of goods and services produced in a country in a given year.

Gross profit (gross margin) How much a firm earned by buying (or making) and selling merchandise.

Hawthorne effect The tendency for people to behave differently when they know they are being studied.

Hierarchy A system in which one person is at the top of the organization and there is a ranked or sequential ordering from the top down of managers who are responsible to that person.

High–low pricing strategy Set prices that are higher than EDLP stores, but have many special sales where the prices are lower than competitors.

Horizontal merger The joining of two firms in the same industry.

Human relations skills Skills that involve communication and motivation; they enable managers to work through and with people.

Human resource management (HRM) The process of determining human resource needs and then recruiting, selecting, developing, motivating, evaluating, compensating, and scheduling employees to achieve organizational goals.

Hygiene (maintenance) factors In Herzberg's theory of motivating factors, job factors that can cause dissatisfaction if missing but that do not necessarily motivate employees if increased.

Identity theft Obtaining personal information about a person and using that information for illegal purposes.

Implied warranties Guarantees legally imposed on the seller.

Import quota A limit on the number of products in certain categories that a nation can import.

Importing Buying products from another country.

Income statement The financial statement that shows a firm's profit after costs, expenses, and taxes; it summarizes all of the resources (called revenue) that have been earned, all of the resources that were used up, and the resulting net income.

Incubators Centres that provide hands-on management assistance, education, information, technical and vital business support services, networking resources, financial advice, as well as advice on where to go to seek financial assistance.

Independent audit An evaluation and unbiased opinion about the accuracy of a company's financial statements.

Industrial design A form of intellectual property that protects the owner's exclusive right to use the visible features of a finished product that identify it.

Industrial policy A comprehensive, coordinated government plan to guide and revitalize the economy.

Industrial union Consists of unskilled and semi-skilled workers in mass-production industries such as automobile manufacturing and mining.

Inflation A general rise in the prices of goods and services over time.

Informal organization The system of relationships and lines of authority that develops spontaneously as employees meet and form power centres; that is, the human side of the organization that does not appear on any organization chart.

Information technology (IT) Technology that helps companies change business by allowing them to use new methods.

Initial public offering (IPO) The first public offering of a corporation's stock.

Injunction A court order directing someone to do something or to refrain from doing something.

Insider trading An unethical activity in which insiders use private company information to further their own fortunes or those of their family and friends.

Insurable interest The possibility of the policyholder to suffer a loss.

Insurable risk A risk that the typical insurance company will cover.

Insurance policy A written contract between the insured and an insurance company that promises to pay for all or part of a loss.

Intangible assets Long-term assets (e.g., patents, trademarks, copyrights) that have no real physical form but do have value.

Integrated marketing communication (IMC) A technique that combines all promotional tools into one comprehensive and unified promotional strategy.

Integrity-based ethics codes Ethical standards that define the organization's guiding values, create an environment that supports ethically sound behaviour, and stress a shared accountability among employees.

Intensive distribution Distribution that puts products into as many retail outlets as possible.

Intermittent process A production process in which the production run is short and the machines are changed frequently to make different products.

Internal customers Individuals and units within the firm that receive services from other individuals or units.

International Monetary Fund (IMF) An international bank that makes short-term loans to countries experiencing problems with their balance of trade.

Internet2 The new Internet system that links government supercomputer centres and a select group of universities; it runs more than 22,000 times faster than today's public infrastructure and supports heavy-duty applications.

Intranet A companywide network, closed to public access, that uses Internet-type technology.

Intrapreneurs Creative people who work as entrepreneurs within corporations.

Intrinsic reward The good feeling you have when you have done a job well.

Inverted organization An organization that has contact people at the top and the chief executive officer at the bottom of the organization chart.

Invisible hand A phrase coined by Adam Smith to describe the process that turns self-directed gain into social and economic benefits for all.

Involuntary bankruptcy Bankruptcy procedures filed by a debtor's creditors.

ISO 14000 A collection of the best practices for managing an organization's impact on the environment.

ISO 9000 The common name given to quality management and assurance standards.

Job analysis A study of what is done by employees who hold various job titles.

Job description A summary of the objectives of a job, the type of work to be done, the responsibilities and duties, the working conditions, and the relationship of the job to other functions.

Job enlargement A job enrichment strategy that extends the work cycle by adding related tasks to the job description.

Job enrichment A motivational strategy that emphasizes motivating the worker through the job itself.

Job rotation A job enrichment strategy that involves moving employees from one job to another.

Job sharing An arrangement whereby two part-time employees share one full-time job.

Job simulation The use of equipment that duplicates job conditions and tasks so that trainees can learn skills before attempting them on the job.

Job specifications A written summary of the minimum qualifications required of workers to do a particular job.

Joint venture A partnership in which two or more companies (often from different countries) join to undertake a major project.

Journal The record book where accounting data are first entered.

Just-in-time (JIT) inventory control A production process in which a minimum of inventory is kept on the premises and parts, supplies, and other needs are delivered just in time to go on the assembly line.

Knowledge management Finding the right information, keeping the information in a readily accessible place, and making the information known to everyone in the firm.

Last in, first out (LIFO) An accounting method for calculating cost of inventory; it assumes that the last goods to come in are the first to go out (this method is not allowed in tax accounting by governments).

Law of large numbers Principle that if a large number of people are exposed to the same risk, a predictable number of losses will occur during a given period of time.

Leading Creating a vision for the organization and guiding, training, coaching, and motivating others to work effectively to achieve the organization's goals and objectives.

Lean manufacturing The production of goods using less of everything compared to mass production.

Ledger A specialized accounting book in which information from accounting journals is accumulated into accounts and posted so that managers can find all of the information about a specific account in one place.

Leverage Raising needed funds through borrowing to increase a firm's rate of return.

Leveraged buyout (LBO) An attempt by employees, management, or a group of investors to purchase an organization primarily through borrowing.

Liabilities What the business owes to others (debts).

Liability For a business, it includes the responsibility to pay all normal debts and to pay because of a court order or law, for performance under a contract, or payment of damages to a person or property in an accident.

Licensing A global strategy in which a firm (the licensor) allows a foreign company (the licensee) to produce its product in exchange for a fee (a royalty).

Limited liability The responsibility of a business's owners for losses only up to the amount they invest; limited partners and shareholders have limited liability.

Limited Liability Partnership (LLP) A partnership that limits partners' risk of losing their personal assets to only their own acts and omissions and to the acts and omissions of people under their supervision.

Limited partner An owner who invests money in the business but does not have any management responsibility or liability for losses beyond the investment.

Limited partnership A partnership with one or more general partners and one or more limited partners.

Line of credit A given amount of unsecured funds a bank will lend to a business.

Line organization An organization that has direct two-way lines of responsibility, authority, and communication running from the top to the bottom of the organization, with all people reporting to only one supervisor.

Line personnel Employees who are part of the chain of command that is responsible for achieving organizational goals.

Liquidity How fast an asset can be converted into cash.

Lockout An attempt by management to put pressure on unions by temporarily closing the business.

Logistics Those activities that focus on getting the right amount of the right products or services to the right place at the right time at the lowest possible cost.

Long-term financing Borrowed funds that are needed for a period more than one year.

Long-term forecast Forecast that predicts revenues, costs, and expenses for a period longer than one year, and sometimes as far as five or ten years into the future.

Loss When a business's expenses are more than its revenues.

Macroeconomics The part of economic study that looks at the operation of a nation's economy as a whole.

Management The process used to accomplish organizational goals through planning, organizing, leading, and controlling people and other organizational resources.

Management by objectives (MBO) A system of goal setting and implementation that involves a cycle of discussion, review, and evaluation of objectives among top- and middle-level managers, supervisors, and employees.

Management development The process of training and educating employees to become good managers and then monitoring the progress of their managerial skills over time.

Managerial accounting Accounting used to provide information and analyses to managers inside the organization to assist them in decision making.

Market People with unsatisfied wants and needs who have both the resources and the willingness to buy.

Market orientation Focusing efforts on (1) continuously collecting information about customers' needs and competitors' capabilities, (2) sharing this information throughout the organization, and (3) using the information to create value, ensure customer satisfaction, and develop customer relationships.

Market price The price determined by supply and demand.

Market segmentation The process of dividing the total market into groups whose members have similar characteristics.

Marketing A set of business practices designed to plan for and present an organization's products or services in ways that build effective customer relationships.

Marketing boards Organizations that control the supply or pricing of certain agricultural products in Canada.

Marketing concept A three-part business philosophy: (1) a customer orientation, (2) a service orientation, and (3) a profit orientation.

Marketing intermediaries Organizations that assist in moving goods and services from producers to business and consumer users.

Marketing mix The ingredients that go into a marketing program: product, price, place, and promotion.

Marketing research The analysis of markets to determine opportunities and challenges, and to find the information needed to make good decisions.

Maslow's hierarchy of needs Theory of motivation that places different types of human needs in order of importance, from basic physiological needs to safety, social, and esteem needs to self-actualization needs.

Mass customization Tailoring products to meet the needs of individual customers.

Mass marketing Developing products and promotions to please large groups of people.

Matching principle Revenues are recorded with earned and expenses are recorded when incurred.

Materials Requirement Planning (MRP) A computer-based production management system that uses sales forecasts to make sure that needed parts and materials are available at the right time and place.

Matrix organization An organization in which specialists from different parts of the organization are brought together to work on specific projects but still remain part of a line-and-staff structure.

Maturity date The exact date the issuer of a bond must pay the principal to the bondholder.

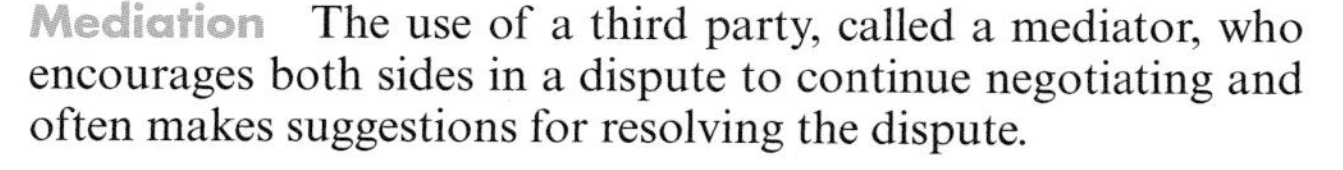

Mediation The use of a third party, called a mediator, who encourages both sides in a dispute to continue negotiating and often makes suggestions for resolving the dispute.

Mentor An experienced employee who supervises, coaches, and guides lower-level employees by introducing them to the right people and generally being their organizational sponsor.

Merger The result of two firms forming one company.

Microeconomics The part of economic study that looks at the behaviour of people and organizations in particular markets.

Micro-enterprise A small business defined as having fewer than five employees.

Micropreneurs Small-business owners with fewer than five employees who are willing to accept the risk of starting and managing the type of business that remains small, lets them do the kind of work they want to do, and offers them a balanced lifestyle.

Middle management The level of management that includes general managers, division managers, and branch and plant managers, who are responsible for tactical planning and controlling.

Mission statement An outline of the fundamental purposes of an organization.

Mixed economies Economic systems in which some allocation of resources is made by the market and some by the government.

Monetary policy The management of the money supply and interest rates.

Money Anything that people generally accept as payment for goods and services.

Money supply The amount of money the Bank of Canada makes available for people to buy goods and services.

Monopolistic competition The market situation in which a large number of sellers produce products that are very similar but that are perceived by buyers as different.

Monopoly A market in which there is only one seller for a product or service.

Motivation A person's internal drive to act.

Motivators In Herzberg's theory of motivating factors, job factors that cause employees to be productive and that give them satisfaction.

Multinational corporation An organization that manufactures and markets products in many different countries and has multinational stock ownership and multinational management.

Mutual fund A fund that buys stocks and bonds and then sells shares in those securities to the public.

Mutual insurance company A type of insurance company owned by its policyholders.

National debt (federal debt) The accumulation of government surpluses and deficits over time.

National policy Government directive that placed high tariffs on imports from the United States to protect Canadian manufacturing, which had higher costs.

Negligence In tort law, behaviour that does not meet the standard of care required and causes unintentional harm or injury.

Negotiable instruments Forms of commercial paper (such as cheques) that are transferable among businesses and individuals and represent a promise to pay a specified amount.

Negotiated labour–management agreement (labour contract) Agreement that clarifies the terms and conditions and sets the tone under which management and labour agree to function over a period of time.

Net income or net loss Revenue left over after all costs and expenses, including taxes, are paid.

Network computing system (client/server computing) Computer systems that allow personal computers (clients) to obtain needed information from huge databases in a central computer (the server).

Networking between firms Using communications technology and other means to link organizations and allow them to work together on common objectives.

Networking between individuals The process of establishing and maintaining contacts with key managers in one's own organization and other organizations and using those contacts to weave strong relationships that serve as informal development systems.

Niche marketing The process of finding small but profitable market segments and designing or finding products for them.

Non-banks Financial organizations that accept no deposits but offer many services provided by regular banks.

Non-profit organization An organization whose goals do not include making a personal profit for its owners or organizers.

North American Free Trade Agreement (NAFTA) Agreement that created a free-trade area among Canada, the United States, and Mexico.

Notes payable Short-term or long-term liabilities that a business promises to repay by a certain date.

Objectives Specific, measurable, short-term statements detailing how to achieve the organization's goals.

Observation Involves watching, either mechanically or in person, how people behave.

Offshoring Sourcing part of the purchased inputs outside of the country.

Off-the-job training Training that occurs away from the workplace and consists of internal or external programs to develop any of a variety of skills or to foster personal development.

Oligopoly A form of competition in which just a few sellers dominate the market.

One-to-one marketing Developing a unique mix of goods and services for each individual customer.

Online training Training programs in which employees "attend" classes via the Internet.

On-the-job training Training in which the employee immediately begins his or her tasks and learns by doing, or watches others for a while and then imitates them, all right at the workplace.

Open shop A workplace in which employees are free to join or not join the union and to pay or not pay union dues.

Operating (master) budget The budget that ties together all of a firm's other budgets and summarizes the business's proposed financial activities.

Operating expenses Costs involved in operating a business, such as rent, utilities, and salaries.

Operational planning The process of setting work standards and schedules necessary to implement the company's tactical objectives.

Operations management A specialized area in management that converts or transforms resources (including human resources) into goods and services.

Organization chart A visual device that shows relationships among people and divides the organization's work; it shows who is accountable for the completion of specific work and who reports to whom.

Organizational (or corporate) culture Widely shared values within an organization that provide coherence and cooperation to achieve common goals.

Organizing A management function that includes designing the structure of the organization and creating conditions and systems in which everyone and everything work together to achieve the organization's goals and objectives.

Outsourcing Assigning various functions, such as accounting, production, security, maintenance, and legal work to outside organizations.

Owners' equity The amount of the business that belongs to the owners minus any liabilities owed by the business.

Participative (democratic) leadership Leadership style that consists of managers and employees working together to make decisions.

Partnership A legal form of business with two or more parties.

Partnership agreement Legal document that specifies the rights and responsibilities of each partner

Patent A form of intellectual property that gives inventors exclusive rights to their inventions for 20 years.

Pay equity Equal pay for work of equal value.

Penetration price strategy A strategy in which the product is priced low to attract many customers and discourage competitors.

Pension funds Amounts of money put aside by corporations, non-profit organizations, or unions to cover part of the financial needs of their members when they retire.

Perfect competition The market situation in which there are many sellers in a market and no seller is large enough to dictate the price of a product.

Performance appraisal An evaluation in which the performance level of employees is measured against established standards to make decisions about promotions, compensation, additional training, or firing.

Personal selling The face-to-face presentation and promotion of goods and services.

Phishing E-mails embellished with a stolen logo for a well-known enterprise (often from financial institutions) that make the messages look authentic, but which are used to collect personal data and use it to commit fraud.

Planning A management function that includes anticipating trends and determining the best strategies and tactics to achieve organizational goals and objectives.

PMI Listing all the pluses for a solution in one column, all the minuses in another, and the interesting in a third column.

Podcasting A means of distributing audio and video programs via the Internet that lets users subscribe to a number of files, also known as feeds, and then hear or view the material at the time they choose.

Precedent Decisions judges have made in earlier cases that guide the handling of new cases.

Preferred shares Stock that gives its owners preference in the payment of dividends and an earlier claim on assets than common shareholders if the company is forced out of business and its assets are sold.

Premium The fee charged by an insurance company for an insurance policy.

Price The money or other consideration (including other goods and services) exchanged for the ownership or use of a good or service.

Price leadership The procedure by which one or more dominant firms set the pricing practices that all competitors in an industry follow.

Primary boycott When a union encourages both its members and the general public not to buy the products of a firm involved in a labour dispute.

Primary data Data that you gather yourself (not from secondary sources such as books, journals, and newspapers).

Prime rate The interest rate that banks charge their most creditworthy customers.

Principle of motion economy Theory developed by Frank and Lillian Gilbreth that every job can be broken down into a series of elementary motions.

Private accountant An accountant who works for a single firm, government agency, or non-profit organization.

Private corporation Corporation that is not allowed to issue stock to the public, so its shares are not listed on stock exchanges; it is limited to 50 or fewer shareholders.

Privatization The process of governments selling Crown corporations.

Problem solving The process of solving the everyday problems that occur. Problem solving is less formal than decision making and usually calls for quicker action.

Process manufacturing That part of the production process that physically or chemically changes materials.

Producers' cartels Organizations of commodity-producing countries that are formed to stabilize or increase prices to optimize overall profits in the long run.

Product Any physical good, service, or idea that satisfies a want or need.

Product differentiation The creation of real or perceived product differences.

Product liability Part of tort law that holds businesses liable for harm that results from the production, design, sale, or use of products they market.

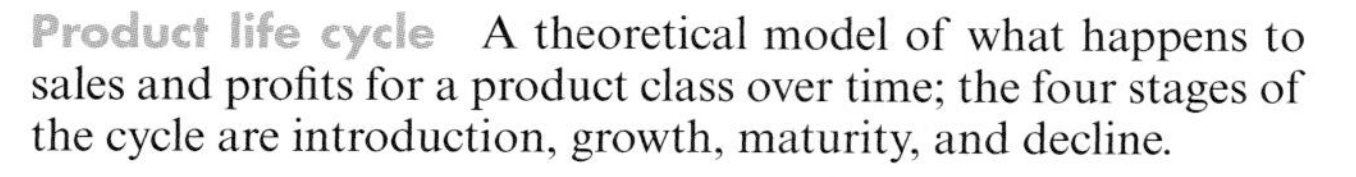

Product life cycle A theoretical model of what happens to sales and profits for a product class over time; the four stages of the cycle are introduction, growth, maturity, and decline.

Product line A group of products that are physically similar or are intended for a similar market.

Product mix The combination of product lines offered by an organization.

Production The creation of finished goods and services using the factors of production: land, labour, capital, entrepreneurship, and knowledge.

Production management The term used to describe all of the activities that managers do to help their firms create goods.

Productivity The amount of output that is generated given the amount of input.

Profit The amount a business earns above and beyond what it spends for salaries and other expenses.

Program evaluation and review technique (PERT) A method for analyzing the tasks involved in completing a given project, estimating the time needed to complete each task, and identifying the minimum time needed to complete the total project.

Promissory note A written contract with a promise to pay.

Promotion All of the techniques sellers use to motivate customers to buy their products.

Promotion mix The combination of promotional tools an organization uses.

Prospectus A condensed version of economic and financial information that a company must make available to investors before they purchase a security.

Psychographic segmentation Dividing the market using the group's values, attitudes, and interests.

Psychological pricing Pricing goods and services at price points that make the product appear less expensive than it is.

Public accountant An accountant who provides his or her accounting services to individuals or businesses on a fee basis.

Public corporation Corporation that has the right to issue shares to the public, so its shares may be listed on a stock exchange.

Public domain software (freeware) Software that is free for the taking.

Public relations (PR) The management function that evaluates public attitudes, changes policies and procedures in response to the public's requests, and executes a program of action and information to earn public understanding and acceptance.

Publicity Any information about an individual, product, or organization that is distributed to the public through the media and that is not paid for or controlled by the seller.

Pull strategy Promotional strategy in which heavy advertising and sales promotion efforts are directed toward consumers so that they'll request the products from retailers.

Purchasing The functional area in a firm that searches for quality material resources, finds the best suppliers, and negotiates the best price for goods and services.

Pure risk The threat of loss with no chance for profit.

Push strategy Promotional strategy in which the producer uses advertising, personal selling, sales promotion, and all other promotional tools to convince wholesalers and retailers to stock and sell merchandise.

Quality Consistently producing what the customer wants while reducing errors before and after delivery to the customer.

Quality of life The general well-being of a society in terms of its political freedom, natural environment, education, health care, safety, amount of leisure, and rewards that add to the satisfaction and joy that other goods and services provide.

Ratio analysis The assessment of a firm's financial condition and performance through calculations and interpretations of financial ratios developed from the firm's financial statements.

Real time The present moment or the actual time in which something takes place; data sent over the Internet to various organizational partners as they are developed or collected are said to be available in real time.

Recession Two or more consecutive quarters of decline in the GDP.

Recruitment The set of activities used to obtain a sufficient number of the right people at the right time.

Re-engineering The fundamental rethinking and radical redesign of organizational processes to achieve dramatic improvements in critical measures of performance.

Regulations Restrictions that provincial and federal laws place on businesses with respect to the conduct of their activities.

Reinforcement theory Theory that positive and negative reinforcers motivate a person to behave in certain ways.

Relationship marketing Marketing strategy with the goal of keeping individual customers over time by offering them products that exactly meet their requirements.

Research and development (R&D) Work directed toward the innovation, introduction, and improvement of products and processes.

Resource development The study of how to increase resources and the creation of the conditions that will make better use of those resources (e.g., recycling).

Resources A general term that incorporates human resources, natural resources, and financial resources.

Restructuring Redesigning an organization so that it can more effectively and efficiently serve its customers.

Retailer An organization that sells to ultimate consumers.

Retained earnings The accumulated earnings from a firm's profitable operations that remains in the business and not paid out to shareholders as dividends.

Revenue The total amount of money that is received during a given period for goods sold, services rendered, and other financial sources.

Reverse discrimination The unfairness that unprotected groups (say, whites or males) may perceive when protected groups receive preference in hiring and promotion.

Revolving credit agreement A line of credit that is guaranteed but usually comes with a fee.

Risk The chance of loss, the degree of probability of loss, and the amount of possible loss (i.e., time and money).

Risk/return trade-off The principle that the greater the risk a lender takes in making a loan, the higher the interest rate required.

Rule of indemnity Rule saying that an insured person or organization cannot collect more than the actual loss from an insurable risk.

Sales promotion The promotional tool that stimulates consumer purchasing and dealer interest by means of short-term activities.

Sampling A promotional tool in which a company lets consumers have a small sample of a product for no charge.

Scientific management Studying workers to find the most efficient ways of doing things and then teaching people those techniques.

Secondary boycott An attempt by labour to convince others to stop doing business with a firm that is the subject of a primary boycott.

Secondary data Information that has already been compiled by others and published in journals and books or made available online.

Secured loan A loan backed by collateral, something valuable such as property.

Securities commission A government agency that administers provincial securities legislation.

Securities dealer A firm that trades securities for its clients and offers investment services.

Selection The process of gathering information and deciding who should be hired, under legal guidelines, to serve the best interests of the individual and the organization.

Selective distribution Distribution that sends products to only a preferred group of retailers in an area.

Self-insurance The practice of setting aside money to cover routine claims and buying only "catastrophe" policies to cover big losses.

Self-managed teams Groups of employees from different departments who work together on a long-term basis.

Services Intangible products (i.e., products that can't be held in your hand) such as education, health care, insurance, recreation, and travel and tourism.

Shareware Software that is copyrighted but distributed to potential customers free of charge.

Shop stewards Union officials who work permanently in an organization and represent employee interests on a daily basis.

Short-term financing Borrowed funds that are needed for one year or less.

Short-term forecast Forecast that predicts revenues, costs, and expenses for a period of one year or less.

Sinking fund A reserve account in which the issuer of a bond periodically sets aside some part of the bond principal prior to maturity so that enough capital will be accumulated by the maturity date to pay off the bond.

Six Sigma quality A quality measure that allows only 3.4 defects per million events.

Skimming price strategy A strategy in which a new product is priced high to make optimum profit while there's little competition.

Small and medium-sized enterprises (SMEs) Refers to all businesses with fewer than 500 employees.

Small business A business that is independently owned and operated, is not dominant in its field, and meets certain standards of size in terms of employees or annual revenues.

Social audit A systematic evaluation of an organization's progress toward implementing programs that are socially responsible and responsive.

Social media The term commonly given to Web sites and online tools that allow users to interact with each other in some way—by sharing information, opinions, knowledge, and interests.

Social media marketing Consumer-generated online-marketing efforts to promote brands and companies for which they are fans (or conversely, negatively promoting brands and companies for which they are non-fans), and the use by marketers of online tools and platforms to promote their brands or organizations.

Socialism An economic system based on the premise that some, if not most, basic businesses should be owned by the government so that profits can be evenly distributed among the people.

Sole proprietorship A business that is owned, and usually managed, by one person.

Span of control The optimum number of subordinates a manager supervises or should supervise.

Speculative risk A chance of either profit or loss.

Staff personnel Employees who advise and assist line personnel in meeting their goals.

Stagflation A situation in which the economy is slowing but prices are going up regardless.

Stakeholders All the people who stand to gain or lose by the policies and activities of a business.

Standard of living The amount of goods and services people can buy with the money they have.

Statistical process control (SPC) The process of taking statistical samples of product components at each stage of the production process and plotting those results on a graph. Any variances from quality standards are recognized and can be corrected if beyond the set standards.

Statistical quality control (SQC) The process that some managers use to continually monitor all phases of the production process to ensure that quality is being built into the product from the beginning.

Statutory law Federal and provincial legislative enactments, treaties of the federal government, and bylaws and ordinances—in short, written law.

Stock certificate Evidence of stock ownership that specifies the name of the company, the number of shares it represents, and the type of stock being issued.

Stock exchange An organization whose members can buy and sell (exchange) securities for companies and investors.

Stock insurance company A type of insurance company owned by shareholders.

Stock split An action by a company that gives shareholders two or more shares of stock for each one they own.

Stockbroker A registered representative who works as a market intermediary to buy and sell securities for clients.

Stocks Shares of ownership in a company.

Strategic alliance A long-term partnership between two or more companies established to help each company build competitive market advantages.

Strategic planning The process of determining the major goals of the organization and the policies and strategies for obtaining and using resources to achieve those goals.

Strict product liability Legal responsibility for harm or injury caused by a product regardless of fault.

Strike A union strategy in which workers refuse to go to work.

Strikebreakers Replacement workers hired to do the jobs of striking employees until the labour dispute is resolved.

Supervisory management Managers who are directly responsible for supervising workers and evaluating their daily performance.

Supply The quantity of products that manufacturers or owners are willing to sell at different prices at a specific time.

Supply chain The sequence of firms that perform activities required to create and deliver a good or service to consumers or industrial users.

Supply chain management The integration and organization of information and logistics activities across firms in a supply chain for the purpose of creating and delivering goods and services that provide value to customers.

Surplus An excess of revenues over expenditures.

Sustainable development Implementing a process that integrates environmental, economic, and social considerations into decision making.

SWOT analysis A planning tool used to analyze an organization's strengths, weaknesses, opportunities, and threats.

Tactical planning The process of developing detailed, short-term statements about what is to be done, who is to do it, and how it is to be done.

Tall organization structure An organization structure in which the pyramidal organization chart would be quite tall because of the various levels of management.

Target costing Designing a product so that it satisfies customers and meets the profit margins desired by the firm.

Target marketing Marketing directed toward those groups (market segments) an organization decides it can serve profitably.

Tariff A tax imposed on imports.

Tax accountant An accountant trained in tax law and responsible for preparing tax returns or developing tax strategies.

Taxes payable Sales taxes and GST or HST collected, and income tax payable.

Technical skills Skills that involve the ability to perform tasks in a specific discipline or department.

Technology Inventions or innovations from applied science or engineering research.

Telecommuting (telework) Using computers linked to the company's network, mobile employees can transmit their work to the office from anywhere.

Telemarketing The sale of goods and services by telephone.

Term-loan agreement A promissory note that requires the borrower to repay the loan in specified instalments.

Test marketing The process of testing products among potential users.

Time deposit The technical name for a savings account; the bank can require prior notice before the owner withdraws money from a time deposit.

Time-motion studies Studies, begun by Frederick Taylor, of which tasks must be performed to complete a job and the time needed to do each task.

Top management Highest level of management, consisting of the president and other key company executives, who develop strategic plans.

Tort A wrongful act that causes injury to another person's body, property, or reputation.

Total fixed costs All expenses that remain the same no matter how many products are made or sold.

Total product offer Everything that consumers evaluate when deciding whether to buy something.

Total quality management (TQM) Striving for maximum customer satisfaction by ensuring quality from all departments.

Trade credit The practice of buying goods and services now and paying for them later.

Trade deficit An unfavourable balance of trade; occurs when the value of a country's imports exceeds that of its exports.

Trade protectionism The use of government regulations to limit the import of goods and services.

Trade surplus A favourable balance of trade; occurs when the value of a country's exports exceeds that of its imports.

Trademark A brand that has been given exclusive legal protection for both the brand name and the pictorial design.

Training and development All attempts to improve productivity by increasing an employee's ability to perform. Training focuses on short-term skills, whereas development focuses on long-term abilities.

Transactional leadership Leadership style where the leader is given the power to assign tasks and their successful completion leads to rewards and reinforcement.

Transfer payments Direct payments from governments to other governments or to individuals.

Transformational leadership Leadership style that occurs when leaders can influence others to follow them in working to achieve a desired outcome or goal.

Transparency The presentation of a company's facts and figures in a way that is clear, assessible, and apparent to all stakeholders.

Trial balance A summary of all of the data in the account ledgers to show whether the figures are correct and balanced.

Triple-bottom line (TBL, 3BL, or People, Planet, Profit) A framework for measuring and reporting corporate performance against economic, social, and environmental parameters.

Trust company A financial institution that can administer estates, pension plans, and agency contracts, in addition to other activities conducted by banks.

Turnover rate A measure of the percentage of employees that leave a firm each year.

Uninsurable risk A risk that no insurance company will cover.

Union An employee organization that has the main goal of representing members in employee–management bargaining over job-related issues.

Union density A measure of the percentage of workers who belong to unions.

Union security clause Provision in a negotiated labour–management agreement that stipulates that employees who benefit from a union must either officially join or at least pay dues to the union.

Union shop A workplace in which the employer is free to hire anybody, but the recruit must then join the union within a short period, perhaps a month.

Unlimited liability The responsibility of business owners for all of the debts of the business.

Unsecured loan A loan that does not require any collateral.

Value Good quality at a fair price. When consumers calculate the value of a product, they look at the benefits and then subtract the cost to see if the benefits exceed the costs.

Values A set of fundamental beliefs that guide a business in the decisions they make.

Variable costs Costs that change according to the level of production.

Venture capital Money that is invested in new or emerging companies that are perceived as having great profit potential

Venture capitalists (VCs) Individuals or companies that invest in new businesses in exchange for partial ownership of those businesses.

Vertical merger The joining of two companies involved in different stages of related businesses.

Vestibule training Training done in schools where employees are taught on equipment similar to that used on the job.

Virtual corporation A temporary networked organization made up of replaceable firms that join and leave as needed.

Virtual private network (VPN) A private data network that creates secure connections, or "tunnels," over regular Internet lines.

Virtualization A process that allows networked computers to run multiple operating systems and programs through one central computer at the same time.

Virus A piece of programming code inserted into other programming to cause some unexpected and, for the victim, usually undesirable event.

Vision An encompassing explanation of why the organization exists and where it is trying to head.

Voluntary bankruptcy Legal procedures initiated by a debtor.

Web 2.0 The set of tools that allow people to build social and business connections, share information, and collaborate on projects online (including blogs, wikis, social networking sites and other online communities, and virtual worlds).

Whistleblowers People who report illegal or unethical behaviour.

Wholesaler A marketing intermediary that sells to other organizations.

Wildcat strike An unauthorized (by the union) work stoppage while a labour contract is still in effect.

Word-of-mouth promotion A promotional tool that involves people telling other people about products they've purchased.

World Bank (International Bank for Reconstruction and Development) An autonomous United Nations agency that borrows money from the more prosperous countries and lends it to less-developed countries to develop their infrastructure.

World Trade Organization (WTO) The international organization that replaced the General Agreement on Tariffs and Trade, and was assigned the duty to mediate trade disputes among nations.

PHOTO CREDITS

Chapter 1

p. 3, Used with permission of Carolyn Foxcroft; p. 5, © image 100/Corbis; p. 6, © Jack Hollingsworth/Getty Images; p. 8, Used with permission of Canadian Blood Services 2009; p. 11, © Jon Feingersh/zefa/Corbis; p. 13, © AP Photos; p. 14, © Getty Images; p. 16, © *The Toronto Star*/Colin McConnell/The Canadian Press; p. 20, © Yellow Dog Productions; p. 23, © Keith Weller/US Department of Agriculture.

Chapter 2

p. 43, © ILD Photo by Flavia Gondolfo; p. 44, © Maria Teijeiro/age fotostock; p. 45, Used with permission of the Department of Fisheries and Oceans Canada; p. 48, © Photodisc; p. 49, © Frank Gunn/The Canadian Press; p. 52, © Icholakov/GetStock.com; p. 54, © Francis Dean/The Image Works; p. 57, © Dynamic Graphics/Jupiter Images; p. 59, © Photodisc Collection/Getty Images; p. 60, © AP Photos.

Chapter 3

p. 67, © AP/Mikhail Metzel/The Canadian Press; p. 70, © Adrian Wyld/The Canadian Press; p. 71, © Scott Barbour/Getty Images; p. 72, © ZUMA Press, Inc./Alamy; p. 75, © Tetra Images; p. 77, © AP Photos; p. 78, Courtesy of Domino's Pizza; p. 79, © Steve White/The Canadian Press; p. 81, Courtesy of Bombardier Transportation; p. 83, © Photoguy707/GetStock.com; p. 85, © canadabrian/Alamy; p. 86, © Bruce Heinemann/Getty Images; p. 87, © Prakash Singh/AFP/Getty Images; p. 88, © Mark Gabrenya/Shutterstock; p. 91, © Karen Su/Getty Images.

Chapter 4

p. 99, © John Lehmann/*The Globe and Mail*/The Canadian Press; p. 101, Reproduced with the permission of the Public Service Commission of Canada, 2012; p. 102, © Tim Stevens Photography; p. 103, Courtesy of Petro-Canada; p. 104 (top), © McGraw-Hill Ryerson/Alison Derry; p. 104 (bottom), © Library of Parliament/Bibliothèque du Parlement; p. 106, © John Lund/Marc Romanelli/Blend Images LLC; p. 108 (top), © The McGraw-Hill Companies/Barry Barker, photographer; p. 114 (top), © Graham Hughes/The Canadian Press; p. 114 (bottom), Courtesy of the Bank of Canada; p. 116, Courtesy of Stephen Hui; p. 117, © Ford of Canada Public Affairs; p. 120, © National Research Council.

Chapter 5

p. 141, © AP Photos; p. 142, © Crowle Art Group; p. 144, © Corbis/Veer; p. 150, © Erproductions Ltd./Blend Images LLC; p. 151, © Flickr.com/Timhortonsmktg; p. 152, © Dick Hemingway; p. 153, © Deborah Baic/*The Globe and Mail*/The Canadian Press; p. 154, Used with permission of Sun Media Corporation; p. 155, © Nathan Denette/The Canadian Press; p. 156, © US Coast Guard Photo/Alamy; p. 161 (top), Used with permission of Fairtrade Canada, www.fairtrade.ca; p. 161 (bottom), © Deanne Fitzmaurice/*San Francisco Chronicle*/Corbis.

Chapter 6

p. 171, Courtesy of Brian Scudamore, founder and CEO of 1-800-GOT-JUNK?; p. 172, Courtesy of BDC; p. 173, © *What's Up Yukon*; p. 174, © Brand X Pictures/Getty Images; p. 176, © Newscom Photos; p. 179, Used with permission of Chapman's Ice Cream; p. 180, © Mario Beauregard/The Canadian Press; p. 184, © Andersen Ross/Blend Images LLC; p. 186, © Daniel Acker/Bloomberg News/Landov; p. 187, © Supperworks 2009; p. 189, © Steve White/The Canadian Press; p. 190, © InterContinental Hotels Group; p. 192, Used with permission of Mountain Equipment Co-op, © 2009.

Chapter 7

p. 199, © Marlene Ross, Marlene Ross Design; p. 201, Courtesy McCain Foods (Canada); p. 202, Courtesy of Company's Coming; p. 204, Used with permission of Mabel's Labels Inc.; p. 206, © Deborah Baic/The Canadian Press; p. 208, © Aaron Harris/The Canadian Press; p. 210, © Bill Varie/Corbis; p. 211 (top), Courtesy of the Business Development Center, Wasau, WI; p. 211 (bottom), © National Research Council Canada; p. 216, Courtesy co-founder and president, Tal Delatiar, MBAs Without Borders, www.mbaswithoutborders.org; p. 218, © Kevin Frayer/The Canadian Press; p. 223 (top), © Greg Paupst/Canadian Broadcasting Corporation; p. 223 (bottom), © Darren Calabrese/The Canadian Press; p. 226, Used with permission of Jennifer Ger, co-owner, Foxy Originals Inc.

Chapter 8

p. 237, Used with permission of John Baker; p. 240, © Nruboc/Dreamstime.com; p. 240, © Dave and Les Jacobs/Blend Images LLC; p. 250, © Pemotret/Dreamstime.com; p. 251, © Jose Luiz Pelaez Inc./Blend Images LLC.

Chapter 9

p. 261, © ZUMA Wire Service/Alamy; p. 262, © Getty Images for John Deere; p. 265, Courtesy of the German Information Center, New York; p. 270, © McGraw-Hill Ryerson; p. 273, © Dave Carpenter, www.cartoonstock.com; p. 277, © Larry MacDougal/The Canadian Press; p. 281, Courtesy of Creation Technologies; p. 282, © Peter Macdiarmid/Getty Images.

Chapter 10

p. 289, © Bombardier Inc.; p. 293, Courtesy of Demetria Giannisis; p. 295, © Graham Hughes/The Canadian Press; p. 296, © Nyul/GetStock.com; p. 297, © Lonnie Duka/age fotostock/photolibrary; p. 299, © Richard Jones/Rex Features/The Canadian Press; p. 300, Courtesy CAW; p. 301, © Gary Reyes/*San Jose Mercury News*; p. 304, © 2011, SAS Institute Inc. All Rights Reserved. Reproduced with permission of SAS Institute Inc., Cary, NC, USA; p. 305 (top), © Ryan McVay/Getty Images; p. 305 (bottom), © Jeff Sciortino; p. 306, © National Quality Institute, 416-251-7600, www.nqi.ca; p. 310, © Aly Song/Reuters/Landov; p. 312, © Benoit Decout/REA/Redux Pictures.

Chapter 11

p. 323, © Moe Doiron/*The Globe and Mail*/The Canadian Press; p. 324, © RF/Corbis; p. 326, Property of AT&T Archives. Reprinted with permission of AT&T; p. 329, © Digital Vision; p. 331, Courtesy of Alberta-Pacific Forest Industries Inc.; p. 333, © Robyn Beck/AFP/Getty Images; p. 334, © Bruce Ayres; p. 335, Courtesy of Mini Maids; p. 336, © Purestock; p. 338, © Stockbyte/Getty Images; p. 340, © Gabriel Bouys/AFP/Getty Images; p. 342, © PRNewsFoto/Travelocity/AP Photos; p. 344, © Getty Images.

Chapter 12

p. 351, Courtesy of Certes Financial Pros, www.certespros.com; p. 354 (top), © Michael Kappeler/AFP/Getty Images; p. 354 (bottom), "Prevent Discrimination—Cultivate Diversity" poster. Canadian Human Rights Commission. Reproduced with the permission of the Ministry of Public Works and Government Services, 2009; p. 357, Courtesy of *Jobpostings* Magazine, Canada's lifestyle magazine for students and a top source for student jobs and internship listings, www.jobpostings.ca; p. 359, © fStop; p. 360, © Yuri Arcurs/Getty Images; p. 362, © Photodisc/Getty Images; p. 363, © Keith Brofsky/Getty Images; p. 364, © Erin Wigger for the *New York Times*/Redux Pictures; p. 367, Courtesy of Canadian Labour Congress; p. 370, © Stand Honda/AFP/Getty Images; p. 371, © 2010 Mediacorp Canada Inc. "Canada's Top 100 Employers" logo used with permission; p. 373 (top), © VEER Mark Adams/Getty Images; p. 373 (bottom), © Royalty-Free Corbis; p. 375, © Steve Cole/Getty Images; p. 377, © ColorBlind Images.

Chapter 13

p. 385, Courtesy of Gerry Varricchio; p. 386, Courtesy CAW; p. 387, © Bettman/Corbis; p. 388, Courtesy City of Toronto Archives (Fonds 1568, Item 314); p. 389, © Kellydt/Dreamstime.com; p. 391, © James Hardy/PhotoAlto; p. 393, Courtesy of UFCW Canada; p. 400, Courtesy of CUPE National; p. 402, Courtesy of the Public Service Alliance of Canada. Ad created by West Star Communications and Working Design for a boycott campaign during a strike at BHP Billiton's Ekati diamond mine in the Northwest Territories in June 2006; p. 403, Walter Tychnowicz/*The Edmonton Sun*/The Canadian Press; p. 404, *The Toronto Star*/GetStock.com; p. 405, Courtesy of Cosmo Mannella, director of LIUNA's Canadian Tri-Funds, 416-245-9520; p. 406, © Canadian Human Rights Commission. Reproduced with the permission of the Ministry of Public Works and Government Services, 2009; p. 407, © AP Photos.

Chapter 14

p. 419, Courtesy of Sofia Colucci; p. 420, © Curves International Inc.; p. 421, © Bettman/Corbis; p. 423, Courtesy of Erik Qualman; p. 424, © Advertising Standards Canada; p. 427, © Burke/Triolo/Brand X Pictures; p. 428 © The McGraw-Hill Companies, Inc./Lars Niki, photographer; p. 431, Courtesy RDA Group, Bloomfield Hills, Michigan; p. 433, Courtesy Telelatino; p. 434, © Siri Stafford/Getty Images; p. 435 (left), © age fotostock/SuperStock; p. 435 (right), © age Comstock/SuperStock; p. 436, © Keith Beaty/GetStock.com; p. 439 (left), Courtesy of Brad Pattison, "The End of My Leash"; p. 439 (right), Courtesy of Frantic Films and Gail Vaz-Oxlade, "Til Debt Do Us Part"; p. 440 (top), Used with permission of Ron Foxcroft, founder and CEO, Fox 40 International Inc.; p. 440 (bottom), © Kuttig—Travel—2/Alamy; p. 442, © Noel Hendrickson/Getty Images.

Chapter 15

p. 451, © Dick Loek/GetStock.com; p. 452, © Art Directors & TRIP/Alamy; p. 453 (left), © Eduardo Penna; p. 453 (right), © Christopher Kerrigan; p. 455, Used with permission of Ron Foxcroft, founder and CEO, Fox 40 International Inc.; p. 456, Courtesy of Victoria School of Business and Technology; p. 457, Courtesy of Greenpeace; p. 460, © Newscom Photos; p. 461, © Air Canada Vacations and Sandals Resorts, 2011–2012 Caribbean & Mexico Collection brochure. Used with permission of Air Canada Vacations; p. 462, © AP Photos; p. 463, Courtesy of The Home Depot Canada; p. 467, © Image Source/Getty Images; p. 468 (top), © Newscom Photos; p. 468 (bottom), Courtesy of Cupcake Diner; p. 471, Courtesy of Adbusters Media Foundation; p. 475, © Jeff Greenberg/Photo Edit; p. 476, © Laurence Mouton/age fotostock; p. 477, Used with permission of Ron Foxcroft, founder and CEO, Fox 40 International Inc.

Chapter 16

p. 489, © Alan Dean Photography; p. 491, © Michael Rosefeld/Getty Images; p. 492, © Stockbyte/PunchStock; p. 495, Reproduced with the permission of the Canadian Institute of Chartered Accountants; p. 497, © *Harvard Business Review*, 2002; p. 510, © age fotostock/SuperStock.

Chapter 17

p. 519, Courtesy of Steven Glover; p. 521, © Image Source Black; p. 523, © Jeff Greenbert/PhotoEdit; p. 527, © Comstock Images; p. 531, © Vic Bider/PhotoEdit; p. 532, © SuperStock/photolibrary; p. 540, © Steve Kagan/*The New York Times*/Redux Pictures.

Appendix D

p. 548, © AP Photos; p. 550, © RF/Corbis.

Chapter 18

p. 559, Courtesy of Anish Chopra; p. 564, Used with the permission of the Bank of Canada; p. 568, © Boris Lyubner/Getty Images; p. 569, © Gvictoria/Dreamstime.com; p. 572, © Christian Lagereek/Getty Images; p. 575, © AP WideWorld Photo; p. 579, Courtesy of Sprott Asset Management.

ORGANIZATION INDEX

SUBJECT INDEX

F

Q

R

URL INDEX